THE PEC

The People's Wars

*Histories of Violence in the German Lands,
1820–1888*

MARK HEWITSON

OXFORD
UNIVERSITY PRESS

OXFORD
UNIVERSITY PRESS

Great Clarendon Street, Oxford, OX2 6DP,
United Kingdom

Oxford University Press is a department of the University of Oxford.
It furthers the University's objective of excellence in research, scholarship,
and education by publishing worldwide. Oxford is a registered trade mark of
Oxford University Press in the UK and in certain other countries

First Edition published in 2017

Impression: 1

Published in the United States of America by Oxford University Press
198 Madison Avenue, New York, NY 10016, United States of America

British Library Cataloguing in Publication Data
Data available

Library of Congress Control Number: 2016950080

ISBN 978–0–19–956426–2

Printed in Great Britain by
Clays Ltd, St Ives plc

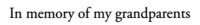

In memory of my grandparents

Preface

Like many academic books, this one has been a long time in the making. That it didn't take even longer is largely due to a timely and generous fellowship from the Arts and Humanities Research Council. During this period of leave, I was able to complete the research for and to write up most of the present volume. The award also gave me the opportunity to meet and discuss the work of a large number of specialists in the field at two workshops—one on nineteenth-century wars and one on the Second World War—and at an international conference funded by the grant. Since I am not a military historian and, in addition, because the project covers a long period, parts of which were unfamiliar to me, it was helpful and stimulating to hear such a wide range of voices on the topic in so short a space of time. I would like to thank Sönke Neitzel and the LSE for co-organizing one of the workshops and Matthew D'Auria for organizing—and contributing so generously to—much of the rest. I should also thank Sebastian Gehrig and Jochen Hung for providing such excellent teaching and administrative cover while I was away, and all my colleagues at UCL for putting up—mostly without complaint—with a long series of absences.

Those absences were spent, for the most part, under the feet of my family (or families) in London, Yorkshire, and France. However difficult it is to separate work from life in academia, it remains a privilege to have such a flexible occupation and to be paid for doing something that most of us would do anyway. For Cécile, the concealed requirements of the associated piecework are very familiar. I thank her for her support and for our life together. For our girls and other members of our families, the same requirements are not self-evident. I thank them for tactfully—and, in the case of Anna and Camille, boisterously—ignoring 'work' altogether.

Children like ours are growing up in a world, notable for its 'war on terror', that has diverged from that of the Cold War in which my parents and I grew up. For none of us, however, has war been more than a half-repressed, half-waking foreboding. My grandparents' expectations were quite different, conditioned by two world wars and the international crises which preceded them. It is a challenge to imagine what they—and their parents—faced. This book is dedicated to them.

MH

London
April 2016

Acknowledgements

The author and publishers wish to thank the following for the use of copyright material:

Map 8.1: The Prussian–Austrian War of 1866, from C. Clark, *Iron Kingdom: The Rise and Downfall of Prussia, 1600–1947* (London, 2006), 527, reproduced with the permission of Penguin Books Ltd.

Map 9.1: Moltke Strikes Back, 5–6 August 1870, from G. Wawro, *The Franco-Prussian War: The German Conquest of France in 1870–1871* (Cambridge, 2003), 109, reproduced with the permission of Cambridge University Press.

Figure 1.1: Wilhelm Camphausen, *Blüchers Rheinübergang bei Caub am 1. Januar 1814* (1860), reproduced with the permission of Mittelrhein-Museum, Koblenz.

Figure 7.1: Wilhelm Camphausen, *Die Erstürmung der Insel Alsen durch die Preußen* (1866), reproduced with the permission of the Deutsches Historisches Museum, Berlin.

Figure 9.1: Paul Sinner, *Straßburg vom Steintor aus, 28. September 1870* (1870), reproduced with the permission of Rheinisches Bildarchiv Köln.

Figure 9.2: Anton von Werner, *Moltke mit seinem Stabe vor Paris* (1873), reproduced with the permission of the Kunsthalle zu Kiel. Photo: Martin Frommhagen.

Figure 10.1: Wilhelm Camphausen, *Der Siegeseinzug in Berlin am 16.6.1871* (n.d.), reproduced with the permission of the Bildarchiv Foto Marburg.

Figure 10.2: Eugen Adam, *Des Todes Rundschau in der Silvesternacht von 1870 auf 1871* (1870/1), reproduced with the permission of the Stadtmuseum, Munich.

Every effort has been made to trace the copyright holders, but if any have been inadvertently overlooked, the publishers will be pleased to make the necessary arrangements at the first opportunity.

Contents

List of Figures

List of Maps

List of Tables

Introduction

Military Violence in German History

> What Sorel remarked sixty years ago, 'The problems of violence still remain very obscure', is as true today as it was then.
>
> Hannah Arendt, *On Violence* (1969)[1]

For Georges Sorel, the former civil servant and engineer who published his revolutionary, syndicalist *Réflexions sur la violence* in 1908, the uses of violence in domestic politics had been subject during the course of the nineteenth century to so many limitations that even the threat of revolution seemed to have been extinguished in favour of peaceful evolution and reform.[2] According to 'the ideas disseminated by middle-class philosophers', he maintained, 'violence is a relic of barbarism which is bound to disappear under the influence of the progress of enlightenment'.[3] Sorel wanted to stimulate the French proletariat to undertake acts of violence in order to overturn the fallacious idea of a supposedly automatic 'progress' and the perpetuation of social inequality with which it was connected.[4] Interestingly, his attempt to salvage violence as an instrument of working-class politics—in the form of 'class war'—rested on an implicit distinction between its use 'internally', which was prohibited, and 'externally', which continued to be mythologized and glorified. 'This belief in "glory" which Renan praised so much quickly fades away into rhapsodies when it is not supported by myths', the renegade revolutionary ideologue wrote of the historian Ernest Renan's *Histoire du peuple d'Israël* (1887–93):

In my opinion, this limited historical outlook is, on the contrary, not a cause but a consequence; it results from the weakening of the heroic myths which had such great popularity at the beginning of the nineteenth century, [when] the Revolution appeared to be essentially a succession of glorious wars, which a people famished for liberty and carried away by the noblest passions had maintained against a coalition of all the powers of oppression and error.[5]

---

[1] H. Arendt, *On Violence* (New York, 1969), 35.
[2] G. Sorel, *Reflections on Violence* (New York, 1950), 80–118.
[3] Ibid., 80.   [4] Ibid., 64–79.
[5] Ibid., 49, 100. His reflections on Renan come from his letter to Daniel Halévy, which became the introduction of his *Reflections*.

It was crucial to remember, claimed the syndicalist thinker, that 'revolutionary war' had played 'an important part...in our history': 'an enormous number of our political ideas originated from war'.[6] The 'analogy' between 'strikes accompanied by violence', which he advocated, and war, which 'provided the republics of antiquity with the ideas [forming] the ornament of our modern culture', was 'prolific of consequences'.[7] In endeavouring to restore violence—by means of 'social war'—to a central place in domestic politics, in an age when 'civil war has become very difficult since the discovery of new firearms', Sorel—who was born in 1847—realized that he would have to reverse one of the most significant dichotomies of the nineteenth century; namely, the distinction between internal exercise of violence, which appeared illegitimate, and its external use, which continued to be revered.[8]

The dichotomy between internal and external forms of violence was defined most sharply in Germany. In a series of lectures on politics which he wrote in the mid-1870s, the historian and publicist Heinrich von Treitschke famously argued that 'every state known to us was created by war; the protection of its citizens with weapons remains the state's first and most essential task'.[9] Citizens were protected by states from violence at home through the exercise or threat of violence abroad. As a consequence, states had come to be legitimated historically by violent actions against enemies. 'Without war, there would be no state', wrote the historian, before going on to add that 'war would persist until the end of history, as long as there is a multitude of states', which he held to be inevitable.[10] Historians have generally taken Treitschke's pronouncements to be proof of bellicosity and subservience to the new German nation-state.[11] However, as the Saxon scholar made plain, he was not uttering a commonplace but attempting to dislodge contrary, popular conceptions of war and statehood.

Treitschke's contemporaries, it seemed, trembled at the prospect of military violence. The Berlin historian feared that 'the Germans' had too little 'political pride' and 'are always in danger of losing their nationality', having become too used to a world of small states and the cosmopolitanism of the Holy Roman Empire.[12] A 'hateful', enlightened belief in the possibility of a world state, the 'reactionary', static idea of a perpetual peace, the misreading of voluntary and limited international law as binding and enforceable, social-contract theory, natural law, fashionable and new legal theories, the illusions of 'the old free-trade school', and too avid a faith in the progressive impact of technology all militated against Treitschke's theses

---

[6] Ibid., 67.

[7] Daniel Halévy, 'Apology for Violence', appended to the 1913 edition of *Reflections*, ibid., 274–5.

[8] Ibid., 275, 81.

[9] H. v. Treitschke, *Politik*, 2nd revised edn (Leipzig, 1899), vol. 1, 72.   [10] Ibid.

[11] James Sheehan, *Where Have All the Soldiers Gone? The Transformation of Modern Europe* (Boston, 2008), 3, starts with these statements by Treitschke in order to show the fundamental shift from an acceptance of war as an integral part of the states' system before 1914 and the re-founding of 'states without war' after 1945, after the disastrous interlude of a 'world made by war' between 1914 and 1945. Another historian of Germany, Richard Bessel, *Violence: A Modern Obsession* (New York, 2015), has recently made and extended similar sets of arguments.

[12] H. v. Treitschke, *Politik*, vol., 29. He devotes a significant part of the first lecture to a debunking of the idea that small states are viable, other than through the precarious courtship of Great Powers.

about the character of and relationship between *Krieg* and *Staat*.[13] Unlike the Greeks, 'modern peoples lead an overwhelmingly social existence', devoting 'the greater part of their work to scientific or industrial interests' and only coming into contact with the state during elections.[14] To understand 'the majesty of the state' and its powerful role, 'modern man has…to distance himself from a whole series of inculcated assumptions'.[15] Economic activity, social interests, and political division regularly obscured contemporaries' view of the higher, power-political purposes of states. 'Only during wartime does politics step directly before us', he continued: 'in their peaceful, tranquil lives, most think little of the state and they are therefore well inclined to underestimate it'.[16]

The state was defined by 'power', which was maintained through war, but few Germans appeared to recognize this fact, Treitschke implied.[17] Military conflict was 'terrible', as recent experience had demonstrated, even for those who regarded it as a necessary 'medicine'.[18] The 'refined, educated person' who went to war in the 1860s 'sees that he must kill the enemy, whose courage he respects', and 'he feels that murders are being committed without passion', which revealed 'the majesty of war', yet 'this struggle required him to overcome much more than the barbarian did'.[19] Scepticism of 'heroism' and the 'bloody' nature of war, its 'economic depredations', and its seemingly immoral, un-Christian injunctions made it difficult to accept: 'Just as the sudden alternation between sensitivity and asceticism which the Middle Ages had made its own is no longer natural to people today, so war, which constitutes a complete break with our habits, appears to us, for this very reason, to be terrifying.'[20] Even Treitschke was concerned that his modern compatriots might balk at the prospect of future wars.

This study re-evaluates nineteenth-century Germans' attitudes and responses to the violence and suffering of war. It asks how far the establishment of mass warfare—or Clausewitz's notion of 'absolute war'—between 1792 and 1815 affected contemporaries' conceptions and expectations of military conflict as the omnipresent, if occasionally concealed, challenge facing the states of the German Confederation.[21] To answer this question, it is necessary to investigate the nature and reform of German armies; subjects' experiences of military service; citizens' sensitivity to violence, hardship, and death; political debates about the military and warfare; writers' and artists' representations of conflict; press reportage of varying types of war; and combatants' and civilians' reactions to those conflicts which involved their own states. After the conflagrations of the revolutionary and Napoleonic eras, the possibility of war remained the primary challenge confronting governments and their subjects, with armies consuming the greater part of most states' budgets and the onset of hostilities menacing the very existence of the

---

[13] Ibid., vol. 1, 29, 36, 38, 54, 65, 75.
[14] Ibid., 1.   [15] Ibid.   [16] Ibid.   [17] Ibid., 32.
[18] Ibid., 76.   [19] Ibid., 76–7.   [20] Ibid., 74, 76–7.
[21] See the first volume in this series: M. Hewitson, *Absolute War: Violence and Mass Warfare in the German Lands, 1792–1820* (Oxford, 2017). On the incorporation of the lessons of the Napoleonic Wars, see D. E. Showalter, 'The Retaming of Bellona: Prussia and the Institutionalization of the Napoleonic Legacy, 1815–1876', *Military Affairs*, 44 (1980), 57–63.

state and the lives of individual citizens. The term 'people's war' (*Volkskrieg*), which was used at the time, hinted at the shifts which had taken place.[22] In these respects, a re-evaluation of contemporaries' responses to war entails a rereading of the history of the German lands in the nineteenth century.[23]

From a reading of the historiography, with some exceptions, the period of 'restoration' appears to have been marked by divergent practices of military recruitment and differing attitudes to the army and to the prospect of future wars.[24] Gradually, by the 1850s and 1860s, similar commemorations and histories of the Napoleonic Wars had been established throughout much of Germany, replacing veterans' and civilians' handed-down stories of their own contrasting experiences of war (and peace), as allies or opponents of France.[25] At the same time, the governments of individual states continued to resist unification and to fashion their own 'federative' forms of nationalism.[26] Their competing policies—together with

[22] Karen Hagemann, *Revisiting Prussia's Wars against Napoleon: History, Culture and Memory* (Cambridge, 2015), 15, distinguishes between monarchic–conservative *Befreiungskriege* (wars of liberation), liberal and German national *Freiheitskriege*, and Marxist 'people's wars', yet the term *Volkskrieg*, or people's war, was used throughout by commentators from different constituencies. See also, D. Langewiesche and N. Buschmann, '"Dem Vertilgungskriege Grenzen setzen', in D. Beyrau, M. Hochgeschwender, and D. Langewiesche (eds), *Formen des Krieges. Von der Antike bis zur Gegenwart* (Paderborn, 2007), 163; S. Förster, 'Facing "People's War": Moltke the Elder and Germany's Military Options after 1871', *Journal of Strategic Studies*, 10 (1987), 209–30.

[23] This is not to contend that the history of warfare and the military was central to all aspects of history in the nineteenth century. Rather, it is to posit the centrality of the question of war—and the military organization of societies in preparation for war—as an important component (perhaps the primary one) of 'politics' (*Politik*) in its nineteenth-century sense; namely, in the sense of overlapping, intimately connected spheres of domestic and foreign policy. As such, this study belongs to an increasing number of investigations of the social, cultural, and political aspects of warfare and the military: see T. Kühne and B. Ziemann (eds), *Was ist Militärgeschichte?* (Paderborn, 2000); J. Bourke, 'New Military History', in M. Hughes and W. Philpott (eds), *Palgrave Advances in Modern Military History* (Basingstoke, 2004), 258–80; P. H. Wilson, 'Defining Military Culture', *Journal of Military History*, 72 (2008), 11–41; P. H. Wilson, 'War, Political Culture and Central European State Formation from the Late Middle Ages to the Nineteenth Century', in N. Garnham and K. J. Jeffery (eds), *Culture, Place and Identity* (Dublin, 2005), 112–37; R. M. Citino, 'Military Histories Old and New: A Reintroduction', *American Historical Review*, 112 (2007), 1070–90; M. Moyar, 'The Current State of Military History', *Historical Journal*, 50 (2007), 225–40; W. Wette (ed.), *Der Krieg des kleinen Mannes* (Munich, 1992); B. Ulrich, '"Militärgeschichte von unten"', *Geschichte und Gesellschaft*, 22 (1996), 473–503.

[24] U. Frevert, *A Nation in Barracks: Modern Germany, Military Conscription and Civil Society* (Oxford, 2004), 47–157. One important exception is J. Leonhard, *Bellizismus und Nation. Kriegsdeutung und Nationsbestimmung in Europa und den Vereinigten Staaten 1750–1914* (Munich, 2008), 181–281, 419–55, who emphasizes the long-standing entanglement of belligerence and nationalism in Germany.

[25] Above all, K. Hagemann, *Revisiting Prussia's Wars against Napoleon*. Also, U. Planert, *Der Mythos vom Befreiungskrieg. Frankreichs Kriege und der deutsche Süden 1792–1841* (Paderborn, 2007); U. Planert, 'From Collaboration to Resistance: Politics, Experience and Memory of the Revolutionary and Napoleonic Wars in Southern Germany', *Central European History*, 39 (2006), 676–705; K. Aaslestad, *Place and Politics: Local Identity, Civic Culture and German Nationalism in North Germany* (Leiden, 2005).

[26] D. Langewiesche, 'Föderativer Nationalismus als Erbe der deutschen Reichsnation: Über Föderalismus und Zentralismus in der deutschen Nationalgeschichte', in D. Langewiesche and G. Schmidt (eds), *Föderative Nation* (Munich, 2000), 215–44; A. Green, *Fatherlands: State-Building and Nationhood in Nineteenth-Century Germany* (Cambridge, 2001); A. Green, 'The Federal Alternative? A New View of Modern German History', *Historical Journal*, 46 (2003), 187–202; A. Green, 'How Did Federalism Shape German Unification?', in R. Speirs and J. Breuilly (eds), *Germany's Two Unifications* (Basingstoke, 2005), 122–38.

continuing disagreements between liberals, democrats, and conservatives about a reform of the *Bund*, foreign policy, the organization of the army, and the necessity of military intervention—ensured that the wars of 1848–51 in Schleswig, south-west Germany, Italy, and Hungary, 1853–6 in Crimea, 1859 against France and Piedmont, 1864 against Denmark, and 1866 in western Germany, Thuringia, and Bohemia, which resulted in the majority of German states fighting against Prussia, remained divisive.[27] Only the Franco-German War of 1870–1 brought the disunited states of Germany together. Unlike previous conflicts, it was underpinned—the argument runs—by various forms of nationalism, including those relying on nega-tive mechanisms of enmity, demonization, racial stereotyping, expansionism, and cultural superiority, which had been visible long before 1870.[28] The foundation of a German nation-state through war in these circumstances at once reinforced such mechanisms and ensconced the position of the army and a national mythology of war-making in the *Kaiserreich*, which were now associated with the middle classes and with popular expressions of 'folklore militarism', it is held.[29]

In such accounts of contemporaries' attitudes to warfare in the German lands during the nineteenth century, the relationship between nationalism and military conflict is close, characterized by regional diversity and a fitful peace in the period before 1848, division between states and mixed reactions to wars between 1848 and 1866, and an uneven convergence of states, popular belligerence, and national unification during and after the war against France in 1870–1. By contrast, this volume, which is the second in a series of studies of the violence of war in Germany, examines the unlikely romanticization of warfare itself, independently of wider sets

---

[27] D. Langewiesche, 'Germany and the National Question in 1848', in J. Breuilly (ed.), *The State of Germany: The National Idea in the Making, Unmaking and Remaking of a Modern Nation-State* (London, 1992), 60–79; D. Langewiesche, 'Kulturelle Nationsbildung im Deutschland des 19. Jahrhunderts', in M. Hettling and P. Nolte (eds), *Nation und Gesellschaft in Deutschland* (Munich, 1996), 46–64; D. Langewiesche, *Nation, Nationalismus und Nationalstaat in Deutschland und Europa* (Munich, 2000); D. Langewiesche, *Reich, Nation, Föderation* (Munich, 2008); N. Buschmann, *Einkreisung und Waffenbruderschaft. Die öffentliche Deutung von Krieg und Nation in Deutschland 1850–1871* (Göttingen, 2003); N. Buschmann, 'Volksgemeinschaft und Waffenbruderschaft. Nationalismus und Kriegserfahrung in Deutschland zwischen "Novemberkrise" und "Bruderkrieg"', in D. Langewiesche and G. Schmidt (eds), *Föderative Nation*, 83–111; N. Buschmann, '"Moderne Versimpelung" des Krieges. Kriegsberichterstattung und öffentliche Kommunikation an der Schwelle zum Zeitalter der Massenkommunikation (1850–1870)', in N. Buschmann and H. Carl (eds), *Die Erfahrung des Krieges. Erfahrungsgeschtliche Perspektiven von der Französischen Revolution bis zum Zweiten Weltkrieg* (Paderborn, 2001), 97–123.

[28] N. Buschmann, '"Im Kanonenfeuer müssen die Stämme Deutschlands zusammen geschmolzen werden". Zur Konstruktion nationaler Einheit in den Kriegen der Reichsgründungspase', in N. Buschmann and D. Langewiesche (eds), *Der Krieg in den Gründungsmythen europäischer Nationen und der USA* (Frankfurt, 2004), 99–119.

[29] F. Becker, *Bilder von Krieg und Nation. Die Einigungskriege in der bürgerlichen Öffentlichkeit Deutschlands 1864–1913* (Munich, 2001); F. Becker, 'Strammstehen vor der Obrigkeit? Bürgerliche Wahrnehmung der Einigungskriege und Militarismus im Deutschen Kaiserreich', *Historische Zeitschrift*, 277 (2003), 87–113; J. Vogel, *Nationen im Gleichschritt. Der Kult der 'Nation in Waffen' in Deutschland und Frankreich 1871–1914* (Göttingen, 1997), 45–91, 210–26; J. Vogel, '"En revenant de la revue". Militärfolklore und Folkloremilitarismus in Deutschland und Frankreich 1871–1914', *Österreichische Zeitschrift für Geschichtswissenschaften*, 9 (1998), 9–30; J. Vogel, 'Der "Folklorenmilitarismus" und seine zeitgenössische Kritik—Deutschland und Frankreich 1871–1914', in W. Wette (ed.), *Militarismus in Deutschland 1871 bis 1945* (Münster, 1999), 277–92.

of national aims and ambitions, on the part of journalists, academics, writers, artists, political leaders, ministers, officers, and, even, ordinary soldiers, after the ordeals and turbulence of the period between 1792 (the War of the First Coalition) and 1820 (the Vienna Final Act).[30] It goes on to show how many soldiers' and some civilians' romantic images of military conflict were dispelled by the realities of combat during the 'wars of unification', leaving contemporaries with a contradictory and volatile set of expectations of war during the imperial era. This trajectory, which proceeded from a fundamental transformation of recruitment and the ways of making war before 1815 (*contra* Ute Planert's thesis of continuity), led to a clear distinction between war and peace and to a widespread acceptance throughout Germany of the possibility of mass warfare in the future, with universal levies *en masse* (against the claims of Ute Frevert).[31]

The romantic mythologies of war which emerged in the first half of the nineteenth century have to be understood and explained in such a context: why were the horrors of the Revolutionary and Napoleonic Wars not translated into public fear of or scepticism about military conflict after 1819–20, once the post-war settlement had been worked out? Because of its emphasis on continuity, diversity, and the relationship between war and the nation, much of the recent historiography neglects this question. The years of international instability after 1848—and especially after 1853—are then seen as the era when the menace and actuality of war helped to overcome the deeply entrenched differences—or federal nationalism and particular traditions (Dieter Langewiesche)—of individual German states.[32] The linkages between popular nationalism and 'militarism' which were established during such years, especially in 1870–1, are held to have altered conceptions of military conflict in Germany for good (Nikolaus Buschmann, Frank Becker, Jakob Vogel). Here, I argue—on the contrary—that conscripts proved willing to go to war and civilians were prepared to support military intervention during the nineteenth century even though they remained uncertain of their governments' national or political objectives. Military conflict itself had become acceptable or, for some conscripts, volunteers, and civilians, desirable. The actuality of modern warfare in 1864–71, which saw masses of German troops subjected to new technologies of killing (breechloading rifles, machine guns, and long-range artillery with explosive shells), shook combatants' earlier expectations of warfare and destabilized national myths of the 'wars of unification' after 1871.

In the following analysis, I separate myths of war, which spread rapidly after the epochal events of the Napoleonic era, and expressions of national sentiment and the aspiration to form a nation-state, which were articulated by journalists and

---

[30] On similar processes elsewhere, see L. Peter, *Romances of War: Die Erinnerung an die Revolutions- und Napoleonischen Kriege in Großbritannien und Irland 1815–1945* (Paderborn, 2012).

[31] See the next section.

[32] On the significance of the Crimean War in the weakening of the Concert of Europe, see P. W. Schroeder, *Austria, Great Britain, and the Crimean War* (Ithaca, 1972). Schroeder argues that key elements of the Concert, as opposed to a defunct Holy Alliance, continued to exist until their destruction during the Crimean War. P. W. Schroeder, 'The Nineteenth-Century International System', *World Politics*, 39 (1986), 1–26. For the case made by Dieter Langewiesche, see footnote 35 of this chapter.

academics from the late eighteenth century onwards and which were turned into better defined political projects within associations and parties during the 1840s, 1850s, and 1860s.[33] What was most striking about the military conflicts and international crises after 1848 was the readiness of conscripts, volunteers, and their families to go to war (or, at least, their unwillingness to avoid the call-up or voice opposition), whether or not a conflict was perceived to be 'national'. Only the far-reaching mythologizing of war itself from the turn of the century onwards—and above all after 1813—can account for such readiness, given the clear, increasing, and unavoidable indications of the suffering caused by modern warfare, particularly in the decade or so after 1854.[34] Paradoxically, this open fear of war became most vocal in and after 1870–1, as national narratives of the conflict were being fashioned and disseminated. Jubilant national justifications of events, to which veterans contributed through the publication of letters and memoirs, could not banish contemporaries' simultaneous 'horror' of war.

THE HISTORIOGRAPHY OF WARFARE IN GERMANY

Recent histories of warfare in nineteenth-century Germany, although predicated on the assumption of a close relationship between war and the nation, have generally sought to qualify the case made by proponents of a German *Sonderweg* about the instrumentalization of nationalism and war-mongering.[35] The staging-posts of the historical debate about a putative 'special path' for Germany are well known, deriving from a dispute about the causes of the First World War (Fritz Fischer) and ending in a controversy about eliminationist anti-Semitism and the Holocaust

---

[33] I have explored the second set of developments in more depth in M. Hewitson, *Nationalism in Germany, 1848–1866: Revolutionary Nation* (Basingstoke, 2010).

[34] Although the Crimean War began in 1853, German or Austrian involvement seemed likely from 1854 onwards.

[35] See H. Schulze, *The Course of German Nationalism: From Frederick the Great to Bismarck, 1763–1867* (Cambridge, 1991), which is a translation of *Der Weg zum Nationalstaat*, originally published in 1985; and H.-U. Wehler, *The German Empire, 1871–1918* (Providence, RI, 1985), published as *Das Deutsche Kaiserreich 1871–1918* in 1973; H.-U. Wehler, *Deutsche Gesellschaftsgeschichte, 1849–1914* (Munich, 1995), 221–376, 873–85, 938–99, 1066–84, 1109–68; H.-U. Wehler, *Nationalismus. Geschichte, Formen, Folgen* (Munich, 2001); and H. A. Winkler, *Der lange Weg nach Westen* (Munich, 2000), vol. 1, 213–65. The studies, collaborative projects, and research students of Dieter Langewiesche have been important in qualifying the case made by advocates of a *Sonderweg*: D. Langewiesche, *Nation, Nationalismus und Nationalstaat in Deutschland und Europa* (Munich, 2000); D. Langewiesche, *Reich, Nation, Föderation* (Munich, 2008); D. Langewiesche, 'Zum Wandel von Krieg und Kriegslegitimation in der Neuzeit', *Journal of Modern European History*, 2 (2004), 5–27; D. Langewiesche, 'Eskalierte die Kriegsgewalt im Laufe der Geschichte?', in J. Baberowski (ed.), *Moderne Zeiten? Krieg, Revolution und Gewalt im 20. Jahrhundert* (Göttingen, 2006), 12–36; D. Langewiesche and N. Buschmann, '"Dem Vertilgungskriege Grenzen setzen". Kriegstypen des 19. Jahrhunderts und der deutsch-französische Krieg 1870/71', in D. Beyrau, M. Hochgeschwender, and D. Langewiesche (eds), *Formen des Krieges. Von der Antike bis zur Gegenwart*, 163–95; N. Buschmann and D. Langewiesche (eds), *Der Krieg in den Gründungsmythen europäischer Nationen und der USA* (Frankfurt, 2004).

(Daniel Goldhagen).[36] One of the most interesting versions of the case has been put forward by the historical sociologist Norbert Elias, who had grown up in the *Kaiserreich*. His thesis about increasing inhibition, the internalization of norms and domestic pacification, which I investigate in this series of studies, appeared to have been brought into question by the violent history of Germany in the twentieth century, which was reaching its apogee as the sociologist's seminal work *Über den Prozess der Zivilisation* was first published in 1939.[37] For this reason, Elias devoted much time to the study of his country of origin in a succession of essays and lectures, later published as *Studien über die Deutschen* (1989).[38] The essays saw the violence of the 1930s and 1940s as the culmination of a long historical process in Germany extending back to the nineteenth century.

The principal focus of *Studien über die Deutschen* is the 'breakdown of civilization' under the Nazis, which was unique in its scale and horror. 'The attempt to wipe out the entire population of Jews in the lands under German rule...was not by any means the only regression to barbarism in the civilized societies of the twentieth century', asserts the sociologist: 'Others could easily be pointed out. But of all these regressions, it was perhaps the deepest.'[39] National Socialism oversaw the removal of even 'the most minimum rules of civilized conduct', which had become typical of European societies, including during wartime: 'In the attitude of the National Socialists towards the Jews none of this survived. At least on a conscious level, the torment, suffering and death of Jews did not appear to mean more to them than that of flies.'[40] Thus, Elias no longer stresses the maintenance of bureaucratic routine and the mechanization of technological killing as he had in *Über den Prozess der Zivilisation*: during the Nazi era, that 'kernel of self-esteem which prevents the senseless torturing of enemies and allows identification with one's enemy', which had characterized modern wars, had been abandoned.[41] Instead, he points to the long-term causes which had led to the gradual undermining of civilization or had prevented its emergence. To put it another way, Elias's response to the challenge presented by the German case to his theory of civilization is to argue that the country was still in important respects uncivilized and that it was subjected to an

---

[36] On the Fischer debate and later Bielefeld-school analysis of the German Empire, see M. Jefferies, *Contesting the German Empire, 1871–1918* (Oxford, 2008), 7–46; A. Mombauer, *The Origins of the First World War: Controversies and Consensus* (London, 2002); D. Blackbourn and G. Eley, *The Peculiarities of German History* (Oxford, 1984). For more on the Goldhagen debate, see D. Goldhagen, *Hitler's Willing Executioners: Ordinary Germans and the Holocaust* (New York, 1996); C. Browning, *Ordinary Men: Reserve Battalion 101 and the Final Solution in Poland* (New York, 1992); C. Browning, *The Path to Genocide* (Cambridge, 1992). On the *Historikerstreit* of the 1980s, which preceded the Goldhagen affair, see P. Baldwin, *Hitler, the Holocaust and the Historians' Dispute* (Boston, 1990); G. Eley, 'Nazism, Politics and the Image of the Past: Thoughts on the West German Historikerstreit', *Past and Present*, 121 (1988), 171–208; R. Evans, *In Hitler's Shadow: West German Historians and the Attempt to Escape the Nazi Past* (New York, 1989); K. H. Jarausch, 'Removing the Nazi Stain? The Quarrel of the Historians', *German Studies Review*, 11 (1988), 285–301; special issue of *New German Critique*, 44 (1988).

[37] N. Elias, *The Civilising Process: The History of Manners* (New York, 1978), vol. 1, and N. Elias, *The Civilising Process: Power and Civility* (Oxford, 1982), vol. 2. Also, J. Fletcher, *Violence and Civilisation: An Introduction to the Work of Norbert Elias* (Oxford, 1997).

[38] Translated as N. Elias, *The Germans* (Cambridge, 1996).

[39] Ibid., 308.   [40] Ibid., 309.   [41] Ibid.

unusual set of circumstances which very slowly whittled away those elements of civilization already attained.

Germany supposedly lacked civilization, in comparison to other European countries, because of its historical legacy of division and internal conflict, the persistence of absolutist forms of government, the incomplete conversion of a warrior caste of Junkers into a courtly aristocracy, selective imitation of the nobility by the upper middle classes, an aversion to parliamentary democracy, and a yearning for a strong ruler. Domestically, this legacy helped to prevent the peaceful resolution of differences and the internalization of norms. Violent disputes between contesting parties were eradicated later and more partially under the Holy Roman Empire than in the centralizing monarchies of France and Britain. Pacification under such conditions was enforced externally by the state rather than internally through 'conscience' or 'reason'. Authoritarian government was preferred to self-government. 'Parliamentary states can only function among people who have, to a degree, learned to bear and deal with conflicts in their midst', writes Elias: 'Many Germans, however, in correspondence to their traditions of thinking and behaving, experienced conflicts and fights between social strata, the parliamentary struggles between different parties, as emotionally repellent or unbearable.'[42] Such feelings, together with 'the longing for external control by a strong ruler, which often grew stronger in critical situations', were 'closely bound up with the insecure standards of self-control which were passed on to the Germans by their traditions'.[43]

In particular, the middle classes, which in France and Britain had overseen the establishment of representative parliamentary government, had in Germany been excluded from aristocratic circles: 'So whereas in France and England a fusion of bourgeois morality and aristocratic good manners had occurred, in Germany the barrier between the two was much higher.' Consequently, 'the German national character was shaped far more by the middle classes', yet the latter remained 'uncivilized': 'The German super-ego and ego ideal always left the middle classes, the lower classes and the peasants more room for outbreaks of violence than the English or French patterns, for example.'[44] What was more, after German unification in 1871—the principal 'middle-class dream'—had been brought about 'under the leadership of a court and military aristocracy', much of the *Bürgertum* 'gave up the domestic struggle against the hegemony of the nobility' and 'acquiesced in their position as a social stratum of the second rank', imitating and exaggerating aristocratic belligerence and aggression.[45] The 'idealistic component of the German middle-class cultural tradition', which had been predominant at the turn of the nineteenth century and which included anti-aristocratic attitudes, 'began to ebb': 'In its place, there occurred in other segments of the middle class, especially the high civil service and the entire academic world, an adoption of aristocratic values, namely the values of a class with a strongly warlike tradition and which was orientated to the politics of international relations.'[46] 'In other words', Elias concludes, 'parts of the German middle class were assimilated into the higher-ranking stratum

---

[42] Ibid., 318.   [43] Ibid., 319.   [44] Elias, *Reflections*, 58.
[45] Elias, *The Germans*, 180.   [46] Ibid.

and made its warrior ethos their own.'⁴⁷ Because of this partial lack of civilization, the threshold of violence in Germany—largely as a result of domestic causes—was lower than elsewhere in Europe.

Germany's international position, and the relationship between its position abroad and the formation of a 'national character' and 'super-ego', led to the erosion and eventual breakdown of civilization.⁴⁸ Such erosion derived above all from the late formation in Germany of a nation-state, which in turn was manifested in the fragility of 'national pride', the absolute nature of loyalty to the nation, the fanatical exclusiveness of a 'we-ideal' as a secular form of self-worth, and a heightened fear of enemies as a consequence of relative weakness. The inhibitions and moral principles typically associated with civilization—particularly those preventing violence—were frequently superseded by the irresistible arguments of 'national interest'. National Socialism, as the most extreme form of exclusive, expansionist nationalism, was popular because it restored the possibility of greatness to a recently unified nation-state which was, in terms of its resources, in decline, compared to other powerful states. 'The Nazis revived among the Germans the belief that they were still a first-rank power and had the necessary resources that, like the medieval emperors, Germany's masters would rule over wide stretches of Europe', proposes Elias: 'The degree of oppression, violence and barbarism which they used corresponded to the degree of effort which was necessary to give Germany once more the appearance of greatness and to avoid the shock of discovery that the days of German pre-eminence and the dream of a Reich were over.'⁴⁹

Such a fanatical sense of a national mission, which tended to override individual or collective moral scruples, assumed a prominent place in domestic politics during the 1920s, after the Weimar Republic was seen by a significant proportion of the middle and upper classes to have colluded with the enemy in Germany's defeat in 1918. The *Freikorps* and other paramilitary groups are treated by Elias as the forerunners of the Nazis—and as a sign that the main defences of civilization had already been breached as a consequence of long-term causes. Admittedly, these long-term, 'de-civilizing' processes had been brought to a head by the destruction of the First World War and the collapse of the German Empire. The critical changes, however, had taken place during—and to a lesser extent before—the nineteenth century. 'If one inquires into the conditions in a society under which civilized forms of behaviour and conscience begin to dissolve, one sees [that]...it is a process of brutalisation and dehumanisation which in relatively civilized societies always requires considerable time', concludes the sociologist: 'In such societies, terror and horror hardly ever manifest themselves without a fairly long social process in which conscience decomposes.'⁵⁰ The causes of violence in Germany were, therefore, largely domestic, with unrealistic national ambitions and inadequate civilizing constraints permitting perpetrators to commit violent crimes and atrocities at home and abroad.

---

⁴⁷ Ibid.
⁴⁸ Accordingly, Elias's chapter on the Nazis and the 'breakdown of civilization' in *The Germans* concentrates on the impact of Germany's international weakness and lack of a nation-state on the construction of national identity.
⁴⁹ Ibid., 402.   ⁵⁰ Ibid., 196.

Historians have been eager, over the last three decades, to qualify or reject the most significant elements of this case about Germany's nineteenth- and early twentieth-century 'special path'. Many have emphasized the diversity of the political traditions and social milieux of the German lands and the continuity of their traditions. In the realm of military violence, continuity was purportedly—according to Ute Planert's analysis—the result of the maintenance of existing practices of recruitment, deployment, supply, and depredation within the German armies of the Napoleonic campaigns and—according to Ute Frevert's influential account—it was a consequence of the *Bürgertum's* continuing scepticism about the army and military service after 1815, effectively insulating it from the risks of war.[51] In Germany, the Hohenzollern monarchy remained an exception. Here, the 'strange duty' of military service 'imposed by the state did eventually become largely accepted, to the extent that people even found it to have positive aspects, and advantages in social, political and gender-specific terms'.[52] 'In *Vormärz* Prussia, a rhetoric developed that had a sustained effect—a rhetoric praising military service not purely as a civic duty, but vindicating it as a means of social integration and cultural socialization', Frevert contends, in keeping with much of the existing literature on the army as a putative 'school' for loyal subjects, active citizens, or, even, a German nation.[53] In the rest of Germany, the question, which inspired 'many heated debates on the pros and cons of various military models' and which engendered 'fierce and profound disagreements' until the late 1860s, was whether there were 'any viable alternatives to the Prussian model of universal conscription across all social classes'.[54] The consensus in the third Germany—the lands outside Prussia and Austria—was affirmative, despite numerous internal differences of opinion, leading to a rejection of 'the Prussian model' and an insistence on the medium-sized and small states' 'own system of conscription and substitutions'.[55] After a 'brief revolutionary intermezzo', 'all the states permitting substitution [paying for a replacement to do military service] prior to 1848 retained it in the 1850s and 1860s', filing away 'the idea of an armed citizenry'.[56] Doubts about '"the" people's readiness to take up arms' lingered on, with the idea of a '*Volksbewaffnung*', 'that notion evoked so persistently and with such pathos', reduced to a rhetorical device.[57]

In a certain sense, the eighteenth-century critique of the military appeared to have survived in the majority of German states during the nineteenth century, limiting their ability and willingness to countenance armed conflict. Even in

---

[51] For the first set of arguments about continuity, see M. Hewitson, *Absolute War*; U. Planert, *Der Mythos vom Befreiungskrieg*; U. Planert, 'Innovation or Evolution? The French Wars in Military History', in R. Chickering and S. Förster (eds), *War in an Age of Revolution, 1775–1815* (Cambridge, 2010), 69–84; U. Frevert, *Nation in Barracks*.

[52] U. Frevert, *Nation in Barracks*, 47.

[53] Ibid., 70–82. W. Wette, *Militarismus in Deutschland*, 39; like Frevert, Markus Ingenlath, M. Ingenlath, *Mentale Aufrüstung. Mlitarisierungstendenzen in Frankreich und Deutschland vor dem Ersten Weltkrieg* (Frankfurt, 1998), 59–60, shows how such aims existed and how, even in Prussia, 'the middle-class striving for privileges' had a significant effect, exempting many sons from full military service as one-year volunteers.

[54] U. Frevert, *Nation in Barracks*, 101.

[55] Ibid., 102.   [56] Ibid., 132.   [57] Ibid.

Prussia, 'criticism of the army' and 'the quest for alternative policy models—that *leitmotif* of early nineteenth-century German military history'—had been vocal in 1848 and was 'still widespread in the 1850s'.[58] The wars of the 1860s, during which Prussian deputies 'made their peace' with the army 'at the latest by 1866–7', therefore 'represented a tectonic shift in domestic and military policy'.[59] Elsewhere, 'it took the Franco-Prussian war in 1870–1 to finally put an end to this incessant wrangling in the southern German states over their internal policies on the form and purpose of their military organizations,' concludes Frevert:

> a military institution scrupulously avoided by the middle classes and exclusively reserved for lower-class men... no longer reflected the *Zeitgeist*. With the substitution system abolished, the educated and propertied members of the middle classes would also see their male offspring having to serve personally in the army; they too would have to pass through the same 'training school for the entire nation' that their Prussian peers had been attending since 1814.[60]

The relationship between criticism of the army, on the one hand, and armed readiness and belligerence, on the other, is not fully clarified in Frevert's account, yet the latter are often treated as if they are merely rhetorical.

Given the persisting diversity of military organization, particularistic affiliations, and competing forms of 'federative' nationalism, historians of nineteenth-century German conflicts have devoted much of their attention to the mechanisms which made war possible. Their conclusions have underlined the role of national sentiment, symbolism, stereotyping, and antagonism in the justification and prosecution of military conflicts. Thus, in his study of 'encirclement' (*Einkreisung*) and a 'brotherhood of arms' (*Waffenbruderschaft*) in public representations of war and the nation between 1850 and 1871, Nikolaus Buschmann examines 'the nationalization of religious depictions of war', 'dying for the fatherland', 'threat and enmity', 'power and territory', 'national–political yearnings', and 'racial struggle'.[61] The processes which he describes purportedly occurred during conflicts in which most German states were involved directly (1866 and 1870–1) and those in which many were not belligerents (1848–51, 1859, 1864). Buschmann's findings supplement and modify those of Michael Jeismann's study of a '*Vaterland der Feinde*', which examines long-standing stereotypes of the 'enemy' from the revolutionary wars to the First World War, and Jörn Leonhard's analysis of the articulation and semantics of belligerence and nationalism from 1750 to 1914.[62] The implication of such arguments is both that military conflicts helped to overcome national differences and that national sentiment, however heterogeneous before the outbreak of hostilities, helped to legitimize, maintain, and commemorate the war effort. Even scholars such as Jakob Vogel and Frank Becker, who strive to distinguish popular or 'folklore' militarism from soldiers' and civilians' experiences and ideologies of war,

---

[58] Ibid., 149.   [59] Ibid.   [60] Ibid., 140–1.
[61] N. Buschmann, *Einkreisung und Waffenbruderschaft*, 114–19, 174–315.
[62] M. Jeismann, *Das Vaterland der Feinde. Studien zum nationalen Feindbegriff und Selbstverständnis in Deutschland und Frankreich 1792–1918* (Stuttgart, 1992); J. Leonhard, *Bellizismus und Nation. Kriegsdeutung und Nationsbestimmung in Europa und den Vereinigten Staaten 1750–1914* (Munich, 2008).

continue to stress the mutually sustaining relationship between the depiction of military conflicts and national mythology.[63] Becker's 'synthetic militarism' is founded on the premise that

> the Prussian–German military system of 1870–71 constitutes a synthesis in which the concept of the arming of the nation is *'aufgehoben'* in the threefold meaning of this concept in Hegel:... in the sense of 'overcome' but at the same time in the sense of 'preserved' and 'raised up'; that is, brought to a form of existence which helps to translate the original form into one of a new, elevated and improved quality.[64]

The 'polyvalence' of such militarism did not detract from the idea that 'the nation was created, not in war, but already on the threshold of war', making 'the military confrontation with the western neighbour the first common action of an awakened Germany'.[65] It also encompassed 'a second popular scheme of interpretation'— which was 'omnipresent' in the 'culture of representation of the Franco-German War'—resting on the analogy of 1870–1 and the 'wars of liberation'.[66]

In some respects, such depictions of the wars of unification are the opposite—or a mirror image—of current studies of the revolutionary and Napoleonic conflicts, which associate a *lack* of nationalism in the late eighteenth and early nineteenth centuries with continuity in the prosecution and representation of war. Many historians of war in the second half of the nineteenth century might be inclined to agree—in contrast to those of the late eighteenth and early nineteenth centuries—with Otto Dann's contention that national 'wars of freedom' had become one of the most successful political recipes of the modern era.[67] Nonetheless, both sets of scholars remain wedded to frameworks of investigation which assume close ties to have existed between war and nationalism. The continuation of eighteenth-century forms of warfare and military organization in the 1800s went alongside—and was tied to—traditional attitudes to authority, 'patriotic' support for individual states, and limited discussion of a German nation. The advent of modern warfare and the

[63] J. Vogel, *Nationen im Gleichschritt*, 45–91, 210–26; J. Vogel, '"En revenant de la revue". Militärfolklore und Folkloremilitarismus in Deutschland und Frankreich 1871–1914', *Österreichische Zeitschrift für Geschichtswissenschaften*, 9 (1998), 9–30; J. Vogel, 'Der "Folklorenmilitarismus" und seine zeitgenössische Kritik—Deutschland und Frankreich 1871–1914', in W. Wette (ed.), *Militarismus in Deutschland*, 277–92; F. Becker, *Bilder von Krieg und Nation*; F. Becker, '2. September 1870 / 18. Januar 1871: Selbstbestätigung einer labilen Nation?', in E. Conze and T. Nicklas (eds), *Tage Deutscher Geschichte. Von der Reformation bis zur Wiedervereinigung* (Stuttgart, 2004), 156–76. See also M. Ingenlath, *Mentale Aufrüstung*, 86–134, and B. Ziemann, 'Sozialmilitarismus und militärische Sozialisation im deutschen Kaiserreich 1870–1914. Ergebnisse und Desiderate in der Revision eines Geschichtsbildes', *Geschichte in Wissenschaft und Unterricht*, 53 (2002), 487–504.

[64] F. Becker, 'Synthetischer Militarismus. Die Einigungskriege und der Stellenwert des Militärischen in der deutschen Gesellschaft', in M. Epkenhans and G. P. Groß (eds), *Das Militär und der Aufbruch in die Moderne 1860 bis 1890. Armeen, Marinen und der Wandel von Politik, Gesellschaft und Wirtschaft in Europa, den USA sowie Japan* (Munich, 2003), 125–41.

[65] Ibid., 130.   [66] Ibid., 135.

[67] O. Dann, 'Der deutsche Bürger wird Soldat', in R. Steinweg (ed.), *Lehren aus der Geschichte?* (Frankfurt, 1990), 72. For more on this debate, see M. Hewitson, 'On War and Peace: German Conceptions of Conflict, 1792–1815', *Historical Journal*, 57 (2014), 450–1.

premonition of revolutionary conflicts from the mid-nineteenth century onwards were connected to novel types of national justification and demonization in the political and public spheres. 'The short, less-than-two-hundred-year-long era of limited war in Europe seemed to be over, and many claim to be able to foresee in the "*Volkskrieg*" of the late eighteenth century the "total" war of the twentieth', Dieter Langewiesche and Nikolaus Buschmann have written: 'We argue against them that, despite all the nationalization of societies in nineteenth-century Europe, most wars—also those from which new nation-states emerged—were conducted as limited state wars but were perceived by nations as people's wars (*Volkskriege*). That changed them. They threatened to escape state control.'[68] This study insists on the analytical separation of war and nationalism, contending that many instances of the romanticization of military conflict in the nineteenth century occurred independently of processes of national justification and political unification. The approach favoured here does not deny the manifold connections, in specific historical circumstances, between the waging and remembrance of wars, on the one hand, and national disputes and appeals to the nation, on the other. It merely treats the imagination, representation, and commemoration of nineteenth-century wars and a German nation-state as potentially separable.

REASSESSING NINETEENTH-CENTURY CONFLICTS

Since the 'vanishing points' of German history, which still structure the field and dictate the issues scholars debate, 'belong to the twentieth century' (whether located in 1914, 1918, 1933, 1939, 1945, or 1989), in Helmut Walser Smith's opinion, historians of wars and military violence in particular have tended to ask twentieth-century questions about nineteenth-century events.[69] In respect of the Second World War, they have—until recently—focused on a minority of 'perpetrators' and their atrocities rather than on the majority of 'non-perpetrators', or soldiers who more or less carry out orders and continue to fight, despite rapidly changing and often deteriorating conditions which are completely different from those they had experienced as civilians.[70] Scholars' emphasis on killing, war crimes, ideology, the role of occupation or colonization, and overlap between domestic and foreign

---

[68] D. Langewiesche and N. Buschmann, '"Dem Vertilgungskriege Grenzen setzen', in D. Beyrau, M. Hochgeschwender, and D. Langewiesche (eds), *Formen des Krieges*, 163.

[69] H. W. Smith, 'The Vanishing Point of German History', in H. W. Smith, *The Continuities of German History: Nation, Religion and Race across the Long Nineteenth Century* (Cambridge, 2008), 16.

[70] This emphasis has altered considerably in recent years, as soldiers' experiences have been studied in a similar way to those of the First World War: F. Römer, *Kameraden. Die Wehrmacht von innen* (Munich, 2012); S. Neitzel and H. Welzer, *Soldaten. Protokolle vom Kämpfen, Töten und Sterben* (Frankfurt, 2011); U. Herrmann and R.-D. Müller (eds), *Junge Soldaten im Zweiten Weltkrieg. Kriegserfahrungen als Lebenserfahrungen* (Munich, 2010); C. Rass, '*Menschenmaterial*'. *Deutsche Soldaten an der Ostfront* (Paderborn, 2003); K. Latzel, *Deutsche Soldaten—nationalsozialistische Krieg? Kriegserlebnis, Kriegserfahrung 1939–1945* (Paderborn, 1998). Understandably, residues of older debates about killing and war crimes remain: see, for instance, C. Hartmann, J. Hürter, and U. Jureit (eds), *Verbrechen der Wehrmacht. Bilanz einer Debatte* (Munich, 2005); F. Römer, *Der Kommissarbefehl. Wehrmacht und NS-Verbrechen an der Ostfront 1941/42* (Paderborn, 2008).

threats and transgressions helps them make sense of the Second World War, but it can hinder their understanding of nineteenth-century conflicts. True, historians of the First World War have, in addition to such questions, continued to ask their own about conscripts' and volunteers' 'endurance' and 'breakdown', highlighting the atrociousness of war instead of individual or collective atrocities.[71] Yet many of their emphases, too, seem out of place or marginal in a nineteenth-century context.[72]

The questions addressed in this study are closer to those asked by historians of the American Civil War. Given the nature of mass warfare from the revolutionary wars onwards and modern warfare, with the introduction of new types of weaponry after the 1850s, why did conscripts and civilians go to war with so little opposition or resistance, why did they carry on fighting, and what was the long-term impact of their participation in military conflicts? It is worth enquiring whether something analogous to Michael Barton's notion of 'character' or Gerald Linderman's concept of 'courage' played a part, where a 'constellation of values' including those of duty, honour, godliness, chivalry, and masculinity initially permitted courageous acts, or 'heroic action undertaken without fear', at least on the part of educated middle-class volunteers.[73] For such men and for others, how important was the cause for which they were fighting and what did it consist of?[74] Critics of Linderman have pointed out that his sources were limited—fifty-seven records from middle-class volunteers out of 2.64 million men in arms—and that his conclusions are inapplicable to the majority of troops.[75] Partly in response to criticisms of this kind, James McPherson's *For Cause and Comrades* uses a sample of 1,076 men: 647 Union and 429 Confederate soldiers, of whom 24 per cent were immigrants and 9 per cent were African American.[76] Did the causes for which they fought continue to motivate soldiers until the end of the conflict or were they replaced by varying phases of disillusionment, as troops were worn down by the firepower of breech-loading rifles and the randomness of

---

[71] For an influential extension of the literature on atrocities to the First World War, see J. Horne and A. Kramer, *German Atrocities, 1914: A History of Denial* (New Haven, 2001). On endurance, see A. Watson, *Enduring the Great War: Combat, Morale and Collapse in the German and British Armies, 1914–1918* (Cambridge, 2008); on breakdown and the psychiatry of war, see P. Lerner, *Hysterical Men: War, Psychiatry and the Politics of Trauma in Germany, 1890–1930* (Ithaca, NY, 2003).

[72] It is worth noting that much of the current literature on combat motivation and morale in the First World War has been heavily influenced by US studies of the Second World War: A. Watson and P. Porter, 'Bereaved and Aggrieved: Combat Motivation and the Ideology of Sacrifice in the First World War', *Historical Research*, 83 (2010), 146–64; A. Watson, 'Culture and Combat in the Western World, 1900–1945', *Historical Journal*, 51 (2008), 529–46; A. Watson, 'Self-Deception and Survival: Mental Coping Strategies on the Western Front, 1914–18', *Journal of Contemporary History*, 41 (2006), 247–68.

[73] G. F. Linderman, *Embattled Courage: The Experience of Combat in the American Civil War* (New York, 1987), 17. M. Barton, *Goodmen: The Character of Civil War Soldiers* (University Park, PA, 1981).

[74] J. M. McPherson, *What They Fought For, 1861–1865* (Baton Rouge, LA, 1994); J. M. McPherson, *For Cause and Comrades: Why Men Fought in the Civil War* (Oxford, 1997).

[75] Even positive reviews pointed this out: for instance, James Kirby Martin, *Journal of Social History*, 22 (1989), 559–62.

[76] See also J. McPherson, *The Negro's Civil War: How American Blacks Felt and Acted during the War for the Union* (New York, 2003).

death resulting from the exploding shells of distant artillery?[77] The evaluation of the longer-term effects of such combat has proved more difficult than for that of twentieth- and twenty-first-century conflicts for which more evidence exists, including extensive psychiatric records.[78] All of these questions and difficulties apply to the nineteenth-century wars in which German soldiers participated.[79] In addition to an assessment of the conditions of war itself, which—as Mark Neely, Jr, has pointed out—remain contested, they entail the investigation of experiences, emotions, psychological impact, memory, history, autobiography, writing, visual representation, and public debate.[80]

This study examines such sensations, states of mind, and forms of inscription in order to assess how subjects' conceptions of war changed during and after two major periods of military conflict (1792–1815 and 1864–71) and during the long and uneven time of 'peace' which followed them. It is based on soldiers' published accounts of wars (memoirs, diaries, and correspondence), which are treated as contributions to wider public discussions and disputes about the nature of warfare. As such, the accounts can be interpreted in the same way as other interventions in the public sphere, with due attention given to the intentions of the author, the discursive context of the writing, its production, distribution, readership, and reception. Yet these sources also refer to, and often derive from, a swirl of individual experiences, strong feelings, physiological reactions or 'nerves', nightmares, 'joy', and 'horror' which, in the words of many veterans and some civilians, they would never forget. Such responses appear to have been typical of most modern conflicts. 'Those who haven't lived through the experience may sympathize as they read, the way one sympathizes with the hero of a novel or a play, but they certainly will never understand, as one cannot understand the inexplicable', wrote one German soldier after the Second World War.[81] Many of his readers, though, had experienced similar conditions and many more felt that they should get to know of them in order to comprehend what had just befallen them—as citizens of a warring state—or what might threaten them in future. War during an era of conscription demanded the greatest sacrifice—of life, limb, or occupation, as a result of wounding—and it occasioned the greatest costs, accounting for between 34 per cent and 82 per cent of central government expenditure in Prussia (and Germany after 1871) from 1792 to 1888.[82] It seemed imperative to contemporaries to understand what

---

[77] James Lee McDonough, *American Historical Review*, 94 (1989), 219, agrees with Linderman's account of the transition, as soldiers became hardened.

[78] See especially M. S. Micale and P. Lerner (eds), *Traumatic Pasts: History, Psychiatry and Trauma in the Modern Age, 1870–1930* (Cambridge, 2001), 1–30.

[79] Some questions and hypotheses stem from research into wars in which Germans participated: for example, John A. Lynn's outline in *Bayonets of the Republic: Motivation and Tactics in the Army of Revolutionary France, 1791–1794* (Boulder, CO, 1996), of three phases of initial patriotism and ideological commitment, a sustaining phase, and the phase of combat itself, in which group loyalty was more important than ideology.

[80] M. Neely, Jr, *The Civil War and the Limits of Destruction* (Cambridge, MA, 2007).

[81] Cited in S. Hynes, *The Soldiers' Tale* (London, 1997), 2.

[82] M. Mann, *The Sources of Social Power: The Rise of Classes and Nation-States, 1760–1914* (Cambridge, 1986), vol. 2, 373. As a proportion of total government spending, the figure was lower, but it was also offset by debt repayments, which Mann does not tabulate but which were increased disproportionately by wars.

military conflicts were really like. For later historians, the comprehension of what veterans meant and how they were understood by readers rests on an understanding of their experiences, emotions, and memories, not merely as literary narratives or visual representations, but as entangled bundles of feelings, images, and words, and as lacunae, silences, and emptiness.

The orthodox way to think about the effects of wartime experiences is either as an individual 'trauma', replicated across a cohort of soldiers, survivors, or civilians, or as an object of memory and commemoration.[83] Some of the symptoms described by combatants during the wars of unification resemble, in a modified form, those of troops showing signs of trauma in the Second World War or Post-Traumatic Stress Disorder—a term officially recognized in the United States in 1980—in the Vietnam War and Gulf War, but their afterlife during the reintegration of soldiers into civilian society was not studied after 1870–1 and is difficult to gauge.[84] Post-war memories and commemorations in nineteenth-century Germany have been studied in detail, as an extension of the so-called 'memory boom' of the late twentieth and early twenty-first centuries.[85] The epilogue of Karen Hagemann's recent book *Revisiting Prussia's Wars against Napoleon: History, Culture and Memory*

[83] For a range of cases, see H. Berding, K. Heller, and W. Speitkamp (eds), *Krieg und Erinnerung. Fallstudien zum 19. und 20. Jahrhundert* (Göttingen, 2000). Also, P. Fritzsche, *Stranded in the Present: Modern Time and the Melancholy of History* (Cambridge, MA, 2004).

[84] See Chapter 13, note 178. On the Second World War, see S. Goltermann, *Die Gesellschaft der Überlebenden. Deutsche Kriegsheimkehrer und ihre Gewalterfahrungen im Zweiten Weltkrieg* (Munich, 2009); P. Fritzsche, 'Volkstümliche Erinnerung und deutsche Identität nach dem Zweiten Weltkrieg', in K. H. Jarausch and M. Sabrow (eds), *Verletztes Gedächtnis* (Frankfurt, 2002), 75–97; A. Förster and B. Beck, 'Post-Traumatic Stress Disorder and World War II: Can a Psychiatric Concept Help Us Understand Postwar Society?', in R. Bessel and D. Schumann (eds), *Life after Death: Approaches to a Cultural and Social History of Europe during the 1940s and 1950s* (Cambridge, 2003), 15–38; B. Shephard, *A War of Nerves: Soldiers and Psychiatrists, 1914–1994* (London, 2000); H. Binneveld, *From Shellshock to Combat Stress: A Comparative History of Military Psychiatry* (Amsterdam, 1997). On Vietnam, see R. J. Lifton, *Home from the War: Learning from Vietnam Veterans* (Boston, 1973); M. Sturken, *Tangled Memories: The Vietnam War, the Aids Epidemic and the Politics of Remembering* (Berkeley, CA, 1997); A. P. Haas, *Wounds of War: The Psychological Aftermath of Combat in Vietnam* (New York, 1984); J. Shay, *Achilles in Vietnam: Combat Trauma and the Undoing of Character* (New York, 1994). On recent wars, including the Gulf War, see A. Young, *The Harmony of Illusions: Inventing Post-Traumatic Stress Disorder* (Princeton, NJ, 1995); R. Leys, *Trauma: A Genealogy* (Chicago, 2000); R. J. McNally, *Remembering Trauma* (Cambridge, 2003).

[85] Again, many of the models and assumptions have been transferred from the literature on the Second World War, some of which combines the study of trauma, memory, and history: see Andreas Huyssen, 'Trauma and Memory: A New Imaginary of Temporality', in J. Bennett and R. Kennedy (eds), *World Memory* (New York, 2003), 16–29; R. N. Lebov, W. Kansteiner, and C. Fogu (eds), *The Politics of Memory in Postwar Europe* (Durham, 2006); N. Frei and V. Knigge (eds), *Verbrechen erinnern. Die Auseinandersetzung mit Holocaust und Völkermord* (Munich, 2002); P. Lagrou, *The Legacy of Nazi Occupation: Patriotic Memory and National Recovery in Western Europe, 1945–1965* (Cambridge, 2000); R. G. Moeller, *War Stories: The Search for a Usable Past in the Federal Republic of Germany* (Berkeley, 2001); B. Niven (ed.), *Germans as Victims: Remembering the Past in Contemporary Germany* (New York, 2006); A. Assmann, 'Von kollektiver Gewalt zu gemeinsamer Zukunft. Vier Modelle für den Umgang mit traumatischer Vergangenheit', in K. Lingen (ed.), *Kriegserfahrung und nationale Identität in Europa nach 1945. Erinnerung, Säuberungsprozesse und nationales Gedächtnis* (Paderborn: Schöningh, 2009), 42–51; A. Assmann, 'On the (In)Compatibility of Guilt and Suffering in German Memory', *German Life and Letters*, 59 (2006), 187–200; S. Behrenbeck, 'Between Pain and Silence: Remembering the Victims of Violence in Germany after 1949', in R. Bessel and D. Schumann (eds), *Life after Death*, 37–64.

is, accordingly, subtitled 'Historicizing War and Memory, 2013—1813—1913'.[86] It starts with a three-page description of the bi-centennial anniversary celebrations of the battle of Leipzig, before going back to 1813, then on to 1913, in order to historicize and contextualize the 'interplay of factors that shaped the contested memories of Germany's and Prussia's wars against Napoleon and their trans-formations'.[87] Through an investigation of practices of commemoration, the literary market, history-writing, the publication of memoirs and novels in the long nineteenth century, the volume—like others of its kind—'explores how competing discourses and cultural practices influenced both historical events and the percep-tion and collective memory of them, how these memories changed over time and which factors influenced the changes'.[88] Its theoretical and methodological under-pinnings rest on the work of Aleida Assmann.[89]

The differentiation of overlapping 'formats' and media of memory which Assmann has outlined is itself founded on Maurice Halbwachs's notion of 'collective memory' and Pierre Nora's distinction between the past, memory, and history.[90] The underlying purpose of much of this work, which has focused above all on post-war Europe (and especially Germany), has been to show that memories are 'living' and contestable sets of assumptions, ideas, and images, entangled in the controversies of art, history, and politics.[91] Whereas Nora had attempted to reveal the antithetical workings of history and memory, as the quest for 'objective' historical knowledge banished the mystery, biases, meaningfulness, and individuality of personal recollections, Assmann has sought to demonstrate their continuing symbiosis.[92] 'Over the last two decades, our approach to the past has become ever more complex and controversial', she writes in an essay on 'History, Memory and the Genre of Testimony':

[86] K. Hagemann, *Revisiting Prussia's Wars against Napoleon*, 397–416.

[87] Ibid., 399.

[88] Ibid., 22. See also A. Forrest, E. François, and K. Hagemann (eds), *War Memories: The Revolutionary and Napoleonic Wars in Modern European Culture* (Basingstoke, 2012).

[89] In particular, A. Assmann, *Erinnerungsräume. Formen und Wandlungen des kulturellen Gedächtnisses* (Munich, 1999).

[90] The German literary critic repeatedly acknowledges her debt to Nora: for instance, starting with a reconsideration of the French historian's work in A. Assmann, *Erinnerungsräume*, 11. See also A. Assmann, 'Four Formats of Memory: From Individual to Collective Constructions of the Past', in C. Emden and D. Midgley (eds), *Cultural Memory and Historical Consciousness in the German-Speaking World since 1500* (Bern, 2004), 20–37; A. Assmann, 'Texts, Traces, Trash: The Changing Media of Cultural Memory', *Representations*, 56 (1996), 123–34.

[91] A. Assmann, 'Wem gehört die Geschichte? Fakten und Fiktionen in der neueren deutschen Erinnerungsliteratur', *Internationales Archiv für Sozialgeschichte der deutschen Literatur*, 36 (2011), 213–25; A. Assmann, 'On the (In)Compatibility of Guilt and Suffering in German Memory', *German Life and Letters*, 59 (2006), 187–200; A. Assmann, 'Two Forms of Resentment: Jean Améry, Martin Walser and German Memorial Culture', *New German Critique*, 90 (2003), 123–33. Also, A. Erll and A. Nünning (eds), *A Companion to Cultural Memory Studies* (Berlin, 2010); C. Gudehus (ed.), *Gedächtnis und Erinnerung. Ein interdisziplinäres Handbuch* (Stuttgart, 2010); C. Cornelißen, 'Was heißt Erinnerungskultur? Begriff, Methoden, Perspektiven', *Geschichte in Wissenschaft und Unterricht*, 52 (2003), 548–63.

[92] P. Nora, 'General Introduction: Between Memory and History', in P. Nora (ed.), *Realms of Memory: Rethinking the French Past* (New York, 1996), vol. 1, 1–20.

One of the reasons for this development in the social and cultural sphere is the continuous impact of the Holocaust and the experience of living in the shadow of a historical event that in many ways maintains its presence. The Holocaust, it turns out, is an event both in history and memory.[93]

Thus, Saul Friedländer, one of the main historians of the Holocaust and himself a survivor, has acknowledged that memory 'is the initiating impulse for the reconstruction of the past in general and for the Holocaust in particular'.[94] Despite warning against the conflation of memories, public memory, and history, Friedländer had published his own memoir, *Quand vient le souvenir*, in 1979.[95] For Assmann, such examples are proof that 'history and memory...are no longer considered to be rivals and more and more are accepted as complementary modes of reconstructing and relating to the past'.[96] Individuals, with their unique, experiential, and embodied memories, verbalize or visualize their autobiographical memories and 'become part of an intersubjective symbolic system', akin to Halbwachs' definition of 'collective memories' deriving from 'social frames'.[97] In theory, 'formats of memory' as 'collective representations of the past' are multifarious and overlapping, taking the form of individual memories, social memories (or generational ones, with a 'common frame of beliefs, values, habits and attitudes' resting on the witnessing of 'the same incisive historical events'), cultural memories ('media of memory, forms of transmission and techniques of storing information'), and political memories ('the role of memory on the level of ideology formation,...collective identity formation and political action').[98] In practice, a focus on memory has led to the neglect of politics and a preoccupation with Nora's history of *lieux de mémoire*, in keeping with Assmann's 'interesting' observation that the term 'ideology', 'after a period of heavy usage in the 1960s and 1970s,...has dropped from contemporary discourse': 'As it declined and disappeared, the term collective memory rose to take its place.'[99]

Ideology is largely forward-looking and memory is backward-looking. This book investigates a representative sample of the hundreds of thousands of conscripts' and volunteers' individual experiences and memories of seismic sets of conflicts, comparing and linking them to official histories and other representations of war. Its focus, however, is wider, encompassing the panoply of actions, discourses, policies, and political debates which affected when, how, and why nineteenth-century Germans' conceptions of war altered.[100] War, after all, did not belong to the past,

---

[93] A. Assmann, 'History, Memory and the Genre of Testimony', *Poetics Today*, 27 (2006), 261–2.

[94] S. Friedländer, 'Im Angesicht der "Endlösung". Die Entwicklung des öffentlichen Gedächtnisses und die Verantwortung des Historikers', in D. Borchmeyer and H. Kiesel (eds), *Das Judentum im Spiegel seiner kulturellen Umwelten* (Neckargemünd, 2002), 207–23.

[95] Ibid. S. Friedländer, *Quand vient le souvenir* (Paris, 1979). See also S. Friedländer, *Memory, History and the Extermination of the Jews in Europe* (Bloomington, IN, 1993).

[96] A. Assmann, 'History, Memory and the Genre of Testimony', 264.

[97] A. Assmann, 'Transformations between History and Memory', *Social Research*, 75 (2008), 50–1.

[98] A. Assmann, 'Four Formats of Memory', 20–31.

[99] A. Assmann, 'Transformations between History and Memory', 53.

[100] For a critique of recent works on memory and history, see A. Confino, 'Collective Memory and Cultural History: Problems of Method', *American Historical Review*, 102 (1997), 1386–403.

but loomed over the future, menacing the lives of subjects and offering the prospect of renewal and change. The army remained the largest institution of the state and was the biggest item in the budget. Military service, the culture of the regiments, army reform, shifting strategies, technology, domestic policing, revolution, international crisis, and the reportage of foreign wars all affected nineteenth-century subjects' imagination of war in the broadest sense. Most commentators agreed that the states' system, even if not an international anarchy, was voluntary and precarious, permitting and sanctioning destructive wars. For Friedrich Gentz, one of the conservative architects of the international order of the 'restoration', the system was intended only to avoid 'constant and great danger and violent shocks'.[101] After 1848, as wars between Great Powers, revolution, and civil war were played out on an international stage, 'the dynamic basic law of the state order'—in the words of Ludwig August von Rochau, the liberal advocate of *'Realpolitik'*—appeared undeniable.[102] War posed a threat to individual persons and to states. It was a matter of critical importance to governments, to high politics, to public opinion, and to the private lives of citizens and their families. How contemporaries' understanding and visions of war had changed depended on a myriad of memories, emotions, experiences, policies, institutions, events, and media, the interactions and transformations of which occurred—and can only be made sense of—over a long period, involving multiple generations. Here, I aim to examine those interactions in order to explain the most important shifts of contemporaries' attitudes during an era of a long but deceptive peace and during periods of 'mass' or 'modern' warfare.

---

[101] F. v. Gentz, 'Fragmente aus der neuesten Geschichte des politischen Gleichgewichts in Europa' (1806), in F. v. Gentz, *Ausgewählte Schriften*, ed. W. Weick (Stuttgart, 1836–8), vol. 4, 42–3.
[102] L. A. v. Rochau, *Grundsätze der Realpolitik* (Frankfurt, 1972), 26. The first volume was published in 1853.

THE ROMANCE OF WAR, 1820–64

1

Histories of Conflict

Veterans' and civilians' memories of the revolutionary and Napoleonic campaigns shaped their image of war after 1815 but they were soon obscured—not least because few were published before 1830 (only nineteen memoirs and autobiographies according to Karen Hagemann)—by a welter of official or patriotic histories, heroic cults, military traditions, and dynastic commemorations and distortions of the reality of combat.[1] The historical imagery and narrative of the 'wars of freedom' or 'liberation' constituted part of a wider history of warfare which served to make military conflicts seem natural or inevitable. In the eighteenth century, this historical understanding of war, which was shaped by publicists and writers of all kinds not merely by university historians, had been contested, with proponents of patriotic struggles such as Johann Wilhelm von Archenholz and Thomas Abbt opposed by critics of warfare or, even, advocates of a 'perpetual peace' such as Immanuel Kant.[2] In the nineteenth century, there were fewer outright opponents of war, with the lessons learned—or allegedly learned—from the revolutionary and Napoleonic eras producing a broad shift in the ways in which military conflict was represented.[3] The sponsorship of official histories and the rise of academic historians within the public sphere, with Rotteck, Welcker, Ranke, Dahlmann, Droysen, and Sybel enjoying national reputations, contributed to this shift.[4]

HISTORY AND THE WARS OF THE *VÖLKER*

The commentators' new conceptions of war owed much to the myth of 1813, with military conflicts seen as an exceptional but legitimate form of national consolidation and defence. The 'rebirth' (*Wiedergeburt*) of Germany could be traced back to 'the momentous years of decision' in 1813–15, when it had been incumbent on 'the princes and peoples of Germany' to ensure that '*Deutschland* could again figure among the peoples of Europe', 'younger, more vital and united' because it drew its strength from the 'primordial spirit of the German people', recorded Brockhaus's

---

[1] K. Hagemann, *Revisiting Prussia's Wars against Napoleon*, 304. See Tables 1.1 and 1.3.
[2] Also, Leonhard, *Bellizismus*, 207–15.
[3] See the first volume of this series: M. Hewitson, *Absolute War*.
[4] W. Hardtwig, 'Geschichtsstudium, Geschichtswissenschaft und Geschichtstheorie in Deutschland von der Aufklärung bis zur Gegenwart', in W. Hardtwig, *Geschichtskultur und Wissenschaft* (Munich, 1990), 13–34.

Conversations-Lexikon in 1832.[5] Accordingly, war was a 'state of actually manifest enmity between two peoples (*Völker*)', not merely states, in which 'the peoples stood in the same relationship with each other' as 'individual people (*einzelnen Menschen*)', the same publication continued in the late 1830s: 'Each *Volk* has its own property, its particular character, its specific interests', but whereas individuals' conflicts were regulated internally by the laws of the state, clashes between the opposing interests of peoples usually led to 'self-help, i.e. war', since there was no overarching structure to resolve their differences.[6] 'Cultured states' (*die gebildeten Staaten*) were believed to safeguard the interests of peoples, as well as to maintain order domestically, and they had drawn up treaties ensuring that 'war would be very disadvantageous for both parties'.[7] War, though, continued to be necessary, waged for goods so 'worthy' that 'the disadvantages of the war do not come into question'.[8] The types of conflict alluded to by the *Conversations-Lexikon* were in keeping with a national understanding of warfare and diplomacy: 'wars of freedom' (*Freiheitskriege*), 'defence' (*Vertheidigungskriege*), 'conquest' (*Eroberungskriege*), and 'civil war' (*Bürgerkrieg*).[9] Not all almanacs and encyclopaedias defined war in such a pronouncedly national fashion after 1815—it was referred to in Brockhaus itself as 'a violent struggle between peoples and states, and also between inimical parties in the same state', by 1857—but all seemed to accept that a national component, introduced between 1792 and 1815, had altered the nature of combat.[10] Thus, the thirty-first revised edition of Hübner's *Conversations-Lexikon* qualified its definition of war as a state of violence between 'independent' states in 1828 and warned against the increased risk of triggering a civil war after 1792 through 'violent intervention in the internal politics of the peoples'.[11] Similarly, although describing 'Krieg' as 'an act of violence to force an opponent to carry out our own will' prosecuted 'by the armies of relevant states' (not individuals), Ersch and Gruber's *Allgemeine Enzyklopädie der Wissenschaften und Künste* conceded in 1828 that 'the more [the motives of war] involved the entire existence of peoples, the more war will approach its abstract form, the more it will concern the defeat (*Niederwerfen*) of the enemy [and] the more warlike aims and political purposes coincide'.[12]

The majority of academic historians, as has been seen in the case of the 'wars of freedom', justified military conflict on national grounds.[13] This reading of history

[5] F. A. Brockhaus (ed.), *Conversations-Lexikon der neuesten Zeit und Literatur* (Leipzig, 1832), vol. 1, 663. The article was on 'Deutschland'.

[6] F. A. Brockhaus (ed.), *Bilder Conversations-Lexikon der neuesten Zeit und Literatur* (Leipzig, 1837–41), vol. 2, 669. The quotation comes from an article on 'Krieg'.

[7] Ibid.   [8] Ibid.   [9] Ibid.

[10] F. A. Brockhaus (ed.), *Kleineres Brockhaus'sches Conversations-Lexikon* (Leipzig, 1854–7), vol. 3, 378. Against this definition, see the earlier one of the *Rheinisches Conversations-Lexikon oder encyclopä-disches Handwörterbuch für gebildete Stände* (Cologne, 1824–30), vol. 7, 106, which described war as 'the state of personal and deadly violent acts amongst peoples'.

[11] F. A. Rüder (ed.), *J. Hübner's Zeitungs- und Conversations-Lexikon*, 31st revised edn (Leipzig, 1824–8), vol. 2, 419.

[12] J. G. Ersch and J. G. Gruber (eds), *Allgemeine Enzyklopädie der Wissenschaften und Künste* (Leipzig, 1828), 380.

[13] See the first volume of this series: M. Hewitson, *Absolute War*, Chapter 5.

Table 1.1 First Editions of Autobiographies and Memoirs by Publication Date

Up to 1829	1830–49	1850–69	1870–89	1890–1909	1910–15	Total
19	61	66	37	43	38	269

Source: Derived from data in K. Hagemann, *Revisiting Prussia's Wars against Napoleon: History, Culture and Memory* (Cambridge, 2015), 304.

extended far beyond a recognition that the revolutionary and Napoleonic eras, with the introduction of the *levée en masse*, had altered the character of warfare—and the state—to the creation of wider national historical mythologies. Virtually all scholars took the existence of 'German tribes' or '*Stämme*' as their starting-point, going back to the '*Germanen*' during the era of the Roman Empire and the *Völkerwanderung*, and they followed—or reconstructed—the military fortunes of these tribes in the medieval, early-modern, and modern periods. Even Leopold von Ranke, who was unusually anxious to keep the concepts of 'state' and 'nation' separate (not least to maintain his emphasis on the Great Powers), perceived history primarily in national terms, observing in 1825 that 'three factors must not be lost from sight: the human species, the nations, the individual'.[14] Humanity gained consciousness of itself only when 'individual nations unite in systems of nations which, for a certain period, dominate the world', he wrote eight years later as he published his well-known essay on 'Die großen Mächte' (1833), yet nationality also corresponded to a group's consciousness of a shared historical spirit and shared fate.[15] 'All states which counted in the world and meant something are permeated by their own particular tendencies', or national spirit: they did not merely function as insurance societies for individuals.[16] 'Our fatherland is not simply to be found at that point at which it finally goes well', he wrote in his imagined 'politisches Gespräch' with Karl von Savigny published in the *Historisch-politische Zeitschrift* in 1836:

> Germany lives in us; we constitute it, whether we can or want to or not, in every country...We have relied on it, from the beginning on, and cannot emancipate ourselves from it. This secret something which imbues the least important thing as well as the most noble one—this spiritual air which we breathe in and out—precedes every constitution and animates and gives substance to all its forms.[17]

What mattered to historians, went on Ranke, was not the futile quest for distant origins and principles, but the study of more immediate 'rules of becoming' in accordance with which 'the forceful raises itself up out of the improbable' and 'new forms, which are nevertheless durable, emerge on their own account, if also—it is

[14] L. v. Ranke, cited in E. Schulin, 'Universal History and National History, Mainly in the Lectures of Leopold von Ranke', in G. G. Iggers and J. M. Powell (eds), *Leopold von Ranke and the Shaping of the Historical Discipline* (Syracuse, NY, 1990), 71.
[15] Cited ibid.; also, R. Vierhaus, *Ranke und die soziale Welt* (Münster, 1957), 68–72.
[16] L. v. Ranke, *Die großen Mächte—Politisches Gespräch* (Göttingen, 1955), 60.
[17] Ibid., 57.

true—amidst convulsions'.[18] A given course of history was the product of 'the nature of things' and of 'opportunity, genius and chance', defined as 'the moment at which independence is fought for and acquired': 'To be something, one has to raise oneself by one's own strength, develop a free independence, and we must fight for the rights which will not otherwise be granted to us.'[19] In Ranke's opinion, history was not dictated by 'raw violence' but by the necessary combination of 'bloody military labour' and 'moral energy', which 'our ancestors' had recognized, resisting the Romans for the sake of an 'empty land': 'In fact, you will be able to name few important wars for me where true moral energy did not gain victory.'[20] Initially, 'in the beginning of existence, for the epoch when it was a question of fighting for independence', this priority entailed more emphasis 'on struggle and movement', making 'the state great and powerful' (at the risk of 'military tyranny'), than 'on peace and leisure', even if, 'gradually, the peaceful needs of human nature made themselves felt'.[21]

For Ranke, as for other scholars, the *Germanen*—a term which he took from Tacitus—played a critical part in the violent, early struggle for the independence of the 'German tribes', creating one of 'three different world developments' in the form of an 'influx of *Germanen*' during 'the age of the *Völkerwanderung*', after the Roman era and before the emergence of a 'Carolingian and German Reich' (the other two developments), which itself was the continuation of a history involving the Germans.[22] Characterized by a *Kriegsverfassung* (system of war) based on 'personal and heritable loyalty' and opposing a Roman system founded on 'strict military discipline', the *Germanen* fought for their freedom by means of more or less constant combat.[23] As the German tribes competed, cooperated, and metamorphosed within the Carolingian and Holy Roman Empires, their history continued to be encompassed by a continuous series of battles.[24] There were, of course, disputes between historians about the precise nature of the German Reich and different German wars. One of the main foci was the Thirty Years' War (1618–48), since it constituted the culmination of the Reformation and the prelude to the formation of nation-states (see Table 1.2). It had also been popularized by Friedrich Schiller's famous plays about Wallenstein, to which most scholars referred.[25]

Protestant and other 'enlightened' or national-minded authors such as Johann Christian von Pfister (1772–1835), Friedrich von Raumer (1781–1875), Friedrich Förster (1791–1868), Gustav Freytag (1816–95), Gustav Droysen (1838–1908), the son of Johann Gustav Droysen, and Ranke himself (1795–1886) all sought to depict, in various religious and scientific inflections, Wallenstein as a victim and opponent of the Habsburg Emperor Ferdinand II and the unifier of 'Germany'

[18] Ibid., 58.   [19] Ibid., 59.   [20] Ibid.   [21] Ibid., 60.

[22] Ranke's eleventh lecture to Max of Bavaria from 6 Oct. 1854, in L. v. Ranke, *Über Epochen der neueren Geschichte*, ed. T. Schieder and H. Berding, (Munich, 1971), 203.

[23] Ibid., 126–7.

[24] On the relative importance of epochs in Ranke's lectures, see G. Berg, *Leopold von Ranke als akademischer Lehrer. Studien zu seinen Vorlesungen und seinem Geschichtsdenken* (Göttingen, 1968), 78–82.

[25] K. Cramer, *The Thirty Years' War and German Memory in the Nineteenth Century* (Lincoln, NE, 2007), especially 94–140, 161–2, 190–1.

against foreign, often French, designs.[26] Catholic, Austrian, Bavarian, or anti-Prussian writers such as Lorenz von Westenrieder (1748–1829), Karl Maria von Aretin (1796–1868), Friedrich Emanuel von Hurter (1787–1865), and Onno Klopp (1822–1903) backed Ferdinand's policy and championed the Holy Roman Empire as a means of preserving peace and order in Germany, absolving the commander of the Catholic League's forces Johann Tserclaes, Count of Tilly, of the responsibility for the brutal sacking of Magdeburg, in which—both sides agreed—the majority of the population, largely Protestant, had been slaughtered.[27] Between such broad camps, Protestant authors like Karl Ludwig von Woltmann (1770–1817), Karl Adolf Menzel (1784–1855), Friedrich Wilhelm Barthold (1799–1858), and August Friedrich Gfrörer (1803–61) challenged the idea that Gustavus Adolphus (1594–1632) was a German liberator, and Catholics such as Johann Sporschil (1800–63), Joseph von Hormayr (1781–1848), and Julius Schottky (1794–1849) portrayed the Swedish king in national colours (see Table 1.2).

Such historians' disputes overlapped with those between Heinrich von Sybel and a vaguely defined 'historical school', the diverse adherents of which had looked back to a purportedly primordial German constitution, on the one hand, and Julius Ficker and sundry supporters of the Habsburg monarchy and the Holy Roman Empire, who contended that it was anachronistic to portray most aspects of the Reich in national terms, on the other.[28] As its name suggested, the *Kaiserreich* was both imperial, stretching over a large territory containing a diverse population, and universal, resting on the religious claims of the Roman Catholic church, contended Ficker. The *Germanen*, on which the empire was supposedly based, appeared, 'on their entry into history, completely to have lacked a feeling of close national ties; at least, any consciousness of common state tasks was lacking'.[29] The individual tribes acted for themselves, 'just as ready to oppose a tribe of brothers as a foreign one'.[30] Within the Reich, although each kingdom corresponded to a major *Stamm*, the empire remained intact, with no movement towards nation-states and without the *Germanen* gaining the ascendancy. All the same, the existence of battling German tribes was accepted by Ficker, Leo, and Klopp, as it was by members of the 'historical school'.[31] In his disagreement with both parties, Sybel stressed the role of the state and the 'fluidity' of the 'factors of nationality (blood, language, history)' at the same time as accepting that nationality, though

[26] Ibid., 50–140.   [27] Ibid., 141–216.

[28] One of Sybel's main opponents was Georg Waitz, who was not in the 'historical school' but accepted similar premises about a German constitution: see G. Waitz, 'Zur deutschen Verfassungsgeschichte', *Allgemeine Zeitschrift für Geschichte*, 3 (1845), 13–41; G. Waitz, *Deutsche Verfassungsgeschichte* (Kiel, 1847), vol. 2; H. v. Sybel, 'Germanische Geschlechtsverfassung', *Allgemeine Zeitschrift für Geschichte*, 3 (1845), 293–348.

[29] J. Ficker, *Das Deutsche Kaiserreich in seinen universalen und nationalen Beziehungen* (Innsbruck, 1862), 17.

[30] Ibid.

[31] H. Leo, *Lehrbuch der Universalgeschichte*, vol. 1, 1–24; the second volume, ibid., vol. 2, 1–374, which is dedicated to Jacob Grimm, examines the establishment of 'a Christian–German world in the West' during the Dark and Middle Ages.

Table 1.2 Pro- and Anti-Imperial Accounts of the Thirty Years' War

Protestant, pro-Wallenstein, or anti-Imperial	**Nikolaus Vogt** (1756–1836), *Gustav Adolph, König in Schweden* (Frankfurt, 1790); *Europäische Staats-Relationen*, 3 vols (Frankfurt, 1805); *Historische Darstellung des europäischen Völkerbundes* (Frankfurt, 1808).
	Johann Christian von Pfister (1772–1835), *Geschichte der Teutschen* (Hamburg, 1829–33), vol. 4.
	Friedrich von Raumer (1781–1875), *Geschichte Deutschlands von der Abdankung Karls V bis zum westphälischen Frieden*, 3 vols (Leipzig, 1831–2).
	Friedrich Förster (1791–1868), *Gustav Adolph* (Berlin, 1832); *Wallenstein Herzog zu Mecklenburg, Friedland und Sagan* (Potsdam, 1834); *Wallensteins Prozess vor den Schranken des Weltgerichts und des k. k. Fiscus zu Prag* (Leipzig, 1844).
	Leopold von Ranke (1795–1886), *Geschichte Wallensteins* (Leipzig, 1869).
	Richard Roepell (1808–93), *De Alberto Waldsteino, Friedlandiae duce Proditore* (Halle, 1834); 'Der Verrath Wallenstein's an Kaiser Ferdinand II', *Historische Taschenbuch*, 6 (Leipzig, 1845), 239–306.
	Karl Gustav Helbig (1808–75), *Wallenstein und Arnim, 1632–1634* (Dresden, 1850); *Der Kaiser Ferdinand und der Herzog von Friedland während des Winters 1633–34* (Dresden, 1852).
	Karl Biedermann (1812–1901), *Deutschlands trübste Zeit, oder der dreißigjährigen Krieg* (Berlin, 1862).
	Gustav Freytag (1816–95), 'Bilder aus der deutschen Vergangenheit', *Grenzboten*, 17 (1858), 3–21; *Bilder aus der deutschen Vergangenheit* (Leipzig, 1859–60), vol. 4.
	Gustav Droysen (1838–1908), 'Studien über die Belagerung und Zerstörung Magdeburgs 1631', *Forschungen zur deutschen Geschichte*, 3 (1863), 435–69; *Gustav Adolf*, 2 vols (Leipzig, 1869–70).
Catholic or Pro-Imperial	**Lorenz von Westenrieder** (1748–1829), *Geschichte des dreyßigjährigen Kriegs*, 3 vols (Munich, 1804–6); 'Wie Gustav Adolph die religiöse Freiheit der Katholiken verstand', *Historisch-politische Blätter für das katholische Deutschland*, 11 (1844), 580–4.
	Peter Philipp Wolf (1761–1808), *Geschichte Maximilians I. und seiner Zeit*, 4 vols (Munich, 1807–11).
	Johann Mailath (1786–1855), *Geschichte des österreichischen Kaiserstaates* (Hamburg, 1842), vol. 3.
	Friedrich Emanuel von Hurter (1787–1865), *Geschichte Kaiser Ferdinands II. Und seiner Eltern bis dessen Krönung in Frankfurt*, 11 vols (Schaffhausen, 1850–64); *Zur Geschichte Wallensteins* (Sahffhausen, 1855); *Wallensteins vier letzte Lebensjahre* (Vienna, 1862).
	Joseph Schuegraf (1790–1861), 'Auszüge aus der Geschichte des 30jährigen Krieges in baierischen Wald', *Eos. Zeitschrift aus Baiern*, 57–9 (April 1825), 229–30, 233–4, 237–8; *Belagerung, Eroberung und Zerstörung der Veste Donaustauf durch die Schweden im Jahre 1634* (Regensburg, 1831).
	Karl Maria von Aretin (1796–1868), *Bayerns auswärtige Verhältniße seit dem Anfang des sechzehnten Jahrhunderts* (Passau, 1839); *Geschichte des bayerischen Herzogs und Kurfürsten Maximilian des Ersten* (Passau, 1842), vol. 1; *Tilly und Wrede* (Munich, 1844); *Wallenstein. Beiträge zur näheren Kenntniß seines Charakters, seiner Pläne, seines Verhältnisses zu Bayern* (Regensburg, 1846).
	Albert Heising, 'Brand Magdeburgs im Jahre 1631', *Historisch-politische Blätter für das katholische Deutschland*, 3 (1839), 43–51; *Magdeburg nicht durch Tilly zerstört. Gustav Adolph in Deutschland* (Berlin, 1846).

Heinrich Bensen (1798–1863), *Teutschland und die Geschichte* (Stuttgart, 1844); *Der Verhängniß Magdeburgs. Eine Geschichte aus dem großen Zweispalt der teutschen Nation im 16ten und 17ten Jahrhundert* (Schaffhausen, 1858).

Carl Adolph Cornelius (1819–1903), *Zur Geschichte der Gründung der detuschen Liga* (Munich, 1863).

Onno Klopp (1822–1903), 'Magdeburg, Tilly und Gustav Adolf', *Historisch-politische Blätter für das katholische Deutschland*, 46 (1860), 845–78, 913–42; 47 (1861), 72–118, 193–212, 245–69; *Tilly im dreißigjährigen Kriege*, 2 vols (Stuttgart, 1861); *Die Katastrophe von Magdeburg 1631* (Freiburg, 1874).

'Revisionist' Protestant accounts critical of Gustavus Adolphus

Karl Ludwig von Woltmann (1770–1817), *Leben, Thaten und Schicksale Wallensteins* (Zofingen, 1804); *Oesterreichs Politik und Kaiserhaus* (Frankfurt, 1815); *Friedrich Schiller's Geschichte des dreyßigjährigen Krieges* (Leipzig, 1816), vols 3–4; *Politische Blicke und Berichte* (Leipzig, 1816), vol. 1.

Karl Adolf Menzel (1784–1855), *Neuere Geschichte der Deutschen von der Reformation bis zu Bundes-Acte* (Breslau, 1833–7), vols 5–7; *Geschichte des dreißigjährigen Krieges in Deutshcland*, 3 vols (Breslau, 1835–9).

Friedrich Wilhelm Barthold (1799–1858), *Geschichte des großen deutschen Krieges vom Tode Gustav Adolf's ab*, 2 vols (Stuttgart, 1842–3).

August Friedrich Gfrörer (1803–61), *Gustav Adolph, König von Schweden, und seine Zeit*, 3rd edn (Stuttgart, 1852).

Catholic or Austrian accounts sympathetic to Gustav Adolphus's 'national' mission

Joseph von Hormayr (1781–1848), 'Die Schweden vor Brunn 1645', *Archiv für Geographie, Historie, Staats- und Kriegskunst*, 3, 12, 26 Jan. and 9 and 14 Feb. 1816; 'Versuch Albrecht's von Waldstein, eine ständische Verfassung in seinem Herzogthume Friedland einzuführen', *Taschenbuch für vaterländische Geschichten*, 1 (1830), 29–45.

Julius Schottky (1794–1849), *Ueber Wallensteins Privatleben* (Munich, 1832).

Johann Sporschil (1800–63), *Wallenstein. Historischer Versuch* (Leipzig, 1828); *Der dreißigjährige Krieg* (Brunswick, 1843).

Source: Adapted from K. Cramer, *The Thirty Years' War and German Memory in the Nineteenth Century* (Lincoln, NE, 2007), 315–36.

'capable of development and education', was 'something fixed'.[32] As such, it was worth fighting for.

Heinrich Luden's *Geschichte des teutschen Volkes* (1825) demonstrated the extent to which the fate of the Germans—like that of other peoples—was connected by academic historians—and other writers—to war. 'Such a land [as Germany], provided with such rich offerings, attributes and resources, is unmistakably destined by nature to nurture a great and strong people in all simplicity and virtue, and to produce, maintain and promote a higher education of the spirit in this *Volk* through practice and effort', he began his twelve-volume history of 'the German people': 'The land is also not deprived of distinct borders for nothing... The inhabitants can rely on nothing to counter the envy and greed of foreign peoples

---

[32] H. v. Sybel in 1847–8 and 1864–5, respectively, cited in V. Dotterweich, *Heinrich von Sybel: Geschichtswissenschaft in politischer Absicht 1817–1861* (Göttingen, 1978), 106. For Sybel's response to Ficker, see H. v. Sybel, *Die deutsche Nation und das Kaiserreich* (Düsseldorf, 1862).

other than their own strength.'[33] A written record of the Germans dated back to the Roman era and the writings of Tacitus, at which point it was difficult to ascertain how far 'German *Volks-Stämme*' had pushed south 'into the interior of Germany'.[34] It was as 'Rome had reached the height of its power' that 'the Germans (*die Teutschen*) came forth', breaking through 'the old darkness which had previously concealed their life and their strength' and creating 'in the Romans such great anxiety that it seemed to be a portent of the danger which would overcome the eternal city from this people'.[35] The war in Germany between the Gauls, the Romans, and the Germans became ever more 'entangled', with the latter pushed to save themselves and to gain revenge by the 'cruelty' of the invading army.[36] Although the Roman army defeated the Teutons, it had gained the 'experience that the North was the home of great forces which no one could calculate'.[37] The next decades were largely devoted to subjugating Gaul, leaving the Rhine—in 38 BC—as 'the border between the German peoples and Roman rule': 'Octavian Caesar, now named Emperor Augustus, soon introduced new relations, and a heavy fate threatened the German *Völker*. Freedom was in danger and was only saved through a new, ugly struggle of life and death.'[38] After a long series of wars, the Romans had established a dominion in Germany, imposing their law on the Germans, to whom 'it must have been an unspeakable cruelty'.[39] Arminius's resistance against such rule led to the deeds of the 'terrible battle' of the Teutoburger Wald in 9 AD,

> great and wonderful in origin and kind because they were rooted in the being of human nature, comprehensible in their course for human reason, honourable for the Germans, without shame for the Roman men, who paid for their earlier sins with their lives and fell as the victims of unfortunate circumstances.[40]

The victory was portrayed as a form of redemption: 'The German Volk had avenged its earlier disgrace, carried away by the force of the spirit, and it had defended its freedom, brought to a decision and into action by the holiest feelings of the human heart.'[41] A further series of wars marked the years until 70 AD, by which time the Rhine had again become the north-eastern border of the Roman Empire, and indeed until the fall of Rome in the years after 376 AD, with the 'complete conquest of the western Roman Empire by the Germans', who included Goths, Huns, and other tribes.[42]

After the collapse of Rome in the West, Luden's narrative focused on the 'gradual uniting of the German peoples into a German *Volk*', which in turn was characterized by constant warfare: Clovis's wars (466–511) against the Alemannen; those between the Franks, the Burgundians, and the Goths; the wars of Clovis's sons against Burgundy; 'the fight to the death of the Ostrogoths'; the campaigns of the Franks in Italy; civil war under the Merovingians; 'the fight against the Slavs'; Charles Martell's campaigns against the Frisians, Saxons, Burgundians, and Muslims; Charlemagne's wars against the Saxons and the collapse of the Reich of the Lombards, all of which took place before the establishment of the Holy Roman Empire.[43] The

---

[33] H. Luden, *Geschichte des teutschen Volkes* (Gotha, 1825), vol. 1, 5.
[34] Ibid., 8.   [35] Ibid., 25.   [36] Ibid., 37.   [37] Ibid., 57.   [38] Ibid., 156.
[39] Ibid., 229.   [40] Ibid., 238.   [41] Ibid., 242.   [42] Ibid., vol. 2, 217–458.
[43] Ibid., vol. 3, 49–93, 106–86, 451–585; vol. 4, 113–26, 285–320.

founding of a German Reich from the debris of Charlemagne's empire (768–814), as his sons fought for pre-eminence, was portrayed as a period of a 'confused struggle and battles to form national states'.[44] The reign of Otto I (936–73), which helped to consolidate a durable Reich, was punctuated by wars against invading Magyars, eventually defeated in 955 AD, and by conflicts with 'the Slavs'.[45] The wars against the Slavs, Danes, French, and Italians continued under Otto II, degenerating into internal wars under the child-emperor Otto III, with Heinrich III of Bavaria defeating his rivals to become Emperor Heinrich II in 1014.[46] Under his successors, wars took place against Poles, Magyars, and Slavs, and against a newly assertive Papacy, becoming an 'open struggle between religious and temporal power' and leaving Germany 'in the greatest disorder'.[47] With the death of Heinrich V without an heir in 1125, the *Kaisertum* passed—after a brief and contested interlude under Lothair III, the Duke of Saxony—to Friedrich I, the Hohenstaufen ruler known as Barbarossa, in 1152, who arrived at a truce between his own dynasty and that of the Welfs (Saxony) 'creating order and terror' in Germany.[48]

Crusades and continuing conflict with Rome dominated much of Barbarossa's reign, leading to the 'complete neglect of the German *Volk* on the part of its king' and a 'secret enmity' between Friedrich and the Welf (Guelph) Duke of Saxony and Bavaria Heinrich (the Lion).[49] The 'long neglect of the Reich' under Heinrich IV, Otto IV, Philipp, and Friedrich II left Germany exposed to the incursions of neighbouring peoples (Danes, for instance) but also permitted the establishment of free cities and the *Landesherrlichkeit*, or autonomy, of German princes.[50] Luden ended his history with the return of Friedrich II from Italy to quell the unrest of Germany's plotting princes, abetted by his own son Heinrich. Having defeated them, occupying Austria and making it part of the *Reich*, he appointed his second-oldest son the future Kaiser of the Reich:

> His second son Konrad, a nine-year-old boy already named as King of Jerusalem because of his mother, was acknowledged in Vienna as his successor, as Roman king and future Kaiser. And soon after this election, in the month of August, Emperor Friedrich went back over the Alps, as if everything had now been arranged, to face his own fate, unconcerned about Germany's own fortune.[51]

After Friedrich's death in Italy in 1250, the Hohenstaufen dynasty was quickly deposed and replaced, but the Jena historian's implicit conclusion was that the foundation of a Reich of the German nation was complete. Future wars would be between Wittelsbach, Habsburg, and Hohenzollern contenders, together with interfering foreign powers, for ascendancy within a Germany and a Holy Roman Empire which had already been established.

Almost all historians treated military conflicts as an ineluctable and heroic component of narratives about peoples and states. This was also true of radical

---

[44] Ibid., vol. 5, 231–478.   [45] For the latter, ibid., vol. 6, 427–57.
[46] Ibid., vol. 7, especially 196–234.   [47] Ibid., vol. 8, 3–371.
[48] Ibid., vol. 10, 390–409.   [49] Ibid., vol. 11, 3–280.
[50] Ibid., vol. 12, 414–88.   [51] Ibid., 596.

historians such as Georg Gottfried Gervinus, who compared the history of modern 'development' (*Entwicklung*) to that of ancient Greece, where the bearing of arms was closely related to the creation of the polity. 'In the oldest times, as Homer described them, when the population was still small, education and wealth, and also the use and possession of weapons, were only to be found amongst the few', serving to prop up the rule of patriarchal kings, he maintained, before passing to an aristocracy, 'as the number of educated, rich and armed people grew over time':

> With the increasing well-being of the middling strata of the people and the simultaneous degeneration of the aristocracy into self-interest and selfishness, and as foot soldiers became more necessary for training in the arts of war and as the military service of the lowest classes became necessary for war at sea, the rule of the people (*Volksherrschaft*), a democratic form of government, took the place of an aristocratic one; or mixed constitutions emerged, in which the nobility, *Mittelstand* and lowest classes (*unteres Volk*) were related to each other via specific rights and laws, as states became more powerful and extensive and as the bodies of the state and military became more entangled and artificial.[52]

The 'development of European states' had proceeded in the same way, 'although in much wider relations of mass, space and time'.[53] At the start, 'with the first spread and consolidation of Germanic tribes of peoples in Europe', patriarchal kings also ruled, both in 'heathen' times and in early Christian ones.[54] Aristocracies had assumed power as a consequence of the 'introduction of broader education, greater properties and the importance of the horse in the art of war'.[55] Since the end of the medieval era, history had been dominated by the 'struggle of democratic ideas', facilitated amongst other things by the superiority of Swiss infantry, 'with the aristocratic institutions of the Middle Ages', between which 'absolutism' oscillated, sometimes favouring the nobility and at other times the *Bürgertum*.[56] The necessity of wars for freer trade, ending colonial restrictions through the wars of independence in America for instance, and of revolutions—in Germany, the Netherlands, and Britain—and associated external conflicts was accepted by Gervinus without further comment.[57]

On different grounds, the necessity of military conflict was also accepted by conservative authors such as Carl Ludwig von Haller, who argued that a prince went to war and signed treaties in his own name, as part of 'his own private affair' and 'his natural freedom to defend his own property and all his natural and acquired rights against the attacks of inimical neighbours or against menacing threats'.[58] According to Haller's conception of estates and hierarchies, in which the state was the mere expression of the historical rights of monarchs, nobilities, and corporations, 'clever' rulers had explained the reasons for conflicts to their populations, without affecting their prerogatives, in order to 'create enthusiasm and to

---

[52] G. G. Gervinus, *Einleitung in die Geschichte des neunzehnten Jahrhunderts* (Leipzig, 1853), 14.
[53] Ibid.   [54] Ibid., 14–15.   [55] Ibid., 15.
[56] Ibid., 19.   [57] Ibid., 123, 136.
[58] C. L. v. Haller, *Restauration der Staats-Wissenschaft oder Theorie des natürlich-geselligen Zustands der Chimäre des künstlich-bürgerlichen entgegengesetzt* (Winterthur, 1820–5), vol. 2, 71–2.

assure themselves complaisant and fuller support' on the part of their people.[59] Conservative historians such as Heinrich Leo, who contended—like the constitutional lawyer Friedrich Julius Stahl—that the state was a moral entity above the monarch or individual subjects, similarly recognized the 'natural' or 'divine' right of states to go to war. Just as conflicts were acknowledged by Gervinus as necessary constituents of 'development', they were accepted by Leo as 'events', coloured by national particularities, with a deeper significance within a religious 'universal history'.[60]

States, nations, societies, and dynasties were treated differently by liberal and conservative, Protestant and Catholic, Prussian, Austrian, Bavarian, and other historians. Few, if any, scholars challenged the momentous, formative role of military conflicts in their emergence, persistence, and collapse, however. Such conflicts constituted turning points in the fortunes, not merely of 'Germany' within the Holy Roman Empire and beyond it (Häusser, Ficker, Sybel), but also of all the Great Powers, including Prussia (Ranke, Droysen), France (Sybel), and Britain (Dahlmann).[61] They also seemed to threaten the very existence of states, following the partitions of Poland in 1772, 1793, and 1795, just as the empires of antiquity had risen and fallen as a consequence of military conquests and defeats (Droysen, Niebuhr, Mommsen).[62] Thus, even Jacob Burckhardt, who paid more attention to the cultural history of civilizations—for example, in his *Die Zeit Constantins des Grossen* (1853)—than to their wars, accepted unthinkingly that the 'downfall' (*Untergang*) of a people was inevitable, comparable to that of an individual insofar as it was unforeseeable yet certain.[63] Violence was the foundation of the state, either as the corollary of 'the inequality of human dispositions' or as the result of 'a highly violent historical process'.[64] States were given such an 'enormous, absolute prerogative', in Burckhardt's opinion, because of 'the terrible crises surrounding the emergence

[59] Ibid., 77. See also F. de la Motte Fouqué, *Etwas über den deutschen Adel, über Ritter-Sinn und Militär-Ehre* (Hamburg, 1819).

[60] H. Leo, *Lehrbuch der Universalgeschichte* (Halle, 1850), vol. 1, 1–24.

[61] Leopold Ranke, *Deutsche Geschichte im Zeitalter der Reformation* (Berlin, 1839–47); Leopold Ranke, *Neun Bücher preußischer Geschichte* (Berlin, 1847–8); Leopold Ranke, *Französische Geschichte, vornehmlich im sechzehnten und siebzehnten Jahrhundert* (Berlin, 1852–61); Leopold Ranke, *Englische Geschichte, vornehmlich im sechzehnten und siebzehnten Jahrhundert* (Berlin, 1859–69); Wilhelm von Giesebrecht, *Geschichte der deutschen 'Kaiserzeit'* (Brunswick, 1855–95); Julius Ficker, *Das Deutsche Kaiserreich in seinen universalen und nationalen Beziehungen* (Innsbruck, 1862); Ludwig Häusser, *Deutsche Geschichte vom Tode Friedrichs des Großen bis zur Gründung des Deutschen Bundes* (Leipzig, 1854–7); Heinrich von Sybel, *Die deutsche Nation und das Kaiserreich* (Düsseldorf, 1862); Heinrich von Sybel, *Geschichte der Revolutionszeit* (Düsseldorf, 1853–79); Johann Gustav Droysen, *Geschichte der preußischen Politik* (Leipzig, 1855–86); Friedrich Christoph Dahlmann, *Geschichte der französischen Revolution* (Leipzig, 1847); Friedrich Christoph Dahlmann, *Geschichte der englischen Revolution* (Leipzig, 1844).

[62] Barthold Georg Niebuhr, *Römische Geschichte* (Berlin, 1811–32); J. G. Droysen, *Geschichte Alexanders des Großen* (Hamburg, 1833), and J. G. Droysen, *Geschichte des Hellenismus* (Hamburg, 1836–43); Theodor Mommsen, *Römische Geschichte* (Berlin, 1854–56). On Poland, see F. v. Gentz, *Ausgewählte Schriften*, vol. 4, 50; W. T. Krug, 'Polens Schicksal, ein Wahrzeichen für alle Volker, welche ihre Freiheit bewahren wollen' (1831), in W. T. Krug, *Gesammelte Schriften* (Brunswick and Leipzig, 1830–41), vol. 5, 91–136.

[63] J. Burckhardt, 'Unsere Aufgabe' (1868–72), in J. Burckhardt, *Weltgeschichtliche Betrachtungen*, ed. J. Oeri (Basel, 1978), 9.

[64] J. Burckhardt, 'Von den drei Potenzen', ibid., 22.

of the state', as a distant memory of 'what it originally *cost*'.[65] The Swiss historian disputed the right of modern states to invade and annex weaker neighbours on the spurious grounds that other powers would otherwise threaten them by doing the same and he questioned whether wars could be said to embody or bring about 'world-historical purposes', but he appeared to concede that 'civilized states' had been justified in countering the danger of 'barbarism' and nullifying 'its potential power to attack'.[66] To most nineteenth-century authors, peoples, states, and their leaders had been compelled throughout history to defend themselves against attack and to prevail by means of military force against their rivals and opponents.

The Revolutionary and Napoleonic Wars constituted a fundamental juncture in the history of warfare, as far as many commentators were concerned, but not one which de-legitimized military conflict per se (see Table 1.3). A conservative like Gentz saw 'the past swimming before my eyes' more than ten years after the French Revolution and Napoleonic era, with the 'affairs of the world' having assumed 'too serious and tragic a form', yet he continued to believe that war against the revolutionary threat had been justified at the time and would be so in future, within a European system of states—or 'an armed coalition for the re-creation of independence'—which he had helped to design.[67] War in 1813, he had written at the time, had extended everywhere except to the North Pole, only to be contained subsequently within a system which had successfully prevented the escalation of war in the first conflict after 1815 involving two or more Great Powers—that between Russia and the Ottoman Empire in 1828—and which had tended towards 'the likelihood of peace' during the revolutions of 1830.[68] In Ludwig von Haller's opinion, the ruin and corpses of the period before 1815 could have been avoided altogether, if the Coalition had declared war earlier and prosecuted it more determinedly.[69] Similarly, a liberal commentator such as Carl von Rotteck conceded that 'the weight of the army had oppressed Europe, and even brought it to despair', with 'still greater masses' being added to each state's forces as a consequence of France's successful *levée en masse*, but he defended German states' right to go to war, deploying mass armies on behalf of the nation, in order to vanquish the neighbouring state:

> The grand army—in fact, the strongest which Europe had ever seen—was defeated by the arms of the sons of the North, fighting for their country, and a second one which advanced suffered the same fate on the fields of Leipzig at the hands of the national armies—or, if also serving for pay, at the hands of armed men enthused by national sentiment—of Prussia, Russia and Austria.[70]

[65] Ibid., 23.   [66] Ibid., 26.

[67] F. v. Gentz to R. Levin, 28 Sept. 1825 and 10 Feb. 1828, in G. Schlesier (ed.), *Schriften von Friedrich von Gentz* (Mannheim, 1838–40), vol. 1, 187–94; G. Schlesier, 'Von Pradt's Gemälde von Europa' (1819), in G. Schlesier, *Ausgewählte Schriften* (Stuttgart, 1836–8), vol. 5, 268.

[68] F. v. Gentz to R. Levin, 1 Aug. 1813, in G. Schlesier (ed.), *Schriften von Friedrich von Gentz*, vol. 1, 133–4; G. Schlesier, 'Beim Friedenschluss von Adrianopel' (1829) and 'Argumente für die Wahrscheinlichkeit des Friedens' (1830), in G. Schlesier (ed.), *Schriften von Friedrich von Gentz*, vol. 5, 168–70, 175–80.

[69] C. L. v. Haller, *Restauration der Staats-Wissenschaft*, vol. 3, 126.

[70] C. v. Rotteck, 'Über stehende Heere und Nationalmiliz' (1816), in C. v. Rotteck, *Sammlung kleinerer Schriften* (Stuttgart, 1829), vol. 2, 187.

Table 1.3 Accounts of the Revolutionary and Napoleonic Wars by Decade

---

J. J. O. A. Rühle v. Lilienstern, *Bericht eins Augenzeugen von dem Feldzug* (Tübingen, 1807)

C. v. Plotho, *Tagebuch während des Krieges zwischen Russland und Preussen einerseits und Frankreich andrerseits in den Jahren 1806 und 1807* (Berlin, 1811)

C. v. Plotho, *Die Kosaken, oder Geschichte derselben von ihrem Ursprunge bis auf die Gegenwart* (Berlin, 1811)

C. v. Plotho, *Der Krieg in Deutschland und Frankreich in den Jahren 1813 und 1814*, 2 vols (Berlin, 1817)

C. v. Plotho, *Der Krieg des verbündeten Europa gegen Frankreich im Jahre 1815* (Berlin, 1818)

F. C. F. v. Müffling, *Die preussisch-russische Campagne im Jahr 1813* (Breslau, 1813)

F. C. F. v. Müffling. *Geschichte des Feldzugs der englisch-hanövrisch-niederländisch-braunschweigischen Armee unter Herzog Wellington und der preußischen Armee unter dem Fürsten Blücher von Wahlstadt im Jahr 1815* (Stuttgart, 1817)

J. W. v. Goethe, *Aus meinem Leben* (Stuttgart, 1811–14)

C. v. Clausewitz, *Der Feldzug von 1813 bis zum Waffenstillstand* (Berlin, 1813)

C. Niemeyer, *Die Schlachten des Heiligen Krieges* (Leipzig, 1817)

Anon., *Rück-Erinnerungen an die Jahre 1813 und 1814* (Munich, 1818)

F. C. F. v. Müffling, *Betrachtungen über die grossen Operationen und Schlachten der Feldzüge von 1813 und 1814.* (Posen, 1825)

E. Heusinger, *Ansichten, Beobachtungen und Erfahrungen* (Brunswick, 1825)

Büttner, *Beschreibung der Schicksale und Leiden des ehemaligen Korporals Büttner* (Nennsling, 1828)

K. W. F. v. Funck, *Erinnerungen aus dem Feldzuge des sächsischen Corps* (Dresden, 1829)

C. v. Clausewitz, *Vom Kriege* (Leipzig, 1832)

A. Böck, *Leben und Schicksale des ehemaligen Musikmeisters* (Halle, 1832)

W. Krimer, *Erinnerungen eines alten Lützower Jägers* (Stuttgart, 1833)

F. Peppler, *Schilderung meiner Gefangenschaft vom Jahre 1812 bis 1814* (Darmstadt, 1834)

C. L. Marter, *Fünf Marter-Jahre: Schicksale eines deutschen Soldaten in Spanien und Sicilien* (Weimar, 1834)

J. Schrafel, *Merkwürdige Schicksale des ehemligen Feldwebels im königl. Bayer. 5ten Linien-Infanterie-Regiment* (Nuremberg, 1834)

J. Meyer, *Erzählung der Schicksale und Kriegsabenteuer des ehemaligen westfälischen Artillerie-Wachtmeisters Jakob Meyer* (Dransfeld, 1836)

H. Steffens, *Was ich erlebte* (Leipzig, 1838)

K. A. Varnhagen v. Ense, *Denkwürdigkeiten* (Berlin, 1838)

E. M. Arndt, *Erinnerungen* (Berlin, 1840)

F. de la Motte Fouqué, *Lebensgeschicthe des Barons de la Motte-Fouque* (Halle, 1840)

C. R. v. Schäffer, *Denkwürdigkeiten*, ed. by G. Muhl (Pforzheim, 1840)

F. Bersling, *Der böhmische Veteran* (Schweidnitz, 1840)

F. Harkort, *Die Zeiten des ersten Westphaelischen Landwehrregiments. Ein Beitrag zur Geschichte der Befreiungskriege* (Essen, 1841)

K. Müchler, *Doppelflucht um den Verfolgungen der Franzosen zu entgehen* (Cottbus, 1841)

W. T. Krug, *Krug's Lebensreise in sechs Stazionen* (Leipzig, 1842)

K. A. Varnhagen v. Ense, *Denkwürdigkeiten des eigenen Lebens* (Leipzig, 1843)

C. v. Pichler, *Denkwürdigkeiten aus meinem Leben* (Vienna, 1844)

A. Vater, *Was wir erlebten im Oktober 1813* (Leipzig, 1845)

F. Steger, *Der Feldzug von 1812* (Essen, 1985), first published in 1845

G. Kirchmayer, *Veteranen-Huldigung oder Erinnerungen an die Feldzugsjahre 1813, 1814 und 1815. Wahre Schilderung von Leistung und Verdienst des Soldaten* (Munich, 1846)

W. L. V. Henckel v. Donnersmarck, *Erinnerungen aus meinem Leben* (Zerbst, 1846)

(continued)

Table 1.3 Continued

W. v. Bismarck, *Aufzeichnungen des Genrallieutenants Friedrich Wilhelm Grafen von Bismarck* (Karlsruhe, 1847)

H. v. Luden, *Rückblicke in mein Leben* (Jena, 1847)

A. v. Keyserling, *Aus der Kriegszeit* (Berlin, 1847–55)

K. G. v. Raumer, *Erinnerungen aus den Jahren 1813 und 1814* (Stuttgart, 1850)

F. C. F. v. Müffling, *Aus meinem Leben* (Berlin, 1851)

L. v. Wolzogen, *Memoiren* (Leipzig, 1851)

F. A. L von der Marwitz, *Lebensbeschreibung* (Berlin, 1852)

T. D. Goethe, *Aus dem Leben eines sächsischen Husaren* (Leipzig, 1853)

W. Meier, *Erinnerungen aus den Feldzügen 1806 bis 1815* (Karlsruhe, 1854)

M. Burg, *Geschichte meines Dienstlebens* (Berlin, 1854)

F. Mändler, *Erinnerungen aus meinen Feldzüge in den Jahren 1809 bis 1815* (Nuremberg, 1854)

G. F. Bärsch, *Erinnerungen aus meinem vielbewegten Leben* (Aachen, 1856)

L. v. Reiche, *Memoiren* (Leipzig, 1857)

H. v. Chézy, *Unvergessenes. Denkwürdigkeiten aus dem Leben von Helmina von Chézy* (Leipzig, 1858)

A.v. Blumröder, *Erlebnisse im Krieg und Frieden in der grossen Welt und in der kleinen Welt meines Gemüths* (Sondershausen, 1857)

J. D. v. Dziengel, *Geschichte des Koeniglichen Zweiten Ulanen-Regiments* (Potdam, 1858)

F. L. A. v. Meerheim, *Erlebnisse eines Veteranen der Grossen Armee während des Feldzuges in Russland* (Dresden, 1860)

W. Mente, *Von der Pieke auf. Erinnerungen an eine neun und vierzigjährige Dienstzeit* (Berlin, 1861)

L. Rellstab, *Aus meinem Leben* (Berlin, 1861)

K. v. Suckow, *Aus meinem Soldatenleben* (Stuttgart, 1862)

C. E. V. Krieg (ed.), *Vor fünfzig Jahren. Tagebuch eines freiwilligen Jägers der Jahre 1813 und 1814* (Wesel, 1863)

M. Prell, *Erinnerungen aus der Franzosenzeit* (Hamburg, 1863)

C. v. Martens, *Vor fünzig Jahren. Tagebuch meines Feldzuges in Sachsen 1813* (Stuttgart, 1863)

L. v. Hoffmann, *Erinnerungen eines alten Soldaten und ehemaligen Freiwilligen* (Berlin, 1863)

C. F. C. Pfnor, *Der Krieg, seine Mittel und Wege, sowie sein Verhältniss zum Frieden, in den Erlebnissen eines Veteranen* (Tübingen, 1864)

Wilhelm, Markgraf v. Baden, *Denkwürdigkeiten* (Karlsruhe, 1864)

H. v. Brandt (ed.), *Aus dem Leben des Generals der Infanterie z. D. Dr Heinrich von Brandt* (Berlin, 1868)

F. A. Brockhaus, *Brockhaus, Friedrich Arnold. Sein Leben und Wirken* (Leipzig, 1872–81)

E. v. Stockmar (ed.), Denkwürdigkeiten aus den Papieren des Freiherrn Christian Friedrich von Stockmar (Brunswick, 1872)

J. v. Hüser, *Denkwürdigkeiten aus dem Leben des Generals der Infanterie von Hüser* (Berlin, 1877)

A. L. v. Ardenne, *Bergische Lanciers Westfälische Husaren Nr. 11* (Berlin, 1877)

L. v. Ranke (ed.), *Denkwürdigkeiten des Staatskanzlers Fürsten von Hardenberg* (Leipzig, 1877)

C. C. Zimmermann, *Geschichte des 1. Grossherzoglich Hessischen Dragoner-Regiments* (Darmstadt, 1878)

A. Adam, *Aus dem Leben eines Schlachtenmalers*, ed. H. Holland (Stuttgart, 1886)

C. E. W. v. Canitz und Dallwitz, *Denkschriften* (Berlin, 1888)

H. v. Boyen, *Erinnerungen aus dem Leben des Generalfeldmarschalls Hermann von Boyen*, 3 vols (Leipzig, 1889–90)

Since the nation and, potentially, the state were the main safeguards of culture and morality in modern Europe, national and state wars were often warranted, claimed the Freiburg historian:

> if we...leave aside the campaigns of robbery and murder of those hordes who, in accordance with their level of culture or character, are nearer to animals than to humans, there are only a very few unjust *Volkskriege*! And even if they were unjust in respect of their object, they could still be just in respect of their disposition and form.[71]

Entire peoples rarely decided on war other than in the 'case of an emergency' or of a 'passion agitated to the greatest degree'.[72] National wars, therefore, were typically limited, lawful, and controllable. The Revolutionary and Napoleonic Wars had witnessed a 'return' to an arming of the people (*Volksbewaffnung*), with corresponding changes in the ways in which wars were fought (requiring rapid marches, living off the land, skirmishing, and decisive battles), the fearful effects of which appeared to have been countered by the need—for conservatives—to restore peace and a working system of states or the hope—for liberals and others—of establishing popular participation and 'patriotic' or 'national' politics. Military conflict as such seemed morally acceptable and historically unavoidable to most parties.

THE ANTHROPOLOGY OF WARFARE

The broader questions about conflict were anthropological: what was war and how was it connected—in nineteenth-century terminology—to the 'human condition'? Many writers, especially but not exclusively military ones, linked combat to more or less unchanging forms of violence, aggression, and power. Thus, although assuming that 'the human world was more than a mere animal one', since people should 'also be guided by moral laws' not just physical ones, even a philosopher such as Wilhelm Traugott Krug thought of war as comparable in some respects to the struggle of animals to mark out territory and to survive: 'War in the wider sense is every violent struggle of opposing forces in the human or, indeed, animal world—[which is] why one also talks of women's wars (*Weiberkriege*), wars of words (*Federkriege*) and the wars of animals (*Thierkriege*)'.[73] Most authors seem to have made similar assumptions, albeit in combination with other, more significant premises and qualifications, to which they devoted much of their attention. Humans were at once part of nature, with the power to compete and destroy, and

---

[71] Ibid., 202.   [72] Ibid.

[73] W. T. Krug, *Allgemeines Handwörterbuch der philosophischen Wissenschaften nebst ihrer Literatur und Geschichte* (Leipzig, 1827), vol. 2, 560. Also, see the account of the former Prussian *Landwehr* officer and critic of the army Karl Heinzen, *Dreißig Kriegsartikeln der neuen Zeit für Officiere und Gemeine in despotischen Staaten* (Neustadt, 1846), 3–5, who makes the comparison between nature, animals, and humanity while also distancing them from each other, in an implied contrast with other authors.

separate from it, creating their own distinct 'histories'.[74] As the former general Rudolph Eickemeyer wrote at the time of the wars of liberation and Congress of Vienna:

> A state of war appears so natural to people that we find both the most savage as well as the most educated *Völker* almost always caught up in a feud, and a people can only expect quiet and peace for as long as it is armed and is in a position to repel its enemies...When wild people then unite, from conditions of animal savagery, this occurs under a leader, who has established himself through daring and cunning, and just as the social bond becomes closer between them, so their enmity against other tribes (*Völkerschaften*) grows. The wars which then take place between them are conducted with cruelty, with the conqueror slaying and often consuming the conquered.[75]

In contrast to 'barbarians or savage peoples', among whom a 'martial spirit' was 'natural', peoples 'with a higher culture, where the wandering shepherd becomes a farmer, artist and city-dweller', could only maintain such an attitude 'through an appropriate state constitution, through morals and education'.[76] There was, however, no alternative for cultured peoples but to encourage bellicosity and to retain adequate military forces, unless they were willing to risk being invaded and destroyed by 'unspoiled peoples', as Egypt, Persia, and the Roman Empire had demonstrated.[77] Accordingly, the history of all human societies had been characterized by their military rise and fall:

> Nature has always been the same for millennia but countless changes have taken place amongst the peoples. How many peoples have not replaced another or have not based their growth on the other's downfall and their well-being on the other's destruction, only to be pushed aside by yet another or to be destroyed by such? The most powerful nations of antiquity have disappeared, the most populous cities have turned into ruins and countries which contained the most prosperous empires have become deserts; barbarism has taken the place of art and sciences, ignorance that of enlightenment. By contrast, we see many prosperous states where there were once savage peoples, and arts and sciences flourish where only barbarism used to be known.
>
> This steady transformation of things seems inseparable from the crimes of humans, but history also teaches us, from the most distant to the most recent times, that states may only expect lasting independence for as long as they are belligerent.[78]

War seemed to be an inevitable part of the human predicament. One of the most famous military writers Carl von Clausewitz, whose works were known

---

[74] For explicit statements and treatments, see the following military writers: H. Beisler, *Betrachtungen über Staatsverfassung und Kriegswesen insbesondere über die Stellung des Wehrstandes zum Staat* (Frankfurt, 1822), 1; C. v. Gersdorff, *Vorlesungen über militairische Gegenstände* (Dresden, 1827), 7–38, 104–5; H. v. Brandt, *Grundzüge der Taktik der drei Waffen. Infanterie, Kavallerie und Artillerie* (Berlin, 1842), 1–6.

[75] R. Eickemeyer, *Abhandlungen über Gegenstände der Staats- und Kriegs-Wissenschaften* (Frankfurt, 1817), vol. 1, 155. Like many other officers, Eickemeyer had fought on the French side.

[76] Ibid., 168.   [77] Ibid., 222.

[78] Ibid., 153–4. Also, H. E. W. Lühe (ed.), *Militair Conversations-Lexikon* (Leipzig, 1833–7), vol. 3, 679–83; Beisler, *Betrachtungen*, 1–77; C. v. Gersdorff, *Vorlesungen*, 27–38.

within army and governing circles and, to an extent, within a wider public, conceived of military conflicts as a necessary consequence of the struggle for, and logic of, power.[79] 'Now, philanthropists may easily imagine there is a skilful method of disarming and overcoming an enemy without causing great bloodshed, and that this is the proper tendency of the art of war,' recorded the Prussian general, referred to by one hostile Austrian reviewer in 1834 as a 'celebrity in the military literature', at the start of his seminal, posthumously published volume *Vom Kriege* (1832–4):

> However plausible this may appear, still it is an error which must be extirpated; for in such dangerous things as war, the errors which proceed from a spirit of benevolence are the worst. As the use of physical power to the utmost extent by no means excludes the co-operation of the intelligence, it follows that he who uses force unsparingly, without reference to the bloodshed involved, must obtain a superiority if his adversary uses less vigour in its application. The former then dictates the law to the latter, and both proceed to extremities to which the only limitations are those imposed by the amount of counteracting force on each side.
>
> This is the way in which the matter must be viewed, and it is to no purpose, it is even against one's interest, to turn away from the consideration of the real nature of the affair because the horror of its elements excites repugnance.
>
> If the wars of civilized people are less cruel and destructive than those of savages, the difference arises from the social condition both of states in themselves and in their relations to each other. Out of this social condition and its relations war arises, and by it war is subjected to conditions, is controlled and modified. But these things do not belong to war itself, they are only given conditions; and to introduce into the philosophy of war itself a principle of moderation would be an absurdity.[80]

Clausewitz's treatise on war and his other writings in the 1810s and 1820s outlined an 'absolute' idea of military conflict as a 'duel', characterized by three 'extremes' of 'reasoning in the abstract' (where 'the mind cannot stop short of an extreme'): 'that war is an act of violence pushed to its utmost bounds'; 'that the aim of all action in war is to disarm the enemy' in order to ensure that an opponent would 'comply with our will' because his situation 'is more oppressive to him than the sacrifice which we demand'; and that, 'if we desire to defeat the enemy, we must proportion our efforts to his powers of resistance', which in its 'pure conception' led to an escalation of effort and violence to a maximum on each side.[81] The military publicist was anxious to demonstrate, as a 'historicist', how conflicts only existed 'in reality' and were subject to different historical 'modifications', and how war could not be compared to science or measured mathematically, as had begun to happen in the eighteenth century 'until the facts of the last war taught [us] better': 'reasoning in the abstract...has to deal with an extreme, with a conflict of forces left to

---

[79] On the scope and limits of Clausewitz's influence, see P. Paret, *Clausewitz and the State* (Oxford, 1976), 331, 339, 362–3. Other works citing Clausewitz included H. v. Brandt, *Grundzüge der Taktik der drei Waffen*, 2, 473, 532–3; F. v. Prondzynski, *Theorie des Krieges*, 2nd revised edn (Bielefeld, 1849), vol. 1, 23, 73, 128–34.

[80] C. v. Clausewitz, *Vom Kriege* (Berlin, 1832–4). Here, the English version of *On War* (Ware, 1997), 6, unless otherwise stated.

[81] Ibid., 5–9.

themselves, and obeying no other but their own inner laws', which 'would be nothing but a play of ideas' and a 'kind of logical chimera'.[82] Combat was 'always the shock of two hostile bodies in action, not the action of a living power upon an inanimate mass', with the hostile bodies themselves comprising individual states, governments, soldiers, and civilians and succeeding or failing as a result of 'the *military power, the country*, and *the will of the enemy*'.[83] Nonetheless, although these vagaries of history determined the outcomes of conflicts and, therefore, constituted a large part of Clausewitz's analysis, war itself—in all its variations—was still compared to and derived from an 'elemental' individual or human act of violence to force an opponent to carry out one's will:

> We shall not enter into any of the abstruse definitions of war used by publicists. We shall keep to the element of the thing itself, to a duel. War is nothing but a duel on an extensive scale. If we would conceive as a unit the countless number of duels which make up a war, we shall do so best by supposing to ourselves two wrestlers. Each strives by physical force to compel the other to submit to his will.[84]

In other words, wars were viewed anthropologically as typical of all societies and analogous to acts of individual violence. On this reading, 'educated nations', despite refraining from devastating towns and putting their prisoners to death, were not fundamentally different from 'savage peoples' who resorted to 'rude acts of mere instinct'.[85] 'The invention of gunpowder, the constant progress of improvements in the construction of firearms, are sufficient proofs that the tendency to destroy the adversary which lies at the bottom of the conception of war is in no way changed or modified by improving education (*Bildung*)', Clausewitz averred.[86] War was a basic fact of human life, deriving from the realities of power.

The armed conflicts of 'barbarians' or 'savage peoples' were comparable in important respects with those of contemporary European states, Clausewitz—like many of his contemporaries—suggested. Here, it was significant that the *Germanen*, the putative forerunners of nineteenth-century Germans, had belonged, in common with much of 'the human race' over the previous 6,000 years, to a period of 'profound barbarism' and 'a very low level of education', typified by 'lawless conditions' and constant warfare, with one power 'drunk with the most glorious victory today' and 'knocked down by the most humiliating defeat the next day', in Krug's words.[87] Many authors, it is true, emphasized what Rotteck termed the equality of 'duties as well as rights' and the existence of a common 'national' cause amongst the Germanic tribes who had stormed the Roman Empire, but he also conceded that 'the *Germanen—Wehrmänner, Waffenmänner—*were a *Volk* of warriors'.[88] Rome

---

[82] Ibid., 7, 9. See especially Paret, *Clausewitz and the State*, 331–55.

[83] Clausewitz, *On War*, 8, 25.　　　[84] Ibid., 5.

[85] Ibid., 7: I have altered the translation of 'gebildete Völker' (in the original German version) from 'civilised nations' in the English version.

[86] Ibid., with 'zunehmende Bildung' rendered as 'the progress of civilisation' in the English translation.

[87] W. T. Krug, *Gesammelte Schriften*, vol. 6, 534–5.

[88] C. v. Rotteck, 'Über stehende Heere und Nationalmiliz' (1816), in C. v. Rotteck, *Sammlung kleinerer Schriften*, vol. 2, 172.

had been 'overpowered, coerced and destroyed by poor and barbaric tribes which were loosely bound together but which fought with the undiminished force of nature and in national masses', he continued in 1816.[89] From this point of view, Georg Waitz's claim in 1844 that 'the Germans were not raw savages' in 'the oldest times', at the start of their history, was an attempt to confront an orthodoxy which—as has been seen—had been established by historians.[90] Certainly, for military writers like Wilhelm Rüstow, violence had been typical during the dislocations and struggles of the *Völkerwanderungen*, as one nomadic people after another pushed from Asia towards Asia Minor and Europe from 1200 BC onwards, culminating in 'the migration of the Huns from the steppes of Asia in the first centuries of our time' and in the animation 'of the entire European world': 'the *Germanen* threw themselves on the sinking Roman Empire and brought new life to an almost decadent Europe'.[91]

Much of the literature on the *Germanen* struck a similar balance between 'the hospitality, humility, integrity, loyalty and friendship unto death, the humanity, mildness and courage in the emergency of battle' of a 'German character', on the one hand, and the 'wild passions and dark forces of revenge, anger, fury, rage and a cruel desire to kill' of the archaic, heroic epic, on the other hand, in the judgement of Friedrich Heinrich von der Hagen, the first translator of the *Nibelungenlied*—rediscovered in the mid-eighteenth century—into High German in 1807.[92] Some critics such as Georg Wilhelm Friedrich Hegel contended, in his *Vorlesungen über die Ästhetik* (1818–20), that 'the Burgundians and King Attila are so cut off from all the conditions of our present level of culture (*Bildung*) and associated patriotic interests that we can feel much more at home, even without learning, in the poems of Homer' than in the *Nibelungenlied*, in spite of the fact that 'we are on home ground geographically'.[93] Others claimed that the interest of German readers and playwrights in the epic—it was dramatized by Friedrich de la Motte Fouqué in *Der Held des Nordens* (1810), Ernst Raupach in *Der Nibelungenhort* (1834), Emanuel Geibel in *Brunhild* (1858), and Friedrich Hebbel in *Die Nibelungen* (1862)—rested on the romance of Kriemhild and Siegfried rather than on the heroism, action, and violence of popular Greek epics or the Scandinavian *Edda*, which recounted the same story from Nordic sources. Thus, Friedrich Theodor Vischer wrote in 1844 that 'Our heroic saga has not taken the storms of the *Völkerwanderungen*, the great victory over the Romans as its material; with German stubbornness, it has been housed in a family history and seeks in vain to widen this narrow interest into a world-historical one.'[94] Even before Richard Wagner used the *Edda* to underpin his own monumental and forceful *Ring des Nibelungen*, writing the text between 1849 and 1853 and most of the music in

---

[89] Ibid., 171.

[90] G. Waitz, *Die Verfassung des Deutschen Volkes in ältester Zeit*, 3rd edn (Kiel, 1880), 32. The first edition was published in 1844.

[91] W. Rüstow, *Untersuchungen ueber die Organisation der Heere* (Basel, 1855), 2.

[92] F. H. von der Hagen, preface to the *Niebelungenlied*, cited in K. v. See, *Barbar, Germane, Arier* (Heidelberg, 1994), 99.

[93] Ibid., 98.   [94] Ibid., 98–9.

the mid-1850s, the various adaptations of the *Nibelungenlied* for the stage had
continued to make unthinking references to the fighting (Siegfried's vanquishing
of Brunhild), killing (Hagen's slaying of Siegfried, the slaughter of the Burgundians or
Nibelungen at the court of Attila), beheadings (Hagen's decapitation of Kriemhild's
son and Kriemhild's of Gunther and Hagen), and dismemberment (Kriemhild at
the hands of Dietrich's lord) of the various *Germanen* in the original story. The
same mixture of violence and national edification could be found in Christian
Dietrich Grabbe's *Die Hermannschlacht* (1838), which recounted Arminius's defeat
of the Romans in the Teutoburger Wald in 9 AD, and in Heinrich von Kleist's
Die Hermannschlacht (1809), which had been published in 1821 and contained a
portrayal of the German hero's duplicity and violent frenzy, in an angry denial of
the superiority of the enemy's culture and in his call to beat his prisoner-of-war
Septimus to death.[95] Germanic wars, in particular, had been brutal, it seemed to
contemporaries.

Modern states were not fully protected from the extremes of older types of
warfare because international law and the states' system were incapable of guaranteeing peace, as even a conservative architect of the post-war order such as Gentz
admitted in 1830.[96] Certainly, few commentators, except for some on the left
such as Moses Heß, bothered to contest the inevitability or necessity of military
conflicts.[97] Krug, one of the main early nineteenth-century critics of 'unjust'

---

[95] F. J. Lamport, 'A Prussian Meteor: Heinrich von Kleist', in F. J. Lamport, *German Classical Drama* (Cambridge, 1990), 167–8; E. Krimmer, *The Representation of War in German Literature, 1800 to the Present* (Cambridge, 2010), 46–64.

[96] F. v. Gentz, 'Argumente für die Wahrscheinlichkeit des Friedens' (1830), in G. Schlesier (ed.), *Schriften von Friedrich von Gentz*, vol. 5, 178–9.

[97] M. Heß, 'Die europaeische Triarchie' (1841), in M. Heß, *Philosophische und sozialistische Schriften*, ed. W. Mönke, 2nd edn (Vaduz, 1980), 43–70; see also J. G. A. Wirth, *Die politische Reform Deutschlands* (Strasbourg, 1832), 35–8. For support for various kinds of war amongst radicals and democrats, combined with criticism of 'princes'' wars' and 'state wars', see A. Ruge, 'Eine Selbstkritik des Liberalismus' (1843), in H. Fenske (ed.), *Vormärz und Revolution 1840–1849* (Darmstadt, 1976), 74–80; F. Engels, 'Rede in Elberfeld' (1845), in K. Marx and F. Engels, *Werke* (Berlin, 1956–68), vol. 2; F. Engels, *Po und Rhein* (1859), ibid., vol. 13, 225–68; K. Marx, 'Cobdens Pamphlet' (1853), ibid., vol. 8, 510; F. Lassalle, 'Der italienische Krieg und die Aufgabe Preußens' (1859), in F. Lassalle, *Nachgelassene Briefe und Schriften*, ed. G. Mayer (Berlin, 1922), vol. 3, 214–22. On the right, see F. v. Gentz, 'Betrachtungen über die politische Lage von Europa' (1831), in G. Schlesier (ed.), *Schriften von Friedrich von Gentz*, vol. 5, 196–206; F. A. L. von der Marwitz, *Ein märkischer Edelmann im Zeitalter der Befreiungskriege*, ed. F. Meusel (Berlin, 1908–13), vol. 1; F. de la Motte Fouqué, *Etwas über den deutschen Adel*, 34; G. W. v. Valentini, *Abhandlung über den Krieg* (Berlin, 1821), vol. 1, 1; A. H. D. v. Bülow, *Geist des neuern Kriegssystems*, 3rd edn (Hamburg, 1837), xiii; C. H. G. v. Venturini, *Rußlands und Deutschlands Befreiungskriege von der Franzosen-Herrschaft unter Napoleon Buonaparte in den Jahren 1812–1815* (Leipzig, 1816), vol. 1, vi–xviii; J. J. O. A. v. Lilienstern, *Aufsätze über Gegenstände und Ereignisse aus dem Gebiete des Kriegswesens* (Berlin, 1818), vol. 1, 180, 190–1, 277. For liberals, see C. v. Rotteck, 'Über stehende Heere und Nationalmiliz' (1816), in C. v. Rotteck, *Sammlung kleinerer Schriften*, 156–239; C. v. Rotteck, 'Krieg', in C. v. Rotteck and C. T. Welcker (eds), *Staatslexikon* (Altona, 1834–43), vol. 9, 491–501; C. T. Welcker, 'Heerwesen', ibid., vol. 7, 593–7; W. Schulz, 'Frieden', in C. v. Rotteck and C. T. Welcker (eds), *Staatslexikon*, 2nd edn (Altona, 1847), 198, 227–33; A. F. v. Liebenstein, *Über stehende Heere und Landwehr mit besonderer Rücksicht auf die deutschen Staaten* (Karlsruhe, 1817); J. v. Theobald, *Die rechte Wehrverfassung. Ein Versuch, der auf die neueste, für Deutschland entworfene Kriegsverfassung Rücksicht nimmt* (Stuttgart, 1819); J. Weiske, *Rechtslexikon für Juristen aller Teutschen Staaten* (Leipzig, 1840–61), vol. 6, 221; O. v. Platen, *Wehrverfassung, Kriegslehren und Friedensideen im Jahrhundert der Industrie* (Berlin, 1843), 59;

eighteenth-century wars, evinced how—and to what extent—assumptions about the international order, state sovereignty, and military conflict were linked. Thus, although he was sympathetic to the idea of securing peace in Europe via a newly established balance of power, the Leipzig philosopher doubted that the international system would be able to exclude the possibility of conflict in all cases or in all areas of the world. 'History has taught us, in sufficient measure, how little a state of peace on this basis would deserve the name of a perpetual peace', he wrote in 1818: 'Fear of each other can seldom or never stop great and powerful states daring to wage war with each other as soon as an important interest comes into play for both of them, for each strong power trusts in its own strength and, besides, also hopes for good fortune.'[98] War could only be ruled out if a 'universal monarchy' could be founded, yet history had proved 'irrefutably' that such a world state or confederation of states (*Staatenbund*) was unrealizable, because 'the further that states expand in space and the more diverse the elements which they incorporate, the more they hasten towards their own ruin' as a consequence of the division of the peoples of the world, 'not only by great rivers, chains of mountains, deserts and seas, but much more by language, *mores*, religion etc.'[99]

States were sovereign, requiring a defensible territory and a population large enough to sustain a powerful army 'for the maintenance of their independence'.[100] What was more, they relied on 'the strength of the nation (*Nazionalkraft*) as the actual foundation of their political independence, and such strength is nothing more than the sum of the military forces to be found in the entirety of the *Volk*'.[101] As the German 'vassal states' had demonstrated when they had, 'over time, extricated themselves from the unnatural relations' of dependency under the Kaiser and the Holy Roman Empire, states had become more independent in recent times, not less so, making foreign intervention more difficult and armament for self-defence more likely.[102] For Krug, given the lessons of the Napoleonic Wars and the necessary shortcomings of the states' system, it went without saying that 'defensive' wars and conflicts of 'honour' were justified in the name of either states or peoples,

---

H. v. Gagern, *Deutscher Liberalismus im Vormärz. Briefe und Reden 1815–48*, ed. P. Wentzcke and W. Klötzler (Göttingen, 1959), 291; J. G. Droysen, *Vorlesungen über die Freiheitskriege* (Kiel, 1846), vol. 1, 5–7; J. G. Droysen, 'Zur Charakteristik der europäischen Krisis' (1854), in J. G. Droysen, *Politische Schriften*, ed. F. Gilbert (Munich, 1933), 328–41; G. Waitz, *Über den Frieden mit Dänemark* (Göttingen, 1849), 4; L. Wienbarg, *Krieg und Frieden mit Dänemark* (Frankfurt, 1848), 16; T. Mommsen, 'Der Kampf der Nationalitäten', *Schleswig-Holsteinische Zeitung*, 21 Apr. 1848; A. L. v. Rochau, *Grundsätze der Realpolitik*, ed. H.-U. Wehler (Frankfurt, 1972), 57; C. Rössler, *System der Staatslehre* (Leipzig, 1857), 547; L. Bamberger, *Juchhe nach Italien* (Frankfurt, 1859), in L. Bamberger, *Gesammelte Schriften* (Berlin, 1913), vol. 3, 159–92; J. C. Bluntschli and C. Brater (eds), *Deutsches Staatswörterbuch* (Stuttgart, 1857–70), vol. 6, 100.

[98] W. T. Krug, 'Kreuz- und Querzüge eines Deutschen auf den Steppen der Staats-Kunst und Wissenschaft' (1818), in W. T. Krug, *Gesammelte Schriften*, vol. 4, 79.

[99] Ibid., 82.

[100] W. T. Krug, *Versuch einer systematischen Enzyklopädie der Kriegswissenschaften* (Leipzig, 1815), ibid., vol. 10, 421–3.

[101] Ibid., 425.

[102] W. T. Krug, *Dikäopolitik oder neue Restaurazion der Staatswissenschaft* (Leipzig, 1824), ibid., vol. 6, 501.

which in turn made it harder to distinguish between defensive and offensive wars, since the latter could often be presented as 'preventative' campaigns designed to protect the threatened interests or reputation of the nation.[103] Under these conditions, it appeared, the principal support for peace was the 'gradual improvement of the physical, political and moral conditions of the peoples' within their own states.[104] However, this improvement itself had been—and would be—brought about amongst other things by war, which fostered self-sacrifice and invention at home and which permitted the conquest of decadent peoples abroad:

> Thanks to the advantages which it creates,...it must be war itself that contributes to the gradual betterment of the circumstances of the *Völker*; [war] is, accordingly, a monster which in its fury eats itself, and, therefore, the peoples will and must wage war against each other for as long as they need war for the improvement of their conditions.[105]

Unlike in domestic life and politics, where violence had been curbed by legislation enforced by legitimate states, in the realm of diplomacy it could continue—in certain circumstances—more or less unchecked.

Violence was integral to states, not so much because state institutions had come to exercise a monopoly over it internally, but because they had been constituted and maintained externally by means—or threats—of violent acts against others. In Krug's opinion, 'stately arts' and 'the arts of war' were 'twins' with the same aim; namely, 'the general good', so that 'the sole, reasonable purpose of the art of war' became 'defence of the state, i.e. resistance against external, enemy forces and the deflection of the danger with which these forces threaten the general good'.[106] Modern states had become 'civil societies' (*bürgerliche Gesellschaften*), with laws which precluded an animal-like 'right of the stronger' operating between individuals, yet they had not been able to impose such civility on their relations with each other, with each faced with at least the prospect of its own downfall, wrote the philosopher in his treatise on the supposed renaissance of a distinct *Staatswissenschaft* in 1824:

> People themselves are, as a rule, the destroyers of states. At one moment, a conqueror goes to war with neighbouring states and takes parts of it as his own; at another moment, his sons or generals divide this state, which had become large as a result of conquest, and create smaller ones again; sometimes, wild tribes of people pour out of their original areas of settlement over distant states, reduce them to rubble and build new ones out of that debris; sometimes, superstition and fanaticism push people to spread their beliefs through violence, as a result of which old states fall and new

---

[103] W. T. Krug, *Allgemeines Handwörterbuch*, vol. 2, 560–2.

[104] W. T. Krug, 'Kreuz- und Querzüge eines Deutschen auf den Steppen der Staats-Kunst und Wissenschaft', 85–6.

[105] Ibid. Krug's arguments about decadence and the benefits of war can be found in W. T. Krug, *Versuch einer systematischen Enzyklopädie der Kriegswissenschaften*, 387. See also G. W. F. Hegel, *Grundlinien der Philosophie des Rechts* (Stuttgart, 1970), 482. Originally published in 1820.

[106] W. T. Krug, 'Kreuz- und Querzüge eines Deutschen auf den Steppen der Staats-Kunst und Wissenschaft', 22.

ones rise up; at other times, colonies tear themselves away from the mother state, which, whilst it might not bleed from the wound, still has to give up a great part of its territory for the formation of one or several new ones; finally, a poor administration can cause an absolute dictatorship and resultant misery, uprisings and civil war, so that the state either is completely dissolved, splits into several other states or is eaten up by a neighbouring state, which cunningly has realized how to use this internal ferment. All these cases have occurred more than once in history.[107]

Like Krug, other early nineteenth-century *Staatswissenschaftler* saw war-making as one of the principal constituents of the state. For Hegel, it was closely related to 'autonomy' (*Selbständigkeit*) and 'the self-confidence that a people has in its own independence': 'the first power with which states emerge historically is thus this independence itself'.[108] The 'negative' aspect of belonging to a state was 'external', deriving from 'the entanglement in chance events which come from outside'; the 'positive' aspect was the 'relationship and acknowledgement' of the individuality of the state 'in-and-for-itself', and of the need to maintain its independence through 'the duty of facing danger and sacrificing property and life'.[109] 'In this fact lies the ethical *moment of war*, which is not to be seen as an absolute evil and as a merely external hazard', concluded the Berlin philosopher at the end of his *Philosophie des Rechts* (1820), before returning to the claim which he had made during the Napoleonic era that military conflicts strengthened a people by introducing 'movement' and 'uncertainty' into the ossified social and political relations of peacetime.[110] Not all academics—the mixture of historians, philosophers, lawyers, and economists who taught *Politik* or *Staatswissenschaft*—were as straightforward as Hegel. Dahlmann, for instance, never wrote the second part of his theory of the state 'as a member of a *Staatengesellschaft*', including diplomacy and warfare, which he had promised in the introduction to the first volume of *Die Politik* in 1835.[111] Likewise, a founder of a separate study of 'society' (*Sozialwissenschaft*) in the 1850s such as Lorenz von Stein or a constitutional lawyer such as Johann Caspar Bluntschli often seemed to pay little attention to the external relations and bellicose histories and functions of states.[112] By the same token, however, they—along with most of their colleagues—did not deny the significance of such histories.[113]

---

[107] W. T. Krug, *Dikäopolitik oder neue Restaurazion der Staatswissenschaft*, 329, 496, 555–6.
[108] G. W. F. Hegel, *Philosophie des Rechts*, 479.   [109] Ibid., 480.
[110] Ibid., 482.   [111] F. C. Dahlmann, *Die Politik* (Frankfurt, 1997), 15.
[112] L. v. Stein, *System der Staatswissenschaft* (Stuttgart, 1856), vol. 2, on 'Die Gesellschaftslehre'; J. C. Bluntschli, *Allgemeines Statsrecht* (Munich, 1863).
[113] J. C. Bluntschli, *Allgemeines Statsrecht*, 229–68; J. C. Bluntschli, 'Zur Revision der statlichen Grundbegriffe', in J. C. Bluntschli, *Kleine Schriften* (Nordlingen, 1879), vol. 1, 287–317; G. Waitz, *Deutsche Verfassungsgeschichte*, 3rd edn (Kiel, 1880), vol. 1, 401–17; vol. 2, 531–633; vol. 4, 95–215; R. v. Mohl, *Encyklopädie der Staatswissenschaften* (Tübingen, 1859), 158–69, 402–60; A. Schäffle, *Das gesellschaftliche System der menschlichen Wirtschaft*, 3rd edn (Tübingen, 1873), vol. 1, 12; K. Knies, *Die politische Oekonomie vom geschichtlichen Standpuncte* (Brunswick, 1853), 433–4; K. Knies, *Die Dienstleistung des Soldaten und die Mängel der Conscriptionspraxis* (Freiburg, 1860); K. Knies, 'Finanzgeschichtliche und volkswirtschaftliche Betrachtungen über den Krieg', *Deutsche Vierteljahrsschrift*, 22 (1859), 1–60; K. Knies, *Das moderne Kriegswesen* (Berlin, 1867); A. Wagner, 'Die Entwicklung des deutschen Staatsgebiets und das Nationalitätsprincip', *Preußische Jahrbücher*, 21 (1868), 290–312, 379–402; H. v. Treitschke, *Die Gesellschaftswissenschaft* (1859), in H. v. Treitschke, *Aufsätze, Reden und Briefe* (Meersburg, 1929), vol. 2, 779–80. Although sceptical in general, even

Humanity was subject to 'other relations, which are not exhausted by a social order', wrote Stein: 'Here belong the phases of the shift from the non-settled, the conquests, the formation of states; here, too, belongs that so often named and so rarely investigated fact of the spiritual life of the whole which we call the *Volksgeist*.'[114] States faced many 'struggles', at once internal and external, which threatened to make them 'go under'.[115] Military conflict played an important part in those struggles.

War was an ineluctable eventuality abroad, with the potential to create exceptional conditions at home, as isolated critics occasionally pointed out. Humans, unlike animals, were not 'natural' killers, lacking sharp teeth and claws, 'yet man murders more than animals do', killing his own species and then not eating his prey, wrote one disaffected former officer of the Prussian *Landwehr* in 1846: 'Mankind', although 'not born to murder', had been brought to commit murderous acts in wartime, which in fact constituted 'a terrible degradation', as if they were a matter of 'duty' and 'law'.[116] For the majority of nineteenth-century commentators, civil war—rather than conflicts *tout court*—had become the site of such transgression and excess.[117] 'The most terrifying war is civil war', declared Brockhaus's *Bilder Conversations-Lexikon* in 1841, because it was 'led by factions in a single state':

> Here, opponents are closely connected by national and family ties, and the more difficult it is to tear apart such natural ties, the greater will be the bloodthirstiness with which war is habitually waged; the vanquished are not only subject to the severity of the victor, but also to harsh, bloody laws; they are not only treated as the defeated, but also as criminals; friends and foes don't split up, the trust of people in each other is destroyed and legal conditions cease to obtain, even amongst those parties which keep together, because everyone can make themselves immune from prosecution by going over to the other party.[118]

Civil wars had been marked by such violence, recorded the same lexicon in 1857, as a consequence of the propinquity of the warring factions and the collapse of the state and law, with the members of a single state taking over 'the entire life of the state' in an 'extended, all-encompassing mass': 'They are, as a rule, particularly cruel because opponents do not see each other as legal enemies, but as evildoers, and they act in hatred and passion, and frequently have everything at stake.'[119] For Catholic commentators especially, the Thirty Years' War had come to symbolize

---

Julius Fröbel admitted the force of this argument in the past, *System der socialen Politik* (Mannheim, 1847), vol. 2, 459. See also A. Lees, *Revolution and Reflection: Intellectual Change in Germany during the 1850s* (The Hague, 1974).

[114] Stein, *System der Staatswissenschaft*, vol. 2, 19.

[115] Ibid., 431.   [116] Karl Heinzen, *Dreißig Kriegsartikeln*, 1–3.

[117] For literary depictions of civil war, revolution, and uprising, see P. M. Lützeler, 'Bürgerkriegsliteratur. Der historische Roman im Europa der Restaurationszeit', in J. Kocka (ed.), *Bürgertum im 19. Jahrhundert. Deutschland im europäischen Vergleich* (Munich, 1988), vol. 3, 232–56.

[118] Article on 'Krieg' in F. A. Brockhaus (ed.), *Bilder Conversations-Lexikon* (Leipzig, 1837–41), vol. 2, 669.

[119] F. A. Brockhaus (ed.), *Kleineres Brockhaus'sches Conversations*, vol. 1, 678.

the dangers of such civil conflict, as a 'time of annihilation' (*Vertilgungszeit*), 'nameless tortures', and 'cold-blooded crimes', in the opinion of one author, referring to the plundering of German villages by the Swedes during the early 1630s.[120] This 'gothic' horror continued to leave its imprint on Protestant accounts, too, despite the ubiquity of narratives of Protestant (and German) redemption. 'This was a time that men, created in the image of God, became accomplices of the devil', wrote the Protestant historian Otto Schmidt: 'Everything good died under their hand; they brought death and fire and bestiality; lamentation and misery followed in their footsteps.'[121] Many on the right and some in the centre saw revolution in a similar light. Thus, for Haller, it was obvious that 'internal disputes and wars are much more dangerous than external ones'.[122]

The question was whether the bloodshed typical of civil wars could be limited and controlled in other types of conflict. For Krug, civil war was, at least in some respects, 'an analogue of a war of the peoples (*Völkerkrieg*)', with different sections of a single *Volk* and state fighting against each other 'because of the lack or weakness of the highest power'.[123] 'Sections of the population (*Volkstheile*) come to oppose each other as if they were enemy peoples,' the philosopher continued: 'But reason can only approve of this because, as long as peoples persist in a state of nature (i.e. as long as they have not set up amongst themselves an association aiming at a lasting peace), they cannot settle their legal disputes, in the last instance, other than through war.'[124] Like Haller and others on the right, who distinguished between the 'actual illness' of 'existing division, impeded justice and the alienation of people's attitudes' in revolutions, on the one hand, and the potentially surgical, healing effects of war itself, on the other, Krug assumed that it was possible to guard against the worst consequences of war in Europe, partly through the establishment of a balance of power and partly as a result of the moral constraints placed on the conduct of the armies of 'cultured states'.[125] Although most peoples were still 'barbaric' and war—even between cultured states—was inevitable, 'some peoples have raised themselves up to a higher level and have learned, at least in their own midst, to secure for the law—through the establishment of a fixed and well-ordered citizenry (*Bürgertum*)—the rule which it deserves', he maintained.[126] The very 'being' (*Wesen*) of a modern state was its function as a 'civil' and 'legal society' (*Rechtsgesellschaft*), ensuring that laws enjoyed a universal application within its territory.[127]

---

[120] F. Ferchel, foreword to M. Freisenegger, *Chronik von Erling und Heiligenberg während dem dreißigjährigen Kriege* (1833), cited in K. Cramer, *The Thirty Years' War and German Memory*, 205.
[121] O. Schmidt, *Geschichte des dreißigjährigen Krieges* (1853), in K. Cramer, *The Thirty Years' War and German Memory*, 182.
[122] C. L. v. Haller, *Restauration der Staats-Wissenschaft*, vol. 3, 113.
[123] W. T. Krug, 'Versuch einer systematischen Enzyklopädie der Kriegswissenschaften' (1815), in W. T. Krug, *Gesammelte Schriften*, vol. 10, 385.
[124] Ibid., 385–6.
[125] C. L. v. Haller, *Restauration der Staats-Wissenschaft*, vol. 3, 111; W. T. Krug, 'Kreuz- und Querzüge eines Deutschen auf den Steppen der Staats-Kunst und Wissenschaft', 77–9; W. T. Krug, *Restauration der Staatswissenschaft*, 533–47.
[126] W. T. Krug, *Restauration der Staatswissenschaft*, 534–5. [127] Ibid., 328–33.

Some 'theoretical, as well as practical, politicians' (*Politiker*) wanted to ignore the existence of a law—'or, at least, natural law'—regulating the external relations of states: 'it only relates to internal laws; there [in foreign affairs], only cunning, attention to advantages and losses, at most a certain equity, is decisive'.[128] Others argued that states merely had to come to a 'mutual agreement'.[129] In Krug's opinion, neither position was tenable. 'Reason' dictated that 'people, and therefore states as great associations of people, should order their mutual relations through law and equity', yet natural law was 'not sufficient' and 'positive' legal restraints lacked a means of enactment and enforcement, given the absence of an 'external law-maker'.[130] In these circumstances, cultured states relied on *de facto* agreements, to which common 'morals and conventions also belong', or on formal treaties, which depended on each other and consequently changed in scope and significance over time.[131] Although agreements and treaties could be overridden by more pressing *raisons d'état*, since states still existed in the last resort in a 'state of nature', they did constitute a series of guidelines for diplomats and their governments.[132] The complexity of the right of states to intervene in the affairs of another and the existence of laws of war, covering the conduct of combat, demonstrated to Krug's satisfaction that a 'legal relationship between states is never completely abolished, not even during wars': 'However just the war may be, it must also be waged in a just way.'[133] In other words, European states had found ways of avoiding the worst effects of war. States' wars were not comparable with civil wars.

Europe would not experience another Thirty Years' War or even a Seven Years' War, claimed Krug in 1835, because 'one has less money to wage war today and yet one needs more than in the past'.[134] His argument was directed at German liberals such as Rotteck, who had claimed that such a conflict might be necessary in order to bring about a constitutional order: 'We might be required to fight our way through a new Thirty Years' War (to continue our simile)... in order to attain the final consolidation of the constitutional principle through a new peace, just as religious peace was first consolidated through the Westphalian one', the liberal historian had written, with a note from the philosopher explaining that the comparison was 'between the earlier era of religious Reformation and a later one of political revolution'.[135] Rotteck, it seemed, not only believed that much of the continent was divided, within 'lands, provinces, communes and families', between constitutionalists and absolutists, as it had been split between Protestants and Catholics in the sixteenth and seventeenth centuries, but he also assumed that a 'world war' constituted an acceptable, if costly, resolution of a political conflict.[136] In 1840, in an article on 'war' in the *Staatslexikon*, Rotteck went further, justifying

---

[128] Ibid., 495.   [129] Ibid., 495–6.   [130] Ibid., 497–9.
[131] Ibid., 498.   [132] Ibid.   [133] Ibid., 543.
[134] W. T. Krug, 'Über Oppositionsparteien in und ausser Deutschland und ihr Verhältniss zu den Regierungen. Nebst einem Nachworte über eine merkwürdige politische Prophezeiung' (1835), in W. T. Krug, *Gesammelte Schriften*, vol. 4, 191.
[135] Ibid., 186.   [136] Ibid., 186–92.

military conflicts in the name of the nation and making individual citizens responsible for their conduct and aims:

> Where and inasmuch as war seems to flow from the real, general will of the nation (*Nation*), all citizens enter personally, in their own role as elements of that general will, into an inimical relationship with the state against which they are fighting; whereas the subjects of a ruler who decides on war autocratically cannot be responsible for it.[137]

From this Rousseauian, national point of view, military conflict could appear 'beneficial', bolstering the independence of individual nations and stiffening the resolve of individual citizens.[138]

Even civil war appeared to be warranted in such circumstances, since citizens would be able to exercise control themselves and prevent escalation:

> Because the flag which the individual follows has usually been chosen by him, so that he also can be regarded as a personal or voluntary participant in the struggle, more things and harsher ones are permitted in respect of him than of either the mercenary of an enemy power, completely without his own will, or of a warrior entering onto the battlefield out of duty, i.e. out of obedience to a legal state power.[139]

International and domestic laws remained in force, argued Rotteck, in most civil and military conflicts.[140] Many other liberals agreed, backing wars—as Heinrich von Gagern did—which established nations or championing—in the manner of Droysen—those which created or defended national 'independence' or 'freedom'.[141] For liberals of the 1850s such as the philosopher and publicist Constantin Rößler, the governments of nations had a duty to protect the *Volk*, if necessary through war: 'A people which subjects itself to foreign rule in order to avoid war would be contemptible.'[142] 'War decides which peoples rule', he wrote in 1857: 'There have been wars for as long as the world has existed, and for as long as there has been war, there have been well-meaning litanies about the arbitrariness and sinfulness which allegedly bring it about.'[143] A small number of liberals such as the Rhinelander David Hansemann believed that trade would make wars rarer in future, but few doubted that certain types and instances of military conflict were justified.[144]

Some conservatives, like liberals, had come to accept that states, and therefore wars, had become national in character by the nineteenth century.[145] Many, at

[137] C. v. Rotteck, 'Krieg', in C. v. Rotteck and C. T. Welcker (eds), *Staatslexikon*, vol. 9, 497.

[138] Ibid., 508. [139] Ibid., 494. [140] Ibid., 493.

[141] H. v. Gagern to H. C. v. Gagern, 9 Apr. 1845, in P. Wentzcke and W. Klötzer (eds), *Deutscher Liberalismus im Vormärz. Heinrich von Gagern, Briefe und Reden, 1815–1848* (Göttingen, 1959), 291; J. G. Droysen, *Vorlesungen über die Freiheitskriege*.

[142] C. Rößler, 'Der Kampf der Nationalitäten un dder Krieg', in C. Rößler, *System der Staatslehre* (Leipzig, 1857), 546.

[143] Ibid., 546–7.

[144] D. Hansemann, 'Denkschrift über Preußens Lage und Politik' (1840), in J. Hansen (ed.), *Rheinische Briefe und Akten zur Geschichte der politischen Bewegung 1830–1850* (Essen, 1919–76), vol. 1, 220–1, argued that Prussia had needed wars to establish itself.

[145] J. J. O. A. Rühle v. Lilienstern, *Aufsätze über Gegenstände und Ereignisse aus dem Gebiete des Kriegswesens*, vol. 1, 180, 193–4, 277; C. H. G. v. Venturini, *Rußlands und Deutschlands Befreiungskriege*, vi–xviii, 14, 78–9.

least until 1848, had not, yet they continued to support wars in the name of their monarch, state, nobility, or, especially, army, whose accounts of combat remained influential.[146] As was to be expected, these accounts of war, propagated by officers acting as publicists, tended to be positive, viewing military conflicts as necessary, meaningful, and heroic instruments of policy. Nearly all military writers concentrated on the supposedly legitimate wars of states rather than on civil wars.[147] 'Earlier, there were incessant feuds and civil wars in all lands, from the Ebro to the Ganges', where governments had 'neither reputation nor power' and armed bands were often misused, wrote one of the few commentators to mention civil conflicts at all: 'But this is scarcely possible, given the organization of the current army', which was drawn from the 'civil relations' of 'the *Volk* itself' and which offered effective protection for the government.[148] Under such predictable and limited conditions, which were characteristic of the conflicts of 'cultured states', armies should continue to counsel and wage war. Accordingly, even the most pessimistic and radical military writers such as Clausewitz, who had been profoundly affected by the contortions and killing of the Napoleonic Wars, assumed that combat should take place and that it could serve 'political objectives'.[149] 'We know, certainly, that war is only called forth through the political intercourse of governments and nations; but in general it is supposed that such intercourse is broken off by war, and that a totally different state of things ensues, subject to no laws but its own', Clausewitz wrote in the concluding section of *Vom Kriege*: 'We maintain, on the contrary, that war is nothing but a continuation of political intercourse, with a mixture of other means.'[150]

In practice, Clausewitz wrote, military conflicts did not tend towards logical 'extremes' of power: they were hampered by unforeseeable obstacles such as 'imperfect knowledge of circumstances' or 'friction', resulting from the fact that 'the military machine' was 'composed entirely of individuals, each of which keeps up its own friction in all directions'; they never led to a 'final decision' that could be regarded as 'absolute', meaning that they could be used strategically, with 'the conquered state' often seeing defeat 'only as a passing evil, which may be repaired at a later date by means of political combinations'; and they remained subordinate to wider political aims, despite 'the peculiar nature' of the means which they used and which merely led to a 'modification' of 'political views', 'for the political view is the object, war is the means, and the means must always include the object in

---

[146] The prominence of proponents of a 'patrimonial' monarchy or 'monarchy of estates' such as Haller, de la Motte Fouqué, Carl von Voss, Carl von Canitz, Carl Wilhelm von Lancizolle, Carl Ernst Jarcke, and Victor Aimé Huber bore witness to this fact. See M. Levinger, *Enlightened Nationalism: The Transformation of Prussian Political Culture, 1806–1848* (Oxford, 2000), 163–90, and L. Dittmer, *Beamtenkonservatismus und Modernisierung. Untersuchungen zur Vorgeschichte der Konservativen Partei in Preussen 1810–1848/49* (Stuttgart, 1992).

[147] H. F. Rumpf, *Allgemeines Kriegswörterbuch für Offiziere aller Waffen* (Berlin, 1821), vol. 1, 489, mentions civil war (termed '*bürgerlicher Krieg*') as a type, but only in passing; no work on civil war appears in the bibliography of the work. 'Bürgerkrieg' is also mentioned in H. E. W. von der Lühe (ed.), *Militair Conversations-Lexikon*, vol. 1, 794–6, but is treated summarily.

[148] H. E. W. von der Lühe (ed.), *Militair Conversations-Lexikon*, vol. 1, 796.

[149] C. v. Clausewitz, *On War*, 12–14, 23–4, 357–63.   [150] Ibid., 357.

our conception'.[151] 'Even if war was perfect war', the general went on, it would be inseparable from 'political intercourse' because of 'the circumstances on which it rests, *viz.*, our own power, the enemy's power, allies on both sides, the characteristics of the people and their governments respectively, etc.', which were 'of a political nature'.[152] In fact, though, 'real war is no such consistent effort tending to an extreme...but a half-and-half thing', which 'must be looked upon as a part of another whole—and this whole is policy'.[153] The limited aims of policy constrained 'the all-overpowering element of war' and helped to determine how military campaigns were conducted. They, in turn, were connected to 'culture' and 'education', so that 'the wars of cultured people are less cruel and destructive than those of savages', with the difference arising 'from the social condition both of the states in themselves and in their relations to each other'.[154] For these reasons, Clausewitz—like other military and conservative observers—assumed that war was a controllable and acceptable undertaking.

The violence experienced by soldiers such as Clausewitz during the Napoleonic era was present in many early nineteenth-century representations of warfare but it was rarely explicit or dominant. In the drawings and watercolours of Adam and Faber du Faur, depicting the abandoned corpses and huddled, freezing soldiers of the *Grande Armée* during its disastrous invasion of Russia in 1812, the horrifying

Figure 1.1 Wilhelm Camphausen, *Blüchers Rheinübergang bei Caub am 1. Januar 1814* (1860)

Source: Mittelrhein-Museum in Koblenz.

<hr />

[151] Ibid., 18, 67, 12, 22. [152] Ibid., 358. [153] Ibid. [154] Ibid., 358, 6.

consequences of violence were unmistakable. They were also visible in retrospective battle scenes from the same campaign, such as Feodor Dietz's *Übergang der badischen Husaren in der Schlacht an der Beresina 1812* (1842), in which disordered masses of unidentified soldiers fight against each other and against the snow in a desperate bid to return home, and they were detectable in depictions of other campaigns, such as Adam's *Die Verteidigung des Blockhauses von Malborghetto und der Heldentod des Kommandanten der Besatzung K. K. Hauptmann Friedrich Hensel am 16. und 17 März 1809* (1843), which showed a mass of soldiers fighting their way up the terraces of a rocky Italian mountainscape and being bayonetted by the 'heroic' Austrian defenders of the distant garrison. In these frenetic battles and in the quiet before and after the fighting, which is reflected in the hushed, snowbound gorge of Wilhelm Camphausen's painting of *Blüchers Rheinübergang bei Caub am 1. Januar 1814* (1860), the toiling of the masses and the suffering of individual soldiers were often juxtaposed (see Figure 1.1). At the same time, however, they were contained within approving accounts of patriotic or national redemption, where the sacrifices of individuals—whose bodies and faces are visible—were tied to the successful endeavour of a state, embodied in the person of the commander among the ranks (Hensel and Blücher), or a people, whose massed movement dominates the canvas. Violence in these portrayals has a social meaning. It was viewed in both images and words as a natural part of human activity, which could be trained and harnessed under the conditions of combat and by the institutions of the army. The next chapter examines changing attitudes to violence and war in the context of such institutions.

2

Life in the German Armies

The ways in which war was understood and remembered depended, in part, on how wartime acts of violence were viewed by civilians and, in part, on the peacetime role and significance of the armies which had sanctioned such violence. To what extent did soldiers' actions offend civilians' and, especially, commentators' and officials' sensibilities, making future conflicts less likely? The fact that a long period of peace at the core of the European pentarchy between 1815 and 1848 was followed by a quick succession of wars (in 1848–51, 1853–6, 1859, 1864, 1866, and 1870–1) seems to leave the question open, as do contemporaries' varied justifications of violence in revolutions, civil conflicts, and national and state wars during the same era. On one level, the 'pacification' of civil society during the nineteenth century could be expected to make conscript soldiers and civilians more reluctant to countenance the type of violence which had characterized the Napoleonic Wars. On another level, myths of 1813 and a continuing acceptance of warfare in general, combined with the legitimacy of patriotic or national campaigns and the persistence—at least in theory—of an 'arming of the people' (*Volksbewaffnung*), seemed to render military conflicts less objectionable.[1] The precise balance of such countervailing arguments and conditions in different German lands is the subject of this chapter. Above all, it concerns negotiations and contradictions which existed between citizens' and soldiers' (and citizen-soldiers') values, attitudes, and expectations.

THE ARMING OF THE PEOPLE

From a historical standpoint, the trajectory of Germany's armies seemed difficult to describe and predict. Beyond the power struggles of rising and falling dynasties, states, and peoples, many commentators perceived the gradual historical transformation of armies and warfare, characterized by the passage from a general arming of all men via standing armies towards conscription. 'Initially, every man capable of bearing arms in a *Volk* was also a combatant on its behalf, a warrior,' noted Brockhaus's *Bilder Conversations-Lexikon* in the late 1830s: 'But after trade, occupations and sciences had raised themselves to a higher level amongst the

---

[1] This seems to have been the case even in new provinces: B. Schmitt, *Armee und Staatliche Integration. Preußen und die Habsburgermonarchie 1815–1866* (Paderborn, 2007), 285, 288, commenting on responses in the Rhineland, Lombardy, and Venetia.

peoples, it soon transpired that a separate estate of warriors was formed, which was kept separate from other estates and which therefore assumed the duty for its part of protecting them in cases of emergency.'[2] At a 'higher cultural level', the complex requirements of states meant that it was neither desirable nor possible 'to interrupt all economic activity through a general arming of the population during wartime' or 'to continue a training in arms during peacetime', not least because 'the art of war itself demanded a higher level and scope of training'.[3] Aristocracies usually took over the functions of the old '*Heerbann*' (general call to arms) and in turn 'received people who were trained in arms', with compensation by landowners formerly responsible for the provision of men soon turning into an 'army tax' (*Heersteuer*).[4] 'In these ways, standing armies emerged', went on the same *Conversations-Lexikon*, but only very slowly, with the Germanic tribes relying entirely on a general call to arms and with both the Roman army and late-medieval noble retinues still requiring an 'arming of the people' (*Volksbewaffnung*) for at least part of their forces.[5] Well before the French Revolution, noble-led armies had been partly replaced as a consequence of aristocracies becoming too 'independent and self-interested', protecting themselves more than their prince and people and prompting the latter to recruit their own mercenaries, who had comprised the first standing armies, narrowly defined.[6] 'Since the war with France or, in fact, since the French Revolution, the armies of the European states have again approached the original position of a general arming of the *Volk*', the lexicon recorded:

> It has generally been recognized once more that the citizens of a state are the sole, born, worthy defenders of it, and not only have standing armies been constituted from the citizens of states and these armies been given an integral, corresponding institution in accordance with their higher worth, but also most citizens in greater or lesser degree have been entrusted with the duty of military service.[7]

During the revolution itself, France—attacked from 'all sides'—had been forced to make 'extraordinary efforts', amassing an army of 1,169,000 troops, it was claimed.[8] During the 'restoration', the same system of *Volksbewaffnung* had remained in place, even though the peacetime strengths of 'standing armies' had been reduced, with the German *Bund* totalling 303,484, Prussia 122,000, Austria 270,000, France 250,000, and Russia 612,000 troops. In wartime, it was assumed, these totals could rapidly expand, as they had done during the Napoleonic Wars. As has been seen, this potential to create mass armies, with corresponding shifts in strategy (mobility, skirmishing, decisive battles, annihilation), was rarely seen to have rendered wars threatening or illegitimate.

The combination of standing armies and volunteers or militia was usually seen to have characterized the Revolutionary and Napoleonic Wars, begging the question of their relative significance and the nature of their relationship with the societies

---

[2] 'Krieg', in F. A. Brockhaus (ed.), *Bilder Conversations-Lexikon der neuesten Zeit und Literatur*, vol. 2, 669.
[3] Article on 'Heer', ibid., 353.   [4] Ibid., 354.   [5] Ibid., 353–4.
[6] Ibid., 354.   [7] Ibid.   [8] Ibid.

from which they were drawn. After 1815, the military no longer conscripted the majority—or a large minority—of young men, but in the larger German states it continued to claim the right to do so. In most cases, laws of conscription from the Napoleonic era remained in place but the number of soldiers recruited was reduced during peacetime, not least because of the cost of maintaining large armies. In Prussia, the standing army counted 124,000 troops and the *Landwehr* a first levy of 180,000 in 1826, from a population of 11 million, compared to a total force of 280,000 from a population of just over 4.5 million in 1813, albeit supplemented by 'Prussians' from outside the territories left intact by the Treaty of Tilsit (1807).[9] The *Wehrgesetz* drafted by Boyen and Grolman, which was promulgated in September 1814 and remained in effect until the early 1860s, stipulated that all Prussian men were liable for military service from their twentieth birthday, to serve in the army of the line for three years (reduced to two years between 1837 and 1852 by royal decree) with a further two years in active reserve, before passing for the next seven years to the first levy of the *Landwehr*, which was intended for use in the field, and for the last seven years to the second levy, which was to be deployed in fortresses and for the purposes of home defence during wartime. The reformers' aim was to create an army of 500,000 men, with 130,000 on active duty—and therefore paid for—during peacetime.[10] The total contingent of conscripts and reservists fell short of these expectations, yet annual conscription remained high: 40,888 in 1820; 35,512 from a population of 13 million in 1837; 40,363 from 15.5 million in 1846; and 41,469 from 18 million in 1858.[11]

Although historians such as Ute Frevert and Ralf Pröve have rightly argued that such figures were lower than those of the early twentieth century, with up to half of those liable being rejected on physical or medical grounds, conscription continued, in comparison to that of other periods and states, to be significant in the Hohenzollern monarchy: in 1820, approximately 40 per cent of 20-year-olds were conscripted and, in the late 1850s, about 25 per cent.[12] It was for this reason that

---

[9] This was the population of the reduced territories after the Peace of Tilsit (1807). Some soldiers were drawn from the traditional territories of Prussia, which counted 9.75 million inhabitants. U. Frevert, *Nation in Barracks*, 50.

[10] G. Craig, *Politics of the Prussian Army, 1640–1945* (Oxford, 1955), 69.

[11] U. Frevert, *Nation in Barracks*, 54. This yearly intake would have created a force of about 500,000 men, but each cohort was depleted through illness, death, imprisonment, and emigration. Heinz Stübig, 'Die Wehrverfassung Preußens in der Reformzeit. Wehrpflicht im Spannungsfeld von Restauration und Revolution 1815–1860', in R. G. Foerster (ed.), *Die Wehrpflicht. Entstehung, Erscheinungsformen und politisch-militärische Wirkung* (Munich, 1994), 49, provides different figures for the period immediately after 1815: 127,000 for the active army of the line in 1819; 28,000–30,000 conscripts for the army of the line from 82,000 per year who were liable for conscription; and about 20,000 per year who went straight into the ranks of the *Landwehr*.

[12] U. Frevert, 'Das jakobinische Modell. Allgemeine Wehrpflicht und Nationsbildung in Preussen-Deutschland', in U. Frevert (ed.), *Militär und Gesellschaft im 19. und 20. Jahrhundert* (Stuttgart, 1997), 33. Frevert herself argues that the standing army of the 'restoration' was small, with many avoiding military service at will: U. Frevert, *Nation in Barracks*, 50. At the same time, she accepts, almost in passing, that Prussia's was 'the strictest conscription system in Europe at the time' (U. Frevert, *Nation in Barracks*, 101). Figures such as those provided by Ralf Pröve, *Militär, Staat und Gesellschaft im 19. Jahrhundert* (Munich, 2006), 15, to show that 'the percentage of the active military in the population clearly diminished' are misleading in this respect, since the 1786 figure of 194,000 troops from a population of 5.7 million (or 3.5 per cent) amounted to the entire standing army, including

many contemporaries—for example, seventy-one landowners who signed a letter to the Chancellor in 1818—complained that the *Wehrgesetz* had created conditions, 'in the midst of peace', which differed 'little from those of war'.[13] It was self-evident, wrote Berlin's councillors late in 1815, that everyone would defend the fatherland, as they had in 1813, but 'that everyone would also become a soldier in times of peace' was likely to militate 'against the prosperity of civilian industry and, thus, the prosperity of the entire state'.[14] Until 1833, extra recruits were enlisted, in addition, directly into the *Landwehr*, whose regiments would otherwise have been too small, since the regular supply of former standing-army conscripts required twelve years to reach a normal state. Despite undermanning and extensive leave, which meant that three-year military service after 1820 effectively amounted to two-and-a-half years (mainly for reasons of cost), the majority of Prussian men had faced the possibility of conscription, with those who served being chosen by lot.[15]

In other German states, which were sometimes distinguished by their subjects from the 'military' monarchy of Prussia, wartime laws of conscription stayed in place.[16] Bavaria's conscription law of 1812 established the terms of its military constitution until 1868.[17] In Baden, the conscription law of 1812 and, in Württemberg, the 1806 law and 1809 royal order, removing exemptions, remained decisive. Article 23 of Württemberg's constitution of September 1819 declared that 'the duty to defend the fatherland and the liability of military service is general', with 'no other than the exceptions established via the acts of the *Bund* and existing laws'.[18] Similar provisions were contained in the constitutions of other German states: for example, Articles 28 and 29 of the constitution of the Grand Duchy of Hesse (1820) stated that 'every Hessian has the duty to defend the fatherland' and that 'every Hessian, for whom there is no constitutional exception, has the duty of

---

'foreigners' (about half the contingent), who served—like Prussian recruits—for life (until 1792, when the length of service was reduced to twenty years), whereas the figure for 1840, 135,000 soldiers from a population of 14.9 million inhabitants (or 0.9 per cent), refers only to Prussian conscripts serving in the army of the line, not to reservists, including both levies of the *Landwehr* (fourteen year groups in total).

[13] Cited in U. Frevert, 'Das jakobinische Modell', 31.   [14] Ibid.

[15] Dierk Walter, *Preußische Heeresreformen 1807–1870. Militärische Innovation und der Mythos der 'Roonschen Reform'* (Paderborn, 2003), 343, stresses exceptions and limits to military service, arguably also swayed by comparisons with later periods.

[16] For criticism of Prussia in the aftermath of the Napoleonic campaigns, see the conservative Badenese landowner and later Austrian minister, Johann von Wessenberg, in a letter to his brother on 21 July 1815, in I. H. v. Wessenberg, *Unveröffentlichte Manuskripte und Briefe*, ed. K. Aland (Freiburg, 1968), K. Aland, vol. 2, 149: 'The Prussians have made themselves much hated by their arbitrary use of power. Their passion and hatefulness borders on madness, and the military despotism which is developing in opposition to monarchical power in Prussia can still have damaging consequences. All monarchs and their ministers should now concentrate exclusively on creating tranquility in the world—only a long period of quiet can save them—their current state of fever is terrible and self-consuming.'

[17] W. D. Gruner, *Das bayerische Heer 1825 bis 1864. Eine kritische Analyse der bewaffneten Macht Bayerns vom Regierungsantritt Ludwigs I. zum Vorabend des deutschen Krieges* (Boppard am Rhein, 1972), 42.

[18] *Verfassungs-Urkunde für das Königreich Württemberg vom 23. September 1819* (Stuttgart, 1843), 18; T. M. Schneider, *Heeresergänzung und Sozialordnung. Dienstpflichtige, Einsteher und Freiwillige in Württemberg zur Zeit des Deutschen Bundes* (Frankfurt, 2002).

participating in regular military service', decided by lot and 'with permission given for substitution'.[19]

The effective strengths of the majority of such states were set by the *Kriegsverfassung* (military constitution) of the German Confederation, Article 1 the 'Precise Specifications' of which stipulated that 'the usual contingent of each *Bundesstaat* comprises one hundredth part of its population'.[20] This contingent was made up of soldiers on active service, with a further part of the population—no more than 0.5 per cent per year—of a state held in reserve during wartime (Article 5).[21] As a consequence, the *Mittelstaaten* maintained sizeable active forces, conscripted annually: Württemberg, 13,955 in 1822 and 21,083 in 1859; Baden, 10,000 and 15,028; Saxony, 12,000 and 18,000; and Hanover, 13,054 and 19,728.[22] Correspondingly, states' military spending remained significant, accounting for 37.8 per cent of Prussia's overall budget in 1850, 30 per cent of Hessen-Kassel's, 27.7 per cent of Mecklenburg-Schwerin's, 25.4 per cent of Bavaria's, and 25.4 per cent (1848) of the Habsburg monarchy's expenditure.[23] As was to be expected, the spending of the small states was much lower—with Lippe-Detmold devoting only 9.6 per cent to its military, Schaumburg-Lippe 9.1 per cent, Anhalt-Dessau 7.7 per cent, and Schwarzburg-Sondershausen 6.7 per cent—but their military contribution was also insignificant, providing fewer than 700 troops each to a total confederal force of 301,637 in 1822.

By contrast, for the medium-sized and larger states, yearly conscription entailed military training—or a real prospect of military training—for a considerable part of the male population, as could be seen in Bavaria, whose forces—like those of all other German states except Austria (with a confederal contingent of 95,000 and an overall active force of 270,000 in the 1820s) and Prussia (80,000 and 125,000, plus the *Landwehr*, in 1822)—came largely under the jurisdiction of the *Bund* (see Table 2.1).[24] Thus, between a quarter and two-thirds of Bavarians liable for conscription each year were actually conscripted: 10,000 soldiers were conscripted from 14,933 in 1821; 9,812 from 41,293 in 1831; 13,380 from 44,994 in 1841; 13,000 from 38,580 in 1851; and 20,009 from 41,141 in 1861.[25] Legal exemptions—about 2,000 per year—accounted for a small proportion of the total, whereas exemptions on grounds of height (about 1,500 per year in the 1840s, about half only being exempted temporarily) and health (10,000–12,000 per year, including 1,000–1,500 temporary cases) were more significant, making up between a quarter

[19] H. Dippel (ed.), *Verfassungen der Welt vom späten 18. Jahrhundert bis Mitte des 19. Jahrhunderts* (Munich, 2007), 225–6.

[20] J. Angelow, *Von Wien nach Königgrätz. Die Sicherheitspoltiik des Deutschen Bundes im europäischen Gleichgewicht 1815–1866* (Munich, 1996), 292; E. Wienhöfer, *Das Militärwesen des Deutschen Bundes und das Ringen zwischen Österreich und Preußen um die Vorherrschaft in Deutschland 1815–1866* (Osnabrück, 1973).

[21] J. Angelow, *Von Wien nach Königgrätz*, 293.

[22] Ibid., 324–8. The figures for 1859 include troops used for manning the fortresses of the *Bund*.

[23] Ibid., 85.

[24] The official figure for the Habsburg monarchy's full strength, referred to here, overstates the state's effective forces: J. G. A. Galletti (ed.), *Allgemeine Weltkunde oder Encyklopädie für Geographie, Statistik und Staatengeschichte*, 5th edn (Pesth, 1822), 139.

[25] W. D. Gruner, *Das bayerische Heer*, 360–2.

Table 2.1 Conscription, Eligibility, and Suitability in Bavaria and Prussia

Year (state)	Eligible	Conscripts	Legal exemptions	Unsuitable: size	Unsuitable: disabled/ health	Temporarily unsuitable
1820 (Pr)	—	**40,888**	—	—	—	—
1820 (Bav)	15,647	15,647	—	—	—	—
1831 (Bav)	41,293	9,812	—	518	10,632	—
1837 (Pr)	—	**35,512**	—	—	—	—
1837 (Bav)	41,441	9,812	—	778	10,892	—
1846 (Pr)	—	**40,363**	—	—	—	—
1846 (Bav)	41,100	9,812	2,296	899	10,578	2,161
1851 (Bav)	38,580	13,000	2,292	825	8,009	2,095
1860 (Bav)	41,169	17,389	—	—	—	—
1862 (Pr)	—	**63,000***	—	—	—	—

*After army reform under Albrecht von Roon.

Source: Derived from W. D. Gruner, *Das bayerische Heer 1825 bis 1864* (Boppard am Rhein, 1972), 360–7; U. Frevert, *A Nation in Barracks* (Oxford, 2004), 54, 153.

and a third of the entire year group.[26] In 1851, 2,292 were legally exempt, 8,834 were deemed permanently 'unsuitable' (825 because of their size, 8,009 because of ailments or physical incapacity), 2,095 were reported to be temporarily unsuitable (returning to the muster the following year), and 28,781 were held to be fit for service, with 13,000 of these being conscripted by lottery. Although they only spent around eighteen months in barracks and had long periods of furlough, when they worked and pursued trades at home, they nonetheless served a total of six years, as in Baden and Württemberg, during which time they were subject to military law and were prohibited from marrying, starting a business, or receiving communal land.[27] As a result, the army loomed large in the 'third Germany' as well as in Prussia and—despite the continuation of different laws of conscription in different territories and the dissolution of the *Landwehr* in 1831—in Austria.[28]

The continuing importance of the prospect of military service in the majority of German states provided a link between peacetime and wartime—in the past and in future—and maintained contemporaries' sense that war was at once legitimate and

[26] Ibid., 363–7.   [27] U. Frevert, *Nation in Barracks*, 109.
[28] The case presented here militates against much of the recent historiography, which tends to stress exemptions, substitutions, and other limitations: U. Frevert, 'Citizen-Soldiers: General Conscription in the Nineteenth and Twentieth Centuries', in E. Krimmer and P. A. Simpson (eds), *Enlightened War: German Theories and Cultures of Warfare from Frederick the Great to Clausewitz* (Rochester, 2011), 219–37; D. Walter, 'Roonsche Reform oder militärische Revolution? Wandlungsprozesse im preußischen Heerwesen vor den Einigungskriegen', in Karl-Heinz Lutz, Martin Rink, and Marcus von Salisch (eds), *Reform—Reorganisation—Transformation. Zum Wandel in deutschen Streitkräften von den preußischen Heeresreformen bis zur Transformation der Bundeswehr* (Munich, 2010), 181–98; D. Walter, 'Was blieb von den preußischen Militärreformen 1807–1814?', in Jürgen Kloosterhuis and Sönke Neitzel (eds), *Krise, Reformen—und Militär. Preußen vor und nach der Katastrophe von 1806* (Berlin 2009), 107–27; W. D. Gruner, 'Die Position der Armee in Staat, Wirtschaft und Gesellschaft Bayerns 1848–1866', *Oberbayerisches Archiv*, 97 (1973), 13–31.

inevitable. The extent to which armies affected Germans' attitudes to war differed, however, depending on individuals' exposure to army life, their educational and social background, and their regional, confessional, and political affiliations. Conservatives tended to be closer to aristocratic milieux, which still dominated the officer corps of the majority of German armies. Democrats were more aware of the reports and complaints of the rank and file. Whatever their allegiances, though, most officials, deputies, journalists, and writers had no direct experience of full military service, either as a regular officer or as a conscript. Outside Prussia, wealthier families were allowed to pay for a replacement for their sons, if their attempts to persuade their doctor failed. Many gained exemptions on medical grounds, in the manner of the Leipzig publisher Friedrich Arnold Brockhaus, whose son was released from military service in 1823 'without any further inconvenience'.[29] Others availed themselves of a clause exempting first-born sons who were needed 'to preserve the family's well-being and civic standing', in the words of one deputy in 1822, debating a provision which was later included in Baden's Conscription Law (1825).[30] In 1827, more than a quarter of those fit for military service in Baden, or 1,190 cases, were granted exemptions on these grounds. Even in states like Württemberg which refused to grant general exemptions, it has been estimated that one in seven sons was being released in this way by the 1850s and early 1860s.[31] For 'respectable' progeny who were not exempted on either medical or family grounds, parents usually took the option of paying for a substitute, who had to sign an officially stamped contract that he was willing to serve and who received a lump sum, paid by the family and administered by the army, at the end of his six-year period of service. In Baden, the sum was negotiated privately—generally 450 guilders for infantrymen and 500 for cavalrymen during the 1830s, or the amount of a labourer's yearly earnings—while in Württemberg, it was set by the government at 400 guilders, with substitutes supplied from an official list. Although the sums involved were considerable, amounting to about a third of a mid-ranking civil servant's salary, most burghers and a number of others were able to provide them: 400–500 per annum out of 2,000–3,000 conscripted in Baden during the 1840s and about 450 per annum, or 16 per cent, in Württemberg during the same decade, rising to 22 per cent during the 1850s.[32]

In Prussia, where there were few exemptions (clergy and, initially, teachers) and there was less chance of influencing doctors since they were employed by the military, the sons of the middling strata were left the option of serving 'voluntarily' for one year instead of three, often registering—until the early 1860s, when the practice was banned—after they had been conscripted by lot. Approximately 800 volunteers, who were required to have completed the *Klein-Tertia* at *Gymnasium* and to pay for their own lodging and equipment, served as 'one-year volunteers' (*Einjährig-Freiwilliger*) every year in Prussia during the 1840s alongside 40,000 or so ordinary conscripts. The War Ministry asked that they be treated 'with

---

[29] H. Brockhaus, *Aus den Tagebüchern* (Leipzig, 1884–7), vol. 1, 66.
[30] Ibid. For the debate in Baden, see U. Frevert, *Nation in Barracks*, 104.
[31] U. Frevert, *Nation in Barracks*, 107.   [32] Ibid., 107–9.

'forbearance', sparing them 'all the common soldiers' hardships'.[33] Although they were frequently despised by NCOs and ridiculed by noble officers, as Theodor Fontane amongst others noted in his memoirs, volunteers ate separately (with access to the officers' *Casino*), lodged in private quarters, became 'vice-non-commanding officers' (*Vizeunteroffiziere*), and enjoyed more free time, living apart from the ordinary troops.[34] Certainly, Fontane, who went on an impromptu two-week trip to England with a friend in the middle of his period of service, spoke largely of other *Freiwillige*, not the rank and file, in his account of that episode of his life.[35] On his return from London, he imagined his captain saying to himself:

> Yes, the young man there, ... when this year is behind him, his life lies before him once more. And even now he was over there and has seen a part of the world and has broadened his chest. And me? I'm now forty-five and I'm going nowhere. Nothing but recruits and parade and manoeuvres. And then more recruits.[36]

In Fontane's opinion, volunteers were different from career soldiers and conscripts. The officials, courtiers, middle-class commentators, and notables who defined and discussed the nature of war and the military had had little direct experience of combat or life in the army. In Mannheim, the Bassermann family, who were the city's most prominent merchants, simply paid for substitutes for their sons until Baden entered the North German Confederation in 1867, when that generation of Bassermanns served as one-year volunteers.[37] In Saxony, Karl Biedermann recounted his time at school, as a student and as a journalist during the 1830s and 1840s without any mention of military service.[38] The same was true of Otto Elben, the son of Stuttgart's principal newspaper proprietor.[39] Unexpectedly, this lack of experience appears to have made them less critical of modern warfare and more supportive of the military, accepting many of the myths of 1813 and ignoring much of the suffering which had been borne by the combatants of the Napoleonic Wars. In some states, different versions of events were remembered. For instance, the later democrat Ludwig Bamberger recalled of Hesse-Darmstadt that 'the old ones told us much about the times of war and something of the times of the Kurfürsten', but nothing of the 'wars of freedom', since their stories focused on 'the return from Russia, the battle of Hanau, the terrible war plague which raged amongst soldiers and citizens during the "blockade", and finally the arrival of the Germans [and] the appearance of the Russians'.[40] Such stories remained the exception to a dominant mythology of '1813'. In this respect, Fontane's year of voluntary

[33] Cited ibid., 54. Max von Schinckel called his volunteer year, in 1868, the 'most delicious', 'carefree', and 'beautiful' year of his life: E. Rohrmann, *Max von Schinckel. Hanseatischer Bankmann im wilhelminischen Deutschland* (Hamburg, 1971), 42.

[34] T. Fontane, *Von Zwanzig bis Dreißig* (Hamburg, 2012), 137–42. Karl Helfferich, *Georg von Siemens. Ein Lebensbild aus Deutschlands großer Zeit* (Berlin, 1921), 23, noted that the volunteer used to come home for lunch, despite belonging to the 1st Company in Berlin, which did an extra two hours of training per day.

[35] T. Fontane, *Von Zwanzig bis Dreißig*, 137–42, 155–9.   [36] Ibid., 155.

[37] L. Gall, *Bürgertum in Deutschland* (Berlin, 1989), 394–5.

[38] K. Biedermann, *Mein Leben und ein Stück Zeitgeschichte* (Breslau, 1886), vol. 1.

[39] O. Elben, *Lebenserinnerungen 1823–1899* (Stuttgart, 1931).

[40] L. Bamberger, *Erinnerungen* (Berlin, 1899), 3–4.

service in the Kaiser-Franz regiment was typical, revealing how closely myths of the wars of liberation were connected to the army itself, even in the 1840s:

> The regimental commander was Colonel von Hirschfeld, the son of General *Karl Friedrich von Hirschfeld*, who dated from the era of Friedrich the Great and who successfully conducted the encounter that became famous as the '*Landwehrschlacht*' on 28 August 1813 near Hagelsberg, and the brother of General *Moritz von Hirschfeld*, who fought in Spain against Napoleon from 1809 until 1815—later commanding general of the Eighth Corps—and who has left very interesting sketches of his Spanish experiences.
>
> I was allocated to the second battalion, on the Neue Friedrichstraße, and reported to Major von Wnuck, an old campaign soldier from 1813...My captain, in the sixth company, was the soul of a man. He had, although still a captain, participated at Ligny and Waterloo, scarcely fifteen years old at the time. At Ligny, he shot at a French lancer and missed, upon which the Frenchman approached him, laughing, and took his *Tschako* off his head with his lance. Such stories were often told.[41]

Few contemporaries except volunteers, conscripts, and officers in the Prussian army were exposed so systematically to the mythology of 1813, it can be held, but many seem to have been influenced by the broader reconceptualization of war and military life with which it was associated.

THE POLITICS OF THE GERMAN ARMIES DURING THE 'RESTORATION'

Nearly all commentators after 1815 accepted that a strong army was required in order to defend a state against external enemies, with the possibility of mobilizing the 'nation'—through a *levée en masse*—during wartime. The point at issue was how best to achieve such mobilization within different forms of polity and civil society. Thus, although the Heidelberg professor Carl Theodor Welcker confessed to the Badenese assembly in 1831 that he would 'give up the last penny that I had hidden away, just as all other fathers in my situation would, in order to free my son from the sacred duty of defending his country, if he were not interested in a career in the officer class', he remained adamant that a free constitution rested on a 'martial spirit' and a 'citizens' army'.[42] Welcker's co-editor of the *Staatslexikon*, Carl von Rotteck, had written one of the most important statements of the liberal position in his treatise *Über stehende Heere und Nationalmiliz* in 1816: his apparent rejection of 'conscription' and his distinction between 'standing armies' and 'militias' create a misleading impression, concealing the fact that he was advocating universal military training for the 'whole nation'—'i.e. the part of it capable

---

[41] Ibid., 137–8.
[42] C. T. Welcker's speech in *Verhandlungen der Ständeversammlung des Großherzogtums Baden im Jahre 1831* (Karlsruhe, 1831), supplementary vol. 4, 37; C. T. Welcker, 'Heerwesen', in C. v. Rotteck and C. T. Welcker (eds), *Staatslexikon*, vol. 7, 589–607.

of fighting'—and a 'standing national defence force'.[43] 'The current state of the art of war and a necessary caution about suddenly occurring dangers command imperiously that, beside the universal and normally constituted national defence force (*Nationalwehr*), a special, more fully trained and immediately deployable force of fighters exists', he wrote, which would consist of 'a small number of infantry and a larger group of cavalry, artillery and engineer corps, and training schools for leaders'.[44] The banning of foreigners (even 'legally nationalized' ones), numbers inferior to those of the 'national' army, an oath to the fatherland and government, and the national representative assembly's sanctioning of the government, which in turn controlled the standing military power, were all designed to guarantee 'that this standing national army, too, always remains truly national in spirit and effect'.[45]

What was critical, in Rotteck's opinion, was that the standing army was subordinate to a nation in arms, which was embodied in the principle that 'Every citizen, as soon and for as long as he is capable of defending himself, is a part of the national army.'[46] Such an army would be made up of the 'entire youth of the Reich—without distinction'—and trained in the use of weapons for a time and in a manner which was 'legally determined', 'without a break in civil occupations'.[47] 'Conscription' was deplored because it was associated with the drafting of populations into standing armies for a long period of time, making 'the whole nation *soldierly*, i.e. imbued with the attitude of a hireling and mercenary', and permitting their use in domestic acts of repression and offensive wars of adventure and expansion: 'A single state of this kind—we have seen it with France—can fill an area of the world with rubble and corpses.'[48] If several powers adopted this type of conscription and pursued offensive wars, a 'perpetual war of everyone against everyone else' resulted, under 'the conditions of the highest civilization (*Civilisation*)', akin to that of 'our very oldest, most bestial ancestors', who were cannibals, and 'the wild hordes of the Irokesen and Ilinesen today', 'only more terrifying because of greater measures of force and a richer range of goods'.[49] History—from the Greeks to the Dutch and Swiss—had shown, however, 'that neither physical force nor masses bestow victory, but spirit and morale'.[50] In such circumstances, the arming of the nation could be more effective in defence—but not attack—than a standing army, while at the same time guarding against external wars and preventing internal tyranny and the thwarting of domestic industry and prosperity. Rotteck's model for this form of militia was an idealized republic in which even 'conscripted republican youths' could be 'a noble idea'.[51]

Rotteck was a deputy of the first chamber of the Badenese *Ständeversammlung*, which was one of the main forums of parliamentary politics and liberalism in early

---

[43] C. v. Rotteck, *Über stehende Heere und Nationalmiliz* (1816), in C. v. Rotteck, *Sammlung kleinerer Schriften*, vol. 2, 234–6. For accounts which take Rotteck more literally, giving too little weight to the ambiguity of terms such as 'Konskription' in this early period, see R. Pröve, *Militär, Staat und Gesellschaft im 19. Jahrhundert*, 17. Jürgen Angelow's account is more nuanced: Jürgen Angelow, *Der Deutsche Bund* (Darmstadt, 2003), 17–18, as is that of Jörn Leonhard, *Bellizismus*, 430–1.

[44] C. v. Rotteck, *Über stehende Heere*, 236.   [45] Ibid., 237.   [46] Ibid., 234.

[47] Ibid., 235.   [48] Ibid., 209.   [49] Ibid., 209–10.   [50] Ibid., 194.

[51] Ibid., 230.

nineteenth-century Germany. This milieu, it has been contended, remained sceptical of the army, partly as a result of enlightened criticism of 'absolutism' and of 'barbarity' and partly because of Baden's history as a *Rheinbund* state which joined the Coalition only after the battle of Leipzig in October 1813. 'The propaganda *über*-myth of burgeoning German patriotism across all social classes culminating in common war efforts in 1813 largely found no resonance here—despite each government's best efforts to reconstitute it for its own state', writes Frevert: 'the middle classes in Baden, Württemberg, Bavaria or Saxony saw no reason to relinquish their traditional distance from military affairs'.[52] Yet liberal and other deputies in Baden's second chamber all started from the premise, in the debate about a new conscription law in the autumn of 1822, that a defence of the fatherland by every able-bodied man was a self-evident principle and that the Revolutionary and Napoleonic Wars had made *Konskription* inevitable. Unlike Rotteck, the head of the assembly's commission on military service, Johann Adam von Itzstein, had 'not found a new word for the word "conscription law"' and had therefore let it stand.[53] Conscription was to be understood in the context of a subject's willing defence of the fatherland, requiring the replacement of the government's preferred term '*Aushebung*' (levy) with '*Aufruf*' (call-up), which implied a voluntary decision. 'One doesn't usually say that the law calls on one, but that it demands', retorted the *Staatsminister* Karl Christian von Berkheim: 'The word "*Aufruf*" appears to make it a matter of free will whether one wants to follow or not.'[54] Ludwig Georg Winter, the state counsellor, agreed: 'There was a call, for example, to give assistance, with each having it in his power to do it or not.'[55] By contrast, '*Aushebung*' implied a 'duty', decided not arbitrarily but by lot.[56] The 'great majority' of deputies rejected the government's terminology and adopted the idea of a call-up precisely, in the words of one liberal manufacturer, because 'it is truly a word which betrays a certain worth', whereas 'levy means, in my opinion, a forced act', redolent of the 'press-gang'.[57] To Ludwig von Liebenstein, the 'word *levy* no longer belongs in our current constitutional order of things', for it recalled, 'all too much, earlier forms, by means of which our youths were summoned to military service—the old canton rules, which were always founded on arbitrariness'.[58] '*Aufruf*' pointed towards equality before the law and was 'more suited to the honour of the military estate, of which I am as much in favour as any member of this chamber'.[59] The chamber decided by vote to call potential conscripts '*kriegsdienstpflichtig*', or those with the duty of doing war service.[60] The assumption of every deputy who voiced an opinion was that such military service was justified.

The dispute between Badenese deputies and officials in 1822 about whether military service was a 'burden' (*Last*) or not took place against this 'patriotic' background.

[52] U. Frevert, *Nation in Barracks*, 106. Most of Frevert's evidence for such scepticism comes from Baden, which she rightly considers a test case.

[53] J. A. v. Itzstein, 7 Nov. 1822, *Verhandlungen der Ständeversammlung des Großherzogthums Baden 1822* (Karlsruhe, 1822), vol. 8, 77.

[54] K. C. v. Berkheim, 7 Nov. 1822, ibid., 83.   [55] L. G. Winter, ibid., 7 Nov. 1822, ibid., 81.

[56] Ibid.   [57] F. Buhl, ibid., 82.

[58] L. v. Liebenstein, ibid., 82–3.   [59] Ibid., 83.   [60] Ibid., 84–5.

Thus, when the army advisor to the government accused him of misrepresenting military service as a great 'load' rather than extolling it as 'a benevolent act' or 'a sacred duty', Itzstein issued a long denial:

> I, too, hold it to be a sacred duty to defend the fatherland, but it is nevertheless also a burden, just as medicine remains a burden, even when it heals. No one would doubt, by the way, that it is a burden when I have to serve for six years during peacetime, a burden when a father has to give up his son, his only support, for six years, a burden when he has to sacrifice—frequently—400 florins or, in wartime, 800 florins in order to place a man in the stead of his son. That the duty to do military service is a real burden also can be seen, sadly and tellingly, from the depiction of the government commission itself, according to which so many people have deserted who would scarcely have sought to avoid a good turn...If this standpoint is correct which I have outlined here, then it appears truly odd that something should not be a burden which the government itself, in the speech with which it introduced the law, has declared a heavy burden. The speaker at this point read out the observation, from the speech of Herr Geh. Referendär v. Saur of April 1822..., that examines the great sacrifices which the state demands through military service, of the heavy state burden, of the harsh duties and the pressing troubles of the military estate, and thus showed that the government had claimed just the same as the [parliamentary] commission's report.[61]

Other deputies concurred that it was necessary 'to portray military duty to the fatherland as a burden', but one which 'itself promotes the honour and value of the military', for 'it cannot be denied that standing armies are an evil, a burden for the *Volk*':

> It is a burden, a burdensome duty, to defend ourselves and, if one observes it from this angle, if one declares it a burden of this estate that one has to sacrifice one's life for us, that one has to be torn from one's usual occupation in life even in peacetime by standing armies corresponding to current conditions, in order to carry out a duty which must always be recognized as pressing, so the worth of the military estate, and mutual respect and love, will be promoted rather than diminished in this fashion.[62]

Although it was true that some youths had been known to cry when called to the service of the fatherland, conceded Gottlieb Bernhard Fecht, these actions were 'a source of shame for our *Volk*' which would be eradicated by establishing a more workable system of conscription.[63] 'In a just war, in conditions of emergency for the fatherland, who would not give up even their only son with joy for the defence of the most sacred rights?' asked another speaker on 22 November: 'I would even call someone...unworthy of living in this country, if he wanted to evade this sacred duty.'[64] For Joseph Kern, a citizen of Freiburg and a liberal civil servant, defence of the state was the 'most sacred' good: although the question before the chamber was what to do 'in times of profound peace', when 'only a small part of the male population capable of bearing arms is required to supplement

---

[61] J. A. v. Itzstein, ibid., 78–9.   [62] F. Buhl, ibid., 81–2.
[63] G. B. Fecht, ibid., 371. Fecht wanted to pay compensation to those who served, but this was rejected by the chamber as impracticable.
[64] L. Hüber, ibid., 378.

the standing army', it remained incontestable—'Who would deny this basic principle?'—that, 'in a war for the fatherland, every burgher has a duty to serve', without exceptions or replacements.[65] Consequently, when the liberal merchant Johann Ludwig Bassermann asked why exceptions, which were allowed during peacetime, should not also be allowed in wartime, the majority of his fellow liberals opposed him, voting to conscript those who had previously been freed—by payment or exemption—from military service, albeit after the conscription of all those who had not been freed.[66] With the state at war, the principle of conscription was a general one.

In theory, the authorization of substitution, which distinguished most German states from Prussia, revealed more about the attitudes of the ministers of *Mittelstaaten* and about the relative significance of notables in representative assemblies than about popular conceptions of military service and warfare. The purchase of replacements, many of whom were old soldiers, could be seen to benefit the state by providing experienced, physically fit, and reliable troops, whilst also giving the substitutes themselves the equivalent of a year's wages on leaving the army after six years. It corresponded, in spite of his concern to establish a system 'without distinctions', to Rotteck's plan in 1816 to divide citizens into several classes 'according to age or estate or other just grounds for distinguishing them', which would determine in what order they were recruited and for what purpose.[67] Little time was spent discussing substitutions in the Badenese second chamber in 1822 because they were not controversial, enjoying what one deputy described as 'the justified praise of the replacement system of recent years', since it was acknowledged to be 'one of the best'.[68] The majority of European states had such a system, including France, which was widely cited as the most relevant point of reference, not least because Baden had retained a Napoleonic civil code. More challengeable, it seemed to many deputies, were exemptions, even on religious grounds, with Mennonites and other small sects which 'may not bear arms' being advised by Johann Georg Duttlinger to buy replacements as a community.[69] The main exemptions were justified by the needs of individual families: only sons were to be freed from military service, it was decided by thirty-seven votes to fifteen, because the citizen whose 'only son is ripped away from him becomes helpless and inconsolable', because 'nobody supports him in his industry in old age, and his savings, often bitterly acquired and carefully saved up for his child pass into foreign hands', as Joseph Ruth put it as he introduced the case for this limited form of exemption.[70]

The fact that the purpose of the military estate was to protect citizens and their property did not make the former subordinate to the latter, given that it was required for external defence, but it did warrant the freeing of an exceptional

---

[65] J. Kern, ibid., 378–9.   [66] Ibid., 554–7.

[67] C. v. Rotteck, *Über stehende Heere*, 234–5.

[68] D. Völker, 30 Nov. 1822, *Verhandlungen der Ständeversammlung des Großherzogthums Baden 1822*, vol. 9, 7.

[69] J. G. Duttlinger, 29 Nov. 1822, ibid., vol. 8, 530.   [70] J. Ruth, 22 Nov. 1822, ibid., 356.

category of young men, who were required to keep families, their farms, and businesses intact. 'Why should the blood of an only son be spilled, if his family, deprived of its last and sole support, is laid to waste and its goods pass into foreign hands?' asked Ruth on 22 November 1822:

> The giving up of only sons is not a favour to the fatherland; it leads to its destruction, since the downfall of every family is a loss for the state; thus, a father does not make this sacrifice for the state; he makes it, frequently, for the freeing of a good-for-nothing, who still has six brothers who are a burden for the country, their communes and their parents.[71]

For Ruth, the measure was not against equality per se, but it was directed against indiscriminate, revolutionary levelling on the French model. 'We have been eye witnesses of the abominations, of the acts of cruelty which were carried out in France under the banner of this sacred name', he went on: 'Which despots, which tyrants can history name under whose government so much innocent blood has been spilled, so many people have been robbed of freedom and property, as has happened within a few years in the French Revolution under the empire of freedom and equality.'[72] Other deputies were anxious to prove that exemptions made no distinction between 'the noble, just like the burgher, the millionaire and the beggar, the educated and the day labourer, the professional and the peasant farmer', and they were therefore not a reversion to 'the old realm of privileges' and were compatible with a desire for equality.[73] The second chamber should imagine the 'scene of wailing', if a blind mother had her last remaining son, having sacrificed six, torn away from her, leaving her without anyone to feed and care for her, declared Kern to opponents like Itzstein, who could see no reason for the consequences of one set of exemptions to be visited on the majority which was not exempt.[74] The dispute was one between proponents of equality and supporters of the family rather than between—in Frevert's words—'civil' interests and patriotism or *raisons d'état*.[75] The task of the Badenese second chamber in 1822, which it carried out successfully, was to create a conscription law suitable for a hierarchical, largely agricultural society. Debates amongst liberals in other *Mittelstaaten* were less vociferous, with less opportunity for politicians and journalists to challenge the government, but they involved similar considerations.[76]

There is little evidence that German liberals' perceptions of the military changed fundamentally between the early 1820s and 1848. Many liberals and democrats—including Rotteck, Heinrich von Gagern, Droysen, Wilhelm Schulz, and Julius Weiske—supported the deployment of existing armies for national ends during the 1840s.[77] Carl Theodor Welcker, who was a *Staatswissenschaftler* at Freiburg as

---

[71] Ibid., 353–4.   [72] Ibid., 356.   [73] J. Kern, 22 Nov. 1822, ibid., 382.
[74] Ibid., 380, 376.   [75] U. Frevert, *Nation in Barracks*, 104–5.
[76] N. Pütter, *Teilnahme und Staatsbürgertum. Von der Etablierung und Verwandlung des 'politischen Bürgers'. Das Beispiel Württemberg* (Münster, 2001), 70–4, 250–308; P. Sauer, *Revolution und Volksbewaffnung. Die württembergischen Bürgerwehren im 19. Jahrhundert* (Ulm, 1976), 36–73.
[77] C. v. Rotteck, 'Krieg', in C. v. Rotteck and C. T. Welcker (eds), *Staatslexikon*, vol. 9, 491–509; H. v. Gagern to H. C. v. Gagern, 9 Apr. 1845, in P. Wentzcke and W. Klötzer (eds), *Deutscher Liberalismus im Vormärz*, 291; W. Schulz, 'Frieden', in C. v. Rotteck and C. T. Welcker (eds), *Staatslexikon*, 2nd edn,

well as a co-editor of the *Staatslexikon*, showed how some positions had altered and many fundamental principles had remained the same in his 'appendix' to the article on the '*Heerwesen*' in the first edition of the *Staatslexikon* in 1839.[78] Almost two decades after the debates about conscription at the time of and immediately after the Vienna Final Acts (1820), the Badenese liberal had come to believe that 'the first, basic principle of a military constitution which is not incorrigibly unjust is the exclusion of exemptions and substitutions'.[79] He distanced himself from existing systems of military recruitment in the third Germany—where 'only the poorer citizens' offered 'the highest of all earthly goods' and sacrificed 'the most energetic time of their life'—and he championed the system of the Hohenzollern monarchy.[80] Yet Welcker's interpretation of Prussia's military emphasized the *Landwehr*, understood as a form of militia, 'the most glorious and happiest institution of this state'.[81] The essence of the system, which the Freiburg academic wanted to introduce into other German states (especially those of South Germany, where the *Staatslexikon*'s readership was concentrated), was its universality:

> Each year, the whole cohort of young men of the relevant year group capable of bearing arms would be conscripted, according to constitutional laws and decisions, as the first levy, without exceptions and without buying one's way out, for as short a period as possible, to complete the education and training of their military service.[82]

Like most commentators, Welcker saw the need for a fully trained, enduring army of the line—or standing army—as the 'kernel' of his plan, providing 'direction and a school for the entire national defence force (*Nationalwehr*)'.[83] The laws of the German Confederation, which set the level of recruitment in most states, insisted that a high proportion of troops—half of the contingent, or 5,000 conscripts annually per million inhabitants—became troops of the line, with the other half free to join the *Landwehr*, both components of which conformed to the liberal's scheme. The first cohort of the *Landwehr*, made up of conscripts, would serve unpaid for short spells of a longer period of service, trained by former officers and NCOs from the army of the line, alongside conscript soldiers who had finished their stint in the regular army. That stint, the example of Prussia had demonstrated, could be short, training soldiers in all branches of the army within three years and volunteers within a year. The Hohenzollern monarchy, 'in order to maintain its

---

vol. 5, 197–255; J. Weiske, *Rechtslexikon für Juristen aller Teutschen Staaten enthaltend die gesammte Rechtswissenschaft*, vol. 6, 221. This is not to argue that German liberals counselled war on all occasions, even during the 1840 Rhine crisis, when liberal periodicals were varied in their response: J. Brophy, 'The Rhine Crisis of 1840 and German Nationalism: Chauvinism, Skepticism and Regional Reception', *Journal of Modern History*, 85 (2013), 17–25.

[78] U. Frevert, *Nation in Barracks*, 116, claims that 'Welcker's positive reading of military service deviates radically from the unfavourable attitude dominant in the southern German states, prevalent in their assemblies and widespread in public opinion during the *Vormärz* period', but she musters little evidence in support of this assertion beyond her examination of the debates in Baden in 1822, her reading of which I have contested.

[79] C. T. Welcker, 'Anhang zum Artikel Heerwesen (Landwehrsystem)', in C. T. Welcker and C. v. Rotteck (eds), *Staatslexikon*, vol. 7, 589, 594–5.

[80] Ibid.   [81] Ibid., 592.   [82] Ibid., 590.   [83] Ibid.

European position with barely a third of the population of the other great empires', had had to recruit three times as many soldiers as other states, dispatching them as paid troops to the army of the line.[84] The *Mittelstaaten* did not need to do this, allowing them to send more conscripts to the *Landwehr* in order 'to reduce costs and disturbances to domestic industry and occupations very considerably'.[85] For 'smaller states' in particular, 'the greater size of the army and the greater military and patriotic strength of the whole *Volk* is worth immeasurably more, indeed all': a state of a million inhabitants could only maintain 10,000 soldiers of the line 'with very great, previously and elsewhere unheard-of effort', serving as a mere part of a foreign-led corps, but under the *Landwehr* system it could maintain its own corps of 30,000–40,000 soldiers, 'with a trained, military population behind it!'[86]

Welcker was convinced that small standing armies, with their preoccupation with parades and noble co-optation, were ineffective against larger patriotic armies open to talent, as Prussia—with a well-stocked treasury and 'such well-drilled troops'— had proven in 1806.[87] His models of successful 'popular armies' (*Volksheeren*) were Swiss, Dutch, British, the French at the start of the revolution in 1792–4, and the Germans in 1813–15, 'in their immortal victory for freedom and a more noble education'.[88] Central to such a conception was the belief that wars were protracted, granting 'a training period of months' between the approach and declaration of conflict, and that they depended on numbers and morale more than technology and technique, which could be left to the standing 'core' of an army:

> Even if, despite everything hitherto, some technical military advantages are granted to troops of the line and a reserve, as Theobald [the writer of the original article on the 'Heerwesen' in the *Staatslexikon*] suggests, are these not *vastly outweighed*, especially since our system still retains a kernel of troops of the line and training by them? Would they not be outweighed, first, by the disproportionately greater strength of this army, as well as by their more patriotic attitude and spirit and their higher, more noble education, and, third, by the unequally more military, more patriotic and self-sacrificing attitude and virtue *of the entire Volk* and the *reliable support* that the army finds in it, and, fourth and finally, by the greater prosperity of the state coffers and the citizens, which unpaid service in the *Landwehr* offers in peacetime, through greater monetary savings and a gain in labour, in comparison with standing, paid, garrison duty?[89]

Critically, for Welcker, war was not threatening. Indeed, it could give a national fillip to a population, imbuing it with a sense of vitality: 'The true force of life, the nourishing, supportive and rejuvenating ground for the defence force of an army is the patriotic (*vaterländisch*), freedom-giving, courageous, war-like attitude of one's nation'.[90] 'Without this, every protection on the part of the best-equipped army is a game of chance', he went on.[91]

Defence of the nation against foreign enemies and civic well-being were closely linked, with an 'organic connection and exchange' between the military and the civilian population not simply perceived as a means of avoiding despotism through

---

[84] Ibid., 591.   [85] Ibid.   [86] Ibid., 600–1.   [87] Ibid., 601.   [88] Ibid., 602.
[89] Ibid., 600.   [90] Ibid., 596.   [91] Ibid.

the deployment of a praetorian guard, but of building the foundation for 'a strong, virtuous life in a healthy constitutional state'.[92] The relationship was reciprocal: 'The army, here, makes the *Volk* and the people makes the army virtuous and strong, and both support and complement each other, just as they harm each other under a poor military order.'[93] Ordinary soldiers, when they were no longer merely 'mercenaries and the poorest' but 'the sons of the most noble and respectable', all felt 'elevated', provided they were treated equally, sharing a 'more noble, higher sense and education' as 'defenders of the fatherland and citizens capable of bearing arms'.[94] What was more, they had faced the same 'struggles and dangers', bestowing on them a sense of 'manly' independence and precluding 'softening, pettiness, weakness and cowardice': 'Even truly fresh, decisive moral courage in life would, at least, be more rarely nurtured in those who do not somehow strengthen their bodies and who do not train themselves physically to look death and danger in the face.'[95] It was, as a consequence, a condition of Welcker's 'harmonious' connection between civil society and the military—comprising both a standing army and a militia—that war was not an object of fear and remained an affair of men rather than machines.

The sense that war was not, in Welcker's term, merely a 'technical' affair, to be left to military experts, gave democrats and radicals, who were often not clearly distinguishable from 'liberals' before 1848, the opportunity to put forward their own schemes for arming the people. Some left-wing critics were content to oppose existing monarchical states and 'absolutism', together with a corresponding international order resting on dynastic 'envy' and 'glory'.[96] The creation of states based on the principle of national sovereignty rather than on the monarchical principle would mean that 'foreign policy has the promotion of the interests of the peoples themselves as its purpose', wrote the Bavarian journalist Johann Georg August Wirth in 1832: 'These, however, come together as one, according to the order of nature, and for this reason world peace, not war, is the determining feature of the human race, according to the eternal order of things.'[97] Most radicals were less utopian, acknowledging the existence of violence and the realities of a distribution of power, and justifying the formation of popular militias and the prosecution of revolutions and civil wars.[98] In Arnold Ruge's 'self-criticism' of an abstract and ineffectual liberalism, overlapping with philosophical Hegelianism, contemporary liberals were deemed to be doing little to defend freedom in a practical sense,

---

[92] Ibid., 598.   [93] Ibid.   [94] Ibid.   [95] Ibid., 597–8.

[96] J. G. A. Wirth, *Die politische Reform Deutschlands*, 35. For a succinct summary of radicals' positions, on which this paragraph draws, see J. Leonhard, *Bellizismus*, 441–7.

[97] J. G. A. Wirth, *Die politische Reform Deutschlands*, 35.

[98] See, for instance, the early socialist Wilhelm Weitling's, *Garantien der Harmonie und Freiheit* (Vivis, 1842), 39, in addition to the texts below: 'We hold war to be an evil, but not for an eternally necessary one, and we seek to use it as an antidote against other greater evils; for as long as injustice rules on earth, war is necessary, war must be waged on it', Wilhelm Weitling, *Die Menschheit, wie sie ist und wie sie sein sollte*, 2nd edn (Berne, 1845), in H. Brandt (ed.), *Restauration und Frühliberalismus 1814–1840* (Darmstadt, 1979), 485–6, imagined an 'industrial army' of civil conscripts (between 15 and 18 years old) organized like a regular army.

despite their claims to be its sole guarantors. Instead of indulging in a 'flight from the world', was 'not the direct way [to gain freedom]—to make all citizens into people and then to let each freely defend the others—infinitely easier and more certain than an undertaking to bring into being a protective police order—which is now the ideal—from the outside, whereby it is falsely implied that these servants of order are the embodiment of reason and all the rest of humanity is irrational?'[99] Ruge's preference was to combine the education and the arming of the people— *Volkserziehung* and *Volksbewaffnung*—to form 'a single, insuperable power' in the state and to render 'armies' (*Heeren*), which were always 'standing' (and, indeed, a 'standing bog'), redundant.[100] 'Only public life and the combination of school and the military can heal these wounds [caused by the long history of standing armies], from which once again, as before, a deadly evil threatens to spring', he concluded in 1843.[101]

Although they were more sceptical than Ruge about the existing order, accusing the Pomeranian journalist of trusting naively in the ability of the state to emancipate citizens, many early socialists and communists sought to extend his injunction to arm the people in order, in Moses Heß's words, to ignite 'a world fire, against which the uniformed firemen of the palace owners would be able to do nothing'.[102] Like many of his collaborators, Heß had been impressed by French 'revolutionaries of the blood', who had fought since 1830 'against the legitimists, against the current government, initially for the republic and now for socialist ideas'.[103] Their 'bloody, life-and-death struggle' and 'practical experiments' stood a chance of realizing 'the truth of socialism sooner than our philosophers can allow themselves to dream'.[104] As such, they were worth emulating, effectively inciting a 'veritable civil war', or a 'struggle of class against class', as Karl Marx put it in a letter to a Russian correspondent in December 1846.[105] Agreeing with Heß that the national wars of states were the by-product of the self-interested competition of capitalists and their states, Marx advocated the use of violence and a different type of war—revolutionary civil war—in order to topple existing structures of power, in direct opposition to liberal, capitalist pacifists such as Richard Cobden.[106] Marx's sponsor and colleague Friedrich Engels, an industrialist and a reserve officer in the Prussian army, went furthest in this respect in a speech at Elberfeld in 1845, advocating the creation of a militia in imitation of the armies of the French Revolution, both to defend the gains of a communist revolution and to foster 'the enthusiasm' of 'these countless masses of the labour

---

[99] A. Ruge, 'Selbstkritik des Liberalismus' (1843), in A. Ruge, *Gesammelte Schriften* (Mannheim, 1846), vol. 3, 113.

[100] Ibid.   [101] Ibid.

[102] M. Heß, 'Die Folgen einer Revolution des Proletariats', *Deutsche-Brüsseler Zeitung*, 14 Oct. 1847, in M. Heß, *Philosophische und sozialistische Schriften*, 432.

[103] M. Heß, 'Über die Not in unserer Gesellschaft und deren Abhilfe' (1845), in M. Heß, *Sozialistische Aufsätze 1841–1847*, ed. T. Zlocisti (Berlin, 1921), 157.

[104] Ibid.

[105] K. Marx to P. W. Annenkow, 28 Dec. 1846, in K. Marx and F. Engels, *Werke* (Berlin, 1956–68), vol. 4, 180–1.

[106] K. Marx, 'Cobdens Pamphlet' (1853), ibid., vol. 8, 510.

force', who had been 'taken from civilized peoples by armies' and who could be enlisted in the communist cause.[107]

The idea of a militia or *Landwehr* was not dismissed out of hand by conservatives after 1815, not least because such forces had been established in most German states between 1813 and 1815 and they continued to play an important part in the Hohenzollern monarchy.[108] Thus, although hardly anyone amongst the circles of conservatives at court, in the administration, and in the army openly opposed the movement after the Congress of Vienna (1815), Carlsbad Decrees (1819), and Vienna Final Acts (1820) towards armies of the line, which were required by the military apparatus of the German Confederation, relatively few spoke out publicly against the *Landwehr*. In Prussia, reactionaries around the Minister of Police, Wilhelm zu Sayn-Wittgenstein-Hohenstein, had persuaded the king to disband thirty-four *Landwehr* battalions and incorporate the sixteen *Landwehr* brigades— now with regular officers holding all field commands—into divisions of the line in December 1819, provoking Boyen's resignation as War Minister. Nonetheless, the myth of a separate *Landwehr*, embodying the principle of an 'arming of the people', persisted amongst conservatives, and the officers and military writers to whom they referred, as well as amongst liberals and some radicals.[109]

Many civilian conservatives such as Ernst Ludwig von Gerlach, one of the most prominent journalists and thinkers in this milieu in the 1830s and 1840s and a founder of the conservative 'party' in Prussia after 1848, had fought in the Napoleonic campaigns—he was injured several times as a volunteer *Jäger* in 1813–15—which they continued to call 'wars of freedom'.[110] Starting from premises different from those of liberals, albeit also regularly critical of state 'absolutism' (on the grounds of an organic social and political hierarchy of estates), conservatives usually seem to have accepted the institution of the *Landwehr* and the memory of a popular war effort in 1813. When Otto von Bismarck-Schönhausen, who later found himself—in his twenties—surrounded by 'a more numerous than interesting clique of Pomeranian squire-bumpkins, Philistines and Ulan officers' on one of his father's estates in the early 1840s, had imagined in a letter to his 'corps brother' at Göttingen Gustav Scharlach in 1834 what it would be like to devote his life to the running of such an estate, he prophesied that he would become 'a well-fed *Landwehr* officer with a moustache, who curses and swears a justifiable hatred of Frenchmen and Jews until the earth trembles, and beats his dogs and his servants in the most brutal fashion, even if he is tyrannized by his wife'.[111] For those Junkers deciding

---

[107] F. Engels, 'Rede in Elberfeld' (1845), ibid., vol. 2, 543.

[108] The *Landwehr* continued to exist in other states, too, although less prominent than in Prussia: see, for instance, F. Münich, *Geschichte der Entwicklung der bayerischen Armee seit zwei Jahrhunderten* (Munich, 1864), 426, on the significance of the *Landwehr-Ordnung* of 1826 in Bavaria.

[109] For the concerted action against Boyen and its aftermath, see G. A. Craig, *Politics of the Prussian Army*, 70–81. The argument here tempers Craig's stark distinction between liberals such as Rotteck, who are said to have seen the standing army merely as 'a tool of despotism', and conservatives in the army and state, who favoured an aristocratic, professionalized army of the line.

[110] H.-C. Kraus, *Ernst Ludwig von Gerlach. Politisches Denken und Handeln eines preussischen Altkonservativen* (Göttingen, 1994), 61–73.

[111] O. v. Bismarck to O. v. Arnim-Kröchlendorff, Oct. 1843, and O. v. Bismarck to G. Scharlach, 7 Apr. 1834, cited in J. Steinberg, *Otto von Bismarck: A Life* (Oxford, 2011), 56, 42–3.

against a career as an officer in the army of the line, which is what Bismarck—according to an anecdote of a family friend—had initially wanted to do before being redirected to the civil service by his mother, the role of *Landwehr* officer, as part of a local social and political elite rather than the command structure of the Prussian army, was an honourable one, at once mythologized and derided by the later judicial official, diplomat, and Chancellor.[112] After trying to avoid it for reasons of health (a minor duelling injury), the young noble completed his one-year voluntary service in 1838.[113] In such family histories, the *Landwehr* was an extension of a noble genealogy of officers, most of whom knew each other or knew of each other and who considered themselves born to lead their localities to war in the service of the king, as their relatives had done in 1813. Militias in this restricted sense, subordinate to the army of the line, were acceptable to many Prussian conservatives.

Prussian military writers such as Rühle von Lilienstern, who became Chief of the General Staff in 1819 and head of the *Kriegsschule* in Berlin in 1837, continued to treat the military as the 'armed wing of the nation', which carried out the will of the people and benefited from the interlocking of the 'arts of war and peace' within the realm of policy-making.[114] All inhabitants of a state had to contribute to its defence on military grounds, since the standing armies of 'absolutism' were more expensive and less efficacious than national ones, tending to become a foreign body in the organism of the state.[115] War, Rühle von Lilienstern believed, would cleanse and invigorate the nation, creating forces which states had to harness and control by educating their populations and instilling patriotism:

> All institutions must be constructed in such a way that they are, at the same time, fit for war and peace, so that the outbreak of a necessary war does not cause the collapse, with deadly force, of the entire existing order, but, rather, that war itself intervenes as the principle of life in the organism of the state, that it becomes a means of making popular liberty grow stronger, of revitalizing the spirit of the *Volk*, of tightening the ties binding the people together and of broadly promoting the well-being of the people.[116]

A standing army was still required in order to protect the Hohenzollern monarchy against surprise attacks, but it was to be reduced in size.

Such changes resulted from a transformation of warfare, contended the military writer Carl von Decker in 1817, in a work based on the writings of the Napoleonic general Joseph Rogniat and resulting from a series of lectures given to the Prussian

---

[112] Ibid., 53.   [113] Ibid., 50–1.

[114] J. J. O A. Rühle v. Lilienstern, *Aufsätze über Gegenstände und Ereignisse aus dem Gebiete des Kriegswesens*, vol. 1, 180. The author also reviewed the 'die der Volksbemannung' of other German states, which he held 'belongs indisputably to the most important and interesting phenomena of our times': J. J. O A. Rühle v. Lilienstern, *Die deutsche Volksbewaffnung* (Berlin, 1815), iii.

[115] J.-J. Langendorf, 'Rühle von Lilienstern und seine Apologie des Krieges', in J. Kunisch and H. Münkler (eds), *Die Wiedergeburt des Krieges aus dem Geist der Revolution* (Berlin, 1999), 211–24.

[116] Cited ibid., 221. Also, A. Lüdtke, '"Wehrhafte Nation" und "innereWohlfahrt": Zur militärischen Mobilisierbarkeit der bürgerlichen Gesellschaft. Konflikt und Konsens zwischen Militär und ziviler Administration in Preußen zwischen 1815 und 1860', *Militärgeschlichtliche Mitteilungen*, 19 (1981), 7–56.

General Staff in 1816–17. 'There was a time when armies were viewed as machines without will,' he wrote: 'The army is an organic body, and therefore not a machine. Its organism rests as much on human as mechanical organisms, and we may not mistake the moral and spiritual element in the army, and not forget it, above and beyond the physical element.'[117] The Napoleonic Wars, it appeared, had posed new problems for the organization of armies, which could not be ignored: 'This kind of war has an altogether different character from that of war with regular armies', with *Volksheeren* (armies of the people) unable to provide for themselves for more than a few days and proving ineffective in attack.[118] Such armies would become 'more useful, as soon as they limit themselves to attacking the supply lines of the enemy in order to inflict small but all the more regular losses', as had occurred in the Vendée.[119] Their organization lay 'in the mass of the people itself', and must be arranged according to basic principles different from those of regular armies, including a more extensive network of arsenals and a less oppressive regime of discipline, which 'would only be damaging here': 'Discipline must only tend to set in motion spiritual elements and moral levers.'[120] Officers were generally elected, often from those in positions of authority in civilian life, and service remained voluntary. Regular armies, which necessarily coexisted with *Volksheeren* in people's wars, could only defeat such forces if they were unable to persuade them to lay down their arms voluntarily, through 'the annihilation of the *Volk* or the taming of the same by means of columns', leading to a long and unpredictable conflict like that of the French in Spain after 1808.[121] After 'the almost unceasing war of the last twenty-five years [had] offered the opportunity, often at a high price, of collecting so many experiences', *Volksheeren* and *Volkskriege* seemed unavoidable, according to one Prussian military dictionary in 1821, leaving open the question of how they could be combined with armies of the line.[122] By 1848–50, many conservative politicians and writers had become more suspicious of unreliable militias, after civil guards in some cities had supported the revolution and the standing armies of Prussia and Austria had quashed it, but until that point commentators had been less critical.[123]

Military writers in other German states were as receptive to the idea of militias, which they linked to the broader principle of *Volksbewaffnung*, as their Prussian counterparts (see Map 1 for the configuration of 'Restoration' states). Although not as closely connected to circles of conservatives or nobles as in the Hohenzollern

---

[117] C. v. Decker, *Ansichten über die Kriegführung im Geiste der Zeit* (Berlin, 1822), 11.
[118] Ibid., 418.   [119] Ibid., 419.   [120] Ibid., 70.   [121] Ibid., 424–5.
[122] H. F. Rumpf, *Allgemeines Kriegswörterbuch für Offiziere aller Waffen*, vol. 1, 500: the dictionary uses the same text as Decker on the actual organization of *Kriegsheeren*.
[123] For a critique of militias, see the Prussian infantry officer Ferdinand von Prondynski, *Theorie des Krieges*, 2nd revised edn (Bielefeld, 1849), vol. 1, 204; also, Wilhelm, Crown Prince of Prussia, *Bemerkungen zu dem Gesetz ueber die deutsche Wehrverfassung* (Berlin, 1849), 26–77. For those more sympathetic to the revolution, militias were useful for exactly the same reason, as a source of protection for the revolutionary German regime: see the retired Prussian artillery officer F. W. Lehmann, *Grundzüge zur Bildung einer deutschen Bürgerwehr und eines deutschen Heerwesens mit Rücksichten auf die preussische Heerverfassung* (Bonn, 1848). In favour of the *Landwehr* and volunteers, C. v. Decker, *Über die Persönlichkeit des preussischen Soldaten festgestellt durch die Militärverfassung seines Vaterlandes* (Berlin, 1842), 8–17.

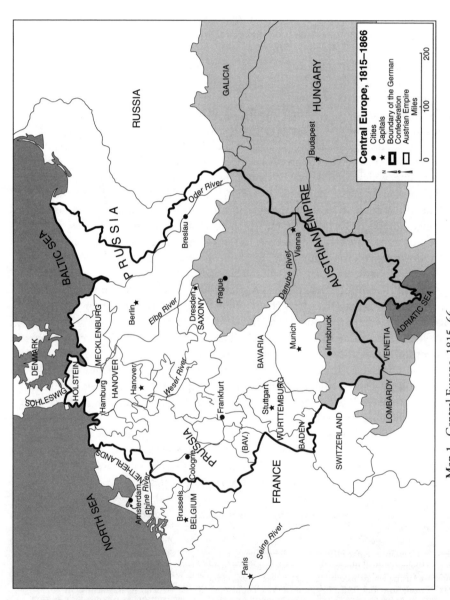

Map 1. Central Europe, 1815–66

Source: J. Sperber (ed.), *Short Oxford History of Germany, 1800–1870* (Oxford, 2004), 288.

monarchy, such officers were part of the ruling elite of the Habsburg empire and the German *Mittelstaaten*, with regular contact with ministers and the court.[124] In other words, they belonged to the conservative-minded establishments of restoration states, keeping them informed of military developments after the widely acknowledged rupture caused by the French Revolution.[125] After 1789 in France, 'the military forces used until then no longer sufficed', recorded the author of the article on the 'army (standing)' in Hanns Eggert Willibald von der Lühe's *Militair Conversations-Lexikon*, published by the retired Saxon officer in Leipzig during the 1830s: by mobilizing 'forces of all kinds', perpetuated by enthusiasm and fear of enemies 'on all sides', 'France gained the ascendancy and maintained it for so long that the German princes used the same means', further refining 'what an emergency had created'.[126] 'Except for the English army,... there is no standing army of the type of the previous century in the whole of Europe', the article continued:

> The law makes it the duty of each citizen, with few exceptions, to do their military service, which—in addition—must be done in person in most states, although only for a short time. The standing army is therefore only a practical war academy; those who have done their course enter the *Landwehr*, military reserve or whatever it is called, for a specified number of years.[127]

Armies after the French Revolution amounted to an enduring structure of regiments and officers, through which the 'mass of fighters' passed, in the context of 'a purposefully established arming of the people', which was the sole means of levying troops in peacetime, given that voluntary service—and the enthusiasm underpinning it— had proved successful 'only in times of a threatening danger' and had not been 'long-lasting'.[128]

The majority of military writers from German *Mittelstaaten* seem to have agreed with this combination of standing and popular elements, with some such as Josef von Xylander defending 'the Prussian military system with great acuity', as the *Militair Conversations-Lexikon* put it.[129] Modern armies had become matters of public discussion and concern: 'What was a simple determination of arbitrary will has now become a difficult object of legislation, and what was the favourite affair of an individual has now become a *national matter*, in which everyone is more or less implicated, in their own person or through a member of their family', noted the

---

[124] I. Deák, *Beyond Nationalism: A Social and Political History of the Habsburg Officer Corps, 1848–1918* (Oxford, 1990), 25–42, 78–92; G. Gahlen, *Das bayerische Offizierkorps 1815–1866* (Paderborn, 2011), 159–264, 517–58.

[125] A good example of such a conservative in Baden was the Catholic landowner and former vicar general of Constance, Ignaz Heinrich von Wessenberg, who was at once close to the ruling dynasty of Baden and who accepted the need for patriotic constitutionalism, since a small state could not rely, in the manner of Austria where his brother Johann was a minister, on a standing army: Vienna could muster a 200,000-strong army but Baden needed a patriotic population. I. G. v. Wessenberg, fragment from 1827, I. G. v. Wessenberg, *Unveröffentliche Manuskripte und Briefe*, ed. K. Aland (Freiburg, 1968), vol. 1, 90.

[126] H. E. W. von der Lühe (ed.), *Militair Conversations-Lexikon* (Leipzig, 1833–37), vol. 3, 682.

[127] Ibid. Also on Saxony, see C. v. Gersdorff, *Vorlesungen*, 170: 'Both sides [after 1789] saw that a rebirth of their [military] systems was necessary.'

[128] H. E. W. von der Luhe (ed.), *Militair Conversations-Lexikon*, vol. 3, 682, and vol. 2, 246.

[129] Ibid., vol. 3, 683.

Bavarian officer and publicist.[130] The *Landwehr* had not been solely responsible for the defeat of Napoleon, contrary to the supposition of some popular accounts:

> This cannot and should not detract from the well-won reputation of the devotion, stamina and courage of all these members of the *Landwehr* and *Landsturm* from those days, for no one can or will deny that they were brave and therefore contributed significantly to the victory, but the fact that this bravery alone did not lead to victory and that they would not have been led to it without the *war-tested leaders* of those armies and without relying on *troops of the line*, who were just as *brave* as they were *war-trained*, will hopefully be recognized as true in 1830, even by the brave ones themselves.[131]

Other Bavarian authors such as Hermann Beisler and Albert von Pappenheim likewise backed the 'evil' or 'tax' of conscription ('the harshest [tax] thinkable', in Pappenheim's words), which would remain necessary 'for as long as state relations exist as they do today'.[132] Armies needed a long period of training—with Prussia, 'a purely military state' unsuitable for imitation, not merely having three years of military duty but a much longer stint in the *Landwehr* afterwards—but they also needed a general system of conscription (in accordance with Beisler's 'civic' *Wehrverfassung* and *Wehrinstitut*) and a general reserve or *Landwehr*, which could halt the enemy at the borders and which could provide 'masses' of soldiers under the conditions of 'popular' (*populair*), post-revolutionary 'wars of the people'.[133] After 1815, then, few military writers or journalists from different political milieux and individual states thought that standing armies alone were sufficient. The majority favoured an 'arming of the *Volk*' and a *Landwehr* or militia of some kind, in addition to a more intensively trained army of the line. The violence of war had, in this sense, become a matter for the people. The next section considers the extent to which military training in the use of violence affected conscripts' and civilians' lives.

ARMY LIVES

What was it like to serve in an early nineteenth-century army? The Hessian academic, medic, radical, and playwright Georg Büchner left one unfinished portrait, which remained an undiscovered fragment until 1879, in his play about the soldier Franz Woyzeck, written in exile in Zurich in 1836–7. The meanings of Büchner's fragment are manifold and include an exploration of self-consciousness under the material conditions of an oppressive society.[134] Woyzeck, who ends up murdering

[130] J. v. Xylander, *Untersuchungen über das Heerwesen unserer Zeit* (Munich, 1831), iv.

[131] Ibid., 16.

[132] A. v. Pappenheim, *Militairische Fantasien über Heerbildung, Heerverfassung und was auf das Soldatenwesen Bezug hat* (Augsburg, 1832), vol. 1, 21, 24; H. Beisler, *Betrachtungen über Staatsverfassung und Kriegswesen insbesondere über die Stellung des Wehrstandes zum Staat* (Frankfurt, 1822), 68–85.

[133] H. Beisler, *Betrachtungen über Staatsverfassung und Kriegswesen insbesondere über die Stellung des Wehrstandes zum Staat*, 85; A. v. Pappenheim, *Militairische Fantasien über Heerbildung*, vol. 3, 20, 10.

[134] See Michael Minden's excellent account in Michael Minden, *Modern German Literature* (Cambridge, 2011), 57–60. On the difficulty of interpreting Büchner's work, see Helmut Müller-Sievers,

his girlfriend—with whom he has had a child out of wedlock after she has had an affair with an army drum-major—expresses and follows his feelings—his love for Marie as well as communion with nature—within an urban world ('the city in the distance' contrasted with the 'free fields'), which contains and torments him.[135] One symbol of such social control is medicine, to which—in the person of the 'doctor'—the soldier has subjugated himself in order to earn more money to pay for his child and common-law wife. Thus, when the doctor reveals that he has seen him 'piss in the street, piss on the wall, like a dog', and Woyzeck's reply is that he was succumbing 'to nature', the medical practitioner prescribes chemicals against such 'disgusting superstition': 'There has been a revolution in science, I'll blow it up, urea 0.10, salt-sour ammonium, hyperoxydul—Woyzeck, must *he* not piss again? He should go and try it!'[136] The other symbol of social control is the army, which 'drums' Andres and Woyzeck away from the open fields towards the city, just as it had drummed into the soldier—through the sound of the drum-major in the street—the fact of Marie's betrayal.[137]

The main agent of military domination is the 'Captain', whom Woyzeck serves, shaving him with a cut-throat razor, without being able to slit his throat, whilst the officer gives a running commentary on his orderly's fate:

HAUPTMANN: Slowly, Woyzeck, slowly; one thing after another! He makes me feel quite giddy. What should I do with the ten minutes by which he is too early today? Woyzeck, think about it; he has his thirty good years to live, thirty years! That makes three-hundred-and-sixty months, and days, hours, minutes! What will he do with all that monstrous amount of time? Split it up a bit, Woyzeck.

WOYZECK: Yes, sir.

HAUPTMANN: It makes me anxious about the world when I think of eternity. Keeping busy, Woyzeck, keep busy! Eternal, that is eternal, eternal—you can see that; now, though, it's not eternal, and that is just a moment, yes, a moment, Woyzeck, it frightens me when I think about it, that the world turns in a single day. What a waste of time! What does it amount to? Woyzeck, I can't look a mill-wheel any more, or I become melancholic.

WOYZECK: Yes, sir.

HAUPTMANN: Woyzeck, he always looks so agitated. A good person doesn't do that, a good person who has a clear conscience. Say something, Woyzeck. How is the weather today?

WOYZECK: Bad, Captain, sir, bad; wind!

'Interpreting: German Textual Criticism and the Case of Georg Büchner', *Modern Philology*, 103 (2006), 498–518.

[135] G. Büchner, *Woyzeck* (Stuttgart, 1975), 5: in some versions, the play begins with this scene. On the theme of love, see Erwin Theodor, 'Büchners Grundgedanke. Sehnsucht nach Liebe', *Revista de Letras*, 3 (1962), 201–17.

[136] G. Büchner, *Woyzeck*, 8, 'Beim Doktor'. See also P. D. Smith, *Metaphor and Materiality: German Literature and the World-View of Science 1780–1955* (Oxford, 2000), 93–150.

[137] G. Büchner, *Woyzeck*, 6.

HAUPTMANN: I feel it, there is such a strong wind outside; such a wind makes me feel like a mouse is running up and down on me. (Slyly.) I should says it was north-southerly, wouldn't you?

WOYZECK: Yes, sir.

HAUPTMANN: Ha, ha, ha! North-southerly! Ha, ha, ha! Oh, he is stupid, so horribly stupid. (Touched.) Woyzeck, he is a good person—but (solemnly) Woyzeck, he has no morals! Morality, that is, when one is moral, you understand. It's a good word. He has a child, without the blessing of the church, as our reverend army chaplain says, without the church's blessing; that's his expression, not mine.

WOYZECK: Captain, sir, dear God is not going to worry whether Amen is said or not before the poor worm has been created. The Lord said: 'Suffer little children to come unto me.'

HAUPTMANN: What is he saying there? What an odd answer. He is confusing me with his answer. When I say 'he', I mean him.

WOYZECK: We poor people—do you see, Captain—money, money! Those with no money—you try getting one of that kind into the world in a moral way. We are flesh and blood as well, though. We never get much luck, in this world or the next. If we went to heaven, I expect, we would be made to help with the thunder.

HAUPTMANN: Woyzeck, he has no virtue. He is not a virtuous person. Flesh and blood? When I am lying by the window, after it has been raining, and I look at a pair of white stockings skipping down the street—damn it, Woyzeck, then I feel desire. I'm also flesh and blood. But virtue, Woyzeck, virtue! What do I do? I always say to myself: you are a virtuous man, (touched) a good man, a good man.

WOYZECK: Yes, Captain, sir, I don't think that I have so much virtue. You see, common people like me don't have virtue, we only have what is natural to us; but if I were a gentleman with a hat and a pocket-watch and all the right words, I would be virtuous alright. Virtue must a great thing, Captain, but I'm just a poor man.

HAUPTMANN: Well, Woyzeck. You are a good fellow, a good fellow. But you think too much, which eats away at you; you always look so over-wrought. The discussion has upset me completely. Go now and don't run; slowly, nice and slowly down the street.[138]

The captain is a cipher for a facile but perhaps necessary self-constraint (if murder is to be avoided), encapsulated in morality and virtue, which is connected to existential as well as merely social forms of alienation. He also stands for a social system which unthinkingly infantilizes and seeks to control the poor and their passions.[139]

[138] Ibid., 4–5, 'Zimmer'.
[139] Jost Hermand, 'Extremfall Büchner. Versuch einer politischen', *Monatshefte*, 92 (2000), 395–411, rightly emphasizes the provocative, rebellious, and critical proclivity of Büchner's play. On the critique

Woyzeck is at once a metaphysical reflection on the gap between language, rhetoric, and morality, typical of liberals as well as conservative elites, and harsh social and material conditions, and it is a folk tale about the *Volk*, with motifs like the red mouth of Marie and the murder in the wood typical of folk songs.[140] The 'military' in the play, alluded to through the characters of the captain and drum-major and through scenes set in the 'guard-room', the 'barracks', and the 'courtyard of the barracks', serves as a device, representing the grinding repetition and material domination of an unjust social order. Büchner's references to life in the army, therefore, were not purely descriptive, although they were intended to be credible, as a result of 'immersing himself in the life of the most humble individual and rendering that life in its finest nuances', as he put it in his novella *Lenz*, published posthumously in 1839.[141] The mechanical replies of Woyzeck ('yes, sir'), despite the agitated state of his mind, and the dull routine of his activity, being forced to shave his captain 'slowly', were indicative of all 'poor men', the playwright implies, not just soldiers. The automatic response of the protagonist as he lapses into madness, leading his comrade Andres—in a scene in the barracks—to warn that he will be going to hospital if he cannot 'kill' his fever with 'schnapps and gunpowder', is to repeat his rank and then the details of his life—'Friedrich Johann Franz Woyzeck, *Wehrmann*, fusilier in the 2nd Regiment, 2nd Battalion, 4th Company, born on Annunciation, 20 July; I am, today, 30 years, 7 months and 12 days old'—yet his mechanical reflex is shared by all manual workers—as the scene in the inn depicting labourers hints—and, possibly, by all people, as the captain's reference to the grinding, endlessly turning mill-wheel suggests. In private correspondence, beset by typhoid of which he died one month later, Büchner himself imagined that he was on such a mill-wheel, despite his lack of energy, turning 'without rest or quiet'.[142]

Similarly, the crass condescension of social betters, denying their inferiors 'morality', 'virtue', and self-restraint at the same time as denying their own 'natural' feelings and 'flesh and blood', was perhaps especially pronounced in the army but was present in all hierarchical societies of the early nineteenth century, in Büchner's view. Thus, in his call in 'Der Hessische Landbote' (1834) for the peasantry to carry out a revolution, the playwright conceived of all social struggle as a 'war' to be waged on the palaces: in the Grand Duchy of Hesse, a 'tyrant'—one of thirty in Germany as a whole—and a political elite of 10,000 'oppressors' sucked the 'blood' of 700,000 inhabitants, helping to turn 'the German earth' into 'a great

of science and enlightenment, and the dilemma in which Woyzeck finds himself, see R. T. Gray, 'The Dialectic of Enlightenment in Büchner's *Woyzeck*', *German Quarterly*, 61 (1988), 78–96; J. M. Harding, 'The Preclusions of Progress: *Woyzeck*'s Challenge to Materialism and Social Change', *Seminar: A Journal of Germanic Studies*, 29 (1993), 28–42; J. Crighton, *Büchner and Madness: Schizophrenia in Georg Büchner's Lenz and Woyzeck* (Lewiston, NY, 1998).

[140] M. Perraudin, 'Towards a New Cultural Life: Büchner and the "Volk"', *Modern Language Review*, 86 (1991), 627–44.

[141] G. Büchner, *Lenz* (1839), cited ibid., 628.

[142] Cited in J. A. McCarthy, 'Some Aspects of Imagery in Büchner's Woyzeck', *Modern Language Notes*, 91 (1976), 545.

field of corpses', as if a battle had just been waged.[143] As he went on to point out in the same tract:

> Your sons [at a cost of 914,820 Gulden paid annually to the military] get a colourful coat on their body, a gun or a drum on their shoulder and they are allowed to shoot it blindly every autumn and tell how the lords from the court and the ill-advised boys from the nobility go in front of all the children of honest people and wander around the thoroughfares of the cities with them, drumming and blowing their trumpets. With their drums, they drown out your sighs and with the butts of their guns they smash your skulls, if you dare to think that you are free people.[144]

Conscription had turned 'your brothers and your children' into 'murderers of brothers and fathers', but only as part of a wider social struggle in which 'legal murderers', or soldiers, were asked to protect 'legal robbers', or ruling elites.[145] Anyone raising their 'sword against the *Volk*' would die 'by the sword of the *Volk*'.[146] Some soldiers were caricatures of human vanity, virility, and brutality, as the market-crier in *Woyzeck* intimates, in turning the world upside down, as he displays his wife in trousers and his monkey decorated in the uniform of a soldier: 'The ape is a soldier; it's not much, the lowest level of the human race.'[147] Yet humanity as a whole was susceptible to weakness, lust, and violence. 'Why do humans exist?' asks a journeyman in the tavern, as Marie and the drum-major dance in front of Woyzeck:

> Truly, I ask you, what would the farmer, the cooper, the shoemaker or the doctor live off, if God had not created man? What should the tailor live on, if he had not planted the feeling of shame in people, and what should the soldier do, if he had not armed him with the need to kill and destroy himself?[148]

Although in an extreme form in the army, human exploitation and self-destruction were present, pointing to the futility of existence, throughout contemporary society.

The impression that Büchner gives is that soldiers were part of a variegated, colourful, often oppressive society of estates rather than constituting a separate caste. Even though he lived in barracks, Woyzeck was free to leave and participate in the life of the garrison town, maintaining a family, frequenting taverns and fleeing to the countryside. The Grand Duchy of Hesse, where Büchner had grown up and about which he wrote, only boasted a small contingent of troops—close to its confederal quota of 6,195 men in the first half of the nineteenth century—which meant that about one-third of those fit for military service were conscripted (or approximately 1,600 conscripts per year), with a further 400 or so of these

---

[143] G. Büchner and L. Weidig, *Der Hessische Landbote. Texte, Briefe, Prozeßakten* (Frankfurt, 1974), 5, 18.
[144] Ibid., 9.   [145] Ibid.   [146] Ibid., 18.
[147] G. Büchner, *Woyzeck*, 10, 'Buden, Lichter, Volk'. L. Martin, '"Schlechtes Mensch/Gutes Opfer": The Role of Marie in Georg Büchner's *Woyzeck*', *German Life and Letters* 50 (1997), 429–44; E. Boa, 'Whores and Hetairas. Sexual Politics in the Works of Büchner and Wedekind', in *Tradition and Innovation*, ed. Ken Mills and Brian Keith-Smith (Bristol, 1990), 161–81.
[148] G. Büchner, *Woyzeck* 20, 'Wirtshaus'.

conscripts going on to pay for a replacement.[149] The *Landwehr* had been abolished in 1819 as a suspected site of disloyalty and rebellion. Most soldiers of the line were lodged in barracks, unlike in some other German states. Nonetheless, they were stationed in many of the larger towns, in addition to the confederal fortress of Mainz which was manned by Austrian and Prussian troops, and they played an active part in urban life, not least because their barracks were typically close to town centres and allowed the regular movement of soldiers and burghers in and out, in contrast to the newly built, sealed, and outlying barracks of the later nineteenth century. As elsewhere in the third Germany, Hessian troops served for six years in total but spent most of this time on leave, normally serving for less than two years. Their ties to their families, localities, and civilian society, therefore, were rarely severed. Likewise, the relations of civilians and soldiers could be close, as the banker's son and later democrat Ludwig Bamberger—born in 1823—recalled of his childhood and youth in Mainz. His early memories and experiences were made up of 'tales of the times of revolution and war and of the actuality of a garrison town', he wrote in his memoirs: 'The French soldiers of the past and the Austrian and Prussian soldiers of the present provided a boy's fantasy with its main nourishment.'[150] The soldiers of the Grand Duke were not in themselves widely revered, since most inhabitants of Mainz resented the Congress of Vienna's transfer of the city from the *Kurfürstentum* of Hesse to the Grand Duchy, whose leader was notorious—mocked decades later in the common saying, 'Have you seen the Emperor?'—for waiting in vain for hours on his horse on the banks of the Rhine for the arrival of Napoleon: 'We boys viewed the company of his soldiers, who were in the fortress and had the duty merely of guarding the gaol, with pity.'[151] Soldiery, however, was an object of fascination and respect:

> The body of soldiers of the garrison naturally formed the central point of our games and distractions. We spent long hours on the exercise ground, and the cuffing, pushing and torturing of the Prussian recruits by the young officers provoked our childish indignation. The more 'measured' Austrian appeared less reprehensible to us, although gauntlets were often run or shots fired off badly. He helped citizens in his free time in all manner of things in exchange for a small payment and he contributed considerably as a 'treasure' of female service to the growth of the population. Though Prussian and Austrian soldiers brawled with each other, there was never any talk of excesses directed at burghers by officers.[152]

The position of soldiers in most German states resembled that of their counterparts in the Grand Duchy of Hesse.[153] The military of the Habsburg monarchy

[149] B. Sicken, 'Landstreitkräfte in Deutschland 1815–1914. Beobachtungen zur Struktur und zu den militärisch-zivilen Beziehungen', in B. Sicken (ed.), *Stadt und Militär. Wirtschaftliche Impulse, infrastrukturelle Beziehungen, sicherheitspolitische Aspekte* (Paderborn, 1998), 126–7; B. Sicken, 'Das großherzoglich-hessische Militär, Struktur, Rekrutierung, Disziplinierung', in *Georg Büchner 1813–1837. Revolutionär, Dichter, Wissenschaftler* (Basel, 1987), 57–9.
[150] L. Bamberger, *Erinnerungen*, 3.   [151] Ibid.   [152] Ibid., 5.
[153] See, for instance, neighbouring Kurhessen: M. Arndt, *Militär und Staat in Kurhessen 1813–1866. Das Offizierskorps im Spannungsfeld zwischen monarchischem Prinzip und liberaler Bürgerwelt* (Marburg, 1996); U. Vollmer, *Die Armee des Königreichs Hannover. Bewaffnung und Geschichte von 1803–1866* (Schwäbisch-Hall, 1978); P. Wacker, W. Rosenwald, and G. Müller-Schellenberg, *Das*

constituted an exception: its forces were large, nominally about 400,000 and actually 250,000 once those on unpaid furlough were subtracted, but its system of recruitment and types of service varied—for life in Hungary, eight years in Lombardy-Venetia, and fourteen years in the 'German' lands except the Tyrol, whose recruits served an extra six years in reserve, according to the service law of 1827. Its deployment was 'imperial' in nature, with ten out of thirty-five 'German' regiments serving in Hungary and Italy, and ten out of fifteen Hungarian regiments in Italy and Austria.[154] A typical infantry regiment such as the Hoch-und-Deutschmeister, Nr. 4, was to be found in Milan in 1815, passing to St Pölten in 1816, Bergamo in 1820, Naples in 1822, Capua in 1825, Linz in 1830, Görz in 1831, Verona in 1833, Kaisers-Ebersdorf in 1836, Vienna in 1840, and Tarnów and Lemberg in 1846.[155] The regiments of other states were less mobile and contained more local conscripts than Austrian units of 'foreign' career soldiers. In Prussia, Boyen had wanted to form mixed regiments, drawing conscripts from all areas of the kingdom as a means of using the army as a patriotic or national 'school', but he had been defeated by the king and his conservative advisors, leaving most regiments—apart from elite guards in Potsdam and Berlin—rooted in particular localities.[156] Thus, although rural recruits themselves regularly found urban life disorienting, at least when they arrived, the populations of the towns themselves were used to the officers and troops of 'their' regiments.

In the absence of significant police forces before 1848, such troops were largely responsible for maintaining order, intervening against rioters and manning guardposts: for instance, in Berlin in 1816, there were fifty-four military guards at the Königswache, fifty-seven at the Schloß-Hauptwache, thirty-four at the Neue Markt-Wache, thirty at the Brandenburger Tor, twelve at the Hallescher Tor, and nineteen at the Neustädter Wache.[157] Fontane gave an account of guard duty and the seriousness with which it was treated, particularly in 'insecure' areas of the

herzoglich-nassauische Militär 1806–1866. Militärgeschichte im Spannungsfeld von Politik, Wirtschaft und sozialen Verhältnissen eines deutschen Kleinstaates (Taunusstein, 1998).

[154] G. E. Rothenberg, *The Army of Francis Joseph* (West Lafayette, IN, 1976), 19; G. Schmitt, *Armee und staatliche Integration*, 43–61, 116–46. The marches of the empire, where the conditions and terms of recruitment were quite different, also provided many troops: K. Kaser, *Freier Bauer und Soldat. Die Militarisierung der agrarischen Gesellschaft an der kroatisch-slawonischen Militärgrenze 1535–1881* (Vienna, 1997).

[155] G. E. Rothenberg, *The Army of Francis Joseph*, 19.

[156] On the limitations of any attempt to use the army as a 'school of the nation', not least because such an idea was rejected by many officers, see U. Frevert, *Nation in Barracks*, 70–82. G. Gahlen, *Das bayerische Offizierkorps*, 291, shows that Maximilian II had a similar intention in Bavaria, as can be seen in correspondence with the War Minister on 26 July 1852, but one which was only very partially realized and which—he implied—had barely begun by the 1850s: 'I see the army as a school for the propagation of national sentiment, national pride and the education of the *Volk*. With a purposeful organization...and the correct nourishment and promotion of a military spirit, the sons of different territories will be fused through it into a whole and be permeated by a common spirit which will outlast their period of service. Their military years will thus serve as a school for their entire lives.'

[157] G. Wittling, 'Zivil-militärische Beziehungen im Spannungsfeld von Residenz und entstehenden großstädtischen Industriezentrum. Die Berliner Garnison als Faktor der inneren Sicherhiet 1815–1871', in B. Sicken (ed.), *Stadt und Militär 1815–1914*, 224; B. R. Kroener (ed.), *Potsdam. Staat, Armee, Residenz in der preußisch-deutschen Militärgeschichte* (Berlin, 1993).

capital like the *Pulvermühlen*.[158] 'Suddenly a couple of civilians came into the guardhouse greatly agitated and asked for help', he wrote in his memoirs: 'The tavern where [the violence] was taking place was quite a long way away, but I had no choice and sent three men there, who then came back with a great big fellow... The hooligan was delivered to the city governor at daybreak.'[159] According to the military governor, in a letter to the Minister of Justice in 1839, incidents involving guards were common.[160] They were indicative of the proximity of soldiers and civilians in many German cities, the large majority of which had garrisons. In Prussia, more than 50 per cent of the 3.8 million urban population lived in a town with a garrison, with those who did not often coming from smaller towns and large villages.[161] In the western Hohenzollern provinces of Westphalia and the Rhineland around 1820, for example, there were twenty-six garrison towns for a contingent of 30,000 troops, with Wesel, Cologne (Deutz), Coblenz (Ehrenbreitstein), Düsseldorf, Trier, Minden, and Münster each having forces of 2,000 or more.[162] In Bavaria, Munich had an 'army population', including wives and children, of 13,464 and a civilian one of 79,971 in 1837, Augsburg 4,369 and 29,904, and Bayreuth 3,397 and 13,552.[163] Once Ingolstadt's long-awaited barracks were in use, by the 1850s, its military population (8,821) actually outnumbered its civilian one (6,320). Because of the economic significance of such soldiers, who were usually stationed near town centres, 134 other Bavarian villages and small towns applied for their own barracks during the long nineteenth century.[164] As was apparent in contemporary painters' depictions of German city streets, military figures were stock characters of urban life. They were 'omnipresent' in Munich, in the words of one British visitor in 1860.[165] They were not isolated from civilian society.[166]

In many garrison towns, officers participated in the life of local elites.[167] Whilst it was true that their colourful, decorative uniforms and stricter codes of honour

---

[158] Theodor Fontane, *Sämtliche Werke*, ed. Edgar Gros (Munich, 1959–75), vol. 20, 144.

[159] Ibid., 145–6.

[160] P. F. C. F. v. Müffling to H. G. v. Mühler, 24 Apr. 1839, cited in B. Sicken (ed.), *Stadt und Militär*, 225.

[161] A. Lüdtke, 'The Role of State Violence in the Period of Transition to Industrial Capitalism: The Example of Prussia from 1815 to 1848', *Social History*, 4 (1979), 199: centres of population with more than 2,000 inhabitants were defined as 'urban'.

[162] B. Sicken, 'Landstreitkräfte in Deutschland 1815–1914, in B. Sicken (ed.), *Stadt und Militär*, 116.

[163] R. Braun, 'Garnisonswünsche 1815–1914. Bemühungen bayerischer Städte und Märkte um Truppen oder militärische Einrichtungen', ibid., 329. Also, C. Lankes, *München als Garnisonsstadt im 19. Jahrhundert* (Berlin, 1993); T. Bruder, *Nürnberg als bayrische Garnison von 1806 bis 1914* (Nuremberg, 1992); W. Schmidt, *Regensburg als bayrische Garnisonsstadt im 19. und frühen 20. Jahrhundert* (Regensburg, 1993); U. Hettinger, *Passau als Garnisonsstadt im 19. Jahrhundert* (Augsburg, 1994).

[164] R. Braun, 'Garnisonswunsche', 323.

[165] E. Wilberforce, *Social Life in Munich* (1863), cited in C. Lankes, 'Bürgerliche Revolution und militärische Reaktion. München und seine Garnison zur Zeit König Maximilians II.', in B. Sicken (ed.), *Stadt und Militär*, 337.

[166] See the cloth-maker Friedrich Lehmann's references to soldiers billeted in his home town of Hainichen in Mittelsachsen: F. G. Lehmann, *Lehmanns Tagebuch 1826–1828* (Marbach, 1999), 15–19.

[167] This intermingling was arguably made easier by the long-term shift towards 'native' rather than 'foreign' officers and towards—or, at least, not away from—aristocratic officers, who were more regularly

were designed to mark out their estate, or *Stand*, they were part of the fabric of occupations, corporations, and orders, many of which could be distinguished by their clothing and rules. 'The respect which the estate of warriors enjoyed appeared, even to the educated man, to be represented visually by the uniform, since humanity seeks to decorate everything which it loves and holds to be valuable', wrote the Prussian military publicist and officer Ferdinand von Prondzynski, at the same time as conceding that officers were beginning—by the mid-nineteenth century—to stand out: 'As far as our regulation clothing is concerned, it is probably as little of an ideal as those ways of dressing which are mocked because the eye is no longer accustomed to them.'[168] Military values were, recorded Pappenheim of Bavaria, an extension of civilian ones: 'Where true honour is present, the burgher will having nothing to fear from the soldier', enjoying friendly relations.[169] Although civil and military laws usually prohibited duels, it was widely accepted that officers would not deserve to wear their uniform if they allowed insults to go 'unpunished'.[170] They would, Pappenheim averred, be 'damned by public opinion'.[171] For disputes between soldiers and civilians, military 'courts of honour' should be established to restore the reputation of officers in cases where burghers refused a duel.[172]

Amongst other things, such elaborate provisions betrayed the close connections between military and civilian hierarchies and the regularity of civil–military disputes about women, money, and etiquette. In an age of conscription, the 'destiny of officers' was all 'the greater and more difficult' to define, wrote Prondzynski, yet the fact that commanding officers had to distinguish themselves from the mass of soldiers as well as to lead them did not mean that they had greater honour than civilians, merely a subtly different kind of honour.[173] 'Our predecessors, who lived under more divided and separate conditions, during an era in which the order of warriors was more self-contained, had, it cannot be denied, a simpler position', the Prussian officer continued: by contrast, contemporaries had the advantage of dealing with 'the true warriors of the fatherland', or citizens-as-soldiers, rather than with 'a raw *Soldateska*'.[174] Officers in Prussia and other German states were aware that they were responsible for—and lived together with—their fellow subjects.[175] In the Habsburg monarchy, this feeling was often less pronounced. Here, military writers, as István Deák has put it, 'customarily described the life of an officer as a near-Calvary; poor pay and an even poorer pension, onerous and dull service, exile

able to marry and have families, in most German states: G. Gahlen, *Das bayerische Offizierkorps*, 163–227, 266–85; 437–76.

[168] F. v. Prondzynski, *Theorie des Krieges*, vol. 1, 12. K. Helfferich, *Georg von Siemens*, 24: Siemens, as one-year volunteer in Berlin in 1858, was proud to wear his uniform outside the barracks, 'for the uniform is meant to look good on me' and it gave him concessionary rail fares.

[169] A. v. Pappenheim, *Militairische Fantasien*, vol. 6, 125.   [170] Ibid., 126.

[171] Ibid.   [172] Ibid., 135–42.   [173] F. v. Prondzynski, *Theorie des Krieges*, vol. 1, 27–8.

[174] Ibid., 29.

[175] M. Funck, *Feudales Kriegertum und militärische Professionalität. Der Adel im preußisch-deutschen Offizierkorps 1860–1935* (Berlin, 2005); K.-H. Lutz, *Das badische Offizierskorps 1840–1870/71* (Stuttgart, 1997); G. Gahlen, *Das bayerische Offizierskorps 1815–1866* (Paderborn, 2010); U. Breymayer (ed.), *Willensmenschen. Über deutsche Offiziere* (Frankfurt, 1999); K. Demeter, *Das Deutsche Offizierkorps in Gesellschaft und Staat, 1650–1945* (Frankfurt, 1962).

from home, involuntary celibacy and loneliness, a wandering restless existence, social isolation, public hostility and, last but not least, the prospect of a violent death'.[176] These conditions did not necessarily undermine the loyalty and sense of identity of the Austrian officer corps, as was demonstrated in 1848, but they did mean that it was usually isolated from the localities to which it was posted.[177]

Other German officers enjoyed different conditions from those of their Habsburg counterparts. Nevertheless, they, too, sought to justify their activities and maintain their status and honour through appeals to bravery, self-sacrifice, and *esprit de corps*. To the majority of military commentators, their calling was a special one and required a specific, 'higher' set of values and attributes. In an era of mass armies, the officer corps was entrusted more than ever, it seemed to many military observers, with perpetuating the traditions, purpose, and morale of regiments. 'The more changeable armies have become, as a result of recent military organizations resting on the principle of general military service, the more difficult and greater the destiny of the order of officers has become', wrote Prondzynski of Prussia in 1840: 'It is, especially in our case, the only genuine group (*Genossenschaft*) of warriors, in the narrower sense of the word, in the entire belligerent nation (*Nation*); it emerges as a common, higher-order category from the mass of individuals who constitute the army.'[178] Officers received two or three times as many demands on them as 'the estate of warriors as a whole'.[179] They also had specific duties imposed on them, in addition to those imposed on all soldiers: 'We hold all members of the order of officers to be the thinking cogs of the army machine and we therefore demand of every officer not merely action but also his free goodwill and his involvement in the sense of the action', which in turn could be equated in most circumstances with a 'free, unforced acceptance of the will of the commander-in-chief and king'.[180]

In Bavaria, the cultivation of this *esprit de corps* and code of honour was likewise believed to be central to the functioning of the army, in Pappenheim's opinion: 'Without this honour of soldiers, we shall never achieve anything great', he wrote: 'It includes everything—loyalty, devotion to one's prince and fatherland, sacrifices of every kind, stamina, courage, decisiveness, in short everything that one can think of in this respect. It must be kept sacred and pure.'[181] The invasion of Russia in 1812 had shown that patriotism, 'however great the spirit of the French warriors was', was insufficient on its own in coping with 'the greatest emergency and danger', with the result that the army 'dissolved' during the crossing of the Beresina river.[182] What was needed in addition was a 'common spirit' (*Gemeingeist*) and 'feeling of honour' (*Ehrgefühl*), particularly amongst officers.[183] 'Whoever enters

---

[176] I. Deák, *Beyond Nationalism*, 128. Also R. A. Kann, 'The Social Prestige of the Officer Corps in the Habsburg Empire from the Eighteenth Century to 1918', in R. A. Kann, *Dynasty, Politics and Culture* (Boulder, CO, 1991), 237–41.

[177] I. Deák, *Beyond Nationalism*, 22; J. C. Allmayer-Beck, 'Die bewaffnete Macht in Staat und Gesellschaft', in A. Wandruszka and P. Urbanitsch (eds), *Die Habsburgermonarchie 1848–1918. Die Bewaffnete Macht* (Vienna, 1987), vol. 5, 99–110; A. Schmidt-Brentano, *Die Armee in Österreich. Militär, Staat und Gesellschaft 1848–1867* (Boppard am Rhein, 1975), 433–57.

[178] F. v. Prondzynski, *Theorie des Krieges*, vol. 1, 26.   [179] Ibid.   [180] Ibid.

[181] A. v. Pappenheim, *Militairische Fantasien*, vol. 6, 120–1.

[182] Ibid., 48.   [183] Ibid., 118.

the army should have a feeling for this spirit within them', regarding his honour as 'untouchable' and becoming a link in a chain which 'should be firm and unbreakable', Pappenheim declared:

> We wish to nurture this common spirit in our army; we perceive it to consist in awe of a high, exalted feeling produced by the true and genuine feeling of honour (*point d'honneur*) that is the basis on which the happy success of military reputation, all illustrious feats of arms and all glorious efforts and endeavours should rest.[184]

To the Bavarian officer, 'the honour of the soldier' and the 'honour of weapons' was 'the highest thing that there is', proven over the previous 2,000 years and not endangered by 'the frivolous pens of many writers of today'.[185] Any attempt wrongly to impugn the honour of a 'soldier'—that is, an 'officer'—should be punished more severely than was the case for a civilian, since officers were subject to a 'moral opinion which applies more strictly' than the law and which ensured that they were 'lost' when accused of a dishonourable act.[186] Officers, in other words, acted as a corps, imposing their own rules on each other and requiring 'moral' protection from civilians who did not share their code of honour but with whom they were in regular contact. One external sign of their special status was their right to wear swords in public.

Most officers and, certainly, the military leadership of the individual states wanted to instil such military values in the rank and file, prompting many of them to contend that a long period of service was required in order to change conscripts' attitudes. 'If one accuses us, too, of belonging to those who see the salvation of education for war only in a long period of service, we cannot deny that we recognize a longer period of service to be very advantageous for a soldierly spirit', wrote Pappenheim: 'What we understand under soldierly spirit (*Soldatengeist*)', in common with Napoleon and many others, lies 'in the recognition of the worth of the soldier and in the right idea of his honour as part of an estate'.[187] New recruits were 'sworn in', taking an oath to the king, fatherland, and, in some southern German states, the constitution, usually on 'the officer's sword or sabre' or 'on the colours or cannon', as the Prussian regulations put it, in the courtyard of the barracks and in the presence of a Catholic or Protestant chaplain, who prepared the soldiers for the ceremony separately.[188] 'The soldier's primary duty', recorded the Prussian oath, 'is to serve his royal majesty and the fatherland loyally.'[189] In order to ensure their loyalty in times of emergency at home and abroad, officers in other states agreed, conscripts needed to learn to accept a panoply of military virtues unconditionally. In the Saxon military writer Carl von Gersdorff's view, these 'moral foundations' of the military included obedience, fear of God, order, discipline, subordination, a willingness to serve, harmony, honour, and a common spirit.[190]

---

[184] Ibid., 117–18.   [185] Ibid., 118.
[186] Ibid., 124. Pappenheim refers to 'the soldier (officer) who is insulted', making clear that this part of his work refers principally to officers.
[187] Ibid., vol. 1, 41–2.
[188] See U. Frevert, *Nation in Barracks*, 71.   [189] Ibid.
[190] C. v. Gersdorff, *Vorlesungen über militairische Gegenstände*, 77–85.

The foundations could be built through the maintenance and adaptation of a separate military sphere which most young men—except those from the *Bürgertum* of the third Germany and a wider range of exempt groups in Austria—believed that they might have to pass through in the transition from adolescence to adulthood.

The army was, in Decker's estimation, a 'moral institute', with recruits 'treated like a member of the family'.[191] Training encompassed 'not only military goals, as used to be the case in the past, but it begins instead with one's duties to oneself and to others, as subjects and Christians, as well as one's duties to brothers in arms and superiors'.[192] The principal aim was to make sure that 'the young soldier gets used to a regular routine of life and gives his body the attention which any moral individual would demand', the Prussian military publicist continued: 'Neglect of cleanliness and decency are not tolerated', with soldiers—often the sons of peasants—learning to set up 'home' in barracks or private quarters and to look after themselves, their weapons, and their clothing.[193] Conscripts completed a 'course of practical ethics', which was tested by examination by the leader of the company, then the major, and then the commander and inspector, guaranteeing that 'superficial, unfounded or erroneous teaching cannot occur'.[194] For those who had not internalized ethical self-restraint there was a carefully graded system of military punishments, from warnings via arrests to military courts, which imposed discipline without stocks or corporal punishment, bringing it into 'doubt in the eyes of foreigners'.[195] The picture that Decker and other Prussian authors painted of the army was that of a well-run, morally motivated body of men, whose 'real principle of life' was 'the spirit of a corporation', in Prondzynski's words.[196] Officers outside the Hohenzollern monarchy produced similar portraits, contending that soldiers' motives extended beyond what Pappenheim termed 'hope of reward or fear of punishment'.[197]

Identification with one's regiment and with the army in general was necessary, it was held, for the fashioning of reliable troops from raw conscripts.[198] It was natural to run away from danger, conceded Prondzynski, so armies had to devise ways of countering such instincts:

> With the majority of people, reasoned arguments—which, in addition, are not always encouraging—do not prevail in the struggle against impulses of mood, and so it is a swing of mood, which proves stronger in all circumstances than the urge of self-preservation, that is for the officer a pressing need. He shares his enthusiasm for the object of a campaign, enmity, a feeling for the honour of arms, devotion to one's commander-in-chief with the whole mass of troops, for whom all these levers of courage, if they are not sufficient to secure the higher position for him, which he urgently needs, leave him with only a single motivation able to achieve this: namely,

---

[191] C. v. Decker, *Über die Persönlichkeit des preußischen Soldaten*, 23.   [192] Ibid., 30.
[193] Ibid.   [194] Ibid., 33.   [195] Ibid., 54–5.
[196] F. v. Prondzynski, *Theorie des Krieges*, vol. 1, 28.
[197] A. v. Pappenheim, *Militairische Fantasien*, vol. 6, 126.
[198] For more on the mechanisms of regimental belonging in 1870–1, see Wencke Meteling, *Ehre, Einheit, Ordnung. Preußische und französische Städte und ihre Regimenter im Krieg, 1870/71 und 1914–19* (Baden-Baden, 2010), 35–198.

a feeling for one's personal honour, which is deeply rooted in him and closely related to the honour of his estate, combined with a clear personal awareness that this honour demands that the officer gives an example of devotion and self-sacrifice in all circumstances.[199]

The 'common man' in such circumstances was moved more by his feelings than by higher motives of honour, requiring the guidance and leadership of his officer.[200] Soldiers were willing to engage an enemy when moved by the hope of 'revenge, a feeling of superiority, enthusiasm for something or a devoted trust in their leaders', but they tended to hesitate when they began 'to hold a danger to be insuperable', when they believed their enemy to be stronger, or when they were 'close to the exhaustion of their physical powers'.[201] Rules of honour had been developed from the Middle Ages onwards, contended Prondzynski, precisely to counter such feelings, when 'cunning, which is not unknown even to animals', began to dictate the course of a battle or campaign.[202] Individual honour itself was inadequate, however, 'where the common interests of entire peoples [were being] fought for'.[203] 'Civilized nations' had come to despise cunning in wars, since it was—on its own—ineffective, and they had developed systems of ethics, international law, and, above all, codes of honour to guide, motivate, and limit their actions.[204]

The challenge, Prondzynski mused, was to maintain such mechanisms of command, obedience, sacrifice, and honour, which were necessary for war, during periods of peace, when an 'overestimation of one's abilities or an unsatisfied yearning for gratification' could be observed, undermining 'the conviction...that all these conditions [of discipline] are needed and unalterable'.[205] In other words, military writers like Prondzynski were more worried by peace than by war, presuming that nineteenth-century German armies could—by means of military training and the example of officers—prepare conscripts for killing and death. One of the reasons for such a belief appears to have been that the conditions experienced by soldiers during wartime were not thought to be fundamentally different from those encountered during peacetime. The main purpose of military training, it can be held, was to guarantee soldiers' loyalty at home as well as abroad rather than to inure them to the effects of violent acts, as both victims and perpetrators.

THE POLITICS OF GERMAN ARMIES DURING AND AFTER THE REVOLUTION

In the event, the boundary between violence at home and abroad was maintained during the revolution of 1848–9, partly because conservative courtiers and officers eventually triumphed and partly because liberals, who controlled the majority of

---

[199] F. v. Prondzynski, *Theorie des Krieges*, vol. 1, 32.
[200] Ibid., 34.   [201] Ibid.   [202] Ibid., 35.   [203] Ibid.
[204] Ibid., 36. Also, R. Eickemeyer, *Abhandlungen über Gegenstände der Staats- und Kriegs-Wissenschaften*, vol. 2, 7.
[205] F. v. Prondzynski, *Theorie des Krieges*, vol. 1, 30.

'revolutionary' governments, refrained from enforcing a fundamental reform of the armies of the German states.[206] In Prussia, many reactionaries were poised to use force against the revolution, if necessary without the king's permission, arguing like Roon in a private letter to his wife that 'the army is now our fatherland, because there alone the impure and violent elements who put everything into turmoil have failed to penetrate'.[207] The Prussian army itself was being threatened with reforms which the majority of officers were not willing to countenance. Many left-wing deputies agreed with Georg Gottlieb Jung's claim in the opening sessions of the Berlin National Assembly that Scharnhorst's original plan of creating a 'volkstümliches Heer' had been corrupted, in the common distinction between a necessary 'army' and a despised 'military', by the emergence of 'das unvolkstümliche Militär', which acted as a praetorian guard and pursued the interests of a noble caste.[208] The left wanted to abolish the regular army altogether. Although its designs were blocked, a majority of the Assembly backed a resolution on 9 August 1848 calling on officers to 'abstain from reactionary agitation', avoiding 'conflicts of any kind with civilians' and giving 'evidence of their desire to co-operate, with honesty and devotion, in the realization of a constitutional legal system'.[209] Any officers unable to comply were to resign.

Faced with Friedrich Wilhelm IV's blank refusal to allow interference with the 'inviolable rights' of the crown, David Hansemann attempted to dissuade deputies from insisting on the implementation of the resolution, leading to the re-passing of the measure on 7 September and the ministry's resignation on the 10th. Ernst von Pfuel, Rudolf von Auerswald's successor as Minister-President, passed on an order complying with the Assembly's wishes to army commanders on 23 September, provoking outrage. Two days earlier, Helmuth von Moltke, a junior officer at the time, wrote to his brother that 'We now have 40,000 men in and around Berlin; the critical point of the whole German question lies there.'[210] 'They now have the power in their hands and a perfect right to use it', he went on: 'If they don't do it this time, then I am ready to emigrate with you to Adelaide.'[211] The king and his military advisors did not act immediately (and Moltke did not set sail for Australia), but they waited instead for Alfred von Windischgrätz's counter-revolutionary bombardment of Vienna on 28 October before initiating their own army-backed change of ministry on 2 November. Until that point, Hohenzollern commanders had been deterred from taking direct action by a shifting coalition of forces within the court, with the monarch vacillating between moderate conservatives and reactionaries, and in Prussia's—and the *Reich*'s—government, assembly, and streets. From that date onwards, they had less need to act *in extremis*, since the army's interests were protected by 'its' government in Berlin, headed by the former military commander Friedrich Wilhelm von Brandenburg.

There was, until Friedrich Wilhelm IV's rejection of the title of 'Kaiser of the Germans' on 28 April 1849, a fundamental debate at the level of the Reich about

---

[206] See Chapter 7.
[207] A. v. Roon, *Denkwürdigkeiten*, 5th edn (Berlin, 1905), vol. 1, 152.
[208] Cited in G. A. Craig, *The Politics of the Prussian Army*, 111.   [209] Ibid., 115.
[210] Ibid., 117.   [211] Ibid.

a reform of the army. The *Reichsverfassung* (imperial constitution), which had been passed and promulgated by the Frankfurt Parliament on 28 March 1849 and which had been recognized formally by the Prussian second chamber on 21 April, stated that the executive of the Reich had an exclusive right to declare war and peace (Art. 2, §10) and had 'the entire armed forces of Germany at its disposal' (Art. 3, §11), with the *Reichsheer* composed of 'the entire armies, intended for the purposes of war, of the individual German states' (§12) and subject to the legislation, organization, and 'continuing control' of the Reich (§13).[212] The 'strength and nature' of the *Reich*'s forces were to be determined by a 'law on the constitution of the army', which was to be passed separately (§12). The perceived importance of this law was such that Wilhelm, the Crown Prince of Prussia and a leader of moderate conservatives at court by 1849, published a detailed commentary on its provisions. The legislation's rationale of creating a unified army to meet external risks was likely to fail, wrote the heir to the throne: 'Is it conceivable that Great Powers like Austria and Prussia will subordinate their armies in the case of a war exclusively to the Central Power and, even in peacetime, will allow the dislocation of their troops?'[213] The liberal and democratic sponsors of the law claimed in its preface to 'have taken the Prussian system as a model', with the intention of

> creating a good impression...since Germany has looked trustingly [at the Prussian model] for a long time and foreign states have acknowledged a war readiness in which Prussia has solved the problem, at little cost and with a relatively weak peacetime force, of raising not only a numerous but also a well-trained and fully disciplined army for war.[214]

The actual provisions of the law, however, which reduced the training of conscripts in the infantry to six months, were held by Wilhelm to be 'untenable': 'This is not the Prussian system!'[215] The election of officers in the *Landwehr*, the abolition of 'all military educational establishments' and courts of honour, and the transfer of soldiers who had committed crimes during peacetime to civil courts were likewise denounced as un-Prussian. Interestingly, though, Wilhelm was prepared to accept that the Central Power appointed a military overlord and commanders in times of war, as long as it had the prior agreement of the states, and he was willing to go along with two-year military service for the infantry.[216] The question of conscription and the overall size of the army was a practical and financial one: the new law's provision that 'all available conscripts (*Wehrpflichtige*) are to be drafted and trained' entailed the raising of a German army of 2.7 million men and an effective doubling in size of the Prussian army from 500,000 to 1 million, which was unaffordable and unrealizable, leading to a 'hunt for conscripts,...unheard-of burdens, disputes, abuses and deceptions'.[217] A figure of 3 per cent of the population at arms during wartime was more realistic, in Wilhelm's opinion. Although his priority was to preserve the loyalty and discipline displayed in 1848–9 ('Never has an

---

[212] *Reichs-Gesetz-Blatt* (Frankfurt, 1849), 103.
[213] Wilhelm, Crown Prince of Prussia, *Bemerkungen zu dem Gesetz über die deutsche Wehrverfassung* (Berlin, 1849), v.
[214] Ibid., vii.   [215] Ibid.   [216] Ibid., 8, 26.   [217] Ibid., 15–17.

army had to tolerate such a burden of fate as the Prussian one in this critical year! Despised, mocked, led astray by all possible artifice, it stood firm as a rock and unshaken in its attitude and discipline'), he was nonetheless ready to consider his opponents' suggestions and to compromise, as the very publication of his pamphlet bore witness.[218] The officers around Lieutenant-Colonel Karl Gustav von Griesheim who had established the *Deutsche-Wehrzeitung* in July 1848 revealed a similar readiness to supply the Frankfurt and Berlin assemblies with technical responses and critiques as well as disseminating reactionary propaganda.[219]

The other side of the argument about military reform was provided by commentators and deputies on the left, who criticized—in the words of the democratic deputy Johann Jacoby—the reactionary 'party' for maintaining 'the military in its privileged position... as an *instrument for its own plans*'.[220] To what extent could citizens' militias, which had been permitted by law in most states in March and April 1848, form the basis of a new army? At the start of the revolution, declared Jacoby on 26 August 1848, 'the general, unanimous cry' had been for a 'reduction of the standing army and the introduction of a general arming of the people'.[221] 'The people had rightly recognized that the standing army had been the main bulwark of absolutism, the main bulwark of the police and bureaucratic state and that, by contrast, a general arming of the people offered the most secure, even the only guarantee of civic freedom', he continued.[222] In part, the creation of militias brought to an end 'the artificially created division between armed and unarmed citizens' by entrusting 'the tranquility and order of the state to independent citizens', rather than leaving it to 'paid police servants' and to the 'military', and by distributing arms to them so that they could enforce it.[223] In part, the *Bürgerwehr* was expected by democrats such as Jacoby to become a 'general national defence force' (*eine allgemeine Volkswehr*), replacing the external functions of the regular army: 'I have, above all, taken up a position because I hold it to be my duty in this matter to draw attention to the pressing need for a thorough-going reform, a radical restructuring of our entire army organization.'[224]

Because the draft law on the *Bürgerwehr* in Prussia did not institute a general arming of the *Volk* and a corresponding abolition of—or reduced role for—the army of the line and the *Landwehr*, it could 'only be a provisional, mere emergency law', noted Jacoby in August.[225] For the moment, the Prussian militia, like other similar German forces, existed alongside the old army:

> As a result of the draft of the law which lies before us, citizens are provided with weapons but the entire army organization is left completely in its old form, which no longer accords with the needs of the age. Beside the army of the line and the *Landwehr* is a third, fully isolated institution, which has no inner connection to the other two institutions at all: the *Bürgerwehr* has been created, and has been created in such a way, so that we must deny the new institution a priori any capacity to develop into a general national defence force.

[218] Ibid., 41.
[219] G. A. Craig, *The Politics of the Prussian Army*, 112–13.
[220] 'Rede vor den Berliner Wählern', 12 Sept. 1848, in J. Jacoby, *Gesammelte Schriften und Reden* (Hamburg, 1872), vol. 2, 49–50.
[221] 'Über das Bürgerwehr-Gesetz', 26 Aug. 1848, ibid., 39.   [222] Ibid.
[223] Ibid., 39–40.   [224] Ibid., 40.   [225] Ibid., 42.

> Our *Landwehr* system, which in its time and in its original purity was outstanding, has not delivered one thing: it has not managed to bring about a fusion of soldiery and citizenry. The present *Bürgerwehr* law will not achieve this. Only a general arming of the people (*eine allgemeine Volksbewaffnung*) will make soldiers into armed citizens, whereas our *Landwehr* system makes the citizen into an unarmed soldier.[226]

To radicals like Jacoby, all citizens had to be issued with and allowed to take home weapons as part of a national militia composed of units at local, state, and Reich levels, which simultaneously guaranteed freedom at home and a defence against foreign enemies. The more reactionaries, using existing armies, gained the upper hand in late 1848 and early 1849, the more radicals were convinced that 'the unconscionable spirit of absolutism', which had re-emerged 'not just in Prussia but in the whole of Germany', together 'with Junkerdom and a system of police', had to be countered by a genuine arming of the people.[227]

Military critics of the left found considerable support amongst moderate conservatives and liberals confronted by the perceived failings of militias, whose recruitment proved inadequate and whose bourgeois fancy-dress parades were widely ridiculed.[228] The establishment during the revolution of *Bürgerwehren* 'in all the cities of Germany' had convinced many, following 'such favourable results at the start', that the role of a popular *Volksbewaffnung* could be extended to encompass the defence of 'freedom against external as well as internal foes', wrote F. W. Lehmann, a former artillery officer in 1848.[229] Options being discussed, including the reduction of the standing army to a 'dependent appendage' or the complete subsumption of the army within a general arming of the people, ignored the overriding purpose of any army, however, which was 'the defence of the fatherland'.[230] A 'great Germany, with its 45 million inhabitants and lying at the centre of Europe', differed from the United States, which furnished the most common examples of successful militias: it 'will as a result also constitute the political centre of gravity of this part of the world and will often be required to act as an arbiter of the different, surrounding nations or to defend itself against their provocations'.[231] Given such external circumstances, 'Germany needs a strong, well-ordered and manoeuvrable army in order to clear a military power of trained soldiers from each point of its borders at any time, if German soil is not to yield the terrain for the battlefields of every conflict and be constantly threatened by the invasions of enemy armies', the pamphlet continued.[232]

The viability of the *Bürgerwehr* as an external force was hindered by the fact that about three-quarters of Germany's population lived 'on the land', which caused them to resent the 'disagreeable aspects and sacrifices' of military service and which would provoke opposition to universal participation in a militia: 'It follows from

---

[226] Ibid., 40.

[227] J. Jacoby, 'Rede vor den Wahlmänner und Wählern des vierten Berliner Wahlbezirks am 14 April 1849', ibid., 60.

[228] See Chapter 7.

[229] F. W. Lehmann, *Grundzüge zur Bildung einer deutschen Bürgerwehr und eines deutschen Heerwesens mit Rücksicht auf die preußische Heerverfassung* (Bonn, 1848), 4.

[230] Ibid.   [231] Ibid., 4.   [232] Ibid.

this antipathy of the great majority that an arming of the people is likely to be anything but general and that the maintenance of the legal order will fall exclusively
on the inhabitants of the cities', who made up only a quarter of the population.[233]
Even these burghers' enthusiasm for the militia, which had derived 'from pure love
of the fatherland' when it had been faced with 'the dangers of the moment', would
wane over time, coming to be seen as a 'restriction of their freedom to pursue a
profession'.[234] Lehmann's practical solution was to leave the army of the line in
place and to make service in it or in the *Bürgerwehr* voluntary for town-dwellers,
which would create a pool of 562,000 men (with 187,000 going to the regular
army). The rest of the army would be drawn from the land, contributing to an
overall wartime contingent of 956,900. 'The *Landwehr* and the *Bürgerwehr*
together will form the overwhelming majority of this army and make it into a truly
popular one, in which examples of virtuous military training, order and discipline
have a place and are adequately represented,' the officer concluded.[235] His aim,
which was shared by many liberals and moderate conservatives, was not to replace
or reduce the size of the army but to adapt it to post-revolutionary domestic conditions at the same time as maintaining its traditional function—confronted by
new revolutionary and counter-revolutionary menaces—abroad.

Given that there had been such a profound and divisive debate about the nature
of the army in 1848–9, aggravated by the use of military force on the side of the
revolution (Baden, Hungary) and counter-revolution (Austria, Prussia), the return
to the *status quo ante* during the post-revolutionary era was unexpected. From reactionaries' point of view, the deployment of the army, not oratory (in the words of
a speech by Bismarck in 1849), had settled the dispute between bourgeois and
Junker, liberal and conservative.[236] The Hohenzollern army had, as the Prince of
Prussia had put it, 'stood firm' in the revolutionary chaos: few conservatives wanted
to tamper with it or expose it to a new debate about reform.[237] Such caution was
more marked in the middle-sized and smaller states, whose armies had proved less
reliable and effective. In Baden, most of the army had backed a republican 'executive commission' established after the flight of the Grand Duke on 13 May 1849,
despite the attempt of the War Minister to lead a 'loyal' army across the border
into Württemberg; in Saxony, Prussian troops—merely accompanied by Saxon
soldiers—had had to put down a revolutionary uprising there early in the same
month; in Württemberg, the authorities had consciously used loyal troops from
the 'old territories', fearing soldiers from the capital, to force the evacuation of the
deputies of the 'Rump Parliament' from Stuttgart on 18 June; and in Bavaria, more
than a third of the troops stationed in the Palatinate had deserted as a secessionist
provisional government was declared.[238] All these forces had to be won over anew,
with the King of Bavaria's injunction not to pursue measures which were 'too strict'

[233] Ibid., 5.   [234] Ibid., 6.   [235] Ibid., 16.

[236] O. v. Bismarck, cited in O. Pflanze, *Bismarck and the Development of Germany: The Period of
Unification, 1815–1871* (Princeton, NJ, 1963), vol. 1, 66.

[237] Wilhelm, Crown Prince of Prussia, *Bemerkungen zu dem Gesetz über die deutsche Wehrverfassung*, 41.

[238] S. Müller, *Soldaten in der deutschen Revolution*, 261–9.

setting the tone for other regimes.[239] Only one mutinying or deserting soldier was executed in Bavaria in 1849.[240]

The opposition to conservative supporters of the states' armies came largely from radical quarters, not liberal ones, in spite of the criticism that middle-class burghers had initially directed at the 'military' and 'soldiery' (*Soldatentum*) and the backing that they had given to militias, for which they often supplied officers and men.[241] Liberals throughout Germany had been worried by workers storming arsenals and building barricades, with their leaders in Frankfurt calling for assistance from Prussian troops against demonstrators on 18 September 1848. Unlike many democrats, few liberals had contemplated the use of *Bürgerwehren* against regular armies and few protested as they were disbanded throughout Germany in the middle of 1849.[242] By that time, Otto Elben's retrospective verdict that the militia had become a 'humorous sideshow' of 'a genuine tragedy', with the 'great idea' underpinning it eclipsed by 'comic' execution, was widely held.[243] For radicals like Arnold Ruge, such inactivity was further proof of the 'childish games' of Gagern and other '*Spiessbürger*' or their collusion with 'reaction', as he wrote to his wife from Frankfurt on 22 September 1848.[244] As he looked back on his letters from the revolutionary period, it was evident to Ruge that the conservative enemies of a radical 'new order' had 'kept the soldiers and the money'.[245] If democrats had seized and retained power in 1848–9, they would have altered the structure of the army. Apart from a few fleeting weeks in Saxony, the Palatinate, and Baden in May–June 1849, however, they did not come to power in the German lands and, therefore, were unable to put their ideas into practice.

Radicals' championing of organizational reform (military law, promotion, training), universal conscription, and the formation of militias persisted in the 1850s and 1860s, resurfacing—for instance—in the General German Workers' Association's (ADAV) call for a 'citizens' militia force' in the mid-1860s and Wilhelm Liebknecht's advocacy of Switzerland's 'democratic' model of a 'universally armed nation' at the fifth congress of the German workers' associations at Nuremberg in 1868, yet it was muted as a consequence of their exile or disappearance from the assemblies of German politics and the newspapers of the public sphere during a post-revolutionary 'reaction'.[246] Many leading democrats had called for armed intervention with existing military organizations on the side of the western powers and Austria in

---

[239] Max II, marginal comment, 29 June 1849, ibid., 302.

[240] J. Calliess, *Militär in der Krise. Die bayerische Armee in der Revolution 1848/49* (Boppard, 1976), 189.

[241] Ludwig Friedrich Seyffardt, *Erinnerungen* (Leipzig, 1900), 9–10, commented laconically that he had joined the *Bürgerwehr* in 1848—as a 21-year-old, former one-year volunteer—just as he had joined all the other associations in Krefeld.

[242] See Chapter 7.   [243] O. Elben, *Lebenserinnerungen*, 117.

[244] A. Ruge to his wife, 22 Sept. 1848, in A. Ruge, *Briefwechsel und Tagebuchblätter aus den Jahren 1825–1880*, ed. P. Nerlich (Berlin, 1886), vol. 2, 18–19.

[245] Ibid., 24.

[246] W. Liebknecht, cited in U. Frevert, *Nation in Barracks*, 136. Also, R. Jaun, 'Die Schweizer Miliz als Inspirationsquelle republikanischer Streitkräfte. Von Rüstow zu Wilhelm Liebknecht und Jean Jaurès', in R. Bergien and R. Pröve (eds), *Spießer, Patrioten, Revolutionäre. Militärische Mobilisierung und gesellschaftliche Ordnung in der Neuzeit* (Göttingen, 2010), 347–60.

the Crimean War (1854–6) and on the Austrian or Italian side in 1859.[247] Faced with a modern reliance on rifles and artillery and with the alleged failure of the *Bürgerwehr* in 1848–9, Friedrich Engels, who had covered the Crimean and Franco-Austrian Wars as a journalist and who later became the most famous commentator on military affairs in socialist circles, renounced the possibility of militias as a 'fantasy' in states like Prussia.[248] His stance showed how far radicals were prepared to compromise on specific points of the 'military question' with their political opponents. Until 1865, when he wrote 'Die preußische Militärfrage und die deutsche Arbeiterpartei', the debate about the army had taken place 'exclusively between the government and the feudal party on the one side and the liberal and radical bourgeoisie on the other side', with representatives of workers having had little to say.[249] Engels' contention was that a 'workers' party' could 'treat such questions completely in cold blood and impartially', or 'scientifically', 'historically', and 'anatomically', since it stood beyond 'the actual conflict'.[250] What this impartiality amounted to, however, was an appreciation of the Hohenzollern state's 'actually existing political and military conditions' (as opposed to those of future socialist states) and its objective of reversing a long period of under-investment and the 'fiasco' of 'attempts at mobilization' in 1850 (Olmütz) and 1859 (Franco-Austrian War).[251] Thus, Albrecht von Roon's controversial reorganization and expansion of the Prussian army in the early 1860s, which sparked a constitutional crisis under the Minister-Presidency of Bismarck, was said 'not to be pitched too high', in line with 'the increase of the population of Prussia from 10 million in 1815 to 18 million in 1861', with the monarchy's prosperity (which had 'grown faster than its population') and with the precedent set by 'the other European great states', which had 'strengthened their armies to a far greater extent since 1815'.[252]

In order to maintain its 'position as a Great Power', in Engels' opinion, Prussia needed 'as strong a first field army as possible for the commencement of a war', as recent experience had demonstrated: Roon had therefore decided to increase the size of the cohort in active service and in reserve at the expense of the *Landwehr*, which was manned by older former conscripts for the most part, since it was a 'defensive institution', only suited to an offensive in the case of a counter-attack during a longer war, 'as in 1814 and 1815'.[253] The weakness of the War Minister's plan, which was otherwise justified in the exiled socialist's view, was its flawed attempt to combine a French 'cadre system', which relied on the recruitment of a smaller group of professional soldiers for a long period, and a Prussian system which rested on '*die allgemeine Wehrpflicht*', 'temporarily the sole democratic institution' of the Hohenzollern monarchy, 'even if it only exists on paper'.[254] Although

---

[247] See Chapter 8.
[248] U. Frevert, *Nation in Barracks*, 137, claims that Engels's argument 'found no echo either in the democratic movement or in the emerging socialist workers' grouping', but this is difficult to prove, given the positions and silences of other radicals of the period. F. Engels, 'Die preußische Militärfrage und die deutsche Arbeiterpartei' (1865), in K. Marx and F. Engels, *Werke*, vol. 16, 51–78.
[249] F. Engels, 'Die preußische Militärfrage', 41.   [250] Ibid.   [251] Ibid., 54, 42.
[252] Ibid., 44–5.   [253] Ibid., 42–3.   [254] Ibid., 50–1.

all types of conscription derived from—and were 'merely very imperfect forms' of—general military service (*allgemeine Wehrpflicht*), the Prussian law of 1814 had perpetuated the idea 'that every citizen who is bodily capable of it also has the duty, whilst he is able to do so, of bearing arms for the defence of the country' more effectively than 'all other lands of conscription', where 'the principle of substitution' had been established.[255] Because a cadre system would permit Prussia, with its 18 million inhabitants, an army of 300,000–400,000 rather than the minimum of 500,000–600,000 'for any serious war' against France (35 million), Austria (34 million), or Russia (60 million), Engels' suggestion, 'on military and political grounds', was 'the expansion of the cadres in the way already carried out, the strengthening of the peacetime army to 180–200,000 men, the pushing back of the first cohort of the *Landwehr* in the great army reserves or the second field army or fortress duty'. Yet this was on condition 'that general military service would be strictly enforced, that the length of service would be set legally at two years under the banner, three in reserve and until one's 36th year in the *Landwehr*, and, finally, that the cadres of the first cohort of the *Landwehr* would be reinstated'.[256] It was necessary to choose between 'many trained people with a shorter period of service and longer duty of bearing arms or fewer, with a longer period of service and shorter duty'.[257] Engels preferred as large a number of citizens as possible (and a majority of workers) to be trained intensively over two years, in order to equip them for the defence of their state under conditions of modern warfare (and, later, to permit them to bear arms in a revolution). Despite criticizing the Prussian bourgeoisie for compromising with the monarchy and noble elites rather than forging an alliance with the working class, which alone could provide soldiers for a reorganized army with middle-class officers, the exiled socialist continued to trust in the political loyalty and effectiveness of a universally conscripted '*Kriegsarmee*', which could 'never' be used in a coup (in contrast to a 'peacetime army').[258] He argued in favour of the perpetuation, in an expanded and politically modified form, of Prussia's existing military system of recruitment, training, and service. He neglected even to consider a militia system.

Other radicals did consider such a system.[259] The best known was Wilhelm Rüstow, a Prussian officer who was suspended, imprisoned, and cashiered in 1848–50 and who later became an instructor in the Swiss army (in 1853) and Garibaldi's Chief of the General Staff (1860).[260] He was also associated with the *Nationalverein*'s campaign to set up voluntary defence associations across Germany during the early 1860s, which were designed to teach single men without military experience between 18 and 35 years old how to use weapons. For this task, a mere eleven days of drill would be required, in Rüstow's opinion.[261] Yet the revolutionary

---

[255] Ibid., 44–5.   [256] Ibid., 50, 55.   [257] Ibid., 51.   [258] Ibid., 56–7, 62–3.

[259] See R. Jaun, '"Das einzige wahre und ächte Volksheer". Die schweizerische Miliz und die helvetische Projektion deutscher Radikal-Liberaler und Demokraten 1830-1870', in C. Jansen (ed.), *Bürger und Soldat* (Essen, 2004), 69–82.

[260] The radical Wilhelm Schulz-Bodmer, *Militärpolitik* (Leipzig, 1855), 24, refers approvingly to Rüstow, for example.

[261] U. Frevert, *Nation in Barracks*, 134 and 137, uses this statement to show the depth of Rüstow's commitment to the militia principle. In fact, his position was more nuanced.

exile, who had been arrested by the Prussian authorities in 1850 for his critique of the Hohenzollern monarchy in *Der deutsche Militärstaat vor und während der Revolution* (1850), gave a realistic appraisal of army reform in *Der Krieg und seine Mittel* (1856), which devoted the majority of its 730 pages to technical questions, and in other similar works.[262] His support for militias was qualified: they were feasible when war was rare, but historically they had been accompanied, preceded, or succeeded by other forms of military organization:

> When war is only—or is only seen to be—a rare break in the peace, it is clear what to do: to select men during peacetime who should form the army during wars, to prepare them for this vocation through training, but not to have them permanently gathered together as an army and to call them together only at certain points and for short periods. Where you have these practices a militia army (*Milizheer*) results.
>
> By contrast, when purposes of state demand the continuous conduct of war and war is, at the very least, always imminent, it is necessary to have as many troops gathered together as correspond to the regular needs of warfare. Thus, one arrives at a standing army (*stehender Heer*).
>
> Between these two extremes stands the cadre army (*Kadresheer*). This is designed to correspond to the needs of both a constant readiness for war and the training of an armed group. A relatively large number of men are kept on active service continuously; after a certain period of service, the length of which differs, as a rule between three and fifteen years, the people are relieved of their ties to the army, whilst new recruits fill the place of each person who has left; those who have left, however, are not completely freed from military duty but are called up again and strengthen the army if a war threatens to break out. This system now predominates in most of the states of Europe.[263]

Rüstow recognized that states were unlikely to give up war as a means of realizing their goals: 'Far from being reduced in number and being made milder by the progress of culture, purposes of state which could possibly lead to war and which, according to all human reckoning, must lead to it have multiplied and have gained in strength.'[264] The increased proximity of peoples and states had increased 'the mass of possible causes of war and, indeed, war with a positive purpose, or offensive war'.[265] There was 'no prospect' of a perpetual peace or a 'tribunal which could preside over disputes between peoples as a court with a decisive voice'.[266] Certainly, the formation of militias meant that states found it harder to wage unjustified military conflicts, but even the adoption of a militia system by all states, which was unlikely, would not rule out war: 'The general introduction of the militia system would not abolish war but it would make it rarer, because these systems limit the independent disposal of the powers of the state over the forces of the people for the purposes of war and make any mere play with the same impossible.'[267] States could refuse to wage offensive wars yet, in existing and foreseeable circumstances of mutual mistrust and mixed forms of military organization and government, they could not ensure that they would not be attacked.[268]

---

[262] W. Rüstow, *Der deutsche Militärstaat vor und während der Revolution* (Königsberg, 1850).
[263] W. Rüstow, *Der Krieg und seine Mittel* (Leipzig, 1856), 50.
[264] Ibid., 39.   [265] Ibid., 39–40.   [266] Ibid., 40.   [267] Ibid., 60.
[268] Ibid., 40.

Rüstow's historical understanding of why states went to war was similar to that of other nineteenth-century authors. War was, as the sub-title of the first chapter of *Der Krieg und seine Mittel* stated, 'a means of achieving the purposes of a state', the most general of which was 'public well-being' (*das öffentliche Wohl*), through the use of violence (*Gewalt*).[269] It had begun with 'wars of looting and slavery' and of 'conquest' undertaken for the 'public good' against 'foreigners' and 'barbarians', of whose public well-being there was no talk and whose land could be taken for the benefit of one's own people.[270] Such conflicts had been present from the 'beginnings of history' and were waged 'by those peoples which, as far as we can see, made world history'.[271] They did not come to an end with the intervention of 'the civilized, in other words with today's world', for

> if this new world exchanged its people and its labour like its goods partly under the protection of peaceable and propertied contracts and wise laws, wars of conquest continued, with the subjugation of the vanquished, wherever it occurred to one of the civilized peoples (*civilisierte Völker*), in the interests of civilization or its own internal tranquility or trade, to found a colony on the territory of poor savages.[272]

Between these two historical points, different types of warfare had developed—commercial wars (*Handelskriege*), wars of honour (*Ehrenkriege*), dynastic conflicts and wars of succession (*Erbfolgekriege*), wars of hegemony in a states' system, and wars of intervention or for a balance of power (*Gleichgewichts- und Interventionskriege*)—but they had all been tied to the workings and interests of states:[273]

> The first need of a state is its own existence, for this is the necessary condition for the realization of all the goals towards which it strives. The existence of a state can be threatened in three ways: first, through enemy attacks from outside, which diminish its borders or impose extra-national rule, wanting to make it dependent so that, in the case of success, it could no longer pursue the aims of its life and effects which it had pursued up to that point; second, through movements in its interior, which neither subject to un-national rule nor diminish its borders but which want to give its constitution—that means the goals which the state has pursued until then—a different direction and form; third, by means of historical developments—over-population, new inventions, new ideas—which emerge in the state itself or in neighbouring states and which alter the relationship of the state to neighbouring lands, leading it to an unfavourable position if it remains on its old historical course.[274]

As a consequence of their entanglement with the policies and activities of states, military conflicts were difficult to control, much less banish.

Domestic movements and developments could be countered by 'good constitutions' and 'material violence' at home by physical improvements, but 'the military organization of a state' would still be required for 'the highest purpose' of the 'repulsion of an enemy', 'which is attempting an intrusion within state borders', wrote Rüstow in 1855: 'thus, an attack outwards, demanded by history itself,...has its natural justification'.[275] Armies and fleets were required in order to counter these

---

[269] Ibid., 13–14.   [270] Ibid., 14, 18–19.   [271] Ibid., 19.
[272] Ibid., 20.   [273] Ibid., 26–39.
[274] W. Rüstow, *Untersuchungen über die Organisation der Heere*, 1.   [275] Ibid., 2.

harsh historical facts. After aristocracies had become the core of European armies (partly because of grants of occupied land) and after a general call to arms (*Heerbann, Lehnsystem*) or simple payment had become impracticable, only conscription remained as a means of recruiting the large armies needed by modern states: 'Currently, conscription (*die Konskription*) is predominant in the whole of Europe', defined as the imposition of 'the duty to do military service', subject to 'the most manifold nuances in practice'.[276] The French Revolution had altered the 'sense' of such conscription, followed 'in the first decade of the nineteenth century [by] all the civilized states of the European mainland', noted Rüstow, but even French regimes had subsequently had to revert to the cadre system during peacetime, lacking the means and will to maintain 'the great army masses which universal conscription was able to deliver'.[277] Within the cadre system, too, there was considerable variation, with Russia before the Crimean War having a ratio of those in active service to those in reserve of 4:1 (closer to a standing army) and Prussia the reverse ratio of 1:4 (more similar to a militia).[278] Only democracies like Switzerland could raise actual militias, which were based on the notion of a legally voluntary 'contract', yet they too were subject to the realities of modern warfare and the life of modern states; most notably, the need to train recruits, since the martial disposition and military skills of citizens were not acquired otherwise, and to field large armies, the extent of which during wartime was uncertain, as the Napoleonic campaigns—relying tactically on the 'massing' of troops—had proved.[279] In these respects, militias were no different from other forms of conscript army.

The reforms of the revolution of 1848 in military affairs, which—in an unexpectedly moderate form—Rüstow perpetuated, were widely ignored in liberal circles. Abolishing the *Bürgerwehr* and reintroducing substitution, the conservative, post-revolutionary regimes of the German states (except Prussia) sought to reverse the revolutionary shift towards citizens' armies. They relied, above all, on the support of a reactionary system reinstalled by Austria, Prussia, and Russia after 1849. They also sought to court 'respectable' middle-class opinion, which—Frevert has claimed—had always resisted the actual implementation of universal military service, even if some of its political representatives, including Rotteck and Welcker, had backed it in principle.[280] A focus on the 'incessant wrangling in the southern German states over their internal policies on the form and purpose of their military organizations' obscures the extent to which conservatives, liberals, and, even, democrats agreed with each other on some of the most important questions of military policy, reinforced by the pre-eminence of moderate conservatives and liberals in the political and public sphere during the 1850s and early 1860s.[281] All were, after all, in favour of an extensive military apparatus, with maintained or increased funding. Thus, liberals on Württemberg's military commission in 1851, like their successors in 1865, contended that military training should be extended

[276] Ibid., 39, 8.   [277] Ibid., 59.   [278] W. Rüstow, *Der Krieg und seine Mittel*, 51.
[279] W. Rüstow, *Untersuchungen*, 5, 7, 43.   [280] U. Frevert, *Nation in Barracks*, 132–3.
[281] Ibid., 140.

to civil society; until that point, though, substitution and cadres, from which non-commanding officers could be drawn, would be necessary:

> In a state in which military education and training has not been introduced from early adolescence onwards, through gymnastics, shooting, marching and exercises, and is not carried on until the age of military service, but which must first be put in motion at a late, almost stiffened age, when a military spirit must first be inculcated, then it is impossible to take a fit group of leaders from the ranks of recruits, for they have barely entered the school of weapons themselves.[282]

Like the militia system, universal military service and a shorter period of military training seemed to require more military exercises and the inculcation of a martial spirit on the part of civilians. The reasons cited for the reintroduction of substitution in the army of Württemberg in 1850 were typical of other *Mittelstaaten* (the preface to the bill remarked that Saxony had already passed a similar measure), emphasizing the overstretching of the 'state's coffers' and an insistence on continuity, recalling that the *Kammer der Abgeordneten* had voted for the law by seventy-three to nine on 17 February 1843.[283] As was to be anticipated, the government appealed to the self-interest of middle-class deputies in the chamber, with the king himself noting that 'the abolition of substitution in military service' had 'brought with it disadvantages for individual conscripts' as well as for 'the active army'.[284] 'At no time' had 'complaints been raised' against the old law, declared the War Minister, whereas 'many reputable voices of the *Volk* have been raised for its reintroduction'.[285]

Generally, the government stressed the organizational benefits of substitution, given that no state except the Hohenzollern monarchy claimed to have a system of universal conscription in peacetime. 'If the basic rights [of the 1849 *Reichsverfassung*] included the statement that substitution will not take place, so a German system of defence was being thought of, in which all those eligible would have to go through the school of active service in the army', concluded the government's justification: 'Such a system of defence has as little basis in law, at present, in Württemberg as it has in the other German states, with the exception of Prussia, and the highly significant financial sacrifices which it demands alone place import-ant obstacles in the way of its introduction.'[286] Even in Prussia, the costs to the economy and to the state had rendered universal conscription unworkable, neces-sitating some form of exemption, yet a system which allowed individuals not to serve, either by voluntary decision or by lot, but did not allow substitution, appeared to contain a 'contradiction'.[287] In Württemberg, the preamble went on, it seemed better to let those families who needed their sons for 'the running of a farm or trade' to foot the bill, not the state, so that 'a disadvantage accrues for no

---

[282] *Verhandlungen der Württembergischen Kammer der Abgeordneten 1851/52* (Stuttgart, 1852), vol. 1 (*Beilagenband*), 194.

[283] *Verhandlungen der dritten verfassungberathenden Versammlung des Königreichs Württemberg im Jahre 1850* (Stuttgart, 1850), 100. For a fuller statement of the same arguments, see *Verhandlungen der Württembergischen Kammer der Abgeordneten 1851/52*, vol. 1 (*Beilagenband*), 95–6.

[284] *Verhandlungen der dritten verfassungberathenden Versammlung des Königreichs Württemberg im Jahre 1850*, 101.

[285] Ibid., 100.   [286] Ibid., 102.   [287] Ibid.

one, because no other person eligible for military service has to stand in place of the one being substituted', who were generally replaced by seasoned soldiers and non-commanding officers.[288] Without this means of recruiting and retaining non-commanding officers, the enduring structure of the army was threatened with dissolution over the longer term. 'The non-commanding officers no longer have any desire to remain in the military if they are to do without the advantages which substitution had earlier bestowed on them', ran the opening section of the justification for the law: 'The expectation that these will be replaced by young men from the educated strata, if these can no longer permit themselves to be represented by others, may well not be realized according to our experiences so far.'[289] By contrast, substitution spared Württemberg's economy the costs of universal conscription, and 'the propertyless substitutes, especially when they substitute several times, receive a capital sum … from the propertied who are substituted, from which they are in a position to create a living for themselves on their return to civilian life'.[290] For their part, the propertied did not have 'to suffer too heavy a sacrifice'.[291] Between 1817 and 1849, 15,000 men had benefited in this way, effectively transferring about 6 million gulden 'from the hands of the rich into the hands of the propertyless'.[292] All these arguments had been put forward from the early 1820s onwards. They still seemed relevant in the 1850s and early 1860s, especially to liberals, because the conditions of military organization did not seem to have changed fundamentally: mass armies—and, therefore, universal conscription—would be needed in wartime, but they were unaffordable in peacetime. What was important was to preserve the basic organization of the army—its cadres, in the terminology of Rüstow and others—to allow a quick expansion during wars.

The commission of the second chamber of the reconstituted *Landtag*, the franchises of which had been restricted but which retained a liberal majority of thirty-five to forty seats compared to just over thirty seats for the 'government' party (and eighteen for the democrats), recommended that the law reintroducing substitution be passed at the end of October 1851, reiterating many of the government's arguments.[293] Unlike the government, the commission did review the case in favour of an abolition of substitution, which was believed by its opponents to contradict 'the basic principle of equality in the fulfilling of general duties to the land'.[294] The commission's report stated:

> Through the authorization of substitution, it is objected, those without means are excluded from a good which the well-off benefit from because they find themselves precisely in the favourable position of being able to buy themselves out of the most noble but also heaviest duty of the citizen, as a result of which the lives of poor sons of the fatherland are sacrificed in wars for its very existence.[295]

---

[288] Ibid., 101–2.
[289] Ibid., 101.   [290] Ibid., 102.   [291] Ibid.   [292] Ibid.
[293] On the strength of the liberals, see M. Hewitson, *Nationalism in Germany, 1848–1866*, 165, and H. Brandt, *Parlamentarismus in Württemberg 1815–1870* (Düsseldorf, 1987), 159, 630, 668.
[294] *Verhandlungen der Württembergischen Kammer der Abgeordneten 1851/52*, vol. 1 (*Beilagenband*), 194.
[295] Ibid.

Table 2.2 War Strength of the Army of the German Confederation in 1859*

Austria	Prussia	Bavaria	Württemberg	Baden	Gr Hesse	Saxony	Hanover
145,855	137,652	42,716	15,255	8,004	9,620	18,063	19,728

* The table refers only to Feldtruppen of the large and medium-sized states, not replacement troops or those carrying out duties behind the lines.

Source: Adapted from J. Angelow, *Von Wien nach Königgrätz. Die Sicherheitspolitik des Deutschen Bundes im europäischen Gleichgewicht 1815–1866* (Munich, 1996), 326–7.

Since 'the poor also usually comprise the less intelligent and educated part of male youth', it continued, substitution could be held to discredit military service itself.[296] Yet any system based on a lottery, such as the 'Napoleonic systems of conscription' of the German states were, could not be said to be equal, since it placed 'the burden of military service on the shoulders of a certain number of individual conscripts chosen by lot'.[297] What was more, life itself could be viewed as 'a game of chance', with the poor unfortunately experiencing an 'unequal distribution of goods at each stage'.[298] Wealthier recruits' ability to pay for a substitute was therefore comparable to their ability to use their money to secure better circumstances for themselves in other aspects of their lives. The cost of an alternative to substitution—here, the government's figures concerning expenditure on non-commanding officers were cited—was too high.[299] 'If substitution has not been introduced in the army in Prussia, this is solely because there a system of army training for the entire male population has long been implemented, so that all those capable of bearing arms remain in military service in the regular army and in the *Landwehr*,' the report maintained: 'Such a system of defence, which the Frankfurt National Assembly also wanted to introduce for the whole of Germany as it proclaimed the abolition of substitution, can be brought into effect by a state such as Prussia, which has been able to propel itself into the ranks of the Great Powers by means of this military system', but was not suitable for a 'small state' (*Kleinstaat*) like Württemberg, which was not in a position to defend—and benefit from—the balance of power through the deployment of military forces.[300]

Partly because democrats had strengthened their position in the second chamber during the 1860s, the debate about military organization in Württemberg continued until 1868, when a 'Prussian' system was introduced. In January 1865, the democratic forty-eighter Karl August Fetzer put forward a motion calling for 'the creation of a system of defence resting on a general duty to serve and to bear arms on the part of the entire people'.[301] Amongst other things, he alluded to the War Minister's claim before the second chamber on 27 November 1863 that the state's army was incapable of defending the territory because of its 'small forces'.[302]

[296] Ibid.   [297] Ibid.   [298] Ibid.   [299] Ibid., 195.   [300] Ibid.
[301] K. A. Fetzer's motion, *Verhandlungen der Württembergischen Kammer der Abgeordneten auf dem Landtag 1862/65* (Stuttgart, 1866), vol. 1 (*Beilage*), 2110.
[302] Ibid., 2112.

His answer was to create a Swiss-type militia, which was equated with universal service, and to abandon a system of conscription which had been in place since 1806:

> The acceptance of a system of conscription in 1806 was itself a complete change of the military system which had existed until then: the government can again, without being untrue to its traditions, if it is convinced, allow that it [the military system] is in no way adequate to existing conditions, as they have developed during the course of half a century.
>
> That great difficulties are associated with every change of system, in particular with the one being advanced here, cannot be denied. Established rights must not be undermined, officers and other officials in the military body, must not have their entitlements impaired, even if they cannot all be used in the new organization; a great part of any savings would, then, in any event first occur over a long period. It is also not to be disputed that the proposed new organization will need new establishments and acquisitions for arms, the keeping of weapons, the accommodation of the men and other things, and will thus, temporarily, require a not inconsiderable expenditure; likewise, organizers, instructors and military officials will have to develop activities whose ways and means are not familiar to them.[303]

In Württemberg, the existing 'standing army' was composed, 'with the exception of officers, mostly from the less well-off classes of the people'.[304] In 'particular, so-called "conservative" circles of society', observers might think that standing armies were justified for the enforcement of domestic order.[305] Most, though, adhered more closely to the 'original and principal definition' of an army and had to recognize that such an unequal and ineffective distribution of the burden was unsustainable in a country like Württemberg where officers and men came from the same nationality and 'class hatred does not exist'.[306] In these circumstances, only a fuller, more equal type of recruitment and service could harness the resources of the state and make it fit the purposes of foreign policy, Fetzer continued:

> The poor conditions and shortcomings depicted here can only be avoided in that system, starting from a general duty of service and training the entire *Volk* to defend itself, which places an organized *Volksheer* in the stead of a conscripted army and which allows, in other words, the *Volk* to take up arms. It is scarcely necessary to add that a disciplined army is being thought of here, not an undisciplined one characterized only by the loose military ties of popular troops.
>
> The Bavarian chamber of deputies has also raised this issue, namely the exchanging of the present system of conscription with a militia system, with the system to train a people's army (*Volksheer*) on the basis of universal military service . . .
>
> Switzerland, . . . with a population about a quarter larger than that of Württemberg, . . . managed to muster 258,000 men, when a Prussian attack was threatened . . . How completely different, militarily and politically, the significance of Switzerland is, with such an army power, from that of a German *Mittelstaat*! . . . Württemberg, too, . . . could increase its defensive forces four or fivefold and would, in this way, increase its security, its independence and its reputation in a military and political sense in an extraordinary fashion.[307]

---

[303] Ibid., 2113.   [304] Ibid., 2114.   [305] Ibid., 2113.
[306] Ibid., 2113–14.   [307] Ibid., 2115–16.

A small majority of deputies—forty-five to forty-one—voted to reject Fetzer's motion.

Despite talk of a 'change of system', most deputies continued to agree on certain basic propositions. Unlike in the 1820s, substitution was divisive, regularly tied by democrats—albeit as a matter of secondary importance in terms of policy—to the existence of an unequal and unjust society. Moreover, 'in public opinion, the idea has gained ground', declared the democrat Gottlob Tafel, that standing armies could be 'misused all too easily as the blind instruments of coups d'état' and that they had come to occupy 'a special position', answerable only to themselves ('and, rightly, this is criticized most strongly in a constitutional state').[308] Even for Tafel, though, 'what makes standing armies unpopular, above all, is the thought, which must trouble so many, that when our armies are defeated' no one stands behind them 'who is in a position to defend our homes'.[309] For many democrats and most conservatives and liberals, despite rarely challenging the rhetoric of equality, the efficacy of the army abroad—against the backdrop of a purportedly imminent French attack—was more important in the 1860s than its role at home. Thus, the left-wing deputy Moritz Mohl was a familiar opponent of Fetzer and supporter of a 'standing army', as he put it in April 1865, on the grounds 'that the country prefers to arm for war in peacetime than to go on paying contributions for its humiliation'.[310] The example given by Fetzer of the defeat of Britain's standing army by American militias in the Wars of Independence was discounted by Mohl as a misplaced comparison: 'such a relatively small army' as the British one was, 'I would prefer to say, already rendered impotent by space alone'.[311] In the American Civil War, the armies of the North and the South had both been militias, accounting for the conflict's 'enormous loss of men and money'.[312]

The Revolutionary Wars had been cited but they were carried out by standing armies, led by an alumnus of a war academy (Napoleon), Mohl went on.[313] For its part, the Swiss military had not been tested in a war against the standing army of another power and 'the conditions of Switzerland can clearly not be considered', since it was 'a neutral state in international law' and could count on the backing of other states, if it were threatened or attacked.[314] More significantly, Fetzer's claim that neither Switzerland nor Württemberg would want to wage an offensive war, to which militias were less well-suited, was false—confirmed by 'the most capable military men'—in the case of a conflict conducted alongside other German states: 'It is an acknowledged fact that Germany can only be defended by means of an offensive and, I believe, the whole history of 1814 and 1815 has taught that, if the Allied armies had not marched towards Paris, they would not have been able to master Napoleon.'[315] Whilst it was obvious that 'a state of two million people loses if it is attacked alone by the first military power in the world (France), with 36 million people', it was also true—and 'we must remind ourselves of it, because it is a fact'—that 'we in Germany can only defend ourselves with success if Germany

---

[308] G. Fetzer, 4 Apr. 1865, *Verhandlungen der Württembergischen Kammer der Abgeordneten auf dem Landtag 1862/65* (Stuttgart, 1866), vol. 4 (*Protokoll*), 3082.
[309] Ibid., 3083.   [310] Moritz Mohl, 4 Apr. 1865, ibid.   [311] Ibid., 3084.
[312] Ibid., 3085.   [313] Ibid., 3084.   [314] Ibid.   [315] Ibid.

is united'.[316] For this task, 'standing armies' of conscripts were better suited, in Mohl's opinion, than militias, since they were better trained, had a more enduring structure, and could be used offensively. Given such a state of affairs, it was neither necessary nor practicable for every man to serve and it made no sense, 'if the entire cohort is not needed', to make 'the whole cohort into soldiers', with economic disadvantages for wider society (see Table 2.2 for the strengths of the German armies).[317] It was preferable to apportion the burden randomly by lottery and to continue to use funds from substitution to offset the burden for some of those—particularly the poor—who did have to do military service, 'the disadvantages of which [had] been exaggerated'.[318]

The terminology of the military debate concealed points of agreement, as some deputies pointed out. 'The words *"allgemeine Wehrpflicht, Wehrhaftmachung des ganzen Volks, die Herstellung eines Volksheeres"* have a certain force, they sound a certain note which can have a seductive effect', declared the spokesperson of the parliamentary commission on the question, the moderate liberal Alois Wiest: 'But we should not be misled by this train of thought; we must break down such reform ideas into their real parts and, above all, test whether they are realizable and work out how, in fact, their realization would occur.'[319] 'Only in this way do such ideas emerge from nebulous conditions of generality, lack of clarity and confusion; then, reservations manifest themselves, the dark sides become visible and obstacles appear', he went on: the aim of Fetzer's motion, when regarded from this standpoint, was evidently 'the introduction of the so-called militia system'.[320] Yet what was a 'militia system'? In theory, the label could denote the arming of all citizens, who would take their weapons home, and the spontaneous formation of armed bands, as the need arose, which was what some radicals had advocated during the revolution of 1848–9. By the 1860s, in Württemberg and elsewhere, few if any deputies appear to have had this revolutionary conception of a militia in mind. Rather, they referred to a closely regulated Swiss model of pre-military 'training', the storage of ammunition in local arsenals, fewer professional officers (instructors trained and coordinated by the Swiss *Bund* not the cantons), and shorter initial periods of service and training, followed by regular military exercises. Even this form of militia was, for most deputies, considered an 'extreme', as Rüstow had put it, akin to the other extreme of the small standing armies of absolutism.[321]

The actual questions being addressed in 1865 fell between the two extremes and concerned the number of those recruited, the means by which they were recruited, and the length of their military service. The War Minister Moritz von Miller had conceded that, 'for Switzerland, such an army [a militia] might be appropriate because this army only has to fulfil defensive purposes', whereas in Württemberg it would quickly be defeated, given the different geography and legal position of the two states, and it would be prevented from playing a part, including participation in joint offensives, in the army of the German Confederation.[322] Far from desiring

[316] Ibid.   [317] Ibid., 3086.   [318] Ibid.   [319] A. Wiest, 4 Apr. 1865, ibid., 3075.
[320] Ibid.   [321] W. Rüstow, *Der Krieg und seine Mittel*, 50.
[322] M. v. Miller, 4 Apr. 1865, *Verhandlungen der Württembergischen Kammer der Abgeordneten auf dem Landtag 1862/65*, vol. 4 (*Protokoll*), 3082.

a full arming of the people as Fetzer contended, the minister continued, Joseph Radetzky had 'merely wanted a well-organized *Landwehr*, which was to back up the standing army', as it had in 1813 and 1814 in Miller's own experience of a company 'mixed with older men' and commanded by officers who had 'already taken part in campaigns'.[323] Progressives like Julius Hölder, who had helped to establish the liberal and democratic *Fortschrittspartei* as the largest party in Württemberg after 1862, rejected the War Minister's arguments but admitted that the state already had a system which combined—unsuccessfully in his view—elements of both a standing army and a militia: 'When the minister said that he would never give his agreement to the introduction of the militia system, I say that our current state of affairs already constitutes a rapprochement with the militia system', although it remained a 'halfway house'.[324] In the opinion of other progressives such as Rudolf Probst, who put forward a weaker motion than Fetzer's—accepted by a large majority—calling for pre-military training, 'the transition from what exists at present to that which must be aimed for in future' (more extensive, shorter military service) was not likely to happen 'at the moment or over the short term'.[325] The majority of deputies in Württemberg, including conservative supporters of the government such as Johann Leonhard Bayrhammer, were in favour, in principle, of a shift towards pre-military training and universal military service, merging different elements of a standing army with experienced officers and technical experts and a *levée en masse*, the necessity of which had been proved by the Revolutionary and Napoleonic Wars.[326] In mid-nineteenth-century Germany, notwithstanding allusions to 'questions of principle' (Hölder), disagreements about army reform were matters of degree, with deputies and other observers comparing their own systems with the more extensive ones of Switzerland and Prussia.[327]

The debate in the Hohenzollern monarchy itself during the early 1860s was marked by a similar heterogeneity, flexibility, and, even, convergence vis-à-vis the principal military questions and by conflict and inflexibility in respect of connected political and constitutional disputes.[328] Frevert has depicted the conflict between Wilhelm I, reactionary ministers, and senior generals, on the one hand, and liberals and democrats in the Prussian *Abgeordnetenhaus*, on the other, as one of 'content', pitting Roon's aim of 'an expanded army, efficient and disciplined, led by an aristocratic officer corps and having sworn an oath of loyalty directly to the person of the king', which resulted from 'more precise notions about the coming challenges in military technologies and the army's tasks', against liberals' 'pathos, invoked tradition and illusions', 'drawing largely on retrospective arguments' about the *Landwehr* 'in memory of the old civilian militia dream'.[329] In fact, however, the

---

[323] Ibid.   [324] J. Hölder, 4 Apr. 1865, ibid., 3091.   [325] R. Probst, ibid., 3090.
[326] J. L. Bayrhammer, ibid., 3094.   [327] J. Hölder, ibid., 3091.
[328] R. Helfert, *Der preußische Liberalismus und die Heeresreform von 1860* (Bonn, 1989); P. Baumgart, B. R. Kroener, and H. Stubig (eds), *Die preußische Armee zwischen Ancien Régime und Reichsgründung* (Paderborn, 2006).
[329] U. Frevert, *Nation in Barracks*, 156. See also W. Petter, 'Die Roonsche Heeresreorganisation und das Ende der Landwehr', in P. Baumgart, B. R. Kroener, and H. Stubig (eds), *Die Preußische Armee*, 215–28.

terms of the debate were unstable, as in other German states, and grounds for compromise existed, usually undermined by broader disagreements about Prussia's system of government and by political posturing deriving from fear of revolution (from the point of view of those on the right) or 'absolutism' and coups d'état (those in the centre and on the left). Initially, as Dierk Walter has pointed out, the impetus for reform came from within the army prior to and at the start of the 'New Era' of the Prince Regent (from October 1858 onwards), before the escalation of a political conflict between reactionaries and liberals and the construction of entrenched positions of military principle.[330]

The army reform bill which was presented to the House of Deputies on 10 February 1860 raised the number of troops conscripted annually from 41,469 in 1858 (approximately 25 per cent of the year group) to a projected 63,000 (40 per cent), increasing the size of the standing army from about 140,000 to 200,000. It also abolished the second levy of the *Landwehr* and reassigned some of its younger recruits to the reserves of the regular army, with conscripts now serving for three years in the army of the line, five years in the reserve, and eleven years in the *Landwehr*, which had been reduced to 116 battalions and relegated to fortress and other duties behind the lines without offensive weapons.[331] The 1814 law which had been in place until then had stipulated three years with the line (reduced to two years in 1837–52), two years in the reserve, and fourteen years in the two levies of the *Landwehr*. In public, the reform was justified by its fairer division of the burden of military service, since the number of conscripts was to be increased, and by its less severe economic impact, since older taxpaying members of the *Landwehr* were effectively to be replaced by younger conscripted recruits to the regular army. The *Landwehr* would 'continue to share in the dangers and honours of our armed forces', declared the preface to the bill:

> Only reduced by three year groups, it is reverting to a relationship similar to that conceived of during its establishment through the ideas of Scharnhorst and Boyen. It is not to give up its connection with the line; rather, it is to remain in a closely interwoven, organic relationship with it.[332]

In private, as was made plain in a series of internal reports by Friedrich Adolf von Willisen (1855), Karl von Clausewitz (reworked by the War Ministry in February 1858), Roon (July 1858), and Konstans Bernhard von Voigts-Rhetz and Julius von Hartmann on behalf of the *Allgemeiner Kriegsdepartement* (January–March 1859), the hierarchy of the Prussian army had other motives and priorities.

---

[330] D. Walter, *Preußische Heeresreformen 1807–1870*, 442–8.

[331] D. Walter, 'Roonsche Reform oder militärische Revolution? Wandlungsprozesse im preußischen Heerwesen vor den Einigungskriegen,' in K.-H. Lutz, M. Rink, and M. v. Salisch (eds), *Reform, Reorganisation, Transformation. Zum Wandel in deutschen Streitkräften von den preußischen Heeresformen bis zur Transformation der Bundeswehr* (Munich, 2010), 183; Anon, *Die preußische Heeres-Reform* (Berlin, 1867), 36, gives figures of 151,000 in 1858 and 212,000 after the implementation of the reform; G. A. Craig, *Politics of the Prussian Army*, 145.

[332] Anon, *Die preußische Heeres-Reform*, 15.

The different groupings within the hierarchy all wanted to expand the size of the regular army, make mobilization easier, lower the average age of soldiers during wartime, and integrate and weaken the *Landwehr*. Some of their aims were related to the technological and strategic transformations of modern warfare, with Willisen for instance seeking during the Crimean War to tie the issuing of needle guns to a fundamental reform of the Prussian infantry which would have abolished *Landwehr* regiments of fusiliers.[333] Other aims resulted from direct experiences of combat and revolution in Schleswig-Holstein, Baden, Saxony, and Prussia (1848–50) and of mobilization during the stand-off at Olmütz (1850) and the Franco-Austrian War (1859). It is difficult to separate military objectives from political ones, as Walter attempts to do, given that officers' attitudes to guns, cannon, conscription, the standing army, and the *Landwehr* were regularly linked to their view of the balance of cavalry, infantry, and artillery, their conception of the relationship between civil society and the military, their memories of revolution, and their differing allegiances and sympathies in the recent wars of the Great Powers.[334] Political judgements in these respects complicated military evaluations, reinforcing differences of opinion about the incorporation of the *Landwehr* and, especially, the scope, cost, and duration of military service. Thus, although it was true that the *Landwehr* had been progressively subjected to the command and conduct of the army of the line in 1819 (when *Landwehr* brigades had been put under regular divisional commanders rather than being directly answerable to commanders-in-chief) and in 1859 (when *Landwehr* regiments had been placed under the tutelage of regular brigades), more liberal-minded army reformers such as the War Minister (1852–4, 1858–9) Eduard von Bonin were much more sensitive to its continuing symbolic importance than reactionaries were. They criticized Roon's memorandum of July 1858 ('Bemerkungen und Entwürfe') for the separation of 'the army from the country' and for risking the destruction of 'the foundations of [Prussia's] existence', which was the trust of the people in the military.[335]

For their part, reactionaries like Edwin von Manteuffel, the Chief of the Military Cabinet, had confirmed the Regent in his view—articulated in an extraordinary meeting of the *Staatsministerium* on 3 December 1859, two days before the official appointment of Roon to the post of War Minister and almost a month after the resignation of Bonin—that

> no one doubts any longer that the *Landwehr* in its present form does not correspond to the demands of military discipline, that justice pressingly demands, at the current level of population, the protection of the older cohorts of the *Landwehr*, that these older people also no longer have the necessary bodily aptitudes to match modern, more mobile tactics and, lastly, that the cavalry of the *Landwehr* is not fit for war.[336]

[333] D. Walter, *Preußische Heeresreformen*, 399–400.

[334] Ibid., 445: 'man wird doch nicht ernsthaft daran zweifeln können, dass die rein militärischen Aspekte bei Weitem überwogen'.

[335] Ibid., 374–9. Bonin is cited in E. Marcks, *Wilhelm I*, 9th edn (Berlin, 1943), 166.

[336] Cited in D. Walter, *Preußische Heeresreformen*, 431.

Manteuffel also insisted that 'combined regiments', the formation of which was authorized by Wilhelm before the army reform bill was put before the House of Deputies in February 1860, should be maintained, despite the stipulation of the assembly in May—consented to by the Finance Minister Robert von Patow—that their provisional grant of 9 million thaler was not intended to be used for reform, which was to remain in abeyance, but merely to strengthen existing regiments referred to in the service law of 1814 and the *Landwehrordnung* of 1815. The Chief of the Military Cabinet's response, in a letter to Roon on 29 May 1860, was to ask 'whether the King or Minister Patow is war lord'.[337] 'I consider the state of army morale and its inner energy imperiled and the position of the Prince Regent compromised, if these [combined] regiments are not established definitively and at once', he wrote in another letter on the same day.[338]

Arguably, as Bonin suggested, there was room for manoeuvre as far as the *Landwehr* was concerned, for it had already been integrated with the army of the line (from 1819 onwards) and remained a necessity for demographic and fiscal reasons: to replace it altogether would mean a doubling of conscription to the standing army rather than the increase of a third proposed in the army reform bill and it would entail correspondingly higher expenditure, which would be required to accommodate, arm, and train such conscripts, compared to the minimal cost of a fortnight of exercises for the veterans of the *Landwehr*.[339] All the military's plans put forward in 1858–9 retained the *Landwehr* in some form, even Roon's 'Bemerkungen und Entwürfe', which had labelled it a 'politically false institution' of 'dubious significance for external as well as internal policy'.[340] On the other question of the length of military service, there was less room for obfuscation and compromise. In February 1859, the War Ministry, basing its recommendations on those of Karl von Clausewitz, proposed a reduction of military service, by law not decree, from three years to two.[341] Wilhelm, Manteuffel, and Roon all opposed the reduction, arguing in the words of the latter for 'military discipline' and the need to be able to withstand 'a war of manoeuvre', retreats and defeats without 'dissolution'.[342]

Roon had been given the chairmanship of a special military commission by the regent in September 1859 in order to allow him to circumvent the War Minister, who was held to be too wedded to the 'so-called constitutional method of doing business', citing popular opposition to a simultaneous increase in conscription to

[337] G. A. Craig, *The Politics of the Prussian Army*, 151.

[338] E. v. Manteuffel to A. v. Roon, 29 May 1860, ibid.

[339] D. Walter, *Preußische Heeresreformen*, 4435; D. Walter, 'Roonsche Reform oder militärische Revolution?' Wandlungsprozesse im preußischen Heerwesen vor den Einigungskriegen', 181–98; W. Petter, 'Die Roonsche Heeresorganisation und das Ende der Landwehr', 215–28.

[340] Königlich Preussischer Kriegsministerium (ed.), *Militärische Schriften weiland Kaiser Wilhelms des Großen Majestät* (Berlin, 1897), vol. 2, 349–50.

[341] G. A. Craig, *The Politics of the Prussian Army*, 139. D. Walter, *Preußische Heeresreformen*, 444, mistakenly suggests that Craig had assumed military service already to have been reduced to two years.

[342] A. v. Roon 'Bemerkungen und Entwürfe', in D. Walter, *Preußische Heeresreformen*, 409–10.

the standing army and the maintenance of three-year service. Bonin rightly countered that the provisions outlined by the commission, which added 9.5 million
thaler per year to the military budget, would be unacceptable to the Prussian
Landtag. Wilhelm's blunt reply, which led to Bonin's resignation as War Minister,
was that, 'in a monarchy like ours, the military point of view must not be subordinated to the financial and economic, for the European position of the state
depends upon it'.[343] Manteuffel's advice to Roon, as Bonin's successor, was never
to give in to public opinion:

> I have always found in my twelve years of experience in revolutionary life [after the
> establishment of a representative assembly in Prussia in 1848] that when a question of
> principle arises, all the world counsels concession and compromise and advises against
> bringing matters to a head; and that when this or that minister has acted upon these
> rules of prudence and the momentary mood has passed, then everyone says, 'How
> could he have given in like that?'[344]

Yet such intransigence, which merged with other political fears (of revolution) and
hopes (of the restoration of the *ancien régime*), led to an exaggeration of the significance of three-year service, dividing the military hierarchy itself, part of which—
the War Ministry—had after all proposed a reduction and another part of which
would have accepted the practical shortening of service as a result of winter leave.[345]
In 1849, faced with the prospect of a six-month period of service, Wilhelm had
been willing to advocate a two-year one, which had been instituted by Friedrich
Wilhelm IV in 1834 and remained in place until 1852.[346] As late as October
1862, Roon and Bismarck had drafted a plan splitting the army into two types of
recruit: long-term volunteers (*Capitulanten*), comprising a third of the total; and
two-year conscripts, making up two-thirds. Manteuffel helped to ensure that the
proposal was never submitted to the *Abgeordnetenhaus*, portraying it as a backdown
over three-year service and an unwarranted restriction of the monarch's right to
determine the size and form of the army.[347]

Bismarck, appointed to the Minister-Presidency in September 1862, greeted the
news that the plan had been shelved with the rejoinder that 'two-year service with
Capitulanten would be sufficient for the infantry, but, if the king makes a stand
on ten-year service, I shall not withdraw my obedience to him in the matter'.[348]
His conservative colleagues in the House of Deputies did not follow his example,
backing the call for two-year service on the grounds of cost. The call came mainly
from liberals. One was Karl Twesten, who had backed two-year service in a pamphlet

---

[343] Wilhelm, Prince Regent of Prussia, cited in G. A. Craig, *The Politics of the Prussian Army*, 143.
[344] E. v. Manteuffel to A. v. Roon, 11 Mar. 1860, ibid., 150.
[345] D. Walter, *Preußische Heeresreformen*, 436–7, for instance, stresses the importance of
Beurlaubung as a potential means of avoiding an impasse over the length of service and associated
expenditure.
[346] W. Petter, 'Die Roonsche Heeresorganisation und das Ende der Landwehr', 224, characterizes
Bonin's decision to put forward two-year service and to enlist the support of the *Landtag* for it was a
'mistake', given the opposition of the regent, but the different positions and their relative weight were
difficult to calculate between 1858 and 1862.
[347] E. v. Manteuffel to A. v. Roon, 5 Dec. 1862, G. A. Craig, *The Politics of the Prussian Army*, 163.
[348] O. v. Bismarck, *Die gesammelten Werke* (Berlin, 1924), vol. 14, 628.

(*Was uns noch retten kann*) in 1861. He was challenged to a duel and shot in the arm by Manteuffel, who had 'made his career at the court' and had 'not seen much of the army for a long time' in the liberal lawyer's estimation.[349] The Chief of the Military Cabinet was said to be a member of the most 'damaging' and 'dangerous' institution, which cut off the king even from his ministers and reinforced the proclivity of the 'military' (*das Militair*), not least because of its 'size and the fixed structure of its organism, its important position in the state, whose security and strength rest on its military development of power, and its resultant consciousness as an estate' had inclined it, 'more than any other bureaucracy, exclusively to shut itself off and not to take notice of anything else', allowing it to forget 'that the army cannot be strong if the country is weak'.[350] 'The haughtiness of the officer corps, the link with the court and the aristocracy makes the special position [of the army] all the more conspicuous and dangerous, summons up an atmosphere of disfavour and enmity between the military and civilians, as it existed in its fullest flower in the years before 1806', the pamphlet continued.[351] Before shooting him, Manteuffel had defamed Twesten, a member of the judiciary of Berlin, accusing him of belonging to a secret revolutionary party which wanted to overthrow the Hohenzollern state.[352] The later co-founder of the Progressive Party, however, was prudent and sympathetic to the government of the old liberal forty-eighter Rudolf von Auerswald (*Staatsminister* until March 1862) in *Was uns noch retten kann*, taken as a whole.[353]

Twesten's reflections, more than half of which were devoted to foreign affairs, were published after the Franco-Austrian War in 1859 and in expectation of a European war in the near future. Like many liberals and democrats, he was mindful of the need for a strong army, looking back to 'the traditions of 1813' as evidence of the interdependence of military strength and popular enthusiasm.[354] 'Admittedly, the many will not achieve much, if they do not find leaders and organization, but outstanding individuals, for their part, not only need trust and joyful agreement, but they also derive their own effective power from the spirit and the mood of their age', he wrote: 'Discipline must give it [the army] resoluteness and posture, training must bestow technical preparedness; but the greatest war-like virtues and those leading to the greatest achievements—vital initiative, enterprising drive, active decisiveness . . .—only flow from the spirit of the whole into the army and its leadership.'[355] Although the influence and power of the state abroad depended on its 'real forces', which were economic (and therefore social and political) as well as military, 'one was generally ready in the country, without a doubt, to take on increased burdens', Twesten conceded: 'As sad as it is that a vast armament for war demands disproportionate means and lames the development of all elements of

---

[349] K. Twesten, *Was uns noch retten kann* (Berlin, 1861), 81.

[350] Ibid., 77, 80.   [351] Ibid., 80.

[352] E. Schmitz, *Edwin von Manteuffel als Quelle zur Geschichte Friedrich Wilhelms IV* (Munich, 1921), 42–3.

[353] Manteuffel demanded as a condition of avoiding the duel that Twesten retract all his claims in the entire work, not just the couple of direct references to the Chief of the Military Cabinet.

[354] K. Twesten, *Was uns noch retten kann*, 60.   [355] Ibid.

life, the necessity of a heightened readiness for war is widely recognized under the present political conditions.'[356] The liberal publicist and politician accepted 'the necessity and habit of military command, unconditional discipline and rapid action', yet he rejected the idea, given the precedent of 'earlier practice' in the 1830s, 1840s, and 1850s when 'an even shorter period regularly sufficed', that three years of training were required for their inculcation and facilitation within the infantry.[357] Unwittingly echoing Bismarck, albeit to different effect, Twesten reiterated the inevitability of compromise in setting the level of military effectiveness, spending, and economic activity:

> One can admit fully that the current plan [of Roon's commission] makes the army far stronger and more flexible. If it were possible to keep all those eligible under arms for tens of years and instead of ten more millions yearly hundreds of millions, then without doubt a far more outstanding army could be set up. We are ready, under the current conditions here, as is happening in other countries, to make greater sacrifices in men and money for the sake of the defence of the state. But it should not lead to a lasting imbalance.[358]

The escalation of the crisis in Prussia during the early 1860s was the consequence of a constitutional dispute, initially about the nature and extent of the monarch's 'power of command' (*Kommandogewalt*) but quickly bringing into question the monarchy's entire system of government, rather than the result of a stand-off over the reorganization of the army.[359] Progressives could have accepted the plan of Bonin and the Auerswald ministry, Twesten implied.[360] Even after the submission (and immediate withdrawal) of Roon's proposal in February 1860, the House of Deputies had granted provisional, increased funds in 1860 and 1861 on the understanding that the proposal would be revised and resubmitted. As such, the controversy about the Prussian military only came to a head slowly, overtaken after the appointment of Roon as War Minister on 5 December 1859 and, especially, Bismarck as Minister-President on 23 September 1862 by a wider political crisis. The programme of the German *Fortschrittspartei*, which was founded in June 1861 in the midst of the crisis and which went on to gain 109 seats in the *Abgeordnetenhaus* in December and 133 (285 with other 'opposition' parties) out of 352 in May 1862, spelled out its different priorities, most notably the 'the strict and consequential creation of a constitutional *Rechtsstaat*' and the 'binding unification of Germany', with 'a strong central power in the hands of Prussia'.[361] The military components of the programme were secondary, listed towards the end. They combined the desire to achieve 'the greatest economies in the military budget during

---

[356] Ibid., 62.   [357] Ibid., 79, 84.   [358] Ibid., 82.

[359] H. A. Winkler, *Preussischer Liberalismus und deutscher Nationalstaat. Studien zur Geschichte der Deutschen Fortschrittspartei 1861–1866* (Tübingen, 1964), 4, argues that the *Fortschrittspartei* had a welter of primary constitutional objectives and was, in part, reacting against the Ministry, which 'expended real energy...only in one field: army reform'.

[360] Ibid.

[361] 'Gründungsprogramm der Deutschen Fortschrittspartei, 6 June 1861', in H. Fenske (ed.), *Der Weg zur Reichsgründung 1850–1870* (Darmstadt, 1977), 212–13.

peacetime' and the need to preserve 'the honour and position of power of our fatherland' during wars, for which 'a sacrifice will never be too great'.[362]

In the event, many progressive deputies were willing to countenance army increases. Even democrats like Hermann Schulze-Delitzsch, one of the main critics of Bismarck, were convinced that Germany needed 'Prussia as the most militarily capable state, deploying the whole strength of its *Volk* to take the lead' in struggles against its many enemies, 'France in the West, Russia in the East, perhaps Italy in the South, Denmark and Sweden with England in the North'.[363] The Progressive Party's aims were 'the maintenance of the *Landwehr*, physical training for youth, to be introduced universally, and an increased drafting of those men capable of bearing arms, which guarantees, with a two-year period of service, the complete war-readiness of the Prussian *Volk in Waffen*'.[364] They could only be attained, however, 'as must unconditionally be clear to the most obtuse eye, after the history of the last three years', by means of more thorough-going reforms, including that of the *Herrenhaus*, 'in constitutional ways'.[365] The implementation of two-year service and a defence of the *Landwehr* were always subordinated, as far as democrats and liberals were concerned to their political struggle against Bismarck, Roon, the monarch, the court, and the nobility. Though they had become points of principle, they did not lead to a fundamental alteration of progressives' conception of the military. Indeed, relatively high and increasing spending, 'universal' conscription by lottery, and a combined standing army and *Landwehr*, not a militia, remained unquestioned elements of the 'Prussian system' throughout.[366] In the Hohenzollern monarchy, as in other German states, service in the army, in peacetime or at war, was a widely accepted fact of life. The next chapters investigate the relationship between civilians' experience of military life and military action (during the revolution of 1848–9) and their attitudes towards violence, killing, and death.

---

[362] Ibid., 213–14.

[363] Schulze, speech to *Nationalverein*, 16 Oct. 1863, and 31 Oct. 1864, in F. Thorwart (ed.), *Hermann Schulze-Delitzch's Schriften und Reden* (Berlin, 1910), vol. 3, 212 and 233.

[364] Ibid., 214. Such ideas, of course, had backers from different constituencies: J.-K. Zabel, *Das preußische Kadettenkorps. Militärische Jugenderziehung als Herrschaftsmittel im preußischen Militärsystem* (Frankfurt, 1978).

[365] Schulze-Delitzsch, in Thorwart (ed.), *Schulze-Delitzsch's Schriften und Reden*, vol. 3, 214.

[366] The argument here runs against the gravamen of that put forward by Frank Lorenz Müller, 'The Spectre of a People in Arms: The Prussian Government and the Militarisation of German Nationalism, 1859–1864', *English Historical Review*, 122 (2007), 82–104.

3

Domestic Violence

Karl Heinzen was one of very few commentators, even amongst democrats and radicals, who were critical of military violence and killing per se. He was in the unusual position, as a former *Landwehr* officer, an adventurer (serving in the Dutch East Indies), and a political radical (as a contributor to the *Rheinische Zeitung*), of knowing what was going on in the Prussian army from the inside but being detached from it, offering an oppositional, civil, middle-class critique of army affairs (as the son of a forestry inspector and a former Prussian civil servant).[1] Humans in armies 'murdered' other humans, he wrote in his 'thirty articles of war for a new era' in 1846, for 'any number of possible reasons': from passion, speculation, or, even, duty, killing 'legally' and making it a 'virtue'.[2] His initial question was: 'who could have brought mankind to so terrible a degradation?'[3] Part of his explanation was historical, depicting a cycle of domination and resistance:

> On all sides, people took possession of the earth, as far as they wanted to, and made their earlier seizure of land, which was by chance, into a planned action. Thus, seizure turned into robbery [–] there were *wars of conquest*. Conquest from one side presupposed defence on the other, on the part of those whose property was to be conquered. Thus, this led to *wars of freedom*.[4]

Such 'toing and froing' made murder 'necessary, as long as humanity had not worked its way out of a state of savagery'.[5] Now, however, after the development of culture, contemporaries were beginning to ask whether humanity would not 'throw away its instruments of murder', leaving a world without 'guns and cannon' as well as the 'living machines of murder who fire them', so that a later generation would look back on 'the official economy of murder, which is called a military organization, as we look back on the cannibals of Nukahiwa and New Zealand'.[6] 'People of our time' said such things, but 'wherever we look, we see murder weapons and the science of murder [pursued] with mad eagerness'.[7] In answer to his own enquiry as to why this was the case, he pointed to the establishment of standing armies, in which leaders became 'lords of their helpers', forcing them to do

---

[1] See K. Heinzen, *Erlebtes. Vor meiner Exilierung* (Boston, 1864), in which he recounts his early life, his time in the East Indies (*Reise eines teutschen Romantikers nach Batavia*), and his service as an official (*Acht Jahre Staatsdienst, oder: ein Stück Beamtenleben*).

[2] K. Heinzen, *Dreißig Kriegsartikeln der neuen Zeit für Officiere und Gemeine in despotischen Staaten*, 3.

[3] Ibid.   [4] Ibid., 4.   [5] Ibid.   [6] Ibid., 5.   [7] Ibid.

their killing.[8] As culture increasingly 'reduced the opportunity to murder', the 'instruments of murder abroad', or 'tools of despotic ambition', became 'instruments of protection at home', or 'tools of despotic security', concealing their true purposes behind the guise of 'popular security' (*Volkssicherheit*).[9] The principal legitimation of standing armies was external but their main use was internal. Partly as a consequence, neither the people—'*Volk*, where are you?'—nor officers were conscious of their real function, in Heinzen's view: 'Do the uniformed murderers come to look at themselves and test their own destiny and acknowledge their key position? The power of habit has blunted them and they even carry their weapons with pride.'[10] Some states—Prussia was implied but not mentioned by name—went as far, without realizing that they were admitting they were 'murder and hanging states', as to call themselves 'military states'.[11]

Within such states—and only countries with purely defensive militias like Switzerland and the United States were exempted—soldiers stopped being 'human'.[12] For Heinzen, who came from a middle-class background and had attended *Gymnasium* and university, the shock of military service was considerable:

> Before I became a soldier, I had not thought at all what it meant to wear a uniform. Habit, via the example of so many others, had rendered me unreflective, and as the time arrived when I was to follow, my youthful outlook even lent the prospect of a colourful coat and life in the garrison city the appeal of novelty. A troubling premonition was also present, but I was not aware what it meant. I drank a lot of brandy at the swearing-in, insolently sang brave tavern songs and marked out my last free moments by using the short grace of the transition to my new state almost unconsciously for the purposes of self-deception. I believe that even the slave manages for a short time to find the comforting appeal of change in the passage to the new world with its opportunities, when he begins the fateful voyage from the African to the American coast. This appeal did not last long for me… The clothes of my free youth were taken off me and they put me in a colourful doublet, which still smelled of the angst-ridden sweat of its previous wearer. Weighed down by bag and baggage and with an unceremonious instrument of murder in my hand, to which I would remain chained for years, I was shown into a room where, in the company of strange 'comrades', I was to get ready for the start of 'the highest service of all'. They ordered me… to clean my instrument of murder and to acquire a 'love for one's weapon'. Love for a weapon! That was a terrifying idea for me. I knew what love for one's parents or one's bride meant, but love for a weapon, for a piece of iron with which one murders one's fellow men seemed worse to me than love for one's jailer. I began to understand that a relationship in which such unnatural demands are made of man in order to frighten him out of his natural assumptions must be an inhuman relationship which is founded only on the overturning of all reasonable thinking… They read out the articles of war to me. Where was I? Talk of summary arrest and shooting dead rang in my ears, I appeared to myself a criminal guilty of capital crimes towards whom the fist of the hangman or beadle stretched out from all sides.
> … The commanding faces, which crowded round me as if for a hanging, the articles of war, the garrison walls all seemed so loving that I would rather have procured a love

---

[8] Ibid. [9] Ibid., 6. [10] Ibid., 8. [11] Ibid. [12] Ibid., 10.

of weapons in order to banish the whole business from the world. Yet these revolutionary thoughts were soon laid to rest. On the next day, so-called 'exercise' began. I was put in a line with a crowd of other 'comrades' and then they began preparing my limbs for 'the highest service of all'. I had previously stood on my healthy, straight legs here and there, in this way and that, but all this had not happened in the right way. Now I learned to 'stand up straight', i.e. like a living walking stick. Previously, I had seen a lot, this and that...But none of this had happened in the right way. Now I learned to look 'straight forward'...Now I learned a 'military bearing'. I had to balance on my big toes, as if it were the highest duty of a 'loyal subject' to fall on his nose at the first command; had to pull in my stomach, as if visited by patriotic stomach cramps; had to stick out my backside, as if ready to receive a caning; had to stick out my chest, as if enemy bullets were about to bounce off it; had to push my head into my neck, as if they wanted to shave me, and above all—in fact, the fatherland would have collapsed, if I had not done this—I had to stretch out my hands alongside my legs, 'so that the little finger touched the seam of the trousers, precisely'....Parents, friends, relatives, loved ones, *Volk*, humanity, help me to find a single reason why I should go through this humiliation, this breaking-in, this de-humanization, this yawning, deadening, brain-destroying absence of spirit for several years...[13]

As a radical, Heinzen was examining military service with deliberately unaccustomed eyes, asking conscripts to revolt against the fact that their 'life', 'profession', and 'family' were 'not present' during the long, pointless years of service when they were 'machines of sweat, without occupations'.[14] Yet his question remains a valid one: why did virtually all his contemporaries—from his parents to humanity as a whole—not see life in the army, during peacetime and at war, as an existence resting on 'murder'?

One reason was that the majority of soldiers, despite being trained to kill, had no direct experience of war. Heinzen's admission that he was willing to fight in a *Volkskrieg*, though not in any other type of conflict, can be seen in this light.[15] He, like most other troops, had little comprehension of what war was like, partly because combatants' accounts of the actual conditions of Napoleonic campaigns had barely filtered through to the public sphere and had been widely ignored by the journalists, artists, academics, and other writers who had fashioned the dominant representations of the conflict after 1815. Even in the army, as Fontane intimated in the 1840s, the most common account of the 'wars of freedom' consisted of a roll call of heroes and heroic actions, which was not openly contradicted by the remaining Prussian officers who had served in the wars.[16] In Bavaria and in other states formerly allied to France, the disastrous invasion of Russia in 1812, from which only about one-tenth of soldiers from southern Germany returned, was removed from the public record and, it seems, gradually erased from most contemporaries' memories, notwithstanding its direct impact on local communities and families at the time.[17] The suffering of returning troops in 1812 was still visible to

---

[13] Ibid., 18–22.   [14] Ibid., 23.   [15] Ibid., 141.   [16] Ibid., 137–8.
[17] Popular almanacs and lexicons tended to treat 1812 as a 'French' catastrophe, without reference to German troops: for example, *Rheinisches Conversations-Lexikon oder encyclopädisches Handwörterbuch für gebildete Stände* (Cologne, 1824–30), vol. 2, 757. For the public whitewashing of 1812, see J. Murken, 'Von "Thränen und Wehmut" zur Geburt des "deutschen Nationalbewußtseins". Die Niederlage des Russlandfeldzugs von 1812 und ihre Umdeutung in einen nationalen Sieg', in H. Carl,

an educated post-war public, for instance in the prints of Albrecht Adam and Christian Wilhelm Faber du Faur published in the 1820s and 1830s, but it appears to have been understood in the context of redemption, brought about by wars of liberation.[18] To Wilhelm, Margrave of Baden, writing in the early 1860s, the invasion of Russia would remain 'forever memorable', yet it was inserted—in his memoirs—into a victorious narrative in which Baden eventually joined Prussia, Austria, and the rest of 'Germany' in the vanquishing of France.[19] Given such popular mythology and the long period of peace after 1815, few soldiers seem to have feared combat. Urban, middle-class contemporaries had not for the most part, outside Prussia, served in the army, with the result that they not only remained ignorant of warfare, but also of military training. Although more burghers had been conscripted in the Hohenzollern monarchy than in other German states, many of them had gone on to become one-year volunteers and had been shielded from the harsh conditions experienced by the majority of conscripts. The same was true of aristocratic career officers, whose outlook as representatives of an order of 'warriors' (*Krieger*) and whose life in private quarters and privileged 'casinos' differed fundamentally from those of regular recruits.

PACIFICATION AND EVERYDAY VIOLENCE

Another reason that war and military service were widely accepted in Germany during the early and mid-nineteenth century derived from the varying responses of different social groups to the very idea of violence, wounding, killing, and death. To what extent had 'pacification'—defined by Giddens as 'the progressive diminution of violence in the internal affairs of nation-states'—taken place within the *Bürgertum*, which furnished most of the readers and commentators making up a German public sphere, the nobility, which dominated the officer corps of the individual states, and the urban and rural poor, which comprised the mass of conscripts?[20] Of these conscripts, it was often said that their background, including 'the hard work that a farmer or journeyman has to put up with in the fields and in the workshop', was compatible with the conditions of service within the military.[21] 'Should I be a farmer's slave, earn my bread by my sweat each day?' asked one Swabian soldier's song from the 1850s: 'No, my friend, that's not my way. I'd rather live where the cannon cry, under canvas and the open sky, where we talk of guns all day. No, I won't be a

---

H.-H. Kortum, D. Langewiesche, and F. Lenger (eds), *Kriegsniederlagen. Erfahrungen und Erinnerungen* (Berlin, 2004), 107–22; W. Schmidt, 'Denkmäler für die bayerischen Gefallenen des Russlandfeldzuges von 1812', *Zeitschrift für bayerische Landesgeschichte*, 49 (1986), 303–26; U. Schlie, *Die Nation erinnert sich* (Munich, 2002), 28–9; T. Nipperdey, 'Nationalidee und Nationaldenkmal im 19. Jahrhundert', *Historische Zeitschrift*, 210 (1968), 529–85.

[18] See the previous chapter. S. Parth, *Zwischen Bildbericht und Bildpropaganda. Kriegskonstruktionen in der deutschen Militärmalerei des 19. Jahrhunderts* (Paderborn, 2010), 252–6, 280–1.

[19] Wilhelm Markgraf v. Baden, *Denkwürdigkeiten*, ed. K. Obser (Heidelberg, 1906), vol. 1, 126.

[20] A. Giddens, *The Nation-State and Violence* (Cambridge, 1985), 187.

[21] C. v. Decker, *Über die Persönlichkeit des preußischen Soldaten*, 31.

farmer's slave.'[22] Throughout the German lands, conscription rested above all on the lower orders and artisanal trades of the towns and on the small farmers and landless agricultural workers of the country. The balance and boundary between the different groups was difficult to discern. In some areas, for example in the *Landgerichte* of Moosburg and Alt Ötting in Bavaria, approximately three-quarters of conscripts in the mid-nineteenth century came from the agricultural sector.[23] By contrast, in Reichenhall, farmers and farm workers made up less than half of the cohort, although many of those with a trade, who comprised much of the rest, also lived in villages and small towns.[24] In the 1840s, the 9th Bavarian Infantry Regiment, recruiting in the Palatinate, counted 24.9 per cent farmers and other agricultural occupations, 21.5 per cent day labourers from both town and country, and 44.2 per cent artisans; the 14th Infantry Regiment recruited 25.8 per cent farmers, 16.5 per cent 'without a trade', and 48.7 per cent artisans; and the 15th Infantry Regiment, based in central Franconia, was composed of 1.5 per cent farmers, 51 per cent from manufacture and trade, and 44.5 per cent 'without a trade'.[25] A similar constituency of recruits existed in other states. In Nassau in the 1840s, 24 per cent came from agriculture and forestry, 37 per cent from trade and industry, and 23.7 per cent had no trade. In Württemberg in 1848, 31.7 per cent of recruits came from agriculture and forestry, and 62.6 per cent from trade and industry.[26] It appears from the conscription statistics that each army chose the fittest—or least well-connected—recruits from varying sections of the peasantry and artisanate. Acceptance of military service and war rested largely on their members' attitudes.

Agricultural workers and farmers had good cause to resent the burden of conscription and the harshness and occasional arbitrariness of military discipline. Overall, however, they seem to have resigned themselves to it, positively revelling in its lustre and purported heroism.[27] 'He was a handsome, slim lad with a defiant face, which had a particular distinction because of a red moustache,' recorded one village tale by the German–Jewish author Berthold Auerbach:

> Jörgli, as the boy was called, was a cavalryman and almost always wore his soldier's cap. When, on Sundays, he went through the village, with his upright, jaunty gait, his feet pointing outwards, his spurs allowed to clink, his soldier's cap on his head and his leather-bound riding trousers on, his whole being said, 'I know that all the girls are looking at me'.[28]

---

[22] Cited in U. Frevert, *Nation in Barracks*, 110.

[23] W. Gruner, *Das bayerische Heer 1825 bis 1864*, 376.   [24] Ibid., 377.

[25] S. Müller, *Soldaten in der deutschen Revolution von 1848/49* (Paderborn, 1999), 134–5.

[26] Ibid., 136–7.

[27] The lustre of military life was widely shared: Georg von Siemens was happy to wear his uniform as a volunteer in Prussia in the 1850s, since it was meant to look good. Even his mother, who was more sceptical, admitted that her son 'plays the soldier externally with a very good figure'. She was only worried that he had begun to swear and pose disgracefully: K. Helfferich, *Georg von Siemens*, 24–6.

[28] Berthold Auerbach, *Der Tolpatsch*, in H. Kircher (ed.), *Dorgeschichten aus dem Vormärz* (Cologne, 1981), vol. 1, 44.

The same tale, from Auerbach's *Schwarzwälder Dorfgeschichten* (1843), hinted at the mixture of resentment, resignation, and fascination with which military service was frequently viewed:

> The mayor waited in the 'Angel' tavern for his local children and, when they were all there with him, he went with them to the town hall. The major was a dumb and presumptuous farmer. He had previously been a non-commanding officer and he invested a lot in his 'commission'; he liked to treat all farmers, old and young, like recruits...
>
> As Aloys approached the lottery wheel, his behaviour was almost challengingly defiant. Several lots came into his hand as he put it into the wheel; he shut his eyes tightly, as if he didn't want to see what he was taking and he took one out; trembling, he gave it in, for he feared that it could be a high number. As he heard the call 'number 17', he roared so loudly that he had to be calmed down.
>
> Now the lads bought bunches of flowers with red ribbons on and, after they had had an honest drink, they made their way home. Our Aloys yelled and sang the loudest...
>
> It was six weeks until the doctor's visit, and everything depended on this. Mother Marei took a great ball of butter and a basket full of eggs and went to the doctor's wife; the butter spread really well, despite the cold winter. Mother Marei received the assurance that Aloys should be freed; 'for', said the conscientious doctor, 'your Aloys is in any case unfit, he can't see long distances, and this is why he is sometimes so clumsy'.
>
> Aloys, however, cared nothing for all these stories; he was completely changed; he swayed and always whistled when he went about the village.
>
> The day of the visit came and the lad went to the town somewhat more quietly this time.
>
> As Aloys was called into the consulting room and had to undress, he said defiantly: 'Just look at me; you'll find no blemishes on me; I have no flaws; I can be a soldier.' He had to stand before the measure, and since he was of full size, he was taken as a soldier; the doctor forgot short-sightedness, butter and eggs confronted with Aloys's defiant speech...
>
> With the certainty of their status as soldiers, the lads made up with drinking, singing and yelling for what they believed they had done too little of beforehand.
>
> As Aloys came home, Marannele gave him a rosemary bunch with a red ribbon on it and sewed it onto their caps. But Aloys whistled, smoked his way smartly through the whole village and tippled deep into the night with his comrades...A third painful day was to be overcome: it was the day when the recruits had to make their way to Stuttgart...
>
> Jörgli had his horses harnessed to the wagon, ready to take the recruits a few hours away, and so they went through the village now, singing; Konrad the baker, who blew on a clarinet, sat with them on the leading wagon...They were marching in step. Friends pushed towards them from all sides and extended a hand or a parting drink, too.[29]

Such ritualized and common occasions elicited various reactions from the different parties involved, including the fears (of unknown destinations) and regrets (of labours lost) of other family members, yet for the recruits themselves, the excitement of leaving the village, the anticipation of life in a distant town, and the hazy prospect of fighting alongside their comrades in a powerful army often appear

---

[29] Ibid., 51–3.

to have overshadowed other thoughts and feelings.[30] How these recruits adapted to the realities of military service and, even, combat was a separate matter.

It is not easy to determine how violent nineteenth-century German peasants and artisans were and, therefore, how straightforwardly or hesitatingly they adjusted to the violence—and training in the use of violence—of the military during peacetime and wartime. There are few statements from farmers and labourers themselves, whose experiences seem to have varied from region to region and from year to year, with peaks in acts of collective violence during the political and economic crises in 1817–20, 1830–2, and 1846–50.[31] Some wealthier rural areas had marginally lower rates of violent crime than poorer ones.[32] What is evident is that violence remained commonplace in the countryside, with one official in Galicia claiming, and perhaps fantasizing, that 'The peasantry...delights in violence and dreams about it.'[33] In the eastern territories of the Habsburg and Hohenzollern monarchies especially, landowners, civil servants, and the military were notorious for using force to enforce labour contracts and—in Galicia until 1848—serfdom. To take one case from the record of Austrian Galicia, that of Hrynko Liush, a peasant who brought his complaint before the *Kreis* authorities in 1848, his lord had beaten him or imprisoned him in a manorial gaol (for a total of eighty-eight days) every year between 1835 and 1840, and every other year between 1840 and 1848, over petty disputes about common land and the length of his *corvée*.[34] The cudgel used to hit such alleged miscreants was typically 'an oak stick covered with lead', with doctors being called in to work out how many blows could be administered, with more than fifty on the same day being considered 'cruel'.[35] When manorial punishment failed to quell unrest, the army was sometimes called in, for example in the *Kreis* of Zolochiv in 1847–8, where several communes had refused to carry out excessive *corvées*. 'Urged on by the manor, these soldiers bullied us as much as they wished', ran one peasant's description: 'They ordered us to catch flies and fry them in butter. Then they threw [peasants] on dung-heaps. They forced the women to make prostrations in the roads. One woman was beaten to death, another had a miscarriage as a result of a beating.'[36] Incidents like these were exceptions, occur-

---

[30] See I. Weber-Kellermann, *Landleben im 19. Jahrhundert* (Munich, 1987), 193–8. She draws—justifiably in my view—on the semi-autobiographical sketches of Auerbach, which are cited here, in order to supplement her other evidence of the daily practices of rural life.

[31] R. Wirtz, 'Widersetzlichkeiten, Excesse, Crawalle, Tumulte und Skandale'. *Soziale Bewegung und gewalthafter sozialer Protest in Baden 1815–1848* (Frankfurt, 1981), 202; H.-G. Husung, *Protest und Repression im Vormärz. Norddeutschland zwischen Restauration und Revolution* (Göttingen, 1983), 212.

[32] Robert von Friedeburg, *Ländliche Gesellschaft und Obrigkeit. Gemeindeprotest und politische Mobilisierung im 18. und 19. Jahrhundert* (Göttingen, 1997), 167, takes the localities of Ziegenhain and Frankenberg in Kurhessen, demonstrating that the former, which was wealthier overall, had a lower percentage of violent crimes ('Drohungen', 'Schlägereien', and 'Exzesse'), at 6 per cent of the total of recorded crimes in 1839, 1842, and 1843, than the latter, at 10 per cent, but the difference is small and unreliable as an indicator.

[33] Cited in J.-P. Himka, *Galician Villagers and the Ukrainian National Movement in the Nineteenth Century* (Basingstoke, 1988), 10.

[34] Ibid., 11.   [35] Ibid., 12, citing peasant and official documents from 1846–8.

[36] Ibid., 13.

ring in the frontier provinces of the Austrian empire, but they revealed how violence itself was unexceptional.[37]

In Prussia, the General Law Code of 1794 had forbidden specific dishonouring corporal punishments—often involving devices such as the 'fiddle' or 'Spanish cloak'—and the legislation of 1807 and 1811 abolishing serfdom had limited the discretion and powers of patrimonial courts, yet caning remained popular amongst Prussian landowners, formally backed by the authorities in Breslau in 1818 and reported still to be in use in Silesia as late as 1832, not least because 'it is not so much the farmhands who are punished by having to sit in the local gaol...as their lords, who are forced to do without their labour'.[38] Manorial justice, whose jurisdiction over minor infractions covered just under a quarter of Hohenzollern subjects, remained in place until 1848. Beyond such courts, various drafts of the Prussian Criminal Code (1827, 1830, 1833, and 1845) restricted corporal punishment, reversed to a limited degree by the drafts of 1836 and 1843, before such punishment was rejected outright by the *Vereinigter ständischer Ausschuß* (United Corporative Committee) of nobles on 30 December 1847 and abolished by royal rescript on 6 May 1848. The eagerness of noble *Landräte* and landowners to reinstate corporal punishments during the 1850s 'in areas where the people in general are at a very primitive level of civilization', in the words of one administrator, betrayed their continuing fear of and hopes for violence.[39] 'Through the abolition of corporal punishment it has come to a pretty pass here', wrote the district administrator of Neumark, 'for the landowners now fear their servants and their people more than they do [their masters]'.[40] Apart from the Rhineland, where the rod was outlawed by the Napoleonic code, 'In earlier times many petty misdemeanours were not brought to the attention of the courts at all, but immediately punished by the landlord and the police authorities by imprisonment or beating', lamented another official in the early 1850s.[41] In Prussia, Austria, and elsewhere, the continuing practice of corporal punishment in the countryside during the early nineteenth century hints at widespread, occasionally contested, toleration of violence.

The willingness of large groups of villagers and burghers to resort to violence, although linked to a variety of ends, does betray amongst other things the regular and unexceptionable nature of violent acts, fuelled from the 1830s by the rising consumption of *Schnapps* and of alcohol in general during the 1850s and 1860s.[42] Some instances of 'tumult' involved political aims—with a majority of cases occurring during moments of political tension—and others were caused by perceived

---

[37] See also K. Verdery, *Transylvanian Villagers: Three Centuries of Political, Economic and Ethnic Change* (Berkeley, CA, 1983), 141–94; S. Kieniewicz, *The Emancipation of the Polish Peasantry* (Chicago, 1969), 72–169.

[38] Citing the Breslau authorities in 1818, R. J. Evans, *Tales from the German Underworld* (New Haven, 1998), 100.

[39] Ibid., 107.   [40] Ibid.   [41] Ibid.

[42] On the wide variety of ends of protests, rendering quantification problematic, see R. J. Evans, 'The Crowd in German History', in R. J. Evans, *Proletarians and Politics: Socialism, Protest and Working Class in Germany before the First World War* (London, 1990), 38–9. On alcohol consumption, which reached its nineteenth-century peak around 1870, see J. S. Roberts, *Drink, Temperance and the Working Class in Nineteenth-Century Germany* (London, 1984), 16–18, 42–8.

challenges to corporate or local rights, issuing in 'social protest', yet most evolved
haphazardly in an era before political parties and—in Prussia until 1848 and in
Austria until 1861—without representative assemblies.[43] Usually, violence erupted
unexpectedly from a single, petty incident. In northern Germany, almost 80 per
cent of riots ended within six hours and attracted a large number of rioters, suggesting that they were triggered more or less spontaneously and drew support from
crowds which were willing to fight. According to Hans-Gerhard Husung, three
out of sixty protests in Hamburg, Bremen, Hanover, Brunswick, and Oldenburg
between 1815 and 1847/8 had more than 2,000 participants, ten had more than
500 and forty had more than 100.[44] In Baden, the pattern was similar, with conflicts escalating rapidly.[45] Rainer Wirtz concentrates on three sets of case studies in
1819, 1830–2, and 1839–47, including anti-Semitic riots in Heidelberg and
Karlsruhe (1819), which showed—in the opinion of the official report—'how easily excesses can be provoked through devilment and lack of reflection' in spite of
the fact that 'the greater part of the participants did not think of it until just before
its actual commencement'; a conflict over press freedom in Mannheim, after the
editor of the *Wächter* Franz Strohmeyer had been placed under arrest in 1832,
prompting a 'great crowd' of 500 people, as the half-official *Karlsruher Zeitung* put
it, to gather in front of Strohmeyer's house; the 'goldsmiths' revolution' in
Pforzheim (1839), which was sparked by the contravention of 'supposed rights'
and ended in the gathering of 'masses' loudly proclaiming their 'contrary opinion'
and uniting '400–500 strong to commit criminal acts of violence' (*Karlsruher
Zeitung*); and, lastly, the Mannheim 'military excesses' of 1845, which had begun
with a brawl between soldiers and dockworkers and had culminated in the injury
of at least four troops and five civilians in a protest of 1,500, 'mostly from the lower
classes', in the estimation of the *Mannheimer Journal*.[46] About fifty of the 101
illegal or violent protests were economic and twenty-two political, with the remainder academic (nine), military (seven), religious (four), or arising from sundry other
causes, in Wirtz's classification.[47] In much of the press and most official reports, a
'mob'—referred to as '*Pöbel*', '*Volksmasse*', '*Haufe*', or '*Menge*'—of 'street urchins'
(*Strassenjungen* or *Gassenjungen*), journeymen, 'the lower class of the *Volk*', and,
sometimes, students and 'strangers' was blamed for the disorder, but not 'local
burghers', as one Karlsruhe policeman expressed it in 1830.[48]

   In the Rhineland, investigated by James Brophy and Jonathan Sperber, there
were more conflicts between soldiers and civilians, given the recent annexation of
the territory by Prussia and the correspondingly high concentration of garrisons
there, but they resembled other types of 'tumult' in respect of the transition to

[43] Anti-Semitism was quite frequently a component of such 'political' and 'social' protest:
S. Rohrbacher, *Gewalt im Biedermeier. Antijüdische Ausschreitungen in Vormärz und Revolution
1815–1848/49* (Frankfurt, 1993).

[44] H.-G. Husung, *Protest und Repression*, 235. The sample does not include protest in the revolution
of 1848 itself.

[45] R. Wirtz, '*Widersetzlichkeiten, Excesse, Crawalle, Tumulte und Skandale*', 52–168; J. M. Brophy,
Popular Culture and the Public Sphere in the Rhineland, 1800–1850, 216–52.

[46] Wirtz, *Widersetzlichkeiten*, 68, 100, 122, 156.   [47] Ibid., 52.

[48] Ibid., 62, 78–9, 85–6, 100–1, 134–6, 160–1.

violence (from legality to criminality), which was rapid, extensive, and, to contemporaries, unremarkable.[49] Three cases illustrate how easily violence could escalate.[50] The first, in the Rhenish village of Beek in November 1831, started with civilians taunting and attacking a lone *Jäger* in a tavern, followed by fighting a week later, when soldiers had refused to remove their weapons whilst dancing. A day later, twenty soldiers had returned to the village and became embroiled in a pitched battle, with swords and daggers, during which eighteen were wounded.[51] The second case took place in the village of Closterchumbd, after a failed attempt to arrest two youths who had fought with a soldier at a parish festival in June 1835. The fighting had commenced when the commanding officer of the local regiment had sought to prevent a soldier from another regiment, who came from Closterchumbd and was home on furlough, from attending the festival in order to avoid resentment amongst his own troops. The officer chose to enforce the ban by posting sentries outside the local tavern, stirring up villagers' anger about unwarranted outside military interference in their affairs. More than 200 people had mobilized 'with pickaxes, branches and poles' to stop the youths being arrested, at which point the officer of the regiment had distributed live rounds to his men, only to be dissuaded from using them by the last-minute intervention of village notables.[52] The third case occurred in Cologne in the summer of 1846, initiated by a duel between a civilian and a soldier over the courtship of a local woman, turning into a violent scrum before becoming, on the second day of the festival of St Martin in early August, a cavalry charge through a disobedient crowd, which left seven badly injured and dozens hit by rifle butts. A subsequent report by a citizens' commission was prohibited but was nonetheless read aloud, printed in Mannheim and circulated to the German and foreign press, permitting the French newspaper *Siècle* to rejoice in the 'disturbances, which stained Cologne with blood', since they showed that 'Rhinelanders are tired of military rule'.[53] All three instances of 'excess'—out of at least 109 recorded conflicts between the authorities and the population in the Rhineland between 1815 and 1848—demonstrated how quickly civilians were prepared to fight or take up arms, as a spontaneous 'mob' (Beek), a community mobilized against external interference (Closterchumbd), or a half-politicized

---

[49] J. Sperber, *Rhineland Radicals: The Democratic Movement and the Revolution of 1848–1849* (Princeton, 1991), 53–184; J. Sperber, 'Echoes of the French Revolution in the Rhineland, 1830–1849', *Central European History*, 22 (1989), 200–17.

[50] On the wider connections between criminality and protest, see D. Blasius, 'Sozialprotest und Sozialkriminalität in Deutschland. Eine Problemstudie zum Vormärz', in H. Volkmann and J. Bergmann (eds), *Sozialer Protest. Studien zu traditioneller Resistenz und kollektiver Gewalt in Deutschland vom Vormärz bis zur Reichsgründung* (Opladen, 1984), 212–27; D. Blasius, *Bürgerliche Gesellschaft und Kriminalität. Zur Sozialgeschichte Preußens im Vormärz* (Göttingen, 1976); D. Blasius, *Kriminalität und Alltag. Zur Konfliktgeschichte des Alltagslebens im 19. Jahrhundert* (Göttingen, 1978); D. Blasius, '"Diebshandwerk" und "Widerspruchsgeist". Motive des Verbrechens im 19. Jahrhundert', in R. van Dülmen (ed.), *Verbrechen, Strafen und soziale Kontrolle* (Frankfurt, 1990), 215–37. Blasius pits his arguments against those of Charles, Richard and Louise Tilly, *The Rebellious Century, 1830–1930* (Cambridge, MA, 1975), who wish dispel the idea that political violence was connected to other forms of violence and criminality; also, R. Tilly, 'Popular Disorders in Nineteenth-Century Germany', *Journal of Social History*, 4 (1970), 1–40.

[51] J. M. Brophy, *Popular Culture and the Public Sphere*, 240–1.   [52] Ibid., 245.
[53] Ibid., 249–50.

group of protesters (Cologne). Such events were characteristic of both towns and villages: thirty-one of the conflicts took place in larger cities, thirty-three in small towns, and forty-five in rural areas.[54] In Baden, about 40 per cent of protests occurred in the main cities (Karlsruhe, Mannheim, Heidelberg, Freiburg, and Pforzheim) and 60 per cent in the countryside, whereas the corresponding figures for northern Germany were 80 per cent urban and 20 per cent rural.[55] These outbursts of collective violence were often limited but regular, with individual thresholds and taboos being affected by the dynamics and politics of groups.

Much of the evidence about civilian violence derives from police and judicial reports and statistics concerning urban criminality, which had come to be seen as the main form of violence, as gangs of 'bandits', deprived of support in their rural hinterland, had started to disappear at the turn of the nineteenth century.[56] To an extent, these statistics refer to the discovery, recording, and prosecution of felonies, which improved during the nineteenth century, as much as the actual committing of crimes, yet—despite their weaknesses—they nonetheless suggest, first, that violent crime was separable from other types of criminality, depending more on longer-term cultural shifts and less on shorter-term economic conditions, and, second, that rates of violent crime did not drop—and may have increased—during the early and mid-nineteenth century.[57] Thus, according to the Bavarian criminologist Georg von Mayr, assault and battery increased in the Wittelsbach monarchy from forty-six per 100,000 annually in 1834–9 to forty-nine in 1840–9 and sixty-two in 1850–9.[58] Similarly, in Prussia (excluding the Rhineland), the figures for the same crimes—*leichte Körperverletzung* rather than *gefährliche Körperverletzung*, or serious assault—rose from twenty-five to twenty-seven per 100,000 in 1836–49 to thirty-three to thirty-four in 1850–9 and forty-four in 1860–5.[59] Homicide was much less common, with 279 criminal investigations launched in the Hohenzollern monarchy excluding the Rhineland in 1846, together with 263 into arson, and between 165 and 309 investigations annually into homicide between 1847 and 1865, together with 196–345 per year into arson.[60] From

[54] Ibid., 218.
[55] R. Wirtz, *Widersetzlichkeiten*, 226–7; R. Wirtz, 'Bemerkungen zum "Sozialen Protest" in Baden 1815–1848. Determinanten, Motive und Verhaltensmuster', and H.-G. Husung, 'Zu einigen Problemen der historischen Protestforschung am Beispiel gemeinschaftlichen Protests in Norddeutschland 1815–1847', in H. Volkmann and J. Bergmann (eds), *Sozialer Protest*, 36–55, 21–35; R. J. Evans, 'The Crowd in German History', 36.
[56] C. Küther, *Räuber und Gauner in Deutschland* (Göttingen, 1976), 138–49.
[57] H. Zehr, *Crime and the Development of Modern Society: Patterns of Criminality in Nineteenth-Century Germany and France* (London, 1976). Eric A. Johnson points out the shortcomings of the statistics and of Zehr's thesis about the disjunctions of 'modernization' (rising property crime and standards of living) but he accepts the two points made here: Eric A. Johnson, 'The Crime Rate and Longitudinal and Periodic Trends in Nineteenth- and Twentieth-Century German Criminality, from *Vormärz* to Late Weimar', in R. J. Evans (ed.), *The German Underworld: Deviants and Outcasts in German History* (London, 1988), 159–88; also, A. Moses, *Kriminalität in Baden im 19. Jahrhundert. Die 'Übersicht der Strafrechtspflege' als Quelle der historischen Kriminologie* (Stuttgart, 2006).
[58] H. Zehr, *Crime and the Development of Modern Society*, 36.
[59] D. Blasius, *Kriminalität und Alltag*, 81–2.
[60] W. Fischer, J. Krengel, and J. Wietog (eds), *Sozialgeschichtliches Arbeitsbuch. Materialien zur Statistik des Deutschen Bundes 1815–1870* (Munich, 1982), 235.

1818 to 1848, between fifteen and thirty-nine people were sentenced to death every year.[61] In the 1850s, the figure rose to between twenty-five and sixty, corresponding to a larger population. In Bavaria from 1815 to 1847, between one and twelve death sentences were passed annually, rising to thirty-nine in 1849–50 and then fluctuating between three and twenty from 1851 to 1866.[62] Most convicted murderers were manual workers from towns: between 1854 and 1865 in Prussia, ninety-six artisans (or 24 per cent) and seventy-seven labourers (19 per cent) were condemned to death out of a total of 398, with 40–44 per cent of them being executed.[63] They were joined by thirty-two members of the *Mittelstand* (8 per cent), made up of shopkeepers, petty clerks, and other tradesmen, totalling 51 per cent of those convicted of homicide. Fifty-seven farmers (14 per cent) and forty-nine servants or *Dienstknechte* (12 per cent), most of whom lived in rural Prussia, were also condemned to death, making up 26 per cent jointly at a time when the rural population comprised more than 70 per cent of the whole. No aristocrats, lawyers, doctors, or academics were convicted of homicide. Overall, cases of murder and arson remained more or less constant in Prussia, despite an increasing population, instances of 'rebelliousness' (*Widersetzlichkeit*) decreased, and those of assault and battery rose.[64] All such crimes were widely associated with the 'mob', 'lower mass of the *Volk*', or '*Proletariat*', separated even by socialists and communists from the law-abiding working class.[65] In 1850, Marx defined the 'ragged working class' or *Lumpenproletariat*, which was not politically conscious, as 'thieves and criminals of all kinds, living on the crumbs of society, people without a definite trade, vagabonds, people without a hearth or home'.[66] How common violence was beyond well-known, often extreme cases which were associated with the lower orders and came to the attention of the judicial authorities is hard to divine.

'Beatings' were certainly common. When they were administered within the family, even if they were severe enough to be reported, they were registered by the police as a separate class of felony from assault. Wives were formally equal in the relevant sections of the law but they were widely believed, in Dorothea Mendelssohn's words, to be under the 'rule of men', without whom they would be 'lost forever', meaning that cases referred to local courts tended to stress the unreasonable or excessive use of force rather than the resort to violence in itself.[67]

---

[61] R. J. Evans, *Rituals of Retribution*, 918–19.   [62] Ibid., 922–3.   [63] Ibid., 301.

[64] F. Fischer, J. Krengel, and J. Wietog (eds), *Sozialgeschichtliches Arbeitsbuch*, 235.

[65] R. J. Evans, 'The "Dangerous Classes" in Germany from the Middle Ages to the Twentieth Century', in R. J. Evans, *Proletarians and Politics*, 1–15. D. Blackbourn, *History of Germany, 1780–1914: The Long Nineteenth Century*, 2nd edn (Oxford, 2003), 90, points out that the term 'proletariat' began to be used from the 1830s onwards to mean 'the urban equivalent of the rural underclass', embracing 'causal workers, labourers, servants, apprentices, unemployed journeymen and impoverished masters, as well as the floating population of knife-grinders, messengers, hawkers and the dangerous classes of beggars, vagrants, prostitutes and criminals'.

[66] K. Marx, *Class Struggle in France* (1850), in K. Marx and Engels, *Selected Works* (Moscow, 1935), vol. 1, 155.

[67] Cited in U. Frevert, *Women in German History: From Bourgeois Emancipation to Sexual Liberation* (Oxford, 1988), 52. D. W. Sabean, *Property, Production and Family in Neckarhausen, 1700–1870* (Cambridge, 1990), 124–46, shows that the number of cases coming to court in a single village in Württemberg increased dramatically after 1820, from sixteen (1790–1819) to sixty-six (1820–50),

The *Allgemeines Landrecht* of 1794, which still formed the basis of the Prussian code, stated that the 'head of the house' had the right to punish his wife and children with the rod, as long as the chastisement was 'moderate'.[68] Masters, land-owners, employers, and teachers were granted the same right vis-à-vis their servants, peasants, apprentices, and pupils. The corporal punishment of juveniles under 16 years of age continued to be sanctioned by draft Criminal Codes in Prussia after 1815.[69] The majority of domestic and much other violence went unreported, often mentioned in passing without being treated as a mitigating cir-cumstance in the reportage and sentencing of more serious cases. One example concerned 50-year-old Marianna Warszawski, who was executed for murdering her younger husband after a long, 'violent and quarrelsome relationship': 'The accused admitted that she and her children had decided to murder Warszawski because of the frequent beatings they had suffered from him.'[70] Another example from the same year was Karoline Frederike Henseling's killing of her husband, who was said by the legal administration 'to be a respectable man', irrespective of the fact that he 'sometimes beat her'.[71]

For those unfortunate members of the lower orders who belonged to the large urban 'proletariat'—or those without a secure livelihood in the contemporary meaning of the term, constituting more than half of some towns' populations by the 1840s—'structural violence' did not merely entail hunger, impotence, and incarceration, but also bodily violation: the radical Ernst Dronke's *Polizei-Geschichten* (1847) recounted one instance of a Hamburg baker, Johann Hanemann, who was expelled from the city in 1832 for using false documents to obtain citizenship.[72] Despite acquiring legal papers, he was expelled from Hanover as an undesirable alien as a consequence of his earlier conviction in Hamburg. He then set up a business in Altona but, in 1839, he was deprived of his citizenship there, too, on the grounds of the same conviction in the Hanseatic city, to which he was sent back and where he was eventually arrested in 1841, after a period in hiding. After serving his time, Hanemann was returned to Altona and was subsequently

---

with violence accounting for 29 per cent of complaints, drinking 22 per cent, scolding and swearing 18 per cent, and other causes 32 per cent, in 1820–50.

[68] P. Gay, *The Cultivation of Hatred* (London, 1994), 188; U. Gerhard, 'Die Rechtsstellung der Frau in der bürgerlichen Gesellschaft des 19. Jahrhunderts. Frankreich und Deutschland im Vergleich', in J. Kocka (ed.), *Bürgertum im 19. Jahrhundert*, vol. 1, 452–68.

[69] R. J. Evans, *Tales from the German Underworld*, 102.

[70] R. J. Evans, *Rituals of Retribution*, 291–2.   [71] Ibid., 291.

[72] R. J. Evans, *Tales from the German Underworld*, 95–6. In Prussia as a whole in 1846, 45 per cent of men over 14 were dependent labourers with an uncertain existence: the Prussian statistician Wilhelm Dieterici estimated that 50–60 per cent of the population lived in needy circumstances, which turned into hunger and, possibly, starvation during economic crises. K. F. W. Dieterici, *Der Volkswohlstand im preussischen Staate* (Münster, 1986), first published in 1846; F.-W. Henning, *Handbuch der Wirtschafts- und Sozialgeschichte Deutschlands* (Paderborn, 1996), vol. 2, 282–305, 426–515; W. Köllmann, *Sozialgeschichte der Stadt Barmen im 19. Jahrhundert* (Tübingen, 1960); F. D. Marquardt, 'Sozialer Aufstieg, sozialer Abstieg und die Entstehung der Berliner Arbeiterklasse 1806–1848', *Geschichte und Gesellschaft*, 1 (1975), 43–77. A. Lüdtke, 'The Role of State Violence', 189–90, claims that 57 to 70 per cent of Berlin's population in 1846 belonged to the 'dangerous classes', and 90 per cent of Barmen's.

sent back to Hamburg, to be rearrested and condemned to spend a second spell on the treadmill. Expelled once more, he ended up back in Altona, where he received twenty-five strokes of the cane and deportation back to the neighbouring city, whose plan of transporting him overseas was foiled in 1842 by the Great Fire of that year. More expulsions and incarceration followed for a man whose principal misdemeanour had been to use false documents in the early 1830s. In jail, he and other unfortunates could be subjected legally to corporal punishment, as the Prussian Justice Ministry confirmed in 1855, after the abolition of corporal punishment in most German states in 1848: 'Corporal punishment may be used in *penal institutions* (penitentiaries) and *Rhenish houses of correction* as a disciplinary measure in the case of infringements of the prison rules according to the criteria of the rules laid down for these institutions and only against *condemned* prisoners held therein.'[73] The whipping of prisoners in front of other inmates could still take place, according to the Prussian Criminal Code of 1851, because prisoners had been excluded from the doctrine of equality before the law, which existed for free subjects. In Austria, corporal punishment was reintroduced into civil society— beyond the prison and schoolroom—in 1852, after abolition in 1848, with thirty lashes authorized for reoffenders and twenty for particular offences by servants, apprentices, and labourers.[74] Such practices, together with domestic beatings and fights in taverns and on the street, helped to ensure that those belonging to the 'underworld' of Germany's towns were regularly exposed to violence.

Through the intervention of neighbours, guilds, the clergy, the police, and the judiciary, contemporaries, including those in the lower orders, carefully regulated their behaviour, distinguishing between acceptable and unacceptable forms of violence. Many, like the Rhenish blacksmith Johann Kirchgaesser as he began his *Wanderschaft* as a journeyman in 1839, sought religiously to stay away from 'poor associations and contact with bad people'.[75] His father's advice before his departure was unambiguous: 'If you fear God, love your parents and listen to their warnings, you will do well.'[76] As he left, Kirchgaesser was overcome 'with great homesickness', sitting down on a pile of stones at the side of the road and 'crying his eyes out'.[77] His regular references in his diary to his religious faith, as a Catholic, and to his feelings for his wife and family, provide ample proof that Kirchgaesser's life was far from being brutish, marked out by self-restraint and sentimental attachment. Yet, like his own forebears and other contemporary labourers, artisans, and farmers, he continued to suffer hunger, hardship, harsh living and working conditions, illness, and early mortality, arguably hardening his attitude to pain and death.[78] By the time that they reached their early thirties in the 1850s and 1860s,

---

[73] Cited in R. J. Evans, *Tales from the German Underworld*, 119.

[74] P. Gay, *The Cultivation of Hatred*, 189.

[75] J. Kirchgaesser, *Aus meinem Leben* (Ratingen, 1990), 8, 26. On *Wanderungen*, see F. Lenger, *Zwischen Kleinbürgertum und Proletariat. Studien zur Sozialgeschichte der Düsseldorfer Handwerker 1816–1878* (Göttingen, 1986), 65–93.

[76] Kirchgaesser, *Aus meinem Leben* 26.   [77] Ibid.

[78] Hans Medick, *Weben und Überleben in Laichingen 1650–1900* (Göttingen, 1996), 355–77 gives a good micro-history of increasing mortality during the late eighteenth and early nineteenth centuries. Also, I. Weber-Kellermann, *Landleben im 19. Jahrhundert*, 271–81.

he and his generation had already experienced the death of half of their peers, help-ing to consolidate a stoical, religious, or matter-of-fact outlook.[79] Thus, when the labourer Christian Petersdorff, born in Neu Hardenberg near Frankfurt an der Oder, began to write a diary at the age of 18 in 1837, he aimed to describe 'what has happened to me from childhood on, what I have done, what I have suffered from, what illnesses and dangers I have survived in the world and how God has protected me and kept me alive'.[80] Kirchgaesser seemed to share a similar view, praying that God would save him 'from all the dangers of body and soul', as he left home at the age of 20.[81] On his travels around north-west Germany and the Netherlands, he went on to experience 'hard work', with insufficient nourishment: 'Often I was so tired on an evening that I could scarcely climb to the attic, where my bed stood under a roof which was so leaky that I could make snowballs on my bed on mornings when it had snowed'.[82] He happily left that particular house, where the married couple 'lived in almost constant discord', and went to seek work in Kreuznach, where his brother worked in a bakery.[83] His new master was indus-trious but also bad-tempered: 'The two apprentices were mishandled in the most brutal way.'[84]

In 1841, Kirchgaesser returned to St Goar to be mustered for the army but he was rejected because of too narrow a chest, only to return in 1842 to be passed as fit for military service, which he began in October 1843. He returned to civilian life in 1846 to marry in 1849 and have a daughter in 1850. Despite his effort to avoid it, he was mobilized as a soldier in 1848 and 1850. There is no sign that Kirchgaesser's passage from civilian to military life was strenuous or uncomfort-able, notwithstanding his anti-Prussian opinions. In common with many others, he had left his home town of Ratingen accompanied by 'all my friends', stopping for 'departure' drinks at various taverns, singing songs along the route, and having 'their hands shaken heartily' by those whom they met.[85] Having taken two ferries up the Rhine, meeting his brother and other family members on the way, he was shown his quarters in Coblenz and, starving, 'like an officer', was served 'pea soup with ham', which tasted so good that he went to the kitchen and got another por-tion.[86] He was less impressed by drill starting the next day, when 'we learned that one is first made into a person in the military and we learned how to move'.[87] He was relieved as 'the heavy procedure' was over after six weeks, but he made no further complaint about it.[88] He went on to note that guard duty in winter was

[79] R. Böckh, *Sterblichkeitstafel für den Preußischen Staat im Umfange von 1865* (Jena, 1875), 54. In villages such as Laichingen, in the Schwäbische Alb, only 45 per cent of those born between 1850 and 1869 lived beyond 15 years of age: H. Medick, *Weben und Überleben*, 356.

[80] F. Nespethal, *Erlebtes und Aufgeschriebenes aus dem 19. Jahrhundert* (Petersburg, 1999), 15.

[81] J. Kirchgaesser, *Aus meinem Leben* (Ratingen, 1990), 6.

[82] Ibid., 27. The ease with which these conditions could lead to begging and criminalization is indicated by Andreas Gestrich, *Traditionelle Jugendkultur und Industrialisierung. Sozialgeschichte der Jugend in einer ländlichen Arbeitergemeinde Württembergs, 1800–1920* (Göttingen, 1986), 119–20, who shows how one weaver apprentice, Fridolin Bolay from Ohmenhausen, was arrested and impris-oned fourteen times between 1846 and 1855.

[83] J. Kirchgaesser, *Aus meinem Leben*, 6.   [84] Ibid.   [85] Ibid., 36.   [86] Ibid.
[87] Ibid., 37.   [88] Ibid.

cold and a three-day military arrest was irritating, but otherwise meant 'nothing'.[89] His existence was 'bearable'.[90] Manoeuvres, which sometimes took place next to the French border within earshot of the neighbouring state's guns, were described as if they were adventures.[91] When he got home, he chopped up his 'hated king's tunic', which symbolized Prussia, yet he showed no sign of having been marked by his time in the army, returning obediently to 'the hated barracks' in 1848 and, despite protesting, in 1850.[92] As a Rhinelander who, in 1848, had become an increasingly fractious 'democrat', Kirchgaesser displayed no affection for the Prussian army but also no open opposition to, or shock at, the purposes and conditions of military service.[93]

SQUEAMISHNESS AND SELF-CONTROL

By the 1850s and 1860s, Kirchgaesser had established his own business and had begun to prosper, taking up civic office and identifying, to an extent at least, with the 'authorities'. It is uncertain how many labourers and peasants were 'civilized', 'pacified', or 'disciplined' in this fashion, as the ranks of an urban underclass and the number of landless agricultural workers swelled in the 1830s, 1840s, and 1850s.[94] In Saxony, only 22 per cent of peasant households were reckoned to support themselves from their own landholdings by 1843.[95] What was evident, however, was the desire of governments, civil servants, and the middle classes to control and change the behaviour of such groups, as Victor von Andrian-Werburg reported from Austria in 1843:

> When has there been greater material misery, when has humanity bled from deeper, more terrible wounds than just now? Thousands of people are being orphaned, forgotten and sacrificed to a nameless misery in the midst of wealthy, steadily growing civilization; they don't know from one day to the next where they will lay their head, where they will find a meagre bit of bread, which will mark out their lamentable life—and through these homeless proletarians, without means, whose numbers grow every day, an upheaval is being prepared, rapidly and threateningly.[96]

The *Bürgertum*, town-dwelling nobility and sections of the broader *Mittelstand* of masters, innkeepers, tradesmen, shopkeepers, minor clerks, and schoolteachers, who came to dominate politics and the public sphere in the early and mid-nineteenth century, were fearful of the 'menace' or 'dangers' arising from the growth of an urban 'proletariat' or 'mob'.[97] These strata had direct experience of the riots and

---

[89] Ibid.   [90] Ibid., 38.   [91] Ibid., 42–3.   [92] Ibid., 43.   [93] Ibid., 45.

[94] On the divisions of rural society and the hatred of rural 'wage labourers' (*Tagelöhner*) for farmers, see G. Schildt, *Tagelöhner, Gesellen, Arbeiter. Sozialgeschichte der vorindustriellen und industriellen Arbeiter in Braunschweig 1830–1880* (Stuttgart, 1986), 89–91.

[95] D. Blackbourn, *History of Germany, 1780–1914*, 111.

[96] V. v. Andrian-Werburg, *Oesterreich und dessen Zukunft* (Hamburg, 1843), vol. 1, 29.

[97] The seminal definition of *Bürgertum* and associated terms remain Jürgen Kocka's, 'Bürgertum und bürgerliche Gesellschaft im 19. Jahrhundert. Europäische Entwicklungen und deutsche Eigenarten', in Jürgen Kocka (ed.), *Bürgertum im 19. Jahrhundert*, vol. 1, 11–78. On the porous

daily violence of German and Austrian towns, which were the forms of social or political protest most troubling to the authorities. They tended, partly as a consequence, to back states' and municipalities' attempts to counter them and establish 'order'.[98] They were also at the forefront of overlapping movements of civic improvement and educational and penal reform, which informed public discussions about how best to alleviate popular suffering, reduce criminality, and impose restraints on the perpetrators of violence.

The fears of middle-class onlookers do not appear, primarily, to have been political. Many students and burghers sympathized with or took part in political festivals, protests, and uprisings in 1830–2 and in 1848–9. In Heinrich Volkmann's sample, just under 30 per cent of those injured in protests in 1830 belonged to the body of students, *Bürgerwehr* or the *Bürgertum*, in the broad sense of citizens but excluding manual workers and the lower orders.[99] The report of the *Augsburger Allgemeine Zeitung* on 11 October 1830 about unrest in Meisenheim, near Mainz, was typical:

> Towards evening, the entire *Bürgerschaft* assembled, not merely the mob but also the better-off classes, and it went to the residence of the judicial official, demanding of him the release of the arrested man [who had started the protests over previous evenings], which had to be granted, upon which the armed burghers took up guard duty. The establishment of order could be attributed to this measure.[100]

Even when confronted with the revolt of the weavers in Silesia in 1844, which exposed the poverty and desperation of labourers in the eastern marches of the Hohenzollern monarchy, organs of the middle-class press registered 'a cry of disgust throughout the whole of Germany', as the *Kölnische Zeitung* remarked.[101] 'Here in Berlin, where there is certainly no proclivity towards unrest, public opinion amongst all orders is expressed in such stormy phrases, with such warm affection, that we don't feel called upon to reproduce them', recorded the pro-government *Deutsche Allgemeine Zeitung*.[102] In this case, it appeared to many middle-class commentators and readers that the grievances of the weavers were justified and that the authorities had acted precipitately and disproportionately.

In general, however, the same 'public' backed the police forces which were being established in German cities during the course of the nineteenth century, in part because the police were mindful of the need, as the Prussian Minister of Police

nature of these social boundaries, see R. Stadelmann and W. Fischer, *Die Bildungswelt des deutschen Handwerkers um 1800. Studien des Kleinbürgers im Zeitalter Goethes* (Berlin, 1955), 148–245; F. Lenger, *Zwischen Kleinbürgertum und Proletariat*, 94–116, 133–49.

[98] See above all A. Lüdtke, *Police and State in Prussia, 1815–1850* (Cambridge, 1989), 32–66.

[99] H. Volkmann, 'Protestträger und Protestformen in den Unruhen von 1830 bis 1832', in H. Volkmann and J. Bergmann (eds), *Sozialer Protest*, 61.

[100] Cited ibid., 56.

[101] *Kölnische Zeitung*, 21 June 1844, cited in L. Kroneberg and R. Schloesser (eds), *Weber-Revolte 1844. Der schlesische Weberaufstand im Spiegel der zeitgenössischen Publizistik und Literatur* (Cologne, 1980), 186.

[102] *Deutsche Allgemeine Zeitung*, June 1844, cited in C. v. Hodenberg, *Aufstand der Weber. Die Revolte von 1844 und ihr Aufstieg zum Mythos* (Bonn, 1997), 78.

expressed it to the director of police in Wetzlar in 1816, 'to ensure the safety of persons and property...and the wealth, the comfort and enjoyment of life of the same', and in part because they represented the presence of a more or less constant disciplinary force, which operated within the towns themselves as a component of civilian 'administration' (*Verwaltung*), not a separate, external apparatus of occasional violent coercion, which was how the army was often seen.[103] 'The necessary institution for maintaining public quiet, safety and order, and for warding off danger to the public as a whole or individual members of it, is the office of the police', stated the passage of the *Allgemeines Landrecht* (1794) most commonly alluded to by nineteenth-century legal manuals.[104] Its task, in the words of Ludwig von Rönne's *Staatsrecht der preussischen Monarchie* (1856), was 'official attendance to the everyday requirements of public safety and welfare'.[105] Although they were not always achieved in practice, such objectives were widely accepted by an educated public, as the Göttingen law professor and liberal constitutionalist Heinrich Zachariä made plain in his *Deutsches Staats- und Bundesrecht* (1842): 'Wherever the issue becomes one of securing civil order in general, including in a certain respect *religion* and *morals*, against injury, and surmounting existing or potential dangers, the use of means of coercion is justified.'[106] On this reading, the use of force—or state violence—was legitimate as long as it restored or safeguarded public order. To liberals like Zachariä, protest and opposition should occur in ordered or peaceable conditions, if not always within the law, which could be unjust or oppressive.[107]

The shift from military intervention and physical force to police surveillance and discipline, which was variable and incomplete, corresponded to a shared official and middle-class desire to avoid violence.[108] Police forces were small and frequently ineffective or corrupt, composed of former NCOs and soldiers between 30 and 70 years of age.[109] On the eve of 1848, Berlin had only 112 policemen and 121 gendarmes for a population of over 400,000, whilst expanding cities in the

---

[103] W. L. zu Sayn-Wittgenstein, 1 Nov. 1816, cited in A. Lüdtke, 'The Role of State Violence', 204. Also, W. Siemann, 'Heere, Freischaren, Barrikaden. Die bewaffnete Macht als Instrument der Innenpolitik in Europa 1815–1847', in D. Langewiesche (ed.), *Revolution und Krieg. Zur Dynamik historischen Wandels seit dem 18. Jahrhundert*, (Paderborn, 1989), 87–102.

[104] Cited in A. Lüdtke, *Police and State in Prussia, 1815–1850*, 23. [105] Ibid.

[106] Cited ibid., 30, 228.

[107] See R. Roth, *Stadt und Bürgertum in Frankfurt am Main. Ein besonderer Weg von der ständischen zur modernen Bürgergesellschaft 1760–1914* (Munich, 1996), 372–439; A. Schulz, *Vormundschaft und Protektion. Eliten und Bürger in Bremen 1750–1880* (Munich, 2002), 247–460; F. Möller, *Bürgerliche Herrschaft in Augsburg 1790–1880* (Munich, 1998), 155–209, 261–328; N. Pütter, *Teilnahme und Staatsbürgertum* 29–194; G. Mettele, *Bürgertum in Köln 1775–1870. Gemeinsinn und freie Association* (Munich, 1998), 226–91; all show the willingness of middle-class elites to lead a politics of 'opposition' and their relative openness to the lower orders in political affairs.

[108] On discipline and self-discipline within the civil service, see S. Brakensiek, *Fürstendiener, Staatsbeamte, Bürger. Amtsführung und Lebenswelt der Ortsbeamten in niederhessischen Kleinstädten 1750–1830* (Göttingen, 1999), 176–92, 380–2; in education, see F.-M. Kuhlemann, *Modernisierung und Disziplinierung. Sozialgeschichte des preußischen Volksschulwesens 1794–1872* (Göttingen, 1992), 107–34, 210–76, 342–52.

[109] E. Glovka Spencer, 'Police–Military Relations in Prussia, 1848–1914', *Social History*, 19 (1985), 305–17.

industrial regions of the Rhineland such as Elberfeld and Barmen, which together constituted the fifth-largest urban concentration in Prussia, had thirteen policemen— or one for every 3,318 inhabitants—and six policemen, respectively—or one for every 5,788 inhabitants.[110] In such circumstances, officials regularly appealed directly to local military commanders to intervene. In the Hohenzollern monarchy, a request for support was supposed to pass from the police to one of the 313 *Landräte* via one of the twenty-three *Regierungspräsidenten* (district) to one of the eight *Oberpräsidenten* (province), who requested assistance from the general in charge of the regional army corps. At the same time, the police were obliged, following a regulation of 1819, to inform the local military commander as soon as they intervened in matters of public order so that the army could 'observe the way the police action went and... make the necessary preparations'.[111] Whenever 'there was a danger that the [civilian authorities] should delay too long with their request for help', the military authorities were 'obliged to intervene without waiting for the request'.[112] In other states, the arrangements were more makeshift, though relying on the army, as in Prussia, in cases of 'tumult' or 'riot': in Württemberg, for instance, a network of *Landjäger* had been established, recruiting soldiers with a good army record between the age of 25 and 40, yet they were restricted in their activities within towns, where local police, who were regularly 'indolent and ignorant' (in the words of one official in Ulm), were in charge, aided by civilian militias; in Hanover, a similar division of competencies and internal competition between municipal police, rural gendarmes, urban civil militias (*Bürgerwehr*), and the army could be observed; in Baden, gendarmes, state-funded local police, and—in Heidelberg and Freiburg—university police jostled with each other for pre-eminence; and, in Bavaria, the gendarmerie existed alongside the military, with which it enjoyed a close relationship.[113]

Beyond this patchwork of authorities and practices was a movement, visible to contemporaries, towards urban police forces whose purpose was, as the mayor of Breslau put it in 1828, to keep the 'indigent folk', representing a 'dangerous threat', under their 'watchful eye'.[114] In theory, as a Prussian circular enactment formulated

---

[110] E. Glovka Spencer, 'State Power and Local Interests in Prussian Cities: Police in the Düsseldorf District, 1848–1914', *Central European History*, 19 (1986), 296–7.

[111] Cited in A. Lüdtke, 'The Role of State Violence', 205.

[112] Ibid. This happened often: James Brophy, *Popular Culture and the Public Sphere*, 218–19, points out that the military was involved in 64 per cent of disturbances in the Rhineland and the gendarmes 23 per cent, whereas the police were only involved in 11 per cent of incidents and civil servants only 9 per cent.

[113] B. Wirsing, '"Gleichsam mit Soldatenstrenge". Neue Polizei in süddeutschen Städten', in A. Lüdtke (ed.), *'Sicherheit' und 'Wohlfahrt'. Polizei, Gesellschaft und Herrschaft im 19. und 20. Jahrhundert* (Frankfurt, 1992), 65–96; P. Sauer, *Revolution und Volksbewaffnung*, 36–73; N. Pütter, *Teilnahme und Staatsbürgertum*, 250–308; D. Riesener, *Polizei und politische Kultur im 19. Jahrhundert. Die Polizeidirektion Hannover und die politische Öffentlichkeit im Königreich Hannover* (Hanover, 1996), 123–40; F. Möller, *Bürgerliche Herrschaft in Augsburg 1790–1880*, 210–17.

[114] A. Lüdtke, *Police and State in Prussia*, 81; A. Lüdtke, 'The Role of State Violence', 190. Also, E. Glovka Spencer, *Police and the Social Order in German Cities: The Düsseldorf District, 1848–1914* (De Kalb, IL, 1992), 3–75.

it in September 1815, 'all those persons who, either on account of their previous way of life or voluntary or involuntary lack of a legal means of subsistence, endangered public or private safety' should be observed by the police to ascertain how they earned their upkeep, whom they were friends with, how much alcohol they consumed and how much money they gambled, and in which taverns.[115] The authorities were to seek outsiders, in particular, 'on the streets and in hidden crannies', pursuing those who harboured them 'with the greatest vigour', with the exception of 'families completely above suspicion and of the first order', the mishandling of whom would provoke 'much unpleasantness', according to the instructions given to the police responsible for passes and aliens.[116] Few such families of the first order would have challenged the distinction made by the editor of the *Polizei-Archiv* between the 'respectable' classes, who were to be protected, and the poor, who could be beaten by the police with great 'enthusiasm'.[117] They ought merely to be thankful that, 'whereas their grandfathers may have had fifty to a hundred beatings, they receive only twenty to twenty-five—a difference of 75–80 percent'.[118] 'And who could complain about such a trifling matter as that?' the editor asked provocatively.[119]

Members of the middling strata usually avoided the beatings of the police and, when they did receive them, for example in Heidelberg in the late 1830s, they complained with disbelief that they had been treated 'not as students, but as vagabonds and slovenly manual-working apprentices'.[120] Most had been beaten as children, by parents and teachers, and many continued to mete out similar punishments themselves.[121] 'Surely nothing more humiliates the proud master of the earth, the high spirit who dominates the seas and investigates the laws of the stars, than corporal punishment', declared Heinrich Heine in 1828, recalling how Latin and French had been beaten into him as a boy: 'The gods, in order to dampen down the blazing arrogance of humans, created flogging.'[122] Nevertheless, immunity from physical manhandling had become an important, if precarious, element of bourgeois sensibility and autonomy by the nineteenth century, colouring contemporaries' attitudes to penal reform. As the Prussian Justice Minister Heinrich Gottlob von Mühler noted in 1833,

> Many and weighty objections have recently been raised against the corporal punishments which are still employed as legal means of chastising criminals from the lowest classes of people and of punishing minors, and the majority of votes in the deliberations held on the revision of the law up to this point have even been in favour of the complete abolition of this means of punishment.[123]

[115] A. Lüdtke, 'The Role of State Violence', 197.

[116] A. Lüdtke, 'Staatliche Gewalt und polizeiliche Praxis: Preußen im Vormärz', in L. Niethammer (ed.), *Bürgerliche Gesellschaft in Deutschland* (Frankfurt, 1990), 181.

[117] Cited in A. Lüdtke, *Police and State in Prussia*, 119, 121.   [118] Ibid.   [119] Ibid., 121.

[120] Students' petition to the Senate of Heidelberg University, 1838, in B. Wirsing, '"Gleichsam mit Soldatenstrenge", 73.

[121] S. Kesper-Biermann, *Staat und Schule in Kurhessen 1813–1866* (Göttingen, 2001), 131–2, on discipline in schools.

[122] H. Heine, 'Nachbemerkung zu dem Aufsatz: Körperliche Strafe' (1828), cited in P. Gay, *The Cultivation of Hatred*, 188.

[123] R. J. Evans, *Tales from the German Underworld*, 102.

The Prussian draft Criminal Code of 1827 had retained corporal punishment 'as a principal punishment against juveniles under the age of 16, and also in certain offences as a substitute for an eight-day to three-month prison or workhouse sentence', which was the term normally given to vagabonds, beggars, and other petty criminals at the discretion of the police.[124] The draft of 1836 specified that beating could be used 'as an independent punishment and as an additional punishment for the lower classes of the population', ignoring the principle of equality before the law. The draft of 1843 went further, allowing the whipping of 'persons of the male sex and indeed not only for the offences and misdemeanours listed in the specific sections but also as a police measure in cases of gross public nuisance'.[125] By contrast, the drafts of 1830, 1833, and 1845 dropped corporal punishment 'in consideration of the regard one must have for the maintenance and increase of the sense of honour even amongst the lower orders'.[126] Although still fearing the 'dangerous classes' and assuming that they needed to be controlled, many reforming bureaucrats and middle-class commentators and political leaders believed that their own mutually respectful and legally guaranteed independence and self-discipline could be transferred to others.

The same combination of moral improvement, in accordance with the religious and reasonable precepts of the *Bürgertum*, and a tacit acceptance that the lower classes of the towns were different, subject to base passions and violent impulses, was apparent in the reform of capital punishment. Many reformers seemed to agree with Goethe that the death penalty averted private vendettas and with Hegel that the punishment should fit the crime, allowing the execution of murderers to deter rational beings from killing and, following the logic of dialectics, to negate the negation.[127] In Württemberg, when capital punishment was debated in the Chamber in 1838, fifty-three deputies opposed abolition and twenty-nine backed it. In 1824, only one deputy had spoken in favour of abolition.[128] State executions continued to take place across the German lands, but in reduced number, as the death penalty was removed from crimes other than homicide and treason: in the Hohenzollern monarchy, an average of seven to eight executions per year were carried out in 1818–27 from an annual average of twenty-one condemnations, five executions from twenty-three per year in 1828–32, four from twenty-two per year in 1833–7, six from twenty-four per year in 1838–42, and seven from thirty-three per year in 1843–7; in Bavaria, three to four executions from seven condemnations per year took place in 1818–27, one execution per year in 1828–37, and one every two years in 1838–47; in Württemberg, two executions per year occurred between 1816 and 1848; in Baden, four per year between 1829 and 1848; and, in Austria, an average of ten executions per year were carried out between 1803 and 1848. In England and Wales, whose 'bloody code' retained the death penalty for a plethora of property crimes, sixty times as many felons were executed between 1816 and

[124] Ibid.   [125] Ibid.   [126] Ibid.

[127] J. W. v. Goethe, 'Maximen und Reflexionen', in R. Trunz (ed.), *Goethes Werke* (1948–69), vol. 12, 379; G. W. F. Hegel, *Grundlinien der Philosophie des Rechts* (Berlin, 1821), 72–9.

[128] R. J. Evans, *Rituals of Retribution*, 256.

1835 as in Prussia.[129] In August 1848, deputies in the Frankfurt Parliament abolished the death penalty altogether, except in military law, by 288 votes to 146, incorporating their decision in Paragraph 7 of the Basic Rights. The states' rejection of the Reich constitution in April 1849 effectively reversed this decision, with executions in Prussia rising to twenty-six per year in the early 1850s before dropping to between two and five per year in 1858–62. The shifts in other German states were less pronounced.

More visible to contemporaries, who were rarely aware of the changing statistics, was the ending of public executions in Prussia in 1848, Württemberg in 1853, Hamburg and Brunswick in 1854, Saxony in 1855, Baden in 1856, Hanover in 1860, and Austria in 1868. They were replaced by executions within prisons, attended only by officials and 'respected people who, because they do not occupy any office of state, can be expected to possess a greater degree of independence', as the memorandum of the Prussian Justice Minister Karl von Uhden and the Minister for the Revision of Legislation Friedrich Karl von Savigny presented the matter to the king on 17 November 1847.[130] It was widely believed by this time in educated circles that 'the moral effects which could be expected from the public nature of executions are not brought about as one would wish', in the opinion of the Central Rhine district authorities of the Grand Duchy of Baden in 1854:

> Only a few people among the numberless crowd which is gathered in the wide open space manage to bring about in themselves the serious and worthy state of mind in which they can receive and store up the moral impressions which the act taking place in front of their eyes would be suited to evoke; the vast majority only sees a spectacle, the satisfaction of coarse carnal desires in front of them, and instead of feeling revulsion at a crime which has to find its human expiation, and respect for the law and the undeviating path of justice, they feel sympathy for the criminal.[131]

With executions continuing to draw thousands of spectators—35,000 in Bremen in 1831 and 12,000–15,000 in Breslau in 1841, for instance—and popular attitudes allegedly becoming less God-fearing and more bloodthirsty, governments resolved to remove them from public view, relying on 'respectable' witnesses, who were not likely to be inflamed in the same manner, to provide a guarantee that the penalty had been applied and justice done. The distinction between the 'respectable' classes, who were supposedly inured to both violent passions and actions, and the rest of the population was evident in these modifications of the means of state violence, as executions became a matter of administration rather than public spectacles for the edification of society as a whole.

Many contemporaries commented on the hypocrisy of middle-class men condemning violence in public, as they continued to abuse their families and prostitutes in private, their employees in the workplace, and their political enemies and 'inferiors' at home and abroad. The cartoonist Wilhelm Busch, who published in the *Fliegende Blätter* and *Münchener Bilderbogen* in the 1860s, made a career out of

---

[129] Ibid., 228–31.   [130] Ibid., 265.
[131] Grossherzoglich Badische Regierung des Mittel-Rheinkreises to the Ministry of Justice, 9 May 1854, ibid., 312–13.

»Ach!« – spricht er – »die größte Freud'
Ist doch die Zufriedenheit!! –«

Rums!! – Da geht die Pfeife los
Mit Getöse, schrecklich groß.
Kaffeetopf und Wasserglas,

Tabaksdose, Tintenfaß,
Ofen, Tisch und Sorgensitz –
Alles fliegt im Pulverblitz. –

Figure 3.1 Wilhelm Busch, 'Max und Moritz'
Source: Wilhelm Busch, *Max und Moritz. Eine Bubengeschichte in sieben Streichen* (Munich, 1865), 4th series.

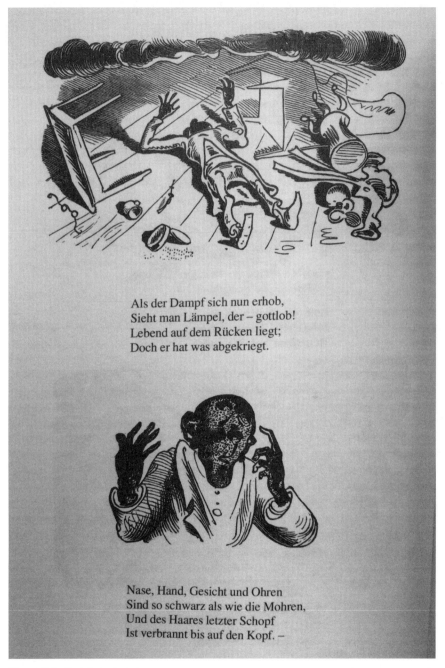

Als der Dampf sich nun erhob,
Sieht man Lämpel, der – gottlob!
Lebend auf dem Rücken liegt;
Doch er hat was abgekriegt.

Nase, Hand, Gesicht und Ohren
Sind so schwarz als wie die Mohren,
Und des Haares letzter Schopf
Ist verbrannt bis auf den Kopf. –

Figure 3.1 Continued

Wer soll nun die Kinder lehren
Und die Wissenschaft vermehren?
Wer soll nun für Lämpel leiten
Seine Amtestätigkeiten?
Woraus soll der Lehrer rauchen,
Wenn die Pfeife nicht zu brauchen??

Mit der Zeit wird alles heil,
Nur die Pfeife hat ihr Teil.

Dieses war der vierte Streich,
Doch der fünfte folgt sogleich.

Figure 3.1 Continued

drawing pugilistic fathers and teachers, beating their unfortunate charges, just as peasants and children tormented their animals. In *Max and Moritz* (1865), the mischievous boys garrotte widow Bolte's chickens and taunt the tailor, Herr Böck, to such an extent that he runs out of his house brandishing a cane.[132] Max and Moritz place explosive in the pipe of the teacher, Herr Lämpel, who blows himself up, and they are themselves, in the last scene, put through a flour mill and ground into small pieces (see Figure 3.1).[133] In *Bilderpossen* (1864), the cartoonist recounts the story of Eispeter, a boy who goes skating despite being warned not to, falls through the ice, and is frozen into an ice statue, only to be melted down by his well-meaning parents and turned inadvertently into a broth, which ends up being stored in a container beside the gherkins.[134] Busch's cartoons tell of a world in which disobedient children and evil adults—for example, the witch and 'people-eater' in his version of Hänsel and Gretel in *Bilderpossen*—might or might not get their violent comeuppance, as if links in a rough, natural, and never-ending chain of misguided or misleading human actions and reactions. Yet his picture stories also evoke scenes from a past, bucolic life of villages and stock characters, deriving from folk tales and eighteenth-century caricature. They poke fun at practices which his largely middle-class readership was aware of—like most children of his generation, Busch was probably caned at school—but which they did not necessarily perpetuate.[135] As such, the cartoons created violent fantasies for a passive public, which satirized the didactic *Kinderbuch* and deliberately overturned adult notions of order, standing alongside the topsy-turvy fantasies of crime literature, sensational newspaper reportage, and bloody accounts of war.[136]

Nineteenth-century '*Bürgerlichkeit*' consisted, to a striking degree, of the exclusion of disharmony and violence from the domestic sphere, as sexual relations were romanticized and marriage, the family, and childhood were sentimentalized.[137] 'The mind of the man is more creative, emerging from itself and having effects in the distant world', whereas 'the woman is limited to a small sphere, which she has a clearer view of', noted *Brockhaus*—the '*Allgemeine deutsche Real-Encyklopädie für die gebildeten Stände*'—in 1834: 'Man must acquire things, the woman seeks to retain; the man through violence and force (*Gewalt*), the woman through goodness or cunning.'[138] Busch delighted in subverting these myths, mocking middle-class ideals of courtship ('Das gestörte Rendezvous'), temperance ('Der vergebliche Versuch', 'Der hastige

---

[132] W. Busch, *Gesammelte Werke* (Hamburg, 1982), vol. 1, 197–251.   [133] Ibid.

[134] Ibid., 154–65.

[135] E. Weissweiler, *Wilhelm Busch. Der lachende Pessimist* (Cologne, 2007), 22.

[136] G. Ueding, *Wilhelm Busch. Das 19. Jahrhundert en miniature* (Frankfurt, 1977), 11–13.

[137] An analysis of the *Journal des Luxus und der Moden*, one of the most popular periodicals of the late eighteenth and early nineteenth centuries with up to 2,250 subscribers and about 25,000 readers, shows that approximately 24 per cent of articles were about love, 16 per cent about marriage, 12 per cent about education (*Bildung*), 8 per cent about current affairs, 6 per cent about virtue, and 6 per cent about money: W. Greiling, 'Zeitschriften und Verlage bei der Vermittlung bürgerlicher Werte', in H.-W. Hahn and D. Hein, *Bürgerliche Werte um 1800* (Cologne, 2005), 222; A. Borchert and R. Dressel (eds), *Das Journal des Luxus und der Moden. Kultur um 1800* (Heidelberg, 2004).

[138] F. A. Brockhaus (ed.), *Bilder Conversations-Lexikon*, vol. 4, 669.

Rausch'), chivalry ('Der schöne Ritter'), modesty ('Der unfreiwillige Spazierritt'), and piety ('Das Teufelswirtshaus').[139] In 'Trauriges Resultat einer vernachlässigten Erziehung' ('The Sad Result of a Neglected Education'), which appeared in the *Fliegende Blätter* in the 1860s, the caricaturist showed what could happen, allegedly, when a well-off couple, with only one son, failed to go to church and give their progeny 'good advice': little Fritz used to annoy a certain tailor called Böckel, who ended up luring the boy into his house in order to chop off his head with a giant pair of scissors; the tailor undressed Fritz, using the clothes for his trade, and threw his corpse into the river; later, as Fritz's mother was beginning to wonder where he was, she cut open a fish and found her son's body in it, causing her to fall down in a faint and impale herself on a kitchen knife; shocked, Fritz's father took a pinch of snuff and, in a sneezing fit, fell out of the window onto a passing aunt, whereupon, 'from both dear relatives, the soul gently departed'.[140] Subsequently, 'the astute police' found 'the true cause of the thing', noticing that Fritz had no clothes on and spotting the material from his breeches on the patchwork of a Jewish pedlar's trousers. After the scapegoat, portrayed in stereotypical fashion, had been hanged for his crime, a receipt from Böckel was found in his trouser pocket, implicating the tailor, who was arrested by a gendarme and sentenced to death by the wheel. Not liking this prospect and still having his 'great tailor's scissors', he cut off his own head: 'So it goes with evil people:/ Finally, they receive their reward./ Therefore, you dear parents,/ Pay attention to your son.'[141] In the manner of a carnival, the 'moral' of the story differed from its real—and visual—meaning, just as the violent consequences of the characters' actions were meaningful but not real. Much of the humour of Busch's work rests on its incongruity, referring to violent feelings—the cartoonist's and the reader's—not to actual actions.[142] As he assured a friend in 1863, 'The happiness of the individual, in so far as it is attainable at all, lies in his own head, in the harmonious cultivation of his personal capacities.'[143]

Burghers regularly covered their base, aggressive impulses, and their oppressive, unequal relationships with a veneer of 'virtue', 'faith', and 'culture'.[144] However deceptive or ambiguous, one consequence of such ideals of *Bürgerlichkeit* appears to have been the marginalization of physical violence. Yet how can such pacification have been compatible with the morally sanctioned violence of middle-class and aristocratic duels, which remained common in nineteenth-century Germany?

---

[139] W. Busch, *Gesammelte Werke*, vol. 1, 43–149, referring to cartoons appearing the *Fliegende Blätter* during the 1860s.

[140] Ibid., 54–61.   [141] Ibid., 61.

[142] Peter Gay, *The Cultivation of Hatred*, 182–3, 408–23, initially treats the cartoons literally, but then in a more nuanced way, as an example of humour and ridicule, if also aggression.

[143] W. Busch to O. Bassermann, 12 Dec. 1863, ibid., 419.

[144] See especially U. Frevert, 'Bürgerliche Familie und Geschlechterrollen. Modell und Wirklichkeit', in L. Niethammer (ed.), *Bürgerliche Gesellschaft in Deutschland*, 90–8; G. Budde, 'Das Öffentliche des Privaten. Die Familie als zivilgesellschaftliche Kerninstitution', in A. Bauerkämper (ed.), *Die Praxis der Zivilgesellschaft* (Frankfurt, 2003), 57–75; C. v. Hodenberg, 'Der Fluch des Geldsacks. Der Aufstieg des Industriellen als Herausforderung bürgerlicher Werte', and M. Kessel, '"Der Ehrgeiz setzte mir heute wieder zu…". Geduld und Ungeduld im 19. Jahrhundert', in M. Hettling and S.-L. Hoffmann (eds), *Der bürgerliche Wertehimmel. Innenansichten des 19. Jahrhunderts* (Göttingen, 2000), 79–104, 129–48.

To an extent, such duels were the residue of a society of estates—especially the military estate—and its codes of honour. Prince Wilhelm, later King of Prussia and Kaiser of Germany, articulated the case for the army in 1846, contending that 'honour and, thus, also the offending of honour amongst the officer corps' had 'a quite different character and a completely different meaning from that of other orders':

> Honour and honourableness are the first requirement for the officer corps, the first and highest condition of its vocation. In this sense, besmirching the honour of an officer, attacking the condition of his very being and existence, must be seen as a particularly heinous crime, which comprises all the more serious a punishment, since legislation, namely that of the Prussian state, has to take into account the maintenance and realization of the feeling of honour of the estate of officers, to which it owes its power, above all. The interest of the state in the honour of the estate of officers, which is not the case to such a degree in respect of any other estate, because the honour of the estate of officers is the basis of the security and existence of the state, seems to be an absolutely compelling reason to treat insults against officers in a different way from insults against other people.[145]

Officers, it was widely believed, had no choice but to defend their honour, to the point where Württemberg's military 'courts of honour' (*Ehrengerichte*), which had been established there in the early nineteenth century as elsewhere in Germany, had the right in serious cases to recommend recourse to arms.[146] Officers were also a warrior caste, it was held, legitimated by their exercise of violence and closely tied to the aristocracy, whose need to protect its honour had been recognized in law: for example, the *Allgemeines Landrecht* (1794) had provided for the duels of officers and nobles in the Hohenzollern monarchy to be treated as an offence (Paragraph 694) separate from murder, with much more lenient sentences. Officers and nobles, it was implied, stood apart from the estate of burghers and civil society. 'If the duel is held to be a *bulwark* of the estate of officers, can—I ask you—the convergence of the estate of the military and that of burghers be encouraged in this way?' demanded the Rhenish liberal and opponent of duelling Hermann von Beckerath in the first united Prussian *Landtag* in 1847: 'Can we also view the duel as the bulwark of the estate of burghers? The foundation of the estate of burghers is respect for the law, but the law says, "You must not kill".'[147]

Beckerath's and some other liberals' assumption was that the military and aristocracy were less 'cultured' and more 'backward', subject to the 'prejudices' of their past and a purported 'officer and noble mystification', as one 'democratic' officer, thrown out of the Prussian officer corps in a notorious case in 1846, described it.[148] A number of aristocrats, including Otto von Bismarck, seem to have agreed with the substance, if not the wording, of this verdict, going out of their way to prove their belligerence—the later Chancellor claimed to have fought and won twenty-five

---

[145] U. Frevert, *Ehrenmänner. Das Duell in der bürgerlichen Gesellschaft* (Munich, 1991), 93.

[146] Ibid., 107: this was not the same in Prussia, which served as a model for Bavaria and other states.

[147] Ibid., 91.   [148] Ibid.

duels—and their aggression, or the 'choleric element' in their nature.[149] However, the majority of the thousands of duels fought in the German lands during the nineteenth century—70 per cent in Prussia, 82 per cent in Bavaria, and 86 per cent in Baden—were recorded as *bürgerlich*.[150] All kinds of burghers fought. They included democrats such as the lawyer and later forty-eighter Heinrich Simon, who shot a friend and colleague in 1828, claiming at the time that 'only one in a hundred thousand people would not have ended up, in this case, where I now stand', and Carl Twesten, who accepted the challenge of the Chief of the Prussian Military Cabinet Edwin von Manteuffel in 1861 after refusing to withdraw political criticism, 'because he had to acknowledge that he would lose the esteem of his peers (*Standesgenossen*)', if he were to turn it down.[151] Even socialists such as Ferdinand Lassalle took part in duels, shot dead at the age of 39 in 1864 by a noble who had rejected the activist's marriage proposal to his daughter. Four years earlier, Lassalle had refrained from taking up the challenge of a Berlin official, but only, as he wrote to Karl Marx in London, with great difficulty: 'As soon as the demand was handed over to me, I experienced an extremely strong urge, seizing pistols, to accept it.'[152] Not all socialists, democrats, and liberals shared Lassalle's feelings, with the Rhenish bankers David Hansemann and Gustav Mevissen, for example, asserting that only the contravention of civilian law brought dishonour. 'Any attempt to discover other criteria' would be 'unfortunate and dangerous', the latter intoned in 1847.[153] His position, notwithstanding the abolition of honour courts in 1848, remained a minority one in educated circles.

Paradoxically, the violent social practice of duelling persisted up to and beyond the First World War because it was connected to an honour code which was perceived, in different guises, to uphold order, individual integrity, and culture. As Goethe himself had proclaimed, in conversation with the Weimar Chancellor Friedrich von Müller in 1827, 'What did a human life matter?': 'It is more important that the principle of a point of honour, a certain guarantee against crude actions, is kept alive.'[154] As shots were about to be exchanged or a sword fight begun, duellists were confronted with what Wilhelm von Humboldt, challenged by Boyen in 1815, called 'strange and peculiar' feelings, as they contemplated injury and death.[155] Yet it was, as Heine's publisher remarked after the author had challenged the banker Salomon Strauss to a duel in 1841, better to be 'dead than dishonoured'.[156] Heine, like many other duellists, had been prepared for his ordeal at university, as a member of a student club (*Burschenschaft, Corps*, or *Landsmannschaft*), which

[149] O. v. Bismarck to his sister, 26 Aug. 1848, cited in P. Gay, *The Cultivation of Hatred*, 258.

[150] The overall figure is impossible to calculate accurately: Ute Frevert has found 520 duels in archives between 1770 and 1925, but at least three times as many cases ended up in civil courts as left traces in archives, it appears from more reliable figures for the period between 1869 and 1873. Duels between officers were brought before military 'Ehrengerichte', but these records only exist for Bavaria and Württemberg. It is likely that many more cases, especially those where neither party was seriously injured, were not reported at all. See U. Frevert, *Ehrenmänner*, 269–70.

[151] H. Simon and C. Twesten, cited ibid., 168–9.

[152] Ibid., 133. Also, U. Frevert, *Emotions in History: Lost and Found* (Budapest, 2011), 48–9.

[153] U. Frevert, *Ehrenmänner*, 90.   [154] Ibid., 55.

[155] U. Frevert, *Emotions in History*, 55.   [156] Cited in P. Gay, *The Cultivation of Hatred*, 14.

staged sword-fights (*Mensuren*) between members as rites of initiation and belong-ing. Although formally banned, seventeen secret clubs existed in a university such as Göttingen during the mid-1820s by the poet's reckoning, organizing 'not only many duels, as never before, but also dangerous ones'.[157] These staged acts of vio-lence left some combatants with a revered facial scar and one with 'his nose hacked off', before a crowd of boisterous fellow students, as Heine's close friend and later liberal politician Eduard Wedekind recalled in 1824.[158] The purpose of such *Mensuren* was to reinforce the identity of the group and its code of honour. To this end, its rituals of violence were highly formulaic and fiercely observed. In a similar fashion, duels were only possible between members of the officer corps, nobility, and 'educated orders', who were '*satisfaktionsfähig*' or worthy as opponents. They could be distinguished from reprehensible street fights by their strict rules and serious consequences. Thus, the historian and *Burschenschafter* Heinrich von Treitschke had been careful to select pistols, after he had been insulted 'in the roughest possible way' by another student at Bonn university in the mid-1850s, in order to mark it out as a 'matter of honour' separate from the '*Schlägerpaukerei*' of the corps.[159] Although they were the subject of conversation and frequently grue-some, with one student combatant describing in 1847 how the bullet had 'pene-trated to the back of the skull' of his opponent 'after the smashing of the temple', they were generally carried out in good order—at a set number of paces, with the offended party firing first up until the middle of the nineteenth century—and they took place in secret at dawn, with only the seconds and doctors present, well away from the gaze of the public.[160] As such, they comprised one aspect of a moralizing and controlling of emotions which was characteristic of the educated and respect-able classes of nineteenth-century societies.[161]

The moral and emotional controlling of violence and the marginalization of violent acts took place in the context of a much broader attempt to banish natural and bodily effusions and odours, promoting squeamishness or a nauseous reac-tion to what was experienced as an assault on the senses. This changing sensibility was connected to the sanitization and privatization of bourgeois homes and daily life. Every well-off woman and, even, every child was now expected to have their own room, recorded the *Hannoverscher Magazin* in 1817, whereas forty years earl-ier 'many women and their children lived in the same room in which the husband had his work desk'.[162] Increasingly, kitchens and latrines, from which odours continued to emanate, were placed at the back of apartments and in the base-ments of houses along with servants' staircases, facing the courtyard, with its

---

[157] Ibid., 23–4.   [158] Ibid.   [159] U. Frevert, *Ehrenmänner*, 150–3.
[160] Ibid., 202.
[161] M. Kessel, 'Das Trauma der Affektkontrolle. Zur Sehnsucht nach Gefühlen im 19. Jahrhundert', in C. Benthien (ed.), *Emotionalität. Zur Geschichte der Gefühle* (Cologne, 2000), 156–77; N. Verheyen, 'Alter(n) mit Gefühl', in U. Frevert (ed.), *Gefühlswissen. Eine lexikalische Spurensuche in der Moderne* (Frankfurt, 2011), 161–18.
[162] H. E. Bödeker, 'Die "gebildeten Stände" im späten 18. und frühen 19. Jahrhundert', in J. Kocka (ed.), *Bildungsbürgertum im 19. Jahrhundert* (Stuttgart, 1989), vol. 4, 36.

deliveries and horses.[163] They were often not mentioned in contemporary descriptions of bourgeois homes. Reception rooms and the rooms of the family faced outwards in order to catch the light and fresh air. The division was naturally stricter in urban villas, which were built from the 1830s onwards.[164] In city centres, sanitation was much more challenging: Hamburg was the first German city to gain a water and sewerage system in 1842, after much of the centre had been destroyed by fire; Berlin and other German cities did not acquire extensive sewers until the 1870s.[165] In the early nineteenth century, water still had to be fetched from the street by servants. From the mid-century onwards running water was available in most middle-class homes, but insufficient water pressure and volume prevented the installation of flushing toilets.[166] Urine and faeces, therefore, had to be carried in a wooden container or bucket to street level and emptied there into open sewers between buildings and in streets, which often got blocked and ran—'completely dark-coloured'—through the gutters, as one contemporary recalled of his grandparents' apartment in the prestigious Königsstraße in Berlin.[167] Even in Hamburg, despite its early construction of a system of sewers, thousands of self-contained privies continued to exist. When their pervasive odour of excrement was added to the smell of animals and manure and of offal and waste, which were stored in thousands of pits throughout the city—Munich had 2,700 in 1854—and which only had to be cleared once a year, burghers' desire for cleanliness and sanitary conditions frequently remained more of an ideal than a reality. In Cologne in the 1820s, 'a town of monks and bones,/...And rags, and hags, and hideous wenches', Samuel Taylor Coleridge counted 'two and seventy stenches, / Ah well defined, and several stinks!'[168] All the same, many—perhaps most—members of the *Bürgertum* were attempting to banish such assaults on their senses from their mind and, through the improvement of housing, sanitation, and hygiene (which was a word coming into common German usage in the early nineteenth century), from their cities, as 'health' became a 'task for the life of the state', in Lorenz von Stein's assessment.[169] They themselves

---

[163] R.-H. Guerrand, 'Private Spaces', in M. Perrot (ed.), *A History of Private Life: From the Fires of Revolution to the Great War* (Cambridge, MA, 1990), vol. 4, 370; A. v. Saldern, 'Im Hause, zu Hause. Wohnen im Spannungsfeld von Gegebenheiten und Aneignungen', in J. Reulecke (ed.), *Geschichte des Wohnens. Das bürgerliche Zeitalter 1800–1918* (Stuttgart, 1997), 176.

[164] W. Brönner, *Die bürgerliche Villa in Deutschland, 1830–1890* (Düsseldorf, 1987).

[165] A. Lees and L. Hollen Lees, *Cities and the Making of Modern Europe, 1750–1914* (Cambridge, 2007), 123; D. Inglis, 'Sewers and Sensibilities: The Bourgeois Faecal Experience in the Nineteenth-Century City', in A. Cowan and J. Steward, *Cities and the Senses: Urban Culture since 1500* (Aldershot, 2007), 108.

[166] P. Münch, *Stadthygiene im 19. und 20. Jahrhundert. Die Wasserversorgung, Abwasser- und Abfallbeseitigung unter besonderer Berücksichtigung Münchens* (Göttingen, 1993), 41.

[167] C. A. Ewaldt, cited in G. Böhmer, *Die Welt des Biedermeier* (Munich, 1968), 70.

[168] Cited in D. Inglis, 'Sewers and Sensibilities', 115. See also D. Inglis, *A Sociological History of Excretory Experience: Defecatory Manners and Toiletry Technologies* (Lewiston, NY, 2001); D. Laporte, *A History of Shit* (Boston, MA, 2002); R. A. Lewin, *Merde: Excursions in Scientific, Cultural and Sociohistorical Coprology* (London, 1999); W. I. Miller, *The Anatomy of Disgust* (Cambridge, MA, 1997); A. Corbin, *The Foul and the Fragrant* (Leamington Spa, 1986).

[169] L. v. Stein, *Die Innere Verwaltung*, 2nd revised edn (Stuttgart, 1882), vol. 2, 89; first published in 1867. See also F. Osterlein, *Handbuch für Hygiene für den Einzelnen wie für eine Bevölkerung*

washed more frequently and expected others to do the same, criticizing those who failed to do so for being 'dirty'.[170] As a consequence, the physical effusions and suffering of the human body—and violence done to it—could appear less palatable.

Like its effusions and infusions, the human body was to be hidden away beneath modest or respectable clothes, which were only to be removed in private rooms, if decorum—outlined in manuals of manners—were to be preserved. Although fashions carefully maintained the clear and in some respects increasing separation of the 'sexes', they also concealed the physicality of the body, just as contemporaries, especially women, sought to suppress physical functions such as blushing, sweating, belching, and farting.[171] In cases of illness, as bodily functions became uncontrollable during fevers, coughing, sneezing, suppuration, urination, defecation, and bleeding, the sick retreated—in order to avoid lapses of decorum as well as to prevent infection—to private rooms, where closed doors, bed-sheets, and curtains could be used to hide their bodies. Maladies were still common, with overall rates of urban mortality increasing in the 1830s, 1850s, and 1860s in contrast to lower and falling rates in the countryside, but for the middling orders they were less visible and less regular than for the poor, who died early primarily of intestinal and respiratory diseases.[172] Although it is true that epidemics such as typhus—with outbreaks in 1823, 1825, 1835–6, 1839–40, 1845, and 1855 in Stuttgart, for instance—and pandemics such as cholera (1826–37, 1841–59, 1863–75, 1881–96), which emptied the body of a quarter of its fluids within several hours as a result of vomiting and diarrhoea, created panic amongst the middle classes, the diseases were nonetheless believed to be afflictions of the poor, if also spreading beyond impoverished social milieux and areas of the city.[173] The wealthy, or the 5 per cent or so of the population in the liberal professions, the upper reaches of the civil service, manufacture, and trade (together with nobles residing in cities), had already begun to create an environment for themselves in the nineteenth century, with running water, better sanitation, and spacious, well-heated apartments, town houses, and villas, which seemed to offer some protection against the ravages of illness and suffering.

Sickness occurred at home still, but in more discreet conditions, with better chances of survival. Hospitals, the number of which had risen from 155 in 1822 to 1,122 in 1876 in Prussia, were intended principally for the poor, with surgery

(Tüingen, 1851). On the literature of 'hygiene', see P. Sarasin, *Reizbare Maschinen. Eine Geschichte des Körpers 1765–1914* (Frankfurt, 2001), 95–172; N. Bullock and J. Read, *The Movement for Housing Reform in Germany and France, 1840–1914* (Cambridge, 1985), 13–51.

[170] G. Vigarello, *Wasser und Seife, Puder und Parfüm* (Frankfurt, 1988), 187–226; R. Jütte, *A History of the Senses: From Antiquity to Cyberspace* (Cambridge, 2005), 170–2.

[171] A. Corbin, 'Backstage', in M. Perrot (ed.), *A History of Private Life*, vol. 4, 475–9.

[172] J. Vögele, 'Die Entwicklung der Gesundheitsverhältnisse in deutschen Städten während der Industrialisierung', in J. Vögele and W. Woelk (eds), *Stadt, Krankheit und Tod. Geschichte der städtischen Gesundheitsverhältnisse während der Epidemiologischen Transition vom 18. bis ins frühe 20. Jahrhundert* (Berlin, 2000), 99–114.

[173] See, especially, S. Schraut, 'Krankheit und Tod in der sich industrialisierenden Residenz. Stuttgart im 19. Jahrhundert', in J. Vögele and W. Woelk (eds), *Stadt, Krankheit und Tod*, 115–40; R. J. Evans, 'Epidemics and Revolutions: Cholera in Nineteenth-Century Europe', *Past and Present*, 120 (1988), 123–46.

being associated with barber surgeons until a reorganization of the profession during the early nineteenth century—in 1825 in the Prussian case—and being equated
with minor incisions of tumours, cysts, and gangrene—to be avoided because of a
high death rate—until the development of anaesthetics (ether and chloroform)
and antisepsis from the mid-nineteenth century onwards.[174] For most burghers,
medical treatment occurred in private, with Cologne's sixty doctors and twenty
surgeons paying home visits to about 4,000 families—out of a population of
75,000—who were able to pay their fees.[175] The improving 'scientific' reputation of
such doctors, along with better living conditions, helped to insulate the middle
classes, to a limited degree, from the corporeal realities of sickness and dying. Death
itself remained a matter of public display, with religious ceremonies and distinctive
clothing and conventions of mourning, but it had become, in cities, a more private
affair, with fewer neighbours viewing the corpse and the local community more
distant from acts of mourning and the rituals of burial.[176] None of these changes,
the incidence of which was patchy, meant that 'refined' or 'finely educated' middle-
class and noble recruits, in the gymnast leader Johann Christian Friedrich
GutsMuths's phrase, would react negatively to the conditions of combat or, indeed,
military service.[177] They do, though, help to explain the appalled reactions of at
least some combatants in the conflicts of 1848–51 and 1864, 1866, and 1870–1.

---

[174] On hospitals, see J. Bleker, 'To Benefit the Poor and Advance Medical Science: Hospitals and
Hospital Care in Germany, 1820–1870', in M. Berg and G. Cocks (eds), *Medicine and Modernity:
Public Health and Medical Care in Nineteenth- and Twentieth-Century Germany* (Cambridge, 1997),
17–34; U. Frevert, *Krankheit als politisches Problem 1770–1880. Soziale Unterschichten in Preußen
zwischen medizinischer Polizei und staatlicher Sozialversicherung* (Göttingen, 1984), 36–44, 116–84.
On surgery, R. Porter, 'Hospitals and Surgery', in R. Porter (ed.), *The Cambridge History of Medicine*
(Cambridge, 2006), 176–202.

[175] J. Bleker, 'To Benefit the Poor and Advance Medical Science', 26. Claudia Huerkamp, *Der
Aufstieg der Ärzte im 19. Jahrhundert* (Göttingen, 1985), 149, shows that the number of such doctors
did not increase in line with population in the nineteenth century, suggesting that home visits
remained the privilege of the middle classes.

[176] See Philippe Ariès, *L'Histoire de la mort* (1978) and Armin Nassehi and Georg Weber, *Tod,
Modernität und Gesellschaft* (1989), who take issue with Werner Fuch's denial in *Todesbilder in der
modernen Gesellschaft* (1969) that 'Todesverdrängung' had taken place. More specifically, M. Fischer,
Ein Sarg nur und ein Leichenkleid. Sterben und Tod im 19. Jahrhundert (Paderborn, 2004); F. J. Bauer,
'Von Tod und Bestattung in alter und neuer Zeit', *Historische Zeitschrift*, 254 (1992), 1–31.

[177] J. C. F. GutsMuths, *Turnbuch für die Söhne des Vaterlandes* (Frankfurt, 1817), xx–xxi.

4

Revolution and Civil War

The ambivalence of many 'educated' subjects to violence was revealed during the revolutions and wars of 1848–9. At the outbreak of revolution in March 1848, 303 civilians and an estimated sixty-three soldiers died in Berlin and forty-eight civilians in Vienna.[1] Inspired by revolutionary conflicts in Paris on 22–24 February, the uprisings had spread from the west (Mannheim, Karlsruhe, Mainz, Wiesbaden, and Hanau) in early March, affecting towns and some rural areas in Baden, Hesse-Darmstadt, Kurhessen, Nassau, Württemberg, Hanover, Bavaria, Oldenburg, Brunswick, and Saxony, but generally issuing in protests and petitions rather than violence.[2] Travelling from Heidelberg to Strasbourg and Mainz, where 'the agitation had naturally already seized this mercurially-tempered population', Ludwig Bamberger had the impression in early March that 'voices were being raised in most small states which demanded from the government fundamental improvements in the constitution and institutions, above all press freedom'.[3] 'The form in which the demands were expressed normally consisted of public meetings or a peaceful but somewhat stormy procession to the palace and administration (*Residenz*), with liberal notables placed at its head', he went on.[4]

The worst of the violence in Vienna and Berlin occurred between 13 and 19 March, followed by an armed insurrection in Baden in April. Here, a multitude of uncoordinated forces—6,000 fighters recruited by the republican revolutionary Friedrich Hecker in Constance, 3,000 raised by the former officer Franz Sigel, 1,000 rallied by the veteran of the Swiss *Sonderbund* war Johann Philipp Becker, and 1,000 following the writer Georg Herwegh from Strasbourg—were defeated by the Eighth Federal Corps, comprised of Hessian soldiers and backed by troops from Baden and Württemberg, at Kandern and Niederdossenbach on 20 and 27 April. The numbers involved in the battles were small—between 1,200 sup-

---

[1] W. Siemann, *German Revolution, 1848–49* (Basingstoke, 1998), 63–5. The figure for Prussian soldiers killed in Berlin is contested. The former Minister President Bodelschwingh disclosed the figure of fifty-six soldiers and seven officers in April 1848, which is accepted as the best estimate by Rüdiger Hachtmann, *Berlin 1848. Eine Politik- und Gesellschaftsgeschichte der Revolution* (Bonn, 1997), 188. Manfred Messerschmidt, 'Die preussische Armee während der Revolution in Berlin 1848', in Manfred Messerschmidt, *Militärgeschichtliche Aspekte der Entwicklung des deutschen Nationalstaates* (Düsseldorf, 1988), 51, gives a figure of twenty to thirty-six military dead. Contemporary estimates of military deaths ranged from 400 (*Vossische Zeitung*) to 1,105 (*Spenersche Zeitung*) or, even, 1,800, according to rumours at the time.

[2] W. Siemann, *The German Revolution*, 58.

[3] L. Bamberger, *Erinnerungen*, 27.

[4] Ibid. Bamberger's comments were, of course, written up and published long after the event.

porters of Hecker and 2,200 confederal troops at Kandern, for instance, with approximately ten deaths, including that of Friedrich von Gagern, the commander-in-chief and brother of the liberal President of the Frankfurt Parliament Heinrich von Gagern—but the perceived threat was much greater. Although Hecker's boast that he could muster 60,000 fighters was widely contested, onlookers such as Siegmund von Arnim, the Prussian envoy in Baden, acknowledged as early as 24 March that the danger was real: 'With one word, which might already have been given, he could unite under his command an army of more than 20,000 desperate and rabid proletarians from southern Germany and Alsace, where, according to the latest news, countless German factory workers have been sacked.'[5] Many of the early uprisings and protests in March and April followed a traditional pattern ('rough music', rural riots, labour disputes) or, at least, retained traditional elements. Later incidents between May 1848 and July 1849, though, were much more frequently understood to be 'political' or 'revolutionary'.[6]

REVOLUTIONARY VIOLENCE AND CIVIL WAR

Many lives were lost in such revolutionary events. Eighty people were killed and about 160 injured as confederal troops, requested by the Reich Minister of Internal Affairs Anton von Schmerling on 17 September, had cleared the square in front of the Paulskirche and had fought revolutionaries manning barricades in Frankfurt on 18 September, after more than 15,000 democrats had demonstrated against the Frankfurt Assembly's acceptance of the Truce of Malmö on 16 September.[7] More than 843 civilians and 189 soldiers died and 1,745 were wounded in Vienna in late October 1848, as Prince Alfred zu Windischgrätz deployed Czech and Croat troops to defeat a mixture of students (in the Academic Legion) and workers (in democratic associations, the Workers' Club, and Mobile Guard) prior to the imposition of the counter-revolutionary government of Felix Fürst zu Schwarzenberg on 21 November.[8] Two hundred and fifty civilians and thirty-one soldiers lost their lives and about 500 were injured in Saxony in May 1849, after the king and his ministers—refusing to accept the Reich Constitution despite votes in favour on the part of both chambers—had been replaced by a provisional government, whose forces—of between 3,000 and 6,000 fighters—were defeated by Prussian troops by 9 May. Lastly, 1,092 Prussian and confederal soldiers were killed or injured according to official statistics in battles in Baden and the Palatinate in June and July between the supporters of the Reich Constitution and National Assembly, on the

[5] Cited ibid., 70.

[6] M. Gailus, 'Soziale Protestbewegungen in Deutschland 1847–1849', in H. Volkmann and J. Bergmann (eds), *Sozialer Protest*, 98–9; W. Siemann, *The German Revolution of 1848–49*, 181, 175.

[7] F. Engehausen, *Die Revolution von 1848/49* (Paderborn, 2007), 201–2.

[8] This death toll is taken from the list of recorded medical cases: Ludwig von Welden, who reported the figures to Schwarzenberg in February 1850, estimated that the death toll could have been as high as 2,000, when unrecorded—or 'private'—deaths were also added: A. Schmidt-Brentano, *Die Armee in Österreich*, 386.

one hand, and the forces of Prussia and the *Bund*, on the other.[9] It is likely that a larger number of 'revolutionaries' died, with forty-three deaths at Waghäusel, fifty-one official executions after the various capitulations—the last at Rastatt on 23 July, involving about 6,000 irregulars—and numerous summary executions in the course of the campaign.[10]

These casualties occurred alongside those incurred in the national and imperial wars waged between 1848 and 1851, to which they were frequently—and increasingly— connected. In the war over Schleswig-Holstein (1848–51), between 1,250 and 2,500 confederal and Prussian soldiers were killed and 4,675 were injured.[11] In the Habsburg monarchy's wars in Italy between May and August 1848 and March and August 1849, 3,887–5,600 Austrian troops died and, in its campaigns against Hungarian revolutionaries, 16,600 were killed or wounded.[12] If one estimate is to be believed, there were approximately 66,000 military and civilian deaths in Italy and Hungary in 1848–9.[13] Given that some of the soldiers and commanders from these campaigns—Radetzky, Windischgrätz, Jellačić, Schwarzenberg, Wrangel—were also active in suppressing revolution in the lands of the *Bund*, it is likely that their experiences of wars 'abroad' affected their counter-revolutionary activities in the German-speaking lands.[14] Certainly, in Austria, the army had a dual role of carrying out external campaigns to maintain the 'empire' and quashing 'insurrectionary cities in the interior of the monarchy', as one officer put it.[15]

Remarkably, in the minds of the majority of civilians, however, 'revolution' and 'war' appear to have been kept separate in 1848–9, despite the fact that many soldiers were conscripts and were of a generation and social background similar to those of revolutionaries.[16] The distinction between revolutionary events and 'civil war' (*Bürgerkrieg*), which was defined by Brockhaus's *Bilder Conversations-Lexikon* at the end of the 1830s as 'the most horrific' type of conflict conducted by 'factions (*Parteiungen*) in a single state', was not clear-cut.[17] In early 1848, radicals such as Hecker had elided the terms, partly in allusion to developments in France and 'the

---

[9] B. Mann, 'Das Ende der Deutschen Nationalversammlung im Jahre 1849', *Historische Zeitschrift*, 214 (1972), 265–309.

[10] A. Lüneberg, *Mannheim und die Revolution in Baden 1848–1849* (Mannheim, 2004), 181–2.

[11] The higher figure comes from Michael Clodfelter, *Warfare and Armed Conflict: A Statistical Reference to Casualty and Other Figures, 1494–2007*, 3rd edn (Jefferson, NC, 2008), 191.

[12] Ibid., for the casualty figures for Hungary and the lower figure for the Italian wars, and M. Small and J. D. Singer, *Resort to Arms: International and Civil Wars 1816–1980* (London, 1982), for the higher figure for Italy.

[13] M. Clodfelter, *Warfare and Armed Conflict*, 190–1. István Deák claims that 100,000 were killed: István Deák, *Beyond Nationalism*, 40.

[14] See, for instance, A. Sked, *The Survival of the Habsburg Empire: Radetzky, the Imperial Army and the Class War, 1848* (London, 1979).

[15] E. Krtschek, *Der Italienische und Ungarische Krieg 1848–1849* (Olmütz, 1853), 90.

[16] S. Müller, 'Soldaten, Bürger, Barrikaden. Konflikte und Allianzen während der Revolution von 1848/49', in C. Jansen and T. Mergel (eds), *Die Revolutionen von 1848/49. Erfahrung, Verarbeitung, Deutung* (Göttingen, 1998), 37, rightly points out that the questions of allegiance and separation have rarely been problematized in the literature, with most authors assuming that soldiers simply considered it their 'job' to put down revolutions.

[17] F. A. Brockhaus (ed.), *Bilder Conversations-Lexikon der neuesten Zeit und Literatur* (Leipzig, 1837–41), vol. 2, 669.

smoking corpses of Italians and Frenchmen who [had] died for their *Volk*.[18] 'In order to live up to the other nations, they now, for their part, had to make a German revolution', the Badenese republican declared to the state's *Landtag* on 29 February 1848: 'German corpses, too, had to smoke. And they have since smoked and they are still smoking, for on the sacred plain of the Neckar, civil war hides its victims in the fields of tall corn.'[19] Few deputies or commentators followed Hecker's example. German revolutionaries, they agreed, had deliberately avoided civil war. Droysen, who was a deputy as well as an historian, wrote in a memorandum of April 1848:

> If Frankfurt had been a city like Paris or if that assembly had been convoked in Vienna or Berlin, in places of central administration, then an extemporized new founding of Germany could possibly have arisen out of it, although admittedly a new foundation which would have provoked more than one Vendée... and would have descended into the complete destruction of Germany in a terrible civil war.[20]

Liberals and constitutionalists rarely mentioned the possibility of a *Bürgerkrieg*. Even Varnhagen von Ense, who was closer to the Prussian nobility, the court, and the officer corps, only referred to it briefly and hypothetically after the September 'uprising' and killing of democrats in Frankfurt:

> I slept little during the night, for public affairs still troubled my soul. How would this German confusion end? Freedom in the end, I'm certain of that, but freedom on top of graves and debris! And beforehand, a long civil war. This would by no means be necessary, the governments could avoid it, but their lack of integrity ensures that everything is torn up in a common act of destruction. The aristocracy still has all the power, but it uses it for evil ends. The constitutions are a comedy, the *Volk* feels and sees it, and its mistrust is decisive, since nothing pushes it more violently to rage and revenge than the feeling of being deceived and lied to.[21]

Most liberals tended to discount the eventuality of civil war in Germany, associating it with the unjustified anxieties and machinations of the reactionary right. Romantics and conservatives who had little sympathy for realistic expectations of representative government regularly said that 'We are in a party struggle! We are in a bloody civil war!' reported Fanny Lewald, who was close to middle-class circles in Berlin and to the moderate democrats of Heinrich Simon's faction in Frankfurt.[22] 'Yet they are taking fright at symptoms of the evil from which they already know themselves to be ailing', she went on in October 1848 from Frankfurt, referring implicitly to

[18] F. Hecker, speech to the Badenese Landtag, 29 Feb. 1848, cited in F. D. Bassermann, *Denkwürdigkeiten 1811–1855* (Frankfurt, 1926), 51.

[19] Ibid.

[20] F. Gilbert (ed.), *Johann Gustav Droysen. Politische Schriften* (Munich, 1933), 125. Capital cities played an important part, especially in the early stages of the revolution (with the fall of Metternich in Vienna and the violence of 18 March in Berlin) and in the transition to counter-revolution (in November and December 1848): R. Hachtmann, 'The European Capital Cities in the Revolution of 1848', in D. Dowe, H.-G. Haupt, and D. Langewiesche (eds), *Europe in 1848: Revolution and Reform* (New York, 2000), 341–70.

[21] K. A. Varnhagen v. Ense, diary entry, 24 Sept. 1848, in K. A. Varnhagen v. Ense, *Tagebücher* (Leipzig, 1862), vol. 5, 204.

[22] F. Lewald, *Erinnerungen aus dem Jahre 1848* (Brunswick, 1850), vol. 2, 245.

her time in Paris: 'They are amazed that cold and heat come during a fever. They wonder at what is already there, at conditions which other peoples have already lived through, only because they themselves have not lived through them.'[23] The murder of two deputies—Prince Felix von Lichnowsky and General Hans von Auerswald—by radicals during the September insurrection was reprehensible but it was not tantamount to civil war. The main danger in Lewald's opinion was the overwrought anxieties of those on the right and their plans to use violence to wrest power from the legitimate liberal governments of Prussia, Austria, and the Reich. When reactionaries succeeded in taking power in early November 1848 in Berlin, the Prussian novelist refused to summon up the spectre of civil war, preferring instead to talk of a 'coup' or '*Staatsstreich*', which everyone was 'united' in condemning as 'a misfortune for the country', 'whether they hold it to be warranted because of the excesses of the National Assembly or to be an injustice of the government [of Brandenburg] and an act of irresponsible arbitrariness'.[24] As the Berlin militia (*Bürgerwehr*) surrounded the Prussian National Assembly, threatening to defend it against the advancing forces of General Friedrich von Wrangel, the writer used military terminology, describing the military drums and a battlefield, but she never seriously contemplated a military clash or conflict.[25]

One reason that contemporaries were confident in 1848 that civil war could be averted was that they were accustomed to the idea of 'revolution', which was at once different from and less menacing than a *Bürgerkrieg*.[26] As was to be expected, the term was contested, passing in and out of favour within various constituencies, but it was widely used, with 'enthusiasm for what, at the time, was called the revolution', in Bamberger's words.[27] 'Revolution', recorded Lewald on 6 June 1848, had 'again become "unloved"', with the Minister-President of Prussia Gottfried Ludolf Camphausen already referring in the Constituent Assembly to 'the struggle for freedom' as an '"occurrence" (*Begebenheit*), in order to avoid the word "revolution"'.[28] At the same time, however, the National Assembly in Berlin passed a resolution recognizing the revolution's achievements.[29] Students and others had continued to stage pilgrimages to the graves of revolutionaries 'in order to show the ministry how the memory of the *Volk* is more loyal, how the revolution is viewed as an event worthy of esteem and how they honour the victims of freedom, who have fallen for its sake'.[30] The 'fallen of March' had sacrificed their lives for a revolution and a new political and social order, not for the sake of victory in a war.[31] The public

[23] Ibid., 246.   [24] F. Lewald, 8 Nov. 1848, ibid., 307.   [25] Ibid., 322.

[26] Some historians have called this assumption into question, asking—like U. Frevert, 'Nation und militärische Gewalt', in C. Dipper and U. Speck (eds), *1848*, 344–6—whether the conflicts of the revolution amounted to a civil war, or were perceived to be a civil war. V. Valentin, *Geschichte der deutschen Revolution von 1848–49* (Berlin, 1931), vol. 2, 448–544, refers to the struggle to save the Reich Constitution in Baden and elsewhere as a *Bürgerkrieg*.

[27] L. Bamberger, *Erinnerungen*, 33.   [28] Ibid., 39.

[29] D. E. Barclay, *Frederick William IV and the Prussian Monarchy, 1840–1861* (Oxford, 1995), 165.

[30] Ibid., 40.

[31] From a radical point of view, 'revolution' meant that 'the mass of the *Volk* was infused with the conviction that the moment had come in which the eternal and inextinguishable rights of humanity could be recognized', in Gustav Struve's words: G. Struve, *Geschichte der drei Volkserhebungen in Baden* (Berne, 1849), 7.

commemoration of their deaths on 22 March in Berlin, which involved a crowd of 20,000 people and a procession of coffin-bearers 7.5 km long, was pronouncedly '*bürgerlich*' in tone, referring both to 'burghers' and 'civilians', with members of workers' associations, the *Bürgerwehr*, and student clubs wearing top hats and black frock-coats. There were no military uniforms or decorations on display except those of 1813.[32] The king played only a marginal part, viewing the procession from the balcony of the royal palace in a bare-headed gesture of deference, as the funeral train made its way from the Gendarmenmarkt, where 183 coffins had been laid out on the steps of the Neue Kirche, to the burial place of Friedrichshain. 'The whole celebration [took] place in the greatest order, we might say, in reverence', reported the *Vossische Zeitung*: 'No gendarme, no police, no soldier was to be seen, and yet there wasn't the slightest disturbance, since everyone was moved by the same good will and the same sense of unity.'[33]

In the liberal painter Adolf Menzel's unfinished depiction of the occasion, burghers are shown solemnly paying their respects to the dead, arrayed in a black mass in front of the dark portico of the church. Although these middle-class citizens—with the exception of students—played a minor part in the fighting on the barricades, they participated in the creation of a cult of fallen revolutionaries and contributed most to funds for widows, orphans, and the wounded.[34] The main speeches of the commemoration were given by the liberal evangelical pastor Adolf Sydow, who talked about martyrs of 'freedom and rights' spilling 'their blood for us to guarantee us, the survivors, the highest goods', and by the democrat Georg Jung, who saw 18 March as the adumbration of social harmony— 'If you can die united on the barricades, then you will be able to live in unity'—and as proof that soldiers had been separated from their 'fatherland', encouraged by unnamed leaders into committing 'acts of cruelty'.[35] In Prussia and beyond it, since newspapers like the *Leipziger Illustrirte Zeitung* described the event at length and depicted it in lithographs, the cult of the dead helped to reinforce a set of 'revolutionary' traditions which rested on well-known French antecedents, myths of 1813, and widespread hopes of reform.[36] As a consequence, few liberals renounced the term 'revolution'

[32] M. Hettling, *Totenkult statt Revolution. 1848 und seine Opfer* (Frankfurt, 1998), 32.

[33] Cited ibid., 42. Hettling gives an excellent description of and commentary on the event.

[34] R. Hachtmann, 'Die Revolution von 1848. Kulte um die Toten und die Lebenden', *Zeitenblicke*, 3 (2004), 3–17. R. Hachtmann, *Berlin 1848. Eine Politik- und Gesellschaftsgeschichte der Revolution* (Bonn, 1997), 71; M. Hettling, *Totenkult*, 26–7.

[35] Cited in M. Hettling, *Totenkult*, 38–41.

[36] See, especially, J. Sperber, 'Echoes of the French Revolution in the Rhineland, 1830–1849', *Central European History*, 22 (1989), 200–17; J. Sperber, 'Eine alte Revolution in neuer Zeit. 1848/49 in europäischer Perspektive', in T. Mergel and C. Jansen (eds), *Die Revolutionen von 1848/49*, 14–36; J. Sperber, 'Germania mit Phrygiermütze. Zur politischen Symbolik der Revolution von 1848/49 in den Rheinlanden'; I. Götz v. Olenhusen, '1848/49 in Baden. Traum und Trauma der Französischen Revolution'; and P. Kurth and B. Morgenbrod, 'Wien 1848 und die Erinnerung an die Französische Revolution von 1789', in I. Götz v. Olenhusen (eds), *1848/49 in Europa und der Mythos der Französischen Revolution* (Göttingen, 1998), 63–133; M. Hettling, '1848. Illusion einer Revolution', in M. Hettling (ed.), *Revolution in Deutschland? 1789–1989* (Göttingen, 1991), 27: 'the concept of "revolution" had remained largely unchanged in its semantic content since around 1800. Two elements constituted its core. On the one hand, an attack on the old order in the name of popular sovereignty. The *Volk*—whatever was understood by it—appeared as an active agent and claimed competence over

altogether.[37] For Varnhagen von Ense, reflecting on the then re-enacting of the commemoration of 22 March at the start of June 1848, 'our revolution' had 'long been in train before 18 March', having been 'the constant companion—loud or quiet—of all government actions for thirty years'.[38] Revolution was, remarked the reactionary Ludwig von Gerlach with regret, 'attractive rather than repellent' in Germany.[39]

For radicals like the poet Ferdinand Freiligrath, who had worked for the *Neue Rheinische Zeitung* under the editorship of Karl Marx during the 1840s, the revolution was a struggle, which could be described in military phrases, but it was not a civil war between two parties. In the best-known poem about 1848, 'The Dead to the Living' ('*Die Todten an die Lebenden*'), written in July, he imagined a dialogue between those killed on 18 March 1848 and those who survived, with thinly veiled accusations levelled against Friedrich Wilhelm IV: 'High in the air you [the bullet in the breast] lifted us, that every writhing of pain / Might be an endless curse to *him*, at whose word we were slain!'[40] Having been arrested for *lèse-majesté*, Freiligrath was acquitted in Prussia's first jury trial, increasing the notoriety of his work. While the monarch 'turns his Bible's leaf, or quaffs his foaming wine', the poet hoped that 'the dread memory' of the dead 'on his soul should evermore be burned', with 'every mouth with pain convulsed, and every gory wound / . . . round with him in the terror-hour, when his last bell shall sound'.[41] Although he described how 'his army fled the field, which dying we had taken', Freiligrath's imagery was drawn predominantly from the iconography of previous revolutions, envisaging that the king's head should be laid 'on bloody scaffold down!'[42] In such circumstances, foreign wars were made objects of ridicule by radicals, subordinated to a political struggle at home in which the Prussian government—that is, the 'March ministry' of Camphausen—had squandered the legacy of 18 March that had been 'so bravely won':

> Like waves came thundering every sound of wrong the country through: -
> The foolish war with Denmark! Poland betrayed anew!
> The calling back of banished troops! The prince's base return!
> Wherever barricades were built, the lock on press and tongue!
> On the free right of all debate, the daily-practised wrong!
> The groaning clang of prison-doors in North and South afar!
> For all who plead the People's right, Oppression's ancient bar!
> The bond with Russia's Cossacks! The slander fierce and loud,

state and society. On the other, the concept of "revolution" was always associated with the idea that this conflict would be carried out with violence and that the conflict would not be peacefully resolved.'

[37] For further references, see M. Hewitson, '"The Old Forms are Breaking Up,. . . Our New Germany is Rebuilding Itself": Constitutionalism, Nationalism and the Creation of a German Polity during the Revolutions of 1848–49', *English Historical Review*, 125 (2010), 1174–214.

[38] K. A. Varnhagen v. Ense, diary entry, 6 June 1848, in K. A. Varnhagen v. Ense, *Tagebücher*, vol. 5, 56.

[39] H.-C. Kraus, *Ernst Ludwig von Gerlach* (Göttingen, 1994), 395.

[40] F. Freiligrath, *Poems from the German* (Leipzig, 1871), 220.

[41] Ibid.   [42] Ibid., 220–1.

Alas! That has become your share, instead of laurels proud –
Ye who have borne the hardest brunt, that freedom might advance,
Victorious in defeat and death—June warriors of France!
Yes, wrong and treason everywhere, the Elbe and Rhine beside,
And beat, oh German men! Your hearts with calm and sluggish tide?
No war within your apron's folds?! Out with it, fierce and bold!
The second, final war with all who freedom would withhold!
Shout: 'the Republic!' till it drowns the chiming minster bells,
Whose sound this swindle of your rights by crafty Austria tells![43]

The revolution was faced with decay, but wrath, like 'chance poppies' could still blossom in the land:

And yet, it *does* remain: it springs behind the reaper's track;
Too much had been already gained, too much been stolen back;
Too much of scorn, too much of shame, heaped daily on your head—
Wrath and revenge *must* still be left: believe it, from the dead!
It *does* remain, and it awakes—it shall and must awake!
The revolution, half complete, yet wholly forth will break.
It waits the hour to rise to power, like an up-rolling storm,
With lifted arms and streaming hair—a wild and mighty form!
It grasps the rusted gun once more, and swings the battered blade,
While the red banners flap the air from every barricade!
Those banners lead the German Guards—the armies of the free—
Till princes fly their blazing thrones and hasten towards the sea!
The boding eagles leave the land—the lions' claws are shorn—
The sovereign people, roused and bold, await the future's morn!

Now, till the wakening hour shall strike, we keep our scorn and wrath
For you, ye living, who have dared to falter on your path!
Up, and prepare—*keep watch in arms!* Oh, make the German sod,
Above our stiffened forms, all free, and blest by freedom's God;
That this one bitter thought no more disturb us in our graves:
'*They once were free—they fell—and now, forever they are slaves!*'[44]

For radicals, revolution was not a war, since the authorities had already been overturned in a morally legitimate political transformation, but it was a violent event.

Most members of the *Bürgertum* and nobility were less sanguine about the violence of revolution. For many, the events of mid-March in Berlin had been shocking. Hugo Graf Lerchenfeld-Köfering gave a vivid account from a child's standpoint of the reactions of one well-connected noble family. When the revolution started, his mother and the children were walking on Unter den Linden, 'as suddenly a patrol of *Ulanen* rode by us, the *Volk* ran towards the palace and a general disquiet was manifest on the street'.[45] In the evening, shots could be heard and, 'from then on, the city was as though transformed'.[46] 'The streets were mostly empty, yet in them

---

[43] Ibid., 221–2.   [44] Ibid., 223.
[45] H. v. Lerchenfeld-Köfering, *Erinnerungen und Denkwürdigkeiten* (Berlin, 1935), 10.
[46] Ibid.

crowds of haunted-looking people ran about', went on the then 5-year-old son of the Bavarian envoy to Prussia: 'I often heard my parents say, "Today, again, we have seen really bad faces about."'[47] In the street outside his house, Lerchenfeld-Köfering observed the wounded being transported and saw students and the *Bürgerwehr* taking over the guard duties of soldiers, who had left the city: 'Everyone was politicized at that time, even our nanny with her colleagues, amongst whom committed democrats were to be found. "For the king and military", "for the *Volk*", these were opposites. We children were naturally for the military. I remember our joy as the troops came back in again.'[48]

Writing about the same social milieu, Varnhagen von Ense came to the opposite conclusion, blaming the military, government, and court for inciting popular violence but also warning on 14 March 1848 that a popular 'political movement', when it really appeared, would ensure that 'the *Volk* is not defeated'.[49] Even though the Berlin diarist and socialite had lengthy experience of the Napoleonic Wars, he could be found conceding by 18 March that conflict on the streets had become 'more violent and terrible', with artillery and gunfire filling the air.[50] Some fighters went up to 'their posts' on the roofs of houses, knowing 'what danger they were taking on', in the face of an 'ignominious death,... through a fall from the roof, by means of the bayonets of the soldiers or the noose of the hangman'.[51] On the next day, Varnhagen recorded in his diary, 'the events have something wonderful about them', with 'ten, twelve young people, committed and ready for death', defending 'barricades successfully against cannon, cavalry and infantry'.[52] Other middle-class witnesses in the Prussian capital were less optimistic and more panicked: Lewald contrasted Parisian leaders, who were confident that they could control the course of the revolution, with Berliners who were either 'like unpractised ball-players', letting the ball drop 'in delight at their good fortune', or like children, 'standing there clueless, shocked and embarrassed'.[53] Even on 18 March itself, most 'respectable' Berliners disappeared from the streets as the demonstrations became more violent towards the late afternoon and evening, with the teacher Wilhelm Angerstein recording differences of attitude between 'burghers' and 'proletarians' or 'workers'.[54] Later, when they looked back on March, at least some burghers agreed with the elders of the Berlin *Korporation der Kaufmannschaft* that 'current events, which profoundly shook all social relations', had endangered 'the property, prosperity and even the persons of private individuals', presaging 'the terrors of anarchy'.[55]

How burghers viewed 'revolution' depended on where they lived. In a city like Mannheim, which was affected by a rapid transition to violence and revolutionary militias in March and April 1848, the families of liberals such as Bassermann and

[47] Ibid.   [48] Ibid., 10–11.
[49] K. A. Varnhagen v. Ense, *Tagebücher*, vol. 4, 281.
[50] Ibid., 293.   [51] Ibid., 294.   [52] Ibid., 318–19.
[53] F. Lewald, *Erinnerungen*, vol. 1, 7.   [54] Cited in R. Hachtmann, *Berlin 1848*, 155.
[55] Resolution of the elders of the KBB, 12 May 1848, ibid., 357. According to Manfred Gailus, *Strasse und Brot. Sozialer Protest in den deutschen Staaten unter besonderer Berücksichtigung Preussens 1847–1849* (Göttingen, 1990), 495–516, which concludes with reflections on 'Der "Eigensinn" der Strassenpolitik und das Konzept der bürgerlichen Revolution', working-class and popular politics of the street remained separate from the notion of a middle-class, citizens' revolution.

Alexander Soiron, who had been denounced by Hecker for becoming 'contempt-ible lackeys of princes' despite their past as 'proud speakers of the people', were subjected to 'rough music'.[56] By the end of April, Bassermann was complaining to his friend Leopold Ladenburg, a son of the founder of a local bank, of the 'disgust-ing conditions of Mannheim', having learned in Frankfurt of his father's forced resignation from the municipal council and his brother's decision to flee the town with his family, followed by his parents in May.[57] 'All the power of the police' had come to an end, undermining public order, against the backdrop of an 'inter-connected, well-ordered plot' under the leadership of Hecker against the Badenese authorities.[58] 'Bassermann has returned from Mannheim with a heightened dis-gust against the population there,' wrote the deputy and government under-secre-tary Karl Mathy in August: 'Mannheim burghers cannot come to terms with their rabble (*Pöbel*); this is the misery as a consequence of which the city will perish.'[59] The three-hour train ride from Frankfurt to Bassermann's native city had been the most terrifying, 'torturing journey, which I have ever experienced'.[60]

Other cities and regions were less agitated, with some persisting throughout the revolution as 'political quiet zones'.[61] Until September, even Frankfurt itself was relatively insulated—as many correspondents and diarists bore witness—from the types of violence witnessed in Berlin, Vienna, and Baden.[62] To new deputies like the academic and journalist Karl Biedermann, who had arrived on the train and by coach from Saxony, it was known as the staid, old 'election and coronation city of the German Kaisers', which metamorphosed into the home of the Frankfurt Parliament, defended against radicalism and republicanism by the 'resident and well-organized Frankfurt *Bürgerwehr*'.[63] Having been elected as deputy for the constituency of Mergentheim-Gerabronn in Württemberg, Robert von Mohl was pleased to be in Frankfurt because it was far from 'the revolutionary machinations of Heidelberg', where his wife insisted on remaining with their children.[64] Georg Beseler, a liberal deputy from the Baltic town of Greifswald, contrasted Frankfurt, whose citizenry was 'reliable and loyal to the Reich', with the rest of the south-west, where 'order, the public peace, even personal security and property were, in many places, threatened'.[65] Like Greifswald, much of northern Germany outside

[56] L. Gall, *Bürgertum in Deutschland*, 308. For a similar report from Elberfeld, see Paul Theis to 'Rosalie', 17 May 1849, *Kriegsbriefe* Archive, Universitäts- und Landesbibliothek Bonn: 'Under a rule of terror for eight days, we are today breathing easily again. Eight days before yesterday (9 May) was the terrible day, which was followed by an even more terrible one.'

[57] Ibid., 313.

[58] F. D. Bassermann, *Denkwürdigkeiten*, 125, 140. Max Duncker, amongst many others, com-mented on the exceptional nature of Badenese conditions; see for instance M. Duncker to his wife, 9 Aug. 1848, in Johannes Schultze (ed.), *Max Duncker. Politischer Briefwechsel aus seinem Nachlass* (Osnabrück, 1967), 3. Also, P. Nolte, 'Baden', in C. Dipper and U. Speck (eds), *1848. Revolution in Deutschland* (Frankfurt, 1998), 53–68.

[59] Cited in L. Gall, *Bürgertum in Deutschland*, 313.

[60] F. D. Bassermann, *Denkwürdigkeiten*, 123.

[61] K.-J. Hummel, 'Political Quiet Zones', in D. Dowe, H.-G. Haupt, and D. Langewiesche (eds), *Europe in 1848*, 401–15.

[62] See, for example, L. Bamberger, *Erinnerungen*, 51–134.

[63] K. Biedermann, *Mein Leben*, vol. 1, 321, 323.

[64] R. v. Mohl, *Lebens-Erinnerungen 1799–1875* (Stuttgart, 1902), 32–3.

[65] G. Beseler, *Erlebtes und Erstrebtes 1809–1859* (Berlin, 1884), 59.

Berlin was relatively quiet.[66] Even in southern Germany, large parts of the countryside and some towns were little affected by revolutionary violence. Thus, as Lewald made her way across the central German lands to Weimar in October 1848, she was struck not just by the beauty of Franconia, but by 'the peace of its tranquil valleys'.[67] In Munich, according to the biased but in some respects credible retrospective report of its mayor Jakob Bauer, the removal of the king's mistress Lola Montez—'that demon'—was 'the only thing that the masses intended'.[68] A revolutionary party subsequently developed but was supported by less than 5 per cent of the population, in Bauer's opinion. For the inhabitants of such cities and regions, the 'revolution' was not automatically associated with violence.

In the opinion of the majority of German liberals, the essence of a 'revolution' concerned the existence and legality of a break with a previous political order rather than the use of violence.[69] The fact that the violent acts of revolutionaries were believed to be limited and controllable was another reason for the continuing separation of revolution and civil war. Hecker pointed out in August 1848, in a letter read out to the Frankfurt Parliament (to which he had been elected but from which—by a majority vote—he had been banned), that such distinctions were irrelevant:

> You stand with us, who have risen up with weapons for the sovereignty of the people, likewise on the ground of the revolution. That you have expressed the negation of monarchical power, with the motto 'The *Volk* is sovereign', merely through resolutions, whereas we added the means of execution, weapons, to the resolution, does not change the slightest thing.[70]

Most liberals, who initially dominated the Frankfurt parliament and the assemblies of other states, disagreed. Under pressure from the right, which was known to be preparing a counter-revolution in Prussia and Austria from the late summer onwards, some liberals avoided and some actually renounced the term 'revolution'.[71] To the *Kölnische Zeitung*, one of the largest-circulation newspapers in Germany, March 1848 had been 'a moral general insurrection of our people against that despotism and bureaucracy under which it was ignominiously laid low', leaving the new, legitimate, liberal authorities with the task of ensuring order and guarding against anarchy.[72] What should not be forgotten, 'least of all in Frankfurt', the

---

[66] This was even true of Hamburg, especially when compared with other similar cities elsewhere: J. Breuilly and I. Prothero, 'The Revolution as an Urban Event: Hamburg and Lyon during the Revolutions of 1848–49', in D. Dowe, H.-G. Haupt, and D. Langewiesche (eds), *Europe in 1848*, 371–400.

[67] F. Lewald, *Erinnerungen*, vol. 2, 302.

[68] Cited in K.-J. Hummel, 'Political Quiet Zones', 406. Also, K.-J. Hummel, *München in der Revolution von 1848/49* (Göttingen, 1987).

[69] See M. Hewitson, *Nationalism in Germany, 1848–1866: Revolutionary Nation* (Basingstoke, 2010), 5–47; M. Hewitson, '"The Old Forms are Breaking Up"', 1176–81, 1203–14.

[70] F. Wigard (ed.), *Stenographischer Bericht über die Verhandlungen der deutschen consitutierenden Nationalversammlung zu Frankfurt am Main* (9 vols, Frankfurt, 1848–9), 10 Aug. 1848, vol. 3, 1476–7.

[71] A. Schildt, *Konservatismus in Deutschland*, 68, talks of growing signs of a 'counter-revolutionary wave' from summer 1848 onwards.

[72] *Kölnische Zeitung*, 13 Apr. 1848.

newspaper continued in May 1848, 'is the fact that one has to build in Germany from the bottom upwards, and that one must take the path of evolution rather than revolution and sovereign emanation'.[73] Conservative criticism of liberals' dangerous courtship of 'radicalism, revolution and revolt against the order of God', as the *Neue Preußische Zeitung* later put it, helped to reinforce calls for 'moderation', with deputies in Frankfurt sensitive to the reproach that the Provisional Central Power was incapable of maintaining order: Prussians did not require 'the help and guarantees of the Reich power to save ourselves from civil war and to avoid losing our liberties', mocked the same conservative mouthpiece in November 1848, but those in Frankfurt did need external assistance.[74]

Other liberals were more robust in their defence of a moderate 'revolution', in part to undermine the legitimacy of any counter-revolution and in part to regain votes from democrats, who had become the largest grouping in the National Assembly—still made up of various factions named after the taverns where they met—after October 1848.[75] The *National-Zeitung* spelled out the distinction in May, underlining that it did 'not belong to those anxious people who lie down each night full of worries about the next day' and who wanted 'to speak in favour of the rule of so-called bourgeois liberalism', resting merely on a political nation of 'educated' burghers rather than a more broadly based democracy.[76] 'Constitutional' leaders in Frankfurt such as Heinrich von Gagern, Carl Theodor Welcker, Anton von Schmerling, and the *Reichsverweser* Archduke Johann, together with most of their followers and with their counterparts in Prussia Ludolf Camphausen and—from July onwards—David Hansemann, appear to have believed until at least November 1848, when Prussian and Austrian administrations were replaced by reactionary ones, that they could control the violent excesses of the German revolutions. From the point of view of radicals like Struve, writing in 1849, the pattern of moderation and pacification which had been established at the start looked set to continue:

> Similar events to those in the land of Baden took place in most of the other constitutional states of Germany. The specific demands of the *Volk*, which were brought forward in every place in a more or less threatening form, received weakening amendments and limitations from the chambers, and their significance was diminished to that of unending negotiations, instead of being raised to the status of imminent action.[77]

However precariously, liberals seemed to have controlled the violence of the revolution from the very beginning.

Burghers had various grounds for believing that violent revolutionary acts could be contained. First, many of the specific forms of protest had been commonplace

---

[73] Ibid., 19 May 1848.
[74] *Neue Preußische Zeitung*, 17 Mar. 1849 and 28 Nov. 1848, respectively. Press criticism of liberal courtship of radicalism appeared from the summer of 1848 onwards.
[75] W. Siemann, *Die Frankfurter Nationalversammlung 1848/49 zwischen demokratischem Liberalismus und konservativer Reform* (Frankfurt, 1976), 27.
[76] *National-Zeitung*, 20 May 1848.
[77] G. Struve, *Geschichte der drei Volkserhebungen in Baden*, 9–10.

before 1848, more or less accepted by citizens whose attitudes to violence and public order were more rough-and-ready than those of their later nineteenth-century counterparts.[78] Camphausen was therefore unimpressed, though fatigued, by the 'rough music' to which he was subjected in Berlin, according to the contemporaneous account of his brother in a letter to the Minister-President's wife, who was still in Cologne, in May 1848:

> Today, Ludolf is very cheerful and well. On previous days, especially on Friday, his nerves were very frayed. Although he treated the rough music (*Katzenmusik*) directed at him on the first three days of the week with indifference, since it only—in fact— came from street urchins and riff-raff, the prospect of further visits was not exactly very enticing, and on Thursday they allegedly even wanted to carry out a coup de grâce again, which had—as later came to light—had no basis. On Friday, I insisted that Ludolf moved his bedroom to the back and that we also have our studies at the back on an evening. Both changes were not because an immediate danger was threatening us, for this does not exist at present in my opinion because the radical party would be carrying out an extremely stupid act with a personal attack on a minister, but they are intended to allow us to escape the terrible street noise.[79]

For Varnhagen von Ense, writing on 25 May, it was remarkable that such 'terrible *Katzenmusik*', which had been imported into the Prussian capital from other regions of Germany, had not issued in actual violence, yet 'no person has been injured and not a single windowpane smashed', with demonstrations keeping within traditional boundaries of intimidation.[80]

Second, respectable citizens' militias had been formed or expanded in order to maintain order after the army had withdrawn or had been confined to barracks, helping to further weaken cities' police forces.[81] The call for an 'arming of the people' (*Volksbewaffnung*) was one of the principal demands of revolutionaries, heard—in the officer Andreas von Schepeler's view—'in every city in Germany, in every village, indeed in every bar... bubbling forth from the prayers of the political rosary'.[82] In Berlin, order had been restored only when Friedrich Wilhelm IV had agreed to the arming of the people during the night of 18–19 March 1848.[83] Throughout the German lands, militias were designed, in the words of Nassau's

---

[78] See, especially, M. Gailus, *Straße und Brot*, 350–430, for an examination of old and new forms of protest. Also W. Siemann, 'Soziale Protestbewegungen in der deutschen Revolution von 1848/49', in H. Reinalter (ed.), *Demokratische und soziale Protestbewegungen in Mitteleuropa 1815–1848/49* (Frankfurt, 1986), 305–26.

[79] J. Hansen (ed.), *Rheinische Briefe und Akten zur Geschichte der politischen Bewegung* (Osnabrück, 1967), vol. 2, 180.

[80] Cited in M. Gailus, *Straße und Brot*, 394.

[81] Even supporters of the Prussian state such as Theodor Fontane, in an unpublished article written in late autumn 1849, resented the imposition of 'naked and inexcusable effrontery by an inglorious and disobliging police' after the 'coup' of November 1848, contrasted with the welcome change under the regime of the revolution: see A. Lüdtke, *Police and State in Prussia, 1815–1850*, 191–2.

[82] A. v. Schepeler, *Volksbewaffnung und Republik* (Aachen, 1848), cited in R. Pröve, 'Civic Guards in the European Revolutions of 1848', in D. Dowe, H.-G. Haupt, and D. Langewiesche (eds), *Europe in 1848*, 686.

[83] Ibid.

law of 11 March, as a 'people's guard for the guarantee of public liberties'.[84] However, they usually received official sanction, with the governments of Baden and Württemberg passing laws in April 1848 which attempted to establish civic guards in all districts, and they frequently remained bourgeois in organization and outlook, despite being allowed by law to recruit 'all citizens of the state', in the phrase of the Austrian draft law, or even non-citizens, in Hanover's law of 16 April.[85] Thus, in Berlin, although it was accepted that the very discussion of limiting entry to the civic guard 'could have led in the worst direction, if not to ruin', it was also assumed that the *Bürgertum* would provide officers and recruits: seventy-eight out of 108 *Hauptleuten* of the city's *Bürgerwehr*, including thirty-six merchants and seventeen manufacturers, belonged to the middle classes in the spring of 1848.[86] The militias were largely urban, with less than a third of Saxony's rural districts having civic guards on paper in 1848–9 but with a single city like Leipzig having a large contingent of 12,000 men, and they regularly stood, in their own estimation, between the forces of 'anarchy' on the left and 'reaction' on the right, as the Prussian commentator Carl Schwebemeyer acknowledged in 1848:

> Which role will the civic guard play here? Will it join in with the rebellion? Then it will be acting against its purpose... of protecting the public peace and legal order. Will it suppress the rebellion? Then, however, it would be acting according to purpose but against the liberties of the people, and supporting absolutism and tyranny.[87]

Notwithstanding contemporary fears that the civilian militia had metamorphosed from 'a bourgeois formation for the protection of legal order' to 'a sort of praetorian guard for the party of revolt', which had been articulated by the *Neue Preußische Zeitung* on 7 November 1848 at the time of the conservative 'coup' in Prussia, burghers seem on the whole to have continued, with some reservations and considerable ridicule, to trust in the *Bürgerwehr* as a safeguard against a radical revolution.[88]

Third, most liberals and many democrats understood themselves to be engaged, not in a violent contest, but in a struggle for power. Correspondingly, the threat of military force from the right, with army regiments gathered menacingly in

---

[84] Ibid. On the shift that occurred, compared to past practices, see also R. Pröve, *Stadtgemeindlicher Republikanismus und die 'Macht des Volkes'. Civile Ordnungsformationen und kommunale Leitbilder politischer Partizipation in den deutschen Staaten vom Ende des 18. bis zur Mitte des 19. Jahrhunderts* (Göttingen, 2000).

[85] R. Pröve, 'Civic Guards in the European Revolutions of 1848', 686–7.

[86] The quotation comes from Carl Philipp Nobiling, *Die Berliner Bürgerwehr in den Tagen vom 19. März bis 7 April 1848* (Berlin, 1852), cited in R. Hachtmann, *Berlin 1848*, 248, 251.

[87] C. Schwebemeyer, *Die Volksbewaffnung, ihr Wesen und Wirken* (Wriezen, 1848), in R. Pröve, 'Civic Guards in the European Revolutions of 1848', 689. The figures come from U. Frevert, *A Nation in Barracks*, 126.

[88] There was a growing polarization, given the perceived overturning of the status quo and the continuing disorder of the revolution in specific localities, between 'order' and 'disorder' (and associated terms, in some accounts, such as 'revolution' and 'anarchy'), but there were also persisting differences of opinion about what was meant by 'order'. This to temper H.-G. Haupt's claims about the Manichean outlook of the various parties in 1848–49 in H.-G. Haupt, 'Ordnungsentwürfe und Erfahrungen von Unordnung. Bemerkungen zu der 1848er Revolution in Deutschland und Frankreich', in M. Grüttner (ed.), *Geschichte und Emanzipation* (Frankfurt, 1999), 217–32.

Innsbruck, Potsdam, Schleswig-Holstein, Bohemia, and Moravia, was to be countered primarily by the establishment of legitimate governments in Frankfurt, Berlin, Munich, Stuttgart, Dresden, Hanover, Karlsruhe, and, even, Vienna, which would then secure the backing of their monarchs and control of their armies.[89] Few ministers, deputies, journalists, or civic guards thought that militia could be deployed against the military of their own state or those of neighbouring states, in spite of repeated but secondary references to a possible external function: the *Bürgerwehr* was conceived of largely as an auxiliary police force or—for democrats—as a 'constitutional guard' (*Verfassungswacht*), with the Saxon decree of April 1849 typical in aiming at 'a universal arming of the people to protect the fatherland internally and, if need be, externally'.[90] Militiamen such as the 47-year-old actor Eduard Devrient from Dresden might have criticized his comrades—'Those male mollies!'—in May 1848 for wanting 'to go home and let their weapons be taken off them', but he felt obliged to do the same when confronted by the Saxon and Prussian armies, reduced to tears at his own 'cowardice': 'If there were not so many lives dependent on me, I know what use I'd make of mine.'[91]

Some militiamen, especially 'young men, robust and courageous', as Devrient put it, did join in a military campaign against the armies of counter-revolutionary states, arguing that they were defending a legal National Assembly and Reich Constitution.[92] A significant number took part in the campaign against Prussia in the Palatinate and Baden, where republican governments had been proclaimed in May and the army—or significant parts of it—and militias put themselves at their disposal.[93] In the latter, after the exiled Grand Duke had requested the intervention of Prussian and 'confederal' troops, the republican supporters of the provisional government could count on 20,000 men in the so-called 'Rhein-und-Neckararmee', of which only two-thirds were capable of fighting and half were battle-ready, in the opinion of Ludwig von Mieroslawski, their French-trained, Polish commander.[94] Up to 45,000 fighters were available in Baden in May–June 1849, according to

---

[89] This is not to suggest that many deputies and ministers overlooked the importance of armed force, through the establishment of civic guards or a general 'arming of the people', or the leverage deriving from the menace of further acts of violence by revolutionaries, which had led to the installation of March ministries and the flight of governments and armies in the first place. On the significance of the question of legitimacy, see M. Hewitson, '"The Old Forms are Breaking Up"', 1173–214; J.-D. Kühne, *Die Reichsverfassung der Paulskirche. Vorbild und Verwirklichung im späteren deutschen Rechtsleben*, 2nd edn (Neuwied, 1998); J.-D. Kühne, 'Eine Verfassung für Deutschland', in C. Dipper and U. Speck (eds), *1848*, 355–65; J.-D. Kühne, 'Die Revolution von 1848/49 als Umbruch für Recht und Juristen', *Zeitschrift für Neuere Rechtsgeschichte*, 18 (1996), 246–59.

[90] Cited in U. Frevert, *A Nation in Barracks*, 125. On the disputes between liberals and democrats about the role of the civic guard as a form of *Hilfspolizei* or *Verfassungswacht*, see R. Pröve, 'Alternativen zum Militär- und Obrigkeitsstaat? Die gesellschaftliche und politische Dimension ziviler Ordnungsformationen im Vormärz und Revolution', in W. Rösener (ed.), *Staat und Krieg. Vom Mittelalter bis zur Moderne* (Göttingen, 2000), 216–18. Some of the early references to an external role might have been linked to fears of French invasion or, even, the arrival of a mob of outsiders, arriving to plunder German localities, especially those in border regions: R. C. Canevali, 'The "False French Alarm": Revolutionary Panic in Baden, 1848', *Central European History*, 18 (1985), 119–42.

[91] U. Frevert, *A Nation in Barracks*, 130.   [92] Ibid.

[93] W. Real, *Die Revolution in Baden 1848/49* (Stuttgart, 1983).

[94] Rulers argued that the revolutionary Reich had effectively lapsed, reverting to the German Confederation.

one estimate, including 20,000 troops of the line.[95] They were no match for the 50,000 Prussian soldiers advancing down both banks of the Rhine, together with Bavaria's 15,000–16,000 troops in Aschaffenburg, Donaueschingen, and Nuremberg and Württemberg's 8,000 troops near Heilbronn. After fighting near Waghäusel, in which—to follow Gottfried Keller, writing from Heidelberg—'the Prussians have had to purchase their victory at a high price, although they had superior forces', most troops fled or retreated, with some withdrawing to the fortress of Rastatt, where they surrendered on 23 July.[96] Certainly, those like Friedrich Engels who took part in the fighting saw it as a 'war', defined by the 'whistling of bullets' and a military 'campaign'.[97] For most militiamen, though, the experience of the Breslau merchant Karl Friedrich Hempel was more characteristic of the end of the revolution: 'the *Bürgerwehr* was ordered via placards to give up its weapons by two o'clock in the afternoon and was threatened, if this did not happen, with the prospect of them being picked up by the military', he wrote in May 1849: 'Since this order was only adhered to in a dawdling fashion, the armed forces went with wagons through the city at half-past four and demanded that weapons be given up with the beat of a drum, and now the delivery went much better.'[98] For Hempel, as for most contemporaries, whether revolutionaries, militiamen, deputies, or ministers, there was little expectation that militias would be used against armies. Rather, it was assumed that armies would obey their governments.

COUNTER-REVOLUTIONARY WARFARE AND THE RESTORATION OF ORDER

In fact, armies did not always obey revolutionary governments, not least because the monarchs to whom soldiers had sworn allegiance remained in place, and the governments themselves were replaced, usually through a combination of dynastic and conservative plotting backed up by the threat or exercise of military force. From February 1848 onwards, as conservative elites began to worry about the impact of revolution in France, there were those who wanted to use force to quash protests and revolts and those who were wary of using it. Although they were central to events in Germany and Europe, with Berlin immediately dispatching Radowitz to discuss the reform of the *Bund* with Metternich in return for Prussian military support in the case of a French attack, civilian and military authorities in

---

[95] V. Valentin, *Geschichte der deutschen Revolution von 1848–49*, vol. 2, 527.

[96] Gottfried Keller cited ibid., 528.

[97] F. Engels to J. Marx, 25 July 1849, in F. Engels and K. Marx, *Werke*, vol. 27, 501–2. He is writing from Switzerland, where he has retreated to with the 'Badenese army'. It seems from his correspondence that Engels' sense of participating in a war derived from his experiences rather than from his—and Marx's—ideological position, which foresaw a revolutionary class struggle being waged in the form of a *Bürgerkrieg*: see W. Wette, *Kriegstheorien deutscher Sozialisten. Marx, Engels, Lassalle, Bernstein, Kautsky, Luxemburg* (Stuttgart, 1971), 72–8.

[98] Cited in R. Pröve, 'Politische Partizipation und soziale Ordnung. Das Konzept der "Volksbewaffnung" und die Funktion der Bürgerwehren 1848/49', in W. Hardtwig (ed.), *Revolution in Deutschland und Europa 1848/49* (Göttingen, 1998), 109.

the Habsburg empire faced a unique set of challenges and responded in ways which diverged from those of other German states.

The decisions leading to the resignation of the Austrian chancellor on 13 March, which was critical for the fortunes of the revolution in Germany as a whole (and especially that in Prussia), were unremarkable: a crowd of students noisily presented a petition calling for the ending of censorship, freedom of conscience, and the establishment of a representative system of government to the Lower Austrian Estates, which were meeting in the *Landhaus*—near the Chancellery—to consider a petition drafted by one of its own members, the lawyer and later minister Alexander Bach; refused entry, some students tried to force their way into the *Landhaus* whilst others gave speeches and chanted slogans outside, watched by many middle-class onlookers. Unable to continue their business, the Estates sent a delegation to the Hofburg, followed by the crowd, to relay the demands of the '*Volk*' to Archduke Ludwig, who was chair of the Conference of State (*Staatskonferenz*). After an unsuccessful attempt by Archduke Albrecht to fetch reinforcements into the centre of the city from the *Vorstadt*, during which he was hit by a missile and three demonstrators were shot dead by Italian troops, triggering riots and arson, a faction including Archdukes Franz Karl, Johann, and Ludwig, together with the minister of state Franz von Kolowrat-Liebsteinsky, agreed to the ultimatum delivered by members of the Civic Guard and deputies from the Lower Austrian Estates at five o'clock, which demanded that the students be armed, the *Bürgerwehr* entrusted to keep the peace, the military withdrawn, and Metternich dismissed by nine o'clock on the same day. Johann and Kolowrat cut short the Chancellor's hour-and-a-half-long speech about the difficulties which would be faced in Hungary, Italy, Germany, and Europe by any successor. 'I have sat in conference with Prince Metternich for twenty-five years and I have always heard him go on in this way, never coming to the point', commented the Archduke.[99] Emperor Ferdinand, who was held to be incapable and dominated by his brothers and advisors, gave in and retired for the night: 'Tell the people I agree to everything.'[100]

This chain of events, taking place in the capital, was similar to those elsewhere in Germany, as was the mixture of caution and resolve demonstrated by Austrian leaders. Metternich, according to the later testimony of Archduke Johann, 'was firmly convinced that he could handle the situation with written memoranda and speeches' and, when this strategy failed, he was confident that he could retain control by investing Windischgrätz with plenipotentiary powers on 13 March to take charge of the 14,000 soldiers in and around Vienna in order to restore order.[101] The general had gone home at six o'clock to change out of his civilian clothes, since he had been on a private visit from Prague (where he was military commander), only to return in full military uniform just after nine to find that the plan had been

---

[99] Cited in A. Palmer, *Metternich: Councillor of Europe* (London, 1972), 311.

[100] Ibid. See also W. Siemann, *Metternich. Staatsmann zwischen Restauration und Moderne* (Munich, 2010), 108–14.

[101] Ibid., 308. See also H. v. Srbik, *Metternich, der Staatsmann und Mensch* (Munich, 1925), vol. 2, 258–77. See G. Rothenberg, *The Army of Francis Joseph*, 22–3, for the size of the forces.

abandoned. His impotent exclamation 'This must not be!' was characteristic of military commanders elsewhere—for example, the Prince of Prussia in Berlin—and reveals how precariously balanced the various forces and calculations of generals, courtiers, ministers, and monarchs were in March 1848.[102]

What was unusual about the Habsburg empire in 1848 was the degree of entanglement of 'national' and 'domestic' political affairs, blurring the boundaries between 'revolution', 'civil war', and 'state war' and implicating the military in a series of contradictions, as it attempted to fulfil its 'internal' and 'external' duties (see Map 2 for the configuration of territories in 1848–9). On 3 March 1848, the leader of the Opposition Party and deputy for Pest Lajos Kossuth had called in the lower house of the Hungarian Diet for 'general constitutional institutions which recognized the different nationalities'.[103] Metternich had attempted to prevent the address being received officially in Vienna, but the text had circulated widely and was read out in German translation during the demonstrations on 13 March. In the last week of March, the Hungarian Diet had passed bills creating Hungarian ministers of finance and war, as well as a minister 'resident around the king's person', having gained the emperor's consent to form a separate government on 17 March.[104] In theory, these reforms, all thirty-one of which Ferdinand con-firmed in the 'April laws' during a journey by steamer to Pressburg to mark the closing of the Diet, appeared to be compatible with the new constitution being drafted by the Minister-President-in-waiting Franz von Pillersdorf in April, yet they were quickly perceived as a threat by much of the governing elite, as they were subject to the pressures of radicalization in Vienna and the competing demands of 'national' representatives. Thus, the actions of the capital's revolutionaries—their protest in early May against the 'Pillersdorf constitution', which issued in its effect-ive replacement by the *Reichstag* as a constituent assembly, or their decision in the same month to place the Hofburg under the protection of the National Guard, pushing the court to leave stealthily for Innsbruck rather than be 'held like a mouse in a trap', in Archduchess Sophie's words—seemed to be rendered more serious by the threat of secessions and the wars which they occasioned.[105]

In northern Italy, the army of King Carlo Alberto of Piedmont-Sardinia had invaded Lombardy on 23 March, with the Milanese—following the withdrawal of Habsburg troops on the same day after five days of fighting—calling for Piedmont's assistance and with the Venetians setting up an independent republic under Daniele Manin. In Bohemia and Moravia, Czechs and Slovaks had sponsored the convoca-tion of the Panslav Congress in Prague in early June, attended by 385 delegates, two-thirds of whom were Czech or Slovak. From Croatia, a delegation had been

---

[102] A. Palmer, *Metternich*, 311; R. Okey, *The Habsburg Monarchy, c. 1765–1918* (Basingstoke, 2001), 134. See also A. Palmer, *The Twilight of the Habsburgs: The Life and Times of Emperor Francis Joseph* (London, 1994), 31–2: Archduke Franz Karl effectively took over from Ludwig and argued in favour of a constitution on 14 March, which Ferdinand promised publicly the next day, partly to postpone further political concessions until the constitution had been agreed. See also D. E. Barclay, *Frederick William IV and the Prussian Monarchy*, 143, on the split between Friedrich Wilhelm IV and his younger brother, the Prince of Prussia, on the question of resistance, violence, and concessions.
[103] Cited ibid., 29.   [104] Ibid., 32.   [105] Ibid., 37.

Map 2. Central Europe in 1848–9

Source: R. J. W. Evans and H. Pogge v. Strandmann (eds), *The Revolutions in Europe, 1848–1849* (Oxford, 2000), xii–xiii.

sent on 17 March to ask the emperor to appoint Josip Jelačić, a well-known officer of the *Grenzer*, as Croatian Ban. They also called for the convening of a Diet designed to bring about the merger of Croatia, Dalmatia, and the Military Frontier. In addition, Slovaks had called for a Slovak territory in northern Hungary on 10–11 May, Serbs for their own duchy or *Vojvodina* on 13 May, and Romanians for participation in an autonomous Transylvania on 15 May. A Supreme Ruthenian Council, founded on 2 May, had demanded a division of Galicia, leaving Ruthenians in a majority in the eastern half of the territory. Habsburg elites, especially military leaders, reacted to these national developments in an ad hoc but ruthless way, conscious that the existence of the monarchy and empire was at stake.[106]

Rather than planning a counter-revolution, the main military commanders— Windischgrätz, Jelačić, and Radetzky, referred to misleadingly at the time as the trinity 'WJR', as if they were closely connected—sought to reconquer northern Italy, Hungary, Serbia, and some of the cities of Bohemia, Moravia, and *Niederösterreich* for the Habsburg empire.[107] As was to be expected, given his role in March 1848, Windischgrätz was the closest of the three generals to the reactionaries at court, corresponding with Archduchess Sophie—the mother of Franz Joseph—and Empress Maria Anna, and advising Joseph von Lobkowitz, the emperor's adjutant-general, on 29 May that the monarch, at the first sign of danger in the capital, should retire to the Moravian garrison town of Olmütz with as many soldiers as possible, where he would be protected by the general's corps: 'After that, I shall seize Vienna, His Majesty will abdicate in favour of his nephew the Archduke Franz and we will take Pest.'[108] Following the 'Whitsun Uprising' in Prague on 12 June, which had seen students, workers, and artisans taking inspiration from the Panslav Congress, erecting barricades and using guns (with an eventual death toll of forty-three), Windischgrätz began shelling the city, forcing its surrender by 16 June and proving that urban insurrections could be defeated, if commanders were brutal enough. Yet even the 61-year-old general had been obliged to seek permission from the War Minister Theodor de Baillet Latour, who was a member of the moderate administration of Pillersdorf. He then had to wait for mediators to arrive from Vienna on 14 June, attempting but failing to change the course of events by proffering his resignation. Only when his own wife was killed, hit by a stray bullet whilst watching the uprising through an upstairs window, and when mediation had failed, was Windischgrätz able to proceed.

For his part, Radetzky, who was 82 years old, was less overtly political, initially accepting the Pillersdorf constitution in April as 'a guarantee' for 'the best part of

---

[106] Much of the German-speaking *Bürgertum* also feared for the existence of the empire as a result of national conflicts, distancing themselves from Frankfurt and, at times, withholding criticism of the army and monarch: H. Rumpler, *Österreichische Geschichte 1804–1914. Eine Chance für Mitteleuropa* (Vienna, 1997), 282.

[107] Steven Beller, *Francis Joseph* (London, 1996), 48, rightly points out that this dilemma was what the dramatist Franz Grillparzer had in mind: '"In deinem Lager ist Österreich." In your camp is Austria. As with many clichés, Franz Grillparzer's over-used adage about the Habsburg army in 1848 is over-used because it is so accurate.'

[108] Cited in G. Rothenberg, *The Army of Francis Joseph*, 27.

the nation' of 'all the wishes and ideas with which they believe their happiness is bound'.[109] His attitude hardened once a majority in the Reichstag had rejected a motion of thanks to the army in Italy after its victory at the battle of Custozza on 24–25 July, but his priority was still northern Italy and the territorial integrity of the empire, as he spelled out in late September after Latour had sent a circular to army commanders warning them to uphold and respect 'the constitutional institutions and arrangements in the state':

> The hostile feeling against the army in Italy which has often been voiced in the Reichstag and which has found an echo in many other parts of the monarchy—although the best and greatest part of the population thanks God that through the victories won by its misguided support they are spared the need to enter public mourning and that the fatherland has not been dragged through the mire—makes me suspect that the content of Your Excellency's dispatch...was primarily directed against the troops under my command.
>
> The army has no reason to retain any predilection for the system which has fallen. This system was, if it can be called a despotism, a civil not a military despotism. The army was neglected, slighted; it, therefore, expressed no spirit of hostility at all towards the free institutions which His Majesty conferred upon his peoples. The army of Italy was far too occupied with its great and heavy duty to pay any special attention to political goings-on; but when political leadership passed from the hands of experienced statesmen and true patriots to those of adolescents and treacherous rabble-rousers, when the emperor had to leave his capital and seek refuge amongst a loyal race of people, then the army's resentment was aroused.[110]

Like Windischgrätz, Radetzky had had to follow Latour's advice and had fought hard to counter the Foreign Minister Ludwig von Ficquelmont's and his successor Johann von Wessenberg's preference of negotiating a peace with Piedmont-Sardinia and ceding territory in Lombardy. His warning to Latour that indications of Austrian weakness would prolong the war by giving encouragement to Italian forces—'I will negotiate with these people only with a sword in my hand'—eventually prevailed but was met initially by the War Minister's plea to the general 'to think of my position as minister of a constitutional state', despite—'as a soldier'—sharing 'completely the feelings and views which Your Excellency expressed'.[111] Confronted with large-scale desertions of Italian soldiers and fearing future desertion of Hungarians and Croats, because of their conflicting loyalties as a consequence of national conflicts, Radetzky became more and more dismissive of government hesitation and constitutionalism, exacerbated by compromises with the left: 'If the general loses too much time through negotiations, the noose will tighten steadily around me and the survival of my army will become even more difficult.'[112] 'We cannot lose sight of the fact that our authority in this country only extends as far as our weapons',

---

[109] A. v. Windischgrätz to P. Zanini, War Minister, 29 Apr. 1848, cited in A. Sked, *The Survival of the Habsburg Empire*, 158.

[110] A. v. Radetzky to T. Baillet de Latour, 30 Sept. 1848, ibid., 159–60.

[111] Radetzky to Latour, 9 May, and Latour to Radetzky, 14 May 1848, ibid., 137.

[112] A. v. Radetzky to L. v. Ficquelmont, 3 May 1848, ibid.

he wrote to Latour on 26 May, betraying his assumption that northern Italy was another—half-foreign—land.[113] Increasingly buoyed up by support from German-speaking, middle-class, or noble public opinion—'the best...part of the nation', who applauded Johann Strauss's *Radetzky March* (15 August 1848)—and irritated by left-wing politicians and constitutional ministers, who showed little comprehension of the realities of warfare in other parts of the empire, Radetzky and other officers who served in Italy—including Schwarzenberg and Franz Joseph—transferred some of the practices and dispositions of combat back to Vienna.[114]

The conflation of war and revolution in Hungary was much greater than elsewhere in the empire, as Radetzky intimated in his reply to Latour on 30 September 1848:

> Let us cast a painful glance over the desperate position of our army in Hungary; there, Austrian soldiers are fighting one another in the name of the same monarch, which one lot call emperor and the other king. I am bold enough to assert that only the Austrian army is in a position to give such an example of self-abnegation and sacrifice. But from where is the army supposed to derive its love for institutions that can bring forth into the world such moral and political abortions? May this unnatural situation reach a speedy end for otherwise the splendid spirit of the army will be lost.[115]

Far from ending speedily, the 'unnatural situation' persisted, remaining closely tied to events in Vienna, for almost a year. Members of the Habsburg and Hungarian ruling elites had long been suspicious of each other's motives, with Karl von Grünne resigning from the Archduke Stephan's service as Chamberlain because of the Palatine's alleged Magyar sympathies only to be welcomed into that of Archduchess Sophie as an advisor for Franz Joseph, for example. The immediate cause of the Hungarian war, however, was the national conflict between Serbs and Hungarians in the south of the kingdom, encouraging Jelačić—who had been removed as *Ban* on 10 June before being reinstated in September—to invade southern Hungary with his army of 45,000 men on 11 September, without formal dispensation to do so but with the tacit support of Latour and much of the court. On the same day, the moderate liberal Prime Minister of Hungary and former officer in the Habsburg army Lajos Batthyány resigned together with most of his government, leaving Kossuth—who had refused to stand down from office—to push a bill authorizing the creation of a 200,000-strong army of 'home defence' through the Hungarian Diet. Batthyány's attempt to enlist the support of the Palatine or to receive the emperor's sanction for his new government on 25 September failed, leading Ferdinand to send the Hungarian-born Field Marshal Lieutenant Franz Philipp von Lamberg to take charge of the Hungarian army as a royal commissioner. He was lynched as he arrived in Pest on 28 September by a mob which had been

---

[113] Radetzky to Latour, 26 May 1848, ibid., 138.

[114] As a result of his experiences in Italy, Franz Joseph was convinced that the Habsburg required firmness from the monarch and government: A. Wheatcroft, *The Habsburgs: Embodying Empire* (London, 1995), 261.

[115] Radetzky to Latour, 30 Sept. 1848, in Sked, *The Survival of the Habsburg Empire*, 160.

informed of his arrival, his mutilated body subsequently being paraded through the streets impaled on scythes.

The emperor refused to compromise with Batthyány, who resigned for a second time on 2 October. On the next day, Ferdinand issued an imperial manifesto declaring war and appointing Jelačić, who had already engaged the Hungarian army in battle at Pákovd-Velence on 29 September, as imperial representative and commander of all troops in Hungary. From 3 October onwards, approximately 50,000 soldiers who chose—or were compelled—to fight in the Hungarian army of home defence were guilty of treason. Before that date, officers such as Friedrich von Blomberg, a colonel in charge of a Polish cavalry regiment in the Banat, had been ordered by their commanders—in the name of Ferdinand, King of Hungary—to attack *Grenzer* who themselves claimed to have the official author-ization of Ferdinand as Emperor of Austria. Implored by his opposing officer Ferdinand Mayerhofer, Blomberg withdrew his troops, leaving German civilians in the region, who remained loyal to Hungary, at the mercy of Serb forces. Having written to Latour, asking him 'to have pity on us' and to 'recall us from this place of uncertainty', since 'we can no longer bear this terrible dilemma', he was told merely 'to consult his conscience', for the War Minister was 'in no position to exer-cise any influence whatever on the Hungarian situation' after the creation of a separate Hungarian War Ministry in April 1848, as he had explained to Radetzky on 28 June.[116] Both before and after 3 October, the choices facing soldiers were confused by political, national, and imperial allegiances.

The radicalization of the revolution in early October 1848, which prepared the way for a counter-revolution and the imposition of the administration of Schwarzenberg on 21 November, was closely tied to events in Hungary, whose border was just over 30 miles from Vienna. On 6 October, the Richter Grenadier Battalion mutinied rather than board a train in the capital to the neighbouring territory, where they would have had to fight troops whom they considered 'imperial'. A crowd, including units of the National Guard, took control of Vienna, hunting for the Minister of Justice Alexander Bach, who escaped in disguise, and besieging the War Ministry, from which Latour was taken, stabbed, stripped, and hung up on a lamp-post on a central square. The royal family left the Hofburg, only a quar-ter of a mile away, the next morning with a large military escort, making its way to Olmütz, as Windischgrätz had advised in May. The 8,000 troops left in Vienna withdrew to positions on the edge of the city and awaited the forces of Jelačić, who had used the opportunity to extricate himself from an unsuccessful campaign in Hungary, and of Windischgrätz, who arrived from Bohemia in mid-October to assemble a force of fifty-nine battalions, sixty-seven squadrons, and 200 guns. The revolutionaries in Vienna, who had about 50,000 badly trained men at their disposal, hoped for Hungarian assistance, although never officially requesting it, despite the fact that Hungarian soldiers crossed the border on three occasions and

---

[116] Blomberg cited in I. Deák, *Beyond Nationalism*, 34–5; also, I. Deák, *The Lawful Revolution: Louis Kossuth and the Hungarians, 1848–1849* (New York, 1979), 140–1. Latour to Radetzky, 28 June 1848, in A. Sked, *The Survival of the Habsburg Empire*, 72.

were repelled by Austrian forces at Schwechat—only 7 miles from the city—as late as 30 October, after which the remaining revolutionary fighters capitulated. Contemporaries commented that order was preserved inside the city, with the Reichstag continuing to meet until the 22nd. As in Prague, Windischgrätz was less restrained than the revolutionaries, ordering a full military assault on Vienna on 28 October, resulting in three to five times more deaths amongst civilians than amongst soldiers from a total of 1,200 military casualties and 3,000 civilian ones, according to one estimate.[117] The attack honoured the promise which he had given in his proclamation to the Viennese on 20 October to declare a state of siege, place civilian authorities under military ones, and allow the imposition of summary justice, threatening the 'rebels with the full severity of military law'.[118]

Such killing and wounding was unprecedented in the German revolutions of 1848–9 and resulted, at least in part, from military tactics and deployments characteristic of warfare, which had already taken place in Italy and Hungary, rather than from the suppression of revolts, which had traditionally corresponded to the internal policing function of the army.[119] Amongst many other reactionary observers, Schwarzenberg, who had been promised the minister-presidency in secret on 19 October by Emperor Ferdinand, showed in a report to Radetzky on the 22nd how external concerns informed internal policy in the empire: on the one hand, revolutionaries were understood to belong to a 'European party of insurrection', who had selected Vienna because of its 'easily moved, wholly politically immature and, in part, morally corrupt population'; on the other hand, it was necessary 'to maintain the undiminished integrity of the Reich', not least by intervening in Hungary to 'place it in a relationship corresponding to this basis'.[120] The new ministry's programme would be 'suppression of insurrection everywhere and at any cost, defence of the rights of the dynasty against the attacks of the revolution, recognition of the freedom granted by the emperor to his peoples, regulation of this freedom internally and the maintenance of the integrity of the monarchy externally'.[121] Unbridled ruthlessness against the insurrectionaries was tied, it appeared, to the safeguarding of the monarchy abroad. To an extent, the German public's appalled reaction to the execution on 9 November of Robert Blum, who had travelled to Vienna in an official delegation from the Frankfurt Parliament, revealed the gap which had emerged between thresholds of violence in the German states and in the Habsburg empire.[122] 'Something like this', recorded the publisher

---

[117] J. Polišensky, *Aristocrats and the Crowd in the Revolutionary Year 1848* (Albany, NY, 1980), 195. Note that the total of casualties includes the wounded as well as the dead.

[118] Cited in Peter Reichel, *Robert Blum. Ein deutscher Revolutionär 1807–1848* (Göttingen, 2007), 160, who calls the proclamation 'a declaration of war against the Viennese population'.

[119] The question of deaths as a result of military operations is separate from that of later reprisals and executions, which are said by Rothenberg to have been 'moderate', although still exceeding those elsewhere in Germany: G. E. Rothenberg, *The Army of Francis Joseph*, 31.

[120] Schwarzenberg to Radetzky, 22 October, cited in S. Lippert, *Felix Fürst zu Schwarzenberg. Eine politische Biographie* (Stuttgart, 1998), 165.

[121] Ibid.

[122] Schwarzenberg, of course, also intended Blum's execution to be a symbol of the seriousness of a European counter-revolution: M. Hettling, *Totenkult statt Revolution*, 58.

Heinrich Brockhaus, a political critic of Blum, 'may not and cannot happen'.[123] Nowhere was the gap more salient than in Hungary, with the intermingling of national independence, moderate constitutionalism, revolution, civil war, and inter-state conflict, as 170,000 men and 508 field guns were arrayed on the Hungarian side against Habsburg forces by the summer of 1849. On Austria's victory, achieved after the intervention of 150,000 Russian troops in June, 490 Hungarian officers were courtmartialled and 231 given death sentences, which were generally commuted into prison terms except for those of the leaders, thirteen of whom were executed on 6 October; 114 civilians, including Batthyány, were executed and 1,765 were imprisoned, with a further 4,628 military and civilian cases being passed on to the Central Military Investigating Commission in Vienna, which continued its work until December 1850. Even Tsar Nicholas I, who was worried about the outcry in European presses and diplomatic establishments, complained about the scope of Austrian prosecutions and executions.[124] Nothing similar was witnessed in other German states.

Conservative elites in Germany were certainly not critical of Austria's actions, as Schwarzenberg was aware.[125] Even in Blum's native state of Saxony, whose liberal government had sent a protest note to Vienna, Friedrich Ferdinand von Beust, the country's envoy in Berlin, could be found on 21 November 1848 warning against criticism which could damage diplomatic relations with the Habsburg monarchy.[126] In Prussia, the army and the reactionary camarilla around Friedrich Wilhelm IV broadly approved of Schwarzenberg's and Windischgrätz's actions, noting—in the words of the Chief of the General Staff Helmuth von Moltke in Magdeburg—that 'the three bullets on the Prater have not only hit Robert Blum, but also many others in Germany'.[127] Yet they paid relatively little attention to those actions beyond unspecified references to 'the impact of Viennese news', as Ludwig von Gerlach recorded without further elaboration in his diary on 11 October, not least because they appeared distant from and inapplicable to conditions in the Hohenzollern monarchy.[128] The Gerlach brothers, Friedrich Wilhelm von Rauch, Edwin von Manteuffel, Ludwig von Massow, Alexander von Keller, Ernst Senfft von Pilsach, Marcus Niebuhr, and Heinrich Leo were planning to impose a 'military ministry' under General Friedrich Wilhelm von Brandenburg—commander of the Sixth Army Corps in Breslau—from September onwards, backed by ultras such as Hans Hugo von Kleist-Retzow and Otto von Bismarck-Schönhausen in the Berlin National Assembly and in the so-called '*Junkerparlament*', which was the permanent general assembly of the *Verein zur Wahrung der Interessen des Grundbesitzes und zur Förderung des Wohlstands aller Klassen*, founded on 24 July 1848.[129] This imposition

---

[123] Cited ibid., 60. Also, P. Reichel, *Robert Blum. Ein deutscher Revolutionär*, 178–99.
[124] M. Hettling, *Totenkult statt Revolution*, 264.
[125] Ibid., 58.   [126] Ibid., 59.   [127] Ibid.
[128] Ibid.; E. L. v. Gerlach, *Von der Revolution zum Norddeutschen Bund. Politik und Ideengut der preussischen Hochkonservativen 1848–1866*, ed. H. Diwald (Göttingen, 1970), vol. 1, 121. There are very few references in Gerlach's diary or correspondence to events in Austria, despite his political sympathy for his counterparts in Vienna and his championing of close cooperation between Austria and Prussia.
[129] E. L. v. Gerlach, 9 Sept. 1848, in E. L. Gerlach, *Von der Revolution*, vol. 1, 111–12.

involved the use of force, with Friedrich Heinrich Ernst von Wrangel having deployed 50,000 soldiers around Berlin and having organized a military parade into the centre of the city from his headquarters in Charlottenburg on 9 October, after his appointment as military governor of the 'Marches' in mid-September. As Brandenburg and his ministers appeared in front of the National Assembly in the capital's *Schauspielhaus* exactly one month later, prior to Wrangel's occupation of Berlin with 13,000 troops at two o'clock on the 9th, they were protected, as Bismarck recalled, by a 'strong posse of police' and 'about thirty of the best shots in the light infantry battalions of the guard', who 'were so disposed that they could appear in the body of the house and the galleries at a given signal; they were unerring marksmen, and could cover the ministers with their muskets if they were actually threatened'.[130]

According to Ludwig von Gerlach, the King of Prussia needed strong ministers who could stand up to large-scale popular unrest.[131] Gerlach's programme for those ministers, which he had passed on to Friedrich Wilhelm IV on 19 October, had been designed to show that 'the king *and his ministers* are independent vis-à-vis the assembly', which was to be prevented from undertaking 'the reshaping of the entire country'.[132] 'On a count of heads', the conservative leader declared, the assembly was in 'the greatest fever of revolution'.[133] 'This completely altered position of the *Ministerii* must not simply be adopted, but it must be made clear to the assembly and the country', he went on: 'This path could and *probably would* lead to a *break* with the assembly and to its dissolution', corresponding to the monarch's 'full, formal and material right', to be maintained 'by force of arms, if need be, for which we must be prepared'.[134] Given the perceived illegality and extremism of his opponents, Brandenburg was expected to throw out all measures encroaching on 'the royal prerogative' and undermining public order, such as the hindering of 'police and the judiciary through the *habeus corpus* acts' and through 'the abolition of *the death penalty*' during a period when 'murder gains the upper hand to a previously unknown degree'.[135] Instead, the new Minister-President was to guarantee security:

> The securing of the assembly against the terrorism of the mob through a law like the Frankfurt one [prohibiting demonstrations near the parliament] or the displacement of the assembly—the dissolution of the same as the measure of last recourse—arming for this case, countering insurrectionary enterprises and maintaining legal conditions through the force of arms—and, in the event that the ministry retains a majority in this way, the laying of the constitutional foundations which make the throne and fatherland secure.[136]

Now that a 'strong, loyal, pugnacious army' stood 'in and around Berlin', reactionaries were willing to contemplate the use of violence.[137]

---

[130] Cited in J. Steinberg, *Bismarck*, 98.
[131] D. E. Barclay, *Frederick William IV and the Prussian Monarchy*, 175.
[132] E. L. v. Gerlach, 'Regierungsplan für Graf Brandenburg', 19 Oct. 1848, in E. L. v. Gerlach, *Von der Revolution*, vol. 2, 591.
[133] Ibid.   [134] Ibid.   [135] Ibid., 590.   [136] Ibid., 592.   [137] Ibid., 590.

Few Prussian conservatives envisaged warlike conditions or an escalation of violence akin to that experienced in the Habsburg empire, however. Occasionally, they fantasized about emulating the French general and War Minister Louis Eugène Cavaignac, who had put down the June uprising in Paris at the cost of 4,000 workers' and 1,600 soldiers' lives before being granted all executive powers by the French assembly, but they seem not to have planned for such an eventuality. Thus, Leopold von Gerlach—Ludwig's brother and a major-general in the Prussian army—argued in late July 1848 that a 'military (reactionary) ministry' had 'to be avoided, if at all possible', for 'something like that can only go ahead, once the sovereign *Volk* has been cavaignacked', which had not occurred and did not, in most foreseeable scenarios, seem likely to occur.[138] Sometimes, members of the camarilla used military terms, with Ludwig von Gerlach, for example, encouraging Friedrich Wilhelm IV in early October to consider an 'alteration of the entire ministry and of the system' and 'the widening prospects' of a 'war', by which he meant 'an *internal* war' (as he specified in a marginal comment), to bring the alteration about.[139] Yet reactionaries' campaigns were directed at domestic political opponents on the ground of a 'revolution', not against external or demonic 'enemies'. 'Revolutionary tyranny' was to be 'resisted', as Gerlach had expressed it in a manifesto 'for Bismarck and others' on 26 March 1848, because it threatened 'property,... German law, a German constitution, German freedom, and everything which is dear and holy for us on this earth', but it was necessary to stay within the law, emphasizing the illegality of the Frankfurt and Berlin National Assemblies' 'usurpation' of monarchs' and states' powers.[140] On 19 October Gerlach wrote:

> Within the limits of strict *legality*—with affectionate attention given to the March words of the king, which, although not legal norms, are still not to be separated from the person of the king—and carried out with just as much *principled firmness* as practical *prudence* and *calm*, the undertaking to free the throne and fatherland from usurpation will appeal to all loyal hearts.[141]

For similar reasons, reactionaries were anxious to avoid the term 'coup' (*Staatsstreich*), 'which no loyal subject...would wish or suggest'.[142] They were also unwilling to contemplate the possibility of a 'dictatorship', other than in desperation, since it was tantamount to an acceptance of illegality or illegitimacy: 'we are not yet so far', Ludwig assured his brother in September.[143] For much of the year, reactionaries were competing with more moderate conservatives, including the Minister-President Ernst von Pfuel and the Catholic officer, diplomat, and courtier Joseph Maria von Radowitz, for their vacillating monarch's attention. With hindsight, Leopold von Gerlach was convinced that 'Rauch, Massow, Ludwig and I were the only ones

---

[138] L. v. Gerlach, *Denkwürdigkeiten* (Berlin, 1891), vol. 1, 179–80.
[139] E. L. v. Gerlach, 11 Oct. 1848, in E. L. v. Gerlach, *Von der Revolution*, vol. 1, 121.
[140] Cited in H.-C. Kraus, *Ernst Ludwig von Gerlach*, 399.
[141] E. L. v. Gerlach, 11 Oct. 1848, in E. L. v. Gerlach, *Von der Revolution*, vol. 2, 589.
[142] E. L. v. Gerlach, cited in H.-C. Kraus, *Ernst Ludwig von Gerlach*, 441–2. They were not always consistent, mentioning 'coup' in private from time to time.
[143] Ibid., 456.

from April 1848 to November 1848' forming the consistent core of the camarilla and preventing the triumph of the revolution: 'Leopold says, without our activity since 7 September, Waldeck [the democratic chair of the Berlin National Assembly's constitutional committee, who amended the government's draft, limiting monarchical powers] would be minister.'[144] They were unlikely to win support for radical, counter-revolutionary repression, notwithstanding Friedrich Wilhelm IV's militant assertions on 11, 15, and 19 September that he would compel the abandonment of the draft constitution by dissolution and force, if necessary.[145] Although 'ready to take on everything that is asked of him', Brandenburg, too, was wary of being seen as a puppet of the camarilla, showing himself to be 'calm, clear, with a very healthy human understanding, modest and, in the best sense, ambitious'.[146] His aim in late November was 'to save the country, which has been revolutionized from above, from anarchy', and to reverse the 'disrespect' to which the 'world of civil servants and, almost, the army' had been subjected, but in an incremental way, concentrating on what was possible not on what was best.[147] This desire to avoid extremes was, it can be held, visible at the height of the crisis on 9 November in the widely shared assumption amongst conservatives—in Bismarck's account— 'that at the first shot', if it were required, 'all who were present would speedily vacate the body of the house', just as 'it was assumed that even large masses, meeting there [in front of the *Schauspielhaus*], would scatter as soon as shots were fired'.[148] The king had left open the issue of 'a bloody or unbloody victory in Berlin' in his letter to Brandenburg of 27 October.[149] The Minister-President himself, like his monarch, preferred and expected to avoid mass killing.

There were many reasons for civilian and military elites' restraint in Prussia, compared to the lowering or absence of interdictions against killing in the Habsburg empire during 1848–9. One reason derived from an earlier lack of restraint in March 1848, which had led to an unexpectedly large number of casualties, galvanizing the resistance of the population—burghers as well as workers—in Berlin and other cities and regions, and dividing the ruling elites themselves. If Varnhagen von Ense is to be believed, the Prince of Prussia, who had favoured further military action to crush the revolutionaries on 18–19 March, had shouted at Friedrich

---

[144] Cited in D. E. Barclay, *Frederick William IV and the Prussian Monarchy*, 157; E. L. v. Gerlach, 18 Oct. 1848, in E. L. v. Gerlach, *Von der Revolution*, vol. 1, 128.

[145] G. Grünthal, 'Zwischen König, Kabinett und Kamarilla. Der Verfassungsoktroi in Preußen vom 5 Dezember 1848', *Jahrbuch für die Geschichte Mittel- und Ostdeutschlands*, 32 (1983), 179–219, suggests that the king was still undecided and subject to many other forces, affecting his decision. For the king's promemoria on 15 Sept. 1848, see Friedrich Wilhelm IV, *Revolutionsbriefe 1848*, ed. K. Haenchen (Leipzig, 1930), 175–8.

[146] L. v. Gerlach to E. L. v. Gerlach, 10 Oct. 1848, cited in H.-C. Kraus, *Ernst Ludwig von Gerlach*, 447.

[147] E. L. v. Gerlach, *Aufzeichnungen aus seinem Leben und Wirken 1795–1877*, ed. J. v Gerlach (Schwerin, 1903), vol. 2, 29.

[148] Cited in J. Steinberg, *Bismarck*, 98.

[149] Friedrich Wilhelm IV to F. W. v. Brandenburg, 27 Oct. 1848, in Friedrich Wilhelm IV, *Revolutionsbriefe 1848*, 219, reiterating his reference to 'the use of victory, whether it is a peaceful one (which God wishes to grant!) or a bloody one', after the deployment of troops: '*I* am prepared for this [the attempt by the Berlin National Assembly to sit permanently rather than be dissolved] through the concentration of 30,000 men around Berlin.'

Wilhelm IV at the height of the crisis: 'I've always known that you're a babbler, but not that you're a coward!'[150] The camarilla's caution, with the Gerlachs warning against precipitate action during the summer and early autumn of 1848, resulted partly from a desire to avoid a repetition of such division and partly from a fear of provoking further revolution, which 'is becoming weaker from day to day', according to Ludwig von Gerlach on 27 August, but which remained powerful, not least because of the backing of Frankfurt.[151] Bismarck was not alone, after the event, to be surprised at the ease with which revolutionaries were disarmed on 10 November, with the army conducting house-to-house searches and seizing 'eighty to ninety percent of the weapons': 'Passive resistance turns out more and more to be a cover for weakness. The military in addition to ensuring calm and order turns out to be popular and the number of the angry reduces itself to the fanatics, the rogues and the barricadists.'[152] Before the event, reactionaries were more hesitant.

Another reason for reactionaries' hesitancy was furnished by the moderation of the Camphausen (29 March to 20 June), Auerswald-Hansemann (25 June to 8 September), and Pfuel ministries (21 September to 1 November), which refrained from forcing a showdown between conservatives in the court and army and liberals and democrats in the government and National Assembly. Thus, although reactionaries were dismissive of the designs of all liberal governments, despite the presence of Rudolf von Auerswald (a Hussar officer and childhood friend of the king) and Ernst von Pfuel (the military governor of Berlin between 11 and 18 March), they and their more moderate conservative colleagues were not obliged to choose between 'revolution' and 'counter-revolution', to the point where it became difficult for the camarilla to demonstrate that ministers had functioned as 'servants, not—as they claim—of an impotent crown, but of an all-powerful assembly'.[153] For its part, the Provisional Central Power in Frankfurt refused to endorse a campaign in Prussia to withhold taxes in protest at the prorogation and exile of Berlin's National Assembly, even after the imposition of Brandenburg's 'military ministry' on 2 November and of a new constitution on 5 December, which was less liberal but retained universal manhood suffrage and the assembly's veto over legislation, allowing pragmatic deputies in the Frankfurt Parliament to banish the thought of a counter-revolution and to continue their business as usual. As in Frankfurt itself, where Prussian troops had overcome radical protesters in September 1848, deputies could be thankful that a more damaging escalation of violence had been avoided, though no liberal or democrat would have gone so far—as the *Kreuzzeitung* did—as to label it 'the first great work of German unity and harmony'.[154]

The principal reason for the comparative restraint of the Prussian army within the borders of the Hohenzollern monarchy during 1848–9, it could be contended, was related to the continuing distinction made by elites between revolution and

---

[150] D. E. Barclay, *Frederick William IV and the Prussian Monarchy*, 143.
[151] Cited in in H.-C. Kraus, *Ernst Ludwig von Gerlach*, 433.
[152] O. v. Bismarck to his brother, 11 Nov. 1848, in J. Steinberg, *Bismarck*, 98.
[153] E. L. v. Gerlach, 'Regierungsplan für Graf Brandenburg', 19 Oct. 1848, in E. L. v. Gerlach, *Von der Revolution*, vol. 2, 590.
[154] *Neue Preußische Zeitung*, 22 Sept. 1848.

warfare, despite their prosecution of a war against Denmark over Schleswig-Holstein between 24 March and 26 August. Unlike in the Habsburg empire, Prussia's 'national' war, which it conducted in the name of the *Bund* and subsequently the Reich, remained external and peripheral, a source of agreement and strength rather than division, secession, and collapse. Initially, the conflict had garnered the support of German liberals and democrats for the Prussian state, giving the kingdom's old elites the opportunity to regroup. Consequently, there was no risk that the tactics and imperatives of a life-or-death struggle abroad would affect the deployment of the military against revolutionaries at home. Indeed, at least some officers did not consider the conflict over Schleswig-Holstein a 'war' at all, reduced to a 'sad episode', in Leopold von Gerlach's phrase in April, akin to the restoration of order in Posen.[155] Liberals and democrats were critical of Prussia's withdrawal from the conflict and its signature of a truce at Malmö on 26 August without the agreement of the Central Power and Frankfurt Parliament, which went on to reject the convention in early September—since the war had been declared the affair of the Reich—before changing its mind a few days later in the face of Prussian intransigence, with narrow majorities on both occasions and the 'September uprising' following the second occasion. However, their objections made little impression on Prussian conservatives, who appear to have viewed the intervention as a traditional, anti-revolutionary form of confederal 'execution'. 'The Holstein-Schleswig affair is in truth a sad entanglement', wrote Gerlach on 15 July:

> The land of Holstein has been agitated into resistance against its rulers, on the ground of genuine contraventions of the law in my opinion, to the point of war; it is natural, after these events, that it cannot now be deterred, and so Prussia, Hanover and Mecklenburg must provide troops in order to prevent the constitution of a republic in Holstein. And this land was the most tranquil in the whole of Germany![156]

Most conservatives in Prussia seem to have understood military intervention in the Palatinate and Baden in the same way, even if sometimes styled as a war, as Gerlach had suggested at the beginning of the conflict on 2 May 1849: 'So, now a war against the Paulskirche is coming; that is, against the revolution, which a year ago we certainly could not have hoped.'[157]

In late 1849, Friedrich Wilhelm IV, who had railed against remaining revolutionaries as 'rebellious murderers and bloodhounds' in May, approved the erection of a 'memorial monument to the Baden campaign' at Babelsberg, next to the Prince of Prussia's palace. In 1850–1, he oversaw the construction of another memorial at Sanssouci, which boasted friezes representing the return of Prussia's victorious warriors.[158] Nevertheless, as the campaign occurred in the summer of 1849, it was widely seen in conservative circles as a limited intervention within the terms set by the treaties of the German Confederation, as one Prussian counsellor testified in a justificatory statement intended to reassure the *Mittelstaaten* on 4 June:

---

[155] L. v. Gerlach, 13 Apr. 1848, in L. v. Gerlach, *Denkwürdigkeiten*, vol. 1, 151: the real war which the king, Wilhelm von Willisen, and he were worried about was with Russia, in alliance with France.
[156] Ibid., 174.   [157] Ibid., 317.
[158] D. E. Barclay, *Frederick William IV and the Prussian Monarchy*, 195–6.

Prussia has, in its various moves, largely had in view the moral pacification of Germany. True to its principles, . . . it will limit itself to remain in a political relationship of alliance with these lands [Bavaria, Württemberg, Baden, Hohenzollern, Liechtenstein] which emanates from the body of the *Bundesakte* of 1815. At the same time, however, Prussia declares that it is ready, immediately and fully, to maintain all those South German states which ask for its military support for the taming of the revolution, in the spirit and on the basis of the Acts of Confederation of 1815.

Prussia would thus appear before the world in a light of the greatest selflessness and its troops, which are pushing into South Germany in order to restore order, may encounter comparatively less resistance from the populations there.[159]

In correspondence with Otto von Manteuffel on 28 June, the same counsellor reiterated that it had been 'important' for Prussia 'to act against the South German revolutionary movement' in the manner that it had, demonstrating its 'moral superiority, in war as in politics, to the other German states'. 'It has been evident for weeks that this movement or, more accurately, this open uprising would limit itself to Baden and the Palatinate', he went on, just as 'the success of its violent suppression was beyond doubt', as a consequence of the actions of the Prussian 'army of execution'.[160] Conservative elites in Prussia were deliberately restoring order in Germany as a whole within the boundaries and in accordance with the precedents—adapted to new revolutionary conditions—of the German Confederation. This self-understanding helped to ward off a further escalation of violence and the prospect of 'civil war'.

Prussian elites were able to act as they did because they could rely on the army, which gave them control of the most effective means of violent coercion.[161] In the Rhineland, some *Landwehr* units—in Aachen, Cologne, Elberfeld, and Trier, for instance—criticized the administration in Berlin and supported the Frankfurt and Berlin National Assemblies in November 1848 and in May–July 1849, but the army of the line remained loyal to the monarch and his newly imposed conservative government, with Westphalian and Saxon as well as East Elbian regiments being deployed successfully during the tax boycott in late November and being used in the occupation of the Palatinate and Baden during the following summer.[162] Conservative elites in other German states were in a weaker position. In Baden, which became the focus of the campaign for the Reich Constitution and the locus

---

[159] H. C. W. Küpfer to O. v. Manteuffel, 4 June 1849, in O. v. Manteuffel, *Unter Friedrich Wilhlem IV*, ed. H. v. Poschinger, 3 vols (Berlin, 1901), 136–7.

[160] Küpfer to O. v. Manteuffel, 28 June 1849, ibid., 140.

[161] Otto von Mülmann, 1849, *Kriegsbriefe* Archive, Universitäts- und Landesbibliothek Bonn, gave a revealing account of the way 'rebels' were viewed: troops occupying Iserlohn were ordered not to fire unless they were fired upon from behind the desultory barricades which had been erected. Once firing began, the troops remained in a vastly superior position, acting like forces of order rather than soldiers at war: more than seventy civilians were estimated to have died but only two soldiers.

[162] S. Müller, *Soldaten in der deutschen Revolution*, 294–300, contesting Jonathan Sperber's thesis, *Rhineland Radicals*, 366–86. Paul Theis to 'Rosalie', 17 May 1849, *Kriegsbriefe* Archive, Universitäts- und Landesbibliothek Bonn, reported on events in Elberfeld: 'Even a few days beforehand, popular assemblies had met, in which rebellion and insurrection were preached under the pretext of German unity and, in particular, the *Landwehr* which had been called up was asked to disobey their king, to whom they had sworn an oath of loyalty.' Shortly afterwards, however, order had been restored.

of the end of the revolution in Germany, the Grand Duke had been forced to flee in May 1849, obliging soldiers to make a choice between their ruler and a new republican 'executive commission'. The chances of a descent into civil war seemed to have been increased by the occurrence of a mutiny at the fortress of Rastatt on 11 May, which triggered civil unrest, and the support of soldiers for the democratic *Volksversammlung* at Offenburg, which was attended by 20,000 and framed a series of demands for new elections, a constituent assembly, and the establishment of a radical republic.

As the mutiny took place, the War Minister General-Lieutenant Friedrich Hoffmann rushed to Rastatt with mounted artillery and troops from the 1st Dragoon Regiment in order to talk to the mutineers. 'They all declared that they supported the Reich Constitution, that they stood by the *Volk* in this respect, and they asked that the government do everything in its power to achieve the full implementation of the *Reichsverfassung*', he wrote to the Reich War Ministry in Frankfurt on 12 May: 'They also declared that they would regard the troops of those governments which had not recognized the Reich Constitution as enemies.'[163] When soldiers subsequently paraded through the streets shouting 'we demand our rights' and calling for a reckoning with their 'officer dogs' and for the incarceration of the War Minister in Struve's cell in the fortress, Hoffmann attempted to intervene with the soldiers who had accompanied him from Karlsruhe, but more than half of them, after being overpowered, defected to the camp of the mutineers.[164] On his return to Karlsruhe, the War Minister's attempts to avert dissent by permitting troops to swear an oath to the Reich Constitution came to nothing, with half of the Life Guard Infantry Regiment gathering with civilians in front of the barracks and calling for 'Prisoners out! Up with Hecker! Republic!'[165] After the revolt had spread to Mannheim, implicating troops who had put down demonstrations for the Reich Constitution only days earlier, Hoffmann fled to Württemberg with a small number of loyal soldiers. A large majority of troops, however, remained in Baden on the 'revolutionary' side, accepting the new authorities. They therefore avoided the dilemma of Habsburg soldiers in Hungary, many of whom had been moved or compelled to fight against their own incumbent government. By contrast, the small band who had marched to Württemberg with the War Minister had divided loyalties, with some escaping back to Baden and with the remainder reduced to tears, fixated on 'the idea that we would be massacred' by two to three thousand *Freischärler*, who were rumoured to be in pursuit.[166] Civil war had been avoided because most of the army accepted the legitimacy of the new republic.

The uprising in Baden had the potential to provoke a civil war in Germany, not because of 'the example which the Badenese *Volk*, united with the Badenese army, gave to the entire German fatherland', as Struve put it, but because of the pitting of regular and irregular troops on the side of the 'revolution', Reich Constitution, and National Assembly against regular soldiers, spearheaded by the Prussian army

---

[163] Cited in S. Müller, *Soldaten in der deutschen Revolution*, 261.
[164] Ibid., 262–4.　　　[165] Ibid., 266.　　　[166] Ibid., 268–9.

and accompanied by the Hessian and Prussian forces of the *Bund*, on the side of a 'counter-revolution'.[167] Friedrich Wilhelm IV was not alone in characterizing the revolutionary fighters who had ended up in Baden by May 1849 as 'the filth of all the nations', to be combated in a campaign which extended beyond individual states.[168] 'Only *action* can help the old regime back to life', the king wrote to Radowitz on 29 May: 'Action is the main thing. And we understand each other— the action which *I* am talking about—is *victory over an armed revolution*.'[169] The campaign did not metamorphose into a German *Bürgerkrieg* because the armies of the 'reactionary' states were overwhelmingly stronger than those of their oppon- ents, encouraging commanders and their governments to stay within the bounds of a confederal 'execution', and because they remained loyal, rendered obedient by their training, the threat of court martial, indoctrination by officers, and the fact that they were operating in another land, which was perceived by many recruits to be 'foreign'.[170]

In some states, officers acknowledged that such loyalty was limited and precarious. In Stuttgart, the soldiers who cleared the streets of demonstrators—as deputies of the 'Rump Parliament' were forced to leave Württemberg on 18 June 1849—came, not from the capital, but from the 'old territories' around Ludwigsburg and Cannstatt and from the 'new' and largely peaceable area of the Donaukreis. In Munich, the king was visibly anxious on 29 June not to reverse 'the outstanding spirit of the soldiers' through 'too strict a set of measures', which might redound to the advantage of 'those with bad intentions'.[171] Only a fortnight earlier, a secessionist provisional government had still exercised power in the Bavarian Palatinate, supported by 13,000 fighters, after more than a third of the kingdom's troops stationed there—2,341 out of 6,500 men—had deserted.[172] Yet the same fighters had capitulated to a Prussian army of 30,000 by 14 June with little bloodshed, suggesting that few were willing to sacrifice their lives for a doomed revolutionary cause; 333 insurrectionaries, a third of whom came from outside the state, were tried by the Bavarian authorities for treason or armed rebellion but none is executed. Some escaped to Baden, where the fighting was much bloodier and punishments were much harsher. Court martials and civilian law courts issued 1,000 verdicts, in addition to summary justice dispensed during the campaign itself, with about 80,000 revolutionaries—or one in eighteen of the population in Baden—eventually emigrating.[173] Here too, though, most fighters surrendered and the death toll, compared to that in the Habsburg

---

[167] G. Struve, *Geschichte der drei Volkserhebungen in Baden*, 289. Most Prussian forces had not belonged to the *Bund*, and therefore not to the Reich under the Provisional Central Power, which was understood by the Prussian government and military to have collapsed by May 1849. Contemporaries like Varnhagen von Ense referred to a 'counter-revolution' and 'attempts at reaction' from autumn 1848 onwards: for instance, K. A. Varnhagen v. Ense, diary entry, 1 Nov. 1848, in K. A. Varnhagen v. Ense, *Tagebücher*, vol. 5, 259.

[168] D. E. Barclay, *Frederick William IV and the Prussian Monarchy*, 195–6.

[169] Friedrich Wilhelm IV to C. M. v. Radowitz, in S. Müller, *Soldaten in der deutschen Revolution*, 98.

[170] Ibid., 121–91, 288–310.

[171] Maximilian II, marginal comment, 29 June 1849, ibid., 302.   [172] Ibid., 280.

[173] The estimate comes from Veit Valentin, *Geschichte der deutschen Revolution von 1848–49*, vol. 2, 448–544.

monarchy, was limited. Revolution and war had not remained separate but they were still distinguishable from each other in the eyes of most contemporaries. What was more, the war waged by Prussian, Hessian, and Bavarian troops was perceived to be a specific type of confederal intervention, which imposed historical constraints on commanders and rulers, albeit within the new context of a European and German struggle between revolutionaries and counter-revolutionaries. In this qualified sense, German soldiers and other fighters had little direct experience in 1848–9, outside Austria, of the violence of inter-state conflicts and, especially, civil war. The next chapter examines how soldiers and civilians of the German states experienced such warfare vicariously, through the reportage of other states' wars.

5

War Reports

Were the years after 1815 a period of peace? To Julius von Wickede, the principal war correspondent of *Die Gartenlaube* and one of the most famous military writers of the 1850s and 1860s, the early nineteenth century had been characterized by a series of 'struggles' and 'campaigns' in South America, Greece, Poland, Spain, and Algeria, in which the subjects of his books had fought as adventurers, mercenaries, and professional soldiers.[1] To many other observers of European affairs, like a 'former Bavarian officer' writing anonymously in the *Allgemeine Zeitung* in 1851, 'thirty-three years had elapsed and Europe had enjoyed a peace which, it appeared, would never end'.[2] If this 'golden peace' had continued, contemporaries would again have been faced with the spectacle, as in the Holy Roman Empire, of having pictures of grenadiers painted onto their guard-houses, since real guards would no longer be needed, he went on.[3] Yet peace had not proved durable, with wars involving European Great Powers breaking out in northern Italy, Hungary, and Schleswig-Holstein in 1848, in the Crimea in 1853, and in Italy again in 1859.[4] Together, such conflicts occupied a prominent place in eight of the sixteen years between 1848 and 1863, after which the wars of German unification began. Although later widely understood to constitute an historical caesura, these wars, too, were seen by most contemporaries as the extension of a single era of international instability, in which the years of conflict outnumbered those of peace.

The escalation of each conflict seemed likely, reawakening fears of a European conflagration—which had never entirely disappeared—akin to those of the revolutionary and Napoleonic periods.[5] Britain had threatened to join the conflict in

---

[1] J. v. Wickede (ed.), *Ein Soldaten-Leben. Erinnerungen aus den napoleonischen, südamerikanischen, griechischen, polnischen, spanischen und algerischen Feldzügen*, 2nd edn, (2 vols, Stuttgart, 1854), vol. 1, viii. Also, J. v. Wickede, 'Kriegerleben in Algerien', *Gartenlaube*, 1854, vol. 18, 206–8, and vol. 19, 219–21.

[2] *Allgemeine Zeitung*, 4 Apr. 1851. See also *Grenzboten*, 1855, vol. 13, no. 4, 58: 'This period of peace has been a long one and, in a certain sense, first ended with the Crimea expedition.'

[3] *Allgemeine Zeitung*, 4 Apr. 1851.

[4] The best work on the destabilization of the states' system after 1848—especially given the impact of the Crimean War—remains P. W. Schroeder, *Austria, Great Britain and the Crimean War: The Destruction of the European Concert* (Ithaca, NY, 1972). See also W. E. Mosse, *The European Powers and the German Question, 1848–71* (New York, 1969); A. Doering-Manteuffel, *Die deutsche Frage und das europäische Staatensystem 1815–1871*, 2nd edn (Munich, 2001); F. R. Bridge, *The Habsburg Monarchy among the Great Powers, 1815–1918* (Oxford, 1990); J. Angelow, *Vom Wiener Kongress zur Pariser Konferenz* (Göttingen, 1991); and F. J. Müller, *Britain and the German Question* (Basingstoke, 2002).

[5] Even Great Powers on the 'right side' were criticized in the German press: see, for example, *Kladderadatsch*'s depiction (1855, vol. 8, 196) of a French eagle and a British lion feeding on the carcass of Sevastopol and throwing tidbits to Turkey and Sardinia.

northern Germany in 1848–51; Russia had given military assistance to Austria in Hungary in 1849; and the Habsburg and Hohenzollern monarchies had been poised to join France, Britain, and the Ottoman Empire against Russia in 1853–6, which had appeared to offer 'a chance of a war of all Europe against Russia', as Marx and Engels eagerly put it.[6] Prussia and other German states had anticipated participation in the war between Piedmont, France, and Austria in 1859. What was more, colonial, national, and civil wars outside Europe had become increasingly difficult to ignore, with the American Civil War, in particular, appearing as an augury of the worst effects of modern warfare in general. Eventually, wrote Wickede from a more optimistic point of view, 'the mythical idea of a perpetual peace', which—he claimed—had 'dominated so many minds' before 1848, had disappeared forever, along with 'that mad notion of the dispensability or even burden of an army which is well-trained and ready for war, even in peacetime'.[7] The 1850s and 1860s seemed to prove, as historians and other commentators had continued to believe throughout the years after 1815, that war was inevitable.

Contemporaries' impressions of such wars were, to a large extent, the product of press reportage, which was combined with an eclectic stock of pictures, personal accounts, and historical narratives of conflict.[8] Given that revolutionary violence had been kept separate in onlookers' minds from military combat, few Germans could claim to have had direct experience of warfare. At its height in 1850, Schleswig-Holstein's army numbered 860 officers and 43,288 men, joined in 1848 and 1849 by much smaller contingents of Prussian and confederal troops. As in 1848–9, many German–Austrian combatants were to be found amongst the Habsburg monarchy's 242,000 troops deployed in northern Italy in 1859 but their experiences, and the communities to which they were relayed, remained isolated to an extent from a wider German public sphere, as a consequence of the different internal and external priorities of the Austrian state and its German-speaking political constituencies. 'I can only lament that Austria manages to have so little effect in the press at this time', the publisher of the *Allgemeine Zeitung* Georg von Cotta had written to an Austrian official and occasional journalist in August 1857: 'The A. Z. neglects it and, since Austrian newspapers are not read at all in Germany, it is only the Frankfurt *Oberpostamtszeitung* through which Austria speaks for itself, but this only has 2,000 subscribers and no influence at all on public opinion.'[9] In contrast to the experiences of their predecessors during the Revolutionary and Napoleonic Wars, which had often been first- or second-hand, Germans' conceptions of warfare by the 1850s were closely connected to received ideas, mediated

---

[6] K. Marx and F. Engels, 'Progress of the War', *New York Daily Tribune*, 1 Jan. 1855, in K. Marx and F. Engels, *Gesamtausgabe* (Berlin, 1985), vol. 13, 567.

[7] J. v. Wickede, *Die militärischen Kräfte Deutschlands und ihre Fortschritte in den neueren Zeit* (Stuttgart, 1855), 1.

[8] See N. Buschmann, 'Auferstehung der Nation? Konfession und Nationalismus vor der Reichsgründung in der Debatte jüdischer, protestantischer und katholischer Kreise', in H.-G. Haupt and D. Langewiesche (eds), *Nation und Religion in der deutschen Geschichte* (Frankfurt, 2001), 333–88.

[9] G. Cotta to J. C. v. Zedlitz, 23 Aug. 1857, in E. Heyck, *Die Allgemeine Zeitung, 1798–1898* (Munich, 1898), 290.

images, and reported events. Thus, although reporters were anxious, in the words of one correspondent of the *Allgemeine Zeitung* after the battle for Eckernförde in April 1849, to establish the 'sources of their portrayals' (in this case, the 'tales of a bombardier from Holstein and the testimony of captured Danes' as well as the journalist's own 'eye- and ear-witness account'), they posted their articles alongside historical recollections and visual depictions of previous conflicts.[10] This chapter investigates the extent to which such traditional representations of warfare were reinforced or contradicted by the varied reporting of modern military conflicts after 1815.

THE COVERAGE OF WAR IN THE PRESS

A transformation of the press and public sphere took place in the German lands during the mid-nineteenth century which had the potential to alter the way in which readers conceived of military conflicts.[11] Much of the debate about a reading public has concerned its extent and significance, not the expansion of the press, which was more or less constant: in 1826, there were 371 separate German language newspapers, 688 in 1848, 845 in 1858, and 1,217 in 1867.[12] The lifting of censorship and interest in politics during the revolution had led to a sudden mushrooming of titles—1,102 by 1850—but this figure remained as exceptional as the circumstances which had produced it. Although there was a quantitative leap in circulation after the adoption of rotary printing presses—making it possible to produce cheap copy for a mass market—from the 1870s onwards, the readership of the principal newspapers and periodicals had increased markedly before then.[13] In 1813, the *Vossische Zeitung* had had 4,000 subscribers for its three weekly editions, the *Leipziger Zeitung* 5,000, and the *Hamburgische Correspondenten* 10,000; by the 1850s and 1860s, the best-selling newspapers had subscriptions for daily issues of 10,000–15,000, with popular publications such as the *Volkszeitung* (Berlin) reaching 26,450.[14] Illustrated periodicals such as the satirical *Kladderadatsch* had 24,550 subscribers (1854) and the family magazine *Gartenlaube* 42,000

---

[10] *Allgemeine Zeitung*, 15 Apr. 1849.

[11] See N. Buschmann, '"Moderne Versimpelung" des Krieges. Kriegsberichterstattung und öffentliche Kriegsdeutung an der Schwelle zum Zeitalter der Massenkommunikation', 97–123; U. Daniel, 'Der Krimkrieg 1853–1856 und die Entstehungskontexte medialer Kriegsberichterstattung', in U. Daniel (ed.), *Augenzeugen. Kriegsberichterstattung vom 18. zum 21. Jahrhundert* (Göttingen, 2006), 40–67, on Britain; also, G. Maag, W. Pyta, and M. Windisch (eds), *Der Krimkrieg als erster europäischer Medienkrieg* (Berlin, 2010).

[12] A. Green, 'Intervening in the Public Sphere: German Governments and the Press, 1815–1870', *Historical Journal*, 44 (2001), 159.

[13] K. Dussel, *Deutsche Tagespresse im 19. und 20. Jahrhundert* (Münster, 2004); K. Koszyk, *Deutsche Presse im 19. Jahrhundert* (Berlin, 1966).

[14] E. Widdeke, *Geschichte der Haude- und Spenerschen Zeitung 1734 bis 1874* (Berlin, 1925), 104–5; O. Groth, *Die Zeitung. Ein System der Zeitungskunde* (Berlin, 1928), vol. 1, 245–7; H.-D. Fischer (ed.), *Deutsche Publizisten des15. bis 20. Jahrhunderts* (Munich, 1971); H.-D. Fischer (ed.), *Deutsche Zeitungen des 17. bis 20. Jahrhunderts* (Munich, 1972); H.-D. Fischer (ed.), *Deutsche Zeitschriften des 17. bis 20. Jahrhunderts* (Munich, 1973); H.-D. Fischer (ed.), *Deutsche Presseverleger des 15. bis 20. Jahrhunderts* (Munich, 1975); K. Hagemann, *Mannlicher Mut und teutsche Ehre. Nation, Krieg und Geschlecht in der Zeit der antinapoleonischen Kriege Preussens* (Paderborn, 2001), 151, 154.

(1856), rising to 100,000 in 1860 and 155,000–160,000 in 1863.[15] The majority of publications appealed largely to middle-class readers, with the *Deutsche Zeitung*, for instance, drawing subscribers predominantly from the civil service (21.5 per cent), educated professions (35.8 per cent), and commerce (12 per cent) between 1847 and 1850, yet they also extended beyond such circles.[16] 'News' was not only discussed within the family, as newspapers were passed from one relative to another, but within reading societies, lending libraries, taverns, and coffee houses, extending a knowledge of domestic and foreign affairs to a calendar and almanac-reading public, which encompassed a significant part of the literate 80 per cent or so of men and 50 per cent or more of women of early nineteenth-century western German towns—even if it also excluded the lower orders from regular daily or weekly exposure to state or national politics.[17] The proliferation of titles and expansion of circulation for each title meant, by the 1860s, that most educated Germans and Austrians regularly read a newspaper or periodical. In Prussia, it has been estimated that weekly newspaper sales in the mid-1850s amounted to one copy for every fifteen householders and one for every two or three voters.[18] The actual number of readers of newspapers and periodicals was probably between three and five times this figure.[19]

The press in the German lands remained varied and central to political life, despite censorship, aided by the patchwork of individual states with their twenty-seven different sets of press laws.[20] In some states such as Hanover, official activity was significant, with 54 per cent of Hanoverian papers controlled by the government and a further 26 per cent occasionally influenced by it, according to one estimate.[21] Even here, however, the chief of the Press Bureau Oskar Meding did not believe the liberal and other milieux of the larger cities to be susceptible to government influence.[22] Elsewhere, the press was less restricted, despite common

[15] K. Belgum, *Popularizing the Nation: Audience, Representation and the Production of Identity in 'Die Gartenlaube', 1853–1900* (Lincoln, NE, 1998), 200; E.-A. Kirschstein, *Die Familienzeitschrift: Ihre Entwicklung und Bedeutung für die deutsche Presse* (Berlin, 1937); D. Barth, *Zeitschrift für Alle—Blätter fürs Volk. Das Familienblatt im 19. Jahrhundert* (Münster, 1974).

[16] U. v. Hirschhausen, *Liberalismus und Nation. 'Die Deutsche Zeitung' 1847–1850* (Düsseldorf, 1998), 302.

[17] From 1770–1820, 597 reading societies were founded, and 656 lending libraries in Prussia by 1846. J. M. Brophy, 'The Common Reader in the Rhineland', *Past and Present*, 185 (2004), 119–58. See also R. Schenda, *Volk ohne Buch* (Munich, 1977); O. Dann, *Lesegesellschaften und europäische Emanzipation* (Munich, 1981); G. Jäger and J. Schönert (eds), *Die Leihbibliothek als Institution des literarischen Lebens im 18. und 19. Jahrhundert* (Hamburg, 1980); M. Knoche, *Volksliteratur und Volksschriftenvereine im Vormärz* (Frankfurt a. M., 1986); R. Engelsing, 'Zur politischen Bildung der deutschen Unterschichten 1789–1863', in R. Engelsing, *Zur Sozialgeschichte deutscher Mittel- und Unterschichten*, 2nd edn (Göttingen, 1978); R. Pröve and N. Winnige (eds), *Wissen ist Macht* (Berlin, 2001).

[18] K. Wappler, *Regierung und Presse in Preussen. Geschichte der amtlichen preussischen Pressestellen 1848–1862* (Leipzig, 1935), 59.

[19] R. Engelsing, *Analphabetentum und Lektüre* (Stuttgart, 1973).

[20] W. Siemann, 'Ideenschmuggel. Probleme der Meinungskontrolle und das Los deutscher Zensoren im. 19. Jahrhundert', *Historische Zeitschrift*, 245 (1987), 71–106; S. Spiegel, *Pressepolitik und Pressepolizei in Bayern unter der Regierung von König Maximilian II* (Munich, 2001).

[21] Abigail Green, 'Intervening in the Public Sphere: German Governments and the Press, 1815–1870', *Historical Journal*, 44 (2001), 172–3, cites Alfred Hildebrandt's figures from 1862.

[22] J. F. M. O. Meding, *Memoiren zur Zeitgeschichte* (Leipzig, 1881–4), vol. 1, 66–7.

practices such as the seizure of individual editions of newspapers, the withdrawal of licences to publish or sell, the lodging of sizeable deposits with the authorities, interference with postal subscriptions, collective liability for the contents of a publication on the part of authors, publishers, printers, and sellers, and the banning of 'foreign' papers.[23] Partly because it did not have a system of deposits and had retained jury trials for cases involving the press, which had been introduced in 1848, Bavaria was notorious for seizing copies of newspapers, with Karl Brater, the Bavarian deputy and newspaper publisher, estimating that the power had been used on 2,520 occasions between 1850 and 1858, making it virtually a daily occurrence, yet it generally took place without further penalty or charge.[24] The Bavarian Ministry of Justice itself seemed to doubt the efficacy of press controls, most notably in a fifteen-page memorandum published in 1869, which looked back to the 1850s and 1860s:

> At different times, and namely at times of agitation, the demand resurfaced to again exercise influence over the press, which was usual in the old legal order. The permissibility of confiscation gave a helping hand towards this end. There was at times the fullest and, it cannot be denied, also a barely permitted use of this method. With what success? Individual evil-intentioned voices in the press were silenced, and the admirers of the past were almost and temporarily satisfied, but only by summoning forth in this fashion, and giving actual credence to, new storms and, at the same time, by making the well-intentioned institution of confiscation, which was not incidentally intended to extend beyond the sphere of penal legislation, into the object of unanimous antipathy.[25]

The President of the *Ministerrat* Ludwig von der Pfordten confessed in 1857 that 'the judgement of charges against the press by juries does not safeguard effective repression of the excesses of the press'.[26]

With states like Saxe-Coburg-Gotha and Sachsen-Weimar—where politics could be discussed openly—constituting 'a happy oasis in the middle of the political desert that covered the greater part of Germany', in Karl Biedermann's words, it proved difficult for any German government to stifle press opinion, especially in the sphere of foreign policy, which had traditionally been subject to fewer controls.[27] At the time of the constitutional crisis in Kurhessen, which provoked a stand-off between Vienna and Berlin, precipitating the Olmütz Punctation on 29 November 1850, the press had demonstrated how unwieldy it was, in the words of the *Allgemeine Zeitung*: 'What the Bavarian papers are silent about, the Swabian ones report on, and in Frankfurt, where the routes of the world and the telegraph lines converge and where one is so close to the site of Kurhessen, the press produces

[23] W. Siemann, *Gesellschaft*, 67–77.

[24] L. Kuppelmayr, 'Die Tageszeitungen in Bayern 1849–1972', in M. Spindler (ed.), *Handbuch der bayerischen Geschichte* (Munich, 1975), vol. 4, 1147.

[25] R. Kohnen, *Pressepolitik des Deutschen Bundes. Methoden staatlicher Pressepolitik nach der Revolution von 1848* (Tübingen, 1995), 185.

[26] Pfordten to Schrenck, 10 Oct. 1857, R. Kohnen, *Pressepolitik*, 121.

[27] The forty-eighter Karl Biedermann, *Mein Leben*, vol. 2, 116, had gone there in 1855 to edit the *Weimarer Zeitung*.

the most extensive and newest reports every day.'[28] Even in Prussia, 'public opinion' refused 'blindly to trust' in government policy, to the chagrin of Friedrich
Wilhelm IV, but instead wanted 'to make itself independent', in Varnhagen von
Ense's opinion.[29] When the king was attacked by the *Vossische Zeitung* for sacking
Gustav von Bonin as War Minister in 1854, Karl Ludwig Friedrich von Hinckeldey,
the *Generalpolizeidirektor* of Berlin, reportedly shrugged his shoulders and said that
the courts usually acquitted journalists in such circumstances.[30] The obverse of
such press independence was the ability of editors to shape the political agenda and
actively to call for war or to depict—or misrepresent—it as inevitable, which is
what the *National-Zeitung* had done on 8 November 1850, in its eagerness to push
a purportedly pro-German Prussia into a war against a reactionary Habsburg monarchy, when it had wrongly reported that the bellicosity of the Prussian public had
prompted the government to mobilize troops.[31] With 1,160,214 newspapers sold
every week in Prussia by 1855, the Prussian state lacked the means to control the
press.[32] Throughout Germany, the expansion of the press and the legacies of 1848
left a diverse public sphere in place: by the mid-1850s, it has been estimated that
34.3 per cent of newspapers were 'oppositional', mainly liberal or democratic,
4.4 per cent Catholic, 6.7 per cent neutral, 14.2 per cent conservative, and
40.4 'governmental', with a higher tally of official publications in rural regions
(72.7 per cent in Silesia) and a lower one in urbanized ones (34.7 per cent in the
Rhineland), where liberal organs such as the *Kölnische Zeitung* (12,250 copies in
1854) and the *Elberfelder Zeitung* (3,200) were dominant.[33]

The bulk of newspapers' coverage had been devoted traditionally to foreign
affairs, with diplomatic and military conflicts occupying many column inches. In
the *Allgemeine Zeitung*, the balance between international and national reports had
been 87:13 in 1824 and 74:26 in 1842.[34] The recollection of the Badenese journalist and revolutionary J. G. A. Wirth that he had gained his political education
from the French press, the articles of which were reprinted in German newspapers,
was not unusual.[35] Even major publications like the *Allgemeine Zeitung* had not
begun to print articles by their own editors until 1836, preferring to use pieces
from other publications and occasional correspondents until that point.[36] From
eight o'clock in the morning, when the daily newspapers arrived at the office, the
editor-in-chief Karl Joseph Stegmann had himself worked his way through
Le Moniteur, Journal des débats, and *The Times* in order to see what would form the

---

[28] *Allgemeine Zeitung*, 12 Nov. 1850, cited in N. Buschmann, *Einkreisung und Waffenbruderschaft*, 46.

[29] 21 Mar. 1854, K. A. Varnhagen v. Ense, *Tagebücher*, vol. 11, 1.

[30] 10 May 1854, ibid., 63–4. Hinckeldey was, according to Varnhagen, also acting to get his own
back for unpunished attacks on him by the *Kreuzzeitung*, but he made the argument only because it
was credible.

[31] *National-Zeitung*, 8 Nov. 1850, cited in Buschmann, *Einkreisung*, 45.

[32] K. Wappler, *Regierung und Presse*, 59.   [33] Ibid., 60.

[34] E. Blumenauer, *Journalismus zwischen Pressefreiheit und Zensur. Die Augsburger* Allgemeine
Zeitung *im Karlsbader System 1818–1848* (Cologne, 2000), 116.

[35] Ibid., 124.

[36] M. Breil, *Die Augsburger* Allgemeine Zeitung *und die Pressepolitik Bayerns. Ein Verlagsunternehmen
zwischen 1815 und 1848* (Tübingen, 1996), 31–2.

kernel of the publication's news agenda and what could be used as articles.[37] By 1824, the journalists of the Augsburg publication were gutting forty-five newspapers—most of which were foreign—in this fashion, extending the practice under Stegmann's successor after 1835, Gustav Kolb, to include the merging and rewriting of pieces from other newspapers within single *AZ* articles.[38] A network of contacts in Bavaria, the rest of Germany, and abroad was developed simultaneously, growing from fourteen correspondents in 1799 to 150 in the years between 1807 and 1819, with the publishers Johann Friedrich and Georg von Cotta helping to select them and arranging their fees.[39] By 1845, the 'directory of all correspondents of the *Allgemeine Zeitung*' registered 250 writers, some of whom submitted only occasional reports: twenty-three in Paris and thirteen in Vienna, with a smaller number in other European capitals and single correspondents further afield in China, the East Indies, Mexico, and Peru.[40] Like the majority of other major newspapers and periodicals, most of which had networks of their own correspondents (albeit less extensive ones), the *AZ* also relied on *Wolff's Telegraphisches Bureau* (WTB), which started to send news to Berlin publications at the end of 1849 and to those of other cities during the 1850s, drawing largely on articles from the foreign press.[41] After using British cables during the Crimean and Franco-Austrian wars, WTB signed an agreement with Reuters (Britain) and Havas (France) to share information in August 1859.[42]

All these changes in the reporting of news ensured that foreign affairs remained central to the growth of the press during the 1850s and 1860s, accounting for 60 per cent of lead articles in Prussia between 1854 and 1857.[43] In part, a foreign focus was the corollary of censorship, with lead articles on domestic policy rising from 10–20 per cent in Prussia during the 1850s to 50 per cent in the first year of the 'New Era' in 1858 to 80 per cent in 1862, before dropping back to 20–30 per cent in 1864–6.[44] In part, the focus was structural, as an article in the *Gartenlaube*, entitled 'A Workshop of Contemporary History', revealed in 1866, as it looked behind the façade of the offices of the *Kölnische Zeitung*—emblazoned in large gold letters—in 'the great building at 76–78 Breitestraße':

> Journalism in our time has achieved so much in respect of the speed of dissemination of the most recent and latest news from all areas of the world that the astonishment of the layman seems to be justified, and the traveller who is not used, with only a Bädeker in his hand, to allow place after place to fly past will certainly not miss the opportunity of having a look at those institutions of a newspaper which create the pleasure of informing himself of everything important that happens in the world from day to day...

[37] Ibid., 34.   [38] Ibid.   [39] Ibid., 35–6.
[40] J. Requate, *Journalismus als Beruf* (Göttingen, 1995), 279.
[41] D. Basse, *Wolff's Telegraphisches Bureau 1849 bis 1933* (Munich, 1991), 17–18.
[42] Ibid., 26.
[43] J. Fröhlich, 'Repression und Lenkung versus Pressefreiheit und Meinungsmarkt. Zur preussischen Pressegeschichte in der Reichsgründungszeit', in B. Sösemann (ed.), *Kommunikation und Medien in Preußen vom 16. bis zum 19. Jahrhundert* (Stuttgart, 2002), 374.
[44] Ibid., 381.

Walking down a long corridor, covered with carpet, we find ourselves, in following the production of the newspaper systematically, initially in the editors' office, less to examine the inner being of a newspaper's editors...as to get to know its external activities. It is just eight o'clock in the morning but all the editors are fully occupied. The French and English post has already come in; the correspondence which has arrived is being edited; ruthlessly, the red pen, this sentence-killing, feared instrument of our gentlemen-colleagues, moves across individual sections which are marred by sweeping statements, lack of clarity, an undesirable proclivity or other incurable, organic defect. Other letters meet with a still worse fate: they go straight into the grave of the waste-paper basket...With the speed of the wind, the editors let their pencils and quills fly across the paper in order to arrive at their own ideas, whether in the form of a lead article or as an introduction and notes to reports sent in from every region of the world.[45]

The established practices of the newspaper business ensured that various perspectives of German and foreign wars were presented to readers, with reports from publications' own editors and correspondents placed alongside those of the foreign press. Such juxtaposition did not prevent newspapers adopting unambiguous political and diplomatic positions, however, which became an object of official interest. Thus, although Kolb wanted to be 'a disinterested observer' in the manner of his predecessor, the *Allgemeine Zeitung* under his stewardship was known as a liberal, pro-Austrian publication.[46] The editor 'reined himself and his paper in so that the many-sided content of each question was fully expressed', wrote the publicist Julius Fröbel of the editor's apparently unrealizable ideal: 'One had usually known for a long time on which side he stood, but he allowed opinions which diverged from his own to be printed without contradicting them.'[47] Editors like Kolb were instrumental in determining the direction of editorial policy, prompting the press offices of the Habsburg and Hohenzollern monarchies to analyse and attempt to influence their decisions. Kolb was 'always strongly courted by diplomats and statesmen', as one contemporary recalled.[48] At the end of 1851, Schwarzenberg himself had complained through an intermediary that the 'A. Z.', despite not belonging 'to the detractors of Austria', had 'no political conviction' and therefore 'no common sentiment' in support of Vienna, effectively sharing the principles of men like Heinrich von Gagern, who were set on pursuing their plans for Germany even at the risk of 'civil war'.[49] During the Crimean War, the Habsburg *Presseleitungskomitee*, which had been founded in 1852, reported that Kolb was 'inclined toward Austria', with the newspaper 'elastic' as a consequence of its 'almost impossible programme' of being 'impartial' but also accessible 'directly' through its publisher Georg von Cotta, who—mindful of the 'circumstance that the *Allgemeine Zeitung* has the greater part of its sales in the Austrian monarchy'— had assured Vienna 'in a private letter' that the publication would, 'in the face of all eventualities in the oriental question and its ramifications in Germany, hold

[45] 'Eine Werkstatt der Zeitgeschichte', *Gartenlaube*, 1866, vol. 48, 752–3.
[46] G. Kolb cited in E. Heyck, *Die Allgemeine Zeitung*, 117.
[47] Ibid., 119.   [48] Ludwig Steub cited ibid., 124.
[49] J. C. v. Zedlitz to G. Cotta, 19 Oct. 1851, ibid., 285–6.

true to Austria'.[50] Yet the editors of newspapers such as the *AZ* were not always to be swayed even by their owners: during the Franco-Austrian War in 1859, both Cotta's and Kolb's preferences were overridden by another of the five editors in Augsburg, Hermann Orges, 'who lets himself be beaten to death for Austria'.[51] Looking back on the war and the crisis which preceded it, the publisher lamented the lack of 'North German' points of view in the newspaper's columns.[52] Editors of newspapers and periodicals were protected by self-contained, reputable organizations—what the article on the '*Werkstatte*' of the press in the *Gartenlaube* called an 'institute', divided spatially into the functions of editing, typesetting, printing, and distribution—and by a distinct 'journalistic life', with Kolb and others preferring to surround themselves 'with their own kind'.[53]

It was obvious to many observers after 1848 that 'newspapers in their entirety – the "press"'—were 'one of the main organs of public opinion'.[54] This state of affairs was new, as the journalist and later academic Wilhelm Heinrich Riehl had noted: in the first half of the nineteenth century, some journalists and many public figures had challenged the idea that newspapers and periodicals should 'lead' the public—hence, the disputed nature of the term '*Leitartikel*'—or that states should seek to form 'a free governmental press' and 'a government party'.[55] For C. P. Berly, the editor of the *Oberpostamtszeitung* (which was owned by the Thurn and Taxis family and was answerable to Vienna), 'the public articulation of an opinion' was always 'a matter of daring', which he sought to conceal through 'the quotation of recognised authorities', preferably 'from the literature of a distant time or a foreign land'.[56] Riehl was sympathetic to Berly's views, which already appeared antiquated by the 1850s, as the editor of the conservative *Nassauische allgemeine Zeitung* (1848–51) and later editor of the Augsburg *Allgemeine Zeitung* (1851–4) was aware. Most journalists were less understanding, particularly those of the largest popular, liberal or unaligned publications like the *Vossische Zeitung*, *Volkszeitung*, *Schlesische Zeitung*, *Magdeburger Zeitung*, *Hamburger Nachrichten*, *Weser-Zeitung*, *Kölnische Zeitung*, *Hannoversches Tageblatt*, *Frankfurter Journal*, *Schwäbischer Merkur*, *Stuttgarter Neues Tageblatt*, *Münchner Neueste Nachrichten*, *Nürnberger Correspondent*, and *Allgemeine Zeitung*, which dominated Berlin, Silesia, and the urban centres of northern, western, central, and southern Germany, respectively. The editors and owners of these publications tended to be trenchantly liberal, like Riehl's own immediate superior Gustav Kolb, who had been a member of a *Burschenschaft* at Tübingen and who had travelled to Piedmont and learned Italian as a 23-year-old, returning to join a secret society and to be imprisoned by the

[50] The committee's annual report for 1854 was presented to the Austrian government on 7 June 1855, K. Paupié, *Handbuch der österreichischen Pressegeschichte* (Vienna, 1960), vol. 2, 24–5.
[51] G. Kolb to G. Cotta, 18 June 1857, in W. Gebhardt, *Die deutsche Politik der Augsburger Allgemeinen Zeitung* (Diss., Dillingen-Donau, 1935), 14.
[52] Ibid., 27.
[53] 'Eine Werkstatt der Zeitgeschichte', *Gartenlaube*, 1866, vol. 48, 752–3; L. Steub on G. Kolb, E. Heyck, *Die Allgemeine Zeitung*, 117.
[54] W. H. Riehl, *Kulturgeschichtliche Charakterköpfe*, 3rd edn (Stuttgart, 1899), 90.
[55] Ibid.   [56] Ibid.

confederal *Zentraluntersuchungskommission* in the 1820s.[57] Characters such as Kolb or his namesake Georg Friedrich Kolb, a forty-eighter from the Bavarian Palatinate who became the political editor of the *Neue Frankfurter Zeitung* in 1859, articulated their own, independent, sometimes idiosyncratic stance on war, willing to attack both allies and opponents, with Georg Friedrich Kolb opposing the anti-Austrian policies of North German democrats—including Vogt and Lassalle—in 1859 but then proceeding—in a retrospective article in 1860—to advocate a 'struggle for unity, not against those abroad, but against the small and great states of Germany', especially Austria.[58]

In general, liberal editors were belligerent in the name of a 'German' and 'western' cause. Karl Heinrich Brüggemann, the editor-in-chief of the *Kölnische Zeitung*, and Otto Elben, the editor and publisher of the *Schwäbischer Merkur*, were cases in point. The latter came from a well-known family of liberals in Stuttgart; the former had been imprisoned for eight years in Prussia during the 1830s, having been influenced by 'the ramifications of the French Revolution' in Germany during his time as a student at Bonn, most notably the causes of 'the freedom of the press and the political unity of the German fatherland'.[59] During the revolution of 1848–9, Brüggemann had demanded 'measures for a *timely war readiness* on the part of Germany' and had backed Prussia's drawing of 'the Reich's sword for Schleswig-Holstein', since 'the opportunity was there':

> Europe's inimical main powers had been lamed by fear of revolution and the desire burned in all hearts in Germany for Prussia to stand at the head of a national rebirth and to see an end brought to the growing anarchy of spirits through the violent jolt of a glorious decision.[60]

When Prussia failed to act on behalf of the revolutionary cause, the journalist had reminded the government via the columns of the newspaper that, 'in times of danger, right lies with might, not with contracts'.[61] 'In Schleswig, Poland, at home, every-where, one wants, above all, courage and decisive action', he went on in April 1848:

> The *Volk*…will be ready for every sacrifice as soon as you tell it what sacrifices you require of it! And it will be enriched by such sacrifices, for they procure for it the bul-wark of all prosperity, the treasure of trust in itself, in the states which it bears and which it will be borne by![62]

Because the 'powers of the Reich' were 'rather theoretical and fictional', he had advised—against those revolutionaries, including 'much-respected Dahlmann', who wanted 'to mediatize or dissolve the armies of Prussia and Austria'—in favour of making the Prussian army 'the actual point of crystallization of a future Reich executive'.[63]

---

[57] E. Heyck, *Die Allgemeine Zeitung*, 112–14.

[58] 'Rückblick', *Neue Frankfurter* Zeitung, in K. Stoll, *Die politische Stellung der* Frankfurter Zeitung *in den Jahren 1859 bis 1871* (Frankfurt 1932), 31.

[59] K. H. Brüggemann, *Meine Leitung der Kölnischen Zeitung und die Krisen der preußischen Politik von 1846–1855* (Leipzig, 1855), 6.

[60] Ibid., 37.   [61] Ibid., 38.   [62] Ibid.

[63] Ibid., 47.

After the 'failure of the Frankfurt Parliament', the same wish for the Hohenzollern monarchy to countenance war for the sake of 'Germany', 'as long as it has not improved its mastery of state fragmentation', led Brüggemann to criticize Berlin's 'isolation' during the Crimean War, warning it in a series of five articles in February 1855 that it faced a repeat of 1806, following its decision not to back Vienna (as in 1805).[64] Although the editor was dismissed, after Joseph DuMont—the owner of the *Kölnische Zeitung*—was threatened with the withdrawal of the newspaper's licence by the Prussian authorities, his replacement Heinrich Kruse continued to criticize Prussia for having missed 'the most favourable opportunity' of entering the war against Russia, which 'unborn generations would have to regret'.[65] The Rhineland would maintain its western outlook, as it had 'twenty or thirty years ago, when we had no press at all' and when the *Kölnische Zeitung*, 'the most widely spread paper of the province, was merely a harmless collection of novelties of the day'.[66] Kruse's point, in spelling out the implications of 'editorial change' on 1 April 1855, was that the press was now much more significant. He went on to advance an equally independent line of argument during the Franco-Austrian war of 1859, hinting that the Habsburg monarchy was pursuing a war for its own ends, not those of 'Europe'.[67] 'Germany' should 'remain vigilant and arm itself', ready to enter a 'German war', if one should break out.[68] Elben followed a similar line, 'not for Austria, not against Italy, but, if the German hereditary enemy [France] interferes again, against it and for Germany!'[69]

What picture or pictures of war did the *Schwäbischer Merkur*, *Kölnische Zeitung*, and other publications propagate and how might readers have interpreted them? 'Public opinion', which was discussed extensively in the mid-nineteenth century, was not to be equated with the press, as one article on 'die öffentliche Meinung' in the Catholic *Historisch-politische Blätter* reminded its readership in 1848: it was a 'great and profound misconception' amongst private individuals and in government to 'hold public opinion to be a product of recent times' or to be interchangeable with the press.[70] Instead, it referred to 'the whole *Volk*', describing the point at which 'many individuals judge something in the same way at the same time' so that 'an agreement of judgement, a kind of general judgement (*Gesammturtheil*) results, either in individual or wider circles or even in whole lands, irrespective of the existing means of mental communication'.[71] Such agreement did not imply that a single 'public opinion' obtained, invalidating unqualified injunctions for governments to enlist 'public opinion on its side', since 'within the educated and reading world opinions on many issues are divided and not all are sufficiently represented by the press', continued the Bavarian periodical.[72] Beyond the educated world of readers, 'the non-reading classes' had their own views and prejudices, which were more difficult to gauge and to influence: 'Each [the group of readers and non-readers] is a world in itself; different ideas are in circulation in each; the

[64] Ibid., 73, 77.
[65] K. Buchheim, *Die Geschichte der Kölnischen Zeitung* (Cologne, 1976), vol. 3, 193.
[66] Ibid., 236.   [67] *Kölnische Zeitung*, 1 May 1859, ibid., vol. 4, 96.
[68] Ibid.
[69] O. Elben, *Geschichte des Schwäbischen Merkurs 1785–1885* (Stuttgart, 1885), 91.
[70] 'Die öffentliche Meinung', *Historisch-politische Blätter*, 1848, vol. 2, 595.
[71] Ibid.   [72] Ibid., 596.

exchange of ideas is mediated in different ways in each', with word of mouth, rumour, and jokes being more central to one than the other.[73]

Nevertheless, the very occasion for the article in the *Historisch-politische Blätter*, which was more critical of what it called 'the bad press' and which was sympathetic to governments' need to thwart or eliminate excesses, was a perceived transformation of the means of communication, opinion formation, and governance, in which 'the most important means for the circulation of ideas, the easiest and most quickly effective', was, 'in truth, the press'.[74] As such, it was 'to be treated as a great power, which admittedly only has a direct effect on a small part of the population but which affects all classes indirectly', the article went on: 'What the reading public thinks, believes and desires metamorphoses over a certain period into the juices and life of the *Volk* and completes, like blood, its circulation of the entire organism.'[75] Governments had come to rely on the press as a forum for the articulation of public opinion, which was needed to achieve public goods such as the provision of financial 'credit'. Thus, they could no longer view 'public opinion as an unjustified interference of the public in public affairs', nor could they put themselves 'in tow to public opinion', either by setting up 'an unworthy, dishonest system of spies and agents' or by subjecting themselves to 'the terrorism of those who claim, by crying the loudest, to represent the most powerful public opinion'.[76] In practice, the governments of most German states, in contrast to that in Austria, had availed themselves of limited, justified censorship to control the worst elements of the press at the same time as encouraging—via education and appeals to culture—the best elements, the article concluded. In an era of international crisis and war such as that between 1848 and 1871, it was expected that the best elements would prevail, with newspapers and periodicals informing subjects objectively and responsibly of the serious matters at hand.

There are many indications that readers took a close interest in military conflicts and looked to the press to relay the 'facts'.[77] Wars abroad led to increased sales for popular and liberal publications. In Vienna, *Die Presse* had seen its subscriptions increase from 15,000 in 1850 to 30,000 in 1854–6 and 38,000 in 1859, before dropping to 25,000 by 1865.[78] Although growing less dramatically, since the other German states were not implicated in hostilities, the circulation of newspapers such as the *Allgemeine Zeitung*, which had fallen from 11,155 to 7,064 between 1848 and 1851, revived during the Crimean and Franco-Austrian wars.[79] At the height of the conflicts in Schleswig-Holstein, Crimea, and northern Italy, newspapers reported daily from 'the scene of the war', relying on telegraphs to pass on news as quickly as possible: at the start of the Crimean campaign, for example, it took five days for news to reach London (two days by steamship from Balaklava to Varna, three by horse to Bucharest, where the nearest telegraph was), from where

---

[73] Ibid.   [74] Ibid., 598, 601.   [75] Ibid., 598.   [76] Ibid., 597.
[77] See, for example, the robust defence of the *Allgemeine Zeitung*, 16 Oct. 1853, of its reporting of the 'facts'.
[78] K. Paupié, *Handbuch*, vol. 1, 136.
[79] E. Heyck, *Die Allgemeine Zeitung*, 126.

it was cabled directly by WTB to Berlin and the rest of Germany.[80] By the end of 1854, the French had linked Varna to Bucharest by telegraph, reducing the delivery time to two days, followed by the laying of an underwater cable by the British from Balaklava to Varna, so that news could reach London and the rest of Europe within hours. The speed of such communication created its own problems, with a time lag between short telegraphic bulletins and longer reports travelling by post, which arrived a week or two later from the Crimea and, even, Italy and a month or so later from the United States.[81] Thus, the alleged defeat of Russia at Sevastopol on 2 October 1854—more than ten months before the event—was widely reported on the basis of telegraphs about an Allied victory at the Alma, which were not clarified and corrected fully until William Howard Russell's report reached *The Times* on 10 October.[82] After the Austrian defeat at Solferino on 24 June 1859, there was an eleven-day delay, punctuated by *Die Presse*'s regular complaints that 'detailed news about the great and bloody event of war are still missing' (28 June), until reliable information arrived 'from our own correspondent at military headquarters' (4 July).[83]

It seems likely, however, that the speed and immediacy of the reportage helped to captivate readers, who weighed up for themselves the variety of sources—the War Ministry, commanders, officers, ordinary soldiers, civilians, foreign or war correspondents, other publications at home and abroad—that newspapers were anxious to evaluate and confirm.[84] Journalists assumed that their readership would be familiar with the intricate details of a campaign—'the general course of the battle...will already be known to you from the newspapers'—even in the case of the American Civil War, which was covered less intensively.[85] Occasionally, they pointed out 'that no branch of literature' was handled 'as ruthlessly as daily newspapers', which were discarded like old household implements, and they voiced doubts that war correspondents, who were still relatively rare—Wickede being one of the best known in Germany—were guilty of sensationalizing or falsifying the events of a conflict in their desperation to produce interesting copy, but most of them were content to go on feeding a popular hunger for war reports.[86]

---

[80] O. Figes, *Crimea* (London, 2010), 305. See also S. Kaufmann, *Kommunikationstechnik und Kriegführung 1815–1945* (Munich, 1996).

[81] Like other reporters, Marx commented on the need to combine the various sources, using 'mails' to substantiate and confirm telegraphs: K. Marx, 'The War in the East', *The Zuid Africaan* (Cape Town), 6 Mar. 1854, written in London on 4 Jan. 1854, in K. Marx and F. Engels, *Gesamtausgabe*, vol. 13, 18.

[82] Ibid.   [83] *Die Presse*, 28 June and 4 July 1859.

[84] One correspondent of *Die Allgemeine Zeitung*, 2 May 1849, was typical of a general concern to confirm the veracity of his report, 'writing down in pencil the oral description of the German officers and soldiers'.

[85] 'Orginalmittheilungen vom Kriegsschauplatze', *Gartenlaube*, 1859, vol. 30, 430. On readers' familiarity with the American Civil War, see the *Preußische Jahrbücher*, 1862, vol. 10, 470.

[86] 'Berliner Bilder. Bürgerliche Kriegsbereitschaft', *Gartenlaube*, 1859, vol. 24, 345; *Grenzboten*, 1850, vol. 9, no. 4, 681–5: there were war reporters in Schleswig-Holstein but their number was small. The first celebrated war reporters were associated with the Crimean War, particularly William Russell, who worked for *The Times*. The number of 'war correspondents' in the American Civil War was much greater, estimated at 500, yet the circumstances of a civil war were different, allowing American journalists and writers who usually worked in other fields to follow the fighting more easily: G. Paul, *Bilder des Krieges, Krieg der Bilder. Die Visualisierung des Modernen Krieges* (Paderborn,

Contemporaries' appetites were stimulated by the novel, visual representation of conflicts in the press from the 1840s onwards. The Crimean War was the first major campaign to be caught on film, with about fifteen photographers from Britain (Roger Fenton, James Robertson), France (Jean-Baptiste-Henri Durand Brager, George Lefèvre Shaw, Jean-Charles Langlois), Italy (Felice Beato), and Russia taking several thousand images of officers, soldiers, camp life, and battle-fields, yet few contemporaries in the German lands saw them at the time, since they could not be reproduced in the press and they were not published in German books.[87] Ten years later, the American Civil War was much more extensively photographed, with up to 1 million images taken. Some were transposed by cohorts of illustrators—*Harper's Weekly* and the *Illustrated Weekly* alone had eighty on their payroll—and others appeared in popular albums such as Timonthy O'Sullivan's *A Harvest of Death* and Alexander Gardner's *Photographic Sketch Book of the War*.[88] However, these images, too, made little impression on the mainstream German press. Photography—including, by the 1860s, images of the Crimean War—was one of several sources available to magazine illustrators, along with the various traditions of military painting, but its effect—particularly its gritty, unflinching realism—was limited until the mid-1860s.[89]

By comparison, the newly developing conventions of magazine illustration vis-ible in the Leipzig *Illustrirte Zeitung* (founded in 1843) and *Gartenlaube* (1853), which focused on exotic landscapes, maps, scenes from daily life, portraiture, and anthropological typologies, were much more important, combined with longer-standing examples of war albums by Albrecht Adam and Christian Wilhelm Faber du Faur, which had revealed the individual suffering and death of the Napoleonic campaigns.[90] *Der Weg zwischen Balaklava und dem englischen Lager*, which appeared in the *Gartenlaube* in 1855, resembled paintings such as Adam's *Auf der Straße nach Moskau 8. September 1812* (1827) and Faber du Faur's *Die Brücke über die Kolotscha bei Borodino, den 17. September 1812* (1831–43) (see Figure 5.1).[91] *Französische Scharfschützen in ihren Feldschanzen*, which was published in the same periodical at the end of 1854, showed French soldiers firing from entrenched positions as if

2004), 66. R. W. Desmond, *The Information Process: World News Reporting to the Twentieth Century* (Iowa City, 1978).

[87] Ulrich Keller, 'Schlachtenbilder, Bilderschlachten. Zur visuellen Kultur des Krimkriegs', in G. Maag, W. Pyta, and M. Windisch (eds), *Der Krimkrieg als erster europäischer Medienkrieg*, 31–40, suggests that photographs were relevant in the construction of 'panoramas' in Paris (Langlois's 'Sevastopol-Panorama')—and there was also exhibitions—which seem to have affected magazine illustration in France and Britain and, subsequently, in the German lands, too. J. Hannavy (ed.), *The Camera Goes to War: Photographs from the Crimean War, 1854–56* (Edinburgh, 1974); U. Keller, *The Ultimate Spectacle: A Visual History of the Crimean War* (Amsterdam, 2001); A. Rouillé, 'Ein photog-raphisches Gefecht auf der Krim', in S. Germer and M. Zimmermann (eds), *Bilder der Macht—Macht der Bilder. Zeitgeschichte in Darstellungen des 19. Jahrhunderts* (Munich, 1997), 361–70.

[88] G. Paul, *Bilder des Krieges*, 66–7; J. D. Horan (ed.), *Timothy O'Sullivan, America's Forgotten Photographer* (New York, 1966).

[89] S. Parth, *Zwischen Bildbericht und Bildpropaganda*, 242–52.

[90] Ibid., 252–61. For the effects of illustrated and *Familienzeitschriften* on newspapers, see E.-A. Kirschstein, *Die Familienzeitschrift*, 131–45. See also Chapters 4 and 5.

[91] *Gartenlaube*, 1855, vol. 10, 137. S. Parth, *Zwischen Bildbericht und Bildpropaganda*, 258–9.

Figure 5.1 'Der Weg zwischen Balaklava und dem englischen Lager'
Source: *Gartenlaube*, 1855, vol. 10, 137.

they were completing a working day in a factory or workshop. It, too, had ante-cedents—in addition to the mid-century realism of painters such as Adolph Menzel—in depictions of daily life during the Napoleonic Wars.[92] Other illustra-tions were closer to those of traditional military portraiture (*Pelissier: Befehlshaber der französischen Armee im Orient*, for instance, posed the commander in front of admiring officers and distant troops) or romantic endeavour (*Garibaldi'scher Volontair, Die Wiedereroberung einer Fahne in der Schlacht von Magenta*).[93] All such images, together with bird's-eye-view maps showing the topography of battlefields (the siege of Sevastopol) and theatres of combat (the Black Sea), gave readers the impression that they were close to the war and the fighting. The images were juxta-posed in the press with graphic correspondence and memoirs, which stood alongside the miscellany of nineteenth-century reportage. How significant such representa-tions were—as a means of assessing their impact on subjects' readiness to go to war—is the subject of the following sections.

THE GERMAN STRUGGLE FOR SCHLESWIG-HOLSTEIN IN 1848–51

The military campaigns of Prussia and the *Bund* against Denmark involved small numbers of troops, but they had the potential to become a popular 'German' war on behalf of a beleaguered national population and territory against a traditional enemy. Jahn had termed the Low Countries and Denmark in their entirety a '*Nordreich*', anticipating their eventual inclusion in a greater German nation-state.[94] The so-called 'Kiel circle' of academics, which included Dahlmann and

---

[92] P. Paret, 'Adolph Menzel from Different Perspectives', in P. Paret, *German Encounters with Modernism, 1840–1945* (Cambridge, 2001), 7–44; P. Paret, *Art as History: Episodes in the Culture and Politics of Nineteenth-Century Germany* (Princeton, NJ, 1988), 11–60, 77–130.

[93] Pelissier, *Gartenlaube*, 1855, vol. 27, 345; *Garibaldi'scher Volontair, Gartenlaube*, 1859, vol. 24, 341; *Die Wiedereroberung einer Fahne in der Schlacht von Magenta, Gartenlaube*, 1859, vol. 28, 405.

[94] Cited in W. Carr, *Schleswig-Holstein, 1815–1848: A Study in National Conflict* (Manchester, 1963), 9.

Karl Theodor Welcker, had helped to establish the idea that Schleswig was a 'German' land, connected by legal, linguistic, and institutional ties to Holstein and therefore—since the duchy was a confederal territory—to the German *Bund*. In 1815, Dahlmann, who had been born in Wismar under Swedish rule in 1785 but who was a professor at Kiel University between 1812 and 1828, remarked:

> Even if the people of Schleswig have never been in the German Confederation, they belong to it through their brothers, the people of Holstein, to whom they have extended the hand of friendship over the centuries and with whom they are most intimately united in their constitution, their liberties and their rights...May they [the people of Schleswig and Holstein] grasp each other's hand more firmly still.[95]

National claims and the call for an autonomous Schleswig-Holstein remained limited in scope and resonance, however, until the late 1840s. Under the conditions of the 'restoration', conceded Welcker in the *Kieler Blätter*, 'our national aspirations will now have to become more or less provincial...so that in general the Germans will have to seek that which is good and true in the special circumstances of their own locality'.[96] In the circumstances of the two duchies, with a handful of nationalists putting forward a case for the incorporation of Schleswig in Denmark or the German Confederation by the 1840s, both liberals and conservatives continued to believe that some form of autonomy within the constitutional arrangements of the *Helstat*, which itself had been granted by and fell under the prerogative of the Danish crown, permitted the maintenance of necessary historical, legal, and cultural linkages between the two territories. Even to a German nationalist like Droysen, who founded what became the *Neue Kieler Blätter* (originally bearing the historian's preferred title of the *Norddeutsche Blätter*) and who taught students such as Karl Samwer, Lorenz Stein, and Theodor Mommsen at Kiel in the 1840s, a personal dynastic union with Denmark remained acceptable until 1848. Outside the duchies, the cause of Schleswig-Holstein became known to a wider German public from the mid-1840s onwards, with the song '*Schleswig-Holstein meerumschlungen*' achieving popularity after the Würzburg festival of 1845, yet the complicated issues involved were barely understood until the eve of the revolution: the *Allgemeine Zeitung* was one of the first German publications to examine them in depth in a series of articles, to which so-called 'Eider Danes'—who favoured extending Denmark's border to the river Eider—also contributed, in 1845 and 1846.[97] Consequently, when the question became a pressing national one, after King Frederik VII of Denmark had announced his intention of annexing Schleswig on 21 March 1848, in order to appease Danish nationalists and forestall the full independence of the duchy (along with Holstein), many German commentators could be found seeking answers and fashioning policies more or less from scratch.

Initially, there was broad support for the 'national' resistance of Schleswig and Holstein—or, at least, that of elites and other sections of the population of the

---

[95] Ibid., 55.   [96] *Kieler Blätter*, vol. 2, cited ibid., 45.
[97] *Allgemeine Zeitung*, 1845, nos 2828, 297, 359, 360; 1846, nos 12, 43, 59, 66, 95, 96, 121, Ibid., 239.

main towns—against Danish aggression, after calling for assistance from the *Bund* and replacing the red, white, and blue flags of the duchies with the black, red, and gold ones of liberal 'Germany'. With Frederik VII still a minor, ran the commentaries of the German press, it was not legitimate to try to banish doubts over his succession in Schleswig and Holstein by means of annexation.[98] The estates of Schleswig-Holstein, meeting in Rendsburg on 18 March, had called for a separate constitution for the duchies and for Schleswig to join Holstein in the German Confederation. A provisional government had been set up by conservatives, national liberals, and radicals on 23 March in order to protect the rights of the duchies against the 'unfree duke', who had been constrained, as King of Denmark, by Danish nationalists.[99] 'With all our might and main we associate ourselves with the German struggle for unity and freedom', ran the provisional government's proclamation, written by Droysen: 'Let us show the German fatherland by our staunch demeanour and dignified bearing that the spirit of true patriotism fills the hearts of those who live in Schleswig-Holstein.'[100] Prompted by his old student friend from Bonn Christian August, the Duke of Augustenburg, who was a contender in the succession to the duchies, Friedrich Wilhelm IV, issued a proclamation on 24 March pledging Prussia's support for the duchies against a Danish attack in accordance with the Confederation's decision in September 1846. On 12 April, the *Bundesversammlung*, which had previously recognized the provisional government of Schleswig-Holstein, as had other German states, declared that the war between Denmark, the duchies, and Prussia, which had begun at the end of March, was a *Bundeskrieg*, involving Germany as a whole, through the Confederation. Accordingly, the Tenth Federal Army Corps, with troops from Hanover, Mecklenburg, Oldenburg, Brunswick, and the Hansa cities, was deployed alongside the Prussian army. The Provisional Central Power and the National Assembly established by revolutionaries in Frankfurt formally endorsed the conflict as a 'German' or 'Reich' war. Deputies from both Schleswig and Holstein were elected in May to the Frankfurt National Assembly, despite the fact that the former territory lay outside the old Confederation. Dahlmann made their case to the newly gathered Frankfurt Parliament on 9 June, to applause from all sides of the chamber: 'The balance of power in Europe may be upset, but if what is right does not occur in the matter of Schleswig, the German business itself will have been defeated'.[101] Germans, he went on, would continue the fight 'until the last drop of blood has streamed out of us'.[102]

After Prussia, under pressure from Britain and Russia, unilaterally ended the war with the truce of Malmö on 26 August 1848, in contravention of the Central Power's conditions, the same deputies in the Frankfurt Parliament objected strongly, rejecting Berlin's action by 238 votes to 221 in early September, even though General Friedrich von Wrangel, the Prussian commander of all German

[98] See, for instance the retrospective account of *Grenzboten*, 1849, vol. 8, 357.
[99] W. Carr, *Schleswig-Holstein*, 279–90.   [100] Cited ibid., 291.
[101] V. Valentin, *Geschichte der deutschen Revolution*, vol. 2, 144.
[102] Cited in B. E. Vick, *Defining Germany: The 1848 Parliamentarians and National Identity* (Cambridge, MA, 2002), 181.

troops in Schleswig-Holstein, had already begun a withdrawal. Those on the left such as Jakob Venedey contended that the diplomacy of the Great Powers, doing deals separately with the German princes—in this case Friedrich Wilhelm IV—had been characteristic of the years after the 'humiliating peace' of Westphalia in 1648: history had proved that—in order to avoid repeated humiliations, of which Malmö was the most recent instance—'we need to create a new Reich, that we must create it even at the risk of entering into a war with the entire world in order to become a single, united Germany'.[103] For his part, the radical Carl Vogt criticized Prussia for being 'dragged along by Russia' and recalled the successful defence of French revolutionaries against enemies on all sides during the 1790s.[104] These calls for a renunciation of Berlin's actions seemed to correspond to the Central Power's expression of dissatisfaction on 3 September:

> It is evident that Prussia, by concluding the present treaty, has overstepped its powers and that the Central Power, as the contracting party, as well as third powers can take on no responsibilities vis-à-vis Prussia before the approval of the Reich government is given. This can only be given by the Central Power as a result of a decision of the National Assembly.[105]

However, the resignation of the Reich ministry of Prince Karl von Leiningen after parliamentarians' vote against the withdrawal of troops from Schleswig-Holstein and the subsequent failure of Dahlmann, who was against the truce, to form a government led to a *volte-face* in the National Assembly, with 258 deputies versus 237 voting against a continuation of the war on 16 September. Despite the demonstration of at least 15,000 people on the Pfingstweide in Frankfurt, followed by the erection of barricades in the centre of the city, liberal deputies had already indicated in the debates and votes of 5 and 16 September that they backed a ceasefire: the centre–right 'Casino' faction voted by eighty-nine to twelve in favour on the first occasion and by 103 to nine on the second; the constitutional–liberal 'Landsberg' faction by thirty-four to five and thirty-nine to four; and the independents by fifty-nine to forty and sixty-eight to thirty-five.[106] To whistles from the left of the chamber, Arndt himself, who had been elected as the voice of Germany's national struggle since 1813, argued for peace on the grounds that deputies were so divided on the issue as to be unable to form a government and that the Danes, as a 'fraternal tribe', would respect the terms of the treaty.[107] All such actions demonstrated that liberals—supported by the right, who voted for a 'Prussian' ceasefire by 30 to 0 and 33 to 0—were not willing to prosecute the war in Schleswig-Holstein at the expense of the domestic purposes of the revolution.[108] Their stance was in keeping with a press response in Germany to the war in the

---

[103] F. Wigard (ed.), *Stenographischer Bericht*, vol. 3, 2048–9.
[104] Ibid., 2094.
[105] Cited in V. Valentin, *Geschichte der deutschen Revolution*, vol. 2, 150–1.
[106] W. Ribhegge, *Das Parlament als Nation. Die Frankfurter Nationalversammlung 1848–49* (Düsseldorf, 1998), 85.
[107] F. Wigard (ed.), *Stenographischer Bericht*, vol. 3, 2049–50.
[108] W. Ribhegge, *Das Parlament als Nation*, 85.

duchies which was supportive but muted, with newspaper coverage often eclipsed by a preoccupation with revolutionary events at home. This proclivity was reinforced during the second phase of the conflict between April and July 1849, after the truce had come to an end on 23 February, and during the third between July 1850 and April 1851. The Catholic *Historisch-politische Blätter*, which was published in Munich, did not devote a single article to the war during the entire period.[109]

Other newspapers and periodicals, including conservative ones, paid more attention to events in Schleswig-Holstein, but they tended to treat them like the strategic manoeuvres of a cabinet war. The fact that the contingents of troops from each state were small—with 64,000 men overall on the side of the Confederation in 1848, 82,000 in 1849, and only 28,000 defending Schleswig-Holstein at the start of 1850, according to one correspondent of the *Grenzboten*—encouraged this proclivity.[110] For conservative publications, which had warned of the dangers of unbridled nationalism and a neglect of the realities of Great Power politics from the start, such reportage seemed natural. The unrealistic 'German' dreams of Frankfurt had come to nothing, gloated the *Kreuzzeitung*, since Prussia alone had been in a position to defend Schleswig-Holstein in March 1848, which it had done on behalf of the *Bund*, not the subsequently formed Provisional Central Power, National Assembly, or Reich.[111] Because 'the whole of Germany except Prussia' had fallen into 'defenceless impotence' at the commencement of the conflict, it was now up to Friedrich Wilhelm IV and his government to decide whether to agree a ceasefire in accordance with their evaluation of the policies of the other Great Powers.[112] There was little mention in the conservative press of casualties and killing, nor in unaligned newspapers which were further from government circles such as the *Königlich-privilegirte Berlinische Zeitung* (known also as the *Vossische Zeitung*). Here, the correspondence of soldiers and 'reliable' local sources was relayed, as well as that of the government and army, but only passing references were made to blood-letting, which was usually linked to the attainment of military goals: thus, as 'His Majesty's troops' achieved 'possession of the whole fixed position before the town of Schleswig', reported the newspaper on 26 April 1848, they met with a 'bloody encounter', about which no further details were given.[113] The style of much of the reporting was characteristic of a military dispatch:

> One wanted on the 23rd only to advance against the Danish positions. However, during the march, General Wrangel decided to carry out a decisive attack on Schleswig itself. Whilst the avant-garde itself now attacked Schleswig, where the Danes continued to hold the fort of Gottorp, the position of the Danes was at the same time outflanked on the western side, upon which they gave up Gottorp and retreated to

---

[109] On the general proclivities of the periodical, see K.-H. Lucas, *Joseph Edmund Jörg. Konservative Publizistik zwischen Revolution und Reichsgründung 1852–1871* (Diss., Cologne, 1969). The same was true of the satirical magazine *Kladderadatsch*, which concentrated on domestic affairs and other aspects of foreign policy.

[110] *Grenzboten*, 1850, vol. 9, no. 4, 683.

[111] *Neue Preussische Zeitung*, 13 and 14 Sept. 1848.   [112] Ibid.

[113] *Königlich-priviligirte Berlinische Zeitung*, 26 Apr. 1848.

Flensburg. The Prussian avant-garde took Königswill on the evening of the 23rd. The fighting lasted three hours and was very lively (*lebhaft*). The Danes fought bravely.[114]

Two days later, Wrangel's own report was printed, passing on details of troop movements in a similar vein: 'The pursuit of the Danes was continued on the 24th, and the avant-garde was composed of troops of the 10th [Federal] Corps (especially Hanoverians and Brunswickers) in order to give them the opportunity to take part in the honour of fighting.'[115] 'The rear-guard consisted of Danish hussars and *Jäger*', the same article went on:

> The Hanoverian hussars captured the enemy's regimental commander, several officers and 80 men and took control of their banner; the Braunschw. *Jäger* forced the Danish defence opposite them, after their heroic counter-fire under Hauptmann von Schafenberg, to lay down their arms. The fighting stopped at this point. It was too late to reach Flensburg, especially since the troops of the 10th Corps had just put five miles behind them in unrelenting rain. Bivouacs were put up and the attack on Flensburg was set for the next day, the 25th.[116]

Local correspondence was interspersed with that of the military, giving a more immediate sense of the conflict but barely diverging from the official narrative:

> The following report from the war front came to us from a reliable source in Rendsburg at 10 o'clock in the evening on 25 April—I am now entering Rendsburg and learn on registering my arrival with the Provisional Government [of Schleswig-Holstein] that the Prussians have already taken the city of Flensburg at 10 o'clock this morning. The Danes have been chased out completely and the route to their ships via Holnis cut off; if they have not got onto the water at Apenrade, they will be found by our troops and, hopefully, be completely destroyed...Apart from small individual contingents of troops from Holstein, the Prussians were again alone on the battlefield and have been gloriously victorious.[117]

The assumption that Prussia, and therefore 'Germany', would win this relatively small war with ease characterized much of the reportage in the conservative press during 1848.

Correspondents of liberal newspapers were less blasé about the aims and outcome of the war in Schleswig, but they, too, frequently overlooked its bloodshed. In southern Germany (but not in Austria), liberals were, if one correspondent in the *Allgemeine Zeitung* were to be believed, more enthusiastic about the conflict precisely because they were less directly implicated in it and, therefore, had less to lose.[118] 'The war with Denmark is comprehended here in the North from a

---

[114] Ibid.   [115] Ibid., 28 Apr. 1848.   [116] Ibid.   [117] Ibid.

[118] *Allgemeine Zeitung*, 6 Sept. 1848, 3977. *Die Presse* (Vienna), 12 Sept. 1848, by contrast, was scathing: 'Nothing has been so overexploited theoretically and so hollowed out by democratic phrases as this Schleswig-Holstein business.' Since Schleswig had not, before March 1848, belonged to the *Bund*, 'despite its historical union with Holstein', the 'one-sided incorporation' of Schleswig in the Confederation by means of arms was, with some justification, seen by Denmark, Russia, and England as a 'war of conquest'. The Viennese newspaper treated the question of Schleswig-Holstein peripherally and exclusively as a matter of high politics.

completely different point of view than in the South as an unjust and, on the whole, senseless one', wrote one 'traveller' in 'the German North' on 6 September 1848: 'Many families have relations, often sons, on both sides, as in the case of people personally known to me. Thus, their interests are thoroughly divided and there is little trace of the enthusiasm which exists amongst us [in the South].'[119] Like their counterparts elsewhere, South German liberals were critical of conservatives—'the party which now wants peace at any price', as the *Allgemeine Zeitung* put it in August 1848—who were more concerned 'not to bring the Danes to a point of desperation' than to avoid driving the Schleswig-Holsteiner to despair and provoking an 'unpredictable war', instead of establishing peace.[120]

The conflict was at once a legal and a national one, 'not at all just a war of nationalities, but also a war of defence on the side of a loyal, German Schleswig-Holstein for the male line of the house of Oldenburg'.[121] It was a question not merely of money, rendering redundant the Hansa cities' claim that they had already lost 'many more millions than Schleswig is worth', but a matter 'of the honour, of the existence of Germany and the German princes': 'it is morally impossible that Schleswig-Holstein again be brought under Danish jurisdiction', for it would create such poor conditions that they would 'become the cause of a new war'.[122] 'The Prussian, the Hanoverian fighters, the warriors of the Hansa cities and those from the Rhine were not fighting alone in Schleswig, not mainly for Schleswig, but for the defence of the left bank of the Rhine', declared the *Allgemeine Zeitung* on 18 August.[123] Although 'it is true that we respected the enemy too little at the beginning of the German–Danish war', the national war was worth waging, with 'tens of thousands of good Germans ready [to give] their blood for a part of Germany'.[124] It was better to have 'either peace, as will soon occur, or war in God's name against any enemy' rather than 'this indeterminate, in-between stage, which has the evil consequences of war for all of us, without being war, allowing the soldiers, who come ready to fight, to despair of their own strength'.[125] Accordingly, the same newspaper supported deputies' rejection of the Malmö ceasefire on 5 September, citing Dahlmann's speech approvingly, and it went on to back the National Assembly's acceptance of a truce on 16 September, calling on the moderate conservative deputy Georg von Vincke as a witness that the truce's terms exceeded Germany's original war aims—the prevention of Danish annexation—and that the Provisional Central Power had no means to impose a more humiliating peace on its opponent.[126] It was 'practical' to end a war which, because of Prussia's unilateral withdrawal and the machinations of the other Great Powers, had become 'costly' and 'unnavigable'.[127] Despite adopting a very different stance from that of conservatives and portraying a national war undermined by neighbouring states, South

---

[119] *Allgemeine Zeitung*, 6 Sept. 1848.   [120] Ibid., 18 Aug. 1848, 3693.
[121] Ibid., 3692.   [122] Ibid.   [123] Ibid.   [124] Ibid.
[125] Ibid., 6 Sept. 1848, 3977.   [126] Ibid., 8 and 25 Sept. 1848, 4002, 4257–8.
[127] Ibid., 12, Sept. 1848. The issue also recorded that news of Prussia's ceasefire landed 'like a bomb' in the Frankfurt Parliament.

German liberals—like deputies and observers on the right—generally perceived the conflict in abstract political and diplomatic terms in 1848.[128]

As the conflict was reignited in April 1849, with confederal forces—including Prussians—under the command of the Prussian officer Eduard von Bonin, southern German liberal publications like the *Allgemeine Zeitung* began to focus on the actual fighting rather than on political manoeuvring, not least because it now appeared possible that the war would be lost. Consequently, the outbreak of fighting was marked by disbelief and foreboding:

> The Danes have really started hostilities! News has just arrived, which I am sharing with you as fully certain, that the Danes, coming over from Alsen at 3, attacked outposts in the Sundewitt'schen peninsula, drew the entire Third *Jäger* Corps into battle and have bombarded it violently with artillery. The loss on our side from the rather tough fighting amounts to 17 wounded and one dead.[129]

'Our young troops' could only withdraw from the fighting 'with difficulty', preceded by 'very many refugees, especially officials'.[130] Large numbers of soldiers and guns—sixty pieces of artillery, Bavarians, Hanoverians, three battalions of Prussians, and 6,000 Saxons—had already been seen making their way north to the fighting front, reported witnesses in worried ignorance.[131] Nonetheless, the *Allgemeine Zeitung*'s coverage focused on German victories at Eckernförde on 5 April, where batteries built by Werner von Siemens incapacitated Danish warships—with a loss of over 100 dead, sixty injured, and 1,000 taken prisoner—as they attempted to land troops and form a bridgehead, and at Kolding on 23 April, as Schleswig-Holstein's troops attacked and took control of a town harbouring the famous Danish nationalist—'the lunatic fanatic'—Orla Lehmann.[132]

On the first occasion, 'the town of Eckernförde suffered a lot', as 'the thunder of the guns' in the afternoon could be heard 'in a radius miles wide, in Schleswig, Rendsburg and even Kiel'.[133] On the second occasion, which was 'one of the most violent and bloodiest instances of fighting' with 'the character of a battle', Kolding's population fled and buildings were set ablaze, as the Danes incurred a 'very significant loss' of 800 dead, wounded, and taken prisoner, compared to 400 'on the German side', including 'many volunteers from the best families of the land'.[134] Such losses did not lead to a reconsideration of the war's purpose, but were the result of 'this shameful, unnatural hatred' of Danes against 'a kindred *Volk*' of

---

[128] B.-C. Padtberg, *Rheinischer Liberalismus in Köln während der politischen Reaktion in Preussen nach 1848/49* (Cologne, 1985); H. Brandt, *Parlamentarismus in Württemberg 1815–1870*; D. Langewiesche, *Liberalismus und Demokratie in Württemberg von der Revolution bis zur Reichsgründung* (Düsseldorf, 1974); L. Gall, *Liberalismus als regierende Partei* (Wiesbaden, 1968); S. Wolf, *Konservatismus im liberalen Baden* (Karlsruhe, 1990); M. Hanisch, *Für Fürst und Vaterland* (Munich, 1991); T. Schieder, *Die kleindeutsche Partei in Bayern in den Kämpfen um die nationale Einheit 1863–1871* (Munich, 1936); A. Neemann, *Landtag und Politik in der Reaktionszeit* (Düsseldorf, 2000) and 'Models of Political Participation in the Beust Era', in J. Retallack (ed.), *Saxony in German History* (Ann Arbor, 2000), 119–34.

[129] *Allgemeine Zeitung*, 10 Apr. 1849.   [130] Ibid., 9 Apr. 1849.
[131] Ibid.   [132] Ibid., 11 Apr. 1849, 1542–3.
[133] Ibid.   [134] Ibid., 2 May 1849, 1877.

Germans in Holstein and Schleswig. They were the consequence of the courage of 'our brave soldiers', who faced the attacks of the Danes with their bayonets:

> 'Forwards! Forwards!' cried the fiery volunteers and they ran at an attacking pace against the Danes, who soon emerged everywhere from the smoke. The street battle lasted nearly an hour. Although very bitter at the cowardly murderers who, secure in the rear, shot down many German fighters from behind, they still spared their life.[135]

This and other reports helped to perpetuate a narrative of an heroic, romantic struggle—with 'the setting of Kolding even more picturesque than that of Eckernförde'—against a familiar and similar enemy:

> The brave *Jäger*..., the dragoons with their shining steel helmets, the handsome martial figures of the Tann'schen *Freiwilligen* from the Ninth Battalion—they make good use today of the looted casks of wine, they sing and laugh and look so fresh, so good-natured, so ready for battle that the first day of fighting could have been a mere happy gymnastic exercise. In addition, it is finally nice weather again![136]

The same narrative was maintained in the unsuccessful campaigns of 1850, as a purported 29,000 troops of Schleswig-Holstein faced 43,000 Danes (and an army of 60,000, according to the testimony of prisoners of war) at the battle of Idstedt (24–25 July), in 'a quite terrible bloodbath', leaving a rumoured 10,000 corpses on the battlefield and leading to the troops' expulsion from Schleswig.[137] Even then, the 'mood of the army' was said to be 'outstanding', with 'no man . . . downhearted about the mishap near Idstedt'.[138] Much was made of the 'fact' that the Danes, who had also fought heroically, had suffered 'more than double the number of dead and wounded' of the army of Schleswig-Holstein.[139] It was sad 'that Germany could not uphold the rights of the duchies in two successful wars', not least because it had lacked sufficient 'feeling for its honour and power', wrote a correspondent of the *Allgemeine Zeitung* from the Baltic Sea on 31 July 1850, but Schleswig-Holstein would in future be able 'to fight for its position vis-à-vis Denmark on its own'.[140]

North German liberals were frequently less sanguine about the prospects of war and more critical of Prussia, Frankfurt, and the Great Powers than their counterparts in the South. They were also closer to the fighting and, particularly in periodicals, gave a more individual account of the wars. 'The daily press has done its duty', laying bare the conditions of the ceasefire, which was a cause of 'shame', and 'criticizing it from a party-political standpoint', wrote one commentator in the *Grenzboten* in 1849.[141] Neither Prussia nor the *Bund* had acted consistently, failing to exploit the circumstance that Denmark had provoked the war, in order to make the duchies 'German': 'The war was waged by us to make a united Schleswig-Holstein into German states.'[142] Notwithstanding the 'repeated question' of

[135] Ibid. Also, ibid., 29 Apr. 1849, on the verification and denial of 'excesses'.
[136] Ibid. See also ibid., 17 Apr. 1849, which also described an idyllic, bucolic landscape in detail.
[137] Ibid., 29 July 1850, 3348–9. Also, ibid., 11 Oct. 1850, 4530.
[138] Ibid., 31 July 1850, 3381.   [139] Ibid., 3 Aug. 1850, 3428.
[140] Ibid., 31 July 1850, 3381.
[141] 'Schleswig-Holstein und Preußen', *Grenzboten*, 1849, vol. 8, no. 3, 215–16.
[142] Ibid., 216.

conservative newspapers in the Hohenzollern monarchy as to whether and how 'the war could have been conducted differently', the Prussian government had 'rightly' received 'the bitter reproaches of the German press' for refusing to oversee the construction of 'our naval forces', for electing not to hold out 'until the end of the winter', and for failing to provide 'an energetic overarching command', preferring to pursue 'its own egotistical advantage and that of its citizens' and to take up 'the struggle for a national interest... half-heartedly'.[143] Most liberal publications agreed with the *Grenzboten* that the population of the duchies 'only wants to be German'; 'the majority, not only of a head count, but also of the educated, the majority of education, is in Schleswig-Holstein decisively German'.[144] What was more, Denmark—it was widely held in such circles—had merely the 'appearance of an independent state' and would not be able to coexist with a strong, unified Germany:

> How would one partition? According to sympathies and antipathies? That is not possible, for only a small part will want to become Danes... Or according to language? The language which is spoken in the northern districts can be called Danish as little as it can be called German; it is a poor bastard.[145]

Whereas German Schleswiger were 'chained to Holstein through the links of the law, all state institutions, the material interests of trade, and so on, Danish Schleswiger are connected to Denmark through none of these things', went on the periodical.[146] The *Kölnische Zeitung* concurred that 'church, school, law and administration, in a word, the whole state, is German', and that 'the educated and propertied in the entire land are almost exclusively German'.[147] Other liberal newspapers made similar claims.[148] These 'German' populations had been let down and a broader national mission had been neglected by Prussia, the states of the Confederation, and the new Reich government in Frankfurt.

Much of the *Grenzboten*'s reportage focused on the war from the perspective of national volunteers, of which there were said to be about 4,000 by 1850.[149] From the very beginning of the conflict, such soldiers were imagined to be 'free fighters' (*Freischärler*), living in the open and defending a cause which they believed in.[150] 'There might be no more enjoyable, carefree life than that of a mounted soldier (*reisiger Landsknecht*)!' wrote one correspondent in 1848:

> The whole of Germany had contributed to the completion of the colourful palette of volunteer corps (*Freischaaren*)... Here, there are bearded *Jäger* and mounted gamekeepers in green hats and with wonderful guns; there, there are black, red and gold students armed with rusting muskets and huge swords—and amongst them young lads for whom their father's rod was perhaps too severe—former assistants of merchants and fashionable barbers' helpers who in the plenitude of their own power had advanced to become doctors of medicine—schoolteachers for whom a posting came

---

[143] Ibid., 220–1.   [144] Ibid., 1848, 496. The article is dated 23 June.
[145] Ibid., 1848, 217, 357.   [146] Ibid., 355.   [147] *Kölnische Zeitung*, 12 Apr. 1848.
[148] For instance, *National-Zeitung*, 14 May 1848.
[149] 'Vom Schleswig-holsteinschen Heere', *Grenzboten*, 1850, vol. 9, no. 4, 682.
[150] 'Aus dem Freischaarenleben in Schleswig-Holstein', ibid., 1848, vol. 7, no. 2, 430–5.

along too late —...also quite a few simple folk from the land...— in short, all strata were thrown together in the most colourful mishmash. Nationalities here were practically submerged in a single German unity—but was it the sense of a German nationality which had brought all these free fighters together in these northern duchies—who can say? Many, especially the educated, the intelligentsia, had certainly been led on by their enthusiasm for the thing, others by a thirst for action typical of youth, which great times powerfully awake; most, however, came for no other reason than to follow an inclination for adventure or because their reckoning with society had been brought to an end. Thus, the most heterogeneous elements were pushed together in tight circles here so that quite often one feared fights breaking out between them. There was no shortage of frictions—but I must say, to the honour of the Schleswig-Holstein volunteer corps, the good element was almost always the dominant one, and the tendency towards roughness and excess, which threatened to develop in many, given any opportunity, was mostly snuffed out powerfully through the influence of the educated majority. The spirit which animated everybody was thus a satisfying one, on the whole, and I confess that I spent happy days in the midst of my comrades, days the memory of which will never pale in my heart.[151]

Following the legend of *Freiwillige* in 1813, the volunteers proved valuable, even though they lacked 'discipline in the sense of the machine of the military of the line', barely understanding how to 'form a front and to distinguish right from left' but knowing how to shoot, to use the bayonet, and shout 'hurrah'.[152] The relationship between volunteers and regular soldiers was strained, with Prussian officers calling them 'bandits', but the different bands of fighters—the largest group being Berliners composed of revolutionaries 'from the barricades' and middle-class men in black coats and gloves—got on well together and were capable of decisive military actions.[153] At Eckernförde, the same correspondent saw 'eighty Berliners, all of them men of the barricades from the days of March, as they called themselves in self-satisfaction, and armed with muskets from the royal arsenal, as they stormed the enemy with bayonets', having discharged their guns at a distance of a thousand paces. The Danes 'could have completely massacred the madly courageous small group, tired out from running', but they were so 'astonished and overcome', once their first volley had been aimed too high and done no damage, that they 'suddenly turned around...and began to run'.[154] Descriptions of similar actions—with volunteers compared to the 'adventurous figures' of an 'attack by robbers' in 'the weak light of the moon' in one report—were common in liberal and other periodicals during 1848–50.[155]

As the fortunes of the war changed in 1850, with the army of Schleswig-Holstein, including its German volunteers, left to fight Denmark alone, reporters modified the tone but not the style or content of their accounts, shielding readers from the harsher realities of combat. Many days were 'quite desperately boring', made up of guard duty on the one-and-a-quarter-mile-wide strip along the border between Schleswig and Holstein, which 'unfortunately is all that we have kept hold of',

---

[151] Ibid., 430–1.   [152] Ibid., 431.   [153] Ibid., 433–4.   [154] Ibid., 431.
[155] For instance, ibid., 'Aroesund. Erinnerungen aus dem Feldzug in Schleswig-Holstein', ibid., 1849, vol. 8, no. 1, 422.

and interspersed with 'episodes' of action which 'help to fill the time', as one article 'from an open-air camp in the field' put it.[156] The 'situation of Schleswig-Holstein and therefore of its army have very few encouraging prospects', noted the same article in 1850, even if the good morale of the troops had 'not entirely disappeared'.[157] The most that could be said was that 'the decision to give the last worldly good and drop of blood in order to fight for an honourable peace' had become 'firmer and more unshakeable' than ever, recorded another article in the *Grenzboten* a few weeks later: 'If the humiliating circumstances of 1850 in Germany are written down in the eternal annals of history, Schleswig-Holstein's page should remain untouched by dirt and shame.'[158] The author was not able to provide 'happy news of victory, for the bloody days of Missunde and Friedrichsstadt remained without successes', with the 'two bloody fights' together costing 'us' almost 700 soldiers, 'dead, wounded or captured'.[159] Each time, 'we had to fight under the most unfavourable conditions, for our enemies were standing safely in front of our guns behind high walls, whereas their bullets smashed devastatingly into the ranks of our soldiers'.[160] However, although they were not victors, they were 'also not defeated', still hoping for volunteers from the rest of Germany and for a successful winter campaign.[161] Soldiers continued to fight for Schleswig-Holstein because it was a just cause, despite the threat of Denmark and the *Bundestag* that they would be treated as 'traitors'.[162] Their dogged resistance, in an army which had been hailed as 'the best that Germany possesses' as late as 1849, was chronicled by reporters, who continued to lurk around the military headquarters and encampments, as heroic acts of defiance.[163] Accounts of combat, humorous interludes (for instance, the taunting of a pompous, shabby actor who arrived to volunteer as an officer, since 'in the realm of my art I have often been more than a lieutenant'), and descriptions of the harshness of the landscape and daily life ('exhausted, frozen and soaked through to the last layer of clothing', buffeted by the 'cold north-west wind' typical of the region) were regular elements of journalists' reports, yet they remained tied to the conventions of an adventure story.[164]

Those journalists who did describe killing and death, such as the *Grenzboten* correspondent Julius von Wickede, stayed within the traditions of the picaresque.[165] A good example appeared in his collection of 'pictures from a life of war', published in 1853, which recounted the story of Liesch, a supplier of milk and other products to the army in Schleswig-Holstein, and Jochen, her fiancé and a

---

[156] 'Aus Schleswig-Holstein', ibid., 1850, vol. 9, no. 3, 433.   [157] Ibid., 435.

[158] 'Vom schleswig-holsteinschen Heere', ibid., no. 4, 681.

[159] Ibid.   [160] Ibid.   [161] Ibid., 681, 683–4.

[162] 'Das Tagewerk eines Adjutanten im schleswig-holsteinschen Heere', ibid., no. 3, 921. Denmark had asked the Confederation, which had just been reinstated by Austria, to act against 'insurgents' in Schleswig-Holstein, to close the 'revolutionary' *Landesversammlung*, and depose the *Statthalter* Friedrich von Reventlow-Preetz in accordance with the terms of Russian-sponsored peace treaty with Prussia in July 1850. See M. Hewitson, *Nationalism in Germany, 1848–1866*, 68, for further details.

[163] *Grenzboten*, 1849, vol. 8, no. 4, 455; ibid., 1850, vol. 9, no. 4, 685.

[164] Ibid., 1850, vol. 9, no. 3, 922, 924–5, 928–9.

[165] Wickede was the author of 'Aus Schleswig-Holstein', ibid., 1850, vol. 9, no. 3, 483–6, for instance.

volunteer in the 'well-known *Bracklowsche Freikorps*'.[166] As soon as 'the just war of independence for Schleswig-Holstein from the Danish yoke' broke out in March 1848, Jochen had gone to his master, the owner of a noble *Gut* in the territory, to ask for his permission to serve, which had been granted willingly, since 'the whole nobility of Schleswig-Holstein were fully convinced of the justice of the struggle, to which [Jochen's landlord] had devoted all his own sons'.[167] A 'quiet, sensible, morally virtuous man', Jochen had soon become an outstanding soldier who was glad to leave behind life in the *Freikorps* with its 'looser morals' (in spite of 'its very good elements') for a regular corps of *Jäger*, with its 'stricter discipline' and 'the care of the officers for their own', which meant that Liesch was able to join him during the campaign.[168] In this idyllic context, combat could seem like a game, with wayward Danish shots met with shouts of 'missed'.[169] As a bullet hit his cap, 'Jochen made nothing of it' and 'showed the Danes, mockingly, that only his cap had been hit, not his head'; as the soldier next to him was shot dead, 'our *Jäger* placed the "Käppis" of the hit man in such a way' that 'the Danes eagerly shot at this deception', filling him with 'delight'.[170]

Although Jochen 'hated the Danes' and looked on 'with great joy' as 'they were hit by his bullets', he insisted on treating them honourably as prisoners, refusing to allow a young Danish dragoon, who refused to give himself up despite being surrounded, to be killed by German soldiers.[171] Such cases, claimed Wickede, 'occurred many times during the course of the war'.[172] In 1850, Jochen was hit by a Danish bullet in the chest, wounding him 'so seriously that he immediately sank to his knees' but not prompting him to call for assistance, as he made his way to the rear.[173] For her part, 'Liesch did not dissolve into tears as she heard of the misfortune of her Jochen...but gave him immediate help', forced to watch 'the wounded man succumb, after terrible pains which he strove to confront as well as possible with manly fortitude', becoming 'a corpse after three weeks'.[174] The pathos of the burial was that of a morality play, revealing the simple goodness and mixed fortunes of its German, peasant protagonists:

> As the small group of pall-bearers, with the dully swirling tambourine at its head, carried the three corpses to the cemetery of Rendsburg, a pale girl followed behind them. She threw the first handful of earth on the coffin, then she sank in silent prayer to her knees and stayed in this posture until the last soldiers had left the cemetery.[175]

Liesch did not go back to supplying the army and could be found in the crowd at Rendsburg, 'a pale, stooped figure of a woman' afflicted by illness, as imperial Austrian troops entered the town, playing a victory march.[176] She died shortly afterwards and was buried 'on the day that Rendsburg was given over fully to the Danes'.[177] The melancholy of Schleswig-Holstein's fate was embodied in the person of Liesch and Jochen, but their own wounding, illness, suffering, and death were barely examined.

---

[166] J. v. Wickede, *Bilder aus dem Kriegsleben* (Stuttgart, 1853), 140–1.
[167] Ibid., 140.   [168] Ibid., 141.   [169] Ibid., 143.   [170] Ibid.
[171] Ibid., 144.   [172] Ibid.   [173] Ibid., 149.   [174] Ibid., 150.
[175] Ibid.   [176] Ibid., 151.   [177] Ibid.

The depiction of the conditions of war in Schleswig-Holstein, which remained subordinated in all publications to reportage of the events of the revolution, did little to revise the heroic conceptualization of warfare which had occurred after 1815. In the opinion of most journalists in and after 1850, a national war over the duchies was worth fighting, not least to make good the failings of Frankfurt and to make amends for the duplicity of the Great Powers, which—in Arndt's words—had proved to be the 'devastators, the exploiters and the predators of Germany'.[178] The abandoned troops of Schleswig-Holstein 'stand, fight and bleed not for themselves alone, but for all Germans, for Germany as a whole', wrote the nationalist proselytizer in the *Kölnische Zeitung* in August 1850: 'Foreigners have had the audacity to do what they liked with it [Germany] and its future, at the same time as anticipating decisions and sealing its fate once and for all.'[179] The victim status of both Schleswig-Holstein and the German nation could only be altered by 'actions', agreed the *Allgemeine Zeitung*, despite its proximity to Vienna and the campaign for a greater Germany.[180] 'Where is Germany?' asked the Catholic, 'greater German' *Deutsches Volksblatt* on 7 August: 'Every shot which falls on Rendsburg's walls brings this question, thunderously, to our ears.'[181] Whereas the Berlin-based, liberal *National-Zeitung* argued that Prussia should back the entire German nation as it joined the uprising of Schleswig-Holstein, the *Volksblatt* saw the same actions as 'the first foundation stone', in 'the far North', of 'the great idea of a central European Reich'.[182] Yet both publications backed the uprising as a worthy national cause, to be prosecuted by means of war.

Conservative newspapers in Prussia were more reluctant to back the insurrection in Schleswig-Holstein, given that at least some of their leaders and journalists still denied the diplomatic significance of a German 'nation' and that most of them advocated a rapprochement with Austria—not war—at the time of the Hohenzollern and Habsburg monarchies' stand-off at Olmütz, which was prompted by the question of intervention in Holstein and, especially, Hesse-Kassel in late November 1850.[183] Nonetheless, even in conservative circles, there were those—like one correspondent in the *Evangelische Kirchenzeitung* in July 1850—who continued to see the conflict in the duchies as a legitimate 'war of defence' on the part of one *Volk* (the Schleswig-Holsteiners) against another (the Danes).[184] Other conservatives, in Prussia and in Austria, opposed the conflict on political and national grounds, not on military ones. Few, if any, onlookers contended that the costs of the war in Schleswig-Holstein had outweighed the potential benefits, partly because combat had been portrayed in such romantic, heroic colours. One lithograph appearing in the *Gartenlaube* in 1863, which displayed a 'picture of a camp in 1850' in an

---

[178] *Kölnische Zeitung*, no. 197, 17 Aug. 1850, cited in N. Buschmann, *Einkreisung und Waffenbruderschaft*, 244.

[179] Ibid.   [180] *Allgemeine Zeitung*, no. 286, 13 Oct. 1850, ibid., 245.

[181] *Deutsches Volksblatt*, no. 185, 7 Aug. 1850, ibid.

[182] Ibid., no. 168, 18 July 1850; *National-Zeitung*, no. 501, 28 Oct. 1850, ibid., 246.

[183] M. Hewitson, *Nationalism in Germany*, 68–72, on the division of opinion, even within the conservative camp in Prussia.

[184] *Evangelische Kirchenzeitung*, nos 54 and 56, 6 and 15 July 1850, in N. Buschmann, *Einkreisung und Waffenbruderschaft*, 249–50.

Figure 5.2 'Schleswig–Holsteinsche Truppen beim Ausrathen des Mittagsfleisches'
Source: Gartenlaube. *Deutsche Blätter*, 1863, 789.

obvious attempt to foster support for the contemporary conflict with Denmark, envisaged well-fed, convivial soldiers from Schleswig-Holstein in smart but casually unbuttoned uniforms enjoying a bounteous midday meal in the bucolic yard of a native farm (see Figure 5.2).[185] This image of the war had been maintained by journalists, historians, and other writers throughout the 1850s and early 1860s.[186]

NEWS FROM ELSEWHERE: FROM GREECE (1821–9) TO THE CRIMEA (1853–6)

The romantic view of war disseminated by press coverage of the conflict in Schleswig-Holstein was reinforced by occasional reporting of wars overseas. Such a view, although qualified, predominated even during the Crimean War, which was

---

[185] 'Schleswig-Holsteinsche Truppen beim Ausrathen des Mittagsfleisches', *Gartenlaube. Deutsche Blätter*, 1863, 789. Special issues, carrying the title *Deutsche Blätter*, were published at the end of 1863.

[186] For instance, A. v. Baudissin, 'Erinnerungen aus dem Schleswig-Holsteinschen Kriege', *Gartenlaube*, 1861, vol. 36, 568–71, and 1862, vol. 4, 53–5. G. Waitz, *Der neueste dänische Versuch in der Geschichte des Herzogthums Schleswig* (Göttingen, 1852); G. Waitz, *Das Recht des Herzogs Friedrichs von Schleswig-Holstein* (Göttingen, 1863); G. Waitz, *Kurze schleswigholsteinische Landesgeschichte* (Kiel, 1864); J. G. Droysen, *Die Herzogthümer Schleswig-Holstein und das Königreich Dänemark*, 2nd edn (Hamburg, 1850); J. G. Droysen, *Kleine Schriften zur schleswig-holsteinischen Frage*, 2nd edn (Berlin, 1863); W. Beseler, *Zur schleswig-holsteinischen Sache im August 1856* (Brunswick, 1856). See K.-O. Hagelstein, *Eine an sich mittelmäßige Frage. Der deutsch-dänische Konflikt 1864* (Frankfurt, 2012), 9–270.

treated as an adventure as well as a conflict between the European Great Powers, with the potential to extend from the periphery of the continent to its centre. 'No place in the wide world catches public attention at this moment more than the Crimea', claimed the *Grenzboten* early in 1854, in large part because it was the site of a war between the Great Powers, carrying the risk of escalation and bringing to an end the long period of 'peace' between the powers since 1815.[187] The war was, in the words of the *Historisch-politische Blätter*, a 'European-Oriental conflict'.[188] Yet, despite contrary predictions in the German press, the fighting neither spread to Europe nor implicated the German states in military action.[189] Throughout the course of the conflict, travel writing, which drew on a long-established tradition of Western Europeans' voyages to the Balkans, the Ottoman Empire, and the 'Orient', was interspersed with descriptions of sieges and battles, to a greater extent than during Napoleon's invasion of Russia in 1812, which initially had been treated by some correspondents and diarists as a foreign adventure but which ultimately had been subsumed within broader military reports of the Napoleonic Wars.[190] One cartoon in the liberal satirical magazine *Kladderadatsch* entitled 'The Newest Post and Travel Map of Europe, from the Kladderadatsch Geographical Institute' (1854), envisaged a jumble of infantry columns, arms manufacturers, and stereotypical national characters moving in different directions in uncoordinated activity, as the Crimea—marked 'Asia'—went up in smoke behind them.[191] In this sense, the Crimean War was cast in the same light as colonial and other wars overseas in South America and China, which were presented to readers as distant, exotic, and exciting events.[192]

---

[187] *Grenzboten*, 1854, vol. 13, no. 4, 361; also, ibid., no. 4, 58. Also, *Gartenlaube*, 1854, vol. 11, 126. *Die Presse* (Vienna), 26 Sept. 1854, commented on the 'extraordinary interest which the expedition to the Crimea is currently enjoying'.

[188] *Historisch-politische Blätter*, 1854, vol. 33, no. 1, 509.

[189] On the possibility of escalation into a European war, see the *Allgemeine Zeitung*, 12 Nov. 1853, 5099, which still doubted that the war would develop into a 'general' one; and ibid., 13 and 24 Oct. 1854, 4561–2, which talk of the war spreading to Germany and Europe. On the transition from the first position to the second, see ibid., 28 Mar. and 7 June 1854. Also, F. Engels, 'The European War', *New York Daily Tribune*, 2 Feb. 1854, in K. Marx and F. Engels, *Gesamtausgabe*, vol. 13, 3–7.

[190] See especially T. Kontje, *German Orientalisms* (Ann Arbor, MI, 2004); S. Mangold, *Eine 'weltbürgerliche Wissenschaft'. Die deutsche Orientalistik im 19. Jahrhundert* (Stuttgart, 2004); S. L. Marchand, *German Orientalism in the Age of Empire. Religion, Race and Scholarship* (Cambridge, 2009); V. G. Liulevicius, *The German Myth of the East, 1800 to the Present* (Oxford, 2009), 44–97; M. Keller (ed.), *Russen und Rußland aus deutscher Sicht*, vol. 3 (Munich, 1992); W. Geier, *Südosteuropea-Wahrnehmungen. Reiseberichte, Studien und biographische Skizzen vom 16. bis zum 20. Jahrhundert* (Wiesbaden, 2006), 116–88; A. Hammond, *The Debated Lands: British and American Representations of the Balkans* (Cardiff, 2007), 1–52; A. Hammond (ed.), *Through another Europe* (Oxford, 2009), 1–19; M. Todorova, *Imagining the Balkans*, new edn (Oxford, 2009), 62–115; B. Jezernik, *Wild Europe: The Balkans in the Gaze of Western Travellers* (London, 2004); W. Bracewell and A. Drace-Francis (eds), *Balkan Departures: Travel Writing from Southeastern Europe* (New York, 2009), 1–24.

[191] 'Neueste Post- und Reisekarte von Europa, aus dem geographischen Institute des Kladderadatsch', *Kladderadatsch*, 1854, vol. 7, 236.

[192] S. Zantop, *Colonial Fantasies: Conquest, Family and Nation in Precolonial Germany, 1770–1870* (Durham, NC, 1997); S. Zantop, 'Domesticating the Other: European Colonial Fantasies, 1770–1830', in J. Brinke-Gabler (ed.), *Encountering the Other(s): Studies in Literature, History and Culture* (Albany, NY, 1995), 269–84; G. Steinmetz, *The Devil's Handwriting: Precoloniality and the German Colonial State in Qingdao, Samoa and Southwest Africa* (Chicago, 2007); G. Brinker-Gabler (ed.), *The Question of the Other(s)* (Albany, NY, 1995), 269–83; M. Fiedler, *Zwischen Abenteuer,*

There was a more or less unquestioned acceptance, including amongst liberals like the economist Friedrich List (who wanted to maintain the existence of 'barbarous nationalities'), that the 'barbaric and half-civilized countries of Central and South America, Asia and Africa' would be subjected to 'pacification' and 'civilizing operations' by European powers, especially Britain.[193] 'The Oriental question', as List labelled it in *Das nationale System der politischen Oekonomie* (1841), encompassed not only the Ottoman Empire and Near East (and, therefore, the Crimea), but also India, China, and the eastern territories of the Russian Empire. 'Sooner or later, Europe will see itself placed before the necessity of taking the whole of Asia into its care and subjected to its discipline', the economist declared:

> In this whole chaos of lands and peoples, there is no single nationality which would be worthy or capable of continuation or rebirth. The complete dissolution of Asiatic nationalities thus seems inevitable and a renaissance of Asia only seems possible through an injection of European energy, through the gradual introduction of the Christian religion and European morals and order, by means of European immigration and paternalistic European governance.[194]

Consequently, wars overseas were usually believed to be legitimate and even natural or beneficial. As the *Allgemeine Zeitung*'s coverage—in the form of reprinted reports from London newspapers—of Britain's intervention in China in 1839–42 and 1856–60 demonstrates, little attempt was made to discover the causes of the conflicts—they were not labelled 'opium wars' at the time—or to get nearer to the fighting.[195] The reporting of revolutions in Naples (1820–1) and Portugal (1820–6), mutiny in Spain (1820–3), and wars of independence in Greece (1821–9) and Belgium (1830–1) was more regular and sympathetic, with the lionization of foreign volunteers in Greece by philhellenic supporters, but it belonged to an era of restricted press activity, which was not comparable to that of the 1850s.[196] Most articles on Greek independence in the 1820s were filed from Constantinople.[197] Like 'the war of Russia against the Porte in 1828 and 1829, the Polish uprising in 1830–31 and the Hungarian, Austrian–Sardinian and Danish–German wars' of 1848–51, which had not seen 'two of the principal powers fight with each other' and which had not therefore constituted 'genuine interruptions' of the peace, these early nineteenth-century conflicts were represented as sets of events in the Austrian

Wissenschaft und Kolonialismus. Der deutsche Afrikadiskurs im 18. und 19. Jahrhundert (Cologne, 2005), 81–174.

[193] F. List, *Das nationale System der politischen Oekonomie* (Stuttgart, 1841). See also M. P. Fitzpatrick, *Liberal Imperialism in Germany: Expansionism and Nationalism, 1848–1884* (New York, 2008), 57–8.

[194] F. List, *Das nationale System*, 213.

[195] *Allgemeine Zeitung*, 13 and 18 Jan. 1840, 7 and 21 Aug., 4 Sept. 1841; ibid., 4 and 17 July 1858, 18 Nov. 1860.

[196] R. Quack-Eustathiades, *Der deutsche Philhellenismus während des griechischen Freiheitskampfes 1821–1827* (Munich, 1984), 90–124, 143–265; M. v. Rintelen, *Zwischen Revolution und Restauration. Die Allgemeine Zeitung 1798–1823* (Frankfurt, 1994), 360–3.

[197] Other articles were sent from the 'Moldavian border' (for example, one written on 10 Mar. 1821, and posted to the *Allgemeine Zeitung*) or from the 'Turkish border' (written on 19 Mar. 1821, also appearing in the *AZ*).

and German press which were secondary or subordinate to those of domestic politics, especially those of the revolution, and to those of diplomacy and foreign affairs more generally.[198]

In contrast to earlier foreign conflicts, the Crimean War was followed closely by German newspapers and periodicals, many of which had correspondents on the spot.[199] Partly because of the emergence of mass-circulation illustrated magazines such as the *Gartenlaube*, which had 5,000 subscribers in its founding year of 1853 and 42,000 by 1856, and partly because it involved Britain, France, and Russia, with Austria also mobilizing troops and forcing a Russian evacuation of Moldavia and Wallachia, the war between Turkey and Russia was reported in a new fashion.[200] For the first time since the Napoleonic campaigns, details of which continued to emerge after 1815, graphic depictions of the suffering and killing of war were disseminated to a wide readership.[201] By early 1855, towards the end of the winter-long siege of Sevastopol by British and French forces, candid descriptions were given of what the *Gartenlaube* called 'the horrible things which come to light in every war and, above all when battles turn into ghastly scenes on the battlefield, which can shake even the most hardened heart'.[202] Although such scenes were counterbalanced by supposed improvements in sanitation and medical care, with the same article going on to describe the invention in the British army of a form of ambulance (a covered carriage carrying three lightly wounded men on a front pinion and two seriously wounded laid out inside), they were no less shocking, as one British-influenced report on the military hospital at Scutari on the Bosphorus, '350 miles away from the Crimea', showed, alongside a 'portrait of Miss Florence Nightingale': '86 English women and girls', mostly 'from the educated classes and good, propertied families', had volunteered to look after '4,200 mutilated soldiers' with 'hideous wounds', which were the result of 'the bloody scenes of horror of the war'.[203]

---

[198] *Grenzboten*, 1855, vol. 13, no. 4, 58.

[199] Part of the press's concern centred on the possibility of the war extending to Germany: see, for example, 'Die neueste deutsche Phase der orientalischen Frage', *Historisch-politische Blätter*, 1854, vol. 34, no. 2, 140–63.

[200] For the circulation of *Gartenlaube*, see K. Belgum, *Popularizing the Nation*, 200.

[201] Memoirs of the Napoleonic Wars continued to appear and were juxtaposed with accounts of contemporary wars: see, for instance, 'Erinnerungen aus dem Jahre 1806', *Gartenlaube*, 1856, vols. 44 and 45, 597–9, 610–12. Nikolaus Buschmann, *Einkreisung und Waffenbruderschaft*, 57, points to an article by Julius von Wickede on Algeria ('Kriegserleben in Algerien', *Gartenlaube*, 1854, vol. 18) as evidence of the existence of 'unleashed warfare', but this was arguably more restricted in its descriptions and was published at the same time as accounts of the Crimean War (including those by Wickede himself).

[202] 'Die Pflege der Verwundeten bei Sebastopol', *Gartenlaube*, 1854, vol. 51, 621.

[203] 'Hospital-Scenen vom Kriegsschauplatze. Mit Portrait der Miß Florence Nightingale', ibid., 1855, vol. 6, 74. *Grenzboten*, 1854, vol. 13, no. 2, 297, also stressed the 'humanity' of at least some of the fighting. On British reporting of the war, which clearly influenced some of the German coverage (as in this case), see A. Lambert and S. Badsey (eds), *The War Correspondents: The Crimean War* (Strand, 1994); S. Markovits, *The Crimean War in the British Imagination* (Cambridge, 2009), 12–62. On France, see L. Case, *French Opinion on War and Diplomacy during the Second Empire* (Philadelphia, 1954).

In 'Pictures from the Current War', 'various eye-witnesses' recounted for the *Gartenlaube* how, in May 1855, they had gone back to Inkerman, the site of one of the war's largest battles on 25 October 1854, to find 'long, dense tufts of grass, weighed down with blossom' indicating—'high above the natural greenery of the plain'—'the mass graves, in which the shot and cut-down from 25 October rest in their hundreds, each in a dug-out hollow':

> The smell of corpses mixed with the herb-like aroma of spring made an indescribably shocking impression, most sensibly on the horses. They snorted and whinnied with their manes erect amongst the grass and flowers, not biting a single stalk, and they could only be guided through the area with the greatest violence.[204]

The birds, too, were still. 'Soon the monuments of that terrible, "glorious" October day piled up along our way', the same correspondent continued:

> The skeleton of an English dragoon lay there between the stalks of grass, where he had fallen. Torn scraps of his red uniform played with gnawed-off bones. His buttons had all been cut off. He must have fallen right at the start of the battle, as the heavy cavalry came under the fire of Russian artillery close by 'Canrobert's hill'. Not far away lay, in friendship, a Russian skeleton, not completely without flesh. They could have got on together just as well in life, if the great stately wisdom of the creators and maintainers of the European balance of power had really settled on four points as men rather than on question marks as diplomats. The small round skull of the Russian had been picked bare and eviscerated by vultures, leaving only its red hair to flutter madly around his deep eye sockets.
>
> Further on, another Russian skeleton seemed to have sprung to the heights out of its grave, between bullets and fragments of cartridges. Only its feet were covered. Its upper body loomed up and an arm was stuck in a position, as if threatening us. Now we had to force our horses with all our strength through labyrinths of half-decayed artillery and cavalry horses, beside and under which single, torn-off human limbs and bits of skull, bleached saddles, rusting bridles, buckles, scraps of clothes etc. were strewn. A terrible labyrinth of fights to the death now laid to rest in the contortions with which death had risen up in them in an act of deliverance. The rain had washed the top layers from countless graves so that the corpses stared upwards grimly and threateningly from the grass and flowers, as if to bring down the vengeance of heaven on their death, their burial and this conduct of the war.
>
> Drums and whistles and our spurs drive us and our horses onwards in the full force of life through the opulence of death and the dawning spring, today still children of the latter, only perhaps to sink under its blooms tomorrow, dismembered and dead.[205]

The representations of war which such eyewitnesses gave were intended, it appeared, both to fascinate and to shock. They were similar to those presented, usually in private correspondence, by combatants themselves.[206]

The same article went on to give a minutely detailed, contemporaneous account of fighting at Mamelon, Taganrog, and Malakhov hill, outside Sevastopol. At the

---

[204] 'Bilder aus dem jetzigen Kriege', *Gartenlaube*, 1855, vol. 27, 356. [205] Ibid., 356–7.

[206] O. Figes, *Crimea*, 230–410; J. Spilsbury, *The Thin Red Line: An Eyewitness History of the Crimean War* (London, 2005); C. Bayley, *Mercenaries for the Crimean: The German, Swiss and Italian Legions in British Service, 1854–56* (Montreal, 1977).

first, on 22 and 23 May 1855, 'about 5,000 French had blown up mines and taken trenches, with the loss of 1,700 men, and they had bayoneted hundreds upon hundreds in the pursuit of fleeing Russians, since no pardon was asked for or granted'.[207] After 'this disgustingly expensive victory, for which General Pelissier was ready to sacrifice 10,000 men', the soldiers prepared to mount an assault on the 'irregular, stony hill of the Mamelon', from which 'heavy cannon and thousands of smaller, gullets of fire, spat out death' to threaten the Allies' positions.[208] The attack would be 'one of the most audacious, bloody acts of war' ever undertaken, the *Gartenlaube* asserted.[209] 'If you think of 12,000 men of the most varied units of the army in a wide, desolate, sullen ravine, menaced from the vantage point of the fearsome Mamelon', which was surrounded by 'desolate hills' stretching away from it and by 'red-coated English, flashing officers,...shouts of triumph from all corners and distances, stormily returned in every accent by the incalculable, dense, closed ranks of the French', 'then you'll be able to paint a pale picture of the scene for yourself', one of the eyewitnesses continued.[210] Once '15,000 yellow Turks and brown Egyptians' under Omar Pasha, the French and British general staffs, and 'a couple of thousand of English below' were added, one would have assembled 'the main motifs of this attack'.[211] When the actual—not the imagined—attack on the Mamelon took place in June 1855, the Russians were taken by surprise and unexpectedly fled, encouraging the French troops, 'without any command', to pursue them and leaving them without cover, exposed to Russian flanking fire, so that 'the greater part of these most daring ones fell during the retreat'.[212] Five to six hundred of every thousand British soldiers, foolishly forced to retreat by their commander Lord Raglan, were also 'mowed down' by the Russians, who had been allowed 'to recover their strength'.[213] 'The fighting which now took place on and around the Mamelon was slaughter of the usual kind, which always occurs in war', the correspondent contended, ignoring the fact that descriptions of such slaughter were not at all commonplace.[214] The sun came up the next morning on 'many thousands of distorted, rigid faces of corpses', with eighty to ninety having 'fallen as victims of the modesty of their commanders'.[215] The assault on Malakhov hill ten days later, on 18 June, was similarly written in 'blood red' ink in 'this shuddering history of war', a 'terrible counterpoint' to the battle of Waterloo exactly forty years earlier.[216] Like the bombardment of Taganrog on the Sea of Azov shortly afterwards, which turned a bustling town of 22,000 'Russians, Tartars, Armenians, Cossacks, Germans and some French' into 'piles of ash', the actions caused the author to doubt the purposes of and consequences wrought by 'the western bearers of civilization'.[217]

---

[207] *Gartenlaube*, 1855, vol. 27, 356, 357.   [208] Ibid.   [209] Ibid.
[210] Ibid.   [211] Ibid.   [212] Ibid., 358.   [213] Ibid.
[214] Ibid. Another similar account can be found in 'Nach der Schlacht an der Traktirbrücke', ibid., vol. 36, 462: 'Near the bridge of Traktir, not far from Sevastopol, another battle was fought and insatiable earth again drank rivers of blood.'
[215] Ibid., vol. 27, 358.   [216] Ibid.   [217] Ibid.

Military technology—one of the products of 'civilization'—also appeared, on some readings, to be one of the principal menaces facing civilized societies.[218] Although such technology encompassed steamships and railways (with the construction of a 7-mile-long stretch from Balaklava to Sevastopol in February–March 1855), it rested above all on what an article in the *Gartenlaube* described as 'the massive use of the gun principle'.[219] Contrary to commonly held expectations, wrote one expert in the *Grenzboten*, the transformation of strategic principles and military technologies had occurred after 1815 during peacetime. 'It may appear surprising but it is nonetheless a fact that wars themselves are not always the periods in which the system of war has made the greatest advances', he noted in 1855: 'More happened in many periods of peace than in the preceding period of fighting, largely because the experiences gained in the latter could only be made useful during the succeeding era of calm.'[220] Those epochs 'dominated by a great reforming spirit' like 'the twenty-three war years that began with the toppling of the French monarchy' were not exempt from the rule, with 'far less' happening 'for the progress of the three branches of the military than during the later period of peace', notwithstanding the prominence of the wartime leadership of the 'military heroes of our century'.[221] The innovations which marked the post-Napoleonic peace were 'the renewal of artillery' in the 1820s and 1830s and the 'improved arms and manner of fighting of the infantry' in the 1830s and 1840s.[222] Both involved the changed shape and material of projectiles— bullets and shells—and the different means of firing them, which meant that they could be projected further and with more devastating effect.[223]

The latter innovation concerned the invention of the so-called 'Minié ball' (more accurately labelled a 'Miniékugel' or 'bullet' in German), which was a conical, soft-lead bullet with grooves and a hollow base designed to spin the projectile and to provide a better seal for the expanding gas from the propulsive explosion, giving it an accurate range of 600 yards or more. The bullet also cleaned the barrel of the gun as it was fired, overcoming the difficulties of jamming and misfiring weapons, which had dogged infantrymen since the early modern period. 'The main point of the Minié casing is obviously its great *range*' and also 'the *safety* of the shot', which propelled the bullet at a speed of 2,000 yards per second, the *Gartenlaube* informed its readers amidst a flurry of technical details.[224] The bullets could be pressed—rather than poured in a molten state—by a machine, which 'now works day and night and can, in a short space of time, deliver a huge pile of such bullets'.[225] The efficacy and ease of use of the rifle ensured that it came to dominate infantry tactics, making sniping, skirmishing, entrenchments, and other forms of protection central parts of warfare, at the expense of cavalry charges and

---

[218] William McNeill, *The Pursuit of Power: Technology, Armed Force and Society since A.D. 1000* (Chicago, 1982), 224–41, 256–61, contends that trench warfare was developed in Crimea alongside the use of new kinds of artillery, which themselves were the product of industrialization.

[219] 'Die Feuerwaffen der Neuzeit', *Gartenlaube*, 1855, vol. 49, 602.

[220] 'Die vier Armeen in der Krim', *Grenzboten*, 1855, vol. 14, no. 2, 58.

[221] Ibid.   [222] Ibid., 58–9.

[223] See the image of 'Die Lancaster-Kanone', *Gartenlaube*, 1855, vol. 49, 602.

[224] 'Die Feuerwaffen der Neuzeit', *Gartenlaube*, 1855, vol. 49, 602.   [225] Ibid.

hand-to-hand combat. Because they were manufactured from soft lead and pene-trated bodies with great force, Minié bullets left terrible, often deadly wounds, far worse than traditional types of shot.

The same was true of the former set of technological innovations, which con-cerned the introduction of lighter field artillery, high-calibre 'bomb cannons', and shrapnel shells. As a result of these changes, some commentators had claimed, from the mid-1830s onwards, that artillery had 'increased its tactical decisiveness to such an extent that the other divisions of the army would no longer be able to counter it in closed formations'.[226] Although such claims were exaggerated, continued the *Grenzboten*'s correspondent, they indicated the centrality of guns and shells as definitive 'fire-arms of modernity', with the capacity to maim, kill, and destroy in a new way.[227] Towards the end of the siege of Sevastopol in the sum-mer of 1855, the Allies fired a daily 75,000 rounds at the small, fortified town, reducing it to rubble and causing 800 Russian casualties per day.[228] Heavy artillery such as the Lancaster cannon, of which drawings were provided in the *Gartenlaube*, could fire conical, 25-pound missiles over 10,000 feet and create breaches in walls at a distance of 7,500 feet.[229] It seemed to have the potential to alter the nature—and combatants' experiences—of modern warfare.

The manner in which such warfare was comprehended in the German lands during the 1850s and the ways in which German contemporaries believed it would be experienced in future depended on the press. Candid literary descriptions, as has been seen, could convey the shock of combatants' and witnesses' sensations and reactions with great immediacy. In illustrated magazines, paintings, and photographs, which—through the sanitized but harsh-toned images of Roger Fenton—became known to at least some members of the public in Britain and elsewhere, the conditions of combat and camp life appeared to become real for the first time.[230] German illustrators and journalists were aware of such photographs, bringing them to the attention of readers.[231] The stark contrasts of their engravings in periodicals, though softer than those of photographs, seemed to coincide with the harshness of the Crimean landscape, which consisted of treeless *karst* or pri-meval mud.[232] 'The current site of war between Inkerman, Balaklava and Chersones

---

[226] *Grenzboten*, 1855, vol. 14, no. 2, 59.

[227] 'Die Feuerwaffen der Neuzeit', *Gartenlaube*, 1855, vol. 49, 599. These innovations forced the *Grenzboten*'s correspondent to revise his earlier evaluation of 'Die vier Armeen in der Krim', *Grenzboten*, 1854, vol. 13, no. 4, 361–70, in which he had treated artillery as if it were no more important than the infantry or cavalry.

[228] O. Figes, *Crimea*, 377.   [229] *Gartenlaube*, 1855, vol. 49, 602.

[230] G. Paul, *Bilder des Krieges*, 61–5; H. and A. Gernsheim (eds), *Roger Fenton, Photographer of the Crimean War* (London, 1954); J. Hannavy (ed.), *The Camera Goes to War: Photographs from the Crimean War, 1854–56*; U. Keller, *The Ultimate Spectacle: A Visual History of the Crimean War*; U. Keller, 'Authentizität und Schaustellung. Der Krimkrieg als erster Medienkrieg', in A. Holzer (ed.), *Mit der Kamera bewaffnet. Krieg und Fotografie* (Marburg, 2003), 21–38.

[231] For example, 'Der Weg zwischen Balaklava und dem englischen Lager', *Gartenlaube*, 1855, vol. 10, 137.

[232] See, for instance, 'Französische Scharfschützen in ihren Feldschützen' and 'Angriff französischer Jäger vor Sevastopol', *Gartenlaube*, 1854, vol. 50, 614–15, and 'Das Innere einer Parallele auf der französischen Linie', ibid., 1855, vol. 15, 201.

[a classical ruin] constitutes on its geological surface a terrible, fitting basis for the winter war and camp scenes', recorded the *Gartenlaube*:

> The earth here really looks like that imagined by geologists long before the first people, as a playground for amphibious enormities and mud monstrosities, ichthyosaurs, plesiorsaurs and sundry other ancestors of crocodiles and alligators. An unremitting, tough mud, without trees or vegetation but with channels and puddles, from which desolate rocks and hills protrude in slovenly disorder. For an eye used to the signs of civilization—paths, fields, welcoming villages and towns, trees and pictures of vegetation of other kinds—there is nothing to behold. The wilderness, as it ruled on earth millennia before the first book of Moses, has returned, and the war between western civilization and eastern barbarism, dirty and ragged, hungry and dismembered, unwashed and unshaved, wades through this wilderness. Yet it doesn't only wade through the mere 'primeval soup' from which the current geological crust of the earth is formed, the soup is richly sown with torn-off limbs of horses and people, half decayed and half dead fallen ones, wheels, bullets, . . . straw, scraps of clothes, blood, bits of weapons, . . . thousands of tiny puddles created by the hooves of horses, whose imprints remain set in the glutinous brew and were filled with water, blood and snow. . . The sky stretches comfortlessly over the corpse-seeking carrion birds and rains, snows and bears down stormily on the dead, the dying, the ailing and the healthy. Here and there, weapons glint, cannons flash and bursts of fire natter, sometimes here, sometimes close by, sometimes further away . . . Here, there is a cadaver-coloured, tattered, wild-bearded fighter who is collapsing, dragging himself with difficulty to a rock in order to rest his head, at least, against something and to die. Other soldiers wind their way past him, throw him a pitying glance and let him lie there, since they can barely drag themselves along.[233]

In such descriptions, there are both literary references—to Moses' flight, to the return from Moscow in 1812, and perhaps to gothic novels—and visual ones, imagining 'scenes' and 'pictures', recalling images of dinosaurs in encyclopaedias and recreating the framing, spaces, and light effects of engravings and photographs ('here', 'there', 'the sky stretches', 'weapons glint').

Literature had been laid bare by photography and art, according to another correspondent of the *Gartenlaube* in a combined article and print representing 'The Road between Balaklava and the English Camp'.[234] Contemporaries owed the fact of their 'nakedness' to 'a welter of pictures, which are true to nature and to the situation, of the great tragedy in the Crimea, old Tauris, which does not look as gentle as the classical "Iphigenia in Tauris" of Goethe'.[235] The depiction of the new road through Tauris showed 'the bogs, valleys and hills, snow and rain, thousands of fallen horses, overturned wagons, buried supplies, frozen soldiers etc.', with figures toiling along a path to nowhere, reminiscent of the hopeless itinerary of returning French and German soldiers in 1812.[236] In one article, the reported eyewitness is a British painter, with readers given a

---

[233] 'Scenen aus dem englisch-französischen Winterlager', *Gartenlaube*, 1855, vol. 3, 34.
[234] 'Der Weg zwischen Balaklava und dem englischen Lager', ibid., vol. 10, 137.
[235] Ibid.   [236] Ibid.

'depiction' (*Schilderung*) of the battle of Chernaia (16 August 1855), as if via the medium of the artist's gaze:

> Dying and dead lay around in all directions and at all angles. Some died with their faces outwards, their hands grasping the air and thus reaching out until they fell flat. Others were dead and stiff with straight uplifted arms, as if they had been turned all of a sudden into stone in the middle of a struggle to the death. Many had in any case immediately fallen and lay with their faces flat on the earth. The wounds and dismemberment of others looked horrible. Two Frenchmen lay close to one another. Each robbed of an arm and shoulder blade by the same shot of a cannon. Elsewhere lay three Russians one behind the other, the first wholly without the front of his head, without a face, the second with a chest with a hole through it, and the third with its torso torn open: the result of a single shot.
>
> Still, the dead were not by far the most horrible thing! No, the dead lay still, even if in the most unnatural positions. But the dying, the dying! That rasping last call for water in a completely incomprehensible language, but made clear enough by some via gesticulations, sticking their tongue out and pointing, and even trying to go through the operation of drinking symbolically during their last breath![237]

The *Gartenlaube* deliberately gave its readers different views of battle. 'The drama of the peninsula [Crimea] continuously calls forth, in bloody flux, new depictions of scenes and situations, which are designed to give us the clearest possible picture of events there', remarked one journalist.[238] Sometimes this striving to find a novel perspective of the action necessitated a bird's-eye view, looking down on the fighting or bombardment below, but often it meant the relaying of sights seen by soldiers themselves amidst fighting or carnage. In the most extreme cases, words were favoured because there were fewer constraints placed on written accounts than on graphic representations of contemporary events, yet they were used increasingly to recreate a shocking visual spectacle.

Such reconstructed spectacles and descriptions were rare and had a limited effect. They do not appear to have prevented most observers from calling for or countenancing war. The majority of newspapers supported the Habsburg monarchy as it moved from the mobilization of a 130,000-strong army of observation in the border areas of Wallachia and Moldavia in the autumn of 1853 via the occupation of the principalities after Russia's withdrawal in August 1854 to more open threats of war.[239] Of the thirty-two German newspapers surveyed by the Austrian *Presseleitungskomitee* in 1855, fourteen supported Vienna's stance in the Crimean War, as it faced the possibility of military hostilities, and ten opposed it.[240]

---

[237] 'Die Schlacht an der Tschernaja', ibid., vol. 39, 521.

[238] 'Der Kampf vor Sevastopol. Mit einer Abbildung des Kampfplatzes vom Fort Konstantin aus', ibid., vol. 24, 317.

[239] G. E. Rothenberg, *The Army of Francis Joseph*, 50–1. Such stances were aided by the positive reporting of the Austrian occupation, even by Vienna's liberal press: see *Die Presse*, 26 Sept. 1854, whose correspondent in Jassy in Moldavia talked of 'the sympathies which the Austrian troops meet with here', with the inhabitants of the city resolving to erect triumphal gate for 'the glorification of the entry of the Austrian troops'.

[240] K. Paupié, *Handbuch*, vol. 2, 23–53. Some newspapers were unaligned.

Most conservative publications, influenced by states which feared being drawn into war, were opposed to Austria's stance, which had been made worse from ministers' points of view by its rapprochement with the western powers.[241] In Saxony, for instance, the *Dresdner Journal* was said to publish 'articles…influenced by the royal Saxon minister Freiherr v. Beust himself', helping to ensure that it was 'decidedly friendly towards Russia', 'hateful towards the western powers', and 'mistrustful of Austria', according to the committee.[242] The official *Leipziger Zeitung* was held, 'in the oriental question', to be 'fully in the direction of the *Kreuzzeitung*, i.e. Russian, and, where this does not seem permissible, collecting everything which speaks against the western powers, with suspicions cast against the k. k. government'.[243] It was joined by the *Freimüthige Sachsenzeitung*, which carried articles originating in Beust's cabinet but which also rested on the 'voluntary contributors in the Saxon noble party' (in effect, 'the Saxon *Kreuzzeitungspartei*'), 'enthusiastic for Russia' and 'constantly warning, and even threatening, Austria'.[244]

For its part, the *Neue Preussische (Kreuz)Zeitung*, whose 'great advantage vis-à-vis all other German papers' was that its 'entire content' was 'permeated by a single tendency', remained at once 'ultra-Prussian up to the point of visible narrow-mindedness' and 'decisively inimical to Austria', piling up 'for this purpose all hateful memories of stock Prussians against Austria' and 'reminiscences of 1813 against France' in order to underline its 'ultra-Russian credentials', in the words of the Austrian press committee report.[245] The conservative mouthpiece 'maintains links for its own ends extending into the king's cabinet (secret counsellor *Illaire*, *Niebuhr*, General *Gerlach*), to the higher circles of the military (Field Marshal Graf *Dohna*, General *v. d. Gröben*, amongst others), with individual ministers (v. *Westphal*, *Manteuffel II*, brother of the Minister-President and an Under-Secretary of State), and finally with the envoys of foreign states, e.g. Baron *Budberg*': 'From Frankfurt, Herr v. *Bismarck-Schönhausen* furnishes it extra-legally with malicious rumours against Austria.'[246] Although it had earlier published 'vituperative anti-government articles, including those from smaller states', it had now stopped opposing Berlin because its position on the Crimean War coincided with that of the Prussian state.[247] Momentarily, the position of the reactionary camarilla tied to the *Kreuzzeitung* and that of the Prussian government and most of the states of the third Germany had converged. In the opinion of the Prussian-born Bavarian ministerial counsellor Wilhelm von Dönniges, expressed in a letter to King Maximilian II on 8 May 1854, 'Prussia can count on having all the main states of the rest of Germany on its side, if it decides to represent German interests through its own mediation with Russia, above all.'[248] This unity soon disappeared, however, with Prussia adopting a policy of armed neutrality, to the annoyance of St Petersburg,

---

[241] S. Meiboom, *Studien zur deutschen Politik Bayerns in den Jahren 1851–59* (Munich, 1931), 65–95.

[242] K. Paupié, *Handbuch*, vol. 2, 30. [243] Ibid., 37. [244] Ibid., 47.

[245] Ibid., 44–5. Also, D. Bussiek, *'Mit Gott fuer König und Vaterland!' Die Neue Preussische Zeitung (Kreuzzeitung) 1848–1892* (Münster, 2000).

[246] K. Paupié, *Handbuch*, vol. 2, 45. [247] Ibid.

[248] Dönniges to Maximilian II, 8 May 1854, S. Meiboom, *Studien zur deutschen Politik Bayerns*, 76.

with the *Mittelstaaten* avoiding committing themselves to either Russia or Austria and with the camarilla—or '*Kreuzzeitung* party'—advocating a 'struggle of the Germans' against 'the Slav-Greek-and-Turkish', which Austria was too 'negative' and lacked the courage to do.[249]

Much of the rest of the press in the German lands was critical of the pro-Russian posturing of the *Kreuzzeitung* and of the pusillanimity of Prussia and the other German states.[250] To Varnhagen von Ense, who was closely connected to Berlin 'society', it was likely that 'the Russian government is giving huge sums of money to the *Kreuzzeitung* people so that their scandal sheet eagerly takes Russia's side': 'Of this money, Wagener, Goedsche, Stahl and Gerlach received the greater part.'[251] Like Prussian conservatives clustered around the *Preußisches Wochenblatt*, edited by the Frankfurt academic Moritz August von Bethmann-Hollweg, Varnhagen wanted Prussia to support Britain and France—'my sympathies are naturally with the western powers in the current conflicts'—and, as it gravitated towards the 'west', Austria. Although he did not favour war, stating that 'it is not my thing which is being fought for here', he struggled not to 'lose [this] from view in the tumult of daily opinion', which generally pushed governments towards a conflict.[252] In this context, the king himself, who 'reads nothing but the *Kreuzzeitung*', was 'very agitated at the proclivity of public opinion, which doesn't blindly trust in his policy but wants to become independent': 'The entire population of Berlin is inflamed and full of indignation over the impudent tirades of Ludwig von Gerlach; everyone repeats the words of Vincke and Bethmann-Hollweg—even in the lowest classes these are known and approved of.'[253] The principal 'western' group of the '*Wochenblatt* party', including the editor Julius von Jasmund and the diplomats Guido von Usedom and Albert von Pourtalès, came to back the Habsburg monarchy's mobilization of troops and threats of military

[249] Diary entry on 23 May 1854, L. v. Gerlach, *Denkwürdigkeiten*, vol. 2, 154.

[250] See, for instance, the *Kölnische Zeitung* in June 1854, which criticized the states of the Confederation for belonging to 'Russia's German *Bund*'; K. Buchheim, *Die Geschichte der Kölnischen Zeitung*, vol. 3, 192. *Kladderadatsch*, 1854, vol. 7, 168, showed a young Prussian 'lad' (*Knabe*) in military uniform being terrified and bullied by a giant Russian ghost; another article from 15 Oct. 1854, carrying the ironic title of 'Good News', *Kladderadatsch*, 189, commented that 'the people of Germany' were 'united', represented at effectively at Frankfurt, and that 'peace' was imminent according to 'a completely trustworthy Tartar'. Some publications such as the *Historisch-politische Blätter*, 1854, vol. 33, no. 1, 607–31, examined the differences between 'old' and 'young' Russia' and between 'western civilization and a Russian *Volkscharakter*' in a relatively nuanced way; also 'Altrußland und die "heilige Allianz"', *Historisch-politische Blätter*, 711–15. J. Froehlich, 'Repression und Lenkung versus Pressefreiheit und meinungsmarkt. Zur preussischen Pressegeschichte in der Reichsbruendungszeit 1848–71', in B. Sösemann (ed.), *Kommunikation und Medien in Preussen vom 16 bis zum 19 Jahrhundert*, 375, points out that most liberal publications in the German lands were happy to use Britain's entry into the conflict as an opportunity to pit liberalism against reaction.

[251] K. A. Varnhagen v. Ense, *Tagebücher*, vol. 10, 464. Hermann Goedsche, the author of *Die Russen nach Constantinopel!*, which had argued that the tsarist regime was warring against 'communist revolution', was especially targeted: H.-C. Kraus, 'Wahrnehmung und Deutung des Krimkrieges in Preußen. Zur innenpolitischen Rückwirkung eines internationalen Großkonflikts', in G. Maag, W. Pyta, and M. Windisch (eds), *Der Krimkrieg als erster europäischer Medienkrieg*, 242.

[252] Diary entry, 16 May 1854, K. A. Varnhagen v. Ense, *Tagebücher*, vol. 11, 71.

[253] Respectively, diary entries on 24 and 21 Mar. 1854 and 10 Apr. 1854, ibid., 8, 1, 57.

intervention, having initially argued—before Vienna had approached Paris and London—that, 'if we must go to war, it would be more advantageous for us to have Austria as an enemy rather than as a friend'.[254] Christian Carl Josias von Bunsen, Prussia's ambassador in London and a close associate of the king's brother and heir Prince Wilhelm, went so far as to advise Friedrich Wilhelm IV in a memorandum of 1854 to back the maritime powers and expand Prussia at Austria's expense.[255] The monarch agreed to his dismissal, believing—or professing to believe—that Bunsen had had a nervous breakdown, yet the diplomat's stand revealed the extent to which the case for the war of the western powers was being made in Prussia and elsewhere.[256] Although discounted in his memoirs by Bismarck as 'childish utopias', such agitation involved figures as orthodox as Albrecht von Roon, the later War Minister under Bismarck, who was stationed at Cologne in the mid-1850s, and who was one of the military correspondents of the *Wochenblatt's* publisher Friedrich Perthes.[257]

The majority of newspapers and periodicals in the Hohenzollern monarchy and other German lands supported the war, pushing their governments to join Austria and the western powers. To Otto Elben, the editor and owner of the *Schwäbischer Merkur*, it was 'almost self-evident' that most of the press was against Russia, given the part that it had played in propping up the Holy Alliance and Metternich's order within the German Confederation.[258] Despite the continuing anti-Habsburg leanings of 'democratic' publications like the *Beobachter* (Stuttgart), *Westfälische Zeitung* (Paderborn), and *National-Zeitung* (Berlin), which nonetheless had been said, 'from various sides', to look on 'Austria with a certain trust or even with secret hopes' as a result of 'the policy followed by the k. k. cabinet in the oriental affair', as the *Presseleitungskomitee* in Vienna put it, many

> 'liberal' papers of Germany—amongst which were the most significant and the most widely spread ones such as the *Kölnische Zeitung*, Bremen's *Weser-Zeitung*, the *Haude- und Spenersche Zeitung* of Berlin etc.—have changed their tone, as a consequence of the decisive policy of the k. k. cabinet in the oriental conflict, or they express their inclination towards, or at least their applause for, Austria more or less openly.[259]

To *Kladderadatsch*, which recalled the words of Schiller's *Wallenstein*, Austria 'came late, but still [it] came!'[260] Of the largest publications in northern and central Germany, copies of which radiated out into their regional hinterlands, the *Kölnische*

[254] *Preussisches Wochenblatt*, 28 Jan. 1854, in R. Müller, *Die Partei Bethmann-Hollweg und die orientalische Krise 1853–1856* (Halle, 1926), 51.

[255] Ibid., 55–6.

[256] Hans-Christof Kraus, 'Wahrnehmung und Deutung des Krimkrieges in Preußen', in G. Maag, W. Pyta, and M. Windisch (eds), *Der Krimkrieg als erster europäischer Medienkrieg*, 238–9, suggests that the *Wochenblatt* party's hold over the monarch was broken by March 1854. Because of the sympathy of the king's brother and successor, this turn of events was not seen to be irreversible at the time.

[257] O. v. Bismarck, *Die gesammelten Werke* (Berlin, 1932), vol. 15, 80–1; M. Behnen, *Das Preußische Wochenblatt 1851–1861. Nationalkonservative Publizistik gegen Ständestaat und Polizeistaat* (Göttingen, 1971), 77.

[258] O. Elben, *Geschichte des Schwäbischen Merkurs*.

[259] K. Paupié, *Handbuch*, vol. 2, 20.

[260] 'Neue Bilder zu alten Texten', *Kladderadatsch*, 1854, vol. 7, 168.

Zeitung (whose circulation in 1855 was 12,000–15,000) was said regularly to take 'Austria's side in the oriental question, especially against the Russian party in Prussia'; the *Hamburger Nachrichten* (11,000–12,000) was believed to follow 'public opinion in the oriental business', backing the war of the western states, 'though always with…reservations'; and the *Frankfurter Journal* (10,000), which was subject to 'Prussian influence', worked 'against the *Bund* and Austria sticking together'.[261]

In southern Germany, the 'Catholic press' had taken up 'such an imposing and patriotic position in the oriental question that the consciousness of a generally affected occidental culture (*abendländische Cultur*), which had earlier been oscillating and unclear, had risen up and been clarified'.[262] Although the states of the third Germany, meeting in the Bavarian town of Bamberg, had been 'terrible' in Varnhagen's opinion, shying away from war (according to the report of the Bavarian Foreign Minister and President of the *Ministerrat* Ludwig von der Pfordten on 26 May 1854), newspapers such as the *Augsburger Postzeitung, Mainzer Journal, Frankfurter Postzeitung, Casseler Zeitung, Hannoversche Zeitung, Leipziger Illustrirte Zeitung, Hamburger Correspondent*, and *Deutsches Volksblatt*, which was published in Stuttgart, all backed Austria's preparations for a military intervention.[263] The *Allgemeine Zeitung*, the second largest southern German publication (after the *Münchner Neueste Nachrichten*, with its 15,000 subscribers), had proved so supportive of the Habsburg monarchy that its publisher Georg von Cotta received a letter of gratitude from the Austrian government, expressing 'the full acknowledgement of the k. k. government for the patriotic and circumspect conduct of this important newspaper in its discussion of the position of Austria and Germany in respect of the oriental question'.[264] The newspaper's position, in its owner's view in October 1854, merely mirrored that of 'the public opinion of the nation', which was 'so little confused, so clearly energetic, that anyone who does not hold to the policy of Austria is depicted as being bribed by Russia'.[265] The public's appetite for war, it seemed to many observers in 1853–6, was undiminished, with many journalists urging the German states to enter the conflict.

Arguably, the presence of a powerful and demonized enemy in the Crimean War, akin to the role played by Napoleonic France in 1813–15 or 1870, might have reinforced German observers' anxieties about the changing nature of warfare by the 1850s. The shifting allegiances of governments and the press, however, militated against such demonization.[266] For the *Allgemeine Zeitung* as for many other German newspapers, the war between Russia and Turkey, which broke out in 1853, had appeared mainly to be about the defence of the rights of Christians in

[261] K. Paupié, *Handbuch*, vol. 2, 27–8, 31–2, 35–6.   [262] Ibid., 19.

[263] Ibid. On Pfordten's report, see S. Meiboom, *Studien zur deutschen Politik Bayerns*, 77–8, noting that Hanover, Kurhessen, Baden, and Hesse-Darmstadt had argued that the *Bund* should join the western powers.

[264] Weil to G. Cotta, 28 Dec. 1854, in E. Heyck, *Die Allgemeine Zeitung*, 289.

[265] G. Cotta to G. Kolb, 21 Oct. 1854, ibid.

[266] The *Historisch-politische Blätter*, 1858, vol. 2, 20, later talked of a revolution in the relations between European states during the Crimean War. Droysen likewise referred to a 'revolution of the European states' system', in F. Gilbert (ed.), *Droysen*, 331.

the Ottoman Empire, recalling—as the *Grenzboten* pointed out in an explicit comparison in 1853—the earlier conflict between the two powers in 1828–9, in which St Petersburg had enjoyed broad support.[267] After Russian troops had occupied Moldavia and Wallachia in July 1853, the *Allgemeine Zeitung* had openly doubted the reassurances of the *Journal de Constantinople* that 'the barbaric times of the old Turks are now over', rendering anachronistic the treaties which continued to grant judicial competencies 'over their subjects to the representatives of the foreign powers'.[268] The maintenance of such competencies was 'a matter for which all Christian Great Powers have to have a concern', the article went on, in part to prevent Russia from 'exploiting' it 'for other reasons' and in part to avert Turkish injustices and atrocities: 'the introduction of laws and courts which treat all Turkish citizens equally impartially, whether believers or unbelievers, does not even appear to be in the realms of possibility as long as Islam is and remains the basis of the state'.[269] Despite the 'objections and reproaches which were directed at the Allg. Ztg. because of the reception of our reports about the internal conditions of Turkey' and 'which gradually became weaker and finally quite silent', noted the newspaper on 16 October 1853, it would continue to bring news of 'abominations' like the boiling and roasting of monks by 'Turkish fanaticism' and the cutting down of notables in 'an open market' by 'armed hordes'.[270] The correspondent declared:

> Our aim in the publication of these facts—which, as long as the Allg. Ztg. is available to you, we shall carry on striving towards in order to clarify European opinion—is and will remain the same, even now that the Turkish question has gone from a state of peace, which was not a true peace, over to a state of war, which is allegedly not yet a war but which must soon become one... One should not forget, in all the political, financial and industrial considerations and calculations in whose bottomless depths this question is swirling around (to the shame of Europe), that the need of assistance of a defenceless Christianity in Turkey lies at the bottom of it, which will soon lead to horrors like those immeasurable outrages committed during the Greek uprising.[271]

Since 'the Russian intention of protecting Christianity' had widely been suspected as a ruse to conceal the 'expansion of the tsars', it had been tempting to shut 'ones eyes and ears to the real fount of the actual evil and the source of all the difficulties and dangers of the situation', viewing 'the independence, greatness and worth of

---

[267] See the *Allgemeine Zeitung*'s reports in support of Russia, dated 18 Oct. 1828 (from the Moldavian town of Jassy), 24 Oct. 1828 (in its *Beilage*, no. 303), 6 June 1829 (citing the *Journal d'Odessa*), and 16 June 1829 (from Jassy). The *Grenzboten*, 1853, vol. 13, no. 4, 241–50, 330–7, printed an extensive report on the earlier campaigns before concluding that Turkey was in a stronger position in 1853 than it had been in 1828–9. For another comparison, see the *Allgemeine Zeitung*, 8 July 1853. The camarilla, in particular, stressed the Christian aspect of the campaign: H.-C. Kraus, 'Wahrnehmung und Deutung des Krimkrieges in Preußen' 241.

[268] *Allgemeine Zeitung*, 6 July 1853.

[269] Ibid. The article mentions the cutting off of Greeks' ears and noses, as they were 'mishandled and dismembered in a barbaric fashion, by Turks during instances of 'disorder', as the *Journal de Constantinople* had put it.

[270] 'Fortsetzung der Mittheilungen über die inneren Zustände der Türkei', ibid., 16 Oct. 1853.

[271] Ibid.

the Ottoman protégé as a European requirement'.[272] For the *Allgemeine Zeitung* in October 1853, it was time for the German states and the European Great Powers 'to join with Russia or take over from Russia' the task of defending 'Christianity in Turkey against the fanaticism of the Muslims'.[273] As Britain and France prepared to declare war on Russia, which they eventually did on 28 March 1854, the Augsburg newspaper's correspondent refused to 'believe that an Anglo-French army will fight for the Turks', not least because 'Russia's victory, supported by the Hellenes, Serbs, Bosnians and Bulgarians, who are mostly Greek Christians and deadly enemies of the Ottomans, is almost absolutely certain, if it pursues no other aim than the freeing of the Christians from the yoke of the [Turkish] crescent.'[274] Even if France and Britain did intervene, they would arrive too late and be overpowered by Russia on the ground.[275] Yet as the Austrian government, too, began to alter its stance, with 'the mood here in the city [of Vienna] for Turkey and against Russia, in accordance with the opinion of the [Viennese] *Lloyd* and most Austrian papers', the *Allgemeine Zeitung* started to qualify its criticism of the Ottoman Empire and Islam, merely stating at the end of March that 'one cannot exactly say that they [the Austrians] are mad about the Turks'.[276] Although traces of the publication's earlier position—with references to 'fanaticism in Constantinople'—could be found later in 1854, its positive coverage of the Habsburg monarchy's defence of Turkey, 'against the greatest danger which menaced [it] from the Russian side on the land bridge in Europe', had come to overshadow its earlier doubts by October.[277] Vienna's actions against Russia and its 'independent position vis-à-vis the entanglements of the Orient' demonstrated that 'Austria feels a rejuvenating force in its limbs', which was worthy of Germany's support and cooperation, even if it entailed war.[278]

North German newspapers were less prone to the demonization of 'Turks' and 'Muslims' than Austrian, Catholic, and other southern German publications— looking back on a long history of conflict in the Balkans and Near East—and they were less likely to be swayed by Vienna's rapprochement with the western powers, with 'well-meaning Christian-Germanic souls in the North' viewing 'Austria as a European China' (in the words of the *Allgemeine Zeitung* in March 1854), but they

[272] Ibid. For more on the Turkish war effort, see C. Badem, *The Ottoman Crimean War, 1853–1856* (Leiden, 2010). For the *Historisch-politische Blätter*, 1854, vol. 33, no. 1, 530, the question hinged on 'the extent to which Russia will be allowed to make use of the Porte's visible decay'. On the speciousness of the Russian claim to protect Christians, see Catholic and conservative commentators like Johann Wilhelm Braun in his *Berliner Briefe über die Orientalische Frage* (Bonn, 1854), for instance.
[273] *Allgemeine Zeitung*, 16 Oct. 1853.   [274] Ibid., 15 Mar. 1854.
[275] Ibid. The same publication declared that Turkey was the 'hereditary and imperial enemy' of the 'West', ibid., 16 Apr. 1854. Other southern German, Catholic publications such as the *Historisch-politische Blätter*, 1854, vol. 33, no. 1, 527, assumed 'that Russia would be forced by victories to wrest the dying Turkish empire from the western powers', with 'incalculable complications' for the constellations of the states' system.
[276] *Allgemeine Zeitung*, 28 Mar. 1854.
[277] For instance, 'Zur historischen Aufhellung der diplomatischen Schachzüge in der orientalischen Frage', ibid., 29 Apr., 7 June 1854. On the newspaper's shift of position by October, see ibid., 24 Oct. 1854.
[278] Ibid., 28 Mar. 1854.

remained similarly undecided about the identity and nature of potential enemies in the Crimean War.[279] The Ottoman Empire was widely regarded at first as a threat to Christians and then, after the western states' declaration of war and the Habsburg monarchy's change of diplomatic course, as a foreign ally and a significant military power. This impression was reinforced by the common practice—especially during the 'reaction', when commentary on domestic politics was riskier—of reprinting articles in German publications from Austria, France, and Britain, where Turkey was treated favourably.[280] As was the case in the *Allgemeine Zeitung*, the Ottoman Empire was still associated with 'Asia' or the 'East' and was subordinated to the machinations and shifting fortunes of European politics. Thus, for Heinrich Kruse, editor-in-chief of the *Kölnische Zeitung* from 1855 to 1872, it was necessary for the rest of Germany to follow the example of Austria—to which his predecessor Karl Heinrich Brüggemann had given 'thundering congratulations' in December 1854—in support of 'the English and the French' in a war to protect 'this communal culture (*Bildung*) of Europe against the push from Asia'.[281] Given the alignment of powers, Turkey was no longer—by 1854—an eastern menace. Rather, it was treated in the same way as the other parties to the conflict or it was made an object of pity.

Like many correspondents, Marx and Engels oscillated between the two modes of representation. 'Amidst all this confusion and uncertainty, one thing alone seems clear, and that is the extinction of the Moslem power as a distinct polity in Europe', they concluded in an article on the 'European War' in the *New York Daily Tribune* on 17 April 1854: 'the emancipation of the Christians of Turkey, whether effected by peaceful concession or by violence, degrades Islamism from a political authority to a religious sect, and utterly uproots the old foundations of the Otttoman Empire'.[282] A few months later, it seemed as though Turkey's army was the principal force, despite being 'very badly cared for' and unable 'to execute rapid movements which would remove it to a distance from its base', with 'nearly a hundred thousand English and French soldiers' merely 'there to assist the Turks or make diversions in their favour'.[283] Notwithstanding its mocking rather than revering tone, the content of the two exiled communists' reportage was similar to

---

[279] Ibid.

[280] J. Fröhlich, 'Repression und Lenkung versus Pressefreiheit und Meinungsmarkt. Zur preussischen Pressegeschichte in der Reichsgründungszeit 1848–71', in B. Sösemann (ed.), *Kommunikation und Medien in Preussen vom 16 bis zum 19 Jahrhundert* (Stuttgart, 2002), 374–5.

[281] Cited in K. Buchheim, *Die Geschichte der Kölnischen Zeitung*, vol. 3, 199.

[282] K. Marx and F. Engels, *Gesamtausgabe*, vol. 13, 179.

[283] Marx and Engels, 'That Bore of a War', *New York Daily Tribune*, 17 Aug. 1854, ibid., 370. Marx made a similar point in 'The War in the East', *The Zuid Africaan* (Cape Town), 6 Mar. 1854, ibid., 21–2, written in London on 4 Jan. 1854, referring to the split nature of the Turkish army: 'We know besides that the Turkish army of Anatolia, recruited as it is from the Asiatic provinces, the seat of old Moslem barbarism, and counting in its ranks a great number of irregulars, unreliable though generally brave soldiers of adventure, fancy warriors, and filibusters of Kurdistan—that the army of Anatolia, is nothing like the staid, disciplined and drilled army of Roumelia, where the commander knows how many and what men he has from day to day under his command, and where the thirst for independent adventure and private plunder is held under check by articles of war and courts martial.'

that of articles in many liberal publications, as the main military evaluation of 'The Four Armies in the Crimea' in the *Grenzboten* made plain. Turkish soldiers were 'in and for themselves incomparably superior' to their Russian counterparts, capable of fitting into 'any tactical formation', the correspondent maintained, denying 'that, in saying this, I am letting myself be affected by considerations of partiality'.[284] Likewise, the Ottoman artilleryman, trained by Prussian officers, 'aims better than the Russian', as 'has been said too often in recent times, so that it must seem redundant to add anything else here'.[285] In this type of report, Turkish troops were treated in a matter-of-fact way alongside Russian, French, and British ones.

At the same time, however, they were cast as 'oriental' objects of European fantasy, transforming the Crimean War into a distant adventure comparable to a colonial expedition.[286] The *Historisch-politische Blätter* was not alone in lamenting the unwillingness of 'our German *Publizistik*' to acknowledge that 'at least America belongs to the questions of *European* politics, not to mention *Asia*'.[287] The affairs of Asia were widely believed to be distinct and distant from those of Europe, as the article's own description of Russia's and Britain's global interests—which would constitute 'the main act of the history of the second half of the nineteenth century'—spelled out, with references to Turkish Armenia and Persia, 'the steppes of the Tartar and Kyrgyz hordes of Central Asia', 'the tents of the Khans of Khiva, Bukhara and Kabul', 'the mountain passes of the Afghans', 'the north-west frontier of India', and the 'great military site of Bombay'.[288] One early article in the *Gartenlaube* on 'Turkish Soldiers', which also conceded that regular troops—from a large total force of 338,260—were 'well trained' and 'used to strict discipline' and that officers were 'very well-informed' and artillery 'excellent', recorded that the soldiers were 'funny, jovial chaps, and one can think of no better travelling companion'.[289] 'Each wears his Stambul fez like a humorous *Bursche* and the blue tassels never rest because of their liveliness', the article continued, before going on to describe the exotic uniform of the soldiers in fetishistic detail: 'Tights are not in fashion, so a part of the foot always peeps out [of their shoes], but they are always well washed.'[290] Such regular troops were portrayed, in words and etchings, beside turban-wearing, mounted Kurds, 'some of whom serve in the Russian, some in the Asiatic-Turkish and some in their own robber armies', or next to fearsome, muscular bashi-bazouks, who functioned as a form of *Landsturm* but 'whole masses of

---

[284] 'Die vier Armeen in der Krim', *Grenzboten*, 1854, vol. 13, no. 4, 365.   [285] Ibid., 369.

[286] Friedrich Engels, 'The Attack on Sevastopol', *New York Daily Tribune*, 14 Oct. 1854, in K. Marx and F. Engels, *Gesamtausgabe*, vol. 13, 550, compared the campaigns in Bulgaria and Africa in derision, exposing the lack of preparedness and disorganization of the Allied armies compared to earlier colonial wars. See also M. Fuhrmann, *Der Traum vom deutschen Osten. Zwei deutsche Kolonien im Osmanischen Reich 1851–1918* (Frankfurt, 2006), 39–47, 111–42, 281–328.

[287] *Historisch-politische Blätter*, 1854, vol. 33, no. 1, 529. There were very occasional references to 'world powers' such as the United States and Russia at the time of the Crimean War: see, for instance, 'Rundschauerlicher Traum', *Kladderadatsch*, 1854, vol. 7, 212.

[288] *Historisch-politische Blätter*, 1854, vol. 33, no. 1, 529–30. Also, 'Rußland in Asien, England als Nachbar', ibid., 852–73; 'Illustrirte-Zeitungs-Notizen', ibid., 220, which showed native Americans wearing ill-fitting 'European' masks and clothes, roasting 'Europa' on a spit.

[289] 'Türkische Soldaten', *Gartenlaube*, 1853, vol. 47, 520.   [290] Ibid.

Figure 5.3 'Irreguläres türkisches Militär'
Source: *Gartenlaube*, 1854, vol. 13, 142.

whom deserted not exactly rarely' and 'roamed around... as robbers'.[291] 'Irregular Turkish Military' were shown as medieval horsemen (see Figure 5.3).[292] As they and their horses waded through a river in a long, arcing column, with the snow-peaked mountains of Asia Minor behind them, the Kurds looked like figures from biblical story or Arabic legend.[293] For their part, the bashi-bazouks were depicted as a single, organic, corporeal mass, similar to drawings of Africans, looking on menacingly and proudly from a mountain ridge.[294]

These anthropological studies of different tribal warriors were supplemented by travel tales of local folklore, topography, peoples, and women, from Georgians, who were 'thin and of the purest proportions, with their chiselled faces and large, enthusiastically shining eyes', via 'the most beautiful girls' in Wallachia, who supposedly lived far from the 'corruption' of Bucharest, to Turkish women, who 'aroused our curiosity' with their veils and their public silence but who were also shown in the 'oriental' fantasy of the Sultan's harem.[295] Readers were presented with 'pictures' of Belgrade, Varna, Sevastopol, Odessa, Kars, Erzerum, and the Balkans and its mountain fastnesses.[296] One article in *Gartenlaube* promised 'Turkish Reflections', including 'walks', 'the Balkans with its narrow passes', 'the Turk with the Christian coat', 'the trading of women', 'Turkish bachelorhood and family life'.[297] It began by inviting 'our readers to accompany us on some walks

[291] 'Türkisches Militär', ibid., 1855, vol. 46, 553; 'Kurden- und Kosaken-Bilder', ibid., 1855, vol. 36, 471–2; 'Die Baschi-Bazuks, der türkische Landsturm', ibid., 1855, vol. 27, 360–2.

[292] 'Irreguläres türkisches Militär', ibid., 1854, vol. 13, 142.

[293] Ibid., 1855, vol. 36, 471.   [294] Ibid., 1855, vol. 27, 361.

[295] 'Am Kaukasus', ibid., 1854, vol. 41, 484; 'Wallachische Schönheiten', ibid., 1854, vol. 34, 404; 'Bilder aus Varna', 1854, vol. 28, 341; 'Blicke in einen türkischen Harem', ibid., 1854, vol. 25, 293.

[296] 'Belgrad', ibid., 1854, vol. 3, 29; 'Bilder aus Varna', ibid., 1854, vol. 28, 327; 'Belagerungsplan von Sevastopol', ibid., 1854, vol. 50, 609; 'Mamelon, Malakoff und Taganrog', ibid., 1855, vol. 27, 357–8; 'Odessa', ibid., 1855, vol. 43, 575; 'Aus den letzten Tagen von Kars', ibid., 1856, vol. 2, 27–8; 'Erzerum', ibid., 1856, vol. 4, 54–5.

[297] 'Türkische Spiegelbilder: Spaziergänge; der Balkan mit seinen Engpässen; der Türke mit dem christlichen Frack; türkisches Junggesellentum und Familienleben; der Türke mit Sprungriemen; Handel mit Mädchen; der Sonntag der Frauen in Constantinopel', ibid., 1853, vol. 46, 500–3.

into the interior of Turkish mores and morals; that is, into those circles on which the "oriental question" largely hinges'.[298] Another article offered a short history and geographical exploration of 'The Crimean Peninsula', which 'even without war, without the English, French and Russians in soldiers' uniforms, is interesting enough', as the old 'seat of the Tartar Empire of the Mongols', who 'once used to dominate the whole of Asia', and as the site of classical ruins and Christian sects.[299] Sticking out into the Black Sea, the peninsula was as large as Saxony, Hanover, Württemberg, and Baden combined, with three-quarters of the territory covered by steppe and one-quarter, on the south coast, an 'attractive mountain land' called 'the Russian Switzerland', noted a guide to 'Rambling in the Crimea' in late 1854.[300] The juxtaposition of and alternation between these types of exotic travelogue and war reports within periodicals and, to a lesser extent, newspapers turned an alien land and culture into a source of fascination and attraction rather than of fear, it appeared.[301] Even gruesome accounts of military killing and hardship such as 'Scenes from the Anglo-French Winter Camp in the Crimea', which was published in the *Gartenlaube* in early 1855, often couched their depictions of corpses— on the battlefield of Inkerman in this case—and 'the dirt, terror, hospitals, graves, dead, dying [and] the stink' of camps (Balaklava) within the conceit of 'a short hike', a trip along a 'road', or a voyage.[302]

In contrast to Turkey, Russia was regularly perceived to be a familiar European power rather than an exotic extra-European one.[303] Until 1848, it had been the guarantor of the Holy Alliance, joining Austrian forces to defeat Hungarian 'revolutionaries' in 1849. Many newspapers reprinted articles from the Russian press, casting the campaign from St Petersburg's point of view and referring to the fortunes of 'our' Russian soldiers. On the left, Engels was unambiguous in viewing the tsarist regime as 'our enemy', which had to be looked at 'straight in the face to see what sort of an opponent he may turn out to be', but he also acknowledged that 'the composition and organisation of the Russian army is known well enough to military men all over Europe', with 'a good deal of valuable matter in our western literatures which requires nothing but sifting and combining', in spite of the existence of 'the most contradictory opinions as to [its] real military strength and capabilities', 'overrated by some, underrated by others'.[304] 'The actual difficulty is merely to know how far this organisation', which was based on an imitation of that introduced in France by Napoleon I, 'has been really carried out, how much of this

[298] Ibid., 500.

[299] 'Die Halbinsel Krimm', ibid., 1855, vol. 37, 436; 'Karaiten von Theodosia auf der Krim', ibid., vol. 16, 216.

[300] 'Wanderungen in der Krim', ibid., 1855, vol. 44, 529.

[301] For such juxtaposition in other periodicals, see 'Sevastopol', *Grenzboten*, 1854, vol. 13, no. 4, 281–8.

[302] 'Scenen aus dem englisch-französischen Winterlager', *Gartenlaube*, 1855, vol. 3, 34–5; 'Der Weg zwischen Balaklava und dem englischen Lager', ibid., vol. 10, 137.

[303] For German representations of Russia, see V. G. Liulevicius, *The German Myth of the East*, 44–97; M. Keller (ed.), *Russen und Rußland aus deutscher Sicht*, vol. 3. For more on Russian perceptions and experiences of the war, see—in addition to Figes's work—J. S. Curtiss, *Russia's Crimean War* (Durham, NC, 1979).

[304] F. Engels, 'The Russian Army', in K. Marx and F. Engels, *Gesamtausgabe*, vol. 13, 173–5.

army exists not merely on paper but can be brought forward against a foreign foe', the journalist and industrialist went on.[305] In principle, at least, Russian forces were large, with 750,000 troops according to Marx and Engels in 1855 (historians now estimate 1.2 million in total), of which only one-third were stationed in the Crimea and two-thirds were 'deployed to menace Austria'.[306] As for many of his contemporaries, war was reduced for Engels to the status of a European strategic game, reminiscent of 1812:

> And there are people who believe that Nicholas will sue for peace if Sevastopol be taken! Why, Russia has not played one-third of her trumps yet, and the momentary loss of Sevastopol and of the fleet is hardly felt at all by the giant to whom Sevastopol and he felt were but a plaything. Russia knows full well that her decisive action does not lie along the sea shores or within reach of disembarking troops; but on the contrary, on the broad interior of the Continent, where massive armies can be brought to act concentrated on one spot, without frittering away their forces in a fruitless coast defence against evanescent enemies. Russia may lose the Crimea, the Caucasus, Finland, St Petersburg and all such appendages; but as long as her body, with Moscow for its heart, and fortified Poland for its sword-arm, is untouched, she need not give in an iota.
>
> The grand actions of 1854 are, we dare say, but the petty preludes of the battles of nations which will mark the annals of 1855. It is not until the great Russian army of the west, and the Austrian army come into play, no matter whether against each other or with each other, that we shall see real war on a large scale, something like the grand wars of Napoleon. And, perhaps, these battles may be the preludes merely of other battles far more fierce, far more decisive—the battles of the European peoples against the now victorious and secure European despots.[307]

In theory, 'the continental force launched against Russia' was stronger in 1854 than in 1812, with Britain on France's and Austria's side, not Russia's.[308] Russia in the latter instance had helped to defend German states. In both instances, it was treated by Marx and Engels as a regular Great Power.

Because of its size, with a land mass of 343,240 square miles compared to the 314,662 square miles of Britain, France, Turkey, and their empires, Russia constituted, for liberal and unaligned publications, a unique site of conflict, with more or less conventional military forces.[309] This positive assessment of the tsarist regime's forces became more, not less, pronounced as the war continued, partly because of Russian resistance during the siege of Sevastopol, where 65,000 soldiers of the tsar had been killed or wounded by the end of July 1855, before the Allies'

[305] Ibid., 174.

[306] K. Marx and F. Engels, 'Progress of the War', 563; O. Figes, *Crimea*, 334.

[307] F. Engels, 'The Military Power of Russia', *New York Daily Tribune*, 31 Oct 1854, in K. Marx and F. Engels, *Gesamtausgabe*, vol. 13, 153. Many publications considered the Crimean War a 'game' between the Great Powers: see, for instance, *Historisch-politische Blätter*, 1855, vol. 35, no. 1, 1030–43.

[308] K. Marx and F. Engels, 'Progress of the War', 566.

[309] 'Die kriegführende Mächte', *Gartenlaube*, 1855, vol. 15, 200.

final assault on the city.[310] Occasionally, the press pointed to the existence of a 'racial conflict' between 'Slavs' and 'Germans', with Austrians fearing 'the national character of this Great Power [Russia]', not merely its military forces, in the words of the *Allgemeine Zeitung* on 7 December 1854, yet the general tenor of newspaper reportage was less stereotypical and more admiring.[311] At the start of the winter of 1854–5, in November, the same publication had underlined the resilience of the Russian troops, against whom 'the Allies cannot boast of any significant progress until now': 'They [the Allies] have underestimated the strength of the defenders and the difficulty of the undertaking', with the 'courage and morale' of the 30,000–35,000 occupiers of Sevastopol 'unbroken' and its defences strong.[312] As the *Gartenlaube* informed its readers, the military fortifications of the port had been designed by a British civil engineer, just as the most opulent of the Crimean palaces of the Russian nobility had been built by a British architect, standing in stark contrast to the wooden huts and freezing living conditions of the British and French armies on the peninsula and begging the question of the two sides' relative 'civilization' and 'humanity'.[313] Initially, in November 1854, the *Grenzboten* had, its military expert conceded, underestimated the strength of the Russian army, emphasizing the 'parade-ground' discipline of its peasant soldiers at the same time as their 'slowness and unwieldiness' in manoeuvres, as they dissolved in disarray under the fire of British artillery.[314] The 'supplement' provided by the same correspondent in the spring of 1855 revised these earlier judgements, praising the tsarist regime for introducing a fundamental reform of the artillery in the 1840s, which had proved effective in the Crimea, in spite of the fact that it lay 'in the nature of the Russian Empire' to lag behind the institutions of 'western Europe'.[315] Its infantry had not been reformed, turning the siege of Sevastopol into 'a school for its army in general', but it nonetheless remained wedded to the military traditions of the European states, having learned from the battles of 'Eylau, Borodino and Leipzig' during the Napoleonic Wars.[316] Unlike in the campaigns of 1812–15, 'Cossacks' were the subject of few reports and, when they did feature, they were often portrayed in an exotic, unmenacing fashion.[317] In such articles, the forces, tactics, and armaments of Russia were compared straightforwardly to those of the other Great Powers.

[310] O. Figes, *Crimea*, 376–7.

[311] *Allgemeine Zeitung*, 7 Dec. 1854. Racial stereotypes remained one element of press reportage, of course, more evident in cartoons than in newspaper reports: see, for instance, 'Der versteckte Freund und einzige Bundesgenosse Rußlands von 1812', *Kladderadatsch*, 1854, vol. 7, 180, or 'Illustrirte Zeitungs-Nachrichten', ibid., 196, which showed a row of characters with stereotypical 'Asiatic' features—with narrow eyes, pig-like or bulbous noses, and long beards—above a caption from the *Journal de Constantinople*, referring to the 'difficult task' of 'distinguishing between officers and rank-and-file soldiers amongst the captured Russians'.

[312] *Allgemeine Zeitung*, 7 Nov. 1854.

[313] 'Fürst Woronzow's Krim-Palast und die Holz-Paläste der Alliirten', *Gartenlaube*, 1855, vol. 7, 96–7.

[314] 'Die vier Armeen in der Krim', *Grenzboten*, 1854, vol. 13, no. 2, 364.

[315] Ibid., 1855, vol. 13, no. 4, 58–63.

[316] 'Die vier Armeen in der Krim', ibid., 1855, vol. 14, no. 2, 143.

[317] 'Kurden- und Kosaken-Bilder', *Gartenlaube*, 1855, vol. 37, 493–4.

To German and Austrian newspaper readers, the Crimean War combined the familiarity of a European crisis with a cast of well-known actors, which had the potential to spread to central and western theatres of war, on the one hand, and an unknown, exotic location, where adventurous or visibly modern forms of combat were being tested and were being covered by the press in a novel way, on the other.[318] In some respects, the exploitation of new technologies of warfare marked out the Crimean campaign from previous wars. More destructive, accurate, and longer-range bullets and shells increased the need for skirmishers and protected positions and reduced the role of infantry formations, hand-to-hand fighting, and cavalry charges, as well as producing more deadly, gruesome wounds and more efficacious medical means of treating such wounds.[319] Steamships criss-crossed the Mediterranean and Black Sea, the routes and ports of which were displayed on countless maps, making a 'European' war—rather than a colonial one, using troops already stationed abroad (in the American War of Independence or the Napoleonic Wars, for instance)—possible for the first time.[320]

From Varna on the Black Sea Coast of European Turkey, where the British and French armies had massed troops in the summer of 1854, to the port of Balaklava was a journey of just two days, giving the town the atmosphere of a staging post, wrote Julius von Wickede, who was in transit with the *Chasseurs d'Afrique* from Algeria.[321] On 7 September, 400 Allied ships led by HMS *Agamemnon*, the Royal Navy's first screw-propelled steamship, set out from the port of Varna bound for the Crimea 'like a vast industrial city on the waters', according to a French observer.[322] 'In the struggle, which threatens to unfold between the European western powers (*Westmächte*) and the Empire of Russia at this time, the art of war appears on the battle scene for the first time with means of violence which have never been seen in previous struggles', one correspondent had written in the *Gartenlaube*, beneath a detailed cross-section of 'The Propeller-Driven Warship *Wellington*', early in 1854:

> We mean the powerful steam-propelled war fleets, and especially the huge propeller-driven steamers which now plough through the seas and which scarcely allow a means

---

[318] One of the main series of articles in the *Allgemeine Zeitung* (22 and 29 April, 3 May 1854) was entitled, 'On the Historical Clarification of the Diplomatic Chess Moves in the Oriental Question', suggesting that the conflict was the result of long-established European rivalries; another (ibid., 21 Oct. 1854) carried the headline 'Prussia's Role in the European War'. 'Ein Schachspiel aus dem 19. Jahrhundert', *Kladderadatsch*, 1854, vol. 7, 200, imagined a chessboard with the different powers on it. For an interesting discussion of the intersection of diplomatic and military considerations in respect of Britain, see H. Strachan, 'Soldiers, Strategy and Sebastopol', *Historical Journal*, 29 (1978), 303–23. Also, W. Baumgart, *The Crimean War, 1853–1856* (Oxford, 1999).

[319] On the strategic shifts, see 'Die vier Armmen in der Krim', *Grenzboten*, 1854, vol. 13, no. 4, 361–70, and 1855, vol. 14, no. 2, 56–63, 143–52.

[320] For typical maps, see *Die Presse*, 26 Sept. 1854, or 'Uebersicht des Kriegsschauplatzes', *Gartenlaube*, 1854, vol. 51, 600–1. The *Allgemeine Zeitung*'s military correspondent cautioned on 24 Oct. 1854 only that 'It must now have become clear to a wider public through the course [of the embarkation] that it is impossible, even under the most favourable conditions, to ship across armies which are completely ready for war.' By implication, armies could be transported which were largely ready for war.

[321] J. v. Wickede, 'Bilder aus Varna', *Gartenlaube*, 1854, vol. 28, 327–9, 340–2.

[322] Cited in O. Figes, *Crimea*, 200.

of resistance to be imagined, given the speed and strength of their attack. The elemental dangers of the sea are more or less vanquished by these steam colossuses.[323]

Yet the destructive potential of such new machines of war was not unleashed, with the Russian fleet remaining in the harbour of Sevastopol where it was destroyed during the siege. Likewise, although the changes wrought by artillery and munitions were recognized, with corresponding use of trenches and protected positions, their full effects were rarely disclosed to a reading public. The nature and extent of shrapnel and bullet wounds were made public infrequently, despite being described more regularly than in the past, following the example of journalists such as William Howard Russell in *The Times*.[324] The use of trenches and artillery was generally incorporated into analyses of siege warfare, with Sevastopol understood to have been 'built for offensive defence' and as a form of 'reinforced battlefield', which could be compared to that used by the French defenders of Danzig in 1813.[325] Thus, the *Grenzboten*, notwithstanding its fear that trench warfare had filled 'Sevastopol's wide field of the dead with new corpses', contrasted the Allies' bombardment of and half-hearted attacks on Sevastopol unfavourably with the French assault on Tarragona in 1811.[326] The human cost of the conflict, with a dozen murderous struggles in 1855 replacing the Napoleonic idea of 'a single, concentrated, genuine assault', was roughly the same as that of its predecessors, it was implied.[327]

The true cost of the Crimean War was only revealed occasionally and partially to a German or an Austrian public. *Kladderadatsch* portrayed the consequences of artillery bombardments and senseless killing, most visible in the chaotic debris and figures of death in 'What the Franco-English Commission Found as It Drew Up an Inventory of Materials at Sevastopol' (1855), yet it more frequently depicted the events in the Crimea as a diplomatic game or a more or less harmless fight between statesmen, national characters, children, or, in one instance, deep-sea divers, who were shown picking up cannon balls from the seabed in order to 'bring this usable munition via Balaklava back to the batteries'.[328] Another cartoon imagined a giant cannon, typical of the siege of Sevastopol, as a 'hearing-aid for those who don't want to hear'.[329] Few lithographs showed dead or wounded soldiers and those which did, such as the drawing of 'French Sharpshooters in their Field Entrenchments' in *Gartenlaube* in 1854, often covered or obscured the bodies.[330] Most pictures

[323] 'Der Kriegsschraubendampfer Wellington', *Gartenlaube*, 1854, vol. 11, 118.

[324] See especially A. Lambert and S. Badsey (eds), *The War Correspondents: The Crimean War*; S. Markovits, *The Crimean War in the British Imagination*; F. Becker, 'Der "vorgeschobene Posten" als "verlorener Posten"? William Howard Russell und die britische Berichterstattung vom Krimkrieg', in G. Maag, W. Pyta, and M. Windisch (eds), *Der Krimkrieg als erster europäischer Medienkrieg*, 221–34.

[325] 'Die Expedition gegen Sebastopol', *Allgemeine Zeitung*, 24 Oct. 1854.

[326] 'Die Belagerung von Sebastopol', *Grenzboten*, 1855, vol. 14, no. 2, 401–10.

[327] Ibid., 402.

[328] 'Was die Französisch-Englische Commission vorfand, als sie das Inventarium des Materials von Sebastopol aufnahm', *Kladderadatsch*, 1855, vol. 8, 180; 'Zur orientalischen Frage', ibid., 1854, vol. 7, 228; 'Ein schlauer Junge!', ibid., 1854, vol. 7, 216.

[329] 'Ende December', ibid., 1854, vol. 7, 240.

[330] 'Französische Scharfschützen in ihren Feld schanzen', *Gartenlaube*, 1854, vol. 51, 614–15.

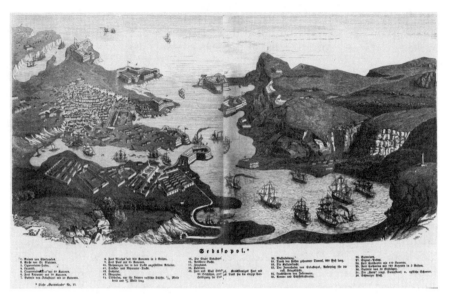

Figure 5.4 'Sevastopol'
Source: Gartenlaube, 1854, vol. 30, 354.

displayed the topography and cultural sites of the various expeditions and the bloodless operations of small groups of soldiers. Three-dimensional maps and aerial views of cities gave readers the impression that they were reconnoitring the scene of a future battle, revealing—in 'Sevastopol' (1854) and 'Siege Plan of Sevastopol' (1854), for instance—the hills, cliffs, escarpments, encampments, army formations, and fortifications surrounding the enclosed harbour in overstated relief in order to suggest the romance of the setting and the entrapment of the Russian fleet (see Figure 5.4).[331] In 'The Crimea from a Bird's Eye View' (1855), the peninsula protruded outwards towards the viewer, hinting at the vast plains of Russia behind, while in 'Pressed Overview Map of the Russian–Turkish War Setting' (1855), the region was portrayed as an organic, rocky integument on which humans would struggle to leave a mark.[332] Other lithographs—such as 'Balaklava (the old Chersonesus)' (1854)—presented landscapes in the Romantic tradition.[333] They were juxtaposed with anthropological images of local peoples and heroic, sometimes mythical ones of soldiers, visible in 'The French Garde-Cuirassiers' (1855), in which they were likened to bearded Germanic gods, and in 'Chasseurs d'Afrique at an Outpost' (1855), where a winding, muscular column of French cavalry made its way along a narrow path around an outcrop of rock.[334] The fascination and adventure of combat overshadowed suffering in these representations. The realities of modern warfare involving 'Germans' in Europe, as Austria went to war with France

---

[331] Ibid., vol. 30, 354, and vol. 50, 609.   [332] Ibid., 1855, vol. 15, 200, and vol. 39, 518.
[333] Ibid., vol. 44, 531.   [334] Ibid., 1855, vol. 41, 543; ibid., 1856, vol. 1, 5.

and Piedmont in northern Italy in 1859, and 'Germans' abroad, as German-speaking correspondents wrote about their experiences of the American Civil War in the early 1860s, tested such heroic mythology more fully.

MODERN WARFARE: THE FRANCO-AUSTRIAN WAR (1859)

Technological, strategic, tactical, and moral changes in the waging of wars during the mid-nineteenth century were likely to have more of an impact in those conflicts involving 'German' soldiers. To a limited extent, an 'internal' view of the American Civil War was provided by correspondents from the German-speaking communities of the northern states (with references to 'our' troops), helping to ensure that admirers of the South such as Heinrich Marquardsen—a lawyer in Erlangen writing for the *Kölnische Zeitung*—were outnumbered by supporters of the North such as the Cologne newspaper's regular reporter in New York, Friedrich Kapp.[335] This form of identification and dissemination occurred more frequently during the Habsburg monarchy's war in northern Italy against France and Piedmont-Sardinia in 1859, when even newspapers traditionally sceptical of Austria and sympathetic to Prussia like the semi-official *Badische Landeszeitung* noted 'the patriotic spirit' permeating 'the whole of Germany'.[336] Other pro-Prussian publications such as the *National-Zeitung* (Berlin) and *Grenzboten* (Leipzig) pointed to the 'agitated mood that today grips the German people', as Vienna strove to secure 'a significant role for our great nation in this European drama'.[337] Southern German newspapers such as the Catholic, pro-Austrian *Freiburger Zeitung* tended to be considerably more positive, declaring as early as January, as the opposing powers jostled for position and threatened the use of force, that 'There are no longer democrats and ultramontanes, backward-looking men and a revolutionary party, but only Germans who are ready to mount a common defence when danger and disadvantage threaten the whole fatherland.'[338] In common with many observers in 1859, Guido von Usedom, the Prussian delegate at the *Bundestag*

[335] On Kapp and Marquardsen, see Karl Buchheim, *Die Geschichte der Kölnischen Zeitung*, vol. 4, 247–8. Examples of reports from German–American commentary included *Allgemeine Zeitung*, 7 Aug. 1862, which referred to 'our sad Civil War'; 'Amerikanische Zustände', *Gartenlaube*, 1861, vol. 39, 574–6, 621–3, by Otto Ruppius, who had 'just returned from America to his *Heimat*', as a footnote to the article explained; 'Briefliche Mittheilungen aus Nordamerika', *Grenzboten*, 1865, vol. 24, no. 1, 477–80. On different aspects of this question, see W. Hochbruck (ed.), *Achtundvierziger/Forty-Eighters. Die deutschen Revolutionen von 1848/49, die Vereinigten Staaten und der amerikanische Bürgerkrieg* (Münster, 2000); J. Nagler, *Frémont contra Lincoln. Die deutsch-amerikanische Opposition in der Republikanischen Partei während des amerikanischen Bürgerkrieges* (Frankfurt, 1984).

[336] *Badische Landeszeitung*, 17 Feb. 1859, cited in F. Fischer, *Die öffentliche Meinung in Baden während der italienischen Krise 1859 und in dern anschliessenden Diskussion um die Bundesreform bis 1861* (Berlin, 1979), 52–3.

[337] *National-Zeitung*, 27 May 1859; *Grenzboten*, 1859, vol. 18, 277. See the attempts of even the conservative *Neue Preußische Zeitung*, 13 Mar. and 15 Apr. 1859, to present itself as the champion of national affairs, which were linked to the international position of the Habsburg monarchy.

[338] *Freiburger Zeitung*, 23 Jan. 1859, in F. Fischer, *Die öffentliche Meinung in Baden*, 52–3.

in Frankfurt, was convinced that 'the whole of South Germany is mad about Austria' and 'identifies Austria with Germany', appearing to push their reluctant governments towards war.[339] Such support seemed to encourage both commentators and readers to empathize with German–Austrian combatants.

As was to be expected, empathy was most pronounced in the Austrian press, which remained influential amongst the political elites of the German lands and whose articles were reprinted in German newspapers. The Habsburg Foreign Minister Karl Ferdinand von Buol-Schauenstein was so confident of the proximity of German and Austrian public opinion in 1859 that he predicted that 'all Germany' would 'gather round a hard-pressed Austria', even if it were defeated.[340] At various points, the 'Franco-Sardinian' campaign was portrayed, not merely as a war against the Habsburg monarchy, but 'an attack on Germany'.[341] As the prospects of the war worsened, Austrian journalists became more convinced than ever that 'the ramifications of the event for Germany appear to be profound and powerful'.[342] The representation of events by the press in Austria was favourable to the Habsburg regime and army, designed in part to garner support in the German states and to push German governments to mobilize the troops of the *Bund*.[343] After the battle of Magenta on 4 June, which issued in a decisive victory for France and Sardinia, the main liberal Viennese newspaper *Die Presse* cast around for positive news. 'French reports about the battle of Magenta already sound more modest', began one article on 11 June: 'They all agree that the fighting has demanded terrible sacrifices from the French.'[344] The figures provided by one newspaper (*L'Indépendance*)—3,000 French dead, 9,000 wounded, and 1,000 captured, which proved to be three to five times too high and which masked Austrian losses twice as great as those of the French and Piedmontese—were seized on as proof that the enemy's victory had been costly and precarious, assured only by MacMahon's arrival at the last minute, preventing an Austrian flanking manoeuvre.[345] The suffering on both sides, even though it was 'not yet possible from official reports and other details to date to give a clear picture', had evidently been 'terribly murderous'.[346] By the end of 'the first act of this bloody drama of war', commented another lead article on 12 June, 'events have taken a different

[339] G. v. Usedom to T. v. Bernhardi, 28 Apr. 1859, in T. v. Bernhardi, *Aus dem Leben Theodor von Bernhardis* (Leipzig, 1893), vol. 3, 194.

[340] J. K. Mayr (ed.), *Das Tagebuch des Polizeiministers Kempen von 1848 bis 1859* (Vienna, 1931), 510. See also K. F. Buol, 5 Feb. and 2 May 1859, in J. Müller, *Deutscher Bund und deutsche Nation 1848–1866* (Göttingen, 2005), 279, 286.

[341] *Die Presse*, 27 June 1859. See also *Bohemia* (Prague), 13 Jan. and 3 May 1859, and the conservative *Oesterreichischer Volksfreund*, 13 Jan. 1859, which called on the support of 'the entirety of the German nation'. For an historical justification of the Habsburg monarchy's 'German' role in Italy and elsewhere, see the historian Ottokar Lorenz's *Österreichs Politik in Italien und die wahren Garantien seiner Macht und Einheit* (Vienna, 1859).

[342] *Die Presse*, 28 June 1859. The liberal *Telegraf* (Graz), 28 Sept. 1859, cited in N. Buschmann, *Einkreisung und Waffenbruderschaft*, 155–6, commented after the event that southern Germans, in particular, had treated Austrian soldiers, including Galician, Czech, and Illyrian ones, 'not as foreigners or as good neighbours, but as brothers'.

[343] The *Oesterreichischer Volksfreund*, 15 July 1859, talked of 'the beautiful and great vocation' of spilling blood for the monarchy even after Solferino and the armistice of Villafranca on 12 July.

[344] *Die Presse*, 11 June 1859.   [345] Ibid.   [346] Ibid.

course from that which we expected, and there has never been a more serious moment for our oft-tested land', but 'our army' had nonetheless done 'everything that daring and a lion's courage could do on their own', despite leaving 'a great, rich province [Lombardy] to the Franco-Sardinian army, which must now be reconquered with the sword'.[347]

When news of Austria's decisive defeat at the battle of Solferino on 24 June began to filter through to Vienna by the end of the month, after days without telegrams or official information, the death toll of the war became impossible to ignore. 'The losses are enormous and Verona is spilling over with wounded', recorded one 'very laconic piece of correspondence' on 30 June: 'Those troops who were active defended Solferino house by house from 10 o'clock in the morning until 8 o'clock in the evening, using bayonets and the butts of their guns, since their ammunition had run out, and at least three times as large a number of the enemy opposed them.'[348] On the evening of the same day, *Die Presse* finally received and printed the fuller report of its own correspondent, which provided more details of the battle and revealed how artillery had been used to devastating effect in hilly terrain, where 'each step forwards' had to be 'bought with rivers of blood', resulting in 'over 20,000 men killed and wounded' on Austria's side.[349] Napoleon III's communication to his own army, in which he congratulated his soldiers for repelling 'the efforts of 150,000 men', was printed in the Viennese newspaper without further comment.[350] By the next day, it had become apparent that the French and Piedmontese had won a 'victory', although 'only with important losses, which were also great on our side'.[351] On 4 July, the newspaper's correspondent continued to ignore the consequences of the Habsburg forces' defeat, passing on 'the decision of the army leadership … to give up the Mincio line' and to adopt a defensive position near Verona', but the same publication had begun to publish long lists of dead and wounded Austrian officers (by name) and soldiers (by number only), which made the extent of the defeat obvious for the first time.[352] The entire second army was, 'as a result of the sick, dead, wounded and missing, unfortunately about half as strong as before'.[353] The empathy, anxiety, and pathos, as well as the ignorance, deceptions, and obfuscations, of such reportage could easily be detected by readers.

Given the effects of artillery and sharpshooters during the Crimean War, the conditions facing combatants in 1859 were foreseeable, even if the 'new factors' of warfare—including the telegraph and 'steam on water and land'—were 'still partly unknown and scarcely studied in theory', in the words of the official *Oesterreichische Zeitung* on 21 June 1859.[354] Modern combat tore 'the manly, youthful strength of the peoples from the arms of their loved ones and from useful work' and pushed

[347] Ibid., 12 June 1859.   [348] Ibid., 30 June 1859.
[349] Ibid., *Abendblatt*, 30 June 1859.   [350] Ibid.
[351] Ibid., 1 July 1859.   [352] Ibid., 4 July 1859.   [353] Ibid.
[354] Cited in *Die Presse*, 29 June 1859. Engels criticized the war for not proceeding, initially, with the speed expected of 'modern' warfare: 'The War: No Progress', *New York Daily Tribune*, 27 May 1859, in K. Marx and F. Engels, *Werke*, vol. 13, 339. The original from the *Tribune* is cited here, not the translation into German.

conscripts, 'with drums and whistles, into the chemically and scientifically studied sphere of war, which spread the instruments of murder afar', leaving thousands dead and 'peace' to be concluded by generals over the bodies of 'cripples and the dismembered', lamented the democratic *Beobachter* (Stuttgart) in May 1859: 'A modern war like this stands before us.'[355] In the ensuing conflict in northern Italy, the consequences of such warfare were occasionally revealed to a mass readership. Thus, one instalment of the *Gartenlaube*'s 'Original Communications from the War Front' gave an account, in the words of its sub-title, of 'the smell of Montebello' and of a 'visit to the battlefield of Palestro' with French forces:

> If we see a corpse, especially someone murdered, in civilian life amongst peaceful people, and the murderer in front of a court, ... no one can very easily guard against a shudder of horror. It is always somewhat shocking. A dead body! Yet hundreds of dismembered and dead bodies around us daily—that is something quite different. One gets used to the horrors of war and takes the hundreds and thousands of those who have been smashed to pieces, even if one sees them at all, as something inevitable, which is self-evident. Even the terrible, tortured, mass death of the wounded appear for those around as for those suffering and dying to become a form of business which one must view and oversee in the coldest blood possible. In Alessandria, I saw long caravans of the wounded and those who died in transit coming from the battle of Montebello, with enough material for the most distressing and cruellest scenes for an entire century of novels, yet those who were lightly wounded sang, smoked and laughed like people who were bringing funny goods to an annual fair. They turned and wrestled and jabbered heart-wrenchingly on their stretchers; others lay completely still and fixed and were dead; but the lightly wounded next to them, who could still make their way, limped and laughed and smoked and sang at their side, and made humorous, well-meaning comments about those who had become completely still. A *zouave* with one smashed leg and one intact one played the formal joker in their midst.
>
> I wasn't able to enter Montebello itself. I was driven far away by a bitterly repellent, unconquerable force: by the smell of the fallen, who had been buried in their hundreds in hastily dug, rectangular pits, densely piled on top of one another and had only been loosely covered by a thin layer of soil—so thin that, as man explained to me on the road, the rain overnight had uncovered heads with fluttering hair and protruding arms and legs, so that grim, frozen faces stared at the sky with white, dead eyes.[356]

Such 'slaughter' was presented by the correspondent of the *Gartenlaube* as proof of the horrors of modern warfare, with 'the scenes of street fighting and "house wars"... sometimes as disgusting and bloody, as fanatical and ruthless as the cruellest instances of revolutionary fighting'.[357] To the satirical journal *Kladderadatsch*, the battles of Magenta and Solferino were feathers in the cap of the grim reaper, the ally of all 'liberators and civilizers', who—'to the relief of all'—was 'now resting from his exertions'.[358]

---

[355] *Beobachter*, 19 May 1859, cited in Buschmann, *Einkreisung und Waffenbruderschaft*, 79.
[356] *Gartenlaube*, 1859, vol. 30, 430.   [357] Ibid., 430.
[358] 'Zum Friedens-Abschluß', *Kladderadatsch*, vol. 12, no. 33, 17 July 1859, 132, depicted the symbol of death in one panel, topped by a greedy, corpulent, comic Napoleon III, whose eyes were 'bigger than his belly', and a vainglorious 'new Italian freedom', half bound to France (Lombardy) and half to Austria (Venice), and dressed half in the military garb of one and half of the other.

The battle of Solferino became famous because it gave rise to the signature of the first Geneva Convention in 1864 and the founding of the International Committee for Relief to the Wounded in 1863 (becoming the International Committee of the Red Cross in 1876), after the publication in 1862 of Jean Henri Dunant's *Un Souvenir de Solférino*, which exposed the conditions experienced by wounded soldiers. Like German coverage of the American Civil War, which eventually saw 2.64 million men in arms and up to one-fifth of combatants killed, press reportage of the war between France, Sardinia, and Austria included few exposés of the effects of modern combat.[359] Military conflict continued to be represented—and, as far as historians can judge, to be understood—as an heroic adventure. There were various reasons why the Habsburg monarchy's war in northern Italy in 1859 did not lead to the abandonment of this conception of military conflict in the German lands. One concerned the unexpectedly short duration of the conflict. Most journalists had foreseen a longer war, which had the potential to become a protracted European conflagration, as the *Gartenlaube* noted:

> The peoples of Europe have become something like a *single* people, through work and trade, railways and telegraphs, and thousands of daily contacts of material and ideal acts of communication. They are a single societal body which suffers as a *whole*, if it is disturbed, wounded or infected in *one* of its parts. This is why we *all* feel, despite the fact that the war has been 'localized' in an exemplary way until now, the misery of it. Now, every war more or less takes on the form and the curse of a *civil war*. Now, the philistine can no longer praise himself for holding forth on Sundays and holidays about war and calls for war when, far away in Turkey, the peoples are fighting with each other. The most distant and most localized war concerns his life and his pocket.[360]

The nature war, on this reading, had changed. The rapid ending of what one journalist of the *Grenzboten* predicted, at the outbreak of hostilities, would become 'at least a European war' and perhaps 'a new thirty years' war' took most commentators by surprise.[361] On 7 June, after defeat on the 4th at Magenta, which was still being referred to six days later as an 'alleged defeat', the *Kreuzzeitung* could be found reiterating the assurance of the *Kölnische Zeitung's* correspondent in Vienna on 1 June that Austrian reinforcements were on their way to Italy.[362] Following the abandonment of Milan a fortnight earlier, the conservative publication prophesied on 21 June, via the reprinting of an article from the *Militär-Zeitung* (Vienna), that the Habsburg forces would soon return.[363] On 24 June, the day of the battle of

---

[359] The death toll comes from Mark Grimsley, 'In Not So Dubious Battle: The Motivations of Civil War Soldiers', *Journal of Military History*, 62 (1998), 176, but the figure is contested; for example, by Mark Neely, Jr, *The Civil War and the Limits of Destruction* (Cambridge, MA, 2007). Much of the literature on the American Civil War has stressed, and sought to explain, the willingness of soldiers to fight, given the conditions and killing rate of modern warfare: G. F. Linderman, *Embattled Courage: The Experience of Combat in the American Civil War* (New York, 1987); Michael Barton, *Goodmen: The Character of Civil War Soldiers* (University Park, PA, 1981); E. J. Hess, *The Union Soldier in Battle* (Lawrence, KA, 1997); J. M. McPherson, *What They Fought For, 1861–1865* (Baton Rouge, LA, 1994); and J. M. McPherson, *For Cause and Comrades: Why Men Fought in the Civil War* (Oxford, 1997); E. Hagerman, *The American Civil War and the Origins of Modern Warfare* (Bloomington, IN, 1988).
[360] *Gartenlaube*, 1859, vol. 24, 341.   [361] *Grenzboten*, 1859, vol. 18, no. 2, 471.
[362] *Neue Preußische Zeitung*, 7 June 1859. On Magenta, see ibid., 10 June 1859.
[363] Ibid., 21 June 1859.

Solferino, the newspaper merely declared that the 'first act' of the war was over, with Austria's early defeats the consequence of bad luck and poor information.[364] The Habsburg army still seemed stronger than those of its enemies. After the gravity of the monarchy's defeat at Solferino had become clear and the armistice of Villafranca had been agreed on 12 July, the *Neue Preußische Zeitung*'s main question was whether 'this pause was the beginning of peace or...the calm before a greater storm'.[365] The conservative mouthpiece found it difficult, like many German newspapers and periodicals, to accept that the war was over.[366] 'The whole of Europe was transported into a state of almost incomparable wonderment by the news that the peace of Villafranca had been signed', stated the principal correspondent of the conflict in the national–liberal *Preußische Jahrbücher* at the end of the war, before going on to provide hasty explanations of it; lack of finances, Hungarian opposition to Vienna, and Austrian anxiety about Prussia's imminent, self-interested involvement.[367] Under such circumstances, there was little opportunity for publications to print accounts of soldiers' experiences of the fighting.

Much of the press coverage of the war was strategic and technical, tracking the advances and retreats of the different armies by telegraph and furnishing detailed reports of their tactics, deployments, and use of weaponry. From these points of view, it seemed to many correspondents that the campaign was comparable to those of the Revolutionary and Napoleonic Wars. Thus, although it was true—as could be seen 'from the reports on the war in the Crimea (which was only a siege war for the most part)'—'that the art of war has developed to a point at which troops trained with the new methods could only be opposed with difficulty or not at all—over the long term—through the use of the old methods', modern warfare appeared to require the extension of Napoleonic techniques, in the words of the main editorial on the Franco-Austrian War in the *Neue Preußische Zeitung*: namely, 'a speed of movement which is very difficult to achieve without particular exercises of this kind'; the ability of infantry, who played 'a great part in the new method', to manoeuvre quickly and then suddenly to stand their ground and to discharge their guns steadily under enemy fire; and the willingness of armies—like Wellington in Spain after 1808—to find and defend fixed positions and strongholds.[368] French forces in Spain, as elsewhere, had had the advantage of speed during the Napoleonic Wars, which other armies had had to imitate and counter.[369] This imperative seemed simply to have increased in the more 'modern' campaigns of Napoleon III. The battle of Magenta, the 'first major battle in the new Austrian–French war', had taken place on 4 June, ten days before the fifty-ninth anniversary of the 'famous

---

[364] Ibid., 24 June 1859.

[365] Ibid., 13 July 1859. The losses in both camps were said to be 'significant' and 'undoubted'.

[366] The *Kölnische Zeitung*'s response to Austria's defeat and Cavour's subsequent resignation was 'Eine Ueberraschung folgt der andern', cited in K. Buchheim, *Die Geschichte der Kölnischen Zeitung*, vol. 4, 104.

[367] 'Frankreich, Oesterreich und der Krieg in Italien', *Preußische Jahrbücher*, 1859, vol. 4, 609. See also *Grenzboten*, 1859, vol. 3, 117, for a similar report.

[368] 'Diplomatisch-militärischer Kriegsschauplatz', *Neue Preußische Zeitung*, 23 June 1859.

[369] Ibid.

battle of Marengo', 'by means of which the first Napoleon commenced his triumphs', wrote the local, conservative *Teltower Kreisblatt* on 11 June 1859: 'The battle at Magenta was bloody but it cannot be seen to be as important as the battle of Marengo once was. The actual work remains to be done.'[370]

Although the precise movements and positions differed, with French forces advancing from the East at Montebello in 1859 and from the West in 1800 for example, the terrain and tactics of the war were similar, with MacMahon concentrating 'all his strength on the right flank of the Austrians' at Magenta, just as the French had once done at Marengo for Napoleon I, in the recollection of the *Grenzboten*.[371] In 1796, the French 'Army of Italy' had stood opposite its Austrian counterpart on the Riviera, making its way under Napoleon I across northern Italy in the following months.[372] Now, 'Napoleon III has, in fact, more chance of imitating the campaign of 1796 and 1797 than seems at first sight to be the case as things stand in Austria and in Germany', warned the military correspondent of the *Grenzboten* on 25 May 1859.[373] The fact—in contrast to the speed and decisiveness—of Austria's defeat at Solferino came as no surprise to the same journalist, reminding him of the battle of Castiglione in 1796.[374] 'We know that this battle was one of the most enormous and bloody of the entire nineteenth century', with each side leading 'at least 150,000 men into battle' and leaving 'about 20,000 men each, dead and wounded, on the field', yet such losses were the same as those of the Napoleonic Wars.[375] They were in keeping with the monarchy's initial mobilization of 650,000 men and an 'external' deployment of up to 450,000 at the start of the campaign, which betrayed 'a strength such as has only been mustered rarely in European wars before' but which had been exceeded by the Coalition's forces in 1813–15.[376] In the *Grenzboten* and other German publications, the war of 1859 was compared in its entirety to the campaigns of 1796–7, 1800, 1813–15, and, even, 1848–9.[377] Though sometimes described as 'new', it appeared to differ in detail alone from earlier military conflicts.

As in previous wars, German and Austrian newspapers presented to their readers a contradictory series of reports of events gleaned from official sources, military journals, and German-language and foreign publications. One article in the *Neue Preußische Zeitung* talked of 'collecting' all available news in order to arrive at a clearer view of what was happening at 'the scene of the war'.[378] Because the conflict lasted just over two months, there was little opportunity for periodicals to counter newspapers' breathless dissemination of information by means of analysis or eyewitness accounts. Even Viennese newspapers with contacts in the Habsburg government and army were frequently obliged to reprint and interpret French reports on the various battles, expressing relief after the battle of Magenta when the

---

[370] *Teltower Kreisblatt*, 11 June 1859.   [371] *Grenzboten*, 1859, vol. 18, no. 2, 485, 495.

[372] Ibid., 387.   [373] 'Ausblicke auf den Kriegsschauplatz', ibid., 390.

[374] Ibid., vol. 18, no. 3, 80.   [375] Ibid.

[376] 'Die Militärmacht Oestreichs in Italien', ibid., 1859, vol. 18, no. 1, 513.

[377] For references to 1848–9, see 'Der Krieg in Italien 1848–1849', ibid., 1859, vol. 18, no. 2, 518–19; ibid., vol. 18, no. 3, 19.

[378] 'Diplomatisch-militärischer Kriegsschauplatz', *Neue Preußische Zeitung*, 26 June 1859.

Parisian press became 'moderate' or when it showed—for instance, on 27 June, via the account of an officer in the French General Staff—the doggedness of Austrian resistance.[379] Sometimes, *Die Presse* was reduced to 'guesses about the position of the Austrian army', given the lack of news arriving by telegraph.[380] At other times, after brief notifications of the battle of Solferino by telegraph had not been corroborated by posted statements from its own correspondents, the newspaper was compelled—for the intervening week—to rely on the Piedmontese, British, and French press, the disclosures of which had been relayed by the *Kölnische Zeitung* and other German publications with well-developed networks of correspondents. 'Today, too, we have not received further details of the battle of the 24th of this month', admitted the lead article 'From the Scene of War' on 28 June: 'The KZ writes of the first impressions [of the battle] in the news in Paris' that the 'fighting must have been terrible and pertinacious, as is shown by its duration alone (16 hours).'[381] When the Viennese publication began to receive articles—initially in fragmentary form—from its own correspondent from 30 June onwards, it continued to print pieces from *Le Moniteur* alongside them.[382] Thus, the claims of its lead article, from 'an authentic source', on 1 July that the French 'success' had only been achieved 'with considerable losses' were juxtaposed on the front page with the commentary of the *Kölnische Zeitung*'s Parisian correspondent on an official French report that the Austrians had been 'chased out of Solferino'.[383] The alleged death of MacMahon was described in parenthesis by the editor as 'not accurate'.[384] The presses of the other German lands, which had less reason to suppress news from France and Piedmont-Sardinia, put forward a similarly eclectic range of views, convinced, like the *Kölnische Zeitung*, that the conflict was not one in which 'Germany can afford to remain indifferent' but, in many cases, remaining unconvinced that it was 'a German war'.[385]

There was considerable sympathy in the German lands for the Habsburg monarchy in its war against Napoleonic France. The resulting 'national feeling' in Germany, which had been given 'the most unambiguous expression' in 1859 according to the Habsburg ambassador in Paris (whose opinion was published in the *Heidelberger Journal*), was not merely the consequence of what the liberal Hermann Baumgarten described as 'Austrian agitation in the South'; it was also the product of political aspirations linked to the struggles of 1848 and an antipathy towards Bonapartism or France (see Figure 5.5).[386] Even a sceptic such as Engels admitted that 'the German nation' was 'fairly roused'.[387] In an official dispatch to

---

[379] *Die Presse*, 11 and 27 June 1859.   [380] Ibid., 12 June 1859.

[381] 'Vom Kriegsschauplatze', ibid., 28 June 1859.

[382] Ibid., 30 June 1859. Also, 'Der Moniteur über die Schlacht von Solferino', ibid., 2 July 1859.

[383] Ibid., 1 July 1859.   [384] Ibid.

[385] *Kölnische Zeitung*, 1 May 1859, cited in K. Buchheim, *Die Geschichte der Kölnischen Zeitung*, vol. 4, 96.

[386] *Heidelberger Journal*, 25 Jan. 1859, cited in E. Portner, *Die Einigung Italiens im Urteil liberaler deutscher Zeitgenossen* (Bonn, 1959), 52–3; H. Baumgarten to M. Duncker, 12 Apr. 1859, in J. Schultze (ed.), *Max Duncker*, 96.

[387] F. Engels, 'War Inevitable', *New York Daily Tribune*, 30 Apr. 1859, in K. Marx and F. Engels, *Werke*, vol. 13, 302.

Vienna, the Austrian envoy in Baden was confident that 'the German nation is beginning to feel its togetherness and its own power', at least 'here in the southwest', where the signs were 'unmistakable'.[388] 'The war, in which one of the German Great Powers would have a part of its territory torn away from it, is a war of German power and German honour; it is a war against Germany, which all Germans have to fight', declared the address of the lower chamber of the Badenese *Landtag* on 2 May 1859:

> And the more powerful the enemy is, which stands opposite us, the more pressing it is that the whole of Germany offers everything in order to meet it with full force... These are the attitudes and opinions which are voiced everywhere in the state and in all classes of the population.[389]

Even though there was 'no enthusiasm for Austria at all' and the 'ultramontanes and absolutists only play very minor violins', the 'rest of the South, the Palatinate and our entire land', except Heidelberg, was 'agitated', in Ludwig Häusser's evaluation on 14 May: 'from the Grand Duke [of Baden] to the smallest Palatinate grower of tobacco, there is only one opinion—hatred against Bonaparte, the desire for an Austrian victory, regret concerning Prussia's fundamental meanness.'[390] In Bavaria, the 'bellicosity of the public' continued, wrote the liberal historian Heinrich von Sybel on 8 May, with the peasantry, 'enthused by the clergy', wanting war 'today rather than tomorrow' and with 'nobles, civil servants and students' streaming to the regiments, 'here as in Swabia and Baden'.[391] In Prussia, Saxony, Hanover, Hesse, and the Thuringian states, too, 'the German question' had again been 'brought into motion', in the testimonies of the Hessian liberal Friedrich Oetker and the Saxon Karl Biedermann.[392] Many liberals and democrats had 'warm feelings for Italy and its emancipation from the Austrian yoke, but a concern for Germany lay closer to their hearts', declared Otto Elben, with everything retreating 'behind the threatening danger from outside'.[393] The 'menace against Austria' was widely considered 'a menace against Germany', recalling the earlier descent from France's war against the Habsburg monarchy in 1805 to that against Prussia in 1806.[394] As the fighting came closer to 'the German border in the Tyrol', the 'Swabian people'—or their representatives—delivered a proclamation 'To Our Fellow Citizens' at the end of June, which constituted 'the actual beginnings of a national party in Württemberg'.[395] In these circumstances, the Stuttgart liberal rejoiced, 'we national-minded ones' were joined by 'those who were later named "Greater German"' at a 'moment of danger', creating 'the agreement, it can be said, of the entire country'.[396]

---

[388] Fürst v. Schönburg-Hartenstein, 3 May 1859, in E. Portner, *Die Einigung Italiens*, 90.

[389] Address of the second chamber of Baden's *Landtag*, 2 May 1859, ibid., 91–2.

[390] L. Häusser to H. Baumgarten, 14 May 1859, ibid., 90.

[391] H. v. Sybel to M. Duncker, 8 May 1859, in J. Schultze (ed.), *Max Duncker*, 101.

[392] F. Oetker, *Lebenserinnerungen*, 3 vols (Stuttgart, 1877–85), vol. 3, 116; K. Biedermann, *Mein Leben und ein Stück Zeitgeschichte*, 2 vols (Breslau, 1886–7), vol. 2, 140–61.

[393] O. Elben, *Lebenserinnerungen 1823–1899* (Stuttgart, 1931), 130.

[394] Ibid.   [395] Ibid.   [396] Ibid., 131.

At the time and later, many contemporaries doubted that such national enthusiasm, which had developed above all in the middling strata during the spring of 1859, betrayed a willingness to go to war or to see the conflict between Austria, France, and Piedmont-Sardinia as their own. Looking back, Elben failed to detect the 'unanimity of all' which had been present in 1848 and 1863, on the eve of the war in Schleswig-Holstein.[397] Certainly, a large number of Catholic politicians and publicists were in favour of a declaration of war by the German Confederation on the grounds, resting on a broad interpretation of Article 47 of the Viennese Final Acts, that Germany—or the territory of the *Bund*—was 'threatened', even if not subjected to an 'attack'.[398] Correspondingly, periodicals such as the *Historisch-politische Blätter* had championed joint Austrian, Prussian, and confederal action throughout the first half of 1859.[399] On this reading of events, which was expounded by the Rhineland Catholic leaders August and Peter Reichensperger, 'the sympathies of millions' would 'accompany and promote the unifying feeling of a common striving' and would 'give the German fatherland the courage and power' to oppose the 'common enemy in the decisive days ahead' but also 'finally to place limits on it', as they had sought to do in 1859.[400] The whole of Germany had opposed an expansionist Bonapartist dictatorship.[401] They had also criticized Italian nationalists such as Mazzini and Garibaldi, who had 'inflicted the deepest wounds on the eternal city', and Italian statesmen like Cavour, who had 'come back from Paris in a very pleased mood' shortly before the outbreak of the war, 'as the newspapers reported' at the time.[402] Even the Reichensperger brothers, however, conceded that 'the confusion of facts corresponds to and serves the confusion of ideas', with 'nationality, unity, humanity, the localization of war, popular will, non-intervention, freedom, civilisation, progress and those sorts of "principles"' clashing with each other and permitting 'no clarification'.[403] Conservatives were also troubled by the confusion of these ideas and by conflicting loyalties, dividing between supporters of Austria within the camarilla, a handful of opponents of Austria such as Bismarck-Schönhausen, and a disquieted majority, including Friedrich Julius Stahl and Hermann Wagener, who backed the Prussian government's policy of armed neutrality.[404]

The majority of other commentators, especially those in the North, had little sympathy for the Habsburg monarchy in the Italian war. For radicals such as Arnold Ruge, mindful of earlier persecution under Metternich and counter-revolution

---

[397] Ibid., 136.

[398] A. und P. Reichensperger, *Deutschlands nächste Aufgaben* (Paderborn, 1860), 42.

[399] For instance, *Historisch-politische Blätter*, 1859, vol. 43, 265, 636. They were supported for the most part by publications with 'Greater German' leanings: 'Die Grenzen Deutschlands', *Stimmen der Zeit*, 1859, vol. 1, 1–28; 'Die nationale Bewegung und ihr Ziel', *Historisch-politische Blätter*, 1859, vol. 43, 316–20; 'Napoléon III et l'Allemagne oder das bevorstehende Attentat auf den europäischen Frieden', *Historisch-politische Blätter*, 1859, vol. 43, 407–41; 'Studien, Kritiken udn Vorschläge in Beziehung auf die gegenwärtige Weltlage', *Historisch-politische Blätter*, vol. 2, 1–51, which was more critical of the *Bund*.

[400] A. and P. Reichensperger, *Deutschlands nächste Aufgaben*, 174, 7, 18.

[401] Ibid.   [402] Ibid.   [403] Ibid., 1.

[404] H.-C. Kraus, *Gerlach*, 706–7. Also, M. v. Moltke, *Nicht für Österreich, aber gegen Frankreich!* (Breslau, 1859); 'Die Politik Preußens. Eine Stimme aus Süddeutschland', *Preußisches Wochenblatt*, 1859, vol. 21, which backed Prussian neutrality and opposed more active support of Austria.

Figure 5.5 'Die Wiedereroberung einer Fahne in der Schlacht von Magenta'
Source: *Gartenlaube*, 1859, vol. 28, 405.

under Schwarzenberg, Prussia, 'with its objectionable love affair with the police', was 'the only salvation for Germany from Jesuits and reactionaries in politics', who were associated with Austria: 'If Germany is not now capable of using this position to free itself from Austrian tyranny, it will be wasting another great opportunity... German freedom means separation from Austria.'[405] In Bamberger's opinion, articulated in his anonymously published pamphlet *Juchhe nach Italia!* (1859),

---

[405] The article in *Das Jahrhundert*, 1859, no. 14, is attributed by Hans Rosenberg to Ruge, in *Die nationalpolitische Publizistik Deutschlands* (Munich, 1935), 33. See also H. Simon, *Don Quixote der Legitimät oder Deutschlands Befreier* (Zurich, 1859); C. Vogt, *Studien zur gegenwärtigen Lage Europas*

the Habsburg monarchy was 'a hundred times deadlier' than France for German freedom and unity.[406] German support for Austria was not the result of national sentiment but an artificially produced, sham patriotism or the 'inculcated roaring of dishonoured subjects'.[407] The 'bulwark of German greatness' lay not on the Po or Mincio Rivers, which had become critical barriers in the military campaign of 1859, but in 'the final realization' of 'German unity' at home.[408] 'Germany' had only awoken and acknowledged this fact on the edge of the abyss of military conflict, if Bamberger were to be believed. In one of the most famous treatises on the war, entitled *Studien zur gegenwärtigen Lage Europas* (1859), the exiled radical Carl Vogt agreed with Bamberger: the Habsburg monarchy was not a 'German' power. Rather, it existed at the expense of nationalities in Italy, Germany, and Eastern Europe, responsible only for 'a series of outrages against Germany's unity, honour, reputation, security, freedom, power and greatness'.[409] The establishment of an independent Italy under Piedmont-Sardinian leadership was to be welcomed by the German Confederation, which ought to remain neutral.[410] Vogt, like many other radicals, was prepared to go to war, not least because he believed that military conflict would be necessary to establish Italian, Hungarian, and German nation-states at the expense of the Habsburg monarchy:

> We call for a mobilization against every attack on Germany, on the development of its people, its national character; against any contravention of its honour or its inner being; but we do not want this to be exploited for self-interested purposes; we want to tear the masks from the faces of the hypocrites and show them that we know how to distinguish between genuine belief and an outrageous abuse of it.[411]

For more extreme radicals such as Karl Blind, 'the moment when Lombardy and Venice, Hungary and Galicia will demand state independence' was 'most keenly' desired: 'We will welcome any true national struggle (*Volkskampf*) of these lands with enthusiasm.'[412] 'By declaring ourselves against Parisian tyrants, we are not preaching sympathy for tyrants in Vienna', declared Blind in a confiscated treatise on 'war risk', before going on to call for the 'arming' of the German people against the danger of a European war which, in the case of 'victory', would 'not bring freedom' and, in the event of a defeat, 'would strike us from the book of nations'.[413] Radicals like Blind were convinced that Austria's war was dynastic, not national.

Not all radicals and socialists toed the line of the majority of their comrades. A few, like Jakob Venedey, initially backed Vienna against Napoleon III, but then changed allegiances, after the peace of Villafranca, to Prussia as the only defence

(Geneva, 1859); H. B. Oppenheim, *Deutschlands Noth und Ärzte* (Berlin, 1859); and H. B. Oppenheim, *Deutsche Begeisterung und Habsburgischer Kronbesitz* (Berlin, 1859).

[406] L. Bamberger, *Juchhe nach Italia!*, 83.
[407] Ibid.   [408] Ibid.
[409] C. Vogt, *Studien zur gegenwärtigen Lage Europas*, 51.
[410] Ibid., 54, 56–7.   [411] Ibid., 118.
[412] K. Blind, *Kriegsgefahr! Deutsche National-Vertretung! Männer von Deutschland!* (Frankfurt, 1859), in H. Rosenberg, *Die nationalpolitische Publizistik Deutschlands*, 42.
[413] Ibid., 42.

against both Austria and France.[414] Johann Baptist von Schweitzer, who was widely suspected in socialist circles of dilettantism as the scion of a wealthy, Catholic family of Italian origin and as the grandson of the editor of the pro-Austrian *Oberpostamtszeitung* (Frankfurt), was exceptional in the degree of his opposition to Vogt, declaring in *Österreichs Sache ist Deutschlands Sache* and *Widerlegung von Carl Vogt's Studien zur gegenwärtigen Lage Europas*—both written at the age of 26 in 1859—that the Habsburg regime was safeguarding the legal treaties of the international order, defending German interests against Italy and France, and furthering natural ties of kinship:

> Where is the cornerstone of a unified national form to be found? Not there, where we calmly look on as a common enemy attacks our fraternal tribe, but there, where we feel ourselves to be a nation (*Nation*) and recognise in the injury of our brotherly tribe the injury of all.[415]

Few other socialists were willing to go so far, even though many were sceptical of Napoleon III's intentions. Marx, indeed, had accused Vogt on 10 May 1859 of being in the pay of the French dictator: 'the pseudo-democratic party...affects to be so exasperated by Austrian brutality, as to discern liberalism on the part of the hero of December [that is, Napoleon III, who launched his coup on 2 December 1851]', pointing to the fact 'that some members of the last mentioned party have positively been bought by *napoléons d'or*, and that the great manager of this trade in consciences resides in Switzerland, being himself not only a German, but an ex-member of the German National Assembly of 1848, and an outrageous Radical'.[416] At the 'the opening of the great and bloody war in which Europe is now involved', Marx and Engels gave their detached backing to Austria as a means of resisting the French and the 'Slavs' and of protecting Germany, with the latter going on to advocate the offensive as 'the true method for Austria to defend herself'.[417]

Like most of their counterparts, Marx and Engels displayed little anxiety about the costs of military engagement, with the latter hailing the first battle at Montebello, in which he reported 1,500 to 2,000 dead or wounded, as 'fighting at last'.[418] Their reports about the battles of Magenta and Solferino betrayed excitement about military technology and strategy, with Engels identifying entrenched or fortified positions and steam as 'two new elements which have significantly changed warfare since Napoleon', and they were apparently indifferent to soldiers' suffering: neither paid much attention to casualty figures other than as a means—as in Engels's passing reference on 21 July to 'losses of approx. 30,000 men since the beginning of the campaign' on the Allied side—of calculating the fighting

---

[414] J. Venedey, *Der italienische Krieg und die deutsche Volkspolitik* (Hanover, 1859), especially 34–55.

[415] J. B. Schweitzer, *Widerlegung von Carl Vogt's Studien zur gegenwärtigen Lage Europas* (Frankfurt, 1859), 42.

[416] K. Marx, 'Austria, Prussia and Germany in the War', *New York Daily Tribune*, 27 May 1859, in K. Marx and F. Engels, *Werke*, vol. 13, 326.

[417] F. Engels, 'The Prospects of the War', *New York Daily Tribune*, 12 May 1859, ibid., 312.

[418] F. Engels, 'Fighting at Last', *New York Daily Tribune*, 6 June 1859, ibid., 344–9.

strengths of the two armies.[419] The 'sudden and unexpected end' of the Italian war made Marx aware that it had been 'costly'.[420] He accepted that it had 'in concentrated form, brought together in a few weeks not only the heroic acts, invasions and counterinvasions, marches, battles, conquests and losses, but also the expenditure of people and money of many wars of considerably longer duration', yet there is little indication that the exiled communist was moved to a more fundamental reassessment of modern warfare.[421] As it became evident that Austria was losing the war (with the 'noble' fool Franz Joseph partly responsible), Marx and Engels moved from disengaged support to specialized criticism.[422] It is doubtful that they ever considered the conflict a 'German' one (or 'theirs'), despite their expectation that Russia and Prussia—'unable to master the national feeling' of the public—would be drawn into it.[423] Other leading socialists in Germany such as Ferdinand Lassalle were more active in calling on the Prussian government to remain neutral, whilst maintaining an armed vigilance and the possibility of attacking Denmark and occupying Schleswig-Holstein, in the unlikely event of a French incursion over the Rhine or a French attempt to redraw Europe's borders along national lines.[424]

Liberals were less worried than radicals about Austrian tyranny and less attracted to Italian nationalism, even though the *Società Nazionale Italiana* served as the model for the *Nationalverein*. Droysen, despite harbouring 'all imaginable sympathies' for the 'unfortunate' Italians, wanted Austria to 'have and rule Italy' so that it was not tempted to 'put even more pressure on Germany', the interests of which were his 'first concern'.[425] 'That the war which has been started in Italy is directly a German affair has not even been claimed by those who have taken it up, notwithstanding the fact that, where Germans fight, the sympathy of all other Germans will always be on their side', proclaimed the rector of Berlin University Heinrich Wilhelm Dove in August 1859.[426] Austria's war, insinuated Constantin Rössler, was the corollary of its unnatural, imperial character, contradicting the imperatives of nation-building: 'Austria hinders natural development. But its nemesis stands before the door... The Schwarzenberg system has been judged and made forever impossible.'[427] Prussia should not be misled into joining Habsburg wars in Italy and the Near East, but should assume the leadership of Germany, after the withdrawal of Austria, and solve the 'German' problem of Schleswig-Holstein,

---

[419] F. Engels, 'Der Feldzug in Italien', *Das Volk*, vol. 4, 28 May 1859, ibid., 358–60; F. Engels, 'Historical Justice', *New York Daily Tribune*, 21 July 1859, ibid., 405.

[420] K. Marx, 'What Has Italy Gained?', *New York Daily Tribune*, 27 July 1859, ibid., 417.

[421] Ibid.

[422] For the reference to the damaging, naive 'Ritterlichkeit' of the Austrian Emperor, see F. Engels, 'Die Schlacht bei Solferino', *Das Volk*, vol. 9, 2 July 1859, ibid., 402. On Marx and Engels's disenchantment with Austria, see F. Engels, 'Progress of the War', 'Military Events', 'The Austrian Events', 'The News from the War', 'The Battle of Solferino', and 'Der Italienische Krieg. Rückschau' and K. Marx, 'The Peace' and 'The Treaty of Villafranca', ibid., 372–439.

[423] F. Engels, 'The News from the War', *New York Daily Tribune*, 8 July 1859, ibid., 402.

[424] F. Lassalle, *Der italienische Krieg und die Aufgabe Preussens. Eine Stimme aus der Demokratie* (Berlin, 1859). 69–73.

[425] Droysen to Duncker, 8 June 1859, in Fenske (ed.), *Reichsgründung*, 161.

[426] Ibid., 106.   [427] C. Rössler, *Preussen und die italienische Frage* (Berlin, 1859), 36.

concluded the publicist.[428] The liberal historian and military commentator Theodor von Bernhardi, writing in the *Preussische Jahrbücher*, went so far as to blame Austria for attacking France as a means of propping up its ailing imperial system of rule and re-establishing a conservative order in Europe:

> What it was actually about was the entanglement of Germany and especially Prussia in a war, the shifting of the war to the Rhine, the invasion of France with a powerful, superior military force, the destruction and banishment of the Napoleonists, and the return of Heinrich V and his befriended clerical coterie to the throne of his ancestors.[429]

Austria's intentions were 'very easy to see through', he explained to Usedom in April 1859: Vienna wanted 'to transfer the war to Germany at any price', meaning that the decisive battles would be fought on the Rhine and that the 'main burden of the war' would pass from Austria to Prussia; 1859 was the last episode in a long history of Habsburg exploitation of both Italy and Germany.[430] Such anti-Austrian rather than pro-Italian sentiment was what linked Italian and German nationalism, in the view of Wilhelm Beseler and many other liberals:

> The German nation has no interest at all in seeing the territorial possessions and influence of the House of Habsburg-Lorraine maintained or even increased. It must be admitted, however difficult this is for many Germans, who have become accustomed—for no reason whatsoever—to looking down on the Italians, that Germany and Italy are largely in the same position vis-à-vis Austria, and that we scarcely suffer less under Austrian pressure in Germany than do our neighbours on the other side of the Alps as a result of the Austrian position in Italy.[431]

In Beseler's view, Prussia had to lead Germany, not Austria. Some North German old liberals—Waitz, Droysen, and Duncker—were less openly against the Habsburg monarchy in 1859, but few were for it. The liberal press displayed a similar disinterest.[432]

The distance of readers from the events of mid-nineteenth-century conflicts was barely altered by the gradual, uneven increase of civilians' sensitivity to violence and by the slow transformation of the technology and practices of military wounding and killing. In these respects, the American Civil War (1861–5), despite its duration, remained closer to a war of movement or adventure than either the Crimean War or the Franco-Austrian War.[433] For much of the century, the United States had, along with Switzerland, provided German commentators with their principal example of a militia (640,000 in the initial Union levy) acting in the

---

[428] See also Aegidi, *Preussen und der Friede von Villafranca*.

[429] T. v. Bernhardi, 'Frankreich, Österreich und der Krieg in Italien', *Preussische Jahrbücher*, 1859, vol. 4, 179–97, 229–52, 457–94, 571–612.

[430] T. v. Bernhardi, *Aus dem Leben Theodor von Bernhardis*, vol. 3, 194–5.

[431] W. Beseler, *Das deutsche Interesse in der italienischen Frage* (Leipzig, 1859), 14–15.

[432] See articles by Hugo Haelschner, *Preußische Jahrbücher*, 1859, vol. 3, 300–9; Hermann Baumgarten, ibid., vol. 3, 738, and vol. 4, 431; Rudolf Haym, ibid., vol. 3, 493; Karl Neumann, ibid., vol. 3, 592 and 734, and vol. 4, 207 and 431.

[433] See S. Förster and J. Nagler (eds), *On the Road to Total War: The American Civil War and the German Wars of Unification, 1861–1871* (Cambridge, 2002).

stead of a regular army (20,000).[434] Thus, George McLellan, the commander of Union forces, was depicted in the *Illustrirte Zeitung* in 1862 in simple, undecorated military dress, only a drawn sabre indicating that he was an officer.[435] In the same year, *Kladderadatsch* imagined 'pictures of the age from America', representing 1822 (when soldiers and taxes were to be found only in Europe), 1842 (when a European being robbed was told there was no police, only freedom), and 1862, when a brutal-looking American, robbed of half of his clothes and facing the prospect of 'conscription' and military drill, was told to go to 'England' if he wanted to avoid the 'overburden of taxation, military rule and lawlessness' which existed in the United States.[436] As war broke out, even though it was initially referred to as a 'civil war', journalists suggested, in the words of one correspondent of the *Allgemeine Zeitung* in May 1861, 'that this war cannot last long', because 'the American army is comprised of people who are dragged away to arms from different occupational groups of civilian life and whose time and work are worth ten times as much in money as in Europe'.[437] The professionalization of Union forces and leadership, with 'Grant and Sherman [coming] from the regular army and [having] completed their military studies at the academy of West Point', took place only in 1864 in the opinion of the *Grenzboten*, replacing the practice of promoting 'more or less political leaders to generals' and involving more extensive training and longer experience of warfare on the part of military volunteers.[438]

Eventually, the mobilization of troops and rates of killing in the American Civil War exceeded those of most European conflicts, with the North widely known to dispose of an army of over 600,000 men.[439] At the beginning of the conflict, though, the number of troops engaged in combat seemed small by European standards, not least because the different battalions of volunteers remained tied to their states: '200,000 men in Virginia, 150,000 on the Mississippi, 100,000 in Tennessee and Kentucky, 100,000 in Louisiana and Missouri, in Minnesota against the Indians, in Texas, North and South Carolina, Florida and the sea forts', with 'the rest in the interior and in California, Maryland and New York', out of a total for the Union army of '600,000 at the most' in 1863, in the judgement of one retrospective article in the *Grenzboten* in 1865.[440] 'The spatial extent of the scene of the fighting in North America offers an offensive front about like that from Memel to the Pyrenees and therefore demands the deployment of forces which are independent of one another at the different points of contact', reported the same publication in 1862:

> These points themselves determine, as a result of general conditions, that the main army is deployed in the direction of the capitals, so between Washington and Richmond,

---

[434] See Chapter 6. The figures come from *Grenzboten*, 1864, vol. 23, no. 4, 458, with an initial Union levy in December 1861 of 682,000.

[435] *Illustrirte Zeitung*, no. 967, 11 Jan. 1862. See also ibid., no. 968, 18 Jan. 1862, which showed disembarking Union troops, in the enthusiastic, disordered state of a militia.

[436] 'Sonst und Jetzt', *Kladderadatsch*, vol. 15, no. 45, 28 Sept. 1862, 180.

[437] *Allgemeine Zeitung*, Beilage, 9 May 1861.

[438] 'Das Ende des Kriegs in Nordamerika', *Grenzboten*, 1865, vol. 24, no. 1, 353.

[439] See, for instance, 'Der Krieg in Nordamerika', ibid., 58.

[440] 'Der Krieg in Nordamerika 1863 und 1864', ibid., no. 1, 229.

the next most important force on the main transport artery, the Mississippi, and a weaker army operates in the enormous space in between these principal points, in Kentucky, Tennessee and southwards.[441]

The largest battle of 1861—Bull Run in Virginia on 21 July—pitted 35,000 Union soldiers against 34,000 Confederates, resulting in less than 2,000 dead and wounded on each side; the battles of 1862 and 1863 were larger, with higher numbers of casualties (approximately 18,000 dead and wounded on each side at Gettysburg, the costliest of the entire war), but no battle exceeded 200,000 men in the field, making them considerably smaller than their Napoleonic equivalents.

Most reports in the German press treated such campaigns strategically, tracking the movements of the two armies across the 'thinly populated landscapes of North America' and weighing up their relative gains and losses: looking back on 'the overall results of the events of the war' in 1864, one article concluded that 'the advantages between Washington and Richmond belong to the South rather than the North, because the former has, with luck, pushed back the considerably greater power of its opponent', whereas 'in the West the North under Grant has achieved domination over the Mississippi river and over the states of both Kentucky and Tennessee'.[442] This form of reportage, which was combined with evaluations of the political significance and causes of the conflict, overshadowed coverage of 'the internal struggle' and 'the bloody wrestling' which had traditionally been understood to characterize civil wars.[443] With the exception of occasional early reports on the '*Bürgerkrieg* in America' or even the '*Sonderbundskrieg*', which hinted at the war between a Swiss federal army and a Catholic *Sonderbund* in November 1847, most German journalists depicted the conflict as a normal 'war' or an 'American war' between two states, rather than a fratricidal conflict which divided families and communities.[444]

The headlines of major articles in the *Allgemeine Zeitung* were telling, betraying the evolution of an unknown 'civil war' into a familiar inter-state conflict combined with a separate and predominant sphere of domestic politics. Thus, there was a transition from 'Der Bürgerkrieg in Amerika' (9 May 1861) and 'Der Sonderbundskrieg in den Vereinigten Staaten von Amerika' (11 May 1861), via 'Der Wendepunkt in dem amerikanischen Krieg' (29 July 1862), 'Die zweite Schlacht am Bull Run' (22 September 1862), and 'Die Schlacht bei Gettysburg' (20 July 1863), to more explicitly political headlines such as 'Petersburg, Atlanta und die Präsidentenwahl in den Vereinigten Staaten' (25 August 1864), 'Der Krieg und die politischen Parteien in den Vereinigten Staaten' (5 September 1864), and

---

[441] 'Der Krieg in Nordamerika. Der Kriegsschauplatz', ibid., 1864, vol. 23, no. 4, 325.

[442] Ibid., 1864, vol. 23, no. 4, 326, and ibid., 1865, vol. 24, no. 1, 238.

[443] Ibid.: here, the reference was left without further commentary at the end of an article which had focused exclusively on the movements of the two armies.

[444] See, for instance, 'Der Bürgerkrieg in Nordamerika und der Untergang der Union', *Historisch-politische Blätter*, 1862, vol. 49, no. 1, 245–79, 'Der Wendepunkt im nordamerikanischen Bürgerkrieg', ibid., 1863, vol. 51, no. 1, 211–42, 'Zeitläufe über Nordamerika', ibid., 1865, vol. 55, no. 1, 476–98, 578–604, and 'Der Feldzug 1862 in Nord-Amerika', in the *Preußische Jahrbücher*, 1862, vol. 10, 470–87, which treated the fighting as a traditional continental 'campaign'.

'Der Präsidentenwahl in den Ver. Staaten' (22 September 1864).[445] Even those correspondents who—early in the conflict—understood it as a 'revolution', which would 'fundamentally reconcile differences of interest and opinion' after further 'sacrifices', generally avoided reference to a 'civil war', with its connotations of uncontrolled brutality and internecine killing.[446] As a war, 'we can say...that the armies still lack a warlike core and nature', wrote the same correspondent in the *Preußische Jahrbücher* in 1862: 'The intensity of the fighting has only reached that of 1849 in Hungary or 1860 in Italy, at most, but not that of the Crimea or the campaign of 1859 in Italy.'[447] As the bloodshed increased in 1863 and 1864, there were descriptions of what the *Allgemeine Zeitung*—at the time of the battles of Petersburg and Atlanta in August 1864—labelled the 'atrocious slaughter' of modern warfare, yet they remained rare.[448] In general, German reports of the American war became more and more disparate over the last two years of the conflict, eclipsed by the 'German' war in Schleswig-Holstein.

Warfare, it seemed from a reading of the press, was changing by the mid-nineteenth century, becoming more destructive, but it still appeared to be a distant adventure or a strategic game for amateurs and experts. Some journalists passed on their anxieties about the suffering and death which they experienced in more explicit reportage of events. The battlefields were a long way away, though, with news of Abraham Lincoln's assassination on 15 April 1865, in one of the final acts of the Civil War, working its way to *Kladderadatsch* 'from far across the ocean', for example.[449] The 'German' wars which occurred either affected few combatants— in Schleswig-Holstein in 1848–51—or they were seen, with some exceptions, to be 'Austrian' affairs, most notably in Hungary in 1849 and Italy in 1859. Many German subjects had served in the military but few had fought in a war, the principal 'memories' of which—by the early 1860s—were historical, dating back fifty years to the Napoleonic campaigns. The public commemorations and histories of these military conflicts were romantic, helping to establish an heroic conception of warfare which military service and the prominence of the army in daily life normalized. News from exotic wars abroad, imagined in visual form, fed readers' existing fascination and did little, despite premonitions of horrifying violence, to deter subjects from going to war. Thus, when conflicts looked likely to escalate in 1848–9, 1854–6, and 1859, political leaders, journalists, and 'public opinion', as far as can be judged, were willing to countenance the possibility of war.

---

[445] These political headlines were accompanied in the latter stages of the war by the continuation of straightforwardly military headlines: for instance, 'Vom amerikanischen Krieg' (22 September 1864), 'Der Krieg in Nordamerika' (9 April 1865), and 'Aus den Vereinigten Staaten' (13 April 1865). Such articles also appeared in periodicals such as the *Preußische Jahrbücher*: 'Der Krieg in Nordamerika seit der Entscheidung im Westen', 1865, vol. 15, 258–91; 'Der Krieg in Nordamerika und die Präsidentenwahl im Herbst 1864', 1865, vol. 16, 324–43.

[446] *Preußische Jahrbücher*, 1862, vol. 10, 487. 'Der Wendepunkt im nordamerikanischen Bürgerkrieg', ibid., 1863, vol. 51, no. 1, 212, was more critical, terming the conflict 'a social war', not a political one or a 'civil war to put down a rebellion'. It nevertheless avoided references of a war of all against all, which had typified historical treatments of civil war and the Thirty Years' War, in particular.

[447] Ibid., 483.   [448] *Allgemeine Zeitung*, 25 Aug. 1864.

[449] 'Zum 15. April', *Kladderadatsch*, vol. 18, no. 20, 30 Apr. 1865, 77.

Their stance was arguably less the consequence of a hardening of attitudes, visible in the liberal Ludwig August von Rochau's championing of *Realpolitik*, than of the consolidation of heroic conceptions of combat.[450] Between 1864 and 1871, this willingness was tested extensively for the first time since 1815.

---

[450] The section on war in L. A. v. Rochau, *Grundsätze der Realpolitik* (Stuttgart, 1853), vol. 1, 100–8, is actually concerned to establish legal and other limits to the use of violence.

THE HORROR OF WAR, 1864–88

6

War and the Nation

After the event, the 'wars of unification' seemed to many commentators to have been a connected, even progressive, series of national conflicts, issuing in the founding of a German *Kaiserreich*.[1] They were comprehended, according to the title of one work from 1879, within a single 'history of three glorious wars'.[2] By the late 1880s, they were being referred to routinely as '*Einigungskriege*' or wars of unification.[3] At the time, however, the conflicts appeared very different from each other, even to supporters of the Hohenzollern monarchy's mission in Germany. The conflict against Denmark in 1864 had been anticipated by liberals as a 'great war', but its very status as a 'war' had been contested by the Prussian and Austrian governments, who preferred to think of it—or to have others think of it—as an 'intervention' on the part of the Great Powers or an 'execution' on behalf of the other German states.[4] 'The two powers [Prussia and Austria] don't want a war above all', noted the *Frankfurter Zeitung* in February 1864: 'they move into Schleswig, they fight with the Danes, they will stage battles and besiege cities—but all that should not be called a war'.[5] The conflict between Prussia, Austria, and the other German states in 1866 was held to be a major war, yet it remained deeply divisive, regularly referred to in the press as a '*Bruderkrieg*' or war of brothers.[6] From the vantage point of many commentators in the South, Germany had been 'ruined' by a war which had been entered into lightly by 'our' parties and courts, in the words of the Catholic, Bavarian *Historisch-politische Blätter*.[7] For Prussians, the reasons for the military conflict had been opaque, with the conservative party's leading ideologue Ernst Ludwig von Gerlach criticizing Bismarck in the *Kreuzzeitung* in May 1866 for his 'patriotic egotism' in the realm of foreign politics and war, 'as if these

---

[1] J. Leonhard, 'Vergangenheit als Vorgeschichte des Nationalstaates? Zur retrospektiven und selektiven Teleologie der deutschen Nationalhistoriographie nach 1850', in H. P. Hye, B. Mazohl, and J. P. Niederkorn (eds), *Nationalgeschichte als Artefakt. Zum Paradigma 'Nationalstaat' in den Historiographien Deutschlands, Italiens und Österreichs* (Vienna, 2009), 179–200.

[2] K. V. Winterfeld, *Geschichte der drei glorreichen Kriege von 1864, 1866 und 1870/71* (Berlin, 1879).

[3] A. Trinius, *Geschichte der Einigungskriege 1864, 1866, 1870/71* (Berlin, 1888), 3 vols; W. Mueller, *Deutschlands Einigungskriege 1864–1871* (Leipzig, 1889). See F. Becker, 'Auf dem Weg zu einer "Kulturgeschichte der Ideen"? Deutung der Einigungskriege und bürgerlicher Militarismus im Deutschen Kaiserreich', in L. Raphael and H.-E. Tenorth (eds), *Ideen als gesellschaftliche Gestaltungskraft im Europa der Neuzeit. Beiträge für eine erneuerte Geistesgeschichte* (Munich, 2006), 267–88.

[4] *National-Zeitung*, 2 Dec. 1863, citing Wilhelm Löwe-Calbe's speech to the Prussian *Abgeordnetenhaus*.

[5] *Frankfurter Zeitung*, 4 Feb. 1864.

[6] N. Buschmann, *Einkreisung und Waffenbruderschaft*, 269–308.

[7] *Historisch-politische Blätter*, vol. 58, 1866, 781.

fields had no higher law'.[8] Prussian liberals were likewise unwilling to trust in the motives of a Chancellor with whom they had been locked in a domestic constitutional struggle since 1862, making it difficult—if the *National-Zeitung* were to be believed—for 'a Prussian and for German liberals in general' to 'follow and stand by our present government'.[9] The war against France in 1870 did have broad 'public' support throughout Germany, reminding the previously critical *Frankfurter Zeitung* of Ferdinand Freiligrath's earlier premonition of 'Swabians and Prussians hand in hand', no longer asking themselves 'what is a German fatherland?'[10] However, this struggle, too, often seemed like a fight for survival or '*Existenzkrieg*', protecting what already existed rather than striving to create something new.[11] During the early stages of the conflict, fear for the continuing existence of the North German Confederation or the Prussian state arguably played a more significant role for different political parties than hopes for the future.[12] What the war was for, other than defence against the aggression of 'Gallic Caesarism', and how it was connected to the preceding conflicts in 1864 and 1866, were questions which were left deliberately open, for fear of exposing internal divisions.[13]

Historians have come to understand the wars of 1864, 1866, and 1870–1 as 'national' conflicts, pitting their arguments against those of both the 'Borussian' tradition, whose linear teleology has long been rejected, and the 'Bielefeld school', which had tended to emphasize the instrumentality of unification from above.[14] Some scholars have reassessed the complex relations between the various groupings of the national movement and proponents (and opponents) of war, asking how they became intertwined after such a long period of peace in the face of government opposition. To an extent, the answer lay in the literary and academic origins of the movement, which encouraged the historical examination of 'German' wars and promoted calls for military intervention without political responsibility for their human and financial consequences.[15] More importantly, the relationship rested on the demonization of enemies—particularly the supposed '*Erbfeind*' France—which had been linked to nationalism since the Revolutionary and Napoleonic Wars and which had been tied more firmly through the development and deployment of national stereotypes and antagonistic discourses of the nineteenth century.[16] As Michael Jeismann has claimed:

> If one follows this genesis and development from national self-understanding and images of the enemy from 1792 to 1918 in Germany and France, it can be seen that

---

[8] *Neue Preussische Zeitung*, 8 May 1866.   [9] *National-Zeitung*, 15 July 1866.

[10] *Frankfurter Zeitung*, 2 Aug. 1870, citing Freiligrath's 'Hurra Germania'.   [11] Ibid.

[12] See, for instance, the *Neue Preussische Zeitung*, 17 July 1870; *Kölnische Volkszeitung*, 20 and 26 July 1870; *Social-Demokrat*, 17, 22, and 24 July 1870.

[13] *Kölnische Volkszeitung*, 7 Sept. 1870.

[14] For a summary, see S. Berger, *Inventing the Nation: Germany* (London, 2004), 66–76.

[15] B. Giesen, *Die Intellektuellen und die Nation* (Frankfurt, 1993); B. Giesen, 'Vom Patriotismus zum völkischen Denken. Intellektuelle als Konstrukteure der deutschen Identität', in H. Berding (ed.), *Nationales Bewußtsein und kollektive Identität* (Frankfurt, 1994), 345–93; H. Gramley, *Propheten des deutschen Nationalismus. Theologen, Historiker und Nationalökonomen 1848–1880* (Frankfurt, 2001), 131–43, 221–46, 333–56.

[16] See, for instance, O. Dann, *Nation und Nationalismus in Deutschland 1770–1990* (Munich, 1993), 57–168.

a principled antagonism lurked beneath the political events and also beneath the multifaceted exchanges of both sides in the cultural sphere which could always be activated when the nation seemed to be threatened.[17]

Other historians such as Jörn Leonhard and Nikolaus Buschmann have focused on the contingent and incremental linkages between belligerence and nationalism, especially during the period of international crisis after 1848, rather than on a purportedly 'irreversible' original fusion between them.[18] 'The more and more entangled perceptions of war since the middle of the 1850s were intensified at the start of the 1860s in what was, in part, a new direction for belligerent discourse', contends Leonhard: 'The reception of the Italian war [of 1859] pushed the question of a *national war* for the creation of a nation-state into the foreground, but reflected at the same time the openness of national–political discourse in Germany and the argumentative pluralism of national designs.'[19] Whereas historians had been tempted to foreshorten 'contemporary awareness of possibilities', 'there was, at the beginning of the 1860s, no linear and inevitable path to a belligerent, *kleindeutsch* form of nation-building, which Borussian historiography had established as a teleological paradigm of German history after the experience of 1866 and 1870–71'.[20] Instead, a 'simultaneity of historically un-synchronic conceptions of war, in which residual and new sediments of experience overlay each other', gradually became apparent.[21] The national and even racial demonization of enemies, Prussian and German expansionism, the simplification of diplomacy and warfare in the press, and the 'sacralization' of 'national wars' were central, in Buschmann's opinion, to the mutual reinforcement of nation-building and the legitimation of warfare in the 1850s and 1860s.[22] With notable qualifications, Jakob Vogel, Markus Ingenlath, and Frank Becker have extended this analysis into the imperial era.[23]

---

[17] M. Jeismann, *Das Vaterland der Feinde*, 382.

[18] Ibid. See, for instance, N. Buschmann, '"Im Kanonenfeuer müssen die Stämme Deutschlands zusammen geschmolzen warden". Zur Konstruktion nationaler Einheit in den Kriegen der Reichsgründungsphase', 99–119.

[19] J. Leonhard, *Bellizismus und Nation*, 590–1.

[20] Ibid., 591. J. Leonhard, 'Vergangenheit als Vorgeschichte des Nationalstaates?', in H. P. Hye, B. Mazohl, and J. P. Niederkorn (eds), *Nationalgeschichte als Artefakt*, 179–200.

[21] J. Leonhard, *Bellizismus und Nation*, 591.

[22] N. Buschmann, *Einkreisung und Waffenbruderschaft*, 83–138, 181–240, 309–36; N. Buschmann, 'Auferstehung der Nation? Konfession und Nationalismus vor der Reichsgründung in der Debatte jüdischer, protestantischer und katholischer Kreise', 333–88; N. Buschmann, '"Moderne Versimpelung" des Krieges. Kriegsberichterstattung und öffentliche Kommunikation an der Schwelle zum Zeitalter der Massenkommunikation (1850–1870)', in N. Buschmann and H. Carl (eds), *Die Erfahrung des Krieges*, 97–123. Also, C. Rak, *Krieg, Nation und Konfession. Die Erfahrung des deutsch-französischen Krieges von 1870/71* (Paderborn, 2004), 137–46, 273–400; C. G. Krüger, *'Sind wir den nicht Brüder?' Deutsche Juden im nationalen Krieg 1870/71* (Paderborn, 2006), 42–91, 189–238; C. G. Krüger, '"Weil nun der Kampf der Völker die jüdischen Bruchstücke gegeneinander schleudert..." Die deutsch-jüdische Öffentlichkeit im Krieg von 1870/71', *Geschichte und Gesellschaft*, 31 (2005), 149–68.

[23] J. Vogel, *Nationen im Gleichschritt*, 45–91, 210–26; J. Vogel, '"En revenant de la revue". Militärfolklore und Folkloremilitarismus in Deutschland und Frankreich 1871–1914', *Österreichische Zeitschrift für Geschichtswissenschaften*, 9 (1998), 9–30; J. Vogel, 'Der "Folklorenmilitarismus" und seine zeitgenössische Kritik—Deutschland und Frankreich 1871–1914', in W. Wette (ed.), *Militarismus in Deutschland 1871 bis 1945* (Münster, 1999), 277–92; M. Ingenlath, *Mentale Aufrüstung*, 86–134; F. Becker, *Bilder von Krieg und Nation*; F. Becker, '2. September 1870 / 18. Januar 1871: Selbstbestätigung einer labilen Nation?', 156–76. Vogel argues that a new cult of a 'nation in arms' was created but that

Becker, in particular, shows how the construction of a civilian mythology of national wars of unification could coexist with continuing opposition to the Hohenzollern monarchy and the imposition of a Prussian-dominated Reich.[24] Thus, in celebrating victory in the summer of 1871, the various dynasties and state governments were content 'merely to combine regional and national symbols with one another', with 'Bavaria' presiding alongside 'Germania' in Munich, and 'Saxonia' in Dresden, as part of a festival led jointly by the local prince and a representative—usually the Crown Prince—of the Hohenzollerns. In the Hohenzollern monarchy, the matter seemed simpler but was, in fact, more complicated, since the King of Prussia was now also a national head of state and 'Prussia no longer only stood for itself but had become the core state of the newly created nation.'[25] At the same time, there were long-standing antipathies to overcome between 'feudal', largely noble elites and new educated and urban ones, and between 'traditional' institutions, including the army, and 'modern' ones such as the Prussian Chamber of Deputies and German Reichstag. The juxtaposition of the unveiling of separate statues of Friedrich Wilhelm III and of Germania in the Lustgarten of the Prussian capital betrayed 'a mixture of feudal and national pathos, . . . a meaningful embodiment of the alliance between the old elites and the resources of the nation'.[26] The prominent display of the symbol of the iron cross, which had been created in 1813, on the stage of the city councillors in the Pariser Platz intimated that the quest for national unity which had begun during the Napoleonic Wars had come to its natural conclusion.

Yet such myths were deceptive, as Becker intimates. Although the idea of 'the war as a midwife of unification' had been 'contested and won by traditional ruling elites and the nation together' and 'this conception of the war, which was at most modified but was hardly questioned in truth, structured the perception of military events in a bourgeois public sphere', such agreement was specific, reciprocal, and precarious, dating back only to the Franco-German war, not earlier conflicts: 'The

---

it can be understood as a form of 'folklore' militarism rather than as an indication of a novel type of 'war ideology'.

[24] See, for instance, F. Becker, '"Bewaffnetes Volk 'oder' Volk in Waffen"? Militärpolitik und Militarismus in Deutschland und Frankreich 1870–1914', in C. Jansen (ed.), *Der Bürger als Soldat. Die Militarisierung europäischer Gesellschaften im langen 19. Jahrhundert: ein internationaler Vergleich* (Essen, 2004), 158–74; F. Becker, 'Synthetischer Militarismus. Die Einigungskriege und der Stellenwert des Militärischen in der deutschen Gesellschaft', in M. Epkenhans and G. P. Groß (eds), *Das Militär und der Aufbruch in die Moderne 1860 bis 1890. Armeen, Marinen und der Wandel von Politik, Gesellschaft und Wirtschaft in Europa, den USA sowie Japan* (Munich, 2003), 125–41. This combination makes Becker's conclusions compatible with historians who stress the limits of the scope and significance of nationalism in nineteenth-century Germany: see especially J. J. Sheehan, 'What is German History?', *Journal of Modern History*, 53 (1981), 1–23; H.-U. Wehler, *Nationalismus. Geschichte, Formen, Folgen*; J. Echternkamp and S. O. Müller (eds), *Die Politik der Nation. Deutscher Nationalismus in Krieg und Krisen 1760–1960*; D. Langewiesche, *Nation, Nationalismus und Nationalstaat in Deutschland und Europa*; D. Langewiesche, *Reich, Nation, Föderation*; J. J. Breuilly, *The Formation of the First German Nation-State* (Basingstoke, 1996); J. J. Breuilly, *Austria, Prussia and the Making of Germany, 1806–1871* (London, 2011); J. J. Breuilly (ed.), *The State of Germany: The National Idea in the Making, Unmaking and Remaking of a Modern Nation-State*.

[25] F. Becker, *Bilder von Krieg und Nation*, 483.   [26] Ibid., 487.

wars of 1864 and 1866 were still commented upon by contemporaries in a very contradictory fashion', with 'their representation only adapted to the myth of the war of 1870/71 after the founding of the Reich, to which they were immediately added as preludes'.[27] This difference in kind was displayed by the 6-km-long parade in 1871, with its four themes (the welcoming of the returning troops, the victory over France, the battles of the autumn and winter campaigns, national unity), which was much more elaborate and more than three times as long as that of 1866. The tensions between Prussia and the *Mittelstaaten*, Catholics and Protestants, nobles and burghers, many of whom had varying attitudes to the military and experiences of conflict, were overcome, however partially, in the unifying events of the Franco-German war, which underpinned 'the foundational political consensus that carried the constitutional edifice of 1871'.[28] Intrinsic to such accounts is the assumption that the military was divisive and that war was hard for civilians— peasants, artisans, democrats, and liberals—to accept, except when it was legitimated by a set of widely held national goals.[29]

By contrast, in this chapter (and in subsequent ones), I argue that patriotic or national goals, though inspiring many noble officers and middle-class recruits (and memoirists), were often less relevant for the actual waging of war than a common acceptance of military conflict amongst civilians, sustained by experience of military service, support for the notion of an arming of the people (*Volksbewaffnung*), and the romanticization of combat during the first half of the nineteenth century.[30] In many instances, the technology of killing, which was closely examined and widely admired by the press, actually reinforced these romantic impressions of fighting, as the predominantly affirmative imagery of the *Illustrirte Zeitung* and *Gartenlaube* hinted.[31] If 'you came to the conclusion' during the recent fighting 'that the modern perfection of weapons, the needle-gun and the chassepot, the *mitrailleuses* and breech-loading artillery made the battle bloodier than they had been in the past, you are mistaken', commented the liberal

---

[27] F. Becker, *Bilder von Krieg und Nation*, 487–8. See also F. Becker, '"Getrennt marschieren, vereint schlagen". Königgrätz, 3. Juli 1866', in S. Förster, M. Pöhlmann, and D. Walter (eds), *Schlachten der Weltgeschichte*, 3rd edn (Munich, 2001), 216–29.

[28] Ibid., 487. On differing attitudes to and policies concerning the military, see U. Frevert, *A Nation in Barracks*, 47–157.

[29] D. Langewiesche, 'Zum Wandel von Krieg und Kriegslegimation in der Neuzeit', 5–27; D. Langewiesche and N. Buschmann, '"Dem Vertilgungskriege Grenzen setzen." Kriegstypen des 19. Jahrhunderts und der deutsch-französische Krieg 1870/71', in D. Beyrau, M. Hochgeschwender, and D. Langewiesche (eds), *Formen des Krieges*, 163–95.

[30] For an example of the routine enthusiasm for war amongst career officers, see A. v. Oertzen, *1870–71. Kriegserinnerungen eines Schwedter Dragoners* (Berlin, 1905), 1, talking of a 'fresh, happy war'.

[31] See, for instance, 'Preußische Belagerungsbatterie Nr. 3 im Park von Naincy vor Paris', *Illustrirte Zeitung*, 21 Jan. 1871; 'Preussisches Belagerungsgeschütz: Krupp'scher 24-Pfünder von Gußstahl', *Illustrirte Zeitung*, 4 Mar. 1871; 'Innere Ansicht des Forts Nogent vor Paris nach der Besetzung durch württembergischen Truppen', *Illustrirte Zeitung*, 11 Mar. 1871. Also, *Kladderadatsch*, 1864, vol. 17, no. 7, which made fun of cannon that could 'break through walls' and argued that all they needed to do was do the same to paper (the London Treaty).

Schwäbischer Merkur on 1 September 1870: 'No, despite all the horror, the casualty numbers decrease while the benefits for the fatherland grow.'[32]

Many conscripts from rural or artisanal backgrounds, together with their families, were less enthusiastic about going to war than were the middle-class volunteers or aristocratic career officers who wrote the public record of 1864, 1866, and 1870–1.[33] To many liberals and democrats, who constituted a majority in most German lower chambers by the early 1860s, the Habsburg and Hohenzollern monarchies had ignored the wishes of the German Confederation and the national movement and they had attempted to conduct a cabinet war against Denmark in 1864. When they had gone to war with each other in 1866, drawing most of the remaining states into the conflict on Austria's side, they had not only divided Prussian liberals, many of whom remained opposed to what they continued to see—in Hermann Baumgarten's 'self-critique' of German liberalism in October 1866—as 'the worst incarnation of the most objectionable Junkerdom' and 'the hated Bismarckian regime'; they had also pitted North against South, placing liberals in the *Mittelstaaten* in an even more invidious position than that of their counterparts in the Hohenzollern monarchy.[34] The Saxon liberal historian Heinrich von Treitschke, who backed Prussia, was opposed by his own brother, who fought for Saxony on the side of Austria. Whereas the *Landtage* of Hanover, Brunswick, Hesse-Darmstadt, Weimar, and Nassau complied with the *Abgeordnetentag's* request in May 1866 for a declaration of neutrality, which benefited Prussia, those of Bavaria, Württemberg, and Baden, all of which had liberal majorities, did not. 'Neutrality was preached among us', wrote Otto Elben of the Swabian monarchy, 'but in vain: blind passion against Prussia was too powerful in the leading circles.'[35]

Few knew exactly why they were fighting in 1866, as the Prussian essayist Theodor Fontane conceded.[36] Nonetheless, they fought: there was little outright opposition to the war on either side and no recorded instance of forceful resistance during mobilization. Compared to previous conflicts, desertion rates were low.[37] War had come to seem unexceptional. What is most striking about contemporaries' reactions to the contrasting conflicts of 1864, 1866, and 1870–1, seen

---

[32] *Schwäbischer Merkur*, 1 Sept. 1870, cited in C. G. Krüger, 'German Suffering in the Franco-German War', *German History*, 29 (2011), 409.

[33] From such accounts of the war, it could appear that national and social unity prevailed in 1870–1: for instance, G. Boschen, *Kriegserinnerungen eines Einundneunzigers 1870/71* (Oldenburg, 1897), 7, claimed that 'All [envy, dispute and egoism] was forgotten; only one thought captivated every heart, young and old, high and low, and a true giddiness of fraternization had seized everyone.' Yet it is clear from other accounts of the later stages of the war that old hierarchies and distinctions continued to exist.

[34] H. Baumgarten, *Der deutsche Liberalismus. Eine Selbstkritik* (1866), 105, 123.

[35] O. Elben, *Lebenserinnerungen*, 141.

[36] T. Fontane, *Der deutsche Krieg von 1866* (Berlin, 1870), vol. 1, 64–5.

[37] As one priest testified in 1870, one reason for this was pressure at home not to seem to be a 'shirker': M. Schall, *Vor vierzig Jahren. Kriegserinnerungen eines Lazarettpfarrers der II. Armee 1870/71* (Spandau, 1910), 14–15; K. Zeitz, *Kriegserinnerungen eines Kriegsfreiwilligen aus den Jahren 1870/71* (Altenburg, 1897), 60. Alexander Seyferth, *Die Heimatfront 1870/71. Wirtschaft und Gesellschaft im deutsch-französischen Krieg* (Paderborn, 2007), 75–104, shows that disquiet was common but active opposition very rare.

from an historical vantage point, is the relative ease with which troops went to war and the casualness of civilians' references to warfare.

POLITICAL MOBILIZATIONS

The romanticization of warfare and the institutionalization of conscription helped to ensure that war had come to appear normal by the 1860s in spite of a long period of peace in the German lands, which was seen to extend back to 1848–50 or 1815.[38] Much of the active support for military intervention, which took contemporaries by surprise, was national or patriotic, associated with the formation of a new German state or support for an existing individual state, as Elben noted after the celebration of the half-centenary of the battle of Leipzig, during which the cause of Schleswig-Holstein had emerged to unite the German *Volk*:

> In great enthusiasm, the mood of the people immediately burst into flames, especially in South Germany. There had been no such movement since 1848; not even in 1859 at the time of the Italian war had such unanimity manifested itself. The gatherings of the years of the reaction had actually only encompassed party members; now, the whole *Volk* once again flowed together when they were called on to advise about the events of the day. As soon as a Schleswig-Holstein committee was formed, it contained, in fact, all relevant political points of view.[39]

All regions, a majority of political parties, and large sections of the population appeared to have been affected. About 900 Schleswig-Holstein committees were established throughout Germany.[40] According to Sybel's calculation, 84.4 per cent of *Landtag* deputies in the third Germany, 53.4 per cent in Prussia, and 7.6 per cent in Austria signed the petition for the duchies' 'rights' in 1864.[41] Unexpectedly, the 'smaller German' *Nationalverein* and the 'greater German' *Reformverein* had converged in a common national cause, criticizing Prussia, Austria, and the Confederation. On 21 December 1863, members of the two organizations met in a specially convened assembly at Frankfurt comprised of 490 deputies. 'Just beforehand, on the occasion of the *Fürstenkongress* in Frankfurt, the "Grossdeutsche" and the "Kleindeutsche" had strongly opposed each other', wrote Karl Biedermann: 'now they both united in the national cause'.[42] Although members of the *Reformverein* later left the assembly, they continued to cooperate in regional Schleswig-Holstein committees throughout the German lands. The movement for the duchies reported one correspondent in the *Wochenschrift des Nationalvereins* had not merely been an aside but a complete act in the drama of Germany's national development, creating a unity of purpose on the part of the previously inimical National and Reform

[38] On the predominance of 'romantic expectations of war', see Thomas Rohkrämer, *Der Militarismus der 'kleinen Leute'. Die Kriegervereine im Deutschen Kaiserreich 1871–1914* (Munich, 1990), 92.

[39] O. Elben, *Lebenserinnerungen*, 136.   [40] A. Biefang, *Bürgertum*, 332.

[41] C. Jansen, *Einheit, Macht und Freiheit. Die Paulskirchenlinke und die deutsche Politik in der nach-revolutionären Epoche 1849–1867* (Düsseldorf, 2000), 482.

[42] K. Biedermann, *Mein Leben*, 221.

Associations which should not be wasted.[43] 'The *Volk* is united to a man in the Schleswig-Holstein affair', commented the *Wochenblatt des Deutschen Reformvereins* on 29 November 1863: 'This is the great favourite bet for the many small German squabbles and German disunity. They completely dissolve in it.'[44]

Such national aims, which were discussed at great length in the press, legitimized the war against Denmark, overriding any doubts about Bismarck's motives, and they sustained the conflict when the death toll, which remained comparatively small, began to mount. The war against Denmark in 1864 was popular, opposed only by a handful of radicals, wrote the liberal historian and forty-eighter Ludwig Häusser in the *Preussische Jahrbücher*, because Schleswig-Holstein had been the principal national question for the preceding twenty years.[45] Many 'patriots', complained Treitschke, had believed 'for years' that 'the Schleswig-Holstein question [was] the German question itself; whoever solves one will bring the other to an end'.[46] There had been broad agreement in 1848–9 that most, if not all, the territories of the duchies should be incorporated into the Reich and there was a corresponding sense of humiliation and dishonour, recalled a retrospective article in the *Grenzboten* in 1864, when Schleswig-Holstein was returned to Denmark in 1851.[47] The Habsburg monarchy's traitorous support for Denmark, the Hohenzollern monarchy's self-interested actions as a Great Power, withdrawing from Jutland by the time of the armistice of Malmö in July 1848, the inefficacy of the Frankfurt Parliament, and the inability of the political parties to act all seemed from the perspective of 1864 to have been responsible for Germany's failure to incorporate the duchies and to protect the German diaspora there in 1848–50.[48] Such a reading of history was widely shared within a limited reading public and political sphere, with much of the press agreeing with Arndt's appraisal at the time—published in the *Kölnische Zeitung*—that Schleswig-Holsteiner were 'fighting for their German life and for their old right of a fatherland'.[49] 'They stand, fight and bleed not for themselves alone, but for all Germans, for the whole of Germany', he continued.[50] The North German liberal *National-Zeitung*, the South German liberal *Allgemeine Zeitung*, and the conservative and Catholic *Deutsches Volksblatt* all concurred in 1850 that the fight for Schleswig-Holstein had been a just national cause on which the fate of Germany itself had depended, derailed by the actions of self-interested Great Powers which had been anxious to maintain the fragmentation of the German lands at the centre of Europe.[51]

Public opinion and the political parties sided largely with the *Mittelstaaten* and the German Confederation as war approached, since they had championed the

---

[43] 'Was nun weiter?', *Wochenschrift des Nationalvereins*, 6 Oct. 1864, in H. Rosenberg, *Die national-politische Publizistik Deutschlands*, 797.

[44] 'Deutschlands Pflicht', *Wochenblatt des Deutschen Reformvereins*, 29 Nov. 1863, in H. Rosenberg, *Die nationalpolitische Publizistik Deutschlands*, 733.

[45] *Preussische Jahrbücher*, 1865, vol. 15, 85.

[46] H. v. Treitschke, 'Herr Biedermann und die Annexion' (1865), in H. v. Treitschke, *Zehn Jahre Deutscher Kämpfe* (Berlin, 1874), 30.

[47] *Grenzboten*, 1864, vol. 23, 161–76.   [48] Ibid., 161–76, 201–14, 260–96.

[49] *Kölnische Zeitung*, 15 Sept. 1850, in Buschmann, *Einkreisung*, 243.   [50] Ibid.

[51] *National-Zeitung*, 15 Sept., 18 and 28 Oct. 1850; *Allgemeine Zeitung*, 16 and 21 Oct. 1850; *Deutsches Volksblatt*, 18 and 21 July, 2 and 7 Aug. 1850, ibid., 244–8.

popular causes of Friedrich Christian, Duke of Augustenburg, and an independent Schleswig-Holstein. Initially, individual governments such as that of Bavaria had coincided in their aims with the most important sections of the political public, especially with what the editor of the *Historisch-politische Blätter* Joseph Edmund Jörg termed 'dominating liberalism'.[52] To the Bavarian Foreign Minister Karl von Schrenck, the Schleswig-Holstein affair was a 'holy cause' and the Schleswig-Holstein-Verein was 'their association', 'composed of very solid people', which aspiring officials like Chlodwig zu Hohenlohe-Schillingsfürst were advised to join, as 'this was the means to become a minister'.[53] The 'question was able to gain so great a significance' in the first instance because of its legal ramifications, and 'the Germans are a legal people', wrote Hohenlohe to Queen Victoria on 4 May 1864: 'Yet, apart from this, everyone in Germany felt the deeper significance of the Schleswig-Holstein question for our internal conditions. Everyone knows that in this question the German question will be decided.'[54] What was more, it appeared to both the ministry and the public 'at the start', 'as if the German *Mittelstaaten*, the truly pure German states, could gain greater political weight through the Schleswig-Holstein affair', he continued: 'Here is the reason why this question has called forth a larger movement in the lands outside Prussia and Austria.'[55] The Bavarian government, parties, and public opinion had comprehended that the defence and formation of an independent, medium-sized Schleswig-Holstein, the most popular national cause since the 1840s, might offer other *Mittelstaaten* and the *Bund*, as the principal champions of Augustenburg and the duchies, a more central role in a reconstructed Germany.

Partly because they could more easily imagine themselves in the position of the Schleswig-Holsteiner, partly because they were threatened by the apparently imminent resolution of the German question, many Bavarians reacted strongly to the occupation of the duchies, to the distaste of self-confessedly more 'conservative' and 'confederal' observers like the Minister-President of Hesse-Darmstadt Reinhard von Dalwigk, who hinted in March 1864 that the former Bavarian Foreign Minister Ludwig von der Pfordten had put 'the subordinate Schleswig-Holstein question' above 'the continuation of the German Confederation' and the individual states' relationship to the Habsburg and Hohenzollern monarchies.[56] This was also the tenor of much early and some later press reportage, which depicted the Treaty of London as a brutal act of violence and called for the establishment of 'Schleswig-Holstein as an independent German land' in 'the interests and for the honour of Germany'.[57] The Augsburger *Allgemeine Zeitung* reported in similar terms that the

[52] 'Die Geschichte der Bundesexekution gegen Dänemark und ihre europäische Umstände', *Historisch-politische Blätter*, 1863, vol. 52, 698–726.

[53] Hohenlohe-Schillingsfürst, 18 Feb. 1864, in F. Curtius (ed.), *Denkwürdigkeiten* (Stuttgart, 1907), vol. 1, 134.

[54] Hohenlohe to Queen Victoria, 4 May 1864, in ibid., 141.

[55] Ibid.

[56] W. Schüssler (ed.), *Die Tagebücher des Freiherrn Reinhard v. Dalwigk zu Lichtenfels aus den Jahren 1860–71* (Osnabrück, 1967), 164.

[57] *Flugblätter des schleswig-holsteinischen Vereins zu Erlangen*, 1863, vol. 1; 1864, vols 3, 4, and 5; *Verhandlungen der am 28. Februar 1864 zu Erlangen abgehaltenen bayerischen Landesversammlung für*

German states, the Confederation, and 'the German *Volk*' should regulate their 'internal affairs' and fight Danish aggression with 'iron and blood', not just words, albeit in a 'nobler sense' than Bismarck.[58] 'The German question does not hinge on Prussia or on Austria, but it has its pivot in the pure German states', declared the Munich periodical *Chronik der Gegenwart*, before proceeding to outline its scheme for a 'West German federation' of middling states, for which Prussia would need to give up the Rhineland.[59] The thrust of Bavarian policy towards Schleswig-Holstein should be to create a counterweight in the *Bund* to the Great Power pretensions of Prussia, wrote the prominent liberal and founder of the Bavarian *Reformverein* Gustav von Lerchenfeld as late as March 1866: on the solution of the question

> rests the continuation or dissolution of the Confederation, the position of its members vis-à-vis the *Bund* authority and amongst themselves; the question of federalism or hegemony, or, more clearly expressed, of complete subjugation and incorporation of the confederal states which are not Great Powers…whether *grossdeutsch* or *kleindeutsch* or, better, *grosspreussisch*, whether through freedom to unification and, temporarily at least, to unity.[60]

To many contemporaries, Schleswig-Holstein seemed, in Hohenlohe's phrase, to be an '*Existenzfrage*' for Bavaria.

In some senses, contemporaries—or those who were following the news in the press—were drawn into a desirable national war via an intervention for the defence of the 'Germans' in Schleswig-Holstein, whose plight they had read about in the newspaper. However, many of their liberal and democratic leaders had also called for war from an early date as a stimulus to the national cause and as a solution to the 'German question'. War, in other words, was an instrument of policy. As Bavaria and the Confederation proved less and less able to act, overshadowed by Prussia and Austria, many contemporaries appear to have become disillusioned with them. Some parties had been sceptical of them throughout the crisis. A minority of Bavarian liberals who were in favour of *Kleindeutschland* were convinced that 'the unworthy role' of the *Mittelstaaten* had been one of 'self-interested denial of national duties' and 'mean-heartedness, incapacity and vacillating cowardice'.[61] For its part, the *Bund* had again shown itself to be the tool of the German Great Powers: 'There is only a Prussian and an Austrian, no *German* policy, in which the *strength of the whole* nation (*Nation*) could be realised', wrote Karl Brater, the editor of the *Süddeutsche Zeitschrift*, co-founder of the Bavarian *Fortschrittspartei* and one of the leading *kleindeutsch* deputies in the Bavarian *Landtag*.[62] Although liberal

Schleswig-Holstein (1864), in H. Rosenberg, *Die nationalpolitische Publizistik Deutschlands*, 725, 757, 759–61.

[58] *Allgemeine Zeitung*, 25 Nov. and 2 Dec. 1863.

[59] 'Die Politik des deutschen Volkes', *Chronik der Gegenwart*, 1865, 289–97; J. Strobel, *Vorschläge zur Neugestaltung Deutschlands oder die deutsche Frage und ihre Lösung* (Munich, 1865), originally published in *Chronik der Gegenwart*, 1865, 913–14.

[60] G. v. Lerchenfeld, *Das Verfahren der deutschen Grossmächte gegen Schleswig-Holstein und den Bund* (Jena, 1866), 1–2.

[61] K. Brater, *Preussen und Bayern in der Sache der Herzogthümer* (Nördlingen, 1864), 2.

[62] K. Brater, *Flugblätter des deutschen Nationalvereins* (1864), in H. Rosenberg, *Die nationalpolitische Publizistik Deutschlands*, 804–5.

politicians like Brater were critical of Prussia as a self-interested Great Power and of Bismarck as a violent adventurer 'without greatness', they believed that 'the German powers [had] been pushed to victory by the pressure of public opinion': 'Through the pressure of the popular movement the allied army was led to Schleswig; under the pressure of military victories Berlin's policy has been obliged to increase its diplomatic demands.'[63] The Prussian Minister-President himself, claimed Brater, had been forced, 'after long toing and froing, to satisfy the desires of the popular assembly and leave the reprehensible path of the policy of 1850. A powerful *liberal* government would have come to the same decisions *without* hesitation.'[64] The mouthpiece of the Bavarian Progressive Party echoed such sentiments, arguing that a Prussian victory 'consolidates the rule of the Junkers' and 'obstructs the internal struggle for freedom', but it was also more dismissive of the 'Austrian *Gesammtstaat*', whose interest was 'not a German interest'.[65] According to this reading of events, 'the nation (*Nation*), as is the essence of cabinet politics, stands beyond the fighting parties'.[66] One part of the democratic party in the southern and central German states, which was made up of 'conscious or unconscious republicans', concurred with such a reading and was similarly detached, waiting for a time 'when a democratic Continental storm would bring down thrones and bring back the happy times of a constituent National Assembly'.[67] The other faction of South German democracy, wrote Hohenlohe, belonged 'in part to the *Nationalverein* and is striving for the organisation of a German *Bundesstaat* under the leadership of Prussia. They hold the government of Herr von Bismarck to be a temporary evil, after the dismissal of which the idea [of *Kleindeutschland*] would nevertheless be implemented.'[68] Some sections of the liberal and democratic milieux of Bavaria—more than is suggested by the sixteen deputies of the *Fortschrittspartei* elected in 1863—rejected Austria's claims and had lost faith in the *Mittelstaaten* and the *Bund*. In such circumstances, cooperation with—or lack of resistance to—a belligerent Prussia, though an object of contempt under Bismarck, could seem to be a lesser evil.

The *Historisch-politische Blätter* exposed the willingness of liberals and democrats to countenance the use of violence and betrayed the support of Bavarian political Catholicism, which constituted—in an undefined form—the second largest political grouping after the liberals, for military intervention. Although its editor Edmund Jörg went on to found the *Bayerische Patriotenpartei* in 1868 and to oppose national unity under Prussian leadership in 1870, the periodical was highly critical of particularist *Mittelstaaten*, which appeared to have forged a *de facto* alliance with liberals and Progressives in support of Augustenburg and against the German Great Powers.[69] All Germans were justified on legal and national grounds in resisting

[63] K. Brater, *Preussen*, 3, 10.

[64] K. Brater, *Flugblätter*, in H. Rosenberg, *Die nationalpolitische Publizistik Deutschlands*, 804.

[65] *Wochenschrift der Fortschrittspartei in Bayern*, 30 June 1866, in ibid., 969.   [66] Ibid.

[67] Hohenlohe, 15 Apr. 1865, in F. Curtius (ed.), *Denkwürdigkeiten*, vol. 1, 144.   [68] Ibid.

[69] 'Ungezählte Fragezeichen zum dritten Deutschland und zur französischen Allianz', *Historisch-politische Blätter*, 1864, vol. 53, 222–38. On Jörg's later career, see E. Fink, 'For Country, Court and Church: The Bavarian Patriots' Party and Bavarian Regional Identity in the Era of German Unification', in R. Speirs and J. Breuilly (eds), *Germany's Two Unifications*, 155–71; and F. Hartmannsgruber, *Die Bayerischer Patriotenpartei 1868–1887* (Munich, 1986).

Denmark's illegitimate attempt to annex the duchies and to oppress their German populations.[70] Yet Progressives had sought to gain a demagogic party advantage from the affair, even mouthing the arguments of monarchical legitimacy in their quest for a revolution at home and abroad.[71] The German Confederation and the middling states had been pushed into a federal execution by the start of 1864 which would be difficult to reverse, 'not least because an ascendant liberalism feels the undemonstrable need to make a heroically active entry somewhere and therefore must hold up the Danish king each time because it believes that it has least to fear from him'.[72] Caught in such a contradictory position, the *Bundestag* and the individual states had been unable to act, demonstrating that the Confederation could not work.[73] 'The hope that the whole of Germany (*Gesammtdeutschland*) would throw itself into the breach, as a European balance, has as good as disappeared', lamented Jörg in 1865.[74] By contrast, Austria and Prussia, whose actions the periodical blessed on 24 January 1864, had circumvented the machinery of the *Bund* in pursuit of more realistic, internationally acceptable goals, motivated by their own self-interest.[75] The editor of the *Historisch-politische Blätter* commented on 24 April 1864:

> It was our view from the start that the snatching of the duchies would be at the cost of a war of conquest against half of Europe and that one would not mount such a war in order to found a new little middling state à la Baden or Coburg for the sphere of domination of the liberal-democratic party and to transfer to a puppet of this party the watch over the most difficult border in Germany... If a great war is to be carried out for Schleswig and Holstein, then it must have the goal of incorporating both lands in Prussia.[76]

Jörg's criticism of the Confederation and his own state of Bavaria was that they had been neither willing nor able to wage such a war: 'an honest German *Bundesreform*' would 'be very well worth a small world war', but it was unlikely to be carried out by a weak *Bund* and feckless *Mittelstaaten*.[77]

Unsurprisingly, North German liberals shared this point of view. The interpretation of events in the duchies provided by a *kleindeutsch* periodical such as the *Grenzboten* illustrated liberal support for a forceful policy and, if necessary, military intervention: the *Bund* had rightly contended that Schleswig and Holstein should not be divided, with the territories belonging by education and culture in a progressive Germany rather than a poor, backward and isolated Danish 'sham state', or *Scheinstaat* (1849); discussion of the duchies by the Great Powers at London in 1852, after Prussia had stood down in 1850, was more important for the area's history than 1848 had been, with Denmark effectively mocking a divided Germany despite the risk of revolutionizing German public opinion, ignoring the

---

[70] *Historisch-politische Blätter*, 1864, vol. 53, 621–36.   [71] Ibid.
[72] 'Die Geschichte der Bundesexekution gegen Dänemark und ihre europäischen Umstände', ibid., 1863, vol. 52, 698–726.
[73] Ibid., 1864, vol. 53, 148–9.   [74] Ibid., 1865, vol. 55, 1–25.
[75] Ibid., 1864, vol. 53, 222–38.
[76] 'Deutschland vor der Londoner Conferenz und der Congress-Ära der Zukunft', ibid., 731–52.
[77] Ibid., 731–52.

fact that Germans dominated both the state and the culture of Denmark, and sealing off Schleswig-Holstein as a bridge for the spread of German culture to the North (1852–3); the 'occupation' of Schleswig-Holstein by Denmark in the 1850s had been the consequence of German, not merely Prussian, impotence, with the duchies—Schleswig in particular, since it was most endangered—remaining a source of national dishonour for large sections of the public, in spite of the continuing dominance and expansion of German culture (1856–61).[78] The reopening of the Schleswig-Holstein question, when it occurred in the early 1860s, had been the consequence of public agitation in the face of Prussia's and Austria's unreliability as Great Powers, the Confederation's continuing ineffectiveness, and international hostility (1863–4), it was suggested.[79] Cross-party support for a beleaguered Schleswig-Holstein as a German '*Lebensfrage*', as various correspondents put it, had a long history.[80] The resulting readiness of 'public opinion' in Germany as a whole to countenance war helped to dictate the course of events in 1864. Even Bismarck, noted Theodor von Bernhardi in May 1864, 'was pushed into the affair against his will'.[81] Only reactionaries in Prussia and Austria, along with Czechs and other nationalities, voiced reservations.[82]

The position of liberals, democrats, conservatives, Catholics, and others in 1866 was different from that of 1864. All the German states except those on Prussia's borders—some Thuringian states, Mecklenburg, Brunswick, and the Hanse cities—went to war in support of the Habsburg monarchy in accordance with the decisive vote in the Confederation for mobilization on 14 June. Much more than in 1864, political and public opinion was divided. In public, most pro-Prussian liberals were still circumspect, with the exception of mavericks such as Treitschke, who had advised readers as early as January 1865 to 'leave the ground of the law' and to carry out 'the *Anschluss* of the small states to Prussia' in order to achieve 'Germany's unity'.[83] One month later, he had alluded to 'the first duty of the German patriot to defend and increase the power of this state', as he had reiterated the case for Berlin's annexation of Schleswig-Holstein.[84] The majority of liberals were more cautious. Rudolf Haym, Treitschke's colleague from the *Preussische*

---

[78] *Grenzboten*, 1849, vol. 8, 215–18, 355–7, 432; 1852, vol. 12, 225–7; 1853, vol. 13, 41–63; 1856, vol. 15, 14, 210–13; 1857, vol. 16, 397–8; 1858, vol. 17, 66–71, 330–3, 440–4, 481–97, pt. 2, 353, 481–90; 1859, vol. 18, 117, 479, pt. 2, 36–9, 78, 356–9; 1861, vol. 20, 341–7.

[79] *Grenzboten*, 1864, vol. 23, 34–6, 77–80, 112–18, 356–60, 518–20, pt. 2, 76–80, 281–7, 348–53, 431–6.

[80] For instance, *Grenzboten*, 1864, vol. 23, 116, or *Preussische Jahrbücher*, 1861, vol. 8, 428.

[81] Diary, 14 May 1864, T. v. Bernhardi, *Aus dem Leben Theodor von Bernhardis* (Leipzig, 1893), vol. 6, 100.

[82] The *Evangelische Kirchenzeitung*, 20 Jan. 1864, deplored any war for a 'modern, un-Christian, nationality swindle'; the Catholic *Österreichischer Volksfreund*, 12 Dec. 1863, argued that a war against Denmark, following the demands of the national movement, should be avoided for it contravened Austria's role as a Great Power, defending law and the European balance of power. See N. Buschmann, *Einkreisung und Waffenbruderschaft*, 252. On the opposition of the Czech *Politik*, see ibid., 262, 266.

[83] H. v. Treitschke, 'Die Lösung der schleswig-holsteinischen Frage', 15 Jan. 1865, in H. v. Treitschke, *Zehn Jahre*, 10, 25.

[84] H. v. Treitschke, 'Herr Biedermann und die Annexion', 22 Feb. 1865, ibid., 29. See the quick historical justification of this position by the national-minded liberal Ludwig Karl Aegidi, *Woher und Wohin? Ein Versuch, die Geschichte Deutschlands zu verstehen*, 4th edn (Hamburg, 1866).

Jahrbücher, organized the first public petition by Prussian liberals in support of Bismarck—the Halle Declaration—on 26 April 1866.[85] In private, pride, triumphalism, and admiration of Bismarck were more common, together with a disdain for *Klein-* and *Mittelstaaten*. 'I am not making up an "ideal Prussia" for myself, as the article which you send me claims', wrote Duncker to a correspondent in Kiel about a piece in the Viennese *Neue Freie Presse* on 26 April 1865: 'My heart is attached to the "real Prussia", whose whole history since 1640 has meant the saving of the German nation and German existence with all its strengths and weaknesses, with its suffering, emergencies and struggles.'[86] Germany's freedom would be created by Prussia's power. 'You know that I don't just want power and success for Prussia's sake; every strengthening of Prussia is a considerable relief for the solution of the German question', he went on: 'The stronger Prussia has become, the less resistance Austria will necessarily offer, the more easily the merger of the smaller German states will occur. To hinder Prussia's growth at a certain point in time so that it can later form an entire *Bundesstaat* is a false doctrine.'[87] If Schleswig-Holstein were made independent, he concluded, it would have a life-long problem with Prussia and particularism.[88] Annexation was desirable, Duncker told Theodor von Bernhardi in January 1866, even if it was necessary to delay it until Hungary seceded from Austria.[89] Droysen, another dinner guest of Bernhardi's, was equally ebullient, having declared 'in a raised voice' in May 1864 that 'the taking of Düppel is...one of those events which are epoch-making in the life of a nation'.[90] He went on:

> The army has won such confidence, such trust in itself, that it is now equal to any enemy; it now knows what it can do. The population has developed a love for and trust in the army; it has shown what part it can play in the public realm, in the honour of Prussian arms...A swing in favour of Bismarck has certainly taken place. Bismarck, too, has truly significant attributes. He [Droysen] had recently said to Gruner: 'If you were at the helm, we would still be standing at the Eider!' Bismarck's impertinent, even cocky, attitude to foreign powers has its advantages.[91]

When Bernhardi took the opportunity to aim a blow at 'Samwer and his like', referring to the Badenese liberal as a cipher for small-state, southern parochialism, Droysen's response was 'Quite right!'[92]

A majority of South German liberals, along with nearly all democrats, conservatives, and Catholics, eventually backed their own states in the war against Prussia in 1866. Some, like one 'old soldier' writing in the *Historisch-politische Blätter*, warned the Prussian government and parties of the dire consequences of waging war without national legitimacy and popular support: 'Under all circumstances, war demands a great willingness for sacrifice amongst the people, but this only exists when the people is convinced that it has to defend its rights and protect its interests through

---

[85] The contradictory pressures on Bismarck as well as on liberals were summarized by 'die Gelegenheit ist günstig', *Kladderadatsch*, 3 June 1866, vol. 19, no. 25, which showed the Minister-President caught between greatness in Prussia or popularity in Germany, which was portrayed as a serious of ghoulish, demagogic, ghost-like figures calling out their particular cause.

[86] Duncker to Francke, 6 May 1865, in J. Schultze (ed.), *Max Duncker*, 388.

[87] Ibid., 389.   [88] Ibid., 390.

[89] Diary, 28 Jan. 1866, T. v. Bernhardi, *Aus dem Leben Theodor von Bernhardis*, 225–6.

[90] 17 May 1864, in ibid., 110–11.   [91] Ibid., 111–12.   [92] Ibid., 111.

the violence of arms', which was not the case in 1866.[93] The experience of Badenese liberals was most revealing of the contradictory imperatives involved, since they not only dominated the *Ständeversammlung* but also ran the government between 1861 and 1866, and they were, until the resignation of Franz von Roggenbach in September 1865, the most consistent proponents in the south of *Kleindeutschland*. What was more, they knew that war was a likely result of the Gastein Convention in August 1865, which adumbrated the annexation of Schleswig-Holstein. Roggenbach eventually decided to back the Hohenzollern monarchy's 'completely new development', the outcome of which was difficult to predict.[94] Friedrich I refused to follow him, helping to precipitate the Foreign Minister's resignation later that month. The Grand Duke refrained until late May 1866, when it was too late, from contemplating the other choice—independence through a war against Prussia—which Roggenbach had put before him. By that time, his own Foreign Minister Ludwig von Edelsheim had already agreed with the other ministers of the *Mittelstaaten* to the *Bund*'s intervention on the side of Austria, provided that Vienna allowed the *Bundestag* to decide the succession to the duchies, which it did on 1 June. 'I was in Karlsruhe over the last few days', wrote Robert von Mohl to his brother on 11 May: 'The Grand Duke is vacillating and not at all a man for clear decisions. There is no real unity; namely, my new minister Edelsheim is going much further towards Austria than is the case with any of his colleagues.'[95]

Many Badenese liberals were as disunited, indecisive, and confused as their monarch and some of their ministers. On 11 April 1866, the second chamber voted almost unanimously—with only three votes against—in support of Bismarck's proposal to reform the *Bund*, which was later rejected even by the *Nationalverein*, yet on 29 May the second chamber voted unanimously for war credits for the Badenese government as it prepared to enter the war on Austria's side. Despite beginning his speech with the statement that virtually no one in the chamber or in the land was in favour of Baden's neutrality or an *Anschluss* with Prussia, Carl Eckhard—one of the leaders of the Badenese *Fortschrittspartei*—went on to claim that there was also no desire in liberal ranks to join an illiberal Austria: rather, it was vital that the individual states ally with each other and with the national movement to create—immediately—a *Volksarmee* and a *Volksvertretung*, elected in accordance with the Reich Constitution agreed in 1849. Friedrich Kiefer—another Progressive leader in Baden—added that, only a few weeks ago as the Prussian *Bundesreform* was put to a vote, he had seen Bismarck as a German Cavour, but he had been disabused of this belief by the current arming of Prussia in order to fight a *Bruderkrieg*.[96] Baden's situation—as a small border state—was certainly awkward, with a decision not to act in concert with the other *Mittelstaaten* likely to issue in the Grand Duchy being surrounded by enemies, as Edelsheim was able to argue in the debate on 28–29 May. Nevertheless, deputies could have opted to remain

---

[93] *Historisch-politische Blätter*, 1866, vol. 57, 911.

[94] H. Oncken, *Grossherzog Friedrich I von Baden und die deutsche Politik von 1854–1871* (Stuttgart, 1877–85), vol. 1, 490–2.

[95] R. v. Mohl to J. Mohl, 11 May 1866, in L. Gall, *Liberalismus in regierende Partei*, 346.

[96] H. Oncken (ed.), *Großherzog Friedrich von Baden*, vol. 1, 490–2.

neutral, as Bluntschli advised, before going on to contend that confederal law—which neutrality contravened—was no longer valid. The constitutional lawyer told the first chamber on 14 May:

> Although Baden, too, has at all times loyally met its obligations to the Confederation and will do so in future, it cannot regard formal confederal law as the highest law at that moment when the entire existence of the present constitution of the *Bund*, which is seen on all sides as untenable, is itself in question . . . and when a break between the two German Great Powers destroys the foundations on which the present law of the *Bund* rests. Rather, in this case, Baden must reserve the right to take its own free decisions as an independent state.[97]

That Baden's government and deputies chose not to pursue such a course of action was an indication that war itself was an acceptable instrument of policy with bearable consequences.

Most parties to the dispute in 1866 were discomfited but few were unduly worried about the human cost of the war. *Kladderadatsch*, which had been critical of Bismarck, betrayed how little armed intervention caused pause for thought, comparing the Prussian Minister-President to Hercules, sweeping smaller and middle-sized states into a single pile before 'sweeping out what doesn't belong (Austria) in good order'.[98] The *Nationalverein's* strategy in May 1866 was to criticize Berlin's policy on Schleswig-Holstein at the same time as guaranteeing the neutrality of states hostile to Prussia, by asking liberal-dominated *Landtage* to refuse them war credits except for purely defensive purposes. The resolutions submitted by the committee of the *Abgeordnetentag* to the general meeting on 20 May were almost identical. They proved unobjectionable to both supporters and opponents of Prussia. 'The core point of the resolutions advanced today' was the neutrality of the third Germany, reported the Prussian envoy in Frankfurt Friedrich Karl von Savigny: 'the other declaration, partly directed against the Prussian policy in Schleswig-Holstein, is only intended to marshal all those towards an acceptance of the core point who have absorbed the widely-held diatribes against Prussia over the years into their political catechism'.[99] The committee's motion had spoken of an 'unnatural war', 'guilty of a serious crime against the nation', and 'a cabinet war serving only dynastic interests', which was 'unworthy of a civilized nation' and which 'endangered all the goods attained in 50 years of peace'.[100] Despite a heated discussion about an alternative resolution which was more critical of Prussia's annexationism, about 170 of the 220 votes cast in the *Abgeordnetentag* supported the committee's wording: the entire delegation from Schleswig-Holstein, who desired a clearer statement of the duchies' independence, made up a good proportion of the fifty or so deputies who voted against the resolution. A similar pattern

---

[97] J. C. Bluntschli, *Denkwürdiges aus meinem Leben* (Nördlingen, 1884), vol. 3, 137–9.

[98] 'Eine Hercules-Arbeit in acht Tagen', *Kladderadatsch*, 15 July 1866, vol. 19, no. 32. I have written about this cartoon and other similar ones as caricature in M. Hewitson, 'Black Humour: Caricature in Wartime', *Oxford German Studies*, 41 (2012), 213–35.

[99] H. Oncken, *Großherzog Friedrich von Baden*, vol. 1, 401–2.

[100] 'Ausschußantrag, Versammlung des Abgeordetentages in Frankfurt, 20 May 1866', in H. Fenske (ed.), *Der Weg zur Reichsgründung 1850–1870* (Darmstadt, 1977), 312.

had been discernible at the general assembly of the National Association in October 1865, where the resolution, again opposed by about fifty votes, had given its support to the constitution of a state in Schleswig-Holstein under Augustenburg, but with Prussian control of its military. This concession to Prussia had been agreed in the so-called 'Berlin compromise' between liberal and national leaders in March 1865 and was a watered-down version of the 'February demands' outlined by Bismarck, which had stipulated economic as well as military cooperation if a separate state were to be set up. As in May 1866, when the terms of the compromise had altered, the *Nationalverein*, after a full-blooded debate, secured the backing of a large majority for its position.[101]

Such a carefully crafted national compromise was doomed to fail when war broke out between Prussia and Austria, backed by most of the *Bund*, on 14 June 1866, for this would not be a straightforwardly national conflict, as Treitschke acknowledged. 'We might well envy the Italians because the national goals of their struggle stood before their eyes infinitely clearer and more certain than ours', he wrote in the *Preußische Jahrbücher* in the summer of 1866.[102] The Hohenzollern and Habsburg monarchies had entered a 'cabinet war', which had the potential 'to become a national war as soon as the nation plucks up the courage to see things as they are' but which had not yet become such a war.[103] One reason was that 'our Progressive men—at least the larger part of them—are anything but patriots', the historian had complained to Bernhardi on 2 April: 'many of them go as far as to desire the humiliation of Prussia because it would also be a humiliation of the currently dominant system!'[104] 'Truly, I am very well aware that party people—unfortunately!—mostly have no fatherland at all—but that things are so bad with such people, that they could be so shameless as to parade those types of opinions in front of foreigners, that I would not have believed!'[105] Another reason was that the courts of the *Mittelstaaten*, 'whose incorrigible, particularistic defiance is well-known', had decided to follow their 'fine instinct for dynastic self-interest', fearing that they would be toppled by Prussian calls for political reform on the national level: 'No one can delude themselves any longer about the attitude of the courts of Stuttgart, Wiesbaden and Darmstadt;…they will, in the best case, wait for a first defeat of Prussia in order, like hungry flies on a bloody wound, to fall upon our state.'[106] Moreover, the populations of the third Germany appeared to be following their governments. In Treitschke's home state of Saxony, 'the smiling despotism

---

[101] Biefang, *Bürgertum*, 310–430, emphasizes the challenges posed by the debates more than the actual votes cast, in line with his thesis about the crisis and disintegration of the movement.

[102] H. v. Treitschke, 'Der Krieg und die Bundesreform', *Preußische Jahrbücher*, June 1866, vol. 17, 687–9.

[103] Ibid.

[104] T. v. Bernhardi, *Aus dem Leben Theodor von Bernhardis*, vol. 6, 266. There were left-wing supporters of Prussian-led unification: A. Ruge, *Aufruf zur Einheit* (Berlin, 1866). Johann Jacoby had argued the opposite, prompting reactions: Anon, *Offener Brief an Johann Jacoby* (Leipzig, 1866). Also against was the democrat Jakob Venedey, *J. Venedey an Prof. Heinrich von Treitschke* (Mannheim, 1866); and Jakob Venedey, *Ave Cäsar, Morituri te salutant!* 3rd edn (Mannheim, 1867).

[105] T. v. Bernhardi, *Aus dem Leben Theodor von Bernhardis*, vol. 6, 266.

[106] H. v. Treitschke, 'Der Krieg und die Bundesreform', 687–9.

of the Beust regime has unnerved the people, made it unaccustomed to any political will'.[107] Here, 'the unfortunate state will tumble, without will, into a ludicrous war', destroying the prosperity which had made them forget their civil duties.[108] 'It is different in the South', he went on, where 'the small cabinets are mistrusted on good grounds', yet 'the antagonism of the *Volk* against Prussia is pronounced', even if less so than during the New Era or that of Stein and Hardenberg.[109] It was still possible that South Germany could take the side of Prussia in 1866, in Treitschke's view, even if such a possibility was more a matter of hope than expectation.

In fact, the governments, parties, and public of the *Mittelstaaten* shifted between different uncomfortable positions. The Bavarian Foreign Minister and Chair of the Ministerial Council Ludwig von der Pfordten had 'no trust at all in Austria', recalled the Saxon Finance Minister Richard von Friesen: Dresden's envoy in Munich had reported that Bavaria was unlikely to back the Habsburg monarchy in a conflict, with von der Pfordten viewing Vienna's actions as 'stupid'.[110] The Bavarian Foreign Minister had already written in March 1866 to Reinhard von Dalwigk zu Lichtenfels, who had been trying to persuade him to give a public declaration of support for Vienna, that 'I have, I confess, completely lost trust in Austria.'[111] In June of the previous year, the Saxon envoy had passed on von der Pfordten's 'bitterest remarks' to the effect that Vienna was

> completely indifferent about how the Holstein question was solved as long as Austria was not 'outplayed' in the matter; in any case, the financial position of Austria was so pitiable, the internal political conditions so fragmented and confused that Austria could not even wage a war against Prussia; thus, if it were to follow such a strong line against Prussia, it would give way at the eleventh hour and would grant as many concessions to the latter, naturally not at its own expense but at that of Germany, as Prussia could wish for.[112]

He repeated this point in 1866.[113] Although 'no German state may sign a separate alliance with one of the conflicting parties', von der Pfordten had warned Dresden early in 1866, 'if war should break out despite everything, then the *Bund*—in the Bavarian view—would be torn apart and every individual German state would then claim full freedom of action and would be able to use its own powers however it wished to do so'.[114] This stance informed Munich's position in the spring and summer of 1866, as it refused—to the chagrin of the ministers of the other *Mittelstaaten*—to commit itself: in March, it told Dresden that it would not enter a war, in April that it would; at the same time, it was trying to organize a single South German army—provoking the mistrust of 'Württemberg, Baden, Hesse, Nassau etc., where in the worst case they would still prefer to subjugate themselves to Prussian rather than Bavarian overlordship'—whilst barely preparing its own

[107] Ibid.   [108] Ibid.   [109] Ibid.
[110] R. v. Friesen, *Erinnerungen aus meinem Leben* (Dresden, 1880), vol. 2, 135, 146–7.
[111] L. von der Pfordten to R. v. Dalwigk, 9 Mar. 1866, in W. Schüssler (ed.), *Die Tagebücher des Freiherrn Reinhard v. Dalwigk zu Lichtenfels*, 279.
[112] Saxon envoy in Munich to F. v. Beust, 12 June 1865, R. v. Friesen, *Erinnerungen aus meinem Leben*, 121–2.
[113] Ibid., 135.   [114] Ibid., 134.

army for war.[115] The Bavarian government only realized that the situation was serious in May 1866, in Friesen's opinion, as it was obliged to mobilize its forces.[116] At a meeting of ministers of the *Mittelstaaten* on 11 May 1866, von der Pfordten ruled out armed neutrality, against the case put forward by Edelsheim and the Badenese delegation, because it was tantamount to giving up Schleswig-Holstein and Saxony, which would be occupied by Prussia, as well as acting against the interests of the *Bund*.[117] He neglected to mention that he was already on record saying that the Confederation would collapse under its own weight in such circumstances. In effect, he preferred to enter a war in the summer of 1866 to maintain or strengthen Bavaria's position than to stand aside whilst it was weakened.

Bavarian political 'parties' and public opinion were subject to similar shifts and moments of indecision, undermining any case for a 'national war'. Briefly, it seemed to the well-known theologian Ignaz Döllinger on 25 June 1866, there was broad patriotic backing for the war:

> Munich and all of *Altbayern* is worthy of admiration. Such an ideal mood, such a burning German-patriotic enthusiasm, such a willingness to sacrifice Mammon and every chattel and good on the altar of the fatherland—I would never have believed that of my dear compatriots. It is even said—it sounds, admittedly, apocryphal—that five people have vowed in future only to drink water in order to place the saved beer money in an account for wounded (or, rather, to-be-wounded) fighters... Everyone is carrying maps in their pockets and they are being sold in huge quantities. Many, it is true, also seem truly worn out; one can see that they are weeping prophylactic tears and, in anticipation, are mourning the men, brothers, sons and fiancés who will be lost in future.[118]

Only a month beforehand, as he continued to hold out the hope of peace despite the aggressive actions of Bismarck (who was making concessions to Napoleon in the expectation that 'he will be able to get them back again at the head of Germany'), Döllinger had merely sought to console himself that, 'whatever might happen, the predicament of the Germans will not be as bad as that of the unfortunate Poles'.[119] The later diplomat Hugo von Lerchenfeld-Koefering, who was a judicial official in Traunstein in 1866, was confident with hindsight that Austria and Bavaria would be victorious:

> It was the case that in Bavaria the conviction was general that the Austrian army was superior to the Prussian one. Only a few military men who knew both armies well thought otherwise, amongst them, of all things, the Chief of the Bavarian General Staff, General von der Tann. Moreover, we had in Bavaria a strongly exaggerated idea of the worth of our own army.[120]

[115] Ibid., 136–7, 173.   [116] Ibid., 143.

[117] R. v. Dalwigk, diary entry 11 May 1866, in W. Schüssler (ed.), *Die Tagebücher des Freiherrn Reinhard v. Dalwigk zu Lichtenfels*, 216. The well-connected aristocrat Hugo von Lerchenfeld-Koefering, *Erinnerungen und Denkwürdigkeiten* (Berlin, 1935), 40, makes the same point.

[118] I. Döllinger to C. Leyden, 25 June 1866, I. v. Döllinger, *Briefwechsel, 1850–1890* (Munich 1963–81), vol. 4, 109–10.

[119] I. Döllinger to C. Leyden, 24 May 1866, ibid., 105.

[120] H. v. Lerchenfeld-Koefering, *Erinnerungen und Denkwürdigkeiten*, 41.

As late as 1 July, Döllinger remained optimistic that 'the few hard blows and defeats which the Austrians and South Germans are suffering will not alter the result overall', for 51 million inhabitants of the Habsburg and German lands were arrayed against 40 million Prussians and Italians.[121]

Like his compatriots, the theologian could cite reports in newspapers such as the Augsburg *Allgemeine Zeitung*, which looked 'calmly upon success in the bloody struggle', not least because 'the mood of the Prussian army' had been affected by 'the embitterment of *Landwehr* men', as a consequence of Roon's reforms, and by 'the impossibility of taking all these armed men away from civilian activity for as little as six months'.[122] Even at the time, however, such prophesies could seem hollow, with journalists of the *Allgemeine Zeitung* and the *Münchner Neueste Nachrichten* openly discussing the need for a reform of the Bavarian army during the conflict itself.[123] By early July, after Austria's defeat at Königgrätz on the 3rd, Döllinger had already turned to blaming the king ('a childlike dreamer') and 'our ministers', who had been told by the Bavarian envoy in Berlin Maximilian von Montgelas more than two years ago 'that the Pruss. army would be put on a great and terrible war footing. V. d. Pfordten also knew this for a long time.'[124] As Lerchenfeld returned to Munich in September 1866, 'I found every circle there in the greatest agitation', he recalled: 'Everyone was criticizing and cursing, and sought above all, as always when something goes awry, the guilty in the wrong places.'[125] In the verdict of the *Historisch-politische Blätter*, 'our' parties and courts had embarked on a 'careless' war and had ruined Germany.[126] What was apparent from such shifting and brittle reactions to the war was that many Bavarian statesmen, politicians, and journalists had no clear national cause for which they were sending troops to fight, beyond what Lerchenfeld termed 'the overwhelming unpopularity of Prussia'.[127]

The predicament of governments and parties in other German states was equally confused. To the surprise of the Saxon government, Hanover and Kurhessen backed Bavaria's motion for the Confederation to mobilize troops, even though they had no money and had not begun military preparations.[128] Kurhessen's best-known liberal Friedrich Oetker, who was a long-standing opponent of his government—as a forty-eighter—and was close to Rudolf von Bennigsen, at once spoke out against Prussian domination, defending his own state's rights with the backing 'of the entire land', even though he was one of only a handful of members who voted in favour of Bismarck in the committee of the *Nationalverein* in Berlin on 13 May 1866.[129] After Austria had 'won the field with the *Kurfürsten*, mostly through the support and advice of the King of Hanover, whereas the ministers were largely of another opinion', the Estates were left 'with nothing to do but warn and reproach

[121] I. Döllinger to C. Leyden, 1 July 1866, I. v. Döllinger, *Briefwechsel*, vol. 4, 118.
[122] *Allgemeine Zeitung*, 17 June 1866, cited in F. Becker, *Bilder von Krieg und Nation*, 142.
[123] *Allgemeine Zeitung*, 3 and 23 July 1866; *Münchner Neueste Nachrichten*, 21 June, 1, 3, 5, 10, and 12 July 1866, ibid., 142–3, 145–7.
[124] I. v. Döllinger, *Briefwechsel*, vol. 4, 126.
[125] H. v. Lerchenfeld-Koefering, *Erinnerungen und Denkwürdigkeiten*, 41.
[126] *Historisch-politische Blätter*, 1866, vol. 58, 781.   [127] Ibid., 40.
[128] R. v. Friesen, *Erinnerungen aus meinem Leben*, 165–6.
[129] F. Oetker, *Lebenserinnerungen* (Cassel, 1885), vol. 3, 423, 529.

once again', recommending that the state join the alliance offered by Prussia.[130] 'The confidence and nonchalance with which the opponents of Prussia, in particular the mainly noble members of the *Ständeversammlung*, behaved was remarkable', he went on: 'I can still see the amazed face of one modest landowner as I called out to him that he could be receiving a Prussian declaration of war in a few hours.'[131]

The level of ignorance in Saxony was similar to that in Kurhessen, if the veteran liberal Karl Biedermann is to be believed. The Foreign Minister and Chair of the *Gesamtministerium* Friedrich Ferdinand von Beust had convinced King Johann that Austria and the *Mittelstaaten* would be victorious in a war against Prussia, moving him to back Vienna in the *Bundestag*.[132] The Saxon first minister, as the principal champion of the *Bund*, had expressed 'his certain conviction', on his return from a meeting at Bamberg with counterparts from Baden, Württemberg, and Bavaria on 13–14 May 1866, 'that Herr von der Pfordten would alter his opinion and Bavaria, if it really should come to war, would in any case come to our aid'.[133] Friesen 'could find nothing' in Beust's report 'other than the sad certainty that we...would be completely isolated and could reckon on no help at all from the side of the Confederation'.[134] The Finance Minister knew that von der Pfordten believed that Austria would be defeated in any future war and he 'saw that a victory of Austria had to be deleterious in its consequences for Germany and also for Saxony', wrote Biedermann: 'And yet he did not break with Herr von Beust.'[135] Friesen himself argued that little could be done, given that, 'in Saxony, public opinion was agitated against Prussia to the highest degree':

if, at the approach of the danger of war, we had quit our loyal, *Bund*-friendly policy, which had been maintained until that point, and had wanted to throw ourselves into the arms of Prussia, we would have been received there with the greatest mistrust and we would have been regarded in Saxony itself as traitors.[136]

For Biedermann, this lack of opposition could be explained by Saxony's 'neo-absolutist' system of government:

He [Beust] was sure of the majority of the old *Stände*, galvanized back into life by his coup d'état of 1850; they sanctioned and agreed what he wanted, including funds for armaments; the small liberal party in the second chamber allowed itself to be satisfied with an obfuscating reply; his own colleagues, the other ministers, he didn't ask at all.[137]

Whatever the diagnosis, however, the result was the same: onlookers were left wondering what Saxon soldiers were fighting for. Even Württemberg, where politics was less restricted and the opposition between a pro-Prussian camp—'the great majority of all the educated, the *Schwäb. Merkur*, the old liberals, the Gothaer, the

---

[130] Ibid., 430–1.   [131] Ibid., 431.
[132] K. Biedermann, *Mein Leben*, 270–1.   [133] R. v. Friesen, *Erinnerungen aus meinem Leben*, 144.
[134] Ibid. For Beust's reply to Friesen's accusations, see F. v. Beust, *Erinnerungen zu Erinnerungen* (Leipzig, 1881), 49–50.
[135] K. Biedermann, *Mein Leben*, 274.   [136] R. v. Friesen, *Erinnerungen aus meinem Leben*, 149.
[137] K. Biedermann, *Mein Leben*, 271.

Nationalvereinler, the Evangelical clergy and their congregations', according to the liberal Gustav von Rümelin—and a 'South German' one—'1. the dynasty with the court, ministry, counsellors, the *Staatsanzeiger* etc.; 2. the democrats... [and] the *Beobachter*...; 3. the Catholic believers and Ultramontanes... [and] their organ... the *Deutsches Volksblatt*'—was more clear-cut, information and decision-making were opaque, characterized by a precarious belief in an Austrian victory and an unwillingness, even after Austria and its allies had been defeated, to remove from office Karl von Varnbüler, the architect of the state's defeat, to the disbelief of critics like Elben.[138]

To the *National-Zeitung* in Berlin, the enmity of Württemberg, Hanover, Kurhessen, and other states against Prussia was the corollary of unreliable princes and the pettiness of small principalities, their assemblies, and their populations.[139] Much of the opposition to Prussia in 1866, however, came from within the kingdom itself, as Progressives and democrats struggled with their own consciences during the constitutional crisis. 'We don't believe there are any thoughts of freedom in this head', wrote Rudolf Haym to Max Duncker on 12 May, avoiding the name of Bismarck:

> the foreign spectacle is to be used to overcome the internal conflict, to conceal the internal embarrassment—the success of a victoriously conducted war will simply lead to the increased arrogance of the reaction and *Soldateska*—... these are roughly the observations and speeches which one hears on every street corner. And the worst thing is that we have nothing directly to answer it with.[140]

For moderate liberals like Georg von Vincke, 'the situation [was] still a really difficult one' even after Austria's defeat at Königgrätz, since they were caught between 'the *Kreuzzeitungspartei* on one flank and an unturning *Fortschritt* on the other'.[141] Viewed from the left, the Progressives seemed weak, undecided about whether to oppose Bismarck or not by the start of July: according to the *Social-Demokrat*, they should have voted against the military budget, but they had not done so.[142]

From their own point of view, however, their position was a principled but increasingly tortured one, leading to the haemorrhaging of Progressive Party votes—from 141 to 83 seats—in the Prussian election on 3 July.[143] In reality, Bismarck was pursuing a national policy, Eduard Lasker agreed with Max Duncker, ensuring 'that the feudal party, the conservatives, took the path that the

[138] G. v. Rümelin to M. Duncker, 7 Aug. 1866, in J. Schultze (ed.), *Max Duncker. Politischer Briefwechsel aus seinem Nachlass* (Osnabrueck, 1967), 230. O. Elben, *Lebenserinnerungen*, 142–3. On the uncertain hope of an Austrian victory, see Walter Seefried, *Mittnacht und die deutsche Frage bis zur Reichsgründung* (Stuttgart, 1928), 48.

[139] *National-Zeitung*, 17 June 1866.

[140] R. Haym to M. Duncker, 12 May 1866, in J. Schultze (ed.), *Max Duncker*, 407.

[141] G. v. Vincke to M. Duncker, 23 July 1866, ibid., 424.

[142] *Social-Demokrat*, 1 July 1866.

[143] A. Heuss, *Theodor Mommsen und das 19. Jahrhundert* (Kiel, 1956), 187: Mommsen—a liberal supporter of Schleswig-Holstein, where he was born—was critical of the Progressives for not pushing the Prussian *Landtag* to devote more money to the war effort.

national party showed them'.[144] 'As things in Prussia stand, the liberal party would only with great difficulty ever have been in a position to bring the army, land-owners and officialdom to a decisive war against Austria', asserted Duncker on 11 July: 'Yet without them the German question cannot be solved.'[145] 'Although the signs of a policy-shift multiplied, a feeling of disbelief was dominant in liberal cir-cles', noted Lasker: 'the mass of the liberal majority in the *Abgeordnetenhaus*, together with virtually all the great leaders, remained, like the great majority of the *Volk*, turned away from the course of the government.'[146] The upshot, which 'was perhaps without historical precedent', was 'that a statesman who had made the realization of the most popular demand into the principal substance of his policy and pursued this goal with unflinching attention and energy kept the healthy ker-nel of his policy secret from the eyes of his *Volk*'.[147] Only 'the war which was break-ing out drew the curtain aside', in Lasker's opinion.[148] Many Progressives disagreed, leading to the splitting of the party over the Indemnity Bill on 3 September (enacted by 230 to 75 votes), which legalized Prussia's budgets since 1862 and indemnified Bismarck in return for recognition of the right of the chamber to sanction and vote on all aspects of government finance. More significant for the waging of the war, though, was the fact that no party in the Hohenzollern mon-archy had felt able to articulate an unambiguous case for a national conflict.

The Franco-German conflict in 1870–1 was different in this respect, with Elben typical in asserting that Germany was carrying out a 'crusade, a holy war', though even here the disagreements between political parties remained marked (see Map 3 for continuing regional divisions).[149] Prussian liberals and conservatives, as was to be expected, backed the campaign. Catholics such as Peter Reichensperger were not prepared to oppose them, as was demonstrated by his support for 'the national feeling of Germany', a 'successfully executed *Volkskrieg*' and 'the well-ordered institution of the North German Confederation' in his speech to the Reichstag on 26 November 1870.[150] For Treitschke, writing in the *Preußische Jahrbücher*, the war was the 'acid test of the North German Confederation', in the words of the article's title, not directed merely against Napoleon but against France as a whole.[151] 'This war is a last, raw expression not of a Napoleonic but of an old French policy', he maintained: 'When has a government ever existed in France over the last eighty years which was friendly to us Germans?'[152] One of the principal questions, 'if God gives us victory', was 'how the French state, not its ruling dynasty, could be weakened in such a way that we could await a new disturbance of the international peace with

[144] M. Duncker to A. Grumbrecht, 11 July 1866, in J. Schultze (ed.), *Max Duncker*, 420. W. Cahn (ed.), *Aus Eduard Lasker's Nachlaß* (Berlin, 1902), 38.

[145] J. Schultze (ed.), *Max Duncker*, 420.

[146] W. Cahn (ed.), *Aus Eduard Lasker's Nachlaß*, 36, 38.

[147] Ibid., 38.   [148] Ibid., 39.   [149] O. Elben, *Lebenserinnerungen*, 156.

[150] P. F. Reichensperger, 26 Nov. 1870, *Stenographische Berichte über die Verhandlungen des Norddeutschen Reichstags 1870* (Berlin, 1871), vol. 2, 9.

[151] H. v. Treitschke, 'Die Feuerprobe des Norddeutschen Bundes', *Preußischer Jahrbücher*, vol. 26, 1870, 240–52.

[152] Ibid., 251.

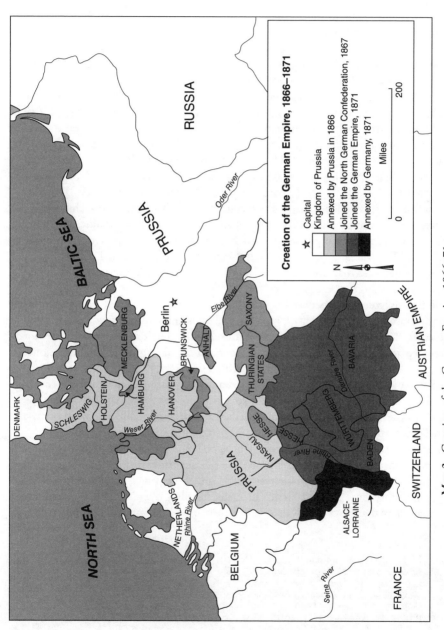

Map 3. Creation of the German Empire, 1866–71

Source: J. Sperber (ed.), *Short Oxford History of Germany, 1800–1870* (Oxford, 2004), 289.

Within the map legend:

Creation of the German Empire, 1866–1871

★ Capital
Kingdom of Prussia
Annexed by Prussia in 1866
Joined the North German Confederation, 1867
Joined the German Empire, 1871
Annexed by Germany, 1871

Miles

0   200

heightened confidence'.[153] In the past, 'if Germany had silently borne the raping of its rights and honour, it did so only because it did not know, in its fragmentation, how strong it was', in Wilhelm I's opinion, but now, Treitschke continued, 'The nation is awakening, the Germans finally understand what they are bearing on their coats of arms.'[154]

After the battles of the summer, 'the thought arose, above all the sacrifices, that a great era has begun, that the great fate of Germany is being fulfilled under the leadership of the wise hero-king', wrote the Rhineland industrialist, financier, and liberal forty-eighter Gustav Mevissen.[155] The 'same noble struggle of all the sons of the fatherland' had been necessary and worthwhile for the founding of the German Reich and the attainment of 'the highest goal, of freedom and independence, and as an expression of both for the education and moralization of the nation', he declared to the annual general meeting of the Schaafhausen Bank on 28 June 1871, offsetting the costs of the conflict against its broader national benefits.[156] As Bismarck had announced the war against France to the Reichstag, recalled the National Liberal deputy for Krefeld Ludwig Friedrich Seyffardt, there were 'stormy cries of bravo and hurrah, which did not want to end, and the shaking of hands on all sides of the house and in the galleries'.[157] 'We trust the experienced leadership of the wise hero-king, of the German commander, whom providence has chosen to lead the great struggle, which he fought as a youngster more than half a century ago, to a decisive conclusion towards the end of his life', ran the 'most beautiful part' of the Reichstag's reply, which was accepted unanimously.[158] As the socialist deputy August Bebel discovered when he stood up in the Reichstag to reject war credits and to challenge the 'nationality principle' as a just ground for war (since, 'were we to want to introduce the nationality principle in Europe truly undistorted, then you will have to concede that no end to war would be visible'), it was dangerous to speak out against this liberal and conservative 'national' consensus.[159] His speech met with 'general disapproval, hissing and calls of "Rubbish! Out! Out with him!"', before the President threatened to withdraw the socialist leader's right to continue, for he had shown that he had 'no feeling at all (and he could value the worth of nationality as high or as low as wanted), so that he has the nerve to insult our own *Volk* in this representation'.[160] When the news was published that Bebel and Wilhelm Liebknecht opposed the war, their windows were smashed.[161]

The parties' responses in South Germany were much less uniform, as Elben admitted. Retrospectively, the Stuttgart liberal described the 'mood at home' in 1870 as 'an elevated, decisive one from the first moment onwards; the party horsetrading was silenced, everyone was ready to stand for the fatherland'.[162]

[153] Ibid., 251–2.   [154] Ibid., 252.

[155] G. v. Mevissen, 28 Sept. 1870, in J. Hansen, *Gustav von Mevissen. Ein rheinisches Lebensbild 1815–1899* (Berlin, 1906), vol. 2, 755–6.

[156] Ibid., 757.   [157] L. F. Seyffardt, *Erinnerungen*, 46.   [158] Ibid., 46–7.

[159] A. Bebel, 26 Nov. 1870, *Stenographische Berichte über die Verhandlungen des Norddeutschen Reichstags 1870*, vol. 2, 11.

[160] Ibid.

[161] F. L. Carsten, *Eduard Bernstein. Eine politische Biographie 1850–1932* (Munich, 1993), 12.

[162] O. Elben, *Lebenserinnerungen*, 155.

'The newspaper was full of the greatest articles, filled with the warmest patriotism', he went on: 'Amongst the *Volk*, there was only one opinion, that we, too, should enter the holy war together with our German brothers.'[163] At the time, however, Elben was much more doubtful about the patriotism of his compatriots. His memorandum to the Prussian envoy at Stuttgart during the Franco-German war therefore contained many qualifications:

> The general enthusiasm at present should not obscure the fact that enemy currents, as they existed before the war, cannot simply be brushed aside but quietly persist and will re-emerge again in time. The eventual establishment of Germany must not therefore be postponed until after the peace, but must immediately proceed to its goal, while the peoples are still united in the field. Now, unification will succeed rapidly, even in Württemberg with its otherwise awkward assembly. Then we will be able to see demonstration and proof on the part of different agencies and parties what their true attitudes are. As far as court circles and the government are concerned, telling conditions are rehearsed and complaints are made about their endless vacillation. The *Volkspartei* is incorrigible and is only waiting for the time when it can be dominant again. The *Großdeutschen* will die out over time, but for the moment they comprise a rump of skilful and stubborn leaders, who give the *Volkspartei* an influence which they would otherwise not have. In broad strata, an undiminished particularistic attitude predominates which, as soon as it is a question of sacrifices, will again make its weight felt. Officials tilt towards the government, so that we don't have a national-minded bureaucracy. [164]

It was with this unruly ensemble of constituencies that Württemberg went to war in 1870.

Varnbüler, the state's first minister, had assured the king repeatedly that it should be possible 'to limit too violent an agitation in favour of entry into the Confederation of the North'.[165] At the beginning of the Franco-German War, he was suspected, partly on the basis of reports from the French envoy in Stuttgart, of hesitating to back the North German Confederation. He was replaced in September 1870 by Hermann von Mittnacht, who had reiterated his support for Berlin on 15 July.[166] For such ministers, even during the conflict, it seemed that there was 'no reason why Württemberg's government and H.M. the King should sacrifice more of their independence up to that point than is necessary for the fatherland, not to mention harbouring a desire to enter the North German Confederation', in the Bavarian Foreign Minister Otto von Bray-Steinburg's estimation.[167] Bray's own motion for the Bavarian *Landtag* in September, which was passed by 101 votes to 47, was to avoid entering the North German *Bund*—'the only right policy'—and to participate in the discussion of 'a refashioning of Germany', with 'a general German *Volksvertretung*' and an army 'organized according to the same principles' but with the right to sign treaties, retain military command over its armed forces in peacetime, and to keep its own laws, administration, and finances.[168] These provisions did not go far beyond the military treaties and

---

[163] Ibid.   [164] Ibid., 159.
[165] W. Seefried, *Mittnacht und die deutsche Frage bis zur Reichsgründung*, 61.
[166] Ibid., 85.   [167] Ibid., 87.
[168] O. v. Bray-Steinburg, *Denkwürdigkeiten aus seinem Leben* (Leipzig, 1901), 131–9.

cooperation within the *Zollparlament*, which had been agreed after 1866, and they were unlikely to be acceptable to Berlin in the new circumstances of 1870.

Such reservations did find an echo in the South German states, where anti-Prussian parties—the newly founded rural People's Party (*Patriotenpartei*) in Bavaria and the democratic *Volkspartei* in Württemberg—had risen to ascendancy after 1866, threatening to limit military service and cut the army's budget. About fifty opponents of Prussia were returned in the first *Zollparlament*, which Bismarck had set up to facilitate unification, out of the eighty-five seats allotted to southern states; twenty-seven opponents to twelve proponents in Bavaria, with a further nine deputies undecided, seventeen to none in Württemberg, six to eight in Baden, and none to six in Hesse. These results were confirmed by elections to the *Landtage* of Bavaria in 1869 (seventy-six liberals versus seventy-nine Catholics, conservatives, and Bavarian *Patrioten*) and Württemberg in 1868 (thirty for the *Volkspartei*, twenty-nine for Catholics and conservatives, and twelve for the pro-Prussian *Deutsche Partei*), though not in Baden in 1869, when the Catholic *Volkspartei* gained only four seats.[169] With a 30 per cent increase in taxation in prospect in order to cover the cost of military reorganization, the *Volkspartei* in Württemberg gained 150,000 signatures—three-quarters of voters in the last election—for a petition to reduce spending on the army. When the party put forward a motion along with the *Großdeutschen*—that is, with a majority of twenty seats—for a reduction of military expenditure and the length of military service in March 1870, the government prorogued the session of the chamber until autumn.[170] Meanwhile, in Bavaria, where Hohenlohe had been forced to resign after receiving a vote of no-confidence in February 1870, a committee of the lower chamber had proposed a similar cut in the military budget and a reduction of military service to eight months, which the new administration of Bray had rejected in July.

Crises in both states were only averted by the Franco-German War. The same events also affected the way in which the states went to war. Thus, in the debate in the Bavarian Chamber of Deputies on 19 July, the leader of the *Patriotenpartei* Edmund Jörg had supported armed neutrality on behalf of the relevant committee of the *Kammer*:

> the committee has not recognized the *casus foederis* in respect of the alliance treaty [with Prussia] of 22 August 1866…If in this case which lies before us, the *casus foederis* were to apply, then, gentlemen, no case would be even imaginable in which the alliance's terms did not bind us to follow the Prussian army.[171]

To Jörg, 'the terrible war which now, from what one hears, might really be ignited' seemed to originate in a petty contravention of court etiquette involving Vincent de Benedetti and Wilhelm I, exploited by Bismarck.[172] It remained a dispute between two Great Powers, with Prussia unable to offer Bavaria protection in the

---

[169] Gall, *Liberalismus in regierende Partei*, 460.

[170] W. Carr, *The Origins of the Wars of German Unification* (London, 1991), 172–3.

[171] E. Jörg, 19 July 1870, *Verhandlungen der Kammer der Abgeordneten des bayerischen Landtags*, cited in H. Fenske (ed.), *Der Weg zur Reichsgründung*, 418–19.

[172] Ibid., 420.

event of a French invasion. For the liberal Catholic deputy Johann Nepomuk Sepp, one of Jörg's main opponents in the debate, the declaration of war had changed everything. 'Yesterday, one could still expect that Prussia might recognize our neutrality', but this was no longer so, with the effect that the warring parties were likely to contravene Bavaria's territorial integrity, and 'we shall be drawn into the war *nolens volens*': 'Whatever the cause of the conflict, when an avalanche is ready to slide, then the slightest disturbance suffices and the catastrophe occurs.'[173] For Sepp, there was a risk that Bavaria's mistake in 1813, when it had failed to take part in the battle of Leipzig, might be repeated: 'If we hold back, as strangers, the wagon of war will roll over us, and we shall harvest no thanks in peacetime, our military youth will gain no honour.'[174] 'We Germans will not allow fate to be determined by a foreign nation', he concluded.[175] Advocates of war like Sepp eventually won the argument. Nonetheless, the political decision to go to war on the side of the North German Confederation was a close and open one in the South German states, notwithstanding calls for a 'national defence' of Germany in the press. The next section examines how widespread and convincing such calls were.

PUBLICITY CAMPAIGNS

Most parts of the press saw 1870 as a national war of defence.[176] As Wilhelm I gave his speech to an extraordinary session of the Reichstag of the North German Confederation in the White Room of the royal palace in Berlin on 19 July, he was met with 'lively applause', mounting to a 'tempest of clapping' and 'joyful acclamation' at the end, after he had alluded to 'the unanimous will of the German governments of the South, as well as of the North'.[177] The 'parliamentary act of state', cheered on by 'a numerous, chosen public', constituted a 'storm-flood of patriotic enthusiasm' for the Franco-German war, in the opinion of the liberal *National-Zeitung*.[178] Johannes Miquel's draft reply to the monarch on the next day, signed by deputies of all factions ('We note merely that the names of the Poles, of Herren Bebel und Liebknecht, of Herren Windhorst, v. Mallinckrodt and Ewald are missing'), affirmed the Reichstag's trust in 'the courage and love of the fatherland of our armed brothers, in the unshakeable resolve of a united *Volk*, to devote all the goods of this earth to it and not to tolerate that the foreign conqueror makes a German man bow down before him'.[179] 'As in the glorious times of the wars of liberation, a Napoleon is again forcing us today into a holy war for our rights and our free-dom', the National Liberal leader's address continued.[180] The most common and powerful memory was that of 1813, concurred Gustav Freytag's *Grenzboten* in

---

[173] J. N. Sepp, 19 July, ibid., 422.   [174] Ibid., 422–3.   [175] Ibid., 423.

[176] Even the generally hostile *Frankfurter Zeitung*, 19 July 1870, accepted this. H. Fenske, 'Die Deutschen und der Krieg von 1870/71. Zeitgenönische Urteile', in P. Levillain and R. Reimenschneider (eds), *La Guerre de 1870/71 et ses consequences* (Bonn, 1990), 167–215.

[177] *National-Zeitung*, 19 July 1870.   [178] Ibid.

[179] *National-Zeitung*, 20 July 1870.   [180] Ibid.

October, but not as a 'liberation'—which was a label (*Befreiungskrieg*) imposed by dogmatists—but an act of 'freedom' (*Freiheitskrieg*), because freedom from foreign domination was the most important freedom of all.[181] Now, Germany had entered an 'age of wars of unity' (*Einheitskriege*), proving that freedom and unity could be combined, despite the contrary earlier claims of German liberals.[182] If only Arndt could have seen what had occurred, commented the *Kölnische Zeitung* on 16 July, he would know that he had not lived in vain: 'Wir wollen sein ein einig Volk von Brüdern, / In keiner Noth uns trennen und Gefahr!'[183]

Berlin would never be a 'capital' in the same dangerous sense as 'the metropolis of our enemies', since, remarked the *Grenzboten*:

> the fate of the fatherland, far away, will never depend on the appearance of these, our lustrous streets; the farmer next to the Pregel, the wine producer from the Moselle, the burgher of Augsburg will never be forced to reach for weapons because of the cry of the masses who throng there... rather, it is the modest, proud task of a German capital that it feels the honour and shame, fortune and emergency of the whole most vitally, that it is the most willing to act and the most tireless in offering aid, that it becomes the first servant of the German nation and, therefore, of the German state.[184]

Businessmen were 'the most downcast', though 'not giving up in an unmanly way', went on the same 'Berlin letter' of July:

> Amongst them, general human reflections are combined naturally with national ones. 'It is a sad indication for our reputed culture (*Cultur*)', one hears them say, 'that wars are possible between such nations, that princes have the power to ignite such wars arbitrarily.' Still, they also know well enough which nation and which prince are guilty; and they, too, assume the standpoint, from which our soldiers, ready for death and the loss of blood, appear as sweet beacons announcing peace, however paradoxical it sounds.[185]

The victories of the war, declared a later 'Berliner Brief' of August, seemed to be on the verge of removing the distinction between northern and southern Germany.[186] The Catholic *Kölnische Volkszeitung* made the same point after the battle of Sedan, when half of the capital's population were said to have come out onto the streets to celebrate.[187] Even in the annexed territory of Hanover, where particularism had worsened between 1866 and 1870, anti-Prussian feeling had been overcome and '*Welfenthum*' expurgated.[188]

There is no doubt that the Franco-German War gave rise to extensive expressions—in the form of poems (10,000–12,000 of them), pamphlets, newspaper articles, speeches, university addresses, and sermons—of national belonging, national interest, and national unity, which had been achieved against the wishes of Great Powers—Austria, then France—as an instance of what would later be termed

---

[181] *Grenzboten*, 1870, vol. 4, 81–2.   [182] Ibid., 84–5.
[183] *Kölnische Zeitung*, 16 July 1870.   [184] *Grenzboten*, 1870, vol. 3, 194.
[185] Ibid., 196.   [186] Ibid., 286.
[187] *Kölnische Volkszeitung*, 3 Sept. 1870.   [188] Ibid., 391–3.

national self-determination.[189] The principal point of historical dispute, however, in addition to the continuity—or discontinuity—of the wars in 1864, 1866, and 1870–1, concerns the nature and significance of such outpourings for different regional, social, and political constituencies.[190] It is evident from a reading of the press that varying types of demonization of the enemies of 'Germany' took place, particularly of France, which was—as Jeismann suggests—the foil for a 'still appreciable German feeling of inferiority'.[191] On hearing the news from Sedan, 'the German nation in arms' was said by the 'Wochenschau' of the *Kölnische Volkszeitung* to have ended a second Gallic *Cäsarenthum*: 'With justified pride, it may now call itself a "*große Nation*"', in the manner of the '*grande nation*' next door.[192] In such reportage, it was common to contrast French 'vices' (civilization, enlightenment, godlessness) with German virtues (culture, humanity, faith, tradition), which journalists fashioned to suit their own and their readers' tastes, as the *Kreuzzeitung* hinted in its summary of 1870: 'Just as the enemy... threatened *our independence*, so its aim was to make us bend before the false gods of *its "civilisation"*; the war which we are waging is therefore a struggle in the full sense of *"with God for king and fatherland!"'*[193]

Given 'the terrible danger with which France confronts the whole of Germany', which had banished 'the hatred of Prussia' in the South (where it was habitually 'alive and well'), in the view of the Viennese *Neue Freie Presse*, stereotypes could easily become brutal and, even, racialized, as Cosima Wagner noted in her diary a few days after Sedan: 'The *Illustrirte Zeitung* brings us pictures of Fr. soldiers (according to nature), in which the misery and the decay of the nation, the entire disgrace of humanity stared out at me. Complete cretinism looks out of the sensual, bestial faces, made dumb by drink.'[194] Sensationalizing reports about the atrocities of *francs-tireurs* and 'turcos' fed the reading public's appetite for violence, as Bismarck realized as he justified the siege of Paris in the press in January 1871: 'The cruelties and sexual bestialities that the *turcos* and Arabs committed against

---

[189] The figure for German poems produced in the war comes from R. Neumann, *Die deutsche Kriegsdichtung von 1870/71* (Diss., Munich, 1911), 12–14. Examples of university addresses and lectures included W. Oncken, *Unsere Lage bei Ausbruch des Krieges. Vortrag, gehalten am 24 Juli 1870 im großen Clubsaale in Gießen* (Gießen, 1870); E. Du Bois-Reymond, *Über den deutschen Krieg. Rede am 3. August 1870 in der Aula der königlichen Friedrich-Wilhelms-Universität zu Berlin gehalten* (Berlin, 1870); W. Baur, *1813 und 1870. Ein Vortrag* (Bremen, 1870); K. J. Diepenbrock, *Deutschlands Sieg und Herrlichkeit in staatlicher, sittlicher und sprachlicher Bedeutung. Patriotische Vorlesung* (Freiburg, 1870); C. G. Bruns, *Deutschlands Sieg über Frankreich. Rede am 15. October 1870 in der Aula der Friedrich-Wilhelms-Universität zu Berlin* (Berlin, 1870); J. C. Bluntschli, *Das moderne Völkerrecht in dem Kriege 1870. Rede zum Geburtstagfeste des höchsteligen Grossherzogs Karl Friedrich von Baden und zur akademischen Preisverteilung am 2. November 1870* (Heidelberg, 1870).

[190] See, for instance, F. Becker, 'Auf dem Weg zu einer "Kulturgeschichte der Ideen"? Deutung der Einigungskriege und bürgerlicher Militarismus im Deutschen Kaiserreich', in L. Raphael and H.-E. Tenorth (eds), *Ideen als gesellschaftliche Gestaltungskraft im Europa der Neuzeit*, 267–88; T. Arand (ed.), *'Der großartigste Krieg, der je geführt worden'. Beiträge zur Geschichtskultur des Deutsch-Französischen Kriegs 1870/71* (Münster, 2008).

[191] M. Jeismann, *Das Vaterland der Feinde*, 250.   [192] *Kölnische Volkszeitung*, 7 Sept. 1870.

[193] *Neue Preußische Zeitung*, 1 Jan. 1871, cited in M. Jeismann, *Das Vaterland der Feinde*, 252.

[194] *Neue Freie Presse*, 17 July 1870, cited in N. Buschmann, *Einkreisung und Waffenbruderschaft*, 235; Cosima Wagner cited in M. Jeismann, *Das Vaterland der Feinde*, 262.

the wounded are according to their stage of civilization, not so much to be imputed to them but to the European government that, knowing about their customs, leads these African hordes to the theatre of war.'[195] According to Buschmann, such racialization could be seen in references to the '*Racen-Krieg*' of 1866, in which, 'should the Prussian and Austrian army enter the field against each other, the war's fire would be ignited in the great majority of Austrian regiments by the age-old hatred of the Slavs and the Magyars against a German nationality privileged in its prosperity and education'.[196] The distinction between the Austro-Prussian and the Franco-German War, on this reading, was that Austrians were still often seen as brothers, whereas French soldiers were seen as enemies, as one article in the periodical *Daheim* put it: 'What can someone do whose leg has just been taken off by a shell...—other than raise his fist menacingly at the enemy, whom he cannot respect, as he could the Austrians in *anno* 66, but whom he hates and despises!'[197] Here, the conflicts themselves were marked by a worsening enmity and, partly in consequence, more extreme depictions of acts of violence.

The emphasis of historians on enmity, demonization, race, and sacralization diverges from contemporaries' understanding of the conflicts.[198] Those contemporaries' reading of the press certainly suggested that the wars were 'national', even that of 1866, but not that the conduct or course of the wars—or, with more qualifications, their causes—depended either on deeply held national sentiments and aspirations or various processes of radicalization, which served to counter or offset the national limitations and contradictions of the conflicts.[199] Thus, even commentators who strongly supported the war of 1870 on national grounds, like those of the *Grenzboten*, also pointed to the apparent normality of the Prussian capital's preparations for war:

> Although Berlin is fuller with all the thousands who usually visit...every green speck of the fatherland, from the sea to deep in the Alps, no one who is uninitiated would in the slightest notice that this is the capital of a great state thrust into a state of war, arming itself energetically.[200]

'Fortunately', there would, continued the correspondent, be no 're-awakening of *Teutschtum* in the style of old Jahn'.[201] It was, at the very least, not certain what

---

[195] *Schwäbischer Merkur*, 18 Jan. 1871, cited in C. G. Krüger, 'German Suffering in the Franco-German War', 415. See especially Heidi Mehrkens, *Statuswechsel. Kriegserfahrung und nationale Wahrnehmung im Deutsch-Französischen Krieg 1870/71* (Essen, 2008), who considers such 'atrocities'—and responses to them—in light of novel and evolving national justifications of war. Few contemporaries were prepared to accept Carl Vogt's argument that the campaign of the *francs-tireurs* was similar to that of Prussian volunteers in 1813: C. Vogt, *Politische Briefe an Friedrich Kolb* (Biel, 1870), 13.

[196] *Preußische Jahrbücher*, 1866, vol. 58, 473, cited in N. Buschmann, *Einkreisung und Waffenbruderschaft*, 294.

[197] *Daheim*, 1870, vol. 6, no. 45, cited ibid., 236.

[198] One example was the manifest empathy of reporters and artists—on some occasions—with the suffering of and mourning for French troops: 'Französische Verwundete aus dem Ausfallsgefecht vom 19. Januar am Quai de la Mégisserie in Paris. Nach einer Skizze aus Paris', *Illustrirte Zeitung*, 25 Feb. 1871, simply reproduced a French illustration of the return of dead and wounded soldiers.

[199] See M. Martin, *Images at War: Illustrated Periodicals and Constructed Nations* (Toronto, 2006).

[200] *Grenzboten*, 1870, vol. 3, 194.   [201] Ibid., 196.

role other manifestations of nationalism would play in the Franco-German War. Impliedly, they had not played this part in the Austro-Prussian War. Many commentators, including those of liberal newspapers like the *National-Zeitung*, were content to note that the North German Confederation's precarious alliances with South German states like Württemberg were 'holding'.[202] The 'unanimity' of Germany was a 'proud monument' in July 1870 because it had not happened before.[203] Yet who was moved to do what in the name of a German nation? The best that could be said of alleged particularists such as the Catholic leader Ludwig Windhorst during the Reichstag's reply to Wilhelm I, declared the *Kölnische Zeitung*, was that he kept tactfully quiet.[204] The Social Democrats limited themselves to remaining seated when the address was read out, while the other deputies stood.[205] What their supporters thought of the war was not easy for journalists to determine. To liberal observers such as the historian Theodor Mommsen, it was obvious 'that death for our fallen'—by which he meant middle-class students and lecturers—'may well have been easier than for the countless ones from lower educational groups, towards whom, in the same flowering years, the same bullet rushed':

> Naturally, life stretched before the former in a more colourful and magnificent way than for the latter; but the former also knew more fully, surely and clearly than their comrades, before as well as in the iron embrace of death itself, for what they were dying and that their blood was not flowing for nothing.[206]

The 'countless others' may not have known, he implied.

There was broad agreement in the press that the wars of 1864–71 were national wars of the people, or *Volkskriege*, but the label seemed self-evident—although still contested by some—rather than millenarian, especially outside Prussian liberal milieux.[207] The term appeared to describe widespread support for and participation in the wars, not to give an exhaustive account of the nature of the conflicts. Thus, when Mommsen referred to 1866 as a cabinet war, he did so in order to provoke and shock, pointing out that Bismarck had not sought popular support for the undertaking, and to avert the possibility of an unlimited, fratricidal war, or

---

[202] *National-Zeitung*, 15 July 1870.   [203] *National-Zeitung*, 23 July 1870.
[204] *Kölnische Zeitung*, 21 July 1870.   [205] Ibid.
[206] T. Mommsen, 'Rede zur Gedächtnisfeier der Universität für die in dem Deutsch-Französischen Kriege 1870 und 1871 gefallenen Dozenten und Studenten' (1875), in T. Mommsen, *Reden und Aufsätze* (Berlin, 1905), 28. The *Deutsche Kriegszeitung*, 1870, vol. 4, 66, made the same point: 'You would think that the pain suffered by an educated man, with a more exquisite nature, moves us more deeply than that of a crude, awkward body. However, the opposite effect occurs. The more spiritual suffering is the more it loses its horrible component; education is power and an educated man has power over himself even in the deepest agonies... How we die, our dissolution into animals, appears to us to be more horrible the less the immortal is developed in a human being.'
[207] F. Becker, *Bilder von Krieg und Nation*, 258, has argued that a distinction was made between a '*Volk in Waffen*' in Germany in 1870 and '*das bewaffnete Volk*' in France, whose own *Volkskrieg* after September 1870 was seen to be illegitimate. There is little sign that the label '*Volkskrieg*' was rendered problematic by the French campaign, however. The term '*bewaffnetes Volk*' continued to be applied to German forces as well as to French ones: for instance, W. Wehrenpfennig, 'Am Schluß des Kriegs', *Preußische Jahrbücher*, 1871, vol. 27, no. 3, 376.

Bruderkrieg, against Austria.[208] As a native of Schleswig, the historian and publicist had long believed, as he made plain in 1848, that a Prussian-led intervention by 'Germany' alone could rescue the cause of Schleswig-Holstein.[209] In the early 1860s, he called for 'all the German states' to back the candidature of Augustenburg, coming to support Prussian annexation of the provinces by 1865. By 18 July 1866, he had modified his earlier statements about the nature of the Austro-Prussian War, given that it had had such spectacular national consequences, attracting the support of the population and prompting criticism of anti-war Progressives: 'It is a wonderful feeling to be present when world history turns a corner. That Germany has a future and that this future will be determined by Prussia is no longer a hope but a fact, a powerful one for all time', he wrote to his brother Tycho.[210]

After the Franco-German War, Mommsen was certain that 'a great time lies behind us; if the harvest comes in as hardily as the seed has been sown, one can be happy with one's life'.[211] Much of the press followed a similar path, occasionally voicing doubts in the run-up to war that the conflicts of 1864 and 1866 were 'wars of the people' but generally labelling them as such in retrospect. By 1870, even Jörg's *Historisch-politische Blätter* was convinced, in anticipation of the coming conflict between Prussia and France, that the war would be a full *Volkskrieg*, notwithstanding the attempt of the Bavarian *Patriotienpartei*, including Jörg, to label the altercation between the two states a matter of courtly etiquette.[212] 'The peoples (*Völker*) themselves are now throwing iron dice over the question as to which one of them will have to stand down, whether it will be Prussia from its newly attained heights or France from its old, established heights as the first power of the continent', commented the Catholic periodical before the outbreak of hostilities: 'Thus, a cabinet war (*Kabinettskrieg*) has become, in a trice, a *Volkskrieg*.'[213] Whereas the two previous wars had 'passed across the political horizon like thunder storms', remaining localized 'before the tranquil gaze of the other powers' and accustoming the world to the idea that 'wars of longer duration might not be possible', the Franco-German War 'seems as though it might want to be otherwise'.[214]

With some qualifications but few exceptions, the presses of the South German states supported a 'national' war of defence in 1870.[215] The *Historisch-politische Blätter* continued to contend that liberals, especially National Liberals, were pursuing their own party interests in 1870 more than national ones, in order to make electoral gains in the South, and to emphasize that the war was between France and

---

[208] A. Heuss, *Theodor Mommsen und das 19. Jahrhundert*, 188–9.

[209] Ibid., 147, 151–2.   [210] Ibid., 190.   [211] Ibid., 191.

[212] E. Jörg, 19 July 1870, *Verhandlungen der Kammer der Abgeordneten des bayerischen Landtags*, cited in H. Fenske (ed.), *Der Weg zur Reichsgründung*, 420.

[213] *Historisch-politische Blätter*, 1866, vol. 66, 314.   [214] Ibid., 313.

[215] See, too, anti-French treatises appearing in the South: Anon, *Die Franzosen in Deutschland*, 6th edn (Munich, 1870); F. C. v. Fechenbach zu Laudenbach und Sommerau, *Deutschland und Frankreich oder: Eine deutsche Antwort auf die französische Herausforderung* (Munich, 1870); V. M. O. Denk, *Die gegenwärtige Stellung des katholischen Clerus Deutschland, Frankreich und Preußen gegenüber* (Munich, 1870); R. Doehn, *Der Bonapartismus und der deutsch-französische Conflict vom Jahre 1870. Eine historische Studie* (Leipzig, 1870); K. J. Diepenbrock, *Deutschlands Sieg und Herrlichkeit in staatlicher, sittlicher und sprachlicher Bedeutung* (Freiburg, 1870).

Prussia, not Germany, according to the title of one of its articles, hinting that Bismarck had provoked Napoleon III into a declaration of hostilities. Yet it also came to accept, by late July, that it was easier to go to war against France, with the other Great Powers having little interest in appeasing Paris (unlike in 1815), than to maintain peace.[216] According to the *National-Zeitung*, in a report on 24 July, the Ultramontanes and the 'so-called patriotic party' in Bavaria were the main exception to the united front behind the war, along with a renegade journalist writing for the *Sächsische Zeitung* and a handful of Hanoverian nobles.[217] On the following day, the *Kölnische Zeitung* commented on the 'wonderful bearing' of southern Germany, which seemed to have overcome its long and tragic history of anti-Prussianism in order to join forces in a national war for Germany: 'Deutschland über alles' was now a common credo.[218] 'Nowhere is the flourishing idealism of the German *Volk* more openly on view than as it now is in the South', wrote the same paper's Munich correspondent on 28 July.[219] Contrary to rumours about 'significant revolts' in Rosenheim, Traunstein, and places in Lower Bavaria, it was now agreed, 'following the testimony of everyone', that the mobilization of the Bavarian army had gone 'completely smoothly', noted the *Grenzboten* 'from Munich'.[220]

Unlike in 1866, when mobilization had still not been completed after two-and-a-half months, it had taken fourteen days in 1870. What was more, the troops were sober, whereas four years earlier 'almost all troops whom I saw billeted were shamefully drunk', so 'that they appeared at the theatre of battle with a physical and moral hangover'.[221] 'How completely public opinion can change in a few years!' exclaimed the same correspondent, noting how 'a normal *Altbayer* thought every Prussian a windbag in 1866' but had come in the meantime to trust in Prussian planning and organization.[222] The first German victories in 1870 had expunged 'many traces of a past, unfortunate period from our "old gentlemen"'; by contrast, 'the younger generation had long ago felt at home with the fruits of '66'.[223] It could be observed 'that even the most pronounced elements of the "patriotic" party have given up their work indefinitely, as far as it is directed against Prussia, partly in their conviction of complete hopelessness, mainly, though, in their hope of a turn for the better'.[224] By September 1870, the *Grenzboten* reported that the Ultramontanes had been defeated and Bavaria was participating fully in the war, with toasts being given to both the Wittelsbach and Hohenzollern monarchs, although no one yet knew the opinion of the '*Landvolk*'.[225] Catholic newspapers like the *Kölnische Volkszeitung*, which had traditionally been more sympathetic to Bavaria, also noted the shift of position there, undermining the French government's assumption of German disunity.[226] Similar comments were made about Württemberg, where a change of public opinion and political direction appeared to have occurred later in the conflict.[227]

---

[216] Respectively, *Historisch-politische Blätter*, 238, 471–4.
[217] *National-Zeitung*, 24 July 1870.   [218] *Kölnische Zeitung*, 25 July 1870.
[219] *Kölnische Zeitung*, 28 July 1870.   [220] *Grenzboten*, 1870, vol. 3, 280.
[221] Ibid., 281.   [222] Ibid., 282.   [223] Ibid., 283.   [224] Ibid., 281–2.
[225] Ibid., 487–90.   [226] *Kölnische Volkszeitung*, 26 July 1870.
[227] Ibid.; *Grenzboten*, 1870, vol. 4, 354, 471–2; *Preußische Jahrbücher*, 1870, vol. 26, 504, which depicted the population and king arrayed against 'decadent party leaders'.

Social–democratic newspapers gave a corresponding picture of opinion in different German lands, printing reports from the South.[228] 'The mood in Germany is better', remarked the *Agitator* on 23 July 1870:

> apart from a quite miniscule number of people whose hatred of Prussia (*Preußenhaß*) pushes them towards treason, everyone in the entire land from the Bodensee to Schleswig, from the Rhine to the Weichsel is only animated by one thought, the honour and freedom of the German nation against a foreign despot, to protect themselves against the pillaging attack of the perjuring tyrant on the Seine.[229]

'War has been declared!' concurred the *Social-Demokrat* on 17 July: 'Louis Napoleon Bonaparte is attacking Germany with his standing army without any relevant ground for war.'[230] As was to be expected, socialists blamed Bonapartism above all for provoking war in 1870, arguing that 'the entire French people is seized by disgust for a fratricidal war', particularly French workers, who 'write socialism and a fraternity of peoples on their banner'.[231] Nevertheless, the readiness of the *Social-Demokrat* and other newspapers to justify a war for 'Germany', under the leadership of Bismarck, Moltke, and the Hohenzollerns, was striking. It differed from August Bebel's later declaration in the Reichstag on 26 November, when he contended that 'the nationality principle is, in my view, a thoroughly reactionary principle', making the war against France, which he conceded was 'a necessity', 'not a national war but a war of freedom against unfreedom'.[232] To 'the organ of the Social Democratic Party', it was evident that the Franco-German conflict was both national and emancipatory:

> The war of 1870 is a war against the German *Volk*, it is a war against socialism. And every German who opposes the disturber of the peace is not only fighting for the fatherland but is also fighting against the principal enemy of the ideas of the future, for freedom, equality and fraternity.[233]

Various French commentators, 'thirsty for war', seemed to think that France would be able to humiliate its opponent, as it had done Russia in the Crimean War and Austria in 1859, yet 'this time the struggle was not against a small reactionary Prussia, but against the whole German nation'.[234] This belief in what the same newspaper called a 'German national struggle' against the 'territorial greed' of Napoleon III persisted beyond the dictator's abdication after the battle of Sedan.[235]

---

[228] See M. Jeismann, *Das Vaterland der Feinde*, 247–8.   [229] Ibid., 248.
[230] *Social-Demokrat*, 17 July 1870.   [231] Ibid.
[232] A. Bebel, 26 Nov. 1870, *Stenographische Berichte über die Verhandlungen des Norddeutschen Bundes 1870* (Berlin, 1871), vol. 2, 11.
[233] *Social-Demokrat*, 17 July 1870. From their vantage point abroad, Marx and Engels also admitted that workers had 'energetically supported' a war they believed to be national and, therefore, justified: cited in J. Leonhard, *Bellizismus und Nation*, 642. In respect of France and the French Commune, Marx argued that 'The highest, most heroic upswing which the old society is still capable of is a *Nationalkrieg*', but 'this reveals itself to be purely a government swindle which no longer has any other purpose than to push the class struggle to one side': K. Marx, *Der Bürgerkrieg in Frankreich* (1850), in K. Marx and F. Engels, *Werke*, vol. 17, 361.
[234] *Social-Demokrat*, 20 July 1870.   [235] Ibid., 3 Aug. 1870.

The impact of the declaration of the Third Republic and calls for an arming of the French people were initially ignored, with social-democratic commentators harking back to the defeat of a tyrant, who had misused a discredited standing army, and rejoicing in the manifest power and superiority of a German *Volkswehr*:

'We can summon up no stronger evidence for the judgement of a standing army than by pointing to the current political situation', we began our lead article on 14 July, at the moment when the world was frightened out of the most profound peace by the Emperor of France and which, in the next instant, brought the most capricious declaration of war. We indicated that it was entirely owing to this standing army, stationed in barracks, that gave that man the power for such an unforeseen attack on Germany, for an attack which not only was to humiliate and rob the German *Volk* but which was also to keep the French one in bondage... In Prussia, there was three-year service in the standing army, in South Germany a much shorter service, in France, by contrast, at least a four-year one, not to mention the numerous French career soldiers serving as substitutes for many a long year... Thus, however great militarism (*Militarismus*) is in Germany, it is insignificant compared to that in France. Whoever expected that the verdict of battles would be delivered by soldiers coming fresh from the barracks, mocking those reservists and *Landwehr* people called up from the work of peacetime for the defence of the fatherland as 'whimpering fathers of families' and 'mounted manual-worker apprentices', were able to hope for the success of the pillaging plans of Napoleon. How contemptibly has such militarism, which was much more fully embodied in the armies of France than in the German ones, ended in ignominy!... Absolutely, no mistrust in the *Volk*! Universal use of weapons, freedom and love of the fatherland, then the *Volk* cannot be defeated! Undeniably, this is the result of the present war. We do not want a defenceless *Volk*, but we oppose a militarism which wants to make the standing army into a tool of 'Reaction' and a means of exhausting the *Volk*... The current war shows that the German armies are so superior to the French ones precisely because they have their main support in the masses of reservists and *Landwehrmänner*, because—in a word—they are much nearer to a *Volkswehr*, as Gneisenau described it, than are their opponents.[236]

Naturally, the *Social-Demokrat* saw events as a justification of its own preference for a militia or, at least, shorter military service. Equally relevant, however, was the publication's discovery of this form of military organization in the German states, including Prussia, and its effort to link it, in a triumphal fashion, to a national war for 'Germany'. 'From the standpoint of socialism, every war is reprehensible', as 'the exploitation of peoples in the crudest form through an act of violence, open murder and looting', which disrupted the peaceful development of the economy and culture necessary for 'the emancipation of the proletariat', the newspaper admitted on 22 July: 'this does not mean, though, that the socialist should put his hands in his pockets with a sigh once a particular war has been sparked'.[237] Despite an awareness of the suffering, economic disruption, cultural damage, and the 'heavy blow' delivered to 'the international unity of peoples' caused by war, social-democratic papers were willing to justify it in 1870 without too much difficulty.

[236] Ibid., 14 Sept. 1870.   [237] Ibid., 22 July 1870.

Amongst other things, their actions betrayed the extent of the romanticization of war in the early and mid-nineteenth century.[238]

The conservative press in Prussia rarely hesitated on humanitarian grounds in its support for war, but it had traditionally harboured reservations about national justifications for armed intervention. By the 1860s, such reservations had been largely dispelled, even though conservatives' nationalism continued to rest on the assumption of Prussian ascendancy in Germany. 'It can never be different in the world', wrote one poet in the *Kreuzzeitung* on 19 July 1870: 'The strongest must be the leader of the strong. / Now, we are united.'[239] Like newspapers close to other political parties, conservative publications emphasized French culpability as a means of establishing German unity without needing to look too closely at war aims (the annexation of Alsace-Lorraine and the form of a future German order or state), which remained divisive: by 14 July, France was insisting that German governments, which had previously been neutral, put pressure on Leopold (a Hohenzollern) to withdraw his candidature for the Spanish throne; by the 17th, France was pushing Prussia to such an extent that peace was no longer possible; by the 20th, it was clear that France's attack was a deliberate attempt to humiliate Prussia, recalling the death of Wilhelm I's mother Queen Luise, who had been forced to beg for leniency from Napoleon I; and by the 24th, it had transpired that France was 'using every pretext to split the forces of Germany', turning the conflict through a common act of resistance into a war for the German nation.[240] At the start of the crisis, it was rarely clear whether references to 'our national independence', which were combined with perceived insults to 'our state's reputation' and to 'our loyalty', alluded to Prussia alone or to both the Hohenzollern monarchy and Germany as a whole.[241] Gradually, though, it became unmistakeable that journalists were equating the two, partly through references to the North German Confederation and the Reichstag, partly as a consequence of the involvement of the South German states.

On 19 July, one correspondent of the *Kreuzzeitung* reported that all were fighting for Germany: 'The *unanimity of mood* which runs *through the whole of Germany* proves this and demonstrates that one has really discovered a *German fatherland* once more, for which it is one's duty to fight.'[242] On 27 July, Wilhelm I's short proclamation (from the 25th) that the will to fight came 'from all the tribes of the German fatherland and all circles of the German *Volk*' was printed without comment as a lead article.[243] Later, after Sedan had signalled victory, the Prussian conservative mouthpiece was more critical of particularists in the South, who had been permitted greater scope amidst the ongoing restructuring of Germany, yet during the pre-war crisis, mobilization, and early campaign it had been much more complimentary.[244]

---

[238] This position altered later: for instance, ibid., 23 Nov. 1870, which noted the 'streams of blood' with which the victories against a 'so-called *Erbfeind* of the nation' had been bought.

[239] *Neue Preußische Zeitung*, 19 July 1870, cited in M. Jeismann, *Das Vaterland der Feinde*, 242.

[240] *Neue Preußische Zeitung*, 14, 17, 20, and 24 July 1870.

[241] Ibid., 14 July 1870.   [242] Ibid., 19 July 1870.

[243] Ibid., 27 July 1870.   [244] Ibid., 14 Sept. 1870, 24 Jan. 1871.

During this period, nothing was to obstruct the sacred duty of going to war, which had long characterized Prussia and was now extended to Germany:

> The danger, the touchstone of genuine trust and loyalty, not only sees the Prussian *Volk*, as at all times, inwardly and indissolubly bound to their king, ready for every sacrifice and waiting for the call of their king—the whole of Germany has become of one voice and the superficial considerations of peacetime, which have often led to painful discord, have been dispersed like trivial shadows before the demands of one's duty to and love of the fatherland.[245]

For Prussian conservatives, war was a holy reaffirmation of the institutions of the Hohenzollern monarch, not those of a future Germany, after the compromises and disputes of a period of peace, which needed to be purged like 'the unhealthy fluids' of a body.[246] Although the *Kreuzzeitung* warned that 'every great, serious war is a great, serious crisis in the life of a *Volk*', it did so to underline the need for a purgation of the German *Volkskörper* and to stress the sacred momentousness of the occasion. Nothing suggested that conservatives in Prussia found it difficult to go to war in 1870. They did not, therefore, require special reasons to do so.

Even during a divisive conflict like that of 1866, when reactionaries around the Gerlach brothers had balked at hostilities against their traditional counter-revolutionary ally Austria, the *Kreuzzeitung* had nonetheless endeavoured to conceal differences of opinion and to continue to back the Bismarck administration's prosecution of the war.[247] The intervention was serious but not exceptional, a regular *Volkskrieg* rather than a cabinet or civil war. 'We have not waged a *Cabinetskrieg*', declared the publication's lead article on 11 July 1866, after Austria's defeat at Königgrätz: 'The war, in which we have stacked up victory after victory until now, was a *Volkskrieg* in the highest and most noble sense of the word; it was a war *for the existence* of our state and *Volk*; a struggle, too, for the future of Germany.'[248] It was a question, now, of 'removing the threat to our fatherland forever; it is a question of creating and consolidating a state of affairs in which the justified desires and needs of our narrower and wider fatherland will find their secure satisfaction'.[249] The conflict was a 'war of brothers' because it pitted German-speaking former allies—in 1864—against each other, but it was not fratricidal: 'We are not so full of hatred and envy that—as has been said—we "are striving, primarily, for the downfall of Austria".'[250] Indeed, the *Kreuzzeitung* had ridiculed liberals and democrats at the start of the crisis in April for deploying the spectre of a *Bruderkrieg* as a way of avoiding a conflict and weakening Bismarck. 'At the head of the movement stand the same people who for fifteen years made the Prussian government's

---

[245] 'Der Krieg is da', ibid., 24 July 1870.   [246] Ibid., 26 July 1870.

[247] *Kreuzzeitung* had also carried E. L. Gerlach's 'Krieg und Bundesreform', in which he criticized Bismarck's attitude to war, nationalism, and liberalism, on 8 May 1866. In general, the publication stood in contrast to the more reactionary *Evangelische Kirchenzeitung*, 20 Jan. 1864, which labelled even the war against Denmark the result of a 'nationality swindle': N. Buschmann, *Einkreisung und Waffenbruderschaft*, 252.

[248] *Neue Preußische Zeitung*, 11 July 1866.   [249] Ibid.   [250] Ibid.

'concessions" towards Austria into the most serious reproach', declared one article
'On the Current Conflict':

> Today, they use talk of an 'avoidance of a war of brothers' in order to keep the govern-
> ment from a firm insistence on very important Prussian interests of state. They are not
> bothered about the humiliation which is a natural consequence of this endeavour.
> What are patriotic interests to them when it is a question of delivering a blow to
> Bismarck's ministry?[251]

For liberals, politicking had superseded diplomacy, bringing them to the cusp of
treason, asserted one *Kreuzzeitung* report on 28 July.[252] As such, war seemed to be
an instrument of policy in liberals' and democrats' domestic constitutional dispute
with the Prussian Minister-President. Partly because it was over so quickly, from
the press's point of view, it was not seen to have run out of control.

Accordingly, the war between Prussia and the northern *Kleinstaaten*, on the one
hand, and Austria and the *Mittelstaaten*, on the other, was rarely seen as a 'civil
war'.[253] Few commentators used the word *'Bürgerkrieg'* in 1866, despite the ubiquity of references in the press and elsewhere to the American Civil War only a year
beforehand. 'The Prussians are coming!' declared *Die Gartenlaube* from its Leipzig
headquarters: 'Do we want to admit with what feelings the majority of the inhabitants
of Leipzig received this news? It was not fear.'[254] Although some 'fatherland-loving
hearts' were weighed down with the possibility of a civil war, 'nobody could think
of the Prussians as an enemy'.[255] Occasionally, Catholic or South German journalists
deployed the term *'Bürgerkrieg'* as a warning, but they were regularly challenged by
others who claimed that any 'civil war' was, in fact, a conflict between the nation
and the dynasties or the church.[256] A larger number of contemporaries, including
liberals and democrats, called the conflict a *'Bruderkrieg'*, or a war of brothers,
acknowledging the consanguinity of their opponents but not their belonging to
the same society or country.[257] The term, of course, carried an element of prohibition or, even, taboo: if the conflict really were a 'war of brothers', remarked
Heinrich von Treitschke in the *Preussische Jahrbücher*, it would be 'a crime'.[258] Yet

---

[251] *Neue Preußische Zeitung*, 13 Apr. 1866.   [252] *Neue Preußische Zeitung*, 28 July 1866.
[253] This interpretation differs from the widely cited thesis about a German Civil War put forward
by James Sheehan, *German History, 1770–1866* (Oxford, 1989), 899–911.
[254] 'Scenen und Bilder aus dem Feld- und Lagerleben: 3. Eine kurze Erinnerung an das erste
Wetterleuchten des Kriegs in Leipzig', *Gartenlaube*, 1866, vol. 28, 446.
[255] Ibid.
[256] *Historisch-politische Blätter*, 1866, vol. 58, 953–72; one correspondent, 'an old soldier', claimed
that Bismarck's *Eroberungskrieg* pitted former 'allies and friends' against each other, ibid., 908.
Preussische Jahrbücher, 1866, vol. 17, 684. The term 'civil war' was sometimes used strategically after
the event. See, for instance, Bennigsen on 12 Mar. 1867: 'It was not a great popular movement but a
civil war which removed the old conditions', in H. Oncken,, *Rudolf von Bennigsen. Ein deutscher liberaler Politiker, von 1867 bis 1902* (Stuttgart, 1910), vol. 2, 46. Likewise, the Crown Prince used the
term just before war broke out, but mainly to deter the King of Prussia from backing a bellicose policy,
in K. A. Lerman, *Bismarck* (London, 2004), 104.
[257] For *Kladderadatsch*, the German states were only 'brothers' in being corralled together by
Prussia: 'Gleiche Brüder, gleiche Kappen', *Kladderadatsch*, 26 Aug. 1866, vol. 19, no. 39.
[258] *Preussische Jahrbücher*, 1866, vol. 17, 573. Nikolaus Buschmann, *Einkreisung*, 269–307, argues
that taboo was the dominant element.

Treitschke's point, like that of the conservative journalists of the *Kreuzzeitung*, was that the war was not a *Bruderkrieg* in the full sense of the term.[259] Bismarck had, four years earlier, referred to the notion of a 'brothers' war' as 'claptrap'.[260] The *Historisch-politische Blätter* condemned the actual war as 'light-headed'.[261] What was remarkable in 1866, an earlier article had stated in the same periodical, was the ease with which Austria was 'shut out definitively from any constitutional involvement in the rest of Germany'.[262] Despite the fact that Prussia's victory was 'an unexpected success', with Austria and the *Mittelstaaten* stronger 'on paper' than the Hohenzollern monarchy, the publication quickly came to terms with the disappearance of the Habsburg monarchy from Germany's affairs: 'there will never again be a German Confederation (*Staatenbund*) with two Great Powers', with Austria as 'the first factor in German affairs', ran one of its editorials in the summer of 1866.[263]

Catholic newspapers in Prussia such as the *Kölnische Blätter* were much more critical of the Habsburg monarchy, charging it with striving for a war against Prussia and with lacking 'any definition', even during the war itself, of 'Austria's place in Germany'.[264] Treitschke agreed, implying that the war could be contemplated without fear. His statement that the platform of the proponents of *Kleindeutschland* aimed 'to push Austria out of Germany and must provoke war sooner or later' was deliberately matter-of-fact.[265] The conflict was warranted because it completed Austria's own self-imposed marginalization from German politics, as far as liberals like Treitschke were concerned, and because wars between states—as opposed to those between citizens (civil war) or brothers—were at once acceptable and necessary.[266] The majority of journalists had anticipated the conflict well in advance; many had more or less accepted its necessity. Although Wilhelm I and Bismarck became more popular, with one correspondent from the *Social-Demokrat* reporting on 1 July that thousands had congregated in front of their residences, there was no sign of the crowds and euphoria in the major cities that accompanied the declaration of war against France in 1870.[267] The mood was more often characterized by resignation, with another correspondent of the social-democratic newspaper, who was touring South Germany in August, writing of an anti-Prussian majority in Württemberg, but an anti-Austrian one in Bavaria.[268] Most were critical of the irresponsible conduct of the war by their governments and yearned for peace and unification, not revenge, the report continued.[269] In such circumstances, the majority of those alluding to a 'war of brothers' were using

---

[259] The accusation of contemplating a 'cabinet war' was sometimes levelled at opponents: *Preussische Jahrbücher*, 1866, vol. 17, 687; *Neue Preussische Zeitung*, 21 June and 11 July 1866; *Social-Demokrat*, 8 July 1866. In May 1866, the *Abgeordnetentag* had 'damned the threatening conflict as a cabinet war serving only dynastic interests', in O. Pflanze, *Bismarck and the Development of Germany*, vol. 1, 319.

[260] Bismarck to Karolyi, Dec. 1862, in L. Gall, *Bismarck*, vol. 1, 214. See also E. Schüller, *Bruder-Krieg? Nein! Prinzipien-Kampf! Von einem Veteranen aus den Jahren 1813–1815* (Berlin, 1866).

[261] *Historisch-politische Blätter*, 1866, vol. 58, 781.   [262] Ibid., 315.

[263] Ibid., 323, 318.   [264] *Kölnische Blätter*, 18–19 June 1866.

[265] *Preussische Jahrbücher*, 1866, vol. 17, 573. This argument militates that proposed by Buschmann, *Einkreisung*, 292–3.

[266] On the marginalization of the Habsburg monarchy from German politics in the 1850s and 1860s, see M. Hewitson, *Nationalism in Germany, 1848–1866*, 113–57.

[267] *Social-Demokrat*, 1 July 1866.   [268] Ibid., 10 Aug. 1866.   [269] Ibid.

a common trope, not anticipating or describing an unthinkable act of fratricide.[270] Most correspondents refrained from calling the conflict either a *Bürgerkrieg* or a *Bruderkrieg*. It was a regrettable but expected event confirming what had long been accepted.[271]

For many commentators, the status of the wars of 1864, 1866, and 1870–1 as *Volkskriege* helped to make them acceptable.[272] The manner in which they were depicted continued in the same traditions of reportage established during the Crimean War and the Franco-Austrian War of 1859. Some accounts were explicit, influenced by soldiers' diaries and eyewitnesses' descriptions typical of war literature. In this respect, the popular war correspondent and writer Hans Wachenhusen's desire in 1866 'to participate in this campaign, too, as a field soldier', accompanying the troops as a journalist, was not unusual.[273] Most, however, conformed either to the factual constraints of newspaper reporting or to the romanticizing conventions of popular history, adventure stories, travel writing, and the illustrated, impressionistic pieces of mass-circulation periodicals such as the *Gartenlaube*.[274] Many journalists languished in military headquarters, where they were 'pushed against [their] will into the background during important actions', in Wachenhusen's view.[275] Few were granted full access to the fighting front by suspicious military commanders and those who were believed to have transgressed—such as Gustav Rasch (*Gartenlaube*) and Eugène d'Arnould (*Le Siècle*) in 1864—were, on occasion, arrested.[276] For the most part, journalists' priority was to establish and corroborate the details of their stories about victories and defeats amidst the tumult of 'the course of the fighting, always in surprising flux, and the continuous change of terrain', which made orientation impossible: 'However many bloody conflicts one has been a witness of, one never gets used to it.'[277] The nature of combatants' experience occasionally intruded into the order of battle but was generally obscured from view. The 'newspaper reading public' imagined that 'special correspondents and artists' spent their time out in the open, dodging shells and riding with the cavalry into battle, mocked *Kladderadatsch*, oblivious to 'how correspondence and drawings are, for the most part, made in reality'; namely, at the desks of journalists and illustrators at home, taking tea in the warmth whilst pontificating

---

[270] Ibid., 16 Aug. 1866.

[271] Even Prussian satirical journals like *Kladderadatsch* (for instance, 'Illustrirte Rückblicke', ibid., 30 June 1866, vol. 19, nos 29 and 30) tended to avoid stereotyping Austria: usually Austrians were shown as actual statesmen (Rechberg, for instance) or as a soldier in uniform, which was very similar to his Prussian counterpart apart from their hats.

[272] This acceptance and use of the term was much more significant than any distinction between 'true' and 'false' *Volkskriege* in 1870–1, after Gambetta had called for an arming of the French people and the continuation of the war: the argument here militates against that of Frank Becker, *Bilder von Krieg und Nation*, 219–49.

[273] H. Wachenhusen, *Tagebuch vom Österreichischen Kriegsschauplatz* (Berlin, 1866), ii.

[274] See K. Belgum, *Popularizing the Nation: Audience, Representation and the Production of Identity in 'Die Gartenlaube', 1853–1900* (Lincoln, NE, 1998), 1–83.

[275] Ibid. See, for instance, Georg Horn, 'Im Hauptquartier des Prinzen Karl', *Gartenlaube*, 1870, vols 35–40, 556–8, 599–603, 612–16, and 655–8.

[276] G. Rasch, 'Von Schleswig nach Rendsburg und meine Gefangennahme bei den Preußen', *Gartenlaube*, 1864, vol. 10, 157–9.

[277] Ibid., 147.

about the storming of Düppel and pretending that they were 'in the middle of a hail of bullets'.[278]

The absence of photography, in contrast to its ubiquity during the American Civil War, helped to maintain the impression that the German wars were being conducted in a traditional fashion. The Prussian General Staff had set up a 'mobile photographic workshop' in 1864, which had been transformed into a 'field photography detachment' of two artists, three photographers, an officer, and ten pioneers by 1870–1, but they were used mainly for reconnaissance and surveying.[279] The prints of private photographers—Friedrich Brandt in Schleswig or August Kampf and Paul Sinner in France—abided by the conventions of military painting— group portraits of soldiers, battlefields cleared of corpses, war spoils—and they were largely unfamiliar to a mass readership.[280] The picture presented by the widely seen lithographs of illustrated magazines, with what one artist termed their 'massive army' (*Riesenarmee*) of readers, remained closer to the idealizing traditions of the historical school of painters favoured by the military hierarchy.[281] The 'special artists' who had appeared 'everywhere over the last twenty years', remarked the *Grenzboten*, did not have 'great battles' as their 'main thing', since the artist 'knew very well that he could see as little as he could sketch in hand-to-hand combat', but rather they concentrated on 'the thousand interesting, always picturesque scenes of marches, camps and look-out posts'.[282] It was notable in 1864, after the decision of Prussian and Austrian military headquarters to ban all newspaper journalists from battle zones (except those of the sympathetic *National-Zeitung* and *The Times*, which was critical for opinion abroad), that the artists of *Die Gartenlaube* and *Die Illustrirte Zeitung* were still allowed full access to the fighting.[283]

The image of the wars which illustrated periodicals disseminated was geographical, historical, and ethnographic, reinforcing the impression that the campaigns were adventurous and unthreatening. The transition from 'newspaper wars' in the Crimea, Italy, and the United States to real ones, involving relatives and friends, in Schleswig, Bohemia, and France was made easier by the limited nature of the first German war in 1864 and by the border region's status as a travel destination and a site of national conflict between 'Germans' and 'Danes'.[284] Historians from the

[278] 'Zur Aufklärung', *Kladderadatsch*, 3 Apr. 1864, vol. 17, no. 16.

[279] G. Paul, *Bilder des Krieges*, 70–1.

[280] U. Steen, *Friedrich Brandt. Ein Pionier der Photographie in Schleswig-Holstein* (Heide, 1989); F. Becker, 'Die Anfänge der deutschen Kriegsfotografie in der Ära der Reichseinigungskriege (1864–1871)', *20th Century Imaginarium*, 2 (1998), 69–102; F. Becker, 'Die "Heldengalerie" der einfachen Soldaten. Lichtbilder in den deutschen Einigungskriegen', in A. Holzer (ed.), *Mit der Kamera bewaffnet. Krieg und Fotografie* (Marburg, 2003), 39–56; F. Becker, 'Deutschland im Krieg von 1870/71 oder die mediale Inszenierung der nationalen Einheit', in U. Daniel (ed.), *Augenzeugen. Kriegsberichterstattung vom 18. zum 21. Jahrhundert* (Göttingen, 2006), 68–86.

[281] G. Paul, *Bilder des Krieges, Krieg der Bilder*, 71; S. Bock, *Bildliche Darstellungen zum Krieg von 1870/71* (Freiburg, 1982); S. Parth, *Zwischen Bildbericht und Bildpropaganda*. For the comment about the mass readership of *Gartenlaube*, see Otto Günther, 'Ein Brief unsers Specialartisten', *Gartenlaube*, 1864, vol. 14, 220.

[282] 'Der Krieg und seine Illustration', *Grenzboten*, 1864, vol. 2, 493.

[283] 'Die Zeichner und Berichterstatter auf dem Kriegsschauplatze', *Gartenlaube*, 1864, vol. 15, 240.

[284] The Swabian liberal Otto Elben, *Lebenserinnerungen*, 140, had been to the duchies five times as a national-minded tourist by 1864.

region—Friedrich Christoph Dahlmann, Georg Waitz, Wihelm Beseler, Johann Gustav Droysen, Theodor Mommsen—had done much to establish the historical rights and national culture of the duchies in the public imagination. The peninsula was portrayed as a 'German arm' reaching out to dominate the North and Baltic seas, extending 'German life, influence and education' to the British Isles, Scandinavia, and the world.[285] It was also the battleground between Scandinavians coming South and Germans advancing to the coast and to the North:

> The archipelago, whose southern half comprises the duchies of Schleswig and Holstein, is the bridge over which the Scandinavian North is connected with the South, with the rest of Europe. Again and again, the Danes—the people of the northern tribe which is furthest forward—have tried to gain both domination of the Baltic and possession of the land up to the Elbe.[286]

'The struggle between the Germans and the Danes here is almost as old as our knowledge of history', asserted Waitz, hinting at the continuity of national conflict.[287] In the modern era, the duchies had gradually become more unified, despite Danish tutelage.[288] Since the seventeenth century, at the latest, they had shared estates, a common law and legal system, and other institutions, much as Prussia and Brandenburg had done: Denmark's connection to Schleswig-Holstein was no greater than that of the King of Prussia to Poland, proposed Waitz in 1852.[289] The relationship had begun to change in the nineteenth century, as Denmark had sought to expand to the South, conflicting with long-established ties—presented as if they were in a chain—between Schleswig and Holstein, and between Holstein and Germany.[290] 'In Schleswig as in Holstein, one lived in full consciousness of the linkage with the German *Volk*... in many respects perhaps too cut off and closed in on themselves, but still advancing along the path of national development', wrote Waitz more than a decade later.[291] 'The fate of the duchies is and remains chained to Germany', wrote Beseler: 'The bonds which nature has created are sacred and indissoluble.'[292] Schleswig-Holstein was small and easily overlooked, he concluded, but its *Volk* was 'immortal', containing a 'higher life force' and offering Germany the enticing prospect of national redemption.[293]

When journalists started to report on the war against Denmark, they did so against this historical and geographical backdrop. 'In the North of *Mitteleuropa*, where the Elbe reaches the sea, the German mainland, as if it is raising an arm towards the North, stretches a peninsular barrier out into the sea', ran the opening lines of Theodor Fontane's *Der Schleswig-Holsteinische Krieg im Jahre 1864* (1866),

---

[285] G. Waitz, *Kurze Schleswigholsteinische Landesgeschichte*, 3.

[286] Ibid., 4.   [287] Ibid.   [288] Ibid., 141–7.

[289] G. Waitz, *Geschichte des Herzogthums Schleswig*, 5–10.

[290] This is the thesis of J. G. Droysen, *Die Herzogthümer Schleswig-Holstein und das Königreich Dänemark*, 2nd edn (Hamburg, 1850), for instance. Also, J. G. Droysen, 'Der Vertrag vom 8. Mai 1852' (1863), in J. G. Droysen, *Kleine Schriften zur Schleswig-Holsteinischen Frage*, 2nd edn (Berlin, 1863), 97.

[291] G. Waitz, *Kurze Schleswigholsteinische Landesgeschichte*, 166.

[292] W. Beseler, *Zur Schleswig-Holsteinischen Sache im August 1856* (Brunswick, 1856), 149.

[293] Ibid., 151.

in a first chapter entitled 'Land und Leute'.[294] The second chapter gave a potted history of 'The History of Schleswig-Holstein', in which Fontane outlined the claims of the contending parties and the 'aggression of the Danes'.[295] Most newspaper reports began with discussion of the historical 'rights' of the duchies, Augustenburg, and the *Bund*, before proceeding to analyse the roots of the national conflict. With political parties and governments preoccupied by the constitutional question in Prussia and the struggle to reform—and resist reform of—the German Confederation, few in Germany were ready for a diplomatic crisis or, even, war in 1863, contended the *Preußische Jahrbücher*.[296] With Danish nationalists forcing the pace of events, 'all the questions which had been at issue between Denmark and ourselves—the independence of the *Bundesland* of Holstein, the authority of its Estates, its right to Schleswig, the equal position of both lands within the monarchy—have now been completely relegated to the background'.[297] What mattered to 'every German man' was 'to save a German land': how far would German princes be able to withstand the force of public opinion?[298] In 1864, during the waging of this national war, historical rights and precedents remained central to the *Preußische Jahrbücher*'s account, however.[299]

For conservative publications like the *Neue Preußische Zeitung*, these disputes about hereditary title, law, and history took precedence, albeit alongside the protections of 'Germans' in the duchies.[300] Although the newspaper was sceptical of 'mass' public opinion, gymnasts, and the *Nationalverein*, all of which had destabilized a precarious international affair of the European powers, it also acknowledged that some conservatives had been led astray by calls for a national war.[301] On the left, too, the *Social-Demokrat* conceded that democrats believed that the conflict was a national one, with a solution to the 'Schleswig-Holstein question' entailing a solution to the German one.[302] Despite finding the question tedious, surpassed only by that of *Kurhessen* (the other component of the stand-off between Austria and Prussia at Olmütz in November 1850), the newspaper's very complaint betrayed the continuing, complicated entanglement of historical, legal, and national affairs in 1864.[303] As the war continued during the first half of 1864, much of the coverage of the liberal press focused on these political questions, beside reports on the actual fighting.[304]

---

[294] T. Fontane, *Der Schleswig-Holsteinische Krieg im Jahre 1864* (Berlin, 1866), 3.   [295] Ibid., 25.

[296] 'Die Entscheidung der schleswig-holsteinischen Sache', *Preussische Jahrbücher*, 1863, vol. 12, 507.

[297] Ibid., 506.   [298] Ibid., 510.

[299] 'Schleswig-Holstein und die preußischen Waffen', ibid., 1864, vol. 13, 173–80.

[300] *Neue Preußische Zeitung*, 2 Dec. 1863 and 12 Jan. 1864.

[301] *Neue Preußische Zeitung*, 12 Jan. 1864.

[302] *Social-Demokrat*, 21 Dec. 1864.   [303] Ibid.

[304] See, for instance, *Grenzboten*, 1864, vol. 1, 'Zur lauenburgischen Successionsfrage: vom historischen Standpunkt aus', 14–28; 'Für Schleswig-Holstein', 34–7, 116–18; 'Schleswig-Holstein und Preußen', 77–80; 'Die preußische Politik in der schleswig-holsteinischen Sache', 201–7; 'Die europäische Lage', 281–4; 'England und die schleswig-holsteinische Frage', 322–4; 'Die preußische Politik', 356–60; ibid., vol. 2, 'Preußen und der Wunsch der Bevölkerung in Schleswig-Holstein', 74–80; 'Preußen, die Conferenz und der Bund', 119–20; 'Die neue Bewegung in Schleswig-Holstein', 193–6; 'Zur schleswig-holsteinischen Frage', 281–7; *Grenzboten*, 1864, vol. 3, 'Der Großherzog von Oldenburg als Prätendent für Schleswig-Holstein', 36–40; 'Die neuen Friedensaussichten', 197–200.

'Diary' accounts of the war in Schleswig likened the experience to that of a 'trip' in the words of one series of articles.[305] In his reports 'From the Lands of the Abandoned Tribe of Brothers' in *Gartenlaube*, Rasch begins with 'a visit to Rendsburg', 'my favourite city between the Elbe and Königsau',[306] 'I love Rendsburg for its history, its position, its typical *Altstadt*, its burghers', he wrote: the city lay 'right in the middle of Schleswig-Holstein', the 'critical node in the line of defence of the Eider, the natural bridge from Holstein to Schleswig'.[307] In Rendsburg and its surroundings, which were 'not at all as blessed by nature as the prosperous districts of the East', 'the kernel of the Nordalbingian Saxon tribe' had combined with 'the most noble part of the original inhabitants of the land', he went on, merging a description of the war with ethnographic, political, and geographical assumptions about nationality: 'From here, the Danes were thrown back towards the North and the Wends to the East.'[308] The violence of the campaign only extruded from Rasch's narrative infrequently. In some respects, the previous oppression of the Danes seemed to be worse than the actual fighting:

> It's two years now since I was in Rendsburg last time. The city was full of Danish troops at that time; Danish officials and Danish police suppressed every civil and individual freedom. In the press, the Danish government knobbled freedom of thought and public opinion. The national, German consciousness of the citizens was to give way to Danishness.[309]

As Rasch was shown the *Dannewerk*, the system of fortifications designed to protect Schleswig from an attack from the South, children were still taunting the Danish soldiers working on the structure. 'Our situation is truly too serious for such a children's game', his guide assured him, yet he was not intimidated by the Danish defences: 'The terrain is hilly. Here, the position is easy to take because of frozen ground and because the fortifications are not armed...It could be taken almost without loss of blood.'[310] When asked why the line had not been provided with the necessary arms, the guide replied that 'The Danes will never be in a position to occupy the line', for they lacked the requisite number of troops.[311]

In his second instalment, Rasch described his voyage through the wall of the *Dannewerk*, which mounted towards the *Riesendamm*, 30 yards high and surrounded by fortifications covered in snow. Beyond it, 'one saw the terrors of war', with buildings in one village 'full of dead Austrian soldiers': 'Most had been shot through the head.'[312] On his way back from Schleswig, he saw the remains of the hard-fought battle between Austrians and Danes at Oeversee:

> They must have fought most fiercely in the copse. There lay the dead in greatest number. The Austrian soldiers had mostly been shot in the head. The faces of the *Jäger* and infantry lying on their backs in the snow were covered with blood. The Danes had still

---

[305] 'Ein Ausflug auf den Kriegsschauplatz in Schleswig-Holstein', *Grenzboten*, 1864, vol. 1, 325–41, 375–81, 426–35, 460–5.

[306] G. Rasch, 'Aus den Landen des verlassenen Bruderstammes: 1. Ein Besuch in Rendsburg', *Gartenlaube*, 1864, vol. 5, 75.

[307] Ibid.   [308] Ibid.   [309] Ibid.   [310] Ibid., 76.

[311] Ibid.   [312] 'Von Rendsburg nach Schleswig', ibid., vol. 9, 143.

fired at a distance of three yards. The Austrians had then turned their guns around and smashed the heads of the Danes with the butts.[313]

The scene was intended to evoke the sympathy of readers and perhaps to shock them, with a description of 'the pools of blood, the corpses with smashed and beaten-in heads, the dead horses—a terrible view!'[314] However, it was preceded by a visit to a notorious spy, whose likely execution was deemed—without further comment—to be justified, and followed by anecdotes about the Austrian commander Ludwig von Gablenz's heroics and the correspondent's own brief imprisonment by the Prussians: he was 'appalled', threatening the offending officer with a later duel, but he went on to declare vaingloriously that 'the fate of war had meant me no ill on this occasion, too'.[315] On his release, after a visit to the celebrated tavern keeper Doris Esselbach, who recounted stories of all the commanders who had waged war in the region, Rasch visited Missunde to the North, which was the key to the entire area: once Missunde was taken, the Danes would have little option but to accept battle or to pull back behind the fortifications at Düppel.[316] The account did not go on to give a description of the killing there.[317] Throughout, it was framed as a heroic and picaresque travelogue. For its part, *Kladderadatsch* imagined the entire campaign in the dunes, which were marked 'Danewirke' and 'Düppel', as a game of cat and mouse.[318]

The lithographs which surrounded *Gartenlaube*'s articles on the war in Schleswig countered the occasional brutality of the text. The fourth instalment of Rasch's account ended with a romantic portrayal ('Bei Missunde, Mitte Februar') of a wagon train struggling up a snow-bound hill, with a large Danish fortification in the background. The white, winter clouds swirl above, filling half of the picture (see Figure 6.1).[319] Other images included the depiction of two soldiers behind the erected brush camouflage of a look-out ('Vorposten bei der Rübler Wassermühle auf der Sonderburger Chaussee') and two nurses caring for a young Prussian soldier in a military hospital ('Im preußischen Hauptlazareth zu Flensburg'). They were drawn by one of the periodical's 'special artists' Otto Günther, who also wrote up his comforting impressions of the campaign.[320] 'All the troops whom I have seen so far, officers as well as common soldiers, are in the best mood, follow Prince Friedrich Karl with true enthusiasm and trust him more than any other general', he recorded in his 'Artist's Journey in Schleswig-Holstein': 'If only he were in charge, they say, then there would soon be no more Danes in Schleswig.'[321] The Prussian army was 'excellently cared for', receiving daily rations of meat, beans, lentil and rice soup, tobacco and cigars, and 'good bread'.[322] The troops put up

---

[313] 'Von Schleswig nach Rendsburg und meine Gefangenschaft bei den Preussen', ibid., vol. 10, 157–8.

[314] Ibid.   [315] Ibid., 159.   [316] Ibid., 188.

[317] 'Von Schleswig nach Missunde', ibid., vol. 12, 187. The curtailment of the account before Düppel is perhaps because Rasch, like many other journalists, was denied access.

[318] 'Katze, Maus und Falle', *Kladderadatsch*, 22 May 1864, vol. 17, no. 24.

[319] *Gartenlaube*, 1864, vol. 12, 189.   [320] Ibid., 218, 221.

[321] O. Günther, 'Künstlerfahrten in Schleswig-Holstein', ibid., vol. 12, 191–2.

[322] Ibid., 192.

Figure 6.1 'Bei Missunde, Mitte Februar'
Source: *Gartenlaube*, 1864, vol. 12, 189.

with the rigours of watch 'with self-sacrifice, even with joy', in their desire to demonstrate 'Prussian courage, the bravery of the battles of the Seven Years' War and from Katzbach and Dennewitz, from Leipzig and Belle-Alliance', if only their commanders would let them storm the fortifications near Missunde:

> 'Without having taken Düppel, we can't go home with honour,' I have heard musketeers and fusiliers, artillerymen and bombardiers say more than once, and not a single one of them recoils from the thought that perhaps the stormtroopers might have to break through to the final victory over their own dead body, twitching in bloody dismemberment.[323]

Such unflinching disclosures were not the result of bitterness, as Günther's next sentence made clear: 'There is something remarkably affecting in this enthusiasm, this lust for battle, this hope of victory, and even your otherwise completely civilian special artist already feels himself infected by these kinds of warlike sentiments.'[324] The artist went on to depict fighting at Veile on 8 March, 'one of the bloodiest [fights] of the present campaign', where many houses had been left 'without roofs, others lacked large sections of their front walls and scarcely a window was to be seen in any of the northern streets'.[325] The main point of the article, however, was to detail the death of Hugo Rathlev, the son of a prominent official

---

[323] 'Ein Brief unsers Specialartisten', ibid., vol. 14, 222.   [324] Ibid.
[325] O. Günther, 'Veile und das Gefecht vom 8. März', ibid., vol. 16, 252.

in Kiel and the 'first Schleswig-Holsteiner to sacrifice his youthful hero's life in the struggle against the hated oppressor'.[326] The young officer had fought at Oeversee on 6 February with his Austrian 'König von Belgien' Regiment, which 'famously played such a glorious part' there.[327] Günther's accompanying sketch displayed soldiers in close combat in dense woodland. Fallen bodies are shown in the foreground, but in the heroic pose of an historical painting, giving an overall impression of human struggle and endeavour.[328] This 'romantic' setting was reproduced in further representations of Kolding ('Chaussee vom Süden nach Fridericia'), which portrayed the ruin of the royal palace under a cloudburst amidst windswept trees, and of typical billets ('Einquartierung in der Küche'), where soldiers were shown warming their feet around a fire in the welcoming kitchen of a Danish farm.[329] Even the depiction of soldiers cowering before the impact of a bomb ('Die Bombe kommt!') stayed carefully within the conventions—in its scale and with its protective natural dunescape—of episodic scenes from military life: indeed, it was intended as 'an amusing piece', one of the conflict's 'agreeable and funny intermezzos', between pictures of hospitals and battle which revealed 'the gruesome seriousness of war'.[330] On such a reading, the conflict with Denmark could be harsh but it was also inspiring and worthwhile. It was not destabilizing.

The wars of 1866 and 1870–1 were much more likely to unsettle the readers of magazines and newspapers than that against Denmark. In periodicals especially, where combatants' and eyewitnesses' reports could be printed at greater length, the scale of the killing seems to have affected the ways in which the conflict was portrayed, albeit within the traditions of conventional war reportage. Long lists of the names of dead and wounded, demonstrated in stark and regular form the human cost of the conflict.[331] After publishing these lists for a dozen editions, the editors of *Die Gartenlaube* were obliged to apologize that 'lack of space' had meant that a register of 'invalids' and 'fallen' would have to be postponed.[332] Modern wars involved millions, creating fear amongst civilians as well as combatants, since the former believed that their cities would be the place where 'the violent acts of war' would 'fight out their horrifying disputes', in the opinion of Gustav Freytag.[333] New technologies such as breech-loading rifles and explosive shells appeared to have increased the dangers of warfare, constituting part—as the Augsburg *Allgemeine Zeitung* put it—of 'a general race towards the most perfect murder weapon, a prize competition of a theme written out by the devil, a world exhibition

---

[326] Ibid.   [327] Ibid.

[328] 'Das Gefecht in der Schlucht auf der Horsenser Chaussee bei Veile', ibid., 253.

[329] The reference to the romantic setting comes from Günther, ibid., 252. E. Wolperding, 'Chaussee vom Süden nach Fridericia' and O. Günther, 'Einquartierung in der Küche', ibid., vol. 15, 236–7.

[330] 'Die Bombe kommt!', ibid., vol. .17, 272.

[331] 'Für die Verwundeten und Hinterlassenen der Gefallenen', ibid., 1866, vol. 29, 464; vol. 30, 480; vols 31/2, 504; vol. 33, 520; vol. 34, 536; vol. 35, 552; vol. 36, 568; vol. 38, 600.

[332] Ibid., vol. 42, 664; vol. 43, 680.

[333] Gustav Freytag, 'Eine deutsche Stadt beim Ausbruch des Krieges', *Grenzboten*, 1866, vol. 2, 486.

of refined barbarity'.[334] For the Saxon *Gartenlaube*, as for many other publications, there was the added complication in 1866 of a multiplicity of perspectives and the proximity of battle. Much of its coverage centred on the defeat of Hanoverian forces at the battle of Langensalza, which had issued in 'the drama of a week of misfortune' beginning on 23 June.[335] After extensive fighting, leaving a battlefield 'sown with human and horses' bodies and limbs' and with blood forming 'true pools', the 'brave Hanoverian army had to lay down its arms', wrote the Thuringian pastor and writer Heinrich Schwerdt (living in Langensalza and 'an eye-witness' of 'these terrible days'), in the face of 18,000 newly arrived troops on the Prussian side. The King of Hanover had overseen 'a useless waste of human life'.[336] His attempt to justify these losses by appeals to God could only 'be damned unconditionally and forever, with the impulse of a shudder, by reasonable insight, humanity and impartial fellow-feeling': 'God and saviour have nothing to do with this reprehensible and pointless human slaughter.'[337] The 'war of "seven days"', wrote the same author later on the eve of peace, had been 'more violent and bloodier than the other one of seven years'.[338] The central panel of the accompanying triptych of scenes showed a melée of barely distinguishable soldiers stabbing and clubbing each other with bayonets and the butts of their rifles.[339] The article ended with a pathos-laden scene of a Prussian soldier bending over an injured Hanoverian in hospital:

> 'Dear brother,' he stammered, 'I truly didn't want to do it, but look, you didn't want it otherwise, and if you have to die, that hurts my heart. The evil bullet! Can you forgive me?' And the dying man pressed his hand gently. A stream of blood came from his lips. 'Tell my wife!'[340]

The lesson that the Prussian soldier took from his experience was a warning, in Schwerdt's view: '"But truly, if you want to drag me into war again, I won't do it, whatever comes of it. My conscience has enough with *one* brother-murder to bear."'[341]

Few other accounts of the war of 1866 were so negative. 'The Catastrophe in Hanover', outlined in the *Grenzboten*, was a political one, precipitating the annexation of the state.[342] Much of the reportage of other aspects of the conflict similarly concerned itself largely with politics and diplomacy.[343] The war received little

---

[334] *Allgemeine Zeitung*, 20 July 1866, cited in N. Buschmann, *Einkreisung*, 71. Most examinations of military technology were laudatory: see, for instance, 'Das Zündnadelgewehr', *Illustrirte Zeitung*, 14 July 1866.

[335] H. Schwerdt, 'Die Schlacht von Langensalza', *Gartenlaube*, vols 28 and 29, 441–6, 457–60.

[336] Ibid., 445, 457, 460. See also 'Scene und Gefecht bei Langensalza am 26 Juni', *Illustrirte Zeitung*, 14 July 1866.

[337] Ibid., 458.

[338] H. Schwerdt, 'Noch einmal vom Langensalzaer Schlachtfelde', ibid., vols 31/32, 499.

[339] A. Sundblad, 'Von und auf dem Langensalzaer Schlachtfelde', ibid., 500.

[340] Ibid., 503.   [341] Ibid.

[342] 'Die Katastrophe in Hannover', *Grenzboten*, 1866, vol. 2, 1–3.

[343] See, for instance, 'Krieg oder Frieden', ibid., 64–7; 'Eine deutsche Stadt beim Ausbruch des Krieges', ibid., 485–92; 'Ein Kriegsbrief aus Nassau', ibid., 41–53; 'Hannover und Kurhessen', ibid., 144–8; 'Die politische Stimmung in Schwaben', ibid., 149–57; 'Die Friedensverhandlungen', ibid., 161–8.

coverage at all in some South German publications.[344] The main Bavarian satirical magazine, the *Fliegende Blätter*, treated the conflict tangentially: one of its few direct references to 'the ominous war' promised to solve 'the whole series of bad conditions' that had come to light by means of modern inventions resulting from 'the relentless progress of the modern era'—a contraption of levers to ensure a good military posture, a metal helmet three-quarters of an inch thick with a lightning conductor on top, a metal knapsack, and a rectangular iron shield attached to various parts of the body with hooks.[345] Reports in *Gartenlaube* were more direct. One soldier's account of the battle of Nachod on 27 June, 'experienced by himself', alternated between the excitement and horror of combat: 'I cannot depict fighting with bayonets for you; it is too terrible. But in the moment one doesn't feel what is terrible, one sprays out destruction.'[346] Although the image of the battle was dark, portraying soldiers creeping through the undergrowth of the forest with their swords and guns raised, the framework of the narrative was epic, with everyone feeling 'proud of the great importance of their task'.[347]

The account of the decisive battle of Königgrätz on 3 July contained more references to corpses—for instance, to an artilleryman, 'both of whose legs had been torn off by a grenade' and were lying in another place still protruding from his boots—but it had been composed by 'a Silesian landowner' who had only seen the events from a distance.[348] His conclusion was redemptive:

> All of you who have bled in this great battle, may you not suffer too badly; may you all return to the arms of your own! Let fate allow you to look on a *great, united Germany* under strong, *unified* leadership and be able to say of yourselves with pride: 'We bought it with our blood!'[349]

Such reports of battle were components of a series of 'scenes and pictures from the life of the field and camp', which followed recruits from mobilization and the transition from civilian society ('Einberufen', with a crowd assembling in a city street), as servants unexpectedly became non-commanding officers, via departure by train ('Der Ausmarsch', with a print of horses being loaded into a wagon) and the anxious waiting for war ('Eine kurze Erinnerung an das erste Wetterleuchten des Krieges in Leipzig', with Prussian cavalry rushing into a tranquil square), to billeting in Bohemia ('Im ersten böhmischen Quartier', with a peasant girl showing soldiers to a rustic barn), and to battle itself.[350] Genuine attempts were made to

---

[344] The *Historisch-politische Blätter*'s main source were three letters from an 'old soldier' in Frankfurt; ibid., 1866, vol. 57, 907–15, 989–98. See also the main article of the Leipzig *Illustrirte Zeitung*, 14 July 1866, after Königgrätz, 'Die ereignissschwere Woche', which concerned itself largely with political questions. It was accompanied by a drawing of a Prussian bivouac in Dresden, where civilians mingled with *Ulanen*. There were, of course, continuing criticisms of Prussia's position: C. Homburg, *Preußische Wegelagerei! Ernster Mahnruf zur Wachsamkeit für ganz Europa* (Mannheim, 1866), which argued for Catholic Great Powers and against 'heathen national religions', supported by 'Unitarismus', which would issue in constant wars.

[345] 'Zum Fortschritt im Militärwesen', *Fliegende Blätter*, 1866, vol. 45, 161–3.

[346] 'Am Saune des Nachoder Wäldchens', *Gartenlaube*, 1866, vol. 30, 471.

[347] Ibid., 469–70.

[348] 'Bei Königgrätz am Tage nach der Schlacht', ibid., vol. 33, 513.   [349] Ibid., 514.

[350] Ibid., vol. 26, 405–9; vol. 27, 428–9; vol. 28, 444, 446–7; vol. 29, 435–5; vol. 30, 468–71.

disclose the 'reality' of war—through the 'self-testimony of a seriously wounded soldier', or a group portrait of individuals' injuries, or a detailed sketch of a railway wagon full of wounded soldiers arriving in Dresden—yet their pain receded (so that 'I am not at all as unhappy about my misfortune', as the injured soldier confessed) and wounds were carefully concealed from view by clean bandages, lending the scene a carnivalesque air.[351] Arms protruding out of the straw in the carriage of wounded soldiers could have been from 'the sleeping' or from 'the seriously wounded'.[352] Likewise, troops who were shown on the grassy earth under trees at Sichrow turned out not to be dead, but merely to be asleep in a bivouac.[353] Those who did die during the campaign were 'remembered' by *Gartenlaube* almost immediately after the fighting had stopped, as Georg Hiltl retraced the soldiers' steps over the battlefield and fashioned 'holy images' out of his experiences.[354] This memorialization took place before the periodical's representation, in words and pictures, of a jubilant homecoming.[355]

The same discourses about war recurred in 1870–1, despite the different circumstances surrounding the outbreak of the conflict. The campaign was longer, more costly, and more difficult to classify, progressing from conventional warfare involving marches, battles, and sieges until the French defeat at Sedan on 2 September 1870, followed by a national call to arms and the use of irregular soldiers, or *francs-tireurs*, under the newly declared Third Republic during the winter of 1870–1.[356] Very occasionally, the suffering and anger of combatants was visible in the press, such as when one poet asked in the *Gartenlaube*, 'Was ist der Krieg?'

> War is a poor position,
> Into which violence presses us;
> War is a modest question,
> Which a *Volk* allows itself to ask.
>
> It is a devilish counsellor,
> Who wants evil and creates evil;
> An unnatural, poor father,
> He undermines the strength of his own children.

[351] 'Selbstbekenntnisse eines Schwerverwundeten', ibid., vol. 43, 672–4; 'Gruppe verschiedener verwundeter Soldaten aus den internationalen Lazarethen in Liepzig', ibid., vol. 29, 461; 'Opfer vom Felde der Ehre', ibid., vols 31/32, 492–3. See also 'Die Pflege der kranken und verwundeten Krieger', *Illustrirte Zeitung*, 21 July 1866, which gave a more specifically Saxon perspective of care for 'our' wounded; 'Ankunft Verwundeter vor dem Cadettenhaus in Dresden', ibid., 28 July 1866.

[352] *Gartenlaube*, vol. 31/32, 492.

[353] 'Am Morgen nach dem Bivouac bei Sichrow', *Gartenlaube*, vol. 35, 541.

[354] G. Hiltl, 'Erinnerungen aus dem deutschen Kriege des Jahres 1866: 1. Heiligenbilder auf dem Schlachtfelde', *Gartenlaube*, vols 40 and 41, 626–8, 643–5.

[355] 'Die Heimkehr der Krieger', *Gartenlaube*, vol. 44, 685, 693, 696. See also 'Die Friedensfeier zu Leipzig: Vor der Germania auf dem Marktplatz am Abend des 5. März', *Illustrirte Zeitung*, 18 Mar. 1871.

[356] This second phase of the war was arguably treated more seriously by the press than by the military: some depictions suggested a rural idyll ('Die Kämpfe am 2. December vor Paris: 2. Württembergische Artillerie auf den Höhen von Villiers', *Illustrirte Zeitung*, 7 Jan. 1871) but others showed bloody fighting ('Die Kämpfe vor Paris: 3. Vertreibung der Franzosen von den Höhen von Villiers und Wegnahme zweier Geschütze durch das k. sächsische Infanterieregiment Nr. 107 am 30. November 1870', *Illustrirte Zeitung*, 14 Jan. 1871; 'Ausfallsgefecht am 21. December 1870 vor Paris', *Illustrirte Zeitung*, 11 Feb. 1871).

War is nothing but a waster,
Whose luxury benefits no one;
A contributor of misery, need and worries
Out of darkness or high spirits…

A book that, with each page,
Only makes you cruder, worse and dumber;
A *Landtag* where, in debate,
Passion acts as president.

A doctor who, instead of curing,
Only makes deeper and deeper wounds;
A judge who, during the trial,
Makes his way off, as a theft, with the prize.

A light which, even in dark times,
Does not light up the smallest room;
A false friend who, in order to be led astray,
Is joined by *Volk* and *Fürst*.[357]

More commonly, the violence of the conflict was betrayed, with varying degrees of intent, in realistic representations of fighting by journalists and artists. Correspondingly, newspapers and magazines contained more descriptions of wounding, dismemberment, and dying in 1870–1 than in 1864 or 1866. Prints of debris and destroyed buildings (in Thionville, Strasbourg, and Paris), the frightening power of modern weaponry, swarming troops and the writhing of the wounded, stretchers, hospitals, and lines of corpses could all be seen in the otherwise respectable and conservative *Illustrirte Zeitung* (see Figure 6.2).[358] The scale of the war was obvious from the different sites—Le Havre, Switzerland, Bordeaux, Marseilles—which were portrayed.[359] All the same, even critical, democratic publications like the *Beobachter*, though fearing that 'the slaughter of thousands has grown into a monster' and remarking that 'our projectiles, shrapnel shells, *mitrailleuses* and needle guns already devour so much human flesh that the forces of the biggest nations hardly permit us to wage war for longer than four weeks', focused on the future rather than a present which was, implicitly, still acceptable: 'What will happen if

---

[357] A. V., 'Was ist der Krieg?', *Illustrirte Zeitung*, 1871, vol. 11, 186.

[358] For debris, see 'Auf dem Marktplatz in Diedenhofen (Thionville) nach Übergabe der Stadt am 25. November', *Illustrirte Zeitung*, 7 Jan. 1871; 'Mein Nachtquartier in Diedenhofen', *Illustrirte Zeitung*, 14 Jan. 1871; 'Einzug der IV. deutschen Armee in St. Denis am 20. Januar', *Illustrirte Zeitung*, 4 Mar. 1871. For cannon, see 'Preußische Belagerungsbatterie Nr. 3 im Park von Naincy vor Paris', *Illustrirte Zeitung*, 21 Jan. 1871; 'Innere Ansicht des Forts Nogent vor Paris nach der Besetzung durch württembergischen Truppen', *Illustrirte Zeitung*, 11 Mar. 1871. On fighting and dying, see 'Die Kämpfe vor Paris: 3. Vertreibung der Franzosen von den Höhen von Villiers und Wegnahme zweier Geschütze durch das k. sächsische Infanterieregiment Nr. 107 am 30. November 1870', ibid., 14 Jan. 1871; 'Ausfallsgefecht am 21. December 1870 vor Paris', ibid., 11 Feb. 1871. The wounded are shown in 'König Wilhelm im Schloßlazareth zu Versailles', ibid., 14 Jan. 1871, and 'Französische Verwundete aus dem Ausfallsgefecht vom 19. Januar am Quai de la Mégisserie in Paris. Nach einer Skizze aus Paris', ibid., 25 Feb. 1871. A line of corpses ready for burial can be seen in 'Vor Paris: Bestattung der gefallenen Franzosen auf dem Mont-Avron', ibid., 11 Feb. 1871.

[359] See, for instance, 'Entwaffnung der auf Schweizerboden übergetretenen Truppen der Bourbaki'schen Armee bei Verrières am 1. Februar', *Illustrirte Zeitung*, 25 Feb. 1871; 'Einfahrt in den Hafen von Havre', 4 Mar. 1871; 'Ansicht der Stadt Bordeaux von der Ostseite', ibid., 4 Mar. 1871.

Figure 6.2 'Vor Paris: Bestattung der gefallenen Franzosen auf dem Mont-Avron'
Source: *Illustrirte Zeitung*, 11 Feb. 1871.

there are further improvements and if with our speed of manoeuvre the war will consume at least a third more flesh than it already has?'[360]

Press 'realism' in 1870–1 continued to exist in a conventional and patriotic framework. 'If the local patriotism of many Germans was painfully injured in 1866, everyone nevertheless was pleased about the increased political importance of the Germans and the yearning for a more complete purification of all the tribes became more pressing and more general with each new year', wrote the international journalist and former revolutionary Otto von Corvin in the late summer of 1870.[361] 'Never in history has there been so general an enthusiasm of the *Volk*, at least not to such an extent and with such rapidity', he wrote of the outbreak of the Franco-German War: 'Other nations will be amazed, most of all because the Germans, who are unfortunately known for constantly bickering and intriguing amongst each other, have risen up as one as soon as their national independence as Germans was threatened.'[362] In Corvin's series of reports for the *Gartenlaube*, which provided the magazine's introduction to the events of the war, to be followed by further series by Georg Horn, Friedrich Gerstäcker, and Friedrich

[360] *Der Beobachter*, 31 Aug. 1870, cited in C. G. Krüger, 'German Suffering in the Franco-German War', 408.
[361] O. v. Corvin, 'Im Lager unserer Heere', Gartenlaube, 1870, vol. 34, 534. Corvin had covered the American Civil War for the *Allgemeine Zeitung* and *The Times*, and he covered the Franco-German War for the *Neue Freie Presse*.
[362] *Gartenlaube*, 1870, vol. 34, 534.

Hofmann, he referred, after the usual depictions of mobilization and departure, to soldiers' suffering only in passing. At the battle of Spicheren on 6 August, he noted that 'the losses of the Germans are very large and perhaps larger than those of the French', yet he went on to add that this 'is quite natural'.[363] 'The battlefield on the plateau between the wood and the road looked like a flea market', he wrote: 'Whoever has not seen one has no idea of it. The dead lay rather densely there, Prussians as well as French.'[364] One soldier had been hit by a bullet in his heart: 'he looked as though he were sleeping and having pleasant dreams'.[365] Four others—two Prussians and two French—'who had been working on each other with the butts of their guns', now—improbably—'lay peacefully close by one another', rather than disfigured beyond recognition.[366] 'I wish you could have seen it', he concluded, as he descended the slopes that the Prussian troops had climbed at the cost of 'a pile of dead'.[367] At Mars-la-Tour, where some of the fiercest fighting had taken place on 16 August, Corvin remarked simply that 'the dead from the 16th were not yet buried, and those of the Eleventh still lay about; but their faces were already black'.[368] In the next paragraph, he derided those journalists who attempted to describe the fighting as it took place, since 'one only ever sees individual moments of a battle, and never enough': 'by contrast, a fresh battlefield is like an opened book, in which one can easily read the history of the battle in the writing of corpses'.[369] At Gravelotte, where the fighting had continued on 18 August, the journalist was less bothered about 'the memory of the butchery that had taken place there' than about the hunger and discomfort which it had brought in its wake: 'Battles are terrible, but their consequences still worse.'[370] Battle for Corvin was a form of travel, during which he collected anecdotes and impressions, and a type of entertainment, which created excitement. He was disappointed on approaching Strasbourg, therefore, because 'a siege, of all martial operations, is for me the most boring and uninteresting'.[371] His subsequent arrival in Versailles, where he met Bismarck for a discussion about German unity, was a relief.[372]

Infrequently, journalists revealed the full horror of what they had seen. Georg Horn, for instance, who was travelling with the staff of Friedrich Karl, visited the battlefield of Vionville, following the 'shot helmets, the scattered guns and dead horses' leading to the site.[373] His description began conventionally: the 'great losses' and 'thickly sown corpses' demonstrated how fierce the fighting had been and how dear 'every foot of ground for the fatherland' was.[374] The picture was still an ideal one: 'Officer and units were loyally united in death there, as they had been in life and during the fighting.'[375] One soldier held his gun to his heart; another had raised his hand in prayer. With no warning, however, the narrative shifts from romantic pathos to medical matter-of-factness: 'Most wounds are head wounds,

---

[363] Ibid., vol. 37, 543.   [364] Ibid., 543–4.   [365] Ibid., 544.
[366] Ibid.   [367] Ibid.   [368] Ibid., vol. 39, 599.   [369] Ibid.
[370] Ibid., vol. 41, 639.   [371] Ibid., vol. 42, 686.   [372] Ibid., vol. 47, 790.
[373] G. Horn, 'Bei Tod und Wunden', ibid., vol. 38, 614–15. Horn subsequently wrote a book on the same subject: G. Horn, *Bei Friedrich Karl. Bilder und Skizzen aus dem Feldzuge der zweiten Armee* (Leipzig, 1872), 2 vols.
[374] *Gartenlaube*, 1870, vol. 38, 614–15.   [375] Ibid.

with running masses of blood marking the place where the life-nerve was hit and destroyed.'[376] Whereas *chassepots* made a small entry wound and French artillery had 'done relatively little damage to our troops', German shells had had a 'terrible' impact on the French troops: it was a 'good thing' that most French relatives 'were spared the sight of the torn-off limbs' that they caused; 'the limbs of most of the French were smashed, ripped off, their heads shot to pieces so that the brain matter flowed out, and the corpses swam in a pool of blood'.[377] Horn carried on across the battlefield, reflecting on the 'bloodthirsty beasts'—the 'hyenas' or 'cannibals'— who had looted and despoiled the bodies of the dead troops.[378] However, by the end of his tour, he had returned to his original pathetic tone, leaving the field 'where so many sleep their last sleep and have sealed the loyalty and manliness of their hearts through death'.[379] For the press, death was meaningful, as that of 'a fusilier of Regiment No. 64', which was consecrated with a poem and sketch in *Die Gartenlaube*, made plain.[380] According to the text, the fusilier had written a poem to his fiancée at home: 'He has truly not forgotten you, Maria, with your gaze of tears. As he sat with your *Lied*, he forgot his death and misfortune', wrote his NCO, in the published letter home.[381] In the accompanying sketch by Fritz Schulz, the fusilier was shown lying slightly twisted—the only sign that he was dead—on a grassy knoll before a line of poplar trees. Behind, horses are grazing tranquilly, obscuring the fact that they are the product of a battle, which gradually becomes visible in the form of a large dismounted wheel and billowing smoke on the far right-hand side of the picture. The poem makes sense of the fusilier's death by referring to the object of his love at home and to his fatherland, for which the victory at Vionville, where he died, was decisive.

Most reports from special war correspondents in 1870–1 combined the styles and tropes of travel writing and military dispatches. These forms and *topoi* at once revealed and informed how the press treated the conflict. Sometimes, as was the case with the portrayal of French colonial troops (or '*turcos*'), the various modes of representation contradicted each other. Thus, the penchant of travel writers for emphasizing the exotic otherness of their objects of study could easily turn into demonization. 'The outrage of German newspapers over the atrocities of the *turcos* is certainly a just one', declared one otherwise well-informed article by Heinrich von Maltzan in *Die Gartenlaube*:

> But whose fault is it that the atrocities of the *turcos* could be committed against Germans? None other than the French government, the most 'civilized nation' on earth. That the Kabyle are cruel by nature, that they martyr their prisoners to death through torture, that their women even compete in the dismemberment of the wounded and fire up their sons to do the same blood-work, the French know this from their Kabyle campaigns. That they use such blood-people in a European war should be a cause of shame.[382]

[376] Ibid.   [377] Ibid.   [378] Ibid.   [379] Ibid., 616.
[380] 'Ein Fuslier vom Regiment Nr. 64', ibid., vol. 39, 632–3.
[381] Ibid.   [382] H. v. Maltzan, 'Meine Turcos-Studien', ibid., vol. 52, 886.

Instead of controlling 'the wild instincts' of *turcos*, the French deliberately inflamed them by recounting 'the most shocking descriptions of the enemy' to these 'unknowing mercenaries'.[383]

However, earlier in the same article, Maltzan had spelled out that the term '*turco*', which was a diminutive of 'Turk' and which was not used by Arab soldiers because they knew that 'not a single Turk now serves in the corps or perhaps had ever served', encompassed a diverse range of groups including 'mixed races' of 'mulattoes' and 'Kuluglis': 'The name "turcos", which is now so often used, is by no means the true term for indigenous Algerian infantry soldiers.'[384] The detailed physiognomical sketches of different 'types' of *turcos*, which accompanied the article, made the same point, recalling the standard images of travel literature and ethnography. Like an earlier report on 'our opponents', which distinguished '*zouaves*' (four long-standing North African regiments and 'the best light infantry of the French army'), '*spahis*' ('a rather reputable troop' of 'indigenous Algerians'), '*chasseurs d'Afrique*' (a 'practised troop, trained under fire'), and '*zephyrs*' (a 'useless troop') from '*turcos*' themselves, Maltzan did not believe that there was a genuine military threat from such troops: 'May our fatherland also in future be protected from this plague, just as has happened until now thanks to the wise military leadership of the German commanders, keeping these wild hordes from German soil.'[385] Viewed 'objectively', it was 'incorrect' to fear 'this rather irregular rump of soldiers': 'This would initially call the bluff of inexperienced German fighters and would even impress them; for their experienced comrades, however, this will soon be exposed as tactical humbug, as a carnival of uniforms.'[386] French colonial troops had become the object of scare stories in the German press but they were also treated as harmless objects of curiosity, as they had been during the Crimean War. For *Kladderadatsch*, they were an object of pity, prodded violently into war by an overbearing (and cruder-looking) French military.[387]

Since the majority of journalists still wrote in the manner of military observers, what mattered most to them was the effectiveness of troops and the progress of the campaign. Colonial and irregular troops were, therefore, usually treated as an indictment of the French government, army, or population rather than a threat to regular warfare.[388] Some observers simply mocked them, labelling Garibaldi's forces—in Felix Dahn's words—'ridiculous'.[389] Others such as the war correspondent and writer of adventures Friedrich Gerstäcker likened *francs-tireurs* to North American 'Indians'.[390] Georg

---

[383] Ibid.   [384] Ibid., 884.

[385] Ibid., 886. Also, 'Unsere Gegner', ibid., vol. 33, 516–19.   [386] Ibid., vol. 33, 516.

[387] 'Aus dem Lande der Civilisation', *Kladderadatsch*, 7 Aug. 1870, vol. 23, no. 36.

[388] This does mean that the press did not voice doubts about an army underestimation of the impact of *francs-tireurs*. Nevertheless, many journalists backed the General Staff: 'Die französische Volksbewaffnung', *Grenzboten*, 1870, vol. 2, 76: 'One cannot doubt in Germany that the leaders of our army, with the self-confidence of career soldiers, underestimate the obstacles which an arming of the people can create.'

[389] F. Dahn, *Moltke als Erzieher. Allerlei Betrachtungen* (Breslau, 1892), 183. See F. Becker, *Bilder von Krieg und Nation*, 232–3. Johannes Scherr, *1870–1871. Vier Bücher deutscher Geschichte* (Leipzig, 1879), vol. 2, 399, called Garibaldi 'the red-shirted Don Quixote of the universal republic'. At the time, the *Allgemeine Zeitung*, 11 Sept. 1870, was one of several publications which pointed out that France's unruly population would not be able to match trained German armies.

[390] F. Gerstäcker, 'Die Franktireurs', in F. Gerstäcker, *Kriegsbilder. Erzählungen und Erinnerungen aus den Kriegsjahren 1870/71* (Leipzig, 1908), 7.

Horn, in an article about 'the victims of fanaticism' which investigated the killing of dragoons by *francs-tireurs* near Verdun, disseminated both the stereotype of irregulars as animals, descending on 'their prey' of two Prussian officers 'like a tiger on a noble savage', and as honourable soldiers, intervening to stop villagers—'cannibals'—killing two more of the dragoons, who were then allowed to return to the German side.[391] When Friedrich Karl sent one of his officers to find out about the 'terrible incident', he discovered that the two officers—'your brave comrades, mein Herr', as the commander of the *francs-tireurs* called them—had been 'buried with full military honours' in graves marked with wreaths.[392] By the end of the article, it was not clear whether Horn was distancing himself from the aspersion of 'fanaticism' altogether or was transferring his accusation from the *francs-tireurs* to the villagers. In either event, the dragoons had had a glorious 'soldier's death', 'dying whilst still fighting' (as the French commander put it).[393]

Such regular, meaningful deaths were acceptable to journalists—the necessary cost and the elevating element of a successful campaign—and they were represented as such, described in words as a pathos-laden 'falling' of comrades and sketched as individual, often imploring, bodies on a battlefield, as the fighting continued. Despite the grisly or anonymous circumstances of most soldiers' demise, death for the fatherland, even one which 'demands much' (in the words of a poem by Friedrich Hofmann), was an important component of a persisting cult of military heroism.[394] For the press, the death toll of 1870–1, like those of 1864 and 1866, did not warrant a shift of focus from the heroes of the conflict: both commanders, who were the subject of extensive reportage and portraiture, and ordinary soldiers, whose feats were recounted through anecdotes, continued to dominate journalists' accounts of the wars. One telling lithograph in the *Gartenlaube* from an original drawing by Wilhelm Camphausen showed 'Prince Friedrich Karl, Commander of the Second Army', galloping at speed across a battlefield alongside a staff officer.[395] His sideways look towards the viewer is contemplative and humane, barely paying attention to the forceful, magnificent forward movement of the horses and the other officer. He also pays no attention to the body of a dead French colonial soldier, lying on his back with his gun dropped beside him, over whom the prince's horse is jumping. Such deaths—of all soldiers, not just colonial ones—were a natural part of war. They rarely caused the press to question its purpose. For many combatants, the changing nature of soldiers' deaths—their own in prospect—did lead to a fundamental re-evaluation of modern warfare. The next chapters examine how, and to what extent, this re-evaluation took place.

[391] G. Horn, 'Opfer des Fanatismus', *Gartenlaube*, 1870, vol. 40, 668. It was common to point to the lawlessness of Gambetta, from Savoy. Gustav Freytag argued that the 'cruel and highly barbaric *Volkskrieg* as a republican means of salvation', which the French leader had unleashed, justified German reprisals: G. Freytag, *Auf der Höhe der Vogesen. Kriegsberichte von 1870/71* (Leipzig, 1914), 76.

[392] G. Horn, 'Opfer des Fanatismus', *Gartenlaube*, 1870, vol. 40, 668. Max von Eelking, *Der Krieg zwischen Deutschland und Frankreuch 1870 bis 1871* (Leipzig, 1871), 319, saw francs-tireurs as 'savages'.

[393] *Gartenlaube*, vol. 40, 668.

[394] F. Hofmann, 'Du forderst viel, o Vaterland!', ibid., 1871, vol. 3, 40. R. Schilling, *'Kriegshelden'. Deutungsmuster heroischer Männlichkeit in Deutschland 1813–1945* (Paderborn, 2002), 126–68.

[395] *Gartenlaube*, 1870, vol. 37, 601.

7

Blood in the Sand

Most of the Prussian and Austrian troops who went to war against Denmark in January 1864, after Berlin and Vienna had issued an ultimatum to Copenhagen on the 16th requiring it to revoke its common constitution, appear not to have questioned the justice and legitimacy of their cause. Despite opposition between the German Great Powers and the German Confederation, which led to a brief stand-off at Rendsburg between confederal and Prussian forces in July 1864, Prussia and Austria quickly became the widely accepted prosecutors of a national war.[1] Even a Hanoverian commander such as Georg Friedrich Ferdinand Dammers, who was posted to Holstein, acknowledged that the Confederation had demonstrated its 'short-sightedness' in leaving it to 'the German Great Powers to seize the Duchy of Schleswig from the Danes and, thus, to protect the rights of the duchies'.[2] He was dismayed by 'the inadequate organization of the German *Bund* and...the misplaced views in which many of the rulers of the middling and smaller states, including their ministers, were caught'.[3] 'The misused soldier' of the Confederation, 'down to the lowest ranks, soon felt the useless and humiliating role which he was forced to play, whereas the Austrians and Prussians gained honour and reputation through battle', Dammers continued.[4] The war was 'inevitable', given Denmark's actions, concurred the Saxon officer Gustav von Schubert, who like his Hanoverian counterpart was critical of the fact that the troops of the *Bund* had been 'condemned to look on', making 1864 'a time full of difficulties and conflicts' from the point of view of confederal commanders.[5] The *Mittelstaaten* had kept narrowly to the maintenance of the *Bund*'s competence in respect of the confederal state of Holstein, which was 'correct and theoretically right' but 'politically impractical', leading 'the two principal powers' simply to push 'the weak decision aside' and to dispatch 60,000 Prussians and Austrians to Holstein on 21 January: 'They proceeded past the *Bund* towards an independent military solution of the question.'[6] 'Remarkably, it was the oldest German national question from 1848, that of Schleswig-Holstein, out of which the long sought-after solution developed by the force of reality', Schubert noted: 'Prussia gave the impulse towards it.'[7] Although it was misleading to suggest that the conflict of 1864 was merely—or even largely—

---

[1] G. F. F. Dammers, *Erinnerungen und Erlebnisse* (Hanover, 1890), 79–80. See also E. v. Friesen, *Erlebnisse des Königlich-Sächsischen 13. Infanterie-Bataillons während der Bundesexekution in Holstein 1863–1864* (Dresden, n.d.).
[2] G. F. F. Dammers, *Erinnerungen*, 40.   [3] Ibid.   [4] Ibid., 42.
[5] G. v. Schubert, *Lebenserinnerungen*, ed. H. v. Schubert (Stuttgart, 1909), 175, 190.
[6] Ibid., 189.   [7] Ibid., 175.

a national one for the majority of mobilized soldiers, it was difficult to deny the war's broad popularity. Certainly, few if any troops voiced open opposition to it.

There were many reasons, in addition to national sentiment, why the fighting in Schleswig appeared tolerable to combatants in 1864. First, the romantic traditions of combat were firmly and widely entrenched by the 1860s. 'Children like to play soldiers', began one poem printed in a picture book at the time of the conflict with Denmark: 'The garden has to be their battlefield; / There, they carry out great acts of heroism, / And beat each other into submission with sticks.'[8] Soldiers, 'shining with the decoration of weapons', hurried to the battlefield, giving 'the enemy much to do' and fighting 'like heroes for the fatherland'.[9] Hopes of glory were common, extending from officers to ordinary soldiers such as 'Casper', a musketeer and former student in the 53rd Regiment of the Prussian army, who decided to publish his 'studies and sketches', not to write a 'military history of the glorious campaign in Schleswig-Holstein', but to provide 'his readers with a true insight into the colourful, animated life' of the troops.[10] 'You know my style of writing by now and I scarcely need to prepare you for what you will meet in these pages, apart from the naked facts', he wrote to his friend Joseph:

> mad dreamscapes, fantastic reflections, small hyperboles here and there, the colours painted thickly in places, statistical reports, learned treatises from the field of *Länder-* and *Völkerkunde* and *Kriegswissenschaft* etc.; and, then, perhaps I'll climb, to your irritation, on a soaring steed and give myself up to magnificent elegies and odes, with which I have so often annoyed you, you dried-up bookworm.[11]

There is evidence that many officers and men anticipated heroism and adventure rather than danger and death in 1864. This expectation helps to explain why 'a mood anything but pleasant reigned amongst these brave troops [of Hanover and Saxony], who would have much rather stormed the fortifications near Friedrichstadt than take up quarters in Altona', through which the Prussian and Austrian armies were moving in January 1864, wrote the journalist Gustav Rasch: 'They, too, could not understand why they should leave the honour of driving the Danes out of Schleswig to the Prussians and Austrians.'[12]

Second, the conflict between Prussia, Austria, and Denmark, all of which were held to be 'civilized' states, was—at least in theory—the first 'humanitarian' war.[13] After publishing *Un Souvenir de Solférino* in 1862, which gave an account of the horrors of the battlefield of 24 June 1859, Jean Henri Dunant had gone on to

[8] G. Holding, *Die Soldaten. Ein Bilderbuch mit Text* (Berlin, n.d.), 1.

[9] Ibid., 15. Leonard Heiners, from the Rhineland, recalled proudly that he had 'always had joy in using weapons': Leonard Heiners, 'Tagebuch und Erlebnisse', *Kriegsbriefe* Archive, Universitäts- und Landesbibliothek Bonn.

[10] Caspar Alexander von Honthumb, *Mein Tagebuch. Erinnerungen aus Schleswig-Holstein* (Münster, 1865), vi. The author was displayed simply as 'Casper' on the title page of the book.

[11] Ibid., 8.

[12] G. Rasch, *Vom verrathenen Bruderstamme. Der Krieg in Schleswig-Holstein im Jahre 1864* (Leipzig, 1864), vol. 1, 191.

[13] F. Loeffler, *General-Bericht über den Gesundheitsdienst im Feldzuge gegen Dänemark 1864* (Berlin, 1867); J. Zechmeister, *Die Schusswunden und die gegenwärtige Bewaffnung der Heere* (Munich, 1864).

found the International Committee for Relief to the Wounded—later becoming the Red Cross—in February 1863 with four other notables from Geneva. Its first conference in October of the same year had been attended by official delegates from Prussia, Austria, Bavaria, Saxony, Baden, and the Electorate of Hesse, as well as Russia, Britain, France, Italy, Spain, the Netherlands, Sweden, and Norway. Amongst other things, it had resolved to protect and guarantee the neutrality of wounded soldiers and to use volunteers, recognizable by the red cross on their white arm band, to provide relief on the battlefield. Dunant had completed a tour of Germany in 1863, meeting the Kings of Prussia and Saxony. When war broke out the following year, the committee sent an envoy, Louis Appia, to Prussian and Austrian headquarters, where he dined with Wrangel, talked to other commanders, and was allowed free access to the fighting front.[14] Prussian military doctors such as the Schleswig-born Friedrich von Esmarch, one of the founders of modern field surgery, were already renowned for their innovations in first aid, bandaging, prostheses, transport for the wounded, and the use of chloroform.[15] They had also encouraged religious associations—most famously, the Order of St John—to tend to soldiers in the field. Although the Danish authorities had been less welcoming of Charles van de Velde, the squeamish Dutch naval officer and explorer who had been dispatched by the International Committee to the Danish front, they were sceptical of the envoy in part because of confidence—which van de Velde labelled insularity and complacency—in their own capacities: 'If there was one thing that is certainly not desired', explained the doctor-in-chief Michael Djørup, 'it is foreign doctors', who would only cause 'delays because of their inadequate knowledge of Danish'.[16] Despite warnings of the impact of modern weaponry and a long and well-known history of the agony of the wounded in battle, it was hoped that the war between Denmark, Prussia, and Austria would be more humane than its European predecessors. No war, remarked Helmuth von Moltke, 'has ever been conducted with more humanity than this one'.[17]

Third, the majority of German onlookers expected the war to be short, limited in scope, and victorious.[18] Prussia's and Austria's ruling elites did not doubt that Germany's two Great Powers, with an initial field army of 61,626, would defeat a small state like Denmark, which had an opposing force of 38,828 at the first encounter at the *Danewerk*. The Prussian officer Franz von Ballestrem spoke for others when he gave a toast in Breslau prophesying that 'The war of the Prussian and Austrian

---

[14] T. Buk-Swienty, *Schlachtbank Düppel. Geschichte einer Schlacht* (Berlin, 2011), 83.

[15] Officers, at least, expected chloroform to be used and were now shocked when it was not available. See, for example, W. v. Gründorf, *The Danish Campaign of 1864: Recollections of an Austrian General Staff Officer* (Solihull, 2010), 23, on the wounding of the Prince of Württemberg at Oeversee: 'His heel-bone was shattered, and the head doctor of the Belgians had to work with very limited means in his personal first-aid kit to resection the bone, or in other words to saw out its splintered part. There was no chloroform, and Württemberg suffered excruciating pain.'

[16] Ibid., 82.

[17] M. Embree, *Bismarck's First War: The Campaign of Schleswig and Jutland, 1864* (Solihull, 2006), 42–3.

[18] This optimism extended to some, but not all, ordinary soldiers: Ike Küppershaus, 5 Apr. 1864, and Johann Meiswinkel, 15 Apr. 1864, *Kriegsbriefe* Archive, Universitäts- und Landesbibliothek Bonn, who hoped that 'the story comes to a good and quick end'.

allies against tiny Denmark can only be the prelude to a greater action which the Germans must be ready for at any time.'[19] In Vienna, Franz Joseph had told the commander of his forces, Ludwig Karl von Gablenz, to use the campaign to 'revive the old Radetzky spirit so as to raise the army's morale, which is still smarting from the defeat of 1859'.[20] In Berlin, all 'are more or less intoxicated and are urging war', wrote Bismarck's close friend Moritz von Blanckenburg in November 1863: 'the worst is the *furor militaris* which goes up to the *highest* circles'.[21] The Minister-President was seen initially as an opponent of war, reluctant to back the *Bund*'s execution in Holstein, yet he was merely anxious to avoid the wrong sort of war in support of the confederal candidate and Wilhelm I's university friend Augustenburg, who would become 'one more grand duke in Germany' and, 'fearful for his new sovereignty', would vote 'against Prussia in the Confederation'.[22] In fact, 'I am prepared for war and revolution combined', Bismarck explained in December 1863 to his ambassador in Paris Robert von der Goltz, who had been encouraging the King of Prussia to back the stance of the *Bund* and German 'public opinion': 'Nor am I the slightest bit afraid of war; on the contrary, I am also indifferent to revolutionary or conservative, as I am to all mere words. You will perhaps very soon be persuaded that war forms part of my programme, too.'[23] His confidence rested on an assessment of the feasibility of a war against Denmark by Helmuth von Moltke, Chief of the General Staff, which he had requested ten days after becoming Minister-President of Prussia on 22 January 1862.[24] Moltke, the son of a lieutenant-general in the Danish army, had estimated that two Prussian divisions, giving a numerical superiority of over 50 per cent, could attack the ancient earthwork defences of the *Danewerk*, on the border between Holstein and Schleswig, from both flanks, before moving northwards to encircle the fortifications of Düppel and the fortress of Fredericia, which protected the islands of Alsen and Fünen and, therefore, the route to Seeland and Copenhagen (see Map 4). Unlike in 1848–50, frontal attacks were to be avoided and gains were to be consolidated, with the whole of Jutland to be seized as a bargaining chip in later peace negotiations. The basis of Prussia's superiority was its numerical advantage, the rapid mobilization of troops, and its decision to carry out a campaign in winter, when frozen coastal waters would limit the effectiveness of the Danish navy.[25] The details of the assessment were kept secret, the work of a relatively obscure, technical organization within the bureaucracy of the Prussian army. Few officers or men, however, seem to have questioned the likelihood of a successful outcome in 1864, possibly without fighting. Wilhelm Steinkamp, a conscript from the village of Varl in Westphalia, was typical

---

[19] W. v. Gründorf, *The Danish Campaign of 1864*, 11. Karl August Kraft zu Hohenlohe-Ingelfingen, *Aus meinem Leben*, 7th edn (Berlin, 1906), vol. 3, 80, wrote retrospectively that 'It was a great good fortune for the Prussian army that it could gather experiences and get rid of all its peacetime rust with impunity in this experimental campaign against an enemy which was not its equal, before it was called to critical struggles against powerful foes.'

[20] Cited in F. Herre, *Kaiser Franz Josef von Österreich* (Cologne, 1978), 196.

[21] K. A. Lerman, *Bismarck* (London, 2004), 100.

[22] Cited in L. Gall, *Bismarck: The White Revolutionary* (London, 1986), vol. 1, 246.

[23] Ibid., 247.   [24] E. Kessel, *Moltke* (Stuttgart, 1957), 359.

[25] A. Bucholz, *Moltke and the German Wars, 1864–1871* (Basingstoke, 2001), 78–9.

in reassuring his father, as his regiment made its way through Holstein in January, that 'all the people here say that not much will come of this war, and I don't think much will come of it either, which is why I am still in a good mood and I have been quite happy until now'.[26]

Not least because it was waged for the sake of a famous national cause and offered the prospect of a glorious victory after a long period of peace for the German states, with the exception of the Habsburg monarchy, Prussia's and Austria's war against Denmark proved popular amongst civilians and soldiers alike at the outset.[27] Even for critical military men like the radical Wilhelm Rüstow, writing from exile in Switzerland, the conflict was 'a holy national-German affair', ensuring 'that German peoples remain within the German *Volk*'.[28] Although he rejected the legitimist claims of Augustenburg ('the Prince of Dolzig') and denied the king's assertion that '"his own idea" of reorganization [of the military] would place Prussia at the summit of the greats', he conceded that Denmark was in the wrong and that the Hohenzollern and Habsburg monarchies had conducted a successful campaign with which he disagreed only in detail.[29] After an early setback at Missunde on 2 February, when Prince Friedrich Karl abandoned his attempt to capture the bridgehead across the Schlei, Austrian and Prussian battalions occupied the *Danewerk*, just to the west of the town of Schleswig on 6 February, only to find that it had been evacuated by Danish troops. The Austrians pursuing the retreating Danes, who were dropping back to the coastal fortification of Düppel, were engaged at Oeversee on the road to Flensburg (due north of Schleswig and south-west of Düppel), where they suffered heavy losses (seventy-seven dead, 309 wounded, and forty-five missing).[30] One attempt to push back Danish outposts at Düppel on 17 March had been indecisive, though occasioning Danish losses four times heavier than Prussian ones (126 killed, 217 wounded, and 303 prisoners against thirty-three Prussians killed and 105 wounded), and another attempt on 28 March had failed, after Danish troops had rallied. From the start, however, these reverses were overshadowed by steady Prussian and Austrian advances, with the invasion of Jutland on 6 March, the taking of Düppel on 18 April, and the forced evacuation of Fredericia on the 22nd. The island of Alsen, opposite Düppel, was occupied successfully on 29 June, after the lapsing of the first armistice on the 26th. By 14 July, the whole of Jutland—mainland Denmark—had been

---

[26] W. Steinkamp to his father, 10 Jan. 1864, in H.-U. Kammeier, 'Der Krieg gegen Dänemark 1864 in Briefen von Soldaten aus dem Kreis Lübbecke', *Zeitschrift der Gesellschaft für Schleswig-Holsteinische Geschichte*, 114 (1989), 75–6.

[27] For local views of the war, which became part of a public stock of images, see P. C. Henrici, *Lebenserinnerungen eines Schleswig-Holsteiners* (Stuttgart, 1897) and W. Frölich, *Vor vierzig Jahren* (Flensburg, 1904).

[28] W. Rüstow, *Der deutsch-dänische Krieg 1864 politisch-militärisch beschrieben* (Zurich, 1864), 62.

[29] Ibid., 62, 546.

[30] For a specifically Austrian perspective, see Anon, *Der Feldzug in Schlewsig im Jahre 1864* (Vienna, 1864); V. Grois, *Geschichte des k. k. Infanterie-Regimentes Nr. 14* (Linz, 1876); L. Pfaundler, *Heldenzüge der Mannschaft des k. k. 27 Infanterie Regiments König der Belgier aus dem Feldzüge 1864* (Vienna, 1864); K. Went v. Römö, *Ein Soldatenleben* (Vienna, 1904); F. v. Wiser, *Die Besetzung der nordfriesischen Inseln im Juli 1864* (Vienna, 1914); L. Schnayder, *Österreichisch-preussischer Krieg gegen Dänemark* (Vienna, 1865).

Map 4. Schleswig–Holstein in 1864

Source: M. Hewitson, *Nationalism in Germany, 1848–1866* (Basingstoke, 2010), 298.

conquered. Arguably, it was the apparently incremental and rapid nature of Prussia's and Austria's victory—after less than four months of fighting—that underlay the positive, if occasionally disapproving, accounts of non-combatants such as Rüstow. Whether combatants themselves continued to hold such positive views and recollections of the conflict, confronted with the transformation of modern warfare, is the subject of this chapter.

JUST WAR

In contrast to later conflicts, few soldiers seem to have gone to war in 1864 in a state of national fervour, even if they also conceived of the justice and aims of the conflict in national terms. Some officers, like Ballestrem, were grandiloquent or melodramatic, proclaiming that 'the blood we will spill on the northern fields will be the cement... [that] will bind the comradeship of the two armies [of Prussia and Austria] and thereby help them perform the difficult task awaiting them in the west'.[31] Others, like the Austrian captain in the General Staff Wilhelm von Gründorf, were professional or matter-of-fact, preoccupied with their immediate tasks (in his case, the transportation of Austrian troops to northern Germany).[32] Many officers were exhilarated at the prospect of military action after a long period of inactivity (in Prussia) or after defeat (Austria). The Prussian infantry captain Carl Bunge wrote of his departure from his posting on the Oder in Brandenburg:

> If one has already known the boring and monotonous life of officers in a small garrison, if one has experienced and seen how they are moved to activity and excitement in departing for a simple peacetime manoeuvre, then one can perhaps get a rough idea of the eagerness, excitement and jubilation which reigns at the announcement of mobilization, before marching out to their first serious clash of arms. On the 13th, great calls to muster were issued in order to check the entire armament of the mobile companies down to the smallest detail, and then we passed to taking leave. The hands of acquaintances and befriended burghers were shaken and the most wonderful promises were made amidst the warmest of jokes; we wanted to send captured *Danskis* to the farms, to lead Swedish bear hunters, who had become figures of fable in all the newspapers, by rings in their nose, and to carry out other atrocities. The married officers and non-commanding officers spent the evening with their wives and families, the young officers and soldiers took their leave of the young beauties of the little town and tried to stem the copiously-flowing tears of separation by means of pledges of eternal devotion and fine gifts; they tried to calm anxious moods with assurances that not every bullet hits its mark and with other grounds for comfort. Later, they met each other again over another glass of wine or beer and experienced their last evening in the garrison, which had become dear to them, in warm, friendly conversation with friends and acquaintances. We, too, sat deep into the night in the hotel together and remained with our civilian friends, who were envious of our excellent prospects, and we were happy, with our glasses of wine and good things. The conversation was lively and warm until we parted in the best of moods and each went back to his still camp to dream in his comfortable bed of icy winter nights, of hunger, thirst and every possible labour, but also of the rage of battle, of heroic acts, glory and honour![33]

On the next morning, the troops departed, 'surrounded and greeted by the entire population of the town and its environs' and followed down the road by a large crowd.[34]

---

[31] W. v. Gründorf, *The Danish Campaign*, 11.   [32] Ibid., 7–12.
[33] C. Bunge, *Aus meinem Kriegstagebuch. Erinnerungen an Schleswig-Holstein 1864* (Rathenow, n.d.), 5.
[34] Ibid., 5–6.

The men who went with officers such as Bunge were less likely to be motivated by the pent-up frustrations of peacetime and a burning desire for military honour. Nonetheless, they appear not to have resisted mobilization, as their predecessors had done in the Revolutionary and Napoleonic Wars. In the Hohenzollern monarchy, most—from an initial total of 39,304—were young conscripts or reservists. The ranks of Third Corps (Brandenburg) and Seventh (Westphalia) were not filled, with battalions of 729 instead of 1,002 men, in order to avoid calling up older *Landwehr* soldiers (between 24 and 29 years old).[35] In the Habsburg monarchy, a single corps (Sixth Corps) of 22,612 men was formed from brigades in Prague, Vienna, Hungary, and Bohemia, which were composed of professional and longer-serving recruits.[36] Because the contingents were made up of serving soldiers, there were few scenes of communities mustering for war. Conscripts received and accepted their marching orders, informing their families after the event by post in the manner of Wilhelm Steinkamp, who had gone from Minden to Hausberge, from where his regiment had taken the train to Harburg: 'We don't yet know where we shall be staying. If we don't stay the night in Harburg, we'll get a warm glass of beer and go on, for it is said that we should be spending a night in quarters in Hamburg, and then where they'll send us, we don't know.'[37] In Berlin with a guards regiment at the end of January 1864, Wilhelm Hafer, who worked on the Steinkamps' farm, noted laconically that his regiment was 'now on a war footing' and that 'we hope every day that we will be mobilized'.[38]

From their letters and diaries, it appears that such soldiers looked forward to the adventure of the campaign, grumbling about the cold rather than worrying about death. 'We want to ask God that it doesn't remain so cold or many of us will remain here', wrote Steinkamp in his first letter home.[39] 'We had to march 8–9 hours every day, Sunday and all', he complained in his second letter, nine days later: 'We just want to beg God that it doesn't become colder, otherwise we'll have to put up with a lot.'[40] For the rest, he seemed to enjoy being a long way from home—'we are now already 70 miles away from you'—and observing different lands: 'What I can tell you about Holstein is that the area here is not particularly good, there are many heaths and dunes, more than where you live, but the people here are all prosperous', not least because they paid less tax.[41] Having left their garrison town and 'familiar *Heimat*' behind to the 'happy notes of brave soldiers' songs', wrote another combatant, the troops were forced to march north 'for eight hours with a full war pack', which was 'really no trivial matter', before arriving at quarters for forty men with nowhere to lie ('forced to remain standing on a patch of ground') and with poor food ('something thin', 'something thick').[42] Yet the same men were marked out by their 'mad talk, stupid jokes and cunning combinations

[35] M. Embree, *Bismarck's First War*, 36.   [36] See Chapter 7.

[37] W. Steinkamp to his parents, 1 Jan. 1864, in H.-U. Kammeier, 'Der Krieg gegen Dänemark 1864' 74–5.

[38] W. Hafer, 26 Jan. 1864, ibid., 76.

[39] Ibid., 75. See also J. Meiswinkel to W. zum Hoff, 15 Apr. 1864, *Kriegsbriefe* Archive, Universitäts- und Landesbibliothek Bonn, complaining of sleeping in trenches of sodden earth.

[40] Ibid.   [41] Ibid.   [42] C. A. v. Honthumb, *Mein Tagebuch*, 11, 25, 37.

of reflections over the coming war', musing during their beer-filled stop-overs that 'we would find ourselves back in our *Heimat* as normal civilian people in 14 days at the most; it could not be otherwise—even the most stubborn only put forward the amendment that the affair might last 6 weeks, but they remained in a minority'.[43] Much of their free time was devoted to the concoction of fantastical, 'correspondingly regular war plans'—'naturally, one had to take Stockholm (probably the capital of Denmark) immediately or to attack Denmark at once from behind'—and to the visiting of some of the 'jewels in the rich crown of our native beauties of landscape' and to the 'ethnographic study' of the peoples of Holstein and Schleswig, 'their ways of life and homes'.[44] As they made their way to the front, such troops were not, for the most part, expecting the worst.

In many respects, the war against Denmark continued, as it unfolded, to conform to soldiers' earlier expectations. Despite the fears of diplomats and military commanders, the conflict did not escalate into a European conflagration. Bismarck's preference in December 1863 had not been openly to repudiate the London Protocol (1852), which had stipulated that Schleswig and Holstein would remain constitutionally independent of Denmark, either by occupying Schleswig militarily or by settling the succession question in Holstein peacefully through the *Bund* (probably in favour of Augustenburg); rather, he had preferred to 'proceed to act in order to enforce the fulfilment of Danish promises in 1852': 'That would mean a war with Denmark which ought to be carried out quickly and energetically; the other powers would have no right to interfere in it.'[45] Wilhelm I had been tempted to follow the *Bund* in installing Augustenburg in Holstein and he had been more concerned about the other powers, fearing the 'threat from France to occupy the Rhine provinces...and a war for the same in which neither England nor Russia could stand by us'.[46] Yet he was also convinced—in a letter of 22 November 1863 to Karl Alexander of Sachsen-Weimar, who was admittedly well disposed to the idea—that 'the Danish question would be an excellent area in which to demonstrate German unity', if Prussia's and Austria's hands were not already tied by the Protocol of 1852.[47]

By July 1864, the King of Prussia showed no sign that the outcome of the conflict was in doubt, merely cautioning against 'the drunkenness of victory' before the war—and, therefore, the risk of reverses—was over.[48] The Crown Prince, Friedrich Wilhelm (later Kaiser Friedrich III), who had been given joint command of the Prussian forces in order to circumvent the erratic and half-senile Wrangel, had written to Bismarck on 5 April, before the battle of Düppel, that, 'seen from the military standpoint, the existing number of troops seems to me

---

[43] Ibid., 11.   [44] Ibid., 12–13, 19–20.

[45] O. v. Bismarck, memorandum, Dec. 1863, in J. Penzler (ed.), *Kaiser- und Kanzler-Briefe. Briefwechsel zwischen Kaiser Wilhelm I. und Fürst Bismarck* (Leipzig, 1900), 50. See J. Steinberg, *Bismarck*, 210–17.

[46] Wilhelm I to Grand Duke Karl Alexander of Sachsen-Weimar, 22 Nov. 1863, in J. Schultze (ed.), *Kaiser Wilhelms I. Weimarer Briefe* (Stuttgart, 1924), vol. 2, 50.

[47] Ibid.   [48] Wilhelm I to Karl Alexander, 9 July 1864, ibid., 55.

adequate'.[49] What mattered was to deliver 'a final decision' and 'a decisive blow against the Danes', which they had long been in a position to do, in the Crown Prince's opinion, but which had been delayed by his cousin Prince Friedrich Karl, the commander of the First Prussian Army Corps and the person in charge of the troops at Düppel.[50] Major Hans Lothar von Schweinitz, whom Wilhelm I had made an aide of Friedrich Wilhelm in 1863 in a futile attempt to coax the Crown Prince away 'from the opposition camp', gave a good account of the decisive storming of Düppel on 18 April from his master's point of view, overlooking the battlefield:

> On 18 April, as is well-known, the well-prepared assault succeeded, at which I was a passive spectator; it was a wonderful feat of arms, in which all the great attributes of our officers and soldiers manifested themselves. Shortly before 10 o'clock, a long column of musicians under the lead of staff oboist Piefke made their way through the trenches to the foremost parallel; as the carefully regulated watches showed ten o'clock, the storm-march sounded, and our storm columns launched themselves at the five or six fortifications; in less than a quarter of an hour, our men were in them; it was a little over twenty minutes before 'Rolf Krake', from whose funnels a column of smoke still ascended, began firing. One scene, which stays with me, was of a Catholic army chaplain, Simon, who wrapped himself in his stole and moved forward immediately behind the storm-troopers.
>
> It was interesting, as the fortifications were taken, to observe our guests: Gablenz, von der Tann and the French military attaché Clermont-Tonnerre. The last could barely keep back his tears, so moved was he by the child-like obedience and heroic behaviour of our young men. Four Danish officers, who had been captured and brought in, looked on darkly and defiantly. Gablenz judged us correctly and made no secret of his favourable judgement later in Vienna; there, however, Graf Gondrecourt was given more attention, who explained... after his return from the Danish war that the Prussians were still in their infancy in the conduct of war.
>
> More important than what foreigners thought of us was the fact that we had gained greater trust in our own power; even if it was no great act of genius to drive out the Danes from a couple of earthworks with our Krupp cannon and Dreyse needle-guns after a couple of months of siege, the reputation of the position of Düppel and the domination of the Danes over the sea, which outflanked each position, made the feat of arms into a wonderful one, which had an effect on the mood of our people.[51]

From the distant observation point of commanders, it was obvious that Prussia and Austria would win, once the danger of escalation had passed.

The war was both offensive and local, taking place outside the territory of the German Confederation but within reach of Lübeck, Hamburg, and Berlin. Thus, as soon as victory at Düppel had been secured, Wilhelm I came by train from the

[49] Friedrich Wilhelm to O. v. Bismarck, 5 Apr. 1864, in G. Schuster (ed.), *Briefe, Reden und Erlasse des Kaisers und Königs Friedrich III.* (Berlin, 1907), 129. On the transfer of command, which remained secret, see W. v. Schweinitz (ed.), *Denkwürdigkeiten des Botschafters General v. Schweinitz* (Berlin, 1927), vol. 1, 164.

[50] G. Schuster (ed.), *Briefe, Reden und Erlasse des Kaisers und Königs Friedrich III.*, 129.

[51] W. v. Schweinitz (ed.), *Denkwürdigkeiten*, 167.

capital 'to the scene of the war in order to greet his troops', recorded Schweinitz.[52] As Bunge recalled, 'our jubilation was spurred on most by the news that our most gracious king and lord himself wanted to come to us, visit us and express his highest gratitude in person'.[53] Having telegraphed in advance, the monarch arrived by train, which was still running to Flensburg in spite of the supposed 'horrors of war', and reviewed the troops on 21 and 22 April.[54] Officers and civilians travelled frequently between Berlin, Hamburg, and Schleswig-Holstein during 1864, with '38 wagons stuffed full of tourists', who had 'made the Düppel fortifications the goal of their various spring trips', coming from the south in April, according to one eyewitness.[55] Many visitors came to the site, 'foreign officers and tourists from all parts of heaven', wanting 'to catch a glimpse of the military activity now dominant there'.[56] They helped to give the impression that the troops, although fighting for victory in a foreign land (and, therefore, avoiding a fight for the survival of their own land), were close to home. During the armistice between 9 May and 26 June 1864, many soldiers enjoyed periods of leave in Prussia, Hamburg, Lübeck, and Kiel, as did the wounded and sick.[57] Although some ordinary soldiers felt to be far from their families, they remained in contact with them, writing regularly and reproving correspondents who failed to reply promptly.[58] They were in a land, as the journalist and author Theodor Fontane put it, which had 'the character of the northern German plain, of which it is a mere extension', albeit one also serving as a 'bridge between Scandinavia and Germany'.[59] For soldiers like Wilhelm Steinkamp, this familiarity of landscape, culture, and language only faded gradually into that of a foreign and enemy territory. In Holstein, 'people are very friendly to us', yet

> it is getting worse and worse as far as language is concerned and one can only understand it very badly here, and once we have gone on for a couple more days, we shall arrive at a place where people cross the street in their dozens to get out of our way.[60]

Unlike in the Revolutionary and Napoleonic Wars, Prussian soldiers did not feel that they had been left to their fate in a distant land. Unlike those in the first Schleswig war in 1848–50, they did not feel forgotten in a contiguous one.

The 'enemy' in the second Schleswig war, though unintelligible, was rarely demonized by combatants. In 'Danish' administrative centres such as Schleswig, 'Danes', 'Germans', and 'Schleswig-Holsteiner' were not easily distinguishable.

[52] Ibid.   [53] C. Bunge, *Aus meinem Kriegstagebuch*, 82.

[54] G. Rasch, *Vom verrathenen Bruderstamme*, vol. 2, 101–2.

[55] H. Mahler, *Über die Eider an den Alsensund. Blätter aus meinem Kriegstagebuch vom 1sten Februar bis zum 20sten April 1864* (Berlin, 1864), 243.

[56] C. Bunge, *Aus meinem Kriegstagebuch*, 85. Also, E. Knorr, *Von Düppel bis zur Waffenruhe* (Hamburg, 1864), 141: 'Von allen Gauen Deutschlands strömte es nach Düppel.' Many allegedly gave up their habitual seaside holiday just to come to Düppel as a 'formal pilgrimage', to see the sites 'where so much blood was spilled'.

[57] For example, C. Bunge, *Kriegstagebuch*, 42–5.

[58] W. Steinkamp to his parents, 1 July 1864, in H.-U. Kammeier, 'Der Krieg gegen Dänemark 1864', 84.

[59] T. Fontane, *Der Schleswig-Holsteinische Krieg im Jahre 1864* (Berlin, 1866), 3–4.

[60] W. Steinkamp to his father, 10 Jan. 1864, in H.-U. Kammeier, 'Der Krieg gegen Dänemark 1864', 75.

Initially, many inhabitants of the duchies had been suspicious of Prussian and Austrian troops as a consequence of their earlier 'betrayal' in 1848.[61] Such suspicions were replaced by broad support for the 'German' troops, as they began to 'free'—in the words of most soldiers' accounts—the towns of Schleswig.[62] As they entered Eckernförde, on the road between Kiel and Schleswig, at 2.00 p.m. on 1 February—at the very start of the campaign—'all the houses were already decorated with German flags and those of Schleswig-Holstein', accompanied by the 'Schleswig-Holstein-Lied' and 'endless jubilation'.[63] A similar sight met Austrian troops as they arrived at the outskirts of the town of Schleswig on 6 February.[64] In the 'liberated city', 'all the Danish officials had been chased out in the first twenty-four hours, when the Danes had left the town'.[65] Those who remained, however, were not unambiguously 'German', notwithstanding the fact that High German was widely used in the town and Low German had become preponderant in much of the surrounding area.[66] In Flensburg, which Prussian soldiers had entered at 7.00 a.m. on 7 February, civilians were not allowed to pursue 'Danes' or Danish-sympathizers (including German-speaking merchants who traded largely with Denmark), which meant that its mixed population remained in place.[67] The rural population of Schleswig, in particular, 'was never uniform', in Fontane's summation, 'and it is not so until the present day', leaving many soldiers confused about who was Danish and who was German.[68] Northern Schleswig was populated by 'Scandinavian elements by language and descent' and central and southern Schleswig by Angles, whose exodus for Britain had encouraged the influx of 'a mixture of Germans with Scandinavian elements', and by Frisians, whose seafaring life had made them quite different from their neighbours and had allowed the emergence of a separate language.[69] As the local writer and *Deichgraf* Adelbert von Baudissin pointed out, despite being in no doubt—as a noble, in contrast to many burghers and peasants—about his own identity as a 'German' and that of others as 'Danes', the differences separating the invading troops—especially the 'Styrians, Viennese, Italians, Hungarians and whatever else the sons of heroes might be called' in the Austrian army—from all inhabitants of Schleswig often seemed greater than those separating the inhabitants from each other.[70]

From the beginning of the campaign, the Prussian and Austrian soldiers' Danish enemy (*Feind*) did not seem alien. The term 'Danski', which was sometimes used, was neither demonic nor demeaning, referring merely to the Danish word for

---

[61] G. Rasch, *Vom verrathenen Bruderstamme*, vol. 1, 192; vol. 2, 212–36. The title of the volumes refers to this 'betrayal'. Rasch had been an officer in the army of Schleswig–Holstein in the first Schleswig war of 1848–50. See also A. v. Baudissin, *Schleswig-Holstein Meerumschlungen. Kriegs- und Friedensbilder aus dem Jahre 1864* (Stuttgart, 1865), 18.

[62] For instance, G. Rasch, *Vom verrathenen Bruderstamme*, vol. 2, 3, 46.　　[63] Ibid., 2.

[64] Ibid., 45. Also, W. v. Gründorf, *The Danish Campaign of 1864*, 19.

[65] Ibid., 46.　　[66] W. Carr, *Schleswig-Holstein, 1815–1848*, 61–73.

[67] Ibid.; J. Kühl, 'Die dänische Minderheit in Preußen und im Deutschen Reich 1864–1914', in H. H. Hahn and P. Kunze (eds), *Nationale Minderheiten und Staatliche Minderheitenpolitik in Deutschland im 19. Jahrhundert* (Berlin, 1999), 121–5.

[68] T. Fontane, *Der Schleswig-Holsteinische Krieg*, 8.　　[69] Ibid., 8–12.

[70] A. v. Baudissin, *Schleswig-Holstein Meerumschlungen*, 20.

Denmark. It tended to be used early on in the conflict and was compatible with sympathy or pity, as the ex-Habsburg, Prussian officer Carl Gottfried von Jena revealed on 27 January 1864 in a letter home:

> At the end of this month, we are going to move to the Eider and we shall see, then, what *Danski* intends to do, and whether or not he will defend himself. It is abomin-able, but everyone believes it here, that we shall attack and then the Danes, who earlier did not want at all to give ground, will immediately retreat, so that the entire history will become a *coup de théatre*. I don't know at all whether that can be believed, but it is a fact that neither hope of victory nor courage for a fight predominates over there, and yet the government, which has no desire—even less than the soldiers—for war, will not give in, if only out of fear of the mob in Copenhagen.[71]

Although few Prussian or Austrian officers had served in the Danish military (Moltke was an exception), some Danish officers had served in a German army.[72] In the Danish ranks, there were a significant number of conscripts from southern Schleswig who sympathized with the Hohenzollern and Habsburg forces, as Antonio Gallenga of *The Times* noted: 'They told me... that their hearts were with the Germans, and that it was very hard they should have to bear arms against their own friends and countrymen; that they should have to follow the standards of those very Danes against whom they fought fourteen years ago.'[73] Many recruits, he went on, would have 'gone over to Holstein' like their friends, 'only... they were not so sure that Schleswig might not remain Danish, after all, when they would find themselves banished from their homes during their lifetime'.[74] These and other Danish troops from Jutland and the islands were encountered mainly on reconnaissance sorties, in which observation was more common than engagement. 'The outposts were disturbed little by the Danes, who felt safe in their secure forti-fications and seemed not to want to undertake anything particular', recorded Bunge of Düppel during the siege.[75] His commanding officer, Jena (who, Bunge went on, had 'already taken part in the Italian campaign of 1859 as an Austrian officer'), was more antagonistic, writing to his family at one moment that the Danes were 'an infamous *Volk*', 'dumb, prejudiced, stubborn, swine-like, a mad nation', compared to the 'magnificent' Holsteiner and Schleswiger.[76] Yet even he admitted, on other occasions, that the Danes, 'who can only manage a little German', were 'completely calm and patient'.[77] As soldiers, the 'Danske' had withdrawn behind their fortifications and would 'defend themselves for as long as they could

---

[71] C. G. v. Jena, *Erinnerungen an einen Heimgegangenen. Briefe des vor den Düppeler Schanzen gefallenen Major von Jena waehrend des schleswig-holsteinischen Feldzuges an seine Familie* (Berlin, 1864), 18.

[72] For instance, Georg Daniel Gerlach, who became commander after the dismissal of Christian Julius de Meza, had served in Holstein's army during the Napoleonic Wars. De Meza himself had travelled widely, undertaking study trips to the Rhineland, France, Italy, and the Netherlands in the 1820s. Branches of the Moltke and Bülow families were also represented in the Danish army hierarchy.

[73] A. Gallenga, *The Invasion of Denmark in 1864* (London, 1864), vol. 1, 105–6.

[74] Ibid.   [75] C. Bunge, *Aus meinem Kriegstagebuch*, 53.

[76] Ibid., 30. C. G. v. Jena, 22 Feb. 1864, *Erinnerungen an einen Heimgegangenen*, 43.

[77] 16 Feb. 1864, ibid., 35.

and then disappear in the night and fog', as they had done at the *Danewerk*.[78] Subject to conscription and four years of service, Danish soldiers seemed to many of their Prussian and Austrian counterparts quite similar to themselves. Given the imbalance of forces and the defensiveness of the Danish campaign, they were rarely objects of fear.[79] Even in the fiercest fighting at Düppel on 18 April, a far higher number of Danes surrendered and were taken prisoner (3,305) than were killed or wounded (882).

The war against Denmark was believed by combatants to be 'civilized'. Prince Friedrich Karl made good behaviour a matter of honour and Christianity, with 'modesty and friendliness' constituting Christian conduct—'a good Christian cannot be a bad soldier'—and honouring the 'Prussian name'.[80] 'The honour of Prussian arms—permit it to be said—consists in being victorious, but also to pardon the vanquished like a brother', the commander's declaration to his troops on 28 January 1864 continued: 'Prussia's name already has a good reputation amongst Danes. It is a fine thing when even our enemies respect us.'[81] Wrangel's proclamation to the people of Schleswig on 1 February likewise called on the inhabitants of the duchy to treat Prussian soldiers with 'friendship and hospitality', not least because they had come 'to protect your rights', yet it also emphasized the rule of law:

> This administration will be undertaken by civil commissioners of the two powers. I call upon you to pay obedience to their orders, and to support them in their efforts for the maintenance of legal and settled conditions. The laws of the country remain valid so far as the security of the troops does not indispensably require momentary and passing exceptions.[82]

An erratic and hardened old veteran like Wrangel did not always keep to his word, partly because he was not bound by international law. The first international codification of the conduct of war took place at Geneva during the conflict itself, ending with the signature of the Geneva Convention on 22 August 1864 by twelve states including Denmark and Prussia (without Austria), yet it only covered care for the wounded on the battlefield by medics and stretcher-bearers, all of whom were to be treated as neutral civilians, not military enemies.[83] Treaties regulating the taking of prisoners, the definition and treatment of civilians, the use and proscription of specified weapons and shells (for instance, projectiles fashioned from soft metals causing maximum harm), and the general conduct of war did not come into existence until the two Hague Conventions of 1899 and 1907. This lack of binding international laws had allowed Wrangel to threaten disproportionate reprisals in May 1848 if the Danish admiralty were to attack the Baltic coast of Prussia. 'My name stands as a guarantee that it would happen', he wrote to

---

[78] 9 Mar. 1864, ibid., 58.

[79] Ike Küppershaus, 5 Apr. 1864, *Kriegsbriefe* Archive, Universitäts- und Landesbibliothek Bonn, was one of many to sympathize with 'the Dane', who had 'lost terribly'.

[80] Prince Friedrich Karl, *Denkwürdigkeiten aus meinem Leben*, 8th edn (Stuttgart, 1910), 282.

[81] Ibid.   [82] Cited in M. Embree, *Bismarck's First War*, 45–6.

[83] J. Ganschow, 'Kriegsvölkerrechtliche Aspekte', in J. Ganschow, O. Haselhorst, and M. Ohnezeit (eds), *Der deutsch-dänische Krieg 1864* (Graz, 2013), 181.

Vice-Admiral Steen Andersen Bille in a typical inversion of the notion of honour and reputation, 'that for every house which the Danish navy shoots into flames on the German coast, a village in Jutland will burn'.[84] Sixteen years later, the substance of Wrangel's reference to 'momentary and passing exceptions' to the validity of 'the laws of the country' became clear as the Prussian commander allowed the taking of supplies and arrested Danish representatives in the assembly of *Hardesvögten* (parish stewards) after they refused to urge unwilling farmers to comply with requisitioning.[85]

The Prussian, Austrian, and Danish armies were constrained by conventions and their own articles of war in the absence of international treaties.[86] According to the influential Heidelberg constitutional lawyer Johann Caspar Bluntschli, 'private law' (*das Privatrecht*)—including provisions concerning property—continued to obtain during wartime, whereas 'public law' (*das öffentliche Recht*) was subject to the enmity of states and replaced by the laws of war: 'As a rule, war is a legal dispute between states-as-warring-parties over public law.'[87] 'Private property is to be respected in war by the victorious power and may only be injured as a consequence of military necessity', he went on.[88] As Wrangel had demonstrated, this exception permitted all manner of injuries. Similarly, Bluntschli's distinction between individuals, who—as private persons—were not to be treated as enemies but who as citizens participated in the inimical relations of their states, begged questions about how civilians were to be treated once they began to help the soldiers of their own side or to fail to cooperate with the military authorities or the regime of occupation.[89] More importantly, how were combatants to be treated? There were cases, as the journalist Heinrich Mahler reported, where 'embitterment led the Danes to infamy': for instance,

> individual groups of Danes put down their weapons and raised their hands, asking for mercy; then, however, as our people approached the prisoners in good faith, often with the intention of sharing their last piece of bread with them, they quickly seized their loaded weapons again in order to deliver a deadly salvo from close range.[90]

Since a 'damning verdict' would be given by the 'existing laws of war of educated nations', the response of the Prussian *Jäger* to shoot them, though they had ceased once more to be combatants, was held to be justified.[91] The conduct of the Danish troops was compared to that of Algerian '*zouaves*', who had pretended to be dead

---

[84] Cited in T. Fontane, *Der Schleswig-Holsteinische Krieg im Jahre 1864*, 44.

[85] J. Ganschow, 'Kriegsvölkerrechtliche Aspekte', 184–5.

[86] J. C. Bluntschli, *Das moderne Völkerrecht der civilisierten Staten als Rechtsbuch dargestellt* (Nördlingen, 1866), 2, 6: this lack of treaties cast doubt on Bluntschli's entire case that 'international law (*Völkerrecht*) also binds the warring parties during wartime and limits them in the use of permitted means of violence', as well as his assertion that 'mere state interest does not in itself justify war'. Given the absence of treaties or means of enforcement, states were reliant on the adherence of the other party to domestic norms of warfare.

[87] J. Ganschow, 'Kriegsvölkerrechtliche Aspekte', 172; J. C. Bluntschli, *Das moderne Völkerrecht der civilisierten Staten als Rechtsbuch* dargestellt, 1.

[88] J. C. Bluntschli, *Das moderne Völkerrecht der civilisierten Staten*, 27.

[89] J. C. Bluntschli, *Die Bedeutung und die Fortschritte des modernen Völkerrechts* (Berlin, 1866), 46–7.

[90] H. Mahler, *Über die Eider an die Alsensund*, 183.   [91] Ibid.

only to rise again and shoot their enemy in the back. The subsequent decision of the Austrian soldiers to 'run them through with a bayonet, whether really dead or pretending', was likewise said by Mahler to be warranted.[92]

The question here, which paralleled the destruction of civilian targets such as the town of Sonderburg opposite Düppel, was how to respond to the contravention of implicit, often one-sided norms of combat and how to define and limit the over-riding military interests—or 'necessities'—of states. Was it true, as Mahler claimed, that 'any other warring nation would have turned Sonderburg into a pile of ash, if it had had the power to do so, as we did'?[93] Prussian and Austrian officers and men believed that such cases were rare and justified exceptions in a conflict in which 'the allied armies are determined to enforce the evacuation of the whole of Schleswig with all the means allowed in war', in Moltke's judgement.[94] After the taking of Düppel, he noted in his diary on 23 April 1864, the Westphalian troops had car-ried 'the Danish as well as their own wounded to the nearest field hospital, where all are treated equally carefully': 'There is scarcely a better disposed *Volk* than our soldiers.'[95] Although 'the Danes shoot until our people are right upon them' before asking for mercy, they were usually granted it, with '20, 50, 100 or, on the 18th [Düppel], 3,145 prisoners' taken, Moltke went on, concurring with Friedrich Karl's opinion that, 'when we are hand-to-hand, they kill only those at the front with their bayonets and take the others prisoner'.[96] Such commanders agreed with Mahler that 'we are conducting a humane war!'[97]

HEROISM AND VICTORY

The Prussian soldiers climb up the sand dune, a tangle of forms silhouetted against the dawn sky. A Prussian flag flaps at its summit, beside a still-lit, night-time bea-con, whose smoke merges with the luminescence behind. Below the dune, which is covered with struggling yet prevailing attackers, hundreds more soldiers descend from packed rowing boats, arriving at the shore, on the left of the picture. On the right, the Danes are huddled tightly together in the crater of their fortification, below the crest of the dune and the triumphant Prussians, desperately protruding their rifles outwards as their attackers overpower them. The lighting of the painting is romantic, from the gloom of the receding darkness at the bottom left of the canvas to the sun's rays obscured by smoke at its centre, behind the looming shape of the dune, which is itself illuminated by the flash of Prussian gunfire and the

---

[92] Ibid., 184.   [93] Ibid., 191.

[94] Cited in W. Vogel, *Entscheidung 1864* (Coblenz, 1987), 121–3. Ordinary soldiers such as Ike Küppershaus from the Rhineland, 5 Apr. 1864, *Kriegsbriefe* Archive, Universitäts- und Landesbibliothek Bonn, talked about 'shooting Sonderborg into flames' without further comment, as if it were entirely justified.

[95] H. v. Moltke, 'Der Deutsch-Dänische Krieg 1864', in *Kriege und Siege*, ed. R. Hoppenheit (Berlin, 1938), 269–70. F. Loeffler, *General-Bericht über den Gesundheitsdienst im Feldzuge gegen Dänemark 1864*, 55, stresses, with some indignation against doubters, that Danes and Prussians were treated in exactly the same way, once taken to field hospitals.

[96] Ibid.   [97] H. Mahler, *Über die Eider an den Alsensund*, 191.

flames of the beacon at the top right. The gaze of the viewer is led from the soldiers on the shore, who are below the standpoint of the onlooker, up the incline to the bugler, flag-bearer, and the leader of the assault. The scene is chaotic but meaning-ful, as the individual figures emerge from the natural landscape of the sea and a tree-lined bay and fade into the smoke-shrouded, 'civilized' form of a damaged building. The mood evoked by the depiction of 'The Storming of the Island of Alsen by the Prussians' (1866), which includes allusions to suffering and confu-sion, is one of hope and ultimate victory (see Figure 7.1).

Wilhelm Camphausen's painting replicated and reinforced the dominant Prussian and, to a lesser extent, Austrian narrative of the Danish campaign. A Rhinelander, Camphausen had made his name as an orthodox historical painter of Friedrich II and the wars of liberation.[98] In 1864, he had had direct, if limited, exposure to combat, having been commissioned by Prince Karl Anton von Hohenzollern on 11 April by telegram to attend and record the imminent storm-ing of the Danish fortifications at Düppel. He arrived just before the battle, having travelled by train via Hamburg to Flensburg. His principal contact was with the military headquarters of Friedrich Karl and the entourage of Karl Anton, with whom he enjoyed 'a wonderful feast of cold roast beef, anchovies, Holstein cheese and strong grog' on his arrival at the front.[99] As a painter, he was close enough to the fighting to be deeply affected by it, but distant enough to be shielded from its worst effects:

> The bare summit of the Spitzberg, which we climbed up, lies in front of the fortifica-tions and is completely exposed to enemy artillery fire. The Dane was polite enough today, too, and thus the repeated visits which we made in the following and last days before the assault became an undertaking quite without danger. From here we enjoyed the interesting spectacle of the bombardment in the closest proximity. In front of us lay the great earthworks of our side, in which the individual batteries with their use of continual fire could be seen magnificently. Today, in addition, colossal black columns of smoke climbed up behind the fortifications on Alsen terribly majestically to the heavens from farms which had been set on fire, a war-like landscape of the most mark-edly individual character. We then climbed down into the trenches and parallels, saw the powerfully constructed walls, which rose to double the height of a man in many places and which were reinforced with bundles of wood, earth-filled cylinders and blocks, strewn erratically there all over the place. While I was busy there with several pencil sketches, a battalion of 24thers moved past me, coming from their night duty, and I stared attentively at their bearded, weather-bronzed faces just as they, almost as wonderingly, gawped at my bandit-like appearance.[100]

Camphausen's illustrated account of his trip, which was published in 1865 as *Ein Maler auf dem Kriegsfelde*, was positive, presenting sketches of various episodes of the conflict: officers in a Flensburg hotel, a view of Düppel across the bay, an artil-leryman posing with his cannon, the transporting of prisoners, the exterior of a

[98] S. Parth, *Zwischen Bildbericht und Bildpropaganda*, 91–6.
[99] W. Camphausen, *Ein Maler auf dem Kriegsfelde* (Bielefeld, 1913), 7. The work was first pub-lished in 1865.
[100] Ibid., 13.

field hospital, the famous destroyed windmill in front of the Sonderburg bridge-head, the attacks on the fortifications of Düppel and Alsen, which became the oil painting of the following year. Camphausen's illustrations, like his paintings and those of contemporaries such as Richard Knötel, Emil Hünten, Georg Bleibtreu, and Louis Braun, combined the immediacy and realism of photography with the story-telling and plasticity of the historical school.[101] Thus, 'Düppel nach dem Sturm' (1867) shows a mass of soldiers in front of a fortification after battle in the form of a photographic group portrait, yet the image is not cold and flat like a photograph, even if the colours are deliberately muted. The figures are three-dimensional, filling the foreground—along with the shining hind legs of a horse—and drawing viewers into the picture from a point of view higher than the figures themselves, so that the centre of the crowd and its animated coteries of characters can be seen clearly.[102] The narrative which the painting relays after battle is the same as during it in 'Die Erstürmung der Insel Alsen': heroic soldiers triumph in a powerful, harmonious, collective effort.

Like many combatants, Camphausen gave a sanguine account of battle. When soldiers heard that the long-awaited assault on Düppel's fortifications would take place, it was 'all too understandable that our carefree conversation gave way to a more serious atmosphere', he wrote: 'In such moments, the easily inflamed fantasy of the artist is transported more than that of any other into stormy activity and it clothes in form and colour, in the inner eye, what to the layman, if also with the same strength of feeling, appears only as a formless idea.'[103] Camphausen, who had—'because of his artistic vocation'—looked eagerly through new and old war stories, was excited 'now to be led close to the immediate reality' of combat: 'In the premonition of the coming day, I was profoundly stimulated, and the most diverse observations and thoughts surged through my soul.'[104] His description of the scene 'out there in the world' was romantic and pathetic, with the night closing 'many hundreds of bright warriors' eyes for their last earthly sleep':

> Like ghosts of the night, the orders for the battalions' assault flew across the dark land and the work of death prepared itself noiselessly and expectantly with a light ghostly step. The great hour of reckoning for Prussia's youthful army, the greatest and most serious baptism of fire of the campaign, draws near. With the silent movement of wings, the angel of death—the earnest valkyrie—sweeps through this land, as in immemorial times, downwards, puts its head by the sleeping warrior and dedicates him with the breath of his kiss to the death of a hero... Then, the waking drum resonated in his ear, he sloughed off the lead shackles of sleep, seized his weapons and stood armed and firm in the ranks of his brothers.[105]

Near a battery about 4,000 paces from the Danish fortifications, 'we made our-selves comfortable and prepared ourselves for the coming spectacle', Camphausen

---

[101] F. Becker, *Bilder von Krieg und Nation*, 412–13; K. Ulshöfer, *Der Schlachtmaler Louis Braun 1836–1916* (Stuttgart, 1976).
[102] S. Parth, *Zwischen Bildbericht und Bildpropaganda*, 246–7.
[103] W. Camphausen, *Ein Maler auf dem Kriegsfelde*, 16.
[104] Ibid.   [105] Ibid., 16–17.

Figure 7.1 Wilhelm Camphausen, *Die Erstürmung der Insel Alsen durch die Preußen* (1866)
Source: Deutsches Historisches Museum, Berlin.

went on.[106] The trenches in front of the fortifications had been 'stuffed full of columns of storm-troopers, their bayonets glinting in the sun', followed by 'lively small-arms fire', which suddenly stopped at ten o'clock in the morning:

Then, suddenly, demonically, as if the earth was spewing them out, thousands jump out of the concealing trenches over the parapet, the storm flags are unfolded and already the whole, terrible yellow field is sown with attacking warriors! What a view! In the most feverish excitement, my heart beating strongly, I call to those standing around who are not armed with a telescope like me: 'there, now it's starting, storm-troopers everywhere!' . . . Not stopping, running at a racing pace, the brave ones storm forwards in a long, exhausted line; in a flash, the free space up to the fortifications is behind them, none of the famous obstacles is noticeable for us for more than a few seconds; now, those furthest forwards are to the wall, and they're going up—now—over forts 6, 4 or 1 . . . the hurrah of ours pierces the air, newly sent hordes attack more and more densely, the eye can distinguish individuals in the knot of people, how they push forwards, here with the bayonet, there with bundles of hay, leaders of the attack with small or big white sacks over their shoulders to fill the trenches or to prepare a path over hundreds of harrows pushed together with sharp iron spikes! Enraged, they greet the Dane with grenades, shrapnel, grapeshot and salvos of flint; fortifications and trenches spew out fire, but nowhere is the advancing wave halted! There, I see those who have been hit fall and remain lying motionless—others rise up again, collapse and waltz onto the yellow sand—still others, lightly wounded or perhaps with the death-lead

---

[106] Ibid., 17.

in their chest, drag themselves off slowly to the next field station... In the unbelievably short time of fifteen minutes, the widely known Sevastopol of the North fell to Prussian youth![107]

Camphausen hinted at the distance between commanders, to whom he was attached, and combatants.

To those outside Prussia and, to a lesser extent, Austria, the victory at Düppel had little resonance at the time, merely referred to by Ernst II of Saxe-Coburg-Gotha, who saw the conflict as part of the German question and who was on a diplomatic mission to Paris, as one of 'the successes at war of the German Great Powers', for instance.[108] To the Saxon officer in Holstein, Gustav von Schubert, the battle was one of a series of events in the more or less inevitable defeat of Denmark:

> After bloody fighting near Oberself, Oeversee and Veile, the Austrians under Field Marshal von Gablenz moved into Jutland, followed by the Prussian division of Mülbe, and they cornered the Danes at Fredericia, whilst the main Prussian army under Prince Friedrich Karl laid siege to the position of Düppel on the Sundewitt peninsula. It was stormed on 18 April, and on 29 April the Danes evacuated Fredericia voluntarily, after which the conclusion of a ceasefire was arrived at between the warring parties on 12 May for four, eventually six weeks. Since Danish diplomats did not want to submit to the stipulated terms of peace but rather still hoped in private—and in vain—for foreign support, hostilities began again on 26 June. Whilst the Austrian corps maintained the occupation of Jutland, the Prussians took the island of Alsen on 29 June, the last piece of German territory which remained in Danish hands. The invasion of the Danish island of Fünen was already planned by the allies, the German navy had already occupied the Frisian islands and the advanced guard of the Austrian corps had already reached the northern spit of Jutland, when the Danes came to see the futility of a longer-lasting resistance.[109]

Liberals and other national-minded observers in the rest of Germany looked on the events of the war in the North with less detachment, but they, too, remained insulated from the effects of the fighting. 'After two months of the hard labour of war, victory was won yesterday by the Prussians over the Danes in Sundewitt', wrote one journalist from Württemberg in his diary: 'All ten fortifications of the enemy at Düppel, including the bridgehead to Sonderburg, are in German hands. The happy jubilation of victory courses throughout Germany, which is proud of its Prussian citizens, who overpowered the Danish bulwark courageously, in the face of death.'[110] For such onlookers, the campaign against Denmark fitted into a narrative of German unification. There was little, at this distance, to cause them to doubt the utility and glory of military action.

[107] Ibid., 18.
[108] Ernst II, *Aus meinem Leben und as meiner Zeit* (Berlin, 1892), vol. 3, 574.
[109] G. v. Schubert, *Lebenserinnerungen*, 191.
[110] Otto Rommel, 19 Apr. 1864, in Otto Rommel, *Aus dem politischen Tagebuch eines Süddeutschen 1863–1884. Festgabe zum hundertjährigen Jubiläum des Schwäbischen Merkurs* (Stuttgart, 1885), 10.

Hohenzollern and Habsburg commanders at the scene of the battle had a differ-ent view of events. From their perspective, the risks, dangers, and precariousness of combat were much more visible. Schweinitz, who had been assigned to the entou-rage of the Crown Prince, had marched against Fredericia and, then, having failed to take it, had returned to Düppel, where he witnessed 'the well-prepared assault' on 18 April as a 'passive spectator'.[111] From his vantage point on higher ground away from the fighting, he observed the columns of stormtroopers advancing to the Danish fortifications at 'running pace' and overcoming the enemy 'in less than a quarter of an hour'.[112] Prince Friedrich Karl, who was in overall command at Düppel, noted that 'the tension was great'.[113] Earlier, he had complained of 'the sickening over-agitation of my nerves': 'How everything rains down on me!... Danish cannon fire regularly woke me during the night... I was anxious for my soldiers, I had worries about all sorts of things in which, decidedly, I had to trust to luck.'[114] Once the fighting began, though, he became less apprehensive. 'Small, light blue clouds along the length of the communication trenches and the natter of Danish small arms fire showed that the assault had begun', to the music—the 'famous Yorck march' and the march from 'Margarete', which was 'so dear to my corps' from the manoeuvres of 1863—of four choirs, he went on: 'Our columns did not hurry, did not run, they raced forwards. Here, an eagerness to attack, an elan which can never have been more beautiful and which has probably never existed before, manifested itself here for the first time and then during the further course of the campaign.'[115]

The older officers were unable to keep up, 'so great' was the haste of ordinary soldiers.[116] To the prince, such eagerness was an indication 'that my principles of training stood the test brilliantly', awakening in 'the common man... a feeling of honour and self-confidence' and making him 'into so complete a soldier that he needs the example of his officers to a lesser extent than before'.[117] After training, 'the soldier must fight like a hero, because he is driven in such a way from within that he can do nothing else': 'This happened and was accompanied by the greatest effects.'[118] Even the armour-plated gunship 'Rolf Krake', which had seemed 'unpredictable' and 'haunting' to officers and men, lost its 'aura' after 18 April, becoming an object of mockery.[119] The commander's only regret, which meant—in Wrangel's words—that 'everyone rejoiced at the victory but not my prince', was that he had been unable to invade Alsen at the start of the campaign, which would have been more decisive and would have brought greater honour than besieging Düppel.[120] Despite his wariness of wasting soldiers' lives, Friedrich Karl's main concerns were personal and strategic. The Chief of the Military Cabinet, Edwin von Manteuffel had commented bluntly in early March that the commander's hesitation at Düppel might be seen as 'wise prudence and concern for soldiers' blood', if he were to act soon, rather than lack of

[111] W. v. Schweinitz (ed.), *Denkwürdigkeiten*, 166.　　[112] Ibid.
[113] W. Förster (ed.), *Prinz Friedrich Karl von Preußen. Denkwürdigkeiten aus seinem Leben* (Stuttgart, 1910), vol. 1, 343.
[114] Ibid., 327.　　[115] Ibid.　　[116] Ibid.　　[117] Ibid., 343.
[118] Ibid., 344.　　[119] Ibid.　　[120] Ibid., 345.

'decisiveness', which is what he was suspected of in Berlin.[121] Manteuffel did not believe that the prince's anxiety actually derived from a fear of spilling the blood of his troops. Correspondingly, Friedrich Karl made no reference in his memoirs to casualties. In July 1864, he recollected that 'the taking of Alsen has been achieved, with God's help, more easily—and with such little loss—than even the most sanguine could have expected'.[122] In spite of his 'nerves', he seems to have been affected little by the killing.

Combatants were much more profoundly affected by the violence of the battle on 18 April but they, too, were sometimes overwhelmed by the immediacy and excitement of it. Through the night and early morning, troops had moved forward through the trenches, where they awaited the signal to go over the parapet at ten o'clock. 'We had to wait here for four long hours' in 'the greatest calmness', conscious of 'the high, holy seriousness of the hour' and betraying 'a fresh, I might almost say, confident-of-victory tone', recalled Caspar Honthumb, who fought as an ordinary musketeer despite his university education:

> We were not remotely bored; the unceasing thunder of the guns, which increased from one minute to the next, the noise of the grenades, which apparently whistled by close to our heads, the thudding of the heavy cannon balls, which chased slowly on their majestic way high above us, leaving light traces of smoke behind them, as well as the entire setting, with its fantastic groups and scenes, offered enough material for our entertainment; amidst all this, it also gave me pleasure to make physiognomic studies, with many faces standing out in which simple anticipation, quiet resignation, happy hopes of victory or even a wild, craving lust for battle was etched.[123]

After receiving absolution from the chaplain, the soldiers—with 'many eyes tearful' and with 'thoughts of mortality and eternity' in mind—heard the call 'Vorwärts' coming along the line.[124] From that point onwards, soldiers' responses were more or less automatic or, at least, reactive:

> In short, 1st Company had climbed over the trench wall, and if many had already sunk, hit, in the thick hail of bullets which immediately burst forth from all fortifications and earthworks, the forwards movement of our brave leader had coursed through the masses like an electric spark, and with these words, with this field cry, 'forwards', 'keep going forwards', which resounded from mouth to mouth through the ranks, confident of victory, they continued irresistibly to advance. At one moment, the company lay on the ground from exhaustion, but it was only a moment; the powerful cry of 'forwards' revived the ranks and they again advanced further, unstoppable; the task which had been allotted to the company was forgotten—one look at the terrain before them sufficed, and each comprehended with the right instincts, as similarly trained strategists, what needed to be done—solely and correctly—in the circumstances obtaining, and it only took a few minutes for that, which everyone understood so correctly, to be carried out—Fort 3 belonged to us![125]

---

[121] E. v. Manteuffel to Friedrich Karl, 10 Mar. 1864, ibid., 317.
[122] Friedrich Karl to Graf von der Groeben, 20 July 1864, ibid., 359.
[123] C. A. v. Honthumb, *Mein Tagebuch*, 83.
[124] Ibid., 84–5. [125] Ibid., 85–6.

The action itself preoccupied many, as another ordinary Prussian soldier, participating in the attack on 'Fort 5', testified:

> Those at the front had to give way. But more and more pushed on from behind so that crest of the parapet was eventually reached. Now, the most fervent, terrible battle took place—man against man. Bayonets clashed against each other, mighty thrusts and strikes were delivered, to which were added curses, cries and fighting, the sighing of those hit, the natter of guns and the crack of exploding shells.[126]

'It would have been terrible', the same soldier continued, 'if every individual had not been in a state of the greatest excitement.'[127] Yet they were in such a state.

Individual bravery seemed to matter in the war against Denmark, where the number of combatants involved was small and single actions made a difference. At Düppel, the circumstances surrounding the fall of each fort—there were ten—appeared crucial. The journalist Heinrich Mahler, who witnessed the battle, recounted how a young officer from a Westphalian battalion (13th and 53rd Regiments) had reacted angrily to the suggestion that the Danes in Fort 10 had capitulated without a fight. His unit, too, had experienced 'solemn hours' before the fighting, asking themselves 'how many comrades, who were now animated and healthy, would be no longer on the next day?'[128] 'Yet we were all convinced of the great victory which would be won by Prussian arms', he went on: 'Our sole desire was to pass the test worthily.'[129] The following morning, when the battle began, 'Danish guns pounded, bringing destruction', but 'we had only one sentiment, as death hollered around us: we wanted to go over!'[130] The 'walls which had defied us for so long and so often' were climbed in an instant, with a cry of 'Hurrah', and the cannon, 'which had also spewed deadly fire on our ranks', was 'entirely ours', and 'many prisoners with them': '18 April was a day of victory for our battalion, too, although it had also cost us heavy casualties.'[131]

At the other end of the line of fortifications on the other coast, between Forts 1 and 2, another junior officer—Carl Bunge—gave a similar account, whilst also admitting that the disorder of the battle and 'the thunder of the guns could scarcely be borne any longer'.[132] Prior to the fighting, the majority of troops had purportedly wanted 'to help to win new laurels for the precious flag':

> Every one of us knew that the thoughts and best wishes of our beloved king and commander were with us, that his blessing as well as that of the beloved fatherland accompanied us. Should such feelings, accompanied by thoughts of the glory of our fathers, of the earlier acts of heroism of the army, not awake enthusiasm in every soldier's breast, not elicit the most loyal and keenest fulfilment of one's duty and the strictest imitation?[133]

---

[126] J. Bubbe, a common soldier in the 24th Regiment, cited in T. Buk-Swienty, *Schlachtbank Düppel*, 258.

[127] Ibid.

[128] H. Mahler, *Wieder in den Krieg. Blätter aus meinem Kriegstagebuche vom 29sten bis zum 1sten August 1864* (Berlin, 1864), 18.

[129] Ibid.   [130] Ibid.   [131] Ibid., 18–19.

[132] C. Bunge, *Aus meinem Kriegstagebuch*, 77.   [133] Ibid.

At 10.00 a.m., as the Prussian guns fell silent, Bunge watched as 'the front ranks of the assault column rushed over the parapet and disappeared on the enemy side', pushing forward 'to be able to follow the brave ones'.[134] When his own regiment 'threw themselves into battle', 'the Danes fired too high, in the first excitement, so that the assault column ran under the fire and arrived almost without loss at the foot of the fortification, where a frenzied struggle began, man against man'.[135] In the carnage of the next few minutes, 'we could not care for the poorest ones' because 'everything was moving forwards with the speed of the wind into the terrible noise, to which was now added the thunder of Danish guns again, which spewed out full rounds of grapeshot deafeningly on the attackers'.[136] However, the rapidity, brevity, and mobility of the action appeared to prevent it from becoming overwhelming, as its heroic purpose was re-established: 'A terrible chaos was all around us, but only for a short span of time, as the first black-and-white flag already fluttered in front of us on the fort, hailed by us with a thunderous "hurrah".'[137] By 11.30 a.m., all ten forts lay 'in our hands', with the 8th Regimental Music Corps blasting out 'Nun danket alle Gott' on the orders of Friedrich Karl from the top of Fort 4.[138] Although the 'most violent fighting' continued, 'this powerful choral music at this moment and in this setting, between dead and wounded, amidst the heavy fire of artillery and guns,... made a strong impression and few eyes stayed dry', Bunge concluded: 'Whoever had lived through this overpowering moment will keep it in thankful memory for his whole life.'[139] Individuals such as Bunge felt that they had derived a personal honour from a collective—regimental and patriotic—enterprise. They were not mere cogs in a military machine.

The romance of the Danish war was connected to a cult of heroes. 'The Red Prince' Friedrich Karl, whose epithet came from the red hussars' uniform which he always wore, and 'Papa' Wrangel, who was almost 80 years old, were unlikely objects of adoration. The former was just 36 years old, appointed lieutenant-general in 1856 and commander of the 3rd Brandenburg Army Corps in 1860. He had retreated after a day's indecisive fighting at Missunde at the start of the campaign, for fear of being defeated outright, and he had been 'heavily criticized' by Manteuffel and others in Berlin for prevaricating in March and April at Düppel: 'It is said that Your Majesty had no independent opinion about what should be done', wrote the Chief of the Military Cabinet in May 1864.[140] The latter—Wrangel—had received the Iron Cross in the Napoleonic Wars and had gone on to carry out the successful crushing of the revolution in Berlin in 1848 and the unsuccessful war against Denmark in 1848–9. By 1864, Wrangel was incapable of command, saying 'Nein' systematically to all his staff officers save his favourite Major Gustav von Stiehle and insisting 'that neither reading nor writing should take place during wartime', which would have rendered the planning of a major campaign impossible, if the order had been brought into effect.[141] Both he and Friedrich

---

[134] Ibid.   [135] Ibid., 78.   [136] Ibid.
[137] Ibid.   [138] Ibid., 79.   [139] Ibid.
[140] E. v. Manteuffel to Friedrich Karl, 10 May 1864, in W. Förster (ed.), *Prinz Friedrich Karl von Preußen*, vol. 1, 306.
[141] F. v. Wrangel, cited in T. Buk-Swienty, *Schlachtbank Düppel*, 167.

Karl quickly became heroes in 1864 to their men and to a wider public.[142] They were joined by Wilhelm I and Franz Joseph, as well as by Gablenz, the commander of the Austrian forces whose effect on his soldiers was said to be 'electrifying', and by other senior officers who were killed or injured.[143] Thus, when the 'god-like' Prussian (and former Austrian) officer Carl von Jena was severely injured during the siege of Düppel, the news 'hit the whole battalion like a muffled peal of thunder', turning 'bright joy at victory into profound and sincere mourning'.[144] When he died of the injury, the mourning became general.[145] In a similar fashion, after Prince Wilhelm of Württemberg had been 'dangerously wounded in the heel by a bullet from the last shot from a Dane lying in a ditch' at Oeversee, in Gründorf's description, the incident was treated in an heroic mode, with his injury deemed 'as dangerous as it was painful'.[146] Wilhelm's own report to his mother continued in the same vein, although admitting that he was not about to die: 'I am quiet and in a good mood, resigned to my fate. I know too well what stands before me to frighten myself about it.'[147] His postscript ran: 'The bravery of the regiment was indescribable.'[148] 'Never had a troop of soldiers fought more resiliently, courageously and enthusiastically than the "König der Belgier" regiment at Oeversee', he wrote to his unit.[149] His own bravery and that of his men were intimately intertwined.

The meaning of individuals' actions derived from a broader narrative. The fact that a war for Schleswig-Holstein was a popular public cause appears to have reassured many soldiers, casting their wartime experiences in a positive light at home. Even beyond Prussia and Austria, 'as the news of victory on the part of the allied armies arrived in quick succession, all internal disputes were forgotten and everyone was suddenly convinced that the spilled blood could mean nothing less than the complete and eternal liberation of the German duchies from the Danish yoke', wrote the Duke of Saxe-Coburg-Gotha: 'The question about whose advantage this occurred for retreated almost completely into the background.'[150] To many members of the reading public at home, the victory of one's state or of Germany mattered. For officers, the army, monarch, and state were usually merged, with the result that any campaign could easily come to seem like a struggle for the existence

---

[142] For example, H. Mahler, *Über die Eider an den Alsensund. Blätter aus meinem Kriegstagebuche vom 1sten Februar bis zum 20sten April 1864*, 193; C. Bunge, *Aus meinem Kriegstagebuch* (Berlin, 1864), 82.

[143] V. v. Baußnern, *Feldmarschall-Lieutenant v. Gablenz und der Deutsch-dänische Krieg in Schleswig-Holstein* (Hamburg, 1864), 41: 'Von Gablenz war fast an allen Punkten mitten unter den Kämpfern und wirkte nicht minder elektrisierend auf sie ein.' See also C. Junck, *Aus dem Leben des k. k. Generals der Cavallerie Ludwig Freiherrn von Gablenz* (Vienna, 1874); G. Rasch, *Vom verrathenen Bruderstamme*, vol. 2, 110–11.

[144] C. Bunge, *Aus meinem Kriegstagebuch*, 71. Jena himself expected to be written about in the newspapers: C. G. v. Jena, *Erinnerungen*, 36.

[145] G. Rasch, *Vom verrathenen Bruderstamme*, vol. 2, 65. For Friedrich Karl's reflections, see W. Förster (ed.), *Prinz Friedrich Karl von Preußen*, vol. 1, 341.

[146] W. v. Gründorf, *The Danish Campaign*, 23.

[147] Wilhelm v. Württemberg to his mother, 8 Feb. 1864, in A. Magirus, *Herzog Wilhelm von Württemberg, k. u. k. Feldzeugmeister. Ein Lebensbild* (Stuttgart, 1897), 155.

[148] Ibid.   [149] W. v. Württemberg, 23 Mar. 1864, ibid., 156.

[150] Ernst II, *Aus meinem Leben*, 560.

of everything which they valued, underpinned by a code of honour, duty, and self-sacrifice. As they awaited an order to attack on 18 April, most were thinking of a moment of 'decision', 'on which the life of thousands and the honour of the father-land depended', according to Emil Knorr, an officer and observer from Hamburg.[151] Wounded and facing death, they purportedly experienced 'joy over the victory' and the thought 'that the forts are ours!'[152] The glory and honour of their under-taking frequently appeared to be self-perpetuating. In January 1864, it had 'smelled like war', wrote Jena, 'and just as the scents of spring do everyone good, so these odours of war enliven every soldier's heart'.[153] 'Men feel themselves to be men', he continued in an affirmation not merely of his masculinity, but also of his position as an army officer.[154] His status depended on the recognition of a social and polit-ical hierarchy, with the majority of officers' accounts—like that of Knorr—returning to the role of monarch: thus, when Friedrich Karl 'seized the hand of the monarch to kiss it', 'the king withdrew it and embraced the prince in front of the troops'.[155] The commander, himself royal, was congratulated as the embodiment of the army by the king, with ordinary soldiers acting as witnesses. In addition, the officer's status was reinforced by wider society and his 'Heimat', from which 'there were many splendid proofs of participation and support', in Knorr's opinion.[156] Replying to messages of congratulation from notables at home, officers were able to reply that their battalions had 'stayed brave during the whole campaign in the old Prussian way and [had] distinguished themselves especially during the attack of 18 April'.[157] Many officers envisaged this communal effort as a broader national one, including Jena, who was famous for his 'audacious, noble, soldierly courage', longing for 'fresh action', rather than for his abstract reflections and ethical stances, as one fellow officer put it, after his death.[158] Even for Jena, the war was for Schleswig-Holstein, which would be a 'bite that I would willingly give to the beloved [Prussian and German] fatherland!'[159] For a large number of ordinary sol-diers, there is evidence that such concerns—though not irrelevant—were less significant.[160]

From their correspondence and other writings, it appears that such soldiers were much more matter-of-fact about their wartime exploits. Wilhelm Steinkamp sent his parents 'a description of our campaign and the storming of Düppel,...com-posed by a fusilier of the 15th Regiment', with the advice that 'instead of fusilier you just have to think of musketeer and instead of Bielefeld Minden', yet the rest of his correspondence was less poetic.[161] Four days before Düppel, he reported

---

[151] E. Knorr, *Von Düppel bis zur Waffenruhe* (Hamburg, 1864), 115.   [152] Ibid., 137.

[153] C. G. v. Jena to his sister, 25 Jan. 1864, in C. G. v. Jena, *Erinnerungen*, 17.

[154] Ibid.   [155] E. Knorr, *Von Düppel bis zur Waffenruhe*, 148.

[156] Ibid., 144.   [157] Ibid., 145.

[158] C. G. v. Jena, *Erinnerungen*, xviii.   [159] Ibid., 26.

[160] See, for instance, one sergeant's fond memory of his 'first German kiss', in a letter printed by the *Magdeburger Zeitung*, from a woman in Schleswig–Holstein in recognition of his defence of the duchies: Anon, *Soldatengeschichten, Anecdoten u. a. aus dem Schleswig-Holstein'schen Kriege* (Nordhausen, 1864), 16.

[161] W. Steinkamp to his parents, 6 June 1864, H.-U. Kammeier, 'Der Krieg gegen Dänemark 1864', 83.

simply that he had been on guard duty as trenches were dug: 'There, one is always in great danger, for nothing but the terrible roar of cannon shells, for our artillery shoots over us and the Dane fires at our artillery.'[162] He showed little interest in what had already happened or what was to follow: 'I don't know what will come of it.'[163] Three days earlier, Carl Holzmeier—from the same locality as the Steinkamps—had written from Düppel to his sister in a similar tone, predicting flatly that his regiment probably would not be needed for the attack on the fortifications but that it might be sent to Alsen, which 'would not be a pleasure either'.[164] What kept such soldiers fighting was not primarily a 'cause' or, even, the romance and adventure of war, but its routine and ineluctability, which were connected to the daily rounds of home: 'I am, thank God, still quite chipper and healthy . . . [God] has helped us until now and will do so again, if we ask him.'[165] Soldiers were often cold and sometimes hungry or unwell, yet they seem to have accepted their fate, rejoicing that their families, too, were 'still all alive and healthy', just as they were, which was 'also to marvel at, since we have stood a lot this winter'.[166]

Army life seems not merely to have been perceived as normal but to have provided combatants with a meaningful set of daily rituals and tasks. 'Soldierly and religious celebrations have always made a very particular impression on me', recalled Bunge during the siege of Düppel in late March:

> It is a beautiful feeling to see thousands of young, fresh, strong men in the midst of a wild life of war humbly bending down before their God. From a thousand lusty throats, the powerful choral rises up to heaven, accompanied by trumpets and trombones, and at the words of the cleric, during prayers and blessings, all these faces can be seen, battered and raw from punishments and the weather, firm and hard from the wild impressions of a life of war, from fighting and horror, listening earnestly and devoutly, with a silent tear running down many a weather-browned cheek. In a fine and elevating fashion, justice is done in our army to this religious feeling and it has a great and powerful effect on the rawest dispositions. Anyone who has seen and experienced the last post being played by all the musicians in a great Prussian camp on an evening, and then heard the evening blessing played by the music corps and seen all the officers and men returning from the front and saying evening prayer with uncovered heads, must have experienced an elevating impression which soothes one's innermost being. These effects on the spirit are especially powerful on those soldiers standing before the enemy, who must be ready at any moment to sacrifice their lives to their duty and loyalty, to make their reckoning with the world and come before the highest judge.[167]

It is difficult to separate the beliefs of the observer and the observed in such accounts. Nonetheless, it does appear that religious faith, military duty, a meaningful

---

[162] Ibid., 78–9.

[163] Ibid., 79. Friedrich Brauweiler wrote on 17 April 1864 from Schleswig to his parents, warning them that the impression at home that 'it would soon be done with the war' seemed false, from his own point of view: Friedrich Brauweiler, *Kriegsbriefe* Archive, Universitäts- und Landesbibliothek Bonn.

[164] W. Steinkamp to his parents, 6 June 1864, in H.-U. Kammeier, 'Der Krieg gegen Dänemark', 81.

[165] Ibid.   [166] W. Vahrenkamp to the Steinkamp family, 23 Mar. 1864, ibid., 78.

[167] C. Bunge, *Aus meinem Kriegstagebuch*, 56.

daily routine, and an unobjectionable political and national objective were frequently combined.

When troops went home during the ceasefire of the summer of 1864, they again 'thought of home and how far they must be there with the cereals, potatoes... etc.', only to have to return immediately to war, which they accepted without demur, as one unnamed, marching soldier put it to Mahler:

> 'To war again', it was said, and we had certainly got to know war. Many did not come back with us to our resting quarters, but rather found an eternal resting quarter, and many more of us will soon find theirs, whether in the water or perhaps in the earth. Is it a wonder, then, if nature appears more beautiful with its green hues and the song of its birds? Now, am I not right?[168]

To journalists like Mahler, 'the modest and thoroughly respectable conduct' of such conscripts was linked to their unquestioning loyalty and their 'high educational level', compared to soldiers in other armies.[169] However, the question of how these troops would react in a longer, more extensive, and more painful war remained unanswered. In this respect, the signs were not encouraging.

MURDEROUS HELL-FIRE

Prussia's and Austria's conflict with Denmark was modern, involving breech-loading needle-guns, new types of bullet and artillery shell, iron-clad steamships, railways, telegraphs, trenches, fortifications, and attrition, all of which had been used during the Crimean War.[170] The number of troops deployed was small, compared to previous and future European conflicts, but the way the war was fought had a long-term impact on many combatants. Much of Moltke's plan of 1862, which had been commissioned by Roon, had been put into effect by the start of the ceasefire on 12 May 1864—the rapid mobilization of a force larger than that of Denmark, the outflanking of the *Danewerk*, and the encirclement of Danish corps at Düppel and Fredericia—yet much of Jutland had not been occupied and the Danish government and army did not consider themselves defeated. During the

---

[168] H. Mahler, *Über die Eider an den Alsensund*, 32.   [169] Ibid., 21.

[170] Some authors such as Robert M. Epstein, 'Patterns of Change and Continuity in Nineteenth-Century Warfare', *Journal of Military History*, 56 (1992), 375–88, have contended that, 'although the mid-nineteenth century saw the advent of technological change regarding strategic deployment and communication on the one hand, and the introduction of new tactical weapons on the other, the operational conduct of warfare remained remarkably consistent with that of 1809–15. This was due to the similarity of the size of the forces committed to operations, their organization and structure.' The physical and psychological impact of technological changes, which is what concerns us here, was much greater, however. See, for instance, Gervase Phillips, 'Military Morality Transformed: Weapons and Soldiers on the Nineteenth-Century Battlefield', *Journal of Interdisciplinary History*, 41 (2011), 579. The debate about the impact of modern military technology and associated transformations of combat is an old one: M. Howard, *War in European History* (Oxford, 1976); J. Gooch, *Armies in Europe* (London, 1980); H. Strachan, *European Armies and the Conduct of War* (London, 1983); G. Wawro, *Warfare and Society in Europe, 1792–1914* (London, 2000). More specifically, see W. Wirtgen (ed.), *Das Zündnadelgewehr. Eine militärtechnische Revolution im 19. Jahrhundert* (Herford, 1991).

ceasefire, Wrangel had been replaced by Friedrich Karl as the commander-in-chief of the joint army and Moltke had been made the prince's Chief of Staff. The latter's recommendation was to take the rest of Jutland and to invade Alsen as soon as possible, annihilating the concentration of Danish forces through the use of every technological advantage available.[171] In the event, the full implementation of the Chief of Staff's plan was partly halted by the opposition of Gablenz, who feared that such conduct would prompt the intervention of other powers, and by the collapse of Danish resistance after the invasion of Alsen. Nevertheless, the use of artillery at Missunde, Düppel, and Fredericia and sharpshooters at Oeversee and elsewhere exposed soldiers to some of the effects of modern warfare.

Prussian and Austrian commanders in 1864 were more sensitive to the spilling of blood than their predecessors. The killing rates of the campaign were comparable to those of other wars, as Rüstow noted, furnishing a casualty rate of 10 per cent (197 dead out of 517 casualties overall) in the early fighting, 2 per cent at Missunde (thirty-three dead out of 195 casualties), and 15 per cent at Oeversee (710 casualties from 5,000 Austrian combatants), which was almost three times the average of previous conflicts.[172] At Düppel, the casualty rate of the fighting on 28 March was 4 per cent (187 from 5,000), which 'belonged to the lower figures', constituting an unprecedently 'tepid' instance of combat for Prussian troops.[173] On 18 April, 16,000 Prussian soldiers participated in 'serious fighting', with a reported 229 dying and 920 being wounded, or about 14 per cent.[174] Although the dead to wounded ratio of 1:4 was low for 'recent conditions, namely for a battle in which artillery played a major part on the Danish side', it was still high in historical perspective, helping to explain the nervousness of Prussian commanders.[175] The overall casualty rate for the war was low—3.8 per cent of the force overall were wounded and 1.2 per cent were killed, according to the Prussian chief medical officer—but it mattered less than the figures for specific battles.[176] Officers were more likely to suffer death or wounding than men.[177] Friedrich Karl admitted after his introduction to combat at Missunde that 'I felt for the first time in reality, before the racing cannon fire of a hundred cannon on each side, the complete weight of responsibility of my position, my conduct, and that I was the cause of blood flowing.'[178] In part, the effects of heavy artillery (grenades) had been direct, with 'a considerable influence on my nerves'.[179] In part, his responsibility for the deaths of others, without which war might still be considered 'a fine sport', wore him down.[180] Earlier, the prince had thought 'that it would be easy for me to

[171] A. Bucholz, *Moltke and the German Wars*, 85.

[172] W. Rüstow, *Der Krieg und seine Mittel*, 194, 201, 237–8.   [173] Ibid., 448.

[174] Ibid., 538. Michael Embree, *Bismarck's First War*, gives the higher figure, including officers, of 263 Prussian dead. F. Loeffler, *General-Bericht*, 3, gives the figure of 217 dead and 1,157 wounded.

[175] Ibid.   [176] F. Loeffler, *General-Bericht*, 4.   [177] Ibid.

[178] W. Förster (ed.), *Prinz Friedrich Karl von Preußen*, vol. 1, 287. This reputation had filtered down to the rank and file, with Friedrich Brauweiler, reporting on 17 April 1864, for example, that 'Prince Carl has said under 6 thousand men could be lost': *Kriegsbriefe* Archive, Universitäts- und Landesbibliothek Bonn.

[179] W. Förster (ed.), *Prinz Friedrich Karl von Preußen*, vol. 1, 288.

[180] Ibid.

bear the responsibility', but 'here, at the start, I found the exact opposite to be the case and almost collapsed under the burden'.[181] As the joint commanders met on 3 February to discuss how to take or circumvent the main fortification on Schleswig's border, Wrangel—an old-school veteran of the Napoleonic Wars—had stated that he wanted to storm the *Danewerk* without siege guns, which Gablenz had requested in order to reduce Prussian and Austria losses.[182]

Faced with their nominal commander's apparent indifference to casualties, Gablenz replied, 'supported by most of those present including myself [Friedrich Karl] giving signs of agreement, that this would mean sacrificing whole hecatombs of soldiers quite uselessly'.[183] The Austrian Field Marshal's stance corresponded to Moltke's original observation in his plan of December 1862 for the Prussian War Ministry, that 'a frontal assault on the fortified position before Schleswig could scarcely be successful, even with the bloodiest sacrifices'.[184] The attack 'decided on by Wrangel, the commander in chief, even though in an *ad hoc* council of war Gablenz had expressed his reservations', was considered as 'bordering on madness' by Gründorf, especially 'when it is understood that the land between us and the Danish defence line was a moor, only half frozen and covered with a foot of snow'.[185] As the Habsburg officer had recalled, 'Wrangel's order read, "In God's name let us go"', which failed to reassure Gablenz: '"It's a pity, a real pity that tomorrow I have to lead these brave troops to be butchered, with the feeling that half of them will be killed."'[186] In the event, Friedrich Karl's First Corps was ordered to cross the Schlei further east, so that it could outflank Danish forces near Schleswig, as Gablenz's Second Corps started to attack the *Danewerk* from the front, resulting in ninety-six deaths and 302 wounded on 3 February alone.[187] The premature evacuation of the fortifications by Danish troops on 5 February averted any stand-off between Wrangel and his commanders, yet the incident had demonstrated that they had different opinions about modern warfare and the incurring of casualties. If the Danes had not withdrawn from the *Danewerk* and 'if it had come to the assault ordered by Wrangel on 7 February, then thousands of our soldiers would have sacrificed their lives in vain', picked off by well-protected, large-calibre Danish guns which the thinly spread heavy artillery of the German forces would not have been able to counter, recorded the artillery officer Prince Karl August Kraft zu Hohenlohe-Ingelfingen.[188]

The deliberate avoidance of casualties—in order to reduce blood-letting rather than to save men as a military resource (which had been more typical of eighteenth-century warfare than of revolutionary and Napoleonic campaigns)—was novel, reflecting—in this form—officers' own changing sensibilities and their heightened awareness of the 'humanity' of the troops. For their part, ordinary soldiers, too, seemed to have become more sensitive to the violence of combat.

---

[181] Ibid., 287. [182] Ibid., 291. [183] Ibid., 292.
[184] H. v. Moltke, *Kriege und Siege*, ed. R. Hoppenheit (Berlin, 1938), 249.
[185] W. v. Gründorf, *The Danish Campaign of 1864*, 17.
[186] Ibid., 17–18. [187] M. Embree, *Bismarck's First War*, 58–81.
[188] K. A. Kraft zu Hohenlohe-Ingelfingen, *Aus meinem Leben*, vol. 3, 90.

This sensitivity appears to have had less to do with fear of hand-to-hand fighting, which was largely mentioned in passing, than with a more generalized anxiety about the perpetration and suffering of violence and death, which had been suppressed at the time and afterwards.[189] 'One has generally been inclined to underestimate the achievements of troops during the campaign of 1864', wrote one young infantryman in his memoirs: 'No great field of operations, always good provisions, nearly always with a numerical superiority in battle—in these circumstances, successes had to be achieved.'[190] Such judgements had often been made, continued the veteran, but 'I believe that, if the beer-swillers at the tavern tables had seen and experienced what was offered up to us..., they would be of a different opinion.'[191] As they waited during the night of 17 April for the attack on Düppel's fortifications the following day, the soldiers of the 24th Regiment watched the moonlight break through the thin, slowly moving cloud cover, noting the silence after the bell tolled midnight.[192] 'An unpleasant feeling came over us in this noiseless stillness, as befalls a sailor when he recognizes a sign of a nearing storm on the horizon and yet sees the wide-open sea flat and calm before him', wrote the same soldier.[193] The troops were moved forward, replacing their heavy helmets with a simple cap and their heavy packs with food rations for three days. They were given ammunition, bushels of straw to mitigate the penetration of water in the trenches at the front, and sacks to fill with sand and use as protection, if the attack stalled; 150 metres before the Danish fortifications, it was 'an eerie situation', the infantryman went on:

> The camp fires [of the Danes] flickered, dying and reigniting; in their uncertain light, shadows darted here and there between the stands of trees, at one moment gigantic, at another in the form of dwarfish, fragmented images; in addition, the call of a tawny owl from the boughs of a tree, like a warning cry for the enemy...Groups stand around together in animated discussion, disputing above all what the dawning day will bring. This is how the situation could be portrayed: the wolf lairs opposite us, the Caesar-like stakes, the barbed-wire barricades, the barbs and, furthermore, a wire fence to overcome, before we get to the fortifications.[194]

The same soldier looked on at the tear-stained face of an experienced, decorated sergeant: 'In his hand, he held the picture of his wife and child.'[195] Another soldier tried to comfort him: ' "Comrade, why are you losing yourself in dark thoughts?" '[196] Yet such words had no effect and 'could not reverse the movement of the brave soul's mood': 'He, who otherwise seemed so manly and unshockable, allowed himself to be led, without will, held by the hand of the well-meaning comrade.'[197] For some troops, waiting to go over the parapet, their fears became unbearable.

---

[189] T. Buk-Swienty, *Schlachtbank Düppel*, 259, cites a Danish corporal who claimed that 'most Prussians preferred to shoot at us from a certain distance' rather than to get involved in 'a sort of hand-fight', with 'bayonet fighting, butt blows, a confused mixture from gunshots, howling, shouting, death-sighs and plaintive cries'.

[190] J. Bubbe, *Ein Düppelstürmer 1864* (1913), cited ibid., 179.

[191] Ibid.   [192] Ibid., 243.   [193] Ibid., 244.

[194] Ibid., 245.   [195] Ibid.   [196] Ibid.   [197] Ibid.

The majority mastered their fear and moved forward in a mixture of excitement and panic. What they encountered during the assault had a profound effect. For some, like Caspar Honthumb, the conditions of combat were paralysing. After storming and taking Fort 3, 'the fire was not spent' and 'the call of "forwards" echoed through the ranks', prompting 'the braver ones to storm from fort to fort in wild, victorious jubilation, more and more audacious, more and more certain of victory and further and further forwards', and to take part 'in the often bitter fighting'.[198] Honthumb was swept forwards in the same movement, yet he quickly fell to the ground, having seen—in his words—'a tremor to the left and to the right': 'As clear as if it had just happened, this moment and the thoughts and experiences which I had then stand before my eyes now.'[199] He 'felt' that he had been wounded in the left hip, but he was not sure whether the bullet had 'grazed it or gone right in'.[200] When he realized that it was 'a rather insignificant glancing blow', he wanted to get up again and advance.[201] 'This attempt failed; I had no more strength to stand up, which I don't attribute to the injury—in itself, small— but largely to my previous endeavours and violent excitement.'[202] His situation, as a consequence, was 'disagreeable in the highest degree', exposed to a 'persistently violent rain of bullets' and surrounded by 'a great number of dead and wounded', whose 'moaning and groaning helped to make up the unpleasantness of his position'.[203] Worst of all, he was forced to watch 'inactively' as his comrades stormed the other forts, before eventually being moved by the sight of Danes retreating with impunity from the fort in front of him to re-enter the battle, 'since I could not forego the pleasure, thirsting for amusement', of sending all 'my bullets...towards the Danes'.[204] 'I can assure you', he wrote to his civilian friend, 'that I now experience as much pleasure in thinking about these manifold acts of killing as I would if I had saved as many human lives as I have now destroyed.'[205] This overpowering combination of emotions was further confused by the disgusting sight of the battlefield, visible as the fighting subsided in the afternoon: 'God, what a view! Wherever the eye looked, corpses; wherever the foot trod, blood. I will not further illuminate these sad groups, these painfully contorted faces, these glassy, broken eyes.'[206] He was only happy 'and first breathed in again' as he finally left 'this site of misery and devastation' at around four o'clock.[207] Few other combatants were completely overcome by their emotions during the fighting itself, to the point of lying motionless on the ground, but many recorded similar types of feeling. 'No one', recalled Honthumb, did not 'have a friend to mourn' after the battle of Düppel.[208] To such veterans, news of more fighting after the lapsing of the armistice in late June 1864 came as a 'message of terror'.[209]

The horror of combat at Düppel appears to have marked even those, like Carl Bunge, whose accounts of the campaign were positive. Thus, despite casting the battle overall in heroic terms, with himself caught up in the motion of the attack, the Prussian captain gave graphic descriptions of injury in the 'chaos' of the fighting,

---

[198] C. A. v. Honthumb, *Mein Tagebuch*, 86.   [199] Ibid., 87.   [200] Ibid.
[201] Ibid.   [202] Ibid.   [203] Ibid.   [204] Ibid., 87–8.   [205] Ibid., 88.
[206] Ibid., 89.   [207] Ibid.   [208] Ibid., 90.   [209] Ibid., 118.

suggesting that the sights and noises had made a deep impression (see Figure 7.2). As his regiment had climbed over the parapet of Fort 2, 'several people were more seriously or more lightly wounded'.[210] Regretting that he could not take care of such 'poor' soldiers as he advanced into the 'thunder of the Danish guns', he went on:

> The flank man of the regiment striding along beside me, a good and brave, very tall, lance corporal, was hit right on the parapet, so that I heard the bullet crunch through his teeth and, clamping his hand on his hurting mouth, he fell to the ground with a gurgling cry, whilst blood streamed out of his mouth and nose in a thick torrent.[211]

For their part, the Danish defenders were 'almost smashed to pieces', as one lieutenant in Fort 1 put it.[212] Many of the Danes attempted to escape, wrote one Prussian infantryman, but artillerymen refused, since they could not take their cannon with them, leaving 'no alternative but to defend their entrusted goods with their swords in their hands until they lay on the ground with their death wound in their chest, overpowered'.[213] On 18 April, 391 Danes were killed and 491 injured, with a further 646 recorded missing, compared to 263 Prussian dead and 909 wounded. The fighting was fiercest in and before Fort 4, where seventy Danish infantry had had time to assume their positions, protected by a further 140 soldiers firing from the trench connecting Forts 3 and 4.

The Prussians incurred 150 casualties, with one-third of the 1st Company of the 53rd Regiment dead or wounded within a few minutes, partly because one Prussian column—quickly followed by another—had mistakenly attacked Fort 3 instead of Fort 4, leaving the remaining Prussian troops exposed, as their commanding officer recounted:

> We had barely climbed over the wall of the parallel when two fell down wounded. Shells of grapeshot hit the earth on the right and left next to us. I was still about 100 paces from Fort IV as most of my men dropped down and said, completely out of breath: 'First a bit of rest, Herr Leutnant.' They protected themselves as well as they could with their sacks. I looked around at my section and realized that several of them already lay wounded or dead on the ground... When I saw that, I urged my men on. They sprang up again, some of them fell back over the so-called Caesar stakes. I also fell, and one of them called in dialect: 'Oh, God! Our lieutenant is also wounded.' Still, I showed them that I was alive. 'Bayonets on!', I shouted to them, and they understood that. 'Now, forwards, forwards,....', and a real storm roar resounded from all sides. Amidst this, the moaning and wailing of the wounded. Our 53rders pushed through four chopped-down palisades into the fort; I squeezed myself through two palisades, probably demolished by our artillery; I was scarcely through with my upper body when a shrapnel shell, lobbed from another fort, smashed the palisade next to me into pieces. A Dane stormed towards me from the side of the fort, thank God with his gun at an angle. I grabbed him by the throat, he let the gun fall and called for pardon. Whoever defended themselves and did not immediately allow themselves to be disarmed was killed... The Danish artillerymen lay dead on the cannon, officers and men.[214]

[210] C. Bunge, *Aus meinem Kriegstagebuch*, 78.   [211] Ibid.
[212] Cited in T. Buk-Swienty, *Schlachtbank Düppel*, 265.
[213] J. Bubbe, *Ein Düppelstürmer 1864*, cited ibid., 259.   [214] Ibid., 272–3.

Figure 7.2 Friedrich Brandt, *Düppeler Schanzen. Nach dem Sturm der preussischen Truppen am 18. April 1864* (1864)
Source: Private collection.

Danish reports suggested that the captain in charge of the fort had called on his troops to lay down their arms, but he was shot or clubbed to death by Prussian attackers.[215] The fighting had lasted for thirty minutes and it had run out of control, although Prussian reports tended to conceal the fact. Other forts, for instance Fort 5, were taken much more quickly—in five minutes—but with considerable loss of life (130 Prussian casualties). For many combatants, it was these brief instances of violence and death which stuck in their minds.

The sight, sound, and smell of soldiers being wounded, dying, and putrefying on the battlefield had been a common staple of the war literature of the Revolutionary

---

[215] Ibid., 273.

and Napoleonic Wars. Yet many earlier authors had also reacted in a matter-of-fact way to, or they had even joked about, such wounding and killing. These types of reaction were much less common by 1864, as a consequence of witnesses' changing sensibilities and the more destructive effect of modern weaponry. As one Prussian soldier put it, as he crossed the battlefield of Düppel, 'Just see what it looked like, here!'[216] 'Doctors and stretcher-bearers were busy putting the first dressings on the wounded and then carrying them off in ambulances and wagons', he continued: 'What misery and suffering converged there on such a small patch of earth. The dead, those fighting with death, lay everywhere, in the position in which they had fallen.'[217] One corpse pointed the soldier to heaven, after 'the enemy's lead' had 'bored through his forehead' without 'a drop of blood' or a 'single noise': 'Gently smiling, he lay on the ground, as if he wanted to show us how beautiful, how peaceful it was on high.'[218] Most of the dead bodies, though, reminded him of the finitude and suffering of life on earth. Four dead Danish soldiers, for instance, were lying in a trench, the signs of their curtailed lives all around them:

> One with his feet on the top of the parapet and with his head on the floor of the trench. His right hand held the loaded gun, still gripping firmly, his finger on the trigger. Death had rushed at him, thus, before he could send his killing lead from its barrel. A bullet had gone through his skull just as he was about to attack. In the room on a primitive table stood the remains of a meagre breakfast; beside it lay two opened letters, a shoe brush and a clothes brush—in front of the entrance of the room, the four corpses.[219]

It was only when soldiers were confronted with the dead and wounded after battle, after their nerves had recovered from combat, that they perceived the consequences of warfare, which were 'dreadful', in Wilhelm Gather's evaluation.[220] 'On the road, whole convoys of wagons loaded with wounded could be seen, from whose faces it was apparent that death played for them the principal part', the 26-year-old guardsman continued.[221] As he marched back to his quarters, he could see dead and wounded everywhere, including a huge pile of Prussian corpses filling a churchyard. 'Five officers also lay there, amongst whom was our major', he reported: 'A foot lay there without a man!'[222]

Non-combatants who saw the battlefield displayed similar reactions. The theologian and Lutheran clergyman Wilhelm Friedrich Besser had travelled north from his parish in Silesia in order to see Düppel for himself. On the train, he had found himself surrounded by relatives of the wounded, including one soldier who had been 'pulled out from under a mountain of corpses, like someone waking from amongst the dead'.[223] As he arrived at the battlefield, a week after the fighting had taken place, pools of blood and, occasionally, corpses could still be seen.[224] Louis Appia, the envoy in Prussia of the International Committee for Relief to the Wounded, had visited the same site seven days earlier, on the afternoon of 18 April, writing to Henri

[216] Bubbe, cited ibid., 306.　　　[217] Ibid.　　　[218] Ibid., 307.
[219] Ibid.　　[220] Ibid.　　[221] Ibid.　　[222] Ibid., 307–8.
[223] W. F. Besser, *Drei Wochen auf dem Kriegsschauplatze* (Halle, 1864), 3.
[224] Ibid., 11–27.

Dunant and the committee that 'the streams are flooded with blood, one finds shreds of uniforms and toiletries', 'here lie all sorts of grenades, spiked grenades, bullets, grapeshot cartridges, and there are shells the size of my head'.[225] 'The landscape is completely ploughed by grenade explosions', he wrote: 'A bit further on, I went past twenty-five corpses, which lay on a plank, ready to be buried in a mass grave. Beside them, there are already two mass graves with a cross, on which was written, "Here rest 308 brave soldiers, who have fallen for the fatherland."'[226]

The painter Wilhelm Camphausen saw an almost identical scene whilst visiting the battlefield the next day—the first time that he had visited one despite making his living as a military painter. He watched as 'corpses were thrown onto a farmer's cart and driven away to specified large burial sites', where one to two hundred of them were laid beside and on top of each other', separated only by straw.[227] He approached the battlefield 'with a certain understandable timidity'.[228] Viewing 'the first laid-out dead bodies hesitantly and gradually, my eye managed to fix onto the terrible sight'.[229] Slowly, he got used to observing the dead, although his asides suggested that he was profoundly moved and repelled by the sight:

> There they [the dead bodies] lay, mostly already ordered into long rows next to each other, pale with bloodless, brown cheeks, blank and motionless, their broken eyes staring at the blue sky, which had again cleared up in the meantime. I saw the first one, the second, and others, and soon I was in a position to observe the next ones for a long time with a fixed gaze. What I would never have held for possible amidst the usual clutter of peaceful daily life, I learned about myself here in a surprising way for the first time: the unbelievably rapid cauterization of the human feeling for the horrible when it manifests itself on such a scale. As I now took the pencil in my hand and began to sketch some of the most characteristic groups of the dead, all my shyness disappeared and I saw in the terrible, violently throttled human bodies only that certain something, that there, coming into being out of straight and bent lines, which was to be fashioned by me and which I sought to bring to the paper with almost the same indifference as if it had been a table or a stool. If this happened in a short amount of time to me, who had grown up in homely tranquility and was quite new to such crass sights, what degree of cauterized coldness do soldiers attain, who have to experience countless repetitions of these scenes in a tiresome campaign! I saw several hundred more dead there in the next two days on the chosen site of Düppel, in part with horrible dismemberment, smashed or completely ripped-off limbs, but most of them by far had been hit in the middle of the head by a reliable Prussian needle-gun. . . . All too atrocious sights were concealed by a tunic or part of a coat in a commendable, natural soldierly aesthetic. I raised one of them gently—a formless, smashed skull without a face—peace to the dead and walk on by![230]

Army doctors, who had started to record causes and types of injury and death, showed how combat had changed. In his *General-Bericht* on the Danish war, the chief medical officer of the Prussian army, Gottfried Friedrich Franz Loeffler, gave

[225] Louis Appia, *Les Blessés dans le Schleswig pendant la guerre de 1864* (1864), cited in T. Buk-Swienty, *Schlachtbank Düppel*, 308.
[226] Ibid., 308–9. [227] W. Camphausen, *Ein Maler auf dem Kriegsfelde*, 26.
[228] Ibid., 24. [229] Ibid. [230] Ibid., 26.

a frank account of the injuries sustained, reproducing the medical notes of 197 cases. Although the campaign of 1864 was 'more limited in its dimensions and was conducted under exceptionally favourable conditions', it nevertheless constituted 'the first large practical test, not only of the increase of the army's ability to strike and its energetic reforms, but also the feasibility of the principles on which the improvement of the military medical establishment rested'.[231] The report itself was explicitly connected by Loeffler to 'the wonderful achievements of a Miss Nightingale in the Crimean War' and by 'the international conference in Geneva in October 1863', the formulation of whose regulations the conflict had actually preceded.[232] Unlike the 'humanist' Henri Dunant, the Prussian medical chief's interest in the incidence of injury was primarily technical, but he betrayed in passing how the physical impact of warfare had altered, with fewer deaths from illness than in the past (about a quarter of cases)[233] and more from shrapnel and bullet wounds (nearly three-quarters of cases); 702 out of 738 Prussian deaths and 2,388 of 2,443 woundings were the result of gun and cannon shot rather than bayonets (one death, twenty-six woundings), swords (one death, twenty-two woundings), or rifle butts and clubs (no deaths, five woundings).[234]

Whereas troops were most likely to die of cold, hunger, or sickness during the Revolutionary and Napoleonic Wars (and during the Crimean War, at least as far as the French army was concerned, Loeffler noted), they were most likely to die outright from artillery and rifle fire or from complications arising from more severe wounding through gunshot.[235] In other words, the soldiers of the wars of liberation frequently died of 'natural' causes, not far removed from those of their daily lives, whilst combatants in 1864 were incapacitated and died in an unaccustomed, more terrifying way, with their wounds rendered worse by new kinds of weaponry and projectiles. The bullet wounds inflicted by round shot had often been shrugged off by seasoned soldiers, but such shot had been 'replaced by extended shot from an extended barrel': 'For hand weapons, this change was complete in 1864...Cylindrical grenades with explosive detonators were already predominant on the Prussian side.'[236] The dominance of these weapons and shells explained, together with improvements in military medicine and 'assured connections to a nearby theatre of war in a rich land', why Prussian casualties were low.[237] Loeffler was well aware that the use of such weaponry on both sides (many Danish artillery shells were still round) in a war of movement and battles of 'annihilation' would be much more destructive.[238] 'With the extraordinary increase in the portability and accuracy of the new precision weapons—cannon as well as guns—the number of hits entered into a new relationship to the number of combatants, and serious injury becomes all the more overwhelming the greater the distances are', he warned.[239]

Much attention had already been devoted to new guns, artillery, bullets, and missiles in the military literature, wrote Loeffler in 1867.[240] Less attention had

[231] F. Loeffler, *General-Bericht*, viii, xvi.   [232] Ibid., ix.   [233] Ibid.
[234] Ibid., 1, 10, 36, 46.   [235] Ibid., 21.   [236] Ibid., 42.
[237] Ibid., 2.   [238] Ibid., 44.   [239] Ibid.
[240] Ibid., 42. For instance, J. Zechmeister, *Die Schusswunden und die gegenwärtige Bewaffnung der Heere* (Munich, 1864).

been given to the bodily impact of such weapons. 'Not only the number, but—much more—the type of wounding could be used to characterize each campaign, and individual actions in each campaign, if one were able to gain and to give a complete overview', he lamented: 'Until now, that has not happened. A view of *the dead on the battlefield* was thought of to such a limited extent that the injuries of the *fallen* could scarcely come into consideration.'[241] Statistics had been collected during the Crimean War and American Civil War, but they remained incomplete, with the best figures for the former deriving from the wounded who were evacuated to Constantinople and with the principal study of the latter ignorant of the 'outcome [of treatment] for thousands' of the 77,775 soldiers suffering from artillery and gunshot wounds.[242] With modern shells, it was common for 'more or less heavy and angular pieces' to splinter, 'which cause the most terrible mutilation'.[243] The majority of Prussian wounds—about 80 per cent—were caused by rifle fire, a figure considerably higher than estimates for the Danish wounded, where dominant and more modern Prussian artillery inflicted a higher proportion of casualties. Like shrapnel, bullets 'change their form on hitting bone, split and, by carrying on their trajectory as separate pieces or by lying between the fragments of bone, make the wound more complicated and make healing more difficult'.[244] Loeffler's individual case studies showed what he meant by complications:

Case 6. Grapeshot shell on the temple. Large brain defect. Healed. Musketeer Fritz Hannemann of the 24th Reg, 24 years old, from Wenzlow in Brandenburg, was wounded on 29 June on Alsen. He arrived half-conscious at the dressing station, but cried about pain and gave his name and regiment number under questioning. At the wound opening, close to the left ear at the level of the helix, an almost thaler-size hole in... the temporal bone was confirmed, from which blood and white brain substance ran. Under the wound, the skin has been ripped open. This pocket is also filled with a bloody brew of brain. An exploratory finger reaches between a pile of bone debris and feels a large defect.... Blood and brain substance runs out of the ear.

Case 9. Shot fracture of the cranial vertex. Profound penetration of a piece of bone in the brain. Death after seven days. Fusilier Leppin from the 24th Reg. was wounded on 18 April... The left vertex bone was drilled through... Brain substance, in which there were some splinters of bone, lay on and near the wound. The bullet could not be found. The wounded man can only slur incomprehensibly, but he remains conscious. He answers questions by nodding his head... L. has a further injury under the right armpit. All soft parts have been ripped off by shrapnel grenade to the extent that the bones are exposed.... On 20 April, the frequency of the pulse increased and the patient complained of headache, he throws himself restlessly around and expels stools

---

[241] F. Loeffler, *General-Bericht*, 35.
[242] Ibid., 53. Jean Charles Chenu, *Rapport au Conseil de santé des armées sur les résultats du service medico-chirurgical aux ambulances de Crimée et aux hopitaux militaires français en Turquie, pendant la champagne d'Orient en 1854—1855—1856* (Paris, 1865); Gaspard Scrive, *Relation medico-chirurgicale de la Campagne d'Orient du 31 mars 1854, occupation de Gallipoli, au 6 juillet, 1856, evacuation de la Crimée* (Paris, 1857). See also the American 'Reports on the Extent and Nature of the Materials Available for the Preparation of a Medical and Surgical History of the Rebellion'.
[243] F. Loeffler, *General-Bericht*, 43.   [244] Ibid., 44.

and urine under him... On 24 April, a fading pulse, throwing about of the head, deep, sighing breathing. Death on 25 April.

Case 86. Deep injury to the soft body tissue of the shoulder by a shrapnel grenade. Festering infiltration. Thrombotic pneumonia. Death. U.-O. Friedrich Schrader of the 4th Guards Reg. was hit by a shrapnel grenade on 4 April before Düppel. The shot had bored its way into the deltoid muscle and was immediately taken out. The reaction was violent. Swelling and painful infiltration spread to the whole arm despite the application of ice. Already on 7 April, thin, liquid pus was emptied through three incisions. Pain and fever subsequently lessen. On 9 April, further incisions were made to the fluctuating areas. The pus was now manure-like... On 16 April, the symptoms of pneumonia appeared, which... led to death on 19 April.[245]

Notwithstanding the clinical language of a curious medic, the gravity, extent, and painfulness of soldiers' injuries were obvious, affecting all combatants, not just victims.

Combatants' experiences and expectations of war in 1864 derived from specific fears of mutilation and an atrocious death and from a more general, ill-defined apprehension about modern warfare. In part, this apprehension was reinforced by the nerve-racking effects of artillery bombardments, which were a feature of the sieges of the campaign in Schleswig and Denmark. Although soldiers were more likely to be hit by a bullet, what frightened them about the fighting, as Wilhelm Steinkamp phrased it, was 'the terrible roar of cannon shells', which was all that could be heard.[246] On the Danish side, the impact of superior Prussian artillery was greater, with a higher killing rate and more extensive destruction, as British observers like Auberon Herbert (who referred to bombardments as a 'tempest') and Edward Dicey of *The Daily Telegraph* spelled out: 'There is not a field, or house, or hollow where shells have not fallen... It is not a battle, but a slaughter.'[247] In part, soldiers' apprehensiveness extended beyond the immediate sounds and sights of battle, issuing in a series of menacing symbols and spectres. One such symbol was the iron-clad Danish gunboat 'Rolf Krake', which regularly steamed into the sound of Alsen to bombard Prussian positions and which had come to embody the superiority of the Danish navy. Ordinary soldiers like Carl Holzmeier from Westphalia feared the ship as 'the sea monster', which had allegedly caused the Prussian forces at Düppel 'the greatest losses'.[248] He assumed that civilians such as his sister and brother-in-law might already know of the ship, about which 'all the papers and journals have been so preoccupied in terms of pictures and descriptions'.[249]

The defensive Danish fortifications at Düppel and the *Danewerk*, in front of Schleswig, came to constitute another set of intimidating symbols or spectres of war. The origins of what Friedrich Karl (reported by Bunge) called 'this fixed

[245] Ibid., 65–6, 70–1, 144.
[246] W. Steinkamp to his parents, 14 Apr. 1864, in H.-U. Kammeier, 'Der Krieg gegen Dänemark 1864', 78–9.
[247] A. Herbert, *The Danes in Camp: Letters from Sonderborg* (London, 1864), 188; E. Dicey, *The Schleswig–Holstein War* (London, 1864), vol. 2, 145–6.
[248] C. Holzmeier to his sister and brother-in-law, 11 Apr. 1864, in H.-U. Kammeier, 'Der Krieg gegen Dänemark 1864', 79.
[249] Ibid. Heinrich Mahler, *Über die Eider an den Alsensund*, 156, on newspapers and journals.

bulwark of the North, behind which the enemy believed itself invincible', dated back as far as the seventh century and had initially loomed above the Austrian and Prussian troops at the start of the campaign.[250] It consisted of a 10-mile cordon of fortified hills and ramparts, including the *Kurgraben*, the central rampart (around 4 miles long), and the *Königshügel*, the largest man-made redoubt (136 feet high). According to the journalist Heinrich Mahler, the *Danewerk* had 'stood there threateningly', as impregnable as the mountain fortress of Zwing Uri in Switzerland.[251] German commanders had generally assumed that 'the taking of the *Dannewerke* would be a dreadful business', as Princess Victoria, the wife of the Crown Prince and daughter of Queen Victoria, had written on 8 February 1864.[252] After the Danes had evacuated the stronghold unexpectedly at the start of the same month, they had dropped back on the fortifications of Düppel, which—although not a 'complete fort'—were 'much more concentrated than that of the position of the *Danewerk*' and were widely known as the 'Malakov of the North'.[253] Subsequently, these redoubts, too, had provoked anxiety amongst the Prussian troops opposite. The scaling of the sandy earthworks of Düppel and those of Alsen depicted by Camphausen, was at once the most heroic and most fearful action of the war in Schleswig and Denmark. The combination of anxiety and confidence amongst Austrian and, especially, Prussian combatants hinted at their sensitivity towards violence and death, even in a supposedly just, national conflict which they expected to win.

The war against Denmark came to an end officially on 30 October 1864. The Danish government of Christian Albrecht Bluhme, which had replaced that of Ditlev Gothard Monrad after his forced resignation on 8 July, had had to accept the payment of compensation to Austria and Prussia and the ceding of Schleswig, Holstein, and Lauenburg in the peace treaty which had been negotiated from 25 July onwards, after the ministry's acceptance of an armistice on 12 July. Approximately 1,000 Prussian, 1,200 Austrian, and 5,600 Danish soldiers had died.[254] The number injured was between two and three times as high.[255] From a Danish point of view, the war was a bloody disaster.[256] From the perspective of most German commentators, it was a much-heralded victory; the Hohenzollern monarchy's first successful campaign since 1815 and a reversal of fortune for its Habsburg counterpart after defeat in 1859. Many Prussian and Austrian combatants had more mixed memories of 1864, yet their reservations and doubts were given little publicity at the time. Thus, Camphausen's pictorial account of the campaign in *Ein Maler auf dem Kriegsfelde* made only fleeting references to wounding and death, with three out of thirty-four sketches in the volume showing human

---

[250] C. Bunge, *Aus meinem Kriegstagebuch*, 45.

[251] H. Mahler, *Über die Eider an den Alsensund*, 171–2.

[252] F. Ponsonby (ed.), *Letters of the Empress Frederick* (London, 1928), 53.

[253] W. Rüstow, *Der Krieg und seine Mittel*, 318. T. Buk-Swienty, *Schlachtbank Düppel*, 219.

[254] O. Haselhorst, 'Der Deutsch-Dänische Krieg von 1864', in J. Ganschow, O. Haselhorst, and M. Ohnezeit (eds), *Der Deutsch-Dänische Krieg 1864*, 145.

[255] F. Loeffler, *General-Bericht*, 3, on the basis of Prussian figures.

[256] This is Tom Buk-Swienty's main argument in *Schlachtbank Düppel* and its sequel on the invasion, and defence, of Alsen, *Dommedag Als. 29 juni 1864* (Copenhagen, 2010).

corpses and one displaying dead horses.[257] 'Sturm auf die Düppeler Schanzen' showed one or two Prussian attackers falling down wounded, but hundreds more running towards and climbing the fortified banks, before planting their flag on a distant mound in anticipation of victory.[258] More daringly, 'Aufräumungsarbeit auf dem Schlachtfeld' displayed rows of dead soldiers, their heads and bodies pointing away from the viewer, except one, whose hollowed-out face looks blankly upwards and whose trunk is aligned in the opposite, more confrontational direction.[259] Even here, though, the form of the sketch—with a horse-drawn cart in the background loaded with corpses looking like hay and with soldiers bearing stretchers and weapons like farm tools—alludes to that of a pastoral idyll, in keeping with the painter's injunction to leave the dead at 'rest'.[260]

Camphausen's narrative, which begins and ends with wholesome, bucolic scenes from Schleswig, corresponded to that of his literary equivalent Theodor Fontane, who had accompanied the troops as a journalist.[261] The writer's account began with a history of the peoples—Germanic tribes such as the Angles and Frisians—inhabiting Schleswig and Holstein and went on to detail the historical and legal legitimacy of the war.[262] He did eventually reflect on the human cost of the conflict, largely through eyewitnesses of 'the day after the storm' on 18 April, but only after recounting at length his travels and adventures, crossing a series of rivers and sounds ('Eider-Uebergang', 'Der Schlei-Uebergang', 'Sundewitt'), lovingly describing 'camp life' and giving an action-by-action summary of the military assault on the fortifications at Düppel.[263] Compared to the excitement and triumph of battle, the brief references of officers to 'the destruction in the redoubts' and the 'murderous' bombardment of the bridgehead seem insignificant.[264] The shelling of Sonderburg in early April, which the British journalist Antonio Carlo Napoleone Gallenga is reported to have labelled 'the first day on which war was waged seriously', was treated by Fontane more or less in passing as a by-product of the Prussian decision not to invade Alsen at that point in time.[265] The invasion of Alsen on 29 June, which left 216 Danes dead, 227 wounded, 536 missing, and 2,113 prisoner, was presented both as a romantic crossing—'Ueber den Alsensund'—and a technical exercise, replete with geometric diagrams and descriptions of dispositions and troop movements.[266] 'The War in Jutland' and 'The War at Sea' were examined perfunctorily, giving the impression of a gradual build-up of military forces from the stand-off at the *Danewerk* until victory at Düppel, which was followed by 'the final act of the war' at Alsen.[267] Like many other observers, even those close to the troops, Fontane's account is Prusso-centric and triumphal. As such, it glosses over combatants' own experiences of conflict. The next chapter investigates whether this type of distortion remained possible in the midst of a large-scale war, which effectively divided opinion in Germany, between the two German Great Powers.

[257] W. Camphausen, *Ein Maler auf dem Kriegsfelde*, 19–27.   [258] Ibid., 19.
[259] Ibid., 25.   [260] Ibid., 26.   [261] For instance, ibid., 9, 43, 47.
[262] T. Fontane, *Der Schleswig-Holsteinische Krieg im Jahre 1864*, 3–38.
[263] Ibid., 55–7, 66–7, 74–8, 99–104, 175–85, 197–243.
[264] Ibid., 245–6.   [265] Ibid., 171.   [266] Ibid., 310–42.   [267] Ibid., 265–306.

8

Brothers-at-War

'The air was thick and hazy, the rain came down steadily, and the wind blew bitterly cold', marking a change from previous days of oppressive summer heat.[1] The troops had been waiting since before dawn. As they crossed the River Bistritz, which was little more than a swollen stream, near the village of Nechanitz, the soldiers of the Prussian Army of the Elbe could see two of the batteries of the First Army already 'firing from wooded heights'.[2] 'About an hour away, far to our left, two villages burned', recorded Georg von Bismarck, a young officer in a *Landwehr* battalion from Siegburg in the Rhineland: 'Troops were not to be seen in the rainy weather, but we learned that the 1st Army of Prince Friedrich Karl stood over there, engaged in violent fighting, and, further, that the Army of the Elbe was going to come to its aid.'[3] 'It was, in any case, a great battle which was in the process of developing, and whoever still doubted it could soon convince themselves after climbing up the heights of Hradek, which allowed a clear overview of the 1st Army through a clearing in the wood', he continued.[4] From this viewpoint, on the far right flank of the Prussian forces, observers could see 'the positions of the armies on both sides quite distinctly from the gunpowder smoke of their lines of artillery, which were obviously in full fire': 'Immediately to the left of us, beginning with the batteries of the Army of the Elbe on Lubno hill, these almost unbroken lines extended far to the north-west, where they disappeared into the mist as a result of the great distance and bad weather.'[5] The battlefield was so extensive that the separate military engagements were barely visible amidst the rolling countryside of cornfields and copses. The hills of Lipa and Chlum, where the Austrians had placed their headquarters and concentrated the forces of the Third Corps, were 'shrouded in thick, white gunpowder smoke, which stood out very distinctly from the thick, grey–black smoke of several burning villages'.[6] The only troops visible were the avant-garde of the Army of the Elbe and, 'beyond the Bistritz in long lines, the masses of Prussian reserve cavalry'.[7] Having been warned by one of his relations, who rode past as they stood waiting, that 'you'll probably get some very hard nuts

---

[1] H. M. Hozier, *The Seven Weeks' War* (Driffield, 2012), 252: the volume was originally published in 1867.

[2] G. v. Bismarck, *Kriegs-Erlebnisse 1866 und 1870/71* (Dessau, 1907), 38.

[3] Ibid.   [4] Ibid.   [5] Ibid.

[6] Ibid. Konrad Sturm, an Austrian lieutenant, spoke of twelve to fourteen villages burning: F. Deitl (ed.), *Unter Habsburg Kriegsbanner. Feldzugserlebnisse aus der Feder von Mitkämpfern und Augenzeugen* (Dresden, 1898), vol. 4, 27.

[7] G. v. Bismarck, *Kriegs-Erlebnisse 1866 und 1870/71*, 38.

to crack', since they were facing Saxons, Bismarck and his fellow-soldiers were ordered into the wood of Ober-Prim at a quick march.[8] Here, with their progress impeded by 'the stand of trees and the steeply climbing slope', they were hit by 'a true hailstorm of grenades', which landed in the trees and on the ground, throwing up 'iron, branches and splinters of wood' and inflicting the brigade's first casualties.[9] For the Army of the Elbe, the battle of Königgrätz—the largest in the modern era—had begun.[10]

The battle was the decisive encounter between a Saxon Army Corps of 23,000 men and the Northern Army of Ludwig von Benedek, which numbered 247,000 including trains and administrative staff, on the one hand, and the Prussian Army of the Elbe (39,000), First Army (85,000), and Second Army (under 100,000), which had united on the battlefield for the first time in the campaign, on the other.[11] The Prussian forces, which had entered Bohemia through the passes and valleys of the *Erzgebirge* and the *Riesengebirge* in the north and east, attacked the corps of the Austrians and the Saxons, which had reinforced their position over the previous two days, on the slopes to the east of the Bistritz, 8 miles to the north-west of the town of Königgrätz. The assault had started at around 7.00 a.m. on 3 July, after reconnoitring parties of the First Army had brought back news of the Austrians' whereabouts at 7.00 p.m. on the 2nd. 'Long before midnight the troops were all in motion', wrote Henry Hozier, one of three *Times* correspondents at the scene: 'The moon occasionally shone out brightly, but was generally hidden behind clouds, and then could be distinctly seen the decaying bivouac fires in the places which had been occupied by the troops along the road.'[12] The vast army moved along the main road from Höritz to Königgrätz, stopping in a hollow before the village of Dub, concealed behind a wood of fir trees. 'Soon after dawn, a person standing between the village of Milowitz and the further hill of Dub could see no armed men, except a few Prussian *vedettes* posted along the Dub ridge, whose lances stood in relief above the summit, against the murky sky', Hozier went on: 'A few dismounted officers were standing below a fruit-tree in front of Milowitz, with their horses held by some orderlies behind them. These were Prince Frederick Charles and his staff.'[13]

Three hours later, Friedrich Karl 'pushed forward some of his cavalry and horse artillery', which 'moved down the slope towards the Bistritz at a gentle trot, slipping about on the greasy ground, but keeping most beautiful lines; the lance flags of the Uhlans, wet with the rain, flapping heavily against the staves'.[14] When they reached the bottom of the hill, where they wheeled about before crossing the river, the trumpets sounded and 'the Austrian guns opened upon them from a battery placed in a field near the village at which the main road crosses the Bistritz',

---

[8] Ibid.   [9] Ibid., 39.

[10] G. A. Craig, *The Battle of Königgrätz: Prussia's Victory over Austria, 1866* (New York, 1964), x.

[11] On the Austrian forces, see G. E. Rothenberg, *The Army of Francis Joseph*, 70–1: 180,000 troops moved north, joining other regiments which were already in Bohemia. On the Prussian army, see Q. Barry, *The Road to Königgrätz: Helmuth Moltke and the Austro-Prussian War, 1866* (Solihull, 2009), 164–73.

[12] H. M. Hozier, *The Seven Weeks' War*, 249.   [13] Ibid.   [14] Ibid., 252.

signalling the commencement of the battle.[15] At a quarter to eight, the King of Prussia arrived at the battlefield along with Bismarck, wearing a cuirassier's helmet (as a major in the *Landwehr* cavalry), and Moltke, who had a cold and was constantly blowing his nose with a red silk handkerchief, but they, like Friedrich Karl, were frustrated by poor visibility and well-prepared Austrian and Saxon positions:

> As soon as the Prussian fire actively commenced Austrian guns seemed to appear, as if by magic, at every point of the position; from every road, from every village, from the orchard of Mokrovous, on the Prussian right, to the orchard of Benatek, on their left, came flashes of fire and whizzing rifle shells, which, bursting with a sharp crack, sent their splinters rattling among the guns, gunners, carriage, and horses, often killing a man or horse, sometimes dismounting a gun, but always ploughing up the earth, and scattering mud in men's faces.[16]

Behind the lines, wrote the special correspondent of *The Times* William Howard Russell from the tower of Königgrätz, Benedek continued to move reserves westwards, 'squares and parallelograms of snowy white, dark green, azure, and blue on the cornfields like the checker work of a patchwork quilt'.[17] Until the arrival of the Second Army under Crown Prince Friedrich Wilhelm at around midday, joining the fighting on the Prussian forces' left flank, the Prussian Seventh Division under Eduard Friedrich Karl von Fransecky had stalled in the face of superior Austrian artillery and larger numbers of troops.[18] When Lieutenant Colonel Karl Walther von Loë returned to headquarters requesting reinforcements, Moltke advised Wilhelm I not to give 'a single man of infantry support' because, as long as 'the Crown Prince has not intervened, which is the only thing that can help the general, we must be on the look-out for an Austrian offensive'.[19] At that point, before the arrival of the Second Army and its subsequent outflanking of Benedek's Northern Army, the outcome of the battle and, therefore, the campaign was uncertain.

In the event, the battle of Königgrätz proved to be the decisive defeat of Austria and its allies, pushing them to agree to the Peace of Prague on 23 August 1866. Six days earlier, fifteen small German states north of the River Main had signed the Treaty of the North German Confederation, along with Prussia. Hanover, Schleswig-Holstein, Nassau, Hesse-Kassel, and Frankfurt were annexed by the Hohenzollern monarchy. The war of 1866 altered the politics of Germany definitively, bringing to an end the contested ascendancy of Austria. The contemporary significance of the conflict for combatants, however, is difficult to disentangle from subsequent myths. Public support in Prussia was mixed initially, as champions of the war effort such as Theodor Fontane acknowledged. Thus, although the mood was said to be 'earnest', with everyone feeling 'the decisiveness of the moment', it was also marked by an absence of belligerence: 'This war-reluctance imbued nearly

---

[15] Ibid.   [16] Ibid., 254.   [17] W. H. Russell, *The Times*, 11 July 1866.

[18] E. v. Fransecky, *Denkwürdigkeiten des Preußischen Generals der Infanterie*, ed. W. v. Bremen (Bielefeld, 1901), 371–9.

[19] F. C. W. D. v. Loë, *Erinnerungen aus meinem Berufsleben 1849 bis 1867* (Stuttgart, 1906), 102–3.

all strata of the people and was quite general, with only their motives differing.'[20] Whereas many prominent conservatives regarded a 'break with Austria as a great political mistake', cementing an 'alliance with revolution' in the form of Italy and permitting 'the man on the Seine' to become the 'arbiter of the fate of Germany', others mistrusted the army and 'the entire Prussian system'.[21] A third party of liberals and democrats—'the most numerous in the country'—'wanted war, which it held to be just and necessary, but they wanted to lead it themselves' and not to leave its prosecution to Bismarck: 'Under existing conditions, war was impossible; the conduct of this war for existence could not be left to a Bismarckian Prussia.'[22] The divisions of public opinion in Prussia were held by Fontane to be one reason for Austria's 'policy of intimidation', which had allegedly been founded on the certainty that 'Prussia cannot fight a war, for the Prussian *Volk* does not want one.'[23]

By contrast, in the Habsburg monarchy, 'never was a war more popular; from all parts of the country, with the sole exception of the Italians, one rushed joyfully to the colours; strict Catholics from confessional antagonism, German-Austrians from a sense of rivalry, Hungarians and Slavs out of racial hatred (*Racenhaß*)', asserted the journalist and essayist.[24] Other commentators, from the vantage points of different states and parties, disagreed. To Treitschke, a Saxon-born liberal supporter of Prussia, 'What Austria is striving for in this war is hidden from view, unclear perhaps to the Hofburg itself.'[25] To Jakob Venedey, one of a minority of radicals backing a *großdeutsch* and confederal solution to the German question,

> while in Prussia everyone knows what they are fighting for, even the educated scarcely know amongst us [on the Austrian side], not to mention the great mass of people, and our soldiers must derive their enthusiasm simply from the pugnacious desire to show the self-important Prussians over there that there are also blokes living over the other side of the mountains who can use force.[26]

Although the 'war was begun against the will of the people', he continued, 'every Prussian heart is currently with the army and the war is decidedly popular', because

---

[20] T. Fontane, *Der deutsche Krieg von 1866*, vol. 1, 64. Wilhelm I himself recognized this fact in a letter to the Archbishop of Cologne on 4 June 1866: E. Berner (ed.), *Kaiser Wilhelm des Grossen. Briefe, Reden und Schriften* (Berlin, 1906), vol. 2, 126.

[21] T. Fontane, *Der deutsche Krieg von 1866*, vol. 1, 64–5. There were also very confused attachments between the rulers of the individual states: H. v. Chappuis, *Bei Hofe und im Felde. Lebenserinnerungen* (Frankfurt a. M., 1902), 21.

[22] T. Fontane, *Der deutsche Krieg von 1866*, vol. 1, 65. See also T. Krieg, *Wilhelm von Doering, königlich preußischer Generalmajor. Ein Lebens- und Charakterbild* (Berlin, 1898), 147: 'Weite Volkskreise wollten, durch die fortschrittliche Presse verhetzt, von dem "Bruderkrieg" nichts wissen.'

[23] T. Fontane, *Der deutsche Krieg von 1866*, vol. 1, 65. For a similar line of argument in the secondary literature, see S. Berger, *Germany: Inventing the Nation* (London, 2004), 72; J. Breuilly, *The Formation of the First German Nation State, 1800–1871* (Basingstoke, 1996), 83.

[24] T. Fontane, *Der deutsche Krieg von 1866*, vol. 1, 53.

[25] H. v. Treitschke, 'Der Krieg und die Bundesreform', *Preußische Jahrbücher*, 17 (1866), 677–96. See also Pieter M. Judson, *Exclusive Revolutionaries: Liberal Politics, Social Experience and National Identity in the Austrian Empire, 1848–1914*, 106–9, who downplays the significance of public opinion in 1866, and Heinrich Lutz, *Zwischen Habsburg und Preussen*, 452, who depicts the conflict as a 'conventional war between the old powers', not a 'national war' or a 'civil war'.

[26] H. v. Srbik (ed.), *Quellen zur deutschen Politik Österreichs* (Oldenburg, 1934–8), vol. 5, 955–7.

the population was a '*Volk in Waffen*' in which 'there is no family, across all classes..., who does not have members up to their fortieth year and remotely capable of bearing arms in the army'.[27] To the Catholic and Bavarian commentator Edmund Jörg, the editor of the *Historisch-politische Blätter*, it seemed that the conflict had been entered into 'blindly', with neither Austria, whose 'opposition would never be led to war in the midst of [the state's] countless difficulties', nor Prussia, given the 'wide-ranging discontentment of the people and the menace of revolution in its own land', able to wage war successfully.[28] The alignments and dispositions of public opinion in the third Germany, many observers agreed, were even more confused and unstable.[29]

How much did the uncertainty of public support for the war of 1866 matter to combatants? It is one of the contentions of this chapter that it mattered less, given the conflict's outcome and short duration, than it would have done if the war had become protracted or if Prussia—where support was at once crucial and precarious—had lost. Such circumstances, which many contemporaries did not foresee, have tended to obscure the actual effects of the conflict, which was hard-fought, bloody, and psychologically destabilizing for many participants. The diplomatic manoeuvres were complicated but the build-up of military pressure was continuous, interpreted by contemporaries as a more or less inexorable movement towards war. The crisis had begun on 26 January 1866, as the Prussian government had lodged a protest against Ludwig von Gablenz's decision, as the Austrian Governor of Holstein, to allow the estates of both duchies to call for a common assembly.[30] Vienna replied angrily to Berlin's protest note on 7 February, with Bismarck going on to raise the prospect of war in a ministerial council on 28 February. Fearing the rapid mobilization of Prussian troops, Franz Joseph ordered the dispatching of twenty infantry battalions and several cavalry regiments to reinforce the Habsburg army in Bohemia on 14 March, to which Wilhelm I responded by placing the five Prussian divisions on Saxony's and Austria's border on a war footing on 27 and 29 March. Berlin signed a three-month offensive alliance with Italy, which contravened Article 11 of the confederal constitution (forbidding binding commitments against other members of the *Bund*), on 8 April, leading—after threatening Italian troop movements—to Austria's mobilization of the Southern Army on 21 April (reversing the prospect of a standing-down of Prussian and Austrian troops in the north, agreed on the same day), the general mobilization of Italy's army on the 26th, and Austrian mobilization on the 27th (since Vienna had learned of the

---

[27] Ibid.

[28] J. E. Jörg, 'Zeitläufe', *Historisch-politische Blätter für das katholische Deutschland*, 58 (1866), 53–6.

[29] Thus, Treitschke, *Preußische Jahrbücher*, 17 (1866), 687–9, admitted that 'the antipathy of the people against Prussia is animated', but not as embittered as during the era of Stein and Hardenberg. In Saxony, by contrast, the regime favoured Austria but not necessarily the *Volk*, which had been 'unnerved' by the 'despotism of the Beustian regime'. In Baden, according to the Grand Duke, public opinion broadly favoured Austria but remained very unpredictable: A. Dove, *Großherzog von Baden als Landesherr und deutscher Fuerst* (Heidelberg, 1902), 142–3. I have written at greater length on the positions of the parties in southern—and northern—Germany in M. Hewitson, *Nationalism in Germany, 1848–1866*, 309–55.

[30] See especially W. Carr, *The Origins of the Wars of German Unification*, 89–143.

alliance between Prussia and Italy). Under pressure from Bismarck, Roon, and Moltke, Wilhelm I gave the order to mobilize all Prussian forces by 7 May.

In the meantime, the Prussian Minister-President had begun to circumvent the German Confederation, sending a note directly to the middling and smaller German states which protested against Austria's military preparations and attempted to ascertain the states' positions. After the governments of the individual states had merely referred the matter, in accordance with Article 11, to the mediation and arbitration of the confederal Diet, the Prussian representative at Frankfurt, Karl von Savigny, had called on 9 April for the election of an assembly by universal manhood suffrage to discuss the reform of the failing *Bund*. Attempts by the *Mittelstaaten* to delay the question of reform in committee on 21 April and to organize a coordinated standing-down of their forces on 24 May failed. Austria referred the dispute of Schleswig-Holstein to the Confederation on 1 June; Prussia objected on the ground that this action contravened the terms of the Austro-Prussian alliance of January 1864, the Peace of Vienna (1864), and the Gastein Convention (1865), all of which had specified that the affairs of Schleswig and Holstein were the preserve of the two powers, not the *Bund*, and it ordered Prussian troops to take control of Holstein. At Frankfurt, Savigny renewed the call for a nationally elected body to solve the issue of the duchies but he was opposed by the Austrian delegate Aloys von Kübeck, who moved successfully for the mobilization of non-Prussian confederal troops by 14 June, contending that the Gastein Convention was an expedient brought into being only temporarily until the matter was resolved by the confederal Diet. Savigny left the chamber and repudiated the Confederation, reiterating that it was in breach of its own constitution, since the administration of Holstein was regulated by the Peace of Vienna, to which the *Bund* was not a party. Prussian forces invaded Hanover, Saxony, and the Electorate of Hesse after the expiry of an ultimatum at midnight on 15 June; Austria pledged its support to states facing invasion, with Franz Joseph issuing a war manifesto on the 17th; and Italy declared war on the Habsburg monarchy on 20 June, commencing hostilities three days later. In Germany, Prussia moved first, deploying most of its forces towards Saxony and Bohemia, following Moltke's maxim that 'the vital thing is to strike down the principal enemy [Austria], the one that is ready, ... in which case the Federal Corps [in western Germany] will probably not do anything'.[31]

There is little evidence that combatants were uneasy about the grounds for going to war. As the Prussian troops crossed the border into Bohemia in late June, recalled one officer, they did so 'with a loud hurrah', although also 'with their eyes looking upwards in concentrated prayer'.[32] The mood of these soldiers and others in Austria and the third Germany appears to have been one of apprehension and excitement rather than fervour or enthusiasm. 'It was a peculiar feeling which

---

[31] H. v. Moltke, cited in Q. Barry, *The Road to Königgrätz*, 202. See also A. v. Blumenthal (ed.), *Journals of Field-Marshal Count von Blumenthal for 1866 and 1870–71* (London, 1903), 31.

[32] L. v. Schönfels (ed.), *Erlebnisse Heinrich von Schönfels als Generalstabsoffizier bei der Avantgarden-Cavallerie 1866 und 1870* (Berlin, 1903), 11. Also, A. v. Voigts-Rhetz (ed.), *Briefe des Generals der Infanterie von Voigts-Rhetz aus den Kriegsjahren 1866 und 1870/71* (Berlin, 1906), 6.

came over us!' recorded Hermann Lüders, a young recruit with the *Gardecorps* from Berlin: 'We were pushing into a foreign land, the people in the quiet village in front of us should have been our enemies, and yet they were all sleeping softly and did not suspect that we were so near.'[33] 'Every single rider seemed to burn with unrest', he went on.[34] Patriotic or national feeling, which was visible in the border region, appeared out of place: the people on one side of the frontier were suddenly 'animated by warm patriotism, they hated the Bohemians from the depths of their hearts, which astonished me all the more, since, in peacetime, many relationships existed between here and there and the neighbouring Austrian inhabitants of the border region are Germans, too', reported Lüders detachedly.[35] Most troops had come by train to Prussia's border with Saxony and Austria in May and early June, proceeding to march through the valleys of the *Erzgebirge* and *Riesengebirge* at separate points in late June, with the Army of the Elbe heading from the north-west towards Rumburg and Münchengrätz, the First Army from the north towards Reichenberg and Podol, and the Second Army from the north-east towards Trautenau, Soor, Nachod, and Skalitz.

Emerging from the passes into Bohemia, they encountered the Austrian and Saxon armies in a series of costly battles at Podol on 26–27 June (with Prussia counting thirty-two killed and eighty-one wounded, and Austria 111 and 432), Nachod on 27 June (Prussia, 283 and 825; Austria, 7,510 losses, including 2,500 taken prisoner), Trautenau on the same day (Prussia, 244 and 1,008; Austria, 5,782 casualties), Skalitz on 28 June (Prussia, 713 losses, of whom 155 were killed; Austria, 207 dead, 311 wounded, 2,908 captured or missing), and Gitschin on 29 June (Prussia, 329 killed and 1,212 wounded; Austria and Saxony, 5,511 losses, including 3,300 taken prisoner).[36] At the battle of Königgrätz, 1,935 Prussians had been killed, 6,959 wounded, and 278 were missing; 24,400 Austrians and Saxons had been killed and wounded, and 19,800 had been taken prisoner.[37] As the same forces moved towards Vienna, they continued to sustain losses—with 247 Prussian casualties and 2,000 Austrian ones at the battle of Tobitschau on 15 July and 207 Prussian and 490 Austrian losses at Blumenau on 22 July, for instance—before the ceasefire on 26 July. Elsewhere, heavy losses were incurred at the battle of Langensalza, in the Prussian Province of Saxony, on 27 June (170 Prussians killed, 643 wounded, thirty-three missing, and approximately 900 taken prisoner; 1,429 Hanoverians killed and wounded), at Kissingen in Bavaria on 10 July (143 Prussians killed, 698 wounded, and fifty-eight missing; ninety-three Bavarians killed, 573 wounded, and 555 missing), and at Frankfurt on 14 July (180 Prussian losses; 2,469 confederal losses, including 707 killed or wounded).[38] In Italy, the Austrian army had been victorious at the battle of Custozza on 24 June,

[33] H. Lüders, *Ein Soldatenleben in Krieg und Frieden* (Stuttgart, 1888), 38.
[34] Ibid., 39.   [35] Ibid., 38.
[36] The figures are taken from official histories, cited in Q. Barry, *The Road to Königgrätz*, 223–89.
[37] Ibid., 381.
[38] See A. v. Goeben, *Das Treffen bei Kissingen am 10. Juli 1866* (Darmstadt, 1868) for a Prussian perspective of the battle.

with losses of 8,407 (of which 6,797 were killed and wounded).[39] Around 1 million troops had been deployed by Prussia (355,000), Austria (528,000), and their German allies (19,000 Hanoverians, 49,147 in the confederal Eighth Corps) and more than 100,000 soldiers had been killed or wounded, from a total adult male population (14–60 years old) of 3,939,264 in Prussia (1867) and 10,431,936 in the German Confederation (1864).[40] How far did these soldiers' experiences of the war in 1866—the impressions and feelings of men like Lüders—alter their conceptions of and attitudes to military conflict?

THE CAMPAIGN: STRATEGISTS AND TECHNICIANS

For commanders, who decided what form the military campaign took and what loss of life was acceptable, the war between Prussia, Austria, and their allies was understood as a life-or-death struggle for their respective states. In this regard, it differed from the conflict with Denmark in 1864, which Prussian and Austrian leaders had occasionally recognized they might not win—after the inconclusive fighting of 1848–51—but had not feared they would lose. The war in 1866 was different, with each power risking defeat, dismemberment, or annexation. 'Today', declared Friedrich Karl to his Brandenburg troops as they went into battle at Königgrätz on 3 July, 'it is either Prussia or Austria!'[41] His uncle, Wilhelm I, had been aware from the beginning of the campaign 'that we are entering into a fight for Prussia's existence, and one which will become a war of brothers if Germany, urged on by Austria, allies itself with this power against me for no reason'.[42] 'That I shall not willingly give up any German territory, the whole world knows, and streams of blood will have to have flowed before this occurs', he had warned the Archbishop of Cologne on 4 June.[43] Two weeks later on 16 June, the king had confided to Bismarck, on going to war after months of hesitation, that 'the dice have been thrown! God alone knows the outcome of what has been started! Let us either win or bear with honour what heaven decides for Prussia!'[44] Such outpourings were not merely rhetorical, for the conflict was not a cabinet war in the eighteenth-century sense.[45] At Königgrätz, one staff officer, who had been

[39] Ibid., 400: Italian total losses were 8,357.
[40] G. A. Craig, *The Battle of Königgrätz*, 7, 17, and Q. Barry, *The Road to Königgrätz*, 441, on the army strengths; W. Fischer, J. Krengel, and J. Wietog, *Sozialgeschichtliches Arbeitsbuch I: Materialien zur Statistik des Deutschen Bundes 1815–1870* (Munich, 1982), 21–3, for the population statistics. The multiplier for the adult male population for both figures is taken from Prussia in 1867.
[41] Friedrich Karl, cited in G. v. Haeseler, *Zehn Jahre im Stabe des Prinzen Friedrich Karl. Erinnerungen* (Berlin, 1915), 156.
[42] Wilhelm I to P. Melchers, Archbishop of Cologne, 4 June 1866, in E. Berner (ed.), *Kaiser Wilhelm des Grossen*, vol. 2, 127.
[43] Ibid.
[44] Wilhelm I to O. v. Bismarck, 16 June 1866, ibid., 128. See also J. v. Hartmann, *Briefe aus dem Feldzuge 1866 an die Gatti geschrieben* (Berlin, 1898), 5, on Wilhelm's hesitation, compared to Bismarck and Roon.
[45] This is not to deny that some commanders viewed war as a royal or noble game: the Austrian commander of the First Army Corps Eduard von Clam Gallas, in whose family seat the Prussian offic-

confident of victory, had been surprised to find his monarch talking, not of Belle-Alliance (Waterloo) but of Auerstädt.[46]

After the defeat of the Habsburg monarchy, the king had wanted to pursue the Austrians to Vienna and to impose an unconditional defeat on them. Bismarck, who sought a peace acceptable to France and Austria, attempted to scotch such ambitions with sarcasm, causing consternation at one military council in July:

> If the enemy army gives up Vienna and withdraws to Hungary, we must follow it. Once we have crossed the Danube, it would be advisable to stay together on the far side; for the Danube is such a formidable obstacle that one cannot march down it whilst bestraddling it. Once we are fully on the other side, however, we lose our connections to the rear; it would then be best to march to Constantinople, to found a new Byzantine empire and to leave Prussia to its fate.[47]

In Berlin, wrote Bismarck's wife on 17 July, 'all conservatives are very concerned that we might be too mild overall towards the enemy *Volk*'.[48] Even she thought her husband was not prepared to punish Austria. In a marginal comment on 24 July, Wilhelm I had written that 'the Minister-President has left me in the lurch', leading him to contemplate replacing Bismarck until a discussion with his son, the Crown Prince, had revealed him to be in agreement with the Minister-President, 'so that I see myself obliged, to my great pain, to bite into this bitter apple and accept such a shameful peace, after such glorious victories of the army'.[49] Except for the loss of Venetia, which was handed—via France—to Italy, Austria was to remain intact, but its dismemberment had been a possibility. The lot of the enemy states north of the Elbe was not so mild, issuing in annexation (Hanover, Hesse-Kassel, Frankfurt) or forced inclusion in the North German Confederation (Saxony).[50]

The Hohenzollern monarchy's war against Austria seemed to many outside observers to be risky.[51] 'Prussia has had no great war for fifty years', Engels warned the readers of the *Manchester Guardian* on 20 June: 'Her army is, on the whole, a peace army, with the pedantry and martinetism inherent to all peace armies. No doubt a great deal has been done latterly, especially since 1859, to get rid of this;

---

ers stayed (as if they were visiting friends), was dismissed by his Prussian counterparts as someone who 'dines more willingly than he fights': Grosser Generalstab (Historische Abteilung), *The Campaign of 1866 in Germany* (London, 1872), 155.

[46] U. v. Stosch (ed.), *Denkwürdigkeiten des Generals und Admirals Albrecht v. Stosch, ersten Chefs der Admiralität. Briefe und Tagebuchblätter*, 3rd edn (Stuttgart, 1904), 93.

[47] O. v. Bismarck, cited in R. v. Keudell, *Fürst und Fürstin Bismarck. Erinnerungen aus den Jahren 1864–1871* (Berlin, 1901), 297.

[48] J. v. Bismarck to O. v. Bismarck, 17 July 1866, ibid., 298.

[49] Wilhelm I marginalia, 24 July 1866, in E. Berner (ed.), *Kaiser Wilhelm des Grossen*, vol. 2, 136.

[50] A. v. Blumenthal (ed.), *Journals of Field-Marshal Count von Blumenthal*, 31.

[51] Even Wrangel was eager to know how Austria could have lost so quickly, quizzing Austrian prisoners of war: F. Deitl (ed.), *Unter Habsburg Kriegsbanner. Feldzugserebnisse aus der Feder von Mitkämpfern und Augenzeugen* (Dresden, 1898–1900), vol. 4, 43–4. Younger Prussian officers also thought that the Austrian army was stronger than it turned out to be: H. v. Clausewitz, *Aus dem Feldzuge des Jahres 1866. Aus dem Tagebuch eines preussischen Jägeroffiziers* (Leipzig, 1868), 6; L. v. Schönfels (ed.), *Erlebnisse Heinrich von Schönfels*, 7, note simply that 'the enemy has a numerical superiority'.

but the habits of forty years are not so easily eradicated.'[52] The battle of Langensalza on 27 June, in which Prussian losses (including 900 soldiers taken prisoner) had exceeded Hanoverian ones by more than 300, appeared to bring into question the Hohenzollern army's effectiveness.[53] By comparison, the Habsburg army—which had defeated the Italian army at Custozza on 24 June—had, by the 1860s, much more experience of combat than its Prussian counterpart, both in its unsuccessful campaign in Italy in 1859 and in its successful ones in Italy and Hungary in 1848–9 and in Schleswig and Denmark in 1864.[54] In addition, it was partly recruited from and deployed in the violent southern marches of the monarchy. Fighting at Oeversee and elsewhere, Austrian regiments had demonstrated their capacity to sustain significant losses without mutiny or desertion. Inside observers of the Prussian army such as Karl Leonhard von Blumenthal were confident that their forces were superior in quality, yet they also conceded that they were inferior in number: 'Yesterday I made an attempt to calculate the number of troops on the opposing sides in Germany', he wrote in his journal on 18 May: 'I make out that if Austria has to leave 150,000 to 180,000 in face of the Italians, and the smaller states remain neutral, we shall not be much weaker than the Austrians. The fortune of war and the excellence of our troops will make up the difference.'[55] Moltke's original war plan, dating back to 1865, had envisaged a Prussian force of 300,000 against 240,000 Austrians, 25,000 Saxons, and about 80,000 southern Germans.[56] Even taking into account the purportedly better training of the former, the Chief of the General Staff was bound to rely on rapid deployment in Saxony and Bohemia in order to overcome his opponents' larger forces.

Moltke's plan, which he outlined to the king in a memorandum on 14 April 1866, relied on the use of nine railway lines—three main lines and six secondary ones—to transport the seven eastern corps from assembly points at Herzberg, Calau, Görlitz, Liegnitz, Landeshut, Schweidnitz, and Neisse down to the railheads north of the *Erzgebirge* and the *Riesengebirge* in Silesia, where the larger Second Army was to assemble, ready to attack on its flank any Austrian force moving north towards Saxony and Berlin (see Map 5).[57] Since the Habsburg Northern Army disposed of only one railway line, the Prussian Chief of Staff calculated that his own forces

---

[52] W. H. Chaloner and W. O. Henderson (eds), *Engels as Military Critic* (Manchester, 1959), 123. August Bebel saw the war as a 'catastrophe' which 'issued, against the expectations of many, in a favourable outcome for Prussia': A. Bebel, *Aus meinem Leben* (Bonn, 1997), 121.

[53] Gerhard Klotten to his sister, 30 June 1866, *Kriegsbriefe* Archive, Universitäts- und Landesbibliothek Bonn, did not go so far as to question the Prussian army but he did note that it had suffered the greatest losses.

[54] Julius von Verdy du Vernois, *Im Hauptquartier der Zweiten Armee 1866 unter dem Oberbefehl Sr. Königlichem Hoheit des Kronprinzen Friedrich Wilhelm von Preußen. Erinnerungen* (Berlin, 1900), 99, noted that the news of both 'the defeat of Langensalza' and 'the victory of the Austrians near Custozza' were 'pieces of news which were hardly pleasant'.

[55] K. L. v. Blumenthal, 18 May 1866, in A. v. Blumenthal (ed.), *Journals of Field-Marshal Count von Blumenthal*, 13.

[56] A. Bucholz, *Moltke and the German Wars*, 112.

[57] H. v. Moltke to W. v. Stülpnagel, 18 June 1866, in W. Bigge (ed.), *Feldmarschall Graf Moltke. Ein militärisches Lebensbild* (Munich, 1901), vol. 2, 179: it was 'not unlikely' that Benedek would seek to attack Berlin immediately.

Map 5. The Prussian–Austrian War of 1866

Source: C. Clark, *Iron Kingdom: The Rise and Downfall of Prussia, 1600–1947* (London, 2006), 527.

would have a numerical superiority between the twenty-fifth day of mobilization, when it would have 118,000–200,000 soldiers already in place (compared to 182,000–223,000 on the thirty-second day), and the fortieth day, when Austria regained its advantage. However, the figures were imprecise and Austrian mobilization had begun much earlier than anticipated, on 27 April, compared to full Prussian mobilization—delayed by Wilhelm I—on 14 May. On 1 June, Moltke told the king that Austria was several weeks ahead of its expected schedule.[58] What was more, Hanover already had a force of 19,000 (two divisions) on manoeuvre in mid-June, which meant that it was ready for war, and Bavaria was threatening to bring up troops from Regensburg to Pilsen and Nuremberg to Prague, effectively giving the Austrian coalition the use of two more railways. In these circumstances, the balance seemed to be tipping back towards Vienna and its allies.

For critics like Engels, who was known by other socialists as 'the general', Moltke's strategy in 1866 was doomed to fail. Any ensign who outlined such a plan in a war academy examination would be told that he 'was not fit to hold even a lieutenant's commission', he declared in an article for the *Manchester Guardian* which was published—unfortunately for its author—on 3 July.[59] Benedek, it appeared to Engels, could use his interior lines to exploit the gap between Prussia's First and Second Armies, defeating one and then the other before they were able to join forces on the southern side of the *Erzgebirge* and *Riesengebirge*. 'It would be completely inexplicable how such a plan could ever be discussed, much less adopted, by a body of such unquestionably capable officers as form the Prussian staff, if it was not for the fact of King William being in chief command', wrote the exiled journalist and industrialist in the same article.[60] Moltke, who had devised the plan without interference, did not give such decisive weight to interior lines, preferring to maintain mobile armies which could attack the enemy's flank and rear, yet he acknowledged that the strategy was dangerous if the armies became separated by more than one day's march.[61] In addition, the progress of the three Hohenzollern armies from the railheads and through the mountains was difficult, running the risk of delay if some units did not spread out and use minor routes away from the main roads. As he waited in Silesia on 22 June for his orders to march south, the Crown Prince's Chief of Staff, Karl Leonhard von Blumenthal, 'pored over the maps' after dinner until his 'eyes streamed'.[62] Working out the order of march, 'there was a terrible lot to do':

> At three o'clock a cipher message came in from General Moltke, directing us to carry out all that we had planned. A good omen! At the same time I cannot conceal from myself the fact that our march over the mountains is a most critical operation and open to failure. It is, however, necessary if we do not wish to lose time.[63]

---

[58] Ibid., 118.

[59] F. Engels, *Manchester Guardian*, 3 July 1866, cited in W. H. Chaloner and W. O. Henderson (eds), *Engels as Military Critic*, 133–4.

[60] Ibid.   [61] G. A. Craig, *Königgrätz*, 46.

[62] K. L. v. Blumenthal, diary, 22 June 1866, in A. v. Blumenthal (ed.), *Journals of Field-Marshal Count von Blumenthal*, 32.

[63] Ibid., 33.

In contrast to Moltke, Blumenthal was convinced that 'warm blood is suited to war'.[64] Both men, though, recognized that the position of the Prussian armies during their march to Bohemia was an exposed one. To the north, 'the armies of Prince Frederick Charles and Herwarth von Bittenfeld appear to have got through the passes almost unopposed', wrote Engels, but

> the various columns of the army of the Crown Prince, as they descended into the valley on the Bohemian side of the hills, were met by the Austrians at favourable points where the valley, widening out, allowed them to offer a larger front to the Prussian columns, and to attempt to prevent them from deploying.[65]

For their part, the Prussians were obliged to 'send troops, wherever practicable, through the lateral valleys, to take their opponents in flank and rear'.[66] Although 'the general result' so far seemed to have been in favour of the Prussians, 'the fighting has been necessarily very much chequered' and 'very severe'.[67] 'The Prussians are now fighting, in Bohemia, a life-and-death struggle', concluded the industrialist.[68]

When the Prussian Second Army started to emerge from the mountains on 26 June 1866, it was still 50 miles away from the First Army, facing the more or less concentrated forces of the Austrian Northern Army. The advance guard of the Prussian Fifth Corps under Karl Friedrich von Steinmetz, who had fought in France in 1814, Schleswig in 1848, Baden in 1849, and Denmark in 1864, arrived on the 26th at the town of Nachod (famous as the birthplace of Wallenstein), which the Austrians quickly abandoned. On the next day, as the rest of the corps arrived from Silesia, the advance guard moved out onto the plateau above the nearby village of Wysokov, where they were met by the Austrian Sixth Corps under Wilhelm von Ramming, which attempted to trap the bulk of the Prussian force before it came out of the valley from the town. About 21,000 Austrians fought 10,000 Prussians for much of the day.[69] By noon, the Crown Prince's troops were being pushed backwards into the hollow behind the plateau, from which they would have had to retreat back into the mountains. Julius von Verdy von Vernois, who was attached to Friedrich Wilhelm's staff and who heard the fighting from a distance, betrayed how its outcome remained in doubt. As they approached Nachod from Branau, a report from Steinmetz came in, explaining 'that he found himself in a fight against a clear enemy superiority and must ask for reinforcements'.[70] Since the guards were also engaged, the heavy cavalry brigade was dispatched southwards but no artillery. In the meantime, over the course of the morning, 'the fire from both fields of battle had strengthened' and 'the thunder of the cannon shots became more and more powerfully and more and more coherently

[64] Cited in G. A. Craig, *Königgrätz*, 31.
[65] F. Engels, *Manchester Guardian*, 3 July 1866, cited in W. H. Chaloner and W. O. Henderson (eds), *Engels as Military Critic*, 134–5.
[66] Ibid., 135.   [67] Ibid.   [68] Ibid., 134.
[69] A. Bucholz, *Moltke and the German Wars*, 125.
[70] J. v. Verdy du Vernois, *Im Hauptquartier der Zweiten Armee*, 98.

audible; both corps were engaged unmistakably in very serious fighting'.[71] Blumenthal turned to Verdy and asked him, 'How many do you think Steinmetz has against him?'[72] His reply hinted at once at the opacity of the information available to commanders and the uncertainty of victory: 'He is surely pushing up against a fresh corps, but there must also be a second one close by, and if the Austrians have deployed correctly, he could even find a third in front of him.'[73] This answer, recorded Verdy, 'was in no way a pleasing one, when one considers the position in which we found ourselves'.[74] As they saw clouds of dust blowing their way during that sweltering hot day, the Prussian commanders assumed that they were coming from 'rapidly retreating troops' and that 'things were bad for the 5th Corps'.[75]

In the event, the clouds were a false alarm, merely revealing the anxieties of the Crown Prince's staff, as Austrian battalions sacrificed themselves in undisciplined fury on round after round of volleys from the needle-guns of the Prussian infantry, leaving more than one thousand Habsburg soldiers dead, more than 1,000 wounded, and 1,000 missing, compared to just over 1,000 Prussian casualties in total. The unruffled demeanour of Hohenzollern commanders, with the Crown Prince showing 'no trace of agitation', concealed the dangers of their undertaking.[76] In his journal, Blumenthal noted simply on 28 June that 'yesterday we fought for four hours at Nachod', 'the fifth army was engaged and drove the enemy back on Jaromir', and 'the Crown Prince was very happy and visited the wounded in hospital, conversing with everyone'.[77] At headquarters on the day, he had been deliberately unperturbed, removing his field cap and running his hand through his hair before saying, 'What a shame that we cannot be with Steinmetz! I'd like to see one more time how the old man deals with them!'[78] Later, on 1 July, he was more sincere:

We have been through an eventful week, and have reached quite an epoch in the war. God was on our side, for without His help the task would have been too hard. The exertion and hardships were terrific, and I have had no time to write up my journal. Our march over the mountains was a most difficult undertaking, for the roads were few and in very indifferent condition.

Our Generals are, for the most part, lacking in war experience, and the way in which they cling to peace traditions greatly increases difficulties. When several Army Corps have to move over hill and down dale, through narrow defiles, woods, and gorges, it should be well understood what care is necessary to prevent the march being hampered with baggage and supply wagons. These should all be left to follow well in the rear, and the troops be made to subsist on provisions which each man can carry on his person, say for three days at least.[79]

---

[71] Ibid., 99.   [72] Ibid.   [73] Ibid.
[74] Ibid.   [75] Ibid., 100.   [76] Ibid.
[77] K. L. v. Blumenthal, 28 June 1866, in A. v. Blumenthal (ed.), *Journals of Field-Marshal Count von Blumenthal*, 36.
[78] J. v. Verdy du Vernois, *Im Hauptquartier der Zweiten Armee*, 99–100.
[79] K. L. v. Blumenthal, 1 July 1866, in A. v. Blumenthal (ed.), *Journals of Field-Marshal Count von Blumenthal*, 37.

Despite appearances, the Prussian armies were improvising and adapting to the realities of modern warfare, with the War Ministry having done little to organize supply trains until mid-June.[80] 'Nothing to live on unless we carry it ourselves', Friedrich Karl had complained to the king on 28 June, after his troops had failed to find sufficient provisions in Bohemia to live off the land.[81]

Moltke's plan required the three armies to move quickly and to travel light, given that they were unable to use railways on Austrian soil. However, by 30 June, the Army of the Elbe and the First Army were already slowing down, as Friedrich Karl admitted: 'First Army completely exhausted. Needs several days' rest.'[82] It remained several days' march from the Second Army, whose own corps were still divided, as Verdy and other commanders had anticipated. 'How far these marches'—of the First Corps to Trautenau, the Guard to Kosteletz, and the Fifth to Nachod, with a *rendezvous* at Königinhof—'are actually carried out simply depends on the intervention of our opponent'.[83] In Verdy's opinion, 'it appeared most probable that the Fifth Corps would come into contact with the enemy', meeting the right flank of Austrian forces coming from the south-east.[84] 'One could estimate this column to be two to three army corps, and the direction of its march led it, at least in part, not far from the Fifth Army Corps, coming out from the mountains', he continued, revealing how little was known about imminent military engagements and their outcomes:

> If the enemy had gained knowledge of the march of our army or at least a part of it, one could anticipate that it would oppose us with strong forces, if this were in any way possible, and would not let the opportunity escape it of using them against the single columns in which we are able to move through the mountains.[85]

The Fifth Corps, he wrote, 'would then face a difficult task', which was proved by events at Nachod on 27 June to be true.[86] Whether the cavalry division and Adolf von Bonin's First Corps, which was on the right flank of the Prussian columns and of which 'we had had no report' as the fighting at Nachod began, would be 'exposed on its march to Trautenau to contact with stronger enemy masses could not with certainty be foreseen'.[87]

As things turned out, the First Corps did meet a superior number of Austrian troops at Trautenau, resulting in a first Prussian defeat, at the same time as the Fifth Corps was being pushed back towards Nachod, recalled Hozier, who saw the fighting from the commanders' point of view:

> The town of Trautenau lies on the River Aupa, in a basin almost surrounded by mountains: by the river the ground is wet and marshy, on the hillsides it is rough and broken, so that it is nowhere particularly favourable for the action of cavalry or artillery.

---

[80] G. A. Craig, *Königgrätz*, 49. See, for instance, the commander of the Second Corps, who wrote about 'very strenuous marches with provisions lacking', in G. v. Haeseler, *Zehn Jahre im Stabe des Prinzen Friedrich Karl. Erinnerungen*, vol. 3, 113.

[81] Grosser Generalstab, *Studien zur Kriegsgeschichte und Taktik*, vol. 6, 100–6, 114, 133.

[82] Ibid.   [83] J. v. Verdy du Vernois, *Im Hauptquartier der Zweiten Armee*, 70.

[84] Ibid., 70–1.   [85] Ibid., 71.   [86] Ibid.   [87] Ibid., 99, 71.

The great heat made the Prussian troops suffer much from fatigue and thirst on their march, and they were weary when they reached the town of Trautenau. But the Austrians were in town, and General von Bonin was forced to attack them...The infantry fight soon began in the streets, and the Austrians were pushed back gradually from house to house...Both sides suffered heavily, and the Prussians gained ground but slowly, for from every house and from every corner hidden marksmen poured bullets into the ranks of the battalions that tried to push along the streets...

When all the Prussian reinforcements had arrived, a general attack was made, and the Austrians were pushed out of the houses into the open country beyond. The Prussians pursued and followed step by step their slowly-retreating enemies. Beyond the town one of Austria's most celebrated cavalry regiments, the Windischgrätz dragoons, stood waiting to sweep the Prussian battalions from the open ground if they issued from the shelter of the houses. These dragoons have long held a high reputation, and, for a record of brave deeds done by the regiment, alone in the Austrian army wear no moustache. The Prussian infantry could not advance, and it seemed that the houses of Trautenau had been won in vain. But assistance was at hand.

The 1st regiment of the Prussian Dragoons came trotting along the main street, deployed into line almost as they debouched from the town, and with their horses well in hand, and their sword-points low, bore in a steady canter straight down upon the Austrian cavalry...When within a few yards of each other, both sides raised a cheer, and, welcoming the hug of battle, the two lines rushed upon each other. Horse pressed against horse, knee against knee, swords went up quick and came down heavily on head-piece or shoulder, points were given and received, blows quickly parried were returned with lightning speed; here an Austrian was borne to the ground, there a Prussian was sent reeling from his seat, and for a few minutes the mass of combatants swayed slowly backwards and forwards. But then, as if some mighty shell had burst among them, the Austrian soldiers flew scattered from the *mêlée*...The Austrians retired a short distance. The Prussian commander ordered eight battalions to advance from Parschnitz, cross the Aupa, and attack the right flank of the Austrian position. These battalions had great difficulties to encounter: the wooded hills close to the Aupa could only be traversed in extended order, and as soon as the open ground was gained they suffered much from some hostile skirmishers concealed in the standing corn.

Notwithstanding these disadvantageous circumstances, they gained ground...It was now three o'clock, the Austrians had retired, and General von Bonin considered that the action was over.[88]

Unfortunately for Bonin, 'the retreat of the Austrians had...been but a tactical manoeuvre' and the Prussian forces were attacked again at 3.30 p.m. by the Austrian Tenth Corps under Gablenz, who 'had advanced from Pilnikau with his whole force'.[89] 'Already weary with a hot march and a lengthened combat', the Prussian troops commenced their retreat at 5.00 p.m.[90] Although the 'terrible disparity in numbers'—196 Austrian officers and 5,536 men lost compared to sixty-three Prussian officers and 1,214 men—meant that success was 'almost as costly as defeat', in Hozier's verdict, 'the Austrian infantry, with a muzzle-loading arm, had indeed gained a victory over an enemy equipped with a breech-loading

---

[88] H. M. Hozier, *The Seven Weeks' War*, 218–20.
[89] Ibid., 220.   [90] Ibid.

weapon'.[91] Bismarck later referred to Trautenau as a blow which rocked the entire Prussian army.[92] At that point, on 27 June, the outcome of the war seemed open and the losses on both sides great.

From the vantage point of commanders, Prussia's position was a precarious one, with its troops having their principal tests before, not behind, them. After Trautenau, Bonin retreated back behind the mountains which he had just traversed, losing contact with the enemy. Consequently, the Crown Prince's order for the Guard to proceed through the pass at Eypel, which was the third route into Bohemia from Silesia, in order to attack Gablenz's Tenth Corps in the flank whilst the First Corps fought it from the front was foiled by the unexpected absence of Bonin's forces on 28 June, which left the Guard redundant and Steinmetz's Fifth Corps exposed to an attack by the 70,000 Austrian soldiers (Ramming's, Archduke Leopold's, and Tassilo Count Festetics de Tolna's corps) arrayed in front of the *Riesengebirge*. Prince Kraft zu Hohenlohe-Ingelfingen met the Crown Prince on his way to Kosteletz:

> He ordered me to ride beside his carriage and oriented me about that which he had kept from the troops. While the Fifth Army Corps repelled the enemy near Nachod, the First was defeated near Trautenau and returned as quickly as possible in flight to Silesia. What would come of today, he did not know.[93]

Only Benedek's stubborn backing of the plan of his operations chief Gideon von Krismanic to move six corps to the west in order to defeat the four-and-a-half corps of Friedrich Karl's First Army, before Friedrich Wilhelm's Second Army could act, prevented the forced retreat or destruction of Steinmetz's corps. 'The 28 June was the hardest day of the whole campaign', wrote Albrecht von Stosch, who was the Crown Prince's Quartermaster General: 'the worry about Bonin and about the link-up with Prince Friedrich Karl pressed down on us'.[94] The Army of the Elbe (under the command of Herwarth von Bittenfeld) and First Army (under Friedrich Karl), which had crossed the border into Saxony on 16 June and into Bohemia on the 23rd, were moving much more slowly than Moltke wanted by the 26th, after the latter had been granted two days' rest at Reichenberg while it established the whereabouts of the former. The Chief of the General Staff's order was terse: 'only a vigorous advance by the First Army [can] disengage the Second'.[95] Although Eduard Friedrich Karl von Fransecky's Seventh Division and Heinrich Friedrich von Horn's Eighth Division had advanced quickly on 26 June, after a minor engagement at Sichrow, to take, respectively, the town of Turnau, which had been abandoned by the Austrians and Saxons, and the village of Podol, which the Austro-Saxons failed to recapture during a night battle, sustaining heavy losses—thirty-three officers and 1,015 men compared to twelve and 118 Prussians—against enemy infantry equipped with needle-guns. Even then, as the Austrians

---

[91] Ibid., 221.　　[92] Cited in G. A. Craig, *Königgrätz*, 64.
[93] K. zu Hohenlohe-Ingelfingen, *Aus meinem Leben*, vol. 3, 241.
[94] U. v. Stosch (ed.), *Denkwürdigkeiten des Generals und Admirals Albrecht v. Stosch*, 87.
[95] H. v. Moltke, *Militärische Werke* (Berlin, 1896), vol. 1, 237.

and Saxons retired to Gitschin, Friedrich Karl refused to move east towards the
Second Army, fearing that his opponent, whom he had neglected to follow with
cavalry reconnaissance rides, would remain at Münchengrätz and attack his flank.
The dangerous corollary of such immobility was that Prussian forces remained
divided.

Moltke separated uncertainty about what would happen in war and risk, which
could be assessed and even, in some circumstances, quantified.[96] Given the
Prussian military's numerical inferiority in a protracted conflict, his planning relied
on rapid mobilization and movement, using railways on the model of the Franco-
Austrian and American Civil Wars, which he had studied in depth.[97] Railroads
permitted the massing of larger armies, but they also encouraged the division of
forces, travelling down roughly parallel lines. For Moltke, it was 'not new' that 'the
Austrians—if we give them time—can assemble as many troops as we can', as he
had said 'in all the conferences that have taken place', as he reassured Roon in April
1866: 'The point is not the absolute number of troops available, it is the time
required on each side to put these troops into a position to fight.'[98] To the king,
whose anxiety about Bavaria's likely intervention in the war had prompted the
Chief of Staff's assurance to Roon, the strategy seemed foolhardy, pitting 'these
60,000 men [that] are all we have against the 100,000 of the South'.[99] Moltke was
counting on the slower mobilization and deployment of Austrian and southern
German troops compared to those of Prussia and on the exploitation of tactical
and technological advantages which would give the other armies time to join the
one being attacked. He spelled out what these advantages were, as they had mani-
fested themselves in the Schleswig war, in an anonymous article in the *Militär-
Wochenblatt* in July 1866 and in the official General Staff history of the conflict:
the Dreyse needle-gun, which was breech-loading and allowed far more shots to be
fired than did Austrian muzzle-loaders, facilitated the creation of strong defensive
positions (a battalion or brigade, not a company), which swash-buckling Austrian
commanders were likely—as a result of a reliance on bayonets, which France had
purportedly used in 1859—to attack with great loss of life and no success, allowing
a decisive Prussian counter-attack.[100] Frontal attacks were to be avoided, because
of probable losses, unless prepared by extensive artillery fire.

Although Austria's artillery and cavalry were perceived to be effective, its infantry was seen to be hampered by the lack of a common language and deficits of
training and education. In such circumstances, a separation of forces, rapid
marches, and flanking movements seemed feasible to the Chief of the General
Staff, but they still appeared reckless to many other Prussian commanders, as
Gustav von Alvensleben, who was close to the king, made plain in three unanswered

[96] A. Bucholz, *Moltke and the German Wars*, 105.

[97] E. Kessel, *Moltke* (Stuttgart, 1957), 321; J. Luvaas, *The Military Legacy of the Civil War*
(Chicago, 1959).

[98] H. v. Moltke to A. v. Roon, 5 Apr. 1866, in H. v. Moltke, *Correspondance Militaire* (Paris,
1900), vol. 5, 108–9; see H. v. Moltke, *Moltkes Militärische Korrespondenz* (Berlin, 1902).

[99] Ibid., 115–17.

[100] E. Kessel, *Moltke*, 426–7; A. Bucholz, *Moltke and the German Wars*, 105–6.

letters in late 1866: since Austria could pick off Prussia's dispersed armies in isolation, it was better to concentrate the Hohenzollern armies further west, occupying Saxony, Hanover, and North Germany with a single concentrated force.[101] In Moltke's opinion, this strategy would have left the Hohenzollern monarchy's principal opponent untroubled, massing its forces and dictating the rest of the campaign. Yet he did not seek to diminish the dangers of his own plan, which required the Second Army to come to the aid of the Army of the Elbe and the First Army (since the Habsburg army was initially expected to move north towards Berlin) during the day of battle, preferably within four hours. Although he was known as a 'decrepit' 66-year-old desk officer, in the words of one of the king's adjutants, Moltke had been marked by his experiences of combat—in addition to witnessing the recent Danish war—as an advisor to the Ottoman army under Hafiz Pasha in 1839.[102] His call to remain in an entrenched position on the Syrian border and to threaten the flank of the Egyptian army was ignored, leading to the rout of the Turkish forces and the flight of the Prussian officers 'riding all night over the mountains, and also all the next day'.[103] As he recalled in a letter to his fiancée two years later, 'Today, I was riding the same horse, and was thinking all the time that, next to God, I owe it to his legs that I am still moving about in the world.'[104] At the battle itself, before which he had asked to be discharged, he had warned Hafiz that 'by tomorrow at sundown you will know what it is to be a commander without an army'.[105] Moltke's intellectual approach to war was founded on an awareness of its dangers and risks, including the possibility of defeat. Thus, when Alvensleben objected on 2 July that the Chief of Staff's planned 'attack, where a river like the Elbe lies between the armies, is dangerous', Moltke replied: 'Yes, war is altogether a dangerous thing.'[106]

As the separated corps of the Second Army pushed forwards towards the First, they remained exposed to attack. Steinmetz's Fifth Corps advanced to Skalitz on 28 June, deprived of support from the Second Guards Division, which had been instructed by Friedrich Wilhelm to go to the aid of Bonin in Trautenau. Instead of ordering the 70,000 Austrian troops in the vicinity to join Archduke Leopold, whose Sixth and Eighth Corps were well positioned on the heights above the town, Benedek—who passed through the town in person—kept to his original plan of concentrating his forces against Friedrich Karl further west. Leopold was told to withdraw from Skalitz by 2.00 p.m., falling back on Josephstadt, if Steinmetz had not marched on it by that time, yet he refused, despite the retreat of the other Austrian corps, and he launched attacks on Steinmetz's advancing columns, which by 3.00 p.m. were engaged in a full-scale assault on Skalitz with 70,000 men against 14,000 Austrians, inflicting 5,570 total losses on the Austrians (compared to 1,365 Prussian losses) and a killing and wounding rate of more than a third (the

[101] E. Kessel, *Moltke*, 426–7.   [102] Ibid., 444.
[103] H. v. Moltke, *Letters to His Wife* (London, 1896), vol. 1, 16.
[104] Ibid.   [105] Cited in F. E. Whitton, *Moltke* (New York, 1921), 38.
[106] W. v. Schweinitz (ed.), *Denkwürdigkeiten des Botschafters General v. Schweinitz*, vol. 1, 226.

highest of the entire conflict).[107] Between three and four o'clock, the Crown
Prince, who had positioned his headquarters between Skalitz in the south and Soor
in the north, 'received the positive report from General Steinmetz that he had
stormed Skalitz, and driven back two of the enemy's corps', according to Hozier's
account: 'He immediately started for Eypel [near Soor] to be present at the action
in which the Guards were engaged', after they had attacked and overrun the main
force of Gablenz, who had been ordered by Benedek to retreat from Trautenau.[108]
'On this day, the 28th, depended whether the Army of Silesia would effect its issue
from the mountains, or fail in the attempt', wrote the British officer and reporter
for *The Times*.[109] Until that point in time, the Austrian and Saxon forces appeared
to have the potential to impose critical defeats on their Prussian opponents, affecting the way in which the conflict was viewed. 'The victories of Skalitz and
Soor... had lifted heavy worries from our brows', wrote Verdy: 'Through them, the
débouches from the mountains were secured and the drawing together of the first
and sixth army corps was no longer brought into question.'[110] 'On the 29th, the
Guard corps stormed Königinhof; and the Prussian fifth corps drove General
Festetics from Schweinschädel', Hozier continued: 'The army of Prince Frederick
Charles that night stormed Gitschen', sustaining half the number of casualties of
the Austrians (1,212 dead and wounded compared to 2,211) and allowing communications to be 'opened between the army of Prince Frederick Charles round
Gitschin and the first corps of the army of the Crown Prince at Arnau'.[111]
Thoroughly disheartened, Benedek sent a telegram of capitulation to Franz Joseph
on 30 June: 'I beg your Majesty urgently to make peace at any price. Catastrophe
for the army is unavoidable.'[112] His request was rejected and his army began to
make preparations for the battle of Königgrätz. The viewpoint of Prussian commanders, however, was quite different: the greatest dangers had been overcome but
the campaign had not been decided.

Prussian commanders' perceptions of the fighting at Königgrätz on 3 July
1866 were coloured by their understanding of the role of the battle in the campaign as a whole. It marked the heroic turning point of the war, bearing witness
to the glory of Prussia and the Hohenzollern dynasty. Commanding officers,
whose published accounts constituted much of the record of the 1866 campaign,
showed how momentary relief and later enthusiasm could merge in narratives of
the conflict. During the day, remarked Verdy, the unfurling of Prussian flags on
the battlefield was 'an elevating moment', reminding 'everyone of their oath of
loyalty unto death'.[113] Likewise, 'the enthusiasm, which the presence of the
Crown Prince awakened, increased all the more as he announced that His
Majesty had arrived and taken up overall command on the field of battle'.[114]
Late in the afternoon, after a 'deathly silence' for a moment along the entire

---

[107] A. Bucholz, *Moltke and the German Wars*, 129.
[108] H. M. Hozier, *The Seven Weeks' War*, 232.   [109] Ibid.
[110] J. v. Verdy du Vernois, *Im Hauptquartier der Zweiten Armee*, 105.
[111] H. M. Hozier, *The Seven Weeks' War*, 235.
[112] H. Friedjung (ed.), *Benedeks nachgelassene Papiere* (Leipzig, 1901), 375.
[113] J. v. Verdy du Vernois, *Im Hauptquartier der Zweiten Armee*, 154.   [114] Ibid.

mile-long front before him, it was as though the Prussian soldiers were seeing 'the agonies of the Austrian army', noted Friedrich Karl's Chief of Staff Konstantin Bernhard von Voigts-Rhetz in a letter on 4 July: 'The short silence...was suddenly interrupted by a hurrah from 100,000 throats and the whole army now pushed forward with its assault, the artillery began its thundering concert again, and one position after another of the enemy was conquered relentlessly.'[115] 'I congratulated the Prince on the battle won', he went on, pointing out that 'the King was also, incidentally, there', after arriving at the battlefield at 8.00 a.m. and giving the order to attack at 9.00 a.m.: 'His Majesty demonstrated great calm and true military insight.'[116]

The fiction of the monarch as an all-conquering commander-in-chief was commonplace, in spite of the fact that high-ranking officers had taken their orders directly from Moltke since 2 June 1866 (six days before the Chief of the General Staff was made a general of infantry).[117] Thus, when Louis Schneider, the actor, royal reader, and editor of the *Soldaten-Freund* (the most popular military periodical of the era), asked Wilhelm I eagerly whether he had actually been in command, the king replied, after allowing the royal counsellor to kiss his hand ('a particularly honouring gesture of favour'): 'Of course, I commanded, although I did not myself draw my sword. How could you believe that I could be with my army without commanding it?'[118] The king was, by his own admission, on his horse between eight in the morning and eight at night:

WILHELM I: It was actually an artillery battle. The 1st Guards Regiment suffered so much that one battalion had to be formed from two. It was moving to see the troops advance. At about one o'clock, everything stood in the balance. I asked Fritz Carl how long he would be able to hold out? He showed me the entire 5th and 6th Divisions still in reserve and also an adequate number of reserve batteries. Go and get an adjutant to explain everything and only report facts, no observations, namely nothing which could debase the enemy. Also, only give the number, not the names, of what you learn of our losses. The names can come later and, even then, they come too soon...

SCHNEIDER: May I ask for another piece of information? Your Majesty was in grenade fire on more than one occasion. Where was that?...

---

[115] A. v. Voigts-Rhetz (ed.), *Briefe des Generals der Infanterie von Voigts-Rhetz*, 12.

[116] Ibid.: Voigts-Rhetz wrote to his wife on 4 July 1866: 'many came to congratulate me. The king himself came to me again in the evening and shook my hand repeatedly and thanked me for my actions. Prince Friedrich Karl could not speak for emotion as I congratulated him and his father, old Prince Carl, embraced me repeatedly.'

[117] H. W. Lucy (ed.), *The Emperor's Diary* (London, 1888), 26: 'I told [Steinmetz] that our King himself was present, and commanded the army.' W. Foerster (ed.), *Prinz Friedrich Karl von Preußen. Denkwürdigkeiten aus seinem Leben* (Stuttgart, 1910), vol. 2, 74: on hearing the news of Friedrich Karl's discovery of the Benedek's forces and his request to attack, Moltke got dressed—it was the middle of the night—and went across to Wilhelm I's billet, where he woke him up and explained the situation: 'It only needed a few words to describe the favourable conditions of the present moment, if it were to be exploited, before the Austrians continued their retreat behind the Elbe.'

[118] L. Schneider, *Aus dem Leben Kaiser Wilhelms, 1849–1873* (Berlin, 1888), vol. 1, 241.

WILHELM I: In grenade fire? As if I didn't know it! In such an extensive battle, grenades fall everywhere. As I rode along the road to the highest hill of Sadowa, I saw several fall and said to the gentlemen following: 'I thank you for that, gentlemen!', but that doesn't need to be made special mention of.[119]

In fact, the monarch had not been able even to see the fighting at first from the relative safety of his military headquarters.[120] On the way to the hill overlooking the battle, he rode through Prussian regiments, 'which greeted me with loud jubilation', he wrote to his wife on 4 July.[121] He spent most of the day watching the unfolding events from a distance, as 'the enemy in the centre continued to make a solid stand despite...the gradual, very slow forward movement of Herwarth [the commander of the Elbe Army]'.[122] The king only left his vantage point as 'the victory began to be decided as a result of the flanking attack of the Second Army' and 'the artillery fire in the centre became weaker and the cavalry were asked for—a sign that the enemy was beginning to yield'.[123] Until then, he was confined to a position which 'was not suited to leading the battle' and which 'in no way permitted a thorough view of the battlefield', in Loë's opinion, as he returned from the front line.[124]

Prince Friedrich Karl, who had begun hostilities on 3 July, was closer to the fighting, having accompanied his troops from before dusk, conscious that they were 'worn-out' after

> almost every planned day of rest became a day of fighting or marching, provisions had been lacking, last night no one had slept longer than a few hours, they had marched in the rain, and no one, apart from the Eighth Division, had even drunk a coffee, not to mention eating.[125]

Yet he, too, was obliged to spend much of the day on the hill near Sadowa, with its 'relatively very limited prospect' of the battle.[126] From here, he directed the movement of his divisions and looked on 'very calmly during the entire time of the battle' at the actions taking place in the distance, feeling the burden of responsibility less than he had in 1864.[127] Although 'the least welcome role had fallen to me, according to the nature of things and in a certain respect as a result of my own choice', with Friedrich Karl playing the part of Wellington (holding the centre against heavy enemy fire) and the Crown Prince playing that of Blücher (arriving later and attacking the flank of the enemy), the commander of the First Army acted as if he were above the battle, gauging 'the use of my forces, the feeding of the fight, the point in time for the use of my reserves of each service' by the

[119] Ibid., 241–2.
[120] Wilhelm I to Queen Augusta, 4 July 1866, in E. Berner (ed.), *Kaiser Wilhelm des Grossen. Briefe, Reden und Schriften* (Berlin, 1906), vol. 2, 132. The experience of battle was different from the vantage point of the military headquarters or from behind the lines, as Heros von Borcke's account, *Mit Prinz Friedrich Karl. Kriegs- und Jagdfahrten und am häuslichen Herd* (Berlin, 1893), 38–53, makes plain.
[121] E. Berner (ed.), *Kaiser Wilhelm des Grossen*, vol. 2, 132.		[122] Ibid.
[123] Ibid.		[124] F. C. W. D. v. Loë, *Erinnerungen aus meinem Berufsleben*, 103.
[125] W. Foerster (ed.), *Prinz Friedrich Karl von Preußen*, 77.
[126] Ibid., 90.		[127] Ibid., 88–9.

progress of the Second Army towards the battlefield.[128] In the same vein, he reported to the king, as the situation of his troops in the centre worsened, 'I can only hold on for another two hours': 'My position is admittedly not yet that of Wellington at Belle-Alliance, but it would be good if your son were to come quickly.'[129] The attitude of the Crown Prince was similar to that of his cousin, showing himself 'perfectly cool and collected, cheerful and bright' throughout 'the whole fight', as his Chief of Staff, Blumenthal, remarked at the time: after the battle, he 'rode now among the troops, praising and congratulating them, caring for the wounded, talking with all he could, and encouraging all'.[130] To a degree, Friedrich Wilhelm was obliged to remain detached from the suffering of the soldiers.[131]

Virtually all officers believed it their duty to lead and set an example, placing themselves above their troops.[132] Their heroic conception of warfare, which usually encompassed the notion of an honourable or glorious death and a dynastic or patriotic purpose, left its imprint on popular narratives of the conflict in 1866.[133] 'It is fine when a Prussian general bleeds', ran the Crown Prince's congratulatory message to Ludwig Karl von Tümpling, who had been hit at the battle of Gitschin on 29 June: 'It brings the army luck.'[134] It is not known whether the general replied. Bravado in the face of danger was regularly displayed by all ranks. Having been shot in the chest during the fiercest fighting on 3 July, as the Seventh Division came under heavy fire in the *Swiepwald* (Svib wood) near the village of Benatek, one major—propped up on an NCO—supposedly exclaimed, 'Now I can gladly die, since I have seen how bravely my battalion has fought.'[135] His commander Fransecky was said by Moltke, advising the king not to send 'a single man of infantry support' to him (since 'we must be on the look-out for an Austrian offensive'), to be indomitable: 'I know General von Fransecky well and I know that he will stand firm.'[136] On the left flank of the Prussian forces, the nineteen battalions of the Seventh Division were opposed by up to fifty Austrian battalions, losing

---

[128] Ibid., 78. See also T. Krieg, *Wilhelm von Doering, königlich preußischer Generalmajor. Ein Lebens- und Charakterbild*, 183: 'We must begin the battle like Wellington and end like Blücher', ran the prophetic saying which Prince Friedrich Karl passed on to his leading officers *en route*.

[129] W. Foerster (ed.), *Prinz Friedrich Karl von Preußen*, 90.

[130] A. v. Blumenthal (ed.), *Journals of Count von Blumenthal*, 42.

[131] The distance between royal commanders and soldiers was visible in all German states, including Austria. See, for instance, C. v. Duncker, *Feldmarschall Erzherzog Albrecht* (Vienna, 1897), 215–56: after the Austrian victory at Custozza, a young Crown Prince Rudolph wrote an enthusiastic letter to his uncle, betraying some of the unspoken attitudes amongst Austrian and German royalty concerning 'their' armies: 'Dear Uncle, how I rejoice that you have won. Mama and Gisela, too, congratulate you from the bottom of their hearts. I prayed to God that we would win and that he would, in addition, protect you. I think very often of our brave army and the poor, wounded soldiers. How many brigades were under fire? Was my regiment already under fire? I read all the telegrams which come from the South and the North. ... Your Rudolph.'

[132] See, for instance, pre-war treatments of the subject such as F. v. Prondzynski, *Theorie des Krieges*, vol. 1, 26, and A. v. Pappenheim, *Militairische Fantasien*, vol. 6, 48, 117–24.

[133] See Chapter 12. Even Wrangel, who was 82 years old, wanted 'to find his death on the battle-field' in 1866, as one Austrian witness who met him as a prisoner confirmed: F. Deitl (ed.), *Unter Habsburg Kriegsbanner*, vol. 4, 45.

[134] Cited in G. A. Craig, *Königgrätz*, 78. [135] E. v. Fransecky, *Denkwürdigkeiten*, 377–8.

[136] F. C. W. D. v. Loë, *Erinnerungen aus meinem Berufsleben*, 102. Also, T. Krieg, *Constantin v. Alvensleben, General der Infanterie. Ein militärisches Lebensbild* (Berlin, 1903), 64.

eighty-four officers and 2,100 men and being reduced to three intact battalions during the course of the morning.[137] During the late morning, 'they had to deal with an enemy which was more than three times as strong', recalled Fransecky: 'From about eleven o'clock, its [the enemy's] first thrusts began, they then became quicker and heavier, and they reached their greatest volume about one o'clock.'[138] These soldiers, together with the Eighth, Third, and Fourth Divisions in the centre, had to pin down Austrian troops until the arrival of the Second Army on their left flank during the early afternoon. 'The Seventh Division is suffering heavily', read one message to the king, 'but it is holding firm.'[139] Earlier, Loë had ridden over from the king's general staff to ascertain how the Prussian left flank was faring and to see the battle at closer quarters. Arriving at Benatek, he learned that 'General v. Fransecky is with the troops of the advance guard in the wood': 'Austrian batteries near Maslowed...and enemy infantry kept the wood strongly under fire and caused numerous losses amongst our companies, which sought cover where possible behind the trees and returned the enemy fire energetically.'[140] Here, he found Fransecky on foot, his horse having been shot from beneath him. At that moment, the Austrians were storming the wood: 'Overpowering fire from nearly one hundred Austrian cannon had prepared the attack and put our troops to a tough test', he wrote: 'Losses increased shockingly, many officers fell, but everyone was firmly decided to defend the wood to the last man, convinced of the importance of the position.'[141] It was difficult to imagine a leader, he went on, 'better suited for this task than General v. Fransecky': 'He stood in heavy fire, mostly in the line of defence, and observed the fighting from here with rapt attention and without any agitation; his intrepidity and calm decisiveness imbued those surrounding him with a firm trust in the outcome of the loss-laden struggle and has remained, for me, unforgettable.'[142] Other officers such as Colonel Franz Friedrich von Zychlinski, commander of the 27th Infantry Regiment, left a similar impression, calling on his men to go '"Vorwärts!" as Vater Blücher used to say! "Drauf!" as Vater Wrangel used to say! "Durch!" as Körner, the poet of the wars of freedom, has sung!'[143] Loë stayed with Fransecky for about an hour and then rode back to deliver the general's request for reinforcements at about 11.00 a.m., reporting at the same time that he was 'firmly resolved to defend the important position to the last man'.[144] Zychlinski was wounded shortly afterwards. His deeds were venerated in many accounts.

Representations of even these acts, however, were often interspersed not merely with pathos but with horror.[145] As the Austrians retook part of the *Swiepwald*,

[137] Grosser Generalstab (Historische Abteilung), *The Campaign of 1866 in Germany* (London, 1872), 169–205; G. A. Craig, *Königgrätz*, 110; G. Wawro, *The Austro-Prussian War: Austria's War with Prussia and Italy in 1866* (Cambridge, 1996), 227.

[138] E. v. Fransecky, *Denkwürdigkeiten*, 378–9.   [139] Ibid., 378.

[140] F. C. W. D. v. Loë, *Erinnerungen aus meinem Berufsleben*, 99.

[141] Ibid., 100–1.   [142] Ibid., 101.

[143] Ibid. F. F. v. Zychlinkski, cited in M. Jähns, *Die Schlacht von Königgrätz* (Leipzig, 1876), 126.

[144] F. C. W. D. v. Loë, *Erinnerungen aus meinem Berufsleben*, 102.

[145] Karl Werner, *Hohlweg der Toten nach der Schlacht auf Chlum* (1866), Muzeum východních Čech v Hradci, is one of very few paintings to show corpses in graphic detail.

Fransecky wrote later, they found the ground 'literally bedecked with dead and wounded of the Prussian Seventh Division'.[146] The call that met the advance guard of the Second Army (which eventually began to relieve the pressure on the left flank at 1.30 p.m.)—'The Crown Prince is coming! No further back! Here we shall die!'—betrayed desperation as well as courage amongst soldiers who had been 'prepared for its arrival since 11.15 a.m.'[147] After the victory, many officers felt like Albrecht von Stosch that the 'day is the finest and greatest in Prussian history', yet they also concurred with him that it had been 'a terribly hard fight', leaving 'exhaustion' in its wake as well as 'contentment and a patriotic mood'.[148] Because he had entered a battle already in progress, the Crown Prince himself was also struck by the ferocity of the fighting. 'The wounded now began to be carried past; the dead were lying about; several villages on our right were all ablaze, but cannon continued to thunder there all the same', he wrote in his diary, published without his permission in 1888:

> As soon as we had perceived the heavy artillery fire, General Blumenthal remarked to me, 'That is the decisive battle', and with the lapse of each quarter of an hour this became all the more plain to us. The action of my army had made the enemy give way on his right flank, and furnished the 1st Army had been making no progress for hours...
>
> Just when we were standing near two battalions of the Queen Elizabeth Grenadier Regiment of the Guards, some routed Austrian cavalry came galloping towards us, and were shot down one after the other by a section (of infantry) post a good way off, so that the horses raced about riderless. Seeing this from a distance, some hussars of the guard galloped up and captured the horses, and after this a considerably stronger body of cavalry began to bear down upon us. Impossible to tell from the white tunics whether they were cuirassiers or dragoons, I was going to ride inside one of our battalions in case they formed square; but this was not necessary, for here again our needle-guns were plied with destructive effect, and secured us from danger...
>
> Arrived on the hills of Masloved, where dead Austrians of all arms lay stretched beside the severely wounded, word came to me that Colonel von Obernitz was lying at a farm hard by with a wound in the head. I at once repaired to him, and found that—as good luck would have it—his head had only been grazed by a bullet; but near him lay Lieutenant von Strantz, of the 1st Foot Guards, with several fingers of his right hand shot away. In the farmyard wounded men belonging to us and the Austrians were lying in heaps, but stay we neither could nor durst, having to fix all our thoughts on the foe...
>
> About a mile from us, on the extreme height, lay the village of Chlum, where independent musketry fire, cheers, and volley-firing alternated, which made it clear to us that the battle there must be of an exceedingly bitter nature.[149]

By the end of the afternoon, it became evident to Friedrich Wilhelm that victory was assured: 'My thoughts were now with my wife, my children, my mother and

·

[146] E. v. Fransecky, *Denkwürdigkeiten*, 383.
[147] Ibid., 379; T. Krieg, *Constantin v. Alvensleben*, 64.
[148] U. v. Stosch (ed.), *Denkwürdigkeiten des Generals und Admirals Albrecht v. Stosch*, 96–7.
[149] H. W. Lucy (ed.), *The Emperor's Diary*, 25–9.

sister' and 'the thought of our little son Sigismund, who has gone to his rest, came into my mind, as if his death had been destined to be the precursor of a great event in my life', yet 'victories do not compensate for the loss of a child; indeed, piercing grief only makes itself all the more terribly felt under the influence of such powerful impressions'.[150] In general, 'the most varied impressions succeeded one another from moment to moment': 'Around us lay or hobbled about so many of the well-known figures of the Potsdam and Berlin garrisons'; 'a shocking appearance was presented by those who were using their rifles as crutches or were being led up the heights by some of their unwounded colleagues'; 'the most horrible spectacle, however, was that of an Austrian battery of which all the men and horses had been shot down'.[151] 'It is a shocking thing to ride over a battlefield, and it is impossible to describe the hideous mutilations which present themselves', the Crown Prince concluded: 'War is really something frightful, and those who create it with a stroke of the pen, sitting at a green cloth table, little dream what horrors they are conjuring up.'[152]

The majority of officers had had more immediate experiences of such horrors. Even Fransecky, who was celebrated for his stoicism, seems to have been affected. Thus, although he consoled himself with the thought that 'every commander, every officer, yes I can say every soldier' knew 'that the wood could not be lost' and that the eventual death toll of the Seventh Division of eighty-nine officers and 2,162 men (or 'one fifth of the entire loss'), who 'covered the battlefield with their dead and wounded bodies', was 'honourable and memorable for all of time', he also recalled in detail the conditions of combat in the *Swiepwald*, which had become an 'individual struggle, man against man' in many instances, and was accompanied by 'terrible fire', rapidly destroying a quarter of some companies (including the musicians of the 67th Regiment).[153] As they made their way out of the wood and up to the village of Chlum, after the Second Army had begun to overcome the Austrian artillery, 'the view of the many dead and wounded' at the side of the path was 'terrifying':

> The defile in front of our wood was literally overflowing—everywhere, mostly with Austrians. Their wounded showed a remarkable contrast with ours—they screamed, sobbed and jabbered and prayed loudly and invoked the sacred. Our wounded bore their pains with still, worthy resignation for the most part.[154]

That night, the troops of the Seventh Division slept on the battlefield, 'on the bare earth, without food and drink and without a warming fire, and if one cast one's gaze beyond the resting troops one met, wherever one turned, the corpses and debris of the beaten army!'[155] Königgrätz had been 'an outstanding victory', Fransecky

[150] Ibid., 34.   [151] Ibid., 37.
[152] Ibid., 39–40. Wilhelm I, too, lamented to his wife in a letter of 4 July, 'How the battlefield looked!': E. Berner (ed.), *Kaiser Wilhelm des Grossen*, 133.
[153] E. v. Fransecky, *Denkwürdigkeiten*, 385, 387, 389.   [154] Ibid., 389–90.
[155] Ibid., 392. Gottlieb von Haeseler, *Zehn Jahre im Stabe ds Prinzen Friedrich Karl*, 161, wrote that the armies slept on the field between 'burning villages', scarcely knowing 'who their neighbours, on left or right', were.

wrote to his wife on 4 July, but also 'a bloody battle', in which the Austrians had lost 'many thousands as prisoners and *many, many* thousands dead and injured' and 'we, too, have had heavy losses'.[156] The casualties on both sides had been 'very important', wrote Voigts-Rhetz at the time to his wife, 'for the Austrians as much as 25,000 men': the victory was a 'glorious' one and 'honestly won after a long struggle', but 'I hope that you never have to see the horrors of such a battlefield!'.[157] For commanders, who had been preoccupied by the technical and tactical elements of combat and had often seen the fighting from a distance, the impact of battle came afterwards. 'Here, on this blood-soaked ground, we gained for the first time the full impression of the violence and seriousness of the struggle, which the foremost divisions of our army, particularly the Guard, had had to stand', wrote Verdy:

> That, on our side, they had fought with the expenditure of all their strength to achieve victory, the layers of the dead, piled up, both from our and the enemy's side, demonstrated,... the masses of wounded, as well as the conquered Austrian guns, but also the view of some of our own cannon, whose entire harnessings lay on the ground and were strewn around in pieces. The earth was, moreover, covered with weapons which had been thrown away or had fallen, helmets and Austrian *Käppis*, the feathered caps of *Jäger*, and manifold bits of equipment and uniforms.[158]

Verdy went to sleep, after drinking with his comrades, feeling 'that today was one of the most important days for Prussia' and praying to God that the king and his advisors would arrive at 'the right results for the welfare and future of Prussia and Germany', yet he was also haunted by the piles of corpses and masses of injured soldiers.[159] Commanders in the Napoleonic Wars had rarely described such visions.

DEFEATS

Unlike their Prussian counterparts, the officers and men of the Austrian, Saxon, Hanoverian, and Bavarian armies were not compensated for their suffering by the honour or glory of a victorious campaign.[160] Defeat at Königgrätz on 3 July marked the turning point of a war which had been going badly before then. 'Catastrophe of the army already prepared the day before yesterday has now happened', ran Benedek's telegram to Franz Joseph on 3 July: 'After more than five hours of brilliant fighting of the entire army and the Saxons, in the partly fortified position of Königgrätz,... the enemy succeeded in establishing itself in Chlum, unnoticed', from where it attacked Austrian troops 'in the flank and rear', causing

---

[156] E. v. Fransecky, *Denkwürdigkeiten*, 393.
[157] A. v. Voigts-Rhetz (ed.), *Briefe des Generals der Infanterie von Voigts-Rhetz*, 13.
[158] J. v. Verdy du Vernois, *Im Hauptquartier der Zweiten Armee*, 172.   [159] Ibid., 190.
[160] Christoph von Degenfeld-Schonburg, *Schweinschädel und Königgrätz. Meine Kriegserinngerungen als Kommandant des 7. Husarenregiments* (Vienna, 1907), 28, makes this point explicitly. Also, M. Hutten v. Klingenstein, *Meine Eindrücke aus dem bayerisch-preußischen Feldzuge im Jahre 1866* (Vienna, 1867).

them to yield.[161] 'Gradually, an unstoppable panic spread to many positions, and all attempts to halt the retreat were in vain', he continued: 'This began slowly but disorder grew and everyone withdrew in complete disarray over the military bridges of the Elbe to Pardubitz. Losses still cannot be made out, but certainly infinitely large.'[162]

On 30 June, after defeat at Skalitz, the *Feldzeugmeister* had written to his wife that he was not going to 'waste a single word', even though she would 'read and hear it a thousand times over in any case', over 'how and why the army, all sections of which have been animated by the greatest courage in the face of death, has come into such a desperate situation'.[163] At that stage of the campaign, he was already hinting that he would rather be dead. Only the need to muster his troops for an imminent major battle made his existence worthwhile: 'It is possible that I shall see you again. It would be better if a bullet were to hit me, but I want to experience even a humiliation, if I can render one last service in this way to the Kaiser and the army.'[164] Six days after the defeat, on 9 July, he wrote to his wife that, although he was 'wonderfully well in his body', 'allow me to stay silent about the state of my mood and soul': 'It would certainly be better for me if a bullet had hit me, and yet I say, "As God wishes".'[165] Fearing that his spouse might have understood his dark forebodings as a desire to commit suicide, he sent a telegram the next day to assure her that 'I have my nerves under control and know how to stand misfortune.'[166] A letter on the same day was more explicit: 'I have never thought of suicide, and I only rode so deliberately into the fire because I had to help. I know my duty and I shall fulfil it for as long as I can, and in every phase of this disastrous war, which I did not propose.'[167] The unexpectedness and rapidity of the Habsburg monarchy's defeat cast what one author called 'a dark gauze'—or 'bloody shadows'—over that 'page of Austrian military history', which not only made it difficult to understand why it had occurred, as Benedek had predicted, but also how soldiers had experienced combat at the time.[168]

Austrian planning for the battle of Königgrätz was poor but it nearly succeeded because of an imbalance of forces during the morning of 3 July, with the Habsburg and Saxon troops outnumbering the Prussians by 2:1 until the arrival of the Second Army after 2.00 p.m. Benedek, who had been a 'political' appointment—appealing to a wider middle-class public as the son of a doctor and the 'hero' of the retreat from Solferino in 1859—and who lacked strategic competence, had failed to prepare the Northern Army for a major battle in front of the Elbe in early July, promising that the coalition's forces would be able to rest near Sadowa for 'several days' at a conference of commanders in the early afternoon of 2 July and dismissing Leopold von Edelsheim's warning that the Prussian armies, which were constantly

---

[161] L. A. v. Benedek to Franz Joseph, 3 July 1866, in H. Friedjung (ed.), *Benedeks nachgelassene Papiere*, 382–3.
[162] Ibid., 383.   [163] L. A. v. Benedek to his wife, 30 June 1866, ibid., 371.
[164] Ibid.   [165] Benedek to his wife, 9 July 1866, ibid., 384.
[166] Benedek to his wife, 10 July 1866, ibid., 385.   [167] Ibid., 386.
[168] B. Kunderna, *Aus bewegten Zeiten. Persönliche Erinnerungen und Erlebnisse aus dem Feldzuge des Jahres 1866 gegen Preussen* (Vienna, 1906), 40. See the long-winded and irritated attempts of Christoph von Degenfeld-Schonburg, *Schweinschädel und Königgrätz*, 15–28, to correct the official record, for instance.

skirmishing with his own hussars, were nearby and might attack on the next day: 'And when did *you* become a prophet?' he laughed, before putting down his objections with a dismissive, 'You youngsters *always* have ideas.'[169] When the *Feldzeugmeister* later referred to the meeting as a war council, Gablenz and others responded that 'That was no *Kriegsrat*': 'At three o'clock on 2 July, when we returned from headquarters to our bivouacs, it was plain that the army commandant still had *no* information on the enemy's position, strength or movements and had *no* intention of fighting a battle on the 3rd.'[170] Karl von Thun, the commander of the Second Corps, recalled in August 1866 that 'the possibility of a battle never came up', with Benedek speaking 'only of disciplinary matters, nothing about operations'.[171] After further reports from Edelsheim and from Crown Prince Albert of Saxony about Prussian reconnaissance for 'an enveloping attack in the early morning hours', Austrian troops watching the Gitschin-Königgrätz road returned in the late evening with Prussian prisoners who confirmed that the First Army was marching through the night to reach the River Bistritz.[172] Thus, at 11.00 p.m. on 2 July, the Austrian chief of operations Gideon von Krismanic began to outline the troop dispositions of the Northern Army for battle, backdating everything written down after midnight to the 2nd and sending out vague instructions—without plans for a retreat or indications of the army's situation or objectives—by 3.00 a.m.

Officers received the instructions by 4.30 a.m., two hours before the Prussian attack, meaning that they could not move battalions far from their encampments and they were unable to protect their left flank by placing artillery at Hradek, as Prince Albert of Saxony had requested, and to guard their right flank by doing the same on the heights of Maslowed and Sendrasitz, which Tassilo Festetics de Tolna and Anton von Mollinary attempted to achieve—without the *Feldzeugmeister*'s permission—during the battle itself. In fact, Krismanic had been dismissed by Franz Joseph at 9.15 p.m. on the previous evening at the suggestion of Benedek, who had sacrificed him in order to save his Chief of the General Staff and close friend Alfred von Henikstein—valued by the *Feldzeugmeister* as a 'paterfamilias, gigolo, gourmand, gambler and stag hunter'—from being summoned immediately back to Vienna for questioning, after he had sent what the emperor had called a 'miserable' telegram to the capital saying matters in Bohemia were 'fast improving'.[173] Henikstein spent the time until 3.15 a.m. on 3 July composing his excuses, which he added to a letter penned by Benedek on the same night: 'I am in the tragic position of being held responsible before the whole world for errors and mishaps that are not *my* fault...I am the Chief of the General Staff *in name alone*...Will there *really* be a court martial?...If only I could shoot myself.'[174] Less than two hours later, at 5.00 a.m., he was sitting down with Benedek and Krismanic in the *Gasthof zur Stadt Prag* on the edge of Königgrätz to brief the new

[169] L. A. v. Benedek, cited in G. Wawro, *The Austro-Prussian War*, 205–6.
[170] L. v. Gablenz, ibid., 205.   [171] Ibid.
[172] Albert of Saxony, 2 July 1866, ibid., 210.
[173] Ibid., 27, 212–13.   [174] Ibid., 213.

chief of operations Alois Baumgarten, the former director of the War Academy in Wiener Neustadt, about the disposition of forces and topography of the area around Sadowa. The *Feldzeugmeister* did not leave the hotel to begin the 10 km ride to his headquarters in Lipa until 7.30 a.m., an hour-and-a-half after the first shots were fired. This was, as many Austrian commanders testified, an inauspicious way to start a 'great, decisive battle'.[175]

Austrian and Saxon corps began the battle of Königgrätz with an inadequate number of prepared battery positions and trenches for troops, especially on their vulnerable left flank, and in a poor location in front of the River Elbe—labelled the Bistritz 'pocket' by Moltke—which had been listed as a site of battle for eighteenth-century armies, with their shorter gun ranges and smaller forces, but which was unsuitable for nineteenth-century ones.[176] 'At first *I couldn't believe it*', wrote one adjutant who had read Krismanic's disposition before it was dispatched to commanders: 'We were offering battle *with a river behind us* and only one line of retreat!'[177] They had no field telegraphs and they were, in Karl von Coudenhove's opinion, 'utterly ignorant' of Prussian troop movements, with some officers believing that the Second Army had joined the First in the West and others believing that it had stayed at Josephstadt.[178] All the same, they disposed of 240,000 men, compared to 135,000 in the First Army and the Army of the Elbe (some of whom had not reached the battlefield) and they had a larger number of rifled cannon with a range of 4,000 yards, which rendered the smooth-bore twelve-pounders of the Prussians—a third of their guns in 1866—obsolete: Austria and Saxony had a total of 450 guns in the field on 3 July, with 320 in reserve, most of which were rifled, compared to Prussia's total in all theatres of war of 492 rifled cannon and 306 smooth-bores.[179] During the course of the day, 672 Austrian and Saxon guns fired 46,535 shots.[180] This superiority allowed Benedek to halt the advance of the Prussian Third, Fourth, and Eighth Divisions in the centre at *Holawald* and the village of Ober-Dohalitz in front of Sadowa, with Prussian troops reportedly cursing 'the dogs' who were 'using measured ranges' against them.[181] 'We sought cover but where could it be found in this kind of fire?' wrote one soldier:

> The shells smashed through the clay walls as if going through cardboard; and, eventually, the crackling guns set the village on fire. We moved to the left into the wood, but it was no better there; hunks of wood and mighty splinters of trees flew around us. At last, something like apathy descended on us.[182]

[175] L. A. v. Benedek to his wife, 3 July 1866, in H. Friedjung (ed.), *Benedeks nachgelassene Papiere*, 376: he wrote in anticipation of such an event.

[176] D. J. Hughes (ed.), *Moltke on the Art of War* (Novato, CA, 1993), 136–7.

[177] Cited in G. Wawro, *The Austro-Prussian War*, 214.

[178] Ibid., 215; C. v. Degenfeld-Schonburg, *Schweinschädel und Königgrätz*, 20. See also C. v. Coudenhove, *Feldmarschall-Lieutenant Graf Carl Coudenhove* (Vienna, 1901).

[179] G. A. Craig, *Königgrätz*, 8, 88–9.   [180] Ibid., 173.

[181] Ibid., 102. From his position on the right flank, Anton von Mollinary, *Sechsundvierzig Jahre im österreich-ungarischen Heere 1833–1879* (Zurich, 1905), vol. 2, 167, noted that, over the course of the morning, 'in the centre of the army the struggle was limited largely to artillery on both sides'.

[182] Cited in T. Fontane, *Der deutsche Krieg von 1866*, vol. 1, 512.

On the Austrian left, the Saxon Corps—using its initial advantage of thirty-eight infantry battalions against the six of the Army of the Elbe—had almost managed to work its way to Hradek in order to protect itself from later flanking manoeuvres, before being driven back by the Fifteenth and Sixteenth Divisions, which began to arrive after 11.00 a.m. On the right, Festetics had used his artillery to move towards the plateau of Maslowed and to fire on troops from Fransecky's Seventh Division coming from Benatek to the *Swiepwald*, where they were attacked by the soldiers of his Fourth Corps. Since 'the needle rifle was unanswerable', the 'only way we could win was with artillery, but our gun emplacements were [too few] and too low-lying', recalled one staff captain: 'To deploy large numbers of guns in dominant positions, we *needed* the plateau of Maslowed (Maslowed) and the heights of Sendrasice (Sendrasitz) and Horenoves (Horenowes)', which would only be protected if the *Swiepwald* could be cleared of Prussian infantry.[183] After Festetics had his foot torn off by shrapnel at 9.30 a.m., Mollinary took over as commander of the Fourth Corps and endeavoured, in concert with the Second and Third Corps, to destroy the Prussian Seventh Division, which was the vulnerable left wing of the Hohenzollern forces before the arrival of the Second Army, and to cut off its lines of retreat at the village of Benatek. At 11.00 a.m., he asked for permission to attack Benatek with a view to outflanking the Prussian First Army and advancing to Dub (behind Sadowa, from where Friedrich Karl had launched his original attack) at the same time as the main corps of the Austrian army (the First, Third, Sixth, and Tenth) moved forward from the centre. 'There I was, standing before the extreme left wing of the Prussian army', wrote Mollinary in August 1866: 'A determined attack would have snapped off the enemy's left wing and put us on the road to victory.'[184] During the morning of 3 July, then, Austrian and Saxon commanders had reason to be confident. 'Until 2.00 p.m., we had excellent prospects for a *victory*', recalled Benedek's adjutant: 'All I heard was talk of an *offensive*.'[185]

Officers in the field were less sanguine than staff officers. The choice facing corps commanders like Mollinary and Gablenz (Tenth Corps), who were urging an attack from the centre on Benedek by late morning, was to launch an offensive to destroy the Prussian armies separately or to retreat behind the Elbe in good order, which was made more difficult by the absence of a workable plan. Mollinary, who had been ordered by the *Feldzeugmeister* to fall back on Chlum-Neдělischt at 11.00 a.m., gave a full account of how distant military headquarters were from the realities of the battle, after he rode up to Chlum to justify an attack on the Prussian flank. The 'order to withdraw seemed incomprehensible to me', he began, for 'it called for the abandonment of a good, easily held position, which was on elevated ground and in keeping with our disposition' (at Maslowed), together with 'the terrain in front'—including the *Swiepwald*—which had been 'well defended until now with heavy fighting', to be exchanged for a weaker one

---

[183] G. Wawro, *The Austro-Prussian War*, 221–2.
[184] Cited ibid., 227.   [185] Ferdinand von Kriz, ibid., 236.

which was difficult to hold, even if strengthened by temporary fortifications in Chlum:

> in short, the renunciation of two factors which had to be of great use in the launching of an offensive, even if it was not to come from the right wing but from the left or the centre; whereas, through the withdrawal of the right wing, the door had been left wide open to the opponent pushing towards it, and an offensive from the centre or from the left wing became futile.[186]

Mollinary had presumed 'that the army leadership was striving, after an initial defensive, for an offensive,... for it was necessary for a victory' and it seemed to follow from 'the decision to accept a battle in front of Königgrätz in the first place', but, after talking to the General Staff at around midday, the commander of Fourth Corps was less certain:

> I found the *Feldzeugmeister*, surrounded by his staff, at the northern end of Chlum... After a short report on the fighting position of the right flank and an allusion to the disadvantages of the position of Chlum-Nedělischt, I began to talk of the prospective offensive but I was interrupted in the middle of the talk by a hand on my arm which was furthest from the *Feldzeugmeister*. Turning round in surprise, I find myself looking at GM. Baumgarten, who begins to share the content of the... telegram from Josefstadt [about an enemy corps, still seven kilometres from the battlefield].
> I didn't know that Baumgarten had been functioning as Chief of the General Staff for a couple of hours... Involuntarily, I turned from him and back to Benedek... Without informing me about Baumgarten's new position and, therefore, about the justification for his interference, he limited himself to demanding that I listen quietly by means of a 'Don't be so nervous!'
> He did me an injustice with this injunction. I was spiritually and physically well on that unfortunate day, in a quiet, normal mood... Baumgarten cut off what I wanted to add by taking up the speech which he had started earlier. He explained that an offensive against the left flank of the opponent standing opposite us in the North-West was no longer permissible, since we knew from that dispatch that an enemy corps was moving along the Elbe from the North-East against our right flank...
> Benedek, who had not spoken about the matter yet, now turned to his chief of artillery, FZM. Archduke Wilhelm, with the following question: 'Imperial Highness, has the moment arrived for an offensive push?'
> For me, what I heard and saw there was a bad dream![187]

The Archduke was a young, ceremonial head of a gun reserve who had no experience of combat and who mumbled 'no' inaudibly, 'in complete cluelessness and helplessness'.[188] The response did not seem to 'remove Benedek's indecision', 'for he turned back towards me sunk in thought'.[189] In desperation, the commander asked the *Feldzeugmeister* what the Fourth Corps was to do, demanding whether the latter's earlier order to withdraw to Chlum-Nedělischt was still valid, which Benedek replied was the case (an 'answer that it was obviously very difficult to give').[190] Supplied with steadily swelling contingents of troops from the Second

---

[186] A. v. Mollinary, *Sechsundvierzig Jahre im österreich-ungarischen*, vol. 2, 164.
[187] Ibid., 165–6.   [188] Ibid., 166.   [189] Ibid.   [190] Ibid., 167.

Army, the Prussian left flank led a successful assault on Chlum between 2.00 and 3.00 p.m., compounding the defeat of the Austrian Eighth Corps by 1.30 p.m. and the opening up of a 'great hole', as Wilhelm von Ramming (Sixth Corps) put it, between the Saxons on the left and the remaining Austrian corps in the centre.[191] The collapse of the Northern Army followed shortly afterwards, with many troops simply taking off their packs and running down the road towards Königgrätz and the far side of the Elbe, 10 km to the south.[192]

The tone of Habsburg officers' accounts was affected by this unexpected military collapse.[193] 'That the battlefield was over-sown with dead and wounded and offered a miserable spectacle is self-evident, but the retreat was more shocking to all of us' wrote Heinrich von Födransperg in his memoirs: 'As far as the eye could see, everything was in disordered, flight-like movement.'[194] Shame at the manner of Austria's defeat compounded—rather than compensated for—the horror of combat. Some officers sought consolation in 'the consciousness of a duty duly carried out' and in 'the rare endurance and cold-bloodedness of all subordinate generals, staff officers and senior officers' and 'the outstanding behaviour of the troops'.[195] Yet their overriding recollection—and experience at the time—seems to have been one of disappointment.

> I am alive and quite healthy, but with a broken heart, for we have been completely beaten despite the great sacrifices which the cavalry, too, had to make in dead and wounded and are in my opinion—to confess—no longer capable now of a great fight; since we lost a load of cannon. Spare me a description of our humiliation. I am not capable of it now—I'll never be able to do it.[196]

Acts of violence were usually intermingled with this broader narrative of the war. Coudenhove's horse had been shot in the throat by 'perfidious small-arms fire' but it had continued to carry him, which was fortunate, for his other horses had been lost forever on that 'fateful day'.[197] 'Many, many are dead and wounded', he went on, flitting from animal to human: 'Such a fight, such a victory, such a defeat— there was never such a thing! The misfortune which will now overcome our Austria is unforeseeable.'[198] As the commander of the Third Reserve Cavalry Division, Coudenhove had been waiting in the bowl behind Chlum, exposed to Prussian shells which he tried to counter by rearranging his squadrons of horses and getting his regimental bands to play as loud as they could.[199] 'By 3.00 p.m., the battle had

---

[191] G. Wawro, *The Austro-Prussian War*, 243. C. v. Degenfeld-Schonburg, *Schweinschädel und Königgrätz*, 22, on the suddenness of the Prussian envelopment of Austrian forces.

[192] On the disorder of the retreat, in which those who fell were simply trampled on, see H. v. Födransperg, *Vierzig Jahre in der österreichischen Armee. Erinnerungen eines österreichischen Offiziers von seinem Eintritte in die Armee bis zur Gegenwart 1854–1894* (Dresden, n.d.), 31.

[193] All soldiers were caught up in this hazardous retreat, with senior figures such as Windischgrätz being injured: F. Deitl (ed.), *Unter Habsburg Kriegsbanner*, vol. 5, 25.

[194] Ibid., 30. H. v. Födransperg, *Vierzig Jahre in der österreichischen Armee. Erinnerungen eines österreichischen Offiziers von seinem Eintritte in die Armee bis zur Gegenwart 1854–1894* (Dresden, n.d.).

[195] C. v. Coudenhove, *Feldmarschall-Lieutenant Graf Carl Coudenhove*, 64–5.

[196] Ibid.   [197] Ibid., 65.   [198] Ibid.

[199] For similar experiences, see C. v. Degenfeld-Schonburg, *Schweinschädel und Königgrätz*, 18–19.

turned', he noted later, with his own division caught up in the chaotic retreat after Chlum and Problus (a Saxon stronghold) had both been taken by advancing Prussian forces.[200] Other commanders like Mollinary, although still removed from combat, had seen more of the fighting, making his own way to the *Swiepwald* after Festetics, 'his face' expressing 'great pain' at the severing of his left foot, and had handed over his command at 9.30 a.m.: 'In the wood, which allowed little overview, friend and foe stood amongst each other.'[201] On their way back, Mollinary and his officers were attacked, with his horse killed by a bullet between the ears and his Chief of Staff by a shot in the chest. As the battalions of his Fourth Corps retreated from Chlum to Rosběritz, they sustained 'enormous losses', going on from village to village until they crossed the Elbe at 7.00 p.m.[202] The corps had lost 6,446 dead, wounded, or missing out of 26,500 men, or more than 24 per cent of its total.[203] According to one contemporary estimate, this casualty rate was precisely the point at which a company—and the majority of companies of the Fourth Corps were well over this level—became incapable of continuing in unfavourable conditions.[204]

The 21-year-old infantry lieutenant Clemens Biegler revealed what the battle of Königgrätz was like for ordinary combatants. Although the campaign before 3 July had been strenuous and bloody, the young officer had had a good night's sleep on the 2nd, not suspecting that a battle was imminent: 'That the cannonade began early in the morning was so usual for us that we didn't notice it.'[205] It was ten o'clock before the officers in his regiment started to worry about what they should do, 'since the troops in front of us were given an alarm signal and left the camp'.[206] The cannonade had 'developed in the meantime to a constant roll of thunder'.[207] As they reached for their guns and advanced to the tune of the Radetzky march, 'wherever one looked immense masses of troops could be seen rolling up, so that one's heart jumped with joy and one would have thought we have to conquer the world with these masses of people'.[208] Biegler and his regiment were placed in the centre of the reserves. As they waited to be deployed, 'all were armed with the greatest contempt of death and were full of courage'.[209] Everywhere, a 'general cheerfulness reigned', with different units greeting each other in their native languages.[210] Benedek and his staff stood in front of them on a hillock, disappearing at midday, which the lieutenant took to be a sign that the Austrian troops were

---

[200] G. Wawro, *The Austro-Prussian War*, 255. See also the account of Bernhard von Ditfurth, who was in the same cavalry division: F. Deitl (ed.), *Unter Habsburg Kriegsbanner*, vol. 5, 17–27.

[201] A. v. Mollinary, *Sechsundvierzig Jahre im österreich-ungarischen Heere*, 160–1.

[202] Ibid., 170–1.   [203] Ibid., 171.

[204] Julius Carl Friedrich Naumann, *Das Regiments-Kriegsspiel* (Berlin, 1877), cited in A. Bucholz, *Moltke and the German Wars*, 124.

[205] C. Biegler, *Meine Erlebnisse während des Kriegsjahres 1866* (St Pölten, 1908), 50–1. This expectation seems to have been widespread: see, for instance, Captain Ferdinand Wikaukal's similar statement in F. Deitl (ed.), *Unter Habsburg Kriegsbanner*, vol. 6, 179; C. v. Degenfeld-Schonburg, *Schweinschädel und Königgrätz*, 15.

[206] C. Biegler, *Meine Erlebnisse*, 51.

[207] Ibid.   [208] Ibid.   [209] Ibid.   [210] Ibid.

advancing and the Prussians were retreating.[211] At about 1.00 p.m., the 'general enthusiasm, with which the thunder of guns and the increasingly audible natter of rifles and the moaning of the wounded and dying were mixed, died down over time, and as the cannon shells started to whizz past and land amongst us, the band also stopped playing and went backwards', Biegler went on.[212] From the *Feldzeugmeister's* harassed expression, it was now obvious that things were not going well, as 'ours withdrew and enemy bullets began to reach us', with the corps of the Crown Prince surrounding them.[213] The Austrian cavalry which were sent to repel them were met with 'rapid fire' (*Schnellfeuer*) from the Prussian infantry, which had maintained a long front rather than forming squares: 'At first, single cavalrymen fell, then an increasing number, more and more as they got closer to the Prussians, and as they came to within about 150 yards, scarcely a third were still sitting on their horses, which fell over and sprang backwards.'[214] Only a few moments beforehand, this regiment had 'launched itself at the enemy with a storming roar'.[215]

By the time his own battalion moved forward, Biegler's earlier confidence had disappeared, viewing the shells and bullets landing on them 'as if they wanted to destroy us completely'.[216] 'I called to my men in Hungarian', he wrote in his memoirs: '"Don't fear, it is better to die here than like old women in bed at home!"'[217] Yet, although their 'hurrah' briefly drowned out 'the cries of those falling like flies' as they stormed forwards, they ran into 'a thick rain of bullets', leading Biegler to 'await death with resignation from one of the rifle bullets whistling past me in every key'.[218] 'We were terribly decimated', recalled another young lieutenant from an adjacent regiment, who was hit five times within fifteen minutes, discovering twenty-two separate bullet holes in his overcoat.[219] Biegler's regiment managed to occupy the village of Rosběritz but failed to keep it, being overrun by a 'general, wild flight' of Austrian soldiers who massed together from different units of the army and made 'all the more certain' that they would be hit by 'enemy shells and bullets'.[220] In the melée, he was pushed into a ditch filled with mud and was unable to get back out again, trodden underfoot by his own comrades, until he objected that he was an officer. 'No longer in a state to run despite every expenditure of effort', he staggered back towards his own lines, using his sword as a crutch.[221] Submitting 'to his fate in complete apathy amidst everything around him', he nonetheless threw himself to the floor to avoid the rapid fire of Prussian infantrymen firing at fleeing Austrians, landing under another soldier and waiting to die, his hearing and sight gone and an 'enormous hail of bullets' flying just over

---

[211] Lieutenant Konrad Sturm gave a similar account from a similar perspective, commenting on the early confidence gleaned from the stance of Benedek's headquarters: F. Deitl (ed.), *Unter Habsburg Kriegsbanner*, vol. 4, 28.

[212] C. Biegler, *Meine Erlebnisse*, 51.

[213] Ibid., 52. F. Deitl (ed.), *Unter Habsburg Kriegsbanner*, vol. 4, 28.

[214] C. Biegler, *Meine Erlebnisse*, 52.

[215] Ibid.   [216] Ibid.   [217] Ibid.

[218] Ibid., 53. On the effects of the Prussian needle-gun on 3 July in the fighting around Rosberitz, see K. Sturm, in F. Deitl (ed.), *Unter Habsburg Kriegsbanner*, vol. 4, 32, 35.

[219] Ibid., 35.   [220] C. Biegler, *Meine Erlebnisse*, 53.   [221] Ibid., 53–4.

him.[222] Any of the 'thousands of bullets', each carrying 'death and destruction' with it, could have hit him.[223] He was captured shortly afterwards and was transported to Prussia, returning home in September. His impression of battle was marked by enthusiasm, fear, despair, the sight of dead and wounded lying in 'masses', and the 'terrible, unarticulated cry of the dismembered dying' in hospital.[224]

Even before Königgrätz, Austrian and Saxon forces had suffered far higher casualties than their Prussian counterparts. The war, of course, had begun in happier circumstances, with officers eager to fight.[225] The promise of Archduke Albrecht, the commander of the Southern Army, that 'the long awaited moment has finally come', with the 'Kaiser and the fatherland'—'your mothers, your wives and brothers'—watching soldiers with expectation and 'enthusiastic participation', was typical.[226] The departure of the Gustav Prinz von Wasa Infantry Regiment Nr. 60 from Olmütz, where it had been based and where Biegler had joined it as a 15-year-old cadet, occurred on 12 May 1866 like many others, 'with the resounding notes of the marching band' and amidst a crowd of local well-wishers.[227] The following month was taken up with marches and billeting, during which soldiers 'certainly did not get bored', before 'news of the declaration of war on Prussia' on 21 June 'was greeted with jubilation'.[228] Likewise, 'individual, audible cannon shots in the far distance provoked joyful excitement amongst us'.[229] In answer to his men, who kept asking where the Prussian border was, Biegler pointed to a mountain on the horizon 'that already belonged to the Prussians', prophesying that 'tomorrow we might already be there and attacking them, whereupon the men expressed their delight'.[230] Their feelings started to change as they approached Nachod a day later, meeting 'more and more compatriots, wailing and wringing their hands, who were moving their goods and chattels towards the interior, either on wagons and carriages or carrying them in their hands', calling out that the Prussians were destroying everything (see Figure 8.1).[231] As they went into battle, they passed the soldiers of the Sixth Corps running back into a wood, 'which did not make a good impression on our men'.[232] Still wearing their coats, so that 'sweat ran over my dust-covered, sun-burned face', the regiment sought cover in a stand of trees, as 'enemy small arms fire became increasingly heavy', causing wonderment, since 'this constant, long-lasting natter', as the 'effect of the Prussian needle-gun as a rapid-firing weapon', was unknown before then.[233] The effects of the Austrian assault were debilitating:

> From the ranks of the Prussians, who were hidden behind fortified positions and in the wood and were not visible to us, came a hail of bullets that made our advance

---

[222] Ibid., 54.   [223] Ibid., 55.   [224] Ibid., 55, 60–1.

[225] C. v. Torresani, *Von der Wasser- bis zur Feuerteufe. Werde- und Lehrjahre eines österreichischen Offiziers* (Dresden, 1900), vol. 2, 265; B. Kunderna, *Aus bewegten Zeiten*, 28; K. Fischer v. Wellenborn, *Erinnerungen aus den Feldzügen 1859 und 1866. Ein Beitrag zur Geschichte des k. und k. Uhlanenregiments Nr. 1* (Vienna, 1894), 172, 187–93.

[226] C. v. Duncker, *Feldmarschall Erzherzog Albrecht* (Vienna, 1897), 219–20.

[227] C. Biegler, *Meine Erlebnisse*, 8.   [228] Ibid., 23.

[229] Ibid.   [230] Diary entry, 26 June 1866, ibid., 30.

[231] 27 June 1866, ibid., 31.   [232] Ibid., 32.

[233] Ibid., 32–3. Also, H. v. Födransperg, *Vierzig Jahre in der österreichischen Armee*, 16.

Figure 8.1 'Am Saume des Nachoder Waldes'
Source: *Gartenlaube*, 1866, vol. 30, 469.

impossible, so that we had to drop back with great losses. We gathered further back and Lieutenant Colonel Teppner himself led the Second Division in a new attack. On this occasion, I ran with some men to a dry ditch about 200 yards in front of us, running parallel with the front, where we could catch our breath a bit and find some cover. But my physical strength was exhausted by this. When I thought that we had been marching since the early morning, despite the sundry obstacles of the greatest heat, and then we had had to climb a mountain and launch two attacks one after the other, not counting the impressions which the continuing howling and groaning of the dying and wounded, the screaming, the noise, the drumming and the thunder of cannon beside the chatter of gunfire and the whistling of shells make on humans, I came to the conclusion that men can stand much more than animals, which at least have the advantage of having no reason.[234]

Trapped in the ditch, Biegler watched one of the many injured and dead, trying to dig a hole in the earth to put his head into in order to escape the relentless sun. Others drank from puddles in which water was mixed with blood.[235] Forced to retreat a second time, the young officer was sure that he would not survive. The same was true of the following day, as the Austrians were defeated at Skalitz as the ground shook under the thunder of cannon and threatened 'to run out of control': 'Because we had seen what a good harvest the guns of the Prussians reaped for the first time yesterday, and the events of the previous day preoccupied our minds, and since we also saw that it was going badly for us today, each of us awaited his death

---

[234] C. Biegler, *Meine Erlebnisse*, 34.   [235] Ibid., 36.

with resignation.'[236] As Biegler dropped to sleep without food after these days of fighting, 'the images of the battle constantly tossed around in his dreams'.[237] Such soldiers were able to carry on fighting but they had been profoundly affected by their experiences of combat.[238]

Those troops of the German *Mittelstaaten* who experienced combat appear to have reacted in a similar fashion, even if their endeavours were cast in a more favourable light in official histories of 1866.[239] For Saxons, there was the consolation of an ordered retreat and brave resistance at Königgrätz, which had 'failed because of the behaviour of Austrian troops', as one account put it.[240] Yet it was difficult to ignore the same facts of defeat which confronted their Habsburg ally. After 1.00 p.m. on 3 July, the Northern Army had begun to collapse, with the dispatching of Saxon troops leading to the loss of 'many men' and failing 'to halt the flight, once it had started', wrote Crown Prince Albert, the commander of the Saxon Corps, to his father the king two days after the battle: although the Saxon retreat took place in 'good order', it did little to counterbalance the 'thoroughly demoralizing and dangerous' chaos of the other troops, fleeing in 'disordered rabbles'.[241] 'I would rather be lying dead on the battlefield', Albert had reportedly told another officer at the time.[242] 'Many found their death near Königgrätz', and 'many came back / From this serious peril!' ran one contemporary Saxon war poem, but to what?[243] 'What is that for a peace for me?' asked another poem, lamenting the forced inclusion of Saxony in the 'northern *Bund*' and the 'downfall' of the 'white and green': 'What use, then, was our bravery?'[244]

The same question confronted Hanoverian soldiers, who had taken part in what one artillery officer called 'a great day' at the battle of Langensalza on 27 June but who were immediately faced with 'the end of the Hanoverian army':

> On the morning of the 28th, the generals and colonels had weighed up our position and passed on the request drafted by Colonel Cordemann to the King, in which it was stated that a capitulation was to be advised, given the superior power of the enemy, the exhaustion of our troops and the impossibility of feeding them any longer, and the

[236] Ibid., 39.   [237] Ibid.

[238] Béla Kunderna, *Aus bewegten Zeiten*, 28–35, described the same transition at Sklalitz from rejoicing to deep disappointment (although not complete demoralization).

[239] Anon, *Zur Beurtheilung des Verhaltens der badischen Felddivision im Feldzuge des Jahrs 1866* (Darmstadt, 1866); Anon, *Der deutsche Bürgerkrieg im Jahre 1866* (Brunswick, 1866); Anon, *Die Operationen des achten deutschen Bundes-Corps im Feldzuge des Jahres 1866* (Darmstadt, 1868); F. Lubojatzky, *Deutschlands Kriegsereignisse im Jahre 1866* (Dresden, 1867); L. Hauff, *Die Geschichte des Krieges von 1866 in Mittel-Europa. Ihre Urasache und ihrere Folgen* (Munich, 1867).

[240] Oskar Häußler, *König Albert von Sachsen und die sächsische Armee* (Leipzig, n.d.), 29–30, also referred to 'the retreat of the Saxons', who maintained 'their tactical unity', in contrast to 'the Austrians, who rushed to Königgrätz in wild flight'. See also Max Dittrich, *Unter König Albert von Sachsen im Felde 1849, 1866 und 1870/1871. Vaterländische Gedenkblätter* (Dresden, 1888), 14, who alluded to 'the toughness, courage and fighting discipline' of 'all Saxon regiments'.

[241] Paul Hassel, *König Albert von Sachsen* (Berlin, 1900), vol. 2, 296–7. Hassel was the Prussian-born royal archivist in Dresden.

[242] Ibid., 301.

[243] 'Sächsisches Kriegslied', in F. Paustka, *Erinnerungen an Garnison und Schlachtfeld. Gedichte und Gesänge für Militair und Militairvereine* (Dresden, 1868), 51.

[244] 'Der Friede', ibid., 54–5.

paucity of the reserves of munitions, meaning that continued blood-letting would be without success.[245]

Because of the wilful incompetence of the commander of the Prussian Army of the Main Eduard Ernst Vogel von Falckenstein, who had disobeyed Moltke's injunction 'to force the Hanoverian army out of the field, and as far as possible to disarm it', preferring initially to head towards Frankfurt to meet the confederal Eighth Corps and then to leave most of his 50,000 troops facing south towards Bavaria, 9,000 Prussians under Eduard von Flies had been repelled by 19,000 Hanoverians at Langensalza.[246] Nevertheless, Hanover's commanders were aware throughout the short campaign, which was subjected to substantial criticism, that Prussia's forces would prevail.[247] Their troops had sustained more than one-and-a-half times the number of casualties (1,429 dead and wounded) suffered by the Prussians, largely as a result of 'rapid fire'.[248] 'The impressions gained on the battlefield must fill even the heart of the victor with pain and distress', wrote Julius Bock von Wülfingen, the commander of a Hanoverian *Jäger* battalion, as he described 'those killed, in the most varied of locations, with an often terrifying expression on their rigid features, the wounded writhing in pain and, amongst them, the medics, ready to help'.[249] The soldiers of other states had more varied experiences of warfare, but they, too, commented on the losses caused by rapid fire.[250] Commanders like Albert von Suckow, who was attached to Bavarian headquarters in 1866, believed that further resistance and spilling of blood after the battle of Königgrätz would be a futile 'crime'.[251]

---

[245] J. Hartmann, *Meine Erlebnisse zu hannoverscher Zeit, 1839–1866* (Wiesbaden, 1912), 217–19. For a fictionalized, heroic account of the battle, see the adventure writer Friedrich Armand Strubberg's *In Süd-Carolina und auf dem Schlachtfelde von Langensalza* (Hanover, 1869), vol. 4, 88–120.

[246] Grosser Generalstab (Historische Abteilung), *The Campaign of 1866 in Germany*, 37. Moltke told Falckenstein on the day of battle that 'All Bavarians and Imperial troops now secondary. Unqualified will of His Majesty that the Hanoverians be at once attacked and disarmed. What arrangements has General Falckenstein made for today? Answer immediately': cited in H. v. Sybel, *The Founding of the German Empire* (London, 1875), vol. 5, 68. See K. Müller, *1866: Bismarcks deutscher Bruderkrieg* (Graz, 2007), 36–73. For criticism of Falckenstein's disobedience, see H. O. v. Meisner (ed.), *Denkwürdigkeiten des General-Feldmarschalls Alfred Grafen von Waldersee* (Stuttgart, 1925), vol. 1, 31.

[247] For criticism of those advising the king, who were wary of fighting or advancing to Saxony or the south because they believed that Prussian forces in the area were larger than was actually the case, see G. F. F. Dammers, *Erinnerungen und Erlebnisse* (Hanover, 1890), 114–46.

[248] See, for instance, J. Bock v. Wülfingen, *Tagebuch vom 11 Juni bis 3 Juli 1866* (Hanover, 1876), 48–9. For an endorsement from the other side, see H. v. Chappuis, *Bei Hofe und im Felde* (Frankfurt, 1902), 54.

[249] J. Bock v. Wülfingen, *Tagebuch*, 50. Armand Strubberg, *In Süd-Carolina und auf dem Schlachtfelde von Langensalza*, 104–20, gives a similarly macabre description of the battlefield.

[250] A. Pfister, *Denkwürdigkeiten aus der württembergischen Kriegsgeschichte des 18. und 19. Jahrhunderts im Anschluß an die Geschichte des 8. Infanterieregiments* (Stuttgart, 1868), 517, commented that 125,000–130,000 bullets must have been fired by Prussians at a single encounter near Impfingen. By contrast, see A. v. Hessen, *Feldzugs-Journal des Oberbefehlshabers des 8ten deutschen Bundes-Armee-Corps im Feldzuge des Jahres 1866 in Westdeutschland*, 2nd edn (Darmstadt, 1867), 1–17, who avoided direct contact with combat, even during heavy fighting near Frankfurt on 14 July; and A. Dove, *Großherzog von Baden*, 145, who points out that Badenese troops did not see fighting on their own soil until 23–25 July 1866.

[251] Diary entry, 9 July 1866, in A. v. Suckow, *Rückschau des Königl. Württembergischen Generals der Infanterie und Kriegsministers*, ed. W. Busch (Tübingen, 1909), 96.

The Bavarians, Hanoverians, Saxons, Austrians, and their allies had been defeated in June and July 1866 because of 'the inferiority of our rifles', 'earlier omissions and mistakes in the organization and training of the army', and 'the inferior tactical training of our infantry', in the opinion of Mollinary.[252] These deficiencies had led to 'bloody defeats' like that at Königgrätz, which the commander of the Fourth Corps—unlike his defender, Heinrich von Hess, the former Chief of the General Staff—later wrote could probably not have been won by means of a flanking manoeuvre early in the battle.[253] They had also produced higher rates of killing and wounding than those experienced by Prussian combatants.[254] On 3 July, Austrian forces lost 64,000 soldiers, killed, wounded, or taken prisoner, which meant 8,000 per hour or 133 per minute on a battlefield which had initially been 60 miles wide and 15 deep (compared to Austerlitz's 8 by 4 miles or Solferino's 11 by 5 miles) but which had shrunk between midday and 4.00 p.m. to a killing zone of 2 square miles.[255] Their Prussian opponents, who fired four to five times per minute in combat compared to the Austrian infantrymen's single shot, sustained losses roughly one-seventh of this level. At the battle of Nachod, the Austrians lost approximately nineteen casualties per minute, or one every three seconds, during five hours of fighting and, at Skalitz on 28 June, almost 800 casualties per hour or thirteen per minute, amounting to just under 40 per cent of their total force, which—according to contemporary estimates—was unsustainable.[256] Even at the battle of Trautenau, where Habsburg forces were victorious on 27 June, they sustained losses close to 20 per cent, or four times those suffered by Prussia.[257] In much more favourable circumstances, Hanoverian losses at Langensalza had amounted to less than 8 per cent of the total, but this proportion was still higher than the contemporary average of 5 per cent.[258] Such levels of wartime violence not only shook the confidence of commanders, with Benedek begging 'urgently' for peace before a full battle had taken place, in the words of Franz Joseph's negative reply; they also appear to have had lasting effects on combatants.[259]

HORROR AND GLORY

How did Prussian soldiers, who were less likely than Austrians to be killed or injured, react to combat? Journalists like Fontane and Hans Wachenhusen attempted to describe what it was like to fight, either by scrutinizing letters and contemporaneous accounts (Fontane) or by accompanying the troops and

---

[252] A. v. Mollinary, *Sechsundvierzig Jahre im österreich-ungarischen Heere*, 172.
[253] Ibid.
[254] For a humane account of the effects of such killing, see the evangelical pastor Christian Thomsen, 'Denkst du daran?', in F. Deitl (ed.), *Unter Habsburg Kriegsbanner*, vol. 4., 234–8.
[255] A. Bucholz, *Moltke and the German Wars*, 121, 135, 137. See also W. F. Besser, *Sechs Wochen im Felde* (Halle, 1866), 52.
[256] A. Bucholz, *Moltke and the German Wars*, 127, 131.   [257] Ibid., 129.
[258] W. Rüstow, *Der Krieg und seine Mittel*, 194, 201, 237–8.
[259] G. A. Craig, *Königgrätz*, 80.

recounting what they saw (Wachenhusen). Most were anxious to combine the evidence of eyewitnesses with the magisterial overview of an historian. Thus, Wachenhusen, who had been a war correspondent in 1854–6, 1859, and 1864 and who was a 'guest of the Army of the Elbe' in 1866, deliberately changed register on 3 July in order to do justice to such a momentous subject: 'I am going over, here, to the style of the serious war historian and I shall start with the commencement of the battle, with the centre of our three armies, the focal point of the entire glorious action.'[260] What the writer of adventures meant was that he would rise above events and depict the movement of the armies as a whole, providing an accurate portrayal of a war which was 'without parallel in history' and constituted a source of 'undying pride for a Prussia that had finally become conscious of its own power'.[261]

For Fontane, who was known principally as a journalist in the 1860s even by other authors such as Theodor Storm (who thought him a 'nice person' despite 'his editorial responsibilities for the *Kreuzzeitung*'), 'the war book' was a work of military history, which a civilian and essayist like himself was well placed to write, since he had 'greater freedom and a less inhibited judgement of extra-military factors' (especially 'so-called imponderables') than did a military historian, as he recalled in his memoirs:

> In the last analysis, the writing of military history is no different from the writing of history in general and is subject to the same laws. How does it go? You are faced with a lot of material and you need to make a decision on the basis of what you have got, 'for or against', 'yes or no'. In addition, the depiction of what concerns the history of war is to a very considerable degree a matter for literary and not merely military criticism.[262]

The author had, as he explained to his publisher Wilhelm Hertz in August 1866, 'a certain talent for such works', with the volume on 1866 enabling him 'to bring the Schleswig-Holstein book'—his first 'war book' on the events of 1864—'to a proper conclusion'.[263] For both Fontane and Wachenhusen, that conclusion was a Prussian and a national one, holding out the prospect of reconciliation with the 'new provinces' and with 'our South German brothers'.[264] The purpose of their works, which were based on the official accounts of the Prussian, Austrian, and other General Staffs, regimental histories (more than twenty of these in Fontane's case), and replies to dozens of letters to commanders, was to chronicle and explain how such a victory had come about.[265] 'The result of our victories was great', wrote Fontane, 'the victories themselves so glorious that the question (aired in the

[260] H. Wachenhusen, *Tagebuch vom Österreichischen Kriegsschauplatz*, 118.

[261] Ibid., i.

[262] T. Fontane, 'Meine Kinderjahre', in T. Fontane, *Sämtliche Werke* (Munich, 1959–75), vol. 14, 119. For the reference to Theodor Storm, see H. Roch, *Fontane, Berlin und das 19. Jahrhundert* (Berlin, 1962), 149; for reference to his 'war book', see T. Fontane to W. Hertz, 11 Aug. 1866, in T. Fontane, *Briefe* (Berlin, 1989), vol. 2, 324–5.

[263] T. Fontane, *Briefe*, vol. 2, 324–5.

[264] T. Fontane, *Der deutsche Krieg von 1866*, vol. 2, 335.

[265] G. A. Craig, *Theodor Fontane: Literature and History in the Bismarck Reich* (Oxford, 1999), 73–4, on sources.

whole of Europe) could not be avoided: "where was the cause of our successes to be sought?" '[266]

In answering his own question, Fontane was affected relatively little by a self-justifying national narrative, preferring to examine a range of reasons for the outcome of the conflict in an unsentimental way. While military writers had tended to emphasize the role played by commanders or the 'tactical training of individual men', political commentators had looked to a 'love of fatherland, which pervades all classes', 'mass education and training', or 'feelings of honour and duty'.[267] Austrian critics of the Habsburg war effort had singled out 'chance, betrayal and the needle-gun', but Fontane's inclination was to blame the 'Austrian system', or the combination of unremarkable deficiencies, and to credit the 'sum of the whole' in Prussia: 'Our *ensemble* was our superiority. Mass education, sentiments of honour, patriotism, the needle-gun, tactics, command—everything did its bit.'[268] The writer's concern to investigate the multiplicity of causes and effects of modern wars, which were affairs of '*masses*' of subjects ('like a *Völkerwanderung* organized by railroads'), encouraged him to describe events from different perspectives—those of Austrians, Saxons, Bavarians, and Prussians—and to use a larger number of memoirs and diaries, military journals (*Militair-Wochenblatt, Oesterreichische militairische Zeitschrift*), and articles and correspondence from sixteen Austrian and German newspapers.[269]

Fontane's work was not academic, 'making books out of books' (as he put it in April 1871), but entailed the historical reconstruction of the campaign, some of the locations of which he went to witness after the cessation of hostilities (Podol, Münchengrätz, Gitschin, Königgrätz, and Langensalza), allowing him to punctuate his narrative with detailed geographical and ethnographic asides.[270] 'Bohemia—the old battleground between Prussia and Austria'—was 'the bastion-like northern part of the imperial state', 'closed off by mountains in all directions' and enclosing 'a pronouncedly hilly and wave-formed terrain', ran Fontane's introduction to the section of *Der deutsche Krieg von 1866* on 'war plans', with the text juxtaposed with the image of a rocky mountain pass and a forested valley in the illustration of Ludwig Burger.[271] Because he had accompanied the troops in June and July 1866, Fontane's illustrator was able to fashion life-like representations of individual combatants and be 'true' to individual events, in his own estimation, using drawings made 'on the spot' and photographs taken at the time.[272] As the soldiers descend from the mountain passes, which were less vertiginous than Burger implied, readers see Bohemia and its inhabitants—and, in the second volume, Bavaria and western Germany—and, then, they read about combat with the enemy in the same locale, partly viewed

---

[266] T. Fontane, *Der deutsche Krieg von 1866*, vol. 2, 334.   [267] Ibid., 334.

[268] Ibid., vol. 1, 364–5, and vol. 2, 334–5.   [269] G. A. Craig, *Theodor Fontane*, 73–4, 77.

[270] Ibid., 74, 90. Craig notes that there were fewer such 'relaxed passages' here than in Fontane's first war book of the events of 1864, which was less mobile and allowed more leeway for asides. Nevertheless, there are many ethnographic and geographical introductions to his treatment of the events of 1866.

[271] John Osborne, *Theodor Fontane: Vor den Romanen. Krieg und Kunst* (Göttingen, 1999), examines Fontane's view of the illustrations and the relationship between the visual and the literary.

[272] Note on the illustrations by Ludwig Burger, in T. Fontane, *Der deutsche Krieg von 1866*, vol. 1, 725.

through the soldiers' eyes, insofar as the author was able to imagine their point of view and re-embody their actions. Fontane claimed to have 'invented, exactly as in my *Wanderungen* [published in 1862 and 1863], a manner of treatment that was simply not there before'.[273] His claim to novelty rested on his examination of the daily life of ordinary soldiers and of the places where they fought.

Fontane's story of the war began like other contemporary accounts with an examination of the murky causes of the conflict, which dated back to the struggle for ascendancy in Germany and the breakdown of trust between Berlin and Vienna in Schleswig-Holstein, with 'the peace of 1864 [giving] birth to the war of 1866'.[274] When Austria armed for war, its population 'fanaticized', the Hohenzollern monarchy's very existence was threatened: 'The one-and-a-half-century-old disturber of the peace of Germany must be rendered harmless, Prussia must be broken up.'[275] Crossing the border into Bohemia, the Prussian troops seemed jubilant, singing 'Heil Dir im Siegerkranz' and the 'Preußenlied', which reverberated in the mountains.[276] The idyll was soon broken as the First Army fought at Podol, an encounter which was described in a letter of a soldier in the 72nd Regiment. Having been separated from other troops, his company of 400 men stood alone under fire for 33 minutes, only 80 yards from the Austrians, who attempted to storm them four times but were repelled by rapid Prussian fire, with his single company using 5,700 cartridges in half an hour, or twenty-two cartridges per man.[277] The Prussians' guns were so hot that they could no longer hold them. The second phase of the battle, which took place in the dark, was more bitter, characterized by 'fire of unusual violence' and a 'great pile of dead and wounded Austrians'.[278]

After the battle of Gitschin on 29 June, more than 4,000 troops lay wounded with very different 'fates', some receiving 'the most loving care' and others languishing untended among the 'full ranks' of the dead, in and around the home town of Wallenstein.[279] 'All of Gitschin was a lazaret', Fontane wrote, deliberately juxtaposing religiosity, romanticism, and realism:

> Everywhere there was a lack of food, bandages and surgical assistance...Wounded Austrians and Prussians, wearing the Schleswig Cross or the Düppel Medal, now, in common misery, revived their old comradeship in arms and supported and comforted each other...The churches offered a particularly gripping and picturesque impression. High procession lanterns, carved in the baroque manner and painted red, between them banners from the Thirty Years' War, dusty, tattered, hung from or stood against the walls. On the steps of the altar crouched Hungarian hussars, some wrapped in blue and gold cloaks, some in white...Italians from the Regiment Sigismund lay around in the aisles and niches, one with a rose between pale lips. Bohemians from the 18th *Jäger* Battalion cowered in the pews and looked pleadingly at the picture of Mary, begging for help—or release. At the side, on the bare tiles and leaning against the pillared wall, sat a Bohemian women, and near to her a mutilated soldier from the Regiment Gyulai. The woman had fallen asleep from exhaustion. The mutilated

---

[273] T. Fontane to H. Kletke, Aug. 1870, cited in W. Paulsen, review of works by and on Fontane, *Monatshefte*, 80 (1988), 239.
[274] T. Fontane, *Der deutsche Krieg von 1866*, vol. 1, 3.   [275] Ibid., 51–2.
[276] Ibid., 138.   [277] Ibid., 157.   [278] Ibid., 159.   [279] Ibid., 243–4.

one didn't move. He had laid his arm around his protectress and drawn her head to his breast.[280]

Further east, the casualties sustained and inflicted by the Prussian Second Army were even greater. At Skalitz, 'the losses were enormous'.[281]

At Trautenau, where the Prussians were defeated, the casualties on the Habsburg side were 'particularly high and exceeded ours more than fourfold'.[282] 'Treason' was allegedly committed by the inhabitants of the town, who were said to have fired at Prussian troops. To Fontane, such acts were 'natural, in their way', in war:

> Whoever has experienced street fighting will have been a witness of it. Without their critical faculties, robbed of their clear-sightedness, given over exclusively to a dark urge and a quaking agitation, an individual believes, in a mixture of heroism and duplicity, self-sacrifice and thirst for revenge, that he is able to dare to throw a rock or fire his rusting gun, blind to the consequences.[283]

At Soor, the Prussian troops emerged into the 'full din of the fighting', 'the natter of small arms fire' and the 'fire of cannons, [which had]...increased with enormous violence', filling the air with shrapnel and grenades.[284] For a while, as one officer expressed it, they seemed to have been 'thundered down'.[285] 'The thunder of the cannon, without reply, the crack of grenades showering to the right and left, the shrill whistle of smaller shots, all that stimulates the genuine soldier in a way that makes every thought of danger fully disappear', wrote one officer idealistically, before going on to describe 'terrible woundings' and a 'bloody march from wood to wood'.[286] Another 'eye witness' who took part was more realistic, admitting that 'we lay, scarcely capable of fighting, in the wood, which had been conquered with so much blood'.[287] Such soldiers had been prepared before 3 July for what Fontane conceded could seem to be a 'chaotic mess' (in the *Swiepwald*, for example) at the battle of Königgrätz itself.[288]

Journalists like Fontane and Wachenhusen were sceptical of soldiers' testimony because it was 'one-sided, like all portrayals of its kind', even if written with 'great liveliness': 'It gives what is immediately experienced and has no eye for what is happening around and beside it.'[289] Nevertheless, they based much of their writing on combatants' reports, relaying an immediate impression of fighting, which contradicted the heroic message of their wider narrative. Thus, Wachenhusen's conclusion that 'the enormous task was done and Prussia's army celebrated the

---

[280] Ibid., 241–2. I have adapted Craig's translation here; Craig, *Theodor Fontane*, 91.

[281] T. Fontane, *Der deutsche Krieg von 1866*, vol. 1, 339.   [282] Ibid., 379.

[283] Ibid., 382. Stories about atrocities in Trautenau were aired in the press, with Fontane here referring to correspondence from both sides in *Grenzboten*. See B. v. Werder, *Erlebnisse eines Johanniter-Ritters auf dem Kriegsschauplatze in Böhmen* (Halle, 1867), 32, who mentions the stories in passing as if they were widely known and accepted; also, W. F. Besser, *Sechs Wochen im Felde*, 10–11. Others referred to the poisoning of wells by 'a Czech people inflamed against us' by the Habsburg authorities, leading it to 'brutalities' of this kind: J. Blänkner, *Die Neunundsechziger bei Kloster und Münchengrätz am 28 Juni 1866* (Berlin, 1868), 49.

[284] T. Fontane, *Der deutsche Krieg von 1866*, vol. 1, 395–6.   [285] Ibid., 400.

[286] Ibid., 400–1.   [287] Ibid., 416.   [288] Ibid., 351.

[289] Ibid., 157. For reporting from the other side, see H. Pollak, *Erlebnisse eines Kriegskorrespondenten aus den Jahren 1859, 1866 und 1870* (Vienna, 1908).

most glorious day of its history', after the Austrians' retreat from Königgrätz on 3 July, stood in sharp contrast to the stories of blood-letting which had filled the preceding pages of the account.[290] Accompanying the Army of the Elbe, he wrote down his own experiences of the combat on the Prussian armies' right flank:

> Until midday, little was achieved, our fortunes were quite similar on each side. Then, finally, a village went up in flames in front of us. Unlamed, the Saxon batteries carried on firing.
>
> Meanwhile, it was becoming hard and bloody on our left. One village, Mekrowans, was burning on our left-hand side, another burst into flames, over there, still further to the left, in Dohalitz and Benatek, the columns of fire were blazing into the misty air; black vortices of smoke tied themselves and became entangled above the battle, we saw the infantry battles, saw the cavalry attacks, then the pall of gunpowder suddenly concealed our entire view until a breeze again blew it away.
>
> Unceasingly, the fire of the guns flashed in our eyes in terrible precision... Scared, our hearts were beating in our breasts... the fighting raged,... leaving a glaring mosaic of corpses on the yellow cornfield...
>
> Death reaped a terrible harvest for more than five hours; as if mowed down by his scythe, the brave ones lay in large piles or in long rows on the field of battle, a gruesome painter's view reminding me of the field of corpses at Magenta.[291]

With grenades exploding in the air above them, 'unfortunately whole sections of our battalions' were ripped apart, 'whole squadrons of our cavalry' were blasted away, with the natter of muskets and horn signals drowning out 'the death sighs of heroes'.[292] Everywhere was 'overfilled with wounded'; the 'wounded were multiplying with every second'; officers staggered away wounded from the fighting, offering 'a painful, heart-rending picture'.[293] 'One also becomes accustomed to the sight of the wounded and one is able in the end to pass by them with an indifference which is, at bottom, unnatural', Wachenhusen continued: 'a familiar and perhaps dear face with the weary, half-extinguished eyes, which look at us so painfully, the bleeding wound, perhaps even a smashed limb—the heart cries before this scene, and yet this is not the place for it'.[294] 'However many bloody conflicts one has been a witness of', he concluded, 'one never gets used to it.'[295]

Although during the fighting itself soldiers could get used to the violent sights and sounds of war, with one of Fontane's 'eye witnesses' suggesting that the explosion of shrapnel and grenades left each combatant feeling himself both 'quiet'— despite 'death around us, before us'—and 'in God's hands', the majority appear to have been affected by the spectre and recollection of killing and wounding after the excitement of battle had passed.[296] 'How many death-pale faces this mist might hide in sympathy', wrote Wachenhusen, in memory of the 800 wounded and 300 dead of the Army of the Elbe on 3 July.[297] The journalist's ride across the battlefield—a 'field of the dead'—revealed 'terrible destruction', hedges on which corpses

---

[290] H. Wachenhusen, *Tagebuch vom Oesterreichischen Kriegsschauplatz*, 157.
[291] Ibid., 145–6.   [292] Ibid., 146.   [293] Ibid., 148.
[294] Ibid.   [295] Ibid.   [296] T. Fontane, *Der deutsche Krieg von 1866*, vol. 1, 513.
[297] H. Wachenhusen, *Tagebuch vom Oesterreichischen Kriegsschauplatz*, 159–60.

were hanging, 'piles of the dead', 'puddles of blood', limbs severed by bits of grenade, and, 'the grisliest thing that I saw, the head of an Austrian soldier which had been separated from his body and stood upright, as if it had grown out of the earth'.[298] Through the evidence given by another witness, Fontane passed on similar sights: in the church of Dohalitz, 'one lay there with a split skull, so that the brain could be seen; the shoulder had been ripped off another—he died'; in Ober-Dohalitz, the wounded who could move had been dragged out into a yard; 'the others were charred'—'it looked atrocious'.[299] Near one Prussian soldier was a blood-spattered 'sacred letter of protection', which he had been holding (in Wachenhusen's reconstruction): 'God be with me! Whoever carries this blessing with him against his enemies will be protected from dangers.'[300] The 'unfortunate who had carried it as a means of protection certainly lay amongst the corpses, of which I counted about sixty, beside and on top of one another', the journalist remarked.[301] Of many other deaths, for instance the 'ravages of the splinters and fragments of grenades' or the 1,300 Austrian wounded who had been left to die after their doctors had fled from a dressing station, he remained more or less silent: 'I had enough of this sad scene and I spare the nerves of the reader, of whom I have perhaps already asked too much.'[302]

Field doctors were less anxious to spare their readers' nerves, revealing for the good of science the diverse nature of soldiers' injuries.[303] Thus, Ernst von Bergmann, an academic surgeon from Dorpat, was delighted finally to see about thirty wounded men in a hospital in Zittau. 'There were very nice wounds there', he wrote: 'we saw a piece of cannon shot, weighing more than three pounds, cutting its way out of a Prussian *Landwehrmann*', causing them such excitement that they had to undergo the subsequent 'pain' of missing their train towards the fighting.[304] For the army doctor Karl-Ludwig August Stahmann, the overriding objective of his work was the 'enrichment of his knowledge', which was hindered by his position in the front line of fighting—as a regimental medic—and his inability to follow up and study the progress of his cases.[305] These cases, as in 1864, were comprised mainly of shot wounds produced by bullets and shells, along with several bayonet and sabre cuts, which—although they were in the face or head in some instances—often healed.[306] The effects of wounding by shells depended on whether the shot was solid (four-pounders, six-pounders, and twelve-pounders) or hollow (grenades), in which case injuries were like those caused by shrapnel and grapeshot. 'Of all these types of shot, fragments are rarely found in the body of the wounded', recorded Stahmann, 'because, naturally, they kill, for the most part, immediately

[298] Ibid., 163–4.   [299] T. Fontane, *Der deutsche Krieg*, vol. 1, 645–6.
[300] H. Wachenhusen, *Tagebuch vom Oesterreichischen Kriegsschauplatz*, 164.   [301] Ibid., 165.
[302] Ibid., 169.
[303] See accounts such as those of K. Fischer, *Militärärztliche Studien aus Süddeutschland und Böhmen* (Aarau, 1866) and C. T. Pelzer, *Militärartzliche Kriegserinnerungen an 1866 und 1870/71* (Berlin, 1914).
[304] A. Buchholtz, *Ernst von Bergmann. Mit Bergmanns Briefe von 1866, 1870/71 und 1877*, 2nd edn (Leipzig, 1911), 207.
[305] K.-L. A. Stahmann, *Militärärztliche Fragmente und Reminiscenzen aus dem österreichisch-preussischen Feldzuge im Jahre 1866* (Berlin, 1868), 1.
[306] Ibid., 90–4.

or soon'.[307] 'That many instances of death occur on the battlefield as a result of such immense wounds, we saw in the fortifications of Lipa', the doctor continued.[308] Splinters of shrapnel could travel up to 200 yards, ranging from invisible shards to large fragments that 'smash and tear bones, vessels and nerves', all of which were common in the lazaret of Sadowa on 3 July (see Figure 8.2 for the military hospital in Leipzig).[309]

Bullet wounds were still more commonplace, creating different incisions on entry and exit, 'in the form of a star, a slit etc.'[310] The Austrian front-loading musket, which was based on the 'Lorenz-Wilkinson system', was effective over a range up to 900 yards. The Prussian needle-gun extended beyond 1,000 yards and could be loaded in a lying position, which meant that infantrymen were more often hit in the head than their Habsburg counterparts, even though less frequently injured overall.[311] Austrian bullets, which more regularly split on impact, caused more tissue damage, which was 'indifferent' from a military point of view (since 'it is a question of making as large a number as possible no longer capable of fighting') but which remained relevant from a medical one.[312] Typical cases included Musketeer K., who was shot in the upper jaw on the right-hand side, with the bullet smashing his palate and taking two incisors with it, boring a hole in the tongue, penetrating down into the left side of the throat and exiting the body near the left shoulder blade.[313] Much of the treatment of such wounds proceeded without chloroform, which was reserved, given the risk of complications, for 'larger operations' like amputation: 'For smaller operations, like the cutting out of superficially embedded bullets, the amputation of fingers and toes, scars from sabre wounds, the extraction of bullets etc., we would not use chloroform because the pain cannot be compared to the dangers which the use of chloroform brings with it.'[314] Doctors like Stahmann seemed to be more or less indifferent to soldiers' suffering and to the horrors of the battlefield.

Not all medics were so detached.[315] One hospital inspector working in Dresden reported to his family on 16 July 1866 that more than fifty amputations per day were being carried out—'for one an arm, for another a leg'—and that 'many, many tears flow here and the groaning and pain is without end'.[316] Julius Naundorff, a doctor working under the aegis of the 'red cross', gave a rambling, quasi-religious account of what it felt like to be in a field sanitation corps. His ideal was to bring to an end the conditions which had characterized battle until then: that soldiers 'remain behind on the bloody battlefield with burning pain, calling out for refreshment and help'; that 'help and care for their wounds would not be lacking, which they need and without delay, which itself is so often deadly or can at least have the loss of the wounded limb as a consequence'; that they should not have 'the worse fate of expecting to become the terrible victim of those

[307] Ibid., 97.   [308] Ibid.   [309] Ibid., 97–9.   [310] Ibid., 103.

[311] Ibid., 152–3. Most of the wounded still had shots to the upper and lower extremities: ibid., 128.

[312] Ibid., 153.   [313] Ibid., 103.   [314] Ibid., 147.

[315] B. v. Werder, *Erlebnisse eines Johanniter-Ritters auf dem Kriegsschauplatze in Böhmen* (Halle, 1867), 30–44, 65–102.

[316] Herr Blittowsky, 16 July 1866, *Kriegsbriefe* Archive, Universitäts- und Landesbibliothek Bonn.

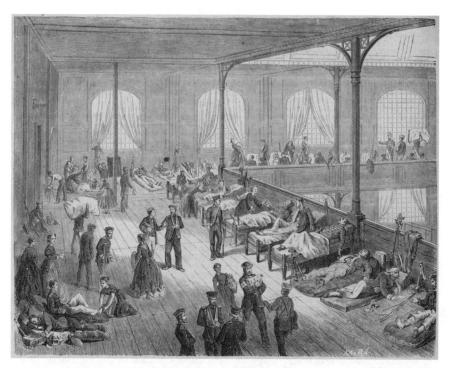

Figure 8.2 'Das international Lazareth in der Leipziger Turnhalle. Nach der Natur aufgenommen' and 'Gruppe verschiedener verwundeter Soldaten aus den internationalen Lazarethen in Leipzig'

Source: *Gartenlaube*, 1866, vol. 29, 460–3.

creatures greedy for booty—the hyenas of the battlefield—who fall on the defence-less for plunder, murdering those still living in order to be able to rob them all the more securely, as they do the dead'.[317] Such conditions were not 'pictures of fan-tasy' or 'from long ago', but 'how it has been in recent times'.[318] 'Whoever has not seen a battle himself can only with difficulty summon up a picture of the apparent disorder, the wild on-top-of-each-other, which predominates within its sphere', kept in check only by 'the power of discipline' of 'good soldiers', degenerating into true chaos with the involvement of 'purely disciplined troops' or with any divergence from the 'mechanical norms' of 'an unchangeable order'.[319] 'Under the impression of indescribable horrors', the soldier began to 'fail in his duty' and the 'machine, whose action is not regulated precisely for every case, starts to falter'.[320]

As they approached the 'hot point of a battle', the group of medics were sur-rounded and passed by all kinds of wounded men. They shared the contents of their water bottle, placed 'a bandage on a flowing artery here, staunched the blood with a tourniquet there', before carrying on across the battlefield:

> Bullets whizz around them so thickly that one thinks one sees them. It is as if they found themselves in the middle of a buzzing swarm of bees. Above them, around them, everywhere the whistling tones, the music of battle, only interrupted by the humming and din of solid and hollow shells which the cannon hurl out.
>
> Closed battalions push forward towards them; soon enough, they will have to pick out their own rubble from the earth...
>
> The earth shakes, as during a raging hurricane...'Forwards, comrades', says an NCO to his men in support—they lower their heads now and then. A bullet glances the arm of one. One puts on a bandage. Who asks anything about it? The bag of ban-dages was ripped from another by grenade splinter. 'Better than if it had been the body', says my comrade...They pay no attention to it, they rush forwards, true to their duty. Past the dead, whom they are no longer able to help, past hills of corpses. Some of these have an expression of calm on their faces. They are the ones who have been given a quick end, the true, ecstatic death of the soldier in 'the joy of battle'. But a far greater number carry the trace of a terrible struggle with death. With rigid, out-stretched limbs, their hands drilled into the earth, their eyes distant and unnaturally wide-open, the hair of their beards bristling on end and covered with a sticky slime, often a haunting and desperate smile on their lips, which allows their teeth to be seen, pressed together—they lie here, there and all over, images of death, which seem to flicker before our spiritual eyes, waking and sleeping, for a long time.
>
> On the rise of the hills and in hollows, they lie piled up, and a sluggish, dark flood seeps from them and collects in the depressions of the ground to form bloody puddles, which steam. It smells of gunpowder and blood, and it is not without reason when one attributes an intoxicating and wild, inflaming energy to this unusual, particular smell

[317] J. Naundorff, *Unter dem rothen Kreuz* (Leipzig, 1867), 73; also, 'Da werden Weiber zu Hyänen', in W. Petsch, *Heldenthaten Preußischer Krieger und Charakterbilder aus dem Feldzuge von 1866* (Berlin, 1867), 19–22.

[318] J. Naundorff, *Unter dem rothen Kreuz*. This was confirmed, amongst others, by officers in F. Deitl (ed.), *Unter Habsburg Kriegsbanner*, vols 1–6.

[319] J. Naundorff, *Unter dem rothen Kreuz*, 108.   [320] Ibid.

of blood. By climbing from the senses to the brain and to the sources of life, it pours into the arteries a feverish excitement.

Wild peoples drink blood before they leap into their cruel battles with the rage and hunger of a tiger.[321]

In parts, Naundorff's account fused fantasy and streams of consciousness, as 'doctors—covered over and again with blood'—could 'no longer carry out their difficult work', since they, too, were humans, and what they were being asked to do was 'beyond the power of humanity'.[322] In other parts, the medic revealed unimagined horrors ('sometimes, from a piled up wall of dead bodies, one sees an arm stretch out and flail around, trying to grab something') and expressed hopes of religious redemption (in a chapter on 'The Coming Dawn', for instance).[323] Citing Dante's vision of hell and Dunant's description of Solferino, he gave a portrayal of a war which was necessary for the existence of the state but which was nerve-shattering and 'unnatural'.[324]

Many soldiers' reports of the fighting in 1866 referred to similar sights and smells. Much of the evidence comes from younger Prussian officers, who were eager to go to war and who believed that the end of a glorious victory justified the nerve-wracking military means of achieving it.[325] A young Alfred von Schlieffen's main regret at the battle of Königgrätz was that he did not participate in an attack.[326] Nonetheless, officers like Schlieffen recognized that the troops were less enthusiastic, with Georg von Bismarck—one of the officers charged with organizing the deployment—noting simply that 'the mobilization proceeded...quietly and steadily': 'Our replacements,...had reached for their arms without any enthusiasm, since they, just as little as the rest of the Prussian population, could not see the deeper grounds for the war. But the teams did their duty in every respect quietly and decisively.'[327] By the time of the battle of Königgrätz, the majority of young officers had already experienced combat and knew what to expect. One of those who had not witnessed combat at close quarters, Heinrich von Schönfels, on the right wing of the First Army, rode to the top of the hill, overlooking the battlefield, where 'a bitter struggle' was taking place:

> It was a great spectacle which lay before us, unfolding. We saw how our infantry stormed towards the strongly held villages of Sadowa and Dohalitz and Dohalicka. We saw their ranks lit up by the murderous fire of the enemy, heard the screams of the wounded, saw the frantic last gasps of the dying. We saw the infantry force their way in and come out again, saw the villages go up in flames—and always between-times

---

[321] Ibid., 120–1.   [322] Ibid., 136.

[323] Ibid., 161, 168–75.   [324] Ibid., 136–7, 165, 177.

[325] Edgar Auer von Herrenkirchen, 'Erinnerungen aus dem Feldzuge gegen Oesterreich 1866', in H. Kufittich (ed.), *Unsere Offiziere vor dem Feinde. Persönliche Erlebnisse aus den Feldzügen 1864, 1866 und 1870/71* (Berlin, 1900), 320: 'Such a wild jubilation and such high spirits had not reigned in the small rooms of the officers' casino in the fortress of Pillau for decades', as at the time of the call for Prussian mobilization in 1866.

[326] A. v. Schlieffen to his bride, 4 July 1866, in E. Kessel (ed.), *Generalfeldmarschall Graf Alfred Schlieffen* (Göttingen, 1958), 194. Viktor von Lignitz, *Aus drei Kriegen. 1866, 1870/71, 1877/78* (Berlin, 1904), 11, noted the same regret, despite his corps (Steinmetz) having sustained heavy losses at Skalitz.

[327] G. v. Bismarck, *Kriegs-Erlebnisse*, 10.

the shouts of hurrah of the attackers and the roaring and whistling of the infernal batteries which the Austrians were directing at us. The shells did not spare our division, either, notwithstanding the fact that it was more than 4,000 yards from the Austro-Saxon cannon...here, I saw the blood flowing on the battlefield close-up for the first time, saw for the first time the groaning and suffering of the seriously wounded immediately in front of me. Doctors and stretcher-bearers were, indeed, on the scene quickly enough, to give assistance. But for wounds by grenade splinters, as was the case here, human help is rarely of much use.[328]

The artillery battle continued, Schönfels recorded, until midday, making 'the earth shake'.[329] The corps of Franseck and Horn were close to giving way, appearing to presage 'an unfavourable turn' for the Prussians, as the Austrians and Saxons refused to relent.[330] Some regiments of the First Army came back from the front, with 'the saddest look of complete exhaustion and shock', causing unrest even in the entourage of Prince Karl Friedrich.[331] Until 3.00 p.m., Schönfels's cavalry corps remained stationary, though the 'infantry masses standing in front of us' continued to be under fire, with Austrian shells 'spreading death and destruction around them'.[332] After 3.00 p.m., the corps was brought into the battle to chase Austrian soldiers, whose 'order in retreat seemed much loosened'.[333] Its losses in the cross-fire were 'not inconsiderable', with over 330 casualties.[334] Although 'it was moving to see [the king's] joy, his happiness, his pride in his creation, his—in truth—outstanding army', when Wilhelm I suddenly appeared amongst the troops during the afternoon, 'the battlefield offered an anonymous, distressing view'.[335] Only a few 'of the great mass of unfortunates lying around were fully dead', he wrote:

Most wrestled with life, in wild convulsions and with sighs, whimpers and moans. Their pleas for help from us, who were not able to assist them—their cries of pain in the face of the jubilation of victory, which resounded against them from our direction—the blood-soaked field, lit by the reflections of burning villages—were impressions which everyone who experienced them will never forget.[336]

These were profoundly ambiguous experiences, compounded by a night of fitful sleep 'among the dying' on the battlefield.[337]

How did it feel to live through the battle of Königgrätz? The 31-year-old captain Albert von Holleben tried to put his emotions into words in a letter of 4 July:

We are still lying here on the battlefield. How should I describe to you the feelings which have moved me over the last days. Thankfulness to the Almighty that he granted such a victory to Prussia, that he kept me alive for you; then the mourning for the severe losses of the regiment (Erkert is still living and perhaps will pull through; Pape's son died yesterday); the feeling of a shudder, not before death itself, but before the terrible prospect of the battlefield in its indescribable misery; the feeling of opposition to the labour of warfare, when it is perhaps used for light-headed designs. But dear God knows humanity. Apart from all the successes for the fatherland, apart from all the glory, the self-confidence which our army will bring home with it, these days of

---

[328] L. v. Schönfels (ed.), *Erlebnisse Heinrich von Schönfels*, 25. [329] Ibid., 26.
[330] Ibid. [331] Ibid., 27. [332] Ibid. [333] Ibid., 29.
[334] Ibid. [335] Ibid., 29–30. [336] Ibid., 30. [337] Ibid.

bloody struggle have brought us one gift which cannot be esteemed highly enough…—religion…The whole officer corps stood in deep earnestness, I prayed to God, I believe each one of us prayed. That is the best thing, in my opinion, about the terrible days for us, the officer corps, the entire army.[338]

Even with the consolation of his religious belief, Holleben believed that the battle-field was 'evil'.[339] Some officers shared this faith in God. 'God will help us further; I trust him and know no fear', wrote Julius von Bose to his wife after Königgrätz: 'He has protected me wonderfully and will do it again, I am told by an inner voice.'[340] Other officers maintained that 'one gets used to' the 'ugly view' of the battlefield, as one became accustomed to privations of all kinds.[341] Few, though, could excise what they had seen from their memory: thus, Georg von Bismarck 'was deeply shaken by the view, beyond all measure', of a field hospital that he visited on the evening of 3 July, commenting that 'whoever sees all that for the first time will be shaken to his core', even those with 'good nerves' like himself.[342]

In common with most Prussian soldiers, Bismarck fell to sleep on the battlefield, waking up in the middle of the night to wander between the corpses, barely caring that he stumbled and fell several times on top of them: 'my receptiveness for other-wise terrifying impressions was so cauterized that I hardly paid attention to the plaintive cries from the nearby dressing station nor the marrow-penetrating shrill neighing of the horses, suffering from open wounds'.[343] He had 'not the slightest sense' of the blood-red horizon and the fires of the twelve burning villages, which cast light on 'the enormous battlefield, the largest of Prussia's history of war'.[344] All the same, 'all the impressions of that night have remained in my memory in the most vital way', he concluded: clearing the field of bodies gave rise to scenes which shook 'even those with the strongest nerves and which stick in the memory forever'.[345] 'All the terror, all the frights of war, all the wild excitement of the most dreadful battle, the sneer of death in a thousand forms—the jubilation and the feeling of victory—all that coursed with the violence of a tempest through my heart over the last few days', wrote the 31-year-old *Freiwillige* and ordnance officer Fred von Frankenberg in his diary on 6 July.[346] In general, officers preferred, like Richard von Strombeck, to 'pass over the individual terrible scenes which mani-fested themselves during the night', yet they did so for the sake of propriety not because they were able themselves to forget them.[347]

---

[338] W. v. Holleben (ed.), *Briefe aus den Kriegsjahren 1866 und 1870/71 des Generals der Inf. Albert v. Holleben* (Berlin, 1913), 26–7.

[339] Ibid., 28. Other soldiers recalled how religious ceremonies were not taken seriously, at least at the start of the campaign: H. Lüders, *Ein Soldatenleben in Krieg und Frieden* (Stuttgart, 1888), 52.

[340] O. Herrmann, *Julius von Bose, Preußischer General der Infanterie. Eine Lebensbeschreibung nach amtlichen Quellen und privaten Mitteilungen* (Berlin, 1898), 79.

[341] F. v. Rauch to his wife, 4 July 1866, in F. v. Rauch, *Briefe aus dem großen Hauptquartier der Feldzüge 1866 und 1870/71 an die Gattin* (Berlin, 1911), 18.

[342] G. v. Bismarck, *Kriegs-Erlebnisse*, 49–50.

[343] Ibid., 51.　　　[344] Ibid.　　　[345] Ibid., 52.

[346] F. v. Frankenberg, *Kriegstagebücher von 1866 und 1870/71* (Stuttgart, 1896), ed. H. v. Poschinger, 35.

[347] R. v. Strombeck, *Fünfzig Jahre aus meinem Leben* (Leipzig, 1894), 129. Rudolph Broecker, *Erinnerungen an die Thätigkeit der 11. Infanterie-Division und ihrer Artillerie während des Feldzuges*

Ordinary soldiers had less to gain from a military campaign than did officers, whose careers had been founded on a mythology of battle honours. From their letters, it appears that some were patriotic, despite the uncertainty surrounding the aims and causes of the war. 'Finally the time has come', wrote Heinrich Baumeister to his family on 16 May 1866, 'when I am lucky enough to seize and bear my weapons for the fatherland.'[348] Yet even these soldiers were aware that others did not feel the same:

> Dear parents, put yourself in good cheer and don't make yourself too sick over me; it is hard for you but remember that there are other families where the husband is away and has had to leave his wife and children behind, for we have two fathers in our company who have had to leave four children sitting at home.[349]

Many probably felt, like one correspondent, that they 'had to leave parents, wife, siblings, father and mother-in-law under the pressure of an iron "must"'.[350] Initially, the fact that they were 'clueless about the dangers standing before them' helped some soldiers to overcome 'the pains of separation in a youthful, happy mood, but now pain and homesickness and, in many still hours, the pain seizes the poor heart so searingly that it could scream out loud'.[351] A considerable number of troops seem to have been like Ferdinand Piel, whose 'heart was overflowing with the misery and the worries' which his family had for him.[352] Virtually all were thinking about death, writing to their relatives to 'help them out of their anxiety' and to reassure them that they were still alive.[353] Even a vocal 'patriot' such as Baumeister was in a sombre frame of mind as he was about to leave 'by rail—where to we don't know yet'.[354] 'You can imagine that it is hard for me perhaps never to see you again in this world', he wrote from Trier.[355]

When they arrived on the battlefields of Bohemia, such troops were usually shocked. The Prussian army had shown its bravery, Baumeister continued on 28 June, describing the early, small-scale fighting of the start of the campaign, yet 'it is a horrible view to see a battlefield covered with corpses. The screaming of the wounded and the stench of the dying enter your marrow'.[356] Some correspondents were tight-lipped, revealing only that 'many were unsettled because it was a question of life and death'.[357] Others were loquacious, unrestrained in their description of the horrors which they were encountering. 'Dear Joseph, it is a terrible thing to take part in a war and the difference between manoeuvres and war cannot be measured', Peter Mertens warned a friend on 29 June who had been looking forward to

---

1866 (Berlin, 1867), 10, expressed similar feelings after the battle of Skalitz; on the same after the battles of Podol and Gitschin, see H. Kufittich (ed.), *Unsere Offiziere vor dem Feinde*, 355.

[348] H. Baumeister to his parents and sister, 16 May 1866, *Kriegsbriefe* Archive, Universitäts- und Landesbibliothek Bonn.

[349] Ibid.   [350] Herr Reis to his father-in-law, 18 July 1866.

[351] Ibid.   [352] F. Piel to his relatives, 31 May 1866, ibid.

[353] Gabriel Schmitz to his parents and sister, 29 June 1866, ibid.

[354] H. Baumeister to his parents and sister, 16 May 1866, ibid.

[355] Ibid.   [356] H. Baumeister to his parents and sister, 28 June 1866, ibid.

[357] G. Klotten to his sister, 30 June 1866, ibid.

'some details'.[358] In his first battle, the Austrians had been 'harvested like ants', bravely—'I am an eye-witness'—getting back up to defend themselves after they had been shot.[359] In his second battle at Königgrätz, their fate was worse: it was 'the most terrible thing I can think of'.[360] His friend was asked to imagine two pictures, as if they were 'photography': in one, which was worth 10 Thaler to each member of our company, 'someone is cooking, someone is eating, someone is digging holes, someone is bringing in the dead, someone is burying them in a grave—oh, what a rare sight, a scene which rarely occurs in life'; in the other imagined photograph, on the next day, enemy corpses had not yet been buried, with the 'smell not to be blocked out in their presence'.[361] 'That was a dreadful picture', he continued: 'it is nice to tell tales about war, but not at all to take part and if I wanted to write down the hardships you would scarcely believe them, now if God is willing you can hear them from my own mouth'.[362] In such circumstances, wrote another soldier to his parents and his aunt, 'many a poor rascal had to leave this life in innocence', yet they were 'the luckiest ones'.[363] Survivors were confronted with 'the dead of both armies', lying 'in piles peacefully beside each other, with smashed limbs and desperately contorted limbs... Many soldiers had been shot into three or four pieces, but were still living despite the gruesome pain.'[364] Since his last letter, the same soldier went on, 'I have experienced repulsive things which father did not experience in five years of military service.'[365] The battle of Königgrätz was merely a 'great murderous battle in which thousands of people lost their lives'.[366] 'I could tell you things which would make the hairs on your head curl', he concluded, 'but I'll keep silent until I come home.'[367]

The majority of ordinary soldiers did the same. During and after the Franco-German war, the legend that educated civilian-soldiers—especially school-masters—had helped to achieve victory came widely to be accepted, founded in part on a panoply of popular memoirs. In 1866, there were comparatively few traces of conscripts' and volunteers' participation in the conflict, which was regularly portrayed only in the form of anecdotes—with titles like 'Two Brave Soldiers' and 'How a Hero Dies'—appearing at the time in the press.[368] Teachers in particular were ridiculed for their ineptitude, 'dumber than the dumbest recruits' and suitable only as 'cannon fodder', according to one captain in Magdeburg.[369] ' "You school-teacher candidate!" was the most shameful swearword that officers could find for a helpless soldier in those days', recalled one school-master.[370] Correspondingly, there were few published accounts of the wartime experiences of rank-and-file conscripts and reservists. One exception was the memoir of Hermann Lüders, a young guardsman and later artist from Halberstadt. As the son of a veteran of the 'wars of liberation',

[358] P. Mertens to J. Rumpen, 29 June 1866, ibid.   [359] Ibid.
[360] P. Mertens to J. Rumpen, 23 July 1866, ibid.   [361] Ibid.   [362] Ibid.
[363] F. Piel to his parents and his aunt, 1 July 1866, ibid.   [364] Ibid.
[365] F. Piel to his parents and his aunt, 6 July 1866, ibid.   [366] Ibid.   [367] Ibid.
[368] Such anecdotes were collected in W. Petsch, *Heldenthaten Preußischer Krieger und Charakterbilder aus dem Feldzuge von 1866* (Berlin, 1867), 40, 49.
[369] P. Stiefelhagen, *Ein Pädagoge im Kriege. Erinnerungen aus den Jahren 1866 und 1870/71* (Strasbourg, 1906), 3.
[370] Ibid., 4.

who 'used to love telling stories of that time in the style of an old warrior', Lüders found it natural that his generation entered war willingly in 1866: 'No wonder that we young ones, when we heard such tales, raged with bright enthusiasm and could barely wait for the time when we were held to be strong enough to wear the so-called coloured tunic.'[371] Accordingly, the guardsman's own story was framed as an adventure, replete with idyllic and heroic imagery. As they crossed into Bohemia with the Second Army, 'every single rider seemed to burn with disquiet', not as a result of fear but 'the desire to engage the enemy'.[372] After 'news of the victory at Nachod' on 27 June, all were 'in the highest spirits'.[373] Yet the good mood began to change at Trautenau, through which they passed the day after the battle:

> We marched for hours through the debris of the fighting of the previous day; a pile of dead and wounded, namely Austrians, still lay in the ditches and on the fields round about, in part offering a distressing view. Many of the dead had already swollen to the point of being unrecognizable; what force was manifest in this process of decay was shown by the fact that the very strong straps on the *Czakos* had been burst by the swelling of the head. I cannot forget the view of an Austrian infantryman, who lay on his back in a ditch at the side of the road; he had stretched out his hands into the air, apparently rigid, and between his fingers were cigars put there in sympathy by passers-by; one wanted to do the poor man a favour and had nothing else to offer. The greatest favour to him would, in truth, have been a bullet in the head, which he had begged for, groaning, from passers-by, but that was not possible.[374]

On 3 July, although they were still eager to fight, the troops around Lüders appeared more apprehensive, advancing in battle formation to join the left flank of the First Army, soaked from the bottom up in thick fields of corn and exhausted by 'the constant up and down' of the march:

> When we were up on a hill, we could see great clouds of gunpowder smoke rise up in the distance, mixed with the black clouds of smoke from burning houses; the thunder of cannon rumbled uninterruptedly now. Our fantasy was already painting a picture of the roar of battle; we thought of the many dead and wounded who must already be lying about over there.[375]

Before he arrived on the battlefield of Königgrätz, Lüders's premonition was one of dead and injured soldiers.

The soldiers of the Second Army joined the battle in the early afternoon. They were immediately overcome by the commotion and seriousness of the fighting. Initially, they went forwards 'as if on the exercise ground', feeling 'that order is the surest kind of protection in the hour of danger'.[376] Soon, however, the 'haunting whistle' of the bullets of the Austrian *Jäger*, 'which became louder and louder', displaced everything else, making the next hours a matter of survival and the

---

[371] H. Lüders, *Ein Soldatenleben in Krieg und Frieden*, 1. It is telling that the same author published his memoir about 1870–1 first: H. Lüders, *Anno 70 mitgelaufen. Erlebnisse eines Berliner Jungen im deutsch-französischen Kriege* (Quedlinburg, 1880).
[372] H. Lüders, *Ein Soldatenleben in Krieg und Frieden*, 39.   [373] Ibid., 45.
[374] Ibid., 50.   [375] Ibid., 55–7.   [376] Ibid., 57.

immediacy of the senses: 'The heart beats a bit, all joking, all frivolity disappears at once, luckily also the fatigue.'[377] Before they entered a wood, the troops saw 'the great battlefield', marked out by 'the flaming shots of cannon and gunpowder smoke miles into the distance'.[378] Once in 'the thick wood, we soon lost all contact with one another; only small groups stayed together, but we heard, from the roar of the battle, that we were in the middle of it'.[379] Emerging from the undergrowth, they had a meadow and, on the hill, a village, which they later discovered to be Lipa, in front of them. By this time, they had become accustomed to 'the whistling of bullets and the cracking of branches' but they were still caught up in the maelstrom of battle, with 'all pushing forwards'.[380] Although the position of the Austrians was becoming 'more and more hopeless', with Habsburg troops 'unable to resist the needle-gun, even with the best will', they continued to fight: 'Against garden fences and in the corners of rooms, the Austrians lay everywhere in piles; some of them were wounded, some threw their weapons and pack down and begged on their knees, wringing their hands for mercy.'[381] The Prussian soldiers 'fired blindly into the village', amidst 'noise and excitement' which were 'indescribable'.[382] One of Lüders' comrades shot an Austrian as he was giving himself up, which was deemed to be 'unchivalrous' but 'pardonable' in the tumult of the fighting.[383] He immediately 'atoned' for it by being shot dead, the guardsman remarked without further comment.[384] With many other Prussians in his company being wounded 'more quickly than can be written down', 'the general urge "forwards" allows no rest'.[385] For the moment, Lüders had no inkling 'where our comrades, the whole battalion, were', meeting up much later as 'the thunder of cannon got weaker and weaker and withdrew further and further into the distance'.[386] Only now was it possible to reflect on what had occurred: 'How much was to be told; every individual had experienced a lot.'[387]

In the telling of the story, Lüders combined the 'jubilation of victory' and the 'appearance of the King near Lipa', which banished any 'sad mood', with mourning for the dead. His battalion alone incurred about eighty casualties.[388] The marches which took place after 3 July, as the Prussian forces pushed south towards Vienna, were 'taxing' but also adventurous, culminating in 'a great and glorious day' on 22 September 1866, when the battalion marched back into Berlin, greeted by 'a welcoming and accompanying mass'.[389] Yet these scenes were juxtaposed with graphic depictions of death, which dominate the middle of the narrative. As cries of 'Vive le roi' subsided against the backdrop of the Austrian forces' disorderly retreat, all that were left 'around us' were 'dead, wounded or captured'.[390] In the large stables of a farm near Lipa lay 'hundreds and hundreds of wounded', amongst whom a large number of Austrian and Prussian doctors went about 'their horrible work', barely able to move.[391] 'An uninterrupted groaning and whimpering' filled the air.[392] The troops slept a few thousand yards from this site, with the 'grey mood

[377] Ibid.   [378] Ibid.   [379] Ibid., 58.   [380] Ibid.
[381] Ibid., 58–9.   [382] Ibid., 59.   [383] Ibid.   [384] Ibid.
[385] Ibid., 60.   [386] Ibid., 61–2.   [387] Ibid., 62.   [388] Ibid., 63.
[389] Ibid., 70, 88.   [390] Ibid., 63.   [391] Ibid.   [392] Ibid.

of the day' returning after the 'agitation of battle'.[393] Even when they were in elevated mood, soon after the fighting, 'nature finally made itself felt': 'Hunger and fatigue fought a grim battle within us.'[394] In the dark, the bivouac fires of 'the entire Prussian army' could be seen on all sides.[395] Most had been marching and fighting without stopping or eating for fourteen hours or more. They went to sleep hungry, ignoring the 'the groaning of the wounded Austrians', and woke up in the same state: 'the main thing again was our hunger'.[396] The arrival of provisions on 4 July was immediately eclipsed, though, by the troops' growing consciousness of their own 'great losses' and the plight of the wounded.[397] ' "Water" was the first thing that everyone called for from every corner', Lüders noted: 'the misery' of the wounded 'was at times dreadful'.[398] As the guardsman made his way across the battlefield towards Chlum, the soldiers still lay on fields and in ditches. One building contained 'hundreds of wounded and dismembered people' lying in the yard and 'in all corners': 'What could one do without any means of assistance?'[399] Lüders' line drawings, which punctuate the text of his memoir, showed a mass of indistinct bodies slumped against each other in the darkness, officers looking forlornly at a dead horse, and infantrymen burying the dead. 'Those who had struggled bloodily yesterday', he concluded, 'now rest here pale and stiff, but also peacefully one beside the other!'[400]

To an extent, soldiers' reflections on the weakness of the flesh and mortality, as they could be witnessed in the field hospital and on the field after battle, had become familiar tropes of combatants' memoirs and of war literature in general.[401] As the old actor Louis Schneider put it, having succeeded in seeing the location of the fighting on 4 July after failing to get there the previous day: 'Three days ago, I was in Berlin, today in the middle of enemy territory close to a bloody battlefield, *au lendemain d'une victoire!*'[402] It is unlikely, however, that such tropes were merely rhetorical devices, for there were many reasons to remain silent, from concern for public decency to a desire to glorify dynastic or patriotic conflict. Even Schneider was struck, after witnessing the screaming of the 'seriously injured', by the way in which 'the most joyful impressions changed places with the saddest ones'.[403] The question concerned the relative significance of joyful and sad impressions over the longer term. It was a question that the following war between France and the German states made at once more pressing and more difficult to answer.

---

[393] Ibid., 64.　　[394] Ibid.　　[395] Ibid., 65.　　[396] Ibid., 66.
[397] Ibid., 67.　　[398] Ibid.　　[399] Ibid., 68.　　[400] Ibid., 69.
[401] W. F. Besser, *Sechs Wochen im Felde*, 62–6, on hospitals, for instance.
[402] L. Schneider, *Aus meinem Leben* (Berlin, 1880), vol. 3, 162–3.
[403] Ibid., 158.

9

The War of the Germans

The conflict of 1870–1 was purportedly the most glorious of German wars but it was also the bloodiest since 1815. Acts of killing and dying were glossed over by painters like Anton Werner, who went on to become the best-known *rapporteur* of the events of the campaign.[1] His most famous work, *Die Proklamierung des Deutschen Kaiserreiches, 18. Januar 1871* (1877), which was based on sketches made during his stay in Versailles at the invitation of the Crown Prince, was probably the most familiar painting in the *Kaiserreich* for two generations of Germans.[2] It helped to establish the connection, which was quickly presented as if it were self-evident, between the war of the North German Confederation and southern German states against France, on the one hand, and the founding of a 'national' German Empire, on the other. Werner's depictions of the conflict itself, which derived partly from drawings made during an earlier trip in October and November 1870 as well as his 'official' visit in January the following year, were varied and realistic, reflecting his desire 'to describe truthfully something I myself had experienced'.[3] Yet they were also invariably congratulatory and distant from the realities of combat. They ranged from *Der 19. Juli 1870* (1881), which showed a pensive Wilhelm I at the tomb of his mother—and the national heroine—Queen Luise prior to his departure for France, and *Graf Moltke in seinem Arbeitszimmer in Versailles* (1872), which portrayed the Chief of the General Staff as a bespectacled, fine-featured academician in a wood-panelled room insulated from the fighting, to episodic depictions of army life such as *Kriegsgefangen, Oktober 1870* (1886), which represented a French soldier embracing his wife in the main street of a barely damaged small town before being made a prisoner by relaxed-looking German troops.[4] *Im Etappenquartier vor Paris, 24. Oktober 1870* (1894) imagined jovial, ruddy-cheeked Prussian soldiers singing and smoking in the resplendent, gilded setting of their billet in a French chateau.[5] The only indication of the conflict outside was the mud on their boots.

[1] D. Bartmann (ed.), *Anton von Werner. Geschichte in Bildern* (Munich, 1993), 470–1.

[2] P. Paret, *Art as History: Episodes in the Culture and Politics of Nineteenth-Century Germany* (Princeton, NJ, 1988), 169. Also, T. W. Gaehtgens, *Die Proklamierung des Deutsche Kaiserreiches. Ein Historienbild im Wandel preußischer Politik* (Frankfurt, 1990).

[3] A. v. Werner, *Erlebnisse und Eindrücke 1870–1890* (Berlin, 1913), 54.

[4] D. Förster, *Der Königin Luise-Mythos. Mediengeschichte des 'Idealbilds deutscher Weiblichkeit' 1860–1960* (Göttingen, 2011).

[5] For commentary on these and other works, see D. Bartmann, *Anton von Werner. Zur Kunst und Kunstpolitik im Deutschen Kaiserreich* (Berlin, 1985); F. Becker, 'Bilder deuten den Krieg: Anton von

Such scenes sometimes blurred the boundary between 'historical documentation' and 'ideal' (or 'monumental') representations of events which Werner had not witnessed and which could be modified for the sake of a 'higher historical truth', as in his series of imagined re-enactments of the attack at Spicheren and the earlier visit of Wilhelm I to Saarbrücken, designed from the late 1870s onwards for the city's *Rathaus*.[6] More importantly, they were defined by the painter's own experiences of a campaign which had come 'unexpectedly... like a lightning strike from a torrid sky' and which he had followed from Kiel 'blow upon blow', with 'messages of victory from Wissembourg, Spicheren und Wörth' transporting 'even the reserved, taciturn Holsteiners into the well-known intoxication of victory of those days', dampened 'only by mourning for our heavy losses in the victorious battles of Colombey, Mars-la-Tour and Gravelotte-St Privat'.[7] As his memoirs make plain, Werner had missed most of the fighting, reduced to documenting the aftermath of combat—debris in Strasbourg, the wounded arriving at railway stations, the burial of soldiers in Versailles—in late autumn and the life of military headquarters and the continuation of political negotiations outside Paris early in 1871.[8] His image of *Moltke mit seinem Stabe vor Paris* (1873), the commissioning of which by the *Kunstverein* of Schleswig-Holstein had been the pretext for his first trip to France in 1870, showed the Chief of Staff in traditional pose on top of a commander's hill, surrounded by his staff officers and looking out over a column of German troops. The picture includes an electric telegraph and soldiers resting, oblivious to the officers behind them, but it makes no reference to actual killing.[9] Similarly, Werner's famous *Sedan-Panorama* (1883), which consisted of a series of large-scale paintings—115 feet long and 15 feet high—for a rotunda in Berlin's Alexanderplatz, overlooks the dismemberment and agony of battle, despite revealing in minute detail the French cavalry charge—a wall of rearing horses—against Prussian infantry at Floing and close combat in the hills above Sedan.[10] More than 1 million visitors saw this version of events.[11]

Not all German painters fashioned such positive images of the war as Werner and Georg Bleibtreu, who had set up a studio in Versailles by October 1870 and introduced the young painter—Werner was only 27 years old—to the military and

Werners Gemälde "Am 19. Juli 1870" ', in T. Arand (ed.), *'Der großartigste Krieg, der je geführt worden'. Beiträge zur Geschichtskultur des Deutsch-Französischen Kriegs 1870/71* (Münster, 2008), 37–48.

[6] P. Paret, *Art as History*, 172. The later, 1885 version of the *Proclamation of the German Empire*, was itself partly imagined, rearranging figures and inserting Albrecht von Roon.

[7] A. v. Werner, *Erlebnisse und Eindrücke*, 4, 6.   [8] Ibid., 3–52.

[9] For a convincing analysis of the way in which the painting continued a movement from aerial and topographical depictions of battles to heroic and episodic scenes of a campaign, see A. Jürgens-Kirchhoff, 'Der Beitrag der Schlachtenmalerei zur Konstruktion von Kriegstypen', in D. Beyrau, M. Hochgeschwender, and D. Langewiesche (eds), *Formen des Krieges*, 454–6; F. Becker, *Bilder von Krieg und Nation*, 458–61.

[10] S. Parth, *Zwischen Bildbericht und Bildpropaganda*, 237–41; F. Becker, *Bilder von Krieg und Nation*, 470–9.

[11] S. Oettermann, *Das Panorama. Die Geschichte eines Massenmediums* (Frankfurt, 1980), 191; F. Becker, 'Augen-Blicke der Größe. Das Panorama als nationaler Erlebnisraum nach dem Krieg von 1870/71', in J. Requate (ed.), *Das 19. Jahrhundert als Mediengesellschaft* (Munich, 2009), 178–91. The figure is a plausible estimate.

political leaders of the German states.[12] Others like Wilhelm Emelé, Franz and Eugen Adam, Otto von Faber du Faur, and Louis Kolitz were more unflinching, displaying dead bodies and exposing the chaos and harshness of the conflict.[13] Yet none broke persisting taboos on the representation of cold or bloated corpses, severed limbs, and obliterated torsos and faces, which were typical sights on battlefields commented on by diarists and memoirists. Arguably, the celebrated realist painter Adolph Menzel, who had already depicted dead bodies in close-up in his illustrations for Franz Kugler's *Geschichte Friedrichs des Grossen* (1842) and during his visit to Bohemia in 1866, confronted the prohibition most starkly, having chosen to stay away from the fighting front in 1870–1, when he sketched a series of decomposing, mummified corpses of eighteenth-century generals exhumed from the *Garnisonkirche* in Berlin in 1873.[14] It is likely that he was influenced by his earlier experience of soldiers dying on the battlefield at Königgrätz. He did not publish the sketches or turn them into paintings, in tacit recognition of contemporary standards of public decency.[15] Paintings were both produced for public exhibition and they presented events as if they were real, in contrast to sketches, which could be kept private, or literary imagery, which was transferred and invented through the different medium of the word. Partly for this reason, photographs were prohibited or restricted as far as possible by the military (see Figure 9.1 for a well-known exception).[16] 'I don't understand where the photographers are!' wrote one correspondent of the *Gartenlaube* in 1870, after the capitulation of Strasbourg: 'In America, they were to hand on every battlefield and we owe to them the most interesting views.'[17] German leaders wanted to keep control of the dominant patriotic and bloodless narrative of the war.

In reality, of course, the Franco-German war of 1870–1 was bloody. French losses from killing, wounding, or disease totalled more than 300,000 from an army of 2 million, German losses up to 140,000 from 1.5 million.[18] According to one estimate, there had been 1,600 Prussian casualties (and 8,000 Danish ones) in the Schleswig War in 1864; 9,000 Prussian dead and wounded (and 44,000 Austrian casualties) in the Austro-Prussian War in 1866; and 116,696 Prussian losses (and

[12] A. v. Werner, *Erlebnisse und Eindrücke*, 16; S. Parth, *Zwischen Bildbericht und Bildpropaganda*, 96–101, on Bleibtreu.

[13] S. Parth, *Zwischen Bildbericht und Bildpropaganda*, 101–8, 117–30, 132–6, 237–40.

[14] P. Paret, 'Adolph Menzel from Different Perspectives', in P. Paret, *German Encounters with Modernism, 1840–1945* (Cambridge, 2001), iii, 12.

[15] This was also the case in later works; for instance, Georg Jacob Wolf's, *Adolf von Menzel. Der Maler deutschen Wesens* (Munich, 1900), which avoids Menzel's depictions of corpses and body parts.

[16] G. Paul, *Bilder des Kriegs*, 70.

[17] Cited in W. Hesse, *Ansichten aus Schwaben. Kunst, Lande und Leute in Aufnahmen der ersten Tübinger Lichtbildner und Fotografen Paul Skinner* (Tübingen, 1989), 67–8.

[18] B. Bond, *War and Society in Europe, 1870–1970* (London, 1984), 16. The figures vary: Michael Howard, *Franco-Prussian War*, 453, gives the following casualty totals for the German Empire: 28,208 dead and 88,488 wounded. Alistair Horne, *The Fall of Paris* (New York, 1967), 268, records 116,696 casualties for the Germans, 300,000 for the French; Larry Addington, *The Pattern of War since the Eighteenth Century* (Bloomington, IN, 1984), 90, reports 133,750 for the Germans, 238,000 for the French. See also Christine Krüger, 'German Suffering in the Franco-German War', 406, who records 180,000 total deaths, including more than 40,000 Germans, 90,000 wounded, and even more who fell ill.

Figure 9.1 Paul Sinner, *Straßburg vom Steintor aus, 28. September 1870* (1870)
Source: Rheinisches Bildarchiv Köln.

370,000 French casualties) in the Franco-German War in 1870–1.[19] Repeatedly, combatants remarked that the battles of August and early September in France were worse than Königgrätz.[20] 'We did not hide from ourselves at all the fact that the war before us against our powerful hereditary enemy, which had played the dominant role in Europe until then, would be much more serious and difficult than that against Austria', recalled the Saxon trainee teacher and common soldier Richard Martin in his memoir of the conflict.[21] Unlike in 1866, when Prussian troops had been more than four times less likely to be hit than their Austrian and Saxon counterparts because of their superior needle-guns and better tactics, they were initially more likely to be killed or wounded than French soldiers in 1870, suffering 4,500 dead and wounded compared to 2,000 French casualties at the battle of Spicheren on 6 August, for example.[22]

[19] A. Bucholz, *Moltke and the German Wars*, 192.
[20] See, for instance, H. Seelmann-Eggebert, *Feldpostbriefe aus dem Kriegsjahre 1870* (Colberg, 1872), 84, who called Königgrätz a 'children's game' beside Mars-la-Tour and Gravelotte.
[21] R. Martin, *Kriegserinnerungen eines 105ers* (Plauen i. V., 1896), 39. Although a Saxon, Martin referred in retrospect to a war 'against' Austria, despite the fact that Saxony had fought on the Habsburg monarchy's side.
[22] M. Howard, *Franco-Prussian War*, 99.

In the main battles at the start of the war—Wissembourg, Spicheren, Froeschwiller, Mars-la-Tour, Gravelotte, and Sedan—the rate of killing was similar to that of the worst of the Napoleonic campaigns. At Mars-la-Tour on 16 August, the Prussians suffered about 16,500 casualties from an initial force of 30,000, which was eventually augmented to 60,000 by arriving infantry divisions throughout the day.[23] 'Almost all our comrades were more or less seriously injured and the whole regiment was worn away to a small rump', recorded one survivor: 'We have seven officers left in the regiment; sergeants are now leading companies; nearly all the corporals have died.'[24] At Gravelotte on 18 August, August von Württemberg's Prussian Guard Corps lost 8,000 men—nearly as many as total Prussian casualties at the battle of Königgrätz—in half an hour, mowed down on the slope up to the village of St Privat by what Paul von Hindenburg, a lieutenant at the time, called a 'hurricane' of fire from French infantrymen's *chassepot* rifles.[25] About 35,943 German soldiers were lost according to official statistics between 16 and 18 August 1870, making such encounters, in the words of a member of the Prussian General Staff, 'amongst the bloodiest and most numerous in losses that have been fought in a long time'.[26] The French casualties with which German troops were confronted in late August and early September were, on occasion, even worse: at the battle of Froeschwiller on 29 August, two Algerian infantry regiments facing the Prussian Eleventh Corps lost thirty-three men per minute around 3.00 p.m. and the second reserve cavalry brigade, ordered forward by Patrice MacMahon at 4.00 p.m. to cover the French retreat, lost 260 men per minute, or 5,000 in less than 20 minutes.[27] Where, asked the writer and war correspondent Hans Wachenhusen, 'should the people come from for wars with these weapons, if they are long-lasting?'[28] As in the early nineteenth century, the battles of the Franco-German War confronted soldiers with extensive scenes of violence and death.

THE ARMY'S WAR: *VOLKSKRIEG* AND *FRANCS-TIREURS*

How could the fighting in 1870–1 be characterized? Any answer was confused at the time, as it has been since, by the succession of two more or less distinct phases of conflict: the first, which lasted until France's defeat at Sedan on 1 September, the surrender of Napoleon III the next day, and the declaration of the Third Republic

[23] G. Wawro, *The Franco-Prussian War: The German Conquest of France in 1870–1871* (Cambridge, 2003), 160.
[24] Cited in O. Haselhorst, 'Operationen der deutschen Heere', in J. Ganschow, O. Haselhorst, and M. Ohnezeit (eds), *Der Deutsch-Französische Krieg 1870/71. Vorgeschichte, Verlauf, Folgen*, 2nd edn (Graz, 2013), 97.
[25] P. v. Hindenburg cited ibid., 176.
[26] F. v. Rauch, *Briefe aus dem grossen Hauptquartier der Feldzüge 1866 und 1870–71* (Berlin, 1911), 53, 56. For the figures, see Großer Generalstab, *The Franco-German War 1870–1871* (London, 1874–84), vol. 1, appendix 24, used by Howard, *Franco-German War*, 161, 181, noting that the General Staff increased the figures for Mars-la-Tour, after investigating French sources.
[27] D. Ascoli, *A Day of Battle: Mars-La-Tour* (London, 1987), 81–2.
[28] H. Wachenhusen, *Tagebuch vom französischen Kriegsschauplatz 1870–1871* (Berlin, 1871), 86.

and a government of 'national defence' on the 4th, was marked by a rapid succession of bloody battles; the second, which ended with the ceasefire of 6 February (preceded by the Interior and War Minister Léon Gambetta's resignation on the 5th and the surrender of Paris brokered by the Foreign Minister Jules Favre on 27 January), consisted of individual acts of sabotage and killing by irregular *francs-tireurs* and disparate fighting on the part of improvised armies of reserves, *gardes mobiles*, and volunteers, which were attempting—until its surrender on 29 October—to reunite with Achille Bazaine's regular army besieged at Metz.[29]

Most soldiers—of all ranks—were convinced that the conflict was a 'people's war' or *Volkskrieg*, involving the pursuit of national interests and the deployment of the troops and economic resources of the entire nation.[30] Moltke himself accepted that the struggle against France was not a 'cabinet war', which is what he had labelled the Crimean War and the Austro-Prussian War, despite also acknowledging that they were 'modern', involving mass armies, together with 'the difficulty of feeding them, the costliness of being at arms and the interruption of trade, craft and agriculture'.[31] The conflicts of 1864 and 1866 had rested on a broad mobilization of states' resources and men, distinguishing them from conflicts of 'past times' when 'small armies of professional soldiers' had been used to pursue 'dynastic ends', occupying 'a city or a stretch of land' before retiring to winter quarters or concluding a peace.[32] They were not 'cabinet' wars in this sense, as the Chief of Staff tacitly acknowledged. Yet they were not *Volkskriege* in the contemporary meaning of the term either—in deliberate contrast to which the notion of a 'cabinet' war had been coined in the mid-nineteenth century—because of limited mobilization (1864) or limited 'political' objectives (1866), which lacked a clear, widely held patriotic or national rationale.[33] The war of 1870–1 would be different, Moltke had warned in 1867: 'A lost battle on French soil would never push France towards peace, but—given the patriotism of the nation (*bei dem Patriotismus der Nation*)—towards the summoning up of all the forces of a land so rich in means

---

[29] Edgar Feuchtwanger's judgement that the 'Franco-Prussian War was in fact a cabinet war that became a national war', with 'events after Sedan, the pursuit of the war by a new French republican regime, growing French radicalism, guerrilla warfare and eventually the Paris Commune' making it 'ever more so', is typical of historians' combination of terms to describe the wars of the 1860s: Edgar Feuchtwanger, *Bismarck* (London, 2002), 173.

[30] D. Langewiesche and N. Buschmann, '"Dem Vertilgungskriege Grenzen setzen". Kriegstypen des 19. Jahrhunderts und der deutsch-französische Krieg 1870/71', in D. Beyrau, M. Hochgeschwender, and D. Langewiesche (eds), *Formen des Krieges*, 165–6. The army chaplain Edmund Pfleiderer, *Erinnerungen und Erfahrungen eines Feldpredigers aus dem Krieg des Jahres 1870/71* (Stuttgart, 1874), 92, echoed the sentiments of many when he wrote that 'this war' was one in which 'the whole *Volk* participated whole-heartedly'. See also the priest Martin Schall, *Vor vierzig Jahren. Kriegserinnerungen eiens Lazarettpfarrers der II. Armee*, 6, who wrote of his wish, after earlier doubts, of not standing behind 'our brothers in this great patriotic time'.

[31] H. v. Moltke, 'Aus den Verordnungen für die höheren Truppenführer vom 24. Juni 1869', D. Langewiesche and N. Buschmann, '"Dem Vertilgungskriege Grenzen setzen"', in D. Beyrau, M. Hochgeschwender, and D. Langewiesche (eds), *Formen des Krieges*, 171.

[32] H. v. Moltke, *Geschichte des deutsch-französischen Krieges von 1870–71* (Berlin, 1891), 1.

[33] On the emergence of the term 'cabinet war' in opposition to the notion of a *Volkskrieg*, see Frank Göse, 'Der Kabinettskrieg', in D. Beyrau, M. Hochgeschwender, and D. Langewiesche (eds), *Formen des Krieges*, 123.

of support.'[34] As the French government of national defence declared its willingness to wage 'une guerre à outrance' in late September, after Favre had published the 'insolent demands' made by Bismarck at Ferrières as the basis of a peace settlement, the question facing the Chief of Staff and other senior German officers was not whether a *Volkskrieg* would revert to a 'cabinet' or 'state' war, but whether it would degenerate into guerrilla warfare or civil war.[35]

For Bismarck, who was in Ferrières and Versailles at military headquarters between September 1870 and early March 1871, it was necessary to end the war as soon as possible, partly to prevent the formation of a coalition of powers against the North German Confederation, partly to settle the German question, and partly to halt France's lurch towards an intransigent revolutionary government.[36] To this end, a wide range of means were justifiable, in the Chancellor's view, including those going beyond contemporary conventions.[37] 'I must express my indignation about newspaper reports which have reached you that it is I who is hindering the firing of our cannon on Paris and that the prolongation of the war is my fault', he wrote to his wife on 21 October 1870: 'The whole matter is enveloped by intrigue, woven by women, archbishops and professors, well known exalted influences are involved, so that the praise of the foreigners and the phrase-making should not diminish.'[38] The Crown Prince, his wife Victoria (who was Queen Victoria's daughter), and the Queen, surrounded by liberals from the *Landtag*, in the diplomatic corps, and at court, were helping to stymie Bismarck's plans at home and abroad, backed by unimaginative and inflexible generals, it seemed. At first, the Chancellor had wanted, as he told his son Herbert in a letter on 7 September, 'to let these people [the French] stew in their own juice, and to install ourselves in comfort in the vanquished provinces before going further. If we go forward too soon, it would prevent them from falling out among themselves.'[39] Once the army had advanced to Paris on Moltke's orders, Bismarck attempted to negotiate with Bazaine, arguing—as he phrased it in an article planted in Rheims' newspapers on 11 September—that 'it is impossible to say what justification the German government would have in treating with a power [the French government of national defence] which up till now represents only a part of the left wing of the

[34] H. v. Moltke, 'Denkschrift vom Januar 1867 über einen Krieg gegen Frankreich und Österreich', in S. Förster (ed.), *Moltke. Vom Kabinettskrieg zum Volkskrieg* (Bonn, 1992), 193.

[35] On France, see S. Audoin-Rouzeau, *1870. La France dans la guerre* (Paris, 1989); F. Roth, *La Guerre de 1870* (Paris, 1993); B. Taithe, *Citizenship and Wars: France in Turmoil, 1870–1871* (London, 2001).

[36] K. A. Lerman, *Bismarck*, 150–3.

[37] Paul von Hatzfeld, *Hatzfelds Briefe, geschrieben vom Hauptquartier Wilhelms 1870–71* (Leipzig, 1907), 48, hinted how blurred such conventions were for Wilhelm I and his staff, too, on 22 August 1870: 'One is very much angered here that so much concern towards French prisoners in Berlin—and this is correct, with even newspapers expressing disapproving opinions about it. These prisoners are stuffed full of every possible good thing whilst our poor soldiers, who spill their blood for the fatherland, must make do with the leftovers... The French truly do not deserve such care; they have disrespected the laws of war and have shot at our doctors and wounded! And then they are shameless enough to talk of civilization!'

[38] O. v. Bismarck to J. v. Bismarck, 21 Oct. 1870, cited in E. Feuchtwanger, *Bismarck*, 174.

[39] O. v. Bismarck to H. v. Bismarck, 7 Sept. 1870, in W. Busch, *Das deutsche Grosse Hauptquartier und die Bekämpfung von Paris im Feldzuge 1870–71* (Stuttgart, 1905), 10.

former legislative assembly': 'The German government could enter into relations with the Emperor Napoleon, whose government is the only one recognized hitherto, or with the Regency he appointed; they would also be able to treat with Marshal Bazaine, who has his command from the Emperor.'[40] Immediately after Sedan, the Chancellor had warned a Bavarian staff officer, who had asked him whether the war was over 'with the capture of the French emperor', that it would only come to an end when 'there is a government in Paris capable of conducting negotiations'.[41]

With the republican provisional government offering an indemnity and a fraction of its fleet, but 'not a piece of territory', as Favre confirmed in his meeting with Bismarck at the Rothschilds' chateau at Ferrières on 18 September, the Prussian leader preferred to entertain the prospect of a restoration of the Bonapartes, backed by Bazaine, as the British ambassador to France pointed out on 16 September: 'Marshal Bazaine might find that it suits his purpose to stand fast by the Emperor. Then, if the Emperor were willing to make peace on the Prussian terms, Prussia would assist him to regain his throne with the aid of Bazaine and the 140,000 troops now prisoners in Germany.'[42] Earlier, Bismarck had revealed to General Philip Sheridan, the American military observer at German headquarters, that he would like to find the 'pliable' 14-year-old Prince Imperial, who had fled to Britain, and put him on the French throne 'under German influences'.[43] On 23 September, a Prussian agent met Bazaine in private and offered safe passage to the 141,000-strong Army of the Rhine, together with their arms and baggage, to a 'neutralized zone', where the deputies of the Second Empire's senate and legislative assemblies could legitimate the formation of a conservative government willing to accept moderate German terms under either the Prince Imperial or a military regency (Bismarck's 'dictature Bazaine').[44] Charles Bourbaki, commander of the Guard Corps, was dispatched to London in secret to hand over the proposal to Empress Eugénie, who refused. Bazaine's own offer on 14 October to withdraw to southern France or Algeria with the Army of the Rhine in order to allow the Prussians to concentrate all their efforts on Paris and its environs and to defeat the republicans quickly was published extensively in the German press, even though it was rejected by Moltke and Bismarck.

Cold and hungry, soaked by constant rain, and beset by dysentery, Bazaine's forces surrendered on 29 October 1870. By that time, Bismarck had redirected his attention to the siege of Paris and the military campaign in the rest of France, which the Chancellor and the Chief of the General Staff had jointly proposed to occupy while national elections took place. The idea of an election had been conceived in order to create a more moderate, amenable government, after Favre had

[40] Cited in M. Howard, *Franco-Prussian War*, 231; see also J. Kühn, 'Bismarck und der Bonapartismus im Winter 1870/71', *Preußische Jahrbücher*, 163 (1916), 51.

[41] O. v. Bismarck to G. Fleschuez, cited in G. Wawro, *The Franco-Prussian War*, 235–6.

[42] R. Lyons to G. G. Leveson-Gower, Earl Granville, 16 Sept. 1870, ibid., 240.

[43] P. H. Sheridan, *Personal Memoirs* (New York, 1888), vol. 2, 414.

[44] See G. Wawro, *The Franco-Prussian War*, 244–5: details of the deal are pieced together from the asides and revelations of Bazaine and the Prussian agent 'Regnier'.

reiterated his resolve to cede 'not a clod of our earth or a stone of our fortresses', to which Bismarck had retorted, 'Find a basis for peace, *propose* something!'[45] Like Friedrich Karl's warning to a British officer in October, when he promised to occupy southern France with 200,000 troops as soon as Bazaine had surrendered, with the local population paying for the occupation 'until a settled government is returned with which peace can be concluded', the Chancellor's priority was to bring every military and political pressure to bear in order to end the conflict.[46] 'Bismarck is furious', wrote Albrecht von Stosch to his wife on 22 December, 'that the military delay disturbs his political combinations very nastily.'[47] At Sedan, the Civil War veteran Sheridan had reproached the Prussians for merely 'defeating' the enemy, which they could do 'like no other army', rather than 'destroying' it.[48] What was required, he went on, was 'more smoke from burning villages, otherwise you will never be finished with the French'.[49] Although Bismarck had not followed his advice, his reaction to alleged atrocities by *francs-tireurs*—for example, reports that 600 Prussian prisoners of war had been killed in November—was to call on the army to execute all suspects and burn the villages where they were being harboured.[50] Male inhabitants of villages refusing requisition orders should be hanged; boys who spat at German troops should be shot; women and children scavenging for food outside Paris should be fired at.[51] From the beginning, he had predicted, 'it will come to this: that we will shoot down every male inhabitant'.[52] There should be no 'laziness in killing'.[53]

During the campaigns in the region of the Loire, as prisoners continued to be taken, the Chancellor complained that 'I should have been better pleased, if they had all been corpses', because it was 'simply a disadvantage to us now to make prisoners'.[54] African soldiers, in particular, were 'beasts of prey, and ought to be shot down', with anyone taking them prisoner to 'be placed under arrest'.[55] According to the Crown Prince,

> Count Bismarck has won for himself the reputation of being the instigator of all the cruel reprisals we have, alas, been forced to carry out; they even say of him that he means to establish a reign of terror in Paris of quite another sort from that of Gambetta's wars. Occasion is certainly given for such suppositions by the monstrous maxims and savage expressions one hears openly given utterance to here, and which his wife repeats in Berlin.[56]

---

[45] Ibid., 253–4.   [46] Ibid., 255.

[47] A. v. Stosch to his wife, 22 Dec. 1870, in U. v. Stosch (ed.), *Denkwürdigkeiten des Generals und Admirals Albrecht v. Stosch,* 17.

[48] A. v. Waldersee, *Denkwürdigkeiten* (Stuttgart, 1922), ed. H. O. Meisner, vol. 1, 100–1.

[49] Ibid.   [50] Cited in G. Wawro, *The Franco-Prussian* War, 279.

[51] O. Pflanze, *Bismarck and the Development of Modern Germany,* vol. 1, 473.

[52] Ibid., 472.   [53] G. Wawro, *The Franco-Prussian War,* 279.

[54] O. Pflanze, *Bismarck and the Development of Germany,* vol. 1, 472.   [55] Ibid., 472–3.

[56] Friedrich Wilhelm, *The War Diary of Emperor Frederick III, 1870–1871,* ed. A. R. Allinson (London, 1927), 292.

In fact, Johanna von Bismarck had called for German soldiers to 'shoot and stab all the French, down to the little babies'.[57] As the 'wretched bombardment' of Paris began on 4 January, the Crown Prince—who was compelled to carry it out by a military council on 31 December 1870—held it to be the damaging culmination of 'the theory, initiated by Bismarck and for years holding the stage, of "blood and iron"': 'We are deemed capable of every wickedness and the distrust of us grows more and more pronounced.'[58] Bismarck himself had been advocating bombardment since October. 'Now that the great army has been tied down for 2 months while our enthusiasm evaporates and the Frenchman rearms, the siege must be carried forward', he wrote to his wife on 16 November: 'but it looks as if the 400 heavy guns and their 100,000 tons of shot are to be left here until after the peace and will then be trundled back to Berlin',[59] The Chancellor did not share Moltke's hesitation about shelling civilians, describing it as posturing 'so that certain people may be praised for saving "civilization"', while 'the men freeze and fall ill, the war is dragging on, [and] the neutrals waste time discussing it with us'.[60]

Like other officers, who ridiculed Bismarck's penchant for wearing his *Landwehr* uniform (one of several 'civilians in cuirassiers' tunics' at military headquarters), Moltke resented the Chancellor's interference in army affairs.[61] 'The question as to when the artillery attack on Paris should or can begin, can only be decided on the basis of *military* views', the Chief of Staff wrote to the king on 30 November: 'Political motives can only find consideration in so far as they do not demand anything militarily inadmissible or impossible.'[62] In conventional military terms, 'the war has actually to be over', he confided to his brother Fritz on 11 October: 'France no longer has an army; one has capitulated and the other, without fail, must capitulate.'[63] Although dogged by many subsequent complications, including the need to keep the First and Second Armies (200,000 men) at Metz until the end of October, Moltke adhered to his conviction that France's military threat, which rested on its regular troops, had been nullified. Surrounding Paris with the 240,000 soldiers of the Third Army and the Army of the Meuse, which were arrayed against the capital's ring of fifteen forts and 400,000 *gardes mobiles* and national guardsmen (only one-fifth were regulars or reservists), the Chief of Staff resolved to starve the 2 million inhabitants of the capital into submission: 'the starvation is proceeding slowly, as Metz demonstrates, but it will achieve its purpose', he assured his other brother Adolf on 12 October.[64] If the government of national defence decided to resist 'until the genuine exhaustion of food, then a situation could arise

[57] G. Wawro, *The Franco-Prussian* War, 279.

[58] Friedrich Wilhelm, *The War Diary of Emperor Frederick III*, 241.

[59] O. v. Bismarck to J. v. Bismarck, 16 Nov. 1870, cited in E. Feuchtwanger, *Bismarck*, 175.

[60] Cited in G. Wawro, *The Franco-Prussian* War, 280. E. Kolb, *Der Weg aus dem Krieg. Bismarcks Politik im Krieg und die Friedensanbahnung 1870/71* (Munich, 1989).

[61] L. Gall, *Bismarck: The White Revolutionary, 1815–1871* (London, 1990), vol. 1, 366.

[62] G. Wawro, *The Franco-Prussian* War, 280.

[63] H. v. Moltke to F. v. Moltke, 11 Oct. 1870, in H. v. Moltke, *Moltke in seinen Briefen* (Berlin, 1902), vol. 2, 220.

[64] H. v. Moltke to A. v. Moltke, 12 Oct. 1870, ibid., 225.

which is terrible to think about', Moltke went on in the same letter, yet such conditions were avoidable and lay beyond the German army's control, attributable to the unwillingness of 'this unfortunate land' to see 'that it is defeated, that its situation is getting worse by the day'.[65] The siege itself was a traditional military tactic and any bombardment would be directed mainly at the forts not the city, as Bismarck was aware.[66] In the event, there were about thirty fires, 500 buildings hit, and under 200 deaths.[67]

Conditions in the rest of the country were certainly confused, with two seats of an ad hoc, internally divided government (the government of national defence in Paris and the 'government delegation' in Tours, to which Gambetta had escaped by balloon on 8 October) and with eight separate and improvised French armies (Paris, Metz, La Motterouge and Aurelle near Orleans, which split into the armies of Chanzy near Blois and Bourbaki near Bourges, Fiereck near Le Mans, Faidherbe's Army of the North near Amiens, and Garibaldi's Corps coming from the South), but Moltke continued to believe that regular military forces and tactics would prevail, sending the 50,000 troops of the Bavarian First Corps and the Twenty-Second Prussian Division under Ludwig von der Tann to meet the much larger forces of the Armies of the Loire (approximately 120,000) in October.[68] A series of German victories against superior enemy numbers followed: at Orleans on 10–11 October; at Beaune-la-Rolande on 28 November, where 9,000 troops under Konstantin von Voigts-Rhetz defeated 60,000 under Louis Aurelle de Paladines; at Loigny on 2 December; and at Le Mans on 10–11 January 1871. Battles at Coulmiers on 9 November and Beaugency on 8–9 December were inconclusive, prompting Moltke to deploy more troops; namely, the 150,000 men of the Mecklenburg Army Section on the first occasion and the 75,000 men of the Second Army under Friedrich Karl on—and after—the second.

Regular warfare was leading inexorably to the defeat of irregular and improvised French forces. 'The railleries of the *francs-tireurs* must be responded to with bloody reprisals, and the war is taking on an increasingly hateful character', the Chief of Staff conceded in late October, before reasserting the need for regular combat: 'It is bad enough when armies have to rip each other apart; still, we should not lead the peoples against each other; that is not progress, but a step

[65] Ibid., 223–4.

[66] H. v. Müller, *Die Artillerieangriff auf Paris und Schlußbetrachtung über den Festungskrieg im Kriege von 1870/71* (Berlin, 1901), 264, citing works by French counterparts in the 1840s, 1850s, and 1860s; O. v. Bismarck to J. v. Bismarck, 16 Nov. 1870, in O. v. Bismarck, *Werke in Auswahl*, ed. E. Scheler (Darmstadt, 1968), vol. 4, 571. Dieter Langewiesche and Nikolaus Buschmann, '"Dem Vertilgungskriege Grenzen setzen"', in D. Beyrau, M. Hochgeschwender, and D. Langewiesche (eds), *Formen des Krieges*, 181–2, provide an effective analysis of this question.

[67] The figures for the damage come from H. v. Müller, *Artillerieangriff*, 127. The number of dead and wounded resulting from the bombardment is disputed: Peter Browning, *The Changing Nature of Warfare: The Changing Nature of Land Warfare from 1792 to 1945* (Cambridge, 2002), records ninety-seven dead and 278 wounded; the German military, according to Dieter Langewiesche and Nikolaus Buschmann, '"Dem Vertilgungskriege Grenzen setzen"', in D. Beyrau, M. Hochgeschwender, and D. Langewiesche (eds), *Formen des Krieges*, 183, noted 111 dead and 142 injured.

[68] G. Wawro, *The Franco-Prussian War*, 266, referring to the troops massing in October and early November.

backward towards barbarity.'[69] Two months later, on 22 December, he was still defending the same position in a letter to his brother Adolf:

The general yearning for the end of this terrible war allows one to forget at home that it has only lasted 5 months; everything is expected from a bombardment of Paris. That this has not already succeeded is ascribed to tender consideration for the Parisians or even to the influence of highly-placed figures, whereas here only what is militarily possible and useful is kept in view. Verses have already been sent to me from three parties:

> Guter Moltke, gehst so stumm
> Immer um das Ding herum,
> Bester Moltke, sei nicht dumm,
> Mach doch endlich bum, bum, bum!

What it means to attack a fortress, for the defence of which an army stands prepared, that can be learned from the example of Sevastopol. Sevastopol first became a fortress during the attack, all materials could be brought by sea, the preparations lasted ten months, and the first assault cost 10,000, the second 13,000 people.

To bombard Paris, we first need the forts. Nothing, indeed, is spared in the use of these means of coercion; I anticipate far more, though, from hunger, which is having an effect slowly but surely...[70]

Moltke's attitude was significant because it helped to ensure, with the backing of Wilhelm I, that the campaign continued to be conducted as a state-led *Volkskrieg*, not a guerrilla war like that in Spain between 1808 and 1814 or a civil war like that in the United States between 1862 and 1865.[71]

Not all officers—not to mention ordinary soldiers—viewed the conflict in this light, however, which encouraged the toleration of unjustified requisitions, penalties, hostage-taking, summary execution, and, it appeared, an escalation of violence between civilians, irregulars, and the occupying forces.[72] Law and convention offered the German military little guidance, as academic lawyers such as Bluntschli acknowledged: 'The deficits and weaknesses of international law first became obvious in this war in shocking measure.'[73] The Swiss academic's hope was to 'tame' and 'control' by means of law the 'wildest passions of people', the 'slumbering or held-back urges', and 'also an original wildness' which had been reawoken by war, as he described the challenge in his rector's speech at

[69] H. v. Moltke to Auguste v. Moltke, 27 Oct. 1870, in H. v. Moltke, *Moltke in seinen Briefen*, vol. 2, 225–6.

[70] H. v. Moltke to A. v. Moltke, 22 Dec. 1870, ibid., 230–1.

[71] This was consistent with press reports which saw the republicans' 'arming of the people' as 'a desperate means': G. Freytag, *Auf der Höhe der Vogesen*, 69.

[72] One anonymous student volunteer from Giessen, *Feldzugs-Erinnerungen eines Kriegsfreiwilligen der 25. Hessischen Division* (Augsburg, 1895), 74, thus reported that 'the francs-tireurs have to take the entire rancour, and not without justification. Without a uniform, they can turn themselves into lowly peasants at any time, only to fetch their hidden guns when the danger has passed and shoot down our patrols.' On the decentralized nature of requisitions, which allowed such practices to continue and to escalate, see M. Steinbach, *Abgrund Metz. Kriegserfahrung, Belagerungsalltag und nationale Erziehung im Schatten einer Festung 1870/71* (Munich, 2002), 87–8.

[73] J. C. Bluntschli, *Das modern Völkerrecht der civilisirten Staten als Rechtsbuch dargestellt*, 2nd edn (Nördlingen, 1872), ix.

the university of Heidelberg on 22 November 1870.[74] Yet he admitted that such attempts, given the focus of the Geneva Convention on the treatment of wounded soldiers, had been limited in scope, leaving areas of uncertainty and points of contestation. One source of conflict concerned the occupation, for which there was no provision by treaty or international agreement and which, as a result, frequently reverted to the practices of previous conflicts, especially those of the Revolutionary and Napoleonic Wars.[75] 'The German commanders who entered France in 1870 seem, for the most part, to have regulated their conduct towards the French by German historical precedents; as for instance in the invasion of 1792,...and in that of 1814', wrote the *Times* journalist Henry Sutherland Edwards: 'If the invasion of 1870 was conducted less harshly than previous invasions, that is to be accounted for, not by any modification of the German Laws of War, but by the general softening of manners during the last half century.'[76]

Initially, the proclamation of Wilhelm I on 11 August 1870 had signalled a deliberate break from the conduct of the Napoleonic Wars, stating unambiguously that he was fighting a war 'with French soldiers and not with French citizens', who were to continue 'to enjoy the security of their own persons and goods as long as they themselves' did not undertake 'enemy actions against German soldiers'.[77] Apart from the removal of military equipment, which was to be handed over to the authorities, plunder and looting were strictly forbidden, as the king's injunction to protect private property and not to tolerate the besmirching of the good reputation of the army through isolated examples of indiscipline made plain.[78] Requisitions were more difficult to regulate, since the army—overstretched in enemy territory—relied heavily on local supplies. In theory, only corps commanders could give the order to requisition food and other goods, which were specified in advance, with each soldier to receive daily '750g of bread, 500g of meat, 250g of ham, 30g of coffee, 60g of tobacco or five cigars, a half litre of wine or a litre of beer or a tenth of a litre of spirits'.[79] Even 'extraordinary deliveries which are found to be necessary in the interests of the army' had to be authorized by 'generals or officers

---

[74] J. C. Bluntschli, *Das moderne Völkerrecht in dem französisch-deutschen Kriege von 1870* (Heidelberg, 1870), cited in H. Mehrkens, *Statuswechsel. Kriegserfahrung und nationale Wahrnehmung im Deutsch-Französischen Krieg 1870/71*, 7. Mehrkens underscores the successes of such attempts to a greater degree than I do here.

[75] This lack of provision betrayed the limited nature of the Geneva Convention. The fact that the Franco-German War was only the second conflict in which both parties had signed the Convention was therefore of little relevance: G. Best, 'Restraints on War by Land before 1945', in M. Howard (ed.), *Restraints on War: Studies in the Limitation of Armed Conflict* (Oxford, 1979), 17–77.

[76] H. S. Edwards, *The Germans in France: Notes on the Method and Conduct of the Invasion, the Relations between Invaders and Invaded, and the Modern Usages of War* (London, 1874), 7–8.

[77] Wilhelm I, 11 Aug. 1870, cited in J. Ganschow, 'Kriegsvölkerrecht im deutsch-französischen Krieg 1870/71', in J. Ganschow, O. Haselhorst, and M. Ohnezeit (eds), *Der deutsch-französische Krieg*, 299.

[78] Großer Generalstab (ed.), *Kriegsbrauch im Landkriege. Kriegsgeschichtliche Einzelschriften* (Berlin, 1902), 55. Some authors attempted to claim that German requisitioning was consistent with international law: A. v. Gordon, *Was trägt und treibt den Soldaten im Felde? Gedanken zum französischen Kriege und Stimmungsbilder aus den Tagen vor Metz* (Berlin, 1896).

[79] Cited in J. Ganschow, O. Haselhorst, and M. Ohnezeit (eds), *Der deutsch-französische Krieg*, 368.

carrying out their orders'.[80] In practice, though, countless exceptions were made, as the Germans exacted monetary contributions and penalties—in the calculation of one contemporary French lawyer—of 239,053,913 francs and contributions in kind of 327,581,506 francs during the course of the war.[81] Such exceptions were regularly justified through assertions of French responsibility for the war.[82]

The principal source of ambiguity and conflict, which did not merely have consequences for the occupation but for the treatment of soldiers and civilians in general, derived from Gambetta's dispatch on 24 October to all prefectures (and other similar proclamations by local authorities throughout France), instructing them to inform each citizen via the country's mayors that he 'has his duty to do' and that 'each city, each commune takes part in the national defence and that each individual is imbued with the duties which have been imposed on France'.[83] German military headquarters quickly issued a 'cabinet order concerning the treatment of irregular French combatants' on 27 August, which formed the basis of later maltreatment of *francs-tireurs*: the status of prisoners as combatants would be granted exclusively to those who had external proof that this was the case; others would be transferred to military courts, where they would be sentenced to death or, in less serious cases, to ten years of forced labour.[84] Many 'disgusting' stories about *francs-tireurs* were relayed to military headquarters, recalled Moritz Busch:

> Their clothing is such that they can scarcely be recognized as soldiers, and what markers they wear, which make them known as such, they can easily remove. Such a lad lies, apparently sunning himself in a ditch beside a tree, as troops of riders go down the street from us. Once they have passed, he fires at them with his gun, which he keeps hidden in the meantime in a bush, and runs into the wood, from which, knowing the way, he comes out again as a harmless man in shirt sleeves. I would almost say that they were not defenders of the fatherland but insidious murderers, who should be hanged without much reading of evidence when they are caught.[85]

The German military was anxious to maintain the distinction between combatants and civilians, ignoring its own practice in the Napoleonic Wars and in coastal regions in 1870, which had been ordered to resist a French invasion by sea, as Edwards pointed out.[86] Thus, at the start of the campaign, it had demanded that anyone taking part voluntarily in the fighting, but not a regular soldier, should carry special authorization from a commander, wear markings showing they were fighting, comply with the laws of war, and be organized hierarchically and militarily, ultimately responsible to the commanders of the army overall.[87]

---

[80] Ibid.

[81] M. A. Ott, in J. L. Klüber, *Droits des gens modernes de l'Europe*, 2nd edn (Paris, 1874), 359.

[82] C. Schepers, *Bilder und Eindrücke au seiner achtwöchentlichen Dienstzeit als freiwilliger Feldprediger im Sommer 1870* (Bonn, 1871), 89.

[83] J. Ganschow, O. Haselhorst, and M. Ohnezeit (eds), *Der deutsch-französische Krieg*, 351.

[84] Ibid., 354.   [85] M. Busch, *Mit Bismarck vor Paris* (Munich, 1942), 38–9.

[86] H. S. Edwards, *The Germans in France*, 13. The wider context of such decision-making was a general refusal on the part of politicians, with the exception of a handful of radicals such as Carl Vogt, to accept that *francs-tireurs* were legitimate fighters, even comparable to German volunteers in 1813: C. Vogt, *Politische Briefe an Friedrich Kolb* (Biel, 1870), 13.

[87] J. Ganschow, O. Haselhorst, and M. Ohnezeit (eds), *Der deutsch-französische Krieg*, 359.

Many French troops, not merely *francs-tireurs*, who were not able to furnish such proof were executed on the spot on the purported grounds that they were simple murderers and that the laws of war allowed such extrajudicial killing in these circumstances. Villages harbouring *francs-tireurs* were regularly punished by means of fines and executions. The French had 'unleashed a *Volkskrieg* and could no longer keep in check the passions they had aroused, which went beyond international law and every convention of war', wrote Moritz Busch in the press, at Bismarck's bidding.[88] Since they had also resorted to 'the use of savages', or West and North African troops, which was widely criticized in Germany—including by lawyers like Bluntschli—as a breach of civilization and as an instrument of barbarity, they were seen to have deserved their harsh treatment.[89] As the American Civil War and, now, the Franco-German war demonstrated, 'the laws made to replace ordinary laws' during wartime were of 'a primitive and barbarous type', in the British journalist Edwards' opinion, consisting of the following maxims: '1. For every offence punish someone; the guilty, if possible, but some one. 2. Better a hundred innocent should suffer than that one guilty man should escape. 3. When in doubt shoot the prisoner.'[90] For the French and Germans alike, such injustice and contested notions of legality increased the violence of the second phase of the war and altered its nature. In a long winter campaign against irregulars, there is evidence that the lack of commonly agreed and enforced laws against summary execution and the arbitrary exercise of power led to abuses. 'It cannot be denied', wrote the Alsatian priest Karl Klein, 'that acts of brutality and unnecessary harshness were manifest.'[91] Usually, the reason given for such abuses was 'revenge' or 'retribution' for alleged contraventions of unspecified 'laws of war'.[92] Reprisals against French colonial troops, who were regularly treated as racially inferior or repellent, were particularly violent.[93]

Many German commanders betrayed greater outrage than Moltke at the supposed excesses and transgressions of *francs-tireurs*, with some such as Alfred von Waldersee condoning the scorched-earth policies of the American Civil War: 'I'm convinced the man is right. If we let our cavalry cut a swathe of destruction through the land à la Sheridan, many Frenchmen would lose the will to play at

---

[88] M. Busch, *Mit Bismarck vor Paris*, 215–16.

[89] The quotation comes from J. C. Bluntschli, *Das moderne Völkerrecht der civilisirten Staten* (Nördlingen, 1868), 315–16.

[90] H. S. Edwards, *The Germans in France*, 285–6.

[91] K. Klein, *Fröschweiler Chronik. Kriegs- und Friedensbilder aus dem Jahr 1870*, 24th edn (Munich, 1906), 130–1.

[92] Such justification extended to extreme punishments like the stringing up of an old woman on a wheel before she was stabbed to death after allegedly gouging out the eyes of a wounded German NCO who had sought refuge in her house: R. Martin, *Kriegserinnerungen*, 159–60. See also S. Husser, *Erlebnisse eines badischen Trainsoldaten im Feldzuge 1870/71*, 60–1: 'we had to behave like that in order to secure our own lives'.

[93] Adolf Fausel, *Ein Ritt ins Franzosenland. Bilder aus dem Kleinleben im Feld 1870/71* (Stuttgart, 1909), 128, talked of the 'disgust' he felt at seeing the 'wild fury and malicious anger' of the face of 'the common negro type'. Another soldier, whose testimony was published in the veterans' newspaper *Parole*, openly admitted to killing a colonial soldier after he had demanded 'pardon' and had raised his hands: 'My bayonet bored into the chest of the black', as the perpetrator was overcome with 'an anger without bounds': cited in T. Rohkrämer, *Der Militarismus der 'kleinen Leute'*, 128.

being *francs-tireurs*.'[94] For other officers closer to the fighting, French irregulars were certainly not pretending and served to compound a military balance of forces which threatened in the Loire to tip against the Bavarians and Prussians in von der Tann's Army Section, as Prince Leopold of Bavaria recorded in his diary: 'We felt horribly exposed, surrounded by far more numerous troops, as if we were sitting at the bottom of a sack, whose opening the enemy had only to grasp and seal shut.'[95] For most officers, however, the fundamental nature of the Franco-German war had not changed in its second phase, with most attention still paid to set-piece battles against more or less regular French forces, as the popular account of the young Bavarian lieutenant Carl Tanera, who fought at Coulmiers and Loigny, testified.[96] At the former on 9 November, the 14,543 infantrymen and 4,450 cavalrymen of von der Tann had faced 75,000 French troops, a 'colossal superiority of the enemy' which had forced a Bavarian retreat—even if it was carried out in 'masterly' good order—and which had demonstrated that war was 'not a game'.[97] Although battalions of *francs-tireurs* had taken 'pleasure in smacking into the weak foreign section', 'no one came too near to the Germans, for hussars, *Jäger* and thirteeners swapped with each other and showed their fangs so decisively that the French gave up, after several failed attempts, any hope of closer acquaintance with such rough-edged fellows'.[98] Instead, what Tanera remembered was fighting in a battle in which the enemy had tried to surround them and 'deliver a type of Sedan' and which had been marked by 'the firing of grenades such as our corps had not experienced before and would not do so afterwards'.[99] The 'crack and natter' of battle left all their 'nerves vibrating', with 'every man in a state of agitation like never before'.[100] For Tanera personally, it entailed 'a piling up of punishments which I almost came close to experiencing on 2 December but which I never experienced again in the exact same form', extinguishing 'any good humour'.[101] At the latter battle of Loigny (on 2 December), the lieutenant was surrounded by similar sights and sounds, with 'grenades and *chassepots* now [hitting] our already thinned-out ranks from all sides' and forcing another retreat.[102] Tanera's own brigade lost thirty-nine

---

[94] A. v. Waldersee, 4 Oct. 1870, in A. v. Waldersee, *Denkwürdigkeiten*, vol. 1, 101.

[95] Cited in G. Wawro, *The Franco-Prussian War*, 263. This feeling seems to have been shared by many ordinary soldiers: C. G. Krüger, 'German Suffering in the Franco-German War, 1870/71', 412; U. Daniel, G. Krumeich, and J. Schröder, *Deutschland und Frankreich im Krieg. Zur Kulturgeschichte der europäischen 'Erbfeindschaft'* (Brunswick, 2004), 108–22.

[96] C. Tanera, *Ernste und heitere Erinnerungen eines Ordonannzoffiziers im Feldzug 1870/71* (Nördlingen, 1887), 53–68, 104–20. G. Wawro, *The Franco-Prussian War*, 309, estimates that *francs-tireurs* were responsible for about 1,000 killings—or about 2 to 3 per cent of the total.

[97] Ibid., 62–5.

[98] Ibid., 55. See also Adolf Kayser, *Erlebnisse eines rheinischen Dragoners im Feldzuge 1870/71* (Nördlingen, 1889), 87, who described the 'first francs-tireurs' that they encountered around the capital as, for the most part, 'next to mobile guards, Parisian volunteers, students and the like in brand new fantasy uniforms'.

[99] C. Tanera, *Ernste und heitere Erinnerungen eines Ordonannzoffiziers*, 60.

[100] Ibid., 61.   [101] Ibid., 56, 66.

[102] Ibid., 109. Another Bavarian soldier, Florian Kühnhauser, *Kriegs-Erinnerungen eines Soldaten des königlich bayerischen Infanterie-Leib-Regiments* (Partenkirchen, 1898), 163–203, described the period of fighting—in battles—around this time as 'the ten worst days'.

out of 115 officers and 765 out of 3,936 men.[103] Beside such experiences, which seemed like an extension of the first phase of the war, encounters with *francs-tireurs* and sentry duty outside Paris were treated as an adventure.[104] Even the reported 45,000 dead and wounded revolutionaries and 20,000 killed and injured men of the Versailles army during the Commune in March–May 1871 were viewed from the detached vantage point of an onlooker, proving that 'these Frenchmen of 1871' were 'truly strange fish'.[105] The tone of such reportage was in keeping with senior officers' accounts of the siege of the French capital, which imposed 'a rather uniform life' on German soldiers, as Hohenlohe described it, after their earlier experiences of battle.[106]

For the majority of officers, the formation of groups of *francs-tireurs* after September 1870 complicated a war which was already considered a *Volkskrieg*, rather than transforming it (see Figure 9.2 for a well-known representation of such conventional warfare). Many *francs-tireurs* wore uniforms, albeit 'fantasy' or 'civilian' ones, in an attempt to avoid summary execution.[107] The *Partisans de Gers*, who fought at Etampes, wore large Calabrian hats, red scarves, and black coats and trousers.[108] Other groups wore blue blouses, which allegedly made it easy for them to merge with the civilian population but which nonetheless constituted a uniform of sorts. The difference between reconstituted regular units, *gardes mobiles*, *corps francs*, and *francs-tireurs* was rarely clear-cut. Thus, although many commanders condoned the treatment of irregulars as 'murderers' (following Bismarck's threat that 'vous serez tous pendus, vous n'êtes pas soldats, vous êtes des assassins'), since they could not be identified unambiguously as soldiers, officers in the field seem to have continued to concentrate on larger-scale fighting and to treat *francs-tireurs* as a source of irritation more often than as a genuine menace.[109] 'The Army of the Loire was thus not a dream of the government of national defence, not a tirade of a systematically agitated passion, and thus not the worthless mass of troops, loosely gathered together, for which we took them', wrote one Prussian soldier of his direct experience of fighting in the Loire valley in November 1870: 'no, it now appeared truly as that "belle armée de la Loire", of which serious men, looking at our weak marching columns with contempt born of confidence of victory, told us that they numbered

[103] C. Tanera, *Ernste und heitere Erinnerungen eines Ordonannzoffiziers*, 105.

[104] Ibid., 161–71. Egmont Fehleisen's lustrous volume on *Der Deutsch-Französische Krieg 1870–71 im Wort und Bild* (Reutlingen, 1872), 212–13, showed bucolic scenes of a cavalryman with a French baby on his knee in front of a peasant woman's hut, and *francs-tireurs* ambushing a German post, similarly before an idyllic rural backdrop. Max Hollnack, *Kriegserinnerungen eine alten 37ers* (Hanover, 1890), 51, was typical in describing the beauty of the sunrise over Paris—'incomparable, unforgettable images!'

[105] C. Tanera, *Ernste und heitere Erinnerungen eines Ordonannzoffiziers*, 171.

[106] K. zu Hohenlohe-Ingelfingen, *Aus meinem Leben*, vol. 4, 274.

[107] A. Kayser, *Erlebnisse*, on the fantasy uniforms of different types of French troops after September 1870.

[108] G. Wawro, *The Franco-Prussian War*, 257.

[109] On Bismarck, see M. Busch, *Mit Bismarck vor Paris*, 40–1. Soldiers commented on summary justice for *francs-tireurs* as if it were a matter of course: A. Fester, *Jugenderinnerungen und Kriegsbriefe eines Altfrankfurters* (Halle, 1911), 50; F. Schäfer, 'Aus meinem Tagebuch von 1870/71', 13–14, *Kriegsbriefe* Archive, Universitäts- und Landesbibliothek Bonn.

Figure 9.2 Anton von Werner, *Moltke mit seinem Stabe vor Paris* (1873)
Source: Kunsthalle zu Kiel.

hundreds of thousands, impressed with the best spirit and very well armed'.[110] It is likely that they paid less attention to uniforms, which were occasionally exchanged with those of dead enemy soldiers as a disguise, than did their commanding officers.[111]

Commonly, 'rough' treatment of irregulars was portrayed as a consequence of the inevitable degradation of manners during a long campaign. 'One becomes somewhat coarse during wars and, in addition, we had become used not to talk with particular respectfulness of any civilians caught with weapons in their hands, which is only natural, given the banditry (*Buschklepperei*) which they carried out', recalled Tanera of his time in the Loire.[112] Small numbers of German troops were wounded or killed in such fighting—perhaps two or three per day around Paris during the winter, according to Hohenlohe—and a limited but indeterminable number of French irregulars were executed.[113] From their diaries and correspondence, illegal killing of this type, for which they were not condemned, sometimes troubled German combatants but it continued to be subordinated in their accounts to other aspects of army life during the winter of 1870–1, both positive

---

[110] G. Friedländer, *Aus den Kriegstagen 1870* (Berlin, 1886), 74.

[111] This practice was generally accepted by both sides and by international lawyers: J. Ganschow, 'Kriegsvölkerrecht', in J. Ganschow, O. Haselhorst, and M. Ohnezeit (eds), *Der deutsch-französische Krieg*, 362.

[112] C. Tanera, *Ernste und heitere Erinnerungen eines Ordonannzoffiziers*, 102.

[113] K. zu Hohenlohe-Ingelfingen, *Aus meinem Leben*, vol. 4, 283: 'Our soldiers meanwhile suffered losses, not exactly as many as the newspapers of the city on the Seine reported vaingloriously, for according to the same a single grenade had supposedly killed 10,000 Prussians, but nevertheless two or three dead or wounded were reported on many days.'

(camaraderie, amorous encounters, sightseeing) and negative (the cold, poor supplies, and illness, with more dying of disease after September than of their injuries).[114]
Quite a few 'outside' observers, such as the later university medic Heinrich Fritsch,
denied that atrocities had occurred at all: 'As for cruelty, murder and manslaughter,
I can only report what I have seen and experienced—this sort of thing never happened, in any event, as far as we were concerned.'[115] In the opinion of the chaplain
Edmund Pfleiderer, 99 per cent of atrocity stories carried by the French press
'belong in the realm of myth'.[116] For officers in particular, the Franco-German War
was a conventional campaign, whose shocking effects they had already experienced
before the second phase of the conflict. Overall, soldiers' deaths comprised 90 per cent
of the total, which made the conflict more like other nineteenth-century wars
than twentieth-century ones, where civilians made up a large proportion of those
killed.[117] On the German side, most of the losses occurred in the battles of August
and early September.

The conditions experienced by soldiers in such battles, including officers who
had been looking forward to combat as an opportunity for heroism, regularly
tempered their enthusiasm for fighting.[118] The violence of the battlefield, precisely because it differed so markedly from the pacified mores of civil society, had
the potential to challenge established narratives about the conflict and overturn
civilized modes of behaviour. The military, of course, was 'a quite specific estate,
far more different as a consequence of its make-up and conduct from all other
strata than it was divided internally', in the opinion of one external observer,
who was critical of its 'feudal-aristocratic' foundation in peacetime (when it was
'not an agreeable phenomenon') but appreciative during wartime ('Completely
different in war!', when its bravery and leadership encouraged the ranks to the
sacrifices of the men).[119] As in the Napoleonic Wars, senior officers, now usually
further from the fighting, showed least emotion in their memoirs, noting casualties as little more than hindrances to the implementation of strategy. The report
of the chief of the Operations Section of the royal headquarters was one of the
coldest, most technical of its kind, making only a passing reference to losses on

[114] T. Vatke, *Feldpostbriefe aus Frankreich 1870–71* (Berlin, 1871), 26.

[115] H. Fritsch, *Erinnerungen und Betrachtungen* (Bonn, 1913), 164.

[116] E. Pfleiderer, *Erinnerungen und Erfahrungen*, 81. See also C. Schepers, *Bilder und Eindrücke au
seiner achtwöchentlichen Dienstzeit als freiwilliger Feldprediger im Sommer 1870*, 81.

[117] J. Ganschow, O. Haselhorst, and M. Ohnezeit (eds), *Der deutsch-französische Krieg*, 309; Mary
Kaldor, *New and Old Wars*, 2nd edn (Stanford, CA, 2007), 9, notes that notes that the civilian–
combatant death ratio was 1:8 in 1900 and 8:1 by the 1990s; M. van Creveld, *The Transformation of
War* (New York, 1991), 33–94. The civilian–combatant ratio for the First World War was 34–40 per cent,
although most civilian deaths were from disease (Spanish flu and starvation-related diseases), some of
which were dissociated by contemporaries from the conflict, as in the nineteenth century. William
Eckhardt, 'Civilian Deaths in Wartime', *Bulletin of Peace Proposals*, 20 (1989), 89–98, gives the dis-
ease-adjusted figure of 25 per cent for the Franco-Prussian War (smallpox killing more French civilians
than soldiers) and 89 per cent for the Austro-Prussian War (cholera killing a large number of Austrian
civilians and accounting for 50 per cent of soldiers' deaths).

[118] This also applied to battles after September 1870: see Ferdinand Düts's account of the winter
campaign, 'Kriegstagebuch 1870–1871', 8, *Feldpostbriefe*, Universitäts- und Landesbibliothek, Bonn,
referring to fighting on 22 October near Champagne: 'none thought they would escape with their life'.

[119] E. Pfleiderer, *Erinnerungen und Erfahrungen*, 92–3.

16 August as 'the battle swung back and forth until the evening'.[120] One officer, called out of retirement, remarked that Helmuth von Moltke, too, was 'eerily' calm.[121]

Other high-ranking officers, however, were more obviously shocked by the scale of the slaughter. 'The fighting on the 16th ended well for us, but was very bloody for the infantry, like all battles now', wrote Julius von Hartmann, a Prussian cavalry general: 'The sacrifices of officers demanded by war is enormous.'[122] The German armies were advancing, but they were also surrounded by 'the horrors of war'; 'devastation and desolation, wherever you look'.[123] By 22 August, the officer's earlier transports of enthusiasm for a 'delicious' 'German war' had completely disappeared:

> You have no idea of the horrors which cover a modern battlefield! These piles of the dead with the most terrible cuts and disfigurements! Each individual would unsettle us in peacetime; the senses are numbed before such masses, and one rides past groups of 10–12 corpses without any emotion at all. The appearance of the French is even ghastlier than that of ours; the red trousers make the overall appearance garish. The mourning for the many who remain [on the battlefield] almost outweighs the joy over the victories gained. They are such terrible losses![124]

Though heralding Sedan as a 'wonderful victory', Hartmann still worried about having lost 'the ability to mourn' because of such large numbers of dead and wounded.[125] 'One becomes as a result of the war a lump of meat, which numbs feelings', confided another officer.[126] 'But it is like a dam whose waters break forth with double the force once the sluice is opened', he went on: 'a single awakening of one's slumbering human feelings and they manifest themselves more strongly than is good for one; I think that I cried the day after.'[127] Many senior officers seem to have alternated in this way between callousness and tenderness.[128] Even Wilhelm I was reported to be 'completely disconsolate over the losses'.[129] For his part, Bismarck, both of whose sons had been injured, complained that commanders were 'misusing' 'the truly tremendous bravery of our troops' and labelled the generals 'blood-spillers' (*Blutverschwender*).[130]

Young, aristocratic career officers demonstrated with particular clarity how expectations of national glory and individual heroism during the Franco-German war collided with domestic interdictions against violence and taboos surrounding

---

[120] P. Rassow (ed.), *Geheimes Kriegstagebuch 1870–1871 von Paul Bronsart von Schellendorf* (Bonn, 1954), 41. See also L. v. Wittich, *Aus meinem Tagebuch 1870–71* (Kassel, 1872), 15–21.

[121] U. v. Stosch (ed.), *Denkwürdigkeiten des Generals und Admirals Albrecht v. Stosch*, 192.

[122] J. v. Hartmann, *Briefe aus dem Deutsch-Französischen Kriege 1870–71* (Kassel, 1893), 16.

[123] Ibid.   [124] Ibid., 23–4.   [125] Ibid., 33–4.

[126] H. v. Kretschmann, *Kriegsbriefe aus den Jahren 1870–1871* (Berlin, 1903), 16.

[127] Ibid.

[128] F. v. Rauch, *Briefe aus dem grossen Hauptquartier*, 49, 53–7, 62; E. E. v. Krause, *Ein deutsches Soldatenleben* (Berlin, 1901), 86–7; A. v. Voigts-Rhetz, *Briefe des Generals der Infanterie von Voigts-Rhetz aus den Kriegsjahren 1866 und 1870–71* (Berlin, 1906), 72, 75; M. v. Berg, *Ulanen-Briefe von der I. Armee* (Bielefeld, 1893), 27.

[129] M. Busch, *Tagebuchblätter* (Leipzig, 1899), vol. 1, 91.   [130] Ibid.

death.[131] Thus, Dietrich Freiherr von Lassberg, a Bavarian noble, had entered the conflict 'with joy' in July 1870, feted by the 'loud cheers and hurrahs' of 'an enormous crowd of people' at Munich train station.[132] At the battle of Froeschwiller (or Wörth) on 6 August, he loaded his gun for the first time except during manoeuvres. It was a 'moment to celebrate'.[133] As the regiment approached the battlefield, he heard the 'eerie' sound of the French *mitrailleuses* in the distance and was eager to get closer. The first two casualties in his unit were almost cause to rejoice—'the first wounded and the first dead in the company!!'—as he rushed forward into enemy fire, shells and bullets ripping up trees around him.[134] During the fighting itself, corpses and injuries constituted part of the adventure, with little time to reflect and every incentive to act: 'from all sides, the horn and drum signal—"Forwards! Attack!"...wounded and dead French...wounded Turkos lying in their own blood'.[135] Yet the next day Lassberg was forced to face the consequences of such military action as he surveyed the battlefield, his tone becoming more muted:

> This great pile of dead—never had I seen so many corpses together—in the most diverse French uniforms, bloody, dusty, disfigured by burns from explosives, with limbs torn off, often half naked, hands regularly clenched convulsively, arms often stretched up stiffly, many with an expression of anger, many with one of pain... – this view was terrible and made...a deep and melancholy impression on us.[136]

On 1 September at Sedan, he witnessed more traumatic scenes as his regiment stormed a village. Despite being part of one of the most heroic assaults of the decisive battle of the war, after which Napoleon III was captured and the German Empire eventually created, Lassberg's descriptions were much more subdued from the start than they had been only a month beforehand. 'They were', he wrote, 'just some of the scenes in the horrible and bitter struggle', littered with 'burned or even roasted bodies'.[137]

To other officers, too, Sedan was 'in fact a terrible picture of destruction and annihilation', with the battlefield 'considerably different in character from that of St Privat': 'Here, death had laid out the field like a careful farmer and the corpses and debris were almost methodically divided equally over a great

---

[131] It was 'highly dangerous', noted the army doctor Heinrich Fritsch, *Erinnerungen und Betrachtungen*, 57, 'for soldiers, and namely for officers, occasionally to betray lack of courage'. Also, F. Koch-Breuberg, *Drei Jahre in Frankreich. Erinnerungen eines Truppenoffiziers aus dem Feldzug 1870/71 und der Occupation 1871–1873* (Munich, 1890), 26–7.

[132] D. v. Lassberg, *Mein Kriegstagebuch aus dem deutsch-französischen Kriege 1870/71* (Munich, 1906), 1, 4.

[133] Ibid., 13.   [134] Ibid., 15.   [135] Ibid., 16–17.

[136] Ibid., 23. Joseph Eisenach, *Erinnerungen an den Feldzug 1870/71. Aus dem Tagebuch eines ehemaligen Angehörigen des Königin Augusta Garde-Grenadier-Regiments Nr. 4* (Coblenz, 1896), 44, recalled the mixed emotions after battle even of his commander, over whose blood-stained cheeks rolled tears over the losses incurred at the same time as congratulations crossed his lips for the 'behaviour' of the troops under fire.

[137] D. v. Lassberg, *Mein Kriegstagebuch*, 55, 57.

space'.[138] A 'massive number of dead' could be seen, wrote the Prussian officer Kurt von Einsiedel:

> A new and peculiar sight for me was repeated regularly in truly terrifying images—these were groups of three or four corpses lying next to each other, which were half burned and with their naked and often green bodies, which in addition were torn apart by grenades and covered with blood, offering a terrible prospect.[139]

During the 'great moment' of victory it seemed to Lassberg that 'after rain comes sunshine', but it was also evident, on inspection of the battlefield, that 'after sunshine comes rain':

> Here one saw the smashed black head of a Turko and under him lay a Bavarian, whose chest had been ripped through by a full grenade; here lay a formless lump of flesh, which one could recognise as a fully shredded French soldier of the line; a grenade probably exploded the moment it hit him, as he was sitting or lying, and tore him up; elsewhere, one saw human bodies which one could have taken for mummies, and others which looked like charcoal... I'll refrain from giving further description, which in any case falls well short of reality. It was a terrible and, at the same time, deeply moving and unsettling view! These are the dark sides of war! It is nice to say of the soldier, and we soldiers like to hear this and say it ourselves: 'The most beautiful death is death on the battlefield'—but truly, the most beautiful dead are not the dead on the battlefield! And how much more do numerous artists fail, who give their dead such a beautiful and ideal appearance that one is almost tempted to wish oneself in their place! These beautiful, ideal soldiers' corpses do not exist.[140]

Like fellow officers, who saw their fantasies 'driven away' by such an 'atrocious reality', Lassberg was left, during such moments, facing an empty and comfortless existence.[141] Only victory and unification seemed capable of restoring soldiers' good spirits. Even then, some found that their 'joy over the great victory was gone'.[142]

A LOVELY WAR? BURGHERS AND WARRIORS

Troops' exposure to violence was countered in 1870 by a much more widely and profoundly felt sense of national belonging and national interest than in 1866, mediated by established traditions of war reportage and correspondence dating back to the conflicts of the 1850s and 1860s.[143] In comparison to coverage of previous conflicts, which were relayed by the reports and memoirs of officers and

---

[138] K. v. Einsiedel, *Tagebuchblätter aus dem deutsch-französischen Krieg* (Berlin, 1907), 82.
[139] Ibid., 85. [140] Ibid., 80.
[141] F. v. Frankenberg, *Kriegstagebücher von 1866 und 1870/71* (Stuttgart, 1896), 166.
[142] Ibid., 169. [143] F. Becker, *Bilder von Krieg und Nation*, 39–76.

the General Staff, the accounts of this war were predominantly *bürgerlich*.[144] Unlike in the wars of 1848–51 and in some of the campaigns of the revolutionary and Napoleonic eras, many social strata and all areas of Germany were now affected by the call to arms in defence of the 'fatherland'.[145] Few doubted that France under Napoleon III was the aggressor.[146] 'War! War with France!' rejoiced a young aristocratic officer in Bavaria, who only four years earlier had backed Vienna in the Austro-Prussian war: 'The enthusiasm was general, and we soldiers were treated on the street with a completely different respect and a certain awe.'[147] A North German student at university in Tübingen had a similar experience, recounting how his lower middle-class landlord, who 'spoke out of that glowing hatred of the Prussians which was still common at the time', had been convinced of France's culpability: 'The landlord remained of this opinion, and all the honest Swabians thought the same as him; they felt the attempted humiliation of Prussia as a dishonouring of the whole of Germany by the Napoleonic clan. The reversal was general and fundamental.'[148] When war was declared, everyone realized 'the full significance of the world-historical moment' and recognized 'the danger that threatened the fatherland'.[149] 'This was the mood of the good people of Tübingen, and so it was in the whole of Germany', concluded the student.[150] Gustav Waltz, a military doctor in the Badenese division, was not

[144] Ibid. The volume and type of memoirs and other records of the war had changed in 1870. This literature was added to the reports of middle-class journalists, as in 1864 and 1866, of course.

[145] Theodor Billroth, *Chirurgische Briefe aus den Kriegs-Lazarethen in Weissenburg und Mannheim 1870* (Berlin, 1872), 7, found 'the participation of the Landvolk in the small stations' which he went through on his way from Austria 'touching'.

[146] Even the left-wing radical Arnold Ruge, exiled in Britain, believed that this was the case: A. Ruge, *Briefwechsel und Tagebuchblätter aus den jahren 1825–1880*, vol. 2, 355. Many, like the doctor Georg Friedrich Louis Stromeyer, *Erinnerungen eins deutschen Arztes*, 2nd edn (Hanover, 1875), 400–1, assumed simply that 'Napoleon III sought, in order to stabilize his tottering throne, salvation in a war with Germany': 'A general enthusiasm [in Germany] for the war was the consequence of French frivolity.'

[147] D. v. Lassberg, *Mein Kriegstagebuch*, 1, 4; on Baden, see the account of the student H. Schmitthenner, *Erlebnisse eines freiwilligen badischen Grenadiers* (Karlsruhe, 1890), 134–7. In Hesse, Richard Schuster, *Erlebnisse und Beobachtungen eines deutschen Feldgeistlichen während des Krieges 1870–71* (Darmstadt, 1871), 1–2, noted that 'War was the object of every conversation at home and in the street.' This was also the case in the Rhineland, where those like Wilhelm Schreiner who 'did not have the opportunity and good fortune...to be able to bear arms for King and Reich', sought to back the campaign in other ways (in his case by participating in a provisioning column): W. Schreiner, 'Meine Erlebnisse in dem Feldzuge 1870/71 als Fahrer der Proviantkolonne', *Kriegsbriefe* Archive, Universitäts- und Landesbibliothek Bonn.

[148] F. Ehrenburg, *Kleine Erlebnisse in grosser Zeit. Aus dem Tagebuche eines Kriegsstudenten von 1870–71* (Strasbourg, 1890), 7, 9.

[149] Ibid., 10. T. Billroth, *Chirurgische Briefe aus den Kriegs-Lazarethen in Weissenburg und Mannheim 1870* (Berlin, 1872), 6–7: this feeling of danger, facing a French invasion, was especially pronounced in western Germany—in Heidelberg and Stuttgart, for instance—but it was also supplemented by broader support for the war, visible in rural areas amongst the *Landvolk* as well as in cities.

[150] F. Ehrenburg, *Kleine Erlebnisse in grosser Zeit*, 10. See also Florian Kühnhauser, *Kriegs-Erinnerungen*, 1–24, whose own enthusiasm contrasted with the more cautious response of villagers in Bavaria; Adolf Kayser, *Erlebnisse eiens rheinischen Dragoners im Feldzuge 1870/71* (Nördlingen, 1889), 1–15, who was a student in Zurich, pointed out that all the Germans there, including those like German–Austrians, supported the war effort; C. L. Hähnel, *Bei den Fahnen des XII. (kgl. Sächsischen) Armeekorps. Aufzeichnungen eines Angehörigen des 107. Regiments im Feldzug 1870/71* (Munich, 1890), 1–3, recalled both the enthusiastic send-off from Leipzig and the support for troops along the way in Erfurt, Weimar, and elsewhere; the

unusual in recording 'the pain of separation, patriotism and that mixture of courage and dependency with which one looks toward an uncertain future', when he set out for France on 24 July.[151] Such sentiments did not rule out the fact that, 'in many respects, a certain tension between South Germans and North Germans' persisted, 'even during the campaign', wrote one army chaplain from Württemberg: 'There were so many 1866ers there from both sides, whose reconciliation against the common enemy lends itself poetically to really beautiful portrayals, but which in reality left much to be desired.'[152] All the same, despite 'the jealous mistrust of a small minority against the majority and the principal power', 'on the whole the great times, lived through and achieved in common, provided a strong, if also at first only instinctive and intermittently effective, tie between all the German tribes'.[153]

In particular, the majority of middle-class liberals, many of whom had continued to oppose Bismarck until 1866, had become the most vocal adherents of a Prussian-led national campaign against France.[154] The Saxon National Liberal historian and publicist Heinrich von Treitschke wrote from Heidelberg to his sister in July 1870 that everyone was 'full of courage and hope'.[155] 'I have the feeling', he went on, 'that all people have become better, as if their pettiness and vulgarity have disappeared.'[156] However hard it seemed, he was pleased that his own relatives were going to war: 'For what can a German soldier wish for that is more beautiful than to take part in this struggle? Oh, dear sister, in such days one must be pious; a higher force rules over us Germans and forces us to become a nation (*Volk*).'[157] The historian was, he assured his sister, ready for anything, 'but we are hoping, after heavy sacrifices, for a great victory, which should compensate us for the sins of three centuries and give Strasbourg back to the Germans'.[158] For another liberal, Rudolf Ihering, who was also happy to send his relatives—in this case his own son—to war, even if 100,000 German soldiers were sacrificed, there would soon be three- or fourfold the number to replace them, so great and tangible was their 'love of the fatherland'.[159] The war against France, it was repeated again and again in the

Hanoverian trainee teacher H. Tiemann, *Mein Feldzug. Erinnerugnen aus dem denkwürdigen Kriege von 1870–1871* (Hanover, 1874), 4, noted that he left for France with 'a tear in his eye' but also 'happily', for 'it was for the fatherland'.

[151] G. Waltz, *Erlebnisse eines Feldarztes der badischen Division im Kriege 1870–71* (Heidelberg, 1872), 1.

[152] E. Pfleiderer, *Erinnerungen und Erfahrungen eines Feldpredigers*, 76.   [153] Ibid., 77.

[154] Even those sceptical of the army, such as the trainee teacher Richard Martin, who had elected to do only his required six weeks of service rather than serving as a one-year volunteer, as his father had wished, were in favour of 'a really imminent, fresh and happy war': R. Martin, *Kriegserinnerungen eines 105ers*, 37.

[155] H. v. Treitschke to his sister, 18 July 1870, in M. Cornicelius (ed.), *Heinrich Treitschkes Briefe* (Leipzig, 1920), vol. 3, 280.

[156] Ibid.   [157] Ibid., 282.   [158] Ibid.

[159] R. v. Jhering to O. Bülow, 5 Aug. 1870, R. v. Jhering, *Rudolf von Jhering in Briefen an seine Freunde* (Leipzig, 1913), 249. For other liberals, see H. Oncken, *Rudolf von Bennigsen*, vol. 2, 176; R. Hübner (ed.), *Johann Gustav Droysen. Briefwechsel* (Osnabrück, 1967), 893–4; J. Schulze (ed.), *Max Duncker. Politischer Briefwechsel aus seinem Nachlass* (Osnabrück, 1967), 451; T. Mommsen, 'To the People of Italy', in T. Mommsen, D. F. Strauss, F. M. Müller, and T. Carlyle, *Letters on the War between Germany and France* (London, 1871), 2–3; H. Rosenberg (ed.), *Ausgewählter*

press, was worth the high price that would probably have to be paid. The names of the dead, whose 'valuable blood' had 'paid the price' of the battles of Wissembourg and Wörth, would not be forgotten, as a journalist of the *Weimarische Zeitung* put it, for they had shown 'a thankful fatherland and an astonished world that a united Germany...is equal to the most feared opponent'.[160] In the light of such reportage and public opinion, most authors implied that the heavy sacrifices of war were to be weighed against the glorious gains made by an incipient German nation-state.[161]

National sentiment and civilization were seen to be complementary. In the words of the same correspondent, 'Our fatherland, after long years of suffering and malaise, has revealed itself to be powerful and overwhelmingly great, and, borne and girded by a spirit of true culture and the highest morality, it has crushed its enemies.'[162] For middle-class participants, the sacred character of a national war— 'the purity of the thing', as one of them termed it—made it imperative to maintain unimpeachable codes of moral conduct and civilized behaviour.[163] The authorities were less convinced that all troops would conform to such norms, which had recently been codified in the Geneva Convention of 1864, yet they were much more concerned than in 1813 to try to enforce them. 'Soldiers!' German troops were warned by royal order as they crossed the French border:

> I expect that the discipline by which you have distinguished yourselves to date will also be maintained on enemy territory. We are not waging war against the *peaceable* inhabitants of the country; it is, rather, the duty of every honour-loving soldier to protect private property and not to tolerate anything which will impinge on the good name of our army, even as the result of isolated incidents of indiscipline (*Zuchtlosigkeit*).[164]

To the authors of the *Bildungsbürgertum*, who—as journalists and diarists—wrote up the events of the war for an avid public, such injunctions already seemed outdated. For them, the campaign in France was the first 'civilian' conflict in modern German history, in which not only peasants had gone off to fight, as in the past, but where 'every man' had been summoned 'from his usual daily work by the

---

Briefwechsel Rudolf Hayms (Osnabrück, 1967), 279; J. Heyderdorff (ed.), *Deutscher Liberalismus im Zeitalter Bismarcks* (Osnabrück, 1967), vol. 1, 473–4.

[160] P. v. Bojanowski, *Geschehenes und Geschriebenes. Tagebuchblätter eines Journalisten aus den Kriegsmonaten der Jahre 1870 und 1871* (Weimar, 1871), 46.

[161] For middle-class soldiers, see G. Morin, *Aus ruhmvollen Tagen. Erinnerungen an den deutsch-französischen Krieg von 1870/71* (Munich, 1882), 13; J. Zaiss, *Aus dem Tagebuch eines badischen Pioniers* (Karlsruhe, 1894), 21; L. Schmitz, *Aus dem Feldzuge 1870/71. Tagebuchblätter eines 65ers* (Berlin, 1902), 3; M. Abel, *Unter der Standarte der Garde Husaren. Kriegserringerungen* (Berlin, 1897), 24–5, 256–7; H. Arnold, *Unter General von der Tann* (Munich, 1896), 35–6; E. Arnold (ed.), *Feldbriefe von Georg Heinrich Rindfleisch*, 2nd edn (Halle, 1889), 1–20; E. Barth, *Kriegserinnerungen eines deutschen Offiziers. Nach Tagebuchblättern* (Kromberg, 1878), 1.

[162] P. v. Bojanowski, *Geschehenes und Geschriebenes*, 66.

[163] H. Arnold (ed.), *Feldbriefe*, 20.

[164] Wilhelm I's order to his troops, 8 Aug. 1870, cited in H. Kohl (ed.), *Deutschlands Einigungskriege 1864–1871 in Urkunden*, 2nd edn (Leipzig, 1917), vol. 1, 97.

trumpets and drums'.[165] 'The world watched in amazement how quickly the transformation from the reservist burgher to battle-ready soldier took place in the German lands', wrote one observer: 'The same burgher, who today as a municipal functionary counts the bricks on a building site and the coppers for the city treasury, is tomorrow the universally feared *Ulan*.'[166] It was essential for such participants that the superior values of a German *Kultur*, which had not yet been distinguished from the word '*Zivilisation*', were proven under the trying conditions of war. Accordingly, all authors were anxious to excuse war crimes, which were committed with increasing frequency as *francs-tireurs* altered the usual rules of engagement during the latter part of the conflict, by alluding to the justified grounds for summary justice. Justifications often included references to heinous acts of arson, the killing of wounded soldiers, and combatants' use of civilian clothing.[167] Many authors, by contrast, attempted to convince their readers that stories of atrocities, even on the French side, were unfounded. 'Nothing that you read in the newspaper is true', wrote one army doctor to his wife: 'I have asked many German soldiers whether they have seen or heard anything of the atrocities that have been attributed to *Turkos* [French colonial troops], but I have learned nothing, so that everything has either been made up or has only occurred in very isolated incidents.'[168] There were few instances of demonization of the French enemy in contemporaries' accounts. A significant number commended their opponents' bravery.[169] Civilization, it appeared, had been upheld.[170]

Many middle-class soldiers experienced similar emotions. At the start of the war, most had harboured great expectations of the conflict, expressing their gratitude that they could be part of such a momentous national event. 'I cannot describe it', rejoiced one participant on his way from Berlin to the Rhineland, 'and I don't

---

[165] A. Buchholtz, *Ernst von Bergmann. Mit Bergmanns Kriegsbriefen von 1866, 1870/71 und 1877* (Leipzig, 1911), 267.

[166] Ibid. For more on the civilian imagery of the war, see F. Becker, *Bilder von Krieg und Nation*, 201–376.

[167] For instance, T. Vatke, *Feldpostbriefe aus Frankreich 1870–71* (Berlin, 1871), 26; A. Fester, *Jugenderinnerungen und Kriegsbriefe eines Altfrankfurters* (Halle, 1911), 50.

[168] T. Billroth, *Briefe*, 9th edn (Hanover, 1922), 103. This downplaying of the atrocities committed by French colonial troops stood in stark contrast to the scare stories concerning them at home: F. Becker, 'Fremde Soldaten in der Armee des Feindes. Deutsche Darstellungen der französischen "Turko"-Truppe im Krieg von 1870/71', in C. Geulen, A. von der Heiden, and B. Liebsch (eds), *Vom Sinn der Feindschaft* (Berlin, 2000), 167–80; C. G. Krüger, 'Die Wahrnehmung der Gewalt im deutsch-französischen Krieg in württembergischen Zeitungen', *Zeitschrift für württembergische Landesgeschichte*, 62 (2003), 319–43.

[169] A. Bornemann, *Kriegs-Tagebuch eines jungen Officiers im Grossherzoglichen Hessischen 2. Jägerbataillon aus den Jahren 1870/71* (Giessen, 1895), 18.

[170] This was the case for those authors who claimed that the 'terror' of the war was the result of *francs-tireurs* acting 'in the name of the republic'. They nevertheless claimed that their own consciences were 'pure': H. Uhde, *Streifzüge auf dem Kriegsschauplatze 1870–1871* (Hamburg, 1871), 39–40. Some commentators argued that even the French-landed population hated the *francs-tireurs*, denigrating them as the 'rabble of the cities': C. Rogge, *Franktireurfahrten und andere Kriegserlebnisse in Frankreich. Kulturbilder aus dem deutsch-französischen Kriege 1870/71* (Berlin, 1907), 36. The General Staff officer Leonhard von Blumenthal, *Tagebücher aus den Jahren 1866 und 1870/71* (Stuttgart, 1902), 128, likened the actions of the *francs-tireurs*, which were despised by wealthier burghers as well as peasants, to a civil war in which social scores were settled under the cover of a war of defence.

need to, for every German heart is filled with the same feeling, pushing everything else into the background.'[171] Another combatant, a middle-aged father and *Obergerichtsrat* in Celle, revealed the extent to which such civilian aspirations and attitudes persisted throughout the war, especially amongst those who did not take part in the major battles. Having been kept back in a reserve unit of the *Landwehr* in Göttingen, the second lieutenant was eager at the end of July 1870 to get to France before the fighting was over, 'for they can't have dragged us old men from wife and children just for peacetime exercises'.[172] News of the 'first great success' in early August helped him get over the unexpected rigour of military training: 'It is truly abominable how one is oppressed by service.'[173] Like others, he was delighted that his own kin had fought at the battle of Wissembourg. 'I don't need to tell you how my mood is constantly improving', he wrote to his wife.[174] 'How painful it is that we can't enjoy these first mighty days together!' he went on:

> We don't yet know enough details to hazard 'expert' opinions. But this much is in any event clear; that we threw them out of naturally fortified, artificially reinforced positions, just as we did the Austrians, and that was the test against the defensive strength of the chassepot, about which I always had secret concerns.[175]

Unfortunately, the civil servant had not found anyone in his regiment to share his passions with and so he had to be content with sketching out his plans and strategies in letters to his wife, whom he advised to consult Treitschke's latest piece in the *Preussische Jahrbücher* in order to keep her nationally inclined spirits up.[176] When he was finally sent to war at the beginning of September, sitting—as he said—'in the middle of events', he saw very little military action and experienced little discomfort, beyond eating stolen chickens for dinner. 'This is how one lives once one has made the leap into a life of war', he bragged to his spouse.[177] The tenor and content of his correspondence were relatively common in memoirs of 1870–1, reporting a middle-aged and often pompous burgher's military adventure in a foreign land. Such accounts of individual duty and national glory showed few signs of transgressing 'civilized' assumptions and codes of behaviour. Virtually all those who witnessed a full battle diverged from this norm, however.[178]

---

[171] T. Vatke, *Feldpostbriefe aus Frankreich 1870–71* (Berlin, 1871), 5.

[172] G. H. Rindfleisch, *Feldbriefe von Georg Heinrich Rindfleisch 1870–71*, ed. E. Arnold, 4th edn (Göttingen, 1895), 1.

[173] Ibid., 3.   [174] Ibid.   [175] Ibid., 5.   [176] Ibid., 11.   [177] Ibid., 20.

[178] It was common for soldiers, especially volunteers, to cast themselves as 'heroes' during their initial deployment, despite the likely consequences. See, for instance, Hermann Tiemann, *Vor fünfundzwanzig Jahren. Feldzugserinnerungen eines Kriegsfreiwilligen* (Brunswick, 1895), 10: 'A thousand-voice hurrah swelled up, linen hung out of every window by way of goodbye, and I saw many, many eyes swimming in tears, for everyone was clear about it—it was not possible to deceive oneself—that many from those who now went to war fresh-faced and healthy would never return, and if they returned, they would be cripples all their lives! This was truly a thought which could make the heart of the bravest stand still for a good while. But in happy, youthful light-headedness we left such considerations on one side. As light as the July sun which fell on us from the sky and was reflected by our weapons, the hope also shone in our hearts that our march to France would be a victory march.'

Many correspondents, it is true, abided by standards of public decency, refusing to divulge what they had seen in battle. 'The peaceable burgher cannot even imagine it', confessed a middle-class reserve officer: 'The impressions which I received here are too horrific for me to want to recollect them in all their details.'[179] Such discretion—as articulated in one later *Justizrat's* claim that 'I have seen scenes the description of which I shall spare you'—was almost routine.[180] Nevertheless, some civilian-soldiers, often despite their best efforts, could not stop themselves from sharing what they had seen and experienced:

> What a sight St Privat was! Is it even possible to give a description of such misery? The nearer we came to the north corner of the village (which had not been burned down), the more the bodies piled up, irregularly beside and on top of one another.... The wounded had been gathered up from the battlefield and lay on the broad village street left and right, one placed close to the other on beds of straw. What a view, everywhere for 300 metres, complaining, moaning, twitching, dying people, some dumb and calm, others with their faces contorted and their limbs dislocated, these screaming loudly, those whimpering, isolated individuals striking their neighbours with fists and elbows in their struggle with death; and these sights! People suffering so! Staring blankly into the heavens, as if they were accusing the originator of the war, as if they were searching for something, perhaps thinking of their own; here, there was no friend and foe any more. Whoever says that war is beautiful did not see St Privat on 19 August!![181]

Having viewed one battlefield, most soldiers tried to avoid going near another, asserted an otherwise proud veteran.[182] It is evident from his and other descriptions, though, that such scenes also fascinated and hardened those who witnessed them. 'It is not a nice sight, such a corpse-filled battlefield; yet people get used to everything', noted one 'civilian' officer, who later became the warden of a workhouse: 'A corpse must contain a sort of magnetic force; at least, I did not manage simply to look away from those dead who lay in our way—I had to look at these poor, often really ugly, dismembered bodies.'[183] For such observers, the comforting defences, prohibitions, and taboos of 'civilized' society had been breached. Yet none of the commentators was moved, for such reasons, publicly to

---

[179] A. Fitze, *Kriegstagebuch eines einjährig-freiwilligen Ulanen aus dem Feldzuge 1870/71* (Rathenow, 1887), 12. See also C. Schepers, *Bilder und Eindrücke*, 55, who shielded his readers from the worst sights of a field hospital: 'Will the reader take a tour through my hospital? He doesn't need to fear. He won't have to see terrible things.' This, of course, was also to acknowledge that readers expected to come across such things.

[180] A. Fester, *Jugenderinnerungen*, 44.

[181] A. Hecker, *Ernstes und Heiteres aus dem Kriegstagebuche eines sächsischen Oberjägers 1870/71* (Dresden, 1895), 22–3. See also B. Berlit (ed.), *Vor Paris und an der Loire 1870 und 1871* (Cassel, 1872); E. Maizier, *Tagebuch aus dem französischen Kriege für die Zeit von Ausmarsch bis zur Waffenruhe* (Magdeburg, 1896); H. Seelmann-Eggebert, *Feldpostbriefe aus dem Kriegsjahre 1870* (Colberg, 1872); H. Abeken, *Ein schlichtes Leben in bewegter Zeit*, 3rd rev. edn (Berlin, 1904); T. Niedermeyer, *Aus meinem Tagebuche: Erlebnisse und Schilderungen aus dem Kriege gegen Frankreich 1870–71* (Hanover, 1871).

[182] H. Bonsack, *Kriegserlebnisse eines Fünfundneunzigers im Feldzug gegen Frankreich 1870–1871* (Gotha, 1906), 17.

[183] A. Bornemann, *Kriegs-Tagebuch*, 12.

question the war effort. The brief duration of their discomfort, their self-conscious participation in an heroic national conflict, and their belief in civilization combined to ensure that virtually all middle-class and noble combatants continued to support Wilhelm I, Bismarck, and the army. Thus, the standard form of memoirs was 'patriotic', starting with the excitement of mobilization and departure and ending with an encomium to regiment, king, and fatherland.[184] When confronted with a high number of casualties, such combatants could claim, with Treitschke, that this would be the last war for a long time.[185] They could continue, therefore, to be 'civilized' advocates of violence and death.

The savage nature of the critical battles of the campaign in 1870 made the balance between patriotism and horror difficult to maintain. The three German armies advanced towards the French border separately in early August (see Map 6). The First Army under Steinmetz (with the First, Seventh, and Eighth Corps comprising 50,000 men) marched from the railhead at Trier down towards Saarlouis, next to the town of Saarbrücken, towards which the Second Army of Friedrich Karl (Third, Fourth, Ninth, Tenth, and Twelfth Corps and the Guard, or 134,000 men) was moving from Mainz and Bingen via Kaiserslautern and St Wendel. Together they formed the right wing of the German forces. Fifty miles to the south, the Third Army of Crown Prince Friedrich Wilhelm (with two Bavarian corps, a division each from Baden and Württemberg, and Fifth and Eleventh Corps, or 125,000 men) constituted the left wing, advancing from Speyer and Landau in the Bavarian Palatinate towards Alsace and Strasbourg. Initially, the armies had been 100 miles apart, spread out between Coblenz in the north and Karlsruhe in the south. Moltke's plan was for the Third Army to attack first, since it was—in Landau—only a day's march from the Alsatian border, making its way northwest to attack the southern flank of the main French forces at Saarbrücken, where the Second Army, having taken several days to cross the hills between the Rhine and the Saar, would be engaging them from the front. The plan was foiled when the Chief of General Staff's order to Blumenthal, the Chief of Staff of the Third Army, to move on the evening of 30 July met with a blank refusal. Verdy du Vernois, sent from military headquarters, confirmed that the Third Army would not be able to march until 4 August. Consequently, Moltke asked the Second Army to attack first, having concentrated its forces north of the Saar. The Third Army would then attack the French flank from the south and the First Army the other flank from the north, having massed its forces near Tholey on 3 August. Steinmetz, who wanted to march rapidly south to Saarlouis and St Avold (in France), objected, turning the experience (he was born in 1796) and stubbornness that had helped to make him a hero of 1866 into a liability in 1870. 'His judgement and activity have been

[184] See, for instance, A. Breithaupt, *Aus dem Lagerleben vor Paris. Erinnerungen eines Kriegsfreiwilligen des Garde-Füsilier-Regiments aus dem Feldzuge 1870/71* (Berlin, 1913), 10–15, 166–9, who was typical of many and who finished his memoir with the following: 'God maintain peace with honour for our dear fatherland! If we must arm again for a great war, however, perhaps even bigger than then, I believe that all its sons will again stand there with the watchword: "With God, for king and fatherland! With God, for the Kaiser and the Reich!" And then be comforted my Volk, my fatherland!'
[185] H. v. Treitschke to S. Hirzel, 1 Sept. 1870, in Cornicelius (ed.), *Heinrich Treitschkes Briefe*, 285.

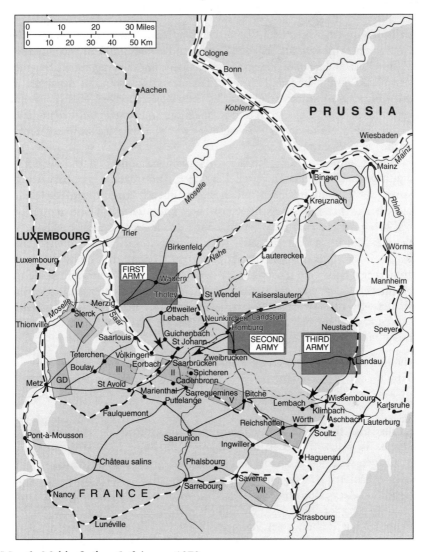

Map 6. Moltke Strikes, 5–6 August 1870

Source: G. Wawro, *The Franco-Prussian War: The German Conquest of France in 1870–1871* (Cambridge, 2003), 109.

impaired', wrote the military writer and General Staff officer Paul Bronsart von Schellendorff: 'his obstinacy alone remains'.[186] On 4 August, he struck south, with his left wing crossing the path of Friedrich Karl's Second Army. Ordered by Moltke not to cross the Saar, Steinmetz retorted, 'I do not understand the strategic ideas which lead to the abandonment of the Saar and which the situation does make at

---

[186] P. Bronsart von Schellendorff, *Geheimes Kriegstagebuch 1870–1871*, ed. P. Rassow (Bonn, 1954), 70.

all necessary.'[187] If he were obliged to take up a position behind the Second Army, he warned Wilhelm I directly on the next day, 'as I have no orders about the offensive movement which would follow, I do not know whether I can play any useful part in it'.[188] The Chief of Staff replied immediately, not the king, telling Steinmetz to clear his troops off the road in front of the Second Army and not to advance to the Saar until 7 August, before adding that 'His Majesty has expressly reserved the giving of orders for the execution of this operation, since the manner of undertaking it, and the direction it is given, will depend upon the turn which events will have taken with the Third Army.'[189]

Steinmetz ignored Moltke's orders and marched south on the evening of 5 August with two of his corps—belonging to the smallest, auxiliary army—across the path of the principal, much larger Second Army towards Spicheren, where Charles Frossard's Second Corps was entrenched on and around the central height of the *Rote Berg*, which looked down towards Saarbrücken to the east. Like Moltke, Friedrich Karl, who had been progressing methodically towards the Saar, preparing to engage the main French armies, was distraught: 'Steinmetz has fatally compromised my beautiful plans.'[190] On 6 August, Georg von Kameke, one of Steinmetz's divisional generals, attacked Frossard's forces at Spicheren with only two brigades, believing wrongly that they were retreating. The terrain was daunting for the German attackers, as one officer in the 12th Infantry Regiment intimated:

Half a mile south of Saarbrücken, a high chain of mountains, wooded and falling steeply in front of Saarbrücken, stretches from west to east. The foreground does not offer the possibility of a hidden approach. This high chain, therefore, appears to constitute an impregnable position.[191]

The Prussians, the same author continued, had disproven that supposition (embodied in Frossard's belief that Spicheren was *une position magnifique*), but with 'great losses'.[192] The action was improvised, risky, and disjointed, running counter to Moltke's strategy and leaving German troops too far from the support of the Second Army. The officer had marched without rest, not eating before battle and not sleeping for three days. He and his men were 'completely exhausted' on 6 August, so that 'it almost seemed impossible to lead them to the crest of the hill, even without their pack'.[193] One brigade, which was made up of Prussians and Hanoverians, made its way along the Forbach railway under heavy artillery fire, followed by the concentrated fire of an entire French brigade's *chassepot* rifles. The rest of the brigade pushed through the woods up towards the *Rote Berg* but they were picked off by French marksmen in the woods and beyond them, augmented by the relentless firing of *mitrailleuses*.

---

[187] K. v. Steinmetz to H. v. Moltke, 4 Aug. 1870, cited in M. Howard, *Franco-Prussian War*, 84.
[188] Ibid.   [189] H. v. Moltke to K. v. Steinmetz, 5 Aug. 1870, ibid.
[190] Friedrich Karl, cited in G. Wawro, *The Franco-Prussian War*, 110.
[191] Cited in T. Fontane, *Der Krieg gegen das Kaiserreich* (Berlin, 1873), vol. 1, 222.
[192] Ibid.   [193] Ibid., 222–3.

By 1.00 p.m., the Prussian assault had been halted, with only Kameke's artillery, pushing up behind, preventing the brigade from being overrun. Reinforced by the arrival of another brigade, an attempt was made to take the *Rote Berg* at around 3.00 p.m. It failed, with French counter-attacks forcing back the remains of both Prussian brigades. One soldier from the 48th Infantry Regiment gave a good account of how disorienting the attack was, even for those arriving in the second wave:

> At about 1 o'clock the alarm sounded; no one thought that he would be standing opposite the enemy within several hours... In St Johann, the sister town of Saarbrücken, we were received with enthusiasm. An old bridge led us across the Saar, and then into Saarbrücken itself; the thunder of cannon echoed across to us, nearer and nearer. Now a command to load our guns; then we were going through the outskirts and gardens; Saarbrücken lay behind us... The gunpowder smoke came across the mountains lying before us, which fell sometimes gently and sometimes steeply down to the Saar... We put our pack down on a meadow and went forward in half battalions. The heights were occupied by the French, as was the wood, composed of low bushes, which covered the left side of the great ravine. The 39th, 40th and 74th were already bedded in under the outcrop. We had barely entered the great wolf's ravine when we received hellish fire from grenades and small arms from the front and from the left, coming from the edge of the wood... The way which the half battalion took was marked by the dead, a long, long way to the next cover, which partly consisted of the wood and partly of defiles and extruding cliffs... There was no question of stopping and orientating ourselves; whoever fell, fell; we went forever forwards up to the heights... Yet to hold what we had gained so strenuously was going to be made difficult for us. Scarcely had we taken the first line of mountains, when—from behind a ridge which had been fully entrenched by the French—such fire was directed at us that the fire of Königgrätz seemed to pale. What could one do in this rain of bullets?[194]

The order was given to advance. Eventually, the French were dislodged from their positions, yet there had been a chance of a decisive French counter-attack, if Frossard had chosen to pursue the Germans after 3.30 p.m. His failure to do so permitted the Third and Eighth Corps of the Second Army, who had marched to the sound of the guns, to outflank the French Second Corps and force it to flee. Nevertheless, the Prussians and Hanoverians lost two men for every French casualty at Spicheren on 6 August, overshadowing the defeat of the much smaller French force of Abel Douay (8,600 men) by the Third Army at Wissembourg in Alsace on the 4th.[195] Such a costly, impromptu battle was disorienting for those involved. It was characteristic of the first phase of the war.

At the same time in the south, the advance units of the Third Army, which were pursuing MacMahon's First Corps towards Strasbourg, unexpectedly bumped into them at Froeschwiller, where the French commander had decided to make a stand, digging in on the three-pronged ridge in front of Wörth—another *position magnifique*—and ordering Pierre de Failly to bring up the Fifth Corps (just under

---

[194] Ibid., 220–1.
[195] Michael Howard, *Franco-Prussian War*, 102, estimates that 6,000 active French combatants faced 50,000 German ones.

30,000 men) in support. If Failly had responded promptly, MacMahon would have disposed of 77,600 soldiers against the advancing Prussian, Bavarian, Swabian, and Badenese corps. As it was, Failly hesitated, refusing to bring his corps south through the Vosges to Froeschwiller until they had been relieved at their border posts by other French troops. MacMahon's own forces therefore numbered 48,000. They were still larger than those of the Germans, who attacked on the orders of Hugo von Kirchbach, the commander of the Prussian Fifth Corps, on the morning of 6 August, against the wishes of the Crown Prince and Blumenthal, the bulk of whose army was still several miles away. Fifth Corps fired first in the early morning, which triggered a similar bombardment, followed by an assault, two miles to the north by the Bavarian Second Corps. Kirchbach, whose own artillery had stopped firing by 8.30 a.m., decided to mount a similar assault in the centre, so that by 10.00 a.m. the three corps—more than half the battle strength of the Third Army—had become embroiled in a battle without any order to do so (indeed, Blumenthal had sent orders 'not to continue the struggle and to avoid everything which might induce a fresh one', which had arrived too late).[196]

With little preparation, the three German corps had to make their way up the valleys and mountain flanks in the crossfire of the French infantrymen and artillery above them. By midday, the Baden-Württemberg Division in the centre was only one-third of the way to Froeschwiller, pinned down by the concealed French marksmen on the ridge and in the woods in front of them. On the right, the Bavarian Second Corps, many of whom were drunk from the wine they had been given—without food—for breakfast, had fallen back, reinforced by a Bavarian First Corps under Ludwig von der Tann who refused to advance, maintaining that 'The Prussians want to sacrifice we Bavarians to spare themselves.'[197] It took four messengers from the headquarters of the Third Army, acting in the name of the Bavarian monarch, to force him to move in the early afternoon: 'In the name of His Majesty the King of Bavaria, the Crown Prince orders that the First Corps deploy all of its forces without further delay to support and exploit the gains made at such heavy cost by the Prussians.'[198] At that stage, the costs were more appreciable than the gains, with the Prussian Eleventh Corps, which was composed largely of Saxons, struggling from midday onwards to outflank the French on the German left wing. Only MacMahon's reluctance to counter-attack in the late morning and continuing reinforcements in the north (Bavarian First Corps) and the south (Eleventh Corps), which saw German numbers swell to 88,000 by the mid-afternoon, allowed the Third Army to outflank the French army and compel it to retreat from the ridge. The French lost 20,000 men, of which more than 9,000 were taken prisoner, and the Germans suffered 10,500 casualties, of which six-sevenths were Prussians.

Educated ordinary soldiers like the Bavarian Florian Kühnhauser, who had been in Vienna in July 1870 and who returned to enter the war with mixed

---

[196] A. v. Blumenthal, cited ibid., 111.
[197] Cited in G. Wawro, *The Franco-Prussian War*, 128.
[198] Ibid.

feelings of trepidation and enthusiasm, revealed how unsettling the battle of Froeschwiller was for reservists like himself. Having served in 1866 on Austria's side, he was at once critical of Habsburg officers' support for France, which he had witnessed in Vienna, and wary of supporting Prussia, preferring to underline his support for Bavaria—'his love for the fatherland'—and the return of his 'soldier's blood', after initial apprehension.[199] 'Within me, a great struggle was going on, for I knew all too well from 1866 what it means to go to war, and now against such a powerful, feared opponent!' he recalled: 'For someone who was not a career soldier, this is certainly excusable; the thought of being torn away again from my profession and from business, and to have to leave Vienna, which had become so dear to me, had a depressing effect on my spirits.'[200] By 6 August, he was in France, rousing himself after spending the night outside in the rain ('I shall never in my life forget this first night in France'), hungry, soaked to the skin, and covered in 'excrement and dirt'.[201] In the distance, they could hear 'dull thuds': 'Was it another storm coming? No, it was the thunder of cannon; the battle near Wörth had already begun. Deep earnestness was visible on every face.'[202] At about 8.00 a.m., the Bavarian columns started to move forwards in hot, humid weather. 'Repeatedly, we heard the thunder of cannon in the west, which, however, kept stopping', he recorded.[203] As they approached the place where they were due to rest that day, they saw adjutants and staff officers springing here and there, 'a sign that something was up'.[204] Meeting someone he knew, their own officer asked, 'How is it looking, Captain?'[205] 'Excellent', replied the staff officer: 'the Second Bavarian Corps is already standing tremendously under fire'.[206] The troops were ordered forward at a quick march, starting off in good order but gradually leaving 'the weaker ones behind', collapsing out of breath and exhausted.[207] As they rested momentarily, they could hear 'the din of battle clearly, the boom of the cannon, the rattle of gun salvos and the haunting noise of the *mitrailleuses*; but nothing could be seen'.[208] They spoke to each other in confidence, passing on messages to give to their 'parents, siblings or bride', if they were to die, before they were interrupted by the order to march.[209] Coming over the ridge from the east, 'the entire picture of the battle unfurled in front of our eyes—the Sauerthal, with the heights opposite, lay before us'.[210] Many would be able to remember 'this ghastly, beautiful view of the turmoil of battle', he wrote, but 'excitement, fatigue, over-exertion and tension blunt the senses' and one's 'mind is not able to comprehend each moment, for there is no time to look or to think', as the command to go 'forwards, forwards' resounded.[211]

The setting of the battle was intimidating, with 'powerful, black clouds' rising up into the air from 'the burning villages of Froeschwiller and Elsaßhausen, on the partly wooded heights' opposite.[212] 'On the left in the valley lay the much fought-for Wörth', with artillery spewing out 'their death-bringing shots from the facing

[199] F. Kühnhauser, *Kriegs-Erinnerungen*, 5.   [200] Ibid.   [201] Ibid., 25.
[202] Ibid.   [203] Ibid., 26.   [204] Ibid.   [205] Ibid.   [206] Ibid.
[207] Ibid.   [208] Ibid.   [209] Ibid.   [210] Ibid., 27.
[211] Ibid.   [212] Ibid.

heights', Kühnhauser noted: 'Below in the valley an infantry battle raged; long lines of marksmen became visible from the gunpowder smoke and, behind on the mountainside, red stripes—the French battalions.'[213] The worst fighting was on the mountainside in front of Froeschwiller, which was 'where we, too, would be taking part'.[214] As they marched towards 'this battle scene', the noise became deafening:

> Salvo upon salvo was sent, needle-guns and *chassepots* competed with one another, the *Pödewils* and *Werder* [makes of Bavarian rifle] would now soon bring victory. What a crack and natter this was that burst the ears! To which was added the hissing of landing grenades, the whirring and whistling of bullets, whilst hundreds of cannon compounded it, so that one would think that the earth was spitting fire and hell was opening up.[215]

Seriously wounded men were already being carried past to a dressing station nearby, serving as 'terrifying examples for the advancing troops'.[216] Shortly afterwards, having come to the crest of the hill, Kühnhauser's own regiment had 'become visible to the enemy and was immediately greeted with artillery fire': 'Who does not remember the small, blue-white clouds in the air?'[217] With the Prussian Fifth Corps on one side and the Bavarian Second Corps on the other, the soldiers of the First Division loaded their guns in 'absolute silence', 'as if everyone had felt the force of this moment at the same time'.[218] As they went into battle, only 'the dull tread of boots was audible', he went on: 'When one goes into battle for the first time, how the pulse vibrates, everyone's heart beats more violently, where are one's thoughts? Many said a prayer in silence, thought of their mother, father or bride, and whether they would ever see them again.'[219] Running up the hill through a wood, they tried to avoid strengthening enemy fire: 'patsch—patsch— cries of pain from all sides, it was the first wounded—splat—and our Lieutenant von Weber collapsed wounded at my side.'[220] In the wood, 'it was haunting': 'shells whistled through the trees, foliage and branches fell down on us and from time to time groups were injured', with some bearing the pain with 'great calm and sanguineness' and others, having had 'a more important part of their body smashed', emitting a 'heart-breaking scream', which cannot have had 'a very encouraging effect on those around'.[221] The French soldiers, lying in shallow trenches, were barely to be seen, as they forced back the united assaults of the Germans, even a bayonet attack, with 'rapid fire and stubborn resistance', inflicting 'great losses'.[222] Even the last successful assault after 3.00 p.m. had to go through an 'enemy rain of fire and the fire of *mitrailleuses*', before the French were eventually routed.[223] The realization that they had won, with the 'drunken jubilation of victory' replacing 'the rage of battle', dawned slowly, banishing 'hunger and thirst, punishments and dangers', at least temporarily.[224]

---

[213] Ibid.   [214] Ibid.   [215] Ibid.   [216] Ibid., 28.
[217] Ibid.   [218] Ibid.   [219] Ibid.   [220] Ibid., 29.
[221] Ibid., 29–30.   [222] Ibid., 30.   [223] Ibid.   [224] Ibid., 31.

Memories of such jubilation, which helped in the framing of patriotic narratives, regularly existed alongside other darker recollections of warfare, which characterized the depiction of battles and their aftermath. For middle-class volunteers like Edmund Metsch, who was a maths student and trainee teacher from Bavaria, the contrast between fear and disgust, on the one hand, and patriotic pride, on the other, was a marked one. Rapidly deployed to France, his first sight of war was the battlefield of Wissembourg, 'the view of which will always remain fresh in my memory my whole life long': 'Germans and French, who were reconciled by the unswayable angel of death, lay peacefully beside one another, and the sight of them cut deep into my heart.'[225] So many had said, 'in their noble, holy enthusiasm', 'Yes, I want to die for my fatherland', but 'here, in view of those who sacrificed their lives on the altar of the fatherland a few hours ago', such 'enthusiasm would disappear from many', as it had gone from Metsch.[226] Before leaving Wissembourg, his regiment had rested near the village, which he had decided to walk around, coming across 'eleven dead in a row' in a vegetable garden, 'their gaping wounds visible to my eye': 'No mourning heart cried over their corpses, no thankful or loving hand closed the eyes of these brave ones, no warm prayer climbed up from their coffins to heaven; lonely, unknown and unmourned, they lay on foreign soil, far from their *Heimat* and their loved ones.'[227] A tear rolled into his beard, as Metsch 'thought that he could meet the same fate, perhaps tomorrow'.[228] At the same time, 'I was brave like a man and called to mind the holy affair for which I was standing in the field; I said to myself that I would fight for the home of my loved ones and for my dear, beloved fatherland.'[229] As they followed a Prussian division, 'in a jovial mood', towards Wörth, he looked at the beautiful landscape and thought about 'home, his parents and siblings, relatives and beloved friends'.[230] The next day, after a night in the open under a thunderstorm, the regiment set off at 8.00 a.m., as the sun broke through, on a six-hour march to battle.

It was about 2.00 p.m. as Metsch's regiment moved into the 'area of bullets and shells'.[231] 'No one will forget the great view of the battle of Wörth, which had already begun, as we marched down the hill into the encounter', he wrote:

> One's chest rose up and one's heart knocked against one's breast with tempestuous beats. The small-arms fire was so violent that it was not possible to distinguish individual shots from one another. In between, there was peculiar 'rrrt' that was made by the *mitrailleuses*, in addition to which the heavy guns bellowed out their thunder incessantly.[232]

It felt as though combatants were being swallowed up by an elemental maelstrom:

> The air was full of smoke and torn apart by millions of bullets; it was turmoil, as if the elements of the earth were going to split apart. I was able to watch this for a few

---

[225] E. Metsch, *Meine Erlebnisse als Einjährig-Freiwilliger beim k. b. Infanterie-Leibregiment im Kriege gegen Frankreich 1870–71* (Munich, 1871), 5.
[226] Ibid.   [227] Ibid., 6.   [228] Ibid.   [229] Ibid., 7.
[230] Ibid., 7–9.   [231] Ibid., 10.   [232] Ibid.

minutes, then we went into the pandemonium, against the enemy. Bullets surrounded us like swarming insects, and only the cracking of hit trees and the collapsing of so many vital, healthy comrades showed that these insects were from another realm of nature. Branches fell down, cracking, and poor wounded soldiers twisted around sighing, groaning and pleading for help, wallowing in their own blood, yet—we kept on going forward—the enemy must give way... The battle raged terribly. The 'hurrah' of the attackers merged with the cries of the Turkos and the gasps of the dying. Four of the five officers of my company were wounded in a very short time, the men were robbed of their leaders, got lost in the wood, and each attached himself to the unit next to him: I came across a regiment of Prussians, with whom I cleared a hill of its current, black inhabitants.

As we passed a small, free plateau north of Wörth, I was able to convince myself of Prussian courage, whilst watching a unit of Prussians storming a wood on a hill to my right... The Prussians, pushing forward onto the meadow, were repelled twice by the French, who were probably entrenched. Twice they had to take up their old protected positions, but they stormed the wood for a third time with a violent 'hurrah', leaving half of these courageous men behind dead or wounded and taking prisoner, as I learned later, a nice part of the French. Thousands of dead and wounded already covered the battlefield, as the French finally ran in flight from them in full disarray towards Niederbronn.[233]

By 7.00 p.m., the battle was over, 'won gloriously'.[234] However, many had paid with 'life, health and limbs'.[235] The sights on the field where they rested were horrific: one soldier had had his foot blown off, left hanging by threads of nerves; another had had 'the right side of his face torn away, from his eye to his chin'.[236] It was a 'terrible prospect', prompting Metsch to go back from his walk across the battlefield to his unit.[237] To see such a 'terrifying picture' banished 'the drunkenness of victory for the most part' and had 'a shaming effect', as soldiers became 'conscious that humans [had] done all this', recalled Kühnhauser of the day after the battle of Froeschwiller.[238] As they wrote their postcards home, distributed by the thousand, the jubilation of victory was mixed with the news, for many 'worried fathers, concerned mothers... and loving brides' that 'an enemy bullet [had] bored through the chest of the warmly loved one'.[239] Metsch, a sensitive man, looked on unmoved as a group of French villagers, accused of cutting off the noses, ears, and tongues of the German wounded were 'worked on with the butts of rifles' by their guards 'to the great joy and happiness' of 'hundreds of our soldiers', sitting passively nearby.[240] The next day, one of them—the village schoolmaster—also received his 'well-deserved reward'—probably death—for 'unheard-of atrocities', committed by 'exceptions to civilized people', noted the trainee teacher without further comment.[241]

The unexpected losses of German armies' unplanned early encounters with the French affected the rest of the campaign. In the northern sector of the theatre of war, Bazaine retreated with 160,000 men towards Metz after the battle of

[233] Ibid., 11–13.   [234] Ibid., 13.   [235] Ibid.   [236] Ibid., 16.   [237] Ibid.
[238] F. Kühnhauser, Kriegs-Erinnerungen, 36.   [239] Ibid., 36–7.
[240] E. Metsch, Meine Erlebnisse, 16–17.   [241] Ibid., 17.

Spicheren on 6 August. Moltke ordered the German First and Second Armies to wheel around these French forces, leaving the corps of the pivot of the movement—the three corps of Steinmetz's First Army and the Third and Tenth Corps of Friedrich Karl's Second Army—near Metz, exposed to a counter-attack in mid-August, before the southernmost corps (Fourth Corps and the Guards) and those in the east (Ninth and Twelfth Corps) could reach them. The Third Army was still too far to the south, after the debilitating battle of Froeschwiller, to play any part in such fighting. The German Chief of the General Staff's gamble was made riskier by the continuing willingness of his field commanders to act independently, disobeying or failing to consult their superiors. Thus, on 14 August, Kuno von der Goltz launched an attack with a brigade of the Seventh Corps—soon joined by the rest of Seventh Corps (Dietrich von Zastrow), First Corps (Edwin von Manteuffel), and, later, the Ninth Corps of the Second Army (Albrecht von Manstein)—in the valleys around Colombey to the east of Metz, against the wishes of Steinmetz, who was unwilling to be reprimanded by Wilhelm I a second time (after Spicheren). The German forces, unable to advance under French fire, were forced to retreat back to the River Nied with the loss of 5,000 men, compared to approximately 3,500 French casualties, which in turn prompted Moltke to slow down the advance of the Second Army to the west of Metz.[242] As a consequence, when Konstantin von Alvensleben attacked much of Bazaine's army (the Guards and the Second, Third, Fourth, and Sixth Corps) with his Third Corps near Mars-la-Tour on 16 August, without being ordered to do so by the General Staff, he could only count on the support of two divisions of the Tenth Corps. An initial German force of about 30,000, reinforced through the day to more than 60,000, met approximately 130,000 French troops who were attempting to drop back on Châlons, where they would be reunited with the army of MacMahon, retreating from Froeschwiller in the south.[243] Bazaine should have won the battle, as Heinrich Antonovich Leer, the Russian war-planner, explained after the event: 'In theory, against a modern fortress like Metz with a 30,000-man garrison and...an army of 100,000 or more on its flank or rear, you would need at least 600,000 men to neutralize the fortress and army.'[244] The pressures which such an imbalance placed on the German troops, fighting against what one combatant termed 'a terrible over-powering force', were immense.[245] With hindsight, some veterans claimed that the battle 'was a day of honour for Prussian arms', in which '60,000 Germans' had been pitted 'against double that number of French'.[246] At the time, 'it developed gradually into the bloodiest battle of the war' between 16 and 18 August, in the countryside to the west of Metz around Mars-la-Tour and Gravelotte.[247] A total of more than 70,000 French and German troops were killed or wounded in two days of hard

[242] M. Howard, *Franco-Prussian War*, 144, 148.
[243] G. Wawro, *The Franco-Prussian War*, 161, gives an estimate of German numbers.
[244] Ibid.   [245] H. Tiemann, *Mein Feldzug*, 17.
[246] H. Ehrenberg, *1870/71. Feldzugs-Erinnerungen eines Fünfunddreissigers*, 15.
[247] Ibid. See also G. Boschen, *Kriegserinnerungen eines Einundzwanzigers 1870/71*, 23.

fighting.[248] 'The path to Metz, a young warrior says simply, as if this path were so easy, as if it did not lead over rivers of blood and walls of corpses!' recalled Georg Horn, who served with Friedrich Karl's staff.[249]

Those fighting at Mars-la-Tour knew that they were likely to be killed. 'Naturally', as one patriotic, 19-year-old, one-year volunteer from Oldenburg put it, the troops were not aware of their precise strategic position or deployment of forces ('What is going on up in front? Who is fighting?'), but they soon realized that their predicament was serious: 'even the bravest were silent, no more jokes were heard'.[250] Rushing to battle through a 'wonderful meadow', whose 'green was so completely fresh' under 'such a blue sky', the soldiers' state of mind contrasted with the 'tranquillity and peace' of the setting.[251] How different these sensations were, wrote Horn, from 'the raging confusion which we had just escaped and the ugly pictures of death and wounds, which we were going step-by-step to confront on this day!'[252] With their path of retreat blocked, the soldiers knew that they would fight to the end, yet they were hopelessly outnumbered.[253] As he approached the battlefield, the young trainee teacher from Brunswick, Hermann Tiemann, came over a small hill 'in the most terrible heat' and saw the broad plain, dotted with villages, in front of him: 'How it bubbled and surged on this plain!'[254] The troops in the volunteer's regiment looked on in 'seriousness' and 'celebration', contemplating the battle raging close to them and knowing 'that today it would count'.[255] Emerging from a wood which they had been using for cover, they were met with 'a murderous rain of bullets', throwing themselves to the ground as the grenades crept towards them.[256] These first experiences of battle were the worst, wrote another volunteer:

> A sinister howling cut through the air, a short metallic bang behind us, the first grenades had reached us...One man in the company, Musketeer J., got cramps and had to stay lying down...My courage, too, began visibly to sink—each time a grenade whistled by my heart beat violently, my breathing stopped; and, in my mind, I was conscious how quickly I, too, could be taken away. I thought of home, of my parents and siblings, whether I would see them again. How many had the same thought?[257]

Many officers in Tiemann's company, as in others, had 'fallen or were wounded', as were nearly all the non-commanding officers.[258] 'The rain of bullets and shells became heavier and heavier, and the enemy pushed more and more violently against us', wrote the volunteer: when it was 'impossible for us to stay', the order came to move 'back, back', but, 'alas, scarcely half could raise themselves from the

[248] For troops at home, too, Mars-la-Tour was notorious for its 'heavy losses'; F. Leo, *Kriegserinnerungen an 1870–71* (Berlin, 1914), 10. Richard Martin, *Kriegserinnerungen eines 105ers*, 159, gave the higher figure of 80,000.

[249] G. Horn, *Bei Friedrich Karl*, vol. 1, 100.

[250] G. Boschen, *Kriegserinnerungen*, 22.   [251] G. Horn, *Bei Friedrich Karl*, 101.

[252] Ibid.   [253] Ibid.   [254] H. Tiemann, *Mein Feldzug*, 16.

[255] Ibid.   [256] Ibid.   [257] G. Boschen, *Kriegserinnerungen*, 26.

[258] H. Tiemann, *Mein Feldzug*, 17.

ground', where they had been cowering; 'only now could we tell how terribly death had affected our ranks'.[259]

In another regiment, one officer upbraided his immobile troops for cowardice and shirking, only to realize that 'all were wounded', moving him to turn away 'with tears in his eyes'.[260] It was common in the early phase of combat to 'get cramp and remain lying down'.[261] Having retreated to the wood, Tiemann's company were unable to find shelter: 'death followed us everywhere.'[262] They crawled through the wood, trying to avoid the bullets by hiding behind trees, but they were caught in the crossfire of a regiment attacking them from the left, leaving them the choice of being taken prisoner or fleeing and meeting an 'almost certain death'.[263] Choosing the latter, they ran, losing 150 out of 250 in their company in a single day. 'As if by a miracle, I was saved; none of the many bullets hit me, one alone tearing my tunic to pieces', he recorded after the battle.[264] Many were not so lucky: the first brigade of the Tenth Corps, for example, lost 60 per cent of its soldiers, with 45 per cent killed, in little more than half an hour, having entered the battle in the late afternoon after a twelve-hour march in sweltering heat. The digging of 'long, long graves' the next day, laying the corpses 'layer upon layer', was at once 'sad' and 'great', in Tiemann's retrospective opinion.[265] Others remembered only the injuries of the dead, with head wounds the most common, the 'running mass of blood and material' marking 'the spot where the life-nerve was hit and destroyed'.[266] Because of the accuracy of Prussian artillery, the bodies of the French, in particular, were often dismembered, 'limbs smashed and severed', 'heads shot to bits, so that the mass of the brain seeped out'.[267]

The night after the battle of Mars-la-Tour, most soldiers slept on the field, surrounded by 'thousands of dead and wounded' and weighed down 'by the remorselessly, heavily depressing consciousness of a lost battle'.[268] They waited, 'with anxiety and terror', for an 'all-destroying struggle of desperation' on the next day.[269] That battle did not materialize because Bazaine and his commanders refused, as on previous occasions, to use their advantage. On the evening of 16 August, the marshal ordered a retreat to the plateau of Plappeville, just to the east of Gravelotte, leaving his officers 'stupefied': 'Now, tonight, after a victorious battle...when the road to Verdun had been secured with the blood of 20,000 men, we *retreated*! Towards Metz!' recalled one of them.[270] As a result, Moltke was able to order the Fourth, Seventh, Eighth, and Twelfth Corps, which had been marching rapidly towards the Meuse, to turn north to Gravelotte, reinforcing Alvensleben's and Voigts-Rhetz's forces with the full strength of the First and Second Armies; 188,332 Germans with 732 guns faced 112,800 Frenchmen with

[259] Ibid.   [260] G. Boschen, *Kriegserinnerungen*, 28.
[261] O. Kopelke, *Kriegserlebnisse eines Veteranen von 1870/71* (Berlin, 1902), 112–13.
[262] H. Tiemann, *Mein Feldzug*, 17.   [263] Ibid.
[264] Ibid., 18. G. Boschen, *Kriegserinnerungen*, 31, makes the same point.
[265] H. Tiemann, *Mein Feldzug*, 19.   [266] G. Horn, *Bei Friedrich Karl*, 103.
[267] Ibid., 105.   [268] G. Boschen, *Kriegserinnerungen*, 33.   [269] Ibid.
[270] Colonel Joseph Andlau, cited in G. Wawro, *The Franco-Prussian War*, 165.

520 guns.[271] Friedrich Karl's orders on 17 August were 'to find the enemy and fight him'.[272] Moving north and east from Mars-la-Tour and Rezonville, however, he found the French arrayed on a plateau, topped by a series of farms (St Hubert, Leipzig, Moscou, Point du Jour) and guarded by a wooded ravine. Friedrich Karl at first thought that he had detected Bazaine's rearguard, assuming that the rest of the army would be retreating to Metz, and he planned to attack it along a narrow front. Moltke corrected his error, extending the corps of the Second Army up to St Privat in the north in an attempt to find the French army's flank, yet there was no consensus about the wisdom of an attack. 'The objective has already been achieved; the French line of retreat has been cut', declared the War Minister Albrecht von Roon: 'To throw them out of their strong positions now will mean a useless loss of blood.'[273]

The German corps attacked regardless, with Manstein—who had lost a son at Spicheren—launching an artillery attack and preparing his infantry for an assault in the centre around midday. At 3.00 p.m., Steinmetz, hearing the cannonade, ordered the Seventh and Eighth Corps (which had been taken from his command) to go through the Mance ravine to both sides of the main road from Verdun (via Gravelotte) to Metz in order to attack the French on the ridge, despite being ordered not to, since the Saxon Twelfth Corps had not reached St Privat to begin a flanking manoeuvre. As Wilhelm I rode up to Steinmetz to ask why his men were not advancing, the 'mad' commander replied: 'They have no more leaders, Your Majesty, their officers are all dead or wounded.'[274] When the king called them cowards, Moltke retorted angrily that 'they are fighting like heroes for Your Majesty', before riding back to Gravelotte in a temper, leaving his monarch alone.[275] German troops were being slaughtered before the Saxons, who were moving north beyond St Privat, were in position. In the event, the Saxons were not allowed to reach their position, for August von Württemberg had used a lull in artillery fire (caused by 270 cannon and approximately 20,000 shells directed at French emplacements) to send columns of the Prussian Guard Corps up the open slope to St Privat at 5.00 p.m. In a 'hurricane' of French rifle fire, 8,000 guards were killed or wounded in just over half an hour.[276] Along the entire front of the battle, the German soldiers had been exposed, by the precipitate actions of individual commanders, to the 'formidable' positions chosen by Bazaine and described by Sheridan:

> Before us, and covering Metz, lay the French army, posted on the crest of a ridge extending north, and about its centre curving slightly westward toward the German forces. The left of the French position was but a short distance from the Moselle, and this part of the line was separated from the Germans by a ravine, the slopes, fairly well wooded, rising quite sharply; farther north, near the centre, this depression disappeared, merged in the general swell of the ground, and thence on toward

---

[271] M. Howard, *Franco-Prussian War*, 167. G. Wawro, *The Franco-Prussian War*, 169, gives the higher figure, with further reinforcements of 200,000 and 160,000.
[272] Friedrich Karl, *Denkwürdigkeiten*, vol. 2, 225.
[273] A. v. Waldersee, *Denkwürdigkeiten*, vol. 1, 89.   [274] Ibid., 90.   [275] Ibid.
[276] A. v. Eberstein, *Erlebtes aus den Kriegen 1864, 1866, 1870–71* (Leipzig, 1899), 40–3.

the right the ground over which an approach to the French line must be made was essentially a natural open glacis, that could be thoroughly swept by the fire of the defenders.[277]

In the absence of a French counter-attack after the disastrous assault by the Guards on St Privat, the Saxon Twelfth Corps was able to carry out its assault on the French flank at 7.00 p.m. and defeat the enemy's forces, but the king was not alone in doubting that the outcome at Gravelotte, given the blood-letting, could have been a victory.[278]

Once again, regiments were assigned positions on the battlefield, where they went to sleep without fires, 'because the possibility of the enemy breaking out from the area around Point du Jour was not ruled out'.[279] 'The results of this bloody struggle could not immediately be perceived', admitted one Saxon combatant.[280] The French Army of the Rhine had withdrawn to Metz, but 'what sacrifices it had cost!' noted one officer and former one-year volunteer.[281] Even from a distance, the casualties of the Guard Corps were shocking: 'It lasted a good two hours; we saw how more and more batteries came up, the *mitrailleuses* made a hellish noise with their marrow and bone-shaking, jarring tone, and behind the walls rising up on the heights the enemy developed the men-murdering fire of *chassepots*.'[282] Arriving in the same area from the north with the Saxon Twelfth Corps, the landscape was 'scattered with villages, individual arms and copses, in and between which large masses of enemy artillery and infantry—both firing—were visible'.[283] 'The hellish din of battle had now reached a terrible high-point and rang out like the ground-shaking growl of an earthquake', wrote one Saxon soldier: 'On both sides, there must have been hundreds of cannon and hundreds of thousands of rifles caught up in this blood-work.'[284] As they entered the battle, the troops felt they were making 'world history', but they were soon overwhelmed by it, as bullets started to whistle past them:

> To the right and left and in front of us, comrades suddenly collapsed...It all happened very suddenly and unexpectedly and was, faced with an invisible enemy, quite eerie. It was, in its particular novelty, so surprising and forceful in the first half minute that the blood of one's heart stopped and a death shudder penetrated to one's innermost recesses.[285]

Such existential panic, however, was 'merely the first zone of hell', as in Dante's vision of it, followed by all manner of 'fire, blood, death and destruction', in the midst of which 'one's whole life flashes before one's soul at lightning speed', ran

[277] P. H. Sheridan, *Personal Memoirs*, vol. 2, 368–9.
[278] G. Wawro, *The Franco-Prussian War*, 184–5.
[279] T. Krokisius, *Erinnerungen aus dem Feldzuge 1870–71* (Berlin, 1907), 31.
[280] C. L. Hähnel, *Bei den Fahnen des XII. (kgl. Sächsischen) Armeekorps. Aufzeichnungen eines Angehörigen des 107. Regiments im Feldzug 1870/71*, 31.
[281] Ibid., 35.
[282] B. Rogge, *Bei der Garde. Erlebnisse und Eindrücke aus dem Kriegsjahre 1870/71* (Hanover, 1895), 36.
[283] C. L. Hähnel, *Bei den Fahnen*, 20.   [284] Ibid., 20–1.   [285] Ibid., 22.

the same soldier's recollection.[286] Similarly, in the ravine in front of the ridge, soldiers who had been nonchalant on entering the battle were reduced to impotence, certain years after the event that their forces 'had been much too weak'.[287] It was only 'thanks to the inactivity of the French' that the German armies were victorious on 18 August, 'but we, who were at the front of the enemy, had to bleed for it', reduced to crawling forwards 'from rock to rock' and lying under a shower of grenades for more than an hour in the vain hope of reinforcement.[288] Later, the victory could be understood as a 'moral' one, connected to the 'historical rebirth of Germany', but as it occurred troops were affected by 'a distinctly elegiac mood', created by the 'forceful quaking of the soul, great bodily exhaustion and the loss of honoured and beloved superiors and close comrades'.[289] The longer-term effects of such contradictory emotions are difficult to assess. Virtually all combatants felt that they were fundamental, however.

Middle-class memoirists' oscillation between, and combination of, pro- and anti-war sentiment reached its apogee at Sedan, to which the 130,000-strong army of MacMahon repaired from Châlons—in an attempt to reach Bazaine's 'Army of Metz'—in late August. The encounter at Sedan on 1 September was 'the most violent, momentous battle of the war, which sealed the end of the Empire and its armies', in the words of one eyewitness.[290] 'Naturally, no Frenchman believed in the capitulation at Sedan', believing that the Germans 'would leave the holy soil of France as soon as possible in unholy flight'; for their part, most Germans thought that 'the war now had to be at an end'.[291] Neither expectation proved accurate. Nonetheless, the battle came to represent the turning point of the entire conflict and the decisive step towards unification, affecting the ways in which it was later portrayed. The Hessian teacher and reservist Johannes Diehl wrote in his lavishly illustrated memoir, recalling how the news reached Metz, where he was stationed, on the same day:

> It is not the battle in and for itself that gives Sedan day such a high value, and that 2 September [the day of the capitulation] is still celebrated today by every good patriot as a day of remembrance for the fatherland, for larger and bloodier battles have been fought, but it is the success of the political turn that gives Sedan day its consecration, on which the French imperial throne foundered and the German imperial throne was founded...At first a silent joy spread amongst individual soldiers, then in a short time joy developed like a hurricane into general jubilation.[292]

[286] Ibid., 23, 25–6.
[287] W. Ernst, *Vom Rhein bis zum Kanal. Erinnerungen aus dem Feldzuge 1870–71* (Rathenow, 1893), 34.
[288] Ibid., 35, 37, 39.
[289] C. L. Hähnel, *Bei den Fahnen*, 30. As Kurt von Einsiedel, *Tagebuchblätter*, 40–1, made plain, what struck eyewitnesses were the piles of corpses and killing that had taken place at Gravelotte. Also, B. Rogge, *Bei der Garde*, 41.
[290] A. Kayser, *Erlebnisse eines rheinischen Dragoners im Feldzuge 1870/71*, 67.
[291] H. Lüders, *Ein Soldatenleben in Krieg und Frieden* (Stuttgart, 1888), 101.
[292] J. Diehl, *Meine Kriegs-Erlebnisse von 1870/71* (Minden, 1904), 42.

These sentiments stood in stark contrast to those of the soldiers who fought on 1 September. For them, the battle of Sedan seemed, in the opinion of one Hanoverian veteran of Gravelotte, like 'one of the bitterest struggles of all time'.[293]

The German forces had pursued MacMahon's army of Châlons to the north, 'as in a hunt', in the words of a Bavarian artillery officer, 'until he is compelled to move in the direction we wish him to take'.[294] Crown Prince Friedrich Wilhelm's Third Army, with 180,000 men, had been ordered to turn and sweep northward by Moltke on 26 August, veering from its course towards Châlons and Paris after reconnaissance reports had indicated that MacMahon might be heading towards Montmédy and Metz. It was joined by Crown Prince Albert of Saxony's newly formed Army of the Meuse, whose 86,000 troops (the Saxon Twelfth Corps and the Prussian Fourth Corps and Guard) had been taken from the Second Army, which was now besieging the forces of Bazaine at Metz. Since MacMahon's cavalry were allowed to run in front of the infantry, rather than hinder the progress of the German troops in the rear, the Army of Châlons was pushed against the Belgian border, prevented from moving south towards Bazaine and given the option of accepting battle around Sedan or laying down its arms in Belgium. The German General Staff were confident of their position, with Moltke telling Wilhelm I on 31 August that 'Now we have them in a mousetrap.'[295] 'How wonderfully the campaign is going and how different from what I had thought', recorded Waldersee in his diary on 30 August: 'No battle on the Moselle, none in Champagne and, instead of this, one in Metz with a reversed front and now the decisive battle on the Belgian frontier. Either we are incredibly skilful or the French strategists are terrible bunglers.'[296]

At Sedan, where MacMahon was trapped, three ridges descended to the Meuse, on which the town and 'small, unimportant fort' stood, surrounded by a valley bottom resembling 'a lake whose waters shimmered quite beautifully blue in the sunshine'.[297] The topography lent itself to the German encirclement which took place on 1 September. Paul Hassel, who—by 1870—was a history *Dozenten* at the University of Berlin and an official compiler of military reports for the Third Army, described the setting of the battle:

Sedan lies on one of the most beautiful points of the valley of the Meuse between ascending, terrace-shaped rows of hills, crowned with deciduous woods. From the heights on the right, narrow meadows lead to the Meuse below. On the left bank, left of Sedan, the town of Donchéry is situated, with its grey tiled roofs, and on both sides a plain extends, but in the middle the landscape rises, in the form of partly wooded, partly clay hills, and is framed on the horizon by the mighty, semi-circular mountain chain of the Ardennes. In the centre-ground, several hamlets can be seen through the

[293] A. Bock, *1870–71. Feldzugserlebnisse und Erinnerungen eines Einjährig-Freiwilligen im 3. Garde-Rgt.*, 2nd edn (Leipzig, 1904), 67.

[294] H. S. Edwards, *The Germans in France*, 98.

[295] H. v. Moltke to Wilhelm I, 31 Aug. 1870, cited in G. Wawro, *The Franco-Prussian War*, 211.

[296] A. v. Waldersee, *Denkwürdigkeiten*, vol. 1, 92.

[297] Louis Leinenweber, *Meine Kriegserlebnisse 1870/71. Erinnerungen aus dem Feldzuge* (Pirmasens, 1911), 81, played a peripheral part in the battle as a Bavarian cavalryman. On the insignificance of Sedan as a fort, see C. L. Hähnel, *Bei den Fahnen*, 75.

bushes and in the woods. On the right, the Meuse meanders…and so goes around the central hills, enclosing a spit of land…MacMahon had divided his army on the evening of 31 August between Bazeilles, Sedan, Floing und Givonne…The strategic task of the German troops was so exactly predetermined by the terrain that they can easily be understood even by a layperson. It was a question of encircling the enemy in the east in such a way that any escape on this side was made impossible, and, in addition, it was a question of keeping it from crossing the Belgian border by going round behind it to block off the northern passes. Once this happened, only one position remained open, the gap towards the west…But in this place, too, care had been given to create a barrier.[298]

Looking at this disposition of forces, Blumenthal believed that it was 'unmistakeably evident' that the Germans would win.[299] For the French, however, Sedan was 'a desperate struggle', where the superiority of the *chassepot* and *mitrailleuse* could be used to good effect.[300] This recollection of the fighting, it can be held, was decisive for German combatants (see Figure 9.3 for Werner's retrospective view).

The sun 'lit up the masses of the French army opposite us glaringly', remembered the Rhinelander Adolf Kayser, who had been posted with the General Staff for the day and who saw the fighting around Donchéry and Sedan at close quarters.[301] The artillery, including the '500 German field guns converging' on the French forces, made 'a deafening noise of hell'.[302] The fighting to the west of Sedan, where Kayser was an 'eye witness', had begun after 7.00 a.m., three hours after the Bavarians had started to move against Bazeilles to the south and two hours after the Saxons to the east.[303] C. L. Hähnel gave a revealing account of what it was like to fight in the Saxon contingent. Waking early in the morning, they left their pack and extra ammunition behind and started to march to an unknown fate: 'No one amongst us had the slightest idea, after this early departure, that the march to a battle that would be counted amongst the most decisive in world history had begun.'[304] Most thought that they were on a forced march in pursuit of the fleeing enemy. As they approached the battle along the valley, their vision was obscured by mist, giving 'everyone the impression that he might fall into an invisible, deep abyss at any moment'.[305] As the mist lifted, the Saxon troops were able to launch a surprise attack—marked with a triumphant 'Ha!' in the text—on the thousands of unsuspecting French infantry opposite them, but they were soon overpowered, with inadequate supplies of bullets, relying on reinforcements who looked increasingly unlikely to arrive in time: 'Where, in God's name, were our comrades?'[306] Facing a superior enemy, they awaited death:

A terrible disappointment now weighed down on our souls with a great load. Until then, the division fighting here with fresh courage had felt to be a closely connected

[298] P. Hassel, *Von der dritten Armee. Kriegsgeschichtliche Skizzen aus dem Feldzuge von 1870–1871* (Leipzig, 1872), 222–5.

[299] A. v. Blumenthal (ed.), *Journals of Field Marshal Count von Blumenthal for 1866 and 1870–71* (London, 1903), 111.

[300] C. L. Hähnel, *Bei den Fahnen*, 82.   [301] A. Kayser, *Erlebnisse*, 68.

[302] Ibid.   [303] Ibid., 69.   [304] C. L. Hähnel, *Bei den Fahnen*, 77.

[305] Ibid., 80.   [306] Ibid., 85.

Figure 9.3 Anton von Werner, *Sedan-Panorama* (1883)

Source: D. Bartmann (ed.), *Anton von Werner: Geschichte in Bildern* (Munich, 1993), 273–5.

part of powerful mass, pushing forwards in the thick fog. These masses could no longer be seen; it was as if the earth had swallowed them up. What was to be found here in the wide gap were weak, torn-apart sections of the 1st and a few men from other companies who had come too far to the right in the thick fog, whom the over-powerful opponent, moving forward in a semi-circle, was seeking to overrun. The division withdrew quickly several hundred yards back up the hill and reached, not without losses, the wide road which went from La Moncelle in a northeasterly direction...Here, the men of the 1st Company, pushed back by enemy superiority, quickly gathered in a violent storm of bullets. They lay in great haste on their stomachs across the road and fired into the advancing swarms of enemy troops...The enemy swarms lying in the valley were being visibly strengthened. Their break-through could only be prevented with extreme effort, above all by artillery...How long the battle just described lasted could not, in the excitement, be determined...In the face of this violent development of the enemy attack, many had to come to the terrible realization, under such conditions, that their bullets were coming to an end and that imminent replacements could not be hoped for...Now, for them, those terrible hours approached that were counted by all those fighting to be amongst the most difficult of their lives and that persist indissolubly as such in their memories.[307]

What made the experience so 'oppressive' and 'horrific' was not merely the 'fear of death', which they had become used to at Gravelotte, but the 'terrifying slowness with which—for hour upon hour—a seemingly certain death, an irredeemable downfall approached'.[308] Although support arrived at the last minute and victory created 'an unspeakably happy and peaceful mood of the soul', it was 'dampened and impaired by the natural reverse which followed the overexertion, going to the most extreme limits, of every mental and physical resource'.[309]

After the battle, the dead, with 'terrible dismemberments', lay 'densely one beside the other', recalled Kayser.[310] 'I am not a man of faint-hearted fear and over-developed sensitivity', he continued: 'Quite the opposite—I departed willingly and happily, although I knew that I would have to deal with the thought of experiencing and seeing terrible things.'[311] 'But truly!' he concluded, he was only able to accept such 'misery' because he was defending 'our most holy goods, our home soil against a brutal enemy'.[312] It was this combination of an heroic, publicly sanctioned victory and privately harboured, often repressed recollections of violence which combatants—especially enthusiastic, patriotic, middle-class memoirists—found precarious.

THE COMBAT EXPERIENCE OF ORDINARY SOLDIERS

Most combatants in 1870–1, as in earlier wars, were not *bürgerlich*. Their reflections on their experiences of warfare were rarely published. They were, however, voluminous, painting a picture of the campaign for millions of anxious, expectant

---

[307] Ibid., 83–8.　　　[308] Ibid., 88.　　　[309] Ibid., 95–6.
[310] A. Kayser, *Erlebnisse*, 79.　　　[311] Ibid., 80.　　　[312] Ibid.

families, friends, relatives, and local communities. 'I and Lang and Jakobi from Dornholzhausen, and Schmit from Großrechtenbach are together', wrote the Hessian Lance Corporal Friedrich Ludwig to his wife and parents on 26 July 1870: 'The others from Niederklee are in 3rd Company.'[313] His subsequent letters contained greetings to 'all those from Niederklee' and to 'all friends and relatives', together with assurances that 'We Niederkleer are all healthy still.'[314] Such correspondence, or the news gleaned from it, was passed around the village. Naturally, ordinary soldiers like Ludwig had written home—as far as they were able—during previous wars, especially during the campaigns of 1864 and 1866, but improving literacy, changing habits, a long campaign, an unprecedented mobilization of conscripts, and the expansion of the military postal service transformed the practice in 1870–1. The Prussian *Feldpost* had carried about 30,000 letters in 1866. Between 16 July 1870 and 31 March 1871, that of the North German Confederation delivered 89,659,000, as well as 2,354,310 newspapers and 1,853,686 packages.[315]

This volume of post created a new expectation that information should pass directly from the theatre of war to home and back. Ludwig's protest in mid-September 1870 that this was his ninth letter to date, after his family had written on 28 August that they had received nothing, was indicative of the appetite for news.[316] Some soldiers devoted much of their letters to a relentless berating of their parents' or wives' lack of contact: 'Have you not had a single hour of time, during the 26 days I have been away from home, to write to me?' asked the Rhenish conscript Johann Overmann on 17 August: 'I cannot get enthusiastic, as it is, about the fact that I still haven't received a letter from you.'[317] Others simply rushed off 'a couple of lines' on postcards, which were regularly distributed in tens of thousands by the army for the first time in 1870.[318] Even barely literate conscripts like Gerhard Becker, writing from Amiens to a wounded comrade, were anxious to pass on their news (*Neuigkeiten*), albeit with excuses for their poor handwriting: 'You will not be angry that the paper is so bad I had it still and the time and chance to write you are worth more to me than a roll of paper.'[319] 'I'll stop one more thing if you can do so much then go to the house of my mother she will be so happy if you tell her something of me just ask for widow Becker', he went on.[320] In this fashion, military post maintained a 'connection for so many hundreds of thousands with their

[313] F. Ludwig to his parents and wife, 26 July 1870, Hessisches Staatsarchiv, Marburg.

[314] F. Ludwig to his parents and wife, 26 July, 5 Aug., and 16 Sept. 1870, Hessisches Staatsarchiv, Marburg.

[315] F. Kühlich, *Die deutschen Soldaten im Krieg von 1870/71*, 207–9.

[316] F. Ludwig to his parents and wife, 16 Sept. 1870, Hessisches Staatsarchiv, Marburg.

[317] J. Overmann to his parents, 17 Aug. 1870, *Feldpostbriefe*, Universitäts- und Landesbibliothek, Bonn. See also J. Overmann, 23 Aug. 1870, *Feldpostbriefe*, Universitäts- und Landesbibliothek, Bonn.

[318] Theodor Vietoris to his brother John, 24 Aug. 1870, *Feldpostbriefe*, Universitäts- und Landesbibliothek, Bonn. The postcards, called 'Feldpost-Correspondenzkarten', were a military version of 'Correspondenzkarten', introduced by the postal service shortly before: F. Kühlich, *Die deutschen Soldaten im Krieg von 1870/71*, 207–9.

[319] J. Becker to 'Comrade Mathis', 19 May 1871, *Feldpostbriefe*, Universitäts- und Landesbibliothek, Bonn.

[320] Ibid.

Heimat', wrote the army chaplain Richard Schuster: its 'blessed effects' were 'easy to behold'.[321]

The impression that ordinary soldiers gave of the Franco-German War, which was generally accepted to be a *Volkskrieg*, differed from that given by many middle-class memoirists. Such 'men between 20 and 30 years old' were often equated with 'the entire *Volk*'.[322] Later, they were seen as model patriots worthy of 'the unshake-able trust' and 'pride' that middle-class comrades had 'in our German *Volk*', feel-ings that were especially heart-felt amongst those who had 'gone on a seven-month campaign with them in the rank and file' as 'ordinary soldiers' and who had had 'the chance to see and to hear how soldiers enjoy themselves, chat and dream'.[323] At the time, such conscripts' attitudes—and those of their relatives—were more difficult to gauge. 'They naturally were more inclined to see the worst, that which pressed and menaced themselves and their families amidst such rapid movements of events over the last few days', wrote Friedrich Rückert, from Hesse-Darmstadt, of the reaction of 'ordinary people' (*die einfache Bevölkerung*) to the outbreak of hostilities: 'The political scope and substance of the coming events was mostly still incomprehensible for them. They held this war too, like every other one, to be a serious misfortune, which intruded into their *Heimat* and well-being.'[324] The response of the parents of the young teacher Karl Schürmann, from the Sauerland, was typical of many, not wanting to expose 'their only son to the changeable dan-gers of a war'.[325] Schürmann himself was sure that 'the Prussians would win', but he conceded that 'there was no lack of anxious voices who said that the French army, with its *chassepots* and *mitrailleuses*, would be superior to ours'.[326]

Such anxiety about the 'much-feared *chassepot*' and 'very good soldiers, who are known everywhere to be victors', as the Rhinelander Friedrich Schäfer recalled his lieutenant saying, was common.[327] In Dresden, 'the mood was depressed rather than joyfully enthusiastic', wrote one officer in his diary on 18 July 1870: 'The simple soldier was not so certain of our cause. Our departure occurred in corres-ponding fashion,... in quite a flat mood before numerous but silent spectators.'[328] In the railway stations of Berlin, the 'send-off is uneasy and oppressive', noted the

---

[321] R. Schuster, *Erlebnisse und Beobachtungen eines deutschen Feldgeistlichen während des Krieges 1870–71* (Darmstadt, 1871), 78.

[322] H. Schmitthenner, *Erlebnisse eines freiwilligen badischen Grenadiers*, 136.

[323] Ibid., 135–6. Schmitthenner was a Badenese student volunteer at the time and later became a pastor.

[324] C. C. Rückert, *Mit dem Tornister. Ungeschminkte Feldzugs-Erinnerungen eines Infanteristen aus dem Jahre 1870* (Frankfurt, 1912), 24. See also the volunteer Karl Zeitz's recollection in *Kriegserinnerungen eines Kriegsfreiwilligen aus den Jahren 1870/71* (Altenburg, 1893), 29, that an old reservist, 'a man in poor circumstances who had to feed his wife and children at home', 'clearly held me to be mad'. Military service for the reservist was nothing but a 'burden'.

[325] K. Schürmann, *Selbsterlebtes. Kriegserinnerungen eines Volksschullehrers* (Remscheid, 1895), 4.

[326] Ibid., 3–4.

[327] F. Schäfer, 'Aus dem Tagebuch von 1870/71', *Feldpostbriefe*, Universitäts- und Landesbibliothek, Bonn.

[328] W. v. Klenck, cited in A. Seyferth, *Die Heimatfront 1870/71. Wirtschaft und Gesellschaft im deutsch-französischen Krieg* (Paderborn, 2007), 25. Karl Klein, *Fröschweiler Chronik. Kriegs- und Friedensbilder aus dem Jahr 1870* (Munich, 1905), 3, reported widespread fear, as well as strong feelings against Prussia, in French Alsace at the start of the war.

illustrator and critic Ludwig Pietsch: 'No happy laughing, no brave joke, few animated faces amongst the departing or the remaining people; in every expression,
the heavy question varying a thousand-fold—what will your return be like?!'[329] By
contrast, in villages like that described by Leonard Heiners, near to Trier, opposition and foreboding were much more openly expressed: during mass,

> no, I have never experienced such a thing, and I'll never experience it again. Women
> wailed loudly. Pastor Antwerpen was himself scarcely in a state to bring the mass to an
> end. After communion, he wanted to give a speech, but impossible. Tears ran down
> his cheeks and his throat as if he was being choked . . . On the parade ground, the scene
> was heart-breaking.[330]

The experiences of such soldiers, and those of the families to whom they wrote,
were less likely to be expressed in patriotic terms and framed in an optimistic way
than those of their middle-class counterparts.

Conscripts seem to have adapted quickly to the routines and structures of the
army, internalizing and reproducing its hierarchical system of values and statuses.
Certainly, many officers' views of their 'men' (*Kerls*), or 'children' (*Kinder*), were
idealized, overlooking unarticulated resentments and regular minor acts of disobedience.[331] The volunteer doctor and 'outsider' Heinrich Fritsch gave a rare,
frank account of such disobedience from an insider's point of view:

> I would like to claim that a soldier, if he is firmly decided to save his dear life and bring
> his limbs safely back home, can easily do so, if he acts with a degree of consistency.
> I knew one of them who regularly sat by the side of the road after two hours of march-
> ing with an affectedly miserable countenance. His handsome, healthy, round face
> betrayed his lies! 'Ah, Herr Doktor, give me something so that I can go a bit further',
> he called in whining complaint. He received Hofmann's drops and promised to go on.
> Not two minutes later—bump—he was lying in the ditch again, as if he had been shot
> dead. Now, his moaning started again: he wanted to advance so much, but he couldn't,
> he was suffocating etc. Finally, one said to oneself that one had better and more
> important things to do than to talk the feeble into doing things. To give courage by
> the spoonful was not something that we carried in our medicine case. On the morning
> after battle or fighting, one could be sure to see the shirker again. Lying in the ditch,
> he inched his way slowly into a wood or field and waited there until the regiment had
> gone by. As soon as it got dark, he slipped back, feigned great exhaustion as troops
> marched by and wound his way back to his company during the night. Although his
> comrades made bad jokes at his expense, his love of life far outweighed any feeling of
> duty. Decades later, I saw the same brave warrior again, chair of every possible veterans'
> association, high-minded patriot, ready at any time to sacrifice his life and blood on
> the altar of the fatherland.[332]

[329] L. Pietsch, *Von Berlin bis Paris. Kriegsbilder 1870–1871* (Berlin, 1871), 3–4.

[330] L. Heiners, 'Tagebuch und Erlebnisse aus meiner Dienstziet beim Königin Augusta Garde
Grenadier Reg. No. 4', *Feldpostbriefe*, Universitäts- und Landesbibliothek, Bonn.

[331] On the terminology used and the values internalized, see F. Kühlich, *Die deutschen Soldaten im
Krieg von 1870/71*, 63–85. T. Rohkrämer, *Der Militarismus der 'kleinen Leute'*, 120, rightly points out
that commanders were often called 'father' by troops.

[332] H. Fritsch, *Erinnerungen und Betrachtungen* (Bonn, 1913), 56–7.

Sometimes, officers too could demonstrate a similar lack of courage, exposing them to 'dangerous' ridicule.[333] 'Undermining discipline', jokes could be directed at an 'unloved officer', 'often quite unjustly'.[334] Thus, the sword of one officer had reportedly been shot from him. He had a servant whom he treated very badly and called him with the three-syllable 'Friederich': 'He was riding one time at the back of the company. All at once, someone called from the front with an anxious voice in a dumb tone, "Friederich, ye shoot". Then, another soldier elsewhere squeaked, "Friederich, ye shoot", in a descant voice. And so it went on for an hour.'[335] When the same officer retired to bed, he found his sheets had been stolen, forcing him to put a guard in front of his hut. Eventually, he went home and 'was seen no more': 'He had not experienced much joy in this campaign.'[336] Such experiences were probably quite common. They were outnumbered, however, by instances of obedience, duty, and 'honourable' behaviour.

Richard Martin, a Saxon student who chose deliberately to remain in the ranks, revealed how even a sceptic like himself had a grudging respect for officers and the military virtues which they embodied. When considering his 'military training', the reader would perhaps expect 'that I did my preparatory studies in a war academy and then began a glorious career as a member of the General Staff or an army commander', he began his memoir, parodying other accounts of this kind.[337] Instead, he did 'not even rise to be a "shiny-buttoned lance corporal"', entering the German army 'as a completely ordinary soldier' and also leaving it as such, despite his education and 'quite extraordinary martial talents', which lay dormant in him and which would 'certainly have pushed him towards an outstanding role as a leader amongst guerrilla fighters'.[338] Although his father wanted him to become a one-year volunteer officer like his brother, Martin stubbornly refused, serving the minimum six weeks reserved for trainee teachers, which later issued in 'all sorts of collisions' as a result of his 'self-denial'.[339] During his training, he was regularly upbraided and punished for refusing to treat officers as his superiors.[340] Nonetheless, during the campaign itself, despite expressing shock at the losses incurred at St Privat and noting with curiosity 'how a great number of ours were made into prostrate servants by the first shots' of battle, he was full of admiration for the courage and heroism of officers and NCOs:

> Admittedly, the *courage* that the *soldier of the modern army* must show is of *a different kind* from that of our ancestors or that of Greek and Roman heroes. For the most part, it can only exist today in *contempt for the risk of death*; in modern battles, it only comes to a struggle of man against man in the rarest cases, for death-bringing bullets reach the majority beforehand from a great distance. Yes, in the battles of the last Franco-German war, many were wounded and killed without ever having seen a single enemy in the face. How should heroic attitudes manifest themselves here other than in the suppression of the fear of death? The weakest and militarily worst schooled man can be greater in this respect than many of gigantic stature who show themselves to be

[333] Ibid., 57–8.　　[334] Ibid., 58–9.　　[335] Ibid.
[336] Ibid., 59.　　[337] R. Martin, *Kriegserinnerungen*, 1.
[338] Ibid.　　[339] Ibid., 9.　　[340] Ibid., 10.

anxious and timid when they think of being shot dead from an unexpected position. I believe that I am right to designate the courage of our modern soldiers as a predominantly *passive virtue*.

Nevertheless, *this type of heroism*, too, deserves our respect, for it betrays a great strength of soul and self-control. It is a question of struggling against the strongest internal urge of man, the urge for self-preservation... The common man, who perhaps will not always find the moral strength in himself, looks in battle to his superiors, to the conduct which they display in a hail of bullets. And, there, I must say that *the conduct of our officers, with very few exceptions, was beyond all praise*...One could assuredly stick a death's head on the helmet of *every* German soldier, as amongst the Brunswick hussars, for every one of them must have seen themselves devoted to death from the moment that they began the career of an officer.[341]

Non-commissioned officers, too, showed similar courage: 'Much virtue and honour can be found in these men', who were characterized in battle by 'great unflappability'.[342] Such officers provided the men with an example to follow and to transmit the values of the regiment and army, conceded Martin. Thus, when the company's flag was unfurled, although it was 'merely a wooden pole with a piece of green and white material on it', it constituted a '*symbol of belonging together* and *loyalty to king and fatherland*'.[343] Many other ordinary soldiers dreamed of getting the iron cross.[344] To them, the army was an accepted institutional framework. It ensured that the majority of conscripts went on doing their duty, wounding and killing the enemy and—themselves—facing injury and death.

Such soldiers were more matter-of-fact than middle-class memoirists. 'With every step, you saw new misery, but in war and in danger you become hardened', commented one conscript simply: 'Although you do everything to ease the situation of an unfortunate comrade, all the misery passes by more quickly than in other times and there is a good side to it.'[345] To Martin, his comrades, marching unsuspectingly to battle on 18 August, were 'dumb blokes', with little idea what they would soon be facing.[346] Some of their accounts, like that of Joseph Hesse, give the impression of troops merely being shunted from one place to another:

On 21 July, we moved from Hanover to Anderten, where we stayed until the 30th; then we went to Bingen, where we arrived on the 31st, and from there we marched to Lauheim, where we stayed the night... On the 15th [August], we came to Ponte-Muoson [*sic*], where we were woken by an alarm at 3 o'clock, and from there marched to Marslatour, where we entered battle around 3 o'clock. In the evening, we went to a bivouac, on the 17th we had a rest. On the 18th, we came under fire

---

[341] Ibid., 175–7. See also Ernst Stier, *Unter Prinz Friedrich Karl. Erlebnisse eines Musketiers vom X. Armeekorps im Feldzug 1870–71* (Munich, 1883), 62, who labelled the troops—himself included— 'leaderless sheep', once their officer had been killed.

[342] R. Martin, *Kriegserinnerungen*, 177.   [343] Ibid., 171.

[344] P. Mertens to J. Rumpen, 24 Nov. 1870, *Feldpostbriefe*, Universitäts- und Landesbibliothek, Bonn.

[345] A. Roese, in his diary, commenting on the battle of Wörth, cited in C. G. Krüger, 'German Suffering in the Franco-German War', 406.

[346] R. Martin, *Kriegserinnerungen*, 166.

again near Gravelotte, we went to a bivouac in the evening, where we stayed for two days.[347]

Hesse's 'Notiz-Buch' gives no indication that he had just experienced some of the bloodiest fighting of the nineteenth century. The emotional content of his record of the war was reserved for the *Soldatenlieder*—'Where courage and strength burn in German souls'—which he had painstakingly written down at the end of his notebook.[348]

Such separation and alternation between sentiment and mundane detail were common, reflecting conscripts' lack of practice and habit as diarists and correspondents, which they overcame because of the perceived momentousness of the events, and hinting at the duality of their attitudes to the campaign, of whose course and causes they had little overview and over whose outcome they had little control.[349] 'The days', wrote one conscript in early August, 'are too long', filled with wearisome marching and other tasks from before dawn until nightfall.[350] 'Our people had, at best, two nights free of guard duty', complained another in November: 'And, in addition, we had rainy weather for at least two-thirds of the entire time.'[351] Bad weather, troubles with money, news and letters from home, and other details of daily life on the campaign made up the bulk of soldiers' correspondence.[352] Reports of battles, with few embellishments, were followed by hopes of an imminent homecoming. 'Dear Parents', wrote Johann Over on 2 February 1871, 'Hopefully, there will now be peace, which Germany as well as France yearns for, and then we shall soon come back to Germany again, if we don't end up with an occupation.'[353] 'The time of the war is over dear friend what I am also happy about thank God', rejoiced Gerhard Becker to his friend on 19 May: 'When we come home then make sure that you are fresh again I think that we are back home for the Duisdorf fair then we want to celebrate together if that is alright.'[354] Such tours of duty came to an end as they had started, with little fuss and fanfare. Many soldiers' overriding feeling seems to have been relief that the campaign was over.

To some soldiers, killing—and risking death—was part of the daily toil of life in the army. Receiving his 'baptism of fire' at Gravelotte on 18 August, Eduard

[347] J. Hesse, 'Notiz-Buch', *Feldpostbriefe*, Universitäts- und Landesbibliothek, Bonn. For a similar account, see F. Ludwig to his parents and wife, 5 Aug. 1870, Hessisches Staatsarchiv, Marburg: 'Wir sind am 4ten August über die Grenze gerückt, des Nachts um zwei Uhr, im furchtbaren Regenwetter des morgens kamen wier an den Feind um 9 Uhr und hat gedauert bis den Mittag 4 Uhr, in welcher die Franzosen geschlagen worden sind. Von unser Companie sind drei gefallen, ich bin aber noch gesund und unverletzt.'

[348] J. Hesse, 'Notiz-Buch', *Feldpostbriefe*, Universitäts- und Landesbibliothek, Bonn.

[349] It was common for soldiers to acknowledge that their correspondents did not like writing: for example, Heinrich Kamphausen to his brother, Wilhelm Kamphausen, 12 Sept. 1870, ibid.

[350] H. Lohmanns, 2 Aug. 1870, ibid.

[351] P. Mertens to J. Rumpen, 24 Nov. 1870, ibid. See also F. Ludwig, 9 Sept. 1870, Hessisches Staatsarchiv, Marburg.

[352] See, for instance, Johann Over, 18 Aug.; 2, 4, 12, 16, 21, 23, and 26 Sept.; 20 and 27 Oct.; 19, 14, 22, and 25 Nov.; 9, 16, 24, and 28 Dec. 1870; 8, 10, 14, and 21 Jan.; 2, 7, 8, 14, 22, and 24 Feb.; 2, 7, 15, 19, 26, and 27 Mar.; 13 and 14 Apr.; 9 and 15 May; 5 and 29 June 1871, *Feldpostbriefe*, Universitäts- und Landesbibliothek, Bonn.

[353] J. Over to his parents, 2 Feb. 1871, ibid.

[354] G. Becker to 'Comrade Mathis', 19 May 1871, ibid.

Merckens wrote to his parents a day after the event that 'we believed at about 11 o'clock there would be no work (*keine Arbeit*) for us today', having heard the guns firing in the distance since early yesterday.[355] Suddenly, though, as they were heating the kettle for coffee, the thunder of cannon sounded and they were given the signal to advance. 'Scarcely had we left the wood before we were noticed by the French and greeted with a shower of shells', he went on: 'We went a few hundred yards further and then the work started.'[356] Because they did not have a good overview from their position, they went further forward for another fifteen to twenty minutes, slowly getting used to the exploding munitions: 'In the meantime, we became accustomed to the hail of shells which had, indeed, caused our hearts to beat faster at the start.'[357] As his artillery unit began to launch shells into the enemy positions in the wood opposite, Merckens was astonished that 'one could remain so cold-blooded during a battle', as if they were on the training ground.[358] As they noticed that they were achieving successes, 'our enthusiasm increased and we took aim and fired more snappily'.[359] Hitting a French munitions wagon, which 'flew in the air', Merckens was praised by his captain: 'this shot was better for me than if someone had given me a gift of a hundred *Thaler*'.[360] Despite setting the notorious Moscow farm on fire and creating a 'terrible rain of iron', which the enemy's 'people could not bear for long', the artilleryman continued to conceive of his task as 'work'.[361] This attitude appears to have been shared by many others, including infantrymen such as Robert Lauermann, who reported from Mainz to his wife on 27 July 1870 that everyone wanted to get the job done. Fearing a French attack and recognizing regretfully ('Thank God if we stay here') that they would not be able to remain where they were, away from danger, 'all are convinced that it will finally come to a battle': 'we are all happy, for the longer the attack is delayed, the longer we must stay here'.[362] Once they themselves had been under fire, however, few soldiers remained so industrious and commonsensical.

Before battle, rank-and-file troops were rarely tempted to dramatize their plight, preferring to note simply—like Carl Ueberfeldt on 22 August—that they would soon be 'under enemy fire'.[363] Even after fighting, many were stoical and taciturn, with Heinrich Becker's postcard home after the battle of Gravelotte on 18 October 1870 typical: 'God did not abandon us. But many a comrade is no longer there.'[364] 'I am', wrote Peter Konen laconically at around the same time, 'healthy, thank God.'[365] The majority, however, were moved by what they had experienced to write at greater length. Johann Hohn had fought on the 18th from 4.00 a.m. to 9.00 p.m. 'I thank God that I remained without injury under a rain of bullets and grenades', he confessed to his father: 'When we go to battle again is not known to

[355] E. Merckens to his parents, 19 Aug. 1870, ibid.   [356] Ibid.

[357] Ibid.   [358] Ibid.   [359] Ibid.   [360] Ibid.   [361] Ibid.

[362] R. Lauermann to his wife, 27 July 1870, ibid.

[363] C. Ueberfeldt to his parents and siblings, 22 Aug. 1870, ibid.

[364] H. Becker to his parents and relative, 19 Aug. 1870, ibid. W. Bührer, 'Volksreligiosität und Kriegserleben. Bayerische Soldaten im Deutsch-Französischen Krieg 1870/71', in F. Böll (ed.), *Volksreligiosität und Kriegserleben* (Munster, 1997), 48–65.

[365] P. Konen to his wife and children, 23 Aug. 1870, *Feldpostbriefe*, Universitäts- und Landesbibliothek, Bonn.

us. God may give his blessing to each.'[366] As he watched the wounded being brought in by stretcher, he found it 'indescribable': 'I would have much more to write but unfortunately for this one has no rest.'[367] Since the French had retreated to Metz, seeking 'support there in a fortress', with us 'behind them', the fighting was likely to recommence immediately.[368] Johann Kochem described the grenades, which 'exploded above us and flew around and over us like doves', obliging his comrades to hide behind a wall.[369] He had been wounded above the eye in the fighting but remained on the field until 10.00 p.m., pushing back the French 'with many losses'.[370] Similarly, Ferdinand Wallmann, who had already witnessed 'terrible fire' before the battle of Gravelotte, gave a fuller, franker report of the fighting on the 18th: 'Yesterday, a great battle was again waged and we were under terrible grenade fire for seven hours in a wood.'[371] Underlining the horror of the fighting, he counted the shells ('at least 200 grenades'), before clamming up: 'I cannot describe this terrible thing for you.'[372] He was hit but not badly wounded. 'Many comrades have gone', he concluded.[373] On the 24th, he repeated the same words: 'I cannot now write for you everything terrible, the battle lasted into the night.'[374] 'How many prayers of thanks climbed up to the heavens that evening?' asked Friedrich Schäfer in his diary.[375] His own company had lost 107 dead and wounded out of 150 or so. As they had marched into battle on the 16th, 'the first already lay there dead and wounded' before the last had entered the fray: 'The reaper had a rich harvest here. It seemed as if the entire French army had trained its guns on us.'[376] When their commander gave a speech amidst the debris of the regiment, 'tears rolled from our eyes'.[377] Schäfer was proud of his company's achievement, but he also 'longed for a quick end to the war'.[378] His sentiments stood in stark contrast to his earlier bravado, as he had 'joyfully answered "yes"' to the prospect of enlistment.[379]

Leonard Heiners had not shown such bravado during mobilization, having already fought in 1864 and 1866.[380] Even for a seasoned soldier like himself, however, the experience of fighting in 1870 proved shocking: 'I took part in the battle near Königgrätz—also a hard-fought battle on a great, nine-mile-long battlefield—but in comparison with the battle near Gravelotte, it only counts as a skirmish.'[381] The preceding marches appear to have been sober, crossing the French border after a speech by his commander—about which he made no comment—and to the tune of 'Ich bin ein Preuße, kennt ihr meine Farben', which he noted without

---

[366] J. Hohn to his father, 21 Aug. 1870, ibid.   [367] Ibid.

[368] Ibid.   [369] J. Kochem to his father and siblings, 19 Aug. 1870, ibid.

[370] Ibid.   [371] F. Wallmann to his parents, 15 and 19 Aug. 1870, ibid.

[372] Ibid.   [373] Ibid.   [374] F. Wallmann to his parents, 24 Aug. 1870, ibid.

[375] F. Schäfer, 'Aus meinem Tagebuch von 1870/71', ibid., 6.

[376] Ibid., 5.   [377] Ibid., 7.   [378] Ibid., 8.   [379] Ibid., 1.

[380] See another soldier from Bochum, now thinking of his family in addition to his previous experiences: 'If I rushed to the colours happily in 1866 as a single man, the departure in July 1870 was very difficult for me. I had married in between times and called two small children, a boy and a girl, my own': cited in T. Rohkrämer, *Der Militarismus der 'kleinen Leute'*, 89.

[381] L. Heiners, 'Tagebuch und Erlebnisse aus meiner Dienstzeit', ibid., 27.

elaboration.[382] That night, 'the rain fell in streams', extinguishing their campfires and leaving them 'soaked to the bone'.[383] By 10 August, the troops were on the Saar, again under heavy rain and 'a tempest-like storm', which blew away helmets, caps, and bread baskets.[384] A week later, they were near the battlefield of Mars-la-Tour, watching the French and German wounded come past them on the road. 'We were now certain that, on the next day, a bloody decisive battle would take place', Heiners wrote of 17 June: 'It was a pitch-black night. Many a man would have had a dark premonition that this night would be his last.'[385] The mood was one of quiet foreboding, far removed from the speech of Prinz Felix Salm-Salm, the commander of Heiners' battalion of fusiliers who had called for Bazaine's head as retribution for the execution of Maximilian in Mexico in 1867.[386] 'To understand this declaration of the prince, one has to know the history of the unfortunate Emperor Maximilian of Mexico', he explained, tacitly acknowledging that his readers would probably not know.[387] Rather than worry about revenge or glory, Heiners immersed himself in 'thoughts of my distant, beloved *Heimat*, where I had left my young wife and all my dear ones, perhaps never to see them again. I drew my rosary towards me and prayed with it more than one time. Perhaps the last time.'[388] In the camp before dawn, the troops ate ham and eggs and drank their coffee, 'like brothers—for the last time'.[389]

When the fighting started in the late afternoon of the 18th, after a lot of waiting around in earshot of the 'thunder of cannon', Heiners' consciousness altered: 'On the battlefield, everything disappears. One thinks of nothing. Before an imminent battle, many do think back to the past, to their beloved at home. During battle, as on the training ground, a feeling of duty and participation.'[390] With the troops advancing, the fusilier saw 'many fall or fly through the air after receiving a shot'.[391] The officers of his company were soon dead, leaving a lieutenant of the reserves alone, blabbering that 'I don't feel myself capable in this important moment of taking over the command of the company'.[392] Scarcely ten minutes later, the corporal who had taken command fell 'in an arc-like movement, with five shots in the chest in an area the size of a hand'.[393] His last words were, 'Heiners, my wife and children, Jesus!'[394] Those 'actively participating in a battle' could not describe it—'that is, its course and state of affairs'—but they could leave a record of their experiences: 'He can only recount what he has himself participated in.'[395] Heiners' own account was mixed: he was impressed by the dutifulness of every soldier, allegedly 'infused with enthusiasm'.[396] Yet he was also overwhelmed by the sensations of battle, which he could recollect—and could not banish—after the event; 'the persistent thunder of cannon from both sides, the peculiar rattle of *mitrailleuse*, the constant small arms fire of the infantry, the roar of the cavalry, the cries of pain of the wounded, the groaning of the dying'.[397] As the 'terrible thunder of the cannon' relented, the soldier was thanking 'his creator in silence' that he had survived when

[382] Ibid., 26. [383] Ibid. [384] Ibid. [385] Ibid., 27.
[386] Ibid. [387] Ibid. [388] Ibid. [389] Ibid., 26–7.
[390] Ibid., 28. [391] Ibid. [392] Ibid. [393] Ibid.
[394] Ibid. [395] Ibid., 27. [396] Ibid. [397] Ibid.

he received 'a knock on the head', causing him to fall down.[398] Getting back up to shoot, he saw that his left arm was 'full of blood': 'Now, I noticed for the first time that I was wounded. I had taken a shot right through my mouth.'[399] Having lost his bandages, 'loss of blood, an empty stomach and over-exhaustion brought me to collapse', only coming round later, 'in the company of other comrades of fortune in a barn, still partly burning'.[400] Tortured by a 'burning thirst', which was almost worse than his wounds, Heiners passed 'the most horrible night of my life, and it will always remain so, as long as I live'.[401] Eleven men died in the barn that night. Looking back on the battle, after which he was sent home wounded, he was unable to find words for it: 'Dear God, the sights of a battlefield cannot be described. They are too terrible.'[402]

Army chaplains did describe such sights.[403] Because they were close to the fighting front and charged with looking after the men, they were able, as one of them phrased it, 'to see behind the scenes' of 'the great, earth-shaking drama'.[404] After most other observers and survivors had passed on to the next confrontation, it was 'interesting', when 'the curtain behind a terrible battle scene was lowered, to look behind the scenes and observe the wounded after the fighting, the sick in the hospitals behind the bivouac', 'the noise of a battle', or the 'wasteland and destruction wrought by fighting'.[405] The same cleric concluded:

> It is clear that much which is behind the scenes is very different from elsewhere, that the battlefield—full of the dead and wounded after fighting—makes a more painful impression than when battalions press forwards with 'hurrahs' and squadrons rattle their way into enemy positions amidst the notes of military music and the thunder of guns.

This was the 'inner history of the war', which often had greater meaning for those conducting it than 'the great actions of the army and the state'.[406] 'The momentous times' seemed slightly different in 'our eyes and hearts', noted another chaplain, because

> much was nearer to us, and we fixed our gaze on what others passed over without noticing; in particular, the behaviour and existence of the common soldier in extraordinary and generally applicable relations were much more uninhibitedly revealed to us, since the hindrance of the immediate subordination of service did not intervene.[407]

What he found, although unwilling to enter into the debate about the 'moral conditions and effects of war' and wanting to steer a course between soldiers as 'saints'

---

[398] Ibid., 28.   [399] Ibid.   [400] Ibid.   [401] Ibid.   [402] Ibid.

[403] See, especially, C. Rak, *Krieg, Nation und Konfession*, 186–210; C. Rak, 'Ein großer Verbrüderungskrieg? Kriegserfahrungen von katholischen Feldgeistlichen und das Bild vom Deutsch-Französischen Krieg 1870/71', in H. Berding, K. Heller, and W. Speitkamp (eds), *Krieg und Erinnerung*, 39–63.

[404] G. Huyssen, *Bilder aus dem Kriegsleben eines Militär-Geistlichen. Ein Beitrag zur Culturgeschichte des deutsch-französischen Krieges von 1870 und 71* (Kreuznach, 1872), ix.

[405] Ibid., ix–x.   [406] Ibid., x.

[407] E. Pfleiderer, *Erinnerungen und Erfahrungen eines Feldpredigers*, 7.

and as 'robbers, murderers and professional thugs', was that wartime conditions and norms diverged from those of peacetime: 'There is no question that a life like that of the campaign could not leave people as they are in their habitual and ordered circumstances.'[408] Everything became more extreme, with 'the steady alternation of security and danger' having an 'enervating' impact, propelling 'one's entire physical and psychic life into a torpor and rage, into a rapid, irregular torrent'.[409] Although there were 'pearls' (comradeship) as well as 'mud' (egoism) to be found in these depths, what clergymen remembered most was arguably the troops' fear, irrationality, and powerlessness before death.[410]

To the Catholic chaplain Gottlob Dettinger, 'one has no conception of the disorder [of war], if one has not seen it with one's own eyes; and these days were just as shocking for one's morale'.[411] Since 'our Christian and un-Christian daily papers one-sidedly stress the humanity with which the war is waged', many at home had 'no idea' of the pain and misery which military conflict brought in its wake.[412] A single day of battle brought 'mass suffering, awful pain and indescribable misery for hundreds and thousands', as 'the most terrifying spectacle' was left 'behind the front of a relentlessly advancing army', thankfully unseen by most soldiers.[413] The wounded seemed to 'relive the terrors of their last hours in wild febrile fantasy'.[414] Some who made their way to field hospitals were a horrible sight: 'the most terrifying which we saw like this', of which 'there were not a few', had had 'his whole face shot away, the nose was fully gone, in the place of his eyes one could see thick, yellow festering areas in the hollows of the bone, . . . and in the entire mass of flesh, the countenance of a human could no longer be recognized at all'.[415] The dead were buried namelessly in mass graves.[416] 'Death on the battlefield has always been praised as a fine soldier's death and has been much lyricized', wrote Schuster:

> Certainly, death for the fatherland has something of the glorious lustre of a sacrificial death. It might be a quick and easy transfer from this life to eternity, if the soldier goes into battle with the blood of Christ and reconciled with God and a bullet bores through his heart, but to suffer from one's severe wounds for days or weeks abroad in the rooms of a field hospital is the hardest lot that can befall a soldier.[417]

The war had not created the 100,000 German widows and 400,000 orphans described in French propaganda, but 'victory . . . had been bought at an expensive, all-too-costly price'.[418] As the Swabian chaplain Heinrich Adolf Köstlin recalled, the 'impressions of cruelty' which war presented observers with were 'too strong for one to insulate oneself completely from them'.[419]

The pain and suffering of ordinary soldiers in the Franco-German War were comparable to those of previous conflicts. Certainly, the Prussian doctor Heinrich

---

[408] Ibid., 47.   [409] Ibid., 48.   [410] Ibid., 48–9, 28–30.
[411] Cited in C. Rak, *Krieg, Nation und Konfession*, 187.   [412] Ibid.
[413] G. Huyssen, *Bilder aus dem Kriegsleben eines Militär-Geistlichen*, 18.
[414] Ibid., 19.   [415] Ibid., 31.   [416] Ibid., 22.
[417] R. Schuster, *Erlebnisse und Beobachtungen eines deutschen Feldgeistlichen*, 105.
[418] Ibid., 101.
[419] H. A. Köstlin, 13/14 Dec. 1870, cited in C. Rak, *Krieg, Nation und Konfession*, 206.

Fritsch, who had received part of his training at Tübingen, was right to note that 'much has got better and will become even better as a result of the Geneva Convention'.[420] Yet military doctors' points of comparison were not encouraging for civilians who, as Fritsch admitted, had become 'better, milder, more compassionate and perhaps softer'.[421] Treatments had improved marginally during the 1860s for some injuries—for example, bullet wounds to the chest—but mortality from other wounds remained high: thus, for hospitalized leg wounds it varied between about 25 per cent and more than 60 per cent.[422] It has been estimated overall that more than 50 per cent of the wounded might eventually have died as a result of their injuries, in spite of official figures suggesting a death rate of 25 per cent.[423] Such statistics militated against anecdotal evidence that 'seriously wounded men [had] returned after healing to duty at the front two or even three times, one after the other'.[424] Some dressing stations and hospitals had improved, with soldiers being treated more quickly (even on trains, as they were transported home), but others were poorly located or deadly.[425] The castle at Sedan, which received more than 2,000 wounded between mid-September 1870 and the end of February 1871, was said to be 'infected' and had an 'unfavourable' overall mortality rate of almost 10 per cent, with more than two-thirds of operations there ending in the death of the patient.[426] Lastly, although some modern weapons were less bloody (the bullets of *chassepots* creating only 'a small hole', for instance), others—such as the Prussian needle-gun, with its long, lead bullets—caused 'enormous wounds' and smashed bones.[427] The British guns supplied to *francs-tireurs* and the troops of Garibaldi left 'quite enormous, great holes in soft tissue' up to 7 cm in diameter.[428]

What was more, the total number of such injuries had increased dramatically in 1870–1 (with between 115,000 and 135,000 dead and wounded on the German side), compared to the shorter war of 1866 and the smaller-scale, less intensive one of 1864.[429] The 'bloody work' of treating these types of cases—'the great amount of blood and the many injuries'—transported even hardened military doctors into 'a painful mood', as Gustav Waltz described his daily experience of a field hospital.[430] In rooms full of corpses, observing barely identifiable bones protruding through tissue, Fritsch's optimistic expectations of war had dissolved: 'I knew of nothing that had affected me more and made me more unhappy in the entire war

---

[420] H. Fritsch, *Erinnerungen und Betrachtungen*, 166.   [421] Ibid., 167.

[422] T. Billroth, *Chirurgische Briefe*, 192–4, 266–75.

[423] M. Steinbach, *Abgrund Metz*, 45.

[424] H. Fritsch, *Erinnerungen und Betrachtungen*, 167.

[425] Theodor Billroth, *Chirurgische Briefe*, 10–14, reported that the *Johanniter* and other volunteer hospitals received casualties 'very much more quickly' than the reserve field hospitals, for instance.

[426] G. F. L. Stromeyer, *Erinnerungen eins deutschen Arztes*, 420.

[427] H. Fritsch, *Erinnerungen und Betrachtungen*, 168.   [428] Ibid., 169.

[429] Matthias Steinbach, *Abgrund Metz*, 45, argues convincingly that many tallies of the dead need to be revised upwards, since initial figures are cited which subsequently increased because of death as a result of wounds. For example, Bazaine estimated 5,000 dead and 23,500 wounded for the Army of the Rhine between 14 August and 7 October 1870, but this number of deaths probably rose by 6,000–10,000.

[430] G. Waltz, *Erlebnisse eines Feldarztes*, 14.

than these conditions' in a field hospital.[431] While 'a fresh battlefield is terrible', soldiers' suffering in a military hospital was worse.[432] 'War, creating hatred, passion and the collision of duties, tore one heart from another', observed Fritsch: 'The misery and misfortune which such a time casts over a true family life together is immeasurable and endless, in great things and small. Oh—wish on no one that a time like this returns!'[433] 'Anyone with any fantasy' would prefer to be blind or to veil 'the cold skeleton of facts', which 'such hardship, suffering and heart-felt pain' had 'spread amongst people'.[434] The painfulness of war was impossible for combatants to ignore.

Injured on a 'meadow of death' at St Privat, Richard Martin described what the physical pain of injury felt like.[435] Earlier in the day, he had received a flesh wound, which he had ignored. Now, running forward towards the enemy, 'I received, all at once, a terrible blow against my body, as if someone had turned a drill through me with unbelievable speed', causing him to fall 'in a turning movement' and to come to rest on his left side.[436] He gasped for breath as everything went dark. The bullet had hit a button and ricocheted through the right side of his chest, 'presumably touching my lung and liver', puncturing his diaphragm and coming back out in the region of his hip.[437] The tunnel bored by the bullet was about 10 inches long. Initially, the main pain had emanated from his chest cavity, where the bullet had hit the button, with 'the pain of the actual wound' superseding it only later: the sensation in his stomach was like that inflicted by running by accident into the shaft of a wagon.[438] Thinking that he had shot himself, he searched for the entry point, finding the hole under his rib cage, with 'the blood of the heart running out, completely black'.[439] The exit wound, which he felt with his thumb, was much larger. As he tried to block the former, to reduce the loss of blood, an increased flow came from the latter, leaving him little option but to lie still in the hope that a clot and scab would slowly form:

> It was replaced by another bad state of affairs, however. The channel of the wound swelled more and more and limited my breathing to such an extent that it was as if my chest had been constricted by a strong leather strap. My lung case lost more and more room to rise and fall, and I felt that I could only breathe from a small corner of my left lung.[440]

His arm swelled up so much around the elbow joint that he could not use it. Because he could barely breathe, Martin was unable to speak or to get up, as the battle around him intensified.

A soldier from the same company, who lay injured beside him and who could speak, blamed him again and again for compelling the soldiers to advance, reminding Martin—an ordinary soldier himself, despite being a teacher—of his comrades' 'urge towards subordination'.[441] Other German troops advanced past him, examined his wound, and left him there: 'Who knows if it will still be worth it with him.'[442] When an NCO later—in the early hours of the morning—forced his men to call

---

[431] H. Fritsch, *Erinnerungen und Betrachtungen*, 133.   [432] Ibid.
[433] Ibid., 263.   [434] Ibid.   [435] R. Martin, *Kriegserinnerungen*, 186.
[436] Ibid., 200.   [437] Ibid., 201.   [438] Ibid.   [439] Ibid.
[440] Ibid., 201–2.   [441] Ibid., 203.   [442] Ibid., 210.

for a stretcher, since there were signs of life, the stretcher-bearer himself could only curse: 'What a heartless speech that was!'[443] 'Comradeship' had, 'here, become a chimera'.[444] Martin was overcome with 'an unending pain of the soul': 'Was *this* the reward for the enthusiasm with which I had left a secure position several weeks ago and voluntarily entered the field, was *this* the thanks for the sacrifice of blood which I had so carelessly made?'[445] After the campaign, he had found out the name of the 'coward'—a miner from Zwickau—and toyed with revealing it in print.[446] In the event, the NCO returned, with two more stretcher-bearers, as Martin's 'saviour', ensuring that he was the last man from his regiment to be carried off the battlefield alive.[447] A long period of recovery in a military hospital helped to restore his faith in humanity, amidst his dying neighbours, but it is doubtful that he ever lost the sense, as one old grenadier of the Napoleonic Wars had expressed it, that war turned a soldier into a 'wild animal'.[448] Every combatant came to feel the same, he contended:

> He might imagine 'God' however he wants to, regaled with all the attributes which religious teachings of the most different directions have bestowed on him, or disrobed of these attributes, as the philosopher does; he is overcome in each case, in the first instance, by a feeling of his insignificance vis-à-vis the majesty of the unforeseeable which pervades the entire battlefield.[449]

How such sentiments coalesced with a longing for home and 'the duty which one has to one's fatherland' was not clear.[450]

The novelist Felix Dahn, perhaps the most prominent literary observer of mass killing in 1870, addressed precisely this question in his reminiscences, helping to explain the juxtaposition of 'civilization' and slaughter. The academic and novelist was 36 years old at the start of the war, when he volunteered in a transport division. Unlike Berthold Auerbach and Gustav Freytag, who had gained permission to join the royal headquarters, he wanted to be close to the fighting.[451] Despite his headlong rush to become involved in combat, which he eventually achieved at Sedan, Dahn was obviously affected by the spectacle of death that he saw on the way. 'The effects of the German grenades were horrible', he reported, as he surveyed a battlefield in late August:

> In the first line of tents, I found five, in the second six, who had been laid out there by a single shot... the main projectile had landed on the very body of the middle one; he was charred from the waist to the knee, flesh and uniform burned to a cinder, the white bones stuck out into the air. The front part of the face and skull of another one had been ripped off, the back part full like a dish with blood and brain; the neck and head of a third had been simply sliced off the rump.[452]

The author's experiences at Sedan, after the excitement of battle, were even more gruesome. Collecting the wounded the following day, he noticed that his foot pushed against

---

443 Ibid., 212.   444 Ibid.   445 Ibid.   446 Ibid.
447 Ibid., 213.   448 Ibid., 175.   449 Ibid., 175–6.   450 Ibid., 176.
451 F. Dahn, *Erinnerungen* (Leipzig, 1894), vol. 4, 286–7.   452 Ibid., 444–5.

something soft, black: I bent down—it was the top part of a skull with the entire crown; two steps away lay the trunk belonging to it. Many of the faces of the dead were distorted by pain or anger, the teeth biting the lips, fingers clawing the earth; the eyes mostly open, blankly, with a look directed towards the heavens.[453]

Dahn claimed, as if to dispel any idea that he was indulging in gothic fantasy, that 'these pictures of horror did not shock' him.[454] He did admit, however, to having been overcome by nausea (*Ekel*) of 'the most extreme' kind, provoked by the 'smell of blood and suppurating wounds'.[455] The writer had, he declared, not shrunk from revealing the 'terrors' of war, using the licence granted to soldiers and war correspondents to transgress the boundaries of good taste. Partly, such transgression was probably designed to accentuate, through contrast, the heroic and picturesque aspects of soldiers' fates, facing death with their weapons 'glinting in the golden light of the sun'.[456] Mainly, though, it seemed to reflect—and here its similarity to the accounts of other combatants is telling—the deeply unsettling nature of the experience itself.

War was, after all, a glorious necessity for Dahn, as for most other observers.[457] His evaluation of the moral rectitude and national significance of the conflict betrayed in explicit form what many middle-class commentators implied; that the muscular, manly defences of civilization, although at times endangered, had been maintained, at least in public:

That war makes warriors wild, that it unfetters the sleeping, ravenous animal in humanity can and should not be denied. According to my fixed conviction, never has a war been waged with such conscience-bound, strict maintenance of international law (*Kriegsrecht*) as the war of 1870 by the German side, especially in the first months...Likewise, it is the height of injustice when the French reproach the German war leaders for regular and serious infractions of international law...Amongst a million men who overran France at that time, there were brutes, even criminals, who in peacetime and at home would also not have gone for seven months without breaking the law. And that war should make people of such a sort wild is no surprise. A certain stubborn fatalism imbues the warrior who, when he reflects, soon gives up the hope of returning home alive and well: it is, so to say, a wonder when this happens; in this mood, in this emotional disposition, the average person will exploit every living hour given to him to fulfil his most desired wishes: he will eat and also drink, as much and as well as he can; and with the less well disposed, there will also be a will to make the nation which had forced on him the suffering and dangers of war suffer to no lesser a degree in this war. Against this, Moltke has recalled...how certain of the most elevated manly virtues can only be fostered by, can only unfold during a war...Granted, all the ideals of humanity hitherto should be given up, not only to the ideas of the Social Democrats, but also to certain filthy tendencies, finally also to a certain womanliness in literature. We, however, hold the heroic death for the fatherland to be the crown of all manly virtues and we recognise with Moltke that the terrible calamity of

---

[453] Ibid., 529–30.   [454] Ibid., 445.   [455] Ibid., 569–70.   [456] Ibid., 335.
[457] See F. Dahn, *Das Kriegsrecht. Kurze, volksthümliche Darstellung für Jedermann zumal für den deutschen Soldaten* (Würzburg, 1870), 2–3, in which Dahn ties 'a great advance of humanity in international law' to the fact that states alone conducted wars, not individuals. Wars could therefore be controlled.

war, besides damaging influences on morality, also has the great effect of inspiring people to this highest act of virtue.[458]

For the majority of ordinary soldiers, it was not obvious that such a balance between wildness and virtue had been maintained. As one combatant recorded in January 1871:

> When I once more consider the very high number of dead and wounded, when I shudder, thinking about the pools of blood that we had to cross on the battlefield, when I remember all the moaning and crying, all my liveliness and all my willingness to remain in this horrible world pass away.[459]

There is considerable evidence that such horror, even when mixed with a continuing belief in the justice or national purpose of the war, had a longer-term significance, altering veterans' attitude to war after 1871.

[458] F. Dahn, *Erinnerungen*, 590–4.
[459] H. Rosenthal, cited in C. G. Krüger, 'German Suffering in the Franco-German War', 406.

10

Shock and Awe
The Aftermath of Conflict

Moltke's speech to the Reichstag on 14 May 1890 appeared to betray the profound impact of 1864, 1866, and 1870–1 on the former Chief of the General Staff's own attitude to war. During the debate on the Army Bill, the 89-year-old deputy warned that the next conflict could become 'a seven-year, a thirty-year war—and woe betide anyone who sets Europe in flames, who first puts a match to the powder keg!'[1] The threat of this type of war—involving 'the greatest powers of Europe, armed as never before'—was a long-standing one, 'which has been hanging over our heads now for more than ten years like the sword of Damocles', extending back to the conflict between Russia and the Ottoman Empire in 1877–8 and beyond.[2] If Germany were drawn into such a conflict through a French desire for revenge or the entanglement of Austria–Hungary in the Balkans, the war's 'duration and its end cannot be foreseen', he warned the Reichstag: none of the Great Powers 'can be defeated so decisively in one or two campaigns that they would declare themselves defeated, that they would be forced to conclude a peace with harsh terms, that they would not rise again, albeit after a period of a year or more, in order to renew hostilities'.[3] When it was

> a question of such great things, when it is a matter of what we have attained with heavy sacrifices, the existence of the Reich, perhaps the continuation of the social order and civilization (*Zivilisation*), in any event hundreds of thousands of human lives, the question of money can only come into account in a secondary way; every pecuniary sacrifice appears here to be justified *a priori*.[4]

Future military conflicts would be difficult to control.

Moltke's image in 1890 of an unlimited future war has often been distinguished from his earlier conception of limited 'cabinet' or 'national' wars. The Chief of the General Staff was 'conscious of the fact that, with European rapid armament and armies of millions,...a changed situation had been created compared to the national wars before 1871', contends Jörn Leonhard.[5] Yet there is little evidence that Moltke's view of warfare had altered fundamentally since the early 1870s. His references to hundreds of thousands of deaths and the difficulty of ending a conflict between Great Powers could easily have been extrapolated from his experience

---

[1] H. v. Moltke, 14 May 1890, cited in S. Förster (ed.), *Moltke*, 639–40.
[2] Ibid., 639. [3] Ibid. [4] Ibid., 640. [5] J. Leonhard, *Bellizismus*, 770.

of the Franco-German War. According to Leonhard, the Second Schleswig War, the Austro-Prussian War, and the Franco-German War were considered to be 'specially directed cabinet wars', which remained 'limited in their form'.[6] The conflict in 1866 was, as Moltke stated, 'not for territorial gain, expansion or material profit', but for 'an ideal good—for a position of power', with Austria compelled 'to renounce its hegemony in Germany'.[7] Nonetheless, the scale of the armies deployed and the uncertainty of the outcome had ensured that the conflict could not simply be likened to an eighteenth-century cabinet war. It was, conceded the Chief of Staff, undeniably 'modern'.[8] The Franco-German War was a modern *Volkskrieg*, a 'great, world-historical struggle' characterized by 'many, in part very painful, actions', which made it 'uncertain and tense' until the end.[9] This model of a people's war arguably dominated Moltke's thinking during the period of peace and relative stability after 1871.[10] Certainly, there were no external wars in this period which would have prompted a fundamental shift of opinion. His assertion in 1890 that 'the time of cabinet wars lies behind us' was the last of a series of such allusions, in which he warned against the unpredictable consequences and high death toll of the new form of warfare: 'we can now only declare a *Volkskrieg*, and one with all its unforeseeable effects; any sensible government would only decide to do this with great reluctance'.[11]

Military conflicts remained unavoidable, even if they would become rarer in an 'advancing culture', Moltke had warned an exiled Russian pacifist in 1881: 'Who would want to deny that all wars, victorious ones too, are a misfortune for one's own *Volk*, for no acquisition of land, no billions can replace human lives and compensate for families' mourning.'[12] On several occasions in the 1870s and 1880s, he raised the possibility of a long conflict akin to the Seven Years' War.[13] As a result, given that 'the time of cabinet wars belongs to the past, there is barely a single leader of a state today who would take the heavy responsibility of unsheathing his sword without serious cause'.[14] The 'humanity of the conduct of wars' might have 'followed the general improvement of morals', as a comparison with 'the barbarization (*Verwilderung*) of the Thirty Years' War' demonstrated, but 'the savage and violent elements' of war had remained, he wrote to Bluntschli in 1880, so that 'the

[6] Ibid., 768.

[7] H. v. Moltke, 'Über den angeblichen Kriegsrat in den Kriegen König Wilhelms I.', cited ibid.

[8] H. v. Moltke, 'Aus den Verordnungen für die höheren Truppenführer vom 24. Juni 1869', in D. Langewiesche and N. Buschmann, '"Dem Vertilgungskriege Grenzen setzen"', in D. Beyrau, M. Hochgeschwender, and D. Langewiesche (eds), *Formen des Krieges*, 171.

[9] H. v. Moltke, 4 Mar. 1871, cited in F. Herre, *Moltke. Der Mann und sein Jahrhundert* (Stuttgart, 1984), 329. He had predicted this change to a *Volkskrieg* in 1867: H. v. Moltke, 'Denkschrift vom Januar 1867 über einen Krieg gegen Frankreich und Österreich', in S. Förster (ed.), *Moltke*, 193. H. v. Moltke, *Geschichte des deutsch-französischen Krieges von 1870–71*, 1. On the term 'cabinet war', see Frank Göse, 'Der Kabinettskrieg', in D. Beyrau, M. Hochgeschwender, and D. Langewiesche (eds), *Formen des Krieges*, 123.

[10] See S. Förster, 'Facing "People's War": Moltke the Elder and Germany's Military Options after 1871', *Journal of Strategic Studies*, 10 (1987), 215.

[11] H. v. Moltke, 14 May 1890, cited in S. Förster (ed.), *Moltke*, 638.

[12] H. v. Moltke, 10 Feb. 1881, ibid., 636.

[13] E. Kessel, *Moltke*, 618.   [14] Ibid.

greatest act of benevolence in war' was still 'the quick ending of the war, and to this end every means must be available which is not completely despicable'.[15] The 'last war against France' had, for this reason, been waged 'with energy', attacking 'all sources of assistance of the enemy government'—'its finances, railways, food, even its prestige'.[16]

Paradoxically, the difficulty of controlling soldiers under the exceptional conditions of war and the inescapable costs of conflict obliged governments to dispose of all means—irrespective of international law, except in respect of the 'wounded, ill, medics and sanitary material'—in order to force a decision and end troops' suffering as quickly as possible.[17] What was needed was that 'governments everywhere be strong enough to master the passions of the *Völker*, which pushed them towards war'.[18] Moltke himself, despite backing the use of force against France during the War-in-Sight crisis of 1875 and sanctioning Alfred von Waldersee's memorandum on Russian armament in 1887, followed such advice, adhering cautiously to the 1 per cent rule (of Germany's population) in discussions of army increases and turning to a strategy of initial defence, partly because the human cost of an immediate offensive had proved so great in 1870.[19] Although the 'Germanic race' was widely known abroad for its 'especially warlike tendency', history showed that this was a myth: 'Germany has achieved its goal of reunification (*Wiedervereinigung*); it does not have the slightest reason to be lured into martial adventures, but it can be forced into defence and it must be prepared for this.'[20] Moltke's caution after 1871 was connected to his fear of a two-front war and to the realities of Bismarck's foreign policy, leading to rejections of the General Staff's war-mongering in 1875 and 1887.[21] It also derived from the 'terrible' experiences—here he cited Wallenstein's 'Der Krieg ist schrecklich.../ Doch ist er gut'—of the Danish, Austrian, and Franco-German Wars.[22]

Moltke was a special case, as a gnarled career soldier and a calculating strategist, 'eerily' calm in the midst of the killing.[23] As the focus of a post-war cult, along with Wilhelm I and Bismarck, he appeared to combine in his person the contradictory

---

[15] H. v. Moltke to J. K. Bluntschli, 11 Dec. 1880, ibid., 633–4.
[16] Ibid., 634.   [17] Ibid.   [18] H. v. Moltke, 10 Feb. 1881, ibid., 637.
[19] E. Kessel, *Moltke*, 595–729.
[20] H. v. Moltke, 10 Feb. 1881, in S. Förster (ed.), *Moltke*, 637.
[21] Stig Förster, 'Dreams and Nightmares: German Military Leadership and the Images of Future Warfare, 1871–1914', in M. Boemeke, R. Chickering, and S. Förster (eds), *Anticipating Total War: The German and American Experiences, 1871–1914* (Cambridge, 1999), 343–76, and Stig Förster, 'Helmuth von Moltke und das Problem der industrialisierten Volkskriegs im 19. Jahrhundert', in R. G. Foerster (ed.), *Generalfeldmarschall von Moltke. Bedeutung und Wirkung* (Munich, 1991), 103–16, stresses the connection between Moltke's defensiveness and the prospect of a two-front war, partly in anticipation of the pre-First World War era. See also K.-E. Jeismann, *Das Problem des Präventivkrieges im europäischen Staatensystem mit besonderem Blick auf die Bismarckzeit* (Freiburg, 1957).
[22] H. v. Moltke, 10 Feb. 1881, in S. Förster (ed.), *Moltke*, 636. The fact that war was an 'element in God's world order' and 'perpetual peace is a dream', as he had written to Bluntschli in 1880, did not demonstrate the redundancy of efforts 'to make milder the suffering which war brings with it': ibid., 633.
[23] U. v. Stosch (ed.), *Denkwürdigkeiten des Generals und Admirals Albrecht von Stosch*, 192.

legacies of war.[24] In Werner's famous depiction of *Moltke mit seinem Stabe vor Paris am 19. September 1870*, painted in 1873 as a commission for the *Kunstverein* of Schleswig-Holstein in Kiel, the Chief of the General Staff is shown erect on his horse, a solitary and contemplative figure looking from a hill over his troops towards the French capital (see Figure 9.2).[25] With his staff leaning towards each other jovially behind, he is both part of an aristocratic officer corps, which itself is characterized by its unpretentious *bonhomie*, and he is separate from it, with the concentrated responsibility of command. Like the rest of his staff, Moltke wears a simple cap and uniform, yet his iron cross marks him out as a patriotic, noble, Prussian officer and natural leader.[26] The German troops on the track below look up at him in wonderment but he does not acknowledge them. He is meditative rather than haughty as he studies his goal on the horizon. This studiousness is the principal theme of Werner's other celebrated portrait, *Moltke in seinem Artbeitszimmer in Versailles 1870*, painted for the first time in 1872.[27] Here, the Chief of the General Staff is revealed in the same simplicity in a wood-panelled study in the French palace. His uniform is the same, with the insignia of the iron cross alone distinguishing his dark tunic, but his posture is that of a professor, immersed in reading, a map, and other documents of war strewn on the desk behind him. Although he is not a representative of the *Bildungsbürgertum*, his class seems unimportant and his task is a technical and educated one, familiar to middle-class enthusiasts of the painter during the imperial era.[28] The victory which Moltke had plotted was a quiet, cerebral, relentless one, in keeping with Werner's own recollection of the commander, whom he had met in October 1870 and dined with repeatedly during his second trip to France in 1871.[29] The very fact that the commander was victorious itself gave him an heroic aura which illuminated

---

[24] For the creation of a Moltke cult, see Felix Dahn, *Moltke als Erzieher. Allerlei Betrachtungen* (Breslau, 1872); Max Dittrich, *Generalfeldmarschall Graf Moltke. Eine Denkschrift für das deutsche Heer und Volk* (Dresden, 1889).

[25] See F. Becker, *Bilder von Krieg und Nation*, 458–9. E. Kolb, 'Gezähmte Halbgötter? Bismarck und die militärische Führung 1871–1890', in L Gall (ed.), *Otto von Bismarck und Wilhelm II* (Paderborn, 2001), 41–60.

[26] Karen Hagemann, *Revisiting Prussia's Wars against Napoleon*, 230–46, and Karen Hagemann, 'National Symbols and the Politics of Memory: The Prussian Iron Cross of 1813, its Cultural Context and its Aftermath', in A. Forrest, E. François, and K. Hagemann (eds), *War Memories*, 215–41, notes that medals were given to a broad cross-section of soldiers and, even, some civilians (with 44,488 agreed for bestowal by the new Federal Decorations Commission of Imperial Germany in July 1871), but with about a quarter going to officers, as after 1813 (when all Grand Crosses went to commanding officers).

[27] Studiousness merged with science in many accounts: Johannes Scherr, *1870–1871. Vier Bücher deutscher Geschichte* (Leipzig, 1880), vol. 1, 194, for instance, talked of Moltke and his staff working 'in complete earnest and in the total thoroughness of scientific research'.

[28] Theodor Lindner, *Der Krieg gegen Frankreich und die Einigung Deutschlands. Zur 25jährigen Wiederkehr der Gedenktage von 1870/71* (Berlin, 1895), 9, pointed out that, although Moltke came from 'an old Mecklenburg aristocratic family', he was not born into 'fortunate goods' but was 'equipped with the most fortunate talents'.

[29] A. v. Werner, *Erlebnisse*, 46–7. The painter comments on the characters of ebullient officers such as Verdy du Vernois and the War Minister Roon, whom he met later, rather than on that of Moltke.

everything around him. Even Moltke's horse, the subject of a majestic portrait by Werner, shared in this aura.[30]

HEROIC HISTORIES OF WAR AND UNIFICATION

'Heroism' typified and complicated the accounts of most of those who wrote about their experiences of the wars of 1864, 1866, and 1870–1.[31] Troops were not 'demobilized'; they were brought home to a series of victory parades. Werner was closely associated with the largest one, held in Berlin on 16 June 1871, after being commissioned to paint a large 20 ft by 18 ft allegory of the Franco-German War, which was suspended between victory columns on Unter den Linden.[32] It revealed, when the white cover was removed on the day of the parade, 'Emperor Napoleon III knocked down to the ground', with Germania looking on at 'the fallen *Imperator* from her chariot'.[33] As Werner went to join the Crown Prince, whose 'knightly figure' he had placed near the centre of the tableau, Berlin's youth could be heard singing, 'Wer kraucht dort auf dem Bauch herum, / Das ist gewiß Napolium.'[34] Unter den Linden was draped in 'the richest jewellery', with the façade of the *Akademie der Künste* bedecked with 'larger-than-life portraits of the German army leaders, painted by Menzel, Gustav Richter, Carl Becker, Otto Heyden, Bleibtreu etc.'[35] Captured French guns lined the central avenue, interspersed with garlands, flags, and inscriptions singing the virtues of 'the different units of troops'.[36] In the Lustgarten, a statue of Germania with Alsace and Lorraine had been erected. 'At the hot midday hour, the brave warriors entered what was now the Reich's capital through the Brandenburger Tor, decorated for the festival, before the indescribable jubilation of the *Volk*.'[37] Wilhelm Camphausen's painting of the occasion, *Der Siegeseinzug in Berlin am 16.6.1871*, displayed crowds packed onto the square, on top of surrounding terraces, extending back through the gate into the Tiergarten as far as the eye could see (see Figure 10.1). The marching soldiers and enthusiastic spectators were indistinguishable from each other. For those at home, this home-coming was one of the main events of the war, as an 11-year-old Marie von Bunsen recalled of Berlin. During the conflict, she and her siblings had gone to Genthiner Straße in order to 'loiter there until the postman came before returning home, swallowing the newspapers with the news of the war': 'Then came the much-desired peace, then the unforgettable *Einzug*.'[38] 'I can still see the happy, proud, young faces', Bunsen wrote in her memoir, decades later.[39] Even local newspapers such as the Thuringian *Eisenbergisches Nachrichtsblatt*, which appeared just twice

---

[30] Ibid., 52. The horse was being led by an out-of-focus stable-hand. Also, D. E. Showalter, 'The Political Soldiers of Bismarck's Germany: Myths and Realities', *German Studies Review*, 17 (1994), 59–77.

[31] R. Schilling, *'Kriegshelden'*, 169–251, on the long afterlife of such heroism.

[32] A. v. Werner, *Erlebnisse*, 53.   [33] Ibid., 58.   [34] Ibid., 59.

[35] Ibid.   [36] Ibid.   [37] Ibid.

[38] M. v. Bunsen, *Die Welt in der ich lebte. Erinnerungen aus glücklichen Jahren 1860–1912*, 3rd edn (Leipzig, 1929), 33.

[39] Ibid.

Figure 10.1 Wilhelm Camphausen, *Der Siegeseinzug in Berlin am 16.6.1871* (n.d.)
Source: Bildarchiv Foto Marburg.

per week, carried their own celebratory poems, enjoining soldiers to 'Take our hand! With sincere welcome / Man and child receive you heartily, / Your wife with a firm, loyal kiss, / Those who win you over today afresh! / You, who found battle as heroes, / Are greeted by every heart in the fatherland, / Take our hand!'[40] The troops were promised the 'golden fruit' of peace on behalf of a thankful individual state and a new German nation-state.[41]

The patriotic mythology of the Franco-German War was established during the conflict and became an orthodoxy after 1871.[42] It rested on several overlapping sets of ideas. First, the idea that the Bonapartist regime had provoked the war, dishonouring the King of Prussia, was widely believed at the time and was maintained by historians and other commentators after 1871.[43] 'The people saw their king and his honour mocked', wrote Hans Wachenhusen in the illustrated wartime periodical *Der Deutsche Volkskrieg* in July 1870: 'To arms! So, a united call resounded through every province. Every dispute came to an end. The other German lands also rose up for Germany's honour.'[44] To conservatives and liberals, it was obvious

---

[40] *Eisenbergisches Nachrichtsblatt*, 20 June 1871.   [41] Ibid.

[42] See especially F. Becker, 'Strammstehen vor der Obrigkeit? Bürgerliche Wahrnehmung der Einigungskriege und Militarismus im Deutschen Kaiserreich', *Historische Zeitschrift*, 277 (2003), 87–113.

[43] See, for instance, the southern German *Allgemeine Zeitung*, 21 July, and 6 Aug. 1870. B. Gödde-Baumanns, 'Ansichten eines Krieges. Die "Kriegsschuldfrage" von 1870 in zeitgenössischem Bewusstsein, Publizistik und wissenschaftlicher Diskussion 1870–1914', in E. Kolb (ed.), *Europa vor dem Krieg von 1870* (Munich, 1987), 175–201.

[44] *Der Deutsche Volkskrieg*, July 1870, vol. 1, cited in F. Becker, *Bilder von Krieg und Nation*, 300.

that 'we have been drawn into war by our hereditary enemy in the most frivolous way', in the words of the Bavarian-born, Göttingen-trained economist Adolph Wagner, writing on 16 July 1870 from the Badenese university city of Freiburg.[45] For the majority of socialists, too, Napoleon III was the guilty party, even if they subsequently admitted—long after the event—that they had been wrong.[46] 'Today there can be no doubt that the war of 1870 was desired by Bismarck, and that he had long laid his plans to bring it about', wrote August Bebel, an opponent of the war, in his memoirs:

> Although in respect of the wars of 1864 and 1866 his pose as the innocent victim, the party attacked was hardly successful, the same could not be said of the war of 1870, when his pose was brilliantly maintained. With the exception of a small inner circle of intimates who knew that Bismarck had worked with might and main to bring about the war—and not even the then King of Prussia, Wilhelm I, belonged to this inner circle—Bismarck duped the whole world, making everyone believe that Napoleon had provoked the war, while poor, peace-loving Bismarck was the aggrieved party. The semi-official and official historians have fostered this belief among the general masses of the population, according to which Germany was acting on the defensive and France was the attacking party. It is true that Napoleon declared war, but the admirable point in Bismarck's policy was that he so shuffled the cards that Napoleon was forced to declare war as though of his own initiative and to appear as the peacebreaker.[47]

Jörg and other Bavarian 'patriots' had argued before the war broke out that the 'misunderstanding' between Benedetti and Wilhelm I at Bad Ems was merely a matter of court etiquette, without consequence for Germany as a whole, yet they were largely silenced during the conflict itself.[48] Bismarck's curt rephrasing of the Ems dispatch sent by Heinrich Abeken at the request of Wilhelm I, which gave the impression that both parties had been insulted at the Hessian spa resort, was not commented on explicitly by historians in Germany until the 1890s.[49] Most historical accounts assumed without further investigation that the honour of the Prussian monarch had been trampled on and that the French government had declared war without good grounds.[50] Some scholars, including Treitschke, continued to assert that France had been the aggressor as a consequence of its long-standing aspiration for hegemony in Europe.[51]

---

[45] A. Wagner, *Briefe, Dokumente, Augenzeugenberichte 1851–1917*, ed. H. Rubner (Berlin, 1978), 82.

[46] See the *Social-Demokrat*, 17 July 1870.

[47] A. Bebel, *My Life* (Westport, CT, 1983), 204–5.

[48] *Grenzboten*, 1870, vol. 3, 487–90.

[49] For instance, by Wilhelm Oncken, *Unser Heldenkaiser. Festschrift zum hundertjährigen Geburtstage Kaiser Wilhelm des Großen* (Berlin, 1897), 130.

[50] W. Müller, *Politische Geschichte der Gegenwart* (Berlin, 1871), vol. 4, 210–11; W. Müller, *Politische Geschichte der Neuesten Zeit 1816–1875* (Stuttgart, 1875), 436; L. Bender, *Der jüngste Franzosenkrieg und die Wiederaufrichtung des Deutschen Reiches*, 4th edn (Essen, 1872), 8; K. Abicht, *Geschichte des deutsch-französischen Krieges und der Wiederaufrichtung des Deutschen Reichs* (Heidelberg, 1873), 7; B. Volz, *Geschichte Deutschlands im neunzehnten Jahrhundert vom Luneviller Frieden bis zum Tode Kaiser Wilhelms I.* (Leipzig, 1890), 541. On this subject, see F. Becker, *Bilder von Krieg und Nation*, 297–8.

[51] H. v. Treitschke, *Zum Gedächtniß des großen Krieges* (Leipzig, 1895), 12–13: 'As soon as Prussia's Bohemian victory threatened to recreate a fair balance of power, every strident Parisian circle, which had always dominated the impotent provinces, attempted to summon up a fantastical state of national

Second, many commentators sought to show at the time and afterwards how a justifiable war against France had been borne by the German people in its entirety. Thus, the King of Prussia had been greeted by a great crowd in Berlin on 15 July, after he had returned from Bad Ems, wrote Oskar Höcker in his history of the 'national war against France': 'more than once the king walked to the window and looked down with greetings to the crowd, which did not tire of hailing him although it was already the midnight hour'.[52] When it was told that the monarch had much more 'work' to do that night, the crowd—recognizing Wilhelm I was working for the common good—quickly dispersed.[53] In keeping with the mythology of '1813', with its youthful, educated volunteers, the war of 1870–1 was perceived by middle-class commentators to have shown that 'we are a warlike people' superior in 'all the virtues of war to the great nation [France]', in the words of Karl Frenzel, 'but we are not at all a people made up of soldiers'.[54] Unlike in 1914, it was not the 'fortress peace' between previously warring parties which struck contemporaries, despite the political conflicts of the 1860s. Rather, it was the union of 'all the German tribes'—after what Georg Hiltl termed the 'fencing off' imposed by Napoleon I—and the coalescence of civilian and military milieux, which had overcome the 'distrust' with which 'military devotion' had been held in the midst of a 'dispute for the free self-determination of the citizen'.[55] The 'loyalty of the Germans', which had contributed to the 'irresistible bravery of our battalions' during the war, did not 'prevent them, in peacetime, from stepping over into opposition for the sake of their interests', the editor and writer continued: returning to 'his civilian occupation', the soldier maintained 'his military sensitivities in a quiet chamber of his heart', countenancing radical measures at home whilst reverting to the 'personal soldierly relationship to his commander' when in the field or 'on great occasions in peacetime'.[56] Civilians could become effective and loyal soldiers, yet they remained active citizens after the war had ended. Their education, industry, morality, and family duties figured prominently in later narratives of the campaign, becoming part of the folklore of military service and commemoration.[57] In

arrogance; the old mad belief reappeared that France's greatness rested on the weakness of its neighbours. Public opinion pushed the sick Emperor into a declaration of war against his will.' See W. Hardtwig, 'Von Preußens Aufgabe in Deutschland zu Deutschlands Aufgabe in der Welt. Liberalismus und borussianisches Geschichtsbild zwischen Revolution und Imperialismus', in W. Hardtwig, *Geschichtskultur und Wissenschaft*, 103–60.

[52] O. Höcking, *Der Nationalkrieg gegen Frankreich in den Jahren 1870 und 1871* (Leipzig, 1895), 45. The argument in this paragraph is made at much greater length by Frank Becker in *Bilder von Krieg und Nation*, 306–76.

[53] O. Höcking, *Der Nationalkrieg gegen* Frankreich, 45.

[54] K. Frenzel, *Deutsche Kämpfe* (Hanover, 1873), 114.

[55] G. Hiltl, *Der Französische Krieg von 1870 und 1871* (Bielefeld and Leipzig, 1884), 61; also, F. Ranke, *Die großen Jahre 1870 und 1871* (Nördlingen, 1873), 12; L. Bender, *Der jüngste Franzosenkrieg und die Wiederaufrichtung des deutschen Reiches*, 13; K. Mewes, *Leiden und Freuden eines kriegsfreiwilligen hallenser Studenten vom Regiment Nr. 86 in den Kriegsjahren 1870–1871* (Magdeburg, 1898), 210. G. Freytag, 'Der Feldzug', *Im Neuen Reich*, 1871, vol. 1, 79.

[56] *Im Neuen Reich*, 1871, vol. 1, 79.

[57] For example, in K. Junck, *Der Deutsch-Französische Krieg 1870 und 1871* (Leipzig, 1876), vol. 1, 117; K. Stieler, *Durch Krieg zum Frieden. Stimmungsbilder aus den Jahren 1870–71* (Stuttgart, 1895), 56–7; K. Köstler, *Geschichte des deutsch-französischen Krieges 1870 und 1871* (Munich, 1881),

these senses, the war could appear socially inclusive as well as nationally unifying. 'The prejudices of class or estate' and 'the narrow egoism of personal interests' had come to seem 'small to our most powerful youths and men compared to the highest interests of the nation', Freytag had written in 1871.[58]

Third, the conflict was interwoven, in the opinion of most commentators, with German unification. For combatants and civilians alike, a German nation-state seemed to have emerged, almost miraculously, from the theatre of war.[59] The wartime experiences of Max von Schinckel, a one-year volunteer in 1868 and later a prominent banker in Hamburg, were typical of many. They had a

> defining influence on my entire life,... because this war taught me to think and feel nationally and placed before my eyes what national sacrifice could achieve, and... because it has shown that even an ordinary reserve officer... was able to contribute a tiny little bit, so that, in the end, the unification of the German lands into a *Kaiserreich* was fought for.[60]

From the more sceptical starting-point of a self-confessed Greater German who had grown up in the Bavarian city of Aschaffenberg near Frankfurt, Lujo Brentano wrote in his memoirs of similar feelings. 'I was... a *Großdeutscher* and an opponent of Prussia because I feared that its policy would lead to the destruction of the dream of the unity of Germany, which had captivated me since childhood', he recollected: 'But the victories on the French battlefields, with the help of the united South German and North German troops, had filled me with the hope that the unity of Germany would emerge from them.'[61] After his mother had reminded him of 'Prussia's previous acts of violence', he had replied on 17 January 1871 that 'The entire history of humanity shows us that everything that we call public law, both in internal and external affairs, is nothing more than the formal fixing of actual power relations.'[62] Since these relations were in 'flux', 'a struggle results between that which was earlier entitled and that which is fated to become entitled', 'for in the life of the human social entity there are natural laws of development just as in the life of nature'.[63] There was, therefore, no point in criticizing or resisting Prussia's bid in 1870 to unite Germany through an act of self-defence against France.

For the majority of deputies in the Reichstag of the North German Confederation, it was evident that 'the German *Volk* will finally find, on the chosen site, the ground—respected by all peoples—of a peaceful and free unification', in the words of the

1. On 'folklore militarism', see J. Vogel, '"En revenant de la revue". Militärfolklore und Folkloremilitarismus in Deutschland und Frankreich 1871–1914', *Österreichische Zeitschrift für Geschichtswissenschaften*, 9 (1998), 9–30; J. Vogel, 'Der "Folklorenmilitarismus" und seine zeitgenössische Kritik—Deutschland und Frankreich 1871–1914', in W. Wette (ed.), *Militarismus in Deutschland*, 277–92.

[58] G. Freytag, 'Kriegsstimmungen im deutschen Volk und Heer', *Im Neuen Reich*, 1871, vol. 1, 76.

[59] J. Diehl, *Meine Kriegs-Erlebnisse von 1870/71*, 42.

[60] E. Rohrmann, *Max von Schinckel. Hanseatischer Bankmann im wilhelminischen Deutschland* (Hamburg, 1971), 45–6.

[61] L. Brentano, *Mein Leben im Kampf um die soziale Entwicklung Deutschlands* (Jena, 1931), 61–2.

[62] L. Brentano to his mother, 17 Jan. 1871, ibid., 62.   [63] Ibid.

address given to the king at the start of the war.[64] On the day that hostilities were declared, the National Liberal deputy and former democrat Ludwig Bamberger wrote in the *Mainzer Zeitung* that 'It had to happen in this way, and because it has happened in this way, it is good that it has happened.'[65] The conflict was necessary, he went on, in order 'to make Germany complete'.[66] The liberal leaders Rudolf von Bennigsen and Eduard Lasker entered into correspondence with politicians such as Otto Elben, Heinrich Marquardsen, Friedrich Kiefer, and Marquard Barth in Württemberg, Baden, and Bavaria. Each individual and party should work to push 'the government to complete the state', ending the division between North and South, Lasker wrote to the Swabian leader of the national–liberal *Deutsche Partei* Julius von Hölder on 18 August 1870.[67] On 6 September, Lasker and Bennigsen set off on a trip to the southern states, meeting with Progressives such as Barth and producing a joint address to the King of Bavaria. Both Ludwig and the Reichstag should have been brought to Versailles, in the liberal leaders' opinion, in order to witness the war and the proclamation of the Kaiser and to participate in the deliberations of Bismarck about the form of the new German *Kaiserreich*.[68] According to the Prussian liberal Max Duncker, Bennigsen and Lasker had concentrated too exclusively on the politics and the constitutional question in Munich, instead of war and annexation, which were more likely to convince the Bavarians. The democratic *Frankfurter Zeitung* agreed.[69] Nevertheless, few if any liberals or democrats denied the close relationship between the struggle against France and the unification of Germany.

Those who opposed the Franco-German War or German unification frequently felt isolated. On the left, August Bebel and Wilhelm Liebknecht, the leaders of the *Sozialdemokratische Arbeiterpartei* (SDAP) founded at Eisenach in August 1869, abstained in the Reichstag vote over war credits on 23 July 1870. They were opposed by the majority of social democrats and their working-class supporters. 'The whole of middle-class society and even broad circles of the working class were inflamed in their enthusiasm for the war, everyone was disgusted by the criminally arrogant act of the French emperor, whom they held to be the main guilty party', wrote a 20-year-old Eduard Bernstein, at the time a left-leaning Progressive from Berlin.[70] 'A complete drunkenness came over the masses', he continued in his memoirs: 'Internal party oppositions seemed to have been overcome, the military

---

[64] Cited in G. Meinhardt, *Eduard von Simson. Der Parlamentspräsident Preußens und die Reichseinigung* (Bonn, 1981), 124.

[65] L. Bamberger, 'Deutschland gegen Frankreich', cited in M.-L. Weber, *Ludwig Bamberger. Ideologie statt Realpolitik* (Stuttgart, 1987), 42.

[66] Ibid.

[67] E. Lasker to J. v. Hölder, 18 Aug. 1870, in J. F. Harris, *A Study in the Theory and Practice of German Liberalism: Eduard Lasker, 1829–1884*, 26.

[68] G. v. Werthern to R. v. Bennigsen, 14 Nov. 1870, and R. v. Bennigsen to his wife, 30 Nov. 1870, in H. Oncken, *Rudolf von Bennigsen*, vol. 2, 200–1.

[69] J. F. Harris, *A Study in the Theory and Practice of German Liberalism*, 26–7.

[70] Cited in F. L. Carsten, *Eduard Bernstein 1850–1932. Eine politische Biographie* (Munich, 1993), 11.

of all ranks enjoyed a popularity as never before.'[71] The larger Lassallean *Allgemeiner Deutscher Arbeiterverein* (ADAV), founded in 1863 and boasting 21,000 members in 1870 compared to the SDAP's 10,000, initially backed the war, with its leader Johann Baptist Schweitzer voting for credits in July. Even in their own party, Bebel and Liebknecht met with the opposition of a majority, particularly former Lassalleans, who held a public assembly at Brunswick—the home town of the party executive—and passed a resolution on 16 July labelling Napoleon III a 'frivolous breaker of the peace' and accepting the 'war of defence as an unavoidable evil'.[72] As Bebel recalled in his memoirs, the assembly had asked 'the whole people to do their utmost to induce the German people to decide in fullest sovereignty upon the question of peace or war', effectively linking the conflict to a call for unification.[73] 'Similar resolutions were passed in many cities, especially in the North', recalled the SDAP leader: 'Thus, a very definite difference of opinion within the party became apparent.'[74]

Liebknecht had already written before the war that he saw no difference between 'Bismarckian and Napoleonic Caesarism', advising his readers to change—through a revolution—the conditions which 'make it possible for any Bonaparte or Bismarck to disturb the world peace and to plunge hundreds of thousands of men into death'.[75] In the Reichstag debate on 23 July, he maintained the same line, denouncing the conflict in a declaration with Bebel as 'a dynastic war in the interest of the Bonaparte dynasty, as the war of 1866 was in the interest of the Hohenzollern dynasty'.[76] 'We cannot vote the monies required for the conduct of this war, as this would imply a vote of confidence in the Prussian government, which prepared the way for this war by its proceedings in 1866', ran the declaration: 'Neither can we vote in an adverse sense, as that would be equivalent to approval of the wicked and criminal policy of Bonaparte.'[77] The executive of the SDAP attempted to force Liebknecht's newspaper, *Der Volksstaat*, to toe the party line set out in the manifesto of 24 July, which promised to defend the fatherland against the French menace and to support 'the striving of the German people for national unity'.[78] When Liebknecht refused, Wilhelm Bracke appealed to Karl Marx and the International Workingmen's Association (or First International), which had published Marx's criticism of Bismarck and championing of a war of national self-defence on 23 July.[79] 'The French need a drubbing', the exiled socialist had confessed to Engels, before going to outline his hope that 'German preponderance will shift the centre of the working-class movement in Western Europe from France to Germany', where the working class was 'theoretically and

---

[71] Ibid.
[72] Cited in R. H. Dominick III, *Wilhelm Liebknecht and the Founding of the German Social Democratic Party* (Chapel Hill, NC, 1987), 194–5.
[73] A. Bebel, *My Life*, 208.   [74] Ibid.
[75] R. H. Dominick III, *Wilhelm Liebknecht*, 190.   [76] A. Bebel, *My Life*, 209.
[77] Ibid.   [78] R. H. Dominick III, *Wilhelm Liebknecht*, 195.
[79] This speech was also infused with what Marx had termed the 'pompous declamations and high-faluting phrases' of socialist internationalism, predicting on 23 July that 'Whatever turn the impending horrid war may take, the alliance of the working classes of all countries will ultimately kill war': F. Wheen, *Karl Marx* (London, 1999), 320–1.

organisationally superior to the French'.[80] Like most others, 'even men like Marx and Engels shared the common opinion' that the French had provoked the war 'and gave public expression thereto, although in their position they ought to have known better', wrote Bebel.[81] For its part, the SDAP executive feared that Bebel and Liebknecht's stance would destroy the party. 'If Liebknecht continues in this way', predicted Bracke, 'at the end of the war we will have a dozen inveterate social republicans and a few Saxon particularists'.[82] The executive altered its position after the declaration of the Third Republic in September 1870, advocating the cessation of hostilities and rejecting the envisaged annexation of Alsace-Lorraine, yet it continued to justify the conflict up to that point as a 'war of defence', a 'war for the independence of Germany'.[83] Although the executive of the SDAP were arrested on 9 September for repudiating the continuation of the war as 'a war of conquest, a war of monarchy against the republic, of counter-revolution against revolution, which is aimed as much at German democracy as at the French Republic', it was Bebel and Liebknecht, imprisoned on 17 December, who were associated with a treasonous opposition to the war and unification. 'The attitude which Liebknecht and I assumed at the outbreak of the war and maintained throughout the course of it, both within the Reichstag and without, has for years been the subject of discussion and the occasion of violent attacks upon us', lamented Bebel, forty years after the event.[84]

Socialist opponents of unification by war were marginal figures, ignored by many contemporaries.[85] 'Particularist' opponents in southern Germany were more important. Yet, here, the early transformation of public opinion at the start of the conflict helped to overcome the resistance of a pre-war majority to unification. Badenese politicians and ministers were the exception, having long been receptive to what the Minister-President Julius Jolly termed a 'German Reich' in the memorandum of support which he handed over to Bismarck on 2 September. The Minister-President of the rump Grand Duchy of Hesse, Reinhard von Dalwigk, was far less receptive, hoping but failing to solicit French and Austrian backing in July 1870, which left him no choice but to fulfil his alliance obligations to Prussia: 'We are completely in the talons of the eagle', he complained.[86] By 15 November, both governments had signed treaties in Versailles to join the North German Confederation in a new Reich. For weeks, it had seemed as if Hermann von Mittnacht, the Minister-President of Württemberg, would do the same. His

[80] K. Marx to F. Engels, July 1870, in D. McLellan, *Karl Marx: His Life and Thought* (London, 1973), 389.

[81] A. Bebel, *My Life*, 205.   [82] R. H. Dominick III, *Wilhelm Liebknecht*, 195.

[83] SDAP manifesto, 5 Sept. 1870, ibid., 200. For Marx's vituperative criticism of annexation, see I. Berlin, *Karl Marx* (London, 1995), 185–6.

[84] A. Bebel, *My Life*, 204.

[85] This is not to say that socialist opposition to the war did not increase after September 1870 nor that it was ignored by other parties, merely that a large majority of citizens were seen to back the war effort throughout. On the undermining of socialist support for the war, see A. Seyferth, *Die Heimatfront 1870/71*, 129–47.

[86] Cited in G. G. Windell, *The Catholics and German Unity, 1866–1871* (Minneapolis, 1954), 249.

predecessor had informed the Prussian government on 13 July that France's conduct had 'deeply wounded' German national feeling in the kingdom, prompting the *Landtag* to vote for war credits with only one deputy dissenting.[87] Such national sentiment influenced the election of a new Chamber on 5 December, as the pro-Prussian *Deutsche Partei* increased its number of seats from fourteen to thirty and the anti-unification *Demokratische Volkspartei* shrank from forty to seventeen. Württemberg's government was less willing to comply with Prussia's plans, preferring to cooperate with Munich.[88] Although Mittnacht had reached an agreement at Versailles by 12 November, the Minister-President suddenly announced that he had been refused permission to sign by the king and that he had to return to Württemberg for further discussions. Bismarck's response, however, betrayed the shift of public mood that had occurred since the start of the war: 'Unless a German storm intervenes, nothing will be accomplished with these diplomats and bureaucrats of the old school, at least not this year.'[89] 'Pressure from below' was needed, he declared to Grand Duke Friedrich of Baden: 'These governments appear to overlook entirely the dangerous elements which surround them.'[90] Through his network of envoys, Bismarck made contact with liberals and the press so that Lasker, in Berlin, was already writing to Bennigsen, in Hanover, by 14 November of 'delays on the part of Württemberg'.[91] By 20 November, he had received a telegram from Otto Elben in Stuttgart reassuring him that 'We are very happy here today and completely satisfied.'[92] Lasker himself had long been confident of Mittnacht's good will.[93] He had written to Hölder, the leader of the *Deutsche Partei*, on 26 September that 'Württemberg really has risen up in the same way as Baden.'[94] If everything 'pushes towards the isolation of Bavaria and a conclusion with the other South German states as quickly as possible', as it seemed to Mittnacht to be doing by 31 October, there was the possibility of 'a desperate struggle' by 'our Greater Germans and democrats' in the forthcoming elections, but it was also likely that these parties would lose.[95] The main problem was not Württemberg but the neighbouring state.

Badenese and Swabian negotiators at Versailles regularly reported that their Bavarian counterparts were opposed to unification. Württemberg's envoy reported on 25 September 1870:

> The impression that the Minister [Bray] wanted to give me about the progress of the talks and the utterances of H. M. the King of Bavaria allow one to conclude that the course of the matter, namely in the last days, was in no way a favourable one insofar

---

[87] O. Pflanze, *Bismarck and the Development of Germany*, vol. 1, 481.

[88] W. Seefried, *Mittnacht und die deutsche Frage bis zur Reichsgründung* (Stuttgart, 1928), 86.

[89] Cited in O. Pflanze, *Bismarck and the Development of Germany*, vol. 1, 486.

[90] Ibid. Such 'German' feelings extended to the court itself, with the heir to the throne Prince Wilhelm, who was at Versailles as a soldier, writing home on 5 September 1870 of the 'unbelievable events' of the previous six weeks and going on to support the declaration of the German Empire as a 'great, world-historical moment': P. Sauer, *Württembergs letzter König. Das Leben Wilhelms II.* (Stuttgart, 1994), 44, 48.

[91] E. Lasker to R. v. Bennigsen, 14 Nov. 1870, in H. Oncken, *Rudolf von Bennigsen*, vol. 2, 197.

[92] Lasker to Bennigsen, 20 Nov. 1870, ibid., 198.

[93] W. Seefried, *Mittnacht*, 93.   [94] E. Lasker to J. v. Hölder, 26 Sept. 1870, ibid.

[95] Ibid., 94.

as Bavaria is adopting a strictly particularistic standpoint, not at all a national one, in several respects.[96]

With Ludwig II and Bray refusing to hand over 'diplomatic leadership' to Prussia and countering 'the character of the North German Confederation and, in the end, any true federal state (*Bundesstaat*)', Bavaria looked unlikely to accept the terms of a new German nation-state.[97] It was possible that the other ministers might circumvent Bray, who was 'constantly tired of his portfolio and internally quite opposed to the new development of things', and convince the monarch directly, yet it seemed that 'King Ludwig is not inclined, of his own free will, to renounce considerable sovereign rights in favour of a national solution of the German question.'[98] Bavarian proponents of German unification like Chlodwig zu Hohenlohe-Schillingsfürst also had to find a two-thirds majority in the *Landtag* from parties which had been largely anti-Prussian before 1870. 'About the treaty of Versailles, the views of the public are still unclear', wrote Hohenlohe on 2 December after the government's signature of the agreement—with its 'special' and 'reserved' rights for Bavaria—on 23 November.[99] 'The supposed shift in the attitude of the land is doubtful, meaning that the Ultramontanes would bring down the treaty if they could', wrote the liberal notable and former Minister-President: 'If the treaty fails and we remain isolated, the Ultramontanes will have enough power in the land to push through isolation and make it plausible', placing Bavaria 'completely in the hands of Austria'.[100] On 21 January 1871, however, the liberal sponsors of the treaty gained a two-thirds majority by two votes in the Bavarian *Landtag*. In this sense, the 'shift of opinion in the land' was real.

In common with other commentators, historians gave their imprimatur to the assumption of contemporaries that the Franco-German War had brought about the unification of Germany, the success of which subsequently served to underscore the putative glory of the campaign. 'How have we earned the grace of God so as to be allowed to experience such great and powerful things and how will we live afterwards?' asked Heinrich von Sybel, who went on to write the official history of *Die Begründung des Deutschen Reiches durch Wilhelm I* (1890–4): 'The content of all our desires and strivings for twenty years has now been realised in so unendingly great ways! From where should we get new meaning in my lifetime for the rest of our lives?'[101] States existed primarily to ensure internal order and to defend populations against external threats, as even liberal historical economists such as Gustav Cohn agreed.[102] In his lectures on 'Die Politik' in 1874–5,

---

[96] J. v. Soden to A. v. Taube, 25 Sept. 1870, W. Seefried, *Mittnacht*, 91.   [97] Ibid.
[98] Ibid. See C. McIntosh, *The Swan King: Ludwig II of Bavaria* (London, 1982) 114–24; O. Hilmes, *Ludwig II. Der unzeitgemäße König*, 2nd edn (Berlin, 2013), 185–201.
[99] C. zu Hohenlohe-Schillingsfürst, diary 2 Dec. 1870, in C. zu Hohenlohe-Schillingsfürst, *Denkwürdigkeiten* (Stuttgart, 1907), vol. 2, 29.
[100] Ibid., 29–30.
[101] H. v. Sybel, *Die Begründung des Deutschen Reiches durch Wilhelm I.* (Munich, 1890–4), 7 vols, cited in U. Schlie, *Die Nation erinnert sich*, 44.
[102] G. Cohn, *System der Nationalökonomie* (Stuttgart, 1885–98), vol. 2, 50: 'the advancing culture of peoples had been preoccupied initially, and for many centuries, with the securing of *domination* and *order*'.

Treitschke elaborated on the obverse of this claim that states waged wars for 'the maintenance of their own power', arguing that wars alone were able to make 'a people into the people (*Volk*)', 'internally held together' through legions of patriotic wartime acts.[103] Wars fostered 'political idealism', associated with 'heroism', against the moral decay of 'materialism'.[104] The background to this analysis of state politics was the German war against France four years earlier, when Treitschke had been one of the most vocal supporters of the North German Confederation and of the annexation of Alsace-Lorraine. 'Finally, the great national movements in Central Europe achieved their breakthrough: in 1859, the rising up of Italy, which led to a unitary state within two short years, and since 1866 the decision in Germany', he wrote in his lecture on the states' system: 'The victory of Germany over France turned the old system on its head', with the map of Europe 'much more natural' as a consequence of its 'strengthened' centre and 'the calming of the international system' through the founding of the German Reich, which had satisfied and appeased the 'ambition' of Prussia.[105]

Ranke, the best-known historian of the previous generation, had been more cautious. Nonetheless, in a speech marking his ninetieth birthday in 1885, he had contended that the wars between France and Germany after 1789 differed fundamentally from earlier conflicts, inaugurating an era of struggle between revolutionary French and anti-revolutionary or anti-Napoleonic German forces, which had come to an end in 1870–1 with the final dissipation of the energy of the revolution and the establishment of a new direction for 'world history'.[106] 'A defeat of revolutionary forces, which made the regular future development of world history impossible, can be seen, above all, in the events which we have experienced', wrote the Berlin historian: 'If they had stayed in place, the advancement of historical forces could not have been talked of, even from an impartial view of the same, making world history impossible in an objective sense.'[107] After defeat in 1806, Prussia had relied on 'new war efforts' against France, contributing 'to the national task' of unification: partly as a result, world history came to rest on 'the reciprocal relations and effects of both nations' of Germany and France.[108] Wars between the two powers were waged at once for the nation and for wider principles. For Burckhardt and other scholars, this duality rested not only on the gradual replacement of a 'revolutionary age' with an 'age of unconditional, ruthless acquisition and trade', characterized by 'modern industry', but also on the internal and external nature of war in conditions of social and economic transformation, where 'the state in the newer sense' found it difficult to cope with 'new social problems' and maintain its position abroad.[109] The principle of nationality was central insofar as it offered 'a further means of agglomeration', yet, externally, 'the national state' could 'not be too all-powerful' and could 'scarcely be powerful enough', given the tasks which

---

[103] H. v. Treitschke, *Die Politik* (Leipzig, 1898), vol. 1, 32, 66, 74–5.
[104] Ibid., 385–6.   [105] Ibid., vol. 2, 540.
[106] L. v. Ranke, 'Rede am neunzigsten Geburtstag, 21. Dezember 1885', in L. v. Ranke, *Sämtliche Werke* (Leipzig, 1888), vol. 51–2, 592–4.
[107] Ibid., 597–8.   [108] Ibid., 592–4.
[109] J. Burckhardt, *Gesamtausgabe* (Stuttgart, 1929–34), vol. 7, 420–37.

faced it.[110] According to this reading, too, war and national unification were intimately connected, conceived of as necessary means of shoring up the state. The 'new great states' of Italy and Germany, it almost went without saying, had come about as a result of 'great wars'.[111]

With few exceptions, the press did little to challenge the mythology of 1870–1 which had been established during wartime and elaborated upon by Borussian and other historians afterwards. Accounts of the conflict in a periodical such as the *Gartenlaube* were infrequent, after an initial run of articles in 1872–3, but they remained celebratory.[112] Rudolf von Gottschall's poem 'Am Sedantag' in 1886 was typical:

> A great day, when the die were cast
> In the misjudged game of chance of Caesar!
> The news was dispatched as in a storm,
> A flash of lightning, which resounded in every heart.
> The heavens shone in the reflection...
> Not cities, engulfed by flames,
> The light of joy alone projected
> Its lustre into the clouds.[113]

Only Napoleon III, imprisoned and crushed by 'the German force of iron', felt—'in anxiety and emergency'—'overcome by terror and death', not the German soldiers, who could take encouragement from the fact that 'North and South are in an alliance' and that 'the Reich came into existence, / A magnificent construction, out of the fire of the war'.[114] Germans kept 'the memory of the bloody battle / Forever young in our hearts', yet the sacrifice appeared to have been given meaning and value, sacralised as 'German heroes' courage' (*Heldenmuth*) and 'German heroes' blood' (*Heldenblut*) by the 'greatness' of the rescue of 'the fatherland from the midst of war'.[115]

The conformity of such coverage of the conflict had already been epitomized by *Gartenlaube*'s publication in 1877–8 of Moritz Busch's experiences as Bismarck's go-between in 1870–1, working with the 'mobilized Foreign Office' which had been assigned to military headquarters.[116] Here, he had 'the opportunity, not only to observe some decisive military actions from a good position, but also to see and hear other important events from close up, too'.[117] It was, above all, the momentousness of the other events which made them appear, for a man from modest circumstances who would 'never have thought that he would come into personal

[110] Ibid. J. Burckhardt, *Weltgeschichtliche Betrachtungen*, ed. J. Oeri (Berlin, 1905), 27–30, 195–206. The volume was based on lectures given in 1868 and, in revised form, in 1870–1.

[111] J. v. Burckhardt, *Weltgeschichtliche Betrachtungen*, 207.

[112] See 'The *Landwehr*'s Bloodiest Day at Metz', 'Memories of the Holy War', 'Parisian Pictures and Histories', 'Hospital Comrades', 'On Guard Duty at Metz', 'In Strasbourg Two Years Ago and Now', all in 1872, and 'Moltke' (1873): *Gartenlaube*, 1872, vol. 1, 11–14; vol. 6, 89–91; vol. 38, 622–4; vol. 43, 705, 716; vol. 46, 753, 764; vol. 47, 777–9; 1873, vol. 43, 705.

[113] *Gartenlaube*, 1886, vol. 35, 614. [114] Ibid. [115] Ibid.

[116] M. Busch, 'Das mobilisierte Auswärtiges Amt', ibid., 1877, vol. 42, 708.

[117] Ibid.

contact with the Chancellor', like 'a dream, almost like a matter of wonder': 'One saw immediately before one's eyes a world-historical event unfolding which has scarcely ever been equalled.'[118] His impressions of the fighting were obscured by the activities of 'crowned heads, princes, ministers, generals, fixers and party leaders of the Reichstag'.[119] Anecdotes of battles were intermingled with those of diplomatic negotiations and the daily lives of great men.[120] In the *Gartenlaube*, this manner of remembering the Franco-German War continued until the death of Wilhelm I in 1888, which was marked by a series of eulogistic articles, illustrated by lithographs with titles like 'On the Evening of the Battle of Gravelotte', 'King Wilhelm's Meeting with Emperor Napoleon after the Battle near Sedan', 'War Council in Versailles', and 'King Wilhelm Visits the Wounded in Versailles'.[121] In the narrative, 'such powerful shocks, issuing in the heights, and such captivating successes of that great time of 1870' constitute the apogee of the monarch's career, followed by the long 'twilight years' of the 1870s and 1880s.[122]

This type of heroic national account had become the norm after 1871. Even in southern German newspapers such as the *Karlsruher Zeitung*, reflecting in July 1889 on the centenary of the storming of the Bastille, the Franco-German War was interwoven in the contrasting foundation myths of Germany and France. The *Kaiserreich*,

> in the first instance, celebrates as its national festival the birthday of its Kaiser, the bearer of its national idea, who keeps alive an awareness that the fate of his dynasty is intimately linked to that of the *Volk* and who cannot—unlike a republican ruler—step down from his responsible office in accordance with his personal desire or comfort, but has to stick it out and struggle alongside his subjects, who have got used to seeing in him the exemplary model of loyalty and patriotic virtue.[123]

Such consciousness of the difference between Germany and its most powerful neighbour derived from the campaign of 1870–1, which itself formed part of a history of conflicts extending back to the Seven Years' War and the Revolutionary and Napoleonic Wars. 'In the hard fight, the German *Volk* won the right to its national existence', the same article went on: 'it has become the powerful pillar of constitutional monarchy in Europe and it is firmly resolved to defend to the last man its position against all desires to the contrary, whether they come from the republican or absolutist side, or from both combined'.[124] Although the mythology of 1870–1 was associated by 'Reich Germans' with different political traditions, not merely with one version of 'constitutional monarchy', it was nearly always tied to the establishment of a German nation-state, which was barely contested during

[118] Ibid.   [119] Ibid.
[120] See, for instance, M. Busch, 'In Rezonville. Eine Schlacht und eine Wahlstatt', ibid., 1877, vol. 46, 776, or M. Busch, 'Tischreden und Theegespräche in Ferrieres. Allerlei Besuch. Fort nach Versailles', ibid., 1878, vol. 2, 26–8.
[121] Ibid., 1888, vols 11–16, 229–32.   [122] Ibid., 249.
[123] *Karlsruher Zeitung*, 16 July 1889, cited in J. Leonhard, *Bellizismus und Nation*, 764.
[124] Ibid.

the imperial era.[125] Friedrich Nietzsche himself, a well-known critic of the crass materialism of the German Empire, accepted in *Die fröhliche Wissenschaft* (1882) that the new German state was the product of the nineteenth-century nexus between military conflict, democratization, and national independence during a 'classic era of war'.[126] Because of national reactions to the Bonapartist order on the Continent, 'for the national movement, out of which this glory of war (*Kriegs-Glorie*) grows, is merely the counter shock against Napoleon', it was possible that 'a couple of warring centuries could follow one another' and that 'man in Europe', who had been threatened with emasculation, could again become 'the boss of the salesman and the philistine'.[127] Eventually, 'who knows', 'this piece of ancient being' ('perhaps the decisive one, the block of granite') could 'also at last become the boss of the national movement' and become a positive creative force in and for himself.[128] For the moment, though, nationalism and bellicosity appeared inseparable.

MEMORIES OF VIOLENCE

In a critical sense, Nietzsche's idiosyncratic treatment of war resembled that of veterans more than the majority of official or public mythologies did. The philosopher had experienced the conflict of 1870–1 as a medical orderly and was sensitive to the 'terrible depths of being' revealed by war, even if he also envisaged it as the principal hope of renewal and destructive creativity.[129] The majority of combatants appear to have experienced similar 'dread' (war was 'schrecklich') and 'horror' (it was 'entsetzlich') during and after the fighting, on the battlefield, in hospitals, and in other contexts. Their physical and psychological reactions to fighting and its aftermath are well documented and often unembellished, in correspondence, diaries, war reports, eyewitness accounts, and memoirs, all of which overlapped with each other. Official narratives, historical research, press memorialization, and, especially, concern for the feelings and sensibilities of those at home conspired to exert pressure on soldiers to suppress or adapt their accounts of what they had seen, heard, smelled, felt, and thought at the time. 'I had the chance to see a great part of the battlefield', wrote the bombardier Richard Gädke from Wörth on 7 November 1870, 'but I shall not describe the view more precisely; it would be bad for Mama's nerves.'[130] In the preceding sentences of the same letter, however, he had detailed 'the traces of the bitter fighting: bombed walls, stamped-on and flattened gardens, pools of blood, the dead all over, the whimpering wounded, scraps

---

[125] I have written about the relationship between political and national traditions at greater length in M. Hewitson, *National Identity and Political Thought in Germany*, 213–59; see also M. Hewitson, 'The *Kaiserreich* in Question: Constitutional Crisis in Germany before the First World War', *Journal of Modern History*, 73 (2001), 725–80.
[126] F. Nietzsche, *Die fröhliche Wissenschaft*, revised edn (Leipzig, 1887), 301–2.
[127] Ibid.   [128] Ibid.
[129] Nietzsche, 7 Nov. 1870, cited in J. Leonhard, *Bellizismus und Nation*, 771.
[130] R. Gädke to his parents, in H. Mehrkens, *Statuswechsel*, 65.

of clothing, thrown-away weapons and knapsacks, in short the traces of dreadful devastation everywhere'.[131] For the priest Martin Schall, it was likewise necessary to look away for his own benefit as well as that of his fiancée: 'I shall spare you and myself a description of the prospect of the suffering in detail.'[132] Yet he was unable to ignore what he had experienced, leaving his future bride wondering why he was not more joyful at the news of Germany's victory, and he subsequently gave a full account of it in his memoirs: 'The daily view of the terrible suffering and pain of the poor wounded, of which I have deliberately depicted little for you, leaves little room for joy in any empathetic heart. These have been difficult, difficult weeks that I have once again lived through here.'[133] It was impossible to banish such impressions, feelings, and reflections in what one doctor, overwhelmed by what he was faced with, called 'stone-age conditions'.[134] These were the conditions experienced by Nietzsche as he accompanied the wounded on the train from Metz: 'Here, given the terrible state of all my sick ones, the constant binding of their often burning wounds, sleeping in cattle wagons in which six heavily wounded men were lying on the straw, I contracted the first signs of dysentery.'[135] The philosopher's extrapolation of these experiences and his aestheticization of warfare, which resembled that of many intellectuals in 1914, found virtually no echo in the 1870s and 1880s. His initial horror, though, was widely shared (see Figure 10.2).

Soldiers of different rank, social background, and locality were, on many occasions, startlingly frank in their description of combat. Their responses to the wars of 1864, 1866, and 1870–1, which diverged markedly in respect of their aims, alliances, and enmities, were similar. In spite of their concern for their families' sensibilities and for public propriety, they regularly referred to dismemberment, the protrusion of bones, effusion of brain matter, the exposure of nerves, and the charring of skin. Although they sometimes limited themselves to euphemisms such as 'difficult hours' and 'terrible battles', at other times they were graphic.[136] Similarly, some soldiers seem to have found it easier to recount examples of injured enemy troops, particularly French ones, yet others scarcely distinguished between them. One purportedly 'humorous' description told of the fate of an outnumbered German cavalryman, for instance, whose body was left on the battlefield near Metz. The soldier had received 'two heavy cuts on his head', leaving his helmet 'open to all directions of the wind'; one in the rear and one in the left arm;

then they cut off three fingers from the left hand and half-way through the forefinger; then he received one cut in the right arm and one in the right cheek, which chased two

[131] Ibid.

[132] M. Schall, 24 Jan. 1871, in M. Schall, *Vor vierzig Jahren. Kriegserinnerungen eines ehemaligen Lazarettpfarrers der II. Armee*, 241.

[133] M. Schall, 17 Feb. 1871, in M. Schall, *Vor vierzig Jahren. Kriegserinnerungen eines ehemaligen Lazarettpfarrers der II. Armee*, 274.

[134] Cited in M. Steinbach, *Abgrund Metz*, 50.

[135] Ibid., 52. Steinbach speculates that Nietzsche's later illness might have dated back to this period.

[136] Theodor Weinreich, diary entry 29 Aug. 1870, cited in H. Mehrkens, *Statuswechsel*, 61.

Figure 10.2 Eugen Adam, *Des Todes Rundschau in der Silvesternacht von 1870 auf 1871* (1870/1). The allegorical figure of death was not new, but its position at the head of column of cavalry and above an open grave was much more unusual. Eugen Adam was the son of Albrecht Adam, the painter of the Napoleonic Wars.
Source: Stadtmuseum, Munich.

teeth down into his throat and thereby kept open the thrust into the throat; and as he fell from his horse, they gave him, for good luck, another four stabs in the back—everything included according to Adam Riese: eleven wounds.[137]

'These are moments that one would not want to relive', wrote the same author: 'One can only bear these impressions hour-by-hour; the suffering will choke and oppress the heart.'[138] Nonetheless, authors recorded such moments. Partly, they used the licence that the authorities and the moral guardians of the 'public' gave to writers of war stories. More significantly, they seem to have been willing to ignore or contravene taboos concerning the graphic description of injuries to the body and death which obtained in most other forms of literature. There is little evidence that their outpourings were merely conventional and stylistic, lapsing into gothic excesses in order to appeal to a fascinated readership.[139] Rather, explicit accounts of battle normally existed within an 'heroic' or a 'patriotic' framework, which they seemed to contradict, suggesting that deaths in combat were anonymous, grisly, or meaningless. Despite the fact that official and public justifications of the 'wars of

---

[137] E. Frommel, *In den Königs Rock. Geschichten aus Krieg und Frieden*, 12th edn (Schwerin, 1915), 115–16.

[138] E. Frommel, 'Die evangelische Feldgeistlichkeit', cited in C. Rak, *Krieg, Nation und Konfession*, 198.

[139] See, for instance, I. Schikorsky, 'Kommunikation über das Unbeschreibbare—Beobachtungen zum Sprachstil von Kriegsbriefen', *Wirkendes Wort*, 42 (1992), 295–315; I. Schikorsky (ed.), *Wenn doch dies Elend ein Ende hätte. Ein Briefwechsel aus dem Deutsch-Französischen Krieg 1870/71* (Cologne, 1999); Y. N. Harari, *The Ultimate Experience: Battlefield Revelations and the Making of Modern War Culture, 1450–2000* (Basingstoke, 2008).

unification' became more pervasive over time, troubling and contradictory revelations about the nature of the conflicts continued to appear, with memoirs drawing heavily on and disseminating the information contained in letters and diaries written during wartime.[140]

Notwithstanding claims to the contrary, such candour encompassed acts of killing and perpetration as well as references to personal suffering and the possibility of injury and death.[141] These disclosures seem to have been easier to make when soldiers believed that they were confronted by dehumanized 'inferiors' or 'enemies'—'*turcos*', 'the negro type', or ill-disciplined, duplicitous *francs-tireurs*— but they also occurred alongside admissions of discomfort or guilt.[142] Retaliatory acts were simple to justify, prompting one officer to congratulate his men with a 'bravo, a head shot', or 'revenge for my NCO whom we buried yesterday'.[143] Other acts seemed like 'unnecessary harshness' or 'savagery', yet they were not routinely concealed.[144] Stories about tying a woman to a wheel before killing her or pointing loaded guns at villagers were well known, appearing in private letters and public chronicles.[145] So were those relating to killing during combat. 'I can't describe to you what it means to take a city where fire is coming from every window', wrote one soldier from Karlsruhe: 'We stormed forwards again and again, houses burned to the left and right, and anything armed standing in our way was shot down.'[146] 'It was completely horrible', reported another combatant to his parents: 'I don't want to take part in another streetfight like it where one is standing looking right into the face of one's enemy, at most 5–10, or 20 paces away, recognizes every facial expression and then has to shoot it to pieces—ghastly.'[147] With long-range weapons, including breech-loading rifles, troops killed and were wounded 'without ever having looked a single enemy in the face', as one combatant in the Franco-German War recalled.[148] For this reason and for others, such as the will to survive, soldiers' accounts tended to concentrate on the risk of being killed or injured and on the consequences of being exposed to such sights rather than on the moral dangers and difficulties of active killing. Modern courage, went on the same combatant, was passive, consisting in 'contempt for the risk of death', not active, involving heroic

---

[140] Thus, Christian Rak, *Krieg, Nation und Konfession*, 199, 202–10, points out that accounts of 'the suffering and terrors of war' became more difficult to portray realistically after the 'triumph' of 1870/1, yet he also shows the ways in which the letters, report, memorial speech, and memoir, published in 1886, of the army chaplain Heinrich Adolf Köstlin, though different in some respects, all gave an explicit account of the battles of Villiers-Champigny, which took up ten out of sixty pages of *Im Felde*.

[141] Ute Frevert, *A Nation in Barracks*, 180, has contended that a taboo on descriptions of killing still obtained: 'Despite the cultural ban on killing being officially suspended in wartime, its impact continued unabated in both war memoirs and the preparation of war.' Heidi Mehrkens, *Statuswechsel*, 60, links the paucity of references to the absence of strongly defined images of the enemy in 1870–1.

[142] For the belittlement of African colonial soldiers, see A. Fausel, *Ein Ritt ins Franzosenland*, 28, for instance.

[143] Cited in T. Rohkrämer, *Der Militarismus der 'kleinen Leute'*, 129.

[144] C. Klein, *Fröschweiler Chronik*, 130.

[145] Ibid. Also, T. Rohkrämer, *Der Militarismus der 'kleinen Leute'*, 109–11, 129.

[146] Cited in C. G. Krüger, *'Sind wir denn nicht Brüder?'*, 240.

[147] Ibid.   [148] R. Martin, *Kriegserinnerungen*, 175–7.

deeds, as in ancient times.[149] Passivity amidst carnage was arguably more unsettling and harder to describe than acts of war, including killing, not least because such actions were a significant element of traditional mythologies of combat. In the conflicts of the 1860s and early 1870s, what was unusual was the combination of soldiers', eyewitnesses', and commentators' unabashed descriptions of both passive and active aspects of warfare and their abhorrence of military slaughter.[150]

Evidently, content could be affected by form.[151] Diaries were most uncompromising, revealing mixed feelings, private doubts, and visual spectacles. To an extent, they were an extension of the practice of keeping a diary during peacetime, which was itself guided by specific conventions, including the possibility of posthumous disclosure. By contrast, memoirs were regularly composed decades after the event, selecting and omitting material in accordance with public taste and retrospective narratives of German unification. Writers of letters were not swayed by such narratives, but they were aware of the expectations of their families and a wider group of neighbours amongst whom their 'news' circulated. They were also conscious of the need to be brave and patriotic, particularly in the widely accepted 'defensive' war of 1870–1. Their lack of familiarity with letter-writing and the circumstances in which they wrote in many cases produced largely formulaic results. 'Who doesn't know about the excellent invention of correspondence cards, those short letters which are completely suited, for our forever-writing species, to accustom them to time-saving, laconic brevity of expression', wrote one commentator in 1871:

> The cards can quickly be got out of a knapsack, can be written in fleeting words in pencil, with an address and report, when the back of a comrade must often serve in the place of a writing desk, then can be given to a passing member of the *Feldpost*, who takes sacks full from the bivouacs, before making their way home in the shortest possible time.[152]

Notwithstanding their diverse audiences and means of production, all three types of ego document—correspondence, memoir, and diary—detailed similar, unsettling descriptions of violence. Partly, such similarity resulted from the use of diaries and letters as the basis of memoirs, partly it appears to have been the consequence of a deeply felt or widely perceived centrality of soldiers' individual experiences.[153]

---

[149] Ibid.

[150] On the treatment of war as 'slaughter', akin to the mass-scale reduction of animals to meat, see D. Pick, *War Machine: The Rationalisation of Slaughter in the Modern Age* (New Haven, 1993), 165–88.

[151] This is germane to the case made by Christine Krüger, 'German Suffering in the Franco-German War, 1870/71', 404–22, who argues that more accurate accounts of the suffering of soldiers, which was revealed in diaries and correspondence above all, was largely kept from public view. Here, I present an opposing argument.

[152] 'Feldpost', *Jahrbücher für ide deutsche Armee und Marine* (1871), cited in F. Becker, *Bilder von Krieg und Nation*, 64.

[153] This sense was already present during the Revolutionary and Napoleonic Wars, but in a much more diluted form: see L. S. James, *Witnessing the Revolutionary and Napoleonic Wars in German Central Europe* (Basingstoke, 2013), 42–67. More generally, D. Wahrmann, *The Making of the Modern Self: Identity and Culture in Eighteenth-Century England* (New Haven, 2004); D. M. Hopkin, 'Storytelling,

These experiences had a direct impact, as just over 100 million postcards and letters were sent back and forth during the Franco-German War, making it the first 'epistolary' conflict of its kind.[154] They were also part of a dynamic public discourse about the character of modern warfare.

Memoirs and collections of letters about the war became popular in their own right after 1871. Hundreds of titles appeared during the imperial era.[155] Frank Kühlich's sample, which is the fullest produced to date, lists 432 published in the fifty years up to 1919 (see Table 10.1). By comparison, 146 titles on the Revolutionary and Napoleonic Wars appeared, according to Karen Hagemann's calculation, in the first fifty-five years between 1815 and 1869.[156] Some memoirs were reissued many times, with Gotthelf Huyssen's *Bilder aus dem Kriegsleben eines Militär-Geistlichen* (1872) running to six editions, Carl Tanera's *Ernste und heitere Erinnerungen eines Ordonnanzoffiziers* (1887) counting twelve editions by 1914, and Carl Klein's *Fröschweiler Chronik* (1870) numbering thirty-four editions by 1914. Even a less well-known work such as Johannes Diehl's *Meine Kriegs-Erlebnisse von 1870/71* (1904) sold 70,000 copies, or nearly as many as Thomas Mann's *Buddenbrooks* (1901), one of the best-selling novels of the period, which had reached 100,000 by 1918.[157] When these works were added to series of articles published in the early 1870s in mass-circulation periodicals like the *Gartenlaube*, *Daheim* (with a circulation of 35,000 in 1867), and *Ueber Land und Meer* (55,000 in 1858), and popular histories of the conflict such as Christlieb Gotthold Hottinger's *Der deutsch-französische Krieg 1870–71* (1876), which had sold 230,000 copies by 1910, and Max Dittrich's *Der Deutsch-Französische Krieg* (1890), which had reached forty editions and around 30,000 copies within five years, the

Table 10.1 Memoirs, Diaries, and Letters by Publication Date

No Date	1870s	1880s	1890s	1900s	1910s	After 1920	Total
60	65	29	124	84	57	20	432

Source: Derived from data in F. Kühlich, *Die deutschen Soldaten im Krieg von 1870/71* (Frankfurt, 1995). I have inserted the publication dates of first editions.

Fairytales and Autobiography: Some Observations on Eighteenth- and Nineteenth-Century French Soldiers' and Sailors' Memoirs', *Social History*, 29 (2004), 186–98; D. M. Hopkin, *Soldier and Peasant in French Popular Culture, 1766–1870* (Suffolk, 2003); K. Moritz, *Das Ich am Ende des Schreibens. Autobiographisches Erzählen im 18. und frühen 19. Jahrhunderts* (Würzburg, 1990); K. v. Greyerz, H. Medick, and P. Weit (eds), *Von der dargestellten Person zum erinnerten Ich. Europäische Selbstzeugnisse als historische Quellen 1500–1850* (Cologne, 2001); M. Fulbrook and U. Rublack (eds), *German History*, 28 (2010), special issue on ego documents.

[154] F. Becker, *Bilder von Krieg und Nation*, 62: the North German Confederation carried 89,659,000 letters and postcards, and the southern German states approximately 11 million.

[155] Ibid., 59.

[156] K. Hagemann, *Revisiting Prussia's Wars against Napoleon*, 304.

[157] E. Boa, 'Mann, Buddenbrooks', in P. Hutchinson (ed.), *Landmarks in the German Novel* (Berne, 2007), 99.

continuing visibility of individuals' experiences of the war becomes apparent.[158] In Kühlich's sample, sixty-five memoirs and other individual accounts about the Franco-German War, together with the majority of a further sixty with no date, were published in the 1870s, followed by a lull in the 1880s (twenty-nine works) and a spike of 124 in the 1890s around the time of the twenty-fifth anniversary of the conflict. The early run of more than a hundred publications within ten years can be contrasted with the nineteen similar works which appeared in the first fifteen years after 1815.[159]

Not all ego documents contained harrowing accounts of combat, but a significant number did. They overlapped with contemporaneous press reportage, which was much more explicit than later, retrospective coverage of the wars. Virtually all newspapers printed letters from soldiers, leading to a dialogue of sorts between journalists and combatants.[160] Although self-censorship existed and occasional bans were placed on letter writing in order to maintain the secrecy of some troops' movements, official censorship was not unusually restrictive and reports were filed and letters printed within three to four days of the events taking place.[161] Letters like that in the *Weimarische Zeitung* from a Prussian officer after the battle of Gravelotte, in which he described his ride through 'the position which we shelled' on the previous day, were common.[162] He had 'the satisfaction of riding over genuine mountains of corpses', he wrote: 'My battery had done all that! It is dreadful, terrible!'[163] 'Our brave people, our courageous comrades, all, all gone, all dead, destroyed, hideously dismembered!' he noted, switching without seeming to realize from an account of the slaughter of the French that he had helped to cause to one of a generalized suffering of his comrades and of others: 'I am truly ashamed still to be living.'[164] If this first-hand account of a pivotal battle was not directly critical of the authorities or of the war, it was also far from being an endorsement. Other letters, some of which were reprinted in the local press, begged similar questions: not whether the war should be waged but whether it should have turned out this way. 'The bullets and grenades hit us from the front and in the right flank', ran the report of a wounded sergeant major, printed in the *Rudolstädter Wochenblatt*: 'The whistling and roaring was terrible. In front and beside me, people fell like flies, some of them still, some screaming in misery. That was the most terrible thing.'[165] When he was hit by a shell—'Sssst, schrumm!'—he twisted around suddenly and sat down 'in dizziness', calling out 'involuntarily': 'Where has my arm gone!'[166] He jumped up, probably in shock, grasping his sword with his left hand,

[158] F. Becker, *Bilder von Krieg und Nation*, 58–60.
[159] K. Hagemann, *Revisiting Prussia's Wars against Napoleon*, 304. The size of the book market had expanded markedly in the interim, of course.
[160] H. Wachenhusen, *Aus bewegtem Leben*, vol. 2, 260.
[161] W. Siemann, 'Ideenschmuggel. Probleme der Meinungskontrolle und das Los deutscher Zensoren im 19. Jahrhundert', *Historische Zeitschrift*, 245 (1987), 71–106.
[162] *Weimarische Zeitung*, Aug. 1870, cited in M. Steinbach, *Abgrund Metz*, 41.
[163] Ibid.   [164] Ibid.
[165] Rudolf Gehring, 23 Aug 1870, in the *Rudolstädter Wochenblatt*, ibid., 49.
[166] Ibid.

and charged, 'but the fire was too thick, too thick'.[167] Waking up from 'deep unconsciousness', he found his clothes cut away and dressings applied to his wounds: 'I stood up, searched again for my arm for a while, which was still dangling near me…and then rushed with mad pain through corpses, the wounded and dead French villains.'[168] It is difficult to know what readers made of the corporal's horrifying streams of consciousness, but it is unlikely that their pre-existing notions of heroism and valour were left unchallenged.

Journalists' and soldiers' reports of 1864, 1866, and 1870–1 were, in all likelihood, mutually reinforcing. There are countless instances of troops referring to newspapers in order to find out what was going on.[169] Their observations seem frequently to have been written in the style of a developing tradition of war reportage which had been given a fillip by the Crimean War, the Franco-Austrian War of 1859, and the American Civil War. Famous foreign journalists like William Howard Russell, who had made careers from the supply of on-the-spot reports of these earlier conflicts filled with interesting anecdotes and unflinching descriptions, also covered the German wars after 1864 and influenced the network of increasingly well-known German war correspondents, who worked alongside them: Hans Wachenhusen for the *Kölnische Zeitung*, Ludwig Pietsch for the *Vossische Zeitung*, Friedrich Wilhelm Hackländer for the *Allgemeine Zeitung*, Gustav Freytag for the *Grenzboten*, and Hans Blum for *Daheim*, amongst many others.[170] Their reporting of events was characterized by speed, a regular flow of exciting actions and an insider's view of individuals' experiences. In their popular books about the wars, they extended and adapted such techniques, combining the testimony of participants and their own perspective of events which they had either witnessed or had reconstructed—sometimes by retracing soldiers' steps—after the conflict. Compared to military experts, Fontane, who wrote for the *Neue Preußische Zeitung*, was in a better position, as he put it, to write about 'extra-military factors'.[171] Like his colleague at the *Kölnische Zeitung* Hans Wachenhusen, Georg Horn self-consciously adopted the standpoint of a diarist in his 'pictures and sketches' of the events of 1870, recounting sights as if he were viewing them as a soldier:

> The first fallen lay there—at first singly, like the sentries of death; then, further, more and more thickly. The numbers of the epaulettes of the uniforms, shot to pieces, indicated that here was the field of battle and victory of the Brandenburg regiments, and the thickly sown corpses showed with great losses every advantage had to be wrung

---

[167] Ibid.   [168] Ibid.

[169] One example was G. v. Siemens, during the Austro-Prussian War: 'I have one more request. We have no newspapers at all here, and I would like to read a Berlin paper in order keep up with both the war news and politics': Karl Helfferich, *Georg von Siemens*, 62.

[170] F. Becker, *Bilder von Krieg und Nation*, 44–5. The *National-Zeitung* alone had ten correspondents following the Franco-German War.

[171] T. Fontane, 'Meine Kinderjahre', in T. Fontane, *Sämtliche Werke*, vol. 14, 119; T. Fontane, *Briefe*, vol. 2, 324–5. In addition to Fontane's three 'war books' on 1864, 1866, and 1870, see H. Wachenhusen, *Tagebuch vom Österreichischen Kriegsschauplatz*; H. Wachenhusen, *Tagebuch vom französischen Kriegsschauplatz 1870–1871*.

from the enemy, how expensive each foot of earth won from the enemy for the fatherland had become.[172]

Although Horn sought reassurance in the fact that, 'on the whole, our troops
did not make the same horror-inducing impression which one got from the
French fallen', his subsequent description of 'the limbs of most Frenchmen
smashed to pieces, separated from the body, heads shot off, so that the brain matter ran out', undermined the reassuring, patriotic case which, on the surface, he
was attempting to make.[173] The more realistically journalists probed the actual-
ities of combat, from soldiers' own points of view, the more unsettling their
accounts became.

The literary representation of the wars of unification by writers such as Theodor
Fontane, Gustav Freytag, and Felix Dahn combined journalistic reportage, the
genre of memoirs, and historical reconstruction and fantasy.[174] All three authors
were moved by the events of the past decade to look for historical parallels, partly
as a means of revealing the momentousness of those events, partly as a form of
escape from them. Thus, even Fontane, who showed the greatest ambivalence of
the three writers about the conduct of the war (demonstrating his readiness to
criticize the crudeness of Germany's occupation of Alsace-Lorraine or the fool-
hardiness of commanders' orders to attack at all costs), decided to go back to the
era of the wars of liberation for his first novel after the publication of the last of his
'war books', *Der Krieg gegen Frankreich*, in 1876.[175] *Vor dem Sturm* (1878) recounts
the story of a noble family in Brandenburg between the Christmas of 1812 and
March 1813, when Prussia joined the war against France. Its purpose amongst
other things was 'to present . . . a large number of figures from the Mark Brandenburg
(i.e. *German-Wendish*, for herein lies their peculiarity), . . . as they existed in those
days and as they, by and large, still exist today', he informed his publisher: 'I was
not interested in conflicts, but rather in showing how the great consciousness born
in those days came upon the most various people and how it affected them.'[176]
Freytag, who had become famous after the publication of *Soll und Haben* in 1855,
was more straightforward and—at least in the scale of his undertaking—ambitious,

---

[172] G. Horn, *Bei Friedrich Karl*, vol. 1, 103, also cited by Heidi Mehrkens, *Statuswechsel*, 66. Horn
also published letters in the *Gartenlaube*, 'Im Hauptquartier des Prinzen Friedrich Karl', 1870, vols 35,
37–40, 556–8, 599–603, 612–16, 655–8, on the same topic.

[173] G. Horn, *Bei Friedrich Karl*, vol. 1, 105.

[174] On the topic in general, see R. Kipper, 'Formen literarischer Erinnerung an den Deutsch-
Französischen Krieg von 1870/71', in H. Berding, K. Heller, and W. Speitkamp (eds), *Krieg und
Erinnerung*, 13–37; G. A. Craig, *Theodor Fontane*; J. Osborne, *Theodor Fontane: Vor den Romanen. Krieg
und Kunst* (Göttingen, 1999); L. L. Ping, *Gustav Freytag and the Prussian Gospel: Novels, Liberalism and
History* (Oxford, 2006); L. L. Ping, 'Gustav Freytag's *Bilder aus der deutschen Vergangenheit* and the
Meaning of German History', *German Studies Review*, 32 (2009), 549–68; M. Nissen, 'Populäre
Geschichtsschreibung im 19. Jahrhundert. Gustav Freytag und seine "Bilder aus der deutschen
Vergangenheit"', *Archiv für Kulturgeschichte*, 89 (2007), 395–425.

[175] See T. Fontane, *Aus der Tagen der Okkupation. Eine Osterreise durch Nordfrankreich und Elsaß-
Lothringen 1871*, 2nd edn (Berlin, 1872). Also, J. Osborne, 'Le Bourget, oder die Garden ach St.
Privat. Zu Fontanes *Der Krieg gegen die Republik*', *Fontane-Blätter*, 58 (1994), 138–54.

[176] Cited in K. Hagemann, *Revisiting Prussia's Wars against Napoleon*, 385.

embarking on the six volumes of *Die Ahnen* (1872–80), which followed the imaginary history of a bourgeois family from the time of the *Germanen* to the nineteenth century. With some embellishment, he recalled in his memoirs how he had seized upon the idea as he was in France with the headquarters of the Crown Prince:

> Already, while I was going along the country roads of France in the bustle of men, horses and wagons, the penetration of our Germanic ancestors into Roman Gaul kept occurring to me again and again. I saw them swimming on rafts and wooden shields above the streams, I heard the 'hara' cry of the old Franks and Alemanen behind the hurrah of my countrymen from the Fifth and Eleventh Corps, I compared German ways of doing things with foreign ones and reflected how the German military commanders and their armies changed in the course of the centuries into the national institution of our system of war, the greatest and most particular edifice of the modern state. From such dreams and a certain historical style, which had entered my imagination through the experiences (*Erlebnisse*) of 1870, the idea for the novel *Die Ahnen* gradually emerged.[177]

In a similar way, Dahn—who was a young specialist of old German legal history at the University of Würzburg—was prompted to go back after 1871 to a novel, begun at the time of the Franco-Austrian War in 1859 but shelved in 1863, about the fall of the Reich of the Ostrogoths in sixth-century Italy. The story about the collapse of a Germanic outpost south of the Alps comparable to that of Austria as a consequence of the scheming of a despotic Latin power, where the Second Empire of Napoleon III was equated with Byzantium, became—in the form of *Ein Kampf um Rom* (1876)—one of the most popular works of the imperial era.[178] Its national parallels and glorification of war contributed to its success.

Like *Die Ahnen*, however, *Ein Kampf um Rom* was not merely an example of escapism.[179] It not only drew on a long-standing mythology of the *Germanen*, which alluded to the savagery and violence of tribes' struggle to survive during and after the *Völkerwanderung*; it was also tied to Dahn's own experiences of the Franco-German War, which he later published as a popular memoir.[180] In this sense, war literature, personal testimony, and reportage were closely linked, bearing the traces of ambiguity—jubilation, fascination, and revulsion—which marked out other records. 'The war, all those great things experienced, had done me good, in my most profound inner self', Dahn wrote in his *Erinnerungen*, confessing his previous lassitude: 'I came back with increased self-esteem, with a somewhat directed self-confidence.'[181] Yet, as has been seen, the author had also been shocked by combat and its effects. Heroism, 'one saw it and experienced it', required ruthlessness, as when 'a couple of hundred barely trained men, who conceptually had

---

[177] G. Freytag, *Erinnerungen aus meinem Leben* (Leipzig, 1887), 347–8.
[178] G. L. Mosse, 'Was die Deutschen wirklich lasen', in R. Grimm and J. Hermand (eds), *Popularität und Trivialität* (Frankfurt, 1974), 101–20; K. V. See, *Die Ideen von 1789 und die Ideen von 1914* (Frankfurt, 1974), 91–5.
[179] *Contra* C. Holz, *Flucht aus der Wirklichkeit. 'Die Ahnen' von Gustav Freytag* (Frankfurt, 1983).
[180] See, especially, R. Kipper, *Der Germanenmythos im Deutschen Kaiserreich* (Göttingen, 2002).
[181] F. Dahn, *Erinnerungen*, vol. 4, 3.

never understood the worth of the state, stormed without hesitation towards an almost inevitable death, over killed and wounded brothers in arms, seized by only one urge—to vanquish'.[182] In part, the 'tragic' components of *Ein Kampf um Rom*, with the demise of the Goths and of Rome itself, are designed to highlight the heroism of the struggle. 'Dark heroes', whose lack of morality contributes to the success of their deeds, were stock characters in the well-known historical novels of Walter Scott, for instance.[183] The struggle was not purely heroic, however, as critics of Dahn were quick to note. The central character of Cornelius Cethegus Cäsarius, the 'heroic' last prefect of Rome, was held to be an 'iron, heartless, cruel and blood-thirsty egotist', in the words of Otto Kraus in *Zeitfragen des christlichen Volkslebens* in 1884.[184] The 'existential' vision of struggle which the novel presented seemed at once threatening and impressive, running parallel to the uncompromising conflict of France and Germany in 1870–1.[185] In this respect, Dahn's notion of a war between *Völker*, in which moral injunctions could be suspended in order to prevail, coincided with that of Freytag and Fontane, whose reports on the conflict were published during its course and aftermath. 'The whole thing has the effect on me of a colossal spectacle, a horrifying, passing, savage hunt', Fontane wrote to his wife: 'A *Völkerwanderung*, regulated by railways, organized masses, ever more *masses*, within which one fluctuates like an atom, not standing outside, dominating, but sacrificed without will to the great train.'[186] The author, who published a memoir of his imprisonment by the French in 1870, felt he was 'a victim of dark urges and violent powers (*Gewalten*)'.[187] 'Many love that because it is an "excitement"', he went on: 'I'm too artistically organized for that to do me any good.'[188] Nonetheless, it had an effect on his treatment of war and on his reputation as a writer, who was known to the public until the 1880s primarily as an historian of the wars of unification, a journalist (for the *Kreuzzeitung*), and a prisoner-of-war, rather than as a novelist. Like that of Freytag, Dahn, and other authors, the 'war literature' of Fontane was a hybrid genre with multiple sources.[189]

The interplay of war literature, which had become a distinct genre after the Napoleonic Wars, and war reports, which had developed in a trans-national setting from the mid-nineteenth century onwards, was not straightforward in the midst of a series of wars after 1864 which differed so markedly from each other and in which so much was at stake, in contrast to the public's response to the Crimean War or

---

[182] Ibid., 593–4.

[183] R. Kipper, *Der Germanenmythos*, 132.   [184] Ibid., 148.

[185] Rainer Kipper characterizes Dahn's portrayal of war as 'existential'; Rainer Kipper, 'Formen literarischer Erinnerung an den Deutsch-Französischen Krieg von 1870/71', in H. Berding, K. Heller, and W. Speitkamp (eds), *Krieg und Erinnerung*, 28–33.

[186] Cited ibid., 23. See also J. S. Cornell, 'Dann weg "mit's Milletär" und wieder ein civiler Civilist: Theodor Fontane and the War of German Unification', in W. Pape (ed.), *1870/71–1989/90: German Unification and the Change of Literary Discourse* (Berlin, 1993), 79–103.

[187] Kipper, 'Formen', 23. Fontane's three-month imprisonment as a journalist (he was accused of spying) became a diplomatic incident: T. Fontane, *Kriegsgefangen. Erlebtes 1870* (Berlin, 1871).

[188] Kipper, 'Formen', 23.

[189] This was also true of earlier war novelists such as Willibald Alexis, Ludwig Rellstab, and George Hesekiel, who were also well-known journalists.

American Civil War. The involvement of German soldiers, implicating nearly all communities and the majority of families, helped to transform the pursuit of news into an all-consuming activity, as the liberal constitutional lawyer Rudolf von Ihering confessed in 1866 in a letter to a friend: 'I have done nothing, nothing at all, for five weeks; for whenever I have an academic book in the hand, my thoughts are not with this but with the war.'[190] During the course of the war, he received the morning edition of the 'old' and 'new' press after 7.00 a.m., followed by the *Allgemeine Zeitung* at 2.00 p.m., and the evening editions at 5.00 p.m.:

> In the meantime, I go into the city [of Gießen] either to read various newspapers in the club or to learn of the newest dispatches which have arrived at one of the coffee houses there. What I do otherwise is eat, drink, sleep and uninterruptedly think about the war and its consequences, and such thinking and brooding has seized hold of me to such an extent that it won't even leave me alone whilst sleeping and in my dreams, for as soon as I wake up in the night (which in my current state of agitation happens often), I find myself at war.[191]

With the press wars of 1866, in which disparaging or accusatory reports from Austria were reprinted in Prussian publications (and vice versa), preparing the ground for the larger-scale and more inimical conflict between France and Germany, many readers found themselves caught up in the events of the campaign. Horror, fascination, fear for their own relatives, and excitement were intermingled, militating against conscious attempts by the government, army, press, and the troops themselves to fashion heroic, national narratives.[192] The dissemination of atrocity stories and public responses to them can be understood in this context, too, not merely as means to stiffen Germans' resolve against a supposedly 'hereditary' enemy.[193] By the same token, the visual representation of the war was double-edged, even though it had been much more carefully controlled by the Prussian military than had been the case in the American Civil War, ensuring that the worst effects of battle were concealed.[194] Certainly, many of the 'realities' of war were

---

[190] Cited in F. Becker, *Bilder von Krieg und Nation*, 49–50.   [191] Ibid.

[192] The focus of much of the literature on such narratives has led to a relative neglect of these aspects of war reportage, with scholars like Nikolaus Buschmann, *Einkreisung und Waffenbruderschaft*, 17, attempting to make sense of 'resistance' to the 'nationalization of the masses' (George L. Mosse) and of 'competing designs for the future', within a broadly 'federative' scheme of unification which places emphasis on wartime enmities, expansionism, and radicalization as means of overcoming internal differences.

[193] Heidi Mehrkens's excellent analysis of the role of reports on the destruction of Bazeilles by Bavarian forces during the battle at Sedan, and on alleged atrocities by French civilians against German troops, is treated as part of a 'process of symbolization', in which 'the events at Bazeilles were judged—sometimes supportively, sometimes critically—as a sign of the resistance of an entire nation against the German advance into France, as the expression of a "Volkskrieg"': Heidi Mehrkens, *Statuswechsel*, 113.

[194] Like Frank Becker, Mehrkens stresses the 'picturesque' and heroic aspects of lithographs in periodicals: ibid., 71. For Becker, *Bilder von Krieg und Nation*, 496, 'the soldiers as a whole appear as *bieder* family figures, full of humour, so that drawings, too, contributed to the bourgeois definition of a national identity deriving from the war'. See also the nuanced judgement of Susanne Parth, *Zwischen Bildbericht und Bildpropaganda*, 362, who likewise stresses 'the forms of trivialization, embellishment and stereotyping of war, the splitting into numerous episodes of battle, overstated pathos, the unique deceptive relation of proximity and distance, but also the painterly dissolution of the pictures and the

excluded, partly on grounds of public decency and partly for other 'propagandistic' purposes, yet a wider striving for 'photographic' realism, which had been glimpsed in previous conflicts, could be detected not merely in the work of illustrators and painters, but in the writings of journalists and diarists alike.[195] The forensic accounts which such developments helped to promote had a long-lasting legacy, notwithstanding later attempts in the press to embellish and heroicize the 'wars of unification'.

The heroic and horrific coexisted in many memoirs about the wars, with the former constituting the framework, by means of which combatants' experiences could be ordered in a meaningful and socially recognized fashion, and with the latter comprising the core or a disruptive element, which could not be ignored or repressed completely.[196] Psychiatrists were not employed by the German armies and psychiatric diagnoses or psychological explanations of the effects of combat played little role in 1864, 1866, or 1870–1, even though the official military report on the medical consequences of the Franco-German War, published in the late 1880s, commented extensively on mental and nervous conditions.[197] Its conclusions were reassuring and indecisive. The concluding section of the report on 'War Psychoses' began:

> The previously very generally held view that great political upheavals and wars are extremely well suited to trouble the life of the soul of those with a less robust psyche, thereby increasing the number of mentally ill in the population of the affected country overall, has recently come to be doubted in many respects.[198]

Given that 'a relatively high number of the mentally ill have come to a demise on the battlefields and barricades, or in prisons for some individuals, one should treat the question of whether wars increase the number of lunatics in the *population as a whole*...as an open one, as previously'.[199] 'In opposition to the tendency to doubt the increase of mental illnesses in the population during the course of wars,

---

deliberate exclusion of the actual battle' on the part of 'realistic' painters of the historical school, yet who also sees such phenomena as 'the artistic expression of an increasing uncertainty'.

[195] Gerhard Paul, *Bilder des Krieges, Krieg der Bilder*, 69–72, rightly states that the potential of photography remained 'unused' in the German wars of 1864 and 1870–1, but he does not go on to look at the wider ramifications on reportage in the 1860s in Germany, even though this is in keeping with his overall argument about a 'war of pictures' occurring in the nineteenth and twentieth centuries.

[196] Christine Krüger, 'German Suffering in the Franco-German War, 1870/71', *German History*, 29 (2011), 417 makes a similar point. The argument here militates against those put forward by Becker and Mehrkens.

[197] Militär-Medizinal-Abtheilung des Königlich Preussischen Kriegsministeriums (ed.), *Sanitäts-Bericht über die deutschen Heere im Krieg gegen Frankreich* (Berlin, 1884–91), 8 vols; see especially, vol. 7: *Erkrankungen der Nervensystem* (1885). M. Lengwiler, 'Psychiatry beyond the Asylum: The Origins of German Military Psychiatry before World War I', *History of Psychiatry*, 14 (2003), 41–62; M. Lengwiler, *Zwischen Klinik und Kaserne. Die Geschichte der Militärpsychiatrie in Deutschland und der Schweiz 1870–1914* (Zurich, 2000). Paul Lerner, *Hysterical Men: War, Psychiatry and the Politics of Trauma in Germany, 1890–1930* (Ithaca, NY, 2003), begins his study twenty years after the end of the Franco-German War and with no reference to it.

[198] Militär-Medizinal-Abtheilung des Königlich Preussischen Kriegsministeriums (ed.), *Traumatische, idiopathische und nach Infektionskrankheiten beobachtete Erkrankungen des Nerven Systemen bei den Deutschen Heeren im Kriege gegen Frankreich 1870/71* (Berlin, 1885), 412.

[199] Ibid., 413.

one finds in the bulletins of psychiatry associations and other publications the conviction voiced, in the main, that the life of the soldier in general, and even more the wartime life of members of the army, tends to cause mental disturbances, and that these develop and are reinforced relatively frequently both during the events of wartime and after them', the report went on.[200] Yet such disagreements were presented as the disciplinary disputation of a handful of experts, with the army summary citing in opposition only a lecture by the Rhenish psychiatrist Karl Friedrich Werner Nasse and the contribution of the Prussian academic Rudolf Arndt—who had served as a military doctor in the war—to the psychiatry section of the meeting of natural scientists in Leipzig in August 1872.[201] The report's own figures for 'the mobile Prussian army', based on admissions to military hospitals, showed that fifty-three per 100,000 of the average strength of the army and thirty-seven per 100,000 of all those mobilized had been admitted for 'mental disturbances' during the period of the war, compared to fifty-one to sixty-four per 100,000 in 1867–9.[202] The statistical analysis of the report confirmed:

> Accordingly, it seems, it is true, as if the gradual decline after the increase in mental illnesses in the army caused by the campaign of 1866 was followed by a new one [increase] in the second half of 1871 and 1872, which was already showing considerable signs of relenting in 1873, whilst 1874 sank far below the average, and then slowly but steadily began to climb again.[203]

The recovery of soldiers seemed to have been rapid, with the majority recorded as 'healed', and the absolute numbers—316 men admitted from a total force of approximately 1.5 million—were small.[204] Taking into account late admissions and other statistical anomalies, 'a moderate increase of mentally ill during the duration of wartime activities could be deduced with considerable probability', ran the *Sanitäts-Bericht*'s cautious conclusion.[205]

The army hierarchy generally ignored psychiatrists' notions of 'war' or 'military psychosis', which were discussed from the 1870s onwards.[206] Nevertheless, some combatants betrayed symptoms of trauma or, at least, acute psychological and physiological distress, unable to pick themselves up or to move on the battlefield, for instance. At the battle of Mars-la-Tour on 16 August 1870, one doctor even claimed to have witnessed 'the first person that I have seen die from anxiety': 'The person screamed out of anxiety and, with contempt, we let him lie where he was. After two hours, he was brought to us at the dressing station, still unwounded but with rasping breath and open eyes which did not blink when one touched the eyeball; he died shortly afterwards.'[207] Most suffered milder reactions but ones which they termed 'terrible' and which they were unable to forget. Many attempted to banish them like the Swabian chaplain Adolph Herzer, who had been outwardly

---

[200] Ibid.   [201] Ibid.   [202] Ibid.   [203] Ibid.

[204] Ibid. The calculations (fifty-three and thirty-seven per 100,000) are taken from the lower totals of the actual fighting force.

[205] Ibid., 414.   [206] M. Lengwiler, 'Psychiatry beyond the Asylum', 48–9.

[207] Paul Hase, *Feldarztbriefe* (Leipzig, 1895), 13.

blasé but who had been diagnosed by his doctors to be ailing 'more from a mental agitation, whose grounds were to be sought in his experiences on the battlefield and in field hospitals', than from a physical one.[208] The 'scenes and experiences' which he had witnessed or lived through were said to have been too strong for his 'nerves', leading to delirium.[209] Another chaplain reassured himself that it was 'good that the implicated relatives at home don't get to see the suffering and misery of their own here', for 'even the doctors admit that the sight of this horror almost wears them down over the long term'.[210] What happened when doctors, priests, and soldiers returned home themselves? It is not known how many experienced 'nervous cramps, in which they broke down in tears', like one evangelical pastor, but it can be surmised that a large number had at least some difficulties, which they endeavoured to conceal.[211] Few, though, made much fuss, rarely referring in writing to their reintegration into interrupted civilian lives. Georg von Siemens, coming back 'in proud virility (*Manneskraft*)' and giving his father his 'last great joy', was probably closer to the norm.[212]

Soldiers' and their relatives' recollections of suffering and mourning of deaths did not issue in pacifism or open criticism of war after 1871. The question of remembrance and shifting attitudes to military conflict is a broader one, however, since the victories of 1864, 1866, and 1870–1, together with their perceived, partly retrospective relationship with unification, rendered public criticism problematic.[213] Unsurprisingly, official histories and monuments were almost entirely positive and triumphal, symbolized by Johann Heinrich Strack's *Siegessäule* (victory column) erected between 1864 and 1873 in *Königsplatz* at the end of the *Siegesallee*. 'From the thankful fatherland to the victorious army', read the inscription.[214] The signification of the 60-metre-high monument, topped by an 8-metre, 40-ton, gold-leaf Victoria, was plain for all to see. Other monuments—most notably, that of 'Hermann' (Arminius) in the *Teutoburger Wald*, financially supported by Prussia at the instigation of Wilhelm I and inaugurated in 1875—were similarly victorious, though not numerous, given the new Kaiser's interdiction on the construction of statues representing his own person.[215] Likewise, schoolbooks, although listing casualties as proof of the willing sacrifices made by German soldiers, generally avoided depictions of wounding and death, concentrating instead on strategy and leadership.[216] References to irregular fighting, breaches of

---

[208] Cited in C. Rak, *Krieg, Nation und Konfession*, 193.   [209] Ibid.

[210] Martin Schall to his bride, 30 Aug. 1870, cited ibid., 190.

[211] Cited ibid., 194.   [212] Karl Helfferich, *Georg von Siemens*, 187–8.

[213] D. Riesenberger, *Geschichte der Friedensbewegung in Deutschland. Von den Anfängen bis 1933* (Göttingen, 1985), 67: although it had grown and increased in prominence, the German Peace Association counted only 7,000 members by 1907.

[214] See U. Schlie, *Die Nation erinnert sich*, 45. The *Siegessäule* was relocated in 1939, now placed in the middle of the *Tiergarten*.

[215] Ibid., 48–51; C. Tacke, *Denkmal im sozialen Raum. Nationale Symbole in Deutschland und Frankreich im 19. Jahrhundert* (Göttingen, 1995); M. Lurz, *Kriegerdenkmaler in Detuschland. Einigungskriege* (Heidelberg, 1985); R. Alings, *Monument und Nation. Das Bild vom Nationalstaat im Medium Denkmal* (Berlin, 1996), 415–532.

[216] C. G. Krüger, 'Im Banne Bismarcks. Der deutsch-französische Krieg (1870/71) in deutschen und französischen Schulgeschichtsbüchern', in M. Furrer (ed.), *Kriegsnarrative in Geschichtslehrmitteln*.

international law, France's use of colonial troops, and the commission of atrocities were also largely expunged from the record. These forms of celebration and omission were to be expected, yet they remained modest compared to the history-writing and monument-building programmes of the Wilhelmine era.[217]

The evidence from veterans' associations, which were formed after 1871 and which quickly attracted a mass membership, suggests that celebrations of victory and unification were combined with a collective recollection of military service and mourning for the dead.[218] Although it is true that early parades could seem triumphal, with the inauguration of the *Siegessäule* in 1873 deliberately timed to coincide with the anniversary of the battle of Sedan, 2 September was left, in accordance with the wishes of Wilhelm I, 'in order to allow it, in its entirety, to come from the people'.[219] For its part, the Prussian *Kultusministerium* organized an annual day of remembrance in all schools and universities. The wider commemoration of *Sedantag* won out against the alternatives of the 'Stiftungstag des Deutschen Reiches' on 18 January and the signing of the peace on 10 May, which had been the preferred date of Berlin's liberals.[220] In most localities, the municipal authorities arranged events, often in cooperation with veterans' associations. They had a 'predominantly internal character', in the words of the *Berliner Tageblatt* in 1878.[221] For the Rhenish cities which had proposed a 'national day' on 2 September in the first place, its purpose was to be a 'day of honour for the living victors', a 'day of joy for our dear hero-Kaiser', and a 'living monument to the unity of *All-Deutschland*'.[222] Yet it was also to be a 'day of remembrance for the fallen heroes', 'a festival of peace, not a festival of victory and triumph over the French, with a challenging character'.[223] Likewise, the *Kaiserparaden*, which were more formal displays of military power, made allusions to peace: an angel of peace, along with Germania, on the picture adorning the tribune at Rostock in 1875; and a large placard on Leipzig's town hall in 1876, with the declaration that 'Unity has been won' and that 'War bound us together with blood and tears!'[224]

Brennpunkte nationaler Diskurse (Schwalbach, Taunus, 2009), 17–29; A. Kelly, 'The Franco-German War and Unification in German Schoolbooks', in W. Pape (ed.), *1870/71—1989/90: German Unifications and the Change of Literary Discourse*, 39; C. Berg (ed.), *Handbuch der deutschen Bildungsgeschichte. Von der Reichsgründung bis zum Ende des Ersten Weltkriegs* (Munich, 1991), vol. 4, 70–3, 136–7, 501–24.

[217] For instance, see J. Düllfer and K. Holl (eds), *Bereit zum Krieg: Kriegsmentalität im wilhelminischen Deutschland, 1890–1914* (Göttingen, 1986); T. v. Elsner, *Kaisertage. Die Hamburger und das Wilhelminische Deutschland im Spiegel öffentlicher Festkultur* (Frankfurt a. M., 1991).

[218] By 1875, 28,000 had joined veterans' associations in Baden, for instance. Although it is true that membership increased rapidly after 1890, with the umbrella organization, the *Kyffhäuserbund*, counting 2.84 million members by 1913, veterans' associations were already mass organizations before then: T. Rohrkrämer, *Der Militarismus der 'kleinen Leute'*, 28; B. Ziemann, 'Militarism', in M. Jefferies (ed.), *The Ashgate Research Companion to Imperial Germany* (Farnham, 2015), 374.

[219] Cited in J. Vogel, *Nationen im Gleichschritt*, 145.

[220] For the ways in which Sedan Day was contested at different points, see U. Schneider, 'Einheit oder Einigkeit: Der Sedantag im Kaiserreich', in S. Behrenbeck and A. Nützenadel (eds), *Inszenierungen des Nationalstaats. Politische Feiern in Italien und Deutschland seit 1860/71* (Cologne, 2000), 27–44.

[221] *Berliner Tageblatt*, 3 Sept. 1878, in J. Vogel, *Nationen im Gleichschritt*, 146.

[222] Cited ibid., 149.   [223] Ibid.   [224] Ibid., 150.

Two decades later during the twenty-fifth anniversary of the Franco-German War, the proceedings were still characterized by remembrance and mourning as well as by patriotic self-aggrandizement and alcohol-fuelled sociability: 'At 12 o'clock the general procession took place, under the military command of the president of the *Kreis* [of the *Kriegerverein*]. The guests of honour [veterans] were fetched from their houses, upon which they marched together to the war memorial which had been decorated for the festival', ran one report about a typical *Kleinstadt*.[225] It was assumed without further comment that civilians who had experienced the war would be honoured by the whole town. At the war monument, 'the memorial celebration (*Gedenkfeier*) began with a performance of the choir and an inaugural speech', continued the mouthpiece of the veterans' association: 'Then, a poem was read out and a wreath for the fallen of 1870/71 was laid before the monument.'[226] The flags were lowered ceremonially and a *Volksfest* began. There was, thus, a strict separation between the contemplative components of the festival, with poems and a choir, and the celebratory ones. The mourning of the dead stood at the centre of the ceremony.

Contemporaries' testimony intimates that there was a close connection between civilians and soldiers in the aftermath of 1870–1, maintained by local regiments, which held ceremonies involving relatives and conscripts, and by veterans' associations, which had become a meeting point for former soldiers of all ranks.[227] Since many members lacked the means to buy a uniform, which they were allowed to wear at the events of the association, the majority wore a dark suit, black hat, and white gloves, together with their decorations. *Das badische Militärvereinsblatt* recorded in 1880:

> Our military associations do not, indeed, have the shiny appearance, the great performances and expensive preparations which accompany shooting festivals, gymnastics festivals and the like, but the consciousness of having already proved themselves in an emergency and in danger and to have looked death in the face pervades them . . . They constantly remember the heavy sacrifices which the German people had to make to secure its national existence, but also the glorious successes, fought for by brave men, to whom the *Volk* owes eternal gratitude.[228]

The 'patriotic feelings' which the veterans' associations were pledged 'to keep alive for a long time' were consequently a mixture of national glory and individual experience (having looked death in the face) and loss (or heavy sacrifices). In the idealized version of the veterans' periodicals, younger generations ask eagerly about their fathers' wartime exploits: 'Tell me, father, how you took the French flag.'[229] Even within the veterans' associations themselves, the reality was different, as

---

[225] Report cited in T. Rohrkrämer, *Der Militarismus der 'kleinen Leute'*, 64.   [226] Ibid.

[227] On regiments, see Wencke Meteling's study, *Ehre, Einheit, Ordnung. Preußische und französische Regimenter im Krieg, 1870/71 und 1914/19* (Baden-Baden, 2010), 119–20: she demonstrates the perceived involvement of 'the men'—'every single man', in the words of one account of the Leibgrenadiere from 1883—and of whole communities where regiments were based, including in later memorials to the fallen, with photographic evidence of the crowd at the unveiling of the war memorial in Frankfurt an der Oder in 1882, for example.

[228] T. Rohrkrämer, *Der Militarismus der 'kleinen Leute'*, 65.

[229] *Parole. Deutscher Kriegerzeitung*, 3 Jan. 1896, ibid., 73.

younger conscripts with no experience of the war came to dominate and alter their agendas during the 1890s, accepting the authorities' endeavour to mobilize their support and to influence their stance.[230] Until that point, which coincided with Wilhelm II's decision to hold traditional military parades in August rather than at the time of *Sedantag*, the associations had maintained an independent position, resisting centralization within the officially backed *Deutscher Kriegerbund* and rejecting the leadership of *Landräte*. Many associations, according to police reports, contained a large number of 'socialists'. Their memorialization of the wars of unification seems to have been correspondingly robust, acknowledging the national (and monarchical) purpose of soldiers' sacrifices but also refusing to 'forget'.[231]

This duality was redolent of the army hierarchy's own inclination after 1871 not to expand and risk war unnecessarily, but to consolidate its existing institutions, practices, and recruitment and to defend what had already been attained.[232] There were many reasons for military conservatism, but one of them appears to have derived from the exhaustion and shock which many officers had felt during the conflicts of the preceding decade.[233] Treitschke himself recognized that the war of 1870–1 had had such an impact on his contemporaries' 'nerves' that a period of cultural stasis was inevitable.[234]

[230] See Robert von Friedeburg, 'Klassen-, Geschlechter- oder Nationalidentität? Handwerker und Tagelöhner in den Kriegervereinen der neupreußischen Provinz Hessen-Nassau 1890–1914', in U. Frevert (ed.), *Militär und Gesellschaft im 19. und 20. Jahrhundert*, 229–44, who criticizes Rohkrämer's sample of evidence and conclusions, though without undermining his principal arguments.

[231] See Thomas Rohkrämer's argument, presented in English in 'Heroes and Would-be Heroes: Veterans' and Reservists' Associations in Imperial Germany', in M. Boemeke, R. Chickering, and S. Förster (eds), *Anticipating Total War*, 189–215; see also K. Saul, 'Der "Deutsche Kriegerbund". Zur innenpolitischen Funktion eines "nationalen" Verbandes im kaiserlichen Deutschland', *Militärgeschichtlichen Mitteilungen*, 6 (1969), 95–159.

[232] Frank Becker, 'Die Folgen des Krieges von 1870/71 für die Organisation der Streitkräfte in Deutschland', in J. Echternkamp (ed.), *Kriegsenden, Nachriegsordnungen, Folgekonflikte. Wege aus dem Krieg im 19. Und 20. Jahrhundert* (Freiburg, 2012), 95–108, draws a similar conclusion but rests his explanation on the integration of the *Volk* within the army rather than examining popular resistance to further military 'adventures' and expansion, which is the case presented here. See also M. Ingenlath, *Mentale Aufrüstung*, 80; M. Schmid, *Der 'eiserne Kanzler' und die Generäle. Deutsche Rüstungspolitik in der Ära Bismarcks 1871–1890* (Paderborn, 2003), 21–272; E. D. Brose, *The Kaiser's Army: The Politics of Military Technology in Germany during the Machine Age, 1870–1918* (Oxford, 2001), 7–68.

[233] Stig Förster (ed.), *Moltke*, has shown how pervasive Moltke's pessimism was, apparently meeting little overt opposition; Stig. Förster, 'Facing "People's War"', 215; S. Förster, 'Dreams and Nightmares', 343–76; S. Förster, 'Helmuth von Moltke und das Problem der industrialisierten Volkskriegs im 19. Jahrhundert', 103–16.

[234] H. v. Treitschke, *Politik*, vol. 1, 47.

Conclusion
Reflections on Violence

> The are so many legal precautions against violence, and our upbringing is directed towards so weakening our tendencies towards violence, that we are instinctively inclined to think that any act of violence is a manifestation of a return to barbarism.
>
> Georges Sorel, *Réflexions sur la violence* (1908)[1]

The connection between violence and warfare seems too obvious to merit further investigation. For Sorel, it went without saying that 'external' military violence continued to be justified. Yet this violence, even though it was carried out by 'civilians' (as conscript soldiers or volunteers), had been separated from 'internal' acts of violence in domestic politics—or political violence—as citizens had been brought up to curb their violent urges and emotions, coming to regard such acts as 'barbaric'. Although the French syndicalist thinker referred to wars as a model for the creation of political myths and the reintroduction of political acts of violence at home, he scarcely paid any attention to the relationship between contrasting internal and external spheres of action.[2] More recent theoreticians of violence also overlook the relationship, albeit for opposing reasons. The majority tend to treat violent acts at home and abroad in a similar fashion, differing little over time, whether the result of symbolic and structural conditions (Slavoj Žižek), enduring physiological, emotional, or psychological attributes (Sigmund Freud), or series of reactions to similar situations (Wolfgang Sofsky, Randall Collins).[3] Recently, historians of twentieth-century conflicts have added to the confusion, it can be contended, by treating military violence during wartime as one of various forms of political violence, neglecting the strict distinction which was made between the different types of violent action by contemporaries.[4]

---

[1] G. Sorel, *Reflections on Violence* (New York, 1950), 180.   [2] Ibid., 64–118.

[3] For more on these theories of violence, see the Introduction of the previous volume of this series of studies: M. Hewitson, *Absolute War*. S. Žižek, *Violence* (London, 2008); S. Freud, *Das Unbehagen in der Kultur*, in S. Žižek, *Gesammelte Werke* (London, 1948), vol. 14; S. Žižek, *Why War?* (1933), in J. Strachey (ed.), *The Standard Edition of the Complete Psychological Works of Sigmund Freud* (London, 1953–74), vol. 22; W. Sofsky, *Violence: Terrorism, Genocide, War* (London, 2003); W. Sofsky, *Traktat über die Gewalt* (Frankfurt, 1996); R. Collins, *Violence: A Micro-Sociological Theory* (Princeton, NJ, 2008).

[4] Donald Bloxham and Robert Gerwarth (eds), *Political Violence in Twentieth-Century Europe* (Cambridge, 2011), 1–2, for instance, define political violence as 'all forms of violence pursuant to

By contrast, this study has focused on the changing historical relationship between citizens' sensitivity to violence, injury, and death at home and abroad in order to explain those citizens' competing, often contradictory, and fluctuating conceptions of war.[5] As Sorel hinted but omitted to spell out, most acts of violence were carried out in wars between states, provoking feelings of revulsion in combatants and challenging romantic conceptions of military conflict, with profound consequences for contemporaries' discussions of culture, progress, and the nation and for the conduct of foreign policy. Only by reinserting nineteenth-century assumptions about violence, which was predominantly external rather than internal, can the excesses and atrocities of the twentieth century—genocide, war crimes, concentration camps, torture, terror, and paramilitary politics—be comprehended.[6]

WAR AND NATIONALISM IN THE NINETEENTH CENTURY

The historical analysis of wartime violence advanced here not only runs counter to the theses put forward by historians of political violence in the twentieth century; it also militates against the historiography of nineteenth-century Germany, pointing to shifts in contemporaries' attitudes to war which were frequently separable from their other national or political objectives (or the presumed causes of a conflict). Such attitudes are difficult to discern because they were regularly embedded in or obscured by public and private accounts of heroism and national enthusiasm. The human sacrifices of the 'wars of unity' (*Einheitskriege*), ran one of the mantras of

---

aims of decisive socio-political control or change', including military conflicts, genocide and ethnic cleansing, terrorism and state repression, revolution and counter-revolution. They also extend their explanation of such violence back into the nineteenth century. See also R. Gerwarth, 'The Central European Counter-Revolution: Paramilitary Violence in Germany, Austria and Hungary after the Great War', *Past and Present*, 200 (2008), 175–209; R. Gerwarth and J. Horne (eds), *War in Peace: Paramilitary Violence in Europe after the Great War* (Oxford, 2012); M. Mazower, 'Violence and the State in the Twentieth Century', *American Historical Review*, 107 (2002), 1158–78; P. Gatrell, 'War after the War: Conflicts, 1919–1923', in J. Horne (ed.), *A Companion to World War One* (Oxford, 2010), 558–75; C. Gerlach, *Extremely Violent Societies: Mass Violence in the Twentieth-Century World* (Cambridge, 2010); C. Gerlach, 'State Violence—Violent Societies', in M. Geyer and S. Fitzpatrick (eds), *Beyond Totalitarianism: Stalinism and Nazism Compared* (Cambridge, 2009), 133–79; C. Gerlach, 'Extremely Violent Societies: An Alternative to the Concept of Genocide', *Journal of Genocide Research*, 8 (2006), 455–71; C. Gerlach, 'Some Recent Trends in German Holocaust Research', in J. M. Diefendorf, *Lessons and Legacies* (Evanston, IL, 2004), vol. 4, 285–99; J. Baberowski, *Räume der Gewalt* (Frankfurt, 2015); J. Baberowski (ed.), *Moderne Zeiten? Krieg, Revolution und Gewalt im 20. Jahrhundert* (Göttingen, 2006); P. Gleichmann and T. Kühne (eds), *Massenhaftes Töten. Kriege und Genozide im 20. Jahrhundert* (Essen, 2004).

[5] This approach is much closer to that of historical sociologists such as Anthony Giddens in *The Nation-State and Violence* (Cambridge, 1985), and Norbert Elias in *The Civilising Process: The History of Manners* (New York, 1978), vol. 1 and *The Civilising Process: Power and Civility* (Oxford, 1982).

[6] I have discussed these questions at greater length in M. Hewitson, 'Introduction: Military and Political Violence in History and Theory', in M. Hewitson (ed.), *Combatants, Civilians and Cultures of Violence*, a special issue of *History*, 101 (2016), 337–61.

the imperial era, resembled those of the 'wars of liberation' (*Befreiungskriege*).[7] In part, this apparent convergence derived from the similar scale and casualty rates of the two sets of conflicts and, in part, from the centrality of myths of '1813', which meant, 'for generations of German historians, the Napoleonic era has marked the origins of modern German nationalism'.[8] The '(war) picture of the era was dominated for a long time by the events after 1813', Ute Planert has written:

> This rests, not least, on the fact that the 'war of liberation' against Napoleon functions in the popular understanding of the nation as in the accounts of certain scholars, now as before, as a foundation myth, comparable to the status of the French Revolution in France or the Risorgimento in Italy.[9]

However, in critical respects, which informed the way conflicts were understood and entered into, the impact of the wars of 1805–15 and those of 1864–71 differed fundamentally.

The divergence between the effects of the Napoleonic Wars and those of the wars of unification was not, primarily, the consequence of German nationalism, or of the relationship between belligerence, war, and nationalism, on which much of the recent historiography has concentrated.[10] Notwithstanding the credible claims made by historians such as James Sheehan, John Breuilly, and Jörn Echternkamp about the small size of the political nation and the limited impact of nationalism in the first half of the nineteenth century, it is likely that publicists' and governments' 'national' portrayal of past wars had an effect.[11] In the years after 1815, official and

---

[7] Gustav Freytag, *Grenzboten*, 1870, vol. 4, 81–2, used the term 'Einheitskrieg' but continued to question that of a 'Befreiungskrieg', arguing that 'wars of freedom' (*Freiheitskrieg*) was more appropriate, since freedom from foreign domination was the most important kind of liberty.

[8] K. Aaslestad and K. Hagemann, '1806 and its Aftermath', *Central European History*, 39 (2006), 564.

[9] U. Planert, *Der Mythos vom Befreiungskrieg*, 19–20: she argues that Wilhelm von Sternburg, *Fall und Aufstieg der deutschen Nation. Nachdenken über einen Massenrausch* (Frankfurt, 1993), Horst Möller, *Fürstenstaat oder Bürgernation. Deutschland 1763–1815* (Berlin, 1998), Erich Pelzer, 'Die Wiedergeburt Deutschlands und die Dämonisierung Napoleons', in G. Krumeich and H. Lehmann (eds), *'Gott mit uns'. Nation, Relgion und Gewalt im 19. und frühen 20. Jahrhundert* (Göttingen, 2000), 135–56, Peter Alter, *Nationalismus* (Frankfurt, 1985), and Hagen Schulze, *Der Weg zum Nationalstaat. Die deutsche Nationalbewegung vom 18. Jahrhundert bis zur Reichsgründung* (Munich, 1985), have all portrayed the Napoleonic wars as an 'initial trigger', with Schulze mistakenly drawing 'an unbroken line from the Prussian events after 1806 to the developments of the 1840s'.

[10] See especially J. Leonhard, *Bellizismus und Nation*, 181–281, 419–55. Also, M. Hewitson, 'Belligerence, Patriotism and Nationalism in the German Public Sphere, 1792–1815', *English Historical Review*, 128 (2013), 839–76, for further literature on this topic.

[11] J. J. Sheehan, 'State and Nationality in the Napoleonic Period', in J. J. Breuilly (ed.), *The State of Germany*, 47–59; J. J. Sheehan, 'What is German History?', 1–23; J. J. Breuilly, 'The Response to Napoleon and German Nationalism', in A. Forrest and P. H. Wilson (eds), *The Bee and the Eagle* (Basingstoke, 2009), 256–83, and J. J. Breuilly, 'Napoleonic Germany and State-Formation', in M. Rowe (ed.), *Collaboration and Resistance in Napoleonic Europe: State-Formation in an Age of Upheaval, c. 1800–1815* (London, 2003), 121–52; S. Berger, *Germany: Inventing the Nation* (London, 2004); J. Echternkamp, *Der Aufstieg des deutschen Nationalismus 1770–1840* (Frankfurt, 1998); U. Planert, 'Wann beginnt der "moderne" deutsche Nationalismus? Plädoyer für eine nationale Sattelzeit', in J. Echternkamp and S. O. Müller (eds), *Die Politik der Nation*, 25–59.

liberal myths of the 'wars of freedom' seem to have been broadly accepted by members of a reading public and they appear to have obscured recent divisions and painful memories. Thus, Bavaria celebrated the twentieth anniversary of the battle of Leipzig on 18 October 1833 with the erection in Munich of an obelisk which mourned the death of 30,000 soldiers in the war but which failed to mention that they had died in the campaign of 1812 as part of the *Grande Armée*, not in 1813.[12] Likewise, Württemberg's Victory Column, finished in 1841, merely referred to the struggle against Napoleon after 1813.[13] Conservatives, Catholics, liberals, and democrats in individual states continued to articulate different interpretations of events, in the restricted political spheres of the early nineteenth century, but few opposed a 'heroic' reading of recent German history outright. Students, gymnasts, and other patriots were most vociferous in their criticism of the corrupt and cowardly princes and courtiers of the Confederation of the Rhine, yet they were repeatedly silenced and, in other respects, they concurred with the legend of a common 'German' resistance against Napoleonic France.[14] The mythology of '1813' was reinforced more often than it was questioned, by historians, journalists, politicians, officials, writers, and artists, throughout the course of the long nineteenth century, constituting the centrepiece of the organized rituals and public festivals of the national movement in 1863 and 1913.[15] It helped governments and political parties to minimize, despite their occasional desire also to exploit, the disagreements between Frankfurt revolutionaries, the Prussian army and government, and sundry governments and publics across Germany, about the conduct, aims, and outcomes of the various warring parties in the first Schleswig war between 1848 and 1851.[16] Liberals and democrats harboured lingering doubts about the intentions of the Prussian government on the eve of the second Schleswig war in 1864, partly as a result of Berlin's alleged duplicity and particularism in 1848, but they quickly put them to one side, forming Schleswig–Holstein associations and supporting the war in the name of 'Germany', even after Prussia and Austria acted in contravention of the Confederation. Such support was strongest in the southern German states.[17]

---

[12] W. Schmidt, 'Denkmäler für die bayerischen Gefallenen des Rußlandfeldzuges von 1812', *Zeitschrift für bayerische Landesgeschichte*, 49 (1986), 303–26; T. Nipperdey, 'Nationalidee und Nationaldenkmal im 19. Jahrhundert', *Historische Zeitschrift*, 210 (1968), 529–85; J. Murken, 'Von "Thränen und Wehmut" zur Geburt des "deutschen Nationalbewußtseins". Die Niederlage des Russlandfeldzugs von 1812 und ihre Umdeutung in einen nationalen Sieg', in H. Carl, H. H. Kortum, D. Langewiesche, and F. Lenger (eds), *Kriegsniederlagen. Erfahrungen und Erinnerungen* (Berlin, 2004), 107–22.

[13] U. Planert, 'From Collaboration to Resistance', *Central European History*, 39 (2006), 700–1.

[14] Chris Clark, 'The Wars of Liberation in Prussian Memory', *Journal of Modern History*, 68 (1996), 550–76, pays more attention to differences than similarities, in contrast to the account given in the previous volume of this series of studies: M. Hewitson, *Absolute War*.

[15] D. Düding, P. Friedemann, and P. Münch (eds), *Öffentliche Festkultur. Politische Feste in Deutschland von der Aufklärung bis zum Ersten Weltkrieg* (Reinbek, 1988), 302–14.

[16] W. Carr, *Schleswig-Holstein, 1815–1848*, 270–90; K.-O. Hagelstein, *Eine an sich mittelmäßige Frage. Der deutsch-dänische Konflikt 1864* (Frankfurt, 2012), 9–270.

[17] C. Jansen, *Einheit, Macht und Freiheit. Die Paulskirchenlinke und die deutsche Politik in der nachrevolutionären Epoche 1849–1867* (Düsseldorf, 2000), 482.

Contemporaries' backing of the war against Denmark in 1864 was—as Frank Becker has noted—conditional, rendered more precarious by the manoeuvring of individual states and party disagreements about the territory and system of government of a reformed German Confederation or future German nation-state.[18] These divisions became manifest in 1866, as the Hohenzollern monarchy went to war against Austria and most of the other German states. Even the National Association, with its base of support in Hanover and other small and medium-sized states as well as in Prussia, was divided by the conflict. Rudolf von Bennigsen, the Hanoverian leader of the *Nationalverein*, was tempted by Bismarck's offer of a German parliament and a reform of the *Bund* in May 1866, but he was opposed to the Chancellor himself and was 'very concerned in respect of the chances in a war', according to Theodor von Bernhardi, who was acting as an intermediary.[19] Although the diarist reassured him that the Prussian army was in 'an outstanding state and good spirit' and that Bismarck was capable of leading Prussia to victory, his argumentation showed how divisive the conflict was: 'only he [Bismarck] can' wage such a war, for a liberal ministry 'would never overcome...the resistance of the Austrian-leaning party in the personal entourage of the king'.[20] Bennigsen remained unconvinced. To the *Abgeordnetentag*, the war was 'unnatural', threatening to damage relations between German states and their populations and to fragment the national movement.[21]

Prussia's victory in 1866 prompted many liberals in the Hohenzollern monarchy to alter their position, yet a majority of deputies in Württemberg and Bavaria, together with their governments, remained opposed to joining the North German Confederation. A common struggle of north and south against a perceived French aggressor in 1870 helped to overcome what Elben labelled 'enemy currents', which had continued to divide his own state of Württemberg from the *Norddeutsche Bund* after the Austro-Prussian War.[22] Such currents could not simply be banished, however, and would re-emerge, the Swabian liberal conceded, meaning that the unification of Germany would have to take place during the Franco-German War itself. Even the shared national sacrifices of 1870–1 could not be assumed, by a supporter of Prussia like Elben, to endure during peacetime. After unification, publicly sponsored and enacted 'memories' of Sedan and other battles of the campaign became founding myths of the *Kaiserreich*, reinforcing national allegiances, just as the mythology of '1813' had created or consolidated the national aspirations of a limited number of German voters and newspaper readers during the first half of the nineteenth century.[23] War, here, was closely tied to early and later forms of nationalism in the German lands. It could also hinder or prevent national unity, leaving

[18] F. Becker, *Bilder von Krieg und Nation*, 487–8.

[19] T. v. Bernhardi, *Aus dem Leben*, 28 Apr. 1866, vol. 6, 302.   [20] Ibid., 302–3.

[21] Ausschußantrag, Versammlung des Abgeordnetentages in Frankfurt, 20 May 1866, in H. Fenske (ed.), *Der Weg zur Reichsgründung*, 312.

[22] O. Elben, *Lebenserinnerungen 1823–1899* (Stuttgart, 1931), 159.

[23] This is not to imply that such 'national' traditions were uniform: A. Confino, 'Localities of a Nation: Celebrating Sedan Day in the German Empire', *Tel Aviver Jahrbuch für deutsche Geschichte*, 26 (1997), 61–74.

behind a legacy—as in the years after 1812–13, 1848–51, 1859, and 1866—of recrimination. What was more, many of the critical transformations and challenges facing national-minded officials, 'party' leaders, journalists, and subjects were the product of political disagreements about the reform of the *Bund*, the extent of the franchise, the balance of powers, and the form of a representative assembly rather than the consequence of military conflict.[24] The dynamics of nationalism and war, as advocates of 'federative' nationalism such as Dieter Langewiesche have pointed out, were varied and complex.[25] However, such 'national' (and regional) understanding of the interplay between politics and warfare is partial, failing to do justice to citizens' own experiences of military conflict.

In an age of conscripts and mass warfare, the nature of the fighting and the wider ramifications of a campaign were more important for the majority of combatants than the aims or causes of a conflict, even if such aims or causes were perceived to be national or patriotic. For soldiers themselves, it was often difficult even for those like Heinrich Schmitthenner who had gone to war with 'the conviction that every good German has to hate our hereditary enemy' to maintain their national antipathy, returning home in 1871 'wholeheartedly won over by the French, not for their institutions but as people'.[26] Under such circumstances, the role of nationalism in the maintenance of morale during wartime and in the recollections of veterans during peacetime—or even in the later commemoration of conflicts—was limited, though still significant. It was typical after 1871 for veterans to harbour contradictory feelings of patriotic pride and physical revulsion when they recalled the campaigns in which they had fought.

POPULAR ATTITUDES TO THE ARMY AND THE WARS OF THE *VOLK*

The military discussions and revisions which took place during the 'restoration' after 1815 and the 'reaction' after 1848 supplemented rather than reversed the transformation in army organization and attitudes to armed conflicts which had occurred during the period of the Revolutionary and Napoleonic Wars. This reading

---

[24] On the independence of these questions for much of the time, see M. Hewitson, *Nationalism in Germany, 1848–1866*, 113–290.

[25] D. Langewiesche, 'Föderativer Nationalismus als Erbe der deutschen Reichsnation: Über Föderalismus und Zentralismus in der deutschen Nationalgeschichte', in D. Langewiesche and G. Schmidt (eds), *Föderative Nation* (Munich, 2000), 215–44; D. Langewiesche, *Nation, Nationalismus und Nationalstaat in Deutschland und Europa* (Munich, 2000); D. Langewiesche, *Reich, Nation, Föderation* (Munich, 2008); D. Langewiesche, 'Zum Wandel von Krieg und Kriegslegitimation in der Neuzeit', 5–27; N. Buschmann and D. Langewiesche (eds), *Der Krieg in den Gründungsmythen*. Also, A. Green, *Fatherlands: State-Building and Nationhood in Nineteenth-Century Germany* (Cambridge, 2001); A. Green, 'The Federal Alternative? A New View of Modern German History', *Historical Journal*, 46 (2003), 187–202; A. Green, 'How Did Federalism Shape German Unification?', in R. Speirs and J. Breuilly (eds), *Germany's Two Unifications*, 122–38.

[26] H. Schmitthenner, *Erlebnisse eines freiwilligen badischen Grenadiers*, 26.

of events is opposed to that of Ute Frevert.[27] Since the French Revolution, recorded Brockhaus's *Bilder Conversations-Lexikon* in the late 1830s, most European states had moved back towards an arming of the people (*Volksbewaffnung*).[28] In most German lands, the conscription laws introduced during the Napoleonic era stayed in place. Although states rarely conscripted a majority of the relevant cohort, their recruitment remained high in historical perspective, with Prussia calling up 25–40 per cent of 20-year-olds and Bavaria 25–66 per cent between 1815 and the early 1860s, for example.[29] In wartime, it was widely assumed (in the words of one liberal deputy in Baden during the debate about military service in 1822) that 'every burgher has a duty to serve' in 'a war for the fatherland'.[30] In these circumstances, as in Prussia between 1813 and 1815, it was expected that a large proportion of young men could be mustered for war using existing laws of universal conscription. This expectation coincided with an acceptance on the part of experts—including the Prussian Chief of the General Staff Rühle von Lilienstern—that war was not merely a technical matter, requiring smaller numbers of well-drilled, career soldiers, but also an affair of the people, necessitating masses of troops in armies of the *Volk* (*Volksheeren*).[31] Most German commentators thought that there should be an army of the line, which would constitute the basic and enduring structure of the military (the officer corps, NCOs, and regiments), and a system of reserves and *Landwehr*, which could provide troops and fulfil auxiliary functions for the regular army during wartime.

Initially, during the 1820s, substitution (or buying a replacement), which was kept separate from exemption on religious or occupational grounds, was not controversial in the third Germany, where it was maintained—apart from the hiatus of the revolution in 1848–9—until the 1860s. Later, it was subject to criticism, labelled 'incorrigibly unjust' by Welcker in 1839, for instance.[32] The liberal academic and editor of the *Staatslexikon* wanted to introduce the 'universal' Prussian system so that the 'whole cohort of young' men would be conscripted 'without exceptions and without buying their way out'.[33] In 1849, liberals and democrats claimed to have incorporated the same system into their 'law on the constitution of the army' of an envisaged German *Reich*, calling for all eligible conscripts throughout Germany to be 'drafted and trained'.[34] The law remained a dead letter. Substitution was abolished and then, by 1851, restored in southern and central German states by conservatives and liberals who continued to argue that no system

---

[27] U. Frevert, *Nation in Barracks*, 47–157.

[28] 'Krieg', F. A. Brockhaus (ed.), *Bilder Conversations-Lexikon der neuesten Zeit und Literatur* (Leipzig, 1837–41), vol. 2, 669.

[29] U. Frevert, 'Das jakobinische Modell', in U. Frevert (ed.), *Militär and Gesellschaft*, 33. W. D. Gruner, *Das bayerische Heer*, 363–7.

[30] J. Kern, 7 Nov. 1822, *Verhandlungen der Ständeversammlung des Großherzogtums Baden*, vol. 8, 77.

[31] J. J. O. A. v. Rühle v. Lilienstern, *Aufsätze über Gegenstände und Ereignisse aus dem Gebiete des Kriegswesens*, vol. 1, 180. See also C. V. Decker, *Ansichten über die Kriegführung im Geiste der Zeit*, 418–25.

[32] C. T. Welcker, 'Anhang zum Artikel Heerwesen (Landwehrsystem)', in C. T. Welcker and C. v. Rotteck (eds), *Staatslexikon*, vol. 7, 589–95.

[33] Ibid., 590.   [34] Wilhelm, Crown Prince of Prussia, *Bemerkungen*, vii.

in peacetime could be fully equal since only part of the cohort could be trained. Some radicals went on to demand the creation of militias during the revolution itself and afterwards. Yet many of them were surprisingly moderate, with Engels broadly agreeing in 1865 with Roon's increase in the size of the Prussian army, for example.[35] For Rüstow, who—unlike Engels—considered militias at length, only democracies such as Switzerland could rely on this type of military organization to meet the actual necessity of war. Most states had to settle for what he termed the 'cadre system', which kept the structure of the army constantly in existence, to be reinforced by reserves during wartime: Russia was closer to a pure standing army within this broad category, with a ratio of those in active service to those in reserve of 4:1, whereas Prussia was nearer to a militia, with a ratio of 1:4.[36]

None of these discussions had much bearing on contemporaries' specific attitudes to war.[37] Tribute was paid throughout the period to the necessity of universal conscription in wartime and the inevitability of people's wars involving mass armies. Burghers' lack of experience of military service in central and southern Germany appears, if anything, to have made it easier for them to expunge memories of the suffering inflicted on soldiers during the Napoleonic Wars and to fashion alternative romantic images of warfare. Such images seem to have been less pervasive amongst ordinary conscripts, yet they were not, for the most part, replaced by fearful or disagreeable expectations of fighting. The majority of recruits appear to have gone to war in 1848–51 and in 1864–71 with a mixture of excitement, ignorance, and enjoyment of public approbation. Patriotism—or allegiance to one's state—was one reason to fight, but it was countered by revolutionary and counter-revolutionary sympathies in 1848–51 and, for some soldiers and civilians, by national aspirations in the 1860s, as the majority of states in the Confederation stayed out of the war against Denmark in 1864, fought with the *Bund* alongside Austria and against Prussia in 1866, before joining the Prussian-led North German Confederation against France in 1870. In 'external' conflicts, whatever their conflicting feelings about fighting for Bismarck, against the Hohenzollern, or alongside the Habsburg monarchy, German troops reported for duty, marched to battle, and fought, without disorder, mutiny, or a significant level of desertion. Recent studies which concentrate on the continuing opposition of individual states (Abigail Green, for instance) or on national mechanisms of enmity (Nikolaus Buschmann) fail to explain soldiers' obedience in such bewilderingly different wars.[38]

In 'internal' conflicts, soldiers' loyalties and actions were more confused, with one-third of Bavarian troops 'deserting' in the Bavarian Palatinate in June 1849 and

---

[35] F. Engels, 'Die preußische Militärfrage, 41–63.

[36] W. Rüstow, *Der Krieg und seine Mittel*, 51. This perspective tempers Frevert's widely cited point about a Prussian military 'exception': U. Frevert, *Nation in Barracks*, 101.

[37] Arguably, some studies of 'militarism' do elide common attitudes to military service and to war: see, for instance, M. Ingenlath, *Mentale Aufrüstung*, 388. Jakob Vogel, *Nationen im Gleichschritt*, presents a differentiated regional and national comparison of military parades and festivals but he leaves the question of the relationship between such 'folklore militarism' and specific attitudes to war largely unexplored.

[38] A. Green, *Fatherlands*, 298–337; N. Buschmann, *Einkreisung und Waffenbruderschaft*, 241–308.

20,000 soldiers of the Badenese army of the line opposing Prussian and confederal forces, who had been asked to intervene by the Grand Duke, in June and July. Yet in these cases, as in Hungary, soldiers had been required to choose sides as political authority splintered under revolutionary conditions: in May 1849, republican governments had been established in the Palatinate and in Baden, after the Grand Duke had fled. With 'revolution' and 'civil war' still kept separate—in contrast to the 1920s—in civilian and military leaders' and in citizens' minds, limiting the violence of domestic conflicts outside the Habsburg monarchy, there was little sign of disobedience or desertion because of soldiers' unwillingness to use force or because of their fear of fighting.[39] Instead, the evidence suggests that the majority of ordinary conscripts were relatively hardy and had a matter-of-fact attitude to war. Many were like Wilhelm Steinkamp, on his way from Westphalia to Schleswig, who appeared to be more concerned about the cold than about killing and dying in 1864.[40] After the fighting had begun, a friend of the same family who was serving in the infantry noted simply that 'we have stood a lot this winter'.[41] The phlegmatic, routine obedience of such soldiers seems to have derived *inter alia* from the legitimacy of the army and the social acceptability of war, both of which distinguished the nineteenth from the eighteenth century. Historians' disputes about the existence of 'wars of liberation' (Ute Planert versus Hagen Schulze), citizen-soldiers (Otto Dann), regional diversity (Michael Rowe, Katherine Aaslestad, Karen Hagemann), and military and political continuities (Planert) have obscured the significance of these changes.[42]

VIOLENCE AND THE MYTHOLOGY OF WAR

The acceptability of armed conflict rested, in turn, on the sensitivity of soldiers and civilians to violence, wounding, and death. Although there are now many studies of soldiers' experiences of warfare, few—if any—explore the ramifications of such

---

[39] This is another reason why twentieth-century studies of 'political violence' are inapplicable in such nineteenth-century settings, *contra* D. Bloxham and R. Gerwarth (eds), *Political Violence*, 4.

[40] W. Steinkamp, 10 Jan. 1864, in H.-U. Kammeier, 'Der Krieg gegen Dänemark 1864 in Briefen von Soldaten', 75.

[41] W. Vahrenkamp, 23 Mar. 1864, ibid., 78.

[42] U. Planert, *Der Mythos*, 19–20; U. Planert, 'Wann beginnt der "moderne" deutsche Nationalismus? Plädoyer für eine nationale Sattelzeit', in J. Echternkamp and S. O. Müller (eds), *Die Politik der Nation: Deutscher Nationalismus in Krieg und Krise 1760–1960* (Munich, 2002), 25–59. H. Schulze, *Der Weg zum Nationalstaat. Die deutsche Nationalbewegung vom 18. Jahrhundert zur Reichsgründung*; O. Dann, 'Der deutsche Bürger wird Soldat', in R. Steinweg (ed.), *Lehren aus der Geschichte* (Frankfurt, 1990), 72; M. Rowe, *From Reich to State: The Rhineland in the Revolutionary Age, 1780–1830* (Cambridge, 2003); K. Aaslestad, 'War without Battles: Civilian Experiences of Economic Warfare during the Napoleonic Era in Hamburg', in A. Forrest, K. Hagemann, and J. Rendall (eds), *Soldiers, Citizens and Civilians* (Basingstoke, 2008), 118–36; K. Aaslestad and K. Hagemann, '1806 and Its Aftermath', *Central European History*, 39 (2006), 568–9; U. Planert, 'Innovation or Evolution? The French Wars in Military History', in R. Chickering and S. Förster (eds), *War in an Age of Revolution*, 69–84, and U. Planert, 'Die Kriege der Französischen Revolution und Napoleons: Beginn einer neuen Ära der europäischen Kriegsgeschichte oder Weiterwirken der Vergangenheit?', in D. Beyrau, M. Hochgeschwender, and D. Langewiesche (eds), *Formen des Krieges*, 149–62.

experiences for subsequent representations of and debates about conflict in the public sphere.[43] Contemporaries' emotional and sensory responses to combat, bombardment, pillaging, requisitioning, and billeting are difficult to compare. From a reading of their testimony, it appears that the majority of troops and civilians at the turn of the nineteenth century had an unsentimental attitude to warfare, even if they saw the Revolutionary or Napoleonic Wars as a watershed. Some civilians like E. T. A. Hoffmann were blasé, treating 'wicked, evil war' as a game; others like Arndt, who witnessed the mass death of the Russian campaign in 1812, were earnest, recalling the 'horror' of 'corpses lying naked here and there…, like cattle'.[44] Most, though, were seemingly able, like Arndt, to turn 'to the living', having already become accustomed through the premature death of parents, children, and spouses to the reality of dying.[45] Combatants had not been fully prepared for what they faced in 1805–6, 1809, and 1812–15. In the midst of extreme conditions and confronted by atrocious sights and smells, some soldiers began to reflect on their capacity to cope with such 'irritability' and 'pain'.[46] The majority, however, got used to such conditions, regarding 'the repeated and multiplied view of lifeless forms' as 'quotidian'.[47] Even the minority of troops who returned from Moscow in the winter of 1812, tramping along roads lined with dead bodies and fending off repeated attacks by Cossacks, rarely seem to have found their experiences unbearable, notwithstanding their awareness of the unprecedented nature of the 'ordeal'. German troops could 'stand a great deal', recorded one officer from Mecklenburg in late November 1812, for they were already 'used to hardship'.[48] Along with many other reasons, including states' interest in suppressing the commemoration of losses incurred on the French side and a lack of continuity because of a high mortality rate and the reconstruction of armies during the Napoleonic period, soldiers' and civilians' own matter-of-fact responses to war before 1815 seem to have affected later portrayals of military conflict.

The absence of a compelling counter-narrative of the Revolutionary and Napoleonic Wars, which could be opposed to heroic official or public depictions of events, played an important part in the romanticization of warfare after 1815. Given the duration and human cost of the wars, there were frank disclosures of the nature of the campaigns, from veterans' published diaries and memoirs to series of prints by painters such as Albrecht Adam and Christian Wilhelm Faber du Faur. There were also widely heeded warnings about the avoidance of war in future, which were taken up especially by conservatives and officials anxious to preserve the political *status quo* and guard against revolution. Thus, Gentz's influential conception of a post-Napoleonic states' system, based on a balance of power in Europe, was

---

[43] See, for instance, S. Müller, *Soldaten in der deutschen Revolution von 1848/49* (Paderborn, 1999); T. Buk-Swienty, *Schlachtbank Düppel. Geschichte einer Schlacht* (Berlin, 2011); F. Kühlich, *Die deutschen Soldaten im Krieg von 1870/71* (Frankfurt, 1995).

[44] E. T. A. Hoffmann, 19 Aug. 1813, in E. Klessmann (ed.), *Die Befreiungskriege im Augenzeugenberichten (Düsseldorf, 1966)*, 133; E. M. Arndt to K. B. Trinius, 12 Dec. 1812, in E. M. Arndt, *Briefe* (Darmstadt, 1972–5), vol. 1, 235.

[45] E. M. Arndt to K. B. Trinius, 12 Dec. 1812, in E. M. Arndt, *Briefe*, vol. 1, 236.

[46] O. A. Rühle v. Lilienstern, *Reise mit der Armee 1809*, ed J.-J. Langendorf (Vienna, 1986), 171–2.

[47] Ibid.

[48] O. v. Raven, 23 Nov. 1812, in O. G. E. v. Raven, *Tagebuch des Feldzuges in Rußland im Jahre 1812*, ed. K.-U. Keubke (Rostock, 1998), 136.

designed to prevent 'contiguous and more or less well-connected states' damaging the independence of another by threatening 'effective resistance from the other side', which would endanger the aggressor's own existence.[49] The fear of a recurrence of uncontrollable Revolutionary Wars was a defining feature of the stable international order presided over by Austria and Russia between 1815 and 1848. It is worth remembering, however, that large-scale conflicts—or *Hauptkriege*—were the consequence of revolution, in Gentz's opinion, not the cause. Wars against revolutionary powers, such as had been undertaken by the coalitions against France since 1792, were justified. To most, if not all, conservative commentators—the Schlegel brothers, Adam Müller, the Gerlach brothers—armed intervention continued to be a necessary, often organic, element of human existence. Liberal writers—Heeren, Luden, Rotteck, or Gervinus—were less willing to agree that war was natural but most of them thought that it was justified as a means of defending the autonomy of civilized states. Such assumptions informed liberals' support for Prussia's war against Denmark over Schleswig in 1848 and their discussion of German intervention in the Crimean War in 1854–6 and the Franco-Austrian War in 1859. The majority of radicals, too, were committed to military intervention in this period of mounting international instability. As their vituperative public clashes in 1859 made plain, they were divided by allegiance—whether to back Italy or Austria—not by the exercise of military force itself. For Carl Vogt, in *Studien zur gegenwärtigen Lage Europas* (1859), the Confederation had to resist Austrian pressure to go to war on Vienna's side, maintaining armed neutrality in favour of Italian unification. For this cause, German states had to be ready to use force against the Habsburg monarchy.[50] Most radicals concurred.[51] Left-wing opponents such as Johann Baptist Schweitzer, who championed the Austrians as a 'fraternal tribe', rarely argued for peace.[52] For his part, Engels encouraged Austria to adopt an offensive strategy as 'the true method' of self-defence.[53] Such politicians and publicists could refer to serried ranks of historians, philosophers, and lawyers who had helped to make war seem inevitable in a world of sovereign states and natural as an extension of individuals' acts of aggression and fight for survival.[54]

The causes of war in the nineteenth century were complex. The changing alignments of political parties, states, social and confessional milieux, officers, soldiers, and civilians (Nikolaus Buschmann, Dieter Langewiesche), together with a shifting set of cultural assumptions and memories (Karen Hagemann), affected individuals' reasons for countenancing conflict.[55] It is these alignments that have been the

---

[49] F. v. Gentz, 'Fragmente' (1806), in F. v. Gentz, *Ausgewählte Schriften*, vol. 4, 39.

[50] C. Vogt, *Studien zur gegenwärtigen Lage Europas*, 118.

[51] See, for instance, L. Bamberger, *Juchhe nach Italia!* (Bern, 1859).

[52] J. B. Schweitzer, *Widerlegung von Carl Vogts Studien*, 42.

[53] F. Engels, 'The Prospects of War', *New York Daily Tribune*, 12 May 1859, in K. Marx and F. Engels, *Werke*, vol. 13, 312.

[54] H. Gramley, *Propheten des deutschen Nationalismus. Theologen, Historiker und Nationalismus. Theologen, Historiker und Nationalökonomen 1848–1880* (Frankfurt, 2001), 131–44, 221–46, 333–57.

[55] K. Hagemann, *Revisiting Prussia's Wars against Napoleon*; A. Forrest, E. François, and K. Hagemann (eds), *War Memories*. N. Buschmann, '"Im Kanonenfeuer müssen die Stämme Deutschlands

focus of historians' attention.[56] Yet, from a later point of view, it is the ease with which the majority of citizens went to war which stands out. If they were not convinced by patriotic or national justifications of war themselves, ordinary conscripts were reassured that the cause for which they were fighting was legitimate and the army was an integral, rarely challenged part of the political order. This acceptance was manifest during wartime, when group loyalty—which was relevant in the 1860s, as it was in 1914–18 and 1939–45—was closely connected to 'the example of leaders', especially at the onset of fighting.[57] Revolts against military recruitment or mobilization were rare compared to the eighteenth century, even during unpopular or ill-explained wars such as the recommencement of hostilities in Schleswig in 1849 or the war in Bohemia in 1866. To Theodor Fontane, most sections of Prussian society were marked out by their 'war-reluctance' in 1866.[58] Jakob Venedey said the same about Austria, not merely about 'the great mass of people', but also about 'the educated'.[59] Hohenzollern and Habsburg soldiers were nonetheless mobilized and went on to fight without significant incident.

Many soldiers preferred the army, claimed a popular refrain, than to be a 'farmer's slave'.[60] The harsh conditions of military service appear to have been tolerable for most conscripts. Likewise, the prospect of war, including the possibility of wounding

---

zusammen geschmolzen warden". Zur Konstruktion nationaler Einheit in den Kriegen der Reichsgründungsphase', in N. Buschmann and D. Langewiesche (eds), *Der Krieg in den Gründungsmythen europäischer Nationen und der USA*, 99–119; N. Buschmann, 'Niederlage als retrospektiver Sieg? Die Entscheidung von 1866 aus Sicht der historischen Verlierer', in H. Carl, H. H. Kortum, D. Langewiesche, and F. Lenger (eds), *Kriegsniederlagen*, 123–43; N. Buschmann, 'Between the Federative Nation and the National State: Public Perceptions of the Foundation of the German Empire in Southern Germany and Austria', in L. Cole (ed.), *Different Paths to the Nation: Regional and National Identities in Central Europe and Italy, 1830–1870* (Basingstoke, 2007), 157–79; N. Buschmann, 'Auferstehung der Nation? Konfession und Nationalismus vor der Reichsgründung in der Debatte jüdischer, protestantischer und katholischer Kriese', 333–88; F. Becker, 'Strammstehen vor der Obrigkeit? Bürgerliche Wahrnehmung der Einigungskriege und Militarismus im Deutschen Kaiserreich', 87–113; D. Langewiesche, 'Fortschrittsmotor Krieg. Krieg im politischen Handlungsarsenal Europas im 19. Jahrhundert und die Rückkehr der Idee des bellum iustum in der Gegenwart', in C. Benninghaus (ed), *Unterwegs in Europa. Beiträge zu einer vergleichen Sozial- und Kulturgeschichte* (Frankfurt, 2008), 23–40; D. Langewiesche, 'Zum Wandel sozialer Ordnungen durch Krieg und Revolution: Europa 1848—Wissenserzeugung und Wissensvermittlung', in J. Baberowski and G. Metzler (eds), *Gewalträume. Soziale Ordnungen im Ausnahmezustand* (Frankfurt, 2012), 93–134.

[56] This is the approach of Jörn Leonhard, *Bellizismus und Nation*, 3–44; Jörn Leonhard, 'Die Nationalisierung des Krieges und der Bellizimus der Nation. Die Diskussion um Volks- und Nationalkrieg in Deutschland, Großbritannien und den Vereinigten Staaten seit den 1860er Jahren', in C. Jansen (ed.), *Der Bürger als Soldat* (Essen, 2004), 83–105; Jörn Leonhard, 'Gewalt und Partizipation. Die Zivilgesellschaft im Zeitalter des Bellizismus', *Mittelweg*, 36 (2005), 49–69. It is also the approach of most other intellectual histories of war: for example, A. Gat, *The Development of Military Thought: The Nineteenth Century* (Oxford, 1992), 46–113; J. Wallach, *Die Kriegslehre von Friedrich Engels* (Frankfurt, 1968); P. Paret, *Understanding War: Essays on Clausewitz and the History of Military Power* (Princeton, NJ, 1992), 167–77.

[57] R. Martin, *Kriegserinnerungen*, ed. F. Bücker (Wiesbaden, 1898), 152.

[58] T. Fontane, *Der deutsche Krieg von 1866*, vol. 1, 64.

[59] J. Venedey, in H. v. Srbik (ed.), *Quellen zur deutschen Politik Österreichs*, vol. 5, 955–7.

[60] Cited in U. Frevert, *Nation in Barracks*, 110.

and death, was sufficiently close to the varied fortunes and commonplace violence of daily life to make it unexceptionable. For the respectable classes of the *Bürgertum* and urban nobility, it was more threatening, given their increasing sensitivity to unpleasant smells, bodily effusions, the sight of blood, pain, dismemberment, and death. As in duels, violence and injury were to be controlled and marginalized or concealed from public view. The laws and conventions of war would limit the consequences of the exercise of armed force and guard against the commission of atrocities, it was anticipated. Not all lawyers trusted in such limitations. For Bluntschli, for example, the Franco-German War of 1870–1 had demonstrated international law's 'deficits and weaknesses'.[61] Yet most commentators believed that armed conflicts were necessary for the defence of the state or nation and that they reinforced civilization rather than undermining it.[62] Even if they did not go as far as Treitschke in labelling war 'beautiful', they would probably have agreed with one correspondent in the *Weimarische Zeitung* in 1870 that the campaign would be conducted in 'the spirit of true culture'.[63] This deeply ingrained sense amongst many subjects that war was at once heroic and just helped to overcome the increasing aversion of 'respectable' society to hardship, suffering, injury, and death at a time when the press coverage of conflicts in the Crimea, Italy, and the United States suggested that the nature of modern warfare was changing, exposing soldiers to the effects of explosive shells, breech-loading rifles, and *mitrailleuses*. That middle-class recruits continued to go to war willingly in 1864, 1866, and 1870 testified to the power and pervasiveness of romantic myths of armed struggle.

THE OPEN SECRET OF MILITARY VIOLENCE

Some soldiers became markedly less willing to continue fighting or to contemplate wars in future once they had experienced the conditions of modern warfare for themselves. Such a conversion had not occurred in 1848–51, in part because 'revolution' had been kept separate from 'civil war' in the minds of the majority of contemporaries and in part because the number of troops involved in the war in Schleswig had been small and instances of combat had been limited. The conflict in Italy in 1859 had differed in these respects, with the modern technologies of mass armies threatening to spill over into German theatres of war, yet it remained for most commentators an 'Austrian' affair.[64] By contrast, the series of German wars after 1864 confronted hundreds of thousands of soldiers and millions of

---

[61] J. C. Bluntschli, *Das moderne Völkerrecht der civilisirten Staaten*, 2nd edn, ix.

[62] For proof of the contrary, see H. Mehrkens, *Statuswechsel. Kriegserfahrung und nationale Wahrnehmung im Deutsch-Französischen Krieg 1870/71* and Daniela L. Caglioti, 'Waging War on Civilians: The Expulsion of Aliens in the Franco-Prussian War', *Past and Present*, 221 (2013), 161–95. The latter finds that 'The Germans...refrained from expelling or interning French subjects, not because they were more "liberal", but because they were clearly less worried about feeding the enemy army with additional forces' (187).

[63] H. v. Treitschke to his sister, 18 July 1870, in M. Cornicelius (ed.), *Heinrich Treitschkes Briefe*, vol. 3, 282; P. v. Bojanowski, *Geschehenes und Geschriebenes*, 66.

[64] M. Hewitson, *Nationalism in Germany, 1848–1866*, 147–53, 192–4.

relatives back home with the realities of combat—355,000 Prussian, 528,000 Austrian, and 68,000 Hanoverian and confederal troops were deployed in 1866; 1.5 million German soldiers were called up in 1870–1. Over 100 million letters and postcards were sent from the front to home and back during the Franco-German War, creating sources of news and maintaining emotional contacts which regularly contradicted the narratives of the government and the press. Whereas periodicals and newspapers continued to disseminate heroic impressions of combat, which were interwoven with contemporaneous and retrospective justification of conflict on national grounds, combatants themselves gave a much more brutal account of events. 'If I now wanted to write that any heroic thought at all had enthused me in the carrying out of this bloody work, I would have to lie, for I was thinking of nothing of the sort', wrote one combatant of the Franco-German War.[65]

The sensations of war seemed physically unbearable, 'as if the elements of the earth were going to split apart', wrote one Bavarian volunteer from Wörth on 6 August 1870.[66] Modern *matériel* dismembered and sliced through human bodies, making soldiers feel defenceless and disoriented. The sight of the battlefield would 'always remain fresh in my memory', recorded the same soldier.[67] The majority of those who experienced fighting appear to have reacted in a similar way. Some claimed that the sights were 'too terrible' to be described, but many others went on to disclose what they had seen.[68] Faced with torsos burnt to charcoal, formless lumps of flesh, limbs torn off, arms stretching up stiffly, and visages marked with 'an expression of anger', even career officers found that they were left feeling empty, their 'joy over the great victory...gone'.[69] The effects of modern weaponry, increasing squeamishness, and fear of death were combined in these responses to combat. Although they were frequently juxtaposed with matter-of-factness and an unsentimental willingness to finish the 'job', especially on the part of ordinary soldiers and staff officers, so that the troops could go home, they were not dislodged or obscured by combatants' readiness to continue. 'Horror' of war remained a *leitmotif* of soldiers' correspondence, diaries, and memoirs. It was rarely displaced or linked to feelings of aggression and reflections on acts of killing by combatants.[70] More regularly, it seemed to lead to hardened indifference, with 'death on the battlefield' bearing 'no terror' and becoming 'a silent companion' seen 'a hundred times but noticed by no one'.[71] There is every indication, though, that what Hänel called 'the night of death' which the majority of combatants had experienced in 1864, 1866,

---

[65] F. Freudenthal, *Von Stade bis Gravelotte. Erinnerungen eines Artilleristen* (Bremen, 1898), 137.

[66] E. Metsch, *Meine Erlebnisse*, 11–13.   [67] Ibid., 5.

[68] L. Heiners, 'Tagebuch', 28, *Feldpostbriefe*, Unversitäts- und Landesbibliothek, Bonn.

[69] D. v. Lassberg, *Mein Kriegstagebuch*, 23, and F. v. Frankenberg, *Kriegstagebücher*, 169.

[70] For more on the comparison with the First World War, where some historians have argued that troops derived pleasure from killing, see M. Hewitson, 'German Soldiers and the Horrors of War in 1870 and 1914', *History*, 101 (2016), 396–424. This downplaying of the role of aggression and displacement runs counter to that presented by Thomas Rohkrämer in *Der Militarismus der 'kleinen Leute'*, 125–40.

[71] F. v. Wantoch-Rekowski, *Kriegstagebuch 1870/71 des jüngsten Offiziers im Königs-Grenadier-Regiment Nr. 7 in Liegnitz* (Munich, 1914), cited T. Rohkrämer in *Der Militarismus der 'kleinen Leute'*, 135.

and 1870–1 remained in their thoughts, however hardened they appeared to have become in the midst of battle.[72]

Circumstances conspired to push soldiers to omit or conceal what they had experienced of battle. Anticipating adventure, travel, heroic action, or simply a change of routine, the majority of troops had not expected to encounter what they did. Their disclosures had regularly met with a lack of understanding or discomfiture on the part of their relatives and friends at home. In both letters and memoirs, many were like the Rhinelander Ferdinand Wallmann, professing to his parents after the battle of Gravelotte that he could not 'describe this terrible thing for you'.[73] The purportedly glorious outcome of the Schleswig and Franco-German wars made it hard for veterans to depart from the tropes of patriotic narratives of the conflicts. Almost all of their accounts had the same national or patriotic framework, ending with a toast, 'with God, for the king, Kaiser and fatherland! Hurrah! Hurrah! Hurrah!'[74] A Bavarian volunteer, twenty-eight years after the event (following a period characterized by 'peace and well-being), concluded:

> May the violent and powerful feats of arms of the German armies in that great time be an illuminating model for the sons of these brave men and for our youth, contemporaries and successors, for then enthusiasm will turn into defence, love for our narrower and wider fatherland will blaze up and we shall again be able to call out in times of danger, 'Dear fatherland, you can rest easy' ... true soldier's blood flows in our veins and we are proud to have taken part in such bloody battles and glorious victories, as co-founders of such a powerful German Reich.[75]

The descriptions of smoking ruins, pools of blood, corpses, half-skulls, deaths of comrades, and mass graves which soldiers provided, often at the heart of their narratives of the war, sat uneasily alongside such patriotic injunctions.[76] Some commented explicitly on the disjunction ('what a contrast!') between 'jubilation in the middle of a field of corpses' and, beside it, 'death, devastation and misery'.[77] Although war literature as it had developed in the nineteenth century commonly evoked danger and the possibility of death as elements of heroism, it had furnished few precedents for this type of description. It is unlikely that such descriptions, which occur repeatedly in private letters and retrospective memoirs, were the corollary of changing literary conventions.[78] Many soldiers refused to divulge what they had witnessed to those at home and many others struggled to find words to depict things which had shocked them. Scholars such as Christine Krüger, who has investigated the press (and the correspondence of clerics), have argued that such

---

[72] C. L. Hähnel, *Bei den Fahnen*, 96.
[73] F. Wallmann to his parents, 15 and 19 Aug. 1870, *Feldpostbriefe*, Universitäts- und Landesbibliothek, Bonn.
[74] F. Kühnhauser, *Kriegs-Erinnerungen*, 264.
[75] Ibid.   [76] Ibid., 34–7, 69–87.   [77] Ibid., 83.
[78] I. Schikorsky (ed.), *'Wenn doch dies Elend ein Ende hätte'*, 7–33; I. Schikorsky, 'Kommunikation über das Unbeschriebene, 295–315.

silence was pervasive.[79] Despite self-censorship, however, a large number of correspondents, diarists, and memoirists did disclose details of their suffering and of the wounding and deaths of friend and foe.[80]

Such imagery, which was often accompanied by allusions to a soldier's feelings of 'disgust' (*Ekel*) or 'fright' (*Erschrecken*), had the power to horrify nineteenth-century readers.[81] It was not new. Reports from the Crimean, Franco-Austrian, and American Civil Wars, following the example of British, French, and American journalists, had revealed the horrors of modern warfare in the 1850s and early 1860s, describing injuries inflicted by exploding shells and massed ranks of entrenched infantrymen. 'One gets used to the horrors of war', wrote one correspondent of the *Gartenlaube* in 1859, before going on to depict 'the hundreds of thousands of those who have been smashed to pieces' and to discuss, for the benefit of a readership which would not automatically understand, how soldiers could become accustomed to such sights and smells.[82] Lithographs in popular periodicals sanitized and domesticated war, representing bucolic, exotic, or humorous aspects of campaigns, but they also showed corpses and hinted at the uncompromising nature of photography, on which some of the etchings were based.[83] The techniques of painting on top of photographs or using them as 'sketches' were already established by the 1860s, with contemporaries gently teasing troops suspected after battle in 1864 of 'arranging the debris themselves' to render it 'painterly'.[84] Photographs and the reality which they were believed to represent were less aesthetically pleasing than the traditional art of war. Yet there was no indication in the diary entries and letters of German soldiers going to war in 1864 and 1866—or in the correspondence of their families—that they had been affected by such reportage or that they harboured specific fears, beyond the usual excitement and sense of general danger, about their fate during the campaign. Such premonitions were much more common in 1914.[85] Without actual experience of modern warfare, most conscripts and civilians appear to have retained an overriding sense that war could be heroic. In this respect, the representation and mediation of conflict (Gerhard Paul, Ute Daniel, Frank Becker, Susanne Parth) remained subordinate to experiences of combat.[86]

---

[79] C. G. Krüger, 'German Suffering in the Franco-German War, 1870/71', 406–7.

[80] This finding contradicts Christine Krüger's claim that 'only a few of them overtly described what they had to endure': Christine Krüger, 'German Suffering in the Franco-German War', 406: by twenty-first-century standards, of course, there was considerable self-censorship, but by nineteenth-century ones, the repeated descriptions of corpses were shocking and were described as such.

[81] The word 'Entsetzen' or 'horror' likewise punctuates this type of description.

[82] *Gartenlaube*, 1859, vol. 30, 430.

[83] On the domestication of war in lithographs, see N. Buschmann, *Einkreisung und Waffenbruderschaft*, 38–9.

[84] Cited in S. Parth, *Zwischen Bildbericht und Bildpropaganda*, 246.

[85] I have written about this at greater length in M. Hewitson, 'German Soldiers and the Horror of War in 1870 and 1914', *History*, 101 (2016), 396–424.

[86] G. Paul, *Bilder des Krieges*; U. Daniel (ed.), *Augenzeugen. Kriegsberichterstattung vom 18. zum 21. Jahrhundert* (Göttingen, 2006); U. Daniel, 'Bücher vom Kriegsschauplatz: Kriegsberichterstattung als Genre des 19. Jahrhunderts', in W. Hardtwig and E. Schütz (eds), *Geschichte für Leser. Populäre Geschichtsschreibung im 20. Jahrhundert* (Stuttgart, 2005), 93–121; F. Becker, 'Kriegsbericht und Vergleich: Krimkrieg 1853–56—Deutsch-Französischer Krieg 1870/71—Südwestafrikanischer Krieg 1904–1907', in A. Epple and

During the previous period of mass warfare in 1805–15, the majority of German troops had faced similar conditions, with higher mortality rates.[87] Some survivors wrote about their experiences in terms which resembled those of later testimony. 'War had left behind the most terrible traces', wrote one Prussian adjutant in August 1813.[88] Even the future Prussian Chief of the General Staff Rühle von Lilienstern could be found reflecting at length about the effects on the 'nervous system' of seeing 'thousands of people dead in a pile'.[89] The German lands were 'already familiar with graphic descriptions of warfare', notes Leighton James: 'Various parts of German-speaking central Europe had been ravaged by warfare since the seventeenth century and many German civilians, the main audience for these soldiers' accounts, were only too familiar with the "horrible figure of war".'[90] The figure changed subtly over the course of the nineteenth century, however. Many memoirists, the majority of whom were officers, accepted the ordeal of war in the manner of Rühle von Lilienstern: 'time and reason', he wrote, mitigated 'all mental discomfort', and bodily pain itself seemed not to exceed 'a certain measure', beyond which 'sensitivity disappears'.[91] As for the 'common soldier', the military writer and Prussian officer was confident that he would, 'with unreflecting indifference', face dangers which would make the 'blood of the peaceful burgher run cold'.[92] A small minority of soldiers were burghers, particularly in companies of volunteers, but their testimony, insofar as it registered horror at the realities of war, was offset by other accounts of military valour, picaresque adventure, and physical toughness. It was obvious to onlookers, as one diarist in 1809 put it, 'that the lot of the soldier in the field is one of the hardest', yet the conditions of the campaign were characterized, not by injury and death in combat, but by 'hunger, thirst, heat and frost', which many troops had already experienced to a lesser degree in their civilian lives.[93] The pictures of suffering presented in the oral traditions and written record of the Napoleonic Wars were more mixed and less visible, in the restricted public spheres of the early nineteenth century, than those of the wars of unification. The 'diversity, intricacy and uncertainty' of veterans' memoirs seemed, in James's phrase, to have been 'overshadowed'.[94]

W. Erhart (eds), *Die Welt beobachten. Praktiken des Vergleichens* (Frankfurt, 2015), 311–35; F. Becker, 'Bildberichterstattung zum Deutsch-Französischen Krieg von 1870/71—eine Kultur der Identifikation', in J. Echternkamp, W. Schmidt, and T. Vogel (eds), *Perspektiven der Militärgeschichte. Raum, Gewalt und Repräsentation in historischer Forschung und Bildung* (Munich, 2010), 213–21; F. Becker, 'Die "Heldengalerie" der einfachen Soldaten. Lichtbilder in den deutschen Einigungskriegen', in A. Holzer (ed.), *Mit der Kamera bewaffnet. Krieg und Fotografie* (Marburg, 2003), 39–56; S. Parth, *Zwischen Bildbericht und Bildpropaganda.*

[87] The campaigns of 1848 did not constitute 'mass' warfare—except in the Habsburg monarchy—given that smaller contingents of troops were deployed in 1848–50.

[88] H. Lem v. Zieten (ed.), *Tagebuch von Heinrich Bolte, Adjutant Blüchers 1813–14* (Berlin, n. d.), 41–50.

[89] J.-J. Langendorf (ed.), *Rühle von Lilienstern. Reise mit der Armee 1809*, 171–2.

[90] L. S. James, *Witnessing the Revolutionary and Napoleonic Wars*, 93–4.

[91] J.-J. Langendorf (ed.), *Rühle von Lilienstern*, 171–2.   [92] Ibid.

[93] Sebastien Koegerl, cited in L. S. James, *Witnessing the Revolutionary and Napoleonic Wars*, 82.

[94] Ibid., 195.

The same effect was not discernible in the decades after the Franco-German War, when reports and recollections of fears, revulsion, and mourning were openly articulated alongside a dominant narrative about an historic, patriotic struggle. This subtext, which corresponded to the emotional responses of a broad cross-section of troops, appears to have played a part in veterans' private memories and subjects' public discussions of the military and of war during the imperial era. It informed the consolidation—rather than expansion—of the army after 1871 and the cautious foreign policy of Bismarck, backed by parties from across the political spectrum, during the 1870s and 1880s. It did not prevent the emergence of bellicose extra-parliamentary leagues (the Society for Germandom Abroad in 1881, the German Language Association in 1886, the Colonial Society in 1887, and the Pan-German League in 1891), nor did it prevent war-mongering within the army, most famously by Colmar von der Goltz, whose book *Das Volk in Waffen* (1883) urged Germans to 'work incessantly' towards 'a final struggle for the existence and greatness of Germany'.[95] Instead, fears and hopes of war were added to the cornucopia of other ambitions and anxieties, including the race for colonies, economic competition, the *Kulturkampf*, opposition to socialism, pan-Germanism, an arms race, and constitutional crisis, which comprised the political life of the *Kaiserreich*. Making sense of what Stig Förster refers to as contemporaries' 'dreams and nightmares' about a future war in such an overheated political atmosphere has proved difficult.[96] Much of the existing historiography has concentrated on the nexus between nation-building and the waging of war which was established through the reporting and more or less official commemoration of the conflicts during and after 1864–71. I have argued here, however, that the Janus-faced images of warfare which had become commonplace in Germany on the eve of the First World War derived above all from the intimate and unstable connections between national myth-making and veterans' own, darker sets of recollections of the 'wars of unification'. Like Moltke in 1890, many citizens appear to have found it impossible to banish the spectre of an unlimited war threatening civilization and costing hundreds of thousands of human lives.[97]

By 1914, the remaining veterans of the wars of unification were old men, their voices largely drowned out by generations who had no experience of military conflict and who had been criticized by at least some members of *Kriegervereine* for their obsequiousness and their sabre-rattling.[98] Some of the succeeding generations evidently regretted that they had missed their opportunity to participate in a glorious war. Many others, though, were less enthusiastic. The previously belligerent

[95] Cited in I. F. Clarke, *Voices Prophesying War, 1763–1984* (Oxford, 1966), 139.

[96] S. Förster, 'Dreams and Nightmares', 343–76; S. Förster, 'Im Reich des Absurden. Die Ursachen des Ersten Weltkrieges', in B. Wegner (ed.), *Wie Kriege entstehen* (Paderborn, 2000), 211–52. For further references, see M. Jefferies, *Contesting the German Empire, 1871–1918*, 179–92, and M. Hewitson, *Germany and the Causes of the First World War* (Oxford, 2004), 85–112.

[97] H. v. Moltke, 14 May 1890, in S. Förster (ed.), *Moltke*, 639–40.

[98] T. Rohkrämer, *Der Militarismus der 'kleinen Leute'*, 37–82.

National Liberal Eugen Schiffer was not alone in noting 'the deadening seriousness which has settled down on the people' during the July crisis.[99] 'Our people had heavy hearts', wrote Theodor Wolff, the left-liberal editor of the *Berliner Tageblatt* in 1916: 'the possibility of war was a frightening giant nightmare which caused us many sleepless nights'.[100] There were many reasons for mass opposition to—or quiet doubts about—the outbreak of hostilities in 1914, ranging from anti-militarism within sections of the SPD to a concern amongst individual newspaper readers that the slaughter of the Russo-Japanese and Balkan Wars would be repeated on a much larger scale. One important reason for doubts about the conflict—perhaps the principal underlying one—was the persistence of ambivalence about the prospect of a future war dating back to the 1860s. In this sense, the apogee of a national struggle coincided with broad scepticism about the romance of war.

[99] Cited in J. Verhey, *The Spirit of 1914: Militarism, Myth and Mobilization in Germany* (Cambridge, 2000), 69.
[100] Ibid., 7.

Select Bibliography

PRIMARY SOURCES[†]

Newspapers and Periodicals

Allgemeine Zeitung
Berliner Tageblatt
Bohemia
Chronik der Gegenwart
Daheim
Deutsche Kriegszeitung
Deutsches Volksblatt
Die Presse
Eisenbergisches Nachrichtsblatt
Evangelische Kirchenzeitung
Fliegende Blätter
Frankfurter Zeitung
Gartenlaube
Grenzboten
Historisch-politische Blätter
Illustrirte Zeitung
Im Neuen Reich
Kladderadatsch
Kölnische Volkszeitung
Kölnische Zeitung
Königlich-priviligirte Berlinische Zeitung
Münchner Neueste Nachrichten
National-Zeitung
Neue Preußische Zeitung
Oesterreichischer Volksfreund
Preußische Jahrbücher
Preussisches Wochenblatt
Schleswig-Holsteinische Zeitung
Social-Demokrat
Teltower Kreisblatt
The Times

PAMPHLETS, TREATISES, ENCYCLOPAEDIAS, AND HISTORIES

K. Abicht, *Geschichte des deutsch-französischen Krieges und der Wiederaufrichtung des Deutschen Reichs* (Heidelberg, 1873).

L. K. Aegidi, *Preußen und der Friede von Villafranca* (Berlin, 1859).

Anon, *Der Bundesfeldzug in Bayern im Jahre 1866* (Jena, 1866).

[†] I have listed only the most useful published primary sources and a selection of the main secondary works. For further works and archival sources, see the notes.

Anon, *Der deutsche Bürgerkrieg im Jahre 1866* (Brunswick, 1866).

Anon, *Die tapferen Preußen, ihr Heldenmuth u. ihre Siege in den blütigen Kämpfen im Böhmen-Lande gegen Österreichs unter Feldzugmeister Benedek fecthenden große Nord-Armee*, 1st edn (Breslau, 1866).

Anon, *Offener Brief an Johann Jacoby* (Leipzig, 1866).

Anon, *Preußens Feldzüge gegen Österreich und dessen Verbündete im Jahre 1866* (Berlin, 1866).

Anon, *Zur Beurtheilung des Verhaltens der badischen Felddivision im Feldzuge des Jahrs 1866* (Darmstadt, 1866).

Anon, *Die preußische Heeres-Reform* (Berlin, 1867).

Anon, *Geschichte der preußischen Invasion und Okkupation in Böhmen im Jahre 1866. Gesammelte Beilage der Zeitschrift* Politik (Prague, 1867).

Anon, *Die Operationen des achten deutschen Bundes-Corps im Feldzuge des Jahres 1866* (Darmstadt, 1868).

Anon, *Von der Elbe is zur Tauber. Der Feldzug der Preussischen Main-Armee im Sommer 1866 vom Berichterstatter des Daheim* (Bielefeld, 1868).

Anon, *Die Franzosen in Deutschland*, 6th edn (Munich, 1870).

E. M. Arndt, *Zur Verständigung ueber den Druck des Kriegsliedes gegen die Wälschen* (Bonn, 1859).

L. Bamberger, *Juchhe nach Italien* (Frankfurt, 1859), in L. Bamberger, *Gesammelte Schriften* (Berlin, 1913), vol. 3.

E. Bartels v. Bartberg, *Kritische Bemerkungen über die Feldzüge in Böhmen, Italien, Sudtirol und am Main*, 1st edn (Leipzig, 1866).

A. v. Baudissin, *Schleswig-Holstein Meerumschlungen. Kriegs- und Friedensbilder aus dem Jahre 1864* (Stuttgart, 1865).

H. Baumgarten, *Historische und politische Aufsätze und Reden* (Strasbourg, 1894).

H. Baumgarten, *Der deutsche Liberalismus. Eine Selbskritik* (Frankfurt, 1974).

W. Baur, *1813 und 1870. Ein Vortrag* (Bremen, 1870).

H. Beisler, *Betrachtungen über Staatsverfassung und Kriegswesen insbesondere über die Stellung des Wehrstandes zum Staat* (Frankfurt, 1822).

L. Bender, *Der jüngste Franzosenkrieg und die Wiederaufrichtung des Deutschen Reiches*, 4th edn (Essen, 1872).

F. v. Bentheim, *Leitfaden zum Unterricht in den Kriegswissenschaften* (Berlin, 1840).

W. Beseler, *Zur schleswig-holsteinischen Sache im August 1856* (Brunswick, 1856).

O. v. Bismarck, *Werke in Auswahl*, ed. E. Scheler (Darmstadt, 1968), vol. 4.

H. Blankenburg, *Der deutsche Krieg von 1866* (Leipzig, 1868).

J. C. Bluntschli, *Allgemeines Statsrecht* (Munich, 1863).

J. C. Bluntschli, 'Zur Revision der statlichen Grundbegriffe', in J. C. Bluntschli, *Kleine Schriften* (Nordlingen, 1879), vol. 1, 287–317.

J. C. Bluntschli and C. Brater (eds), *Deutsches Staatswörterbuch* (Stuttgart, 1857–70), vol. 6.

J. C. Bluntschli and C. Brater (eds), '*Das moderne Kriegsrecht der civilisirten Staten als Rechtsbruch dargestellt* (Nördlingen, 1866).

J. C. Bluntschli and C. Brater (eds), *Die Bedeutung und die Fortschritte des modernen Völkerrechts* (Berlin, 1866).

J. C. Bluntschli and C. Brater (eds), *Das moderne Völkerrecht in dem Kriege 1870. Rede zum Geburtstagfeste des höchsteligen Grossherzogs Karl Friedrich von Baden und zur akademischen Preisverteilung am 2. November 1870* (Heidelberg, 1870).

E. Du Bois-Reymond, *Über den deutschen Krieg. Rede am 3. August 1870 in der Aula der königlichen Friedrich-Wilhelms-Universität zu Berlin gehalten* (Berlin, 1870).

A. Borbstaedt, *Preussens Feldzüge gegen Österreich und dessen Verbündete im Jahre 1866* (Berlin, 1866).

A. Borbstaedt, *The Franco-German War* (London, 1873).

A. Böttger, *Teutsche Kriegslieder* (Leipzig, 1841).

Theodor Bracklow, *Geschichte Schleswig-Holsteins von 1848 bis 1852* (Altona, 1852).

K. v. Brandenstein, *Die Kriegskunst nach den neuesten Erfahrungen und ansichten dargestellt* (Erfurt, 1824).

H. v. Brandt, *Grundzüge der Taktik der drei Waffen. Infanterie, Kavallerie und Artillerie* (Berlin, 1842).

K. Brater, *Preussen und Bayern in der Sache der Herzogthümer* (Nördlingen, 1864).

L. Brentano, *Mein Leben im Kampf um die soziale Entwicklung Deutschlands* (Jena, 1931).

F. A. Brockhaus (ed.), *Allgemeine deutsche Real-Encyclopaedie fuer die gebildeten Stände* (Leipzig, 1817).

F. A. Brockhaus (ed.), *Conversations-Lexikon der neuesten Zeit und Literatur* (Leipzig, 1832).

F. A. Brockhaus (ed.), *Bilder Conversations-Lexikon der neuesten Zeit und Literatur* (Leipzig, 1837–41).

F. A. Brockhaus (ed.), *Kleineres Brockhaus'sches Conversations-Lexikon* (Leipzig, 1854–7).

C. G. Bruns, *Deutschlands Sieg über Frankreich. Rede am 15. October 1870 in der Aula der Friedrich-Wilhelms-Universität zu Berlin* (Berlin, 1870).

G. Büchner and L. Weidig, *Der Hessische Landbote. Texte, Briefe, Prozeßakten* (Frankfurt, 1974).

A. H. D. v. Bülow, *Geist des neuern Kriegssystems*, 3rd edn (Hamburg, 1837).

J. Burckhardt, *Weltgeschichtliche Betrachtungen*, ed. J. Oeri (Berlin, 1905).

J. Burckhardt, *Gesamtausgabe* (Stuttgart, 1929–34), vol. 7.

J. Burckhardt, 'Unsere Aufgabe' (1868–72), in J. Burckhardt, *Weltgeschichtliche Betrachtungen*, ed. J. Oeri (Basel, 1978).

J. C. Chenu, *Rapport au Conseil de santé des armées sur les résultats du service medico-chirurgical aux ambulances de Crimée et aux hopitaux militaires français en Turquie, pendant la champagne d'Orient en 1854–1855–1856* (Paris, 1865).

Karl Joseph von Clam-Martiniac, *Vorlesungen aus dem Gebiet der Kriegskunst* (Vienna, 1823).

C. v. Clausewitz, *Vom Kriege* (Berlin, 1832–4).

G. Cohn, *System der Nationalökonomie* (Stuttgart, 1885–98), vol. 2.

Philipp A. Colombier, *Militaerisches Hand- und Taschenbuch zur Ausbildung vaterlaendischer Krieger* (Erlangen, 1832).

F. C. Dahlmann, *Geschichte der englischen Revolution* (Leipzig, 1844).

F. C. Dahlmann, *Geschichte der französischen Revolution* (Leipzig, 1847).

F. C. Dahlmann, *Kleine Schriften und Reden* (Stuttgart, 1886).

F. C. Dahlmann, *Die Politik* (Frankfurt, 1997).

F. Dahn, *Das Kriegsrecht. Kurze, volksthümliche Darstellung für Jedermann zumal für den deutschen Soldaten* (Würzburg, 1870).

F. Dahn, *Moltke als Erzieher. Allerlei Betrachtungen* (Breslau, 1892).

C. v. Decker, *Ansichten über die Kriegsführung im Geiste der Zeit* (Berlin, 1822).

C. v. Decker, *Grundzüge der praktischen Strategie*, 2nd edn (Berlin, 1841).

C. v. Decker, *Die Shrapnels. Einrichtung und Theorie der Wirkung dieses Geschosses* (Berlin, 1842).

C. v. Decker, *Über die Persönlichkeit des preussischen Soldaten festgestellt durch die Militärverfassung seines Vaterlandes* (Berlin, 1842).

Ludwig Degen, *Zur Beurtheilung der badischen Revolution* (Leipzig, 1850).

V. M. O. Denk, *Die gegenwärtige Stellung des katholischen Clerus Deutschland, Frankreich und Preußen gegenüber* (Munich, 1870).

K. J. Diepenbrock, *Deutschlands Sieg und Herrlichkeit in staatlicher, sittlicher und sprachlicher Bedeutung. Patriotische Vorlesung* (Freiburg, 1870).

M. G. A. v. Ditfurth, *Benedek und die Taten und Schicksale der k. k. Nordarmee 1866* (Vienna, 1911), 3 vols.

M. Dittrich, *Generalfeldmarschall Graf Moltke. Eine Denkschrift für das deutsche Heer und Volk* (Dresden, 1889).

J. v. Dobay, *Der Krieg zwischen Österreich und Preußen im Jahre 1866 und der strategische Kritik desselben* (Pest, 1867–8).

R. Döhn, *Der Bonapartismus und der deutsch-französische Conflict vom Jahre 1870. Eine historische Studie* (Leipzig, 1870).

M. Dragomirow, *Abriß des österreichisch-preußichen Krieges im Jahre 1866* (Berlin, 1868).

J. G. Droysen, *Geschichte Alexanders des Großen* (Hamburg, 1833).

J. G. Droysen, *Geschichte des Hellenismus* (Hamburg, 1836–43).

J. G. Droysen, *Vorlesungen über die Freiheitskriege* (Kiel, 1846), 2 vols.

J. G. Droysen, *Die Herzogthümer Schleswig-Holstein und das Königreich Dänemark*, 2nd edn (Hamburg, 1850).

J. G. Droysen, 'Zur Charakteristik der europäischen Krisis' (1854), in J. G. Droysen, *Politische Schriften*, ed. F. Gilbert (Munich, 1933), 328–41.

J. G. Droysen, *Geschichte der preußischen Politik* (Leipzig, 1855–86).

J. G. Droysen, *Kleine Schriften zur schleswig-holsteinischen Frage*, 2nd edn (Berlin, 1863).

J. G. Droysen, *Politische Schriften*, ed. F. Gilbert (Munich, 1933).

R. Eickemeyer, *Abhandlungen über Gegenstände der Staats- und Kriegs-Wissenschaften* (Frankfurt, 1817), vol. 1.

O. Elben, *Keine Zerreissung Schleswigs!* (Stuttgart, 1864).

O. Elben, *Geschichte des* Schwäbischen Merkurs *1785–1885* (Stuttgart, 1885).

F. Engels, 'Rede in Elberfeld' (1845), in K. Marx and F. Engels, *Werke* (Berlin, 1962), vol. 2, 536–57.

F. Engels, 'Die Niederlage der Piemontesen', *Neue Rheinische Ztg*, 1849, in K. Marx and F. Engels, *Werke* (Berlin, 1961), vol. 6, 385–92.

F. Engels, *Po und Rhein* (1859), in K. Marx and F. Engels, *Werke* (Berlin, 1961), vol. 13, 225–68.

F. Engels, 'The Prospects of the War', *New York Daily Tribune*, 12 May 1859, in K. Marx and F. Engels, *Werke* (Berlin, 1961), vol. 13, 312.

F. Engels, 'Die preußische Militärfrage und die deutsche Arbeiterpartei' (1865), in K. Marx and F. Engels, *Werke* (Berlin, 1962), vol. 16.

F. Engels, 'The European War', 'The Attack on Sevastopol', and 'The Military Power of Russia', *New York Daily Tribune*, 2 Feb. and 14 and 31 Oct. 1854, in K. Marx and F. Engels, *Gesamtausgabe* (Berlin, 1985), vol. 13.

F. Engels, 'Der Feldzug in Italien' and 'Die Schlacht bei Solferino', *Das Volk*, vol. 4, 28 May and 2 July 1859, in K. Marx and F. Engels, *Gesamtausgabe* (Berlin, 1985), vol. 13.

F. Engels, 'Fighting at Last' and 'Historical Justice', *New York Daily Tribune*, 6 June and 21 July 1859, in K. Marx and F. Engels, *Gesamtausgabe* (Berlin, 1985), vol. 13.

Theodor Enslin, *Bibliothek der Kriegswissenschaften* (Berlin, 1824).

J. G. Ersch and J. G. Gruber (eds), *Allgemeine Enzyklopädie der Wissenschaften und Künste* (Leipzig, 1828).

F. C. v. Fechenbach zu Laudenbach und Sommerau, *Deutschland und Frankreich oder: Eine deutsche Antwort auf die französische Herausforderung* (Munich, 1870).

J. Ficker, *Das Deutsche Kaiserreich in seinen universalen und nationalen Beziehungen* (Innsbruck, 1862).

C. B. Fickler, *In Rastatt 1849* (Rastatt, 1853).

T. Fontane, *Der Schleswig-Holsteinische Krieg im Jahre 1864* (Berlin, 1866).

T. Fontane, *Der deutsche Krieg von 1866* (Berlin, 1871), 2 vols.

T. Fontane, *Der Krieg gegen das Kaiserreich* (Berlin, 1873), 2 vols.

S. Förster (ed.), *Moltke. Vom Kabinettskrieg zum Volkskrieg* (Bonn, 1992).

C. Frantz, *Die Quelle alles Übels. Betrachtungen über die preussische Verfassungskrise* (Stuttgart, 1863).

C. Frantz, *Literarisch-politische Aufsätze* (Munich, 1876).

K. Frenzel, *Deutsche Kämpfe* (Hanover, 1873).

G. Freytag, *Auf der Höhe der Vogesen. Kriegsberichte von 1870/71* (Leipzig, 1914).

J. Fröbel, *System der socialen Politik* (Mannheim, 1847), vol. 2.

J. Fröbel, *Theorie der Politik* (Vienna, 1861–4), 2 vols.

F. v. Gentz, *Ausgewählte Schriften*, ed. W. Weick (Stuttgart, 1836–8), vol. 4.

F. v. Gentz, *Schriften von Friedrich von Gentz*, ed. G Schlesier (Mannheim, 1838–40), 5 vols.

E. L. v. Gerlach, 'Regierungsplan für Graf Brandenburg', 19 Oct. 1848, in E. L. v. Gerlach, *Von der Revolution zum Norddeutschen Bund. Politik und Ideengut der preusssischen Hochkonservativen 1848–1866*, ed. H. Diwald (Göttingen, 1970), vol. 2.

C. v. Gersdorff, *Vorlesungen über militairische Gegenstände* (Dresden, 1827).

F. Gerstäcker, *Kriegsbilder. Erzählungen und Erinnerungen aus den Kriegsjahren 1870/71* (Leipzig, 1908).

G. G. Gervinus, *Einleitung in die Geschichte des neunzehnten Jahrhunderts* (Leipzig, 1853).

W. v. Giesebrecht, *Geschichte der deutschen 'Kaiserzeit'* (Brunswick, 1855–95).

G. E. F. v. Glasenapp, *Preussens Feldzug vom militaerischen Sttandpunkt* (Berlin, 1866).

G. E. F. v. Glasenapp, *Der Feldzug von 1870* (Berlin, 1871).

R. v. Gneist, *Berliner Zustände. Politische Skizzen aus der Zeit vom 18. März 1848 bis 18 März 1849* (Berlin, 1849).

R. v. Gneist, *Die Lage der preussischen Heeresorganisation* (Berlin, 1862).

J. C. F. Gutsmuths, *Turnbuch für die Söhne des Vaterlandes* (Frankfurt, 1817).

F. Hackländer, *Bilder aus dem Soldatenleben im Kriege* (Stuttgart, 1849).

C. L. v. Haller, *Restauration der Staats-Wissenschaft oder Theorie des natürlich-geselligen Zustands der Chimäre des künstlich-bürgerlichen entgegengesetzt* (Winterthur, 1820–5), 2 vols.

W. Hammer, *Napoleon als Feldheer, Regent, Staatsmann und Politiker* (Stuttgart, 1833).

D. Hansemann, 'Denkschrift für Friedrich Wilhelm IV, August und September 1840', in J. Hansen (ed.), *Rheinische Briefe und Akten zur Geschichte der politischen Bewegung 1830–1850* (Essen, 1919, and Bonn, 1942), 2 vols.

F. Harkort, *Die Zeiten des ersten Westphälischen Landwehrregiments. Ein Beitrag zur Geschichte der Befreiungskriege*, ed. W. Kollmann. (Hagen, 1964).

L. Hauff, *Die Geschichte des Krieges von 1866 in Mittel-Europa. Ihre Urasache und ihrere Folgen* (Munich, 1867).

L. Häusser, *Deutsche Geschichte vom Tode Friedrichs des Großen bis zur Gründung des Deutschen* Bundes (Leipzig, 1854–7).

G. W. F. Hegel, *Grundlinien der Philosophie des Rechts* (Stuttgart, 1970).

K. P. Heinzen, *Dreißig Kriegsartikel der neuen Zeit für Officiere und Gemeine in despotischen Staaten* (Neustadt, 1846).

L. Herbert, *Zwischen Krieg und Frieden oder nach Custozza und Königgraetz* (Pest, 1868), 3 vols.

M. Heß, 'Korrespondenzen aus der *Kölnischen Zeitung*' (1843), in M. Heß, *Sozialistische Aufsätze 1841–47*, ed. T. Zlocisti (Berlin, 1921).

M. Heß, 'Über die Not in unserer Gesellschaft und deren Abhilfe' (1845), in M. Heß, *Sozialistische Aufsätze 1841–1847*, ed. T. Zlocisti (Berlin, 1921).

M. Heß, 'Die europäische Triarchie' (1841), in M. Heß, *Philosophische und sozialistische Schriften*, 2nd edn (Vaduz, 1980), ed. W. Mönke, 43–70.

M. Heß, 'Die Folgen einer Revolution des Proletariats', *Deutsche-Brüsseler Zeitung*, 14 Oct. 1847, in M. Heß, *Philosophische und sozialistische Schriften*, ed. W. Mönke. 2nd edn (Vaduz, 1980).

G. Hiltl, *Der böhmische Krieg* (Bielefeld, 1867).

G. Hiltl, *Der Französische Krieg von 1870 und 1871* (Bielefeld and Leipzig, 1884).

N. Hocker, *Geschichte der deutschen Krieges im Jahre 1866 und des Krieges in Italien* (Cologne, 1867).

O. Höcking, *Der Nationalkrieg gegen Frankreich in den Jahren 1870 und 1871* (Leipzig, 1895).

F. Hoffmann, *Preussens Krieg für Deutschlands Einheit* (Berlin, 1866).

C. Homburg, *Preußische Wegelagerei! Ernster Mahnruf zur Wachsamkeit für ganz Europa* (Mannheim, 1866).

J. G. v. Hoyer, *Litteratur der Kriegswissenschaften und Kriegsgeschichte* (Berlin, 1832).

J. Jacoby, 'Rede vor den Berliner Wählern', 12 Sept. 1848, and 'Über das Bürgerwehr-Gesetz', 26 Aug. 1848, in J. Jacoby, *Gesammelte Schriften und Reden* (Hamburg, 1872), vol. 2.

F. L. Jahn, *Die Deutsche Turnkunst*, 2nd edn (Berlin, 1847).

G. W. Jahn, *Der deutsche Krieg und Preussens Sieg im Jahre 1866, dem Volke erzählt*, 3rd edn (Halle, 1867).

K. Junck, *Der Deutsch-Französische Krieg 1870 und 1871* (Leipzig, 1876), vol. 1.

O. Kanngeisser, *Geschichte des Krieges von 1866* (Basel, 1892), 2 vols.

F. v. Kausler, *Die Kriege von 1792 bis 1815 in Europa und Ägypten* (Karlsruhe, 1842).

A. Kehrer, *Ereignisse und Betrachtungen während der Verwendung der Grossherzogl. Hessischen Armee-Division in den Jahren 1848 und 1849* (Worms, 1855).

J. L. Klüber, *Droits des gens modernes de l'Europe*, 2nd edn (Paris, 1874).

K. Knies, *Die politische Oekonomie vom geschichtlichen Standpuncte* (Brunswick, 1853), 433–4.

K. Knies, 'Finanzgeschichtliche und volkswirtschaftliche Betrachtungen über den Krieg', *Deutsche Vierteljahrsschrift*, 22 (1859), 1–60.

K. Knies, *Die Dienstleistung des Soldaten und die Mängel der Conscriptionspraxis* (Freiburg, 1860).

K. Knies, *Das moderne Kriegswesen* (Berlin, 1867).

Georg Friedrich Kolb, *Die Nachteile des stehenden Heerwesens und die Notwendigkeit der Ausbildung eines Volkswehrsystems* (Leipzig, 1862).

K. Köstler, *Geschichte des deutsch-französischen Krieges 1870 und 1871* (Munich, 1881).

Königlich Preussischer Kriegsministerium (ed.), *Militärische Schriften weiland Kaiser Wilhelms des Großen Majestät* (Berlin, 1897), vol. 2.

E. Krtschek, *Der Italienische und Ungarische Krieg 1848–1849* (Olmütz, 1853).

W. T. Krug, *Versuch einer systematischen Enzyklopädie der Kriegswissenschaften* (Leipzig, 1815).

W. T. Krug, *Dikäopolitik oder neue Restaurazion der Staatswissenschaft* (Leipzig, 1824).

W. T. Krug, *Allgemeines Handwörterbuch der philosophischen Wissenschaften nebst ihrer Literatur und Geschichte* (Leipzig, 1827).

W. T. Krug, *Gesammelte Schriften* (Brunswick and Leipzig, 1830–41), 6 vols.

F. Lassalle, *Der italienische Krieg und die Aufgabe Preussens. Eine Stimme aus der Demokratie* (Berlin, 1859).

F. Lassalle, *Nachgelassene Briefe und Schriften*, ed. G. Mayer (Berlin, 1922).

J. P. Lefren and Josef von Xylander, *Über Kriegsentwürfe* (Augsburg, 1824).

F. W. Lehmann, *Grundzüge zur Bildung einer deutschen Bürgerwehr und eines deutschen Heerwesens mit Rücksichten auf die preussische Heerverfassung* (Bonn, 1848).

H. Leo, *Studien und Skizzen zu einer Naturlehre des Staats* (Halle, 1833).

H. Leo, *Lehrbuch der Universalgeschichte* (Halle, 1850), 6 vols.

H. Leo, *Vorlesungen über die Geschichte des deutschen Volkes und Reiches* (Halle, 1854–67), 5 vols

G. v. Lerchenfeld, *Das Verfahren der deutschen Grossmächte gegen Schleswig-Holstein und den Bund* (Jena, 1866).

H. O. v. Lettow-Vorbeck, *Geschichte des Kriegs von 1866 in Deutschland* (Berlin, 1896–1902), 3 vols.

A. F. v. Liebenstein, *Über stehende Heere und Landwehr mit besonderer Rücksicht auf die deutschen Staaten* (Karlsruhe, 1817).

T. Lindner, *Der Krieg gegen Frankreich und die Einigung Deutschlands. Zur 25jährigen Wiederkehr der Gedenktage von 1870/71* (Berlin, 1895).

A. Lips, *Der Krieg in Osten* (Nuremberg, 1828).

F. List, *Das nationale System der politischen Oekonomie* (Stuttgart, 1841).

F. Lubojatzky, *Deutschlands Kriegsereignisse im Jahre 1866* (Dresden, 1867).

H. Luden, *Geschichte des teutschen Volkes* (Gotha, 1825–37), 12 vols.

J. G. Luedde, *Gedenkblätter des deutschen Krieges im Sommer 1866* (Berlin, 1866).

H. E. W. Lühe (ed.), *Militair Conversations-Lexikon* (Leipzig, 1833–7).

J. Lukas, *Die Presse, ein Stück moderner Versimpelung* (Regensburg, 1867).

K. Marx, *Der achzehnte Brumaire des Louis Bonarparte* (New York, 1852).

K. Marx, *Der Bürgerkrieg in Frankreich* (Leipzig, 1871).

K. Marx, 'Das Elend der Philosophie', in K. Marx and F. Engels, *Werke* (Berlin, 1956–90), vols 4, 8, 12–13, 17.

K. Marx and F. Engels, *Die Deutsche Ideologie* (Berlin, 1932).

W. Menzel, *Der deutsche Krieg im Jahre 1866* (Stuttgart, 1867).

R. v. Mohl, *Die Geschichte und Literatur der Staatswissenschaften* (Erlangen, 1855–8), 3 vols.

R. v. Mohl, *Encyklopädie der Staatswissenschaften* (Tübingen, 1859).

R. v. Mohl, *Staastrecht, Voelkerrecht und Politik* (Tübingen, 1860–9), 3 vols.

R. v. Mohl, *Politische Schriften* (Cologne, 1966).

H. v. Moltke, *Geschichte des deutsch-französischen Krieges von 1870–71* (Berlin, 1891).

H. v. Moltke, *Militärische Werke* (Berlin, 1896–1911), 4 vols.

H. v. Moltke, *Moltkes Militärische Korrespondenz* (Berlin, 1902).

M. v. Moltke, *Nicht für Österreich, aber gegen Frankreich!* (Breslau, 1859).

T. Mommsen, *Römische Geschichte* (Berlin, 1854–6).

T. Mommsen, *Die Annexion Schleswig-Holsteins* (Berlin, 1865).

T. Mommsen, *Reden und Aufsätze* (Berlin, 1905).

F. de la Motte Fouqué, *Etwas über den deutschen Adel, über Ritter-Sinn und Militär-Ehre* (Hamburg, 1819).

W. Müller, *Politische Geschichte der Gegenwart* (Berlin, 1871), vol. 4.

W. Müller, *Politische Geschichte der Neuesten Zeit 1816–1875* (Stuttgart, 1875).

W. Müller, *Deutschlands Einigungskriege 1864–1871* (Leipzig, 1889).

F. Münich, *Geschichte der Entwicklung der bayerischen Armee seit zwei Jahrhunderten* (Munich, 1864).

H. Nabbat and J. Lemcke, *Die Sieges-Strasse der Preussen im Jahre 1866 durch Böhmen, Mähren, Österreich und Ungarn. Ansichten der vorzüglichsten Hauptquartiere und Panoramen der Schlachtfelder* (Berlin, 1868), 3 vols.

G. Neuhaus, *Geschichte des deutschen Krieges der Jahre 1866 und seiner Folgen* (Mohrungen, 1867).

B. G. Niebuhr, *Römische Geschichte* (Berlin, 1811–32).

B. G. Niebuhr, *Geschichte des Zeitalters der Revolution* (Hamburg, 1845), vol. 1.

C. Niemeyer, *Die Schlachten des Heiligen Krieges* (Leipzig, 1817).

F. Nietzsche, *Die fröhliche Wissenschaft*, revised edn (Leipzig, 1887).

W. Oncken, *Unsere Lage bei Ausbruch des Krieges. Vortrag, gehalten am 24 Juli 1870 im großen Clubsaale in Gießen* (Gießen, 1870).

W. Oncken, *Unser Heldenkaiser. Festschrift zum hundertjährigen Geburtstage Kaiser Wilhelm des Großen* (Berlin, 1897).

H. B. Oppenheim, *Deutsche Begeisterung und Habsburgischer Kronbesitz* (Berlin, 1859).

H. B. Oppenheim, *Deutschlands Noth und Ärzte* (Berlin, 1859).

A. v. Pappenheim, *Militairische Fantasien über Heerbildung, Heerverfassung und was auf das Soldatenwesen Bezug hat* (Augsburg, 1832), vol. 1.

A. Pfister, *Deutscher Zwietracht. Erinnerungen aus meiner Leutnantszeit 1859–1869* (Stuttgart, 1902).

O. v. Platen, *Wehrverfassung, Kriegslehren und Friedensideen im Jahrhundert der Industrie* (Berlin, 1843).

F. v. Prondynski, *Theorie des Krieges*, 2nd revised edn (Bielefeld, 1849), vol. 1.

R. Prutz, *Geschichte des deutschen Journalismus* (Hanover, 1845).

F. Ranke, *Die großen Jahre 1870 und 1871* (Nördlingen, 1873).

L. v. Ranke, *Deutsche Geschichte im Zeitalter der Reformation* (Berlin, 1839–47).

L. v. Ranke, *Neun Bücher preußischer Geschichte* (Berlin, 1847–8).

L. v. Ranke, *Französische Geschichte, vornehmlich im sechzehnten und siebzehnten Jahrhundert* (Berlin, 1852–61).

L. v. Ranke, *Englische Geschichte, vornehmlich im sechzehnten und siebzehnten Jahrhundert* (Berlin, 1859–69).

L. v. Ranke, 'Rede am neunzigsten Geburtstag, 21. Dezember 1885', in L. v. Ranke, *Sämtliche Werke* (Leipzig, 1888), vol. 51–2, 592–8.

L. v. Ranke, *Die großen Mächte—Politisches Gespräch* (Göttingen, 1955).

L. v. Ranke, *Über Epochen der neueren Geschichte*, ed. T. Schieder and H. Berding (Munich, 1971).

F. v. Raumer, *Zur Politik des Tages* (Leipzig, 1859).

R. v. Raumer, *Vom Deutschen Geiste* (Erlangen, 1866).

F. Raveaux, *Mittheilungen ueber die Badische Revolution* (Frankfurt, 1850).

E. Reiche, *Der deutsche Krieg 1866* (Wittenberg, 1866).

A. and P. Reichensperger, *Deutschlands nächste Aufgaben* (Paderborn, 1860).

Rheinisches Conversations-Lexikon oder encyclopädisches Handwörterbuch für gebildete Stände (Cologne, 1824–30).

W. H. Riehl, *Kulturgeschichtliche Charakterköpfe*, 3rd edn (Stuttgart, 1899).

G. Riesser, *Gesammelte Schriften*, ed. M. Isler (Frankfurt, 1867), 3 vols.

A. L. v. Rochau, *Grundsätze der Realpolitik*, ed. H.-U. Wehler (Frankfurt, 1972).

C. Rössler, *System der Staatslehre* (Leipzig, 1857).

C. Rössler, *Preussen und die italienische Frage* (Berlin, 1859).

C. v. Rotteck, 'Über stehende Heere und Nationalmiliz' (1816), in C. v. Rotteck, *Sammlung kleinerer Schriften* (Stuttgart, 1829), vol. 2.

C. v. Rotteck, 'Krieg', in C. v. Rotteck and C. T. Welcker (eds), *Staats-Lexicon* (Altona, 1834–43), vol. 9, 491–501.

F. A. Rüder (ed.), *J. Hübner's Zeitungs- und Conversations-Lexikon*, 31st revised edn (Leipzig, 1824–8).

A. Ruge, 'Selbstkritik des Liberalismus' (1843), in A. Ruge, *Gesammelte Schriften* (Mannheim, 1846), vol. 3.

A. Ruge, *Aufruf zur Einheit* (Berlin, 1866).

J. J. O. A. Rühle v. Lilienstern, *Die deutsche Volksbewaffnung* (Berlin, 1815).

J. J. O. A. Rühle v. Lilienstern, *Aufsätze ueber Gegenstände und Ereignisse aus dem Gebiete des Kriegswesens* (Berlin, 1818).

F. Rümelin, *Aus der Paulskirche. Berichte an den Schwäbischen Merkur aus den Jahren 1848 und 1849* (Stuttgart, 1892).

H. F. Rumpf (ed.), *Allgemeines Kriegswörterbuch für Offiziere aller Waffen* (Berlin, 1821), vol. 1.

H. F. Rumpf, *Allgemeine Real-Encyclopädie der gesammten Kriegskunst* (Berlin, 1827), 2 vols.

W. Rüstow, *Der deutsche Militärstaat vor und während der Revolution* (Königsberg, 1850).

W. Rüstow, *Untersuchungen ueber die Organisation der Heere* (Basel, 1855).

W. Rüstow, *Der Krieg und seine Mittel* (Leipzig, 1856).

W. Rüstow, *Der deusch-dänische Krieg 1864* (Zurich, 1864).

W. Rüstow, *Der Krieg von 1866 in Deutschland und Italien* (Zurich, 1866).

A. Schäffle, *Das gesellschaftliche System der menschlichen Wirtschaft*, 3rd edn (Tübingen, 1873), vol. 1.

M. Schall, *Vor vierzig Jahren. Kriegserinnerungen eines ehemaligen Lazarettpfarrers der II. Armee 1870–71* (Spandau, 1910).

J. Scherr, *1870–1871. Vier Bücher deutscher Geschichte* (Leipzig, 1880), vol. 1.

C. L. v. Schilling, *Die Militärmeuterei in Baden. Aus authentischen Quellen zusammengetragen von einem badischen Offizier* (Karlsruhe, 1849).

F. J. A. Schneidewind, *Allgemeine Geschichte der Kriege der Franzosen und ihrer Allirten vom Anfange der Revoltuion bis zum Ende der Regierung Napoleons* (Darmstadt, 1827).

F. W. v. Schuetz, *Geschichte der Kriege in Europa seit dem Jahre 1792, als Folgen der Staatsveränderung in Frankreich unter König Ludwig XVI* (Leipzig, 1827–53), 16 vols.

E. Schüller, *Bruder-Krieg? Nein! Prinzipien-Kampf! Von einem Veteranen aus den Jahren 1813–1815* (Berlin, 1866).

W. Schulz, 'Frieden', in C. v. Rotteck and C. T. Welcker (eds), *Staatslexikon*, 2nd edn (Altona, 1847).

W. Schulz-Bodmer, *Militärpolitik* (Leipzig, 1855).

W. Schulz-Bodmer, *Die Rettung der Gesellschaft aus den gefahren der Militärherrschaft* (Leipzig, 1859).

J. B. Schweitzer, *Widerlegung von Carl Vogt's Studien zur gegenwärtigen Lage Europas* (Frankfurt, 1859).

G. Scrive, *Relation medico-chirurgicale de la Campagne d'Orient du 31 mars 1854, occupation de Gallipoli, au 6 juillet, 1856, evacuation de la Crimée* (Paris, 1857).

J. Segers, *Über den Zweikampf im Allgemeinen* (Bonn, 1837).

F. W. Siegmann (ed.), *Aphorismen über den Krieg und die Kriegführung* (Dresden 1842).

H. Simon, *Don Quixote der Legitimät oder Deutschlands Befreier* (Zurich, 1859).

J. Sporschil, *Die allgemeine Volksbewaffnung, ihre Organisation und ihre Vorzuege vor den stehenden Heeren* (Leipzig, 1831).

F. A. Staegemann, *Erinnerungen an die preussischen Kriegesthaten* (Halle, 1819).

D. Staroste, *Tagebuch über die Ereignisse in der Pfalz und Baden im Jahre 1849* (Potsdam, 1852–3).

L. v. Stein, *Geschichte der sozialen Bewegung in Frankreich von 1789 bis auf unsere Tage*, 3rd edn (Munich, 1850).

L. v. Stein, *System der Staatswissenschaft* (Stuttgart, 1856), vol. 2.

L. v. Stein, *Die Innere Verwaltung*, 2nd revised edn (Stuttgart, 1882), vol. 2.

K. Stieler, *Durch Krieg zum Frieden. Stimmungsbilder aus den Jahren 1870–71* (Stuttgart, 1895).

J. Strobel, *Vorschläge zur Neugestaltung Deutschlands oder die deutsche Frage und ihre Lösung* (Munich, 1865).

G. Struve, *Geschichte der drei Volkserhebungen in Baden* (Bern, 1849).

H. v. Sybel, 'Germanische Geschlechtsverfassung', *Allgemeine Zeitschrift für Geschichte*, 3 (1845), 293–348.

H. v. Sybel, *Geschichte der Revolutionszeit* (Düsseldorf, 1853–79).

H. v. Sybel, *Die Erhebung Europas gegen Napoleon* (Munich, 1860).

H. v. Sybel, *Die deutsche Nation und das Kaiserreich* (Düsseldorf, 1862).

H. v. Sybel, *Kleine historische Schriften* (Munich, 1863).

H. v. Sybel, *Vorträge und Aufsätze* (Berlin, 1874).

J. v. Theobald, *Die rechte Wehrverfassung. Ein Versuch, der auf die neueste, für Deutschland entworfene Kriegsverfassung Rücksicht nimmt* (Stuttgart, 1818).

F. Thorwart (ed.), *Hermann Schulze-Delitzch's Schriften und Reden* (Berlin, 1910), vol. 3.

C. v. Torresani, *Von der Wasser- bis zur Feuerteufe. Werde- und Lehrjahre eines österreichischen Offiziers* (Dresden, 1900), vol. 2.

H. v. Treitschke, *Die Gesellschaftswissenschaft* (Leipzig, 1859).

H. v. Treitschke, *Historische und politische Aufätze* (Leipzig, 1865).

H. v. Treitschke, *Zehn Jahre Deutscher Kämpfe* (Berlin, 1874).

H. v. Treitschke, *Zum Gedächtniß des großen Krieges* (Leipzig, 1895).

H. v. Treitschke, *Die Politik* (Leipzig, 1898), 2 vols.

A. Trinius, *Geschichte der Einigungskriege 1864, 1866, 1870/71* (Berlin, 1888), 3 vols.

K. Twesten, *Was uns noch retten kann* (Berlin, 1861).

G. W. v. Valentini, *Abhandlung über den Krieg* (Berlin, 1821), vol. 1.

G. W. v. Valentini, *Die Lehre vom Krieg* (Berlin, 1822).

J. Venedey, *Der italienische Krieg und die deutsche Volkspolitik* (Hanover, 1859).

J. Venedey, *J. Venedey an Prof. Heinrich von Treitschke* (Mannheim, 1866).

J. Venedey, *Ave Cäsar, Morituri te salutant!* 3rd edn (Mannheim, 1867).

C. H. G. v. Venturini, *Rußlands und Deutschlands Befreiungskriege von der Franzosen-Herrschaft unter Napoleon Buonaparte in den Jahren 1812–1815* (Leipzig, 1816), vol. 1.

C. v. Vinke, *Die Reorganisation des Preussischen Heerwesens nach dem Schleswig-Holsteinschen Kriege* (Berlin, 1864).

C. Vogt, *Studien zur gegenwärtigen Lage Europas* (Geneva, 1859).

B. Volz, *Geschichte Deutschlands im neunzehnten Jahrhundert vom Luneviller Frieden bis zum Tode Kaiser Wilhelms I* (Leipzig, 1890).

G. Waitz, 'Zur deutschen Verfassungsgeschichte', *Allgemeine Zeitschrift für Geschichte*, 3 (1845), 13–41.

G. Waitz, *Deutsche Verfassungsgeschichte* (Kiel, 1847), vol. 2.

G. Waitz, *Über den Frieden mit Dänemark* (Göttingen, 1849).

G. Waitz, *Der neueste dänische Versuch in der Geschichte des Herzogthums Schleswig* (Göttingen, 1852).

G. Waitz, *Das Recht des Herzogs Friedrichs von Schleswig-Holstein* (Göttingen, 1863).

G. Waitz, *Kurze schleswigholsteinische Landesgeschichte* (Kiel, 1864).

G. Waitz, *Die Verfassung des Deutschen Volkes in ältester Zeit*, 3rd edn (Kiel, 1880).

T. Waitz, *Anthropologie der Naturvölker*, 2nd edn (Leipzig, 1877).

J. Weiske, *Rechtslexikon für Juristen aller Teutschen Staaten* (Leipzig, 1840–61), vol. 6.

W. Weitling, *Garantien der Harmonie und Freiheit* (Vivis, 1842).

W. Weitling, *Die Menschheit, wie sie ist und wie sie sein sollte*, 2nd edn (Berne, 1845).

C. T. Welcker, 'Heerwesen' and 'Anhang zum Artikel Heerwesen (Landwehrsystem)', in C. T. Welcker and C. v. Rotteck (eds), *Staats-Lexicon* (Altona, 1834–43), vol. 7.

J. v. Wickede, *Die militärischen Kräfte Deutschlands und ihre Fortschritte in den neueren Zeit* (Stuttgart, 1855).

L. Wienbarg, *Krieg und Frieden mit Dänemark* (Frankfurt, 1848).

Wilhelm,Crown Prince of Prussia, *Bemerkungen zu dem Gesetz ueber die deutsche Wehrverfassung* (Berlin, 1849).

W. v. Willisen, *Theorie des grossen Krieges* (Berlin, 1849).

K. v. Winterfeld, *Vollständige Geschichte des preussischen Krieges von 1866 gegen Österreich und dessen Bundesgenossen*, 18th edn (Berlin, 1866).

K. v. Winterfeld, *Vollständige Geschichte des deutsh-französischen Krieges von 1870 und 1871* (Berlin, 1871).

K. v. Winterfeld, *Geschichte der drei glorreichen Kriege von 1864, 1866 und 1870/71* (Berlin, 1879).

J. G. A. Wirth, *Die politische Reform Deutschlands* (Strasbourg, 1832).

A. Wolff, *Berliner Revolutions-Chronik* (Berlin, 1851).

H. Wuttke, *Die deutschen Zeitschriften und die Entstehung der öffentlichen Meinung* (Leipzig, 1875).

K. A. J. v. Xylander, *Untersuchungen über das Heerwesen unserer Zeit* (Munich, 1830).

M. v. Xylander, *Das Heerwesen der Staaten des Deutschen Bundes* (Augsburg, 1842).

DIARIES, CORRESPONDENCE, AND MEMOIRS

i. General

E. M. Arndt, *Briefe* (Darmstadt, 1972–5), 3 vols.

E. M. Arndt, *Ein Lebensbild in Briefen*, ed. H. Messner (Berlin, 1898).

L. Bamberger, *Erinnerungen* (Berlin, 1899).

F. D. Bassermann, *Denkwürdigkeiten 1811–1855* (Frankfurt, 1926).

A. Bebel, *Aus meinem Leben* (Bonn, 1997).

E. Berner (ed.), *Kaiser Wilhelm des Grossen. Briefe, Reden und Schriften* (Berlin, 1906), vol. 2.

T. v. Bernhardi, *Aus dem Leben Theodor vor Bernhardis* (Berlin, 1893–1901), 8 vols.

E. Bernstein, *My Years of Exile* (London, 1921).

G. Beseler, *Erlebtes und Erstrebtes 1809–1859* (Berlin, 1884).

W. Beseler, *Das deutsche Interesse in der italienischen Frage* (Leipzig, 1859).

F. v. Beust, *Erinnerungen zu Erinnerungen* (Leipzig, 1881).

F. v. Beust, *Drei Viertel-Jahrhunderten* (Stuttgart, 1887), 2 vols.

K. Biedermann, *Mein Leben und ein Stück Zeitgeschichte* (Breslau, 1886).

W. Bigge (ed.), *Feldmarschall Graf Moltke. Ein militärisches Lebensbild* (Munich, 1901), vol. 2.

T. Billroth, *Briefe*, 9th edn (Hanover, 1922).

O. v. Bismarck, *Die gesammelten Werke* (Berlin, 1924), vol. 14.

O. v. Bismarck, *Gedanken und Erinnerungen* (Essen, 2000), 3 vols.

J. C. Bluntschli, *Denkwürdiges aus meinem Leben* (Nördlingen, 1884), 3 vols.

H. v. Borcke, *Mit Prinz Friedrich Karl. Kriegs- und Jagdfahrten und am häuslichen Herd* (Berlin, 1893).

S. Born, *Erinnerungen eines Achtundvierzigers*, ed. J. Schütz (Berlin, 1978).

O. v. Bray-Steinburg, *Denkwürdigkeiten aus seinem Leben* (Leipzig, 1901).

H. Brockhaus, *Aus den Tagebüchern* (Leipzig, 1884–7), vol. 1.

K. H. Brüggemann, *Meine Leitung der Kölnischen Zeitung und die Krisen der preußischen Politik von 1846–1855* (Leipzig, 1855).

M. v. Bunsen, *Die Welt in der ich lebte. Erinnerungen aus glücklichen Jahren 1860–1912*, 3rd edn (Leipzig, 1929).

M. Busch, *Tagebuchblätter* (Leizig, 1899), 3 vols.

W. Cahn (ed.), *Aus Eduard Lasker's Nachlaß* (Berlin, 1902).

M. Cornicelius (ed.), *Heinrich Treitschkes Briefe* (Leipzig, 1920), vol. 3.

F. Dahn, *Erinnerungen* (Leipzig, 1894), vol. 4.

G. F. F. Dammers, *Erinnerungen und Erlebnisse* (Hanover, 1890).

R. v. Delbrück, *Lebenserinnerungen 1817–1867* (Leipzig, 1905), 2 vols.

I. v. Döllinger, *Briefwechsel, 1850–1890* (Munich 1963–81), vol. 4.

J. G. Droysen, *Briefwechsel*, ed. R. Hübner. (Stuttgart, 1929), 2 vols.

A. Duckwitz, *Denkwürdigkeiten aus meinem öffentlichen Leben von 1841 bis 1866* (Bremen, 1877).

M. Duncker, *Politischer Briefwechsel*, ed. J. Schultze (Stuttgart, 1923).

J. v. Eckhart, *Lebenserinnerungen* (Leipzig, 1910), 2 vols.

O. Elben, *Lebenserinnerungen 1823–1899* (Stuttgart, 1931).

Ernst II, Herzog von Sachsen-Coburg-Gotha, *Aus meinem Leben und aus meiner Zeit* (Berlin, 1889), vol. 3.

H. v. Feder, *Die Revolution und die Partei des gesetzlichen Fortschritts in Baden. Ein Selbstbekenntnis* (Karlsruhe, 1850).

H. v. Födransperg, *Vierzig Jahre in der österreichischen Armee. Erinnerungen eines österreichischen Offiziers von seinem Eintritte in die Armee bis zur Gegenwart 1854–1894* (Dresden, n.d.).

Albert Foerderer, *Erinnerungen aus Rastatt 1849* (Lahr, 1899).

R. G. Foerster (ed.), *Generalfeldmarschall von Moltke. Bedeutung und Wirkung* (Munich, 1991).

T. Fontane, *Sämtliche Werke*, ed. Edgar Groß (Munich, 1959–75), vols 14 and 20.

T. Fontane, *Von Zwanzig bis Dreissig. Autobiographisches* (Frankfurt, 1987).

T. Fontane, *Briefe* (Berlin, 1989), vol. 2.

W. Förster (ed.), *Prinz Friedrich Karl von Preußen. Denkwürdigkeiten aus seinem Leben* (Stuttgart, 1910), vol. 1.

G. Freytag, *Erinnerungen aus meinem Leben* (Leipzig, 1887).

H. Friedjung (ed.), *Benedeks nachgelassene Papiere* (Leipzig, 1901).

Friedich III, *The War Diary of Emperor Frederick III, 1870–1871*, ed. A. R. Allinson. (London, 1927).

Friedrich Wilhelm IV, *Revolutionsbriefe 1848*, ed. K. Haenchen (Leipzig, 1930).

R. v. Friesen, *Erinnerungen aus meinem Leben* (Dresden, 1880), vol. 2.

H. v. Gagern, *Briefe und Reden 1815–48*, ed P. Wentzcke and W. Klötzer (Göttingen, 1959).

E. L. v. Gerlach, *Aufzeichnungen aus seinem Leben und Wirken 1795–1877*, ed. J. v. Gerlach (Schwerin, 1903), vol. 2.

L. v. Gerlach, *Denkwürdigkeiten* (Berlin, 1891), 2 vols.

L. v. Gerlach, *Briefe des Generals Leopold von Gerlach an Otto von Bismarck*, ed. H. Kohl (Stuttgart, 1912).

G. G. Gervinus, *Leben, von ihm selbst* (Leipzig, 1893).

D. Hansemann, 'Denkschrift über Preußens Lage und Politik' (1840), in J. Hansen (ed.), *Rheinische Briefe und Akten zur Geschichte der politischen Bewegung 1830–1850* (Essen, 1919–76), vol. 1, 220–1.

J. Hartmann, *Meine Erlebnisse zu hannoverscher Zeit, 1839–1866* (Wiesbaden, 1912).

G. v. Häseler, *Zehn Jahre im Stabe des Prinzen Friedrich Karl. Erinnerungen* (Berlin, 1915), 3 vols.

W. Hasenclever, *Erlebtes. Erinnerungen 1857–1871* (Arnsberg, 1987).

L. Häusser, *Denkwürdigkeiten zur Geschichte der Badischen Revolution* (Heidelberg, 1951).

R. Haym, *Aus meinem Leben. Erinnerungen* (Berlin, 1902).

R. Haym, *Ausgewählter Briefwechsel Rudolf Hayms*, ed. H. Rosenberg (Stuttgart 1930).

A. Heiberg, *Erinnerungen aus meinem Leben*, 2nd edn (Berlin, 1897).

K. Heinzen, *Erlebtes. Vor meiner Exilierung* (Boston, 1864).

P. Hindenburg, *Aus meinem Leben* (Leipzig, 1920).

L. Höbelt (ed.), *Österreichs Weg zur konstitutionellen Monarchie. Aus der Sicht des Staatsministers Anton von Schmerling* (Frankfurt a. M., 1994).

C. zu Hohenlohe-Schillingsfürst, *Denkwürdigkeiten*, ed. F. Curtius (Stuttgart, 1907), vol. 1.

R. v. Jhering, *Rudolf von Jhering in Briefen an seine Freunde* (Leipzig, 1913).

Johann, König von Sachsen, *Lebenserinnerungen des Königs Johann von Sachsen* (Göttingen, 1958).

Johann Georg, Herzog zu Sachsen (ed.), *Briefwechsel zwischen König Johann von Sachsen und den Königen Friedrich Wilhelm IV. und Wilhelm I von Preußen* (Leipzig, 1911).

J. E. Jörg, *Briefwechsel 1846–1901*, ed. D. Albrecht (Mainz, 1988).

E. Kessel (ed.), *Generalfeldmarschall Graf Alfred Schlieffen* (Göttingen, 1958).

J. Kirchgässer, *Aus meinem Leben* (Ratingen, 1990).

H. Kohl (ed.), *Deutschlands Einigungskriege 1864–1871 in Briefen und Berichten der führenden Männer* (Leipzig, 1912), vol. 1.

G. F. Kolb, *Lebenserinnerungen eines liberalen Demokraten 1808–1884*, ed. L. Merckle (Freiburg, 1976).

K. A. Kraft zu Hohenlohe-Ingelfingen, *Aus meinem Leben*, 7th edn (Berlin, 1906), vol. 3.

T. Krieg, *Wilhelm von Doering, königlich preußischer Generalmajor. Ein Lebens- und Charakterbild* (Berlin, 1898).

Wilhelm von Kügelen, *Bürgerleben. Briefe an den Bruder Gerhard 1840–1867*, ed. W. Killy (Munich, 1990).

F. G. Lehmann, *Lehmanns Tagebuch 1826–1828* (Marbach, 1999).

H. v. Lerchenfeld-Köfering, *Erinnerungen und Denkwürdigkeiten* (Berlin, 1935).

F. Lewald, *Erinnerungen aus dem Jahre 1848* (Brunswick, 1850), 2 vols.

F. C. W. D. v. Loë, *Erinnerungen aus meinem Berufsleben 1849 bis 1867* (Stuttgart, 1906).

H. W. Lucy (ed.), *The Emperor's Diary* (London, 1888).

H. Lüders, *Ein Soldatenleben in Krieg und Frieden* (Stuttgart, 1888).

O. v. Manteuffel, *Unter Friedrich Wilhlem IV*, ed. H. v. Poschinger (Berlin, 1901), 3 vols.

F. A. L. von der Marwitz, *Ein märkischer Edelmann im Zeitalter der Befreiungskriege*, ed. F. Meusel (Berlin, 1908–13), vol. 1.

L. von der Marwitz (ed.) *Vom Leben am preussischen Hofe 1815–1852. Aufzeichnungen von Caroline v. Rochow* (Berlin, 1908).

A. B. Marx, *Erinnerungen* (Berlin, 1865).

K. Mathy, *Aus dem Nachlass von Karl Mathy. Briefe aus den Jahren 1846–1848* (Leipzig, 1898).

J. K. Mayr (ed.), *Das Tagebuch des Polizeiministers Kempen von 1848 bis 1859* (Vienna, 1931).

J. F. M. O. Meding, *Memoiren zur Zeitgeschichte* (Leipzig, 1881–4), vol. 1.

H. O. v. Meisner (ed.), *Denkwürdigkeiten des General-Feldmarschalls Alfred Grafen von Waldersee* (Stuttgart, 1925), vol. 1.

R. v. Mohl, *Lebens-Erinnerungen 1799–1875* (Stuttgart, 1902), vol. 1.

H. v. Moltke, *Letters to His Wife* (London, 1896), vol. 1.

H. v. Moltke, *Moltke in seinen Briefen* (Berlin, 1902), vol. 2.

F. Nespethal, *Erlebtes und Aufgeschriebenes aus dem 19. Jahrhundert* (Petersberg, 1999).

F. Oetker, *Lebenserinnerungen* (Stuttgart, 1877–85), 3 vols.

H. Oncken (ed.), *Grossherzog Friedrich I von Baden und die deutsche Politik von 1854–1871* (Stuttgart, 1877–85), 3 vols.

F. Paulsen, *Aus meinem Leben. Jugenderinnerungen* (Jena, 1909).

F. Ponsonby (ed.), *Letters of the Empress Frederick* (London, 1928).

J. v Radowitz, *Nachgelassene Briefe und Aufzeichnungen zur Geschichte der Jahre 1848–53* (Stuttgart, 1922).

F. v Raumer, *Briefe aus Frankfurt und Paris 1848–49* (Leipzig, 1849).

F. v Raumer, *Lebenserinnerungen und Briefwechsel* (Leipzig, 1861), 2 vols.

W. Real (ed.), *Karl Friedrich von Savigny. Briefe, Akten, Aufzeichnungen aus dem Nachlass eines preussischen Diplomaten der Reichsgründungszeit* (Boppard, 1981), 2 vols.

P. Reichensperger, *Erlebnisse eines alten Parlamentariers im Revolutionsjahre 1848* (Berlin, 1882).

A. v. Roon, *Denkwürdigkeiten*, 5th edn (Berlin, 1905).

A. Ruge, *Briefwechsel und Tagebuchblätter aus den Jahren 1825–1880*, ed. P. Nerlich (Berlin, 1886), vol. 2.

L. Schneider, *Aus meinem Leben* (Berlin, 1880), vol. 3.

L. Schneider, *Aus dem Leben Kaiser Wilhelms, 1849–1873* (Berlin, 1888), vol. 1.

K. Schorn, *Lebenserinnerungen. Ein Beitrag zur Geschichte des Rheinlands im 19. Jahrhundert* (Bonn, 1898), 2 vols.

G. v. Schubert, *Lebenserinnerungen*, ed. H. v. Schubert (Stuttgart, 1909).

J. Schultze (ed.), *Max Duncker. Politischer Briefwechsel aus seinem Nachlass* (Osnabrück, 1967).

T. Schumacher, *Was ich als Kind erlebte* (Stuttgart, 1901).

W. Schüssler (ed.), *Die Tagebücher des Freiherrn Reinhard v. Dalwigk zu Lichtenfels aus den Jahren 1860–71* (Osnabrück, 1967).

G. Schuster (ed.), *Briefe, Reden und Erlasse des Kaisers und Königs Friedrich III* (Berlin, 1907).

W. v. Schweinitz (ed.), *Denkwürdigkeiten des Botschafters General v. Schweinitz* (Berlin, 1927), 2 vols.

L. F. Seyffardt, *Erinnerungen* (Leipzig, 1900).

G. v. Siemens, *Ein Lebensbild aus Deutschlands großer Zeit* (Berlin, 1921–3).

W. v. Siemens, *Lebenserinnerungen* (Berlin, 1892).

U. v. Stosch (ed.), *Denkwürdigkeiten des Generals und Admirals Albrecht v. Stosch, ersten Chefs der Admiralität. Briefe und Tagebuchblätter*, 3rd edn (Stuttgart, 1904).

R. v. Strombeck, *Fünfzig Jahre aus meinem Leben* (Leipzig, 1894).

A. Struve, *Erinnerungen aus den badischen Freiheitskaempfen* (Hamburg, 1850).

G. Stüve (ed.), *Johann Carl Bertram Stüve nach Briefen und persönlichen Erinnerungen* (Hanover, 1900), 2 vols.

A. v. Suckow, *Aus meinem Leben* (Strasbourg, 1894).

A. v. Suckow, *Rückschau des Königl. Württembergischen Generals der Infanterie und Kriegsministers*, ed. W. Busch (Tübingen, 1909).

J. D. H. Temme, *Erinnerungen* (Leipzig, 1883).

H. V. v. Unruh, *Erinnerungen* (Stuttgart, 1895).

K. A. Varnhagen v. Ense, *Tagebücher* (Leipzig, 1861–70), 14 vols.

C. Vogt, *Politische Briefe an Friedrich Kolb* (Biel, 1870).

C. Vogt, *Aus meinem Leben* (Stuttgart, 1896).

H. Wagener, *Erlebtes. Meine Memoiren aus der Zeit von 1848 bis 1866 und von 1873 bis jetzt* (Berlin, 1884), 2 vols.

A. Wagner, *Briefe, Dokumente, Augenzeugenberichte 1851–1917*, ed. H. Rubner (Berlin, 1978).

P. Wentzcke and W. Klötzer (eds), *Deutscher Liberalismus im Vormärz. Heinrich von Gagern, Briefe und Reden 1815–1848* (Göttingen, 1959).

A. v. Werner, *Erlebnisse und Eindrücke 1870–1890* (Berlin, 1913).

I. H. v. Wessenberg, *Unveröffentlichte Manuskripte und Briefe*, ed. K. Aland (Freiburg, 1968), vol. 2.

A. Westphalen, *Lebenserinnerungen 1836–1920*, ed. J. H. Meyer and H. F. Schütt (Flensburg, 1985).

L. v. Westphalen (ed.), *Die Tagebuecher des Oberpraesidenten Ludwig Freiherrn Vincke 1813–1818* (Munester, 1980).

J. v. Wickede, *Bilder aus dem Kriegsleben* (Stuttgart, 1853).

J. v. Wickede (ed.), *Ein Soldaten-Leben. Erinnerungen aus den napoleonischen, südamerikanischen, griechischen, polnischen, spanischen und algerischen Feldzügen*, 2nd edn (Stuttgart, 1854), 2 vols.

J. Wiggers, *Aus meinem Leben* (Leipzig, 1901).

I. Wilhelm, *Briefe an seine Schwester Alexandrine und Grossherzog Friedrich Franz II* (Berlin, 1928).

ii. 1864[‡]

Anon, *Der Befreiung Schlewsig-Holsteins im Jahre 1864. Nach den Berichten des Koenigl. Staats-Anzeigers zusammengestellt* (Berlin, 1864).

Anon, *Der Feldzug in Schlewsig im Jahre 1864* (Vienna, 1864).

Anon, *Illustrierte Kriegs-Berichte aus Schleswig-Holstein* (Leipzig, 1864).

Anon, *Soldatengeschichten, Anecdoten u. a. aus dem Schleswig-Holstein'schen Kriege* (Nordhausen, 1864).

V. v. Baußnern, *Feldmarschall-Lieutenant v. Gablenz und der Deutsch-dänische Krieg in Schleswig-Holstein* (Hamburg, 1864).

D. W. F. Besser, *Drei Wochen auf dem Kriegsschauplatze* (Halle, 1864).

F. M. Braumüller, *Geschichte des Königin Augusta Garde-Grenadier-Regiments Nr. 4* (Berlin, 1901).

J. Bubbe, *Ein Düppelstürmer 1864*, ed. H. F. Bubbe (Cologne, 1914).

C. Bunge, *Aus meinem Kriegstagebuch. Erinnerungen an Schleswig-Holstein 1864* (Rathenow, 1889).

W. Camphausen, *Ein Maler auf dem Kriegsfelde* (Bielefeld, 1913).

A. Cramer, *Geschichte des Infanterie-Regiments Prinz Friedrich der Niederlande Nr. 15* (Berlin, 1910).

V. Dedenroth, *Der Winterfeldzug in Schleswig-Holstein* (Berlin, 1864).

E. Dicey, *The Schleswig-Holstein War* (London, 1864), 2 vols.

A. v. Eberstein, *Erlebtes aus den Kriegen 1864, 1866, 1870–71* (Leipzig, 1899).

E. v. Friesen, *Erlebnisse des Königlich-Sächsischen 13. Infanterie-Bataillons während der Bundesexekution in Holstein 1863–1864* (Dresden, n.d.).

W. Frölich, *Vor vierzig Jahren* (Flensburg, 1904).

E. Frommel, *In den Königs Rock. Geschichten aus Krieg und Frieden*, 12th edn (Schwerin, 1915).

A. Gallenga, *The Invasion of Denmark in 1864* (London, 1864).

[‡] Memoirs or diaries which refer to multiple wars are listed under the first war mentioned in the title.

H. Granier, *Der Feldzug von 1864* (Berlin, 1897).

W. v. Gründorf, *The Danish Campaign of 1864: Recollections of an Austrian General Staff Officer* (Solihull, 2010).

P. C. Henrici, *Lebenserinnerungen eines Schleswig-Holsteiners* (Stuttgart, 1897).

A. Herbert, *The Danes in Camp: Letters from Sonderborg* (London, 1864).

C. A. v. Honthumb, *Mein Tagebuch. Erinnerungen aus Schleswig-Holstein* (Münster, 1865).

F. K. D. Jansen, *Erinnerungen aus meinem Leben*, ed. W. Jansen (Karlsruhe, 2004).

C. G. v. Jena, *Erinnerungen an einen Heimgegangenen* (Berlin, 1864).

C. Junck, *Aus dem Leben des k. k. Generals der Cavallerie Ludwig Freiherrn von Gablenz* (Vienna, 1874).

Heinz-Ulrich Kammeier, 'Der Krieg gegen Dänemark 1864 in Briefen von Soldaten aus dem Kries Lübbecke', *Zeitschrift der Gesellschaft für Schleswig-holsteinische Geschichte*, 114 (1989), 73–5.

E. Knorr, *Von der Eider bis Düppel* (Hamburg, 1864).

E. Knorr, *Von Düppel bis zur Waffenruhe* (Hamburg, 1864).

E. Knorr, *Von Alsen bis zur Frieden* (Hamburg, 1865).

J. Kreipner, *Geschichte des k. und k. Infanterie-Regimentes Nr. 34* (Kaschau, 1900).

H. Kufittich (ed.), *Unsere Offiziere vor dem Feinde. Persönliche Erlebnisse aus den Feldzügen 1864, 1866 und 1870/71* (Berlin, 1900).

L. v. Kusserow, *Geschichte des Brandenburgischen Jäger-Battalions Nr. 3 und des Magdeburgishcen Jäger Battalions Nr. 4 von 1815 bis 1865* (Berlin, 1865).

F. Loeffler, *General-Bericht über den Gesundheitsdienst im Feldzuge gegen Dänemark 1864* (Berlin, 1867).

A. Magirus, *Herzog Wilhelm von Württemberg, k. u. k. Feldzeugmeister. Ein Lebensbild* (Stuttgart, 1897).

H. Mahler, *Über die Eider an den Alsensund. Blätter aus meinem Kriegstagebuche vom 1sten Februar bis zum 20sten April 1864* (Berlin, 1864).

H. Mahler, *Wieder in den Krieg. Blätter aus meinem Kriegstagebuche vom 29sten bis zum 1sten August 1864* (Berlin, 1864).

H. v. Moltke, 'Der Deutsch-Dänische Krieg 1864', in H. v. Moltke, *Kriege und Siege*, ed. R. Hoppenheit (Berlin, 1938).

H. v. Müller, *Kriegerisches und Friedliches aus den Feldzügen von 1864, 1866 und 1870/71*, ed. R. Hoppenheit. (Berlin, 1909).

R. Neumann, *Über den Angriff auf die Düppler Schanzen in der Zeit vom 15. März bis zum 18 April 1864* (Berlin, 1865).

L. Pfaundler, *Heldenzüge der Mannscahft des k. k. 27 Infanterie Regiments König der Belgier aus dem Feldzüge 1864* (Vienna, 1864).

F. Pflug, *Der deutsch-dänische Krieg* (Leipzig, 1865).

G. Rasch, *Vom verrathenen Bruderstamme. Der Krieg in Schleswig-Holstein im Jahre 1864* (Leipzig, 1864), vol. 1.

O. Rommel, *Aus dem politischen Tagebuch eines Süddeutschen 1863–1884. Festgabe zum hundertjährigen Jubiläum des Schwäbischen Merkurs* (Stuttgart, 1885).

E. Rothpletz, *Bericht eines schweizerischen Offiziers über seien Mission nach Dänemark 1864* (Bern, 1924).

L. Schnayder, *Österreichisch-preussischer Krieg gegen Dänemark* (Vienna, 1865).

H. Voigts-Koenig, *Geschicthe des Infanterie-Regiments Grossherzog Friedrich Franz II von Mecklenburg-Schwerin Nr. 24* (Berlin, 1908).

F. J. G. v. Waldersee, *Der Krieg gegen Dänemark im Jahre 1864* (Berlin, 1865).

K. Went v. Römö, *Ein Soldatenleben* (Vienna, 1904).

F. v. Wiser, *Die Besetzung der nordfriesischen Inseln im Juli 1864* (Vienna, 1914).

J. Zechmeister, *Die Schusswunden und die gegenwärtige Bewaffnung der Heere* (Munich, 1864).

ii. 1866

F. v. Bardeleben (ed.), *Erinnerugnen eines Husaren–Offiziers an den Jahren 1866–1871* (Frankfurt, 1904).

E. Beck, *Meine Erlebnisse im Feldzuge 1866* (Freiburg, 1867).

W. F. Besser, *Sechs Wochen im Felde* (Halle, 1867).

C. Biegler, *Meine Erlebnisse während des Kriegsjahres 1866* (St Pölten, 1908).

L. Biergans (ed.), *Erinnerungen des Generals der Kavallerie Gustav Ritter von Fleschuez aus den Jahren 1866 bis 1871* (Berlin, 1914).

G. v. Bismarck, *Kriegs-Erlebnisse 1866 und 1870/71* (Dessau, 1907).

J. Blänkner, *Die Neunundsechziger bei Kloster und Münchengrätz am 28 Juni 1866* (Berlin, 1868).

A. v. Blumenthal (ed.), *Journals of Field-Marshal Count von Blumenthal for 1866 and 1870–71* (London, 1903).

J. Bock v. Wülfingen, *Tagebuch vom 11 Juni bis 3 Juli 1866* (Hanover, 1876).

Rudolph Broecker, *Erinnerungen an die Thätigkeit der 11. Infanterie-Division und ihrer Artillerie während des Feldzuges 1866* (Berlin, 1867).

A. Buchholtz, *Ernst von Bergmann. Mit Bergmanns Breife von 1866, 1870/71 und 1877*, 2nd edn (Leipzig, 1911).

H. v. Chappuis, *Bei Hofe und im Felde* (Frankfurt, 1902).

H. v. Clausewitz, Aus dem Feldzuge des Jahres 1866. *Aus dem Tagebuch eines preussischen Jägeroffiziers* (Leipzig, 1868).

E. K. G. H. W. A v. Conrady, *Das Leben des Grafen August von Werder, königlich preussshcen Generals der Infanterie* (Berlin, 1889).

C. v. Coudenhove, *Feldmarschall-Lieutenant Graf Carl Coudenhove* (Vienna, 1901).

C. v. Degenfeld-Schonburg, *Schweinschädel und Königgrätz. Meine Kriegserinngerungen als Kommandant des 7. Husarenregiments* (Vienna, 1907).

F. Deitl (ed.), *Unter Habsburg Kriegsbanner. Feldzugserebnisse aus der Feder von Mitkämpfern und Augenzeugen* (Dresden, 1898–1900), 6 vols.

M. Dittrich, *Unter König Albert von Sachsen im Felde 1849, 1866 und 1870/1871. Vaterländische Gedenkblätter* (Dresden, 1888).

K. Fischer, *Militärärztliche Studien aus Süddeutschland und Böhmen* (Aarau, 1866).

K. Fischer v. Wellenborn, *Erinnerungen aus den Feldzügen 1859 und 1866. Ein Beitrag zur Geschichte des k. und k. Uhlanenregiments Nr. 1* (Vienna, 1894).

F. v. Frankenberg, *Kriegstagebücher von 1866 und 1870/71*, ed. H. v. Poschinger (Stuttgart, 1896).

E. v. Fransecky, *Denkwürdigkeiten des Preußischen Generals der Infanterie*, ed. W. v. Bremen (Bielefeld, 1901).

D. Fricke, Aus dem Feldzuge 1866. *Briefe aus dem Felde und Predigten und Reden im Felde* (Leipzig, 1891).

H. A. E. v. Gablenz, *Meine Erlebnisse im Feldzuge 1866 als Landwehr-Unteroffizier im 4. Magdeburgischen Infanterie-Regiments Nr. 67*, 2nd edn (Berlin, 1867).

A. v. Goeben, *Das Gefecht bei Dermbach am 4. Juli 1866* (Darmstadt, 1870).

A. v. Goeben, *Das Treffen bei Kissingen am 10. Juli 1866*, 3rd edn (Darmstadt, 1894).

Grosser Generalstab (Historische Abteilung) (ed.), *The Campaign of 1866 in Germany* (London, 1872).

J. v. Hartmann, *Briefe aus dem Feldzuge 1866 an die Gatti geschrieben* (Berlin, 1898).

O. Herrmann, *Julius von Bose, Preußischer General der Infanterie. Eine Lebensbeschreibung nach amtlichen Quellen und privaten Mitteilungen* (Berlin, 1898).

A. v. Hessen, *Feldzugs-Journal des Oberbefehlshabers des 8ten deutschen Bundes-Armee-Corps im Feldzuge des Jahres 1866 in Westdeutschland*, 2nd edn (Darmstadt, 1867).

G. Hilder, Ein friedlicher Feldzug. *Tagebuch-Blätter aus dem Jahre 1866* (Berlin, 1870).

W. v. Holleben (ed.), *Briefe aus den Kriegsjahren 1866 und 1870/71 des Generals der Inf. Albert v. Holleben* (Berlin, 1913).

A. v. Holzhausen-Gablenz, *Erinnerungen einer österreichischen Offiziersfrau aus dem Kriegsjahre 1866* (Gotha, 1891).

J. Horwitz, *Von Berlin nach Nikolsburg. Skizzen aus dem Kriegsjahre 1866* (Berlin, 1866).

H. M. Hozier, *The Seven Weeks' War* (Driffield, 2012).

M. v. Hutten-Klingenstein, *Meine Eindrücke aus dem bayerisch-preußischen Feldzuge im Jahre 1866* (Vienna, 1867).

H. Jacobi, *Im Felde. Erinnerungen eines Einjährigen –Freiwilligen vom Füsilier-Bataillon des Kaiser Franz-Garde-Grenadier-Regiments aus dem Feldzuge in Böhmen und Mähren* (Berlin, 1867).

E. v. Jena, *General von Goeben im Feldzuge 1866 gegen Hannover und der Süddeutschen Staaten und meine Erlebnisse in diesem Feldzuge als Generalstabsoffizier des Division Goeben* (Berlin, 1904).

E. Jentsch, *Erinnerungen nach dem Tagebuch eines Zwanzigers aus dem Main-Feldzuge 1866* (Rathenow, 1899).

H. v. Krosigk (ed.), *General Feldmarschall von Steinmetz. Aus den Familienpapieren dargestellt* (Berlin, 1900).

B. Kunderna, *Aus bewegten Zeiten. Persönliche Erinnerungen und Erlebnisse aus dem Feldzuge des Jahres 1866 gegen Preussen* (Vienna, 1906).

V. W. A. V. v. Lignitz, Aus drei *Kriegen. 1866, 1870/71, 1877/78* (Berlin, 1904).

G. Malden Willis (ed.), *Hannovers Schicksalsjahr 1866 im Briefwechsel König Georg V mit der Königin Marie* (Hildesheim, 1966).

A. v. Mollinary, *Sechsundvierzig Jahre im österreich-ungarischen Heere 1833–1879* (Zurich, 1905), 2 vols.

Fritz Mücke, *1866–1870/71. Erinnerungen eines alten Garde Jägers* (Neudamm, 1899).

J. C. F. Naumann, *Das Regiments-Kriegsspiel* (Berlin, 1877).

J. Naundorff, *Unter dem rothen Kreuz* (Leipzig, 1867).

C. Nissel, *Von Nachod bis Josephstadt, Erinnerungen an der glorreichen Feldzug 1866* (Liegnitz, 1866).

F. Paustka, *Erinnerungen an Garnison und Schlachtfeld. Gedichte und Gesänge für Militair und Militairvereine* (Dresden, 1868).

G. v. Pelet-Narbonne, *Aus den Tagebuch eines preussischen Korpsadjutant im böhmischen Feldzuge 1866* (Vienna, 1908).

C. T. Pelzer, *Militärartzliche Kriegserinnerungen an 1866 und 1870/71* (Berlin, 1914).

H. G. Peter, *Kriegserlebnisse eines preussischen Landwehrmannes 1866* (Meissen, 1871).

W. Petsch, *Heldenthaten Preußischer Krieger und Charakterbilder aus dem Feldzuge von 1866* (Berlin, 1867).

A. Pfister, *Denkwürdigkeiten aus der württembergischen Kriegsgeschichte des 18. und 19. Jahrhunderts im Anschluß an die Geschichte des 8. Infanterieregiments* (Stuttgart, 1868).

H. Pollak, *Erlebnisse eines Kriegskorrespondenten aus den Jahren 1859, 1866 und 1870* (Vienna, 1908).

F. v. Rauch, *Briefe aus dem grossen Hauptquartier der Feldzüge 1866 und 1870–71* (Berlin, 1911).

J. P. Richter, *Am Elbestrand 1866. Erinnerungen* (Gera, 1906).

R. Rostok, *Furchtlos und treu* (Marburg, 1897).

C. H. Schauenburg, *Erinnerungen aus dem preussischen Kriegslazarethleben von 1866* (Altona, 1869).

L. v. Schönfels (ed.), *Erlebnisse Heinrich von Schönfels als Generalstabsoffizier bei der Avantgarden-Cavallerie 1866 und 1870* (Berlin, 1903).

B. Schreyer, *Vor 40 Jahren. Erinnerungen eines alten sächsischen Reiters* (Dresden, 1905).

K.-L. A. Stahmann, *Militärärztliche Fragmente und Reminiscenzen aus dem österreichisch-preussischen Feldzuge im Jahre 1866* (Berlin, 1868).

P. Stiefelhagen, *Ein Pädagoge im Kriege. Erinnerungen aus den Jahren 1866 und 1870/71* (Strasbourg, 1906).

T. Vatke, *Mein Sommer unter der Waffen. Auszeichnungen und Erinnerungen aus dem böhmischen Feldzug im Jarhe 1866* (Berlin, 1867).

J. v. Verdy du Vernois, *Im Hauptquartier der Zweiten Armee 1866 unter dem Oberbefehl Sr. Königlichem Hoheit des Kronprinzen Friedrich Wilhelm von Preußen. Erinnerungen* (Berlin, 1900).

A. v. Voigts-Rhetz (ed.), *Briefe des Generals der Infanterie von Voigts-Rhetz aus den Kriegsjahren 1866 und 1870/71* (Berlin, 1906).

H. Wachenhusen, *Tagebuch vom Österreichischen Kriegsschauplatz* (Berlin, 1866).

B. v. Werder, *Erlebnisse eines Johanniter-Ritters auf dem Kriegsschauplatze in Böhmen* (Halle, 1867).

L. v. Winning, *Erinnnerungen eines preussischen Leutnants aus den Kriegsjahren 1866 und 1870/71* (Heidelberg, 1911).

iii. 1870–1

H. Abeken, Ein schlichtes *Leben in bewegter Zeit*, 3rd rev. edn (Berlin, 1904).

M. Abel, Unter der Standarte der Garde Husaren. *Kriegserringerungen* (Berlin, 1897).

A. v. Adelmann, *Aus dem Felde. Erinnerungen, Skizzen und Noveletten* (Stuttgart, 1871).

C. Angelrodt, *1870/71. Kriegstagebuch des Lehrers Carl Angelrodt Reservist im 3. Thüring. Infant.-Reg. Nr. 71*, ed. H. Heineck (Nordhausen, 1913).

E. Arnold (ed.), Feldbriefe *von Georg Heinrich Rindfleisch*, 2nd edn (Halle, 1889).

H. Arnold, *Unter General von der Tann* (Munich, 1896).

K. W. Augustin, *Kriegserlebnisse eines Fünfundachtzigers* (Kiel, 1898).

E. Barck, Soldatengeschichten. *Aus den Erinnerungen eines Veteranen aus dem deutsch-französischen Krieg 1870/71* (Waldshut, 1909).

E. Barth (E. Clarus), Kriegserinnerungen eines deutschen Offiziers. *Nach Tagebuchblättern* (Kromberg, 1878).

H. Bauer, *Erinnerungen eines Feldgeistlichen aus den badischen Feldlazaretten im Kriege 1870–71* (Heidelberg, 1872).

M. Bauer, *Von der Maas-Armee* (Halle, 1871).

M. Bauer, *Unter Rothgekreuzten Standarten im Felde und Daheim. Jubiläums-Erinnerungen an Kriegsfahrten 1870–71* (Berlin, 1895).

P. Bauriedel, *Meine Erlebnisse während des Feldzugs im Jahre 1870/71* (Nuremberg, 1895).

R. Berendt, *Erinnerungen aus meiner Dienstzeit* (Leipzig, 1894).

M. v. Berg, *Ulanen-Briefe von der I. Armee* (Bielefeld, 1893).

B. Berlit (ed.), *Vor Paris und an der Loire 1870 und 1871* (Cassel, 1872).

E. Betz, *Aus den Erlebnissen und Erinnerungen eines alten Offiziers* (Karlsruhe, 1894).

Theodor Billroth, *Chirurgische Briefe aus den Kriegs-Lazarethen in Weissenburg und Mannheim 1870* (Berlin, 1872).

H. Blum, *Auf dem Wege zur deutschen Einheit. Erinnerungen und Aufzeichnungen eines Mitkämpfers aus den Jahren 1867 bis 1870* (Jena, 1893), 2 vols.

A. Bock, *1870–71. Feldzugserlebnisse und Erinnerungen eines Einjährig-Freiwilligen im 3. Garde-Rgt*, 2nd edn (Leipzig, 1904).

P. v. Bojanowski, *Geschehenes und Geschriebenes. Tagebuchblätter eines Journalisten aus den Kriegsmonaten der Jahre 1870 und 1871* (Weimar, 1871).

H. Bonsack, *Kriegserlebnisse eines Fünfundneunzigers im Feldzug gegen Frankreich 1870–1871* (Gotha, 1906).

A. Bornemann, *Kriegs-Tagebuch eines jungen Officiers im Grossherzoglichen Hessischen 2. Jägerbataillon aus den Jahren 1870/71* (Giessen, 1895).

G. Boschen, *Kriegserinnerungen eines Einundneunzigers 1870/71* (Oldenburg, 1897) 1907.

A. Brandenburg, *Vor dem Feind. Kriegs-Erinnerungen aus dem Feldzug gegen Frankreich im Jahre 1870/71* (Munich, 1913).

A. Breithaupt, *Aus dem Lagerleben vor Paris. Erinnerungen eines Kriegsfreiwilligen des Garde-Füsilier-Regiments aus dem Feldzuge 1870/71* (Berlin, 1913).

P. Bronsart v. Schellendorff, *Geheimes Kriegstagebuch 1870–1871*, ed. P. Rassow (Bonn, 1954).

M. Busch, *Mit Bismarck vor Paris* (Munich, 1942).

W. Busch, *Das deutsche Grosse Hauptquartier und die Bekämpfung von Paris im Feldzuge 1870–71* (Stuttgart, 1905).

J. Campe, *Ein wackerer deutscher Kriegsmann vor dem Feinde. Tagebuch des Oberstleutnants Campe während des Feldzuges 1870–1871* (Berlin, 1904).

A. Conradi, *Vor Paris. Feldzugsbriefe aus dem Kriege 1870/71*, ed. P. Conradi (Berlin, 1909).

F. Daffner, *Erinnerungen an den deutsch-französischen Feldzug 1870–1871* (Stuttgart, 1906).

J. Diehl, *Meine Kriegs-Erlebnisse von 1870/71* (Minden, 1904).

L. Diemer, *Von der Schulbank gegen die Franzosen. Kriegsfahrten eines Freiwilligen 1870/71* (Dresden, 1911).

L. Diestelkamp, *Erlebnisse eines Lazarettpredigers. Erinnerungen aus den Kriegsjahren 1870/71* (Gütersloh, 1903).

M. Dittrich, *Beim Regiment des Prinzen Friedrich August 1870/71. Kriegs-Erinnerungen* (Dresden, 1886).

J. Doering, *Meine Dienstzeit. Friedens- und Kriegs-Erinnerungen 1869–1871* (Marburg, 1891).

P. Dorsch (ed.), *Württembergs Söhne in Frankreich 1870/71*, 2nd edn (Stuttgart, 1911).

R. Eckold, *Kriegserinnerungen*, 2nd edn (Hildburghausen, 1885).

H. S. Edwards, *The Germans in France: Notes on the Method and Conduct of the Invasion, the Relations between Invaders and Invaded, and the Modern Usages of War* (London, 1874).

F. Ehrenburg, *Kleine Erlebnisse in grosser Zeit. Aus dem Tagebuche eines Kriegsstudenten von 1870–71* (Strasbourg, 1890).

H. Ehrenberg, *Feldzugs-Erinnerungen eines Fünfunddreißigers 1870/71*, 2nd edn (Rathenow, 1891).

K. v. Einsiedel, *Tagebuchblätter aus dem deutsch-französischen Krieg* (Berlin, 1907).

J. Eisenach, *Erinnerungen an den Feldzug 1870/71. Aus dem Tagebuch eines ehemaligen Angehörigen des Königin Augusta Garde-Grenadier-Regiments Nr. 4* (Coblenz, 1896).

H. Emerich, *Hinter der Front. Kriegs-Erinnerungen aus den Jahren 1870–71* (Zabern, 1911).

J. W. Emonts, *Unserer Jäger Freud und Leid. Kriegserinnerungen aus dem glorreichen Feldzuge 1870/71 nach dem Tagebuch eines bayerischen Jägers*, 7th edn (Kaiserslautern, 1887).

W. Ernst, *Vom Rhein bis zum Kanal. Erinnerungen aus dem Feldzuge 1870–71* (Rathenow, 1893).

A. Fausel, *Ein Ritt ins Franzosenland. Bilder aus dem Kleinleben im Feld 1870/71* (Stuttgart, 1909).

E. Fehleisen, *Der Deutsch-Französische Krieg 1870–71 im Wort und Bild* (Reutlingen, 1872).

A. Fester, *Jugenderinnerungen und Kriegsbriefe eines Altfrankfurters* (Halle, 1911).

A. Fitze, *Kriegstagebuch eines einjährig-freiwilligen Ulanen aus dem Feldzuge 1870/71* (Rathenow, 1887).

M. Flesch, *1870–1871 und 1914–1918 von der Verwundeten- und Krankenpflege in Zwei Kriegen. Aus Eigenen Erinnerungen* (Frankfurt, 1930).

T. Fontane, *Kriegsgefangen. Erlebtes 1870* (Berlin, 1871).

T. Fontane, *Aus der Tagen der Okkupation. Eine Osterreise durch Nordfrankreich und Elsaß-Lothringen 1871*, 2nd edn (Berlin, 1872).

A. Forbes, *My Experiences of the War between France and Germany* (Leipzig, 1871), 2 vols.

E. v. Fransecky, *Denkwürdigkeiten*, ed. W. v. Bremen (Bielefeld, 1901).

H. Freyer, *Erlebnisse eines Feldbeamten im deutsch-französischen Kriege 1870–71. Nach seinen Erinnerungen niedergeschrieben*, ed. H. Freyer (Darmstadt, 1910).

G. Freytag, *Auf der Höhe der Vogesen. Kriegsberichte von 1870/71* (Leipzig, 1914).

G. Friedländer, *Aus den Kriegstagen 1870* (Berlin, 1886).

Friedrich III, *Das Kriegstagebuch von 1870/71*, ed. O. Meisner (Berlin, 1926).

H. Fritsch, *Erinnerungen und Betrachtungen* (Bonn, 1913).

H. Frobenius, *Vor Französischen Festungen. Erinnerungen an 1870/71* (Berlin, 1911).

F. Gerstäcker, *Kriegsbilder eines Nachzüglers aus dem deutsch-französischen Kriege* (Jena, n.d.).

C. Geyer, *Verwundet und kriegsgefangen in Paris unter dem Schutze des Roten Kreuzes 1870/71. Kriegserlebnisse eines Württembergers* (Berlin, 1910).

A. v. Gordon, *Was trägt und treibt den Soldaten im Felde? Gedanken zum französischen Kriege und Stimmungsbilder aus den Tagen vor Metz* (Berlin, 1896).

K. Gotthilf, *Lustige und traurige Erinnerungen an die große Zeit vor 25 Jahren* (Rathenow, 1895).

C. L. Hähnel, *Bei den Fahnen des XII. (kgl. Sächsischen) Armeekorps. Aufzeichnungen eines Angehörigen des 107. Regiments im Feldzug 1870/71* (Munich, 1890).

G. Hammon, *Einiges aus dem Tagebuche eines Feldgeistlichen im Kriege 1870/71* (Kempten, 1887).

J. v. Hartmann, *Erlebtes aus dem Kriege 1870/71*, 2nd edn (Wiesbaden, 1885).

J. v. Hartmann, *Briefe aus dem Deutsch-Französischen Kriege 1870–71* (Kassel, 1893).

Paul Hase, *Feldarztbriefe* (Leipzig, 1895).

P. Hassel, *Von der dritten Armee. Kriegsgeschichtliche Skizzen aus dem Feldzuge von 1870–1871* (Leipzig, 1872).

P. v. Hatzfeld, *Hatzfelds Briefe, geschrieben vom Hauptquartier Wilhelms 1870–71* (Leipzig, 1907).

W. Haupt, *Erlebnisse unter den Verwundeten aus der Schlacht bei Gravelotte, den 18. August 1870* (Hamburg, 1870).

A. Hecker, *Ernstes und Heiteres aus dem Kriegstagebuche eines sächsischen Oberjägers 1870/71* (Dresden, 1895).

W. Heim, *Vor 25 Jahren. Erinnerungen eines Konstanzer Füsiliers* (Constance, 1895).

F. N. Heimes, *Von der Schulbank ins Feld 1870–71. Ein Lebensjahr aus großer Zeit* (Berlin, 1907).

W. Heye, *Kriegstagebuch*, ed. A. Heye (Oldenburg, 1905).

J. Hoeck, *Meine Erlebnisse als Kriegsfreiwilliger bei den badischen schwarzen Dragonern im Feldzuge 1870/71* (Karlsruhe, 1895).

M. Hollnack, *Kriegserinnerungen eine alten 37ers* (Hanover, 1890).

Karl Homann, *Kriegstagebuch eines deutschen Reservemannes*, 2nd edn (Nuremberg, 1879).

G. Horn, *Bei Friedrich Karl. Bilder und Skizzen aus dem Feldzuge der zweiten Armee* (Leipzig, 1872), vol. 1.

S. Husser, *Erlebnisse eines badischen Trainsoldaten im Feldzuge 1870/71* (Karlsruhe, 1895).

G. Huyssen, *Bilder aus dem Kriegsleben eines Militär-Geistlichen. Ein Beitrag zur Culturgeschichte des deutsch-französischen Krieges von 1870 und 71* (Kreuznach, 1872).

D. Isensee, 'Das Kriegstagebuch von 1870/71 des Georg Friedrich Wilhelm Beckermann', *Oldenburger Jahrbuch*, 86 (1986), 95–122.

H. Jahn, *Aus Deutschlands großen Tagen. Erlebnisse eines 24ers im deutsch-französischen Kriege* (Brunswick, 1895–6), 2 vols.

H. Kadelbach, *Bilder und Erinnerungen aus dem Kriegsleben von 1870/71* (Leipzig, 1871).

Adolf Kayser, *Erlebnisse eines rheinischen Dragoners im Feldzuge 1870/71* (Nördlingen, 1889).

L. Kayßler, *Aus dem Hauptquartier und der Kriegsgefangenschaft* (Berlin, 1871).

A. Keysser, *Frieden im Kriege. Erinnerungen eines vormaligen preußischen Linienofficiers aus dem Feldzuge 1870/71* (Cologne, 1893).

C. Kissel, Mit *den Hessen in Frankreich 1870–71. Nach täglichen Aufzeichnungen eines Mainzer Mitkämpfers* (Mainz, 1904).

K. Klein, *Fröschweiler Chronik. Kriegs- und Friedensbilder aus dem Jahr 1870*, 24th edn (Munich, 1906).

O. Knechtel, *Erinnerungen eines 75ers aus dem Feldzuge 1870/71* (Bremen, 1895).

F. Koch-Breuberg, *Drei Jahre in Frankreich. Erinnerungen eines Truppenoffiziers aus dem Feldzug 1870/71 und der Occupation 1871–1873* (Munich, 1890).

O. Kopelke, *Kriegserlebnisse eines Veteranen von 1870/71* (Berlin, 1902).

E. E. v. Krause, *Ein deutsches Soldatenleben* (Berlin, 1901).

H. v. Kretschmann, *Kriegsbriefe aus den Jahren 1870–1871* (Berlin, 1903).

F. Krohn, *Kriegserinnerungen 1870/71* (Berlin, 1895).

T. Krokisius, *Erinnerungen aus dem Feldzuge 1870–71* (Berlin, 1907).

F. Kühnhauser, *Kriegs-Erinnerungen eines Soldaten des königlich bayerischen Infanterie-Leib-Regiments* (Partenkirchen, 1898).

D. v. Lassberg, *Mein Kriegstagebuch aus dem deutsch-französischen Kriege 1870/71* (Munich, 1906).

K. Legewitt, *Feldpostbriefe eines 79ers. Erinnerungen an den Feldzug 1870/71* (Essen, 1900).

O. Leibig, *Erlebnisse eines freiwilligen Jägers im Feldzuge 1870/71*, 2nd edn (Nördlingen, 1889).

L. Leinenweber, *Meine Kriegserlebnisse 1870/71. Erinnerungen aus dem Feldzuge* (Pirmasens, 1911).

J. E. Lenz, *Meine Kriegserlebnisse 1870–71* (Berlin, 1920).

F. Leo, *Kriegserinnerungen an 1870–71* (Berlin, 1914).

M. Liebermann v. Sonnenberg, *Aus der Glückszeit meines Lebens. Erinnerungen aus dem großen deutschen Kriege 1870/71* (Munich, 1911).

M. v. Liliencron, *Kriegserlebnisse eines preußischen Ulanenoffiziers aus dem Jahre 1870* (Cassel, 1901).

H. Lüders, *Anno 70 mitgelaufen. Erlebnisse eines Berliner Jungen im deutsch-französischen Kriege* (Quedlinburg, 1880).

E. Maizier, *Tagebuch aus dem französischen Kriege für die Zeit von Ausmarsch bis zur Waffenruhe* (Magdeburg, 1896).

R. Martin, *Kriegserinnerungen eines 105ers* (Plauen i. V., 1896).

R. Marty, *Friedensbilder aus dem deutsch-französischen Kriege 1870–71*, 2nd edn (Amberg, 1872).

A. v. Massow, *Erlebnisse und Eindrücke im Kriege 1870/71* (Berlin, 1912).

C. G. A. Mauerhof, *Kriegs-Erinnerungen eines vor dem Feinde verwundeten deutschen Kriegers aus dem deutsch-französischen Feldzuge vom Jahre 1870 bis 1871*, 7th edn (Eilenburg, 1903).

E. Metsch, *Meine Erlebnisse als Einjährig-Freiwilliger beim k. b. Infanterie-Leibregiment im Kriege gegen Frankreich 1870–71* (Munich, 1871).

K. Mewes, *Leiden und Freuden eines kriegsfreiwilligen hallenser Studenten vom Regiment Nr. 86 in den Kriegsjahren 1870–1871* (Magdeburg, 1898).

A. G. Meyer, *Vor fünfundzwanzig Jahren. Feldzugsbriefe eines Kriegsfreiwilligen* (Leipzig, 1896).

G. F. Meyer, *Unter dem rothen Kreuz. Erlebnisse im Feldzuge 1870/71* (Brunswick, 1895).

Militär-Medizinal-Abtheilung des Königlich Preussischen Kriegsministeriums (ed.), *Sanitäts-Bericht über die deutschen Heere im Krieg gegen Frankreich* (Berlin, 1884–91), 8 vols.

A. di Miranda (ed.), *Feldpostbriefe eines Fünfundzwanzigers während des deutsch-französischen Krieges von 1870–1871* (Aachen, n.d.).

T. Mommsen, F. M. Müller, and T. Carlyle, *Letters on the War between Germany and France* (London, 1871).

H. v. Monbart, *Aus ernster Zeit. Erinnerungen aus dem Feldzuge 1870–71*, 2nd edn (Bochum, 1896).

G. Morin, *Aus ruhmvollen Tagen. Erinnerungen an den deutsch-französischen Krieg von 1870/71* (Munich, 1882).

H. v. Müller, *Die Artillerieangriff auf Paris und Schlußbetrachtung über den Festungskrieg im Kriege von 1870/71* (Berlin, 1901).

T. Niedermeyer, *Aus meinem Tagebuche: Erlebnisse und Schilderungen aus dem Kriege gegen Frankreich 1870–71* (Hanover, 1871).

T. Niemeyer, *Aus meinem Tagebuche. Erlebnisse und Schilderungen aus dem Kriege gegen Frankreich 1870–71* (Hanover, 1871).

Georg Niethammer, *Feldzugsbriefe an seine Mutter* (Stuttgart, 1890).

R. Oeri-Sarasin, *Lazarett-Erinnerungen aus dem Kriege von 1870/71* (Basel, 1913).

A.v. Oertzen, *1870–71. Kriegserinnerungen eines Schwedter Dragoners* (Berlin, 1905).

A. Ott, *Bei höheren Stäben. Adjutanten-Erlebnisse aus dem großen Kriegsjahre* (Munich, 1892).

R. v. Pfeil, *Vor vierzig Jahren. Persönliche Erlebnisse und Bilder aus großer Zeit* (Schweidnitz, 1911).

E. Pfleiderer, *Erinnerungen und Erfahrungen eines Feldpredigers aus dem Krieg des Jahres 1870/71* (Stuttgart, 1874).

L. Pietsch, *Von Berlin bis Paris. Kriegsbilder 1870–1871* (Berlin, 1871).

F. Plitt, *Vor dreißig Jahren. Rückerinnerungen eines Dreiundachtzigers*, 2nd edn (Cassel, 1901).

T. Prenzel, *Das Dienst- und Kriegsjahr eines Brandenburgischen Jägers. Persönliche Erinnerungen, Briefe und Tagebuchblätter aus dem deutsch-französischen Kriege* (Rathenow, 1893).

P. Quade, *Mit den Pommern vor Metz, Paris und im Jura. Ernste und heitere Bilder aus dem Kriegsleben von 1870–71* (Munich, 1910).

P. Rassow (ed.), *Geheimes Kriegstagebuch 1870–1871 von Paul Bronsart von Schellendorf* (Bonn, 1954).

F. Ratzel, *Bilder aus dem Kriege mit Frankreich* (Wiesbaden, 1908).

H. Retzlaff, *Aus meinem Tagebuche. Erlebnisse und Erinnerungen aus dem deutsch-französischen Kriege 1870/71* (Berlin, 1897).

C. Richter, *Kriegs-Tagebuch eines Sanitäts-Offiziers beim Stabe des General-Commandos des X. Armeecorps aus den Jahren 1870–71* (Rathenow, 1892).

M. Richter, *Kriegsbriefe eines Feldgeistlichen 1870/71* (Berlin, 1895).

G. H. Rindfleisch, *Feldbriefe von Georg Heinrich Rindfleisch 1870–71*, ed. E. Arnold, 4th edn (Göttingen, 1895).

B. Rogge, *Bei der Garde. Erlebnisse und Eindrücke aus dem Kriegsjahre 1870/71* (Hanover, 1895).

C. Rogge, *Franktireurfahrten und andere Kriegserlebnisse in Frankreich. Kulturbilder aus dem deutsch-französischen Kriege 1870/71* (Berlin, 1907).

F. A. Roth, *Aus dem Tagebuche eines freiwilligen Unteroffiziers des 5. bad. Infanterie-Regiments im Feldzuge 1870/71* (Karlsruhe, 1895).

C. C. Rückert, *Mit dem Tornister. Ungeschminkte Feldzugs-Erinnerungen eines Infanteristen aus dem Jahre 1870* (Frankfurt, 1912).

M. Runze, *Beim Königs-Regiment 1870/71. Feldzugserinnerungen eines Kriegsfreiwilligen vor Metz, vor Paris, im Jura, unter Bezugnahme auf das Tagebuch des Feldwebels Friehmelt* (Berlin, 1896).

W. H. Russell, *My Diary During the Last Great War* (London, 1874).

M. Schall, *Vor vierzig Jahren. Kriegserinnerungen eines Lazarettpfarrers der II. Armee 1870/71* (Spandau, 1910).

C. Schepers, *Bilder und Eindrücke au seiner achtwöchentlichen Dienstzeit als freiwilliger Feldprediger im Sommer 1870* (Bonn, 1871).

R. Scherff, *Kriegs-Tagebuch 1870/71*, ed. K. Scherff-Romain (Berlin, 1982).

H. Schmitthenner, *Erlebnisse eines freiwilligen badischen Grenadiers* (Karlsruhe, 1890).

F. Schmitz, *Erinnerungs-Skizzen aus dem deutsch-französischen Krieg 1870–71*, 4th edn (Frankfurt, 1895).

L. Schmitz, *Aus dem Feldzuge 1870/71. Tagebuchblätter eines 65ers* (Berlin, 1902).

W. Schultze-Klosterfelde, *Weißenburg, Wörth, Sedan, Paris. Heitere und ernste Erinnerungen eines preußischen Offiziers aus dem Feldzuge 1870/71* (Leipzig, 1889).

K. Schürmann, *Selbsterlebtes. Kriegserinnerungen eines Volksschullehrers* (Remscheid, 1895).

R. Schuster, *Erlebnisse und Beobachtungen eines deutschen Feldgeistlichen während des Krieges 1870–71* (Darmstadt, 1871).

H. Seelmann-Eggebert, *Feldpostbriefe aus dem Kriegsjahre 1870* (Colberg, 1872).

P. H. Sheridan, *Personal Memoirs* (New York, 1888), vol. 2.

P. Stiefelhagen, *Ein Pädagoge im Kriege. Erinnerungen aus den Jahren 1866 und 1870/71* (Strasbourg, 1906).

K. Stieler, *Durch Krieg zum Frieden. Stimmungsbilder aus den Jahren 1870–71*, 2nd edn (Stuttgart, 1895).

Ernst Stier, *Unter Prinz Friedrich Karl. Erlebnisse eines Musketiers vom X. Armeekorps im Feldzug 1870–71* (Munich, 1883).

G. F. L. Stromeyer, *Erinnerungen eins deutschen Arztes*, 2nd edn (Hanover, n.d.).

V. Stubenrauch, *Erlebnisse eines bayerischen Kanoniers im Kriege 1870/71* (Munich, 1896).

C. Tanera, *Ernste und heitere Erinnerungen eines Ordonannzoffiziers im Feldzug 1870/71* (Nördlingen, 1887).

H. Tiemann, *Mein Feldzug. Erinnerugnen aus dem denkwürdigen Kriege von 1870–1871* (Hanover, 1874).

H. Tiemann, *Vor fünfundzwanzig Jahren. Feldzugserinnerungen eines Kriegsfreiwilligen* (Brunswick, 1895).

L. Tiesmeyer, *Reiseerinnerungen an den deutsch-französischen Krieg 1870* (Barmen, 1870).

T. Uebe, *Schlichte Erinnerungen aus großer Zeit*, 3rd edn (Berlin, 1912).

H. Uhde, *Streifzüge auf dem Kriegsschauplatze 1870–1871* (Hamburg, 1871).

T. Vatke, *Feldpostbriefe aus Frankreich 1870–71* (Berlin, 1871).

H. Wachenhusen, *Tagebuch vom französischen Kriegsschauplatz 1870–1871* (Berlin, 1871).

F. Wallmann, *Erlebnisse eines Jägers im großen Kriege 1870/71* (Berlin, 1898).

G. Waltz, *Erlebnisse eines Feldarztes der badischen Division im Kriege 1870–71* (Heidelberg, 1872).

R. Wilckens, *Kriegsfahrten eines freiwilligen badischen Dragoners anno 1870/71* (Karlsruhe, 1891).

L. Wilde, *Kriegstagebuch und Erinnerungen aus dem Feldzug gegen Frankreich 1870/71* (Greifswald, 1908).

K. v. Wilmowski, *Feldbriefe 1870/71*, ed. G. v. Wilmowski (Breslau, 1894).

C. A. Winn, *What I Saw of the War at the Battles of Speichern, Gorze and Gravelotte: A Narrative of Two Months' Campaigning with the Prussian Army of the Moselle* (Edinburgh, 1870).

L. v. Winning, *Erinnerungen eines preußischen Leutnants aus den Kriegsjahren 1866 und 1870/71* (Heidelberg, 1911).

L. v. Wittich, *Aus meinem Tagebuche 1870–71* (Cassel, 1872).

R. P. Wülcker, *Fünfzig Feldpostbriefe eines Frankfurters aus den Jahren 1870 und 1871*, 2nd edn (Halle, 1876).

J. Zaiss, *Aus dem Tagebuch eines badischen Pioniers* (Karlsruhe, 1894).

K. Zeitz, *Kriegserinnerungen eines Kriegsfreiwilligen aus den Jahren 1870/71* (Altenburg, 1897).

SECONDARY LITERATURE

The literature on the conceptualization of military conflict is uneven. The seminal work of intellectual history in the field is J. Leonhard, *Bellizismus und Nation. Kriegsdeutung und Nationsbestimmung in Europa und den Vereinigten Staaten 1750–1914* (Munich, 2008), accompanying older studies of individual theorists of war: P. Paret, *Understanding War: Essays on Clausewitz and the History of Military Power* (Princeton, NJ, 1992), J. Wallach, *Die Kriegslehre von Friedrich Engels* (Frankfurt, 1968), and H. Gramley, *Propheten des deutschen Nationalismus. Theologen, Historiker und Nationalökonomen 1848–1880* (Frankfurt, 2001). Studies of the representation of warfare in the press concentrate on the second half of the nineteenth century: notably, N. Buschmann, *Einkreisung und Waffenbruderschaft. Die öffentliche Deutung von Krieg und Nation in Deutschland 1850–1870* (Göttingen, 2003) and F. Becker, *Bilder von Krieg und Nation. Die Einigungskriege in der bürgerlichen Öffentlichkeit Deutschlands 1864–1913* (Munich, 2000). These can be supplemented by works on history and memory: K. Hagemann, *Revisiting Prussia's Wars against Napoleon: History, Culture and Memory* (Cambridge, 2015); F. Akaltin, *Die Befreiungskriege im Geschichtsbild der Deutschen im 19. Jahrhundert* (Frankfurt, 1997); K. Cramer, *The Thirty Years' War and German Memory in the Nineteenth Century* (Lincoln, NE, 2007). Commemoration was also physical: U. Schlie, *Die Nation erinnert sich* (Munich, 2002); C. Tacke, *Denkmal im sozialen Raum. Nationale Symbole in Deutschland und Frankreich im 19. Jahrhundert* (Göttingen, 1995); M. Lurz, *Kriegerdenkmaler in Detuschland. Einigungskriege* (Heidelberg, 1985); R. Alings, *Monument und Nation. Das Bild vom Nationalstaat im Medium Denkmal* (Berlin, 1996). See, in addition, the essays in S. Förster and J. Nagler (eds), *On the Road to Total War: The American Civil War and the German Wars of Unification, 1861–1871* (Cambridge, 2002) and M. Boemeke, R. Chickering, and S. Förster (eds), *Anticipating Total War: The German and American Experiences, 1871–1914* (Cambridge, 1999).

These works usually focus on the relationship between war, belligerence, and nationalism, exemplified—amongst other works—by N. Buschmann and D. Langewiesche (ed.), *Der Krieg in den Gründungsmythen europäischer Nationen und der USA* (Tübingen, 2002) and G. Krumeich and H. Lehmann (eds), *'Gott mit uns'. Nation, Religion und Gewalt im 19. und frühen 20. Jahrhundert* (Göttingen, 2000). These studies differ in respect of the extent to which they discern national considerations in politics and the linkages that they make to belligerence. Many historians dispute the scope of nineteenth-century nationalism and stress the relevance of federalism and regionalism: D. Langewiesche and G. Schmidt (eds), *Föderative Nation* (Munich, 2000); D. Langewiesche, *Nation, Nationalismus und Nationalstaat in Deutschland und Europa* (Munich, 2000); D. Langewiesche, *Reich, Nation, Föderation* (Munich, 2008); J. Müller, *Deutscher Bund und deutsche Nation 1848–1866* (Göttingen, 2005); C. Applegate, *A Nation of Provincials: The Idea of Heimat* (Berkeley, CA, 1990); A. Confino, *The Nation as a Local Metaphor: Württemberg, Imperial Germany and National Memory, 1871–1918* (Chapel Hill, NC, 1997); A. Green, *Fatherlands: State-Building and Nationhood in Nineteenth-Century Germany* (Cambridge, 2001); U. Planert, *Der Mythos vom Befreiungskrieg. Frankreichs Kriege und der deutsche Süden 1792–1841* (Paderborn, 2007); O. Zimmer, *Remaking the Rhythms of Life: German Communities in the Age of the Nation-State* (Oxford, 2013); P. Judson, *Exclusive Revolutionaries: Liberal Politics, Social Experience, and National Identity in the Austrian Empire, 1848–1914* (Ann Arbor, 1996); J. J. Breuilly, *Austria, Prussia and Germany, 1806–1871* (London, 2002); J. J. Breuilly, *The Formation of the First German Nation-State, 1800–1871* (London, 1996); J. J. Breuilly (ed.), *The State of Germany: The National Idea in the Making, Unmaking and Remaking of a Modern Nation-State* (London, 1992). Other historians continue to underline the relevance of the gradual development of 'national' politics: O. Dann, *Nation und Nationalismus in Deutschland 1770–1990* (Munich, 1993); J. Echternkamp, *Der Aufstieg des deutschen Nationalismus 1770–1840* (Frankfurt, 1998); M. Levinger, *Enlightened Nationalism: The Transformation of Prussian Political Culture, 1806–1848* (Oxford, 2000); D. Düding, *Organisierter gesellschaftlicher Nationalismus in Deutschland 1808–1847* (Munich, 1984); W. Hardtwig, *Nationalismus und Bürgerkultur in Deutschland* (Göttingen, 1994); M. Jeismann, *Das Vaterland der Feinde. Studien zum nationalen Feindbegriff und Selbstverständnis in Deutschland und Frankreich 1792–1918* (Stuttgart, 1992); B. E. Vick, *Defining Germany: The 1848 Frankfurt Parliamentarians and National Identity* (Cambridge, MA, 2002); and M. Hewitson, *Nationalism in Germany, 1848–1866: Revolutionary Nation* (Basingstoke, 2010). For a balanced summary, see S. Berger, *Germany: Inventing the Nation* (London, 2004); E. Fehrenbach, *Verfassungsstaat und Nationsbildung 1815–1871* (Munich, 1992).

Such studies overlap with new research into 'militarism' and popular attitudes to the military: U. Frevert, *A Nation in Barracks: Modern Germany, Military Conscription and Civil Society* (Oxford, 2004); R. G. Foerster (ed.), *Die Wehrpflicht. Entstehung, Erscheinungsformen und politisch-militärische Wirkung* (Munich, 1994); B. Sicken (ed.), *Stadt und Militär. Wirtschaftliche Impulse, infrastrukturelle Beziehungen, sicherheitspolitische Aspekte* (Paderborn, 1998); C. Lankes, *München als Garnisonsstadt im 19. Jahrhundert* (Berlin, 1993); T. Bruder, *Nürnberg als bayrische Garnison von 1806 bis 1914* (Nuremberg, 1992); W. Schmidt, *Regensburg als bayrische Garnisonsstadt im 19. und frühen 20. Jahrhundert* (Regensburg, 1993); U. Hettinger, *Passau als Garnisonsstadt im 19. Jahrhundert* (Augsburg, 1994); M. Arndt, *Militär und Staat in Kurhessen 1813–1866. Das Offizierskorps im Spannungsfeld zwischen monarchischem Prinzip und liberaler Bürgerwelt* (Marburg, 1996); P. Wacker, W. Rosenwald, and G. Müller-Schellenberg (eds), *Das herzoglich-nassauische Militär 1806–1866. Militärgeschichte im Spannungsfeld von Politik, Wirtschaft und sozialen Verhältnissen eines deutschen Kleinstaates* (Taunusstein, 1998); J. Vogel, *Nationen im Gleichschritt. Der Kult* der 'Nation in Waffen' in Deutschland und Frankreich 1871–1914 (Göttingen, 1997); T. Rohkrämer, *Der Militarismus der 'kleinen Leute'*. *Die Kriegervereine im deutschen Kaiserreich 1871–1914* (Munich, 1990); W. Wette (ed.), *Militarismus in Deutschland 1871 bis 1945* (Münster, 1999), 277–92; L. Cole, *Military Culture and Popular Patriotism in Late Imperial Austria* (Oxford, 2014); M. Ingenlath, *Mentale Aufrüstung. Militarisierungstendenzen in Frankreich und Deutschland vor dem Ersten Weltkrieg* (Frankfurt, 1998); and N. Stargardt, *The German Idea of Militarism: Radical and Socialist Critics, 1866–1914* (Cambridge, 1994). Ralf Pröve, *Militär, Staat und Gesellschaft im 19. Jahrhundert* (Munich, 2006) gives a concise statement of the state of this research.

The research overlaps with other social, political, and cultural histories of the military: D. Walter, *Preußische Heeresreformen 1807–1870. Militärische Innovation und der Mythos der 'Roonschen Reform'* (Paderborn, 2003); W. D. Gruner, *Das bayerische Heer 1825 bis 1864. Eine kritische Analyse der bewaffneten Macht Bayerns vom Regierungsantritt Ludwigs I. zum Vorabend des deutschen Krieges* (Boppard am Rhein, 1972); A. Wandruszka and P. Urbanitsch (eds), *Die Habsburgermonarchie 1848–1918. Die Bewaffnete Macht* (Vienna, 1987), vol. 5; G. E. Rothenberg, *The Army of Francis Joseph* (West Lafayette, IN, 1976); J. Niemeyer, *Das österreichische Militärwesen im Umbruch* (Osnabrück, 1979); R. Bassett, *For God and Kaiser: The Imperial Austrian Army from 1619 to 1918* (New Haven, CT, 2015); J. Angelow, *Von Wien nach Königgrätz. Die Sicherheitspoltiik des Deutschen Bundes im europäischen Gleichgewicht 1815–1866* (Munich, 1996); and E. D. Brose, *The Kaiser's Army: The Politics of Military Technology in Germany during the Machine Age, 1870–1918* (Oxford, 2001). Part of this literature focuses on the socialization of the officer corps and the question of whether it was exclusive or not: M. Funck, *Feudales Kriegertum und militärische Professionalität. Der Adel im preußisch-deutschen Offizierkorps 1860–1935* (Berlin, 2005); K.-H. Lutz, *Das badische Offizierskorps 1840–1870/71* (Stuttgart, 1997); G. Gahlen, *Das bayerische Offizierskorps 1815–1866* (Paderborn, 2010); U. Breymayer (ed.), *Willensmenschen. Über deutsche Offiziere* (Frankfurt, 1999); I. Deák, *Beyond Nationalism: A Social and Political History of the Habsburg Officer Corps, 1848–1918* (Oxford, 1990); and G. Gahlen, *Das bayerische Offizierkorps 1815–1866* (Paderborn, 2011).

The degree to which such military institutions mediated popular conceptions of war is disputed. That it depends on combatants' and civilians' experiences of warfare is the underlying contention of the growing number of studies of contemporaries' 'experiences' of combat: N. Buschmann and H. Carl (eds), *Die Erfahrung des Krieges. Erfahrungsgeschichtliche Perspektiven von der französischen Revolution bis zum Zweiten Weltkrieg* (Paderborn, 2001); S. Müller, *Soldaten in der deutschen Revolution von 1848/49* (Paderborn, 1999); T. Buk-Swienty, *Schlachtbank Düppel. Geschichte einer Schlacht* (Berlin, 2011); F. Kühlich, *Die deutschen Soldaten im Krieg von 1870/71* (Frankfurt, 1995); C. Rak, *Krieg, Nation und Konfession. Die Erfahrung des deutsch-französischen Krieges von 1870/71* (Paderborn, 2004); M. Steinbach, *Abgrund Metz. Kriegserfahrung, Belagerungsalltag und nationale Erziehung im Schatten einer Festung 1870/71* (Munich, 2002); C. G. Krüger, *'Sind wir den nicht Brüder?' Deutsche Juden im nationalen Krieg 1870/71* (Paderborn, 2006); H. Mehrkens, *Statuswechsel. Kriegserfahrung und nationale Wahrnehmung im Deutsch-Französischen Krieg 1870/71* (Essen, 2008); and W. Meteling, *Ehre, Einheit, Ordnung. Preußische und französische Regimenter im Krieg, 1870/71 und 1914/19* (Baden-Baden, 2010).

Soldiers' and civilians' experience of war also rested on the means of communication and wider attitudes to violence, suffering, and death. The literature on the public sphere, press reportage, and visual representation is stimulating: G. Paul, *Bilder des Krieges, Krieg der Bilder. Die Visualisierung des Modernen Krieges* (Paderborn, 2004); G. Maag, W. Pyta, and M. Windisch (eds), *Der Krimkrieg als erster europäischer Medienkrieg* (Berlin, 2010);

A. Holzer (ed.), *Mit der Kamera bewaffnet. Krieg und Fotografie* (Marburg, 2003); P. Paret, *Art as History: Episodes in the Culture and Politics of Nineteenth-Century Germany* (Princeton, NJ, 1988); S. Bock, *Bildliche Darstellungen zum Krieg von 1870/71* (Freiburg, 1982); S. Parth, *Zwischen Bildbericht und Bildpropaganda. Kriegskonstruktionen in der deutschen Militärmalerei des 19. Jahrhunderts* (Paderborn, 2010); U. Daniel (ed.), *Augenzeugen. Kriegsberichterstattung vom 18. zum 21. Jahrhundert* (Göttingen, 2006); K. Belgum, *Popularizing the Nation: Audience, Representation and the Production of Identity in 'Die Gartenlaube', 1853–1900* (Lincoln, NE, 1998); U. v. Hirschhausen, *Liberalismus und Nation. 'Die Deutsche Zeitung' 1847–1850* (Düsseldorf, 1998); S. Spiegel, *Pressepolitik und Pressepolizei in Bayern unter der Regierung von König Maximilian II* (Munich, 2001); and J. Brophy, *Popular Culture and the Public Sphere in the Rhineland, 1800–1850* (Cambridge, 2007).

On popular attitudes to violence, suffering, and death, the literature is patchy. Protests and revolt, criminality, the emergence of police forces, and discipline or public order have been researched much more extensively than other aspects of the topic: H. Reinalter (ed.), *Demokratische und soziale Protestbewegungen in Mitteleuropa 1815–1848/49* (Frankfurt, 1986); R. Wirtz, *'Widersetzlichkeiten, Excesse, Crawalle, Tumulte und Skandale'. Soziale Bewegung und gewalthafter sozialer Protest in Baden 1815–1848* (Frankfurt, 1981); H.-G. Husung, *Protest und Repression im Vormärz. Norddeutschland zwischen Restauration und Revolution* (Göttingen, 1983); R. v. Friedeburg, *Ländliche Gesellschaft und Obrigkeit. Gemeindeprotest und politische Mobilisierung im 18. und 19. Jahrhundert* (Göttingen, 1997); S. Rohrbacher, *Gewalt im Biedermeier. Antijüdische Ausschreitungen in Vormärz und Revolution 1815–1848/49* (Frankfurt, 1993); J. Sperber, *Rhineland Radicals: The Democratic Movement and the Revolution of 1848–1849* (Princeton, 1991); H. Volkmann and J. Bergmann (eds), *Sozialer Protest. Studien zu traditioneller Resistenz und kollektiver Gewalt in Deutschland vom Vormärz bis zur Reichsgründung* (Opladen, 1984); D. Blasius, *Bürgerliche Gesellschaft und Kriminalität. Zur Sozialgeschichte Preußens im Vormärz* (Göttingen, 1976); D. Blasius, *Kriminalität und Alltag. Zur Konfliktgeschichte des Alltagslebens im 19. Jahrhundert* (Göttingen, 1978); A. Moses, *Kriminalität in Baden im 19. Jahrhundert. Die 'Übersicht der Strafrechtspflege' als Quelle der historischen Kriminologie* (Stuttgart, 2006); R. J. Evans, *Rituals of Retribution: Capital Punishment in Germany, 1600–1987* (London, 1996); R. J. Evans, *Tales from the German Underworld* (New Haven, CT, 1998); A. Lüdtke, *Police and State in Prussia, 1850–1850* (Cambridge, 1989); E. Glovka Spencer, *Police and the Social Order in German Cities: The Düsseldorf District, 1848–1914* (De Kalb, IL, 1992); and D. Riesener, *Polizei und politische Kultur im 19. Jahrhundert. Die Polizeidirektion Hannover und die politische Öffentlichkeit im Königreich Hannover* (Hanover, 1996). Broader attitudes to violence are harder to evaluate: Ute Frevert, *Ehrenmänner. Das Duell in der bürgerlichen Gesellschaft* (Munich, 1991) and Peter Gay, *The Cultivation of Hatred* (London, 1994) look at important aspects of the question.

The year 1848 in many respects constitutes the source or the culmination of such literature, testing citizens' and leaders' willingness to use violence. The excellent collection of essays in D. Dowe, H.-G. Haupt, D. Langewiesche, and J. Sperber (eds), *Europe in 1848: Revolution and Reform* (New York, 2000) are a good starting-point for research in this field. See also D. Langewiesche (ed.), *Revolution und Krieg. Zur Dynamik historischen Wandels seit dem 18. Jahrhundert* (Paderborn, 1989); J. Calliess, *Militär in der Krise. Die bayerische Armee in der Revolution 1848/49* (Boppard, 1976); A. Sked, *The Survival of the Habsburg Empire: Radetzky, the Imperial Army and the Class War, 1848* (London, 1979); R. Pröve, *Stadtgemeindlicher Republikanismus und die 'Macht des Volkes'. Civile Ordnungsformationen und kommunale Leitbilder politischer Partizipation in den deutschen Staaten vom Ende des 18.*

bis zur Mitte des 19. Jahrhunderts (Göttingen, 2000); and M. Hettling, *Totenkult statt Revolution. 1848 und seine Opfer* (Frankfurt, 1998). Many treatments of 1848 examine violence tangentially at most. One exception is Wolfgang Dreßen, *Gesetz und Gewalt. Berlin 1848* (Berlin, 1999).

The wars and diplomatic relations which were entangled with the revolutions of 1848–9 are generally treated separately. For the military inflections of diplomacy, see J. Dülffer, H. Kröger, and R.-H. Wippich (eds), *Vermiedene Kriege. Deeskalation von Konflikten der Großmächte zwischen Krimkrieg und Erstem Weltkrieg 1856–1914* (Munich, 1997); W. Carr, *The Origins of the Wars of German Unification* (London, 1991); P. W. Schroeder, *Austria, Great Britain and the Crimean War* (Ithaca, NY, 1972); W. E. Mosse, *The European Powers and the German Question, 1848–71* (New York, 1969); F. J. Müller, *Britain and the German Question* (Basingstoke, 2002); A. Doering-Manteuffel, *Die deutsche Frage und das europäische Staatensystem 1815–1871*, 2nd edn (Munich, 2001); F. R. Bridge, *The Habsburg Monarchy among the Great Powers, 1815–1918* (Oxford, 1990); H. Rumpler (ed.), *Deutscher Bund und deutsche Frage 1815–1866* (Vienna, 1990). On the course as well as the causes of the wars of unification, see D. Showalter, *The Wars of German Unification* (London, 2004); A. Bucholz, *Moltke and the German Wars, 1864–1871* (Basingstoke, 2001); G. A. Craig, *The Battle of Königgrätz* (Philadelphia, 1964); G. Wawro, *The Austro-Prussian War* (Cambridge, 1996), and *The Franco-Prussian War* (Cambridge, 2003); and M. Howard, *Franco-Prussian War*, 2nd edn (London, 2001).

Index